Kelley Blue Book

KELLEY BLUE BOOK OFFICIAL GUIDE

USED CAR GUIDE
Consumer Edition
2000 – 2014 Models

Vol. 23	April—June 2015	No. 2

LES KELLEY - *Founder*
BRETT NANIGIAN - - *Sr. Product Director, Industry Solutions*
KELLY J. SALAZAR - - - - - - - - - - - *Director, Publications*

Kelley Blue Book Used Car Guide, Consumer Edition is published four times per year in January, April, July and October for $9.95 per issue by Kelley Blue Book Co., P.O. Box 19691, Irvine, CA 92623. POSTMASTER: Send address changes to Kelley Blue Book Auto Market Report, P.O. Box 19691, Irvine, CA 92623.

This publication is distributed to the book trade by NBN (National Book Network), 4501 Forbes Blvd, Ste 200, Lanham, MD 20706.

Published at:

P.O. Box 19691, Irvine, California 92623

We assume no responsibility for errors or omissions.

Official Guidebooks Since 1926

ORDER YOUR BLUE BOOK NOW!

**Kelley Blue Book
P.O. Box 19691
Irvine, California 92623**

Please accept our order for _____ copies of the Kelley Blue Book Used Car Guide Consumer Edition, at $9.95 per copy, including shipping.

NAME _____

ADDRESS _____

CITY _____

STATE _____ ZIP _____

PHONE (_____)_____

VISA or MASTER CARD # _____

EXP. DATE _____ SIGNATURE _____

Visa ☐   MasterCard ☐   Check Enclosed ☐

California residents please add sales tax. Shipping outside U.S. extra.

INTRODUCTION

Since 1926, Kelley Blue Book has provided the automotive industry with used vehicle values. Today we are the trusted resource relied upon by both the automotive industry and consumers. This **Consumer Edition** has been prepared to provide values and information relevant to the different types of consumer transactions.

What is a guidebook?

A guidebook such as this one is just that, a guide. To produce the most timely, accurate and trusted used vehicle values, Kelley Blue Book's pricing analysts constantly collect and review new and used vehicle transaction data, as well as information on each vehicle's current supply and demand. They then meticulously determine and report used car values based on real market information.

This guidebook represents the educated opinion of Kelley Blue Book's staff and each value is determined after carefully studying information we deem complete and reliable. We assume no responsibility for errors or omissions.

Is this book the same as the Kelley Blue Book trade publication?

This book contains the trusted values you have come to expect from Kelley Blue Book. The values in the Consumer Guide represent transactions relevant to consumers including Trade-In, Private Party and used Retail Values.

What is the difference between Trade-In, Private Party and Retail Values?

Kelley Blue Book provides several different values representing different types of transactions.

Trade-In Value is what consumers can expect to receive from a dealer for a Trade-In vehicle assuming an accurate appraisal of condition. This value will likely be less than the Private Party Value because the dealer incurs the cost of safety inspections, reconditioning and other costs of doing business.

Kelley Blue Book factors the following into our Trade-In values:

Safety Inspections — The dealer will incur the cost of inspecting and repairing the vehicle to ensure that it meets government requirements for safety and smog emissions.

Reconditioning — Before reselling a vehicle a dealer can spend hundreds or even thousands of dollars performing repairs, routine maintenance and cosmetic detailing and touch up.

The dealer also hopes to make a fair profit for its efforts.

INTRODUCTION

Private Party Value is what a buyer can expect to pay when buying a used car from a private party. The Private Party Value assumes the vehicle is sold "As Is" and carries no warranty (other than the continuing factory warranty). The final sales price will vary depending on the vehicle's actual condition and local market conditions. This value may also be used to derive Fair Market Value for insurance and vehicle donation purposes.

Suggested Retail Value is representative of dealers' asking prices and is the starting point for negotiation between a consumer and a dealer. This Suggested Retail Value assumes that the vehicle has been fully reconditioned and has a clean Title History. This value also takes into account the dealers' profit, costs for advertising, sales commissions and other costs of doing business. The final sales price will likely be less depending on the vehicle's actual condition, popularity, type of warranty offered and local market conditions.

How does Condition affect the value of the vehicle and what is the difference between "Good," "Very Good," and "Excellent"? There is never a single correct value for a used vehicle. The value of a vehicle depends on several factors, most importantly condition and overall appearance. Supply and demand for a particular vehicle, local market conditions and the economy also play a role in determining a car's value.

Kelley Blue Book provides additional values for used vehicles in each of the following conditions:

"Excellent" condition means that the vehicle looks new, is in excellent mechanical condition and needs no reconditioning. The vehicle has never had any body/paint work, is free of rust, has a clean title history and will pass a smog and safety inspection. The engine compartment is clean and free of visible defects, with no fluid leaks. The vehicle also has complete and verifiable service records. Roughly 3% of all used vehicles fall into this category.

"Very Good" condition means that the vehicle may have minor cosmetic defects, is in excellent mechanical condition, and requires minimal (if any) reconditioning. The vehicle is rust free and has had minor or no body/paint work. A clean title history, minimal signs of wear or visible defects, and will pass a smog and safety inspection. The vehicle also has most of its maintenance records.

"Good" condition means that the vehicle is free of any major defects. The vehicle has a clean title history with only minor (if any) paint, body and/or interior blemishes and no major mechanical problems. There should be little to no rust on the vehicle. The tires match and have substantial tread wear left. Only some reconditioning or routine servicing required to be sold at retail. Most used vehicles fall into this category.

HOW TO USE THE BLUE BOOK

Asterisks (****) may appear in place of values on certain vehicles where due to rarity in the marketplace or extreme special interest we can not yet provide accurate Trade-In or Private Party values. Some of these vehicles may be limited production or rarely traded-in. We have included retail values for these vehicles but asterisks appear in place of Trade-In and Private Party values.

FINDING A VEHICLE

There are two sections in this book, the Automobile or Car section up front and the Truck & Van Section in the back. The Truck & Van section is marked by black tabs on each page. Within each section, the makes are listed alphabetically and models are listed by size within each make. Model years are listed oldest to newest.

EQUIPMENT ADJUSTMENTS

To get the most accurate value, you will need to add or deduct from the base value depending on the equipment. "Adds" and "Deducts" appear underneath individual vehicles and in separate Equipment Schedules. A value in parentheses represents a "Deduct." More generic equipment adjustments appear in the Equipment Schedules. Schedules for cars are at the front of the book. Equipment schedules for trucks and vans are at the back of the book.

You should always add or subtract for each item that is listed separately, even if it is part of a package that you have already added for or if it was considered original standard equipment. If an equipment item is listed both underneath the vehicle listing and in the Equipment Schedule, use the value underneath the vehicle listing because it is specific to that vehicle.

MILEAGE

Mileage must also be taken into consideration to derive the most accurate valuation of a used vehicle. On page 9 we have listed an "acceptable" range of mileage for each model year. The range does not represent the average mileage driven for the model year but the point of resistance where value can be affected. As a vehicle gets older, condition is more important than mileage. Vehicles with more miles may sometimes be worth more than lower mileage vehicles if its condition is better. It is important to note that the values we list are intended for vehicles within the acceptable mileage range.

HOW TO USE THE BLUE BOOK

ABBREVIATIONS USED IN THIS BOOK

VIN — Vehicle Identification Number. The VIN may vary depending on model, engine, transmission and option packages.

W.B. — Wheelbase. This is the distance from the center of the front wheel to the center of the rear wheel.

CID/L — Engine size displacement in cubic inches or liters.

List — This is the original suggested retail price of the vehicle when it was sold new, including destination charges and equipment as indicated on the equipment schedule.

Trucks — Trucks listed in this guide have a smooth exterior with the rear wheel wells inside the bed. Value adjustments for models with the rear wheel wells on the outside of the bed can be found on the Truck Equipment Schedules under the Stepside listing.

Premium Sound — This refers to an upgraded sound system (Bose, JBL, Infinity, etc.) not simply a CD changer, equalizer or an aftermarket receiver.

VEHICLE IDENTIFICATION NUMBERS (VINs)

If you are not sure of the year or model of a vehicle, you can often determine them from the Vehicle Identification Number or VIN. Using VINs can get a bit technical. If you already know the year and the model of the vehicle you can skip this information.

Under 2013 Jaguar, you will see the heading "2013 JAGUAR — SAJ (WA0E7)-D-#." This indicates that all 2013 Jaguars have a VIN starting with SAJ and have a D in the 10th position. The fourth through eighth positions determine the specific Jaguar model and are marked by parentheses. The hyphens indicate positions which can be ignored and the # symbol represents the individual vehicle's serial number.

Please note that we do not have room in this guidebook to list all the VIN information. There are some VINs that you cannot decode using the information provided. Also there are some VINs that indicate two or more possible models. In these cases you must determine the particular model by inspecting the vehicle.

TIPS ON BUYING A USED CAR

DEALER vs PRIVATE PARTY

There are advantages and disadvantages to buying a car from a dealer vs a Private Party. With a dealer, you may get a warranty and some dealerships offer certification programs for late model vehicles that will extend the original factory warranty. While buying from a dealership provides security, buying from a Private Party can save you money. When buying from a private party, ask for all repair and maintenance records and contact information of the previous owner in case you have questions later.

TRADING-IN YOUR VEHICLE

If you are trading your vehicle to a dealer, be sure to check the Trade-In Value and the Private Party Value of your vehicle. You may find it to your benefit to sell the vehicle yourself.

CHECKING OUT A USED VEHICLE

If you are contacting a private party, be sure to ask why they are selling the vehicle. Ask them to describe the condition of the vehicle and how it was used (daily, as a second car, kids car). Ask if they have all of the repair and maintenance records for the vehicle. Ask if you can take the car to a mechanic for an inspection. This is extremely important as private party sales are "As Is" and once you have bought the vehicle, it's yours. If your state requires a smog certificate, insist that the vehicle pass a smog test before buying the car. Smog checks are the current owner's responsibility. Also be certain the vehicle's registration is current and paid to date. It can be costly to reinstate an expired registration. Registration fees vary from state to state, be sure to consult your state's Department of Motor Vehicles.

— Stand away from the vehicle and look at its body panels. Do they all match in color? Do they line up?

— Check the tires for wear. Uneven tire wear, balding on the sides or in the middle, could indicate the need for an alignment or a costly repair to the vehicle's suspension.

— Open the trunk, hood and doors. Look for paint specks or over spray, a sign that all or part of the vehicle has been repainted. If the vehicle has been repainted it is often a sign of some previous damage.

— Check the radiator fluid. If it is very dark or has oil droplets in it, there is a good chance the vehicle has a cracked head gasket meaning that coolant and oil are mixing together.

— Look at the condition of the rubber on each foot pedal and the leather on the steering wheel. Do they show heavy wear? Heavy wear in a low mileage vehicle may indicate that the vehicle has seen more mileage then the odometer indicates.

TIPS ON BUYING A USED CAR

— Spend as much time as you can inside the vehicle. Feel the seat, and we mean really feel it. Take a good long time to sit, because really, the seat is one of the most important parts of the vehicle.

— What about the steering wheel? Is it too high up or too close to the dash? When adjusted comfortably, does it cut off any or all the gauges? Look at the layout of the radio and heater controls. Can they be easily adjusted without taking your eyes off the road? Look over your shoulders, are there any blind spots that you cannot compensate for by using your mirrors? Climb into the seats, front and back. Is there enough legroom and headroom? Do the headrests come up far enough? Do they touch your head or are they raked back at an angle away from you? Does the seatbelt have an adjustable anchor or does it cut into your neck? Check to see how far the rear windows roll down. Some models have windows that only go down a few inches or are sealed in place and don't roll down at all. Take your time to explore all these areas.

— Then take it for a drive. How does it sound? A prolonged tapping could be the valves needing adjustment or a bad hydraulic lifter. Pump the brake pedal a few times and then press hard with your foot. If it slowly sinks all the way to the floor, there is either a leak in the line or the master cylinder/brake booster is dying. Shift into gear. If the vehicle is an automatic, the transmission should engage immediately and shifts should be crisp and quick. With your foot firmly on the brake, shift from drive to reverse; clunks or grinding noises could indicate a worn or broken engine/transmission mount, bad U-joints or differential wear.

— As you drive along, does the steering wheel shake or vibrate? It shouldn't. Vibration in the steering wheel can mean anything from an unbalanced wheel to a loose steering rack. Cars with ABS (anti-lock brakes) will have a slight pulsating action in the brake pedal when the brakes are applied with some force. Cars without ABS should not have a pulsating brake pedal.

— We also recommend that you contact your local Department of Motor Vehicles. Ask them what forms are required to transfer the vehicle title as well as any other required information. For example, some states require a smog certificate while others require the bill of sale from the current owner.

— Lastly, whatever you do, get it in WRITING. This means if you settle with a private party, write up a contract stating what you are paying for the vehicle and under what terms it is to be delivered. Likewise with a dealer, any work they promise to do or options they intend to add, get it in writing before you close the deal.

MILEAGE RANGES

ACCEPTABLE MILEAGE RANGES

The following are acceptable mileage ranges for each model year. They do **not** represent the average miles driven. Rather, they represent an accepted mileage range as demonstrated by market research. If a vehicle's mileage is outside of the accepted range, dollar adjustments may be necessary. Mileage higher than shown on the guidelines below can expect to encounter resistance from a buyer.

YEAR	ACCEPTABLE MILEAGE RANGE
2000 – 2002	146,000 – 151,000
2003	137,000 – 142,000
2004	128,000 – 133,000
2005	119,000 – 124,000
2006	111,000 – 116,000
2007	102,000 – 107,000
2008	91,000 – 96,000
2009	81,000 – 86,000
2010	67,000 – 72,000
2011	52,000 – 57,000
2012	40,000 – 45,000
2013	30,000 – 35,000
2014	21,000 – 26,000

PRIVATE PARTY & RETAIL EQUIPMENT VALUE CONVERSION

Use the chart below to convert Trade-In Equipment Values to Private Party and Retail Values. Simply find your total Trade-In Equipment Value under the Trade-In (TI) column then follow across to the Private Party and Retail (PP/R) column. This new figure will be your Private Party or Retail Equipment Value.

TI	PP/R	TI	PP/R	TI	PP/R	TI	PP/R	TI	PP/R
25	35	225	300	425	565	625	835	825	1100
50	65	250	335	450	600	650	865	850	1135
75	100	275	365	475	635	675	900	875	1165
100	135	300	400	500	665	700	935	900	1200
125	165	325	435	525	700	725	965	925	1235
150	200	350	465	550	735	750	1000	950	1265
175	235	375	500	575	765	775	1035	975	1300
200	265	400	535	600	800	800	1065	1000	1335

2000-2001 FACTORY EQUIPMENT TRADE-IN VALUES

Equipment	1	2	3	4	5	6
Premium Sound	25	25	25	25	25	25
Navigation System	50	—	—	—	—	—
Leather	*	*	100	100	100	100
Rear Spoiler	25	25	25	25	25	25
Parking Sensors	70	—	—	—	—	—
Alloy Wheels	*	*	25	25	25	25
Premium Wheels	100	100	50	50	50	25
Roof Rack (Wagon)	25	25	25	25	25	25
Third Seat (Wagon)	125	50	50	50	50	50
DEDUCT FOR:						
w/o ABS	—	—	(50)	(50)	(25)	(25)
w/o Power Windows	—	—	—	—	(25)	(25)
w/o Power Locks	—	—	—	—	(25)	(25)
w/o Tilt Wheel	—	—	—	—	(25)	(25)
w/o Leather	(100)	(100)	—	—	—	—
w/o Cassette	—	—	—	—	(50)	(50)

* — EQUIPMENT INCLUDED IN BASE PRICE

10   SEE PAGE 9 FOR PVT PARTY & RETAIL EQUIPMENT

2002 FACTORY EQUIPMENT TRADE-IN VALUES

Equipment	1	2	3	4	5	6
Premium Sound	25	25	25	25	25	25
Navigation System	50	110	110	120	120	120
Leather	*	*	100	100	100	100
Rear Spoiler	25	25	25	25	25	25
Parking Sensors	90	65	—	—	—	—
Alloy Wheels	*	*	25	25	25	25
Premium Wheels	100	100	50	50	50	25
Roof Rack (Wagon)	25	25	25	25	25	25
Third Seat (Wagon)	125	50	50	50	50	50
DEDUCT FOR:						
w/o ABS	—	—	(50)	(50)	(25)	(25)
w/o Power Windows	—	—	—	—	(25)	(25)
w/o Power Locks	—	—	—	—	(25)	(25)
w/o Tilt Wheel	—	—	—	—	(25)	(25)
w/o Leather	(100)	(100)	—	—	—	—
w/o Cassette	—	—	—	—	(25)	(25)

* — EQUIPMENT INCLUDED IN BASE PRICE

SEE PAGE 9 FOR PVT PARTY & RETAIL EQUIPMENT

2003 FACTORY EQUIPMENT TRADE-IN VALUES

Equipment	1	2	3	4	5	6
Premium Sound	25	25	25	25	25	25
Navigation System	75	125	125	130	130	130
Leather	*	*	100	100	100	100
Rear Spoiler	25	25	25	25	25	25
Parking Sensors	95	70	—	—	—	—
Alloy Wheels	*	*	25	25	25	25
Premium Wheels	125	125	75	75	50	25
Premium Whls 19"+	390	390	390	390	390	390
Roof Rack (Wagon)	25	25	25	25	25	25
Third Seat (Wagon)	150	75	75	75	50	50
DEDUCT FOR:						
w/o ABS	—	—	(50)	(50)	(25)	(25)
w/o Power Windows	—	—	—	—	(25)	(25)
w/o Power Locks	—	—	—	—	(25)	(25)
w/o Tilt Wheel	—	—	—	—	(25)	(25)
w/o Leather	(100)	(100)	—	—	—	—

* — EQUIPMENT INCLUDED IN BASE PRICE

2004 FACTORY EQUIPMENT TRADE-IN VALUES

Equipment	1	2	3	4	5	6
Premium Sound	25	25	25	25	25	25
Navigation System	100	135	135	140	140	140
Leather	*	*	100	100	100	100
Rear Spoiler	25	25	25	25	25	25
Parking Sensors	100	75	60	—	—	—
Alloy Wheels	*	*	25	25	25	25
Premium Wheels	150	150	100	100	50	25
Premium Whls 19"+	420	420	420	420	420	420
Roof Rack (Wagon)	25	25	25	25	25	25
Third Seat (Wagon)	200	100	100	100	50	50
DEDUCT FOR:						
w/o ABS	—	—	(50)	(50)	(25)	(25)
w/o Power Windows	—	—	—	—	(25)	(25)
w/o Power Locks	—	—	—	—	(25)	(25)
w/o Tilt Wheel	—	—	—	—	(25)	(25)
w/o Leather	(100)	(100)	—	—	—	—

* — EQUIPMENT INCLUDED IN BASE PRICE

SEE PAGE 9 FOR PVT PARTY & RETAIL EQUIPMENT

2005 FACTORY EQUIPMENT TRADE-IN VALUES

Equipment	1	2	3	4	5	6
Premium Sound	50	50	25	25	25	25
Video/DVD	100	100	100	100	100	100
Navigation System	150	150	150	150	150	150
Leather	*	*	125	125	125	125
Panorama Roof	800	—	—	—	—	—
Rear Spoiler	25	25	25	25	25	25
Parking Sensors	125	75	65	—	—	—
Backup Camera	165	165	165	—	—	—
Alloy Wheels	*	*	25	25	25	25
Premium Wheels	175	175	125	125	75	25
Premium Whls 19"+	450	450	450	450	450	450
Roof Rack (Wagon)	25	25	25	25	25	25
Third Seat (Wagon)	250	125	125	125	75	75
DEDUCT FOR:						
w/o ABS	—	—	(50)	(50)	(25)	(25)
w/o Power Windows	—	—	—	—	(50)	(25)
w/o Power Locks	—	—	—	—	(25)	(25)
w/o Tilt Wheel	—	—	—	—	(25)	(25)
w/o Leather	(125)	(125)	—	—	—	—

* — EQUIPMENT INCLUDED IN BASE PRICE

2006 FACTORY EQUIPMENT TRADE-IN VALUES

Equipment	1	2	3	4	5	6
Premium Sound	75	75	25	25	25	25
Video/DVD	135	135	135	135	135	135
Navigation System	200	200	200	200	200	200
Leather	*	*	150	150	150	150
Panorama Roof	850	—	—	—	—	—
Rear Spoiler	25	25	25	25	25	25
Parking Sensors	150	100	70	—	—	—
Backup Camera	175	175	175	—	—	—
Alloy Wheels	*	*	50	50	25	25
Premium Wheels	200	200	150	150	100	50
Premium Whls 19"+	450	450	450	450	450	450
Roof Rack (Wagon)	25	25	25	25	25	25
Third Seat (Wagon)	300	150	150	150	100	100
DEDUCT FOR:						
w/o ABS	—	—	(50)	(50)	(25)	(25)
w/o Power Windows	—	(100)	—	(100)	(75)	(25)
w/o Power Locks	—	(25)	—	(25)	(25)	(25)
w/o Tilt Wheel	—	(75)	—	(75)	(50)	(25)
w/o Leather	(150)	(150)	—	—	—	—

* — EQUIPMENT INCLUDED IN BASE PRICE

SEE PAGE 9 FOR PVT PARTY & RETAIL EQUIPMENT 15

2007 FACTORY EQUIPMENT TRADE-IN VALUES

Equipment	1	2	3	4	5	6
Premium Sound	100	100	50	50	50	50
Video/DVD	200	200	200	200	200	200
Navigation System	250	250	250	250	250	250
Leather	*	*	175	175	175	175
Panorama Roof	900	—	—	—	—	—
Rear Spoiler	25	25	25	25	25	25
Parking Sensors	175	125	75	—	—	—
Backup Camera	190	190	190	—	—	—
Alloy Wheels	*	*	75	75	50	25
Premium Wheels	250	250	175	175	125	75
Premium Whls 19"+	450	450	450	450	450	450
Roof Rack (Wagon)	25	25	25	25	25	25
Third Seat (Wagon)	350	175	175	175	125	125
DEDUCT FOR:						
w/o ABS	—	—	(75)	(75)	(25)	(25)
w/o Power Windows	—	—	—	—	(100)	—
w/o Power Locks	—	—	—	—	(25)	—
w/o Tilt Wheel	—	—	—	—	(75)	—
w/o Leather	(175)	(175)	—	—	—	—

* — EQUIPMENT INCLUDED IN BASE PRICE

2008 FACTORY EQUIPMENT TRADE-IN VALUES

Equipment	1	2	3	4	5	6
Premium Sound	125	125	75	75	75	75
Video/DVD	200	200	200	200	200	200
Navigation System	300	300	300	300	300	300
Leather	*	*	200	200	200	200
Panorama Roof	950	—	705	705	—	—
Rear Spoiler	25	25	25	25	25	25
Parking Sensors	200	150	100	—	—	—
Backup Camera	200	200	200	—	—	—
Alloy Wheels	*	*	100	100	75	50
Premium Wheels	300	300	200	200	150	100
Premium Whls 19"+	450	450	450	450	450	450
Roof Rack (Wagon)	25	25	25	25	25	25
Third Seat (Wagon)	400	200	200	200	150	150
DEDUCT FOR:						
w/o ABS	—	—	(100)	(100)	(50)	(50)
w/o Power Windows	—	—	—	—	(125)	(75)
w/o Power Locks	—	—	—	—	(50)	(25)
w/o Tilt Wheel	—	—	—	—	(100)	(50)
w/o Leather	(200)	(200)	—	—	—	—

* — EQUIPMENT INCLUDED IN BASE PRICE

SEE PAGE 9 FOR PVT PARTY & RETAIL EQUIPMENT

2009 FACTORY EQUIPMENT TRADE-IN VALUES

Equipment	1	2	3	4	5	6
Premium Sound	150	150	100	100	75	75
Video/DVD	250	250	250	250	250	250
Navigation System	325	325	325	325	325	325
Leather	*	*	250	250	250	250
Panorama Roof	950	—	745	745	—	—
Rear Spoiler	50	50	50	50	50	50
Parking Sensors	225	150	100	—	—	—
Backup Camera	200	200	200	—	—	—
Alloy Wheels	*	*	100	100	75	50
Premium Wheels	325	325	225	225	150	100
Premium Whls 19"+	500	500	500	500	500	500
Roof Rack (Wagon)	50	50	50	50	50	50
Third Seat (Wagon)	425	225	225	225	175	175
DEDUCT FOR:						
w/o ABS	—	—	(100)	(100)	(50)	(50)
w/o Power Windows	—	—	—	—	(125)	(75)
w/o Power Locks	—	—	—	—	(50)	—
w/o Tilt Wheel	—	—	—	—	(100)	(50)
w/o Leather	(250)	(250)	—	—	—	—

* — EQUIPMENT INCLUDED IN BASE PRICE

2010 FACTORY EQUIPMENT TRADE-IN VALUES

Equipment	1	2	3	4	5	6
Premium Sound	175	175	125	125	75	75
Video/DVD	300	300	300	300	300	300
Navigation System	350	350	350	350	350	350
Leather	*	*	300	300	300	300
Panorama Roof	950	785	785	785	—	—
Rear Spoiler	75	75	75	75	75	75
Parking Sensors	250	175	100	—	—	—
Backup Camera	200	200	200	—	—	—
Alloy Wheels	*	*	100	100	75	50
Premium Wheels	350	350	250	250	175	100
Premium Whls 19"+	550	550	550	550	550	550
Roof Rack (Wagon)	75	75	75	75	50	50
Third Seat (Wagon)	450	250	250	250	200	200
DEDUCT FOR:						
w/o ABS	—	—	(100)	(100)	(50)	(50)
w/o Power Windows	—	—	—	—	(150)	(75)
w/o Power Locks	—	—	—	—	(50)	(25)
w/o Tilt Wheel	—	—	—	—	(100)	(50)
w/o Leather	(300)	(300)	—	—	—	—

* — EQUIPMENT INCLUDED IN BASE PRICE

SEE PAGE 9 FOR PVT PARTY & RETAIL EQUIPMENT

2011 FACTORY EQUIPMENT TRADE-IN VALUES

Equipment	1	2	3	4	5	6
Premium Sound	200	200	150	150	100	75
Video/DVD	350	350	350	350	350	350
Navigation System	400	400	400	400	400	400
Leather	*	*	350	350	350	350
Panorama Roof	950	825	825	500	—	—
Rear Spoiler	100	100	100	100	100	100
Parking Sensors	275	200	100	—	—	—
Backup Camera	200	200	200	—	—	—
Alloy Wheels	*	*	100	100	75	50
Premium Wheels	400	400	275	275	200	100
Premium Whls 19"+	600	600	600	600	600	600
Roof Rack (Wagon)	—	100	100	100	50	50
Third Seat (Wagon)	—	275	275	275	225	225
DEDUCT FOR:						
w/o ABS	—	—	(100)	(100)	(50)	(50)
w/o Power Windows	—	—	—	—	(175)	(75)
w/o Power Locks	—	—	—	—	(50)	(25)
w/o Tilt Wheel	—	—	—	—	(100)	(50)
w/o Leather	(350)	(350)	—	—	—	—

* — EQUIPMENT INCLUDED IN BASE PRICE

2012 FACTORY EQUIPMENT TRADE-IN VALUES

Equipment	1	2	3	4	5	6
Premium Sound	225	225	175	175	125	75
Video/DVD	400	400	400	400	400	400
Navigation System	450	450	450	450	450	450
Leather	*	*	400	400	400	400
Panorama Roof	975	825	825	—	—	—
Rear Spoiler	100	100	100	100	100	100
Parking Sensors	300	225	125	125	—	—
Backup Camera	200	200	200	200	—	—
Alloy Wheels	*	*	125	125	100	75
Premium Wheels	450	450	300	300	225	125
Premium Whls 19"+	675	675	675	675	675	675
Roof Rack (Wagon)	—	100	100	100	50	50
Third Seat (Wagon)	—	300	300	300	250	250
DEDUCT FOR:						
w/o ABS	—	—	(125)	(125)	(75)	(50)
w/o Power Windows	—	—	—	—	(200)	(100)
w/o Power Locks	—	—	—	—	(75)	(25)
w/o Tilt Wheel	—	—	—	—	(100)	(75)
w/o Leather	(400)	(400)	—	—	—	—

* — EQUIPMENT INCLUDED IN BASE PRICE

SEE PAGE 9 FOR PVT PARTY & RETAIL EQUIPMENT

2013 FACTORY EQUIPMENT TRADE-IN VALUES

Equipment	1	2	3	4	5	6
Premium Sound	250	250	200	200	150	100
Video/DVD	450	450	450	450	450	450
Navigation System	500	500	500	500	500	500
Leather	*	*	450	450	450	450
Panorama Roof	1000	825	825	825	—	—
Rear Spoiler	100	100	100	100	100	100
Parking Sensors	325	250	150	150	—	—
Backup Camera	200	200	200	200	—	—
Alloy Wheels	*	*	150	150	125	100
Premium Wheels	500	500	350	350	250	150
Premium Whls 19"+	750	750	750	750	750	750
Roof Rack (Wagon)	—	100	100	100	50	50
Third Seat (Wagon)	—	350	350	350	275	275
DEDUCT FOR:						
w/o ABS	—	—	(150)	(150)	(100)	(50)
w/o Power Windows	—	—	—	—	(225)	(125)
w/o Power Locks	—	—	—	—	(100)	(50)
w/o Tilt Wheel	—	—	—	—	(125)	(100)
w/o Leather	(450)	(450)	—	—	—	—

* — EQUIPMENT INCLUDED IN BASE PRICE

2014 FACTORY EQUIPMENT TRADE-IN VALUES

Equipment	1	2	3	4	5	6
Premium Sound	275	275	225	225	175	125
Video/DVD	500	500	500	500	500	500
Navigation System	550	550	550	550	550	550
Leather	*	*	525	525	525	525
Panorama Roof	1025	825	825	825	—	—
Rear Spoiler	100	100	100	100	100	100
Parking Sensors	350	275	175	175	—	—
Backup Camera	200	200	200	200	—	—
Alloy Wheels	*	*	175	175	150	125
Premium Wheels	550	550	400	400	275	175
Premium Whls 19"+	825	825	825	825	825	825
Roof Rack (Wagon)	—	100	100	100	50	50
Third Seat (Wagon)	—	400	400	400	300	300
DEDUCT FOR:						
w/o ABS	—	—	(175)	(175)	(175)	(75)
w/o Power Windows	—	—	—	—	(250)	150
w/o Power Locks	—	—	—	—	(175)	(75)
w/o Tilt Wheel	—	—	—	—	(200)	(200)
w/o Leather	(525)	(525)	—	—	—	—

* — EQUIPMENT INCLUDED IN BASE PRICE

SEE PAGE 9 FOR PVT PARTY & RETAIL EQUIPMENT

Body Type	VIN	List	Trade-In Good	Very Good	Pvt-Party Good	Retail Excellent

Automobile Section

ACURA

2000 ACURA — (JH4or19U)(DB765)–Y–#

INTEGRA—4-Cyl.—Equipment Schedule 3
W.B. 101.2", 103.1" (4D); 1.8 Liter.

Body Type	VIN	List	Good	Very Good	Good	Excellent
LS Sedan 4D	DB765	21355	1725	1925	2575	4050
LS Sport Coupe 2D	DC445	20555	1775	1975	2675	4225
GS Sedan 4D	DB766	22755	1875	2075	2800	4375
GS Sport Coupe 2D	DC446	22205	1950	2150	2825	4375
GS-R Sedan 4D	DB859	22955	1925	2125	2825	4425
GS-R Sport Coupe 2D	DC239	22655	2000	2225	2875	4450
Type R Sport Cpe 2D	DC231	24805	****	****	****	8150
Manual, 5-Spd (Sedan)	3,5		(100)	(100)	(135)	(135)

TL—V6—Equipment Schedule 1
W.B. 108.1"; 3.2 Liter.

3.2 Sedan 4D	UA566	28855	1725	1950	2675	4325

RL—V6—Equipment Schedule 1
W.B. 114.6"; 3.5 Liter.

3.5 Sedan 4D	KA965	42455	1475	1650	2450	4050

NSX—V6—Equipment Schedule 2
W.B. 99.6"; 3.0 Liter, 3.2 Liter.

Sport Coupe 2D	NA123	84745	24600	25800	26900	32700
T-Targa 2D	NA126	88745	24800	26000	27000	32900

2001 ACURA — (JH4or19U)(DB765)–1–#

INTEGRA—4-Cyl.—Equipment Schedule 3
W.B. 101.2", 103.1" (4D); 1.8 Liter.

LS Sedan 4D	DB765	21480	2150	2375	3025	4625
LS Sport Coupe 2D	DC445	20680	2225	2450	3125	4775
GS Sedan 4D	DB766	22880	2350	2600	3325	5100
GS Sport Coupe 2D	DC446	22330	2425	2675	3350	5075
GS-R Sedan 4D	DB859	23080	2400	2650	3400	5175
GS-R Sport Coupe 2D	DC239	22780	2525	2800	3475	5250
Type R Sport Cpe 2D	DC231	24930	****	****	****	9625
Manual, 5-Spd (Sedan)	3,5		(175)	(175)	(235)	(235)

CL—V6—Equipment Schedule 1
W.B. 106.9"; 3.2 Liter.

3.2 Coupe 2D	YA424	28460	1850	2075	2675	4100
3.2 Type S Coupe 2D	YA426	30810	2150	2400	3100	4775

TL—V6—Equipment Schedule 1
W.B. 108.1"; 3.2 Liter.

3.2 Sedan 4D	UA566	29030	2025	2275	3000	4725

RL—V6—Equipment Schedule 1
W.B. 114.6"; 3.5 Liter.

3.5 Sedan 4D	KA965	42630	2075	2325	3225	5100

NSX—V6—Equipment Schedule 2
W.B. 99.6"; 3.0 Liter, 3.2 Liter.

Sport Coupe 2D	NA123	84845	26600	27900	28800	34800
Targa 2D	NA126	88845	26800	28100	29000	35000

2002 ACURA — (JH4or19U)(DC548)–2–#

RSX—4-Cyl.—Equipment Schedule 3
W.B. 101.2"; 2.0 Liter.

Sport Coupe 2D	DC548	21350	2600	2875	3550	5275
Type S Sport Cpe 2D	DC530	23650	3275	3600	4325	6325

CL—V6—Equipment Schedule 1
W.B. 106.9"; 3.2 Liter.

3.2 Coupe 2D	YA424	28510	2200	2475	3100	4675
3.2 Type S Coupe 2D	YA426	30860	2650	2950	3675	5525

TL—V6—Equipment Schedule 1
W.B. 108.1"; 3.2 Liter.

3.2 Sedan 4D	UA566	29360	2350	2625	3375	5225
3.2 Type S Sedan 4D	UA568	31710	2725	3050	3850	5900

RL—V6—Equipment Schedule 1
W.B. 114.6"; 3.5 Liter.

3.5 Sedan 4D	KA965	43630	2425	2700	3450	5250

2002 ACURA

Body Type	VIN	List	Trade-In Good	Very Good	Pvt-Party Good	Retail Excellent
NSX—V6—Equipment Schedule 2						
W.B. 99.6"; 3.0 Liter, 3.2 Liter.						
Targa 2D	NA126	89745	28800	30100	31600	38500

2003 ACURA — (JH4or19U)(DC548)-3-#

Body Type	VIN	List	Trade-In Good	Very Good	Pvt-Party Good	Retail Excellent
RSX—4-Cyl.—Equipment Schedule 3						
W.B. 101.2"; 2.0 Liter.						
Sport Coupe 2D	DC548	21375	3400	3725	4475	6525
Type S Sport Cpe 2D	DC530	23770	3900	4275	5150	7350
CL—V6—Equipment Schedule 1						
W.B. 106.9"; 3.2 Liter.						
3.2 Coupe 2D	YA424	28700	2600	2900	3625	5450
3.2 Type S Coupe 2D	YA426	31050	3175	3525	4350	6500
TL—V6—Equipment Schedule 1						
W.B. 108.1"; 3.2 Liter.						
3.2 Sedan 4D	UA566	29480	2750	3075	3725	5575
3.2 Type S Sedan 4D	UA568	31830	3175	3525	4350	6375
RL—V6—Equipment Schedule 1						
W.B. 114.6"; 3.5 Liter.						
3.5 Sedan 4D	KA965	43650	2825	3150	3900	5850
NSX—V6—Equipment Schedule 2						
W.B. 99.6"; 3.0 Liter, 3.2 Liter.						
Targa 2D	NA126	89765	31300	32700	34000	41000

2004 ACURA — (JH4or19U)(DC548)-4-#

Body Type	VIN	List	Trade-In Good	Very Good	Pvt-Party Good	Retail Excellent
RSX—4-Cyl.—Equipment Schedule 3						
W.B. 101.2"; 2.0 Liter.						
Sport Coupe 2D	DC548	21470	4125	4500	5275	7400
Type S Sport Cpe 2D	DC530	23865	4850	5250	6025	8300
TSX—4-Cyl.—Equipment Schedule 3						
W.B. 105.1"; 2.4 Liter.						
Sedan 4D	CL958	26990	4275	4700	5475	7650
TL—V6—Equipment Schedule 1						
W.B. 107.9"; 3.2 Liter.						
3.2 Sedan 4D	UA566	33195	5350	5825	6350	8575
RL—V6—Equipment Schedule 1						
W.B. 114.6"; 3.5 Liter.						
3.5 Sedan 4D	KA965	46100	4025	4425	5400	7775
NSX—V6—Equipment Schedule 2						
W.B. 99.6"; 3.0 Liter, 3.2 Liter.						
Targa 2D	NA126	89765	35900	37400	38100	45100

2005 ACURA — (JH4or19U)(DC548)-5-#

Body Type	VIN	List	Trade-In Good	Very Good	Pvt-Party Good	Retail Excellent
RSX—4-Cyl.—Equipment Schedule 3						
W.B. 101.2"; 2.0 Liter.						
Sport Coupe 2D	DC548	21745	4350	4725	5650	7750
Type S Sport Cpe 2D	DC530	24240	5525	5975	7025	9475
TSX—4-Cyl.—Equipment Schedule 3						
W.B. 105.1"; 2.4 Liter.						
Sedan 4D	CL968	27760	6150	6675	7475	9775
TL—V6—Equipment Schedule 1						
W.B. 107.9"; 3.2 Liter.						
3.2 Sedan 4D	UA662	33670	6250	6775	7500	9850
RL SH-AWD—V6—Equipment Schedule 1						
W.B. 110.2"; 3.5 Liter.						
3.5 Sedan 4D	KB165	49670	6025	6525	7550	10100
NSX—V6—Equipment Schedule 2						
W.B. 99.6"; 3.0 Liter, 3.2 Liter.						
Targa 2D	NA126	89765	40300	42000	42700	50300

2006 ACURA — (JH4or19U)(DC548)-6-#

Body Type	VIN	List	Trade-In Good	Very Good	Pvt-Party Good	Retail Excellent
RSX—4-Cyl.—Equipment Schedule 3						
W.B. 101.2"; 2.0 Liter.						
Sport Coupe 2D	DC548	21840	5150	5575	6625	8850
Type S Sport Cpe 2D	DC530	24460	6825	7325	8425	11150
TSX—4-Cyl.—Equipment Schedule 3						
W.B. 105.1"; 2.4 Liter.						
Sedan 4D	CL968	28505	6925	7475	8275	10750
TL—V6—Equipment Schedule 1						
W.B. 107.9"; 3.2 Liter.						
3.2 Sedan 4D	UA662	33940	7275	7875	8550	11000

Body Type	VIN	List	Trade-In Good	Very Good	Pvt-Party Good	Retail Excellent
RL SH-AWD—V6—Equipment Schedule 1						
W.B. 110.2"; 3.5 Liter.						
3.5 Sedan 4D	KB165	49915	7000	7550	8375	10800
Technology Pkg			675	675	880	880

2007 ACURA — (JH4or19U)(CL968)-7-#

Body Type	VIN	List	Trade-In Good	Very Good	Pvt-Party Good	Retail Excellent
TSX—4-Cyl. VTEC—Equipment Schedule 3						
W.B. 105.1"; 2.4 Liter.						
Sedan 4D	CL968	28760	7675	8250	9300	12050
TL—V6 VTEC—Equipment Schedule 1						
W.B. 107.9"; 3.2 Liter, 3.5 Liter.						
3.2 Sedan 4D	UA662	34295	8550	9175	9775	12300
Type S Sedan 4D	UA755	38795	10450	11200	11950	14950
RL SH-AWD—V6—Equipment Schedule 1						
W.B. 110.2"; 3.5 Liter.						
3.5 Sedan 4D	KB165	46450	8875	9475	10100	12600
Technology Pkg			675	675	860	860

2008 ACURA — (JH4or19U)(CL968)-8-#

Body Type	VIN	List	Trade-In Good	Very Good	Pvt-Party Good	Retail Excellent
TSX—4-Cyl. VTEC—Equipment Schedule 3						
W.B. 105.1"; 2.4 Liter.						
Sedan 4D	CL968	28905	8750	9325	10100	12450
TL—V6 VTEC—Equipment Schedule 1						
W.B. 107.9"; 3.2 Liter, 3.5 Liter.						
3.2 Sedan 4D	UA662	34440	9875	10500	11200	13750
Type S Sedan 4D	UA765	38940	12450	13150	13850	16900
RL SH-AWD—V6—Equipment Schedule 1						
W.B. 110.2"; 3.5 Liter.						
3.5 Sedan 4D	KB165	46995	10550	11200	12050	14800
Technology Pkg			700	700	855	855

2009 ACURA — (JH4or19U)(CU266)-9-#

Body Type	VIN	List	Trade-In Good	Very Good	Pvt-Party Good	Retail Excellent
TSX—4-Cyl. VTEC—Equipment Schedule 3						
W.B. 106.4"; 2.4 Liter.						
Sedan 4D	CU266	29720	10850	11450	12400	15000
Technology Pkg			700	700	895	895
TL—V6 VTEC—Equipment Schedule 1						
W.B. 109.3"; 3.5 Liter, 3.7 Liter.						
Sedan 4D	UA862	35765	13350	14050	14750	17500
Technology Pkg			700	700	845	845
SH-AWD			1750	1750	2090	2090
RL SH-AWD—V6—Equipment Schedule 1						
W.B. 110.2"; 3.7 Liter.						
3.5 Sedan 4D	KB265	47040	14500	15250	16450	19900
Technology Pkg			700	700	820	820

2010 ACURA — (JH4or19U)(CU2F6)-A-#

Body Type	VIN	List	Trade-In Good	Very Good	Pvt-Party Good	Retail Excellent
TSX—4-Cyl. VTEC—Equipment Schedule 3						
W.B. 106.4"; 2.4 Liter.						
Sedan 4D	CU2F6	30070	11950	12550	13650	16400
Technology Pkg			725	725	900	900
V6, VTEC, 3.5 Liter	4		1900	1900	2365	2365
TL—V6 VTEC—Equipment Schedule 1						
W.B. 109.3"; 3.5 Liter, 3.7 Liter.						
Sedan 4D	UA8F2	35915	14750	15450	16300	19050
Technology Pkg			725	725	850	850
SH-AWD			1850	1850	2165	2165
RL SH-AWD—V6—Equipment Schedule 1						
W.B. 110.2"; 3.7 Liter.						
Sedan 4D	KB2F5	47640	17150	17950	18900	22200
Technology Pkg			725	725	830	830

2011 ACURA — (JH4or19U)(CU2F6)-B-#

Body Type	VIN	List	Trade-In Good	Very Good	Pvt-Party Good	Retail Excellent
TSX—4-Cyl. VTEC—Equipment Schedule 3						
W.B. 106.4"; 2.4 Liter.						
Sedan 4D	CU2F6	30470	13850	14450	15600	18300
Wagon 4D	CW2H5	31820	15900	16600	17550	20400
Technology Pkg			750	750	875	875
V6, VTEC, 3.5 Liter	4		2025	2025	2410	2410
TL—V6 VTEC—Equipment Schedule 1						
W.B. 109.3"; 3.5 Liter, 3.7 Liter.						

0415

2011 ACURA

Body Type	VIN	List	Trade-In Good	Very Good	Pvt-Party Good	Retail Excellent
Sedan 4D	UA8F2	36165	16200	16850	17750	20500
Technology Pkg			750	750	860	860
RL SH-AWD—V6—Equipment Schedule 1						
W.B. 110.2"; 3.7 Liter.						
Sedan 4D	KB2F5	48060	20500	21300	21800	24600
Advance Pkg			900	900	980	980
Technology Pkg			750	750	810	810

2012 ACURA — (JH4or19U)(CU2F4)-C-#

TSX—4-Cyl. VTEC—Equipment Schedule 3
W.B. 106.4"; 2.4 Liter.

Body Type	VIN	List	Good	Very Good	Good	Excellent
Sedan 4D	CU2F4	30695	15600	16250	17350	20100
Wagon 4D	CW2H5	32045	17650	18350	19300	22200
Technology Pkg			750	750	885	885
V6, VTEC, 3.5 Liter	4		2150	2150	2510	2510
TL—V6 VTEC—Equipment Schedule 1						
W.B. 109.3"; 3.5 Liter.						
Sedan 4D	UA8F2	36600	18250	18900	19750	22500
Advance Pkg			1300	1300	1500	1500
Technology Pkg			750	750	865	865
TL SH-AWD—V6 VTEC—Equipment Schedule 1						
W.B. 109.3"; 3.7 Liter.						
Sedan 4D	UA9F2	40150	21600	22400	23200	26300
Advance Pkg			1300	1300	1495	1495
Technology Pkg			750	750	865	865
RL SH-AWD—V6—Equipment Schedule 1						
W.B. 110.2"; 3.7 Liter.						
Sedan 4D	KB2F5	48585	24400	25300	26100	29700
Advance Pkg			1300	1300	1410	1410
Technology Pkg			750	750	815	815

2013 ACURA — (JH4or19U)(DE1F3)-D-#

ILX—4-Cyl. VTEC—Equipment Schedule 3
W.B. 105.1"; 2.0 Liter, 2.4 Liter.

Body Type	VIN	List	Good	Very Good	Good	Excellent
2.0L Sedan 4D	DE1F3	26795	16650	17250	18500	21400
2.4L Sedan 4D	DE2E5	30095	17100	17700	18900	21800
Technology Pkg			1425	1425	1620	1620
ILX—4-Cyl. VTEC Hybrid—Equipment Schedule 3						
W.B. 105.1"; 1.5 Liter.						
Sedan 4D	DE3F3	29795	18450	19100	20300	23500
Technology Pkg			1425	1425	1620	1620
TSX—4-Cyl. VTEC—Equipment Schedule 3						
W.B. 106.4"; 2.4 Liter.						
Sedan 4D	CU2F4	31405	18200	18900	19900	22700
Wagon 4D	CW2H5	32775	20500	21200	22100	25100
Technology Pkg			775	775	880	880
V6, VTEC, 3.5 Liter	4		2250	2250	2580	2580
TL—V6 VTEC—Equipment Schedule 1						
W.B. 109.3"; 3.5 Liter.						
Sedan 4D	UA8F2	36800	21200	22000	22700	25600
Special Ed Sedan 4D	UA8F3	38300	22100	22800	23600	26600
Advance Pkg			950	950	1075	1075
Technology Pkg			775	775	875	875
TL SH-AWD—V6 VTEC—Equipment Schedule 1						
W.B. 109.3"; 3.7 Liter.						
Sedan 4D	UA9F2	40350	25600	26500	27300	30700
Advance Pkg			950	950	1075	1075
Technology Pkg			775	775	870	870

2014 ACURA — (JH4or19U)(DE1F5)-E-#

ILX—4-Cyl. VTEC—Equipment Schedule 3
W.B. 105.1"; 2.0 Liter.

Body Type	VIN	List	Good	Very Good	Good	Excellent
2.0L Sedan 4D	DE1F5	27795	17000	17650	18900	21800
Premium Pkg			1250	1250	1400	1400
Technology Pkg			1500	1500	1695	1695
ILX—4-Cyl. VTEC—Equipment Schedule 3						
W.B. 105.1"; 2.4 Liter.						
2.4L Sedan 4D	DE2E5	30095	18200	18850	20000	23000
TSX—4-Cyl. VTEC—Equipment Schedule 3						
W.B. 106.5"; 2.4 Liter.						
Sedan 4D	CU2F4	31530	20100	20800	22500	26300
Wagon 4D	CW2H5	32880	22300	23100	24700	28700

Body Type	VIN	List	Trade-In Good	Very Good	Pvt-Party Good	Retail Excellent
Technology Pkg		------	775	775	905	905
V6, VTEC, 3.5 Liter		------	2375	2375	2750	2750
TL—V6 VTEC—Equipment Schedule 1						
W.B. 109.3"; 3.5 Liter.						
Sedan 4D	UA8F2	36925	24400	25200	25900	28900
Advance Pkg		------	975	975	1085	1085
Technology Pkg		------	775	775	875	875
TL—V6 VTEC—Equipment Schedule 1						
W.B. 109.3"; 3.5 Liter.						
Special Edition Sedan	UA8F3	38425	25300	26100	26900	30000
TL SH-AWD—V6 VTEC—Equipment Schedule 1						
W.B. 109.3"; 3.7 Liter.						
Sedan 4D	UA9F2	40475	28700	29600	30400	33900
Advance Pkg		------	975	975	1085	1085
Technology Pkg		------	775	775	875	875
RLX—V6 i-VTEC—Equipment Schedule 1						
W.B. 112.2"; 3.5 Liter.						
Sedan 4D	KC1F3	49345	30100	31100	32600	37400
Advance Pkg		------	975	975	1065	1065
Technology Pkg		------	775	775	855	855

ASTON MARTIN

2005 ASTON MARTIN — SCF(AD01A)-5-#

DB9—V12—Equipment Schedule 2
W.B. 107.9"; 6.0 Liter.

Body Type	VIN	List	Good	Very Good	Good	Excellent
Coupe 2D	AD01A	160000	****	****	****	68700
Volante Conv 2D	AD02A	173000	****	****	****	74600
VANQUISH S—V12—Equipment Schedule 2						
W.B. 105.9"; 6.0 Liter.						
Coupe 2D	AC243	255000	****	****	****	102400

2006 ASTON MARTIN — SCF(AD01A)-6-#

DB9—V12—Equipment Schedule 2
W.B. 107.9"; 6.0 Liter.

Body Type	VIN	List	Good	Very Good	Good	Excellent
Coupe 2D	AD01A	162350	****	****	****	70500
Volante Conv 2D	AD02A	176250	****	****	****	79000
VANQUISH S—V12—Equipment Schedule 2						
W.B. 105.9"; 6.0 Liter.						
Coupe 2D	AC243	261350	****	****	****	105600
VANTAGE—V8—Equipment Schedule 2						
W.B. 102.4"; 4.3 Liter.						
Coupe 2D	BB03B	108750	****	****	****	63500

2007 ASTON MARTIN — SCF(AD01A)-7-#

DB9—V12—Equipment Schedule 2
W.B. 108.0"; 6.0 Liter.

Body Type	VIN	List	Good	Very Good	Good	Excellent
Coupe 2D	AD01A	163400	****	****	****	84700
Volante Conv 2D	AD02A	176900	****	****	****	93800
VANTAGE—V8—Equipment Schedule 2						
W.B. 102.5"; 4.3 Liter.						
Coupe 2D	BB03B	111950	****	****	****	69700
Roadster 2D	BF04B	125150	****	****	****	79200

2008 ASTON MARTIN — SCF(AD01A)-8-#

DB9—V12—Equipment Schedule 2
W.B. 108.0"; 6.0 Liter.

Body Type	VIN	List	Good	Very Good	Good	Excellent
Coupe 2D	AD01A	168950	****	****	****	99200
Volante Conv 2D	AD02A	182450	****	****	****	116200
DBS—V12—Equipment Schedule 2						
W.B. 107.9"; 6.0 Liter.						
Coupe 2D	AB05D	266350	****	****	****	145500
VANTAGE—V8—Equipment Schedule 2						
W.B. 102.5"; 4.3 Liter.						
Coupe 2D	BF03B	114750	****	****	****	73500
Roadster 2D	BF04B	127750	****	****	****	82700

2009 ASTON MARTIN — SCF(AD01E)-9-#

DB9—V12—Equipment Schedule 2
W.B. 108.0"; 6.0 Liter.

2009 ASTON MARTIN

Body Type	VIN	List	Trade-In Good	Very Good	Pvt-Party Good	Retail Excellent
Coupe 2D	AD01E	184685	****	****	****	127800
Volante Conv 2D	AD02E	198185	****	****	****	144400
DBS—V12—Equipment Schedule 2			****	****	****	2415
W.B. 107.9"; 6.0 Liter.						
Coupe 2D	AB05D	270615	****	****	****	163500
Volante Conv 2D	AB02D	284115	****	****	****	166800
VANTAGE—V8—Equipment Schedule 2						
W.B. 102.5"; 4.3 Liter.						
Coupe 2D	BF03C	122365	****	****	****	82800
Roadster 2D	BF04C	135365	****	****	****	91800
Bang & Olufsen Sound			****	****	****	2390

2010 ASTON MARTIN — SCF(FDAAE)-A-#

DB9—V12—Equipment Schedule 2
W.B. 107.9"; 6.0 Liter.

Body Type	VIN	List	Trade-In Good	Very Good	Pvt-Party Good	Retail Excellent
Coupe 2D	FDAAE	187685	****	****	****	137900
Volante Conv 2D	FDABE	201185	****	****	****	153900
Bang & Olufsen Sound			****	****	****	2545
DBS—V12—Equipment Schedule 2						
W.B. 107.9"; 6.0 Liter.						
Coupe 2D	FDCBD	273615	****	****	****	185700
Volante Conv 2D	FDCCD	287115	****	****	****	189000
RAPIDE—V12—Equipment Schedule 2						
W.B. 117.7"; 6.0 Liter.						
Sedan 4D	HDDAJ	203665	****	****	****	161300
VANTAGE—V8—Equipment Schedule 2						
W.B. 102.5"; 4.7 Liter.						
Coupe 2D	EBBAC	122365	****	****	****	94500
Roadster 2D	EBBBC	135365	****	****	****	105700
N420 Coupe 2D	EBBAC	135315	****	****	****	99000
N420 Roadster 2D	EBBBC	148315	****	****	****	110200
Bang & Olufsen Sound			****	****	****	2520

2011 ASTON MARTIN — SCF(FDAAE)-B-#

DB9—V12—Equipment Schedule 2
W.B. 107.9"; 6.0 Liter.

Body Type	VIN	List	Trade-In Good	Very Good	Pvt-Party Good	Retail Excellent
Coupe 2D	FDAAE	192230	****	****	****	152600
Luxury Ed Coupe 2D	FDAAE	201175	****	****	****	156900
Sports Ed Coupe 2D	FDAAE	201566	****	****	****	157100
Volante Conv 2D	FDABE	205730	****	****	****	168500
Volante Luxury Conv	FDABE	214275	****	****	****	173000
Volante Sports Conv	FDABE	214666	****	****	****	173500
Bang & Olufsen BeoSound			****	****	****	2645
DBS—V12—Equipment Schedule 2						
W.B. 107.9"; 6.0 Liter.						
Coupe 2D	FDCBD	273275	****	****	****	208100
Volante Conv 2D	FDCCD	286910	****	****	****	211300
VANTAGE—V8—Equipment Schedule 2						
W.B. 102.5"; 4.7 Liter.						
Coupe 2D	EBBAK	121965	****	****	****	102200
Convertible 2D	EBBBK	134965	****	****	****	113100
N420 Coupe 2D	EBBAK	133215	****	****	****	106600
N420 Convertible 2D	EBBBK	146215	****	****	****	117500
S Coupe 2D	EKBDL	139615	****	****	****	115000
S Convertible 2D	EKBEL	152615	****	****	****	126300
Bang & Olufsen Sound			****	****	****	2650
VANTAGE—V12—Equipment Schedule 2						
W.B. 107.9"; 6.0 Liter.						
Coupe 2D	EBBCF	185150	****	****	****	150300
Carbon Black Coupe 2D	EBBCF	196610	****	****	****	156800
Bang & Olufsen Sound			****	****	****	2645

2012 ASTON MARTIN — SCF(FDAAE)-C-#

DB9—V12—Equipment Schedule 2
W.B. 108.1"; 6.0 Liter.

Body Type	VIN	List	Trade-In Good	Very Good	Pvt-Party Good	Retail Excellent
Coupe 2D	FDAAE	193730	****	****	****	166400
Luxury Ed Coupe 2D	FDAAE	199975	****	****	****	170700
Sports Ed Coupe 2D	FDAAE	200366	****	****	****	170900
Volante Conv 2D	FDABE	208730	****	****	****	182300
Volante Luxury Conv	FDABE	214975	****	****	****	186800
Volante Sports Conv	FDABE	215636	****	****	****	187300

Body Type	VIN	List	Trade-In Good	Very Good	Pvt-Party Good	Retail Excellent
Bang & Olufsen BeoSound			****	****	****	2775
RAPIDE—V12—Equipment Schedule 2						
W.B. 117.7"; 6.0 Liter.						
Sedan 4D	HDDAJ	212110	****	****	****	175900
Luxe Sedan 4D	HDDAJ	231065	****	****	****	188900
VANTAGE—V8—Equipment Schedule 2						
W.B. 102.5"; 4.7 Liter.						
Coupe 2D	EBBAK	122465	****	****	****	110800
Convertible 2D	EBBBK	135465	****	****	****	121700
N420 Coupe 2D	EBBAK	133715	****	****	****	115200
N420 Convertible 2D	EBBBK	146715	****	****	****	126000
S Coupe 2D	EKBDL	140115	****	****	****	123500
S Convertible 2D	EKBEL	153115	****	****	****	134700
Bang & Olufsen Sound			****	****	****	2775
VANTAGE—V12—Equipment Schedule 2						
W.B. 107.9"; 6.0 Liter.						
Coupe 2D	EBBCF	185650	****	****	****	158600
Carbon Black Coupe	EBBCF	201010	****	****	****	165100
Bang & Olufsen Sound			****	****	****	2775
VIRAGE—V12—Equipment Schedule 2						
W.B. 107.9"; 6.0 Liter.						
Coupe 2D	FDECN	211610	****	****	****	158100
Volante Conv 2D	FDEDN	226610	****	****	****	168600
Bang & Olufsen BeoSound			****	****	****	2775
2013 ASTON MARTIN — SCF(FDAAM)-D-#						
DB9—V12—Equipment Schedule 2						
W.B. 97.2"; 6.0 Liter.						
Coupe 2D	FDAAM	188225	****	****	****	173600
Volante Convertible	FDABM	203225	****	****	****	189500
VANTAGE—V8—Equipment Schedule 2						
W.B. 102.4"; 4.7 Liter.						
Coupe 2D	EBBAK	121225	****	****	****	115600
Convertible 2D	EKBBK	135725	****	****	****	126300
S Coupe 2D	EKBDL	135225	****	****	****	128200
S Convertible 2D	EKBEL	149725	****	****	****	139200
Bang & Olufsen Sound			****	****	****	2900

AUDI

2000 AUDI — (WAUorTRU)(AH28D)-Y-#

Body Type	VIN	List	Trade-In Good	Very Good	Pvt-Party Good	Retail Excellent
A4—V6—Equipment Schedule 3						
W.B. 103.0"; 2.8 Liter.						
Sedan 4D	AH28D	30390	800	900	1650	2850
Quattro AWD	D		1175	1175	1565	1565
Manual, 5-Spd			(125)	(125)	(165)	(165)
4-Cyl, Turbo, 1.8 Liter	C		(475)	(475)	(620)	(620)
A4 AVANT QUATTRO AWD—V6—Equipment Schedule 3						
W.B. 102.6"; 2.8 Liter.						
Wagon 4D	KH28D	33140	1625	1825	2450	3975
Manual, 5-Spd			(125)	(125)	(165)	(165)
4-Cyl, Turbo, 1.8 Liter	C		(475)	(475)	(620)	(620)
S4 QUATTRO AWD—V6 Turbo—Equipment Schedule 3						
W.B. 102.6"; 2.7 Liter.						
2.7T Sedan 4D	DD68D	39625	1725	1900	2600	4025
A6—V6—Equipment Schedule 3						
W.B. 108.7"; 2.8 Liter.						
Sedan 4D	BH24B	34475	575	650	1175	1975
Quattro AWD	G,J		1175	1175	1565	1565
A6 AVANT QUATTRO AWD—V6—Equipment Schedule 3						
W.B. 108.6"; 2.8 Liter.						
Wagon 4D	LH24B	37425	1450	1625	2250	3675
A6 QUATTRO AWD—V6 Turbo—Equipment Schedule 3						
W.B. 108.7"; 2.7 Liter.						
2.7T Sedan 4D	ED24B	39075	1725	1925	2700	4350
A6 QUATTRO AWD—V8—Equipment Schedule 3						
W.B. 108.6"; 4.2 Liter.						
4.2 Sedan 4D	ZL54B	49425	1850	2050	2875	4600
A8 QUATTRO AWD—V8—Equipment Schedule 1						
W.B. 113.4", 118.5" (L); 4.2 Liter.						
Sedan 4D	FL54D	62525	750	850	1475	2450

Body Type	VIN	List	Trade-In Good	Trade-In Very Good	Pvt-Party Good	Retail Excellent
L Sedan 4D	FL54D	68425	**1600**	**1750**	**2525**	**3950**
TT—4-Cyl. Turbo—Equipment Schedule 2						
W.B. 95.4"; 95.6"; 1.8 Liter.						
Coupe 2D	TC28N	31025	**1600**	**1775**	**2400**	**3750**
Quattro AWD	U		**1175**	**1175**	**1565**	**1565**

2001 AUDI — (WAUorTRU)(AH68D)-1-#

A4—V6—Equipment Schedule 3
W.B. 103.0"; 2.8 Liter.

Sedan 4D	AH68D	30890	**1050**	**1175**	**1900**	**3250**
Quattro AWD	D		**1200**	**1200**	**1600**	**1600**
Manual, 5-Spd			(175)	(175)	(235)	(235)
4-Cyl, Turbo, 1.8 Liter	C		(525)	(525)	(695)	(695)

A4 AVANT QUATTRO AWD—V6—Equipment Schedule 3
W.B. 102.6"; 2.8 Liter.

Wagon 4D	KH68D	33640	**2025**	**2250**	**2950**	**4550**
Manual, 5-Spd			(175)	(175)	(235)	(235)
4-Cyl, Turbo, 1.8 Liter	C		(525)	(525)	(695)	(695)

S4 QUATTRO AWD—V6 Turbo—Equipment Schedule 3
W.B. 102.6"; 2.7 Liter.

2.7T Sedan 4D	RD58D	39450	**3050**	**3350**	**3850**	**5425**
2.7T Avant Wagon 4D	XD68D	41050	**3825**	**4175**	**4875**	**6825**

A6—V6—Equipment Schedule 3
W.B. 108.7"; 2.8 Liter.

Sedan 4D	BH54B	34950	**600**	**675**	**1225**	**2075**
Quattro AWD	E		**1200**	**1200**	**1600**	**1600**

A6 AVANT QUATTRO AWD—V6—Equipment Schedule 3
W.B. 108.6"; 2.8 Liter.

Wagon 4D	LH54B	37900	**1500**	**1650**	**2325**	**3800**

A6 QUATTRO AWD—V6 Turbo—Equipment Schedule 3
W.B. 108.7"; 2.7 Liter.

2.7T Sedan 4D	ED54B	40050	**1950**	**2175**	**3050**	**4850**
Sport Pkg			250	250	350	350

ALLROAD QUATTRO AWD—V6 Turbo—Equipment Sch 1
W.B. 108.5"; 2.7 Liter.

2.7T Wagon 4D	YP54B	43450	**2375**	**2650**	**3575**	**5625**

A6 QUATTRO AWD—V8—Equipment Schedule 3
W.B. 108.6"; 4.2 Liter.

4.2 Sedan 4D	ZL54B	49950	**2100**	**2350**	**3250**	**5175**
Sport Pkg			250	250	350	350

A8 QUATTRO AWD—V8—Equipment Schedule 1
W.B. 113.4"; 118.5" (L); 4.2 Liter.

Sedan 4D	FL54D	62750	**775**	**850**	**1550**	**2625**
L Sedan 4D	ML54D	68450	**1750**	**1925**	**2825**	**4425**

S8 QUATTRO AWD—V8—Equipment Schedule 1
W.B. 113.4"; 4.2 Liter.

Sedan 4D	GU54D	73050	**3550**	**3850**	**4775**	**6775**

TT—4-Cyl. Turbo—Equipment Schedule 3
W.B. 95.4"; 1.8 Liter.

Coupe 2D	SC28N	31750	**1750**	**1925**	**2625**	**4050**
Roadster 2D	TC28N	33750	**2200**	**2425**	**3025**	**4525**
Power Folding Roof			250	250	345	345

TT QUATTRO AWD—4-Cyl. HO Turbo—Equipment Schedule 2
W.B. 95.4"; 1.8 Liter.

Coupe 2D	WT28N	36650	**2900**	**3200**	**3850**	**5600**
Roadster 2D	UT28N	39450	**3125**	**3450**	**4225**	**6075**

2002 AUDI — (WAUorTRU)(JC58E)-2-#

A4—V6—Equipment Schedule 3
W.B. 104.3"; 3.0 Liter.

Sedan 4D	JC58E	31965	**1700**	**1875**	**2725**	**4400**
Sport Pkg			150	150	205	205
Quattro AWD	L		**1250**	**1250**	**1665**	**1665**
Manual, 5-Spd			(175)	(175)	(240)	(240)
4-Cyl, Turbo, 1.8 Liter	C		(575)	(575)	(765)	(765)

A4 AVANT QUATTRO AWD—V6—Equipment Schedule 3
W.B. 104.3"; 3.0 Liter.

Wagon 4D	VC58E	34715	**2800**	**3125**	**3800**	**5625**
Sport Pkg			150	150	205	205
Manual, 5-Spd			(175)	(175)	(240)	(240)
4-Cyl, Turbo, 1.8 Liter	C		(575)	(575)	(765)	(765)

Body Type	VIN	List	Trade-In Good	Very Good	Pvt-Party Good	Retail Excellent
S4 QUATTRO AWD—V6 Turbo—Equipment Schedule 3						
W.B. 102.6"; 2.7 Liter.						
2.7T Sedan 4D	RD68D	39475	3075	3375	3950	5625
2.7T Avant Wagon 4D	XD68D	41075	3900	4250	5100	7225
A6—V6—Equipment Schedule 3						
W.B. 108.7"; 3.0 Liter.						
Sedan 4D	JT54B	35975	625	700	1275	2175
Quattro AWD	L		1250	1250	1665	1665
A6 AVANT QUATTRO AWD—V6—Equipment Schedule 3						
W.B. 108.6"; 3.0 Liter.						
Wagon 4D	VT54B	38925	1600	1775	2550	4075
A6 QUATTRO AWD—V6 Turbo—Equipment Schedule 3						
W.B. 108.7"; 2.7 Liter.						
2.7T Sedan 4D	LD54B	40325	2100	2325	3175	5000
Sport Pkg			275	275	365	365
ALLROAD QUATTRO AWD—V6 Turbo—Equipment Sch 1						
W.B. 108.5"; 2.7 Liter.						
2.7T Wagon 4D	YD54B	43325	2450	2700	3675	5775
A6 QUATTRO AWD—V8—Equipment Schedule 3						
W.B. 108.6"; 4.2 Liter.						
4.2 Sedan 4D	ML54B	50225	2450	2725	3625	5650
Sport Pkg			275	275	365	365
S6 AVANT QUATTRO AWD—V8—Equipment Schedule 1						
W.B. 108.6"; 4.2 Liter.						
Wagon 4D	XU54B	61375	9200	9900	12650	18450
A8 QUATTRO AWD—V8—Equipment Schedule 1						
W.B. 113.4", 118.5" (L); 4.2 Liter.						
Sedan 4D	FL44D	62775	925	1000	1625	2675
L Sedan 4D	ML44D	67775	2000	2200	3000	4550
S8 QUATTRO AWD—V8—Equipment Schedule 1						
W.B. 113.4"; 4.2 Liter.						
Sedan 4D	GU44D	74775	3750	4050	5300	7700
TT—4-Cyl. Turbo—Equipment Schedule 2						
W.B. 95.4"; 1.8 Liter.						
Coupe 2D	SC28N	31775	2475	2725	3250	4725
Roadster 2D	TC28N	33775	3075	3375	3925	5600
Power Folding Roof			275	275	370	370
TT QUATTRO AWD—4-Cyl. Turbo—Equipment Schedule 2						
W.B. 95.4"; 1.8 Liter.						
180 Coupe 2D	WC28N	33595	3175	3500	4175	5950
TT QUATTRO AWD—4-Cyl. HO Turbo—Equipment Schedule 2						
W.B. 95.6"; 1.8 Liter.						
225 Coupe 2D	WT28N	36675	3850	4200	4925	6875
225 Roadster 2D	UT28N	39475	4350	4725	5600	7925
225 ALMS Comm Cpe	WT28N	40245	4950	5375	6175	8550

2003 AUDI — (WAU,WUA,WA1orTRU)(JC58E)-3-#

Body Type	VIN	List	Trade-In Good	Very Good	Pvt-Party Good	Retail Excellent
A4—4-Cyl. Turbo—Equipment Schedule 3						
W.B. 104.3", 104.5" (Cab); 1.8 Liter.						
1.8T Sedan 4D	JC58E	26910	2175	2400	3175	4850
1.8T Cabriolet 2D	AC48H	35610	2300	2525	3250	4925
Sport Pkg			150	150	215	215
Manual, 5-Spd			(200)	(200)	(265)	(265)
A4 QUATTRO AWD—4-Cyl. Turbo—Equipment Schedule 3						
W.B. 104.5"; 1.8 Liter.						
1.8T Sedan 4D	LC58E	28660	2450	2700	3550	5425
A4—V6—Equipment Schedule 3						
W.B. 104.3", 104.5" (Cab); 3.0 Liter.						
Sedan 4D	JT58E	32250	2350	2575	3400	5175
Cabriolet 2D	AT28H	42160	2625	2875	3650	5475
Sport Pkg			150	150	215	215
Manual, 5-Spd			(200)	(200)	(265)	(265)
A4 QUATTRO AWD—V6—Equipment Schedule 3						
W.B. 104.5"; 3.0 Liter.						
3.0 Sedan 4D	LT58E	34150	2775	3075	3950	5950
Sport Pkg			150	150	215	215
Manual, 5-Spd			(200)	(200)	(265)	(265)
A4 AVANT QUATTRO AWD—4-Cyl. Turbo—Equipment Schedule 3						
W.B. 104.3"; 1.8 Liter.						
1.8T Wagon 4D	VC58E	29660	3075	3400	4100	6000
Manual, 5-Spd			(200)	(200)	(265)	(265)
A4 AVANT QUATTRO AWD—V6—Equipment Schedule 3						
W.B. 104.3"; 3.0 Liter.						

0415

2003 AUDI

Body Type	VIN	List	Trade-In Good	Very Good	Pvt-Party Good	Retail Excellent
Wagon 4D	VT58E	35000	3475	3825	4575	6650
Sport Pkg			150	150	215	215
Manual, 5-Spd			(200)	(200)	(265)	(265)
A6—V6—Equipment Schedule 3						
W.B. 108.7"; 3.0 Liter.						
Sedan 4D	JT54B	36360	1125	1250	1775	2850
A6 QUATTRO AWD—V6—Equipment Schedule 3						
W.B. 108.7"; 3.0 Liter.						
Sedan 4D	LT54B	38260	2425	2675	3625	5675
A6 AVANT QUATTRO AWD—V6—Equipment Schedule 3						
W.B. 108.6"; 3.0 Liter.						
Wagon 4D	VT54B	39310	2150	2375	3250	5100
A6 QUATTRO AWD—V6 Turbo—Equipment Schedule 3						
W.B. 108.7"; 2.7 Liter.						
2.7T Sedan 4D	LD54B	41510	2825	3125	4150	6450
ALLROAD QUATTRO AWD—V6 Turbo—Equipment Schedule 1						
W.B. 108.5"; 2.7 Liter.						
2.7T Wagon 4D	YD54B	45110	2975	3275	4275	6525
A6 QUATTRO AWD—V8—Equipment Schedule 3						
W.B. 108.6"; 4.2 Liter.						
4.2 Sedan 4D	ML54B	48460	3225	3550	4675	7200
Sport Pkg			275	275	380	380
S6 AVANT QUATTRO AWD—V8—Equipment Schedule 1						
W.B. 108.6"; 4.2 Liter.						
Wagon 4D	XU54B	61060	9575	10250	13000	18800
RS6 QUATTRO AWD—V8 Bi Turbo—Equipment Schedule 1						
W.B. 108.6"; 4.2 Liter.						
Sedan 4D	PV54B	84660	11150	11850	12550	15900
A8 QUATTRO AWD—V8—Equipment Schedule 1						
W.B. 113.4", 118.5" (L); 4.2 Liter.						
Sedan 4D	FL44D	62860	1375	1525	2175	3400
L Sedan 4D	ML44D	67860	2575	2800	3525	5125
S8 QUATTRO AWD—V8—Equipment Schedule 1						
W.B. 113.4"; 4.2 Liter.						
Sedan 4D	GU44D	74460	4175	4525	5600	7850
TT—4-Cyl. Turbo—Equipment Schedule 2						
W.B. 95.4"; 1.8 Liter.						
Coupe 2D	SC28N	33145	2950	3250	3900	5500
Roadster 2D	TC28N	35145	3825	4175	4775	6575
Power Folding Roof			300	300	395	395
TT QUATTRO AWD—4-Cyl. HO Turbo—Equipment Schedule 2						
W.B. 95.4"; 1.8 Liter.						
Coupe 2D	WT28N	36845	4275	4625	5425	7525
Roadster 2D	UT28N	39645	4575	5150	6175	8525

2004 AUDI — (WAU,WA1orTRU)(JC58E)-4-#

Body Type	VIN	List	Trade-In Good	Very Good	Pvt-Party Good	Retail Excellent
A4—4-Cyl. Turbo—Equipment Schedule 3						
W.B. 104.3", 104.5" (Cab); 1.8 Liter.						
1.8T Sedan 4D	JC58E	27420	2675	2950	3625	5350
1.8T Cabriolet 2D	AC48H	35970	3050	3350	4025	5875
Sport Pkg			175	175	225	225
Ultra Sport Pkg			725	725	975	975
A4 QUATTRO AWD—4-Cyl. Turbo—Equipment Schedule 3						
W.B. 104.3"; 1.8 Liter.						
1.8T Sedan 4D	LC58E	29520	3025	3300	4050	5925
Sport Pkg			175	175	225	225
Ultra Sport Pkg			725	725	975	975
A4 AVANT QUATTRO AWD—4-Cyl. Turbo—Equipment Schedule 3						
W.B. 104.3"; 1.8 Liter.						
1.8T Wagon 4D	VC58E	30520	3525	3875	4550	6525
Sport Pkg			175	175	225	225
Ultra Sport Pkg			725	725	975	975
A4—V6—Equipment Schedule 3						
W.B. 104.3", 104.5" (Cab); 3.0 Liter.						
Sedan 4D	JT58E	31840	3150	3450	4175	6050
Cabriolet 2D	AT48H	42490	3300	3625	4475	6450
Sport Pkg			175	175	225	225
Ultra Sport Pkg			725	725	975	975
Manual, 5-Spd			(200)	(200)	(265)	(265)
A4 QUATTRO AWD—V6—Equipment Schedule 3						
W.B. 104.3", 104.5" (Cab); 3.0 Liter.						
3.0 Sedan 4D	LT58E	35010	3525	3825	4600	6625
3.0 Cabriolet 2D	DT48H	44270	3725	4075	4975	7175

Body Type	VIN	List	Trade-In Good	Trade-In Very Good	Pvt-Party Good	Retail Excellent
Sport Pkg		------	175	175	225	225
Ultra Sport Pkg		------	725	725	975	975
Manual, 5-Spd		------	(200)	(200)	(265)	(265)
A4 AVANT QUATTRO AWD—V6—Equipment Schedule 3						
W.B. 104.3"; 3.0 Liter.						
Wagon 4D	VT58E	35480	3925	4325	5150	7350
Sport Pkg		------	175	175	225	225
Ultra Sport Pkg		------	725	725	975	975
S4 QUATTRO AWD—V8—Equipment Schedule 1						
W.B. 104.3", 104.5" (Cab); 4.2 Liter.						
Sedan 4D	PL58E	47490	4425	4775	5475	7400
Cabriolet 2D	RL48H	55720	4550	4925	5925	8100
S4 AVANT QUATTRO AWD—V8—Equipment Schedule 1						
W.B. 104.3"; 4.2 Liter.						
Wagon 4D	XL68E	48490	5050	5450	6350	8525
A6—V6—Equipment Schedule 3						
W.B. 108.7"; 3.0 Liter.						
Sedan 4D	JT54B	36640	1625	1800	2325	3525
A6 QUATTRO AWD—V6—Equipment Schedule 3						
W.B. 108.7"; 3.0 Liter.						
Sedan 4D	LT54B	40170	3025	3325	4100	6075
A6 AVANT QUATTRO AWD—V6—Equipment Schedule 3						
W.B. 108.6"; 3.0 Liter.						
Wagon 4D	VT54B	40840	2700	3000	3750	5600
A6 QUATTRO AWD—V6 Turbo—Equipment Schedule 3						
W.B. 108.7"; 2.7 Liter.						
2.7T Sedan 4D	LD64B	42480	3500	3825	4800	7000
2.7T S-Line Sedan 4D	CD64B	43870	3775	4125	5175	7550
ALLROAD QUATTRO AWD—V6 Turbo—Equipment Schedule 1						
W.B. 108.5"; 2.7 Liter.						
2.7T Wagon 4D	YD54B	44040	3300	3625	4700	7000
ALLROAD QUATTRO AWD—V8—Equipment Schedule 1						
W.B. 108.5"; 4.2 Liter.						
4.2 Wagon 4D	YL64B	47640	3500	3825	4900	7225
A6 QUATTRO AWD—V8—Equipment Schedule 3						
W.B. 108.6"; 4.2 Liter.						
4.2 Sedan 4D	ML54B	49690	3950	4300	5375	7825
Sport Pkg		------	300	300	400	400
A8 QUATTRO AWD—V8—Equipment Schedule 1						
W.B. 121.1"; 4.2 Liter.						
L Sedan 4D	ML44E	69190	6200	6600	7425	9775
TT—4-Cyl. Turbo—Equipment Schedule 2						
W.B. 95.4"; 1.8 Liter.						
Coupe 2D	SC28N	33940	3675	4000	4675	6500
Roadster 2D	TC28N	35940	4550	4900	5625	7700
Power Folding Roof		------	325	325	415	415
TT QUATTRO AWD—V6—Equipment Schedule 2						
W.B. 95.6"; 3.2 Liter.						
Coupe 2D	WF28N	40590	5525	5950	6875	9275
Roadster 2D	UF28N	43590	6225	6675	7650	10300
4-Cyl, HO Turbo, 1.8L	T		(1000)	(1000)	(1335)	(1335)

2005 AUDI — (WAU,WA1 or TRU)(JC58E)—5—#

Body Type	VIN	List	Trade-In Good	Trade-In Very Good	Pvt-Party Good	Retail Excellent
A4—4-Cyl. Turbo—Equipment Schedule 3						
W.B. 104.3", 104.5" (Cab); 1.8 Liter.						
1.8T Sedan 4D	JC58E	32670	3175	3475	4300	6075
1.8T Cabriolet 2D	AC48H	43020	3525	3850	4850	6900
Sport Pkg		------	175	175	235	235
Ultra Sport Pkg		------	775	775	1045	1045
S-Line Pkg		------	550	550	740	740
A4 QUATTRO AWD—4-Cyl. Turbo—Equipment Schedule 3						
W.B. 104.3"; 1.8 Liter.						
1.8T Sedan 4D	LC58E	30070	3500	3850	4800	6750
Sport Pkg		------	175	175	235	235
Ultra Sport Pkg		------	775	775	1045	1045
S-Line Pkg		------	550	550	740	740
A4—V6—Equipment Schedule 3						
W.B. 104.3", 104.5" (Cab); 3.0 Liter.						
Sedan 4D	JT58E	32670	3500	3850	4750	6650
Cabriolet 2D	AT48H	43020	3925	4275	5300	7500
Sport Pkg		------	175	175	235	235
Ultra Sport Pkg		------	775	775	1045	1045
S-Line Pkg		------	550	550	740	740

Body Type	VIN	List	Trade-In Good	Very Good	Pvt-Party Good	Retail Excellent
A4 QUATTRO AWD—V6—Equipment Schedule 3						
W.B. 104.3"; 3.0 Liter.						
3.0 Sedan 4D	JT58E	35510	**4250**	**4625**	**5550**	**7650**
3.0 Cabriolet 2D	DT48H	44970	**4425**	**4800**	**5875**	**8250**
Sport Pkg			175	175	235	235
Ultra Sport Pkg			775	775	1045	1045
S-Line Pkg			550	550	740	740
A4 AVANT QUATTRO AWD—4-Cyl. Turbo—Equipment Schedule 3						
W.B. 104.3"; 1.8 Liter.						
1.8T Wagon 4D	VC58E	31070	**4375**	**4775**	**5700**	**7875**
Sport Pkg			175	175	235	235
Ultra Sport Pkg			775	775	1045	1045
A4 AVANT QUATTRO AWD—V6—Equipment Schedule 3						
W.B. 104.3"; 3.0 Liter.						
Wagon 4D	VT58E	36510	**4550**	**4975**	**5900**	**8150**
Sport Pkg			175	175	235	235
Ultra Sport Pkg			775	775	1045	1045
A4 (2005.5)—4-Cyl. Turbo—Equipment Schedule 3						
W.B. 104.3"; 2.0 Liter.						
2.0T Sedan 4D	AF78E	29270	**3800**	**4150**	**5050**	**6975**
Sport Pkg			175	175	235	235
A4 QUATTRO AWD (2005.5)—4-Cyl. Turbo—Equipment Schedule 3						
W.B. 104.3"; 1.8 Liter.						
2.0T Sedan 4D	AF78E	31370	**4275**	**4650**	**5600**	**7700**
Sport Pkg			175	175	235	235
A4 AVANT QUATTRO AWD (2005.5)—4-Cyl. Turbo—Equip Sch 3						
W.B. 104.3"; 2.0 Liter.						
2.0T Wagon 4D	KF78E	32370	**5075**	**5525**	**6375**	**8675**
Sport Pkg			175	175	235	235
A4 QUATTRO AWD (2005.5)—V6—Equipment Schedule 3						
W.B. 104.3"; 3.2 Liter.						
3.2 Sedan 4D	DG78E	36120	**4600**	**5000**	**6025**	**8350**
Sport Pkg			175	175	235	235
A4 AVANT QUATTRO AWD (2005.5)—V6—Equipment Sch 3						
W.B. 104.3"; 3.2 Liter.						
3.2 Wagon 4D	KG78E	37120	**5525**	**6025**	**7125**	**9700**
Sport Pkg			175	175	235	235
S4 QUATTRO AWD—V8—Equipment Schedule 1						
W.B. 104.3", 104.5" (Cab); 4.2 Liter.						
Sedan 4D	PL58E	47770	**5850**	**6275**	**7200**	**9375**
Cabriolet 2D	RL48H	55870	**7250**	**7750**	**8900**	**11650**
S4 AVANT QUATTRO AWD—V8—Equipment Schedule 1						
W.B. 104.3"; 4.2 Liter.						
Wagon 4D	XL58E	48770	**7075**	**7575**	**8600**	**11150**
S4 QUATTRO AWD (2005.5)—V8—Equipment Schedule 1						
W.B. 104.3"; 4.2 Liter.						
Sedan 4D	GL68E	49320	**6950**	**7425**	**8500**	**11050**
S4 AVANT QUATTRO AWD (2005.5)—V8— Equipment Schedule 1						
W.B. 104.3"; 4.2 Liter.						
Wagon 4D	UL58E	50320	**8625**	**9175**	**10300**	**13200**
A6 QUATTRO AWD—V6—Equipment Schedule 3						
W.B. 111.9"; 3.2 Liter.						
Sedan 4D	DG54F	41620	**5450**	**5900**	**6700**	**8825**
Sport Pkg			300	300	380	380
A6 QUATTRO AWD—V8—Equipment Schedule 3						
W.B. 111.9"; 4.2 Liter.						
4.2 Sedan 4D	DL54F	51220	**6350**	**6850**	**7750**	**10250**
Sport Pkg			300	300	385	385
S-Line Pkg	E		550	550	680	680
ALLROAD QUATTRO AWD—V6 Turbo—Equipment Schedule 1						
W.B. 108.5"; 2.7 Liter.						
2.7T Wagon 4D	YD54B	40970	**5325**	**5750**	**6400**	**8425**
ALLROAD QUATTRO AWD—V8—Equipment Schedule 1						
W.B. 108.5"; 4.2 Liter.						
4.2 Wagon 4D	YL54B	47970	**5750**	**6225**	**7025**	**9225**
A8 QUATTRO AWD—V8—Equipment Schedule 1						
W.B. 115.9", 121.0" (L); 4.2 Liter.						
Sedan 4D	LL44E	67310	**6000**	**6400**	**7500**	**9725**
L Sedan 4D	ML44E	70620	**7200**	**7650**	**8875**	**11450**
A8 QUATTRO AWD—W12—Equipment Schedule 1						
W.B. 121.0"; 6.0 Liter.						
L Sedan 4D	MR44E	118120	**11350**	**11950**	**13750**	**17700**

2005 AUDI

Body Type	VIN	List	Trade-In Good	Very Good	Pvt-Party Good	Retail Excellent
TT—4-Cyl. Turbo—Equipment Schedule 2						
W.B. 95.4"; 1.8 Liter.						
Coupe 2D	SC28N	34220	4550	4925	5925	8000
Roadster 2D	TC28N	36220	5600	6025	7050	9400
Power Folding Roof			325	325	440	440
TT QUATTRO AWD—V6—Equipment Schedule 2						
W.B. 95.4", 95.6" (Cpe); 3.2 Liter.						
Coupe 2D	WF28N	40870	6700	7175	8350	11050
Roadster 2D	UF28N	43870	8175	8725	9975	13150
4-Cyl, HO Turbo, 1.8L	T		(1050)	(1050)	(1385)	(1385)

2006 AUDI — (WAU,WUAorTRU)(HF68P)-6-#

Body Type	VIN	List	Trade-In Good	Very Good	Pvt-Party Good	Retail Excellent
A3—4-Cyl. Turbo—Equipment Schedule 3						
W.B. 101.5"; 2.0 Liter.						
2.0T Wagon 4D	HF68P	26860	4700	5125	5925	7975
Sport Pkg	M		175	175	245	245
A3 QUATTRO AWD—V6—Equipment Schedule 3						
W.B. 101.5"; 3.2 Liter.						
3.2 S-Line Wagon 4D	KD78P	34700	8950	9600	10800	14200
A4—4-Cyl. Turbo—Equipment Schedule 3						
W.B. 104.3", 104.5" (Cab); 1.8 Liter, 2.0 Liter.						
2.0T Sedan 4D	AF78E	29560	4825	5200	6025	8075
1.8T Cabriolet 2D	AC48H	38060	4650	5050	5950	8100
S-Line Pkg	B,E		600	600	800	800
A4 QUATTRO AWD—4-Cyl. Turbo—Equipment Schedule 3						
W.B. 104.3"; 1.8 Liter.						
2.0T Sedan 4D	DF58E	32260	5225	5650	6775	9025
S-Line Pkg	B,E		600	600	800	800
A4—V6—Equipment Schedule 3						
W.B. 104.3"; 3.2 Liter.						
3.2 Sedan 4D	AH78E	34660	5675	6100	7300	9725
S-Line Pkg	E		600	600	800	800
A4 QUATTRO AWD—V6—Equipment Schedule 3						
W.B. 104.3"; 3.2 Liter.						
3.2 Sedan 4D	DG78E	37310	6350	6800	7950	10600
S-Line Pkg	E		600	600	800	800
A4 QUATTRO AWD—V6—Equipment Schedule 3						
W.B. 104.5"; 3.0 Liter.						
3.0 Cabriolet 2D	DT48H	46210	5700	6150	7350	9925
S-Line Pkg	E		600	600	800	800
A4 AVANT QUATTRO AWD—4-Cyl. Turbo—Equipment Sch 3						
W.B. 104.3"; 2.0 Liter.						
2.0T Wagon 4D	KF78E	32660	6100	6600	7525	9875
S-Line Pkg	S		600	600	800	800
A4 AVANT QUATTRO AWD—V6—Equipment Schedule 3						
W.B. 104.3"; 3.2 Liter.						
3.2 Wagon 4D	KH78E	37760	6975	7525	8425	10950
S-Line Pkg	S		600	600	800	800
S4 QUATTRO AWD—V8—Equipment Schedule 1						
W.B. 104.3", 104.5" (Cab); 4.2 Liter.						
Sedan 4D	GL78E	49620	9650	10250	11050	13650
Special Ed Sedan 4D	GL78E	60970	10750	11350	12300	15150
Cabriolet 2D	RL48H	57860	9825	10450	11400	14150
S4 QUATTRO AWD—V8—Equipment Schedule 1						
W.B. 104.3"; 4.2 Liter.						
Wagon 4D	UL78E	50620	11500	12200	13050	16000
A6—V6—Equipment Schedule 3						
W.B. 111.9"; 3.2 Liter.						
3.2 Sedan 4D	AH74F	41540	5325	5775	6775	8950
S-Line Pkg	B		600	600	745	745
A6 QUATTRO AWD—V6—Equipment Schedule 3						
W.B. 111.9"; 3.2 Liter.						
3.2 Sedan 4D	DG74F	44690	6975	7500	8650	11450
S-Line Pkg	E		600	600	745	745
A6 AVANT QUATTRO AWD—V6—Equipment Schedule 3						
W.B. 111.9"; 3.2 Liter.						
3.2 Wagon 4D	KG74F	47590	8675	9275	10450	13700
A6 QUATTRO AWD—V8—Equipment Schedule 3						
W.B. 111.9"; 4.2 Liter.						
4.2 Sedan 4D	DL74F	54490	7550	8100	9375	12450
S-Line Pkg	E		600	600	755	755
A8 QUATTRO AWD—V8—Equipment Schedule 1						
W.B. 115.9", 121.0" (L); 4.2 Liter.						

Body Type	VIN	List	Trade-In Good	Very Good	Pvt-Party Good	Retail Excellent
Sedan 4D	LL44E	68850	**7925**	**8400**	9475	11900
L Sedan 4D	ML44E	72810	**9075**	**9600**	10950	13650
Premium Pkg			**875**	**875**	1060	1060
Sport Pkg			**600**	**600**	720	720
A8 QUATTRO AWD—W12—Equipment Schedule 1						
W.B. 121.0"; 6.0 Liter.						
L Sedan 4D	MR44E	120610	**13350**	**14050**	15750	19850
TT—4-Cyl. Turbo—Equipment Schedule 2						
W.B. 95.4"; 1.8 Liter.						
Coupe 2D	SC28N	34710	**5975**	**6425**	7425	9800
Roadster 2D	TC28N	36710	**7075**	**7575**	8650	11250
Power Folding Roof			**350**	**350**	450	450
TT QUATTRO AWD—V6—Equipment Schedule 2						
W.B. 95.6"; 3.2 Liter.						
Coupe 2D	WD28N	38110	**8375**	**8925**	10000	12950
Special Ed Coupe 2D	PD28N	44259	**9725**	**10350**	11750	15150
Roadster 2D	UD28N	44360	**8925**	**9525**	10900	14050
Special Ed Roadster	RD28N	47259	**10800**	**11500**	12750	16250
4-Cyl, HO, Turbo, 1.8 Liter			**(1100)**	**(1100)**	(1405)	(1405)

Body Type	VIN	List	Trade-In Good	Very Good	Pvt-Party Good	Retail Excellent
A3—4-Cyl. Turbo—Equipment Schedule 3						
W.B. 101.5"; 2.0 Liter.						
2.0T Wagon 4D	HF78P	27540	**5700**	**6175**	7150	9350
S-Line Pkg			**650**	**650**	865	865
A3 QUATTRO AWD—V6—Equipment Schedule 3						
W.B. 101.5"; 3.2 Liter.						
3.2 S-Line Wagon 4D	KD78P	34700	**10250**	**10950**	12050	15350
A4—4-Cyl. Turbo—Equipment Schedule 3						
W.B. 104.3"; 2.0 Liter.						
2.0T Sedan 4D	AF78E	30160	**5600**	**6025**	7050	9200
2.0T Coupe 2D	AF48H	39820	**5825**	**6250**	7300	9550
S-Line Pkg			**650**	**650**	865	865
A4 QUATTRO AWD—4-Cyl. Turbo—Equipment Schedule 3						
W.B. 104.3"; 2.0 Liter.						
2.0T Sedan 4D	DF783	32260	**6350**	**6800**	7850	10200
2.0T Cabriolet 2D	DF48H	41920	**6800**	**7275**	8375	10900
S-Line Pkg			**650**	**650**	865	865
A4—V6—Equipment Schedule 3						
W.B. 104.3"; 3.2 Liter.						
3.2 Sedan 4D	AH78E	38360	**7075**	**7575**	8825	11600
S-Line Pkg			**650**	**650**	865	865
A4 QUATTRO AWD—V6—Equipment Schedule 3						
W.B. 104.3"; 3.2 Liter.						
3.2 Sedan 4D	DH78E	38360	**7825**	**8350**	9600	12550
3.2 Cabriolet 2D	DH48H	47670	**7825**	**8350**	9475	12300
S-Line Pkg			**650**	**650**	865	865
A4 AVANT QUATTRO AWD—4-Cyl. Turbo—Equipment Sch 3						
W.B. 104.3"; 2.0 Liter.						
2.0T Wagon 4D	KF78E	33260	**7025**	**7550**	8400	10800
S-Line Pkg			**650**	**650**	865	865
A4 AVANT QUATTRO AWD—V6—Equipment Schedule 3						
W.B. 104.3"; 3.2 Liter.						
3.2 Wagon 4D	KH78E	39360	**8325**	**8925**	9725	12300
S-Line Pkg			**650**	**650**	845	845
RS 4 QUATTRO AWD—V8—Equipment Schedule 1						
W.B. 104.3"; 4.2 Liter.						
Sedan 4D	RU78E	68820	**19800**	**20800**	21300	25300
S4 QUATTRO AWD—V8—Equipment Schedule 1						
W.B. 104.3", 104.5" (Cab); 4.2 Liter.						
Sedan 4D	GL78E	50720	**11650**	**12300**	12800	15350
Cabriolet 2D	RU48H	58920	**13900**	**14650**	15050	17850
S4 AVANT QUATTRO AWD—V8—Equipment Schedule 1						
W.B. 104.3"; 4.2 Liter.						
Wagon 4D	UU78E	51720	**13300**	**14050**	14550	17350
A6—V6—Equipment Schedule 3						
W.B. 111.9"; 3.2 Liter.						
3.2 Sedan 4D	AH74F	42670	**6825**	**7300**	8200	10500
S-Line Pkg			**650**	**650**	800	800
A6 QUATTRO AWD—V6—Equipment Schedule 3						
W.B. 111.9"; 3.2 Liter.						
3.2 Sedan 4D	DH74F	45820	**8475**	**9025**	10150	13100
S-Line Pkg			**650**	**650**	815	815

Body Type	VIN	List	Trade-In Good	Very Good	Pvt-Party Good	Retail Excellent
A6 AVANT QUATTRO AWD—V6—Equipment Schedule 3						
W.B. 111.9"; 3.2 Liter.						
3.2 Wagon 4D	KH94F	48720	10500	11150	12250	15500
S-Line Pkg			650	650	790	790
A6 QUATTRO AWD—V8—Equipment Schedule 3						
W.B. 111.9"; 4.2 Liter.						
4.2 Sedan 4D	DV74F	56020	8900	9500	10750	13850
S-Line Pkg	B		650	650	810	810
S6 QUATTRO AWD—V10—Equipment Schedule 1						
W.B. 112.1"; 5.2 Liter.						
Sedan 4D	GN74F	72720	12350	13000	13800	16700
A8 QUATTRO AWD—V8—Equipment Schedule 1						
W.B. 115.9"; 121.0" (L); 4.2 Liter.						
Sedan 4D	LV44E	69620	10900	11500	12400	14850
L Sedan 4D	MV44E	73620	12350	13000	13900	16650
Premium Pkg			950	950	1090	1090
Sport Pkg			650	650	745	745
A8 QUATTRO AWD—W12—Equipment Schedule 1						
W.B. 121.0"; 6.0 Liter.						
L Sedan 4D	MR44E	121770	17350	18150	19600	23800
S8 QUATTRO AWD—V10—Equipment Schedule 1						
W.B. 115.9"; 5.2 Liter.						
Sedan 4D	PN44E	92720	19550	20400	21500	25500

2008 AUDI — (WAUorWUA)(HF78P)-8-#

Body Type	VIN	List	Trade-In Good	Very Good	Pvt-Party Good	Retail Excellent
A3—4-Cyl. Turbo—Equipment Schedule 3						
W.B. 101.5"; 2.0 Liter.						
2.0T Wagon 4D	HF78P	28185	7050	7525	8400	10550
S-Line Pkg			700	700	875	875
A3 QUATTRO AWD—V6—Equipment Schedule 3						
W.B. 101.5"; 3.2 Liter.						
3.2 S-Line Wagon 4D	KD78P	35690	11000	11700	12600	15500
A4—4-Cyl. Turbo—Equipment Schedule 3						
W.B. 104.3"; 2.0 Liter.						
2.0T Sedan 4D	AF78E	30975	7250	7725	8750	11100
2.0T Cabriolet 2D	AF48H	40525	7400	7875	8850	11150
S-Line Pkg	B		700	700	925	925
A4 QUATTRO AWD—4-Cyl. Turbo—Equipment Schedule 3						
W.B. 104.3"; 2.0 Liter.						
2.0T Sedan 4D	DF58E	33075	8200	8700	9800	12400
2.0T Cabriolet 2D	DF48H	42625	8650	9175	10200	12750
S-Line Pkg	B		700	700	920	920
A4 AVANT QUATTRO AWD—4-Cyl. Turbo—Equipment Schedule 3						
W.B. 104.3"; 2.0 Liter.						
2.0T Wagon 4D	KF78E	34075	9650	10250	11200	13900
Third Row Seat			200	200	250	250
S-Line Pkg	S		700	700	880	880
A4—V6—Equipment Schedule 3						
W.B. 104.3"; 3.2 Liter.						
3.2 Sedan 4D	AH78E	37075	8850	9375	10500	13300
S-Line Pkg	B		700	700	915	915
A4 QUATTRO AWD—V6—Equipment Schedule 3						
W.B. 104.3"; 3.2 Liter.						
3.2 Sedan 4D	DH58E	39175	9625	10200	11350	14300
S-Line Pkg	B		700	700	910	910
A4 QUATTRO AWD—V6—Equipment Schedule 3						
W.B. 104.3"; 3.2 Liter.						
3.2 Cabriolet 2D	DH48H	48675	9650	10200	11250	14050
S-Line Pkg	E		700	700	890	890
A4 AVANT QUATTRO AWD—V6—Equipment Schedule 3						
W.B. 104.3"; 3.2 Liter.						
3.2 Wagon 4D	KH78E	40175	10600	11250	12100	14900
Third Row Seat			200	200	250	250
S-Line Pkg	S		700	700	880	880
RS 4 QUATTRO AWD—V8—Equipment Schedule 1						
W.B. 104.3"; 4.2 Liter.						
Sedan 4D	RU78E	69785	21600	22600	23100	27100
Cabriolet 2D	YU78E	84775	23000	24100	24600	28800
S4 QUATTRO AWD—V8—Equipment Schedule 1						
W.B. 104.3", 104.5" (Cab); 4.2 Liter.						
Sedan 4D	GL78E	48675	14800	15500	16200	19100
Cabriolet 2D	RL48H	60050	16250	17000	17750	21000

0415

Body Type	VIN	List	Trade-In Good	Very Good	Pvt-Party Good	Retail Excellent
S4 AVANT QUATTRO AWD—V8—Equipment Schedule 1						
W.B. 104.3"; 4.2 Liter.						
Wagon 4D	UL78E	52785	17600	18400	19050	22400
Third Row Seat			400	400	440	440
A5 QUATTRO AWD—V6—Equipment Schedule 1						
W.B. 108.3"; 3.2 Liter.						
Coupe 2D	DH78T	41975	14800	15600	16250	19400
Bang & Olufsen Sound			325	325	395	395
S-Line Pkg	E		700	700	825	825
S5 QUATTRO AWD—V8—Equipment Schedule 1						
W.B. 108.3"; 4.2 Liter.						
Coupe 2D	RV78T	54325	18650	19600	20100	23800
Bang & Olufsen Sound			325	325	390	390
A6—V6—Equipment Schedule 3						
W.B. 111.9"; 3.2 Liter.						
3.2 Sedan 4D	AH74F	43725	8825	9350	10050	12300
S-Line Pkg	B		700	700	830	830
A6 QUATTRO AWD—V6—Equipment Schedule 3						
W.B. 111.9"; 3.2 Liter.						
3.2 Sedan 4D	DH74F	46875	10950	11600	12400	15200
S-Line Pkg	E,S		700	700	830	830
A6 QUATTRO AWD—V6—Equipment Schedule 3						
W.B. 111.9"; 3.2 Liter.						
3.2 Wagon 4D	KH94F	49775	12450	13150	13950	16950
Third Row Seat			200	200	235	235
S-Line Pkg	E,S		700	700	825	825
A6 QUATTRO AWD—V8—Equipment Schedule 3						
W.B. 111.9"; 4.2 Liter.						
4.2 Sedan 4D	DV74F	57075	11450	12100	13000	15950
S-Line Pkg	B		700	700	830	830
S6 QUATTRO AWD—V10—Equipment Schedule 1						
W.B. 112.1"; 5.2 Liter.						
Sedan 4D	DN74F	74425	15200	15950	16600	19550
Adaptive Cruise Control			375	375	425	425
A8 QUATTRO AWD—V8—Equipment Schedule 1						
W.B. 115.9"; 121.0" (L); 4.2 Liter.						
Sedan 4D	LV44E	71465	14700	15350	16050	18700
L Sedan 4D	MV44E	75465	16150	16900	17600	20500
Bang & Olufsen Sound			2250	2250	2510	2510
Adaptive Cruise Control			375	375	420	420
Premium Pkg			1050	1050	1175	1175
Sport Pkg			700	700	785	785
A8 QUATTRO AWD—W12—Equipment Schedule 1						
W.B. 121.0"; 6.0 Liter.						
L Sedan 4D	MR44E	122575	21100	22000	23300	27600
Bang & Olufsen Sound			2250	2250	2620	2620
Adaptive Cruise Control			375	375	440	440
R8 QUATTRO AWD—V8—Equipment Schedule 1						
W.B. 104.3"; 4.2 Liter.						
Coupe 2D	AV342	124200	****	****	****	87800
Bang & Olufsen Sound			****	****	****	340
S8 QUATTRO AWD—V10—Equipment Schedule 1						
W.B. 115.9"; 5.2 Liter.						
Sedan 4D	PN44E	96175	23300	24300	25100	29100
Adaptive Cruise Control			375	375	420	420
TT—4-Cyl. Turbo—Equipment Schedule 2						
W.B. 97.2"; 2.0 Liter.						
Coupe 2D	AF38J	35575	10000	10600	11400	14000
Roadster 2D	MF38J	37575	10900	11500	12350	15100
Power Folding Roof			400	400	485	485
S-Line Pkg			700	700	850	850
TT QUATTRO AWD—V6—Equipment Schedule 2						
W.B. 97.2"; 3.2 Liter.						
3.2 Coupe 2D	DD38J	43675	12850	13550	14550	17800
3.2 Roadster 2D	RD38J	46675	14750	15500	16500	20000
S-Line Pkg			700	700	845	845

2009 AUDI — (WAUorWUA)(HF78P)-9-#

Body Type	VIN	List	Trade-In Good	Very Good	Pvt-Party Good	Retail Excellent
A3—4-Cyl. Turbo—Equipment Schedule 3						
W.B. 101.5"; 2.0 Liter.						
2.0T Wagon 4D	HF78P	29225	9150	9675	10450	12600
Third Row Seat			225	225	270	270
Sport Pkg			250	250	300	300

Body Type	VIN	List	Trade-In Good	Very Good	Pvt-Party Good	Retail Excellent
S-Line Pkg			750	750	900	900
A3 QUATTRO AWD—4-Cyl. Turbo—Equipment Schedule 3						
W.B. 101.5"; 2.0 Liter.						
2.0T Wagon 4D	KF78P	31325	11500	12150	12950	15500
Third Row Seat			225	225	265	265
Sport Pkg			250	250	295	295
S-Line Pkg			750	750	880	880
A3 QUATTRO AWD—V6—Equipment Schedule 3						
W.B. 101.5"; 3.2 Liter.						
3.2 Wagon 4D	KD78P	37800	13050	13750	14650	17450
Third Row Seat			225	225	260	260
Sport Pkg			250	250	290	290
S-Line Pkg			750	750	875	875
A4—4-Cyl. Turbo—Equipment Schedule 3						
W.B. 104.3", 110.6" (Sed); 2.0 Liter.						
2.0T Sedan 4D	AF78E	31525	10150	10700	11700	14300
2.0T Cabriolet 2D	AF48H	41575	11100	11700	12550	15100
2.0T Special Ed Cab 2D	AF48H	41575	11750	12400	13250	15950
Adaptive Cruise Control			375	375	470	470
Premium Plus Pkg			725	725	910	910
Prestige Pkg			1525	1525	1915	1915
A4 QUATTRO AWD—4-Cyl. Turbo—Equipment Schedule 3						
W.B. 104.3", 110.6" (Sed); 2.0 Liter.						
2.0T Sedan 4D	LF78K	33525	11300	11900	12950	15800
2.0T Cabriolet 2D	DF48H	41575	12600	13250	14100	16950
2.0T Special Ed Cab	DF48H	43675	13050	13700	14700	17650
Adaptive Cruise Control			375	375	470	470
Premium Plus Pkg			725	725	905	905
Prestige Pkg			1525	1525	1900	1900
S-Line Pkg			750	750	940	940
A4 AVANT QUATTRO AWD—4-Cyl. Turbo—Equipment Schedule 3						
W.B. 110.6"; 2.0 Liter.						
2.0T Wagon 4D	VF78K	35325	12950	13600	14650	17650
Adaptive Cruise Control			375	375	450	450
Premium Plus Pkg			725	725	870	870
Prestige Pkg			1525	1525	1830	1830
S-Line Pkg		S	750	750	905	905
A4 QUATTRO AWD—V6—Equipment Schedule 3						
W.B. 104.3", 110.6" (Sed); 3.2 Liter.						
3.2 Sedan 4D	LK98K	40825	12900	13550	14600	17750
3.2 Cabriolet 2D	DH48H	49625	15000	15700	16700	19950
3.2 Special Ed Cab 2D	DH48H	49625	15650	16400	17400	20800
Adaptive Cruise Control			375	375	465	465
Prestige Pkg			1525	1525	1885	1885
S-Line Pkg			750	750	930	930
S4 QUATTRO AWD—V8—Equipment Schedule 1						
W.B. 104.5"; 4.2 Liter.						
Cabriolet 2D	RL48H	60450	21700	22600	23400	27300
A5 QUATTRO AWD—V6—Equipment Schedule 1						
W.B. 108.3"; 3.2 Liter.						
Coupe 2D	DK78T	42425	16800	17600	18400	21700
Bang & Olufsen Sound			350	350	400	400
Adaptive Cruise Control			375	375	440	440
S-Line Pkg			750	750	880	880
S5 QUATTRO AWD—V8—Equipment Schedule 1						
W.B. 108.3"; 4.2 Liter.						
Coupe 2D	RV78T	54825	21400	22300	22900	26700
Bang & Olufsen Sound			350	350	395	395
Adaptive Cruise Control			375	375	435	435
A6—V6—Equipment Schedule 3						
W.B. 111.9"; 3.2 Liter.						
3.2 Sedan 4D	AH74F	45925	13200	13900	14550	17100
Premium Plus Pkg			725	725	835	835
A6 QUATTRO AWD—V6 Supercharged—Equipment Schedule 3						
W.B. 111.9"; 3.0 Liter.						
3.0T Sedan 4D	DH74F	50925	15700	16450	17100	20100
Premium Plus Pkg			725	725	835	835
Sport Pkg			375	375	435	435
A6 AVANT QUATTRO AWD—V6 Supercharged—Equipment Schedule 3						
W.B. 111.9"; 3.0 Liter.						
3.0T Wagon 4D	KH94F	54135	17300	18150	18800	22000
Third Row Seat			225	225	260	260
Premium Plus Pkg			725	725	835	835

Body Type	VIN	List	Trade-In Good	Very Good	Pvt-Party Good	Retail Excellent
Sport Pkg			375	375	435	435
A6 QUATTRO AWD—V8—Equipment Schedule 3						
W.B. 111.9"; 4.2 Liter.						
4.2 Sedan 4D	DV74F	61775	17650	18500	19150	22500
Premium Plus Pkg			725	725	835	835
S6 QUATTRO AWD—V10—Equipment Schedule 1						
W.B. 112.1"; 5.2 Liter.						
Sedan 4D	DN74F	76675	21000	21900	22300	25600
A8 QUATTRO AWD—V8—Equipment Schedule 1						
W.B. 115.9", 121.0" (L); 4.2 Liter.						
Sedan 4D	LV44E	74875	22500	23400	23900	27200
L Sedan 4D	MV44E	78725	23900	24800	25400	28900
Bang & Olufsen Sound			2375	2375	2545	2545
Adaptive Cruise Control			375	375	405	405
Sport Pkg			750	750	805	805
A8 QUATTRO AWD—W12—Equipment Schedule 1						
W.B. 121.0"; 6.0 Liter.						
L Sedan 4D	MR44E	122625	28800	29900	30900	35500
Bang & Olufsen Sound			2375	2375	2620	2620
Adaptive Cruise Control			375	375	415	415
R8 QUATTRO AWD—V8—Equipment Schedule 1						
W.B. 104.3"; 4.2 Liter.						
Coupe 2D	AU342	124800	****	****	****	93100
Bang & Olufsen Sound			****	****	****	345
S8 QUATTRO AWD—V10—Equipment Schedule 1						
W.B. 115.9"; 5.2 Liter.						
Sedan 4D	PN44E	99125	31100	32200	32700	37200
Adaptive Cruise Control			2375	2375	2555	2555
Adaptive Cruise Control			375	375	405	405
TT—4-Cyl. Turbo—Equipment Schedule 2						
W.B. 97.2"; 2.0 Liter.						
Coupe 2D	AF38J	36025	12700	13350	14050	16750
Roadster 2D	MF38J	38025	13150	13850	14650	17450
Power Folding Roof			400	400	470	470
S-Line Pkg			750	750	880	880
TT QUATTRO AWD—4-Cyl. Turbo—Equipment Schedule 2						
W.B. 97.2"; 2.0 Liter.						
Coupe 2D	DF38J	38125	14400	15150	15850	18750
Roadster 2D	RF38J	40125	16900	17750	18650	22200
Power Folding Roof			400	400	470	470
S-Line Pkg			750	750	865	865
TT QUATTRO AWD—V6—Equipment Schedule 2						
W.B. 97.2"; 3.2 Liter.						
3.2 Coupe 2D	DD38J	44295	16600	17400	18300	21800
3.2 Roadster 2D	RD38J	47365	18200	19100	19900	23600
S-Line Pkg			750	750	885	885
TTS QUATTRO AWD—4-Cyl. Turbo—Equipment Schedule 2						
W.B. 97.2"; 2.0 Liter.						
Coupe 2D	UF38J	46325	18700	19600	20400	24200
Roadster 2D	WF38J	48325	21400	22400	23200	27500
Power Folding Roof			400	400	465	465

2010 AUDI — (TRUorWAUorWUA)(BFBFM)-A-#

Body Type	VIN	List	Trade-In Good	Very Good	Pvt-Party Good	Retail Excellent
A3—4-Cyl. Turbo—Equipment Schedule 3						
W.B. 101.5"; 2.0 Liter.						
2.0T Wagon 4D	BFBFM	29575	11050	11600	12450	14750
Third Row Seat			250	250	290	290
Premium Plus Pkg			775	775	885	885
Sport Pkg			275	275	315	315
A3 QUATTRO AWD—4-Cyl. Turbo—Equipment Schedule 3						
W.B. 101.5"; 2.0 Liter.						
2.0T Wagon 4D	DFBFM	31675	14800	15500	16350	19150
Third Row Seat			250	250	290	290
Premium Plus Pkg			775	775	885	885
Sport Pkg			275	275	320	320
A3—4-Cyl. Turbo Diesel—Equipment Schedule 3						
W.B. 101.5"; 2.0 Liter.						
2.0 TDI Wagon 4D	BJBFM	30775	14800	15500	16550	19500
Third Row Seat			250	250	290	290
Premium Plus Pkg			775	775	880	880
Sport Pkg			275	275	315	315
A4—4-Cyl. Turbo—Equipment Schedule 3						
W.B. 110.6"; 2.0 Liter.						

Body Type	VIN	List	Trade-In Good	Very Good	Pvt-Party Good	Retail Excellent
2.0T Sedan 4D	AFBFL	32275	12500	13100	14050	16750
Bang & Olufsen Sound			350	350	425	425
Premium Plus Pkg			775	775	935	935
A4 QUATTRO AWD—4-Cyl. Turbo—Equipment Schedule 3						
W.B. 110.6"; 2.0 Liter.						
2.0T Sedan 4D	BFBFL	34375	13800	14450	15500	18500
Bang & Olufsen Sound			350	350	425	425
S-Line Pkg	B		800	800	975	975
Premium Plus Pkg			775	775	935	935
Prestige Pkg			1600	1600	1950	1950
A4 AVANT QUATTRO AWD—4-Cyl. Turbo—Equipment Schedule 3						
W.B. 110.6"; 2.0 Liter.						
2.0T Wagon 4D	SFBFL	36175	16350	17050	18050	21200
Bang & Olufsen Sound			350	350	405	405
Third Row Seat			250	250	290	290
Adaptive Cruise Control			400	400	470	470
S-Line Pkg			800	800	935	935
Premium Plus Pkg			775	775	895	895
Prestige Pkg			1600	1600	1875	1875
S4 QUATTRO AWD—V6 Supercharged—Equipment Schedule 1						
W.B. 110.7"; 3.0 Liter.						
Sedan 4D	BGBFL	48125	22400	23300	24200	27900
Bang & Olufsen Sound			350	350	380	380
Adaptive Cruise Control			400	400	435	435
Prestige Pkg			1600	1600	1750	1750
A5—4-Cyl. Turbo—Equipment Schedule 1						
W.B. 108.3"; 2.0 Liter.						
2.0T Cabriolet 2D	AFAFH	42825	19450	20300	21100	24500
Bang & Olufsen Sound			350	350	400	400
A5 QUATTRO AWD—4-Cyl. Turbo—Equipment Schedule 1						
W.B. 108.3"; 2.0 Liter.						
2.0T Coupe 2D	CFAFR	38025	18450	19250	20000	23300
2.0T Cabriolet 2D	CFAFH	44925	20600	21500	22300	25800
Bang & Olufsen Sound			350	350	405	405
Adaptive Cruise Control			400	400	465	465
Premium Plus Pkg			775	775	885	885
Prestige Pkg			1600	1600	1855	1855
S-Line Pkg			800	800	925	925
A5 QUATTRO AWD—V6—Equipment Schedule 1						
W.B. 108.3"; 3.2 Liter.						
Coupe 2D	LKAFR	44825	20700	21600	22400	26000
Bang & Olufsen Sound			350	350	400	400
Adaptive Cruise Control			400	400	460	460
Premium Plus Pkg			775	775	885	885
Prestige Pkg			1600	1600	1850	1850
S-Line Pkg			800	800	925	925
S5 QUATTRO AWD—V6 Turbo—Equipment Schedule 1						
W.B. 108.3"; 3.0 Liter.						
3.0T Cabriolet 2D	CGAFH	59075	25500	26600	27100	31200
Bang & Olufsen Sound			350	350	395	395
Adaptive Cruise Control			400	400	455	455
Prestige Pkg			1600	1600	1830	1830
S5 QUATTRO AWD—V8—Equipment Schedule 1						
W.B. 108.3"; 4.2 Liter.						
Coupe 2D	CVAFR	54425	25200	26300	26800	30800
Bang & Olufsen Sound			350	350	395	395
Adaptive Cruise Control			400	400	455	455
Prestige Pkg			1600	1600	1825	1825
A6—V6—Equipment Schedule 3						
W.B. 111.9"; 3.2 Liter.						
3.2 Sedan 4D	AKBFB	46025	14400	15100	16050	18850
Premium Plus Pkg			775	775	910	910
Sport Pkg			400	400	475	475
A6 QUATTRO AWD—V6 Supercharged—Equipment Schedule 3						
W.B. 111.9"; 3.0 Liter.						
3.0T Sedan 4D	AGBFB	51025	16950	17750	18750	22100
Premium Plus Pkg			775	775	910	910
Prestige Pkg			1600	1600	1900	1900
A6 AVANT QUATTRO AWD—V6 Supercharged—Equipment Schedule 3						
W.B. 111.9"; 3.0 Liter.						
3.0T Wagon 4D	SGBFB	54135	18700	19550	20500	24000
Third Row Seat			250	250	295	295
Premium Plus Pkg			775	775	905	905

Body Type	VIN	List	Trade-In Good	Very Good	Pvt-Party Good	Retail Excellent
Prestige Pkg			1600	1600	1890	1890
A6 QUATTRO AWD—V8—Equipment Schedule 3						
W.B. 111.9"; 4.2 Liter.						
4.2 Sedan 4D	BVBFB	61775	18750	19600	20600	24200
Sport Pkg			400	400	475	475
S6 QUATTRO AWD—V10—Equipment Schedule 1						
W.B. 112.1"; 5.2 Liter.						
Sedan 4D	BNBFB	78225	28500	29600	29900	33600
A8 QUATTRO AWD—V8—Equipment Schedule 1						
W.B. 115.9", 121.0" (L); 4.2 Liter.						
Sedan 4D	BVAFA	75375	24000	24900	26100	29900
L Sedan 4D	SVAFA	79225	25500	26500	27600	31600
Bang & Olufsen Sound			2500	2500	2655	2655
Adaptive Cruise Control			400	400	425	425
Sport Pkg			800	800	850	850
R8 QUATTRO AWD—V8—Equipment Schedule 1						
W.B. 104.3"; 4.2 Liter.						
4.2 Coupe 2D	AUAFG	126600	****	****	****	103800
Bang & Olufsen Sound			****	****	****	360
R8 QUATTRO AWD—V10—Equipment Schedule 1						
W.B. 104.3"; 5.2 Liter.						
5.2 Coupe 2D	ANAFG	158400	****	****	****	133800
TT QUATTRO AWD—4-Cyl.—Equipment Schedule 2						
W.B. 97.2"; 2.0 Liter.						
Coupe 2D	AFAFK	38625	17600	18400	18900	21800
Roadster 2D	SFAFK	41625	18750	19600	20200	23400
S-Line Pkg			800	800	905	905
Prestige Pkg			1600	1600	1810	1810
TTS QUATTRO AWD—4-Cyl. Turbo—Equipment Schedule 3						
W.B. 97.2"; 2.0 Liter.						
Coupe 2D	B1AFK	46725	21200	22200	22700	26400
Roadster 2D	S1AFK	49725	23500	24500	25200	29300
Prestige Pkg			1600	1600	1820	1820

2011 AUDI — (TRUorWAUorWUA)(BFBFM)-B-#

Body Type	VIN	List	Trade-In Good	Very Good	Pvt-Party Good	Retail Excellent
A3—4-Cyl. Turbo—Equipment Schedule 3						
W.B. 101.5"; 2.0 Liter.						
2.0T Wagon 4D	BFBFM	29625	12800	13350	14550	17200
Premium Plus Pkg			800	800	955	955
Sport Pkg			300	300	355	355
A3 QUATTRO AWD—4-Cyl. Turbo—Equipment Schedule 3						
W.B. 101.5"; 2.0 Liter.						
2.0T Wagon 4D	DFBFM	31725	16650	17300	18600	21900
Premium Plus Pkg			800	800	955	955
Sport Pkg			300	300	355	355
A3—4-Cyl. Turbo Diesel—Equipment Schedule 3						
W.B. 101.5"; 2.0 Liter.						
2.0 TDI Wagon 4D	BJBFM	31125	16650	17350	18550	21800
Premium Plus Pkg			800	800	955	955
Sport Pkg			300	300	355	355
A4—4-Cyl. Turbo—Equipment Schedule 3						
W.B. 110.6"; 2.0 Liter.						
2.0T Sedan 4D	AFBFL	32825	14900	15600	16550	19400
Bang & Olufsen Sound			350	350	425	425
Premium Plus Pkg			800	800	970	970
A4 QUATTRO AWD—4-Cyl. Turbo—Equipment Schedule 3						
W.B. 110.6"; 2.0 Liter.						
2.0T Sedan 4D	BFBFL	35015	16350	17100	18050	21200
Bang & Olufsen Sound			350	350	425	425
Adaptive Cruise Control			425	425	505	505
S-Line Pkg			800	800	955	955
Premium Plus Pkg			800	800	970	970
Prestige Pkg			1675	1675	2005	2005
A4 AVANT QUATTRO AWD—4-Cyl. Turbo—Equipment Schedule 3						
W.B. 110.6"; 2.0 Liter.						
2.0T Wagon 4D	SFBFL	36815	18400	19100	20100	23200
Bang & Olufsen Sound			350	350	410	410
Adaptive Cruise Control			425	425	490	490
S-Line Pkg			800	800	925	925
Premium Plus Pkg			800	800	940	940
Prestige Pkg			1675	1675	1945	1945
S4 QUATTRO AWD—V6 Supercharged—Equipment Schedule 1						
W.B. 110.7"; 3.0 Liter.						

Body Type	VIN	List	Trade-In Good	Very Good	Pvt-Party Good	Retail Excellent
Sedan 4D	BGBFL	48875	24700	25600	26700	30500
Bang & Olufsen Sound			350	350	385	385
Adaptive Cruise Control			425	425	460	460
Prestige Pkg			1675	1675	1820	1820

A5—4-Cyl. Turbo—Equipment Schedule 1
W.B. 108.3"; 2.0 Liter.

Body Type	VIN	List	Good	Very Good	Good	Excellent
2.0T Premium Cab 2D	AFAFH	42875	21600	22500	23300	26700
Bang & Olufsen Sound			350	350	405	405
Adaptive Cruise Control			425	425	490	490
Premium Plus Pkg			800	800	930	930
Prestige Pkg			1675	1675	1930	1930
S-Line Pkg			800	800	920	920

A5 QUATTRO AWD—4-Cyl. Turbo—Equipment Schedule 1
W.B. 108.3"; 2.0 Liter.

Body Type	VIN	List	Good	Very Good	Good	Excellent
2.0T Premium Coupe	CFAFR	38665	20700	21500	22200	25500
2.0T Premium Cab 2D	CFAFH	45065	22900	23800	24600	28200
Bang & Olufsen Sound			350	350	410	410
Adaptive Cruise Control			425	425	490	490
S-Line Pkg			800	800	920	920
Premium Plus Pkg			800	800	935	935
Prestige Pkg			1675	1675	1935	1935

S5 QUATTRO AWD—V6 Supercharged—Equipment Schedule 1
W.B. 108.3"; 3.0 Liter.

Body Type	VIN	List	Good	Very Good	Good	Excellent
3.0T Convertible 2D	CGAFH	59325	28400	29600	30200	34300
Bang & Olufsen Sound			350	350	400	400
Adaptive Cruise Control			425	425	480	480
Prestige Pkg			1675	1675	1895	1895

S5 QUATTRO AWD—V8—Equipment Schedule 1
W.B. 108.3"; 4.2 Liter.

Body Type	VIN	List	Good	Very Good	Good	Excellent
Coupe 2D	CVAFR	55175	27900	29000	29600	33500
Bang & Olufsen Sound			350	350	400	400
Adaptive Cruise Control			425	425	480	480
Prestige Pkg			1675	1675	1890	1890

A6—V6—Equipment Schedule 3
W.B. 111.9"; 3.2 Liter.

Body Type	VIN	List	Good	Very Good	Good	Excellent
3.2 Sedan 4D	AKBFB	46075	19400	20200	21000	24200
Sport Pkg			400	400	470	470
Premium Plus Pkg			800	800	955	955

A6 QUATTRO AWD—V6 Supercharged—Equipment Schedule 3
W.B. 111.9"; 3.0 Liter.

Body Type	VIN	List	Good	Very Good	Good	Excellent
3.0T Sedan 4D	BGBFB	51075	22000	22900	23700	27300
Sport Pkg			400	400	470	470
Premium Plus Pkg			800	800	950	950
Prestige Pkg			1675	1675	1970	1970

A6 AVANT QUATTRO AWD—V6 Supercharged—Equipment Schedule 3
W.B. 111.9"; 3.0 Liter.

Body Type	VIN	List	Good	Very Good	Good	Excellent
3.0T Wagon 4D	SGBFB	54185	23600	24600	25500	29400
Sport Pkg			400	400	470	470
Premium Plus Pkg			800	800	950	950
Prestige Pkg			1675	1675	1970	1970

A6 QUATTRO AWD—V8—Equipment Schedule 3
W.B. 111.9"; 4.2 Liter.

Body Type	VIN	List	Good	Very Good	Good	Excellent
4.2 Sedan 4D	BVBFB	60025	23500	24400	25300	29200
Sport Pkg			400	400	470	470

A8 QUATTRO AWD—V8—Equipment Schedule 1
W.B. 115.9", 121.0" (L); 4.2 Liter.

Body Type	VIN	List	Good	Very Good	Good	Excellent
4.2 Sedan 4D	AVAFD	78925	29100	30100	31100	35100
L 4.2 Sedan 4D	RVAFD	84875	30900	31900	32900	37100
Bang & Olufsen Sound			2625	2625	2885	2885
Adaptive Cruise Control			425	425	470	470
Sport Pkg			800	800	880	880
Premium Pkg			1450	1450	1595	1595

R8 QUATTRO AWD—V8—Equipment Schedule 1
W.B. 104.3"; 4.2 Liter.

Body Type	VIN	List	Good	Very Good	Good	Excellent
4.2 Coupe 2D	AUAFG	126250	****	****	****	112800
4.2 Convertible 2D	VUAFG	139750	****	****	****	120400
Bang & Olufsen Sound			****	****	****	360

R8 QUATTRO AWD—V10—Equipment Schedule 1
W.B. 104.3"; 5.2 Liter.

Body Type	VIN	List	Good	Very Good	Good	Excellent
5.2 Coupe 2D	ANAFG	159950	****	****	****	141900
5.2 Convertible 2D	VNAFG	173450	****	****	****	150700

TT QUATTRO AWD—4-Cyl. Turbo—Equipment Schedule 2
W.B. 97.2"; 2.0 Liter.

Body Type	VIN	List	Trade-In Good	Very Good	Pvt-Party Good	Retail Excellent
Coupe 2D	BFAFK	39175	**21800**	**22700**	**23000**	**26200**
Roadster 2D	SFAFK	42175	**23000**	**24000**	**24300**	**27700**
S-Line Pkg		......	**800**	**800**	**885**	**885**
Prestige Pkg		......	**1675**	**1675**	**1860**	**1860**
TTS QUATTRO AWD—4-Cyl. Turbo—Equipment Schedule 3						
W.B. 97.2"; 2.0 Liter.						
Coupe 2D	F1AFK	47875	**25800**	**26900**	**27200**	**31100**
Roadster 2D	W1AFK	50875	**27800**	**28900**	**29200**	**33200**
Prestige Pkg		......	**1675**	**1675**	**1860**	**1860**

2012 AUDI — (TRUorWAUorWUA)(BFAFM)—C—#

Body Type	VIN	List	Trade-In Good	Very Good	Pvt-Party Good	Retail Excellent
A3—4-Cyl. Turbo—Equipment Schedule 3						
W.B. 101.5"; 2.0 Liter.						
2.0T Premium Wagon	BFAFM	29625	**14300**	**14900**	**16200**	**19100**
Sport Pkg		......	**300**	**300**	**350**	**350**
Premium Plus Pkg		......	**850**	**850**	**990**	**990**
A3 QUATTRO AWD—4-Cyl. Turbo—Equipment Schedule 3						
W.B. 101.5"; 2.0 Liter.						
2.0T Premium Wagon	DFAFM	31725	**19250**	**19950**	**21200**	**24700**
Sport Pkg		......	**300**	**300**	**360**	**360**
Premium Plus Pkg		......	**850**	**850**	**1030**	**1030**
A3—4-Cyl. Turbo Diesel—Equipment Schedule 3						
W.B. 101.5"; 2.0 Liter.						
2.0 TDI Premium Wag	BJAFM	31125	**17800**	**18500**	**19750**	**23000**
Sport Pkg		......	**300**	**300**	**360**	**360**
Premium Plus Pkg		......	**850**	**850**	**1025**	**1025**
A4—4-Cyl. Turbo—Equipment Schedule 3						
W.B. 110.6"; 2.0 Liter.						
2.0T Sedan 4D	AFAFL	33375	**17550**	**18350**	**19200**	**22200**
Bang & Olufsen Sound		......	**350**	**350**	**420**	**420**
S-Line Plus Pkg		......	**800**	**800**	**935**	**935**
Premium Plus Pkg		......	**850**	**850**	**1000**	**1000**
Prestige Pkg		......	**1750**	**1750**	**2055**	**2055**
A4 QUATTRO AWD—4-Cyl. Turbo—Equipment Schedule 3						
W.B. 110.6"; 2.0 Liter.						
2.0T Sedan 4D	BFAFL	35475	**19600**	**20400**	**21300**	**24600**
Bang & Olufsen Sound		......	**350**	**350**	**410**	**410**
Adaptive Cruise Control		......	**450**	**450**	**510**	**510**
S-Line Plus Pkg		......	**800**	**800**	**935**	**935**
Premium Plus Pkg		......	**850**	**850**	**1000**	**1000**
Prestige Pkg		......	**1750**	**1750**	**2060**	**2060**
A4 AVANT QUATTRO AWD—4-Cyl. Turbo—Equipment Schedule 3						
W.B. 110.6"; 2.0 Liter.						
2.0T Premium Wagon	SFAFL	37275	**22000**	**22800**	**23600**	**26900**
Bang & Olufsen Sound		......	**350**	**350**	**410**	**410**
Adaptive Cruise Control		......	**450**	**450**	**510**	**510**
S-Line Plus Pkg		......	**800**	**800**	**910**	**910**
Premium Plus Pkg		......	**850**	**850**	**975**	**975**
Prestige Pkg		......	**1750**	**1750**	**2005**	**2005**
S4 QUATTRO AWD—V6 Supercharged—Equipment Schedule 1						
W.B. 110.7"; 3.0 Liter.						
Premium Plus Sedan	BGAFL	49575	**28500**	**29500**	**30500**	**34400**
Bang & Olufsen Sound		......	**350**	**350**	**385**	**385**
Adaptive Cruise Control		......	**450**	**450**	**480**	**480**
Prestige Pkg		......	**1750**	**1750**	**1890**	**1890**
A5—4-Cyl. Turbo—Equipment Schedule 1						
W.B. 108.3"; 2.0 Liter.						
2.0T Premium Cab 2D	AFAFH	43475	**24600**	**25400**	**26300**	**29900**
Bang & Olufsen Sound		......	**350**	**350**	**410**	**410**
Adaptive Cruise Control		......	**450**	**450**	**510**	**510**
S-Line Pkg		......	**800**	**800**	**910**	**910**
Premium Plus Pkg		......	**850**	**850**	**970**	**970**
Prestige Pkg		......	**1750**	**1750**	**1995**	**1995**
A5 QUATTRO AWD—4-Cyl. Turbo—Equipment Schedule 1						
W.B. 108.3"; 2.0 Liter.						
2.0T Premium Coupe	CFAFR	39175	**22500**	**23300**	**24100**	**27400**
2.0T Premium Cab 2D	CFAFH	45575	**25900**	**26800**	**27600**	**31300**
Bang & Olufsen Sound		......	**350**	**350**	**410**	**410**
Adaptive Cruise Control		......	**450**	**450**	**510**	**510**
S-Line Pkg		......	**800**	**800**	**910**	**910**
Premium Plus Pkg		......	**850**	**850**	**975**	**975**
Prestige Pkg		......	**1750**	**1750**	**2005**	**2005**

Body Type	VIN	List	Trade-In Good	Very Good	Pvt-Party Good	Retail Excellent
S5 QUATTRO AWD—V6 Supercharged—Equipment Schedule 1						
W.B. 108.3"; 3.0 Liter.						
3.0T Convertible 2D	CGAFH	60175	**33400**	**34600**	**35000**	**39300**
Bang & Olufsen Sound		......	350	350	400	400
Adaptive Cruise Control			450	450	500	500
Prestige Pkg			1750	1750	1955	1955
S5 QUATTRO AWD—V8—Equipment Schedule 1						
W.B. 108.3"; 4.2 Liter.						
Coupe 2D	CVAFH	55975	**32400**	**33600**	**34000**	**38100**
Bang & Olufsen Sound		......	350	350	400	400
Adaptive Cruise Control			450	450	500	500
Prestige Pkg			1750	1750	1955	1955
A6—4-Cyl. Turbo—Equipment Schedule 3						
W.B. 114.7"; 2.0 Liter.						
2.0T Premium Sedan	AFAFC	42575	**25100**	**26100**	**26700**	**30200**
Premium Plus Pkg		......	850	850	940	940
Sport Pkg			400	400	440	440
A6 QUATTRO AWD—V6 Supercharged—Equipment Schedule 3						
W.B. 114.7"; 3.0 Liter.						
3.0T Premium Sedan	BGAFC	50775	**28000**	**29000**	**29600**	**33300**
Bang & Olufsen Sound		......	2750	2750	3000	3000
Adaptive Cruise Control			450	450	490	490
Innovation Pkg			1225	1225	1335	1335
Premium Plus Pkg			850	850	935	935
Prestige Pkg			1750	1750	1920	1920
Sport Pkg			400	400	435	435
A7 QUATTRO AWD—6-Cyl. Supercharged—Equipment Schedule 1						
W.B. 114.7"; 3.0 Liter.						
Premium Sedan 4D	SGAFC	60125	**37800**	**39200**	**39400**	**44100**
Bang & Olufsen Sound		......	2750	2750	3000	3000
Adaptive Cruise Control			450	450	490	490
Innovation Pkg			1225	1225	1335	1335
Premium Plus Pkg			875	875	960	960
Prestige Pkg			1750	1750	1920	1920
A8 QUATTRO AWD—V8—Equipment Schedule 1						
W.B. 117.8"; 122.9" (L); 4.2 Liter.						
4.2 Sedan 4D	AVAFD	79625	**36300**	**37500**	**38100**	**42300**
L 4.2 Sedan 4D	RVAFD	85575	**38600**	**39800**	**40400**	**44800**
Bang & Olufsen Sound		......	2750	2750	3010	3010
Adaptive Cruise Control			450	450	490	490
Premium Pkg			1450	1450	1585	1585
A8 QUATTRO AWD—W12—Equipment Schedule 1						
W.B. 112.9"; 6.3 Liter.						
L Sedan 4D	R4AFD	136975	**75100**	**77400**	**76600**	**83700**
Bang & Olufsen Sound		......	2750	2750	2925	2925
Adaptive Cruise Control			450	450	480	480
Premium Pkg			1450	1450	1545	1545
R8 AWD—V8—Equipment Schedule 1						
W.B. 104.3"; 4.2 Liter.						
4.2 Coupe 2D	AUAFG	126250	********	********	********	**116000**
4.2 Spyder 2D	SUAFG	139750	********	********	********	**123500**
Bang & Olufsen Sound			********	********	********	**370**
Ceramic Brakes			********	********	********	**3980**
R8 AWD—V10—Equipment Schedule 1						
W.B. 104.3"; 5.2 Liter.						
5.2 Coupe 2D	ENAFG	161450	********	********	********	**144900**
5.2 Spyder 2D	VNAFG	175150	********	********	********	**153600**
GT Coupe 2D	9NAFG	200150	********	********	********	**189600**
GT Spyder Conv 2D	8NAFG	213650	********	********	********	**204200**
Ceramic Brakes			********	********	********	**3980**

2013 AUDI — (TRUorWAUorWUA)(BEAFM)-D-#

Body Type	VIN	List	Trade-In Good	Very Good	Pvt-Party Good	Retail Excellent
A3—4-Cyl. Turbo—Equipment Schedule 3						
W.B. 101.5"; 2.0 Liter.						
2.0T Premium Wagon	BEAFM	29645	**14500**	**15050**	**16450**	**19300**
2.0T Premium Plus	KEAFM	31645	**19400**	**20100**	**21400**	**24700**
Sport Pkg		......	300	300	350	350
AWD	D		1300	1300	1510	1510
A3—4-Cyl. Turbo Diesel—Equipment Schedule 3						
W.B. 101.5"; 2.0 Liter.						
2.0 TDI Premium Wag	BJAFM	31145	**19350**	**20000**	**21300**	**24600**
2.0 TDI Premium Plus	KJAFM	33145	**21200**	**21900**	**23200**	**26700**
Sport Pkg		......	300	300	345	345

Body Type	VIN	List	Trade-In Good	Trade-In Very Good	Pvt-Party Good	Retail Excellent
allroad QUATTRO AWD—4-Cyl. Turbo—Equipment Schedule 1						
W.B. 110.4"; 2.0 Liter.						
Premium Wagon 4D	9FAFL	40495	**25900**	**26900**	**27300**	**30400**
Premium Plus Wagon	UFAFL	43795	**28800**	**29800**	**30300**	**33700**
Prestige Wagon 4D	VFAFL	49695	**30000**	**31100**	**31500**	**35100**
Bang & Olufsen Sound			**375**	**375**	**405**	**405**
A4 QUATTRO AWD—4-Cyl. Turbo—Equipment Schedule 3						
W.B. 110.6"; 2.0 Liter.						
Premium Sedan 4D	BFAFL	35495	**21400**	**22300**	**23000**	**26300**
Premium Plus Sedan	FFAFL	39659	**23700**	**24600**	**25300**	**28900**
Prestige Sedan 4D	KFAFL	45245	**26600**	**27700**	**28300**	**32300**
Bang & Olufsen Sound			**375**	**375**	**420**	**420**
Adaptive Cruise Control			**475**	**475**	**540**	**540**
S-Line Pkg			**800**	**800**	**915**	**915**
FWD	A		**(1350)**	**(1350)**	**(1560)**	**(1560)**
S4 QUATTRO AWD—V6 Supercharged—Equipment Schedule 1						
W.B. 110.7"; 3.0 Liter.						
Premium Plus Sedan	BGAFL	49895	**33100**	**34100**	**34900**	**38900**
Prestige Sedan 4D	KGAFL	56145	**35900**	**37100**	**37700**	**41800**
Bang & Olufsen Sound			**375**	**375**	**400**	**400**
Adaptive Cruise Control			**475**	**475**	**515**	**515**
A5 QUATTRO AWD—4-Cyl. Turbo—Equipment Schedule 1						
W.B. 108.3"; 2.0 Liter.						
2.0T Premium Cab 2D	CFAFH	46345	**29600**	**30600**	**31400**	**35400**
2.0T Premium + Cab	LFAFH	49895	**31800**	**32800**	**33500**	**37600**
2.0T Prestige Cab 2D	VFAFH	55795	**34500**	**35600**	**36200**	**40500**
Bang & Olufsen Sound			**375**	**375**	**410**	**410**
Adaptive Cruise Control			**475**	**475**	**530**	**530**
S-Line Pkg			**800**	**800**	**895**	**895**
FWD			**(1350)**	**(1350)**	**(1530)**	**(1530)**
A5 QUATTRO AWD—4-Cyl. Turbo—Equipment Schedule 1						
W.B. 108.3"; 2.0 Liter.						
2.0T Premium Cpe 2D	CFAFR	39945	**25400**	**26200**	**27000**	**30500**
2.0T Premium Plus 2D	LFAFR	43495	**28100**	**29100**	**29800**	**33600**
2.0T Prestige Cpe 2D	VFAFR	49395	**30500**	**31500**	**32200**	**36200**
Bang & Olufsen Sound			**375**	**375**	**415**	**415**
Adaptive Cruise Control			**475**	**475**	**530**	**530**
S-Line Pkg			**800**	**800**	**895**	**895**
S5 QUATTRO AWD—V6 Supercharged—Equipment Schedule 1						
W.B. 108.3"; 3.0 Liter.						
Premium Plus Cpe 2D	CGAFR	53195	**37600**	**38900**	**39800**	**43100**
Prestige Coupe 2D	VGAFR	59845	**39200**	**40500**	**40600**	**45000**
Premium Plus Conv	CGAFH	60195	**40200**	**41600**	**41600**	**46100**
Prestige Convertible	VGAFH	66845	**43300**	**44800**	**44700**	**49500**
Bang & Olufsen Sound			**375**	**375**	**400**	**400**
Adaptive Cruise Control			**475**	**475**	**520**	**520**
RS 5 QUATTRO AWD—V8—Equipment Schedule 1						
W.B. 108.3"; 4.2 Liter.						
Coupe 2D	C6AFR	69795	**50800**	**52500**	**52500**	**58100**
Convertible 2D	C6AFH	78795	**53800**	**55600**	**55700**	**61700**
Adaptive Cruise Control			**475**	**475**	**520**	**520**
A6 QUATTRO AWD—4-Cyl. Turbo—Equipment Schedule 3						
W.B. 114.7"; 2.0 Liter.						
2.0T Premium Sedan	BFAFC	45295	**27200**	**28200**	**29400**	**33600**
2.0T Premium Plus	GFAFC	49595	**28900**	**29900**	**31200**	**35700**
Premium Plus Pkg			**900**	**900**	**995**	**995**
FWD			**(1350)**	**(1350)**	**(1500)**	**(1500)**
A6 QUATTRO AWD—V6 Supercharged—Equipment Schedule 3						
W.B. 114.7"; 3.0 Liter.						
3.0T Premium Sed 4D	BGAFC	51295	**30000**	**31100**	**32300**	**36800**
3.0T Premium Plus	GGAFC	55595	**33200**	**34300**	**35500**	**40400**
3.0T Prestige Sed 4D	HGAFC	57845	**36300**	**37600**	**38700**	**44100**
Bang & Olufsen Sound			**2875**	**2875**	**3160**	**3160**
Adaptive Cruise Control			**475**	**475**	**520**	**520**
Innovation Pkg			**1250**	**1250**	**1375**	**1375**
Premium Plus Pkg			**900**	**900**	**990**	**990**
S6 QUATTRO AWD—V8 Twin Turbo—Equipment Schedule 1						
W.B. 114.7"; 4.0 Liter.						
Prestige Sedan 4D	B2AFC	74095	**41700**	**42900**	**43400**	**48000**
Bang & Olufsen Sound			**2875**	**2875**	**3105**	**3105**
Adaptive Cruise Control			**475**	**475**	**515**	**515**
Innovation Pkg			**1250**	**1250**	**1350**	**1350**

2013 AUDI

Body Type	VIN	List	Trade-In Good	Very Good	Pvt-Party Good	Retail Excellent
A7 QUATTRO AWD—V6 Supercharged—Equipment Schedule 1						
W.B. 114.7"; 3.0 Liter.						
Premium Sedan 4D	SGAFC	60995	39000	40400	41500	47100
Premium Plus Sedan	YGAFC	64695	39000	40300	41600	47300
Prestige Sedan 4D	2GAFC	67045	43100	44500	45600	51700
Bang & Olufsen Sound			2875	2875	3105	3105
Adaptive Cruise Control			475	475	515	515
S7 QUATTRO AWD—V8 Twin Turbo—Equipment Schedule 1						
W.B. 114.7"; 4.0 Liter.						
Prestige Sedan 4D	S23FC	79695	55400	57100	56400	61100
Bang & Olufsen Sound			2875	2875	2940	2940
Adaptive Cruise Control			475	475	485	485
Innovation Pkg			1250	1250	1280	1280
A8 QUATTRO AWD—V6 Supercharged—Equipment Schedule 1						
W.B. 117.8", 122.9" (L); 3.0 Liter.						
3.0T Sedan 4D	AGAFD	73095	39200	40400	40800	44900
3.0T L Sedan 4D	RGAFD	79395	42000	43300	43700	48200
Bang & Olufsen Sound			2875	2875	3080	3080
Adaptive Cruise Control			475	475	510	510
A8 QUATTRO AWD—V8 Turbo—Equipment Schedule 1						
W.B. 117.8", 122.9" (L); 4.0 Liter.						
4.0T Sedan 4D	A2AFD	81795	43800	45200	45400	49900
4.0T L Sedan 4D	R2AFD	88095	45300	46600	46900	51500
Bang & Olufsen Sound			2875	2875	3110	3110
Adaptive Cruise Control			475	475	515	515
A8 QUATTRO AWD—W12—Equipment Schedule 1						
W.B. 122.9"; 6.3 Liter.						
L Sedan 4D	R4AFD	137495	84300	86700	85400	92800
Bang & Olufsen Sound			2875	2875	3040	3040
Adaptive Cruise Control			475	475	515	515
S8 QUATTRO AWD—V8 Twin Turbo—Equipment Schedule 1						
W.B. 117.8"; 4.0 Liter.						
Sedan 4D		110895	63500	65300	65000	70800
Bang & Olufsen Sound			2875	2875	3100	3100
Adaptive Cruise Control			475	475	510	510
TT QUATTRO AWD—4-Cyl. Turbo—Equipment Schedule 2						
W.B. 97.2"; 2.0 Liter.						
Premium Plus Coupe	BFAFK	39545	27000	28000	28400	32100
Prestige Coupe 2D	KFAFK	45645	28900	30000	30600	34700
PremiumPlus Rdstr	SFAFK	42545	27700	28800	29300	33100
Prestige Roadster 2D	4FFAFK	48645	31100	32300	32800	37200
S-Line Pkg			800	800	880	880
TT RS QUATTRO AWD—5-Cyl. Turbo—Equipment Schedule 2						
W.B. 97.2"; 2.5 Liter.						
Coupe 2D	B3AFK	58095	41200	42700	43200	48900
TTS QUATTRO AWD—4-Cyl. Turbo—Equipment Schedule 3						
W.B. 97.2"; 2.0 Liter.						
Premium Plus Cpe 2D	B1AFK	48245	30600	31700	32300	36700
Prestige Coupe 2D	K1AFK	51545	33100	34400	35000	39900
PremiumPlus Rdstr	S1AFK	51245	32100	33400	33900	38500
Prestige Roadster 2D	41AFK	54545	35700	37000	37600	42800

2014 AUDI — (TRUorWAUorWUA)(9FBFL)-E-#

Body Type	VIN	List	Good	Very Good	Good	Excellent
allroad QUATTRO AWD—4-Cyl. Turbo—Equipment Schedule 1						
W.B. 110.4"; 2.0 Liter.						
Premium Wagon 4D	9FBFL	41595	27400	28400	28800	32100
Premium Plus Wag	UFBFL	44195	31000	32100	32500	36100
Prestige Wagon 4D	VFBFL	50095	34200	35400	35600	39500
Bang & Olufsen Sound			375	375	410	410
Sensing Cruise Control			500	500	545	545
A4 QUATTRO AWD—4-Cyl. Turbo—Equipment Schedule 1						
W.B. 110.6"; 2.0 Liter.						
Premium Sedan 4D	BFBFL	36795	24600	25500	25900	29200
FWD	A		(1425)	(1425)	(1595)	(1595)
A4 QUATTRO AWD—4-Cyl. Turbo—Equipment Schedule 3						
W.B. 110.6"; 2.0 Liter.						
Premium Plus Sedan	FFBFL	40295	28000	29100	29300	33000
Bang & Olufsen Sound			375	375	415	415
FWD			(1425)	(1425)	(1590)	(1590)
A4 QUATTRO AWD—4-Cyl. Turbo—Equipment Schedule 3						
W.B. 110.6"; 2.0 Liter.						
Prestige Sedan 4D	KFBFL	45595	30500	31700	32000	35900
Dynamic Cruise Control			500	500	555	555

48   DEDUCT FOR RECONDITIONING   0415

Body Type	VIN	List	Trade-In Good	Very Good	Pvt-Party Good	Retail Excellent
Driver Assistance Pkg			675	675	755	755
S4 QUATTRO AWD—V6 Supercharged—Equipment Schedule 1						
W.B. 110.7"; 3.0 Liter.						
Premium Plus Sedan	BGAFL	50395	38700	39900	40400	44600
Bang & Olufsen Sound			375	375	400	400
S4 QUATTRO AWD—V6 Supercharged—Equipment Schedule 1						
W.B. 110.7"; 3.0 Liter.						
Prestige Sedan 4D	KGAFL	56295	41600	42800	43100	47400
Adaptive Cruise Control			500	500	535	535
Driver Assist Pkg			675	675	720	720
A5 QUATTRO AWD—4-Cyl. Turbo—Equipment Schedule 1						
W.B. 108.3"; 2.0 Liter.						
Premium Coupe 2D	CFAFR	41095	28500	29500	30200	33900
Premium Plus Cpe 2D	LFAFR	44195	31800	32800	33400	37300
Bang & Olufsen Sound			375	375	415	415
A5 QUATTRO AWD—4-Cyl. Turbo—Equipment Schedule 1						
W.B. 108.3"; 2.0 Liter.						
Prestige Coupe 2D	WFAFR	50295	35100	36200	36700	40800
Dynamic Cruise Control			500	500	555	555
Driver Assist Pkg			675	675	745	745
S-Line Pkg			800	800	885	885
A5 QUATTRO AWD—4-Cyl. Turbo—Equipment Schedule 1						
W.B. 108.3"; 2.0 Liter.						
Premium Cabriolet 2D	CFAFH	47495	32700	33700	34400	38400
Premium Plus Cab 2D	LFAFH	50595	35500	36600	37100	41300
Prestige Cabriolet 2D	WFAFH	56695	38000	39200	39600	44100
Bang & Olufsen Sound			375	375	415	415
Dynamic Cruise Control			500	500	555	555
S-Line Pkg			800	800	885	885
FWD			(1425)	(1425)	(1590)	(1590)
S5 QUATTRO AWD—V6 Supercharged—Equipment Schedule 1						
W.B. 108.3"; 3.0 Liter.						
Premium Plus Cpe	CGAFR	54295	42500	43900	44000	48400
Premium Plus Cnv 2D	CGAFH	61295	45500	47000	47000	51700
Prestige Coupe 2D	VGAFR	60545	45100	46600	46300	50900
Prestige Convertible	VGAFH	67545	48600	50200	49800	54800
Sensing Cruise Control			500	500	545	545
A6 QUATTRO AWD—4-Cyl. Turbo—Equipment Schedule 3						
W.B. 114.7"; 2.0 Liter.						
2.0T Premium Sedan	FFAFC	46095	30500	31600	32900	37600
2.0T Premium Plus	GFAFC	50395	32300	33400	34900	40000
FWD			(1425)	(1425)	(1575)	(1575)
A6 QUATTRO AWD—V6 Supercharged—Equipment Schedule 1						
W.B. 114.7"; 3.0 Liter.						
3.0T Premium Plus	FGAFC	55995	36600	37900	39300	44900
3.0T Prestige Sedan	HGAFC	58795	39700	41000	42600	48700
Bang & Olufsen Sound			3000	3000	3320	3320
Adaptive Cruise Control			500	500	555	555
A6 QUATTRO AWD—V6 Turbo Diesel—Equipment Schedule 3						
W.B. 114.7"; 3.0 Liter.						
TDI Premium Plus	FMAFC	58395	42500	44000	44200	49200
TDI Prestige Sedan	HMAFC	61195	45000	46500	46600	51700
Bang & Olufsen Sound			3000	3000	3200	3200
Adaptive Cruise Control			500	500	535	535
S6 QUATTRO AWD—V8 Twin Turbo—Equipment Schedule 1						
W.B. 114.7"; 4.0 Liter.						
Sedan 4D		74295	48800	50200	50600	55500
Bang & Olufsen Sound			3000	3000	3215	3215
Sensing Cruise Control			500	500	535	535
A7 QUATTRO AWD—V6 Supercharged—Equipment Schedule 1						
W.B. 114.7"; 3.0 Liter.						
Premium Plus Sedan	WGAFC	65395	47600	49200	50200	56300
Prestige Sedan 4D	2GAFC	68295	50800	52500	53400	59800
Bang & Olufsen Sound			3000	3000	3205	3205
Adaptive Cruise Control			500	500	535	535
Driver Assistance Pkg			675	675	720	720
A7 QUATTRO AWD—V6 Turbo Diesel—Equipment Schedule 1						
W.B. 114.7"; 3.0 Liter.						
TDI Premium Plus	WMAFC	67795	50200	51900	52800	59200
TDI Prestige Sedan	2MAFC	70695	52800	54500	55300	61800
Bang & Olufsen Sound			3000	3000	3200	3200
Adaptive Cruise Control			500	500	535	535
Driver Assistance Pkg			675	675	720	720

Body Type	VIN	List	Trade-In Good	Very Good	Pvt-Party Good	Retail Excellent
Innovation Pkg			1275	1275	1360	1360
S7 QUATTRO AWD—V8 Twin Turbo—Equipment Schedule 1						
W.B. 114.7"; 4.0 Liter.						
Sedan 4D		81095	59900	61700	60800	65600
Bang & Olufsen Sound			3000	3000	3065	3065
Adaptive Cruise Control			500	500	510	510
Driver Assistance Pkg			675	675	690	690
Innovation Pkg			1275	1275	1305	1305
RS 7—V8 Twin Turbo—Equipment Schedule 1						
W.B. 114.8"; 4.0 Liter.						
Prestige Sedan 4D	W2AFC	105795	90900	93900	90800	98800
Bang & Olufsen Sound			3000	3000	3115	3115
Adaptive Cruise Control			500	500	520	520
Driver Assist Plus Pkg			675	675	700	700
Carbon-Optic Pkg			1450	1450	1515	1515
Dynamic Pkg			1000	1000	1035	1035
Innovation Pkg			1275	1275	1325	1325
A8 QUATTRO AWD—V6 Supercharged—Equipment Schedule 1						
W.B. 117.8", 122.9" (L); 3.0 Liter.						
3.0T Sedan 4D	AGAFD	75995	46900	48300	48100	52100
3.0T L Sedan 4D	RGAFD	79695	55100	56800	56000	60400
Adaptive Cruise Control			500	500	530	530
Driver Assistance Pkg			675	675	715	715
A8 QUATTRO AWD—V6 Turbo Diesel—Equipment Schedule 1						
W.B. 122.9"; 3.0 Liter.						
L TDI Sedan 4D	RMAFD	83395	61400	63200	62400	67400
Bang & Olufsen Sound			3000	3000	3145	3145
Adaptive Cruise Control			500	500	525	525
Driver Assistance Pkg			675	675	705	705
Rear Seat Comfort Pkg			1375	1375	1440	1440
A8 QUATTRO AWD—V8 Turbo—Equipment Schedule 1						
W.B. 117.8", 122.9" (L); 4.0 Liter.						
4.0T Sedan 4D	A2AFD	84795	56900	58600	58300	63300
4.0T L Sedan 4D	R2AFD	88495				
Bang & Olufsen Sound			3000	3000	3155	3155
Driver Assistance Pkg			675	675	710	710
S8 QUATTRO AWD—V8 Twin Turbo—Equipment Schedule 1						
W.B. 117.8"; 4.0 Liter.						
Sedan 4D	D2AFD	113395	76900	79100	77900	84300
Bang & Olufsen Sound			3000	3000	3195	3195
Active Cruise Control			500	500	530	530
Driver Assistance Pkg			675	675	720	720
R8 QUATTRO AWD—V8—Equipment Schedule 1						
W.B. 104.3"; 4.2 Liter.						
Coupe 2D	FUAFG	126550	****	****	****	120500
Convertible 2D	WUAFG	140050	****	****	****	128000
Bang & Olufsen Sound			****	****	****	380
Ceramic Brakes			****	****	****	4180
R8 QUATTRO AWD—V10—Equipment Schedule 1						
W.B. 104.3"; 5.2 Liter.						
Coupe 2D	ENAFG	163250	****	****	****	148600
Plus Coupe 2D	3NAFG	182595				
Convertible 2D	VNAFG	176750	****	****	****	158300
Ceramic Brakes			****	****	****	4185
TT QUATTRO AWD—4-Cyl. Turbo—Equipment Schedule 2						
W.B. 97.2"; 2.0 Liter.						
Coupe 2D	BFAFK	40795	30800	32000	32200	36100
Roadster 2D	SFAFK	43795	32100	33300	33700	38100
S-Line Pkg			800	800	870	870
TTS QUATTRO AWD—4-Cyl. Turbo—Equipment Schedule 2						
W.B. 97.2"; 2.0 Liter.						
Coupe 2D	B1AFK	49595	37100	38500	38600	43400
Roadster 2D	S1AFK	52595	39200	40600	40800	46000

BMW

2000 BMW — (4UorWB)(SorA)(AM334)-Y-#

Body Type	VIN	List	Trade-In Good	Very Good	Pvt-Party Good	Retail Excellent
3 SERIES—6-Cyl.—Equipment Schedule 1						
W.B. 107.3"; 2.5 Liter, 2.8 Liter.						
323i Sedan 4D	AM334	32680	1825	2075	2650	4150
323i Wagon 4D	AR334	32985	2100	2350	2950	4575

Body Type	VIN	List	Trade-In Good	Very Good	Pvt-Party Good	Retail Excellent
323Ci Coupe 2D	BM334	34280	2175	2425	2925	4425
323Ci Convertible 2D	BR334	38285	2000	2175	2950	4475
328i Sedan 4D	AM534	37670	2100	2375	3000	4650
328Ci Coupe 2D	BM534	38335	2475	2775	3325	5025
Hard Top (Conv)			300	300	400	400
Premium Pkg			150	150	200	200
Sport Pkg			175	175	235	235
Sport Premium Pkg			200	200	265	265
Manual, 5-Spd (ex 2D)			(300)	(300)	(400)	(400)
Z3—6-Cyl.—Equipment Schedule 1						
W.B. 111.4"; 2.5 Liter, 2.8 Liter.						
Coupe 2D	CK534	38395	4075	4450	5125	7125
2.3 Roadster 2D	CH933	34470	2675	2925	3525	5150
2.8 Roadster 2D	CH334	38445	3700	4050	4825	6875
Hard Top (Roadster)			300	300	400	400
M—6-Cyl.—Equipment Schedule 1						
W.B. 96.8"; 3.2 Liter.						
Coupe 2D	CM934	42670	9175	9825	11000	14700
Roadster 2D	CK934	43270	5725	6175	7150	9800
Hard Top (Roadster)			300	300	400	400
Z8—V8—Equipment Schedule 1						
W.B. 98.9"; 5.0 Liter.						
Roadster 2D	EJ134	130670	****	****	****	55800
5 SERIES—6-Cyl.—Equipment Schedule 1						
W.B. 111.4"; 2.8 Liter.						
528i Sedan 4D	DM634	44595	1675	1875	2675	4325
528iT Wagon 4D	DP634	46545	1200	1350	1900	3125
Premium Pkg			150	150	200	200
Sport Pkg			275	275	380	380
Manual, 5-Spd			(350)	(350)	(465)	(465)
5 SERIES—V8—Equipment Schedule 1						
W.B. 111.4"; 4.4 Liter.						
540i Sedan 4D	DN634	52970	2675	2975	3975	6250
540iT Wagon 4D	DR634	55350	2625	2900	3875	6075
Sport Pkg			275	275	380	380
M5—V8—Equipment Schedule 1						
W.B. 111.4"; 5.0 Liter.						
Sedan 4D	DE934	72070	6225	6725	7850	10850
7 SERIES—V8—Equipment Schedule 1						
W.B. 115.4", 120.9" (iL); 4.4 Liter.						
740i Sedan 4D	GG834	64670	1650	1825	2425	3700
740iL Sedan 4D	GH834	66970	2275	2525	3050	4475
Sport Pkg			275	275	380	380
7 SERIES—V12—Equipment Schedule 1						
W.B. 120.9"; 5.4 Liter.						
750iL Sedan 4D	GJ034	95270	3100	3425	4450	6625

2001 BMW — WBAorWBS(AV334)-1-#

Body Type	VIN	List	Trade-In Good	Very Good	Pvt-Party Good	Retail Excellent
3 SERIES—6-Cyl.—Equipment Schedule 1						
W.B. 107.3"; 2.5 Liter, 3.0 Liter.						
325i Sedan 4D	AV334	30060	2175	2450	2975	4500
325xi AWD Sedan 4D	AV334	31810	2475	2775	3325	4975
325Ci Coupe 2D	BN334	32060	2500	2800	3275	4850
325Cic Convertible 2D	BS534	38010	2400	2625	3475	5225
325iT Wagon 4D	AW334	32470	2400	2675	3325	5100
325xiT AWD Wagon 4D	AW334	34220	2650	2950	3675	5600
330i Sedan 4D	AV534	39280	2650	2975	3550	5275
330xi AWD Sedan 4D	AV534	41030	3075	3450	4050	5975
330Ci Coupe 2D	BN534	39335	2850	3200	3725	5500
330Cic Convertible 2D	BS534	44245	2750	3025	3900	5775
Hard Top (Conv)			300	300	400	400
Premium Pkg			150	150	215	215
Sport Pkg			175	175	235	235
Manual, 5-Spd (ex 2D)			(300)	(300)	(400)	(400)
M3—6-Cyl.—Equipment Schedule 1						
W.B. 107.5"; 3.2 Liter.						
Coupe 2D	BL934	46045	4950	5350	6275	8725
Convertible 2D	BR934	54045	5600	6050	7000	9675
Hard Top (Conv)			300	300	400	400
Z3—6-Cyl.—Equipment Schedule 1						
W.B. 96.3"; 2.5 Liter, 3.0 Liter.						
2.5i Roadster 2D	CN334	34295	2925	3225	3975	5525
3.0i Coupe 2D	CK734	39845	4175	4525	5200	7200

Body Type	VIN	List	Trade-In Good	Very Good	Pvt-Party Good	Retail Excellent
3.0i Roadster 2D	CN534	39745	3875	4225	5000	7050
Hard Top (Roadster)			300	300	400	400
M—6-Cyl.—Equipment Schedule 1						
W.B. 96.8"; 3.2 Liter.						
Coupe 2D	CN934	45635	10950	11700	12700	16600
Roadster 2D	CL934	46635	8025	8600	9450	12450
Hard Top (Roadster)			300	300	375	375
Z8—V8—Equipment Schedule 1						
W.B. 98.6"; 5.0 Liter.						
Roadster 2D	EJ134	130745	****	****	****	60600
5 SERIES—6-Cyl.—Equipment Schedule 1						
W.B. 111.4"; 2.5 Liter, 3.0 Liter.						
525i Sedan 4D	DT334	40195	1975	2175	2875	4475
525iT Wagon 4D	DS334	41995	1325	1475	1975	3150
530i Sedan 4D	DT534	44345	2525	2775	3575	5475
Premium Pkg			150	150	215	215
Sport Pkg			325	325	435	435
Manual, 5-Spd			(375)	(375)	(500)	(500)
5 SERIES—V8—Equipment Schedule 1						
W.B. 111.4"; 4.4 Liter.						
540i Sedan 4D	DN634	51670	3100	3425	4325	6575
540iT Wagon 4D	DR634	54050	3100	3425	4250	6375
Sport Pkg			325	325	435	435
M5—V8—Equipment Schedule 1						
W.B. 111.4"; 5.0 Liter.						
Sedan 4D	DE934	69970	7450	8000	9400	12950
7 SERIES—V8—Equipment Schedule 1						
W.B. 115.4", 120.9" (iL); 4.4 Liter.						
740i Sedan 4D	GC834	63470	2125	2350	3200	4950
740iL Sedan 4D	GH834	67470	2850	3150	3875	5700
Sport Pkg			325	325	435	435
7 SERIES—V12—Equipment Schedule 1						
W.B. 120.9"; 5.4 Liter.						
750iL Sedan 4D	GJ034	92670	3775	4125	5050	7225
Sport Pkg			150	150	215	215

2002 BMW — WBA,WBS,4USor5UM(ET374)-2-#

Body Type	VIN	List	Trade-In Good	Very Good	Pvt-Party Good	Retail Excellent
3 SERIES—6-Cyl.—Equipment Schedule 1						
W.B. 107.3"; 2.5 Liter, 3.0 Liter.						
325i Sedan 4D	ET374	32465	2525	2825	3350	4975
325xi AWD Sedan 4D	EU334	34215	2875	3225	3775	5575
325Ci Coupe 2D	BN334	34465	2900	3225	3700	5375
325Cic Convertible 2D	BS334	39470	3000	3275	4075	5875
325iT Wagon 4D	EN334	34865	2975	3325	3900	5725
325xiT AWD Wagon 4D	EP334	36615	3325	3700	4300	6300
330i Sedan 4D	EV534	38410	3050	3425	3950	5800
330xi AWD Sedan 4D	EW534	40160	3500	3900	4500	6550
330Ci Coupe 2D	BN534	39410	3300	3650	4225	6150
330Cic Convertible 2D	BS534	46820	3350	3650	4625	6625
Hard Top			350	350	465	465
Premium Pkg			175	175	235	235
Sport Pkg			200	200	265	265
Manual, 5-Spd (ex 2D)			(325)	(325)	(435)	(435)
M3—6-Cyl.—Equipment Schedule 1						
W.B. 107.5"; 3.2 Liter.						
Coupe 2D	BL934	49745	5250	5650	6550	9050
Convertible 2D	BR934	55545	5900	6350	7250	9950
Hard Top (Conv)			350	350	465	465
Z3—6-Cyl.—Equipment Schedule 1						
W.B. 96.3"; 2.5 Liter, 3.0 Liter.						
2.5i Roadster 2D	CN334	34370	3075	3375	4075	5750
3.0i Coupe 2D	CK734	39920	4900	5300	6000	8125
3.0i Roadster 2D	CN534	39820	4475	4850	5600	7700
Hard Top (Roadster)			350	350	465	465
Sport Pkg			175	175	225	225
M—6-Cyl.—Equipment Schedule 1						
W.B. 96.8"; 3.2 Liter.						
Coupe 2D	CN934	45635	12050	12800	13800	17750
Roadster 2D	CL934	46635	9250	9875	10750	13950
Hard Top			350	350	435	435
Z8—V8—Equipment Schedule 1						
W.B. 98.6"; 5.0 Liter.						
Roadster 2D	EJ134	132745	****	****	****	68000

Body Type	VIN	List	Trade-In Good	Trade-In Very Good	Pvt-Party Good	Retail Excellent
5 SERIES—6-Cyl.—Equipment Schedule 1						
W.B. 111.4"; 2.5 Liter, 3.0 Liter.						
525i Sedan 4D	DT434	41070	2450	2725	3425	5150
525iT Wagon 4D	DS334	42870	1525	1700	2250	3475
530i Sedan 4D	DT634	44670	3200	3550	4325	6425
Premium Pkg			175	175	235	235
Sport Pkg			350	350	480	480
Manual, 5-Spd			(400)	(400)	(535)	(535)
5 SERIES—V8—Equipment Schedule 1						
W.B. 111.4"; 4.4 Liter.						
540i Sedan 4D	DN634	53145	3500	3850	4800	7100
540iT Wagon 4D	DR634	55545	3575	3950	4900	7200
Sport Pkg			350	350	480	480
M5—V8—Equipment Schedule 1						
W.B. 111.4"; 5.0 Liter.						
Sedan 4D	DE934	72645	8250	8825	10700	15000
7 SERIES—V8—Equipment Schedule 1						
W.B. 117.7", 123.2" (Li); 4.4 Liter.						
745i Sedan 4D	GL634	68495	2900	3175	3925	5750
745Li Sedan 4D	GN634	72495	3500	3825	4750	6850
Sport Pkg			350	350	480	480

2003 BMW — WBA,WBSor4US(EV334)-3-#

Body Type	VIN	List	Trade-In Good	Trade-In Very Good	Pvt-Party Good	Retail Excellent
3 SERIES—6-Cyl.—Equipment Schedule 1						
W.B. 107.3"; 2.5 Liter, 3.0 Liter.						
325i Sedan 4D	EV334	32270	2825	3175	3725	5475
325xi AWD Sedan 4D	EU334	34020	3200	3575	4150	6075
325Ci Coupe 2D	BN334	34070	3250	3625	4175	5925
325Cic Convertible 2D	BS334	40120	3475	3775	4700	6625
325iT Wagon 4D	EN334	33820	3400	3775	4450	6375
325xiT AWD Wagon 4D	EP334	35570	3850	4250	4950	7075
330i Sedan 4D	EV534	39070	3275	3650	4350	6325
330xi AWD Sedan 4D	EW534	40820	3750	4150	4900	7050
330Ci Coupe 2D	BN534	40070	3750	4150	4800	6825
330Cic Convertible 2D	BS534	44870	3975	4300	5275	7400
Hard Top (Conv)			375	375	500	500
Premium Pkg			200	200	265	265
Sport Pkg			175	175	240	240
Performance Pkg			1050	1050	1385	1385
Manual, 5-Spd (ex 2D)			(350)	(350)	(465)	(465)
M3—6-Cyl.—Equipment Schedule 1						
W.B. 107.5"; 3.2 Liter.						
Coupe 2D	BL934	49345	6600	7075	8250	11150
Convertible 2D	BR934	55195	7425	7950	9175	12350
Hard Top (Conv)			375	375	500	500
Z4—6-Cyl.—Equipment Schedule 1						
W.B. 98.2"; 2.5 Liter, 3.0 Liter.						
2.5i Roadster 2D	BT334	37690	3475	3800	4600	6525
3.0i Roadster 2D	BT534	43215	3900	4225	5075	7125
Premium Pkg			200	200	265	265
Sport Pkg			175	175	240	240
Z8—V8—Equipment Schedule 1						
W.B. 98.6"; 4.8 Liter, 5.0 Liter.						
Roadster 2D	EJ134	134295	****	****	****	75300
Alpina Roadster 2D	EJ134	139295	****	****	****	91500
5 SERIES—6-Cyl.—Equipment Schedule 1						
W.B. 111.4"; 2.5 Liter, 3.0 Liter.						
525i Sedan 4D	DT334	41770	2975	3300	4025	5975
525iT Wagon 4D	DS334	43470	1650	1850	2450	3775
530i Sedan 4D	DT534	45370	3600	3950	4900	7175
Premium Pkg			200	200	265	265
Sport Pkg			400	400	535	535
Manual, 5-Spd			(275)	(275)	(365)	(365)
5 SERIES—V8—Equipment Schedule 1						
W.B. 111.4"; 4.4 Liter.						
540i Sedan 4D	DN634	52495	4025	4400	5400	7875
540iT Wagon 4D	DR634	56085	4050	4425	5425	7900
Sport Pkg			400	400	535	535
M5—V8—Equipment Schedule 1						
W.B. 111.4"; 5.0 Liter.						
Sedan 4D	DE934	73195	10450	11100	13050	17800
7 SERIES—V8—Equipment Schedule 1						
W.B. 117.7", 123.2" (Li); 4.4 Liter.						

Body Type	VIN	List	Trade-In Good	Very Good	Pvt-Party Good	Retail Excellent
745i Sedan 4D	GL634	70895	3250	3550	4450	6400
745Li Sedan 4D	GN634	73195	3975	4325	5250	7425
Adaptive Cruise Control			250	250	335	335
Sport Pkg			400	400	535	535

7 SERIES—V12—Equipment Schedule 1
W.B. 123.2"; 6.0 Liter.

760Li Sedan 4D	GN834	118195	8425	9000	10700	14600
Adaptive Cruise Control			250	250	335	335

2004 BMW — WBA,WBSor4US(EV334)-4-#

3 SERIES—6-Cyl.—Equipment Schedule 1
W.B. 107.3"; 2.5 Liter, 3.0 Liter.

325i Sedan 4D	EV334	33265	3275	3625	4350	6250
325xi AWD Sedan 4D	EU334	35015	3650	4025	4775	6825
325Ci Coupe 2D	BD334	34570	4050	4475	5025	6950
325Cic Convertible 2D	BW334	40720	4475	4825	5675	7725
325iT Wagon 4D	EN334	34815	3900	4300	4925	6900
325xiT AWD Wagon 4D	EP334	36565	4500	4950	5575	7775
330i Sedan 4D	EV534	39270	3975	4375	5125	7275
330xi AWD Sedan 4D	EW534	41020	4350	4775	5525	7825
330Ci Coupe 2D	BD534	40770	4725	5175	5775	7975
330Cic Convertible 2D	BW534	45570	4975	5325	6275	8475
Hard Top (Conv)			400	400	535	535
Premium Pkg			225	225	300	300
Sport Pkg			200	200	255	255
Performance Pkg			1125	1125	1505	1505
Manual, 5-Spd (ex 2D)			(375)	(375)	(500)	(500)

M3—6-Cyl.—Equipment Schedule 1
W.B. 107.5"; 3.2 Liter.

Coupe 2D	BL934	51340	7225	7700	8850	11800
Convertible 2D	BR934	56595	8125	8650	9875	13150
Hard Top (Conv)			400	400	535	535

Z4—6-Cyl.—Equipment Schedule 1
W.B. 98.2"; 2.5 Liter, 3.0 Liter.

2.5i Roadster 2D	BT334	37790	4575	4950	5825	8075
3.0i Roadster 2D	BT534	43315	5450	5875	6925	9425
Premium Pkg			225	225	300	300
Sport Pkg			200	200	255	255

5 SERIES—6-Cyl.—Equipment Schedule 1
W.B. 113.7"; 2.5 Liter, 3.0 Liter.

525i Sedan 4D	NA535	43670	4875	5275	5925	8075
530i Sedan 4D	NA735	48670	5625	6075	6950	9425
Adaptive Cruise Control			275	275	365	365
Premium Pkg			225	225	300	300
Sport Pkg			450	450	600	600
Manual, 6-Spd			(325)	(325)	(435)	(435)

5 SERIES—V8—Equipment Schedule 1
W.B. 113.7"; 4.4 Liter.

545i Sedan 4D	NB335	54995	5850	6325	7200	9750
Adaptive Cruise Control			275	275	365	365
Sport Pkg			450	450	600	600

6 SERIES—V8—Equipment Schedule 1
W.B. 109.4"; 4.4 Liter.

645Ci Coupe 2D	EH734	69995	6275	6700	7525	9600
645Cic Convertible 2D	EK734	76995	7850	8350	9325	11800
Adaptive Cruise Control			275	275	320	320
Sport Pkg			450	450	525	525

7 SERIES—V8—Equipment Schedule 1
W.B. 117.7", 123.2" (Li); 4.4 Liter.

745i Sedan 4D	GL634	69195	3900	4225	5150	7275
745Li Sedan 4D	GN634	73195	4725	5100	6275	8725
Adaptive Cruise Control			275	275	365	365
Sport Pkg			450	450	600	600

7 SERIES—V12—Equipment Schedule 1
W.B. 117.7", 123.2" (Li); 6.0 Liter.

760i Sedan 4D	GL834	111795	8475	9025	10800	14800
760Li Sedan 4D	GN834	117795	8650	9225	11200	15450
Adaptive Cruise Control			275	275	365	365

2005 BMW — WBA,WBSor4US(EV334)-5-#

3 SERIES—6-Cyl.—Equipment Schedule 1
W.B. 107.3"; 2.5 Liter, 3.0 Liter.

2005 BMW

Body Type	VIN	List	Trade-In Good	Trade-In Very Good	Pvt-Party Good	Retail Excellent
325i Sedan 4D	EV334	33715	3800	4200	5050	7125
325xi AWD Sedan 4D	EU334	35465	4225	4650	5525	7750
325Ci Coupe 2D	BD334	36115	4725	5175	5800	7825
325Ci Convertible 2D	BW334	42420	5125	5500	6650	8800
325i Wagon 4D	EN334	35615	4450	4875	5600	7700
325xi AWD Wagon 4D	EP334	37365	5100	5550	6325	8625
330i Sedan 4D	EV534	39120	4700	5150	6050	8400
330xi AWD Sedan 4D	EW534	40870	4875	5350	6425	8900
330Ci Coupe 2D	BD534	40720	5350	5850	6675	8975
330Ci Convertible 2D	BW534	46470	5675	6075	7275	9625
Hard Top (Conv)		-------	425	425	565	565
Premium Pkg		-------	250	250	335	335
Sport Pkg		-------	200	200	265	265
Performance Pkg		-------	1225	1225	1630	1630
Manual, 5-Spd (ex 2D)		-------	(400)	(400)	(535)	(535)

M3—6-Cyl.—Equipment Schedule 1
W.B. 107.5"; 3.2 Liter.

Body Type	VIN	List	Good	Very Good	Good	Excellent
Coupe 2D	BL934	51140	9225	9800	10750	13650
Convertible 2D	BR934	56495	10150	10750	11700	14850
Hard Top (Conv)		-------	425	425	520	520
Club Sport Pkg		-------	725	725	905	905
Competition		-------	725	725	905	905

Z4—6-Cyl.—Equipment Schedule 1
W.B. 98.2"; 2.5 Liter, 3.0 Liter.

Body Type	VIN	List	Good	Very Good	Good	Excellent
2.5i Roadster 2D	BT335	38415	4425	4800	6125	8475
3.0i Roadster 2D	BT535	44265	6075	6525	7725	10350
Premium Pkg		-------	250	250	335	335
Sport Pkg		-------	200	200	265	265

5 SERIES—6-Cyl.—Equipment Schedule 1
W.B. 113.7"; 2.5 Liter, 3.0 Liter.

Body Type	VIN	List	Good	Very Good	Good	Excellent
525i Sedan 4D	NA535	44720	5225	5650	6550	8725
530i Sedan 4D	NA735	48820	6275	6750	7700	10150
Adaptive Cruise		-------	300	300	400	400
Premium Pkg		-------	250	250	335	335
Sport Pkg		-------	500	500	665	665

5 SERIES—V8—Equipment Schedule 1
W.B. 113.7"; 4.4 Liter.

Body Type	VIN	List	Good	Very Good	Good	Excellent
545i Sedan 4D	NB335	56495	6300	6775	7725	10250
Adaptive Cruise		-------	300	300	400	400
Sport Pkg		-------	500	500	665	665

6 SERIES—V8—Equipment Schedule 1
W.B. 109.4"; 4.4 Liter.

Body Type	VIN	List	Good	Very Good	Good	Excellent
645Ci Coupe 2D	EH734	70595	9600	10150	11500	14500
645Cic Convertible 2D	EK734	78895	11200	11850	13300	16700
Adaptive Cruise Control		-------	300	300	370	370
Sport Pkg		-------	500	500	615	615

7 SERIES—V8—Equipment Schedule 1
W.B. 117.7", 123.2" (Li); 4.4 Liter.

Body Type	VIN	List	Good	Very Good	Good	Excellent
745i Sedan 4D	GL635	70595	5425	5825	6975	9400
745Li Sedan 4D	GN635	74595	7825	8350	9475	12350
Sport Pkg		-------	500	500	665	665

7 SERIES—V12—Equipment Schedule 1
W.B. 117.7", 123.2" (Li); 6.0 Liter.

Body Type	VIN	List	Good	Very Good	Good	Excellent
760i Sedan 4D	GL835	111895	10100	10750	12250	16050
760Li Sedan 4D	GN835	119295	10300	10900	12750	16850
Adaptive Cruise Control		-------	300	300	400	400

2006 BMW — WBA,WBSor4US(VB135)-6-#

3 SERIES—6-Cyl.—Equipment Schedule 1
W.B. 107.3", 108.7" (Sed & Wag); 2.5 Liter, 3.0 Liter.

Body Type	VIN	List	Good	Very Good	Good	Excellent
325i Sedan 4D	VB135	35315	6075	6600	7425	9800
325xi AWD Sedan 4D	VD135	37215	6525	7075	7925	10450
325Ci Coupe 2D	BD334	36715	5625	6125	6825	8900
325Ci Convertible 2D	BW334	43020	6450	6850	8000	10300
325xi AWD Wagon 4D	VT135	39015	6450	6975	7825	10300
330i Sedan 4D	VB335	40020	7200	7775	8725	11450
330xi AWD Sedan 4D	VD335	41920	7575	8150	9100	11950
330Ci Coupe 2D	BD534	41920	6550	7075	7875	10250
330Ci Convertible 2D	BW534	46870	7025	7450	8725	11250
Adaptive Cruise Control		-------	325	325	435	435
Hard Top (Conv)		-------	450	450	600	600
Premium Pkg		-------	275	275	365	365
Sport Pkg		-------	200	200	265	265

2006 BMW

Body Type	VIN	List	Trade-In Good	Trade-In Very Good	Pvt-Party Good	Retail Excellent
Performance Pkg			1325	1325	1755	1755
M3—6-Cyl.—Equipment Schedule 1						
W.B. 107.5"; 3.2 Liter.						
Coupe 2D	BL934	52640	11600	12250	13350	16600
Convertible 2D	BR934	58295	12600	13350	14350	17800
Hard Top (Conv)			450	450	545	545
Competition Pkg			775	775	955	955
Z4—6-Cyl.—Equipment Schedule 1						
W.B. 98.2"; 3.0 Liter.						
3.0i Roadster 2D	BU335	39135	6675	7150	8425	11100
3.0si Coupe 2D	DU534	40795	8350	8875	10250	13250
3.0si Roadster 2D	BU535	44485	7325	7825	9200	12100
Premium Pkg			275	275	365	365
Sport Pkg			200	200	265	265
Z4 M SERIES—6-Cyl.—Equipment Schedule 1						
W.B. 98.3"; 3.2 Liter.						
Coupe 2D	DU934	49995	13550	14300	15650	19600
Roadster 2D	BT935	51995	11650	12300	13750	17400
Premium Pkg			275	275	330	330
5 SERIES—6-Cyl.—Equipment Schedule 1						
W.B. 113.7", 113.6" (Wag); 3.0 Liter.						
525i Sedan 4D	NE535	43195	6125	6600	7450	9700
525xi AWD Sedan 4D	NF335	45395	7600	8150	9075	11750
530i Sedan 4D	NE735	47495	7100	7600	8650	11350
530xi AWD Sedan 4D	NF735	49695	7400	7925	9025	11850
530xi AWD Wagon 4D	NN735	52095	8550	9125	10300	13450
Adaptive Cruise Control			325	325	430	430
Premium Pkg			275	275	365	365
Sport Pkg			550	550	730	730
5 SERIES—V8—Equipment Schedule 1						
W.B. 113.7"; 4.8 Liter.						
550i Sedan 4D	NB535	58095	8550	9125	10250	13400
Adaptive Cruise Control			325	325	435	435
Sport Pkg			550	550	735	735
M5—V10—Equipment Schedule 1						
W.B. 113.7"; 5.0 Liter.						
Sedan 4D	NB935	84895	13550	14300	15450	19300
6 SERIES—V8—Equipment Schedule 1						
W.B. 109.4"; 4.8 Liter.						
650i Coupe 2D	EH134	72495	11000	11650	12950	15850
650i Convertible 2D	EK134	79495	12750	13400	14850	18350
Adaptive Cruise Control			325	325	385	385
Sport Pkg			550	550	655	655
M6—V10—Equipment Schedule 1						
W.B. 109.5"; 5.0 Liter.						
Coupe 2D	EH934	99795	16750	17600	18800	22700
7 SERIES—V8—Equipment Schedule 1						
W.B. 117.7", 123.2" (Li); 4.8 Liter.						
750i Sedan 4D	HL835	72495	6975	7450	8400	10700
750Li Sedan 4D	HN835	76495	8525	9075	10100	12900
Adaptive Cruise Control			(350)	(350)	(440)	(440)
Sport Pkg			550	550	725	725
7 SERIES—V12—Equipment Schedule 1						
W.B. 117.7", 123.2" (Li); 6.0 Liter.						
760i Sedan 4D	HL035	113895	11750	12400	13800	17600
760Li Sedan 4D	HN035	121295	11800	12500	14100	18050
Adaptive Cruise Control			325	325	425	425

2007 BMW — WBA,WBSor4US(VA335)-7-#

Body Type	VIN	List	Trade-In Good	Trade-In Very Good	Pvt-Party Good	Retail Excellent
3 SERIES—6-Cyl.—Equipment Schedule 1						
W.B. 108.7"; 3.0 Liter.						
328i Sedan 4D	VA335	36815	7250	7800	8700	11250
328xi AWD Sedan 4D	VC935	38715	7725	8300	9200	11900
328i Coupe 2D	WB335	39715	8925	9575	10250	12750
328xi AWD Coupe 2D	WC335	41515	9075	9725	10400	12950
328i Convertible 2D	WL135	43975	10200	10750	11750	14350
328i Wagon 4D	VS135	36815	7175	7700	8600	11100
328xi AWD Wagon 4D	VT735	40515	8000	8575	9500	12250
Adaptive Cruise Control			350	350	465	465
Premium Pkg			300	300	400	400
Sport Pkg			200	200	265	265
3 SERIES—6-Cyl. Twin Turbo—Equipment Schedule 1						
W.B. 108.7"; 3.0 Liter.						

Body	Type	VIN	List	Trade-In Good	Trade-In Very Good	Pvt-Party Good	Retail Excellent
335i Sedan 4D		VB735	39675	8475	9100	10200	13200
335xi AWD Sedan 4D		VD535	41575	8850	9500	10600	13750
335i Coupe 2D		WB735	44020	9925	10600	11300	14050
335i Convertible 2D		WL735	49875	10850	11450	12600	15400
Adaptive Cruise Control			------	350	350	465	465
Premium Pkg			------	300	300	400	400
Sport Pkg			------	200	200	265	265

Z4—6-Cyl.—Equipment Schedule 1
W.B. 98.2"; 3.0 Liter.

Body	Type	VIN	List	Trade-In Good	Trade-In Very Good	Pvt-Party Good	Retail Excellent
3.0i Roadster 2D		BU335	37095	7725	8200	9400	12050
3.0si Coupe 2D		DU535	41095	10150	10750	11900	14950
3.0si Roadster 2D		BU535	43095	9000	9550	10900	13950
Premium Pkg			------	300	300	390	390
Sport Pkg			------	200	200	260	260

Z4 M SERIES—6-Cyl.—Equipment Schedule 1
W.B. 98.3"; 3.2 Liter.

Body	Type	VIN	List	Trade-In Good	Trade-In Very Good	Pvt-Party Good	Retail Excellent
Coupe 2D		DU934	50795	15350	16150	17400	21500
Roadster 2D		BT935	52795	13950	14700	15950	19750
Premium Pkg			------	300	300	355	355

5 SERIES—6-Cyl.—Equipment Schedule 1
W.B. 113.7", 113.6" (Wag); 3.0 Liter.

Body	Type	VIN	List	Trade-In Good	Trade-In Very Good	Pvt-Party Good	Retail Excellent
525i Sedan 4D		NE535	46920	7325	7850	8875	11450
525xi AWD Sedan 4D		NF335	49120	8000	8550	9575	12300
530i Sedan 4D		NE735	50920	8550	9125	10150	13000
530xi AWD Sedan 4D		NF735	53120	9075	9650	10800	13800
530xi AWD Wagon 4D		NN735	55520	10200	10850	12050	15350
Adaptive Cruise Control			------	350	350	460	460
Premium Pkg			------	300	300	395	395
Sport Pkg			------	575	575	760	760

5 SERIES—V8—Equipment Schedule 1
W.B. 113.7"; 4.8 Liter.

Body	Type	VIN	List	Trade-In Good	Trade-In Very Good	Pvt-Party Good	Retail Excellent
550i Sedan 4D		NB535	60485	9700	10300	11550	14800
Adaptive Cruise Control			------	350	350	460	460
Sport Pkg			------	575	575	755	755

M5—V10—Equipment Schedule 1
W.B. 113.7"; 5.0 Liter.

Body	Type	VIN	List	Trade-In Good	Trade-In Very Good	Pvt-Party Good	Retail Excellent
Sedan 4D		NB935	86195	16000	16850	17600	21200

6 SERIES—V8—Equipment Schedule 1
W.B. 109.4"; 4.8 Liter.

Body	Type	VIN	List	Trade-In Good	Trade-In Very Good	Pvt-Party Good	Retail Excellent
650i Coupe 2D		EH135	74595	13000	13650	14850	17950
650i Convertible 2D		EK135	81595	15950	16750	18100	21900
Adaptive Cruise Control			------	350	350	415	415
Sport Pkg			------	575	575	685	685

M6—V10—Equipment Schedule 1
W.B. 109.5"; 5.0 Liter.

Body	Type	VIN	List	Trade-In Good	Trade-In Very Good	Pvt-Party Good	Retail Excellent
Coupe 2D		EH935	101995	17450	18300	19550	23500
Convertible 2D		EK935	108695	19250	20200	21300	25400

7 SERIES—V8—Equipment Schedule 1
W.B. 117.7", 123.1" (Li); 4.8 Liter.

Body	Type	VIN	List	Trade-In Good	Trade-In Very Good	Pvt-Party Good	Retail Excellent
750i Sedan 4D		HL835	75695	9475	10050	11200	13950
750Li Sedan 4D		HN835	78795	10750	11400	12700	15850
Adaptive Cruise Control			------	(350)	(350)	(440)	(440)
Sport Pkg			------	575	575	725	725

7 SERIES—V12—Equipment Schedule 1
W.B. 123.1"; 6.0 Liter.

Body	Type	VIN	List	Trade-In Good	Trade-In Very Good	Pvt-Party Good	Retail Excellent
760Li Sedan 4D		HN035	123795	14250	15000	16350	20300

ALPINA B7—V8 Supercharged—Equipment Schedule 1
W.B. 117.7"; 4.4 Liter.

Body	Type	VIN	List	Trade-In Good	Trade-In Very Good	Pvt-Party Good	Retail Excellent
Sedan 4D		HL835	115695	15000	15800	17200	21400
Adaptive Cruise Control			------	350	350	440	440

2008 BMW — WBA,WBS(UP735)-8-#

1 SERIES—6-Cyl.—Equipment Schedule 1
W.B. 104.7"; 3.0 Liter.

Body	Type	VIN	List	Trade-In Good	Trade-In Very Good	Pvt-Party Good	Retail Excellent
128i Coupe 2D		UP735	33095	8275	8750	9775	12100
128i Convertible 2D		UL735	33875	10050	10550	11550	14150
Premium Pkg			------	300	300	375	375
Sport Pkg			------	200	200	250	250

1 SERIES—6-Cyl. Twin Turbo—Equipment Schedule 1
W.B. 104.7"; 3.0 Liter.

Body	Type	VIN	List	Trade-In Good	Trade-In Very Good	Pvt-Party Good	Retail Excellent
135i Coupe 2D		UC735	39395	11600	12200	13250	16100
135i Convertible 2D		UN935	39875	12050	12700	13800	16800
Premium Pkg			------	300	300	355	355

2008 BMW

Body Type	VIN	List	Trade-In Good	Very Good	Pvt-Party Good	Retail Excellent
Sport Pkg			200	200	235	235

3 SERIES—6-Cyl.—Equipment Schedule 1
W.B. 108.7"; 3.0 Liter.

328i Sedan 4D	VA335	36895	8875	9450	10250	12800
328xi AWD Sedan 4D	VC935	38795	9450	10050	10950	13650
328i Coupe 2D	WB335	39795	10550	11200	11850	14500
328xi AWD Coupe 2D	WC335	41595	10750	11400	12100	14800
328i Convertible 2D	WL135	46800	11950	12500	13500	16150
328i Wagon 4D	VS135	38695	9825	10450	11250	13900
328xi AWD Wagon 4D	VT735	40595	10950	11600	12450	15350
Adaptive Cruise Control			375	375	490	490
Premium Pkg			300	300	390	390
Sport Pkg			200	200	260	260

3 SERIES—6-Cyl. Twin Turbo—Equipment Schedule 1
W.B. 108.7"; 3.0 Liter.

335i Sedan 4D	VB735	42400	10700	11350	12300	15300
335xi AWD Sedan 4D	VD535	44300	11150	11800	12800	15900
335i Coupe 2D	WB335	43400	11850	12550	13300	16250
335xi AWD Coupe 2D	WC735	46100	12500	13250	13950	17000
335i Convertible 2D	WL735	51150	13150	13750	14900	17750
Adaptive Cruise Control			375	375	490	490
Premium Pkg			300	300	390	390
Sport Pkg			200	200	260	260

M3—V8—Equipment Schedule 1
W.B. 108.7"; 4.0 Liter.

Sedan 4D	VA935	56650	20200	21200	21600	25200
Coupe 2D	WD935	59350	21100	22100	22500	26200
Convertible 2D	WL935	68200	22100	23100	23600	27500
Premium Pkg			300	300	325	325

Z4—6-Cyl.—Equipment Schedule 1
W.B. 98.2"; 3.0 Liter.

3.0i Roadster 2D	BU335	40595	10550	11150	12200	14950
3.0si Coupe 2D	DU535	43445	12000	12650	13800	16900
3.0si Roadster 2D	BU535	45445	11750	12400	13600	16700
Premium Pkg			300	300	365	365
Sport Pkg			200	200	245	245

Z4 M SERIES—6-Cyl.—Equipment Schedule 1
W.B. 98.3"; 3.2 Liter.

Coupe 2D	DU935	52870	18900	19800	20900	25100
Roadster 2D	BT935	54870	16650	17450	18600	22500
Premium Pkg			300	300	345	345

5 SERIES—6-Cyl.—Equipment Schedule 1
W.B. 113.7"; 3.0 Liter.

528i Sedan 4D	NU535	46525	9825	10400	11100	13500
528xi AWD Sedan 4D	NV135	48725	10900	11500	12200	14750
Adaptive Cruise Control			375	375	465	465
Premium Pkg			300	300	370	370
Sport Pkg			600	600	745	745

5 SERIES—6-Cyl. Twin Turbo—Equipment Schedule 1
W.B. 113.7", 113.6" (Wag); 3.0 Liter.

535i Sedan 4D	NW135	51625	11000	11650	12350	15000
535xi AWD Sedan 4D	NV935	53825	11450	12100	12850	15550
535xi AWD Wagon 4D	PT735	56225	12750	13450	14200	17150
Adaptive Cruise Control			375	375	460	460
Premium Pkg			300	300	370	370
Sport Pkg			600	600	740	740

5 SERIES—V8—Equipment Schedule 1
W.B. 113.7"; 4.8 Liter.

550i Sedan 4D	NW535	61075	13600	14350	15300	18550
Adaptive Cruise Control			375	375	465	465
Sport Pkg			600	600	750	750

M5—V10—Equipment Schedule 1
W.B. 113.7"; 5.0 Liter.

| Sedan 4D | NB935 | 86675 | 19500 | 20400 | 21300 | 25200 |

6 SERIES—V8—Equipment Schedule 1
W.B. 109.4"; 4.8 Liter.

650i Coupe 2D	EA535	76375	16350	17150	18350	21900
650i Convertible 2D	EB535	84775	19350	20200	21600	25700
Adaptive Cruise Control			375	375	440	440
Individual Comp			2175	2175	2570	2570
Sport Pkg			600	600	705	705

M6—V10—Equipment Schedule 1
W.B. 109.5"; 5.0 Liter.

Body Type	VIN	List	Trade-In Good	Very Good	Pvt-Party Good	Retail Excellent
Coupe 2D	EH935	103075	20400	21300	22700	27100
Convertible 2D	EK935	108875	22700	23700	25100	29700
7 SERIES—V8—Equipment Schedule 1						
W.B. 117.7"; 123.2" (Li); 4.8 Liter.						
750i Sedan 4D	HL835	76575	12200	12800	13950	17000
750Li Sedan 4D	HN835	79675	13400	14050	15350	18750
Adaptive Cruise Control			375	375	455	455
Individual Comp			2175	2175	2665	2665
Sport Pkg			600	600	730	730
7 SERIES—V12—Equipment Schedule 1						
W.B. 123.2"; 6.0 Liter.						
760Li Sedan 4D	HN035	125075	16800	17600	19150	23400
Adaptive Cruise Control			375	375	460	460
Individual Comp			2175	2175	2690	2690
ALPINA B7—V8 Supercharged—Equipment Schedule 1						
W.B. 117.7"; 4.4 Liter.						
Sedan 4D	HL835	117075	17550	18400	20000	24500
Adaptive Cruise Control			375	375	465	465

2009 BMW — WBA,WBS(UP735)-9-#

Body Type	VIN	List	Trade-In Good	Very Good	Pvt-Party Good	Retail Excellent
1 SERIES—6-Cyl.—Equipment Schedule 1						
W.B. 104.7"; 3.0 Liter.						
128i Coupe 2D	UP735	31550	10150	10650	11650	14050
128i Convertible 2D	UL735	36150	11850	12450	13400	16050
Premium Pkg			350	350	425	425
Sport Pkg			250	250	305	305
1 SERIES—6-Cyl. Twin Turbo—Equipment Schedule 1						
W.B. 104.7"; 3.0 Liter.						
135i Coupe 2D	UC735	38000	13400	14000	15150	18050
135i Convertible 2D	UN935	42300	14250	14900	16050	19100
Premium Pkg			350	350	425	425
Sport Pkg			250	250	305	305
3 SERIES—6-Cyl.—Equipment Schedule 1						
W.B. 108.7"; 3.0 Liter.						
328i Sedan 4D	PH735	35750	10750	11350	12250	14850
328i xDrive Sedan 4D	PK735	37750	11500	12150	13050	15800
328i Coupe 2D	WB335	38650	12200	12850	13650	16400
328i xDrive Coupe 2D	WG335	40550	12450	13150	14100	16900
328i Convertible 2D	WL135	46700	14050	14700	15800	18850
328i Wagon 4D	UT935	37550	12350	13050	13900	16600
328i xDrive Wagon 4D	UU335	39550	14000	14750	15600	18600
Adaptive Cruise Control			375	375	470	470
Premium Pkg			350	350	435	435
Sport Pkg			250	250	310	310
M Sport Pkg			1075	1075	1340	1340
3 SERIES—6-Cyl. Twin Turbo—Equipment Schedule 1						
W.B. 108.7"; 3.0 Liter.						
335i Sedan 4D	PM735	41125	13000	13650	14850	18000
335i xDrive Sedan 4D	PL335	43125	13700	14400	15550	18800
335i Coupe 2D	WB735	43025	13950	14700	15700	18850
335i xDrive Coupe 2D	WC735	44925	14750	15500	16500	19750
335i Convertible 2D	WL735	51525	15700	16350	17550	20600
Adaptive Cruise Control			375	375	470	470
Premium Pkg			350	350	440	440
Sport Pkg			250	250	315	315
M Sport Pkg			1075	1075	1355	1355
3 SERIES—6-Cyl. Twin Turbo Diesel—Equipment Schedule 1						
W.B. 108.7"; 3.0 Liter.						
335d Sedan 4D	PN735	44725	13450	14150	15250	18500
Adaptive Cruise Control			375	375	470	470
Premium Pkg			350	350	440	440
Sport Pkg			250	250	315	315
M3—V8—Equipment Schedule 1						
W.B. 108.7"; 4.0 Liter.						
Sedan 4D	PM935	56975	24100	25100	26000	30300
Coupe 2D	WD935	60925	24400	25400	26400	30800
Convertible 2D	WL935	69025	25700	26700	27700	32400
Z4—6-Cyl.—Equipment Schedule 1						
W.B. 98.3"; 3.0 Liter.						
30i Roadster 2D	LM535	46575	15900	16600	17650	20800
Premium Pkg			350	350	405	405
Sport Pkg			250	250	290	290

Body Type	VIN	List	Trade-In Good	Very Good	Pvt-Party Good	Retail Excellent
Z4—6-Cyl. Twin Turbo—Equipment Schedule 1						
W.B. 98.3"; 3.0 Liter.						
35i Roadster 2D	LM735	52475	18150	18950	20100	23800
Premium Pkg		------	350	350	405	405
Sport Pkg		------	250	250	290	290
5 SERIES—6-Cyl.—Equipment Schedule 1						
W.B. 113.7"; 3.0 Liter.						
528i Sedan 4D	NU535	46625	12400	13050	14100	17050
528i xDrive Sedan 4D	NV135	48925	13700	14400	15500	18650
Adaptive Cruise Control		------	375	375	445	445
Premium Pkg		------	350	350	415	415
Sport Pkg		------	700	700	835	835
5 SERIES—6-Cyl. Twin Turbo—Equipment Schedule 1						
W.B. 113.7", 113.6" (Wag); 3.0 Liter.						
535i Sedan 4D	NW135	51925	14200	14900	16100	19450
535i xDrive Sedan 4D	NV935	54225	15100	15850	17100	20700
535i xDrive Wagon 4D	PT735	56625	16550	17350	18750	22800
Adaptive Cruise Control		------	375	375	445	445
Premium Pkg		------	350	350	415	415
Sport Pkg		------	700	700	825	825
5 SERIES—V8—Equipment Schedule 1						
W.B. 113.7"; 4.8 Liter.						
550i Sedan 4D	NW535	61225	18600	19500	21000	25500
Adaptive Cruise Control		------	375	375	450	450
Sport Pkg		------	700	700	840	840
M5—V10—Equipment Schedule 1						
W.B. 113.7"; 5.0 Liter.						
Sedan 4D	NB935	89325	23800	24800	26000	30600
6 SERIES—V8—Equipment Schedule 1						
W.B. 109.4"; 4.8 Liter.						
650i Coupe 2D	EA535	79025	19850	20700	21800	25400
650i Convertible 2D	EB535	87425	23200	24200	25300	29600
Adaptive Cruise Control		------	375	375	440	440
Individual Comp		------	2225	2225	2630	2630
Sport Pkg		------	700	700	820	820
M6—V10—Equipment Schedule 1						
W.B. 109.5"; 5.0 Liter.						
Coupe 2D	EH935	105925	23800	24800	26100	30600
Convertible 2D	EK935	111725	26100	27200	28500	33200
7 SERIES—V8 Twin Turbo—Equipment Schedule 1						
W.B. 120.9", 126.4"(Li); 4.4 Liter.						
750i Sedan 4D	KA835	82125	21300	22200	22700	26100
750Li Sedan 4D	KB835	86025	23700	24700	25200	29000
Adaptive Cruise Control		------	375	375	420	420
Sport Pkg		------	700	700	785	785

2010 BMW — WB(AorS)(UP7C5)-A-#

Body Type	VIN	List	Trade-In Good	Very Good	Pvt-Party Good	Retail Excellent
1 SERIES—6-Cyl.—Equipment Schedule 1						
W.B. 104.7"; 3.0 Liter.						
128i Coupe 2D	UP7C5	34645	11750	12300	13300	15750
128i Convertible 2D	UL7C5	38595	14550	15150	16300	19200
Premium Pkg		------	400	400	490	490
Sport Pkg		------	275	275	335	335
1 SERIES—6-Cyl. Twin Turbo—Equipment Schedule 1						
W.B. 104.7"; 3.0 Liter.						
135i Coupe 2D	UC7C5	40445	16600	17300	18500	21700
135i Convertible 2D	UN9C5	44745	17700	18450	19600	22900
Premium Pkg		------	400	400	485	485
Sport Pkg		------	275	275	335	335
3 SERIES—6-Cyl.—Equipment Schedule 1						
W.B. 108.7"; 3.0 Liter.						
328i Sedan 4D	PH7C5	33675	12550	13150	14100	16750
328i xDrive Sedan 4D	PK7C5	35675	13450	14100	15150	18000
328i Coupe 2D	WB3C5	36575	14000	14650	15700	18550
328i xDrive Coupe 2D	WC3C5	38475	14500	15150	16200	19150
328i Convertible 2D	WL1C5	45375	17650	18350	19550	22700
328i Wagon 4D	UT9C5	36225	14850	15500	16500	19400
328i xDrive Wagon 4D	UU3C5	38225	16550	17300	18250	21400
Active Cruise Control		------	400	400	485	485
Premium Pkg		------	400	400	485	485
Sport Pkg		------	275	275	335	335
M Sport Pkg		------	1100	1100	1340	1340

2010 BMW

Body Type	VIN	List	Trade-In Good	Very Good	Pvt-Party Good	Retail Excellent

3 SERIES—6-Cyl. Twin Turbo—Equipment Schedule 1
W.B. 108.7"; 3.0 Liter.

Body Type	VIN	List	Good	Very Good	Pvt-Party Good	Retail Excellent
335i Sedan 4D	PM7C5	42450	**16600**	**17350**	**18450**	**21800**
335i xDrive Sedan 4D	PL3C5	44450	**17100**	**17850**	**18950**	**22400**
335i Coupe 2D	WB7C5	44350	**17150**	**17900**	**19050**	**22500**
335i xDrive Coupe 2D	WC7C5	46250	**18050**	**18850**	**19950**	**23600**
335i Convertible 2D	WL7C5	52850	**19950**	**20700**	**21900**	**25500**
Active Cruise Control		-------	400	400	485	485
Premium Pkg		-------	400	400	485	485
Sport Pkg		-------	275	275	330	330
M Sport Pkg		-------	1100	1100	1330	1330

3 SERIES—6-Cyl. Twin Turbo Diesel—Equipment Schedule 1
W.B. 108.7"; 3.0 Liter.

Body Type	VIN	List	Good	Very Good	Pvt-Party Good	Retail Excellent
335d Sedan 4D	PN7C5	44725	**16250**	**17000**	**18150**	**21500**
Active Cruise Control		-------	400	400	490	490
Premium Pkg		-------	400	400	490	490
Sport Pkg		-------	275	275	335	335

M3—V8—Equipment Schedule 1
W.B. 108.7"; 4.0 Liter.

Body Type	VIN	List	Good	Very Good	Pvt-Party Good	Retail Excellent
Sedan 4D	PM9C5	56975	**28800**	**29900**	**31100**	**35900**
Coupe 2D	WD9C5	59975	**29100**	**30200**	**31200**	**35900**
Convertible 2D	WL9C5	69025	**30400**	**31500**	**32600**	**37500**

Z4—6-Cyl.—Equipment Schedule 1
W.B. 98.3"; 3.0 Liter.

Body Type	VIN	List	Good	Very Good	Pvt-Party Good	Retail Excellent
30i Roadster 2D	LM5C5	46575	**19550**	**20300**	**21200**	**24400**
Premium Pkg		-------	400	400	450	450
Sport Pkg		-------	275	275	310	310

Z4—6-Cyl. Twin Turbo—Equipment Schedule 1
W.B. 98.3"; 3.0 Liter.

Body Type	VIN	List	Good	Very Good	Pvt-Party Good	Retail Excellent
35i Roadster 2D	LM7C5	52475	**22400**	**23200**	**24100**	**27800**
Premium Pkg		-------	400	400	450	450
Sport Pkg		-------	275	275	310	310

5 SERIES—6-Cyl.—Equipment Schedule 1
W.B. 113.7"; 3.0 Liter.

Body Type	VIN	List	Good	Very Good	Pvt-Party Good	Retail Excellent
528i Sedan 4D	NU5C5	46625	**14750**	**15450**	**16550**	**19650**
528i xDrive Sedan 4D	NV1C5	48925	**16800**	**17550**	**18650**	**22000**
Active Cruise Control		-------	400	400	490	490
Premium Pkg		-------	400	400	490	490
Sport Pkg		-------	800	800	980	980
M Sport Pkg		-------	1100	1100	1345	1345

5 SERIES—6-Cyl. Twin Turbo—Equipment Schedule 1
W.B. 113.7", 113.6" (Wag), 120.7" (Gran Turismo); 3.0 Liter.

Body Type	VIN	List	Good	Very Good	Pvt-Party Good	Retail Excellent
535i Sedan 4D	NW1C5	51925	**16600**	**17350**	**18500**	**21900**
535i xDrive Sedan 4D	NV9C5	54225	**17500**	**18300**	**19500**	**23100**
535i xDrive Wagon 4D	PT7C5	56625	**20400**	**21300**	**22500**	**26600**
535i Gran Turismo Sed	SN2C5	56875	**16700**	**17450**	**18600**	**22000**
Active Cruise Control		-------	400	400	460	460
Premium Pkg		-------	400	400	460	460
Sport Pkg		-------	800	800	925	925
M Sport Pkg		-------	1100	1100	1270	1270

5 SERIES—V8—Equipment Schedule 1
W.B. 113.7", 120.7" (Gran Turismo); 4.8 Liter.

Body Type	VIN	List	Good	Very Good	Pvt-Party Good	Retail Excellent
550i Sedan 4D	NW5C5	61475	**21100**	**22000**	**23400**	**27900**
550i Gran Turismo Sed	SN4C5	65775	**21500**	**22400**	**23500**	**27600**
550i Gran'Turismo xDrv	SP4C5	67075	**23200**	**24200**	**25300**	**29800**
Active Cruise Control		-------	400	400	470	470
Sport Pkg		-------	800	800	940	940
M Sport Pkg		-------	1100	1100	1295	1295

M5—V10—Equipment Schedule 1
W.B. 113.7"; 5.0 Liter.

Body Type	VIN	List	Good	Very Good	Pvt-Party Good	Retail Excellent
Sedan 4D	NB9C5	89325	**27900**	**29000**	**30200**	**34800**

6 SERIES—V8—Equipment Schedule 1
W.B. 109.4"; 4.8 Liter.

Body Type	VIN	List	Good	Very Good	Pvt-Party Good	Retail Excellent
650i Coupe 2D	EA5C5	80325	**24200**	**25200**	**26100**	**29900**
650i Convertible 2D	EB5C5	87425	**29600**	**30800**	**31700**	**36100**
Adaptive Cruise Control		-------	400	400	460	460
Individual Comp		-------	2300	2300	2620	2620
Sport Pkg		-------	800	800	915	915

M6—V10—Equipment Schedule 1
W.B. 109.5"; 5.0 Liter.

Body Type	VIN	List	Good	Very Good	Pvt-Party Good	Retail Excellent
Coupe 2D	EH9C5	105925	**31300**	**32500**	**33400**	**38100**
Convertible 2D	EK9C5	111725	**35300**	**36600**	**37400**	**42500**

2010 BMW

Body Type	VIN	List	Trade-In Good	Very Good	Pvt-Party Good	Retail Excellent
7 SERIES—V8 Twin Turbo—Equipment Schedule 1						
W.B. 120.0", 126.4" (Li); 4.4 Liter.						
750i Sedan 4D	KA8C5	82280	25200	26100	26800	30500
750i xDrive Sedan	KC6C5	85580	26200	27200	27800	31600
750Li Sedan 4D	KC8C5	86180	27700	28700	29300	33300
750Li xDrive Sedan	KC8C5	89480	28700	29700	30300	34500
Active Cruise Control		------	400	400	450	450
Individual Comp		------	2300	2300	2580	2580
Luxury Seating		------	1300	1300	1475	1475
7 SERIES—V12—Equipment Schedule 1						
W.B. 126.4"; 6.0 Liter.						
760Li Sedan 4D	KB0C5	140425	45400	47000	47000	52800
Active Cruise Control		------	(400)	(400)	(450)	(450)
Individual Comp		------	2300	2300	2570	2570

2011 BMW — WB(AorS)(UP7C5)-B-#

Body Type	VIN	List	Trade-In Good	Very Good	Pvt-Party Good	Retail Excellent
1 SERIES—6-Cyl.—Equipment Schedule 1						
W.B. 104.7"; 3.0 Liter.						
128i Coupe 2D	UP7C5	33445	13650	14200	15450	18100
128i Convertible 2D	UL7C5	37445	17600	18250	19600	22800
Premium Pkg		------	450	450	545	545
Sport Pkg		------	300	300	365	365
1 SERIES—6-Cyl. Twin Turbo—Equipment Schedule 1						
W.B. 104.7"; 3.0 Liter.						
135i Coupe 2D	UC9C5	39295	19050	19800	21100	24500
135i Convertible 2D	UN7C5	43795	20700	21500	22900	26400
M Coupe 2D	UR9C5	47010	43900	45400	47100	54100
Premium Pkg		------	450	450	540	540
Sport Pkg		------	300	300	360	360
3 SERIES—6-Cyl.—Equipment Schedule 1						
W.B. 108.7"; 3.0 Liter.						
328i Sedan 4D	PH7C5	37945	17050	17750	18650	21600
328i xDrive Sedan 4D	PK7C5	39945	18350	19050	20000	23100
328i Coupe 2D	KE3C5	40000	17800	18500	19500	22600
328i xDrive Coupe 2D	KF3C5	41900	18500	19200	20200	23400
328i Convertible 2D	DW3C5	47750	21800	22600	23600	27000
328i Sport Wagon 4D	UT9C5	39445	19050	19800	20800	24100
328i xDrive Sport Wag	UU3C5	41445	20800	21600	22600	26200
Active Cruise Control		------	425	425	495	495
Premium Pkg		------	450	450	525	525
Sport Pkg		------	300	300	350	350
M Sport Pkg		------	1125	1125	1310	1310
3 SERIES—6-Cyl. Twin Turbo—Equipment Schedule 1						
W.B. 108.7"; 3.0 Liter.						
335i Sedan 4D	PM5C5	44800	21700	22500	23500	27000
335i xDrive Sedan 4D	PL5C5	46800	22400	23200	24200	27800
335i Coupe 2D	KG7C5	46850	22700	23500	24600	28400
335i xDrive Coupe 2D	KF9C5	48750	23500	24300	25500	29500
335is Coupe 2D	KG1C5	54050	25400	26300	27500	31900
335i Convertible 2D	DX7C5	53950	25100	26000	27200	31000
335is Convertible 2D	DX1C5	61150	28000	29000	30000	34100
Active Cruise Control		------	425	425	495	495
Premium Pkg		------	450	450	525	525
Sport Pkg		------	300	300	350	350
M Sport Pkg		------	1125	1125	1310	1310
3 SERIES—6-Cyl. Twin Turbo Diesel—Equipment Schedule 1						
W.B. 108.7"; 3.0 Liter.						
335d Sedan 4D	PN7C5	46475	22000	22800	23800	27400
Active Cruise Control		------	425	425	500	500
Premium Pkg		------	450	450	530	530
Sport Pkg		------	300	300	350	350
M Sport Pkg		------	1125	1125	1320	1320
M3—V8—Equipment Schedule 1						
W.B. 108.7"; 4.0 Liter.						
Sedan 4D	PM9C5	59575	34000	35200	36200	41200
Coupe 2D	KG9C5	61525	33500	34700	35800	40700
Convertible 2D	DX9C5	69625	34600	35700	36700	41700
Z4—6-Cyl.—Equipment Schedule 1						
W.B. 98.3"; 3.0 Liter.						
30i Roadster 2D	LM5C5	50995	21800	22600	23700	27200
Premium Pkg		------	450	450	510	510
Sport Pkg		------	300	300	340	340
M Sport Pkg		------	1125	1125	1270	1270

2011 BMW

Body Type	VIN	List	Trade-In Good	Very Good	Pvt-Party Good	Retail Excellent
Z4—6-Cyl. Twin Turbo—Equipment Schedule 1						
W.B. 98.3"; 3.0 Liter.						
35i Roadster 2D	LM7C5	55845	25000	25900	27000	30900
35is Roadster 2D	LM1C5	63420	26900	27800	28900	33000
Premium Pkg			450	450	505	505
Sport Pkg			300	300	335	335
M Sport Pkg			1125	1125	1265	1265
5 SERIES—6-Cyl.—Equipment Schedule 1						
W.B. 116.9"; 3.0 Liter.						
528i Sedan 4D	FR1C5	46875	22000	22900	23600	27000
Active Cruise Control			425	425	490	490
Driver Assistance Pkg			600	600	690	690
Premium Pkg			450	450	520	520
Premium Pkg 2			900	900	1040	1040
Sport Pkg			900	900	1040	1040
M Sport Pkg			1125	1125	1300	1300
5 SERIES—6-Cyl. Twin Turbo—Equipment Schedule 1						
W.B. 116.9", 120.9" (Gran Turismo); 3.0 Liter.						
535i Sedan 4D	FR7C5	52425	23600	24600	25400	29200
535i xDrive Sedan 4D	FU7C5	54225	26100	27200	27900	31800
535i Gran Turismo Sed	SN2C5	56875	23800	24700	25500	29200
535i GrnTurismo xDrv	SP2C5	59175	25700	26700	27500	31500
Active Cruise Control			425	425	470	470
Driver Assistance Pkg			600	600	665	665
Premium Pkg			450	450	500	500
Premium Pkg 2			900	900	1000	1000
Sport Pkg			900	900	1000	1000
M Sport Pkg			1125	1125	1250	1250
5 SERIES—V8 Twin Turbo—Equipment Schedule 1						
W.B. 116.9", 120.9" (Gran Turismo); 4.4 Liter.						
550i Sedan 4D	FR9C5	61075	28000	29100	30300	35000
550i xDrive Sedan 4D	FU9C5	62875	32600	33900	34700	39700
550i Gran Turismo Sed	SN4C5	64775	27900	29000	30000	34500
550i GrnTurismo xDrv	SP4C5	67075	28400	29500	30600	35200
Active Cruise Control			425	425	480	480
Driver Assistance Pkg			600	600	680	680
Premium Pkg			450	450	520	520
Premium Pkg 2			900	900	1020	1020
Sport Pkg			900	900	1020	1020
M Sport Pkg			1125	1125	1275	1275
7 SERIES—6-Cyl. Twin Turbo—Equipment Schedule 1						
W.B. 120.9", 126.4" (Li); 3.0 Liter.						
740i Sedan 4D	KA4C5	71525	27900	28800	29800	34000
740Li Sedan 4D	KB4C5	75925	28400	29400	30700	35100
Active Cruise Control			425	425	490	490
Driver Assistance Pkg			600	600	690	690
Individual Comp			2350	2350	2695	2695
M Sport Pkg			1125	1125	1295	1295
Luxury Seating			1325	1325	1525	1525
7 SERIES—V8 Twin Turbo—Equipment Schedule 1						
W.B. 120.9", 126.4" (Li); 4.4 Liter.						
750i Sedan 4D	KA8C5	84375	29800	30800	32200	36900
750i xDrive Sedan 4D	KC6C5	87675	30700	31800	32900	37500
750Li Sedan 4D	KB8C5	88275	32200	33300	34800	39900
750Li xDrive Sedan 4D	KC8C5	91575	32500	33600	34700	39600
Active Cruise Control			425	425	490	490
Driver Assistance Pkg			600	600	690	690
Individual Comp			2350	2350	2695	2695
M Sport Pkg			1125	1125	1295	1295
Luxury Seating			1325	1325	1525	1525
7 SERIES—V8 Twin Turbo ActiveHybrid—Equipment Schedule 1						
W.B. 120.9", 126.4" (Li); 4.4 Liter.						
750i Sedan 4D	KX6C5	103175	31200	32300	33500	38300
750Li Sedan 4D	KX8C5	107075	34300	35400	36600	41600
Driver Assistance Pkg			600	600	685	685
Luxury Seating			1325	1325	1530	1530
7 SERIES—V12 Twin Turbo—Equipment Schedule 1						
W.B. 126.4"; 6.0 Liter.						
760Li Sedan 4D	KB0C5	139975	56300	58100	59100	66500
Active Cruise Control			425	425	480	480
Individual Comp			2350	2350	2655	2655
M Sport Pkg			1125	1125	1275	1275
Luxury Seating			1325	1325	1505	1505

2011 BMW

Body Type	VIN	List	Trade-In Good	Very Good	Pvt-Party Good	Retail Excellent
ALPINA B7—V8 Twin Turbo—Equipment Schedule 1						
W.B. 120.9"; 4.4 Liter.						
Sedan 4D	KA8C5	123875	48200	49700	50900	57400
xDrive Sedan 4D	KC6C5	127175	51100	52800	53600	60100
Active Cruise Control			425	425	480	480
Driver Assistance Pkg			600	600	675	675

2012 BMW — WB(AorS)(UP7C5)–C–#

	VIN	List	Good	Very Good	Good	Excellent
1 SERIES—6-Cyl.—Equipment Schedule 1						
W.B. 104.7"; 3.0 Liter.						
128i Coupe 2D	UP7C5	35320	16250	16900	18350	21400
128i Convertible 2D	UL7C5	39920	19700	20400	22000	25500
Premium Pkg			500	500	610	610
Sport Pkg			325	325	395	395
M Sport Pkg			1150	1150	1405	1405
1 SERIES—6-Cyl. Twin Turbo—Equipment Schedule 1						
W.B. 104.7"; 3.0 Liter.						
135i Coupe 2D	UC9C5	41825	21400	22200	23700	27500
135i Convertible 2D	UN7C5	46575	23100	23900	25500	29500
Premium Pkg			500	500	605	605
M Sport Pkg			1150	1150	1390	1390
3 SERIES—6-Cyl.—Equipment Schedule 1						
W.B. 108.7"; 3.0 Liter.						
328i Sedan 4D	3A5C5	39290	21800	22600	23400	26500
328i Coupe 2D	KE3C5	42870	19900	20600	21600	24600
328i xDrive Coupe 2D	KF5C5	44570	20900	21600	22600	25800
328i Convertible 2D	DW3C5	50820	26100	27000	28000	31700
328i Sport Wagon 4D	UT9C5	41620	23100	23900	24700	27900
328i xDrive Sport Wag	UU3C5	43620	25300	26100	26900	30300
Dynamic Cruise Control			450	450	510	510
Premium Pkg			500	500	580	580
Sport Pkg			325	325	365	365
M Sport Pkg			1150	1150	1335	1335
3 SERIES—6-Cyl. Twin Turbo—Equipment Schedule 1						
W.B. 108.7"; 3.0 Liter.						
335i Sedan 4D	3A9C5	44745	27700	28600	29400	33100
335i Coupe 2D	KG7C5	45775	25000	25900	26900	30600
335i xDrive Coupe 2D	KF9C5	47475	26400	27300	28300	32200
335is Coupe 2D	KG1C5	52775	28900	29800	31100	35500
335i Convertible 2D	DX7C5	54475	29500	30500	31600	35700
335is Convertible 2D	DX1C5	61475	35100	36200	37300	41900
Premium Pkg			500	500	575	575
M Sport Pkg			1150	1150	1325	1325
M3—V8—Equipment Schedule 1						
W.B. 108.7"; 4.0 Liter.						
Coupe 2D	KG9C5	63595	38000	39200	40200	45100
Convertible 2D	DX9C5	73045	39000	40200	41200	46200
Competition Pkg			1150	1150	1280	1280
Individual Comp			2400	2400	2675	2675
Z4—4-Cyl. Twin Turbo—Equipment Schedule 1						
W.B. 98.3"; 2.0 Liter.						
28i Roadster 2D	LL5C5	51790	26400	27300	28200	31800
Premium Pkg			500	500	555	555
Sport Pkg			325	325	360	360
M Sport Pkg			1150	1150	1275	1275
Z4—6-Cyl. Twin Turbo—Equipment Schedule 1						
W.B. 98.3"; 3.0 Liter.						
35i Roadster 2D	LM7C5	56495	31200	32200	33100	37300
35is Roadster 2D	LM1C5	65095	34100	35200	36000	40400
Premium Pkg			500	500	550	550
Sport Pkg			325	325	360	360
M Sport Pkg			1150	1150	1270	1270
5 SERIES—6-Cyl.—Equipment Schedule 1						
W.B. 116.9"; 3.0 Liter.						
528i Sedan 4D	XG5C5	47575	25800	26800	27300	30800
528i xDrive Sedan 4D	XH5C5	49875	27900	28900	29400	33200
Active Cruise Control			450	450	500	500
Premium Pkg			500	500	560	560
Sport Pkg			975	975	1090	1090
M Sport Pkg			1150	1150	1285	1285
5 SERIES—6-Cyl. Twin Turbo—Equipment Schedule 1						
W.B. 116.9", 120.7" (Gran Turismo); 3.0 Liter.						
535i Sedan 4D	FR7C5	53125	30700	31800	32300	36300

Body Type	VIN	List	Trade-In Good	Very Good	Pvt-Party Good	Retail Excellent
535i xDrive Sedan 4D	FU7C5	55425	32100	33300	33800	37900
535i Gran Turismo Sed	SN2C5	58675	28400	29500	30100	34000
535i Grn Turismo xDrv	SP2C5	61275	31300	32400	33000	37200
Active Cruise Control			450	450	500	500
Premium Pkg			500	500	555	555
Sport Pkg			975	975	1085	1085
M Sport Pkg			1150	1150	1280	1280

5 SERIES—6-Cyl. Turbo ActiveHybrid—Equipment Schedule 1
W.B. 116.9"; 3.0 Liter.

Body Type	VIN	List	Trade-In Good	Very Good	Pvt-Party Good	Retail Excellent
Sedan 4D	FZ9C5	61845	31000	32100	32900	37300
Premium Pkg			500	500	560	560
Sport Pkg			975	975	1095	1095

5 SERIES—V8 Twin Turbo—Equipment Schedule 1
W.B. 116.9", 120.7" (Gran Turismo); 4.4 Liter.

Body Type	VIN	List	Trade-In Good	Very Good	Pvt-Party Good	Retail Excellent
550i Sedan 4D	FR9C5	62575	34100	35400	36200	41100
550i xDrive Sedan 4D	FU9C5	64875	38100	39400	40000	45200
550i Gran Turismo Sed	SN4C5	67675	34500	35800	36400	41100
550i Grn Turismo xDrv	SP4C5	70275	34500	35700	36500	41300
Active Cruise Control			450	450	500	500
Sport Pkg			975	975	1090	1090
M Sport Pkg			1150	1150	1285	1285

6 SERIES—6-Cyl. Turbo—Equipment Schedule 1
W.B. 112.4"; 3.0 Liter.

Body Type	VIN	List	Trade-In Good	Very Good	Pvt-Party Good	Retail Excellent
640i Coupe 2D	LW3C5	74475	37300	38600	39400	44400
640i Convertible 2D	LW7C5	81975	40100	41500	42300	47600
Bang & Olufsen Sound			2750	2750	3020	3020
Active Cruise Control			450	450	495	495
Driver Assistance Pkg			625	625	685	685
Individual Comp			2400	2400	2630	2630
M Sport Pkg			975	975	1070	1070

6 SERIES—V8 Twin Turbo—Equipment Schedule 1
W.B. 112.4"; 4.4 Liter.

Body Type	VIN	List	Trade-In Good	Very Good	Pvt-Party Good	Retail Excellent
650i Coupe 2D	LX3C5	83875	41200	42600	43500	48900
650i xDrive Coupe 2D	LX5C5	86875	42300	43700	44600	50100
650i Convertible 2D	LZ3C5	92375	43200	44700	45400	50900
650i xDrive Convertible	LZ5C5	94375	44400	45900	46600	52300
Bang & Olufsen Sound			2750	2750	3020	3020
Active Cruise Control			450	450	495	495
Driver Assistance Pkg			625	625	685	685
Luxury Seating			1350	1350	1475	1475
Individual Comp			2400	2400	2630	2630
M Sport Pkg			975	975	1070	1070

M6—V8 Twin Turbo—Equipment Schedule 1
W.B. 112.2"; 4.4 Liter.

Body Type	VIN	List	Trade-In Good	Very Good	Pvt-Party Good	Retail Excellent
Convertible 2D	LZ9C5	115295	60700	62800	63500	71000
Bang & Olufsen Sound			2750	2750	3035	3035

7 SERIES—6-Cyl. Twin Turbo—Equipment Schedule 1
W.B. 120.9", 126.4" (Li); 3.0 Liter.

Body Type	VIN	List	Trade-In Good	Very Good	Pvt-Party Good	Retail Excellent
740i Sedan 4D	KA4C5	71875	30100	31100	32200	36300
740Li Sedan 4D	KB4C5	76375	32400	33400	34400	38700
Active Cruise Control			450	450	505	505
Driver Assistance Pkg			625	625	705	705
Individual Comp			2400	2400	2695	2695
M Sport Pkg			1150	1150	1295	1295

7 SERIES—V8 Twin Turbo—Equipment Schedule 1
W.B. 120.9", 126.4" (Li); 4.4 Liter.

Body Type	VIN	List	Trade-In Good	Very Good	Pvt-Party Good	Retail Excellent
750i Sedan 4D	KA8C5	86175	35100	36300	37100	41700
750i xDrive Sedan 4D	KC6C5	89475	36100	37300	38200	42800
750Li Sedan 4D	KB8C5	90075	37600	38800	40000	45200
750Li xDrive Sedan 4D	KC8C5	93375	38600	39800	40700	45700
Active Cruise Control			450	450	500	500
Luxury Seating			1350	1350	1495	1495
Individual Comp			2400	2400	2670	2670
Driver Assistance Pkg			625	625	695	695

7 SERIES—V8 Twin Turbo ActiveHybrid—Equipment Schedule 1
W.B. 126.4"; 4.4 Liter.

Body Type	VIN	List	Trade-In Good	Very Good	Pvt-Party Good	Retail Excellent
750i Sedan 4D	KX6C5	97875	35600	36800	37800	42700
750Li Sedan 4D	KX8C5	101875	39600	40900	41800	47000
Luxury Seating			1350	1350	1505	1505
Individual Comp			2400	2400	2665	2665
M Sport Pkg			1150	1150	1280	1280

7 SERIES—V12 Twin Turbo—Equipment Schedule 1
W.B. 126.4"; 6.0 Liter.

Body Type	VIN	List	Trade-In Good	Very Good	Pvt-Party Good	Retail Excellent
760Li Sedan 4D	KB0C5	142375	61700	63600	63900	70800
Active Cruise Control		------	450	450	495	495
Individual Comp		------	2400	2400	2625	2625
M Sport Pkg		------	1150	1150	1260	1260
ALPINA B7—V8 Twin Turbo—Equipment Schedule 1						
W.B. 120.9"; 4.4 Liter.						
Sedan 4D	KB8C5	124475	53500	55200	55800	62000
xDrive Sedan 4D	KC8C5	127775	56500	58200	58900	65400
Active Cruise Control		------	450	450	490	490
Luxury Seating		------	1350	1350	1460	1460

2013 BMW — WB(AorS)(UP7C5)-D-#

1 SERIES—6-Cyl.—Equipment Schedule 1
W.B. 104.7"; 3.0 Liter.

Body Type	VIN	List	Trade-In Good	Very Good	Pvt-Party Good	Retail Excellent
128i Coupe 2D	UP7C5	35590	18850	19500	21200	24700
128i Convertible 2D	UL7C5	41290	23200	24000	25800	29900
Premium Pkg		------	550	550	665	665
M Sport Pkg		------	1175	1175	1420	1420
1 SERIES—6-Cyl. Turbo—Equipment Schedule 1						
W.B. 104.7"; 3.0 Liter.						
135i Coupe 2D	UC9C5	41645	25000	25800	27600	31900
135is Coupe 2D	UC9C5	45595	28400	29300	31300	36100
135i Convertible 2D	UN7C5	46445	26800	27700	29700	34500
135is Convertible 2D	UN7C5	50295	29300	30200	32400	37600
Premium Pkg		------	550	550	650	650
M Sport Pkg		------	1175	1175	1390	1390
3 SERIES—4-Cyl. Turbo—Equipment Schedule 1						
W.B. 104.7"; 2.0 Liter.						
320i Sedan 4D	3B1C5	35945	21200	21900	22700	25600
320i xDrive Sedan 4D	3C1C5	37945	22600	23400	24200	27300
328i Sedan 4D	3A5C5	38845	23900	24700	25600	29000
328i xDrive Sedan 4D	3B3C5	40845	25300	26100	27100	30600
Active Cruise Control		------	475	475	535	535
M Sport Line		------	1175	1175	1330	1330
Premium Pkg		------	550	550	620	620
3 SERIES—6-Cyl.—Equipment Schedule 1						
W.B. 108.7"; 3.0 Liter.						
328i Coupe 2D	KE3C5	42040	22700	23500	24400	27600
328i xDrive Coupe 2D	KF3C5	43740	24600	25400	26400	29800
328i Convertible 2D	DW3C5	50045	28400	29300	30400	34100
Active Cruise Control		------	475	475	545	545
Premium Pkg		------	550	550	630	630
M Sport Pkg		------	1175	1175	1345	1345
3 SERIES—6-Cyl. Turbo—Equipment Schedule 1						
W.B. 108.7", 110.6" (335i xDrive Sed); 3.0 Liter.						
335i Sedan 4D	3A9C5	45145	29900	30900	31900	36000
335i xDrive Sedan 4D	3B9C5	47145	31000	32000	33000	37100
335i Coupe 2D	KG7C5	47445	28000	28900	29900	33700
335i xDrive Coupe 2D	KF9C5	49145	29400	30400	31400	35500
335i Convertible 2D	DX7C5	54695	32600	33600	34700	38900
Active Cruise Control		------	475	475	535	535
Premium Pkg		------	550	550	630	630
M Sport Pkg		------	1175	1175	1340	1340
3 SERIES—6-Cyl. Twin Turbo—Equipment Schedule 1						
W.B. 108.7"; 3.0 Liter.						
335is Coupe 2D	KG1C5	54445	32800	33800	34900	39300
335is Convertible 2D	DX1C5	61695	37800	39000	40000	44700
Premium Pkg		------	550	550	630	630
3 SERIES—6-Cyl. Turbo ActiveHybrid—Equipment Schedule 1						
W.B. 110.6"; 3.0 Liter.						
3 Sedan 4D	3F9C5	51645	28900	29900	30800	34800
Active Cruise Control		------	475	475	535	535
Premium Pkg		------	550	550	620	620
M Sport Pkg		------	1175	1175	1325	1325
M3—V8—Equipment Schedule 1						
W.B. 108.7"; 4.0 Liter.						
Coupe 2D	KG9C5	62295	44400	45700	46400	51500
Convertible 2D	DX9C5	71345	45400	46700	47300	52500
Competition Pkg		------	1200	1200	1295	1295
M3—V8—Equipment Schedule 1						
W.B. 108.7"; 4.0 Liter.						
Lime Rock Park Ed 2D	KG9C5	73190	52200	53700	54700	60900
Frozen Limited Ed 2D	KG9C5	78590	48800	50300	51300	57100

2013 BMW

Body Type	VIN	List	Trade-In Good	Very Good	Pvt-Party Good	Retail Excellent
Z4—4-Cyl. Turbo—Equipment Schedule 1						
W.B. 98.3"; 2.0 Liter.						
28i Roadster 2D	LL5C5	48245	27900	28800	29700	33400
Premium Pkg		------	550	550	605	605
Sport Pkg		------	350	350	385	385
M Sport Pkg		------	1175	1175	1295	1295
Z4—6-Cyl. Twin Turbo—Equipment Schedule 1						
W.B. 98.3"; 3.0 Liter.						
35i Roadster 2D	LM7C5	56045	33400	34400	35400	39600
35is Roadster 2D	LM1C5	65095	36500	37600	38500	43000
Premium Pkg		------	550	550	605	605
M Sport Pkg		------	1175	1175	1295	1295
5 SERIES—4-Cyl. Turbo—Equipment Schedule 1						
W.B. 116.9"; 2.0 Liter.						
528i Sedan 4D	XG5C5	49845	28200	29300	30200	34200
528i xDrive Sedan 4D	XH5C5	52145	30300	31400	32200	36200
Bang & Olufsen Sound		------	2875	2875	3235	3235
Active Cruise Control		------	475	475	535	535
Premium Pkg		------	550	550	620	620
M Sport Pkg		------	1175	1175	1325	1325
5 SERIES—6-Cyl. Turbo—Equipment Schedule 1						
W.B. 116.9", 120.9" (Gran Turismo); 3.0 Liter.						
535i Sedan 4D	FR7C5	53995	33300	34400	35200	39600
535i xDrive Sedan 4D	FU7C5	56295	36100	37400	37900	42500
535i Gran Turismo Sed	SN2C5	58895	31000	32100	32800	37000
535i Grn Turismo xDrv	SP2C5	61195	33800	35000	35700	40200
Bang & Olufsen Sound		------	2875	2875	3225	3225
Active Cruise Control		------	475	475	535	535
Driver Assistance Pkg		------	650	650	730	730
Premium Pkg		------	550	550	615	615
M Sport Pkg		------	1175	1175	1320	1320
5 SERIES—6-Cyl. Turbo ActiveHybrid—Equipment Schedule 1						
W.B. 116.9"; 3.0 Liter.						
5 Sedan 4D	FZ9C5	61995	33500	34700	35500	40000
Bang & Olufsen Sound		------	2875	2875	3250	3250
Premium Pkg		------	550	550	620	620
Sport Pkg		------	1050	1050	1185	1185
5 SERIES—V8 Twin Turbo—Equipment Schedule 1						
W.B. 116.9", 120.9" (Gran Turismo); 4.4 Liter.						
550i Sedan 4D	FR9C5	63295	36900	38200	39000	43900
550i xDrive Sedan 4D	FU9C5	65595	40900	42400	43000	48300
550i Gran Turismo Sed	SN0C5	68395	37200	38500	39300	44300
550i Grn Turismo xDrv	SP0C5	70695	42400	43900	44500	50100
Bang & Olufsen Sound		------	2875	2875	3205	3205
Active Cruise Control		------	475	475	530	530
Dynamic Handling Pkg		------	1000	1000	1115	1115
Executive Pkg		------	2000	2000	2230	2230
M Sport Pkg		------	1175	1175	1310	1310
M5—V8 Twin Turbo—Equipment Schedule 1						
W.B. 116.9"; 4.4 Liter.						
Sedan 4D	FV9C5	92095	55400	57100	57800	63900
Bang & Olufsen Sound		------	2875	2875	3040	3040
6 SERIES—6-Cyl. Turbo (Gran); 3.0 Liter.—Equipment Schedule 1						
W.B. 112.4", 116.9" (Gran); 3.0 Liter.						
640i Coupe 2D	LW3C5	75295	45000	46500	46800	51900
640i Convertible 2D	LW7C5	82795	48000	49600	50200	55800
640i Gran Coupe 4D	6A0C5	76895	46000	47600	48000	53400
Bang & Olufsen Sound		------	2875	2875	3105	3105
Active Cruise Control		------	475	475	515	515
Individual Comp		------	2450	2450	2645	2645
M Sport Pkg		------	1050	1050	1135	1135
6 SERIES—V8 Twin Turbo—Equipment Schedule 1						
W.B. 112.4", 116.9" (Gran); 4.4 Liter.						
650i Coupe 2D	YM9C5	86395	47700	49400	50000	55700
650i xDrive Coupe 2D	YM1C5	89395	49300	51000	51700	57500
650i Gran Coupe 4D	6B2C5	87395	50000	51700	52300	58100
650iGranCpe xDrv4D	6B4C5	90395	51300	53100	53500	59400
650i Convertible 2D	YP9C5	93895	52300	54100	54500	60400
650i xDrive Convertible	YP1C5	96895	51600	53400	53900	59900
Bang & Olufsen Sound		------	2875	2875	3115	3115
Active Cruise Control		------	475	475	515	515
Luxury Seating		------	1350	1350	1455	1455
Individual Comp		------	2450	2450	2655	2655

Body Type	VIN	List	Trade-In Good	Very Good	Pvt-Party Good	Retail Excellent
M Sport Pkg			1050	1050	1140	1140
M6—V8 Twin Turbo—Equipment Schedule 1						
W.B. 112.2"; 4.4 Liter.						
Coupe 2D	LX9C5	108295	67600	69900	70200	78000
Convertible 2D	LZ9C5	115295	68600	70900	71100	79000
Bang & Olufsen Sound			2875	2875	3060	3060
7 SERIES—6-Cyl. Turbo—Equipment Schedule 1						
W.B. 126.4"; 3.0 Liter.						
740i Sedan 4D	YA6C5	74195	38900	40100	41500	46900
740Li Sedan 4D	YE4C5	78195	39500	40700	41500	46300
740i xDrive Sedan 4D	YF4C5	81195	45100	46500	46900	52000
Bang & Olufsen Sound			2875	2875	3120	3120
Driver Assistance Pkg			650	650	705	705
Luxury Seating			1350	1350	1475	1475
Individual Comp			2450	2450	2660	2660
M Sport Pkg			1175	1175	1275	1275
7 SERIES—6-Cyl. Turbo ActiveHybrid—Equipment Schedule 1						
W.B. 126.4"; 3.0 Liter.						
ActiveHybrid 7 Sedan	YE0C5	84895	45100	46500	48000	54200
Bang & Olufsen Sound			2875	2875	3100	3100
Luxury Seating			1350	1350	1465	1465
Individual Comp			2450	2450	2640	2640
M Sport Pkg			1175	1175	1270	1270
7 SERIES—V8 Twin Turbo—Equipment Schedule 1						
W.B. 126.4"; 4.4 Liter.						
750i Sedan 4D	YA8C5	88195	44600	46000	46500	51500
750i xDrive Sedan 4D	YB6C5	91495	45600	47000	48300	54400
750Li Sedan 4D	YE8C5	91895	47100	48500	49200	54800
750Li xDrive Sedan 4D	YF8C5	95195	47800	49200	50900	57300
Bang & Olufsen Sound			2875	2875	3105	3105
Driver Assistance Pkg			650	650	700	700
Luxury Seating			1350	1350	1465	1465
Individual Comp			2450	2450	2645	2645
M Sport Pkg			1175	1175	1270	1270
ALPINA B7—V8 Twin Turbo—Equipment Schedule 1						
W.B. 126.4"; 4.4 Liter.						
Sedan 4D	YA8C5	127495	66200	68100	68600	75900
Bang & Olufsen Sound			2875	2875	3110	3110
Luxury Seating			1350	1350	1470	1470

2014 BMW — WB(AorS)(1Z2C5)—E—#

Body Type	VIN	List	Trade-In Good	Very Good	Pvt-Party Good	Retail Excellent
i3—Electric—Equipment Schedule 1						
W.B. 101.2".						
Hatchback 4D	1Z2C5	42275	30500	30500	33300	35900
2 SERIES—4-Cyl. Turbo—Equipment Schedule 1						
W.B. 105.9"; 2.0 Liter.						
228i Coupe 2D	1F5C5	37075	25400	26200	28000	32200
Premium Pkg			575	575	660	660
M Sport Line			1200	1200	1380	1380
2 SERIES—6-Cyl. Turbo—Equipment Schedule 1						
W.B. 105.9"; 3.0 Liter.						
M235i Coupe 2D	1J7C5	44025	36000	37100	38700	43800
Premium Pkg			575	575	645	645
3 SERIES—4-Cyl. Turbo—Equipment Schedule 1						
W.B. 110.6"; 2.0 Liter.						
320i Sedan 4D	3B1C5	36875	22300	23000	23900	26900
320i xDrive Sedan 4D	3C3C5	38875	23700	24500	25400	28600
328i Sedan 4D	3A5C5	40725	27900	28800	29600	33200
328i xDrive Sedan 4D	3B3C5	42725	29800	30700	31500	35300
328i Grn Trsm xDrive	3X5C5	43825	31800	32800	33600	37600
328i Sport Wagon 4D	3G7C5	43825	32900	33900	34700	38700
Active Cruise Control			500	500	555	555
Premium Pkg			575	575	640	640
Sport Pkg			375	375	420	420
M Sport Line			1200	1200	1335	1335
3 SERIES—6-Cyl. Turbo—Equipment Schedule 1						
W.B. 108.7", 110.6" (335i xDrive Sed); 3.0 Liter.						
335i Sedan 4D	3A9C5	45775	34100	35100	35900	40100
335i xDrive Sedan 4D	3B9C5	47775	35700	36800	37500	41800
335i Gran Trsmo xDrv	3X9C5	49225	36000	37100	37900	42300
Active Cruise Control			500	500	555	555
Premium Pkg			575	575	635	635
M Sport Line			1200	1200	1330	1330

Body Type	VIN	List	Trade-In Good	Very Good	Pvt-Party Good	Retail Excellent
3 SERIES—6-Cyl. Turbo ActiveHybrid—Equipment Schedule 1						
W.B. 110.6"; 3.0 Liter.						
3 Sedan 4D	3F9C5	52275	35000	36100	36800	41000
Active Cruise Control		———	500	500	550	550
Premium Pkg		———	575	575	635	635
M Sport Line		———	1200	1200	1325	1325
3 SERIES—6-Cyl. Turbo Diesel—Equipment Schedule 1						
W.B. 110.6"; 2.0 Liter.						
328d Sedan 4D	3D3C5	42025	29800	30700	31500	35300
328d xDrive Sedan 4D	3D5C5	44025	31700	32700	33500	37400
328d xDrive Sport Wag	3K5C5	45325	35500	36600	37200	41400
Active Cruise Control		———	500	500	555	555
Premium Pkg		———	575	575	635	635
M Sport Line		———	1200	1200	1330	1330
4 SERIES—4-Cyl. Turbo—Equipment Schedule 1						
W.B. 110.6"; 2.0 Liter.						
428i Coupe 2D	3N3C5	41425	31000	32000	32500	36000
428i xDrive Coupe 2D	3N5C5	43425	33100	34200	34600	38400
428i Convertible 2D	3V5C5	49675	40600	41800	42400	46800
428i xDrive Conv 2D	3V9C5	51676	42300	43600	44200	48800
Active Speed Control		———	500	500	550	550
M Sport Line		———	1200	1200	1325	1325
4 SERIES—6-Cyl. Turbo—Equipment Schedule 1						
W.B. 110.6"; 3.0 Liter.						
435i Coupe 2D	3R1C5	46925	36000	37100	37600	41600
435i xDrive Coupe 2D	3R5C5	48925	38200	39300	39800	44100
435i Convertible 2D	3T3C5	55825	46000	47400	47900	52900
Active Cruise Control		———	500	500	550	550
M Sport Line		———	1200	1200	1325	1325
5 SERIES—4-Cyl. Turbo—Equipment Schedule 1						
W.B. 116.9"; 2.0 Liter.						
528i Sedan 4D	5A5C5	51875	34300	35500	35900	40000
528i xDrive Sedan 4D	5A7C5	54175	37200	38500	38700	43100
Bang & Olufsen Sound		———	3000	3000	3300	3300
Active Cruise Control		———	500	500	550	550
Premium Pkg		———	575	575	630	630
M Sport Line		———	1200	1200	1320	1320
5 SERIES—6-Cyl. Turbo—Equipment Schedule 1						
W.B. 116.9"; 3.0 Liter.						
535i Sedan 4D	5B1C5	56025	39200	40600	40900	45600
535i xDrive Sedan 4D	5B3C5	58325	42100	43500	43700	48600
Bang & Olufsen Sound		———	3000	3000	3290	3290
Active Cruise Control		———	500	500	550	550
Luxury Seating		———	1375	1375	1510	1510
Dynamic Handling Pkg		———	1000	1000	1095	1095
Individual Comp		———	2500	2500	2745	2745
Premium Pkg		———	575	575	630	630
M Sport Line		———	1200	1200	1315	1315
5 SERIES—6-Cyl. Turbo—Equipment Schedule 1						
W.B. 116.9"; 3.0 Liter.						
535i Gran Turismo Sed	5M2C5	61125	38000	39300	39600	44100
535i Grn Turismo xDrv	5M4C5	63425	43400	44800	44900	49800
Bang & Olufsen Sound		———	3000	3000	3285	3285
Luxury Seating		———	1375	1375	1505	1505
Dynamic Handling Pkg		———	1000	1000	1095	1095
M Sport Line		———	1200	1200	1315	1315
5 SERIES—6-Cyl. Turbo Diesel—Equipment Schedule 1						
W.B. 116.9"; 3.0 Liter.						
535d Sedan 4D	XA5C5	57525	42800	44300	44300	49000
535d xDrive Sedan 4D	FV3C5	59825	44200	45700	45500	50300
Bang & Olufsen Sound		———	3000	3000	3255	3255
Active Cruise Control		———	500	500	540	540
Luxury Seating		———	1375	1375	1490	1490
Dynamic Handling Pkg		———	1000	1000	1085	1085
Individual Comp		———	2500	2500	2710	2710
Premium Pkg		———	575	575	625	625
M Sport Line		———	1200	1200	1300	1300
5 SERIES—6-Cyl. Turbo ActiveHybrid—Equipment Schedule 1						
W.B. 116.9"; 3.0 Liter.						
5 Sedan 4D	5E1C5	62325	39500	40900	41300	46100
Bang & Olufsen Sound		———	3000	3000	3335	3335
Active Cruise Control		———	500	500	555	555
Premium Pkg		———	575	575	640	640

Body Type	VIN	List	Trade-In Good	Very Good	Pvt-Party Good	Retail Excellent
M Sport Line			1200	1200	1335	1335
Individual Comp			2500	2500	2780	2780

5 SERIES—V8 Twin Turbo—Equipment Schedule 1
W.B. 116.9"; 4.4 Liter.

Body Type	VIN	List	Good	Very Good	Good	Excellent
550i Sedan 4D	KN9C5	64825	44100	45600	45900	51100
550i xDrive Sedan 4D	KP9C5	67125	47500	49100	49200	54700
550i Gran Turismo Sed	5M6C5	69025	43500	44900	45200	50300
550i Grn Turismo xDrv	5M0C5	71325	48400	50000	50600	56400
Bang & Olufsen Sound			3000	3000	3285	3285
Active Cruise Control			500	500	545	545
Luxury Seating			1375	1375	1505	1505
Dynamic Handling Pkg			1000	1000	1095	1095
Executive Pkg			2100	2100	2300	2300
Individual Comp			2500	2500	2740	2740
M Sport Line			1200	1200	1315	1315

M5—V8 Twin Turbo—Equipment Schedule 1
W.B. 116.7"; 4.4 Liter.

Body Type	VIN	List	Good	Very Good	Good	Excellent
Sedan 4D	FV9C5	95125	67600	69600	69700	76600
Bang & Olufsen Sound			3000	3000	3150	3150
Competition Pkg			1250	1250	1310	1310

6 SERIES—6-Cyl. Turbo—Equipment Schedule 1
W.B. 112.4", 116.9" (Gran); 3.0 Liter.

Body Type	VIN	List	Good	Very Good	Good	Excellent
640i Coupe 2D	LW3C5	75795	52000	53700	53800	59300
640i xDrive Coupe 2D	LX9C5	78795	53200	55000	55400	61400
640i Gran Coupe 4D	6A0C5	77995	54900	56800	56800	62700
640i GranCpe xDrive	6B8C5	80995	57100	59000	59100	65300
640i Convertible 2D	LW7C5	83295	55200	57000	57100	63000
640i xDrive Convertible	YP5C5	86295	59700	61600	61600	67900
Bang & Olufsen Sound			3000	3000	3215	3215
Active Cruise Control			500	500	535	535
Driver Assistance Pkg			675	675	725	725
Driver Asst Plus Pkg			675	675	725	725
Executive Pkg			2100	2100	2250	2250
Individual Comp			2500	2500	2675	2675
M Sport Pkg			1125	1125	1205	1205

6 SERIES—V8 Twin Turbo—Equipment Schedule 1
W.B. 112.4", 116.9" (Gran); 4.4 Liter.

Body Type	VIN	List	Good	Very Good	Good	Excellent
650i Coupe 2D	YM9C5	87095	55500	57300	57600	63700
650i xDrive Coupe 2D	YM1C5	90095	58600	60500	60500	66800
650i Gran Coupe 4D	6B2C5	89295	61200	63200	63000	69300
650i GranCpe xDrv 4D	6B4C5	92295	62900	65000	64600	71000
650i Convertible 2D	YP0C5	94595	61500	63500	63300	69600
650i xDrive Convertible	YP1C5	97595	65200	67300	66900	73500
650i Frozen White Cnv	YP9C5	106695				
650i Frzn Wht xDrv Cnv	YP1C5	110095				
Bang & Olufsen Sound			3000	3000	3220	3220
Active Cruise Control			500	500	535	535
Driver Assistance Pkg			675	675	725	725
Driver Asst Plus Pkg			675	675	725	725
Executive Pkg			2100	2100	2255	2255
Individual Comp			2500	2500	2685	2685
M Sport Pkg			1125	1125	1210	1210

M6—V8 Twin Turbo—Equipment Schedule 1
W.B. 112.2", 116.9" (4D); 4.4 Liter.

Body Type	VIN	List	Good	Very Good	Good	Excellent
Coupe 2D	LX9C5	111395	80600	83200	82600	91000
Coupe 4D	6C9C5	115195	84400	87200	86000	94200
Convertible 2D	LZ9C5	117695	84600	87400	86400	95000
Bang & Olufsen Sound			3000	3000	3160	3160
Executive Pkg			2100	2100	2210	2210

7 SERIES—6-Cyl. Turbo—Equipment Schedule 1
W.B. 126.4"; 3.0 Liter.

Body Type	VIN	List	Good	Very Good	Good	Excellent
740i Sedan 4D	YA6C5	74925	49900	51400	52500	58400
740Li Sedan 4D	YE4C5	78925	50500	52100	52500	57800
740Li xDrive Sedan 4D	YE4C5	81925	56200	57900	57800	63100
Bang & Olufsen Sound			3000	3000	3200	3200
Active Cruise Control			500	500	535	535
Driver Asst Plus Pkg			675	675	720	720
Executive Pkg			2100	2100	2240	2240
Luxury Seating			1375	1375	1455	1455
Individual Comp			2500	2500	2670	2670
M Sport Pkg			1200	1200	1280	1280

7 SERIES—6-Cyl. Turbo Hybrid—Equipment Schedule 1
W.B. 126.4"; 3.0 Liter.

Body Type	VIN	List	Trade-In Good	Very Good	Pvt-Party Good	Retail Excellent
ActiveHybrid 7 Sedan	YE0C5	85225	**56300**	**57900**	**59000**	**65700**
Bang & Olufsen Sound			**3000**	**3000**	**3190**	**3190**
Luxury Seating			**1375**	**1375**	**1460**	**1460**
Individual Comp			**2500**	**2500**	**2660**	**2660**
M Sport Pkg			**1200**	**1200**	**1275**	**1275**
7 SERIES—V8 Twin Turbo—Equipment Schedule 1						
W.B. 126.4"; 4.4 Liter.						
750i Sedan 4D	YA8C5	88225	**55700**	**57400**	**57500**	**62900**
750i xDrive Sedan 4D	YB6C5	91225	**57800**	**59500**	**60400**	**66900**
750Li Sedan 4D	YE8C5	91925	**58200**	**59900**	**60200**	**66200**
750Li xDrive Sedan 4D	YF8C5	94925	**59200**	**61000**	**61900**	**68700**
Bang & Olufsen Sound			**3000**	**3000**	**3165**	**3165**
Active Cruise Control			**500**	**500**	**525**	**525**
Driver Asst Plus Pkg			**675**	**675**	**710**	**710**
Executive Pkg			**2100**	**2100**	**2215**	**2215**
Luxury Seating			**1375**	**1375**	**1450**	**1450**
Individual Comp			**2500**	**2500**	**2635**	**2635**
M Sport Pkg			**1200**	**1200**	**1265**	**1265**

BENTLEY

2005 BENTLEY — SCB(LC37F)-5-#

ARNAGE—V8 Twin Turbo—Equipment Schedule 2
W.B. 122.7", 132.5"; 6.8 Liter.

Body Type	VIN	List	Good	Very Good	Good	Excellent
R Sedan 4D	LC37F	219985	****	****	****	**86000**
T Sedan 4D	LF34F	241985	****	****	****	**91900**
RL Sedan 4D	LC37F	250985	****	****	****	**97800**

CONTINENTAL—W12 Twin Turbo—Equipment Schedule 2
W.B. 108.0", 120.7"; 6.0 Liter.

Body Type	VIN	List	Good	Very Good	Good	Excellent
Coupe 2D	CR63W	162285	****	****	****	**80600**
Flying Spur Sedan 4D	BR53W		****	****	****	**77000**

2006 BENTLEY — SCB(LC43F)-6-#

ARNAGE—V8 Twin Turbo—Equipment Schedule 2
W.B. 122.7", 132.5"; 6.8 Liter.

Body Type	VIN	List	Good	Very Good	Good	Excellent
R Sedan 4D	LC43F	220985	****	****	****	**103700**
T Sedan 4D	LF34F	242985	****	****	****	**109700**
RL Sedan 4D	LC37F	251985	****	****	****	**115600**

CONTINENTAL AWD—W12 Twin Turbo—Equipment Schedule 2
W.B. 108.1", 120.7"; 6.0 Liter.

Body Type	VIN	List	Good	Very Good	Good	Excellent
Coupe 2D	CR63W	171285	****	****	****	**88700**
Flying Spur Sedan 4D	BR53W	172125	****	****	****	**85200**

2007 BENTLEY — SCB(LC47J)-7-#

ARNAGE—V8 Twin Turbo—Equipment Schedule 2
W.B. 122.7", 132.5"; 6.8 Liter.

Body Type	VIN	List	Good	Very Good	Good	Excellent
R Sedan 4D	LC47J	229985	****	****	****	**121200**
T Sedan 4D	LF44J	250985	****	****	****	**129300**
RL Sedan 4D	LF37J	271985	****	****	****	**144400**

AZURE—V8 Twin Turbo—Equipment Schedule 2
W.B. 122.7"; 6.8 Liter.

Body Type	VIN	List	Good	Very Good	Good	Excellent
Convertible 2D	DC47L	337085	****	****	****	**169800**

CONTINENTAL AWD—W12 Twin Turbo—Equipment Schedule 2
W.B. 108.1", 120.7"; 6.0 Liter.

Body Type	VIN	List	Good	Very Good	Good	Excellent
GT Coupe 2D	CR73W	176285	****	****	****	**105400**
Flying Spur Sedan 4D	BR93W	176285	****	****	****	**102000**
GTC Convertible 2D	DR33W	196285	****	****	****	**116800**

2008 BENTLEY — SCB(LC47J)-8-#

ARNAGE—V8 Twin Turbo—Equipment Schedule 2
W.B. 122.7", 132.5"; 6.8 Liter.

Body Type	VIN	List	Good	Very Good	Good	Excellent
R Sedan 4D	LC47J	229085	****	****	****	**141100**
T Sedan 4D	LF44J	250085	****	****	****	**153600**
RL Sedan 4D	LE47K	271085	****	****	****	**166000**

AZURE—V8 Twin Turbo—Equipment Schedule 2
W.B. 122.7"; 6.8 Liter.

Body Type	VIN	List	Good	Very Good	Good	Excellent
Convertible 2D	DC47L	338085	****	****	****	**205700**

CONTINENTAL AWD—W12 Twin Turbo—Equipment Schedule 2
W.B. 108.1", 120.7"; 6.0 Liter.

Body Type	VIN	List	Good	Very Good	Good	Excellent
GT Coupe 2D	CR73W	178585	****	****	****	**114200**

Body Type	VIN	List	Trade-In Good	Very Good	Pvt-Party Good	Retail Excellent
GT Speed Coupe 2D	CP73W	202585	****	****	****	131000
Flying Spur Sedan 4D	BR93W	173585	****	****	****	110800
GTC Convertible 2D	DR33W	196585	****	****	****	125500

2009 BENTLEY — SCB(LC47J)–9–#

ARNAGE—V8 Twin Turbo—Equipment Schedule 2
W.B. 122.7", 132.5"; 6.8 Liter.

R Sedan 4D	LC47J	227585	****	****	****	156900
T Sedan 4D	LF44J	249585	****	****	****	173400
RL Sedan 4D	LE47K	270585	****	****	****	184300
Final Series Sedan 4D	LF44J	273585	****	****	****	200900

AZURE—V8 Twin Turbo—Equipment Schedule 2
W.B. 122.7"; 6.8 Liter.

Convertible 2D	DC47L	342085	****	****	****	255400

BROOKLANDS—V8 Twin Turbo—Equipment Schedule 2
W.B. 122.7"; 6.8 Liter.

Coupe 2D	CC41N	348085	****	****	****	257000

CONTINENTAL AWD—W12 Twin Turbo—Equipment Schedule 2
W.B. 108.1", 120.7"; 6.0 Liter.

GT Coupe 2D	CR73W	181795	****	****	****	132000
GT Speed Coupe 2D	CP73W	206195	****	****	****	154100
Flying Spur Sedan 4D	BR93W	176695	****	****	****	124300
Flying Spur Speed Sdn	BP93W	201095	****	****	****	151300
GTC Convertible 2D	DR33W	200095	****	****	****	149600
GTC Speed Conv 2D	DP33W		****	****	****	184800
Adaptive Cruise Control			****	****	****	380

2010 BENTLEY — SCB(DC4BL)–A–#

AZURE T—V8 Twin Turbo—Equipment Schedule 2
W.B. 122.7"; 6.8 Liter.

Convertible 2D	DC4BL	370095	****	****	****	337800

BROOKLANDS—V8 Twin Turbo—Equipment Schedule 2
W.B. 122.7"; 6.8 Liter.

Coupe 2D	CC41N	348085	****	****	****	316100

CONTINENTAL AWD—W12 Twin Turbo—Equipment Schedule 2
W.B. 108.1", 120.7"; 6.0 Liter.

GT Coupe 2D	CR7ZA	189095	****	****	****	137500
GT Speed Cpe 2D	CP7ZA	213995	****	****	****	159000
Supersports Cpe 2D	CU8ZA	272195	****	****	****	215500
Flying Spur Sed 4D	BR9ZA	183895	****	****	****	131500
Flying Spur Speed Sed	BP9ZA	208795	****	****	****	156300
GTC Convertible 2D	DR3ZA	207795	****	****	****	154600
GTC Speed Conv 2D	DP3ZA	237695	****	****	****	188800
Supersports Conv 2D	CU8ZA		****	****	****	246900
Adaptive Cruise Control			****	****	****	410

2011 BENTLEY — SCB(BR9ZA)–B–#

CONTINENTAL AWD—W12 Twin Turbo—Equipment Schedule 2
W.B. 108.1", 120.7"; 6.0 Liter.

Flying Spur Sedan 4D	BR9ZA	186795	****	****	****	136200
Flying Spur Speed 4D	BP9ZA	212195	****	****	****	160600
Supersports Coupe 2D	CU7ZA	272195	****	****	****	218900
GTC Convertible 2D	DR3ZA	211195	****	****	****	159000
GTC Speed Conv 2D	DP3ZA	238695	****	****	****	192700
Supersports Conv 2D	DU3ZA	285595	****	****	****	249900
Adaptive Cruise Control			****	****	****	430

MULSANNE—V8 Twin Turbo—Equipment Schedule 2
W.B. 128.6"; 6.8 Liter.

Sedan 4D	BB7ZH	291295	****	****	****	263400
Adaptive Cruise Control			****	****	****	435

2012 BENTLEY — SCB(BR9ZA)–C–#

CONTINENTAL AWD—W12 Twin Turbo—Equipment Schedule 2
W.B. 108.1", 120.7"; 6.0 Liter.

Flying Spur Sedan 4D	BR9ZA	186795	****	****	****	141300
Flying Spur Speed 4D	BP9ZA	212195	****	****	****	164700
GT Coupe 2D	FR7ZA	192495	****	****	****	146400
Supersports Coupe 2D	CU7ZA	269595	****	****	****	222400
Supersports Conv 2D	DU3ZA	282995	****	****	****	253700
Adaptive Cruise Control			****	****	****	455

MULSANNE—V8 Twin Turbo—Equipment Schedule 2
W.B. 128.6"; 6.8 Liter.

2012 BENTLEY

Body Type	VIN	List	Trade-In Good	Very Good	Pvt-Party Good	Retail Excellent
Sedan 4D	BB7ZH	296295	****	****	****	**271200**
Adaptive Cruise Control			****	****	****	460

2013 BENTLEY — SCB(BR9ZA)–D–#

MULSANNE—V8 Twin Turbo—Equipment Schedule 2
W.B. 128.6"; 6.8 Liter.

Sedan 4D	BB7ZH	302425	****	****	****	**276400**
Adaptive Cruise Control			****	****	****	485

BUICK

2000 BUICK — (1,2or3)G4(WS52J)–Y–#

CENTURY—V6—Equipment Schedule 4
W.B. 109.0"; 3.1 Liter.

Custom Sedan 4D	WS52J	20592	**950**	**1100**	**1675**	**2850**
Century 2000 Pkg			125	125	180	180
Limited	Y		275	275	360	360

REGAL—V6—Equipment Schedule 4
W.B. 109.0"; 3.8 Liter.

LS Sedan 4D	WB52K	22780	**950**	**1075**	**1675**	**2850**
Gran Touring Pkg			50	50	65	65

REGAL—V6 Supercharged—Equipment Schedule 4
W.B. 109.0"; 3.8 Liter.

GS Sedan 4D	WF521	25625	**1350**	**1500**	**2225**	**3750**

LeSABRE—V6—Equipment Schedule 4
W.B. 112.2"; 3.8 Liter.

Custom Sedan 4D	HP54K	24115	**1025**	**1175**	**1775**	**2925**
Limited Sedan 4D	HR54K	27310	**1150**	**1300**	**2025**	**3425**
Gran Touring Pkg			50	50	65	65

PARK AVENUE—V6—Equipment Schedule 4
W.B. 113.8"; 3.8 Liter.

Sedan 4D	CW52K	32395	**975**	**1100**	**1725**	**2875**
Gran Touring Pkg			50	50	65	65

PARK AVENUE—V6 Supercharged—Equipment Schedule 4
W.B. 113.8"; 3.8 Liter.

Ultra Sedan 4D	CU521	37470	**1425**	**1600**	**2300**	**3825**
Gran Touring Pkg			50	50	65	65

2001 BUICK — (1or2)G4(WS52J)–2–#

CENTURY—V6—Equipment Schedule 4
W.B. 109.0"; 3.1 Liter.

Custom Sedan 4D	WS52J	20870	**1175**	**1350**	**1950**	**3250**
Limited	Y		300	300	410	410

REGAL—V6—Equipment Schedule 4
W.B. 109.0"; 3.8 Liter.

LS Sedan 4D	WB52K	23445	**1125**	**1250**	**1900**	**3175**
Abboud Pkg			75	75	100	100
Gran Touring Pkg			50	50	65	65

REGAL—V6 Supercharged—Equipment Schedule 4
W.B. 109.0"; 3.8 Liter.

GS Sedan 4D	WF521	26695	**1450**	**1600**	**2375**	**4000**
Abboud Pkg			75	75	100	100

LeSABRE—V6—Equipment Schedule 4
W.B. 112.2"; 3.8 Liter.

Custom Sedan 4D	HP54K	24762	**1175**	**1325**	**2000**	**3325**
Limited Sedan 4D	HR54K	29451	**1225**	**1375**	**2200**	**3750**
Gran Touring Pkg			50	50	65	65

PARK AVENUE—V6—Equipment Schedule 4
W.B. 113.8"; 3.8 Liter.

Sedan 4D	CW52K	33700	**1250**	**1400**	**2025**	**3350**
Gran Touring Pkg			50	50	65	65

PARK AVENUE—V6 Supercharged—Equipment Schedule 4
W.B. 113.8"; 3.8 Liter.

Ultra Sedan 4D	CU521	38210	**1625**	**1825**	**2650**	**4300**
Gran Touring Pkg			50	50	65	65

2002 BUICK — (1or2)G4(WS52J)–2–#

CENTURY—V6—Equipment Schedule 4
W.B. 109.0"; 3.1 Liter.

Custom Sedan 4D	WS52J	21325	**1525**	**1700**	**2375**	**3925**

Body Type	VIN	List	Trade-In Good	Very Good	Pvt-Party Good	Retail Excellent
Limited .... Y			350	350	460	460
REGAL—V6—Equipment Schedule 4						
W.B. 109.0"; 3.8 Liter.						
LS Sedan 4D........................ WB52K	23840		1500	1675	2275	3700
Abboud Pkg			75	75	105	105
Gran Touring Pkg			75	75	100	100
REGAL—V6 Supercharged—Equipment Schedule 4						
W.B. 109.0"; 3.8 Liter.						
GS Sedan 4D........................ WF521	27895		1600	1775	2575	4275
Abboud Pkg			75	75	105	105
LeSABRE—V6—Equipment Schedule 4						
W.B. 112.2"; 3.8 Liter.						
Custom Sedan 4D.................. HP54K	24975		1550	1725	2375	3850
Limited Sedan 4D.................. HR54K	30675		1650	1850	2675	4325
PARK AVENUE—V6—Equipment Schedule 4						
W.B. 113.8"; 3.8 Liter.						
Sedan 4D............................. CW52K	34165		1600	1800	2475	4025
Gran Touring Pkg			75	75	100	100
PARK AVENUE—V6 Supercharged—Equipment Schedule 4						
W.B. 113.8"; 3.8 Liter.						
Ultra Sedan 4D.................... CU521	38675		2050	2275	3175	5025
Gran Touring Pkg			75	75	100	100

2003 BUICK — (1or2)G4(WS52J)–3–#

Body Type	VIN	List	Trade-In Good	Very Good	Pvt-Party Good	Retail Excellent
CENTURY—V6—Equipment Schedule 4						
W.B. 109.0"; 3.1 Liter.						
Sedan 4D............................. WS52J	21685		1800	2000	2925	4775
Limited .... Y			375	375	515	515
REGAL—V6—Equipment Schedule 4						
W.B. 109.0"; 3.8 Liter.						
LS Sedan 4D........................ WB52K	24230		1800	2000	2775	4375
Abboud Pkg			75	75	115	115
Gran Touring Pkg			100	100	135	135
REGAL—V6 Supercharged—Equipment Schedule 4						
W.B. 109.0"; 3.8 Liter.						
GS Sedan 4D........................ WF521	28175		1925	2125	3125	5050
Abboud Pkg			75	75	115	115
LeSABRE—V6—Equipment Schedule 4						
W.B. 112.2"; 3.8 Liter.						
Custom Sedan 4D.................. HP52K	25730		1850	2050	2800	4375
Limited Sedan 4D.................. HR54K	31360		2000	2225	3100	4900
Celebration Edition			350	350	460	460
PARK AVENUE—V6—Equipment Schedule 4						
W.B. 113.8"; 3.8 Liter.						
Sedan 4D............................. CW54K	34615		1875	2100	2875	4500
Gran Touring Pkg			100	100	135	135
PARK AVENUE—V6 Supercharged—Equipment Schedule 4						
W.B. 113.8"; 3.8 Liter.						
Ultra Sedan 4D.................... CU541	39915		2375	2650	3500	5425

2004 BUICK — (1or2)G4(WS52J)–4–#

Body Type	VIN	List	Trade-In Good	Very Good	Pvt-Party Good	Retail Excellent
CENTURY—V6—Equipment Schedule 4						
W.B. 109.0"; 3.1 Liter.						
Sedan 4D............................. WS52J	22415		2125	2375	3125	4825
Limited			250	250	335	335
Special Edition			425	425	565	565
REGAL—V6—Equipment Schedule 4						
W.B. 109.0"; 3.8 Liter.						
LS Sedan 4D........................ WB52K	24895		2375	2625	3375	5125
Abboud Pkg			100	100	120	120
Gran Touring Pkg			100	100	135	135
REGAL—V6 Supercharged—Equipment Schedule 4						
W.B. 109.0"; 3.8 Liter.						
GS Sedan 4D........................ WF521	28345		2775	3075	3975	6050
Abboud Pkg			100	100	120	120
LeSABRE—V6—Equipment Schedule 4						
W.B. 112.2"; 3.8 Liter.						
Custom Sedan 4D.................. HP54K	26470		2300	2550	3350	5125
Limited Sedan 4D.................. HR54K	32245		2850	3175	4025	6100
Celebration Edition			375	375	500	500
PARK AVENUE—V6—Equipment Schedule 4						
W.B. 113.8"; 3.8 Liter.						

2004 BUICK

Body Type	VIN	List	Trade-In Good	Very Good	Pvt-Party Good	Retail Excellent
Sedan 4D	CW52K	35545	2350	2600	3425	5250
Gran Touring Pkg			100	100	135	135
PARK AVENUE—V6 Supercharged—Equipment Schedule 4						
W.B. 113.8"; 3.8 Liter.						
Ultra Sedan 4D	CU521	40720	3000	3325	4225	6375

2005 BUICK — (1or2)G4(WS52J)-5-#

CENTURY—V6—Equipment Schedule 4
W.B. 109.0"; 3.1 Liter.

Sedan 4D	WS52J	22950	2150	2400	3475	5475
Limited			275	275	360	360
Special Edition			500	500	665	665
LACROSSE—V6—Equipment Schedule 4						
W.B. 110.5"; 3.6 Liter, 3.8 Liter.						
CX Sedan 4D	WC532	23495	2800	3150	3850	5550
CXL Sedan 4D	WD532	25995	3375	3775	4650	6625
CXS Sedan 4D	WE537	28995	3750	4175	5100	7250
LeSABRE—V6—Equipment Schedule 4						
W.B. 112.2"; 3.8 Liter.						
Custom Sedan 4D	HP52K	27270	3050	3375	4225	6150
Limited Sedan 4D	HR54K	32930	3250	3600	4575	6700
Celebration Edition			400	400	540	540
PARK AVENUE—V6—Equipment Schedule 4						
W.B. 113.8"; 3.8 Liter.						
Sedan 4D	CW54K	36350	2575	2900	3850	5750
PARK AVENUE—V6 Supercharged—Equipment Schedule 4						
W.B. 113.8"; 3.8 Liter.						
Special Ed Ultra 4D	CU541	41525	3375	3725	4900	7200

2006 BUICK — (1or2)G4(WC582)-6-#

LACROSSE—V6—Equipment Schedule 4
W.B. 110.5"; 3.6 Liter, 3.8 Liter.

CX Sedan 4D	WC582	23595	3025	3375	4175	5875
CXL Sedan 4D	WD582	26095	3825	4225	5075	7050
CXS Sedan 4D	WE587	29095	4225	4650	5550	7700
LUCERNE—V6—Equipment Schedule 4						
W.B. 115.6"; 3.8 Liter.						
CX Sedan 4D	HP572	26990	3950	4250	5225	7050
CXL Sedan 4D	HD572	28990	4375	4725	5700	7625
V8, 4.6 Liter	Y		550	550	735	735
LUCERNE—V8—Equipment Schedule 4						
W.B. 115.6"; 4.6 Liter.						
CXS Sedan 4D	HE57Y	35990	4600	4950	5975	8000

2007 BUICK — (1or2)G4(WC582)-7-#

LACROSSE—V6—Equipment Schedule 4
W.B. 110.5"; 3.6 Liter, 3.8 Liter.

CX Sedan 4D	WC582	22915	3975	4375	5125	7000
CXL Sedan 4D	WD582	25330	4725	5150	5975	8075
CXS Sedan 4D	WE587	27545	5250	5725	6725	9050
LUCERNE—V6—Equipment Schedule 4						
W.B. 115.6"; 3.8 Liter.						
CX Sedan 4D	HP572	26265	4550	4875	5725	7500
CXL Sedan 4D	HD572	29280	5200	5550	6675	8700
V8, 4.6 Liter	Y		600	600	800	800
LUCERNE—V8—Equipment Schedule 4						
W.B. 115.6"; 4.6 Liter.						
CXS Sedan 4D	HE57Y	35295	5000	5325	6425	8525

2008 BUICK — (1or2)G4(WC582)-8-#

LACROSSE—V6—Equipment Schedule 4
W.B. 110.5"; 3.6 Liter, 3.8 Liter.

CX Sedan 4D	WC582	23995	4950	5350	6100	8025
CXL Sedan 4D	WD582	25995	5800	6250	7225	9400
CXS Sedan 4D	WE587	27995	7025	7525	8875	11700
LACROSSE—V8—Equipment Schedule 4						
W.B. 110.5"; 5.3 Liter.						
Super Sedan 4D	WN58C	31995	8025	8575	10000	13150
LUCERNE—V6—Equipment Schedule 4						
W.B. 115.6"; 3.8 Liter.						
CX Sedan 4D	HP572	26995	5325	5650	6725	8550
CXL Sedan 4D	HD572	29595	6350	6725	7825	9900

Body Type	VIN	List	Trade-In Good	Very Good	Pvt-Party Good	Retail Excellent
CXL Special Ed 4D	HR572	32150	6675	7050	8175	10350
V8, 4.6 Liter			650	650	865	865
LUCERNE—V8—Equipment Schedule 4						
W.B. 115.6"; 4.6 Liter.						
CXS Sedan 4D	HE57Y	36595	6375	6775	8025	10250
Super Sedan 4D	HF579	39395	8075	8525	9850	12400

2009 BUICK — (1or2)G4(WC582)-9-#

Body Type	VIN	List	Trade-In Good	Very Good	Pvt-Party Good	Retail Excellent
LACROSSE—V6—Equipment Schedule 4						
W.B. 110.5"; 3.8 Liter.						
CX Sedan 4D	WC582	25590	5000	5375	6525	8575
CXL Sedan 4D	WD582	27960	7200	7650	8900	11400
LACROSSE—V8—Equipment Schedule 4						
W.B. 110.5"; 5.3 Liter.						
Super Sedan 4D	WN58C	33755	9000	9525	10900	13900
LUCERNE—V6—Equipment Schedule 4						
W.B. 115.6"; 3.9 Liter.						
CX Sedan 4D	HP57M	27520	6975	7350	8475	10450
CXL Sedan 4D	HD57M	30165	7775	8175	9325	11450
CXL Special Ed 4D	HR57M	32980	8275	8700	9875	12100
LUCERNE—V8—Equipment Schedule 4						
W.B. 115.6"; 4.6 Liter.						
Super Sedan 4D	HF579	39395	10150	10600	11900	14550

2010 BUICK — (1,2or3)G4(GB5EG)-A-#

Body Type	VIN	List	Trade-In Good	Very Good	Pvt-Party Good	Retail Excellent
LACROSSE—V6—Equipment Schedule 4						
W.B. 111.7"; 3.0 Liter.						
CX Sedan 4D	GB5EG	27835	9750	10250	11150	13450
CXL Sedan 4D	GC5EG	30395	11000	11550	12500	15150
CXS Sedan 4D	GE5EV	33765	13050	13650	14800	17800
AWD	D		1000	1000	1195	1195
4-Cyl. 2.4 Liter	C		(575)	(575)	(700)	(700)
LUCERNE—V6—Equipment Schedule 4						
W.B. 115.6"; 3.9 Liter.						
CX Sedan 4D	HA5EM	29995	8500	8925	10050	12200
CXL Sedan 4D	HC5EM	33495	9500	9925	11250	13650
CXL Special Ed 4D	HD5EM	33995	9850	10300	11600	14050
CXL Premium Ed.	HC5EM	36390	9775	10250	11650	14200
LUCERNE—V8—Equipment Schedule 4						
W.B. 115.6"; 4.6 Liter.						
Super Sedan 4D	HH5E9	39995	12550	13100	14650	17550

2011 BUICK — (1or2)G4(GN5EC)-B-#

Body Type	VIN	List	Trade-In Good	Very Good	Pvt-Party Good	Retail Excellent
REGAL—4-Cyl.—Equipment Schedule 4						
W.B. 107.8"; 2.4 Liter.						
CXL Sedan 4D	GN5EC	26995	9800	10250	11100	13100
REGAL—4-Cyl. Turbo—Equipment Schedule 4						
W.B. 107.8"; 2.0 Liter.						
CXL Sedan 4D	GV5EV	29495	10650	11100	12050	14250
LACROSSE—V6—Equipment Schedule 4						
W.B. 111.7"; 3.0 Liter.						
CX Sedan 4D	GA5ED	27245	11100	11600	12500	14800
CXL Sedan 4D	GC5ED	30395	12400	12950	13950	16550
AWD	D		1000	1000	1160	1160
4-Cyl. 2.4 Liter	C		(575)	(575)	(680)	(680)
LACROSSE—V6—Equipment Schedule 4						
W.B. 111.7"; 3.6 Liter.						
CXS Sedan 4D	GE5ED	33765	14200	14800	15950	18900
LUCERNE—V6—Equipment Schedule 4						
W.B. 115.6"; 3.9 Liter.						
CX Sedan 4D	HA5EM	29995	10200	10650	11950	14300
CXL Sedan 4D	HC5EM	33495	11250	11700	13150	15700
CXL Premium Sed 4D	HJ5EM	36440	12050	12550	14000	16750
LUCERNE—V8—Equipment Schedule 4						
W.B. 115.6"; 4.6 Liter.						
Super Sedan 4D	HK5ES	45225	14600	15150	16750	19800

2012 BUICK — (1or2)G4(PP5SK)-C-#

Body Type	VIN	List	Trade-In Good	Very Good	Pvt-Party Good	Retail Excellent
VERANO—4-Cyl.—Equipment Schedule 4						
W.B. 105.7"; 2.4 Liter.						
Sedan 4D	PP5SK	23470	10700	11150	12300	14650
Convenience Sedan	PR5SK	24670	11050	11500	12700	15150

Body Type	VIN	List	Trade-In Good	Very Good	Pvt-Party Good	Retail Excellent
Leather Sedan 4D	PS5SK	26850	11550	12050	13150	15500
REGAL—4-Cyl.—Equipment Schedule 4						
W.B. 107.8"; 2.4 Liter.						
Sedan 4D	GR5EK	27530	10750	11200	12250	14500
Premium 1 Sedan 4D	GS5EK	28965	11550	12050	13150	15550
Premium 2 Sedan 4D	GT5EK	30375	12200	12700	13800	16250
REGAL—4-Cyl. Turbo—Equipment Schedule 4						
W.B. 107.8"; 2.0 Liter.						
Premium 1 Sedan 4D	GS5EV	30735	12300	12800	13900	16400
Premium 2 Sedan 4D	GT5EV	32145	13500	14050	15350	18000
Premium 3 Sedan 4D	GU5EV	33395	14500	15050	16300	19150
GS Sedan 4D	GV5EV	35310	15750	16350	17700	20800
LACROSSE—V6—Equipment Schedule 4						
W.B. 111.7"; 3.6 Liter.						
Sedan 4D	GA5ER	30820	12200	12700	14000	16750
Convenience Sedan	GB5ER	31290	13050	13550	14950	17800
Leather Sedan 4D	GC5ER	32755	13600	14150	15550	18500
Premium I Sedan 4D	GD5ER	33300	13950	14500	15900	18950
Premium II Sedan 4D	GF5E3	34725	15050	15600	17050	20300
Premium III Sedan 4D	GH5E3	36145	15850	16450	18000	21400
Touring Sedan 4D	GJ5E3	39130	16250	16850	18450	22000
AWD	L		1100	1100	1305	1305
4-Cyl, eAssist, 2.4 Liter	R		(650)	(650)	(760)	(760)

Body Type	VIN	List	Trade-In Good	Very Good	Pvt-Party Good	Retail Excellent
VERANO—4-Cyl. Flex Fuel—Equipment Schedule 4						
W.B. 105.7"; 2.4 Liter.						
Sedan 4D	PP5SK	23965	11100	11550	12900	15400
Convenience Sedan	PR5SK	25260	11350	11800	13150	15650
Leather Sedan 4D	PS5SK	27640	11950	12400	13650	16100
VERANO—4-Cyl. Turbo—Equipment Schedule 4						
W.B. 105.7"; 2.0 Liter.						
Premium Sedan 4D	PT5SV	29990	13600	14150	15550	18300
REGAL—4-Cyl. eAssist—Equipment Schedule 4						
W.B. 107.8"; 2.4 Liter.						
Sedan 4D	GR5ER	29900	11250	11650	13200	15950
Premium 1 Sedan 4D	GS5ER	31520	12100	12550	14200	17200
Premium 1 Sedan 4D	GT5GR	32930	13800	14300	16100	19300
REGAL—4-Cyl. Turbo Flex Fuel—Equipment Schedule 4						
W.B. 107.8"; 2.0 Liter.						
Premium 1 Sedan 4D	GS5GV	31520	12700	13150	14800	17800
Premium 2 Sedan 4D	GT5GV	32930	14400	14950	16750	20100
Premium 3 Sedan 4D	GU5GV	34100	14950	15500	17350	20800
REGAL—4-Cyl. Turbo—Equipment Schedule 4						
W.B. 107.8"; 2.0 Liter.						
GS Sedan 4D	GV5GV	35865	16650	17250	19200	23000
LACROSSE—V6—Equipment Schedule 4						
W.B. 111.7"; 3.6 Liter.						
Sedan 4D	GA5ER	32535	13800	14350	15800	18750
Leather Sedan 4D	GC5ER	34745	14250	14800	16200	19150
Premium I Sedan 4D	GD5E3	36160	15850	16450	17950	21300
Premium II Sedan 4D	GF5E3	37580	16650	17250	18800	22200
Touring Sedan 4D	GJ5E3	40115	17750	18350	20000	23700
AWD			1200	1200	1435	1435
4-Cyl, eAssist, 2.4 Liter	R		(700)	(700)	(840)	(840)

Body Type	VIN	List	Trade-In Good	Very Good	Pvt-Party Good	Retail Excellent
VERANO—4-Cyl. ECOTEC Flex Fuel—Equipment Schedule 4						
W.B. 105.7"; 2.4 Liter.						
Sedan 4D	PP5SK	24625	12550	13050	14350	16900
Convenience Sedan	PR5SK	25795	13000	13550	14800	17400
Leather Sedan 4D	PS5SK	27825	13900	14450	15700	18350
VERANO—4-Cyl. ECOTEC Turbo—Equipment Schedule 4						
W.B. 105.7"; 2.0 Liter.						
Premium Sedan 4D	PT5SV	29990	15800	16400	17550	20200
REGAL—4-Cyl. Turbo—Equipment Schedule 4						
W.B. 107.8"; 2.0 Liter						
Sedan 4D	GK5EX	30615	14200	14750	16300	19300
AWD	L		1250	1250	1410	1410
4-Cyl, 2.4 Liter	K		(750)	(750)	(845)	(845)
REGAL—4-Cyl. Turbo—Equipment Schedule 4						
W.B. 107.8"; 2.0 Liter						

Body Type	VIN	List	Trade-In Good	Very Good	Pvt-Party Good	Retail Excellent
Premium II Sedan 4D	GR5GX	34685	18700	19350	20600	23800
GS Sedan 4D	GT5GX	37830	20600	21300	22500	25700
AWD	L		1250	1250	1410	1410
REGAL—4-Cyl. Turbo—Equipment Schedule 4						
W.B. 107.8"; 2.0 Liter.						
Premium I Sedan 4D	GN5EX	32485	15100	15650	17200	20200
4-Cyl, eAssist, 2.4 Liter	R		(750)	(750)	(840)	(840)
LACROSSE—V6—Equipment Schedule 4						
W.B. 111.7"; 3.6 Liter.						
Sedan 4D	GA5G3	34060	17750	18400	20100	23800
Leather Sedan 4D	GB5G3	36135	18650	19300	20900	24600
Premium I Sedan 4D	GD5G3	39735	21400	22200	23900	28200
Premium II Sedan 4D	GD5G3	40280	22000	22800	24600	29000
AWD	C		1250	1250	1455	1455
4-Cyl, eAssist, 2.4 Liter	R		(750)	(750)	(890)	(890)

CADILLAC

2000 CADILLAC — (Wor1)(Gor0)6(VR52R)-Y-#

Body Type	VIN	List	Trade-In Good	Very Good	Pvt-Party Good	Retail Excellent
CATERA—V6—Equipment Schedule 2						
W.B. 107.5"; 3.0 Liter.						
Sedan 4D	VR52R	31500	475	550	1075	1875
Sport			200	200	250	250
ELDORADO—V8—Equipment Schedule 2						
W.B. 108.0"; 4.6 Liter.						
ESC Coupe 2D	EL12Y	39790	2900	3225	3875	5775
ETC Coupe 2D	ET129	43365	3575	3925	4725	6975
SEVILLE—V8—Equipment Schedule 2						
W.B. 112.2"; 4.6 Liter.						
SLS Sedan 4D	KS52Y	44550	650	725	1225	2025
STS Touring Sedan 4D	KY529	49150	600	675	1375	2475
DeVILLE—V8—Equipment Schedule 2						
W.B. 115.3"; 4.6 Liter.						
Sedan 4D	KD54Y	40955	900	1000	1650	2800
DHS Sedan 4D	KE54Y	45370	1075	1200	1975	3425
DTS Sedan 4D	KF549	45370	975	1100	1875	3300

2001 CADILLAC — (Wor1)(Gor0)6(VR52R)-1-#

Body Type	VIN	List	Trade-In Good	Very Good	Pvt-Party Good	Retail Excellent
CATERA—V6—Equipment Schedule 2						
W.B. 107.4"; 3.0 Liter.						
Sedan 4D	VR52R	31945	525	600	1150	1975
Sport Pkg			225	225	285	285
ELDORADO—V8—Equipment Schedule 2						
W.B. 108.0"; 4.6 Liter.						
ESC Coupe 2D	EL12Y	40756	3100	3425	4225	6300
ETC Coupe 2D	ET129	44331	3650	4025	5075	7525
SEVILLE—V8—Equipment Schedule 2						
W.B. 112.2"; 4.6 Liter.						
SLS Sedan 4D	KS52Y	42655	700	800	1325	2175
STS Touring Sedan 4D	KY529	48765	625	725	1450	2550
DeVILLE—V8—Equipment Schedule 2						
W.B. 115.3"; 4.6 Liter.						
Sedan 4D	KD54Y	42000	1075	1200	1850	3125
DHS Sedan 4D	KE54Y	46987	1225	1375	2225	3850
DTS Sedan 4D	KF549	46987	1075	1200	2125	3750

2002 CADILLAC — 1G6(EL12Y)-2-#

Body Type	VIN	List	Trade-In Good	Very Good	Pvt-Party Good	Retail Excellent
ELDORADO—V8—Equipment Schedule 2						
W.B. 108.0"; 4.6 Liter.						
ESC Coupe 2D	EL12Y	42610	3575	3925	5000	7425
ETC Coupe 2D	ET129	45745	4275	4675	5875	8700
ECS Coupe 2D	ET129	48405	4700	5125	6425	9475
SEVILLE—V8—Equipment Schedule 2						
W.B. 112.2"; 4.6 Liter.						
SLS Sedan 4D	KS52Y	44269	725	825	1350	2225
STS Touring Sedan 4D	KY529	49825	650	750	1500	2650
DeVILLE—V8—Equipment Schedule 2						
W.B. 115.3"; 4.6 Liter.						
Sedan 4D	KD54Y	43070	1250	1400	2075	3475
DHS Sedan 4D	KE54Y	48000	1400	1550	2400	4050
DTS Sedan 4D	KF549	48000	1200	1350	2250	3950

2003 CADILLAC

Body Type	VIN	List	Trade-In Good	Very Good	Pvt-Party Good	Retail Excellent
2003 CADILLAC — 1G6(DM57N)-3-#						
CTS—V6—Equipment Schedule 2						
W.B. 113.4"; 3.2 Liter.						
Sedan 4D	DM57N	31190	2325	2600	3375	5175
Luxury Sport Pkg			275	275	380	380
SEVILLE—V8—Equipment Schedule 2						
W.B. 112.2"; 4.6 Liter.						
SLS Sedan 4D	KS54Y	45270	875	1000	1525	2475
STS Touring Sedan 4D	KY549	51175	1025	1150	1850	3125
DeVILLE—V8—Equipment Schedule 2						
W.B. 115.3"; 4.6 Liter.						
Sedan 4D	KD54Y	43995	1450	1625	2275	3700
DHS Sedan 4D	KE54Y	48825	1575	1775	2675	4475
DTS Sedan 4D	KF549	48825	1600	1775	2775	4725
2004 CADILLAC — 1G6(DM57N)-4-#						
CTS—V6—Equipment Schedule 2						
W.B. 113.4"; 3.2 Liter.						
Sedan 4D	DM57N	33155	2875	3175	3925	5850
Luxury Sport Pkg			300	300	410	410
V6, 3.6 Liter	7		450	450	610	610
CTS-V—V8—Equipment Schedule 2						
W.B. 113.4"; 5.7 Liter.						
Sedan 4D	DN57S	49995	7200	7750	8600	11400
SEVILLE—V8—Equipment Schedule 2						
W.B. 112.2"; 4.6 Liter.						
SLS Sedan 4D	KS52Y	47955	3175	3475	4275	6275
DeVILLE—V8—Equipment Schedule 2						
W.B. 115.3"; 4.6 Liter.						
Sedan 4D	KD54Y	45445	1725	1925	2575	4075
DHS Sedan 4D	KE54Y	50595	1875	2075	3100	5025
DTS Sedan 4D	KF549	50595	1850	2050	3125	5125
XLR—V8—Equipment Schedule 1						
W.B. 105.7"; 4.6 Liter.						
Hardtop Conv 2D	YV34A	76200	9575	10100	11200	14100
2005 CADILLAC — 1G6(DM56T)-5-#						
CTS—V6—Equipment Schedule 2						
W.B. 113.4"; 2.8 Liter.						
Sedan 4D	DM56T	33595	3450	3825	4850	6950
Luxury Pkg			325	325	440	440
V6, 3.6 Liter	7		475	475	645	645
CTS-V—V8—Equipment Schedule 2						
W.B. 113.4"; 5.7 Liter.						
Sedan 4D	DN56S	49995	8050	8625	9625	12600
STS—V6—Equipment Schedule 2						
W.B. 116.6"; 3.6 Liter.						
Sedan 4D	DW677	40995	3700	4050	5050	7125
AWD			1425	1425	1885	1885
V8, 4.6 Liter	A		600	600	800	800
DeVILLE—V8—Equipment Schedule 2						
W.B. 115.3"; 4.6 Liter.						
Sedan 4D	KD54Y	46490	2275	2525	3475	5275
DHS Sedan 4D	KE54Y	52045	2800	3125	4350	6675
DTS Sedan 4D	KF549	52045	2950	3275	4475	6800
XLR—V8—Equipment Schedule 1						
W.B. 105.7"; 4.6 Liter.						
Hardtop Conv 2D	YV34A	76650	10900	11450	12700	15700
2006 CADILLAC — 1G6(DM57T)-6-#						
CTS—V6—Equipment Schedule 2						
W.B. 113.4"; 2.8 Liter.						
Sedan 4D	DM57T	32435	4350	4750	5750	8000
Luxury Pkg			350	350	470	470
V6, 3.6 Liter	7		525	525	685	685
CTS-V—V8—Equipment Schedule 2						
W.B. 113.4"; 6.0 Liter.						
Sedan 4D	DN57U	51395	10150	10850	11800	15000
STS—V6—Equipment Schedule 2						
W.B. 116.4"; 3.6 Liter.						
Sedan 4D	DW677	41740	4750	5150	5975	8025

2006 CADILLAC

Body Type	VIN	List	Trade-In Good	Trade-In Very Good	Pvt-Party Good	Retail Excellent
AWD			**1525**	**1525**	**2045**	**2045**
V8, 4.6 Liter	A		**800**	**800**	**1055**	**1055**
STS-V—V8 Supercharged—Equipment Schedule 2						
W.B. 116.4"; 4.4 Liter.						
Sedan 4D	DX67D	77090	**10800**	**11500**	**13150**	**17200**
DTS—V8—Equipment Schedule 2						
W.B. 115.6"; 4.6 Liter.						
Sedan 4D	KD57Y	41990	**4700**	**5125**	**6425**	**9175**
Luxury Pkg			**1075**	**1075**	**1435**	**1435**
Performance Pkg			**1075**	**1075**	**1445**	**1445**
XLR—V8—Equipment Schedule 1						
W.B. 105.7"; 4.6 Liter.						
Hardtop Conv 2D	YV36A	77295	**13650**	**14350**	**15450**	**18650**
Star Black Ltd Conv	YV36A	79795	**17900**	**18700**	**19950**	**24000**
XLR-V—V8 Supercharged—Equipment Schedule 2						
W.B. 105.7"; 4.4 Liter.						
Convertible 2D	YX36D	98300	**19350**	**20200**	**21400**	**25800**

2007 CADILLAC — 1G6(DM57T)-7-#

Body Type	VIN	List	Trade-In Good	Trade-In Very Good	Pvt-Party Good	Retail Excellent
CTS—V6—Equipment Schedule 2						
W.B. 113.4"; 2.8 Liter.						
Sedan 4D	DM57T	31390	**5100**	**5525**	**6550**	**8700**
Luxury Pkg			**375**	**375**	**500**	**500**
V6, 3.6 Liter	7		**550**	**550**	**720**	**720**
CTS-V—V8—Equipment Schedule 2						
W.B. 113.4"; 6.0 Liter.						
Sedan 4D	DN57U	53205	**11250**	**11950**	**13100**	**16450**
DTS—V8—Equipment Schedule 2						
W.B. 115.6"; 4.6 Liter.						
Sedan 4D	KD57Y	41990	**5850**	**6350**	**7400**	**9750**
Luxury Pkg			**1175**	**1175**	**1555**	**1555**
Performance Pkg			**1175**	**1175**	**1555**	**1555**
STS—V6—Equipment Schedule 2						
W.B. 116.4"; 3.6 Liter.						
Sedan 4D	DW677	42765	**5925**	**6375**	**7550**	**10050**
Platinum Edition			**1125**	**1125**	**1510**	**1510**
4-AWD			**1650**	**1650**	**2200**	**2200**
V8, 4.6 Liter	A		**975**	**975**	**1305**	**1305**
STS-V—V8 Supercharged—Equipment Schedule 2						
W.B. 116.4"; 4.4 Liter.						
Sedan 4D	DX67D	77485	**12100**	**12850**	**14550**	**18900**
XLR—V8—Equipment Schedule 1						
W.B. 105.7"; 4.6 Liter.						
Hardtop Conv 2D	YV36A	78495	**18200**	**19050**	**19850**	**23300**
Platinum Edition			**1125**	**1125**	**1260**	**1260**
XLR-V—V8 Supercharged—Equipment Schedule 2						
W.B. 105.7"; 4.4 Liter.						
Convertible 2D	YX36D	100000	**23800**	**24800**	**25700**	**30200**

2008 CADILLAC — 1G6(DF577)-8-#

Body Type	VIN	List	Trade-In Good	Trade-In Very Good	Pvt-Party Good	Retail Excellent
CTS—V6—Equipment Schedule 2						
W.B. 113.4"; 3.6 Liter.						
Sedan 4D	DF577	34290	**8625**	**9175**	**10200**	**12800**
Luxury Pkg			**400**	**400**	**515**	**515**
Performance Pkg			**1250**	**1250**	**1615**	**1615**
Premium Pkg			**1250**	**1250**	**1615**	**1615**
AWD	G,H,S,T		**1775**	**1775**	**2285**	**2285**
V6, DI, 3.6 Liter	V		**1150**	**1150**	**1470**	**1470**
DTS—V8—Equipment Schedule 2						
W.B. 115.6"; 4.6 Liter.						
Sedan 4D	KD57Y	42590	**7050**	**7575**	**8600**	**11050**
Luxury Pkg			**1250**	**1250**	**1630**	**1630**
Performance Pkg			**1250**	**1250**	**1630**	**1630**
Platinum Edition			**1200**	**1200**	**1570**	**1570**
STS—V6—Equipment Schedule 2						
W.B. 116.4"; 3.6 Liter.						
Sedan 4D	DW67V	43135	**7325**	**7800**	**8900**	**11350**
Platinum Edition			**1200**	**1200**	**1555**	**1555**
AWD	A,D,B,L		**1775**	**1775**	**2280**	**2280**
V8, 4.6 Liter	A		**1175**	**1175**	**1510**	**1510**
STS-V—V8 Supercharged—Equipment Schedule 2						
W.B. 116.4"; 4.4 Liter.						

2008 CADILLAC

Body Type	VIN	List	Trade-In Good	Trade-In Very Good	Pvt-Party Good	Retail Excellent
Sedan 4D	DX67D	79000	**13450**	**14150**	**15600**	**19400**
XLR—V8—Equipment Schedule 1						
W.B. 105.7"; 4.6 Liter.						
Hardtop Conv 2D	YV36A	79600	**20000**	**20900**	**21800**	**25600**
Platinum Edition			**1200**	**1200**	**1330**	**1330**
XLR-V—V8 Supercharged—Equipment Schedule 1						
W.B. 105.7"; 4.4 Liter.						
Convertible 2D	YX36D	100000	**25900**	**26900**	**28000**	**32600**

2009 CADILLAC — 1G6(DF577)-9-#

CTS—V6—Equipment Schedule 2
W.B. 113.4"; 3.6 Liter.

Body Type	VIN	List	Trade-In Good	Trade-In Very Good	Pvt-Party Good	Retail Excellent
Sedan 4D	DF577	36080	**10450**	**11000**	**12100**	**14800**
Luxury Pkg		------	**475**	**475**	**600**	**600**
Performance Pkg		------	**1325**	**1325**	**1680**	**1680**
Premium Pkg		------	**1325**	**1325**	**1680**	**1680**
AWD	G,H,S,T	------	**1875**	**1875**	**2375**	**2375**
V6, DI, 3.6 Liter	V	------	**1200**	**1200**	**1525**	**1525**
CTS-V—V8—Equipment Schedule 2						
W.B. 113.4"; 6.2 Liter.						
Sedan 4D	DN57P	62595	**23500**	**24500**	**24900**	**28800**
DTS—V8—Equipment Schedule 2						
W.B. 115.6"; 4.6 Liter.						
Sedan 4D	KD57Y	44900	**10050**	**10700**	**11800**	**14750**
Performance Pkg		------	**1325**	**1325**	**1675**	**1675**
Platinum Edition		------	**1275**	**1275**	**1605**	**1605**
STS—V6—Equipment Schedule 2						
W.B. 116.4"; 3.6 Liter.						
Sedan 4D	DW67V	45290	**9850**	**10400**	**11700**	**14600**
Platinum Edition		------	**1275**	**1275**	**1580**	**1580**
AWD	A,D,B,L	------	**1875**	**1875**	**2330**	**2330**
V8, 4.6 Liter	A	------	**1350**	**1350**	**1680**	**1680**
STS-V—V8 Supercharged—Equipment Schedule 2						
W.B. 116.4"; 4.4 Liter.						
Sedan 4D	DX67D	81940	**20600**	**21600**	**23500**	**29000**
XLR—V8—Equipment Schedule 1						
W.B. 105.7"; 4.6 Liter.						
Platinum Conv 2D	YV36A	83530	**25400**	**26400**	**27600**	**32200**
XLR-V—V8 Supercharged—Equipment Schedule 1						
W.B. 105.7"; 4.4 Liter.						
Convertible 2D	YX36D	102530	**31200**	**32400**	**33800**	**39300**

2010 CADILLAC — 1G6(DA5EG)-A-#

CTS—V6—Equipment Schedule 2
W.B. 113.4"; 3.0 Liter.

Body Type	VIN	List	Trade-In Good	Trade-In Very Good	Pvt-Party Good	Retail Excellent
Sedan 4D	DA5EG	37270	**12400**	**13000**	**14100**	**16900**
Wagon 4D	DA8EG	39090	**13000**	**13650**	**14850**	**17800**
Luxury Pkg		------	**550**	**550**	**670**	**670**
4-AWD	C,D,G,H	------	**2000**	**2000**	**2435**	**2435**
CTS—V6 DI—Equipment Schedule 2						
W.B. 113.4"; 3.6 Liter.						
3.6 Sedan 4D	DJ5EV	42390	**14050**	**14700**	**16000**	**19150**
3.6 Wagon 4D	DJ8EV	44190	**14750**	**15450**	**16700**	**19950**
4-AWD	L,M,R,S	------	**2000**	**2000**	**2430**	**2430**
CTS-V—V8 Supercharged—Equipment Schedule 2						
W.B. 113.4"; 6.2 Liter.						
Sedan 4D	DV5EP	64145	**27400**	**28600**	**28900**	**33000**
DTS—V8—Equipment Schedule 2						
W.B. 115.6"; 4.6 Liter.						
Sedan 4D	KA5EY	47200	**12650**	**13350**	**14650**	**17950**
Luxury Collection		------	**1425**	**1425**	**1760**	**1760**
Premium Collection		------	**1225**	**1225**	**1510**	**1510**
Platinum Collection		------	**1350**	**1350**	**1670**	**1670**
STS—V6—Equipment Schedule 2						
W.B. 116.4"; 3.6 Liter.						
Sedan 4D	DU6EV	47670	**12650**	**13250**	**14750**	**17900**
4-AWD		------	**2000**	**2000**	**2385**	**2385**
V8, 4.6 Liter		------	**1550**	**1550**	**1850**	**1850**

2011 CADILLAC — 1G6(DA5EY)-B-#

CTS—V6—Equipment Schedule 2
W.B. 113.4"; 3.0 Liter.

Body Type	VIN	List	Trade-In Good	Very Good	Pvt-Party Good	Retail Excellent
Sedan 4D	DA5EY	37580	**13500**	**14100**	**15300**	**18050**
Sport Wagon 4D	DA8EY	39090	**14900**	**15550**	**16750**	**19750**
Luxury Pkg			**600**	**600**	**725**	**725**
Performance Pkg			**1500**	**1500**	**1820**	**1820**
4-AWD	C,D		**2000**	**2000**	**2425**	**2425**

CTS—V6 DI—Equipment Schedule 2
W.B. 113.4"; 3.6 Liter.

3.6 Sedan 4D	D15ED	42605	**15850**	**16500**	**17750**	**20900**
3.6 Coupe 2D	DJ1ED	39230	**16600**	**17250**	**18450**	**21700**
3.6 Sport Wagon 4D	DJ8ED	44190	**16650**	**17300**	**18550**	**21800**
4-AWD	L,M		**2000**	**2000**	**2420**	**2420**

CTS-V—V8 Supercharged—Equipment Schedule 2
W.B. 113.4"; 6.2 Liter.

Sedan 4D	DV5EP	65820	**29300**	**30400**	**31000**	**35200**
Coupe 2D	DV1EP	65820	**29700**	**30800**	**31400**	**35700**
Wagon 4D	DV8EP	64290	**30000**	**31100**	**31700**	**36000**

DTS—V8—Equipment Schedule 2
W.B. 115.6"; 4.6 Liter.

Sedan 4D	KA5E6	47600	**16350**	**17200**	**18650**	**22500**
Luxury Collection			**1500**	**1500**	**1745**	**1745**
Premium Collection			**1300**	**1300**	**1505**	**1505**
Platinum Collection			**1425**	**1425**	**1660**	**1660**

STS—V6—Equipment Schedule 2
W.B. 116.4"; 3.6 Liter.

| Sedan 4D | DU6ED | 48105 | **15150** | **15800** | **17250** | **20500** |
| AWD | | | **2000** | **2000** | **2370** | **2370** |

2012 CADILLAC — 1G6(DA5E5)-C-#

CTS—V6—Equipment Schedule 2
W.B. 113.4"; 3.0 Liter.

Sedan 4D	DA5E5	36189	**15150**	**15750**	**16900**	**19700**
Sport Wagon 4D	DA8E5	39890	**16950**	**17600**	**18800**	**21900**
Luxury Pkg			**650**	**650**	**775**	**775**
Touring Pkg			**850**	**850**	**1020**	**1020**
AWD	C,D		**2000**	**2000**	**2390**	**2390**

CTS—V6 DI—Equipment Schedule 2
W.B. 113.4"; 3.6 Liter.

3.6 Coupe 2D	DJ1E3	39590	**19350**	**20000**	**21300**	**24800**
Touring Pkg			**850**	**850**	**1015**	**1015**
Performance Luxury			**1200**	**1200**	**1425**	**1425**
Performance Pkg			**1500**	**1500**	**1790**	**1790**
Premium Pkg			**2000**	**2000**	**2385**	**2385**
AWD	L		**2000**	**2000**	**2385**	**2385**

CTS—V6 DI—Equipment Schedule 2
W.B. 113.4"; 3.6 Liter.

3.6 Sedan 4D	DJ5E3	43165	**19550**	**20300**	**21500**	**24900**
3.6 Sport Wagon 4D	DA8E3	45065	**20300**	**21100**	**22300**	**25900**
Touring Pkg			**850**	**850**	**1015**	**1015**
Performance Luxury			**1200**	**1200**	**1425**	**1425**
Premium Pkg			**2000**	**2000**	**2380**	**2380**
AWD	L		**2000**	**2000**	**2380**	**2380**

CTS-V—V8 Supercharged—Equipment Schedule 2
W.B. 113.4"; 6.2 Liter.

Sedan 4D	DV5EP	65390	**31900**	**33100**	**33700**	**37900**
Coupe 2D	DV1EP	66710	**32400**	**33600**	**34200**	**38500**
Sport Wagon 4D	DV8EP	65390	**33800**	**35000**	**35500**	**39900**

2013 CADILLAC — 1G6(AA5SA)-D-#

ATS—4-Cyl.—Equipment Schedule 2
W.B. 109.3"; 2.5 Liter.

| 2.5L Standard Sedan | AA5SA | 33990 | **16200** | **16850** | **18100** | **21100** |
| 2.5L Luxury Sedan 4D | AB5SA | 38485 | **17400** | **18050** | **19400** | **22600** |

ATS—4-Cyl. Turbo—Equipment Schedule 2
W.B. 109.3"; 2.0 Liter.

2.0L Standard Sed	AA5SX	35795	**16900**	**17550**	**18900**	**22000**
2.0L Luxury Sed 4D	AB5SX	40290	**18150**	**18850**	**20200**	**23500**
2.0L Performance Sed	AC5SX	42790	**20100**	**20800**	**22200**	**25800**
2.0L Premium Sedan	AE5SX	45790	**21600**	**22500**	**23900**	**27800**
AWD	J		**2000**	**2000**	**2305**	**2305**

ATS—V6 Flex Fuel—Equipment Schedule 2
W.B. 109.3"; 3.6 Liter.

| 3.6L Luxury Sedan 4D | AB5S3 | 42090 | **19650** | **20400** | **21800** | **25300** |

2013 CADILLAC

Body Type	VIN	List	Trade-In Good	Very Good	Pvt-Party Good	Retail Excellent
3.6L Performance Sed	AC5S3	44590	**21300**	**22100**	**23600**	**27400**
3.6L Premium Sedan	AE5S3	47590	**22800**	**23600**	**25100**	**29100**
AWD	H		**2000**	**2000**	**2305**	**2305**

XTS—V6 Flex Fuel—Equipment Schedule 2
W.B. 111.7"; 3.6 Liter.

Sedan 4D	1N5S3	44995	**21000**	**21800**	**23000**	**26600**
Luxury Sedan 4D	1P5S3	49610	**24100**	**25000**	**26300**	**30300**
Premium Sedan 4D	1S5S3	54505	**24900**	**25800**	**27200**	**31300**
Platinum Sedan 4D	1U5S3	59080	**27900**	**28900**	**30100**	**34500**
AWD	R		**2000**	**2000**	**2245**	**2245**

CTS—V6—Equipment Schedule 2
W.B. 113.4"; 3.0 Liter.

3.0 Luxury Sedan 4D	DE5E5	39990	**17800**	**18450**	**19650**	**22700**
3.0 Luxury Sport Wag	DE8E5	43045	**20400**	**21100**	**22300**	**25700**
3.0 Sport Wagon 4D	DA8E5	40100	**18400**	**19050**	**20300**	**23400**
Touring Pkg			**900**	**900**	**1065**	**1065**
AWD	G,H		**2000**	**2000**	**2365**	**2365**

CTS—V6 DI—Equipment Schedule 2
W.B. 113.4"; 3.6 Liter.

3.6 Coupe 2D	DA1E3	39800	**20700**	**21400**	**22600**	**26000**
3.6 Performance Sedan	DJ5E3	44235	**20800**	**21600**	**22800**	**26200**
3.6 Performance Coupe	DJ1E3	44845	**22600**	**23400**	**24700**	**28400**
3.6 Performance Wag	DJ8E3	45085	**22500**	**23300**	**24600**	**28300**
3.6 Premium Sedan 4D	DP5E3	49185	**22700**	**23500**	**24800**	**28500**
3.6 Premium Coupe	DP1E3	49045	**25500**	**26300**	**27700**	**31800**
3.6 Premium Wagon	DP8E3	50645	**25200**	**26000**	**27400**	**31500**
Touring Pkg			**900**	**900**	**1060**	**1060**
AWD	L,M		**2000**	**2000**	**2350**	**2350**

CTS-V—V8 Supercharged—Equipment Schedule 2
W.B. 113.4"; 6.2 Liter.

Sedan 4D	DV5EP	65410	**35500**	**36700**	**37400**	**42000**
Coupe 2D	DV1EP	65410	**37300**	**38600**	**39200**	**44000**
Sport Wagon 4D	DV8EP	65410	**38000**	**39300**	**39800**	**44600**

2014 CADILLAC — 1G6(AA5RA)-E-#

ATS—4-Cyl.—Equipment Schedule 2
W.B. 109.3"; 2.5 Liter.

2.5L Standard Sedan	AA5RA	33990	**17800**	**18500**	**19650**	**22700**
2.5L Luxury Sedan 4D	AB5RA	38020	**19250**	**20000**	**21200**	**24400**

ATS—4-Cyl. Turbo—Equipment Schedule 2
W.B. 109.3"; 2.0 Liter.

2.0L Standard Sedan	AA5RX	36020	**18850**	**19600**	**20800**	**23900**
2.0L Luxury Sed 4D	AB5RX	40020	**20300**	**21000**	**22200**	**25500**
2.0L Performance Sed	AC5RX	43020	**22200**	**23100**	**24200**	**27700**
2.0L Premium Sedan	AE5RX	46020	**24000**	**24800**	**26000**	**29800**
AWD	G		**2000**	**2000**	**2315**	**2315**

ATS—V6 Flex Fuel—Equipment Schedule 2
W.B. 109.3"; 3.6 Liter.

3.6L Luxury Sedan 4D	AB5R3	42020	**22000**	**22900**	**23900**	**27400**
3.6L Performance Sed	AC5R3	45020	**23800**	**24600**	**25800**	**29500**
3.6L Premium Sedan	AE5R3	48020	**25200**	**26100**	**27200**	**31100**
AWD	H		**2000**	**2000**	**2295**	**2295**

XTS—V6 Flex Fuel—Equipment Schedule 2
W.B. 111.7"; 3.6 Liter.

Sedan 4D	1L5S3	45525	**24300**	**25200**	**26300**	**30000**
Luxury Sedan 4D	1M5S3	50435	**27300**	**28300**	**29400**	**33500**
Premium Sedan 4D	1P5S3	55380	**28300**	**29300**	**30500**	**34700**
Platinum Sedan 4D	1S5S3	62675	**31200**	**32300**	**33400**	**37900**
Sensing Cruise Control			**500**	**500**	**555**	**555**
Driver Assist Pkg			**675**	**675**	**750**	**750**
AWD	N		**2000**	**2000**	**2225**	**2225**

XTS AWD—V6 Twin Turbo—Equipment Schedule 2
W.B. 111.7"; 3.6 Liter.

Vsport Premium Sed	1V5S8	63020	**33600**	**34700**	**35800**	**40600**
Vsport Platinum Sed	1W5S8	70020	**39900**	**41300**	**42400**	**48000**
Adaptive Cruise Control			**500**	**500**	**555**	**555**
Driver Assist Pkg			**675**	**675**	**750**	**750**

CTS—4-Cyl. Turbo—Equipment Schedule 2
W.B. 113.4"; 2.0 Liter.

2.0 Standard Sedan 4D	AP5EX	46025	**26100**	**27000**	**27900**	**31500**
2.0 Luxury Sedan 4D	AR5EX	51925	**30200**	**31200**	**32000**	**36000**
2.0 Performance Sedan	AS5SX	58325	**33300**	**34400**	**35000**	**39100**
Adaptive Cruise Control			**500**	**500**	**555**	**555**

0415   **EQUIPMENT & MILEAGE PAGE 9 TO 23**   **83**

Body Type	VIN	List	Trade-In Good	Very Good	Pvt-Party Good	Retail Excellent
Full Leather			675	675	755	755
AWD	W		2000	2000	2265	2265
CTS—4-Cyl. Turbo—Equipment Schedule 2						
W.B. 113.4"; 2.0 Liter.						
2.0 Premium Sedan 4D	AT5SX	62725	37000	38100	38600	43000
AWD	Z		2000	2000	2220	2220
CTS—V6—Equipment Schedule 2						
W.B. 113.4"; 3.0 Liter, 3.6 Liter.						
3.6 Coupe 2D	DA1E3	40420	24600	25400	26500	30100
3.6 Performance Cpe	DC1E3	44720	26300	27200	28200	32100
3.6 Performance Wagon	DC8E3	45120	25800	26700	27800	31600
3.6 Luxury Sedan 4D	AR5S3	54625	31900	32900	33600	37700
3.0 Luxury Sport Wag	DB8E5	43120	24900	25700	26600	30200
3.6 Performance Sedan	AS5S3	61025	33900	35000	35600	39800
3.6 Premium Sedan 4D	AT5S8	65425	37600	38800	39300	43800
3.6 Premium Coupe 2D	DD1E3	48920	28000	29000	30200	34400
3.6 Premium Wagon	DD8E3	50720	27700	28600	29900	34100
Adaptive Cruise Control			500	500	560	560
Full Leather			675	675	755	755
Luxury Pkg			750	750	865	865
Performance Luxury Pkg			1325	1325	1530	1530
Touring Pkg			950	950	1090	1090
AWD	X		2000	2000	2240	2240
CTS—V6 Twin Turbo—Equipment Schedule 2						
W.B. 113.4"; 3.6 Liter.						
3.6 Vsport Sedan 4D	AU5S8	59995	34700	35800	36600	41000
3.6 Vsport Premium 4D	AV5S8	69995	40900	42200	42700	47600
CTS—V—V8 Supercharged—Equipment Schedule 2						
W.B. 113.4"; 6.2 Liter.						
Sedan 4D	DD5EP	65825	42800	44200	44600	49400
Coupe 2D	DV1EP	65825	44600	46100	46400	51400
Sport Wagon 4D	DV8EP	65825	45300	46800	47000	52000
RECARO Seats			575	575	635	635

CHEVROLET

2000 CHEVROLET — (1,2or3)(C,GorY)1(MR226)-Y-#

Body Type	VIN	List	Trade-In Good	Very Good	Pvt-Party Good	Retail Excellent
METRO—3-Cyl.—Equipment Schedule 6						
W.B. 93.1"; 1.0 Liter.						
Coupe 2D	MR226	10680	550	625	1225	2175
METRO—4-Cyl.—Equipment Schedule 6						
W.B. 93.1"; 1.3 Liter.						
LSi Sedan 4D	MR522	12395	700	800	1400	2450
LSi Coupe 2D	MR222	11530	675	775	1375	2375
PRIZM—4-Cyl.—Equipment Schedule 6						
W.B. 97.1"; 1.8 Liter.						
Sedan 4D	SK528	14246	575	650	1250	2225
LSi Sedan 4D	SK528	16272	750	850	1500	2675
CAVALIER—4-Cyl.—Equipment Schedule 5						
W.B. 104.1"; 2.2 Liter, 2.4 Liter.						
Sedan 4D	JC524	14275	525	625	1300	2325
Coupe 2D	JC124	14175	500	600	1250	2275
LS Sedan 4D	JF524	15225	675	800	1550	2775
Z24 Coupe 2D	JF12T	17560	975	1125	1775	3050
Z24 Convertible 2D	JF32T	21025	1250	1425	2275	3975
MALIBU—V6—Equipment Schedule 5						
W.B. 107.0"; 3.1 Liter.						
Sedan 4D	ND52J	16995	825	950	1775	3200
LS Sedan 4D	NE52J	19625	1225	1400	2300	3800
LUMINA—V6—Equipment Schedule 4						
W.B. 107.5"; 3.1 Liter.						
Sedan 4D	WL52J	19350	525	600	1075	1775
IMPALA—V6—Equipment Schedule 4						
W.B. 110.5"; 3.4 Liter, 3.8 Liter.						
Sedan 4D	WF52E	19787	600	675	1325	2325
LS Sedan 4D	WH52K	22925	900	1000	1725	2975
MONTE CARLO—V6—Equipment Schedule 4						
W.B. 110.5"; 3.4 Liter, 3.8 Liter.						
LS Coupe 2D	WW12E	20090	750	850	1450	2475
SS Coupe 2D	WX12K	22295	1150	1300	2000	3400

2000 CHEVROLET

Body Type	VIN	List	Trade-In Good	Very Good	Pvt-Party Good	Retail Excellent
CAMARO—V6—Equipment Schedule 4						
W.B. 101.1"; 3.8 Liter.						
Coupe 2D	FP22K	19360	1375	1525	1925	2950
Convertible 2D	FP32K	25490	2300	2550	3150	4725
T-Bar Roof			225	225	300	300
Manual, 5-Spd			(175)	(175)	(235)	(235)
CAMARO—V8—Equipment Schedule 4						
W.B. 101.1"; 5.7 Liter.						
Z28 Coupe 2D	FP22G	23515	2300	2550	3150	4725
Z28 Convertible 2D	FP32G	28900	3625	3975	4775	7025
T-Bar Roof			225	225	300	300
SS Pkg			650	650	865	865
CORVETTE—V8—Equipment Schedule 2						
W.B. 104.5"; 5.7 Liter.						
Hard Top 2D	YY12G	39205	4675	5025	5850	7875
CORVETTE—V8—Equipment Schedule 2						
W.B. 104.5"; 5.7 Liter.						
Coupe 2D	YY22G	40085	5025	5375	6025	7925
Convertible 2D	YY32G	46510	6150	6550	7450	9675
Glass Roof Panel			250	250	280	280
Dual Roof Panels			300	300	335	335
Suspension Pkg			200	200	225	225
Manual, 6-Spd			150	150	165	165

2001 CHEVROLET — (1or2)(C,GorY)(MR522)-1-#

Body Type	VIN	List	Trade-In Good	Very Good	Pvt-Party Good	Retail Excellent
METRO—4-Cyl.—Equipment Schedule 6						
W.B. 93.1"; 1.3 Liter.						
LSi Sedan 4D	MR522	12915	750	850	1500	2625
PRIZM—4-Cyl.—Equipment Schedule 6						
W.B. 97.0"; 1.8 Liter.						
Sedan 4D	SK528	14460	600	700	1300	2275
LSi Sedan 4D	SK528	16525	800	925	1550	2675
CAVALIER—4-Cyl.—Equipment Schedule 5						
W.B. 104.1"; 2.2 Liter, 2.4 Liter.						
Sedan 4D	JC524	14480	600	700	1350	2425
Coupe 2D	JC124	14380	575	675	1325	2400
LS Sedan 4D	JF524	15375	750	850	1575	2825
Z24 Coupe 2D	JF12T	17665	1125	1275	2025	3500
MALIBU—V6—Equipment Schedule 5						
W.B. 107.0"; 3.1 Liter.						
Sedan 4D	ND52J	17595	1050	1200	2025	3550
LS Sedan 4D	NE52J	19875	1425	1600	2400	4075
LUMINA—V6—Equipment Schedule 4						
W.B. 107.5"; 3.1 Liter.						
Sedan 4D	WL52J	19490	550	625	1125	1875
IMPALA—V6—Equipment Schedule 4						
W.B. 110.5"; 3.4 Liter, 3.8 Liter.						
Sedan 4D	WF52E	20271	750	825	1425	2450
LS Sedan 4D	WH52K	23825	1150	1275	1975	3325
MONTE CARLO—V6—Equipment Schedule 4						
W.B. 110.5"; 3.4 Liter, 3.8 Liter.						
LS Coupe 2D	WW12E	20410	925	1025	1675	2850
SS Coupe 2D	WX15K	23000	1375	1525	2325	3950
CAMARO—V6—Equipment Schedule 4						
W.B. 101.1"; 3.8 Liter.						
Coupe 2D	FP22K	19635	1550	1725	2150	3300
Convertible 2D	FP32K	25760	2600	2875	3525	5250
T-Bar Roof			225	225	300	300
RS			75	75	105	105
Manual, 5-Spd			(150)	(150)	(200)	(200)
CAMARO—V8—Equipment Schedule 4						
W.B. 101.1"; 5.7 Liter.						
Z28 Coupe 2D	FP22G	23935	2700	2975	3650	5425
Z28 Convertible 2D	FP32G	29325	4300	4700	5750	8400
T-Bar Roof			225	225	300	300
SS Pkg			750	750	1000	1000
CORVETTE—V8—Equipment Schedule 2						
W.B. 104.5"; 5.7 Liter.						
Coupe 2D	YY22G	40475	5450	5825	6600	8500
Z06 Hard Top 2D	YY12G	47500	7500	7950	8750	11050
Convertible 2D	YY32G	47000	6725	7150	7875	9975
Glass Roof Panel			250	250	280	280
Dual Roof Panels			300	300	335	335

2001 CHEVROLET

Body Type	VIN	List	Trade-In Good	Very Good	Pvt-Party Good	Retail Excellent
Suspension Pkg			200	200	220	220
Z51 Handling			200	200	220	220
Manual, 6-Spd			150	150	165	165

2002 CHEVROLET — (1or2)(GorY)1(SK528)-2-#

PRIZM—4-Cyl.—Equipment Schedule 6
W.B. 97.0"; 1.8 Liter.

Body Type	VIN	List	Good	Very Good	Good	Excellent
Sedan 4D	SK528	14815	725	825	1525	2700
LSi Sedan 4D	SK528	16880	850	975	1575	2700

CAVALIER—4-Cyl.—Equipment Schedule 5
W.B. 104.1"; 2.2 Liter, 2.4 Liter.

Sedan 4D	JC524	15280	675	775	1450	2575
Coupe 2D	JC124	15180	650	750	1450	2625
LS Sedan 4D	JF524	16330	850	975	1700	3000
LS Coupe 2D	JS124	16230	800	900	1625	2850
LS Sport Sedan 4D	JF52F	17700	1000	1125	1900	3350
LS Sport Coupe 2D	JS12F	17600	1000	1125	1900	3350
Z24 Sedan 4D	JH52T	17900	1125	1275	1775	2875
Z24 Coupe 2D	JF12T	17800	1250	1425	2225	3825

MALIBU—V6—Equipment Schedule 5
W.B. 107.0"; 3.1 Liter.

Sedan 4D	ND52J	18120	1150	1300	2075	3600
LS Sedan 4D	NE52X	20325	1550	1750	2575	4350

IMPALA—V6—Equipment Schedule 4
W.B. 110.5"; 3.4 Liter, 3.8 Liter.

Sedan 4D	WF52E	20820	975	1075	1675	2775
LS Sedan 4D	WH52K	24270	1475	1650	2350	3850

MONTE CARLO—V6—Equipment Schedule 4
W.B. 110.5"; 3.4 Liter, 3.8 Liter.

LS Coupe 2D	WW12E	20920	1100	1225	1825	3050
SS Coupe 2D	WX12K	23470	1550	1750	2625	4375

CAMARO—V6—Equipment Schedule 4
W.B. 101.1"; 3.8 Liter.

Coupe 2D	FP22K	20640	1850	2050	2500	3675
Convertible 2D	FP32K	26650	3075	3400	3925	5625
T-Bar Roof			225	225	300	300
RS			100	100	120	120
Manual, 5-Spd			(200)	(200)	(265)	(265)

CAMARO—V8—Equipment Schedule 4
W.B. 101.1"; 5.7 Liter.

Z28 Coupe 2D	FP22G	24770	3275	3600	4150	5950
Z28 Convertible 2D	FP32G	30165	5125	5575	6450	9075
T-Bar Roof			225	225	300	300
35th Anniversary			100	100	135	135
SS Pkg			875	875	1165	1165

CORVETTE—V8—Equipment Schedule 2
W.B. 104.5"; 5.7 Liter.

Coupe 2D	YY22G	41650	5950	6350	6975	8775
Z06 Hard Top 2D	YY12G	50350	8000	8450	9175	11400
Convertible 2D	YY32G	48175	7225	7675	8250	10300
Glass Roof Panel			250	250	285	285
Dual Roof Panels			300	300	340	340
Suspension Pkg			200	200	230	230
Z51 Handling			200	200	230	230
Manual, 6-Spd			150	150	170	170

2003 CHEVROLET — (1or2)G1(JC52F)-3-#

CAVALIER—4-Cyl.—Equipment Schedule 5
W.B. 104.1"; 2.2 Liter.

Sedan 4D	JC52F	15520	800	925	1575	2700
Coupe 2D	JC12F	15370	800	925	1600	2800
LS Sedan 4D	JF52F	16920	1100	1250	1925	3275
LS Coupe 2D	JF12F	16770	1100	1250	1975	3350
LS Sport Sedan 4D	JH52F	18120	1250	1425	2100	3525
LS Sport Coupe 2D	JH12F	17970	1200	1375	2100	3575

MALIBU—V6—Equipment Schedule 5
W.B. 107.0"; 3.1 Liter.

Sedan 4D	ND52J	18290	1400	1600	2350	3925
LS Sedan 4D	NE52J	20575	1675	1900	2675	4400

IMPALA—V6—Equipment Schedule 4
W.B. 110.5"; 3.4 Liter, 3.8 Liter.

Sedan 4D	WF52E	21350	1325	1450	2150	3575

2003 CHEVROLET

Body Type	VIN	List	Trade-In Good	Very Good	Pvt-Party Good	Retail Excellent
LS Sedan 4D	WH52K	24460	1675	1875	2750	4450
MONTE CARLO—V6—Equipment Schedule 4						
W.B. 110.5"; 3.4 Liter, 3.8 Liter.						
LS Coupe 2D	WW12E	21350	1375	1525	2200	3625
SS Coupe 2D	WX12K	23665	1925	2125	2975	4750
CORVETTE—V8—Equipment Schedule 2						
W.B. 104.5"; 5.7 Liter.						
Coupe 2D	YY22G	43895	7375	7825	8625	10900
Z06 Hard Top 2D	YY12S	51155	9425	9950	10900	13650
Convertible 2D	YY32G	50370	8325	8800	9775	12350
50th Anniversary			1800	1800	1955	1955
Glass Roof Panel			250	250	270	270
Dual Roof Panels			300	300	325	325
Suspension Pkg			200	200	215	215
Z51 Handling			200	200	215	215
Manual, 6-Spd			150	150	160	160

2004 CHEVROLET — (1,2orK)(GorL)1(TD526)-4-#

Body Type	VIN	List	Trade-In Good	Very Good	Pvt-Party Good	Retail Excellent
AVEO—4-Cyl.—Equipment Schedule 6						
W.B. 97.6"; 1.6 Liter.						
SVM Sedan 4D	TD526	9995	600	675	1250	2100
SVM Hatchback 4D	TD626	9995	600	675	1300	2250
Sedan 4D	TD526	11690	1000	1100	1800	3050
Hatchback 4D	TD626	11690	1025	1125	1850	3100
LS Sedan 4D	TJ526	12635	1125	1250	1950	3275
LS Hatchback 4D	TJ626	13435	1175	1325	2050	3425
CAVALIER—4-Cyl.—Equipment Schedule 5						
W.B. 104.1"; 2.2 Liter.						
Sedan 4D	JC52F	15995	1025	1175	1925	3300
Coupe 2D	JC12F	15810	975	1125	1900	3300
LS Sedan 4D	JF52F	17230	1250	1425	2250	3900
LS Coupe 2D	JF12F	17030	1250	1425	2250	3900
LS Sport Sedan 4D	JH52F	18635	1400	1575	2450	4200
LS Sport Coupe 2D	JH12F	18435	1400	1575	2450	4175
CLASSIC—4-Cyl.—Equipment Schedule 5						
W.B. 107.0" 2.2 Liter.						
Sedan 4D	ND52F	19380	1400	1575	2150	3450
MALIBU—4-Cyl.—Equipment Schedule 5						
W.B. 106.3"; 2.2 Liter.						
Sedan 4D	ZS52F	18995	1650	1850	2450	3925
V6, 3.5 Liter	8		350	350	450	450
MALIBU—V6—Equipment Schedule 5						
W.B. 106.3", 112.3" (MAXX); 3.5 Liter.						
MAXX Hatchback 4D	ZS638	21725	1950	2200	2850	4475
LS Sedan 4D	ZT528	20995	2375	2675	3500	5425
LS MAXX H'Back 4D	ZT638	22225	1975	2225	2975	4675
LT Sedan 4D	ZU528	23495	2200	2475	3275	5100
LT MAXX H'Back 4D	ZU668	24725	2250	2525	3325	5200
IMPALA—V6—Equipment Schedule 4						
W.B. 110.5"; 3.4 Liter, 3.8 Liter.						
Sedan 4D	WF52K	22150	1750	1925	2550	4025
LS Sedan 4D	WH52K	25000	1950	2175	3050	4850
IMPALA—V6 Supercharged—Equipment Schedule 4						
W.B. 110.5"; 3.8 Liter.						
SS Sedan 4D	WP521	27995	2375	2600	3750	6025
MONTE CARLO—V6—Equipment Schedule 4						
W.B. 110.5"; 3.4 Liter, 3.8 Liter.						
LS Coupe 2D	WW12E	22075	1675	1875	2725	4375
SS Coupe 2D	WX12K	24225	2250	2500	3300	5125
V6, Supercharged, 3.8L			450	450	600	600
CORVETTE—V8—Equipment Schedule 2						
W.B. 104.5"; 5.7 Liter.						
Coupe 2D	YY22G	44535	8725	9200	10300	13050
Z06 Hard Top 2D	YY12S	52385	11050	11650	12800	16000
Convertible 2D	YY32G	51535	9950	10500	11750	14850
Commemorative Ed			450	450	530	530
Glass Roof Panel			250	250	290	290
Dual Roof Panels			300	300	345	345
Suspension Pkg			200	200	230	230
Z51 Handling			200	200	230	230
Manual, 6-Spd			150	150	175	175

Body Type	VIN	List	Trade-In Good	Very Good	Pvt-Party Good	Retail Excellent

2005 CHEVROLET—(1,2orK)(GorL)1(TD526)-5-#

AVEO—4-Cyl.—Equipment Schedule 6
W.B. 97.6"; 1.6 Liter.

Body Type	VIN	List	Good	Very Good	Good	Excellent
SVM Sedan 4D	TD526	9995	700	800	1475	2400
SVM Hatchback 4D	TD626	9995	700	800	1525	2500
LS Sedan 4D	TD526	12635	1325	1475	2275	3650
LS Hatchback 4D	TD626	12635	1325	1475	2300	3725
LT Sedan 4D	TG526	12760	1575	1750	2575	4050
LT Hatchback 4D	TG626	13905	1750	1950	2825	4325

COBALT—4-Cyl.—Equipment Schedule 5
W.B. 103.3"; 2.2 Liter.

Sedan 4D	AJ52F	15040	2025	2275	3075	4725
Coupe 2D	AJ12F	15040	2125	2375	3200	4875
LS Sedan 4D	AL52F	17335	2375	2650	3450	5200
LS Coupe 2D	AL12F	17335	2475	2775	3575	5350
LT Sedan 4D	AM52F	18760	2625	2950	3725	5550

COBALT—4-Cyl. Supercharged—Equipment Schedule 5
W.B. 103.3"; 2.0 Liter.

SS Coupe 2D	AP12P	21995	3600	4000	5075	7425

CAVALIER—4-Cyl.—Equipment Schedule 5
W.B. 104.1"; 2.2 Liter.

Sedan 4D	JC52F	16025	1300	1475	2375	3975
Coupe 2D	JC12F	15825	1150	1300	2275	3850
LS Sedan 4D	JF52F	17705	1650	1850	2925	4850
LS Coupe 2D	JF12F	17505	1650	1850	2850	4675
LS Sport Sedan 4D	JH52F	19125	1775	2000	3075	5000
LS Sport Coupe 2D	JH12F	18925	1725	1950	3025	4925

CLASSIC—4-Cyl.—Equipment Schedule 5
W.B. 107.0"; 2.2 Liter.

Sedan 4D	ND52F	20130	2200	2475	3300	5000

MALIBU—4-Cyl.—Equipment Schedule 5
W.B. 106.3"; 2.2 Liter.

Sedan 4D	ZS528	19710	2250	2525	3375	5100
V6, 3.5 Liter	8		375	375	495	495

MALIBU—V6—Equipment Schedule 5
W.B. 106.3", 112.3" (MAXX); 3.5 Liter.

MAXX Hatchback 4D	ZS628	21475	2450	2750	3625	5425
LS Sedan 4D	ZT528	21775	2600	2925	3800	5675
LS MAXX H'Back 4D	ZT628	21975	2750	3075	4000	5950
LT Sedan 4D	ZU548	24570	2925	3275	4200	6250
LT MAXX H'Back 4D	ZU648	25120	3025	3375	4325	6400

IMPALA—V6—Equipment Schedule 4
W.B. 110.5"; 3.4 Liter, 3.8 Liter.

Sedan 4D	WF52E	23130	1900	2125	3250	5125
LS Sedan 4D	WH52K	25990	2475	2775	3900	5975

IMPALA—V6 Supercharged—Equipment Schedule 4
W.B. 110.5"; 3.8 Liter.

SS Sedan 4D	WP521	29085	3350	3700	5250	7950

MONTE CARLO—V6—Equipment Schedule 4
W.B. 110.5"; 3.4 Liter, 3.8 Liter.

LS Coupe 2D	WW12E	23060	2400	2675	3525	5250
LT Coupe 2D	WX12K	25220	3075	3425	4375	6475

MONTE CARLO—V6 Supercharged—Equipment Schedule 4
W.B. 110.5"; 3.8 Liter.

SS Coupe 2D	WZ121	28885	4075	4475	5300	7350

CORVETTE—V8—Equipment Schedule 2
W.B. 105.8"; 6.0 Liter.

Coupe 2D	YY22U	44245	12000	12600	13800	17000
Convertible 2D	YY34U	52245	13200	13850	15250	18750
Glass Roof Panel			250	250	275	275
Dual Roof Panels			300	300	330	330
Suspension Pkg			250	250	275	275
Z51 Handling			250	250	275	275
Manual, 6-Spd			150	150	165	165

2006 CHEVY—(1,2,3orK)(GorL)(1orN)(TD526)-6-#

AVEO—4-Cyl.—Equipment Schedule 6
W.B. 97.6"; 1.6 Liter.

SVM Sedan 4D	TD526	9995	750	850	1600	2575
SVM Hatchback 4D	TD626	9995	750	850	1650	2650

2006 CHEVROLET

Body Type	VIN	List	Trade-In Good	Very Good	Pvt-Party Good	Retail Excellent
AVEO—4-Cyl.—Equipment Schedule 6						
W.B. 97.6"; 1.6 Liter.						
LS Sedan 4D	TD526	12760	**1350**	**1500**	**2400**	**3800**
LS Hatchback 4D	TD626	12760	**1350**	**1500**	**2400**	**3800**
LT Sedan 4D	TG526	13165	**1825**	**2025**	**2975**	**4600**
LT Hatchback 4D	TG626	14180	**1900**	**2100**	**3025**	**4625**
Manual, 5-Spd			**(275)**	**(275)**	**(365)**	**(365)**
COBALT—4-Cyl.—Equipment Schedule 5						
W.B. 103.3"; 2.2 Liter, 2.4 Liter.						
LS Sedan 4D	AK55F	15340	**2125**	**2375**	**3325**	**4975**
LS Coupe 2D	AK15F	15340	**2250**	**2525**	**3450**	**5125**
LT Sedan 4D	AL55F	17640	**2550**	**2875**	**3750**	**5500**
LT Coupe 2D	AL15F	17640	**2625**	**2950**	**3850**	**5625**
LTZ Sedan 4D	AZ55F	18990	**2925**	**3275**	**4150**	**6025**
SS Sedan 4D	AM55B	19640	**3250**	**3600**	**4500**	**6425**
SS Coupe 2D	AM15B	19640	**3450**	**3825**	**4700**	**6675**
COBALT—4-Cyl. Supercharged—Equipment Schedule 5						
W.B. 103.3"; 2.0 Liter.						
SS Coupe 2D	AP15P	21990	**4025**	**4425**	**5625**	**8175**
HHR—4-Cyl.—Equipment Schedule 5						
W.B. 103.5"; 2.2 Liter.						
LS Sport Wagon 4D	A13D	16990	**2700**	**3000**	**3925**	**5600**
LT Sport Wagon 4D	A23D	17990	**2925**	**3250**	**4150**	**5900**
4-Cyl, 2.4 Liter	P		**200**	**200**	**270**	**270**
MALIBU—4-Cyl.—Equipment Schedule 5						
W.B. 106.3"; 2.2 Liter.						
LT Sedan 4D	ZT55F	19990	**2950**	**3300**	**4300**	**6275**
V6, 3.5 Liter	8		**400**	**400**	**535**	**535**
MALIBU—V6—Equipment Schedule 5						
W.B. 106.3"; 3.5 Liter.						
LS Sedan 4D	ZS558	17990	**2850**	**3200**	**4100**	**5925**
4-Cyl, 2.2 Liter	F		**(250)**	**(250)**	**(335)**	**(335)**
MALIBU—V6—Equipment Schedule 5						
W.B. 106.3", 112.3" (MAXX); 3.5 Liter, 3.9 Liter.						
LS MAXX H'Back 4D	ZS658	20835	**2875**	**3225**	**4125**	**5950**
LT MAXX H'Back 4D	ZT658	21650	**3400**	**3800**	**4750**	**6775**
SS Sedan 4D	ZW571	24490	**4200**	**4625**	**5700**	**8050**
SS MAXX H'Back 4D	ZW671	24490	**4425**	**4875**	**5950**	**8375**
LTZ Sedan 4D	ZU578	24830	**4000**	**4425**	**5450**	**7725**
LTZ MAXX H'Back 4D	ZU678	25380	**4425**	**4875**	**5950**	**8400**
IMPALA—V6—Equipment Schedule 4						
W.B. 110.5"; 3.5 Liter, 3.9 Liter.						
LS Sedan 4D	WB55K	21990	**3500**	**3825**	**4975**	**7125**
LT Sedan 4D	WC551	22520	**3750**	**4100**	**5275**	**7525**
LTZ Sedan 4D	WU551	27530	**4300**	**4675**	**5950**	**8500**
IMPALA—V8—Equipment Schedule 4						
W.B. 110.5"; 5.3 Liter.						
SS Sedan 4D	WD55C	27790	**5150**	**5575**	**7125**	**9975**
MONTE CARLO—V6—Equipment Schedule 4						
W.B. 110.5"; 3.5 Liter, 3.9 Liter.						
LS Coupe 2D	WJ15K	21990	**2800**	**3125**	**4275**	**6350**
LT Coupe 2D	WK15K	22520	**3250**	**3600**	**4800**	**7075**
LTZ Coupe 2D	WN151	26635	**4025**	**4400**	**5725**	**8325**
MONTE CARLO—V8—Equipment Schedule 4						
W.B. 110.5"; 5.3 Liter.						
SS Coupe 2D	WL15C	27790	**5000**	**5450**	**6600**	**8975**
CORVETTE—V8—Equipment Schedule 2						
W.B. 105.7"; 6.0 Liter, 7.0 Liter.						
Coupe 2D	YY22U	47345	**13150**	**13800**	**14700**	**17500**
Convertible 2D	YY32U	53585	**14500**	**15150**	**16050**	**19100**
Z06 Coupe 2D	YY25E	65800	**20400**	**21300**	**22500**	**26800**
Glass Roof Panel			**250**	**250**	**270**	**270**
Dual Roof Panels			**300**	**300**	**325**	**325**
Suspension Pkg			**300**	**300**	**325**	**325**
Z51 Handling			**300**	**300**	**325**	**325**
Manual, 6-Spd			**150**	**150**	**160**	**160**

2007 CHEVY—(1,2,3orK)(GorL)(1orN)(TD566)-7-#

AVEO—4-Cyl.—Equipment Schedule 6						
W.B. 97.6"; 1.6 Liter.						
LS Sedan 4D	TD566	13165	**1950**	**2150**	**3075**	**4600**
LT Sedan 4D	TG566	13470	**2350**	**2575**	**3575**	**5300**
Manual, 5-Spd			**(300)**	**(300)**	**(400)**	**(400)**

Body Type	VIN	List	Trade-In Good	Very Good	Pvt-Party Good	Retail Excellent
AVEO5—4-Cyl.—Equipment Schedule 6						
W.B. 97.6"; 1.6 Liter.						
SVM Hatchback 4D	TD666	10045	1100	1225	1950	3000
LS Hatchback 4D	TD666	12515	1725	1925	2775	4175
Automatic			300	300	400	400
COBALT—4-Cyl.—Equipment Schedule 5						
W.B. 103.3"; 2.2 Liter, 2.4 Liter.						
LS Sedan 4D	AK55F	14515	2575	2875	3725	5375
LS Coupe 2D	AK15F	14515	2675	2975	3825	5525
LT Sedan 4D	AL55F	15635	2925	3250	4100	5825
LT Coupe 2D	AL15F	15635	3225	3575	4400	6200
SS Sedan 4D	AM52B	19920	3875	4250	5050	6975
SS Coupe 2D	AM15B	19920	4225	4625	5400	7400
Manual, 5-Spd.			(400)	(400)	(535)	(535)
COBALT—4-Cyl.—Equipment Schedule 5						
W.B. 103.3"; 2.2 Liter.						
LTZ Sedan 4D	AZ55F	18790	3425	3775	4600	6450
COBALT—4-Cyl. Supercharged—Equipment Schedule 5						
W.B. 103.3"; 2.0 Liter.						
SS Coupe 2D	AP18P	21465	4575	5000	6075	8550
HHR—4-Cyl.—Equipment Schedule 5						
W.B. 103.5"; 2.2 Liter.						
LS Sport Wagon 4D	A13D	17470	3300	3625	4575	6425
LS Panel Sport Wag 2D	A15D	17750	3400	3725	4700	6550
LT Sport Wagon 4D	A23D	18470	3525	3850	4825	6725
LT Panel Sport Wag 2D	A25P	19595	3625	3975	4925	6850
Manual, 5-Spd.			(400)	(400)	(535)	(535)
4-Cyl, 2.4L (ex LT Panel)	P		225	225	295	295
MALIBU—4-Cyl.—Equipment Schedule 5						
W.B. 106.3"; 2.2 Liter.						
LT Sedan 4D	ZT58N	18930	3575	3950	4850	6800
V6, 3.5 Liter	N		425	425	580	580
MALIBU—V6—Equipment Schedule 5						
W.B. 106.3"; 3.5 Liter.						
LS Sedan 4D	ZS58N	17495	3475	3850	4750	6650
4-Cyl, 2.2 Liter	F		(250)	(250)	(335)	(335)
MALIBU—V6—Equipment Schedule 5						
W.B. 106.3", 112.3" (MAXX); 3.5 Liter, 3.9 Liter.						
LS MAXX H'Back 4D	ZS68N	20385	3650	4025	4950	6925
LT MAXX H'Back 4D	ZT68N	21130	4075	4475	5425	7550
SS Sedan 4D	ZW571	23965	5000	5450	6475	8925
SS MAXX H'Back 4D	ZW671	24265	5225	5700	6750	9275
LTZ Sedan 4D	ZU57N	24170	4675	5100	6100	8450
LTZ MAXX H'Back 4D	ZU67N	24470	5225	5700	6750	9275
IMPALA—V6—Equipment Schedule 4						
W.B. 110.5"; 3.5 Liter, 3.9 Liter.						
LS Sedan 4D	WB55K	21445	3950	4275	5325	7400
LT Sedan 4D	WT55K	22125	4400	4775	5800	7975
LTZ Sedan 4D	WU551	26935	5375	5800	7125	9725
IMPALA—V6—Equipment Schedule 4						
W.B. 110.5"; 5.3 Liter.						
SS Sedan 4D	WD55C	28540	5625	6050	7525	10250
MONTE CARLO—V6—Equipment Schedule 4						
W.B. 110.5"; 3.5 Liter.						
LS Coupe 2D	WJ15K	21515	3325	3675	4875	7100
LT Coupe 2D	WK15K	23125	4000	4375	5625	8075
MONTE CARLO—V8—Equipment Schedule 4						
W.B. 110.5"; 5.3 Liter.						
SS Coupe 2D	WL15C	28240	5750	6225	7300	9725
CORVETTE—V8—Equipment Schedule 2						
W.B. 105.7"; 6.0 Liter, 7.0 Liter.						
Coupe 2D	YY25U	46245	15200	15900	16500	19200
Convertible 2D	YY36U	54320	16450	17200	17900	20900
Z06 Coupe 2D	YY25E	70000	22900	23900	24600	28700
Glass Roof Panel			250	250	270	270
Dual Roof Panels			300	300	325	325
Suspension Pkg			350	350	380	380
Z51 Handling			350	350	380	380
Indy Pace Car Pkg			1100	1100	1200	1200
Manual, 6-Spd.			150	150	165	165

Body Type	VIN	List	Trade-In Good	Very Good	Pvt-Party Good	Retail Excellent

2008 CHEVY — (1,2,3orK)(GorL)(1orN)(TD566)-8-#

AVEO—4-Cyl.—Equipment Schedule 6
W.B. 97.6"; 1.6 Liter.

Body Type	VIN	List	Good	Very Good	Good	Excellent
LS Sedan 4D	TD566	15255	**2500**	**2775**	**3675**	**5275**
LT Sedan 4D	TG566	15180	**3050**	**3325**	**4300**	**6100**
Manual, 5-Spd w/Overdrive			**(350)**	**(350)**	**(470)**	**(470)**

AVEO5—4-Cyl.—Equipment Schedule 6
W.B. 97.6"; 1.6 Liter.

SVM Hatchback 4D	TD666	10610	**1575**	**1750**	**2425**	**3500**

AVEO5—4-Cyl.—Equipment Schedule 6
W.B. 97.6"; 1.6 Liter.

LS Hatchback 4D	TD666	13620	**2725**	**2975**	**3850**	**5450**
Manual, 5-Spd w/Overdrive			**(350)**	**(350)**	**(470)**	**(470)**

COBALT—4-Cyl.—Equipment Schedule 5
W.B. 103.3"; 2.2 Liter, 2.4 Liter.

LS Sedan 4D	AK58F	15215	**3000**	**3300**	**4100**	**5775**
LS Coupe 2D	AK18F	15215	**3100**	**3400**	**4200**	**5900**
LT Sedan 4D	AL58F	15915	**3350**	**3675**	**4600**	**6400**
LT Coupe 2D	AL18F	15915	**3450**	**3775**	**4675**	**6475**
Sport Sedan 4D	AM58B	20540	**4275**	**4650**	**5525**	**7450**
Sport Coupe 2D	AM18B	20540	**4575**	**4975**	**5825**	**7800**
Manual, 5-Spd			**(425)**	**(425)**	**(555)**	**(555)**

COBALT—4-Cyl. Turbo—Equipment Schedule 5
W.B. 103.5"; 2.0 Liter.

SS Coupe 2D	AP18X	22995	**5750**	**6225**	**7550**	**10250**

HHR—4-Cyl.—Equipment Schedule 5
W.B. 103.5"; 2.2 Liter.

LS Sport Wagon 4D	A13D	17795	**4000**	**4325**	**5275**	**7100**
LS Panel Sport Wag 2D	A15D	18095	**4100**	**4425**	**5400**	**7250**
LT Sport Wagon 4D	A23D	18795	**4400**	**4750**	**5700**	**7625**
LT Panel Sport Wag 2D	A25D	19095	**4500**	**4850**	**5850**	**7850**
Manual, 5-Spd	3		**(425)**	**(425)**	**(555)**	**(555)**
4-Cyl, 2.4 Liter	P		**250**	**250**	**320**	**320**

HHR—4-Cyl. Turbo—Equipment Schedule 5
W.B. 103.5"; 2.0 Liter.

SS Sport Wagon 4D	A83X	22995	**7125**	**7600**	**8900**	**11600**
Manual, 5-Spd			**(425)**	**(425)**	**(555)**	**(555)**

MALIBU CLASSIC—4-Cyl.—Equipment Schedule 5
W.B. 106.3"; 2.2 Liter.

LS Sedan 4D	ZS58F	18495	**3425**	**3750**	**4450**	**6050**
V6, 3.5 Liter	N		**475**	**475**	**620**	**620**

MALIBU CLASSIC—V6—Equipment Schedule 5
W.B. 106.3"; 3.5 Liter.

LT Sedan 4D	ZT58N	20880	**4100**	**4475**	**5325**	**7175**

MALIBU—4-Cyl.—Equipment Schedule 4
W.B. 112.3"; 2.4 Liter.

LS Sedan 4D	ZG58B	19995	**5700**	**6150**	**7150**	**9350**
LT Sedan 4D	ZH58B	20955	**6350**	**6825**	**7925**	**10400**
V6, 3.5 Liter	N		**375**	**375**	**500**	**500**
V6, 3.6 Liter	7		**750**	**750**	**1000**	**1000**

MALIBU—4-Cyl. Hybrid—Equipment Schedule 4
W.B. 112.3"; 2.4 Liter.

Sedan 4D	ZF585	22790	**6650**	**7125**	**8250**	**10850**

MALIBU—V6—Equipment Schedule 4
W.B. 112.3"; 3.6 Liter.

LTZ Sedan 4D	ZK587	26995	**7050**	**7575**	**8725**	**11400**

IMPALA—V6—Equipment Schedule 4
W.B. 110.5"; 3.5 Liter, 3.9 Liter.

LS Sedan 4D	WB55K	21940	**5050**	**5425**	**6450**	**8600**
LT Sedan 4D	WT55K	22550	**5425**	**5825**	**7025**	**9275**
LT 50th Anniv Ed Sed	WV55K	25995	**6375**	**6825**	**8025**	**10500**
LTZ Sedan 4D	WU553	27515	**6550**	**6975**	**8275**	**10900**

IMPALA—V8—Equipment Schedule 4
W.B. 110.5"; 5.3 Liter.

SS Sedan 4D	WD55C	28920	**7075**	**7550**	**8950**	**11800**

CORVETTE—V8—Equipment Schedule 2
W.B. 105.7"; 6.2 Liter, 7.0 Liter.

Coupe 2D	YY25W	47245	**17350**	**18100**	**18850**	**21900**
Convertible 2D	YY36W	55585	**19350**	**20100**	**20900**	**24200**
Z06 Coupe 2D	YY25E	71000	**26000**	**27000**	**27800**	**32200**
Glass Roof Panel			**250**	**250**	**280**	**280**
Dual Roof Panels			**300**	**300**	**335**	**335**

Body Type	VIN	List	Trade-In Good	Very Good	Pvt-Party Good	Retail Excellent
Suspension Pkg		------	400	400	445	445
Z51 Handling		------	400	400	445	445
Indy Pace Car Pkg		------	1150	1150	1285	1285
4LT		------	1750	1750	1955	1955
Manual, 6-Spd		------	150	150	165	165

2009 CHEVY — (1,2,3orK)(GorL)(1orN)(TD56E)-9-#

AVEO—4-Cyl.—Equipment Schedule 6
W.B. 97.6"; 1.6 Liter.

Body Type	VIN	List	Trade-In Good	Very Good	Pvt-Party Good	Retail Excellent
LS Sedan 4D	TD56E	12120	2725	2975	3925	5525

AVEO—4-Cyl.—Equipment Schedule 6
W.B. 97.6"; 1.6 Liter.

LT Sedan 4D	TG56E	15180	3475	3775	4875	6700
Manual, 5-Spd w/Overdrive			(375)	(375)	(500)	(500)

AVEO5—4-Cyl.—Equipment Schedule 6
W.B. 97.6"; 1.6 Liter.

LS Hatchback 4D	TD66E	12120	3025	3300	4150	5725

AVEO5—4-Cyl.—Equipment Schedule 6
W.B. 97.6"; 1.6 Liter.

LT Hatchback 4D	TG66E	14255	3175	3450	4400	6100
Automatic, 4-Spd			350	350	465	465

COBALT—4-Cyl.—Equipment Schedule 5
W.B. 103.3"; 2.2 Liter.

XFE Sedan 4D	AK58N	15710	3375	3700	4500	6200
XFE Coupe 2D	AK18N	15710	3325	3625	4450	6125
LS XFE Sedan 4D	AK58N	15670	3275	3575	4375	6050
LS XFE Coupe 2D	AK18N	15670	3225	3525	4325	6000
LT XFE Sedan 4D	AL58N	16370	3875	4200	5175	7050
LT XFE Coupe 2D	AL18N	16370	4025	4350	5325	7250

COBALT—4-Cyl.—Equipment Schedule 5
W.B. 103.3"; 2.2 Liter.

LS Sedan 4D	AS58N	16595	3750	4075	4975	6750
LS Coupe 2D	AS18N	16595	4125	4450	5325	7100
LT Sedan 4D	AT58N	17295	4325	4675	5675	7675
LT Coupe 2D	AT18N	17295	4425	4775	5775	7825
Manual, 5-Spd			(450)	(450)	(600)	(600)

COBALT—4-Cyl. Turbo—Equipment Schedule 5
W.B. 103.3"; 2.0 Liter.

SS Sedan 4D	AP58X	23435	7100	7575	8975	11850
SS Coupe 2D	AP18X	23435	7175	7675	8700	11100

HHR—4-Cyl.—Equipment Schedule 5
W.B. 103.5"; 2.2 Liter.

LS Sport Wagon 4D	A13D	19590	4550	4875	5825	7625
LS Panel Sport Wag 2D	A15D	19900	4650	4975	5950	7775
LT Sport Wagon 4D	A23D	20590	5100	5450	6450	8425
LT Panel Sport Wag 2D	A25D	20900	5200	5550	6550	8550
Manual, 5-Spd			(450)	(450)	(600)	(600)
4-Cyl, 2.4 Liter	P		250	250	345	345

HHR—4-Cyl. Turbo—Equipment Schedule 5
W.B. 103.5"; 2.0 Liter.

SS Sport Wagon 4D	A83X	25490	8100	8575	9875	12550
SS Panel Sport Wag 2D	A83X	25810	8600	9075	10400	13100
Manual, 5-Spd			(450)	(450)	(600)	(600)

MALIBU—4-Cyl.—Equipment Schedule 4
W.B. 112.3"; 2.4 Liter.

LS Sedan 4D	ZG57B	22090	6550	6975	8075	10350
LT Sedan 4D	ZH57B	22990	7025	7475	8575	10950
LTZ Sedan 4D	ZK57B	27365	7825	8325	9600	12300
V6, 3.5 Liter	N		400	400	535	535
V6, 3.6 Liter	7		800	800	1065	1065

MALIBU—4-Cyl. Hybrid—Equipment Schedule 4
W.B. 112.3"; 2.4 Liter.

Sedan 4D	ZF575	26040	7425	7900	9175	11750

IMPALA—V6—Equipment Schedule 4
W.B. 110.5"; 3.5 Liter, 3.9 Liter.

LS Sedan 4D	WB55K	23795	6075	6450	7600	9775
LT Sedan 4D	WT55K	24650	6275	6675	7825	10050
LTZ Sedan 4D	WU553	29635	7325	7775	9125	11700

IMPALA—V8—Equipment Schedule 4
W.B. 110.5"; 5.3 Liter.

SS Sedan 4D	WD55C	31140	8025	8500	9900	12650

CORVETTE—V8—Equipment Schedule 2
W.B. 105.7"; 6.2 Liter, 7.0 Liter.

Body Type	VIN	List	Trade-In Good	Very Good	Pvt-Party Good	Retail Excellent
Coupe 2D	YY25W	49145	19650	20400	21300	24700
Convertible 2D	YY36W	53800	22500	23400	24200	27900
Z06 Coupe 2D	YZ25E	74955	29300	30400	31500	36400
Glass Roof Panel			275	275	305	305
Dual Roof Panels			350	350	390	390
4LT			1800	1800	2000	2000
Hertz Special Ed			700	700	770	770
Suspension Pkg			450	450	500	500
Z51 Handling Pkg			450	450	500	500
Manual, 6-Spd			175	175	195	195
CORVETTE—V8 Supercharged—Equipment Schedule 2						
W.B. 105.7"; 6.2 Liter.						
ZR1 Coupe 2D	YR25R	105000	****	****	****	67600

2010 CHEVY — (1,2,3,6orK)(GorL)(1orN)(TD5DE)–A–#

AVEO—4-Cyl.—Equipment Schedule 6
W.B. 97.6"; 1.6 Liter.

Body Type	VIN	List	Trade-In Good	Very Good	Pvt-Party Good	Retail Excellent
LS Sedan 4D	TD5DE	12685	3825	4125	5150	6875

AVEO—4-Cyl.—Equipment Schedule 6
W.B. 97.6"; 1.6 Liter.

LT Sedan 4D	TD5DE	15895	4650	4975	5975	7800
Manual, 5-Spd w/Overdrive			(475)	(475)	(625)	(625)

AVEO5—4-Cyl.—Equipment Schedule 6
W.B. 97.6"; 1.6 Liter.

LS Hatchback 4D	TD6DE	12685	3875	4175	5125	6750

AVEO5—4-Cyl.—Equipment Schedule 6
W.B. 97.6"; 1.6 Liter.

LT Hatchback 4D	TD6DE	15745	4450	4750	5825	7675
Manual, 5-Spd w/Overdrive			(475)	(475)	(625)	(625)

COBALT—4-Cyl.—Equipment Schedule 6
W.B. 103.3"; 2.2 Liter.

XFE Sedan 4D	AK58H	15710	4350	4700	5725	7175
XFE Coupe 2D	AK18H	15710	4200	4525	5350	6975
LS XFE Sedan 4D	AA5F5	16990	4550	4900	5725	7450
LS XFE Coupe 2D	AA1F5	16990	4500	4850	5675	7375
LT XFE Sedan 4D	AC5F5	17190	5175	5550	6400	8275
LT XFE Coupe 2D	AC1F5	17190	5550	5950	6825	8775

COBALT—4-Cyl.—Equipment Schedule 6
W.B. 103.3"; 2.2 Liter.

LS Sedan 4D	AB5F5	16390	4575	4925	5850	7700
LS Coupe 2D	AB1F5	16390	4950	5325	6250	8175

COBALT—4-Cyl.—Equipment Schedule 6
W.B. 103.3"; 2.2 Liter.

LT Sedan 4D	AD5F5	17190	5575	5975	7025	9025
LT Coupe 2D	AD1F5	17190	5725	6125	7200	9225
Manual, 5-Spd			(500)	(500)	(655)	(655)

COBALT—4-Cyl. Turbo—Equipment Schedule 5
W.B. 103.3"; 2.0 Liter.

SS Coupe 2D	AG1FX	25255	10250	10850	11650	14100

HHR—4-Cyl.—Equipment Schedule 5
W.B. 103.5"; 2.2 Liter.

LS Sport Wagon 4D	AADB	20440	5200	5525	6675	8550
LS Panel Sport Wag 2D	AADB	20750	5500	5825	7000	8950
LT Sport Wagon 4D	ABDB	21440	5800	6150	7350	9400
LT Panel Sport Wag 2D	ABDB	21750	5850	6200	7375	9400
Manual, 5-Spd			(500)	(500)	(655)	(655)
4-Cyl, Flex Fuel, 2.4L	V		275	275	375	375

HHR—4-Cyl. Turbo—Equipment Schedule 5
W.B. 103.5"; 2.0 Liter.

SS Sport Wagon 4D	ADDM	26975	8750	9200	10600	13300
Manual, 5-Spd			(500)	(500)	(655)	(655)

MALIBU—4-Cyl.—Equipment Schedule 4
W.B. 112.3"; 2.4 Liter.

LS Sedan 4D	ZB5EB	22545	7425	7850	9050	11350
LT Sedan 4D	ZC5EB	23435	8175	8650	9825	12250
LTZ Sedan 4D	ZE5E7	27325	9075	9575	10800	13450
V6, 3.6 Liter	7		850	850	1100	1100

IMPALA—V6—Equipment Schedule 4
W.B. 110.5"; 3.5 Liter, 3.9 Liter.

LS Sedan 4D	WA5EK	24715	7050	7475	8625	10850
LT Sedan 4D	WB5EK	26950	7450	7875	9150	11500
LTZ Sedan 4D	WC5EM	30455	8600	9075	10400	13000

2010 CHEVROLET

Body Type	VIN	List	Trade-In Good	Very Good	Pvt-Party Good	Retail Excellent
CAMARO—V6—Equipment Schedule 4						
W.B. 112.3"; 3.6 Liter.						
LS Coupe 2D	FE1EV	23990	11650	12200	13000	15300
LT Coupe 2D	FF1EV	25625	13000	13650	14600	17150
RS Pkg			1250	1250	1490	1490
CAMARO—V8—Equipment Schedule 4						
W.B. 112.3"; 6.2 Liter.						
SS Coupe 2D	FS1EW	31990	16250	17000	17850	20900
CORVETTE—V8—Equipment Schedule 2						
W.B.105.7"; 6.2 Liter, 7.0 Liter.						
Coupe 2D	YE2DW	49880	22300	23100	23700	26700
Convertible 2D	YE3DW	54530	26100	27000	27600	31100
Grand Sport Cpe 2D	YP2DW	55720	28400	29400	29900	33700
Grand Sport Conv 2D	YP3DW	59530	31200	32400	32900	37100
Z06 Coupe 2D	YJ2DE	75235	36300	37600	38000	42700
Glass Roof Panel			300	300	330	330
Dual Roof Panels			400	400	440	440
Heritage			1400	1400	1540	1540
4LT			1850	1850	2040	2040
Suspension Pkg			500	500	550	550
Manual, 6-Spd			200	200	220	220
CORVETTE—V8 Supercharged—Equipment Schedule 2						
W.B. 105.7"; 6.2 Liter.						
ZR1 Coupe 2D	YM2DT	109130	****	****	****	70500

2011 CHEVY — (1,2,3,6orK)(G1,GAorL1)(TD5DG)–B–#

Body Type	VIN	List	Trade-In Good	Very Good	Pvt-Party Good	Retail Excellent
AVEO—4-Cyl.—Equipment Schedule 6						
W.B. 97.6"; 1.6 Liter.						
LS Sedan 4D	TD5DG	12685	4750	5050	6125	7925
AVEO—4-Cyl.—Equipment Schedule 6						
W.B. 97.6"; 1.6 Liter.						
LT Sedan 4D	TD5DG	15745	5400	5750	6875	8700
Manual, 5-Spd w/Overdrive			(500)	(500)	(665)	(665)
AVEO5—4-Cyl.—Equipment Schedule 6						
W.B. 97.6"; 1.6 Liter.						
LS Hatchback 4D	TD6DG	12835	4950	5275	6200	7850
AVEO5—4-Cyl.—Equipment Schedule 6						
W.B. 97.6"; 1.6 Liter.						
LT Hatchback 4D	TD6DG	15745	5400	5750	6950	8850
Manual, 5-Spd w/Overdrive			(500)	(500)	(665)	(665)
CRUZE—4-Cyl.—Equipment Schedule 5						
W.B. 105.7"; 1.8 Liter.						
LS Sedan 4D	PB5SH	17920	7675	8150	9150	11300
Manual, 6-Spd w/Overdrive	B		(475)	(475)	(620)	(620)
CRUZE—4-Cyl. Turbo—Equipment Schedule 5						
W.B. 105.7"; 1.4 Liter.						
LT Sedan 4D	PF5S9	18895	8375	8875	9900	12200
LTZ Sedan 4D	PH5S9	22695	9600	10150	11200	13750
CRUZE—4-Cyl. Turbo—Equipment Schedule 5						
W.B. 105.7"; 1.4 Liter.						
eco Sedan 4D	PK5S9	19820	8625	9125	10150	12450
Manual, 6-Spd w/Overdrive	K		(475)	(475)	(610)	(610)
VOLT—AC Electric—Equipment Schedule 3						
W.B. 105.7".						
Sedan 4D	RC6S4	41000	12300	12900	13600	16050
HHR—4-Cyl.—Equipment Schedule 5						
W.B. 103.5"; 2.2 Liter.						
LS Sport Wagon 4D	AEFW	19440	6675	7050	8275	10400
LS Panel Sport Wag 2D	AEFW	19750	6925	7300	8550	10700
LT Sport Wagon 4D	AFFW	20440	7050	7425	8725	10900
Manual, 5-Spd	E		(500)	(500)	(665)	(665)
4-Cyl, Flex Fuel, 2.4L	U		300	300	400	400
MALIBU—4-Cyl.—Equipment Schedule 5						
W.B. 112.3"; 2.4 Liter.						
LS Sedan 4D	ZB5E1	22695	8250	8675	9975	12400
LT Sedan 4D	ZC5E1	23545	8925	9375	10700	13250
LTZ Sedan 4D	ZE5E1	27735	9875	10350	11800	14550
V6, 3.6 Liter	7		900	900	1155	1155
IMPALA—V6—Equipment Schedule 4						
W.B. 110.5"; 3.5 Liter, 3.9 Liter.						
LS Sedan 4D	WA5EK	25215	8050	8475	9700	11950
LT Sedan 4D	WB5EK	26430	8625	9075	10350	12750
LTZ Sedan 4D	WC5EM	30755	9625	10100	11450	14050

Body Type	VIN	List	Trade-In Good	Very Good	Pvt-Party Good	Retail Excellent
CAMARO—V6—Equipment Schedule 4						
W.B. 112.3"; 3.6 Liter.						
LS Coupe 2D	FA1ED	24525	12750	13350	14250	16650
LT Coupe 2D	FB1ED	25725	14450	15100	16150	18850
LT Convertible 2D	FB3ED	30995	15800	16500	17550	20500
RS Pkg			1300	1300	1550	1550
CAMARO—V8—Equipment Schedule 4						
W.B. 112.3"; 6.2 Liter.						
SS Coupe 2D	FJ1EJ	32790	18300	19050	20100	23400
SS Convertible 2D	FJ3EJ	38495	19500	20300	21300	24600
CORVETTE—V8—Equipment Schedule 2						
W.B.105.7"; 6.2 Liter, 7.0 Liter.						
Coupe 2D	YA2DW	49900	23600	24500	25200	28500
Convertible 2D	YA3DW	54550	26900	27900	28600	32400
Grand Sport Cpe 2D	YP2DW	55740	30000	31000	31800	35800
Grand Sport Conv 2D	YP3DW	59550	33600	34800	35500	39900
Z06 Coupe 2D	YJ2DE	75255	42000	43400	43800	49000
Dual Roof Panels			450	450	495	495
Glass Roof Panel			325	325	355	355
Heritage			1500	1500	1670	1670
4LT			1500	1500	1670	1670
Magnetic Ride Suspension			1900	1900	2080	2080
Manual, 6-Spd	A		550	550	600	600
			225	225	245	245
CORVETTE—V8 Supercharged—Equipment Schedule 2						
W.B. 105.7"; 6.2 Liter.						
ZR1 Coupe 2D	YM2DT	112050	****	****	****	73000

Body Type	VIN	List	Good	Very Good	Good	Excellent
SONIC—4-Cyl.—Equipment Schedule 6						
W.B. 99.4"; 1.8 Liter.						
LS Sedan 4D	JB5SH	14495	6150	6500	7775	9775
LS Hatchback 4D	JB6SH	15395	6500	6875	8150	10200
LT Sedan 4D	JD5SH	16695	6725	7100	8375	10500
LT Hatchback 4D	JD6SH	16495	7075	7450	8750	10950
LTZ Sedan 4D	JF5SH	17295	7800	8225	9575	11850
LTZ Hatchback 4D	JF6SH	17995	8150	8575	9950	12300
Automatic, 6-Spd	C		475	475	635	635
4-Cyl, Turbo, 1.4 Liter	B		350	350	455	455
CRUZE—4-Cyl.—Equipment Schedule 5						
W.B. 105.7"; 1.8 Liter.						
LS Sedan 4D	PD5SH	17470	8650	9125	10200	12500
Manual, 6-Spd w/Overdrive			(500)	(500)	(650)	(650)
CRUZE—4-Cyl. Turbo—Equipment Schedule 5						
W.B. 105.7"; 1.4 Liter.						
LT Sedan 4D	PL5SC	19225	9300	9800	10850	13200
eco Sedan 4D	PK5SC	19995	9550	10050	11100	13450
Manual, 6-Spd	L,M		(500)	(500)	(645)	(645)
CRUZE—4-Cyl. Turbo—Equipment Schedule 5						
W.B. 105.7"; 1.4 Liter.						
LTZ Sedan 4D	PH5SC	23860	10500	11050	12200	14800
VOLT—AC Electric—Equipment Schedule 3						
W.B. 105.7".						
Sedan 4D	RA6S4	39995	12650	13250	14150	16650
MALIBU—4-Cyl.—Equipment Schedule 4						
W.B. 112.3"; 2.4 Liter.						
LS Sedan 4D	ZB5E0	22755	9350	9775	11200	13850
LT Sedan 4D	ZC5E0	24115	9850	10300	11900	14700
LTZ Sedan 4D	ZE5E0	29245	10850	11350	13000	16050
V6, 3.6 Liter	7		950	950	1210	1210
IMPALA—V6—Equipment Schedule 4						
W.B. 110.5"; 3.6 Liter.						
LS Sedan 4D	WA5E3	26470	9000	9425	10800	13250
LT Sedan 4D	WB5E3	27995	9275	9725	11100	13650
LTZ Sedan 4D	WC5E3	31010	10350	10850	12300	14950
CAMARO—V6—Equipment Schedule 4						
W.B. 112.3"; 3.6 Liter.						
LS Coupe 2D	FA1E3	25095	13250	13800	14950	17450
LT Coupe 2D	FB1E3	27095	15200	15850	17000	19750
LT Convertible 2D	FB3E3	31995	16700	17400	18550	21600
RS Pkg			1350	1350	1595	1595
CAMARO—V8—Equipment Schedule 4						
W.B. 112.3"; 6.2 Liter.						
SS Coupe 2D	FJ1EW	37345	19450	20200	21300	24600

Body Type	VIN	List	Trade-In Good	Very Good	Pvt-Party Good	Retail Excellent
SS Convertible 2D	FJ3EW	39795	20900	21800	22700	26100
CAMARO—V8 Supercharged—Equipment Schedule 4						
W.B. 112.3"; 6.2 Liter.						
ZL1 Coupe 2D	FS1EP	54995	33200	34400	34500	38300
CORVETTE—V8—Equipment Schedule 2						
W.B. 105.7"; 6.2 Liter, 7.0 Liter.						
Coupe 2D	YA2DW	51750	24900	25800	26700	30100
Convertible 2D	YA3DW	58750	27900	28900	29900	33800
Grand Sport Coupe	YP3DW	58150	31300	32400	33100	37200
Grand Sport Conv 2D	YP3DW	61750	36500	37800	38500	43300
Z06 Coupe 2D	YJ2DE	76500	44800	46300	46800	52400
Glass Roof Panel			350	350	380	380
Dual Roof Panels			500	500	545	545
Centennial Edition			5350	5350	5960	5960
Heritage			1600	1600	1785	1785
4LT			1950	1950	2130	2130
Suspension Pkg			600	600	655	655
Manual, 6-Spd	A,B,C,D		250	250	270	270
CORVETTE—V8 Supercharged—Equipment Schedule 2						
W.B. 105.7"; 6.2 Liter.						
ZR1 Coupe 2D	YM2DT	113500	****	****	****	77600

2013 CHEVY — (1,2or3)G1or(6orK)L1(CA6S9)–D–#

Body Type	VIN	List	Trade-In Good	Very Good	Pvt-Party Good	Retail Excellent
SPARK—4-Cyl. ECOTEC—Equipment Schedule 6						
W.B. 93.5"; 1.2 Liter.						
LS Hatchback 4D	CA6S9	12995	6200	6550	7650	9450
LT Hatchback 4D	CC6S9	14495	6875	7250	8375	10300
SONIC—4-Cyl.—Equipment Schedule 6						
W.B. 99.4"; 1.8 Liter.						
LS Sedan 4D	JB5S4	14995	7175	7575	8825	10950
LS Sedan 4D	JB6SH	15595	7550	7925	9275	11500
LT Sedan 4D	JD5SH	16430	7925	8325	9650	11850
LT Hatchback 4D	JD6SH	17030	8175	8575	9825	12000
LTZ Sedan 4D	JF5SH	18040	8825	9275	10550	12850
LTZ Hatchback 4D	JF6SH	18640	9075	9500	10900	13300
Automatic, 6-Spd	C		500	500	665	665
4-Cyl, Turbo, 1.4 Liter	B		350	350	480	480
SONIC—4-Cyl. Turbo—Equipment Schedule 6						
W.B. 99.4"; 1.4 Liter.						
RS Hatchback 4D	JH6SB	20995	10550	11050	12350	14850
Automatic, 6-Spd	G		500	500	635	635
CRUZE—4-Cyl.—Equipment Schedule 5						
W.B. 105.7"; 1.8 Liter.						
LS Sedan 4D	PA5SH	19020	9775	10250	11350	13650
Manual, 6-Spd w/Overdrive	B		(550)	(550)	(680)	(680)
CRUZE—4-Cyl. Turbo—Equipment Schedule 5						
W.B. 105.7"; 1.4 Liter.						
LT Sedan 4D	PC5SB	20450	10300	10800	11950	14400
eco Sedan 4D	PH5SB	21670	10950	11500	12600	15150
LTZ Sedan 4D	PG5SB	24345	11950	12550	13700	16450
Manual, 6-Spd w/OD	D,F		(550)	(550)	(675)	(675)
VOLT—AC Electric—Equipment Schedule 3						
W.B. 105.7".						
Sedan 4D	RA6E4	39995	14050	14650	15550	18150
MALIBU—4-Cyl.—Equipment Schedule 4						
W.B. 107.8"; 2.5 Liter.						
LS Sedan 4D	1B5RA	23150	11300	11750	13200	16000
LT Sedan 4D	1C5RA	24765	12300	12800	14250	17100
eco Sedan 4D	1D5RR	25995	13050	13550	15050	18100
LTZ Sedan 4D	1H5RA	28590	13400	13900	15500	18650
IMPALA—V6—Equipment Schedule 4						
W.B. 110.5"; 3.6 Liter.						
LS Sedan 4D	WA5E3	26685	9825	10300	11850	14550
LT Sedan 4D	WB5E3	28210	10300	10800	12400	15250
LTZ Sedan 4D	WC5E3	31225	11300	11800	13400	16300
CAMARO—V6—Equipment Schedule 4						
W.B. 112.3"; 3.6 Liter.						
LS Coupe 2D	FA1E3	24245	14400	15000	16150	18700
LT Coupe 2D	FB1E3	26660	16800	17450	18650	21600
LT Convertible 2D	FB3D3	31560	18350	19100	20300	23500
RS Pkg			1400	1400	1650	1650
CAMARO—V8—Equipment Schedule 4						
W.B. 112.3"; 6.2 Liter.						

2013 CHEVROLET

Body Type	VIN	List	Trade-In Good	Very Good	Pvt-Party Good	Retail Excellent
SS Coupe 2D	FJ1EJ	33535	21400	22200	23200	26600
SS Convertible 2D	FJ3DJ	39585	24400	25300	26300	29900

CAMARO—V8 Supercharged—Equipment Schedule 4
W.B. 112.3"; 6.2 Liter.

Body Type	VIN	List	Good	Very Good	Good	Excellent
ZL1 Coupe 2D	FL1EP	56550	35200	36500	36400	40100
ZL1 Convertible 2D	FL3DP	61745	40200	41600	41100	45000

CORVETTE—V8—Equipment Schedule 2
W.B.105.7"; 6.2 Liter. 7.0 Liter.

Body Type	VIN	List	Good	Very Good	Good	Excellent
Coupe 2D	YA2DW	51825	26800	27700	28500	32000
Convertible 2D	YA3DW	56825	29400	30400	31400	35300
Grand Sport Coupe	YP2DW	58225	33200	34300	35000	39000
Grand Sport Conv 2D	YP3DW	61825	38400	39600	40300	45100
Z06 Coupe 2D	YJ2DE	76575	46600	48100	48600	54200
427 Convertible 2D	YY3DE	76900	46200	47700	48400	54100
Glass Roof Panel			375	375	405	405
Dual Roof Panels			550	550	595	595
Heritage Pkg			1700	1700	1885	1885
4LT			2000	2000	2170	2170
Suspension Pkg			650	650	705	705
Manual, 6-Spd	A,B,C,D		275	275	300	300

CORVETTE—V8 Supercharged—Equipment Schedule 2
W.B. 105.7"; 6.2 Liter.

Body Type	VIN	List	Good	Very Good	Good	Excellent
ZR1 Coupe 2D	YM2DT	113575	70400	72600	72800	80700

2014 CHEVY — (1,2or3)G1or(6orK)L1(CA6S9)–E–#

SPARK—4-Cyl. ECOTEC—Equipment Schedule 6
W.B. 93.5"; 1.2 Liter.

Body Type	VIN	List	Good	Very Good	Good	Excellent
LS Hatchback 4D	CA6S9	12995	7075	7450	8450	10250
1LT Hatchback 4D	CC6S9	14765	7400	7775	8900	10800
2LT Hatchback 4D	CE6S9	16115	8450	8875	9950	11950
Automatic, CVT	D		525	525	660	660

SPARK EV—Electric Motor—Equipment Schedule 6
W.B. 93.5".

Body Type	VIN	List	Good	Very Good	Good	Excellent
1LT Hatchback 4D	CK6S0	28305	16850	17500	18400	21000
2LT Hatchback 4D	CL6S0	28630	17150	17800	18700	21300

SONIC—4-Cyl.—Equipment Schedule 6
W.B. 99.4"; 1.8 Liter.

Body Type	VIN	List	Good	Very Good	Good	Excellent
LS Sedan 4D	JB5SH	14995	7550	7950	9375	11650
LS Hatchback 4D	JB6SH	15595	7925	8325	9625	11750
LT Sedan 4D	JD5SH	16605	8475	8900	10200	12450
LT Hatchback 4D	JD6SH	17205	8575	9000	10300	12500
LTZ Sedan 4D	JF5SH	18215	9800	10250	11550	13900
LTZ Hatchback 4D	JF6SH	18815	10200	10650	12000	14500
Automatic, 6-Spd	C		525	525	685	685
4-Cyl, Turbo, 1.4 Liter	B		375	375	495	495

SONIC—4-Cyl. Turbo—Equipment Schedule 6
W.B. 99.4"; 1.4 Liter.

Body Type	VIN	List	Good	Very Good	Good	Excellent
RS Sedan 4D	JH5SB	20530	11850	12350	13650	16200
RS Hatchback 4D	JH6SB	21150	12300	12800	14100	16650
Automatic, 6-Spd	G		525	525	645	645

CRUZE—4-Cyl.—Equipment Schedule 5
W.B. 105.7"; 1.8 Liter.

Body Type	VIN	List	Good	Very Good	Good	Excellent
LS Sedan 4D	PA5SG	19180	10500	11000	12100	14600
Manual, 6-Spd w/Overdrive	B		(575)	(575)	(710)	(710)

CRUZE—4-Cyl. Turbo—Equipment Schedule 5
W.B. 105.7"; 1.4 Liter.

Body Type	VIN	List	Good	Very Good	Good	Excellent
LT Sedan 4D	PK5SB	19790	11050	11550	12650	15250
1LT Sedan 4D	PC5SB	20635	11350	11900	12850	15250
eco Sedan 4D	PH5SB	21855	11900	12450	13550	16150
2LT Sedan 4D	PE5SB	23305	12200	12750	13850	16450
LTZ Sedan 4D	PG5SB	24530	13350	13950	15000	17800
Manual, 6-Spd w/Overdrive	D		(575)	(575)	(705)	(705)

CRUZE—4-Cyl. Turbo Diesel—Equipment Schedule 5
W.B. 105.7"; 2.0 Liter.

Body Type	VIN	List	Good	Very Good	Good	Excellent
Sedan 4D	P75SZ	25710	14550	15200	16300	19150

VOLT—Electric—Equipment Schedule 3
W.B. 105.7".

Body Type	VIN	List	Good	Very Good	Good	Excellent
Sedan 4D	RA674	34995	20800	21600	22100	25100

MALIBU—4-Cyl.—Equipment Schedule 4
W.B. 107.8"; 2.5 Liter.

Body Type	VIN	List	Good	Very Good	Good	Excellent
LS Sedan 4D	1B5SL	22965	12150	12650	13900	16450
LT Sedan 4D	1C5SL	24335	13150	13650	15000	17700
eco Sedan 4D	1F5SR	26670	13850	14400	15800	18650

2014 CHEVROLET

Body Type	VIN	List	Trade-In Good	Very Good	Pvt-Party Good	Retail Excellent
LTZ Sedan 4D	1H5SL	28515	14250	14800	16250	19250
4-Cyl, Turbo, 2.0 Liter	X		1800	1800	2105	2105
IMPALA—4-Cyl.—Equipment Schedule 4						
W.B. 110.5"; 2.5 Liter.						
LS Sedan 4D	1Y5SL	27535	15000	15600	17050	20000
LS Eco Sedan 4D	1Z5SR	29945	16900	17550	18950	22100
LT Eco Sedan 4D	135SR	31920	18950	19700	20900	24200
IMPALA—V6—Equipment Schedule 4						
W.B. 110.5"; 3.6 Liter.						
LT Sedan 4D	125S3	30760	17400	18050	19400	22600
LTZ Sedan 4D	155S3	36580	20800	21600	22800	26200
4-Cyl, 2.5 Liter	L		(725)	(725)	(860)	(860)
IMPALA LIMITED—V6—Equipment Schedule 4						
W.B. 110.5"; 3.6 Liter.						
LS Sedan 4D	WA5E3	26655	10850	11300	12850	15650
LT Sedan 4D	WB5E3	27665	11450	11950	13550	16300
LTZ Sedan 4D	WC5E3	31360	12550	13100	14550	17400
CAMARO—V6—Equipment Schedule 4						
W.B. 112.3"; 3.6 Liter.						
LS Coupe 2D	FE1E3	24450	16450	17100	18350	21200
LT Coupe 2D	FB1E3	27935	18550	19250	20400	23400
LT Convertible 2D	FB3D3	33135	20200	21000	22100	25300
RS Pkg			1450	1450	1700	1700
CAMARO—V8—Equipment Schedule 4						
W.B. 112.3"; 6.2 Liter, 7.0 Liter.						
SS Coupe 2D	FJ1EJ	35135	23700	24600	25400	28800
SS Convertible 2D	FJ3DJ	41135	26400	27300	28300	32100
Z/28 Coupe 2D	FS1EE	75000	61000	63000	64600	73200
RS Pkg			1450	1450	1670	1670
CAMARO—V8 Supercharged—Equipment Schedule 4						
W.B. 112.3"; 6.2 Liter.						
ZL1 Coupe 2D	FL1EP	58855	45300	46800	46000	50100
ZL1 Convertible 2D	FL3DP	64055	50900	52600	51900	56600
SS—V8—Equipment Schedule 2						
W.B. 114.8"; 6.2 Liter.						
Sedan 4D	F15RW	45770				
CORVETTE—V8—Equipment Schedule 2						
W.B. 106.7"; 6.2 Liter.						
Stingray Coupe 2D	YB2D7	53345	44400	45800	45400	49700
Stingray Conv 2D	YB3D7	58345	49000	50600	50700	55700
Stingray Z51 Cpe 2D	YH2D7	56145	49200	50800	50400	54900
Stingray Z51 Conv 2D	YH3D7	61145	52500	54100	54100	59400
Glass Roof Panel			400	400	420	420
3LT			2975	2975	3135	3135
Manual, 7-Spd	A,C,E		300	300	315	315

CHRYSLER

2000 CHRYSLER — (1,2,3or4)C3-(U42N)-Y-#

Body Type	VIN	List	Trade-In Good	Very Good	Pvt-Party Good	Retail Excellent
SEBRING—V6—Equipment Schedule 4						
W.B. 103.7", 106.0" (Conv); 2.5 Liter.						
LX Coupe 2D	U42N	19635	550	650	1350	2425
LXi Coupe 2D	U52N	22015	650	750	1500	2675
JX Convertible 2D	L45H	24790	475	550	975	1600
JXi Convertible 2D	L55H	27105	975	1100	1650	2725
Limited			200	200	255	255
CIRRUS—4-Cyl.—Equipment Schedule 4						
W.B. 108.0"; 2.0 Liter, 2.4 Liter.						
LX Sedan 4D	J46B	17675	750	850	1650	2925
Manual, 5-Spd			(175)	(175)	(250)	(250)
CIRRUS—V6—Equipment Schedule 4						
W.B. 108.0"; 2.5 Liter.						
LXi Sedan 4D	J56H	20480	775	875	1700	3050
CONCORDE—V6—Equipment Schedule 4						
W.B. 113.0"; 2.7 Liter, 3.2 Liter.						
LX Sedan 4D	D46R	22550	1000	1125	1800	3075
LXi Sedan 4D	D36J	26480	1375	1525	2175	3600
LHS—V6—Equipment Schedule 2						
W.B. 113.0"; 3.5 Liter.						
Sedan 4D	C56G	28695	775	875	1400	2350

0415

2000 CHRYSLER

Body Type	VIN	List	Trade-In Good	Very Good	Pvt-Party Good	Retail Excellent
300M—V6—Equipment Schedule 2						
W.B. 113.0"; 3.5 Liter.						
Sedan 4D	E66G	29690	**825**	**950**	**1600**	**2750**

2001 CHRYSLER — 1C(4or8)-(Y4BB)-1-#

Body Type	VIN	List	Good	Very Good	Good	Excellent
PT CRUISER—4-Cyl.—Equipment Schedule 4						
W.B. 103.0"; 2.4 Liter.						
Sport Wagon 4D	Y4BB	18415	**625**	**725**	**1200**	**1975**
Limited Sport Wag 4D	Y4BB	21385	**775**	**875**	**1425**	**2375**
SEBRING—4-Cyl.—Equipment Schedule 4						
W.B. 103.7", 108.0" (Sed); 2.4 Liter.						
LX Sedan 4D	L46G	18520	**825**	**925**	**1725**	**3050**
LX Coupe 2D	G42G	20495	**625**	**700**	**1450**	**2625**
V6, 2.7 Liter	R,H		**100**	**100**	**135**	**135**
SEBRING—V6—Equipment Schedule 4						
W.B. 103.7", 106.0" (Conv), 108.0" (Sed): 2.7 Liter, 3.0 Liter.						
LXi Sedan 4D	L66R	21405	**950**	**1075**	**1925**	**3425**
LXi Coupe 2D	G62H	22885	**675**	**775**	**1575**	**2825**
LX Convertible 2D	L55U	24945	**475**	**550**	**1025**	**1700**
LXi Convertible 2D	L65U	27405	**1025**	**1150**	**1825**	**3075**
Limited Convertible 2D	L65U	29490	**1550**	**1725**	**2575**	**4325**
CONCORDE—V6—Equipment Schedule 4						
W.B. 113.0"; 2.7 Liter, 3.2 Liter.						
LX Sedan 4D	D46R	22995	**1125**	**1250**	**1950**	**3300**
LXi Sedan 4D	D36J	27240	**1550**	**1725**	**2400**	**3925**
LHS—V6—Equipment Schedule 2						
W.B. 113.0"; 3.5 Liter.						
Sedan 4D	C56G	29210	**900**	**1025**	**1600**	**2725**
300M—V6—Equipment Schedule 2						
W.B. 113.0"; 3.5 Liter.						
Sedan 4D	E66G	30170	**1075**	**1200**	**1850**	**3150**
PROWLER—V6—Equipment Schedule 1						
W.B. 113.3"; 3.5 Liter.						
Roadster 2D	W65G	45400	**11200**	**11800**	**12300**	**14950**

2002 CHRYSLER-(1,2,3or4)C(3,4or8)-(Y48B)-2-#

Body Type	VIN	List	Good	Very Good	Good	Excellent
PT CRUISER—4-Cyl.—Equipment Schedule 4						
W.B. 103.0"; 2.4 Liter.						
Sport Wagon 4D	Y48B	17590	**850**	**975**	**1575**	**2625**
Touring Sport Wag 4D	Y58B	19305	**950**	**1075**	**1700**	**2825**
Limited Sport Wag 4D	Y68B	21655	**1150**	**1300**	**1975**	**3275**
Dream Cruiser			**400**	**400**	**515**	**515**
Woodie Edition			**150**	**150**	**200**	**200**
SEBRING—4-Cyl.—Equipment Schedule 4						
W.B. 103.7", 106.0" (Conv), 108.0" (Sed); 2.4 Liter.						
LX Sedan 4D	L46X	18535	**825**	**925**	**1725**	**3075**
LX Coupe 2D	G42G	20615	**650**	**725**	**1475**	**2650**
LX Convertible 2D	L55G	23905	**475**	**550**	**1050**	**1775**
V6, 2.7 Liter	R,H		**150**	**150**	**200**	**200**
SEBRING—V6—Equipment Schedule 4						
W.B. 103.7", 106.0" (Conv), 108.0" (Sed): 2.7 Liter, 3.0 Liter.						
LXi Sedan 4D	L56R	20875	**1075**	**1200**	**2075**	**3650**
LXi Coupe 2D	G52H	23130	**750**	**850**	**1625**	**2875**
LXi Convertible 2D	L55R	26755	**1125**	**1250**	**1875**	**3075**
GTC Convertible 2D	L75R	25875	**600**	**675**	**1175**	**1925**
Limited Convertible 2D	L65R	29390	**1725**	**1925**	**2700**	**4400**
CONCORDE—V6—Equipment, Schedule 4						
W.B. 113.0"; 2.7 Liter, 3.5 Liter.						
LX Sedan 4D	D46R	22995	**1225**	**1375**	**2025**	**3350**
LXi Sedan 4D	D36M	25600	**1675**	**1850**	**2600**	**4225**
Limited Sedan 4D	D56G	28495	**2050**	**2275**	**3175**	**5100**
300M—V6—Equipment Schedule 2						
W.B. 113.0"; 3.5 Liter.						
Sedan 4D	E66G	28995	**1350**	**1525**	**2150**	**3525**
Special Sedan 4D	E76K	32595	**1500**	**1675**	**2325**	**3825**
PROWLER—V6—Equipment Schedule 1						
W.B. 113.0"; 3.5 Liter.						
Roadster 2D	W65G	45400	**12600**	**13250**	**13800**	**16650**

2003 CHRYSLER-(1,2,3or4)C(3,4or8)-(Y48B)-3-#

PT CRUISER—4-Cyl.—Equipment Schedule 4
W.B. 103.0"; 2.4 Liter.

2003 CHRYSLER

Body Type	VIN	List	Trade-In Good	Very Good	Pvt-Party Good	Retail Excellent
Sport Wagon 4D	Y48B	18010	825	925	1550	2600
Touring Sport Wag 4D	Y58B	19940	1025	1150	1800	3000
Limited Sport Wag 4D	Y68B	22180	1150	1300	1950	3250
Woodie Edition			200	200	265	265
PT CRUISER—4-Cyl. HO Turbo—Equipment Schedule 4						
W.B. 103.0"; 2.4 Liter.						
GT Sport Wagon 4D	Y78G	23320	1200	1350	2000	3325
Dream Cruiser			425	425	555	555
SEBRING—4-Cyl.—Equipment Schedule 4						
W.B. 103.7", 106.0" (Conv), 108.0" (Sed); 2.4 Liter.						
LX Sedan 4D	L46X	19930	925	1050	1825	3150
LX Coupe 2D	G42G	21560	725	825	1600	2825
LX Convertible 2D	L45X	24560	500	575	1075	1825
V6, Flex Fuel, 2.7 Liter	U,R		200	200	265	265
SEBRING—V6—Equipment Schedule 4						
W.B. 103.7", 106.0" (Conv), 108.0" (Sed); 2.7 Liter, 3.0 Liter.						
LXi Sedan 4D	L56R	21295	1525	1700	2625	4450
LXi Coupe 2D	G52H	23835	825	950	1775	3125
GTC Convertible 2D	L75R	26160	750	850	1400	2325
LXi Convertible 2D	L55T	27410	1250	1400	2025	3300
Limited Convertible 2D	L65R	30045	1725	1925	3000	4975
CONCORDE—V6—Equipment Schedule 4						
W.B. 113.0"; 2.7 Liter, 3.5 Liter.						
LX Sedan 4D	D46R	23510	1575	1750	2500	4125
LXi Sedan 4D	D36M	26240	2050	2275	3250	5225
Limited Sedan 4D	D56G	29135	2500	2750	3850	6100
300M—V6—Equipment Schedule 2						
W.B. 113.0"; 3.5 Liter.						
Sedan 4D	E66G	29245	1675	1875	2550	4150
Special Sedan 4D	E76K	32895	1700	1900	2650	4350

2004 CHRYSLER – (1,2,3or4)C(3,4or8)–(Y48B)–4–#

Body Type	VIN	List	Trade-In Good	Very Good	Pvt-Party Good	Retail Excellent
PT CRUISER—4-Cyl.—Equipment Schedule 4						
W.B. 103.0"; 2.4 Liter.						
Sport Wagon 4D	Y48B	19515	1250	1375	2050	3350
Touring Sport Wag 4D	Y58B	20585	1475	1625	2300	3750
Limited Sport Wag 4D	Y68B	22825	1575	1750	2450	3975
4-Cyl, Turbo, 2.4 Liter	8		450	450	585	585
PT CRUISER—4-Cyl. HO Turbo—Equipment Schedule 4						
W.B. 103.0"; 2.4 Liter.						
GT Sport Wagon 4D	Y78G	26245	1675	1850	2575	4150
SEBRING—4-Cyl.—Equipment Schedule 4						
W.B. 103.7", 106.0" (Conv), 108.0" (Sed); 2.4 Liter.						
Sedan 4D	L66R	19360	1275	1425	2200	3725
Coupe 2D	G42G	22305	850	950	1775	3125
Convertible 2D	L45J	25570	500	575	1125	1900
LX Sedan 4D	L46X	19500	1000	1100	2025	3575
LX Convertible 2D	L45X	25215	725	800	1300	2150
V6, Flex Fuel, 2.7 Liter	T		250	250	335	335
SEBRING—V6—Equipment Schedule 4						
W.B. 103.7", 106.0" (Conv), 108.0" (Sed); 2.7 Liter, 3.0 Liter.						
LXi Sedan 4D	L56R	21840	1975	2175	3175	5125
LXi Convertible 2D	L55T	28140	1500	1675	2300	3675
GTC Convertible 2D	L75R	27045	1000	1125	1750	2925
Touring Sedan 4D	L56R	21200	1775	1950	2900	4725
Touring Convertible 2D	L55T	28370	1600	1775	2525	4025
Limited Sedan 4D	L66R	23490	2075	2300	3350	5450
Limited Coupe 2D	G52H	24580	1375	1525	2300	3875
Limited Convertible 2D	L65R	31180	2175	2425	3475	5575
CONCORDE—V6—Equipment Schedule 4						
W.B. 113.0"; 2.7 Liter, 3.5 Liter.						
LX Sedan 4D	D46R	24130	1800	2000	3050	5025
LXi Sedan 4D	D36M	26860	2450	2700	3875	6200
Limited Sedan 4D	D56G	29755	3025	3350	4600	7250
300M—V6—Equipment Schedule 2						
W.B. 113.0"; 3.5 Liter.						
Sedan 4D	E66G	29865	1875	2075	2900	4600
Special Sedan 4D	E76K	33295	1975	2200	3075	4900
CROSSFIRE—V6—Equipment Schedule 1						
W.B. 94.5"; 3.2 Liter.						
Coupe 2D	N69L	35570	2375	2600	3375	5025

2005 CHRYSLER

Body Type	VIN	List	Trade-In Good	Very Good	Pvt-Party Good	Retail Excellent

2005 CHRYSLER — (1,2,3or4)C(4or8)–(Y48B)–5–#

PT CRUISER—4-Cyl.—Equipment Schedule 4
W.B. 103.0"; 2.4 Liter.

Sport Wagon 4D	Y48B	14820	1325	1475	2225	3525
Convertible 2D	Y45X	21685	1625	1825	2775	4375
Touring Sport Wag 4D	Y58B	13820	1625	1825	2750	4300
Limited Sport Wag 4D	Y68B	18730	1625	1825	2775	4375
4-Cyl, Turbo, 2.4 Liter	E		475	475	620	620

PT CRUISER—4-Cyl.Turbo—Equipment Schedule 4

Touring Convertible 2D	Y55X	25595	2350	2625	3600	5450
4-Cyl, 2.4 Liter	B,X		(425)	(425)	(575)	(575)

PT CRUISER—4-Cyl. HO Turbo—Equipment Schedule 4
W.B. 103.0"; 2.4 Liter.

GT Sport Wagon 4D	Y78S	23935	2100	2350	3300	5075
GT Convertible 2D	Y75S	28595	2200	2450	3400	5175

SEBRING—4-Cyl.—Equipment Schedule 4
W.B. 103.7", 106.0" (Conv), 108.0" (Sed); 2.4 Liter.

Sedan 4D	L46X	19975	1350	1525	2450	4050
Coupe 2D	G42C	22770	1050	1175	2075	3475
Convertible 2D	L45X	26035	800	900	1725	2875
V6, 2.7 Liter	R		300	300	400	400

SEBRING—V6—Equipment Schedule 4
W.B. 103.7", 106.0" (Conv), 108.0" (Sed); 2.7 Liter, 3.0 Liter.

GTC Convertible 2D	L75R	27510	900	1025	1825	3050
Touring Sedan 4D	L56R	20695	1900	2125	3300	5325
Touring Convertible 2D	L55T	28835	1750	1950	2925	4575
Limited Sedan 4D	L66R	22985	2325	2600	3825	6025
Limited Coupe 2D	G52H	25045	1450	1625	2575	4225
Limited Convertible 2D	L65R	31645	2450	2750	3825	5850
TSi Sedan 4D	L56R	24455	2725	3050	4400	6925

300—V6—Equipment Schedule 2
W.B. 120.0"; 2.7 Liter, 3.5 Liter.

Sedan 4D	A43R	24695	4175	4550	5400	7425
Touring Sedan 4D	A53G	27720	4750	5150	6025	8250
Signature Series			175	175	235	235
Limited			700	700	945	945
AWD			575	575	755	755

300C—V8 HEMI—Equipment Schedule 2
W.B. 120.0"; 5.7 Liter.

Sedan 4D	A63H	33495	5000	5425	6400	8825
AWD	K		575	575	755	755

300—V8 HEMI—Equipment Schedule 2
W.B. 120.0"; 6.1 Liter.

SRT8 Sedan 4D	A73W	39995	7975	8625	9025	11400

CROSSFIRE—V6—Equipment Schedule 1
W.B. 94.5"; 3.2 Liter.

Coupe 2D	N69L	29920	2025	2225	3125	4700
Roadster 2D	N65L	34960	3300	3600	4750	6825
Limited Coupe 2D	N69L	35695	3225	3525	4525	6525
Limited Roadster 2D	N65L	39995	4050	4375	5625	7975

CROSSFIRE—V6 Supercharged—Equipment Schedule 1
W.B. 94.5"; 3.2 Liter.

SRT-6 Coupe 2D	N79N	45695	5125	5525	7225	10250
SRT-6 Roadster 2D	N75N	49995	5950	5950	7675	10800

2006 CHRYSLER — (1,2,3or4)C(4or8)–(Y48B)–6–#

PT CRUISER—4-Cyl.—Equipment Schedule 4
W.B. 103.0"; 2.4 Liter.

Sport Wagon 4D	Y48B	15950	1750	1950	2725	4100
Convertible 2D	Y45X	21795	2200	2450	3475	5175
Touring Sport Wag 4D	Y58B	17945	2100	2325	3200	4800
Limited Sport Wag 4D	Y68B	20360	2375	2650	3675	5425
Route 66 Edition			100	100	135	135
Signature Series			150	150	185	185
4-Cyl, Turbo, 2.4 Liter	E,8		500	500	660	660

PT CRUISER—4-Cyl.Turbo—Equipment Schedule 4
W.B. 103.0"; 2.4 Liter.

Touring Convertible 2D	Y55X	26150	2900	3225	4250	6150
4-Cyl, 2.4 Liter	B,X		(450)	(450)	(615)	(615)

PT CRUISER—4-Cyl. Turbo—Equipment Schedule 4
W.B. 103.0"; 2.4 Liter.

Body Type	VIN	List	Trade-In Good	Very Good	Pvt-Party Good	Retail Excellent
GT Sport Wagon 4D	Y78G	24835	2525	2825	3850	5650
GT Convertible 2D	Y75S	30050	2925	3250	4275	6175
SEBRING—4-Cyl.—Equipment Schedule 4						
W.B. 106.0", 108.0" (Sed); 2.4 Liter.						
Sedan 4D	L46X	20380	1800	2025	3075	4875
Convertible 2D	L45X	26440	950	1100	1950	3175
V6, 2.7 Liter	T		350	350	465	465
SEBRING—V6—Equipment Schedule 4						
W.B. 106.0", 108.0" (Sed); 2.7 Liter.						
TSi Sedan 4D	L36R	24665	3350	3700	5100	7675
GTC Convertible 2D	L75R	27915	1250	1425	2275	3625
Touring Sedan 4D	L56R	21100	2250	2525	3700	5800
Touring Convertible 2D	L55R	29240	2025	2275	3325	5025
Limited Sedan 4D	L66R	23390	2700	3000	4350	6700
Limited Convertible 2D	L65R	32050	2750	3050	4150	6125
300—V6—Equipment Schedule 2						
W.B. 120.0"; 2.7 Liter, 3.5 Liter.						
Sedan 4D	A43R	24200	5225	5650	6525	8775
Touring Sedan 4D	A53G	28300	5225	5675	6800	9125
Signature Series			175	175	250	250
Limited			775	775	1020	1020
AWD	K		625	625	845	845
300C—V8 HEMI—Equipment Schedule 2						
W.B. 120.0"; 5.7 Liter.						
Sedan 4D	A63H	34100	6150	6625	7825	10450
Heritage			275	275	365	365
AWD	K		625	625	845	845
300—V8 HEMI—Equipment Schedule 2						
W.B. 120.0"; 6.1 Liter.						
SRT8 Sedan 4D	A73W	42695	9425	10100	10650	13400
CROSSFIRE—V6—Equipment Schedule 1						
W.B. 94.5"; 3.2 Liter.						
Coupe 2D	N59L	30070	2525	2800	3850	5750
Roadster 2D	N55L	35110	3775	4100	5450	7850
Limited Coupe 2D	N69L	36195	3500	3825	5125	7425
Limited Roadster 2D	N65L	40545	4650	5025	6475	9200
CROSSFIRE—V6 Supercharged—Equipment Schedule 1						
W.B. 94.5"; 3.2 Liter.						
SRT-6 Coupe 2D	N79N	46085	5850	6250	8075	11300
SRT-6 Roadster 2D	N75N	50395	6550	7000	8900	12400

2007 CHRYSLER — (1,2,3or4)C(4or4)-(Y48B)-7-#

Body Type	VIN	List	Trade-In Good	Very Good	Pvt-Party Good	Retail Excellent
PT CRUISER—4-Cyl.—Equipment Schedule 4						
W.B. 103.0"; 2.4 Liter.						
Sport Wagon 4D	Y48B	15950	2050	2275	3025	4400
Convertible 2D	Y45X	22045	2650	2950	3750	5425
Touring Sport Wag 4D	Y58B	18295	2375	2625	3425	4975
Limited Sport Wag 4D	Y68B	21740	2925	3225	4200	6025
Signature Series			150	150	200	200
Street Cruiser PCH			300	300	395	395
4-Cyl, Turbo, 2.4 Liter	8,E		525	525	695	695
PT CRUISER—4-Cyl. Turbo—Equipment Schedule 4						
W.B. 103.0"; 2.4 Liter.						
Touring Convertible 2D	Y55X	26350	3225	3550	4550	6450
GT Sport Wagon 4D	Y78G	24835	3475	3800	4800	6775
GT Convertible 2D	Y75S	30250	3825	4175	5175	7225
SEBRING—4-Cyl.—Equipment Schedule 4						
W.B. 108.9"; 2.4 Liter.						
Sedan 4D	C46K	18995	3075	3400	4450	6425
Touring Sedan 4D	C56K	20195	3575	3925	5050	7275
Limited Sedan 4D	C66K	23995	4125	4500	5625	7975
V6, Flex Fuel, 2.7 Liter	R		375	375	500	500
V6, HO, 3.5 Liter	M		525	525	695	695
300—V6—Equipment Schedule 2						
W.B. 120.0"; 2.7 Liter, 3.5 Liter.						
Sedan 4D	A43R	24480	5750	6200	7125	9325
Touring Sedan 4D	A53G	29290	6025	6475	7600	10000
Signature Series			200	200	265	265
Limited			825	825	1100	1100
AWD			700	700	935	935
300C—V8 HEMI—Equipment Schedule 2						
W.B. 120.0"; 5.7 Liter.						
Sedan 4D	A63H	34935	7725	8250	9475	12400

2007 CHRYSLER

Body Type	VIN	List	Trade-In Good	Very Good	Pvt-Party Good	Retail Excellent
SRT Design			275	275	365	365
Heritage			300	300	400	400
AWD	K		700	700	935	935
300—V8 HEMI—Equipment Schedule 2						
W.B. 120.0"; 6.1 Liter.						
SRT8 Sedan 4D	A73W	40970	10750	11500	12050	14900
CROSSFIRE—V6—Equipment Schedule 1						
W.B. 94.5"; 3.2 Liter.						
Coupe 2D	N59L	30435	3150	3425	4500	6350
Roadster 2D	N55L	36595	4900	5250	6450	8850
Limited Coupe 2D	N69L	36560	4550	4875	6075	8350
Limited Roadster 2D	N65L	40955	5825	6225	7700	10450

2008 CHRYSLER — (1,2,3or4)C(4or8)(Y48B)-8-#

Body Type	VIN	List	Trade-In Good	Very Good	Pvt-Party Good	Retail Excellent
PT CRUISER—4-Cyl.—Equipment Schedule 4						
W.B. 103.0"; 2.4 Liter.						
Sport Wagon 4D	Y48B	16780	2625	2900	3700	5250
Convertible 2D	Y55X	19995	3675	4000	4975	6925
Touring Sport Wag 4D	Y58B	19570	3275	3575	4475	6275
Signature Series			175	175	235	235
4-Cyl, Turbo, 2.4 Liter	E		550	550	730	730
PT CRUISER—4-Cyl. Turbo—Equipment Schedule 4						
W.B. 103.0"; 2.4 Liter.						
Limited Sport Wag 4D	Y688	23300	4225	4550	5650	7725
SEBRING—4-Cyl.—Equipment Schedule 4						
W.B. 108.9"; 2.4 Liter.						
LX Sedan 4D	C46K	19365	4050	4425	5350	7300
LX Convertible 2D	C45K	26515	3300	3625	4775	6775
Touring Sedan 4D	C56K	20540	4300	4675	5625	7650
Limited Sedan 4D	C66K	24190	5300	5750	6950	9350
Signature Series			200	200	265	265
AWD	D		1075	1075	1420	1420
V6, HO, 3.5 Liter			550	550	745	745
SEBRING—V6—Equipment Schedule 4						
W.B. 108.9"; 2.7 Liter, 3.5 Liter.						
Touring Convertible 2D	C55R	29115	4300	4675	5900	8250
Limited Convertible 2D	C65M	32730	5750	6200	7675	10400
Power Hard Top			425	425	555	555
300—V6—Equipment Schedule 2						
W.B. 120.0"; 2.7 Liter, 3.5 Liter.						
Sedan 4D	A43R	25270	6025	6450	7475	9650
Touring Sedan 4D	A53G	29265	7050	7500	8550	10950
Limited Sedan 4D	A33G	32295	7825	8325	9425	11950
DUB Pkg			350	350	465	465
Signature Series			275	275	350	350
AWD	K		775	775	1015	1015
300C—V8 HEMI—Equipment Schedule 2						
W.B. 120.0"; 5.7 Liter.						
Sedan 4D	A63H	36070	9125	9675	10850	13800
Adaptive Cruise Control			375	375	490	490
SRT Design			300	300	390	390
Heritage			350	350	460	460
AWD	K		775	775	1000	1000
300C—V8 HEMI—Equipment Schedule 2						
W.B. 120.0"; 6.1 Liter.						
SRT8 Sedan 4D	A73W	44223	12350	13050	13900	16850
CROSSFIRE—V6—Equipment Schedule 1						
W.B. 94.5"; 3.2 Liter.						
Limited Coupe 2D	N69L	36685	6000	6375	7650	10000
Limited Roadster 2D	N65L	41130	7575	8025	9450	12200

2009 CHRYSLER — (1,2,3or4)C(4or8)(Y489)-9-#

Body Type	VIN	List	Trade-In Good	Very Good	Pvt-Party Good	Retail Excellent
PT CRUISER—4-Cyl.—Equipment Schedule 4						
W.B. 103.0"; 2.4 Liter.						
Sport Wagon 4D	Y489	18745	3300	3600	4500	6050
Touring Sport Wag 4D	Y589	20700	3775	4075	5075	6825
Dream Cruiser			550	550	745	745
4-Cyl, Turbo, 2.4 Liter	E		575	575	765	765
PT CRUISER—4-Cyl. Turbo—Equipment Schedule 4						
W.B. 103.0"; 2.4 Liter.						
Limited Sport Wag 4D	Y688	24430	5275	5650	6700	8775

2009 CHRYSLER

Body Type	VIN	List	Trade-In Good	Very Good	Pvt-Party Good	Retail Excellent
SEBRING—4-Cyl.—Equipment Schedule 4						
W.B. 108.9"; 2.4 Liter.						
LX Sedan 4D	C46K	21255	5050	5450	6350	8350
LX Convertible 2D	C45K	28130	4375	4725	5700	7600
Touring Sedan 4D	C56B	21655	5325	5750	6850	9000
Limited Sedan 4D	C66B	26660	6550	7025	8250	10800
V6, HO, 3.5 Liter	V		475	475	635	635
SEBRING—V6—Equipment Schedule 4						
W.B. 108.9"; 2.7 Liter, 3.5 Liter.						
Touring Convertible 2D	C55D	30610	5275	5700	6900	9075
Limited Convertible 2D	C65V	35465	9150	9750	10900	13650
Power Hard Top			450	450	590	590
300—V6—Equipment Schedule 2						
W.B. 120.0"; 2.7 Liter, 3.5 Liter.						
LX Sedan 4D	A43D	27415	7550	8000	9050	11300
Touring Sedan 4D	A53V	29885	8300	8775	9850	12250
Limited Sedan 4D	A33V	35220	9400	9925	11050	13700
AWD	K		825	825	1060	1060
300C—V8 HEMI—Equipment Schedule 2						
W.B. 120.0"; 5.7 Liter.						
Sedan 4D	A63T	37585	10850	11450	12750	15800
Adaptive Cruise Control			375	375	480	480
Heritage			400	400	510	510
AWD	K		825	825	1065	1065
300—V8 HEMI—Equipment Schedule 2						
W.B. 120.0"; 6.1 Liter.						
SRT8 Sedan 4D	A73W	46361	18000	18850	19300	22500

2010 CHRYSLER — (1,2or3)(AorC)(3or4)(Y5F9)–A–#

Body Type	VIN	List	Trade-In Good	Very Good	Pvt-Party Good	Retail Excellent
PT CRUISER—4-Cyl.—Equipment Schedule 4						
W.B. 103.0"; 2.4 Liter.						
Classic Sport Wag 4D	Y5F9	18995	5075	5400	6350	7975
SEBRING—4-Cyl.—Equipment Schedule 4						
W.B. 108.9"; 2.4 Liter.						
LX Convertible 2D	C4EB	28590	5675	6075	6975	8775
Touring Sedan 4D	C4FB	20860	6325	6800	8000	10400
Limited Sedan 4D	C5FB	22855	7275	7775	9100	11750
V6, HO, 3.5 Liter	V		550	550	735	735
SEBRING—V6—Equipment Schedule 4						
W.B. 108.9"; 2.7 Liter.						
Touring Convertible 2D	C5ED	29950	6525	6975	8050	10200
Limited Convertible 2D	C6EV	35445	10900	11550	12600	15450
Power Hard Top			475	475	570	570
300—V6—Equipment Schedule 2						
W.B. 120.0"; 2.7 Liter, 3.5 Liter.						
Touring Sedan 4D	A5CD	28010	9400	9900	10850	13100
Touring Plus Sed 4D	A5CV	29100	9550	10050	11050	13300
Touring Signature Sed	A5CV	31225	9800	10300	11350	13700
Limited Sedan 4D	A3CV	35860	11100	11650	12800	15450
AWD	K		1000	1000	1210	1210
300C—V8 HEMI—Equipment Schedule 2						
W.B. 120.0"; 5.7 Liter.						
Sedan 4D	A6CT	38760	12750	13350	14600	17500
Adaptive Cruise Control			400	400	480	480
AWD	K		1000	1000	1200	1200
300—V8 HEMI—Equipment Schedule 2						
W.B. 120.0"; 6.1 Liter.						
SRT8 Sedan 4D	A7CW	45615	19900	20700	21400	24600

2011 CHRYSLER — (1,2or3)(AorC)(3or4)(C4FB)–B–#

Body Type	VIN	List	Trade-In Good	Very Good	Pvt-Party Good	Retail Excellent
200—4-Cyl.—Equipment Schedule 4						
W.B. 108.9"; 2.4 Liter.						
LX Sedan 4D	C4FB	19995	7700	8200	9100	11200
Touring Convertible 2D	C2EB	27195	7950	8425	9350	11400
Limited Convertible 2D	C7EG	31990	12050	12750	13850	16700
Power Hard Top			500	500	590	590
V6, Flex Fuel, 3.6 Liter	G		850	850	1065	1065
200—V6—Equipment Schedule 4						
W.B. 108.9"; 3.6 Liter.						
Touring Sedan 4D	C1FB	23790	8750	9300	10250	12550
Limited Sedan 4D	C2FB	26290	9325	9900	10900	13400
4-Cyl, 2.4 Liter	B		(600)	(600)	(755)	(755)

2011 CHRYSLER

Body Type	VIN	List	Trade-In Good	Very Good	Pvt-Party Good	Retail Excellent
200—V6—Equipment Schedule 4						
W.B. 108.9"; 3.6 Liter.						
S Sedan 4D	C8FG	26790	10150	10800	11850	14550
S Convertible 2D	C8EG	32490	12900	13650	14750	17650
300—V6—Equipment Schedule 2						
W.B. 120.0"; 3.6 Liter.						
Sedan 4D	A4CG	27995	12100	12650	13550	15850
Limited Sedan 4D	A5CG	31995	13350	14000	15050	17650
Adaptive Cruise Control			425	425	500	500
300C—V8 HEMI—Equipment Schedule 2						
W.B. 120.0"; 5.7 Liter.						
Sedan 4D	A6CT	38995	15450	16100	17200	20100
Adaptive Cruise Control			425	425	495	495

2012 CHRYSLER — (1,2or3)C3-(CBAB)-C-#

Body Type	VIN	List	Trade-In Good	Very Good	Pvt-Party Good	Retail Excellent
200—4-Cyl.—Equipment Schedule 4						
W.B. 108.9"; 2.4 Liter.						
LX Sedan 4D	CBAB	19745	8925	9475	10450	12750
Touring Convertible 2D	CBEB	27325	9400	9950	10900	13250
V6, Flex Fuel, 3.6 Liter	G		875	875	1095	1095
200—V6—Equipment Schedule 4						
W.B. 108.9"; 3.6 Liter.						
Touring Sedan 4D	CBBB	23915	9675	10250	11300	13750
Limited Sedan 4D	CBCB	26615	10150	10750	11850	14400
4-Cyl. 2.4 Liter	B		(650)	(650)	(810)	(810)
200—V6—Equipment Schedule 4						
W.B. 108.9"; 3.6 Liter.						
S Sedan 4D	CBHG	27115	11000	11650	12850	15700
S Convertible 2D	CBGG	32820	14750	15500	16600	19650
Limited Convertible 2D	CBFG	32320	13550	14250	15450	18450
Power Hard Top			550	550	650	650
300—V6—Equipment Schedule 2						
W.B. 120.0"; 3.6 Liter.						
Sedan 4D	CAAG	27995	13850	14450	15550	18150
Limited Sedan 4D	CACG	32995	14350	14950	16000	18600
AWD	H		1100	1100	1280	1280
300S—V6—Equipment Schedule 2						
W.B. 120.0"; 3.6 Liter.						
Sedan 4D	CABG	33995	17700	18450	19600	22700
Adaptive Cruise Control			450	450	520	520
Mopar 12			5500	5500	6370	6370
V8, HEMI, 5.7 Liter	T		1950	1950	2260	2260
300—V8 HEMI—Equipment Schedule 2						
W.B. 120.0"; 5.7 Liter, 6.4 Liter.						
300C Sedan 4D	CAET	38995	15900	16600	17800	20700
300C Luxury Series Sed	CAPT	42895	18950	19700	20800	24000
SRT8 Sedan 4D	CAFJ	47995	27000	27900	28500	31900
Adaptive Cruise Control			450	450	525	525
AWD	G,J		1100	1100	1275	1275

2013 CHRYSLER — (1,2or3)C3-(CBAB)-D-#

Body Type	VIN	List	Trade-In Good	Very Good	Pvt-Party Good	Retail Excellent
200—4-Cyl.—Equipment Schedule 4						
W.B. 108.9"; 2.4 Liter.						
LX Sedan 4D	CBAB	19990	9975	10550	11600	14050
Touring Convertible 2D	CBEB	28095	10800	11400	12200	14350
V6, Flex Fuel, 3.6 Liter	G		925	925	1070	1070
200—V6—Equipment Schedule 4						
W.B. 108.9"; 3.6 Liter.						
LX Z Sedan 4D	CBAG	22385	10200	10800	11850	14350
Touring Sedan 4D	CBBB	22990	10600	11250	12300	14850
Limited Sedan 4D	CBCB	25680	11150	11800	12800	15400
Limited Convertible 2D	CBFG	33090	15200	15950	16750	19500
S Convertible 2D	CBGG	33590	15800	16600	17400	20200
Power Hard Top			600	600	685	685
4-Cyl. 2.4 Liter	B		(700)	(700)	(865)	(865)
300—V6—Equipment Schedule 2						
W.B. 120.0"; 3.6 Liter.						
Sedan 4D	CAAG	30840	15800	16450	17700	20600
Motown Sedan 4D	CAAG	34140	15400	16050	17300	20100
Adaptive Cruise Control			475	475	550	550
AWD	R		1200	1200	1385	1385

Body Type	VIN	List	Trade-In Good	Very Good	Pvt-Party Good	Retail Excellent
300S—V6—Equipment Schedule 2						
W.B. 120.0"; 3.6 Liter.						
Sedan 4D	CABG	33990	18350	19100	20400	23600
Adaptive Cruise Control			475	475	550	550
AWD	G		1200	1200	1390	1390
V8, HEMI, 5.7 Liter	T		2300	2300	2665	2665
300S AWD—V6 Flex Fuel—Equipment Schedule 2						
W.B. 120.0"; 3.6 Liter.						
Glacier Sedan 4D	CAGG	37840	19750	20500	21700	25000
Adaptive Cruise Control			475	475	550	550
V8, HEMI, 5.7 Liter	T		2300	2300	2660	2660
300C—V6—Equipment Schedule 2						
W.B. 120.0"; 3.6 Liter.						
Sedan 4D	CACG	36990	16350	17000	18300	21400
Luxury Series Sedan	CAPG	40990	19550	20300	21500	24700
Varvatos Luxury Sedan	CADG	41490	21000	21800	23200	27000
Varvatos Limited Sed	CADG	44490	23300	24200	25300	29100
Adaptive Cruise Control			475	475	555	555
AWD	K		1200	1200	1400	1400
V8, HEMI, 5.7 Liter	T		2300	2300	2680	2680
300—V8 HEMI—Equipment Schedule 2						
W.B. 120.0"; 6.4 Liter.						
SRT8 Core Sedan 4D	CAXJ	46275	24400	25200	26300	29900
SRT8 Sedan 4D	CAFJ	49845	28100	29000	30200	34100
Adaptive Cruise Control			475	475	535	535

Body Type	VIN	List	Trade-In Good	Very Good	Pvt-Party Good	Retail Excellent
200—4-Cyl.—Equipment Schedule 4						
W.B. 108.9"; 2.4 Liter.						
Touring Convertible 2D	CBEB	28695	13550	14250	15000	17400
V6, Flex Fuel, 3.6 Liter	G		950	950	1095	1095
200—V6—Equipment Schedule 4						
W.B. 108.9"; 3.6 Liter.						
LX Sedan 4D	CBAG	22190	10950	11600	12750	15450
Touring Sedan 4D	CBBG	23660	11450	12150	13350	16200
Limited Sedan 4D	CBCG	26350	12550	13250	14400	17400
Limited Convertible 2D	CBFG	33690	17250	18100	18850	21800
S Convertible 2D	CBGG	34190	18050	18900	19700	22800
Power Hard Top			700	700	795	795
4-Cyl, 2.4 Liter	B		(950)	(950)	(1190)	(1190)
300—V6—Equipment Schedule 2						
W.B. 120.2"; 3.6 Liter.						
Sedan 4D	CAAG	34040	16600	17250	18600	21600
Uptown Ed Sedan 4D	CAAG	34990	16450	17100	18600	21900
Adaptive Cruise Control			500	500	580	580
AWD	R		1250	1250	1445	1445
300S—V6—Equipment Schedule 2						
W.B. 120.2"; 3.6 Liter.						
Sedan 4D	CABG	34540	20000	20700	22000	25400
Adaptive Cruise Control			500	500	575	575
AWD	G		1250	1250	1440	1440
V8, HEMI, 5.7 Liter	T		2650	2650	3050	3050
300C—V6—Equipment Schedule 2						
W.B. 120.2"; 3.6 Liter.						
Sedan 4D	CAEG	37540	17750	18450	19800	23000
John Varvatos Sedan	CADG	42040	24300	25200	26500	30500
John Varvatos Ltd 4D	CADG	45475	25200	26100	27500	31700
Adaptive Cruise Control			500	500	580	580
AWD	K		1250	1250	1455	1455
V8, HEMI, 5.7 Liter	T		2650	2650	3080	3080
300—V8 HEMI—Equipment Schedule 2						
W.B. 120.2"; 6.4 Liter.						
SRT8 Core Sedan 4D	CAXJ	46520	28300	29200	30300	34200
SRT8 Sedan 4D	CAFJ	50520	31700	32700	33800	38100
Adaptive Cruise Control			500	500	560	560

DODGE

NEON—4-Cyl.—Equipment Schedule 6
W.B. 105.0"; 2.0 Liter.

2000 DODGE

Body Type	VIN	List	Trade-In Good	Very Good	Pvt-Party Good	Retail Excellent
Highline Sedan 4D	S46C	13890	550	625	1150	1950
ES Sedan 4D	S56C	14680	675	775	1325	2300
AVENGER—V6—Equipment Schedule 4						
W.B. 103.7"; 2.5 Liter.						
Coupe 2D	U42N	18840	600	675	1250	2150
ES Coupe 2D	U52N	21130	725	825	1450	2525
STRATUS—4-Cyl.—Equipment Schedule 5						
W.B. 108.0"; 2.0 Liter, 2.4 Liter.						
SE Sedan 4D	J46C	17525	500	575	1100	1900
STRATUS—V6—Equipment Schedule 4						
W.B. 108.0"; 2.5 Liter.						
ES Sedan 4D	J56H	20655	875	975	1650	2825
INTREPID—V6—Equipment Schedule 4						
W.B. 113.0"; 2.7 Liter, 3.2 Liter, 3.5 Liter.						
Sedan 4D	D46R	20950	750	850	1425	2400
ES Sedan 4D	D56J	22530	1125	1250	1975	3350
R/T Sedan 4D	D76V	24995	1575	1750	2500	4150
VIPER—V10—Equipment Schedule 2						
W.B. 96.2"; 8.0 Liter.						
RT/10 Roadster 2D	R65E	70925	13350	14050	15800	20200
GTS Coupe 2D	R69E	73425	16350	17150	19300	24800
Competition			950	950	1125	1125

2001 DODGE — (1,2or4)B3–(S46C)–1–#

Body Type	VIN	List	Trade-In Good	Very Good	Pvt-Party Good	Retail Excellent
NEON—4-Cyl.—Equipment Schedule 6						
W.B. 105.0"; 2.0 Liter.						
Highline Sedan 4D	S46C	14275	575	675	1175	1975
ES Sedan 4D	S46C	15095	750	850	1425	2450
Competition Sedan 4D	S66C	15155	650	750	1300	2225
R/T Sedan 4D	S66F	16845	850	975	1550	2625
STRATUS—4-Cyl.—Equipment Schedule 4						
W.B. 103.7", 108.0" (Sed); 2.4 Liter.						
SE Sedan 4D	J46X	18425	500	575	1125	1950
SE Coupe 2D	G42X	19230	425	500	875	1400
Manual, 5-Spd			(200)	(200)	(265)	(265)
V6, 2.7 Liter	U,H		100	100	135	135
STRATUS—V6—Equipment Schedule 4						
W.B. 103.7", 108.0" (Sed); 2.7 Liter, 3.0 Liter.						
ES Sedan 4D	J56U	21010	925	1050	1725	2925
R/T Coupe 2D	G52H	22390	750	850	1475	2525
INTREPID—V6—Equipment Schedule 4						
W.B. 113.0"; 2.7 Liter, 3.2 Liter, 3.5 Liter.						
SE Sedan 4D	D46R	21395	925	1025	1675	2825
ES Sedan 4D	D56J	23090	1250	1400	2100	3500
R/T Sedan 4D	D66V	25460	1750	1950	2825	4625
VIPER—V10—Equipment Schedule 2						
W.B. 96.2"; 8.0 Liter.						
RT/10 Roadster 2D	R65E	67950	14150	14850	16300	20500
GTS Coupe 2D	R69E	70450	16750	17550	19550	24800
Competition			1075	1075	1275	1275

2002 DODGE — (1,2or4)B3–(S26C)–2–#

Body Type	VIN	List	Trade-In Good	Very Good	Pvt-Party Good	Retail Excellent
NEON—4-Cyl.—Equipment Schedule 6						
W.B. 105.0"; 2.0 Liter.						
S Sedan 4D	S26C	10570	425	500	925	1550
Sedan 4D	S26C	13805	425	500	925	1550
SXT Sedan 4D	S66C	15935	800	925	1550	2675
ACR Sedan 4D	S66F	14795	700	800	1400	2400
SE Sedan 4D	S46C	15405	625	725	1300	2225
ES Sedan 4D	S56C	15860	800	900	1525	2625
R/T Sedan 4D	S76F	16680	950	1075	1725	2950
STRATUS—4-Cyl.—Equipment Schedule 4						
W.B. 103.7", 108.0" (Sed); 2.4 Liter.						
SE Sedan 4D	L46X	18290	525	600	1150	2000
SE Coupe 2D	G42X	19340	450	525	925	1525
SXT Sedan 4D	L66X	19345	600	675	1325	2325
SXT Coupe 2D	G42G	19695	375	425	900	1500
Manual, 5-Spd			(200)	(200)	(265)	(265)
V6, 2.7 Liter	R,H		150	150	200	200
STRATUS—V6—Equipment Schedule 4						
W.B. 103.7", 108.0" (Sed); 2.7 Liter, 3.0 Liter.						
ES Sedan 4D	J56R	21255	1050	1175	1875	3150

Body Type	VIN	List	Trade-In Good	Very Good	Pvt-Party Good	Retail Excellent
R/T Sedan 4D	L76R	22150	1250	1400	2175	3675
R/T Coupe 2D	G52H	22490	850	950	1600	2725
INTREPID—V6—Equipment Schedule 4						
W.B. 113.0"; 2.7 Liter, 3.5 Liter.						
SE Sedan 4D	D46R	21230	1050	1175	1800	3025
ES Sedan 4D	D56M	23155	1500	1675	2375	3900
SXT Sedan 4D	D56G	24170	1525	1700	2350	3850
R/T Sedan 4D	D76G	27240	1950	2150	3050	4900
VIPER—V10—Equipment Schedule 2						
W.B. 96.2"; 8.0 Liter.						
RT/10 Roadster 2D	R65E	75500	14800	15550	16750	20800
GTS Coupe 2D	R69E	76000	17750	18600	20300	25400
Competition			1200	1200	1420	1420

2003 DODGE — (1,2or4)B3–(S46C)–3–#

Body Type	VIN	List	Trade-In Good	Very Good	Pvt-Party Good	Retail Excellent
NEON—4-Cyl.—Equipment Schedule 6						
W.B. 105.0"; 2.0 Liter.						
SE Sedan 4D	S46C	13925	750	850	1550	2725
SXT Sedan 4D	S66C	16235	875	1000	1775	3125
R/T Sedan 4D	S76F	17250	975	1100	1925	3375
NEON—4-Cyl. Turbo—Equipment Schedule 6						
W.B. 105.0"; 2.4 Liter.						
SRT-4 Sedan 4D	S66S	19965	2725	3075	3750	5600
STRATUS—4-Cyl.—Equipment Schedule 4						
W.B. 103.7", 108.0" (Sed); 2.4 Liter.						
SXT Sedan 4D	L46X	18340	1000	1125	1775	2950
SXT Coupe 2D	G42G	20680	400	450	925	1525
SE Sedan 4D	L46X	18470	1000	1125	1725	2850
SE Coupe 2D	G42G	20680	475	550	950	1550
Manual, 5-Spd			(250)	(250)	(335)	(335)
V6, Flex Fuel, 2.7 Liter	R,H		200	200	265	265
STRATUS—V6—Equipment Schedule 4						
W.B. 103.7", 108.0" (Sed); 2.7 Liter, 3.0 Liter.						
ES Sedan 4D	J56U	21980	1150	1300	1925	3150
R/T Sedan 4D	L76R	22340	1525	1700	2475	4075
R/T Coupe 2D	G52H	23175	900	1025	1600	2650
INTREPID—V6—Equipment Schedule 4						
W.B. 113.0"; 2.7 Liter, 3.5 Liter.						
SE Sedan 4D	D46R	21720	1325	1475	2250	3800
ES Sedan 4D	D56J	25515	1875	2075	2975	4825
SXT Sedan 4D	D66G	24335	1775	1975	2775	4425
VIPER—V10—Equipment Schedule 2						
W.B. 98.8"; 8.3 Liter.						
SRT10 Roadster 2D	R65Z	83795	15850	16600	17400	21000

2004 DODGE — (1,2or4)B3–(S46C)–4–#

Body Type	VIN	List	Trade-In Good	Very Good	Pvt-Party Good	Retail Excellent
NEON—4-Cyl.—Equipment Schedule 6						
W.B. 105.0"; 2.0 Liter.						
SE Sedan 4D	S46C	14495	975	1100	1850	3200
SXT Sedan 4D	S66C	16805	1175	1325	2175	3775
R/T Sedan 4D	S76F	17895	1250	1400	2275	3975
NEON—4-Cyl. HO Turbo—Equipment Schedule 6						
W.B. 105.0"; 2.4 Liter.						
SRT-4 Sedan 4D	S66S	20995	3275	3650	4400	6500
STRATUS—4-Cyl.—Equipment Schedule 4						
W.B. 103.7", 108.0" (Sed); 2.4 Liter.						
SXT Sedan 4D	L66X	19155	1075	1200	1825	3000
SXT Coupe 2D	G42G	20535	700	800	1350	2250
SE Sedan 4D	L46X	20315	1075	1200	1825	3000
Manual, 5-Spd			(300)	(300)	(400)	(400)
V6, Flex Fuel, 2.7 Liter	T		250	250	335	335
STRATUS—V6—Equipment Schedule 4						
W.B. 103.7", 108.0" (Sed); 2.7 Liter, 3.0 Liter.						
ES Sedan 4D	J56R	22600	1200	1350	1975	3250
R/T Sedan 4D	L76R	23135	1825	2025	2900	4650
R/T Coupe 2D	G52H	23750	925	1050	1650	2725
INTREPID—V6—Equipment Schedule 4						
W.B. 113.0"; 2.7 Liter, 3.5 Liter.						
SE Sedan 4D	D46R	22270	1700	1875	2775	4600
ES Sedan 4D	D56J	24685	2250	2475	3600	5825
SXT Sedan 4D	D66G	24485	2000	2200	3250	5275

Body Type	VIN	List	Trade-In Good	Very Good	Pvt-Party Good	Retail Excellent

VIPER—V10—Equipment Schedule 2
W.B. 98.8"; 8.3 Liter.

| SRT10 Roadster 2D | R65Z | 84795 | 17000 | 17800 | 18500 | 22100 |

2005 DODGE — (1,2or4)B3—(S26C)—5—#

NEON—4-Cyl.—Equipment Schedule 6
W.B. 105.0"; 2.0 Liter.

SE Sedan 4D	S26C	14985	1100	1275	2125	3550
SXT Sedan 4D	S56C	17295	1525	1725	2700	4450
Special Edition			75	75	100	100

NEON—4-Cyl. HO Turbo—Equipment Schedule 6
W.B. 105.0"; 2.4 Liter.

| SRT-4 Sedan 4D | S66S | 21195 | 3450 | 3850 | 4750 | 6750 |

STRATUS—4-Cyl.—Equipment Schedule 6
W.B. 103.7", 108.0" (Sed); 2.4 Liter.

SXT Sedan 4D	L46J	19770	1550	1725	2425	3775
SXT Coupe 2D	G42G	21825	1200	1350	2000	3150
Special Edition			150	150	185	185
Manual, 5-Spd.			(350)	(350)	(465)	(465)
V6, Flex Fuel, 2.7 Liter	T		300	300	400	400

STRATUS—V6—Equipment Schedule 4
W.B. 103.7", 108.0" (Sed); 2.7 Liter, 3.0 Liter.

| R/T Sedan 4D | L76T | 22250 | 2275 | 2525 | 3450 | 5200 |
| R/T Coupe 2D | G52H | 24320 | 1350 | 1500 | 2175 | 3425 |

MAGNUM—V6—Equipment Schedule 4
W.B. 120.0"; 2.7 Liter, 3.5 Liter.

SE Sport Wagon 4D	V48T	22495	3500	3850	4725	6750
SXT Sport Wagon 4D	V48T	22695	3400	3750	4800	6900
Special Edition			150	150	185	185
AWD	Z		600	600	800	800

MAGNUM—V8 HEMI—Equipment Schedule 4
W.B. 120.0"; 5.7 Liter.

| R/T Sport Wagon 4D | V582 | 29995 | 4675 | 5100 | 6225 | 8725 |
| AWD | Z | | 600 | 600 | 800 | 800 |

VIPER—V10—Equipment Schedule 2
W.B. 98.8"; 8.3 Liter.

SRT10 Roadster 2D	Z65Z	85395	19750	20600	21300	25200
Copperhead Edition			1425	1425	1615	1615
Mamba Edition			1225	1225	1390	1390

2006 DODGE — (1,2or4)B3—(L46X)—6—#

STRATUS—4-Cyl.—Equipment Schedule 4
W.B. 108.0"; 2.4 Liter.

| SXT Sedan 4D | L46X | 20140 | 1850 | 2075 | 2775 | 4100 |
| V6, 2.7 Liter | R | | 575 | 575 | 770 | 770 |

STRATUS—V6—Equipment Schedule 4
W.B. 108.0"; 2.7 Liter.

| R/T Sedan 4D | L76R | 24120 | 2500 | 2800 | 3725 | 5400 |

MAGNUM—V6—Equipment Schedule 4
W.B. 120.0"; 2.7 Liter, 3.5 Liter.

Sport Wagon 4D	V47V	22995	3550	3900	4900	6925
SXT Sport Wagon 4D	V47V	25935	4000	4375	5475	7750
AWD	Z		675	675	900	900
V8, HEMI, 5.7 Liter	2		1175	1175	1570	1570

MAGNUM—V8 HEMI—Equipment Schedule 4
W.B. 120.0"; 5.7 Liter, 6.1 Liter.

R/T Sport Wagon 4D	V572	30910	4900	5350	6850	9625
SRT8 Sport Wagon 4D	V773	37995	8825	9475	10600	13700
AWD	Z		675	675	900	900

CHARGER—V6—Equipment Schedule 4
W.B. 120.0"; 2.7 Liter, 3.5 Liter.

Sedan 4D	A43G	22295	5200	5625	6750	9075
SXT Sedan 4D	A43G	25995	5500	5925	7125	9575
V8, HEMI, 5.7 Liter	H		1175	1175	1570	1570

CHARGER—V8 HEMI—Equipment Schedule 4
W.B. 120.0"; 5.7 Liter, 6.1 Liter.

R/T Sedan 4D	A53H	29995	7125	7625	8950	11950
SRT8 Sedan 4D	A73W	38095	10550	11350	11900	14750
Daytona Edition			575	575	765	765
Performance Group			600	600	795	795

VIPER—V10—Equipment Schedule 2
W.B. 98.8"; 8.3 Liter.

Body	Type	VIN	List	Trade-In Good	Very Good	Pvt-Party Good	Retail Excellent
SRT10 Coupe 2D		Z697	86995	25000	26100	26700	31200
SRT10 Convertible 2D		Z65Z	85745	22600	23600	24200	28300
First Edition Group				**750**	**750**	**840**	**840**

2007 DODGE — (1,2or4)B3–(B28C)–7–#

CALIBER—4-Cyl.—Equipment Schedule 6
W.B. 103.7"; 1.8 Liter, 2.0 Liter.

Body	Type	VIN	List	Good	Very Good	Good	Excellent
Sport Wagon 4D		B28C	14985	2950	3300	4200	5975
SXT Sport Wagon 4D		B48C	16985	3225	3575	4525	6375
Manual, 5-Spd				(300)	(300)	(400)	(400)

CALIBER AWD—4-Cyl.—Equipment Schedule 6
W.B. 103.7"; 2.4 Liter.

R/T Sport Wagon 4D		E78K	19985	4725	5175	6250	8700
FWD				(625)	(625)	(835)	(835)
Manual, 5-Spd				(300)	(300)	(400)	(400)

MAGNUM—V6—Equipment Schedule 4
W.B. 120.0"; 2.7 Liter, 3.5 Liter.

Sport Wagon 4D		V47T	23545	4400	4775	5850	8075
SXT Sport Wagon 4D		V47V	27405	4750	5125	6275	8675
AWD		Z		750	750	1000	1000
V8, HEMI, 5.7 Liter		2		1250	1250	1680	1680

MAGNUM—V8 HEMI—Equipment Schedule 4
W.B. 120.0"; 5.7 Liter, 6.1 Liter.

R/T Sport Wagon 4D		V572	31590	7650	8200	9725	13050
SRT8 Sport Wagon 4D		V773	38220	10200	10850	11850	14900
AWD		Z		750	750	1000	1000

CHARGER—V6—Equipment Schedule 4
W.B. 120.0"; 2.7 Liter, 3.5 Liter.

SE Sedan 4D		A43R	23475	5600	6025	7075	9375
SXT Sedan 4D		A43G	26580	6300	6775	7825	10300
AWD		K		750	750	1000	1000
V6, HO, 3.5 Liter (SE)		G		275	275	360	360
V8, HEMI, 5.7 Liter		H		1250	1250	1680	1680

CHARGER—V8 HEMI—Equipment Schedule 4
W.B. 120.0"; 5.7 Liter, 6.1 Liter.

R/T Sedan 4D		A53H	30890	8500	9075	10450	13700
SRT8 Sedan 4D		A73W	38695	12450	13250	13850	17000
Performance Group				625	625	850	850
Daytona Edition				625	625	850	850
Super Bee Special Ed				175	175	220	220
AWD		K		750	750	1000	1000

2008 DODGE — (1,2or3)B3–(B28C)–8–#

CALIBER—4-Cyl.—Equipment Schedule 6
W.B. 103.7"; 1.8 Liter, 2.0 Liter.

SE Sport Wagon 4D		B28C	15485	3650	3975	5000	6950
SXT Sport Wagon 4D		B48C	18180	4100	4450	5525	7625
Manual, 5-Spd w/Overdrive				(350)	(350)	(470)	(470)

CALIBER AWD—4-Cyl.—Equipment Schedule 6
W.B. 103.7"; 2.4 Liter.

R/T Sport Wagon 4D		E78K	21055	5575	6000	7425	10100
FWD				(675)	(675)	(890)	(890)
Manual, 5-Spd w/Overdrive				(350)	(350)	(470)	(470)

CALIBER—4-Cyl. Turbo—Equipment Schedule 6
W.B. 103.7"; 2.4 Liter.

SRT4 Sport Wagon 4D		B68F	23015	6975	7500	8425	10800

AVENGER—4-Cyl.—Equipment Schedule 4
W.B. 108.9"; 2.4 Liter.

SE Sedan 4D		C46K	19265	4200	4550	5475	7325
SXT Sedan 4D		C56K	20195	4650	5025	5975	7950
V6, 2.7 Liter		R		650	650	860	860

AVENGER—V6—Equipment Schedule 4
W.B. 108.9"; 3.5 Liter.

R/T Sedan 4D		C76M	23945	5700	6125	7425	9850
AWD		Z		825	825	1100	1100

MAGNUM—V6—Equipment Schedule 4
W.B. 120.0"; 2.7 Liter, 3.5 Liter.

Sport Wagon 4D		V47T	24095	5550	5975	7225	9575
SXT Sport Wagon 4D		V37V	27900	5750	6175	7525	10100
AWD		Z		825	825	1100	1100
V8, HEMI, 5.7 Liter		2		1350	1350	1795	1795

Body Type	VIN	List	Trade-In Good	Very Good	Pvt-Party Good	Retail Excellent
MAGNUM—V8 HEMI—Equipment Schedule 4						
W.B. 120.0"; 5.7 Liter, 6.1 Liter.						
R/T Sport Wagon 4D	V572	32455	9550	10150	11700	15100
SRT8 Sport Wagon 4D	V773	38580	12400	13150	14400	17850
AWD	Z		825	825	1095	1095
CHARGER—V6—Equipment Schedule 4						
W.B. 120.0"; 2.7 Liter.						
Sedan 4D	A43R	22350	6625	7075	8200	10600
SXT Sedan 4D	A33G	26360	7700	8200	9450	12150
AWD	K		825	825	1100	1100
V6, HO, 3.5 Liter (Base)	G		275	275	380	380
V8, HEMI, 5.7 Liter	H		1350	1350	1795	1795
CHARGER—V8 HEMI—Equipment Schedule 4						
W.B. 120.0"; 5.7 Liter, 6.1 Liter.						
R/T Sedan 4D	A53H	31430	9800	10400	11800	15050
SRT8 Sedan 4D	A73W	38993	13950	14750	15400	18550
Performance Pkg			675	675	895	895
Daytona Edition			675	675	895	895
Super Bee Special Ed.			200	200	235	235
AWD	K		825	825	1090	1090
CHALLENGER—V8 HEMI—Equipment Schedule 4						
W.B. 98.8"; 6.1 Liter.						
SRT8 Coupe 2D	J74W	40158	16300	17100	17950	21000
VIPER—V10—Equipment Schedule 2						
W.B. 98.8"; 8.4 Liter.						
SRT10 Coupe 2D	Z69Z	86496	34500	35800	36600	42300
SRT10 Convertible 2D	Z65Z	85746	32000	33200	34200	39600

2009 DODGE — (1,2or3)(B3orD4)–(B28C)–9–#

Body Type	VIN	List	Trade-In Good	Very Good	Pvt-Party Good	Retail Excellent
CALIBER—4-Cyl.—Equipment Schedule 6						
W.B. 103.7"; 1.8 Liter, 2.0 Liter, 2.4 Liter.						
SE Sport Wagon 4D	B28C	17290	4275	4600	5500	7275
SXT Sport Wagon 4D	B48C	18660	4875	5250	6200	8150
R/T Sport Wagon 4D	B78B	21200	6250	6650	7925	10350
Manual, 5-Spd w/Overdrive			(375)	(375)	(500)	(500)
CALIBER—4-Cyl. Turbo—Equipment Schedule 6						
W.B. 103.7"; 2.4 Liter.						
SRT4 Sport Wagon 4D	B68F	24670	8025	8525	9575	12000
AVENGER—4-Cyl.—Equipment Schedule 4						
W.B. 108.9"; 2.4 Liter.						
SE Sedan 4D	C46B	20505	4750	5100	6050	7925
SXT Sedan 4D	C56B	21790	5575	5975	7200	9400
V6, 2.7 Liter	D		675	675	905	905
AVENGER—V6—Equipment Schedule 4						
W.B. 108.9"; 3.5 Liter.						
R/T Sedan 4D	C76V	25705	6475	6900	8225	10700
CHARGER—V6—Equipment Schedule 4						
W.B. 120.0"; 2.7 Liter, 3.5 Liter.						
Sedan 4D	A43D	24595	7725	8200	9400	11850
SXT Sedan 4D	A33V	26210	8775	9275	10500	13200
AWD			900	900	1155	1155
V6, HO, 3.5 Liter (Base)	V		300	300	385	385
CHARGER—V8 HEMI—Equipment Schedule 4						
W.B. 120.0"; 5.7 Liter, 6.1 Liter.						
R/T Sedan 4D	A53T	32560	11200	11800	13300	16550
SRT8 Sedan 4D	A73W	41121	17700	18600	19050	22200
Performance Pkg			725	725	915	915
Daytona Edition			725	725	915	915
Super Bee Special Ed			200	200	240	240
AWD	K		900	900	1150	1150
CHALLENGER—V6—Equipment Schedule 4						
W.B. 116.0"; 3.5 Liter.						
SE Coupe 2D	J44V	21995	11200	11750	12600	14850
CHALLENGER—V8 HEMI—Equipment Schedule 4						
W.B. 116.0"; 5.7 Liter, 6.1 Liter.						
R/T Coupe 2D	J54T	29995	14900	15600	16600	19400
SRT8 Coupe 2D	J74W	39995	19050	19900	20800	24000
VIPER—V10—Equipment Schedule 2						
W.B. 98.8"; 8.4 Liter.						
SRT10 Coupe 2D	Z69Z	89021	37200	38500	39300	45000
SRT10 Convertible 2D	Z65Z	88271	33200	34400	35500	40800
VOI 10 Edition			6850	6850	7660	7660

Body Type	VIN	List	Trade-In Good	Very Good	Pvt-Party Good	Retail Excellent

2010 DODGE — (1 or 2)B3–(B1HA)–A–#

CALIBER—4-Cyl.—Equipment Schedule 6
W.B. 103.7"; 1.8 Liter, 2.0 Liter, 2.4 Liter.

Body Type	VIN	List	Good	Very Good	Good	Excellent
Express Sport Wag 4D	B1HA	17510	4775	5100	5925	7600
Mainstreet Spt Wag 4D	B3HA	18690	6100	6475	7550	9575
Uptown Sport Wagon	B9HA	20625	7875	8300	9550	12000

CALIBER—4-Cyl.—Equipment Schedule 6
W.B. 103.7"; 1.8 Liter, 2.0 Liter, 2.4 Liter.

SE Sport Wagon 4D	B2HA	18605	5300	5650	6700	8525
Heat Sport Wagon 4D	B5HA	20070	6275	6675	7750	9825
SXT Sport Wagon 4D	B4HA	20370	6350	6750	7850	9925
Rush Sport Wagon 4D	B8HB	21625	7975	8400	9650	12100
R/T Sport Wagon 4D	B7HB	22260	8475	8925	10200	12800
Manual, 5-Spd w/Overdrive			(475)	(475)	(625)	(625)

AVENGER—4-Cyl.—Equipment Schedule 4
W.B. 108.9"; 2.4 Liter.

SXT Sedan 4D	C4FB	20970	6150	6550	7825	10050
V6, 2.7 Liter	D		725	725	955	955

AVENGER—V6—Equipment Schedule 4
W.B. 108.9"; 2.4 Liter.

R/T Sedan 4D	C5FB	22470	7500	7925	9475	12150

CHARGER—V6—Equipment Schedule 4
W.B. 120.0"; 2.7 Liter, 3.5 Liter.

Sedan 4D	A4CD	25140	9025	9525	10750	13200
SXT Sedan 4D	A3CV	26900	9800	10300	11500	14100
Rallye Sedan 4D	A9CV	27395	10500	11050	12250	14950
AWD	K		950	950	1185	1185
V6, HO, 3.5 Liter (Base)	V		325	325	395	395

CHARGER—V8 HEMI—Equipment Schedule 4
W.B. 120.0"; 5.7 Liter, 6.1 Liter.

R/T Sedan 4D	A5CT	32120	13950	14600	16050	19400
SRT8 Sedan 4D	A7CW	38930	19400	20200	20800	24000
Road/Track Pkg			750	750	935	935
AWD	K		950	950	1170	1170

CHALLENGER—V6—Equipment Schedule 4
W.B. 116.0"; 3.5 Liter.

SE Coupe 2D	J4DV	23460	12600	13150	14300	16950

CHALLENGER—V8 HEMI—Equipment Schedule 4
W.B. 116.0"; 5.7 Liter, 6.1 Liter.

R/T Coupe 2D	J5DT	31585	16600	17300	18500	21700
SRT8 Coupe 2D	J7DW	41955	20900	21800	22700	26100

VIPER—V10—Equipment Schedule 2
W.B. 98.8"; 8.4 Liter.

SRT10 Coupe 2D	Z6JZ	94930	38900	40300	41100	46800
SRT10 Convertible 2D	Z6EZ	94180	35000	36200	37300	42600

2011 DODGE — (1 or 2)B3–(B1HA)–B–#

CALIBER—4-Cyl.—Equipment Schedule 6
W.B. 103.7"; 1.8 Liter, 2.0 Liter, 2.4 Liter.

Express Sport Wag 4D	B1HA	17630	6375	6725	7675	9475
Mainstreet Spt Wag 4D	B3HA	18990	8175	8575	9700	11900
Uptown Sport Wagon	B9HA	20835	9250	9700	10950	13350

CALIBER—4-Cyl.—Equipment Schedule 6
W.B. 103.7"; 1.8 Liter, 2.0 Liter, 2.4 Liter.

Heat Sport Wagon 4D	B5HA	19835	8375	8800	9925	12150
Rush Sport Wagon 4D	B8HB	21835	9400	9875	11100	13550
Manual, 5-Spd w/Overdrive			(500)	(500)	(650)	(650)

AVENGER—4-Cyl.—Equipment Schedule 4
W.B. 108.9"; 2.4 Liter.

Express Sedan 4D	D1FB	19995	7600	8000	9475	11950
Mainstreet Sedan 4D	D1FB	21995	7825	8225	9650	12100
LUX Sedan 4D	D2FB	24295	8700	9150	10650	13350

CHARGER—V6—Equipment Schedule 4
W.B. 120.2"; 3.6 Liter.

Sedan 4D	L3CG	25995	13000	13550	14700	17400
Rallye			500	500	605	605

CHARGER—V8 HEMI—Equipment Schedule 4
W.B. 120.2"; 5.7 Liter.

R/T Sedan 4D	L5CT	30995	17150	17850	19250	22700
AWD	M		1000	1000	1185	1185

Body Type	VIN	List	Trade-In Good	Very Good	Pvt-Party Good	Retail Excellent
CHALLENGER—V6—Equipment Schedule 4						
W.B. 116.0"; 3.6 Liter.						
Coupe 2D	J4DG	25495	**13650**	**14200**	**15250**	**17600**
CHALLENGER—V8 HEMI—Equipment Schedule 4						
W.B. 116.0"; 5.7 Liter, 6.1 Liter.						
R/T Coupe 2D	J5DT	30495	**18300**	**19050**	**19950**	**22800**
SRT8 Coupe 2D	J7DJ	45714	**25200**	**26200**	**26900**	**30400**

2012 DODGE — (1,2or3)C3–(DWBA)–C–#

Body Type	VIN	List	Trade-In Good	Very Good	Pvt-Party Good	Retail Excellent
CALIBER—4-Cyl.—Equipment Schedule 4						
W.B. 103.7"; 2.0 Liter.						
SE Sport Wagon 4D	DWBA	18130	**7525**	**7900**	**9000**	**10950**
SXT Plus Sport Wag 4D	DWEA	19480	**8725**	**9125**	**10250**	**12450**
Automatic, CVT			**475**	**475**	**605**	**605**
CALIBER—4-Cyl.—Equipment Schedule 6						
W.B. 103.7"; 2.0 Liter.						
SXT Sport Wagon 4D	DWDA	19515	**8625**	**9025**	**10150**	**12300**
AVENGER—4-Cyl.—Equipment Schedule 4						
W.B. 108.9"; 2.4 Liter.						
SE Sedan 4D	DZAB	19745	**8525**	**8925**	**10300**	**12650**
SXT Sedan 4D	DZCB	22245	**9150**	**9575**	**10950**	**13450**
AVENGER—V6—Equipment Schedule 4						
W.B. 108.9"; 3.6 Liter.						
SXT Plus Sedan 4D	DZEG	24745	**9575**	**10000**	**11500**	**14050**
R/T Sedan 4D	DZBG	26745	**10700**	**11150**	**12850**	**15750**
CHARGER—V6—Equipment Schedule 4						
W.B. 120.2"; 3.6 Liter.						
SE Sedan 4D	DXBG	26320	**13650**	**14250**	**15550**	**18250**
SXT Sedan 4D	DXHG	29320	**15150**	**15800**	**17050**	**19950**
Rallye			**500**	**500**	**600**	**600**
CHARGER—V8 HEMI—Equipment Schedule 4						
W.B. 120.2"; 5.7 Liter, 6.4 Liter.						
R/T Sedan 4D	DXCT	30820	**17900**	**18600**	**20000**	**23500**
SRT8 Superbee Sedan	DXGJ	43350	**25900**	**26800**	**27400**	**30700**
SRT8 Sedan 4D	DXEJ	47650	**27700**	**28600**	**29100**	**32500**
AWD	D		**1200**	**1200**	**1440**	**1440**
CHALLENGER—V6—Equipment Schedule 4						
W.B. 116.0"; 3.6 Liter.						
SXT Coupe 2D	DYAG	25820	**14400**	**14950**	**16050**	**18500**
CHALLENGER—V8 HEMI—Equipment Schedule 4						
W.B. 116.0"; 5.7 Liter, 6.4 Liter.						
R/T Coupe 2D	DYBT	30820	**19300**	**20000**	**20900**	**23700**
SRT8 392 Coupe 2D	DYCJ	46150	**26900**	**27800**	**28600**	**32200**

2013 DODGE — (1,2or3)C3–(DFAA)–D–#

Body Type	VIN	List	Trade-In Good	Very Good	Pvt-Party Good	Retail Excellent
DART—4-Cyl.—Equipment Schedule 6						
W.B. 106.4"; 1.4 Liter, 2.0 Liter, 2.4 Liter.						
SE Sedan 4D	DFAA	16790	**8500**	**8875**	**9975**	**12100**
SXT Sedan 4D	DFBA	18790	**9975**	**10400**	**11450**	**13650**
Rallye Sedan 4D	DFBA	19790	**10450**	**10850**	**11900**	**14100**
Limited Sedan 4D	DFCA	20790	**11300**	**11750**	**12700**	**14950**
GT Sedan 4D	DFEB	22890	**11950**	**12400**	**13450**	**15850**
Automatic, 6-Spd			**500**	**500**	**625**	**625**
4-Cyl, MltiAir Trbo, 1.4L			**175**	**175**	**220**	**220**
DART—4-Cyl. Turbo—Equipment Schedule 6						
W.B. 106.4"; 1.4 Liter.						
Aero Sedan 4D	DFAH	20090	**10650**	**11050**	**12100**	**14300**
AVENGER—4-Cyl.—Equipment Schedule 4						
W.B. 108.9"; 2.4 Liter.						
SE Sedan 4D	DZAB	19990	**9525**	**9950**	**11450**	**14000**
AVENGER—4-Cyl.—Equipment Schedule 4						
W.B. 108.9"; 2.4 Liter.						
SXT Sedan 4D	DZCB	22990	**10150**	**10600**	**12100**	**14750**
V6, Flex Fuel, 3.6 Liter	G		**925**	**925**	**1155**	**1155**
AVENGER—V6 Flex Fuel—Equipment Schedule 4						
W.B. 108.9"; 3.6 Liter.						
SE Sedan 4D	DZAG	22690	**9925**	**10350**	**11900**	**14550**
R/T Sedan 4D	DZBG	26490	**11550**	**12000**	**13700**	**16600**
CHARGER—V6—Equipment Schedule 4						
W.B. 120.2"; 3.6 Liter.						
SE Sedan 4D	DXBG	26790	**14250**	**14850**	**16150**	**18900**
SXT Sedan 4D	DXHG	29590	**16150**	**16850**	**18150**	**21200**

Body Type	VIN	List	Trade-In Good	Very Good	Pvt-Party Good	Retail Excellent
SXT Plus Sedan 4D	DXHG	31590	**16050**	**16700**	**18150**	**21300**
Rallye			**500**	**500**	**605**	**605**
AWD	F		**1100**	**1100**	**1325**	**1325**

CHARGER—V8 HEMI—Equipment Schedule 4
W.B. 120.2"; 5.7 Liter, 6.4 Liter.

Body Type	VIN	List	Trade-In Good	Very Good	Pvt-Party Good	Retail Excellent
R/T Sedan 4D	DXCT	30990	**18600**	**19350**	**20800**	**24300**
R/T Plus Sedan 4D	DXCT	32990	**18800**	**19550**	**21000**	**24500**
R/T Road/Track Sed	DXCT	34990	**18800**	**19550**	**21000**	**24500**
R/T Max Sedan 4D	DXCT	37190	**18550**	**19250**	**20700**	**24200**
SRT8 Super Bee Sedan	DXGJ	43800	**26600**	**27400**	**28300**	**31900**
SRT8 Sedan 4D	DXEJ	47020	**28200**	**29100**	**29900**	**33600**
AWD	D		**1100**	**1100**	**1315**	**1315**

CHALLENGER—V6 Flex Fuel—Equipment Schedule 4
W.B. 116.0"; 3.6 Liter.

Body Type	VIN	List	Trade-In Good	Very Good	Pvt-Party Good	Retail Excellent
SXT Coupe 2D	DYAG	26990	**15050**	**15650**	**16700**	**19000**
SXT Plus Coupe 2D	DYAG	28990	**15900**	**16500**	**17950**	**20900**
Rallye Redline Cpe 2D	DYAG	30890	**16600**	**17200**	**18250**	**20800**

CHALLENGER—V8 HEMI—Equipment Schedule 4
W.B. 116.0"; 5.7 Liter, 6.4 Liter.

Body Type	VIN	List	Trade-In Good	Very Good	Pvt-Party Good	Retail Excellent
R/T Coupe 2D	DYBT	32190	**19800**	**20600**	**21600**	**24500**
R/T Plus Coupe 2D	DYBT	34190	**20200**	**21000**	**22000**	**25000**
R/T Classic Coupe 2D	DYBT	36190	**20400**	**21200**	**22200**	**25300**
SRT8 Core Coupe 2D	DYDJ	42220	**26800**	**27700**	**28600**	**32200**
SRT8 392 Coupe 2D	DYCJ	47120	**29700**	**30700**	**31400**	**35200**

2014 DODGE — (1,2or3)C3–(DFAA)–D–#

DART—4-Cyl.—Equipment Schedule 6
W.B. 106.4"; 2.0 Liter, 2.4 Liter.

Body Type	VIN	List	Trade-In Good	Very Good	Pvt-Party Good	Retail Excellent
SE Sedan 4D	DFAA	18385	**9650**	**10050**	**11150**	**13300**
SXT Sedan 4D	DFBB	19490	**10700**	**11150**	**12150**	**14350**
GT Sedan 4D	DFEB	21990	**12850**	**13350**	**14400**	**16750**
Automatic, 6-Spd			**525**	**525**	**635**	**635**

DART—4-Cyl.—Equipment Schedule 6
W.B. 106.4"; 2.4 Liter.

Body Type	VIN	List	Trade-In Good	Very Good	Pvt-Party Good	Retail Excellent
Limited Sedan 4D	DFCB	23990	**13750**	**14250**	**15250**	**17650**

DART—4-Cyl. Turbo—Equipment Schedule 6
W.B. 106.4"; 1.4 Liter.

Body Type	VIN	List	Trade-In Good	Very Good	Pvt-Party Good	Retail Excellent
Aero Sedan 4D	DFDH	20990	**11750**	**12200**	**13250**	**15550**
Auto 6-Spd Dual Dry Cltch			**525**	**525**	**630**	**630**

AVENGER—4-Cyl.—Equipment Schedule 4
W.B. 108.9"; 2.4 Liter.

Body Type	VIN	List	Trade-In Good	Very Good	Pvt-Party Good	Retail Excellent
SE Sedan 4D	DZAB	20890	**10500**	**10950**	**12450**	**15050**
SXT Sedan 4D	DZCB	23690	**11450**	**11900**	**13550**	**16400**
V6, Flex Fuel, 3.6 Liter	G		**950**	**950**	**1215**	**1215**

AVENGER—V6 Flex Fuel—Equipment Schedule 4
W.B. 108.9"; 3.6 Liter.

Body Type	VIN	List	Trade-In Good	Very Good	Pvt-Party Good	Retail Excellent
SE Sedan 4D	DZAG	22330	**10950**	**11400**	**13000**	**15850**
R/T Sedan 4D	DZBG	26790	**13000**	**13500**	**15300**	**18450**

CHARGER—V6—Equipment Schedule 4
W.B. 120.2"; 3.6 Liter.

Body Type	VIN	List	Trade-In Good	Very Good	Pvt-Party Good	Retail Excellent
SE Sedan 4D	DXBG	27290	**15100**	**15700**	**17000**	**19900**
AWD	F		**1150**	**1150**	**1385**	**1385**

CHARGER—V6—Equipment Schedule 4
W.B. 120.2"; 3.6 Liter.

Body Type	VIN	List	Trade-In Good	Very Good	Pvt-Party Good	Retail Excellent
SXT Sedan 4D	DXHG	30290	**17250**	**17950**	**19400**	**22700**
SXT Plus Sedan 4D	DXHG	32290	**18000**	**18750**	**20200**	**23600**
Adaptive Cruise Control			**500**	**500**	**595**	**595**
Rallye Appearance Group			**500**	**500**	**595**	**595**
AWD	F		**1150**	**1150**	**1385**	**1385**

CHARGER—V6—Equipment Schedule 4
W.B. 120.2"; 3.6 Liter.

Body Type	VIN	List	Trade-In Good	Very Good	Pvt-Party Good	Retail Excellent
SXT 100th Annv Ed	DXHG	34490	**20500**	**21300**	**22800**	**26500**

CHARGER—V8 HEMI—Equipment Schedule 4
W.B. 120.2"; 5.7 Liter.

Body Type	VIN	List	Trade-In Good	Very Good	Pvt-Party Good	Retail Excellent
R/T Sedan 4D	DXCT	31490	**20500**	**21300**	**22700**	**26300**
R/T Max Sedan 4D	DXCT	37990	**19550**	**20300**	**21800**	**25500**
AWD	D		**1150**	**1150**	**1365**	**1365**

CHARGER—V8 HEMI—Equipment Schedule 4
W.B. 120.2"; 5.7 Liter.

Body Type	VIN	List	Trade-In Good	Very Good	Pvt-Party Good	Retail Excellent
R/T Plus Sedan 4D	DXCT	33490	**20700**	**21500**	**22900**	**26600**
Adaptive Cruise Control			**500**	**500**	**585**	**585**
	D		**1150**	**1150**	**1345**	**1345**

2014 DODGE

Body Type	VIN	List	Trade-In Good	Very Good	Pvt-Party Good	Retail Excellent
CHARGER—V8 HEMI—Equipment Schedule 4						
W.B. 120.2"; 5.7 Liter, 6.4 Liter.						
R/T Road/Track Sed	DXCT	34990	20200	21000	22500	26200
SRT8 Sedan 4D	DXEJ	47920	31200	32100	32900	36700
Adaptive Cruise Control			500	500	585	585
CHARGER—V8 HEMI—Equipment Schedule 4						
W.B. 120.2"; 5.7 Liter, 6.4 Liter.						
R/T 100th Anniv Ed Sed	DXCT	35690	18250	19000	20600	24200
SRT8 Super Bee Sedan	DXGJ	44920	29100	30000	30900	34600
CHALLENGER—V6 Flex Fuel—Equipment Schedule 4						
W.B. 116.0"; 3.6 Liter.						
SXT Coupe 2D	DYAG	27290	16050	16650	17750	20200
SXT Plus Coupe 2D	DYAG	29290	17000	17650	19200	22300
SXT 100th Anniv Ed	DYAG	31790				
Rallye Redline Cpe 2D	DYAG	31290	17700	18350	19450	22100
CHALLENGER—V8 HEMI—Equipment Schedule 4						
W.B. 116.0"; 5.7 Liter, 6.4 Liter.						
R/T Coupe 2D	DYBT	31490	21100	21900	22800	25900
R/T Plus Coupe 2D	DYBT	33490	22300	23200	24100	27400
R/T Classic Coupe 2D	DYPT	35490	22500	23400	24400	27700
R/T 100th Anniv Ed Cpe	DYBT	35890				
R/T Shaker Coupe 2D	DYBT	38490				
R/T Mopar '14 Shaker	DYBT	40490				
SRT8 Core Coupe 2D	DYDJ	41020	28800	29900	30700	34500
SRT8 Coupe 2D	DYCJ	46220	31800	32900	33600	37500

FERRARI

2006 FERRARI — ZFF(EW58A)-6-#

Body Type	VIN	List	Good	Very Good	Good	Excellent
F430—V8—Equipment Schedule 2						
W.B. 102.4"; 4.3 Liter.						
Coupe 2D	EW58A	171185	****	****	****	152900
Challenge Coupe 2D	EW58A	228600	****	****	****	179500
Spider Convertible 2D	EW59A	195909	****	****	****	181500
612 SCAGLIETTI—V12—Equipment Schedule 2						
W.B. 116.1"; 5.7 Liter.						
Coupe 2D	AA54A	264134	****	****	****	192900

2007 FERRARI — ZFF(EW58A)-7-#

Body Type	VIN	List	Good	Very Good	Good	Excellent
F430—V8—Equipment Schedule 2						
W.B. 102.4"; 4.3 Liter.						
Coupe 2D	EW58A	174579	****	****	****	156400
Spider Convertible 2D	EW59A	202713	****	****	****	184000
599 GTB FIORANO—V12—Equipment Schedule 2						
W.B. 108.3"; 6.0 Liter.						
Coupe 2D	FC60A	275345	****	****	****	253000
612 SCAGLIETTI—V12—Equipment Schedule 2						
W.B. 116.1"; 5.7 Liter.						
Coupe 2D	JB54A	269381	****	****	****	196900

2008 FERRARI — ZFF(EW58A)-8-#

Body Type	VIN	List	Good	Very Good	Good	Excellent
F430—V8—Equipment Schedule 2						
W.B. 102.4"; 4.3 Liter.						
Coupe 2D	EW58A	191425	****	****	****	157500
Spider Convertible 2D	EW59A	221810	****	****	****	186400
430 SCUDERIA—V8—Equipment Schedule 2						
W.B. 102.4"; 4.3 Liter.						
Coupe 2D	KW64A	261956	****	****	****	164200
599 GTB FIORANO—V12—Equipment Schedule 2						
W.B. 108.3"; 6.0 Liter.						
Coupe 2D	FC60A	317595	****	****	****	254500
612 SCAGLIETTI—V12—Equipment Schedule 2						
W.B. 116.1"; 5.7 Liter.						
Coupe 2D	JB54A	281887	****	****	****	198100

2009 FERRARI — ZFF(EW58A)-9-#

Body Type	VIN	List	Good	Very Good	Good	Excellent
F430—V8—Equipment Schedule 2						
W.B. 102.4"; 4.3 Liter.						
Coupe 2D	EW58A	192925	****	****	****	160700
Spider Convertible 2D	EW59A	223310	****	****	****	189500

0415   **EQUIPMENT & MILEAGE PAGE 9 TO 23   115**

2009 FERRARI

Body Type	VIN	List	Trade-In Good	Very Good	Pvt-Party Good	Retail Excellent
430 SCUDERIA—V8—Equipment Schedule 2						
W.B. 102.4"; 4.3 Liter.						
Coupe 2D	KW64A	287618	****	****	****	169900
Spider 16M Coupe 2D	KW66A	313000	****	****	****	194600
CALIFORNIA—V8—Equipment Schedule 2						
W.B. 105.1"; 4.3 Liter.						
Convertible 2D	LJ65A	197350	****	****	****	183700
599 GTB FIORANO—V12—Equipment Schedule 2						
W.B. 108.3"; 6.0 Liter.						
Coupe 2D	FC60A	326730	****	****	****	256500
612 SCAGLIETTI—V12—Equipment Schedule 2						
W.B. 116.4"; 5.7 Liter.						
Coupe 2D	JB54A	320038	****	****	****	200100

2010 FERRARI — ZFF(67NFA)–A–#

Body Type	VIN	List	Trade-In Good	Very Good	Pvt-Party Good	Retail Excellent
458 ITALIA—V8—Equipment Schedule 2						
W.B. 104.3"; 4.5 Liter.						
Coupe 2D	67NFA	230675	****	****	****	215900
CALIFORNIA—V8—Equipment Schedule 2						
W.B. 105.1"; 4.3 Liter.						
Convertible 2D	LJA5A	196450	****	****	****	187200
599 GTB FIORANO—V12—Equipment Schedule 2						
W.B. 108.3"; 6.0 Liter.						
Coupe 2D	60FCA	326730	****	****	****	258500
612 SCAGLIETTI—V12—Equipment Schedule 2						
W.B. 116.1"; 5.7 Liter.						
Coupe 2D	54JBA	315538	****	****	****	200900

2011 FERRARI — ZFF(67NFA)–B–#

Body Type	VIN	List	Trade-In Good	Very Good	Pvt-Party Good	Retail Excellent
458 ITALIA—V8—Equipment Schedule 2						
W.B. 104.3"; 4.5 Liter.						
Coupe 2D	67NFA	230675	****	****	****	220800
CALIFORNIA—V8—Equipment Schedule 2						
W.B. 105.1"; 4.3 Liter.						
Convertible 2D	65LJA	196450	****	****	****	189100
599 GTB FIORANO—V12—Equipment Schedule 2						
W.B. 108.3"; 6.0 Liter.						
Coupe 2D	60FCA	327130	****	****	****	262900
599 GTO—V12—Equipment Schedule 2						
W.B. 108.3"; 6.0 Liter.						
Coupe 2D	70RCA	416550	****	****	****	474800
612 SCAGLIETTI—V12—Equipment Schedule 2						
W.B. 116.1"; 5.7 Liter.						
Coupe 2D		315538	****	****	****	205900

2012 FERRARI — ZFF(67NFA)–C–#

Body Type	VIN	List	Trade-In Good	Very Good	Pvt-Party Good	Retail Excellent
458 ITALIA—V8—Equipment Schedule 2						
W.B. 104.3"; 4.5 Liter.						
Coupe 2D	67NFA	236182	****	****	****	256300
CALIFORNIA—V8—Equipment Schedule 2						
W.B. 105.1"; 4.3 Liter.						
Convertible 2D	65LJA	201290	****	****	****	199100
FF AWD—V12—Equipment Schedule 2						
W.B. 116.1"; 6.3 Liter.						
Coupe 2D	73SKA	298750	****	****	****	277800

2013 FERRARI — (ZFF)(67NFA)–D–#

Body Type	VIN	List	Trade-In Good	Very Good	Pvt-Party Good	Retail Excellent
458 ITALIA—V8—Equipment Schedule 2						
W.B. 104.3"; 4.5 Liter.						
Coupe 2D	67NFA	239859	****	****	****	269200
458 SPIDER—V8—Equipment Schedule 2						
W.B. 104.3"; 4.5 Liter.						
Convertible 2D	68NHA	263762	****	****	****	274200
CALIFORNIA—V8—Equipment Schedule 2						
W.B. 105.1"; 4.3 Liter.						
Convertible 2D	65TJA	203640	****	****	****	209500
F12BERLINETTA—V12—Equipment Schedule 2						
W.B. 107.1"; 6.3 Liter.						
Convertible 2D	68NHA	263762	****	****	****	274200
FF AWD—V12—Equipment Schedule 2						
W.B. 117.7"; 6.3 Liter.						
Coupe 2D	73SKA	302450	****	****	****	287700

Body Type	VIN	List	Trade-In Good	Very Good	Pvt-Party Good	Retail Excellent

FIAT

2012 FIAT — (3C3)–(FFAR)–C–#

500—4-Cyl.—Equipment Schedule 4
W.B. 90.6"; 1.4 Liter.

Body Type	VIN	List	Good	Very Good	Good	Excellent
Pop Hatchback 2D	FFAR	17000	6675	7050	8025	9900
Sport Hatchback 2D	FFBR	19000	7200	7600	8575	10600
Lounge Hatchback 2D	FFCR	20000	7725	8150	9150	11150
Abarth Hatchback 2D	FFFH	22700	10750	11300	12150	14500
Gucci Hatchback 2D	FFCR	24200	9575	10050	11150	13500

500C—4-Cyl.—Equipment Schedule 4
W.B. 90.6"; 1.4 Liter.

Body Type	VIN	List	Good	Very Good	Good	Excellent
Pop Convertible 2D	FFDR	21000	7925	8375	9350	11350
Lounge Convertible 2D	FFER	24000	9125	9600	10650	12900
Gucci Convertible 2D	FFER	28200	10250	10800	11850	14250

2013 FIAT — (3C3)–(FFAR)–D–#

500—4-Cyl.—Equipment Schedule 4
W.B. 90.6"; 1.4 Liter.

Body Type	VIN	List	Good	Very Good	Good	Excellent
Pop Hatchback 2D	FFAR	16200	7575	7975	9125	11200
Sport Hatchback 2D	FFBR	18200	8225	8650	9750	11900
Lounge Hatchback 2D	FFCR	19200	8275	8700	9800	11950
Sport Cattiva H'Back	FFBR	20400	8875	9325	10500	12800
Gucci Hatchback 2D	FFCR	25250	10750	11250	12400	14900

500—4-Cyl. Turbo—Equipment Schedule 4
W.B. 90.6"; 1.4 Liter.

Body Type	VIN	List	Good	Very Good	Good	Excellent
Hatchback 2D	FFHH	20300	8825	9275	10450	12700
Cattiva Hatchback 2D	FFHH	21150	9225	9675	10800	13100
Abarth Hatchback 2D	FFHH	22700	11300	11850	12850	15300

500C—4-Cyl.—Equipment Schedule 4
W.B. 90.6"; 1.4 Liter.

Body Type	VIN	List	Good	Very Good	Good	Excellent
Pop Convertible 2D	FFDR	20200	8675	9125	10300	12550
Lounge Convertible 2D	FFER	23200	10600	1100	12300	14750
Abarth Convertible 2D	FFJH	26700	12100	12650	13600	16050
Gucci Convertible 2D	FFER	29000	12300	12850	13900	16500

500e—Electric—Equipment Schedule 4
W.B. 90.6".

Body Type	VIN	List	Good	Very Good	Good	Excellent
Hatchback 2D	FFGE	32600	13600	14250	15250	17900

2014 FIAT — (3C3)–(FFAR)–E–#

500—4-Cyl.—Equipment Schedule 4
W.B. 90.6"; 1.4 Liter.

Body Type	VIN	List	Good	Very Good	Good	Excellent
Pop Hatchback 2D	FFAR	18245	9275	9750	10850	13100
Sport Hatchback 2D	FFBR	19550	9925	10400	11450	13750
Lounge Hatchback 2D	FFCR	20550	11000	11550	12550	14900
1957 Ed Hatchback 2D	FFCR	20550	10850	11350	12400	14750

500—4-Cyl. Turbo—Equipment Schedule 4
W.B. 90.6"; 1.4 Liter.

Body Type	VIN	List	Good	Very Good	Good	Excellent
Hatchback 2D	FFHH	21550	11550	12050	13100	15500

500 ABARTH—4-Cyl. Turbo—Equipment Schedule 4
W.B. 90.6"; 1.4 Liter.

Body Type	VIN	List	Good	Very Good	Good	Excellent
Hatchback 2D	FFFH	22895	12000	12550	13500	15950
Cabrio Cabriolet 2D	FFJH	26895	14700	15350	16200	18800

500C—4-Cyl. Turbo—Equipment Schedule 4
W.B. 90.6"; 1.4 Liter.

Body Type	VIN	List	Good	Very Good	Good	Excellent
Pop Convertible 2D	FFDR	20495	10900	11450	12450	14800
Lounge Convertible 2D	FFER	23200	12900	13500	14500	17000
GQ Edition Conv 2D	FFJH	26895	14650	15300	16100	18650

500e—Electric—Equipment Schedule 4
W.B. 90.6".

Body Type	VIN	List	Good	Very Good	Good	Excellent
Hatchback 2D	FFGE	32600	16100	16800	17550	20200

500L—4-Cyl.—Equipment Schedule 4
W.B. 102.8"; 1.4 Liter.

Body Type	VIN	List	Good	Very Good	Good	Excellent
Pop Hatchback 4D	FAAH	19000	10350	10800	12100	14450
Lounge Hatchback 4D	FACH	24995	11900	12400	13650	16100

500L—4-Cyl. Turbo—Equipment Schedule 4
W.B. 102.8"; 1.4 Liter.

Body Type	VIN	List	Good	Very Good	Good	Excellent
Easy Hatchback 4D	FABH	22345	11000	11450	12700	15100
Trekking Hatchback	FADH	23345	11400	11850	13150	15550

Body	Type	VIN	List	Trade-In Good	Very Good	Pvt-Party Good	Retail Excellent

FISKER

2012 FISKER

KARMA—AC Electric—Equipment Schedule 2
W.B. 124.4".

EcoStandard Sed 4D		K12AA	103000	****	****	****	62800
EcoSport Sedan 4D		K14AA	111000	****	****	****	64500
EcoChic Sedan 4D		K16AA	116000	****	****	****	67500

FORD

2000 FORD — (1,2or3)FA-(P33P)-Y-#

FOCUS—4-Cyl.—Equipment Schedule 6
W.B. 103.0"; 2.0 Liter.

LX Sedan 4D		P33P	13335	400	450	925	1550
SE Sedan 4D		P34P	13980	525	600	1275	2250
SE Wagon 4D		P36P	15795	725	825	1425	2425
Sony Special Edition				50	50	55	55
4-Cyl, 16V, 2.0 Liter		3		50	50	80	80

FOCUS—4-Cyl. 16V—Equipment Schedule 6
W.B. 103.0"; 2.0 Liter.

ZX3 Hatchback 2D		P313	13075	400	450	925	1575
ZTS Sedan 4D		P383	15580	675	775	1350	2325
Kona Limited Edition				50	50	55	55

ESCORT—4-Cyl.—Equipment Schedule 6
W.B. 98.4"; 2.0 Liter.

Sedan 4D		P13P	12440	475	550	1075	1875
ZX2 Coupe 2D		P113	12970	600	675	1275	2225
S/R Performance Pkg				50	50	80	80

CONTOUR—V6—Equipment Schedule 5
W.B. 106.5"; 2.5 Liter.

SE Sedan 4D		P66L	17265	750	850	1475	2525
SE Sport Sedan 4D		P66L	18195	1200	1325	1975	3300
SVT Sedan 4D		P68G	23250	1775	1975	2875	4700
4-Cyl, 2.0 Liter		Z,3		(75)	(75)	(115)	(115)

MUSTANG—V6—Equipment Schedule 4
W.B. 101.3"; 3.8 Liter.

Coupe 2D		P404	18410	800	900	1500	2550
Convertible 2D		P444	23260	1225	1375	2025	3350
Manual, 5-Spd				(175)	(175)	(235)	(235)

MUSTANG—V8—Equipment Schedule 4
W.B. 101.3"; 4.6 Liter.

GT Coupe 2D		P42X	22905	1600	1775	2200	3425
GT Convertible 2D		P45X	27160	2325	2600	3175	4775

TAURUS—V6—Equipment Schedule 4
W.B. 108.5"; 3.0 Liter.

LX Sedan 4D		P52U	18995	700	800	1375	2375
SE Sedan 4D		P53U	19295	725	825	1425	2425
SE Wagon 4D		P58U	20450	975	1125	1750	3000
SES Sedan 4D		P55U	20290	875	975	1600	2750
SES Wagon 4D		P55U	20870	975	1125	1750	3000
SEL Sedan 4D		P56U	21565	1000	1150	1800	3050
V6, 24V, 3.0 Liter		S		100	100	135	135
V6, Flex Fuel, 3.0 Liter		2		0	0	0	0

CROWN VICTORIA—V8—Equipment Schedule 4
W.B. 114.7"; 4.6 Liter.

Sedan 4D		P73W	22610	575	675	1200	2075
LX Sedan 4D		P74W	24725	800	925	1500	2525

2001 FORD — (1,2or3)FA-(P33P)-1-#

FOCUS—4-Cyl.—Equipment Schedule 6
W.B. 103.0"; 2.0 Liter.

LX Sedan 4D		P33P	13645	425	475	1100	1925
SE Sedan 4D		P34P	14505	775	875	1650	2875
Street Edition				50	50	55	55
4-Cyl, 16V, 2.0 Liter		3		75	75	95	95

FOCUS—4-Cyl. 16V—Equipment Schedule 6
W.B. 103.0"; 2.0 Liter.

0415

2001 FORD

Body Type	VIN	List	Trade-In Good	Very Good	Pvt-Party Good	Retail Excellent
ZX3 Hatchback 2D	P313	13385	425	500	1125	1975
ZTS Sedan 4D	P383	15725	725	825	1500	2600
SE Wagon 4D	P363	16700	900	1000	1675	2850
Street Edition			50	50	55	55
S2 Feature Car			50	50	55	55
Traction Control			125	125	175	175
ESCORT—4-Cyl.—Equipment Schedule 6						
W.B. 98.4"; 2.0 Liter.						
Sedan 4D	P13P	14230	500	575	1125	1925
ZX2—4-Cyl.—Equipment Schedule 6						
W.B. 98.4"; 2.0 Liter.						
Coupe 2D	P113	13310	625	725	1325	2275
MUSTANG—V6—Equipment Schedule 4						
W.B. 101.3"; 3.8 Liter.						
Coupe 2D	P404	17695	925	1050	1675	2850
Deluxe Coupe 2D	P404	18260	925	1050	1675	2850
Deluxe Convertible 2D	P444	23110	1350	1500	2200	3650
Premium Coupe 2D	P404	19490	1325	1475	2150	3525
Premium Conv 2D	P444	25675	1375	1550	2225	3675
Manual, 5-Spd			(150)	(150)	(200)	(200)
MUSTANG—V8—Equipment Schedule 4						
W.B. 101.3"; 4.6 Liter.						
GT Deluxe Coupe	P42X	23330	1750	1925	2400	3700
GT Deluxe Convertible	P45X	27585	2450	2700	3325	4975
GT Premium Coupe	P42X	24480	1750	1925	2400	3700
GT Premium Conv 2D	P45X	28735	2650	2925	3550	5300
Bullitt Coupe 2D	P42X	26830	2725	3000	3650	5425
Cobra Coupe 2D	P47V	29205	3700	4000	5050	7125
Cobra Convertible 2D	P46V	33205	4825	5200	6375	8650
TAURUS—V6—Equipment Schedule 4						
W.B. 108.5"; 3.0 Liter.						
LX Sedan 4D	P52U	19455	800	900	1500	2550
SE Sedan 4D	P53U	19635	825	925	1525	2600
SE Wagon 4D	P58U	20790	1150	1275	1950	3325
SES Sedan 4D	P55U	20650	1075	1200	1850	3150
SES Wagon 4D	P55U	21225	1200	1350	2025	3450
SEL Sedan 4D	P56U	22135	1300	1450	2175	3675
V6, 24V, 3.0 Liter	S		100	100	135	135
CROWN VICTORIA—V8—Equipment Schedule 4						
W.B. 114.7"; 4.6 Liter.						
Sedan 4D	P73W	22620	625	700	1225	2100
LX Sedan 4D	P74W	24735	875	1000	1625	2775

2002 FORD — (1,2or3)FA—(P33P)-2-#

Body Type	VIN	List	Trade-In Good	Very Good	Pvt-Party Good	Retail Excellent
FOCUS—4-Cyl.—Equipment Schedule 6						
W.B. 103.0"; 2.0 Liter.						
LX Sedan 4D	P33P	13220	650	725	1350	2325
SE Sedan 4D	P34P	15625	1000	1100	1825	3100
SE Wagon 4D	P36P	17015	1350	1475	2150	3550
4-Cyl, 16V, 2.0 Liter	3		75	75	100	100
FOCUS—4-Cyl. 16V—Equipment Schedule 6						
W.B. 103.0"; 2.0 Liter.						
ZX3 Hatchback 2D	P313	13700	675	750	1375	2375
ZTS Sedan 4D	P383	15730	1025	1125	1825	3075
ZX5 Hatchback 4D	P373	16105	975	1075	1675	2775
SVT Hatchback 2D	P395	17995	1550	1725	2400	3900
ZTW Wagon 4D	P363	18195	1350	1475	2150	3550
ESCORT—4-Cyl.—Equipment Schedule 6						
W.B. 98.4"; 2.0 Liter.						
Sedan 4D	P13P	14450	600	675	1250	2175
ZX2—4-Cyl.—Equipment Schedule 6						
W.B. 98.4"; 2.0 Liter.						
Coupe 2D	P113	13655	650	725	1325	2275
MUSTANG—V6—Equipment Schedule 4						
W.B. 101.3"; 3.8 Liter.						
Coupe 2D	P404	18100	1150	1300	1850	3025
Deluxe Coupe 2D	P404	18705	1150	1300	1850	3025
Deluxe Convertible 2D	P444	23955	1550	1750	2425	3850
Premium Coupe 2D	P404	19820	1500	1675	2300	3700
Premium Conv 2D	P444	26210	1725	1925	2625	4150
Manual, 5-Spd			(200)	(200)	(265)	(265)
MUSTANG—V8—Equipment Schedule 4						
W.B. 101.3"; 4.6 Liter.						

Body Type	VIN	List	Trade-In Good	Very Good	Pvt-Party Good	Retail Excellent
GT Deluxe Coupe 2D	P42X	23845	2050	2275	2875	4325
GT Deluxe Convertible	P45X	28430	2775	3100	3725	5500
GT Premium Coupe	P42X	25015	2375	2625	3250	4850
GT Premium Conv 2D	P45X	29270	3000	3325	3975	5850
TAURUS—V6—Equipment Schedule 4						
W.B. 108.5"; 3.0 Liter.						
LX Sedan 4D	P52U	19445	900	1025	1625	2750
SE Sedan 4D	P53U	20070	925	1050	1650	2800
SE Wagon 4D	P58U	22005	1275	1425	2100	3550
SES Sedan 4D	P55U	21085	1200	1350	2025	3400
SEL Sedan 4D	P56S	22995	1425	1600	2300	3875
SEL Wagon 4D	P59S	23265	1325	1475	2175	3675
V6, 24V, 3.0L (ex SEL)	S		125	125	165	165
CROWN VICTORIA—V8—Equipment Schedule 4						
W.B. 114.7"; 4.6 Liter.						
Sedan 4D	P73W	23435	650	725	1275	2150
LX Sedan 4D	P74W	27025	1000	1125	1725	2875
LX Sport Sedan 4D	P74W	28840	1100	1250	1850	3075
THUNDERBIRD—V8—Equipment Schedule 2						
W.B. 107.2"; 3.9 Liter.						
Soft Top Conv 2D	P60A	35495	5225	5750	6325	8575
Hard Top			425	425	575	575

2003 FORD — (1,2or3)FA—(P33P)-3-#

Body Type	VIN	List	Trade-In Good	Very Good	Pvt-Party Good	Retail Excellent
FOCUS—4-Cyl.—Equipment Schedule 6						
W.B. 103.0"; 2.0 Liter, 2.3 Liter.						
LX Sedan 4D	P33P	13505	800	900	1725	3025
SE Sedan 4D	P34P	15175	1275	1425	2300	3950
SE Wagon 4D	P36P	17525	1575	1750	2625	4375
4-Cyl, 16V, 2.3 Liter	Z		75	75	115	115
FOCUS—4-Cyl. 16V—Equipment Schedule 6						
W.B. 103.0"; 2.0 Liter, 2.3 Liter.						
ZX3 Hatchback 2D	P313	13990	875	975	1725	3000
ZX5 Hatchback 4D	P373	15900	1175	1300	2075	3525
ZTS Sedan 4D	P383	16095	1200	1350	2200	3775
ZTW Wagon 4D	P363	17870	1525	1700	2550	4275
ZX3 SVT Hatchback 2D	P395	19100	1750	1925	2675	4200
ZX5 SVT Hatchback 4D	P375	19600	1925	2125	2900	4525
ZX2—4-Cyl.—Equipment Schedule 6						
W.B. 98.4"; 2.0 Liter.						
Coupe 2D	P113	14250	675	775	1400	2400
MUSTANG—V6—Equipment Schedule 4						
W.B. 101.3"; 3.8 Liter.						
Coupe 2D	P404	18345	1700	1900	2500	3850
Deluxe Coupe 2D	P404	19075	1700	1900	2500	3850
Deluxe Convertible	P444	24080	2175	2425	3075	4675
Premium Coupe 2D	P404	20190	2100	2350	3000	4525
Premium Convertible 2D	P444	26665	2575	2875	3575	5350
Manual, 5-Spd			(250)	(250)	(335)	(335)
MUSTANG—V8—Equipment Schedule 4						
W.B. 101.3"; 4.6 Liter.						
GT Deluxe Coupe 2D	P42X	24330	2900	3225	3750	5375
GT Deluxe Convertible	P45X	28670	3700	4075	4800	6800
GT Premium Coupe 2D	P42X	26550	3350	3700	4250	6075
GT Premium Conv 2D	P45X	29840	4050	4450	5200	7325
Mach I Coupe 2D	P42R	29810	5075	5525	6375	8900
MUSTANG—V8 Supercharged—Equipment Schedule 4						
W.B. 101.3"; 4.6 Liter.						
Cobra Coupe 2D	P48Y	34085	6550	6975	7825	10000
Cobra Convertible 2D	P49Y	38460	8225	8725	9525	11900
10th Anniversary			200	200	255	255
TAURUS—V6—Equipment Schedule 4						
W.B. 108.5"; 3.0 Liter.						
LX Sedan 4D	P52U	20230	1325	1500	2300	3900
SE Sedan 4D	P53U	20345	1375	1550	2350	4000
SE Wagon 4D	P582	21995	1575	1750	2750	4675
SES Sedan 4D	P55U	21070	1650	1850	2925	4600
SEL Sedan 4D	P56S	23570	1700	1900	2925	5000
SEL Wagon 4D	P59U	23820	1600	1800	2825	4750
V6, 24V, 3.0 Liter	S		150	150	200	200
V6, Flex Fuel, 3.0 Liter	2		0	0	0	0
CROWN VICTORIA—V8—Equipment Schedule 4						
W.B. 114.7"; 4.6 Liter.						

2003 FORD

Body Type	VIN	List	Trade-In Good	Trade-In Very Good	Pvt-Party Good	Retail Excellent
Sedan 4D	P73W	24510	1225	1375	1875	3000
LX Sedan 4D	P74W	27780	1575	1575	2400	3800
LX Sport Sedan 4D	P74W	29600	1725	1925	2600	4075
THUNDERBIRD—V8—Equipment Schedule 2						
W.B. 107.2"; 3.9 Liter.						
Soft Top Conv 2D	P60A	36895	6025	6575	7150	9550
007 Hard Top Conv 2D	P62A	43995	****	****	****	15050
Hard Top			450	450	600	600

2004 FORD — (1,2or3)FA—(P333)—4-#

Body Type	VIN	List	Trade-In Good	Trade-In Very Good	Pvt-Party Good	Retail Excellent
FOCUS—4-Cyl.—Equipment Schedule 6						
W.B. 103.0"; 2.0 Liter.						
LX Sedan 4D	P333	14640	1000	1125	1900	3250
SE Wagon 4D	P363	18490	1925	2125	3125	5050
4-Cyl, 16V, 2.0L/2.3L	PZ		100	100	120	120
FOCUS—4-Cyl. 16V—Equipment Schedule 6						
W.B. 103.0"; 2.0 Liter, 2.3 Liter.						
ZX3 Hatchback 2D	P313	14180	1100	1225	2000	3350
ZX5 Hatchback 4D	P373	15580	1300	1450	2225	3675
SE Sedan 4D	P34Z	16311	1575	1725	2700	4525
ZTS Sedan 4D	P38Z	16080	1500	1650	2550	4275
ZTW Wagon 4D	P35Z	18290	1800	1975	2975	4800
SVT Hatchback 2D	P395	19375	2250	2475	3075	4550
SVT Hatchback 4D	P375	19630	2750	3050	3625	5250
MUSTANG—V6—Equipment Schedule 4						
W.B. 101.3"; 3.8 Liter, 3.9 Liter.						
Coupe 2D	P404	18775	1975	2200	2900	4425
Deluxe Coupe 2D	P404	19505	2000	2225	2925	4475
Deluxe Convertible 2D	P444	24510	2450	2725	3475	5225
Premium Coupe 2D	P404	20160	2350	2600	3350	5075
Premium Convertible 2D	P444	26635	2950	3275	4075	6075
Manual, 5-Spd			(300)	(300)	(400)	(400)
MUSTANG—V8—Equipment Schedule 4						
W.B. 101.3"; 4.6 Liter.						
GT Deluxe Coupe 2D	P42X	24300	3600	3950	4625	6600
GT Deluxe Convertible	P45X	28640	4475	4875	5800	8200
GT Premium Coupe 2D	P42X	25470	3925	4300	5150	7325
GT Premium Conv 2D	P45X	29810	4825	5250	6200	8750
Mach 1 Coupe 2D	P42R	29875	5925	6400	7500	10350
MUSTANG—V8 Supercharged—Equipment Schedule 4						
W.B. 101.3"; 4.6 Liter.						
Cobra Coupe 2D	P48Y	35485	8225	8725	9550	11950
Cobra Convertible 2D	P49Y	39575	10200	10800	11450	13950
TAURUS—V6—Equipment Schedule 4						
W.B. 108.5"; 3.0 Liter.						
LX Sedan 4D	P52U	20720	1525	1700	2500	4175
SE Sedan 4D	P53U	20855	1600	1775	2700	4475
SE Wagon 4D	P58U	22290	1875	2075	3125	5125
SES Sedan 4D	P55U	22040	1800	2000	2975	4900
SEL Sedan 4D	P56S	23965	1900	2100	3225	5325
SEL Wagon 4D	P59U	24115	1950	2175	3225	5275
V6, 24V, 3.0 Liter	S		175	175	235	235
V6, Flex Fuel, 3.0 Liter	2		0	0	0	0
CROWN VICTORIA—V8—Equipment Schedule 4						
W.B. 114.7"; 4.6 Liter.						
Sedan 4D	P73W	24345	1575	1750	2350	3700
LX Sedan 4D	P74W	27370	1950	2150	2750	4175
LX Sport Sedan 4D	P74W	30890	2225	2475	3150	4850
THUNDERBIRD—V8—Equipment Schedule 2						
W.B. 107.2"; 3.9 Liter.						
Soft Top Conv 2D	P60A	37530	6775	7375	7800	10200
Pacific Coast Conv 2D	P63A	43995	****	****	****	12500
Hard Top			475	475	620	620

2005 FORD — (1,2or3)(FAorZV)—(P31N)—5-#

Body Type	VIN	List	Trade-In Good	Trade-In Very Good	Pvt-Party Good	Retail Excellent
FOCUS—4-Cyl.—Equipment Schedule 6						
W.B. 102.9"; 2.0 Liter, 2.3 Liter.						
ZX3 S Hatchback 2D	P31N	14545	1500	1650	2700	4400
ZX3 SE Hatchback 2D	P31N	15865	2025	2225	3275	5075
ZX3 SES Hatchback 2D	P31N	16965	2250	2475	3575	5550
ZX4 S Sedan 4D	P34N	14965	1900	2100	3150	4975
ZX4 SE Sedan 4D	P34N	16465	2050	2250	3375	5325

Body Type	VIN	List	Trade-In Good	Very Good	Pvt-Party Good	Retail Excellent
ZX4 SES Sedan 4D	P34N	17565	2475	2725	3875	5950
ZX4 ST Sedan 4D	P38Z	18335	2725	3000	4075	6150
ZX5 S Hatchback 4D	P38N	15665	1975	2175	3275	5150
ZX5 SE Hatchback 4D	P37N	17165	2325	2550	3675	5700
ZX5 SES H'Back 4D	P37N	18265	2675	2925	4025	6075
ZXW SE Wagon 4D	P36N	18165	2275	2500	3625	5600
ZXW SES Wagon 4D	P33N	19265	2775	3050	4200	6400
MUSTANG—V6—Equipment Schedule 4						
W.B. 107.1"; 4.0 Liter.						
Deluxe Coupe 2D	T80N	19890	4125	4500	5450	7600
Deluxe Convertible 2D	T84N	24615	4625	5025	6025	8350
Premium Coupe 2D	T80N	20765	4550	4950	5925	8225
Premium Convertible 2D	T84N	25490	4925	5375	6550	9050
Manual, 5-Spd			(350)	(350)	(465)	(465)
MUSTANG—V8—Equipment Schedule 4						
W.B. 107.1"; 4.6 Liter.						
GT Deluxe Coupe 2D	T82H	25815	5850	6325	7225	9600
GT Deluxe Convertible	T85H	30240	7150	7700	8700	11450
GT Premium Coupe 2D	T82H	26995	6400	6900	7825	10350
GT Premium Conv 2D	T85H	31420	7450	8000	8950	11650
TAURUS—V6—Equipment Schedule 4						
W.B. 108.5"; 3.0 Liter.						
SE Sedan 4D	P53U	21145	1650	1850	2925	4725
SE Wagon 4D	P58U	23015	1950	2175	3375	5425
SEL Sedan 4D	P56U	23055	1900	2125	3375	5500
SEL Wagon 4D	P59U	24005	1950	2175	3375	5450
V6, 24V, 3.0 Liter	S		200	200	265	265
V6, Flex Fuel, 3.0 Liter	2		0	0	0	0
FIVE HUNDRED—V6—Equipment Schedule 4						
W.B. 112.9"; 3.0 Liter.						
SE Sedan 4D	P231	22795	2250	2525	3350	5075
SEL Sedan 4D	P241	24795	2525	2825	3700	5525
Limited Sedan 4D	P251	26795	2725	3050	3950	5875
AWD	6,7,8		500	500	665	665
CROWN VICTORIA—V8—Equipment Schedule 4						
W.B. 114.7"; 4.6 Liter.						
Sedan 4D	P73W	24810	1950	2175	2875	4275
LX Sedan 4D	P74W	27945	2400	2675	3350	4900
LX Sport Sedan 4D	P74W	31270	2775	3100	3875	5675
THUNDERBIRD—V8—Equipment Schedule 2						
W.B. 107.2"; 3.9 Liter.						
Soft Top Conv 2D	P60A	38065	7000	7575	8325	10850
50th Anniv Conv 2D	P69A	44430	8575	9250	9975	12950
Hard Top			475	475	650	650
GT—V8 Supercharged—Equipment Schedule 2						
W.B. 106.7"; 5.4 Liter.						
Coupe 2D	P90S	143345	****	****	****	145900

2006 FORD-(1,2or3)(F7, FAorZV)-(P31N)-6-#

Body Type	VIN	List	Trade-In Good	Very Good	Pvt-Party Good	Retail Excellent
FOCUS—4-Cyl.—Equipment Schedule 6						
W.B. 102.9"; 2.0 Liter, 2.3 Liter.						
ZX3 S Hatchback 2D	P31N	14905	2125	2325	3275	4950
ZX4 ST Sedan 4D	P38Z	17585	3100	3400	4575	6675
FOCUS—4-Cyl.—Equipment Schedule 6						
W.B. 102.9"; 2.0 Liter, 2.3 Liter.						
ZX3 SE Hatchback 2D	P31N	16075	2500	2750	3825	5650
ZX3 SES Hatchback 2D	P31N	16835	2850	3150	4225	6175
ZX4 SE Sedan 4D	P34N	15265	2550	2800	3850	5675
ZX4 SES Sedan 4D	P34N	16375	2700	3000	4125	6100
ZX5 S Hatchback 4D	P34N	17135	2950	3250	4375	6425
ZX5 S Hatchback 4D	P37N	15975	2650	2950	3975	5825
ZX5 SE Hatchback 4D	P37N	17080	2950	3250	4350	6325
ZX5 SES Hatchback 4D	P37N	17815	3100	3400	4600	6750
ZXW SE Wagon 4D	P36N	18095	3300	3625	4675	6675
ZXW SES Wagon 4D	P36N	18855	3500	3825	5025	7250
Manual, 5-Spd			(275)	(275)	(365)	(365)
FUSION—4-Cyl.—Equipment Schedule 4						
W.B. 107.4"; 2.3 Liter.						
S Sedan 4D	P06Z	18620	2975	3275	4300	6200
SE Sedan 4D	P07Z	19375	3250	3575	4625	6650
Manual, 5-Spd			(400)	(400)	(535)	(535)
V6, 3.0 Liter	1		575	575	770	770

Body Type	VIN	List	Trade-In Good	Very Good	Pvt-Party Good	Retail Excellent
FUSION—V6—Equipment Schedule 4						
W.B. 107.4"; 3.0 Liter.						
SEL Sedan 4D	P081	22360	4075	4425	5650	8050
Manual, 5-Spd			(400)	(400)	(535)	(535)
4-Cyl, 2.3 Liter	Z		(550)	(550)	(725)	(725)
MUSTANG—V6—Equipment Schedule 4						
W.B. 107.1"; 4.0 Liter.						
Coupe 2D	T80N	19835	4825	5250	6150	8325
Convertible 2D	T84N	24660	5350	5800	6900	9300
Deluxe Coupe 2D	T80N	19935	4825	5250	6150	8325
Deluxe Convertible 2D	T84N	24760	5350	5800	6900	9300
Premium Coupe 2D	T80N	20810	5225	5675	6750	9100
Premium Convertible 2D	T84N	25635	5600	6075	7250	9750
Manual, 5-Spd			(400)	(400)	(535)	(535)
MUSTANG—V8—Equipment Schedule 4						
W.B. 107.1"; 4.6 Liter.						
GT Deluxe Coupe	T82H	25860	6575	7075	8075	10650
GT Deluxe Convertible	T85H	30685	7925	8475	9425	12200
GT Premium Coupe	T82H	27040	7150	7650	8650	11250
GT Premium Conv 2D	T85H	31865	8325	8900	9875	12750
TAURUS—6-Cyl.—Equipment Schedule 4						
W.B. 108.5"; 3.0 Liter.						
SE Sedan 4D	P53U	21515	1900	2125	3150	4950
SEL Sedan 4D	P56U	23665	2175	2425	3675	5700
FIVE HUNDRED—V6—Equipment Schedule 4						
W.B. 112.9"; 3.0 Liter.						
SE Sedan 4D	P231	22930	2475	2775	3700	5425
SEL Sedan 4D	P241	24930	2875	3200	4175	6075
Limited Sedan 4D	P251	27080	3250	3600	4650	6700
AWD	6,7,8		550	550	720	720
CROWN VICTORIA—V8—Equipment Schedule 4						
W.B. 114.7"; 4.6 Liter.						
Sedan 4D	P73W	25285	2325	2600	3350	4775
LX Sedan 4D	P74W	28830	3225	3575	4125	5675
LX Sport Sedan 4D	P74W	31605	3525	3900	4750	6650
GT—V8 Supercharged—Equipment Schedule 2						
W.B. 106.7"; 5.4 Liter.						
Coupe 2D	P90S	153345	****	****	****	166900
Heritage Coupe 2D	P90S	166345	****	****	****	185900

Body Type	VIN	List	Trade-In Good	Very Good	Pvt-Party Good	Retail Excellent
FOCUS—4-Cyl.—Equipment Schedule 6						
W.B. 102.9"; 2.0 Liter, 2.3 Liter.						
S Hatchback 2D	P31N	14985	2600	2850	3700	5375
ST Sedan 4D	P38Z	17690	3875	4200	5275	7375
FOCUS—4-Cyl.—Equipment Schedule 6						
W.B. 102.9"; 2.0 Liter.						
SES Wagon 4D	P36N	18145	4175	4525	5575	7750
Automatic			300	300	400	400
FOCUS—4-Cyl.—Equipment Schedule 6						
W.B. 102.9"; 2.0 Liter.						
S Sedan 4D	P34N	15110	3100	3400	4300	6150
S Hatchback 4D	P37N	15810	3100	3400	4350	6150
SE Sedan 4D	P34N	16375	3300	3600	4700	6700
SE Hatchback 2D	P31N	16075	3100	3400	4250	6050
SE Hatchback 4D	P37N	17080	3600	3925	4950	6950
SE Wagon 4D	P36N	18095	4050	4400	5425	7550
SES Sedan 4D	P34N	17135	3675	4000	5050	7075
SES Hatchback 2D	P31N	16835	3525	3850	4850	6825
SES Hatchback 4D	P37N	17845	3925	4275	5375	7550
Manual, 5-Spd			(300)	(300)	(400)	(400)
FUSION—4-Cyl.—Equipment Schedule 4						
W.B. 107.4"; 2.3 Liter.						
S Sedan 4D	P06Z	18845	3500	3825	4900	6925
SE Sedan 4D	P07Z	19705	3900	4250	5350	7475
AWD	1,2		775	775	1025	1025
Manual, 5-Spd			(425)	(425)	(565)	(565)
V6, 3.0 Liter	1		625	625	815	815
FUSION—V6—Equipment Schedule 4						
W.B. 107.4"; 3.0 Liter.						
SEL Sedan 4D	P081	22675	4850	5225	6425	8900
AWD	1,2		775	775	1025	1025
Manual, 5-Spd			(425)	(425)	(565)	(565)

Body Type	VIN	List	Trade-In Good	Very Good	Pvt-Party Good	Retail Excellent
4-Cyl. 2.3 Liter	Z		(575)	(575)	(775)	(775)
MUSTANG—V6—Equipment Schedule 4						
W.B. 107.1"; 4.0 Liter.						
Deluxe Coupe 2D	T80N	19995	5600	6050	7050	9300
Deluxe Convertible	T84N	24820	6375	6875	7950	10450
Premium Coupe 2D	T80N	20990	6225	6700	7800	10250
Premium Convertible 2D	T84N	25815	6700	7200	8350	10950
Pony Pkg			150	150	205	205
Manual, 5-Spd			(425)	(425)	(565)	(565)
MUSTANG—V8—Equipment Schedule 4						
W.B. 107.1"; 4.6 Liter.						
GT Deluxe Coupe	T82H	26440	8400	8950	9800	12450
GT Deluxe Convertible	T85H	31265	9725	10350	11350	14350
GT Premium Coupe 2D	T82H	27620	9100	9675	10550	13350
GT Premium Conv 2D	T85H	32445	9875	10500	11600	14800
Shelby Pkg			800	800	1010	1010
MUSTANG SHELBY GT500—V8 Supercharged—Equipment Schedule 4						
W.B. 107.1"; 5.4 Liter.						
Cobra Coupe 2D	T88S	42975	17100	17950	18300	21100
Cobra Convertible 2D	T89S	47800	20200	21100	21400	24700
TAURUS—6-Cyl.—Equipment Schedule 4						
W.B. 108.5"; 3.0 Liter.						
SE Sedan 4D	P53U	21745	2475	2750	3750	5650
SEL Sedan 4D	P56U	23895	2900	3225	4300	6400
FIVE HUNDRED—V6—Equipment Schedule 4						
W.B. 112.9"; 3.0 Liter.						
SEL Sedan 4D	P241	23420	3550	3900	4900	6925
Limited Sedan 4D	P251	26995	3925	4300	5375	7625
AWD	7,8		575	575	775	775
CROWN VICTORIA—V8—Equipment Schedule 4						
W.B. 114.6"; 4.6 Liter.						
Sedan 4D	P73W	25390	2800	3100	3775	5200
LX Sedan 4D	P74W	28385	3625	3950	4750	6500

2008 FORD — (1,2or3)(F7,FAorZV)–(P32N)–8–#

Body Type	VIN	List	Trade-In Good	Very Good	Pvt-Party Good	Retail Excellent
FOCUS—4-Cyl.—Equipment Schedule 6						
W.B. 102.9"; 2.0 Liter.						
S Coupe 2D	P32N	14695	3100	3350	4225	5875
FOCUS—4-Cyl.—Equipment Schedule 6						
W.B. 102.9"; 2.0 Liter.						
S Sedan 4D	P34N	15810	3625	3925	4950	6825
SE Coupe 2D	P33N	16510	4075	4400	5475	7475
SE Sedan 4D	P35N	16810	4275	4600	5650	7675
SES Sedan 4D	P35N	17810	4625	4975	6075	8225
SES Coupe 2D	P33N	17510	4525	4850	6000	8175
Manual, 5-Spd w/Overdrive			(350)	(350)	(470)	(470)
FUSION—4-Cyl.—Equipment Schedule 4						
W.B. 107.4"; 2.3 Liter.						
S Sedan 4D	P06Z	19370	4300	4625	5600	7550
SE Sedan 4D	P07Z	20295	5000	5350	6400	8550
AWD	1,2		825	825	1100	1100
Manual, 5-Spd			(450)	(450)	(600)	(600)
V6, 3.0 Liter	1		650	650	860	860
FUSION—V6—Equipment Schedule 4						
W.B. 107.4"; 3.0 Liter.						
SEL Sedan 4D	P081	22875	5775	6200	7475	9925
AWD	1,2		825	825	1100	1100
Manual, 5-Spd			(450)	(450)	(600)	(600)
4-Cyl, 2.3 Liter	Z		(625)	(625)	(835)	(835)
MUSTANG—V6—Equipment Schedule 4						
W.B. 107.1"; 4.0 Liter.						
Deluxe Coupe 2D	T80N	20990	6000	6450	7400	9475
Deluxe Convertible	T84N	25815	7000	7475	8375	10600
Premium Coupe 2D	T80N	21675	6875	7350	8350	10650
Premium Convertible	T84N	26500	7425	7900	9000	11450
Pony Pkg			175	175	210	210
Manual, 5-Spd w/Overdrive			(450)	(450)	(585)	(585)
MUSTANG—V8—Equipment Schedule 4						
W.B. 107.1"; 4.6 Liter.						
GT Deluxe Coupe	T82H	27230	9450	10000	11050	13850
GT Deluxe Convertible	T85H	32055	10800	11400	12500	15650
GT Premium Coupe	T82H	28215	10300	10900	12000	15000
GT Premium Conv 2D	T85H	33040	11300	11950	13050	16300

2008 FORD

Body Type	VIN	List	Trade-In Good	Very Good	Pvt-Party Good	Retail Excellent
Bullitt Pkg			825	825	1030	1030
Shelby GT Pkg			850	850	1075	1075
MUSTANG SHELBY GT500—V8 Supercharged—Equipment Schedule 4						
W.B. 107.1"; 5.4 Liter.						
Coupe 2D	T88S	43975	19300	20100	20300	23000
Convertible 2D	T89S	48800	22100	23000	23100	26200
TAURUS—V6—Equipment Schedule 4						
W.B. 112.9"; 3.5 Liter.						
SEL Sedan 4D	P24W	23995	4900	5275	6250	8350
Limited Sedan 4D	P25W	27980	5375	5775	6850	9175
AWD	7,8		1250	1250	1675	1675
CROWN VICTORIA—V8—Equipment Schedule 4						
W.B. 114.7"; 4.6 Liter.						
Sedan 4D	P73V	26150	3775	4100	4775	6250
LX Sedan 4D	P74V	29145	4675	5050	5725	7450

2009 FORD — (1,2or3)(F7,FAorZV)-(P34N)-9-#

Body Type	VIN	List	Trade-In Good	Very Good	Pvt-Party Good	Retail Excellent
FOCUS—4-Cyl.—Equipment Schedule 6						
W.B. 102.9"; 2.0 Liter.						
S Sedan 4D	P34N	16505	4350	4675	5650	7525
SE Coupe 2D	P33N	17690	5250	5600	6550	8525
SE Sedan 4D	P35N	17690	5175	5550	6700	8750
SES Coupe 2D	P33N	19080	5750	6125	7300	9475
SES Sedan 4D	P35N	19080	5925	6325	7500	9725
SEL Sedan 4D	P35N	19480	5975	6375	7550	9775
Manual, 5-Spd w/Overdrive			(375)	(375)	(500)	(500)
FUSION—4-Cyl.—Equipment Schedule 4						
W.B. 107.4"; 2.3 Liter.						
S Sedan 4D	P06Z	18860	5450	5800	6775	8825
SE Sedan 4D	P07Z	20000	5975	6375	7550	9775
AWD	1,2		875	875	1175	1175
Manual, 5-Spd w/Overdrive			(500)	(500)	(665)	(665)
V6, 3.0 Liter	1		675	675	905	905
FUSION—V6—Equipment Schedule 4						
W.B. 107.4"; 3.0 Liter.						
SEL Sedan 4D	P081	24065	7425	7875	9275	11900
AWD	1,2		875	875	1175	1175
4-Cyl, 2.3 Liter	Z		(675)	(675)	(895)	(895)
MUSTANG—V6—Equipment Schedule 4						
W.B. 107.1"; 4.0 Liter.						
Deluxe Coupe 2D	T80N	21525	7175	7600	8675	10950
Deluxe Convertible	T84N	26350	8075	8550	9750	12250
Premium Coupe 2D	T80N	23315	8075	8550	9750	12250
Premium Convertible 2D	T84N	28140	8625	9125	10350	12950
Pony Pkg			175	175	220	220
Manual, 5-Spd Overdrive			(500)	(500)	(640)	(640)
MUSTANG—V8—Equipment Schedule 4						
W.B. 107.1"; 4.6 Liter.						
GT Deluxe Coupe	T82H	27220	11150	11750	13050	16150
GT Deluxe Convertible	T85H	32045	12550	13200	14450	17750
GT Premium Coupe	T82H	29170	12050	12700	14050	17400
GT Premium Conv 2D	T85H	34780	13050	13700	15050	18450
Bullitt Pkg			850	850	1085	1085
MUSTANG SHELBY GT500—V8 Supercharged—Equipment Schedule 4						
W.B. 107.1"; 5.4 Liter.						
Coupe 2D	T88S	43480	21600	22500	22600	25400
Convertible 2D	T89S	48305	24300	25300	25400	28500
TAURUS—V6—Equipment Schedule 4						
W.B. 112.9"; 3.5 Liter.						
SE Sedan 4D	P23W	24950	6425	6850	7900	10050
SEL Sedan 4D	P24W	26250	6725	7175	8225	10450
Limited Sedan 4D	P25W	30250	7800	8275	9500	12050
AWD	6,7,8		1350	1350	1795	1795
CROWN VICTORIA—V8—Equipment Schedule 4						
W.B. 114.7"; 4.6 Liter.						
LX Sedan 4D	P74V	30080	7550	8000	9075	11400

2010 FORD — (1,2or3)(FAorZV)(P3EN)-A-#

Body Type	VIN	List	Trade-In Good	Very Good	Pvt-Party Good	Retail Excellent
FOCUS—4-Cyl.—Equipment Schedule 6						
W.B. 102.9"; 2.0 Liter.						
S Sedan 4D	P3EN	17505	5375	5750	6800	8675
SE Coupe 2D	P3CN	18385	5875	6250	7250	9125

Body Type	VIN	List	Trade-In Good	Very Good	Pvt-Party Good	Retail Excellent
SE Sedan 4D	P3FN	18385	6225	6625	7725	9800
SES Coupe 2D	P3DN	19995	7125	7550	8600	10750
SES Sedan 4D	P3GN	19995	7025	7450	8475	10600
SEL Sedan 4D	P3HN	19995	7075	7500	8550	10700
Manual, 5-Spd w/Overdrive			(475)	(475)	(625)	(625)

FUSION—4-Cyl.—Equipment Schedule 4
W.B. 107.4"; 2.5 Liter.

S Sedan 4D	P0GA	19995	6550	6950	8150	10350
SE Sedan 4D	P0HA	21270	7400	7825	9175	11600
V6, Flex Fuel, 3.0 Liter	G		725	725	955	955

FUSION—4-Cyl. Hybrid—Equipment Schedule 4
W.B. 107.4"; 2.5 Liter.

| Sedan 4D | P0L3 | 27995 | 10350 | 10850 | 11800 | 14150 |

FUSION—V6 Flex Fuel—Equipment Schedule 4
W.B. 107.4"; 3.0 Liter.

SEL Sedan 4D	P0JG	26310	8550	9025	10450	13150
AWD	C,D		1000	1000	1330	1330
4-Cyl, 2.5 Liter	A		(625)	(625)	(840)	(840)

FUSION—V6—Equipment Schedule 4
W.B. 107.4"; 3.5 Liter.

| Sport Sedan 4D | P0KC | 26550 | 9275 | 9775 | 11350 | 14250 |
| AWD | C,D | | 1000 | 1000 | 1335 | 1335 |

MUSTANG—V6—Equipment Schedule 4
W.B. 107.1"; 4.0 Liter.

Coupe 2D	P8AN	22840	9200	9675	11000	13600
Convertible 2D	P8EN	27840	10000	10500	11850	14650
Premium Coupe 2D	P8AN	25245	10200	10700	12100	14900
Premium Conv 2D	P8EN	30245	10700	11250	12600	15550
Pony Pkg			175	175	235	235
Manual, 5-Spd w/Overdrive			(500)	(500)	(655)	(655)

MUSTANG—V8—Equipment Schedule 4
W.B. 107.1"; 4.6 Liter.

GT Coupe 2D	P8CH	28845	13150	13800	15050	18100
GT Convertible 2D	P8FH	34840	15250	15950	17150	20400
GT Premium Coupe 2D	P8CH	31845	14250	14950	16250	19500
GT Premium Conv.	P8FH	37245	15550	16250	17500	20800

MUSTANG SHELBY GT500—V8 Supercharged—Equipment Schedule 4
W.B. 107.1"; 4.6 Liter.

| Coupe 2D | P8JS | 47575 | 26600 | 27600 | 28100 | 31800 |
| Convertible 2D | P8KS | 52575 | 27200 | 28200 | 28700 | 32400 |

TAURUS—V6—Equipment Schedule 4
W.B. 112.9"; 3.5 Liter.

SE Sedan 4D	P2DW	25995	10050	10600	11600	13950
SEL Sedan 4D	P2EW	27995	10450	11000	12050	14500
Limited Sedan 4D	P2FW	31995	11450	12000	13150	15850
AWD	H,J		1425	1425	1770	1770

TAURUS AWD—V6 EcoBoost Twin Turbo—Equipment Schedule 4
W.B. 112.9"; 3.5 Liter.

| SHO Sedan 4D | P2KT | 37995 | 14400 | 15050 | 16050 | 18850 |

CROWN VICTORIA—V8 Flex Fuel—Equipment Schedule 4
W.B. 114.7"; 4.6 Liter.

| LX Sedan 4D | P7EV | 30780 | 9350 | 9825 | 10700 | 12900 |

2011 FORD — (1,2or3)(FAorZV)(P4AJ)–B–#

FIESTA—4-Cyl.—Equipment Schedule 6
W.B. 98.0"; 1.6 Liter.

S Sedan 4D	P4AJ	13995	5125	5475	6450	8150
SE Sedan 4D	P4EJ	14995	6275	6675	7675	9650
SE Hatchback 4D	P4EJ	15995	6250	6650	7700	9725
SEL Sedan 4D	P4CJ	16995	6625	7025	8100	10250
SES Hatchback 4D	P4FJ	17795	6700	7100	8225	10400
Automatic, 6-Spd w/OD			450	450	600	600

FOCUS—4-Cyl.—Equipment Schedule 6
W.B. 102.9"; 2.0 Liter.

S Sedan 4D	P3EN	18180	5900	6275	7325	9275
SE Sedan 4D	P3FN	18810	6700	7100	8325	10450
SES Sedan 4D	P3GN	20410	7950	8400	9550	11800
Manual, 5-Spd w/Overdrive			(500)	(500)	(655)	(655)

FOCUS—4-Cyl.—Equipment Schedule 4
W.B. 102.9"; 2.0 Liter.

| SEL Sedan 4D | P3HN | 20395 | 7800 | 8250 | 9375 | 11600 |

FUSION—4-Cyl.—Equipment Schedule 4
W.B. 107.4"; 2.5 Liter.

2011 FORD

Body Type	VIN	List	Trade-In Good	Very Good	Pvt-Party Good	Retail Excellent
S Sedan 4D	P0GA	21295	**7900**	**8325**	**9700**	**12150**
SE Sedan 4D	P0HA	22975	**8825**	**9275**	**10750**	**13400**
AWD	C		675	675	860	860
V6, Flex Fuel, 3.0 Liter	G		750	750	980	980
FUSION—4-Cyl. Hybrid—Equipment Schedule 4						
W.B. 107.4"; 2.5 Liter.						
Sedan 4D	P0L3	28825	**11600**	**12150**	**13100**	**15500**
FUSION—V6—Equipment Schedule 4						
W.B. 107.4"; 3.5 Liter.						
SEL Sedan 4D	P0JG	27140	**9975**	**10450**	**12100**	**15000**
AWD	C		675	675	860	860
4-Cyl, 2.5 Liter	A		(675)	(675)	(875)	(875)
FUSION—V6—Equipment Schedule 4						
W.B. 107.4"; 3.5 Liter.						
Sport Sedan 4D	P0KC	27380	**10850**	**11350**	**13050**	**16250**
AWD	D		675	675	865	865
MUSTANG—V6—Equipment Schedule 4						
W.B. 107.1"; 3.7 Liter.						
Coupe 2D	P8AM	23990	**10250**	**10750**	**12150**	**14850**
Convertible 2D	P8EM	28990	**11100**	**11600**	**13050**	**15900**
Premium Coupe 2D	P8AM	26695	**11050**	**11550**	**13000**	**15850**
Premium Conv 2D	P8EM	31695	**11750**	**12300**	**13850**	**16850**
Pony Pkg			200	200	240	240
Manual, 6-Spd w/Overdrive			(550)	(550)	(695)	(695)
MUSTANG—V8—Equipment Schedule 4						
W.B. 107.1"; 5.0 Liter.						
GT Coupe 2D	P8CF	30495	**15750**	**16450**	**17600**	**20700**
GT Convertible 2D	P8FF	35495	**18100**	**18900**	**20000**	**23400**
GT Premium Coupe 2D	P8CF	33695	**17050**	**17750**	**18900**	**22100**
GT Premium Conv 2D	P8FF	38695	**18500**	**19300**	**20400**	**23800**
Brembo Brake Pkg			400	400	465	465
MUSTANG SHELBY GT500—V8 Supercharged—Equipment Schedule 4						
W.B. 107.1"; 5.4 Liter.						
Coupe 2D	P8JS	49495	**30100**	**31200**	**31700**	**35500**
Convertible 2D	P8KS	54495	**32700**	**33900**	**34300**	**38400**
TAURUS—V6—Equipment Schedule 4						
W.B. 112.9"; 3.5 Liter.						
SE Sedan 4D	P2DW	25995	**11200**	**11750**	**12800**	**15200**
SEL Sedan 4D	P2EW	28195	**11500**	**12050**	**13250**	**15800**
Limited Sedan 4D	P2FW	32595	**11700**	**12250**	**13500**	**16100**
AWD	H		1525	1525	1885	1885
TAURUS AWD—V6 EcoBoost Twin Turbo—Equipment Schedule 4						
W.B. 112.9"; 3.5 Liter.						
SHO Sedan 4D	P2KT	38595	**15900**	**16550**	**17500**	**20200**
CROWN VICTORIA—V8 Flex Fuel—Equipment Schedule 4						
W.B. 114.7"; 4.6 Liter.						
LX Sedan 4D	P7EV	30780	**10300**	**10800**	**11850**	**14100**

2012 FORD — (1,2or3)FAor1ZV-(P4AJ)-C-#

FIESTA—4-Cyl.—Equipment Schedule 4						
W.B. 98.0"; 1.6 Liter.						
S Sedan 4D	P4AJ	13995	**5925**	**6275**	**7300**	**9150**
S Hatchback 4D	P4TJ	14895	**6425**	**6800**	**7875**	**9850**
SE Sedan 4D	P4BJ	15195	**7075**	**7475**	**8550**	**10600**
SE Hatchback 4D	P4EJ	16195	**7150**	**7550**	**8675**	**10800**
SEL Sedan 4D	P4CJ	17295	**7625**	**8050**	**9250**	**11500**
SES Hatchback 4D	P4FJ	18195	**7825**	**8250**	**9400**	**11650**
Automatic, 6-Spd			475	475	635	635
FOCUS—4-Cyl.—Equipment Schedule 6						
W.B. 104.3"; 2.0 Liter.						
S Sedan 4D	P3E2	18090	**7650**	**8075**	**9100**	**11100**
SE Sedan 4D	P3F2	19090	**8550**	**9000**	**10150**	**12400**
SE Hatchback 4D	P3K2	19885	**8950**	**9425**	**10500**	**12800**
Titanium Sedan 4D	P3J2	22995	**11000**	**11550**	**12800**	**15550**
Titanium Hatchback 4D	P3N2	23490	**11150**	**11650**	**13000**	**15800**
Manual, 5-Spd			(475)	(475)	(610)	(610)
FOCUS—4-Cyl.—Equipment Schedule 6						
W.B. 104.3"; 2.0 Liter.						
SEL Sedan 4D	P3H2	20995	**9300**	**9775**	**10950**	**13300**
SEL Hatchback 4D	P3M2	21790	**9600**	**10100**	**11250**	**13700**
FOCUS—AC Electric—Equipment Schedule 6						
W.B. 104.3".						
Hatchback 4D	P3R4	39995	**12800**	**13350**	**14350**	**16650**

EQUIPMENT & MILEAGE PAGE 9 TO 23

Body Type	VIN	List	Trade-In Good	Very Good	Pvt-Party Good	Retail Excellent
FUSION—4-Cyl.—Equipment Schedule 4						
W.B. 107.4"; 2.5 Liter.						
S Sedan 4D	P0GA	20645	**9300**	**9750**	**11250**	**13850**
SE Sedan 4D	P0HA	23625	**10150**	**10600**	**12150**	**14950**
AWD	C		700	700	880	880
V6, Flex Fuel, 3.0 Liter	G		750	750	955	955
FUSION—4-Cyl. Hybrid—Equipment Schedule 4						
W.B. 107.4"; 2.5 Liter.						
Sedan 4D	P0L3	29395	**12200**	**12750**	**13750**	**16150**
FUSION—V6—Equipment Schedule 4						
W.B. 107.4"; 3.5 Liter.						
SEL Sedan 4D	P0JG	27480	**11300**	**11800**	**13550**	**16600**
AWD	C		700	700	880	880
4-Cyl, 2.5 Liter	A		(700)	(700)	(905)	(905)
FUSION—V6—Equipment Schedule 4						
W.B. 107.4"; 3.5 Liter.						
Sport Sedan 4D	P0KC	27945	**12450**	**13000**	**14850**	**18200**
AWD	D		700	700	885	885
MUSTANG—V6—Equipment Schedule 4						
W.B. 107.1"; 3.7 Liter.						
Premium Coupe 2D	P8AM	27890	**12550**	**13100**	**14750**	**17900**
Premium Convertible	P8EM	32890	**13150**	**13700**	**15450**	**18700**
MUSTANG—V8—Equipment Schedule 4						
W.B. 107.1"; 5.0 Liter.						
GT Premium Coupe 2D	P8CF	34505	**18500**	**19250**	**20400**	**23700**
GT Premium Conv 2D	P8FF	39505	**20100**	**20900**	**22000**	**25400**
Boss 302 Coupe 2D	P8CU	40995	**27300**	**28300**	**28800**	**32300**
Brembo Brake Pkg			450	450	525	525
MUSTANG SHELBY GT500—V8 Supercharged—Equipment Schedule 4						
W.B. 107.1"; 5.4 Liter.						
Coupe 2D	P8JS	49495	**32700**	**33900**	**34400**	**38400**
Convertible 2D	P8KS	54495	**35600**	**36900**	**37300**	**41600**
TAURUS—V6—Equipment Schedule 4						
W.B. 112.9"; 3.5 Liter.						
SE Sedan 4D	P2DW	26350	**12450**	**12950**	**14100**	**16550**
SEL Sedan 4D	P2EW	28550	**12650**	**13200**	**14400**	**17000**
Limited Sedan 4D	P2FW	32950	**12950**	**13500**	**14800**	**17450**
AWD	H		1600	1600	1930	1930
TAURUS AWD—V6 EcoBoost Twin Turbo—Equipment Schedule 4						
W.B. 112.9"; 3.5 Liter.						
SHO Sedan 4D	P2KT	38950	**17950**	**18600**	**19800**	**22900**
2013 FORD — (1,2or3)FAor1ZV–(P4AJ)–D–#						
FIESTA—4-Cyl.—Equipment Schedule 6						
W.B. 98.0"; 1.6 Liter.						
S Sedan 4D	P4AJ	13995	**7100**	**7500**	**8650**	**10750**
S Hatchback 4D	P4TJ	14995	**7600**	**8025**	**9225**	**11450**
SE Sedan 4D	P4BJ	15995	**7950**	**8375**	**9600**	**11900**
SE Hatchback 4D	P4EJ	16995	**8300**	**8725**	**9975**	**12350**
Titanium Sedan 4D	P4CJ	17995	**9200**	**9675**	**10850**	**13250**
Titanium Hatchback 4D	P4FJ	18995	**9650**	**10150**	**11300**	**13750**
Automatic, 6-Spd			500	500	665	665
FOCUS—4-Cyl.—Equipment Schedule 6						
W.B. 104.3"; 2.0 Liter.						
S Sedan 4D	P3E2	16995	**9075**	**9525**	**10650**	**12900**
SE Sedan 4D	P3R2	18995	**9950**	**10450**	**11700**	**14150**
SE Hatchback 4D	P3K2	19995	**10350**	**10850**	**12000**	**14450**
Titanium Sedan 4D	P3J2	23995	**12550**	**13150**	**14400**	**17200**
Titanium Hatchback 4D	P3N2	24995	**12850**	**13450**	**14700**	**17600**
Manual, 5-Spd			(500)	(500)	(635)	(635)
FOCUS ST—4-Cyl. Turbo EcoBoost—Equipment Schedule 6						
W.B. 104.3"; 2.0 Liter.						
Hatchback 4D	P3L9	24495	**15800**	**16450**	**17350**	**19800**
FOCUS—AC Electric—Equipment Schedule 6						
W.B. 104.3".						
Hatchback 4D	P3R4	39995	**13750**	**14300**	**15350**	**17700**
C-MAX—4-Cyl. Hybrid—Equipment Schedule 4						
W.B. 104.3"; 2.0 Liter.						
SE Wagon 4D	P5AU	25995	**11700**	**12200**	**13300**	**15500**
SEL Wagon 4D	P5BU	28995	**13700**	**14300**	**15450**	**17900**
C-MAX ENERGI—4-Cyl. Hybrid—Equipment Schedule 3						
W.B. 104.3"; 2.0 Liter.						
SEL Wagon 4D	P5CU	33745	**14200**	**14800**	**15900**	**18400**

Body Type	VIN	List	Trade-In Good	Very Good	Pvt-Party Good	Retail Excellent
FUSION—4-Cyl.—Equipment Schedule 4						
W.B. 112.2"; 2.5 Liter.						
S Sedan 4D	P0G7	22495	11550	12050	13200	15600
SE Sedan 4D	P0H7	24495	12750	13300	14550	17150
4-Cyl EcoBoost Turbo 1.6L	R		150	150	170	170
4-Cyl EcoBoost Turbo 2.0L	9		175	175	215	215
FUSION—4-Cyl. Hybrid—Equipment Schedule 4						
W.B. 112.2"; 2.0 Liter.						
SE Sedan 4D	P0LU	27995	15500	16150	17200	19850
FUSION—4-Cyl. Turbo EcoBoost—Equipment Schedule 4						
W.B. 112.2"; 2.0 Liter.						
Titanium Sedan 4D	P0K9	30995	15250	15900	17350	20400
AWD	D		725	725	855	855
FUSION ENERGI—4-Cyl. Plug-In Hybrid—Equipment Schedule 4						
W.B. 112.2"; 2.0 Liter.						
SE Sedan 4D	P0PU	39495	18300	19000	20000	22900
Titanium Sedan 4D	P0SU	40995	19800	20500	21600	24700
MUSTANG—V6—Equipment Schedule 4						
W.B. 107.1"; 3.7 Liter.						
Coupe 2D	P8AM	22995	13000	13550	15000	17750
Convertible 2D	P8EM	27995	13800	14350	15850	18750
Premium Coupe 2D	P8AM	26995	14000	14550	16050	18950
Premium Conv 2D	P8EM	31995	14700	15300	16800	19850
MUSTANG—V8—Equipment Schedule 4						
W.B. 107.1"; 5.0 Liter.						
GT Coupe 2D	P8CF	32290	19650	20400	21100	23800
GT Convertible 2D	P8FF	37290	22400	23300	23900	27000
GT Premium Coupe 2D	P8CF	35095	21200	22000	22600	25500
GT Premium Conv 2D	P8FF	40095	23000	23900	24500	27600
Boss 302 Coupe 2D	P8CU	42995	31500	32600	32700	36000
Brembo Brake Pkg			500	500	550	550
MUSTANG SHELBY GT500—V8 Supercharged—Equipment Schedule 4						
W.B. 107.1"; 5.4 Liter.						
Coupe 2D	P8JZ	54995	43700	45200	45100	49700
Convertible 2D	P8KZ	59995	46600	48200	48000	52900
TAURUS—V6—Equipment Schedule 4						
W.B. 112.9"; 3.5 Liter.						
SE Sedan 4D	P2D8	27395	13100	13650	14950	17400
SEL Sedan 4D	P2E8	29595	13350	14100	15500	18150
Limited Sedan 4D	P2F8	33795	14250	14800	16250	19050
AWD			1650	1650	1985	1985
4-Cyl EcoBoost Turbo 2.0L	9		175	175	215	215
TAURUS AWD—V6 Twin Turbo EcoBoost—Equipment Schedule 4						
W.B. 112.9"; 3.5 Liter.						
SHO Sedan 4D	P2KT	39995	21900	22600	23700	27000

Body Type	VIN	List	Trade-In Good	Very Good	Pvt-Party Good	Retail Excellent
FIESTA—4-Cyl.—Equipment Schedule 6						
W.B. 98.0"; 1.6 Liter.						
S Sedan 4D	P4AJ	14795	7375	7775	9025	11200
S Hatchback 4D	P4TJ	15395	7675	8100	9400	11700
SE Sedan 4D	P4BJ	16245	8450	8900	10150	12500
SE Hatchback 4D	P4EJ	16845	8950	9425	10550	12900
Titanium Sedan 4D	P4CJ	18995	9400	9875	11150	13600
Titanium Hatchback 4D	P4FJ	19595	9800	10300	11500	14000
Auto, 6-Spd SelectShift			525	525	690	690
FIESTA—4-Cyl. Turbo EcoBoost—Equipment Schedule 6						
W.B. 98.0"; 1.6 Liter.						
ST Hatchback 4D	P4GX	22195	15000	15650	16550	19200
FOCUS—4-Cyl.—Equipment Schedule 6						
W.B. 104.3"; 2.0 Liter.						
S Sedan 4D	P3E2	17105	9950	10450	11700	14150
SE Sedan 4D	P3F2	19310	10850	11400	12550	15050
SE Hatchback 4D	P3K2	19910	11050	11600	12750	15250
Titanium Sedan 4D	P3J2	24310	13350	13950	15250	18100
Titanium Hatchback 4D	P3N2	24910	13650	14250	15550	18400
Manual, 5-Spd			(525)	(525)	(650)	(650)
FOCUS ST—4-Cyl. EcoBoost Turbo—Equipment Schedule 6						
W.B. 104.3"; 2.0 Liter.						
Hatchback 4D	P3L9	24495	16800	17450	18450	21200
FOCUS—AC Electric—Equipment Schedule 6						
W.B. 104.3".						
Hatchback 4D	P3R4	39995	14650	15250	16250	18700

Body Type	VIN	List	Trade-In Good	Very Good	Pvt-Party Good	Retail Excellent
C-MAX—4-Cyl. Hybrid—Equipment Schedule 4						
W.B. 104.3"; 2.0 Liter.						
SE Wagon 4D	P5AU	25995	13700	14250	15300	17600
SEL Wagon 4D	P5BU	29280	15950	16600	17600	20200
C-MAX ENERGI—4-Cyl. Hybrid—Equipment Schedule 3						
W.B. 104.3"; 2.0 Liter.						
SEL Wagon 4D	P5CU	33745	17150	17800	18700	21300
FUSION—4-Cyl.—Equipment Schedule 4						
W.B. 112.2"; 2.5 Liter.						
S Sedan 4D	P0G7	22695	12400	12950	14900	18250
FUSION—4-Cyl.—Equipment Schedule 4						
W.B. 112.2"; 1.5 Liter.						
SE Sedan 4D	P0H7	24650	13750	14300	16700	20700
4-Cyl EcoBoost Turbo 1.5L	D		125	125	160	160
4-Cyl EcoBoost Turbo 1.6L	R		150	150	195	195
4-Cyl EcoBoost Turbo 2.0L	9		200	200	250	250
FUSION—4-Cyl. Hybrid—Equipment Schedule 4						
W.B. 112.2"; 2.0 Liter.						
S Sedan 4D	P0UU	26995	15750	16350	17550	20300
SE Sedan 4D	P0LU	27995	17550	18250	19350	22300
Titanium Sedan 4D	P0RU	33295	18700	19450	20600	23700
FUSION—4-Cyl. Turbo EcoBoost—Equipment Schedule 4						
W.B. 112.2"; 2.0 Liter.						
Titanium Sedan 4D	P0K9	31295	16100	16750	19600	24400
AWD	D		750	750	1000	1000
FUSION ENERGI—4-Cyl. Plug-In Hybrid—Equipment Schedule 4						
W.B. 112.2"; 2.0 Liter.						
SE Luxury Sedan 4D	P0PU	39495	20300	21000	21700	24400
Titanium Sedan 4D	P0SU	41295	21800	22700	23300	26200
Adaptive Cruise Control			500	500	540	540
MUSTANG—V6—Equipment Schedule 4						
W.B. 107.1"; 3.7 Liter.						
Coupe 2D	P8AM	24190	14900	15450	17000	20100
Convertible 2D	P8EM	29190	15700	16250	17800	21000
Premium Coupe 2D	P8AM	28190	15900	16450	18000	21200
Premium Convertible	P8EM	33190	16750	17350	18850	22100
Pony Pkg			200	200	240	240
Manual, 6-Spd			(625)	(625)	(755)	(755)
MUSTANG—V8—Equipment Schedule 4						
W.B. 107.1"; 5.0 Liter.						
GT Coupe 2D	P8CF	31545	21100	21900	22800	25900
GT Convertible 2D	P8FF	37740	23600	24500	25300	28600
GT Premium Coupe 2D	P8CF	35545	22800	23600	24500	27700
GT Premium Conv 2D	P8FF	41740	24600	25500	26400	29900
Brembo Brake Pkg			550	550	615	615
MUSTANG SHELBY GT500—V8 Supercharged—Equipment Schedule 4						
W.B. 107.1"; 5.8 Liter.						
Coupe 2D	P8JZ	55445	45400	46900	46900	51700
Convertible 2D	P8KZ	60445	47900	49500	49800	54900
TAURUS—V6—Equipment Schedule 4						
W.B. 112.9"; 3.5 Liter.						
SE Sedan 4D	P2D8	27495	13850	14350	15900	18700
SEL Sedan 4D	P2E8	29695	15600	16150	17700	20700
Limited Sedan 4D	P2F8	34995	16250	16850	18350	21400
AWD	H		1700	1700	1995	1995
4-Cyl EcoBoost Turbo 2.0L	9		200	200	220	220
TAURUS AWD—V6 Twin Turbo EcoBoost—Equipment Schedule 4						
W.B. 112.9"; 3.5 Liter.						
SHO Sedan 4D	P2KT	40595	22200	22900	24300	27900
Adaptive Cruise Control			500	500	575	575

HONDA

<u>**2000 HONDA**</u> — (1HG,2HGorJHM)(ZE137)-Y-#

Body Type	VIN	List	Trade-In Good	Very Good	Pvt-Party Good	Retail Excellent
INSIGHT—3-Cyl. Hybrid—Equipment Schedule 3						
W.B. 94.5"; 1.0 Liter.						
Hatchback 2D	ZE137	20495	1500	1700	2050	3150
CIVIC—4-Cyl.—Equipment Schedule 6						
W.B. 103.2"; 1.6 Liter.						
CX Hatchback 2D	EJ632	11165	825	925	1475	2425
DX Sedan 4D	EJ652	13300	1225	1375	1950	3125

2000 HONDA

Body Type	VIN	List	Trade-In Good	Very Good	Pvt-Party Good	Retail Excellent
DX Coupe 2D	EJ612	13095	1125	1250	1825	2925
DX Hatchback 2D	EJ634	12615	1025	1150	1700	2725
VP Sedan 4D	EJ661	15145	1525	1700	2300	3700
HX Coupe 2D	EJ712	13915	1275	1425	2000	3225
LX Sedan 4D	EJ657	15345	1350	1500	2100	3375
EX Sedan 4D	EJ854	17245	1625	1800	2450	3900
EX Coupe 2D	EJ814	15965	1575	1750	2375	3800
Si Coupe 2D	EM115	17960	1850	2100	2850	4575

ACCORD—4-Cyl.—Equipment Schedule 3
W.B. 105.1", 106.9" (Sed); 2.3 Liter.

Body Type	VIN	List	Trade-In Good	Very Good	Pvt-Party Good	Retail Excellent
DX Sedan 4D	CF864	16565	825	900	1575	2725
LX Sedan 4D	CG564	19755	1250	1375	2150	3650
LX Coupe 2D	CG324	19755	850	950	1725	3050
SE Sedan 4D	CG567	20905	1425	1575	2375	4025
EX Sedan 4D	CG565	22265	1700	1875	2775	4600
EX Coupe 2D	CG325	22265	1275	1425	2325	4075
Manual, 5-Spd			(175)	(175)	(235)	(235)
V6, VTEC, 3.0 Liter			100	100	135	135

PRELUDE—4-Cyl.—Equipment Schedule 3
W.B. 101.8"; 2.2 Liter.

Body Type	VIN	List	Trade-In Good	Very Good	Pvt-Party Good	Retail Excellent
Coupe 2D	BB614	23915	1725	1925	2600	4125
Type SH Coupe 2D	BB615	26415	2000	2225	3000	4725
Automatic			125	125	165	165

S2000—4-Cyl.—Equipment Schedule 2
W.B. 94.5"; 2.0 Liter.

Body Type	VIN	List	Trade-In Good	Very Good	Pvt-Party Good	Retail Excellent
Convertible 2D	AP114	32415	4200	4600	5400	7750
Hard Top			425	425	565	565

2001 HONDA — (1HGorJHM)(ZE135)-1-#

INSIGHT—3-Cyl. Hybrid—Equipment Schedule 3
W.B. 94.5"; 1.0 Liter.

Body Type	VIN	List	Trade-In Good	Very Good	Pvt-Party Good	Retail Excellent
Hatchback 2D	ZE135	20620	1725	1925	2375	3675

CIVIC—4-Cyl.—Equipment Schedule 6
W.B. 103.1"; 1.7 Liter.

Body Type	VIN	List	Trade-In Good	Very Good	Pvt-Party Good	Retail Excellent
DX Sedan 4D	ES152	13400	1350	1475	2050	3300
DX Coupe 2D	EM212	13200	1250	1375	1925	3100
HX Coupe 2D	EM217	14000	1400	1525	2125	3400
LX Sedan 4D	ES165	15450	1725	1875	2550	4050
LX Coupe 2D	EM225	15250	1675	1825	2475	3950
EX Sedan 4D	ES267	17350	1925	2125	2925	4625
EX Coupe 2D	EM229	16850	1875	2075	2875	4525
GX Sedan 4D	EN264	20670	1875	2075	2525	3875

ACCORD—4-Cyl.—Equipment Schedule 3
W.B. 105.1", 106.9" (Sed); 2.3 Liter.

Body Type	VIN	List	Trade-In Good	Very Good	Pvt-Party Good	Retail Excellent
DX Sedan 4D	CF864	16640	875	975	1650	2850
VP Sedan 4D	CF866	17640	1075	1175	1925	3275
LX Sedan 4D	CG564	20030	1425	1575	2375	4000
LX Coupe 2D	CG324	20030	975	1100	1850	3200
EX Sedan 4D	CG565	22640	1900	2075	3125	5125
EX Coupe 2D	CG325	22640	1500	1675	2575	4400
Manual, 5-Spd	1,5		(200)	(200)	(265)	(265)
V6, VTEC, 3.0 Liter			100	100	135	135

PRELUDE—4-Cyl.—Equipment Schedule 3
W.B. 101.8"; 2.2 Liter.

Body Type	VIN	List	Trade-In Good	Very Good	Pvt-Party Good	Retail Excellent
Coupe 2D	BB614	24040	2150	2375	3075	4725
Type SH Coupe 2D	BB615	26540	2450	2700	3525	5425
Automatic			125	125	165	165

S2000—4-Cyl.—Equipment Schedule 2
W.B. 94.5"; 2.0 Liter.

Body Type	VIN	List	Trade-In Good	Very Good	Pvt-Party Good	Retail Excellent
Convertible 2D	AP114	32740	5150	5625	6525	9050
Hard Top			450	450	615	615

2002 HONDA — (1HG,SHHorJHM)(ZE135)-2-#

INSIGHT—3-Cyl. Hybrid—Equipment Schedule 3
W.B. 94.5"; 1.0 Liter.

Body Type	VIN	List	Trade-In Good	Very Good	Pvt-Party Good	Retail Excellent
Hatchback 2D	ZE135	21720	1700	1925	2525	3950

CIVIC—4-Cyl.—Equipment Schedule 6
W.B. 101.2", 103.1" (Sed & Cpe); 1.7 Liter, 2.0 Liter.

Body Type	VIN	List	Trade-In Good	Very Good	Pvt-Party Good	Retail Excellent
DX Sedan 4D	ES151	13450	1550	1725	2375	3800
DX Coupe 2D	EM212	13250	1450	1600	2375	3900
HX Coupe 2D	EM217	14050	1625	1800	2475	3925
LX Sedan 4D	ES166	15550	1900	2100	3050	4875

Body Type	VIN	List	Trade-In Good	Trade-In Very Good	Pvt-Party Good	Retail Excellent
LX Coupe 2D	EM225	15350	1850	2050	2925	4675
EX Sedan 4D	ES267	17450	2250	2475	3375	5250
EX Coupe 2D	EM229	16950	2200	2425	3300	5150
Si Hatchback 2D	EP335	19440	2325	2625	3325	5150
ACCORD—4-Cyl.—Equipment Schedule 3						
W.B. 105.1", 106.9" (Sed); 2.3 Liter.						
DX Sedan 4D	CF864	16740	1075	1175	1825	3025
VP Sedan 4D	CF866	17740	1400	1525	2225	3650
LX Sedan 4D	CG564	20130	1775	1950	2825	4525
LX Coupe 2D	CG324	20130	1300	1450	2175	3650
SE Sedan 4D	CG567	21290	2100	2300	3250	5150
SE Coupe 2D	CG320	21290	1600	1800	2575	4250
EX Sedan 4D	CG566	22740	2400	2625	3650	5750
EX Coupe 2D	CG324	22740	1825	2050	2975	4875
Manual, 5-Spd	1,5		(200)	(200)	(265)	(265)
V6, VTEC, 3.0 Liter.			175	175	235	235
S2000—4-Cyl.—Equipment Schedule 2						
W.B. 94.5"; 2.0 Liter.						
Convertible 2D	AP114	32840	5700	6200	7075	9725
Hard Top			500	500	660	660

2003 HONDA — (1HG,SHHorJHM)(ZE135)-3-#

	VIN	List	Good	Very Good	Good	Excellent
INSIGHT—3-Cyl. Hybrid—Equipment Schedule 3						
W.B. 94.5"; 1.0 Liter.						
Hatchback 2D	ZE135	21740	1925	2150	2925	4650
CIVIC—4-Cyl.—Equipment Schedule 6						
W.B. 101.2", 103.1" (Sed & Cpe); 1.7 Liter, 2.0 Liter.						
DX Sedan 4D	ES151	13470	1800	1975	2700	4200
DX Coupe 2D	EM212	13270	1800	1975	2875	4600
HX Coupe 2D	EM217	14170	2025	2225	2975	4575
LX Sedan 4D	ES166	15670	2475	2700	3625	5575
LX Coupe 2D	EM225	15470	2375	2600	3450	5300
EX Sedan 4D	ES267	17520	2800	3075	3925	5925
EX Coupe 2D	EM229	17270	2850	3125	4000	6025
Si Hatchback 2D	EP335	19460	3125	3475	4100	6050
CIVIC—4-Cyl. Hybrid—Equipment Schedule 6						
W.B. 103.2"; 1.3 Liter.						
Sedan 4D	ES966	19990	1800	2000	2850	4650
ACCORD—4-Cyl.—Equipment Schedule 3						
W.B. 105.1", 107.9" (Sed); 2.4 Liter.						
DX Sedan 4D	CM551	17060	2875	3175	3950	5850
LX Sedan 4D	CM564	20460	3200	3500	4350	6400
LX Coupe 2D	CM712	20560	2325	2575	3500	5475
EX Sedan 4D	CM556	22860	3975	4325	5450	7950
EX Coupe 2D	CM716	22960	2900	3225	4225	6525
Manual, 5-Spd	1,5		(250)	(250)	(335)	(335)
V6, VTEC, 3.0 Liter.			250	250	335	335
S2000—4-Cyl.—Equipment Schedule 2						
W.B. 94.5"; 2.0 Liter.						
Convertible 2D	AP114	33060	6125	6650	7600	10450
Hard Top			525	525	695	695

2004 HONDA — (1HG,SHHorJHM)(ZE135)-4-#

	VIN	List	Good	Very Good	Good	Excellent
INSIGHT—3-Cyl. Hybrid—Equipment Schedule 3						
W.B. 94.5"; 1.0 Liter.						
Hatchback 2D	ZE135	21870	2100	2325	3200	5050
CIVIC—4-Cyl.—Equipment Schedule 6						
W.B. 101.2", 103.1" (Sed & Cpe); 1.7 Liter, 2.0 Liter.						
DX Sedan 4D	ES151	13500	2375	2625	3350	5025
Value Sedan 4D	ES163	14900	2975	3275	4075	6025
Value Coupe 2D	EM221	13900	2725	3025	3775	5625
HX Coupe 2D	EM217	14200	2675	2950	3700	5525
LX Sedan 4D	ES166	15850	3225	3525	4350	6350
LX Coupe 2D	EM225	15650	3125	3425	4250	6275
EX Sedan 4D	ES267	17750	3500	3825	4750	6875
EX Coupe 2D	EM229	17350	3525	3850	4675	6775
Si Hatchback 2D	EP335	19560	3850	4275	4950	7000
GX Sedan 4D	EN264	21250	2825	3150	3900	5900
CIVIC—4-Cyl. Hybrid—Equipment Schedule 6						
W.B. 103.1"; 1.3 Liter.						
Sedan 4D	ES966	20140	2100	2325	3200	5050

2004 HONDA

Body Type	VIN	List	Trade-In Good	Very Good	Pvt-Party Good	Retail Excellent
ACCORD—4-Cyl.—Equipment Schedule 3						
W.B. 105.1", 107.9" (Sed); 2.4 Liter.						
DX Sedan 4D	CM551	17190	3300	3600	4275	6100
LX Sedan 4D	CM553	20590	3625	3950	4825	6875
LX Coupe 2D	CM712	20690	3000	3325	4150	6175
EX Sedan 4D	CM556	22990	4575	4950	5925	8350
EX Coupe 2D	CM716	23090	3625	4000	4900	7225
Manual, 5-Spd	1,5		(300)	(300)	(400)	(400)
Manual, 5-Spd	1,5		(300)	(300)	(400)	(400)
V6, VTEC, 3.0 Liter			300	300	400	400
S2000—4-Cyl.—Equipment Schedule 2						
W.B. 94.5"; 2.2 Liter.						
Convertible 2D	AP214	33290	6675	7225	8225	11150
Hard Top			575	575	725	725

2005 HONDA — (1HG,SHHorJHM)(ZE137)-5-#

Body Type	VIN	List	Trade-In Good	Very Good	Pvt-Party Good	Retail Excellent
INSIGHT—3-Cyl. Hybrid—Equipment Schedule 3						
W.B. 94.5"; 1.0 Liter.						
Hatchback 2D	ZE137	22045	2275	2525	3475	5300
CIVIC—4-Cyl.—Equipment Schedule 6						
W.B. 101.2", 103.1" (Sed & Cpe); 1.7 Liter, 2.0 Liter.						
DX Sedan 4D	ES151	13675	2850	3150	3975	5725
Value Sedan 4D	ES163	15075	3550	3875	4725	6700
Value Coupe 2D	EM221	14075	3200	3500	4425	6350
HX Coupe 2D	EM217	14375	3150	3450	4225	5975
LX Sedan 4D	ES166	16025	3725	4075	5025	7050
LX Coupe 2D	EM225	15825	3625	3975	4975	7025
LX Special Ed Sed 4D	ES155	16775	3625	3975	4975	7025
LX Special Ed Cpe 2D	EM215	16575	3525	3850	4875	6925
EX Sedan 4D	ES267	17925	4175	4550	5475	7575
EX Coupe 2D	EM220	17525	4275	4650	5575	7675
EX Special Ed Sed 4D	ES257	18375	4425	4800	5725	7825
EX Special Ed Cpe 2D	EM219	17975	4325	4700	5625	7725
Si Hatchback 2D	EP335	19735	4600	5075	5825	8000
GX Sedan 4D	EN264	20910	3350	3700	4550	6575
CIVIC—4-Cyl. Hybrid—Equipment Schedule 6						
W.B. 103.1"; 1.3 Liter.						
Sedan 4D	ES966	20315	2425	2700	3700	5675
ACCORD—4-Cyl.—Equipment Schedule 3						
W.B. 105.1", 107.9" (Sed); 2.4 Liter.						
DX Sedan 4D	CM561	17510	3550	3875	5000	7125
LX Sedan 4D	CM564	20990	4325	4700	5650	7750
LX Coupe 2D	CM723	21090	3625	4000	4950	6975
LX Special Ed Cpe 2D	CM723	25065	4125	4525	5525	7750
EX Sedan 4D	CM567	23415	5150	5550	6725	9300
EX Coupe 2D	CM726	23650	4225	4625	5625	7900
Manual, 5-Spd			(350)	(350)	(465)	(465)
V6, VTEC, 3.0 Liter			350	350	465	465
ACCORD—V6 Hybrid—Equipment Schedule 3						
W.B. 107.9"; 3.0 Liter.						
Sedan 4D	CN364	30655	5875	6325	7775	10750
S2000—4-Cyl.—Equipment Schedule 2						
W.B. 94.5"; 2.2 Liter.						
Convertible 2D	AP214	33465	9425	10150	10950	14150
Hard Top			600	600	740	740

2006 HONDA — (1HG,SHHorJHM)(ZE137)-6-#

Body Type	VIN	List	Trade-In Good	Very Good	Pvt-Party Good	Retail Excellent
INSIGHT—3-Cyl. Hybrid—Equipment Schedule 3						
W.B. 94.5"; 1.0 Liter.						
Hatchback 2D	ZE137	22080	3350	3700	4575	6475
CIVIC—4-Cyl.—Equipment Schedule 6						
W.B. 104.3", 106.3" (Sed); 1.8 Liter, 2.0 Liter.						
DX Sedan 4D	FA162	15110	3725	4050	4925	6775
LX Sedan 4D	FA165	17060	4825	5200	6100	8250
LX Coupe 2D	FG126	16860	4575	4950	5850	7975
EX Sedan 4D	FA168	18810	5325	5725	6600	8825
EX Coupe 2D	FG128	18810	5225	5625	6525	8725
Manual, 5-Spd			(275)	(275)	(365)	(365)
CIVIC—4-Cyl.—Equipment Schedule 6						
W.B. 104.3", 106.3" (Sed); 1.8 Liter, 2.0 Liter.						
DX Coupe 2D	FG112	14910	3450	3750	4625	6550
Si Coupe 2D	FG215	20540	6125	6650	7475	9775

2006 HONDA

Body Type	VIN	List	Trade-In Good	Trade-In Very Good	Pvt-Party Good	Retail Excellent
GX Sedan 4D	FA465	24990	4325	4725	5575	7675
CIVIC—4-Cyl. Hybrid—Equipment Schedule 6						
W.B. 106.3"; 1.3 Liter.						
Sedan 4D	FA362	22400	3525	3900	4775	6725
ACCORD—4-Cyl.—Equipment Schedule 3						
W.B. 105.1", 107.9" (Sed); 2.4 Liter.						
VP Sedan 4D	CM561	19575	4325	4675	5550	7525
LX Sedan 4D	CM564	21375	5375	5775	6575	8725
LX Coupe 2D	CM723	21725	4375	4750	5600	7600
SE Sedan 4D	CM563	22075	5575	5975	6900	9250
EX Sedan 4D	CM567	23800	6125	6575	7825	10450
EX Coupe 2D	CM726	23945	5100	5525	6400	8625
Manual, 5-Spd			(400)	(400)	(535)	(535)
Manual, 6-Spd			0	0	0	0
V6, VTEC, 3.0 Liter			400	400	535	535
ACCORD—V6 Hybrid—Equipment Schedule 3						
W.B. 107.9"; 3.0 Liter.						
Sedan 4D	CN364	31540	7725	8250	9700	12950
S2000—4-Cyl.—Equipment Schedule 2						
W.B. 94.5"; 2.2 Liter.						
Convertible 2D	AP214	34600	9925	10650	11700	15050
Hard Top			625	625	775	775

2007 HONDA — (1HG,SHHorJHM)(GD384)-7-#

Body Type	VIN	List	Trade-In Good	Trade-In Very Good	Pvt-Party Good	Retail Excellent
FIT—4-Cyl. VTEC—Equipment Schedule 6						
W.B. 96.5"; 1.5 Liter.						
Hatchback 4D	GD384	14445	3925	4350	5025	6900
Sport Hatchback 4D	GD386	15765	4550	5025	5725	7775
Manual, 5-Spd			(300)	(300)	(400)	(400)
CIVIC—4-Cyl. VTEC—Equipment Schedule 6						
W.B. 104.3", 106.3" (Sed); 1.8 Liter, 2.0 Liter.						
DX Sedan 4D	FA162	15605	4250	4600	5450	7350
LX Sedan 4D	FA165	17555	5400	5800	6650	8825
LX Coupe 2D	FG126	17355	5350	5725	6625	8775
EX Sedan 4D	FA168	19305	5800	6225	7225	9475
EX Coupe 2D	FG128	19305	5725	6150	7150	9400
Manual, 5-Spd			(300)	(300)	(400)	(400)
CIVIC—4-Cyl. VTEC—Equipment Schedule 6						
W.B. 104.3"; 1.8 Liter.						
DX Coupe 2D	FG112	15405	3675	4000	4975	6875
Automatic	2,6		300	300	400	400
CIVIC—4-Cyl. VTEC—Equipment Schedule 6						
W.B. 104.3", 106.3" (Sed); 1.8 Liter, 2.0 Liter.						
Si Sedan 4D	FA555	21885	7025	7575	8375	10750
Si Coupe 2D	FG215	21685	6925	7475	8250	10550
CIVIC—4-Cyl. Hybrid—Equipment Schedule 6						
W.B. 106.3"; 1.3 Liter.						
Sedan 4D	FA362	23195	4350	4725	5525	7475
CIVIC—4-Cyl. NGV—Equipment Schedule 6						
W.B. 106.3"; 1.8 Liter.						
GX Sedan 4D	FA465	25185	5175	5625	6650	8825
ACCORD—4-Cyl. VTEC—Equipment Schedule 3						
W.B. 105.1", 107.9" (Sed); 2.4 Liter.						
VP Sedan 4D	CM561	20020	4925	5300	6125	8150
LX Sedan 4D	CM564	21520	5650	6075	7100	9325
LX Coupe 2D	CM723	21870	5450	5875	6600	8650
SE Sedan 4D	CM563	22220	6025	6450	7675	10200
EX Sedan 4D	CM567	23945	7000	7475	8650	11300
EX Coupe 2D	CM826	24085	6225	6700	7625	9925
EX-L Sedan 4D	CM665	25685	7700	8200	9525	12500
EX-L Coupe 2D	CM726	25785	6750	7275	8275	10750
Manual, 5-Spd			(425)	(425)	(565)	(565)
V6, VTEC, 3.0 Liter			450	450	600	600
ACCORD—V6 Hybrid—Equipment Schedule 3						
W.B. 107.9"; 3.0 Liter.						
Sedan 4D	CN364	33585	8750	9300	10750	14050
S2000—4-Cyl. VTEC—Equipment Schedule 2						
W.B. 94.5"; 2.2 Liter.						
Convertible 2D	AP214	34845	11350	12150	13000	16450
Hard Top			650	650	800	800

2008 HONDA

Body Type	VIN	List	Trade-In Good	Very Good	Pvt-Party Good	Retail Excellent

2008 HONDA — (1HG,SHHorJHM)(GD384)-8-#

FIT—4-Cyl. VTEC—Equipment Schedule 6
W.B. 96.5"; 1.5 Liter.

Body Type	VIN	List	Good	Very Good	Good	Excellent
Hatchback 4D	GD384	15385	**4825**	**5250**	**5950**	**7850**
Sport Hatchback 4D	GD386	16705	**5300**	**5775**	**6650**	**8750**
Manual, 5-Spd w/Overdrive			**(350)**	**(350)**	**(470)**	**(470)**

CIVIC—4-Cyl. VTEC—Equipment Schedule 6
W.B. 104.3", 106.3" (Sed); 1.8 Liter, 2.0 Liter.

DX Sedan 4D	FA162	15645	**4825**	**5200**	**6025**	**7925**
LX Sedan 4D	FA165	17595	**6050**	**6475**	**7475**	**9600**
LX Coupe 2D	FG126	17395	**5825**	**6225**	**7250**	**9400**
EX Sedan 4D	FA168	19345	**7100**	**7575**	**8500**	**10800**
EX Coupe 2D	FG128	19345	**7175**	**7650**	**8625**	**10900**
EX-L Sedan 4D	FA169	20545	**7175**	**7650**	**8625**	**10900**
EX-L Coupe 2D	FG129	20545	**7250**	**7700**	**8675**	**11000**
Manual, 5-Spd w/Overdrive			**(350)**	**(350)**	**(470)**	**(470)**

CIVIC—4-Cyl. VTEC—Equipment Schedule 6
W.B. 104.3"; 1.8 Liter.

DX Coupe 2D	FG112	15445	**4275**	**4625**	**5575**	**7500**
Automatic, 5-Spd	2,6		**300**	**300**	**400**	**400**

CIVIC—4-Cyl. VTEC—Equipment Schedule 6
W.B. 104.3", 106.3" (Sed); 2.0 Liter.

Si Sedan 4D	FA555	21925	**8300**	**8850**	**9625**	**12050**
Si Coupe 2D	FG215	21725	**8100**	**8625**	**9425**	**11800**
Si Mugen Sedan 4D	FA555	30135	**12400**	**13150**	**13800**	**16850**

CIVIC—4-Cyl. Hybrid—Equipment Schedule 6
W.B. 106.3"; 1.3 Liter.

Sedan 4D	FA362	23235	**5225**	**5625**	**6675**	**8750**

CIVIC—4-Cyl. NGV—Equipment Schedule 6
W.B. 106.3" (Sed); 1.8 Liter.

GX Sedan 4D	FA465	25225	**6425**	**6875**	**7825**	**10100**

ACCORD—4-Cyl. VTEC—Equipment Schedule 3
W.B. 107.9", 110.2" (Sed); 2.4 Liter.

LX Sedan 4D	CP253	21795	**7250**	**7700**	**8550**	**10750**
LX-P Sedan 4D	CP254	22795	**7525**	**8000**	**8950**	**11250**
LX-S Coupe 2D	CS113	23295	**6675**	**7150**	**8050**	**10200**
EX Sedan 4D	CP257	24495	**8625**	**9125**	**10250**	**12950**
EX Coupe 2D	CS117	24594	**7525**	**8025**	**9075**	**11550**
EX-L Sedan 4D	CP258	26495	**9125**	**9650**	**10800**	**13650**
EX-L Coupe 2D	CS118	26595	**8475**	**9000**	**10100**	**12800**
Manual, 5-Spd w/Overdrive			**(450)**	**(450)**	**(570)**	**(570)**
V6, i-VTEC, 3.5 Liter			**0**	**0**	**0**	**0**

S2000—4-Cyl. VTEC—Equipment Schedule 2
W.B. 94.5"; 2.2 Liter.

Convertible 2D	AP214	34935	**12650**	**13450**	**14350**	**17700**
CR Convertible 2D	AP212	37935	**14200**	**15050**	**15800**	**19250**
Hard Top			**650**	**650**	**790**	**790**

2009 HONDA — (1HG,SHHorJHM)(GE882)-9-#

FIT—4-Cyl. VTEC—Equipment Schedule 6
W.B. 98.4"; 1.5 Liter.

Hatchback 4D	GE882	16020	**6150**	**6625**	**7375**	**9300**
Sport Hatchback 4D	GE884	17580	**6825**	**7325**	**8100**	**10200**
Manual, 5-Spd w/Overdrive			**(375)**	**(375)**	**(495)**	**(495)**

CIVIC—4-Cyl. VTEC—Equipment Schedule 6
W.B. 104.3", 106.3" (Sed); 1.8 Liter, 2.0 Liter.

DX Sedan 4D	FA162	16175	**5475**	**5850**	**6850**	**8750**
VP Sedan 4D	FA163	16925	**6300**	**6700**	**7675**	**9675**
LX Sedan 4D	FA165	18125	**7025**	**7450**	**8450**	**10650**
LX Coupe 2D	FG126	17925	**6875**	**7300**	**8275**	**10450**
LX-S Sedan 4D	FA166	18765	**7100**	**7525**	**8575**	**10750**
EX Sedan 4D	FA168	19975	**7925**	**8400**	**9375**	**11650**
EX Coupe 2D	FG128	19975	**7950**	**8425**	**9425**	**11700**
EX-L Sedan 4D	FA169	21525	**8275**	**8750**	**9700**	**12000**
EX-L Coupe 2D	FG129	21525	**8275**	**8750**	**9700**	**12000**
Manual, 5-Spd w/Overdrive			**(375)**	**(375)**	**(500)**	**(500)**

CIVIC—4-Cyl. VTEC—Equipment Schedule 6
W.B. 104.3"; 1.8 Liter.

DX Coupe 2D	FG112	15875	**5150**	**5500**	**6425**	**8350**
Automatic, 5-Spd	2,6		**350**	**350**	**465**	**465**

2009 HONDA

Body Type	VIN	List	Trade-In Good	Very Good	Pvt-Party Good	Retail Excellent
CIVIC—4-Cyl. VTEC—Equipment Schedule 6						
W.B. 104.3", 106.3" (Sed); 2.0 Liter.						
Si Sedan 4D	FA555	22775	9625	10150	11000	13400
Si Coupe 2D	FG215	22575	9425	9975	10850	13200
CIVIC—4-Cyl. Hybrid—Equipment Schedule 6						
W.B. 106.3"; 1.3 Liter.						
Sedan 4D	FA362	24320	6375	6775	7800	9900
CIVIC—4-Cyl. NGV—Equipment Schedule 6						
W.B. 106.3"; 1.8 Liter.						
GX Sedan 4D	FA465	25860	7675	8150	9150	11400
ACCORD—4-Cyl. VTEC—Equipment Schedule 3						
W.B. 107.9", 110.2" (Sed); 2.4 Liter.						
LX Sedan 4D	CP253	22225	8150	8650	9675	12050
LX-P Sedan 4D	CP254	23415	8500	9000	10050	12550
LX-S Coupe 2D	CS113	23275	7650	8125	9250	11600
EX Sedan 4D	CP257	24925	9450	9975	11200	13950
EX Coupe 2D	CS117	24925	8700	9200	10400	13050
EX-L Sedan 4D	CP258	27115	9950	10500	11750	14600
EX-L Coupe 2D	CS118	27215	9400	9925	11250	14050
Manual, 5-Spd w/Overdrive			(500)	(500)	(635)	(635)
V6, i-VTEC, 3.5 Liter.			575	575	735	735
S2000—4-Cyl. VTEC—Equipment Schedule 2						
W.B. 94.5"; 2.2 Liter.						
Convertible 2D	AP214	35665	13950	14800	15650	18950
CR Convertible 2D	AP212	38665	15850	16800	17450	21000
Hard Top			675	675	815	815

2010 HONDA — (1HG,SHHorJHM)(GE8H2)–A–#

Body Type	VIN	List	Trade-In Good	Very Good	Pvt-Party Good	Retail Excellent
FIT—4-Cyl. VTEC—Equipment Schedule 6						
W.B. 98.4"; 1.5 Liter.						
Hatchback 4D	GE8H2	16410	7250	7700	8400	10200
Sport Hatchback 4D	GE8H4	17970	7900	8400	9100	11050
Sport VSA Hatchback	GE8H6	19820	8550	9075	9775	11800
Manual, 5-Spd w/Overdrive			(475)	(475)	(585)	(585)
INSIGHT—4-Cyl. VTEC Hybrid—Equipment Schedule 3						
W.B. 100.4"; 1.3 Liter.						
LX Hatchback 4D	ZE2H5	20510	7725	8150	9225	11400
EX Hatchback 4D	ZE2H7	22010	8250	8700	9925	12300
CIVIC—4-Cyl. VTEC—Equipment Schedule 6						
W.B. 104.3", 106.3" (Sed); 1.8 Liter, 2.0 Liter.						
DX Sedan 4D	FA1F2	16365	6475	6875	7825	9775
VP Sedan 4D	FA1F3	17115	7225	7650	8650	10700
LX Sedan 4D	FA1F5	18315	8125	8575	9575	11800
LX Coupe 2D	FG1B6	18115	7925	8375	9375	11550
LX-S Sedan 4D	FA1F6	18915	8225	8675	9650	11850
EX Sedan 4D	FA1F8	20165	9150	9650	10650	12950
EX Coupe 2D	FG1B8	20165	9075	9575	10500	12800
EX-L Sedan 4D	FA1F9	21715	9350	9875	10900	13250
EX-L Coupe 2D	FG1B9	21715	9250	9775	10800	13150
Manual, 5-Spd w/Overdrive			(475)	(475)	(625)	(625)
CIVIC—4-Cyl. VTEC—Equipment Schedule 6						
W.B. 104.3"; 1.8 Liter.						
DX Coupe 2D	FG1A2	16165	5875	6250	7350	9375
Automatic, 5-Spd	2,6		400	400	520	520
CIVIC—4-Cyl. VTEC—Equipment Schedule 6						
W.B. 104.3"; 1.8 Liter.						
Si Sedan 4D	FA5E5	22965	11400	11950	12800	15250
Si Coupe 2D	FG2A5	22765	11200	11750	12650	15100
CIVIC—4-Cyl. Hybrid—Equipment Schedule 6						
W.B. 106.3"; 1.3 Liter.						
Sedan 4D	FA3F2	24510	8000	8425	9500	11650
CIVIC—4-Cyl. NGV—Equipment Schedule 6						
W.B. 106.3"; 1.8 Liter.						
GX Sedan 4D	FA4F5	26050	9300	9775	10800	13100
ACCORD—4-Cyl. VTEC—Equipment Schedule 3						
W.B. 107.9", 110.2" (Sed); 2.4 Liter.						
LX Sedan 4D	CP2E3	22565	9350	9850	10750	13050
LX-P Sedan 4D	CP2E4	23405	9700	10200	11150	13550
LX-S Coupe 2D	CS1A3	24065	9100	9575	10500	12700
EX Sedan 4D	CP2E7	25340	10550	11100	12150	14700
EX Coupe 2D	CS1A7	25390	9950	10450	11450	13800
EX-L Sedan 4D	CP2E8	27580	11100	11650	12800	15500
EX-L Coupe 2D	CS1A8	27630	11050	11600	12650	15300

2010 HONDA

Body Type	VIN	List	Trade-In Good	Very Good	Pvt-Party Good	Retail Excellent
Manual, 5-Spd w/Overdrive			(500)	(500)	(625)	(625)
V6, i-VTEC, 3.5 Liter			650	650	805	805

2011 HONDA — (1,2,5orJ)(9,HorK)(B,G,MorX)ZF1C4–B–#

CR-Z—4-Cyl. VTEC Hybrid—Equipment Schedule 6
W.B. 95.9"; 1.5 Liter.

Coupe 2D	ZF1C4	20115	8175	8625	9625	11600
EX Coupe 2D	ZF1C6	21675	8725	9175	10150	12200

FIT—4-Cyl. VTEC—Equipment Schedule 6
W.B. 98.4"; 1.5 Liter.

Hatchback 4D	GE8H3	16650	8725	9200	9900	11750
Sport Hatchback 4D	GE8H5	18460	9325	9825	10600	12600
Manual, 5-Spd w/Overdrive			(500)	(500)	(600)	(600)

INSIGHT—4-Cyl. VTEC Hybrid—Equipment Schedule 3
W.B. 100.4"; 1.3 Liter.

Hatchback 4D	ZE2H3	18950	8200	8600	9700	11800
LX Hatchback 4D	ZE2H5	20650	8850	9275	10400	12650
EX Hatchback 4D	ZE2H7	22240	9575	10050	11150	13400

CIVIC—4-Cyl. VTEC—Equipment Schedule 6
W.B. 104.3", 106.3" (Sed); 1.8 Liter.

DX Sedan 4D	FA1F2	16555	7325	7750	8725	10700
VP Sedan 4D	FA1F3	17305	8425	8900	9850	12000
LX Sedan 4D	FA1F5	18505	9175	9675	10750	13050
LX Coupe 2D	FG1B6	18305	8925	9425	10400	12600
LX-S Sedan 4D	FA1F6	19105	9375	9875	10900	13150
EX Sedan 4D	FA1F8	20355	10450	11000	11950	14350
EX Coupe 2D	FG1B8	20355	10350	10850	11850	14250
Manual, 5-Spd w/Overdrive			(500)	(500)	(645)	(645)

CIVIC—4-Cyl. VTEC—Equipment Schedule 6
W.B. 104.3"; 1.8 Liter.

DX Coupe 2D	FG1A2	16355	6675	7075	8125	10150
Automatic, 5-Spd	B		450	450	570	570

CIVIC—4-Cyl. VTEC—Equipment Schedule 6
W.B. 104.3", 106.3" (Sed); 1.8 Liter, 2.0 Liter.

EX-L Sedan 4D	FA1F9	22705	10700	11250	12200	14600
EX-L Coupe 2D	FG1B9	22705	10500	11000	12000	14400
Si Sedan 4D	FB2A5	23155	12400	12950	13900	16400
Si Coupe 2D	FG2A5	22955	12200	12750	13750	16200

CIVIC—4-Cyl. Hybrid—Equipment Schedule 6
W.B. 106.3"; 1.3 Liter.

Sedan 4D	FA3F2	24700	8925	9350	10400	12500

CIVIC—4-Cyl. NGV—Equipment Schedule 6
W.B. 106.3"; 1.8 Liter.

GX Sedan 4D	FA4F5	26240	10200	10700	11750	14000

ACCORD—4-Cyl. VTEC—Equipment Schedule 3
W.B. 107.9", 110.2" (Sed); 2.4 Liter.

LX Sedan 4D	CP2F3	22730	10250	10800	11600	13800
LX-P Sedan 4D	CP2F4	23730	10700	11250	12150	14450
LX-S Coupe 2D	CS1B3	24330	10350	10850	11700	13800
SE Sedan 4D	CP2F6	24480	11150	11700	12550	14900
EX Sedan 4D	CP2F7	25655	11550	12100	13100	15600
EX Coupe 2D	CS1B7	26005	11200	11700	12650	15000
EX-L Sedan 4D	CP2F8	28105	12050	12650	13650	16300
EX-L Coupe 2D	CS1B8	27855	11950	12450	13550	16000
Manual, 5-Spd w/Overdrive			(550)	(550)	(645)	(645)
V6, i-VTEC, 3.5 Liter			865	865	865	865

2012 HONDA — (1,2,5orJ)(9,HorK)(B,G,MorX)ZF1C4–C–#

CR-Z—4-Cyl. i-VTEC Hybrid—Equipment Schedule 6
W.B. 95.9"; 1.5 Liter.

Coupe 2D	ZF1C4	20315	9750	10250	11250	13350
EX Coupe 2D	ZF1C6	21875	10350	10850	11850	14050

FIT—4-Cyl. VTEC—Equipment Schedule 6
W.B. 98.4"; 1.5 Liter.

Hatchback 4D	GE8H3	16745	9475	9925	10750	12700
Sport Hatchback 4D	GE8H5	18530	10500	11000	11800	13950
Manual, 5-Spd	G		(475)	(475)	(565)	(565)

INSIGHT—4-Cyl. VTEC Hybrid—Equipment Schedule 3
W.B. 100.4"; 1.3 Liter.

Hatchback 4D	ZE2H3	19120	8900	9325	10400	12450
LX Hatchback 4D	ZE2H5	20895	9450	9875	11100	13300
EX Hatchback 4D	ZE2H7	22585	10850	11300	12350	14550

2012 HONDA

CIVIC—4-Cyl. VTEC—Equipment Schedule 6
W.B. 105.1"; 1.8 Liter.

Body Type	VIN	List	Good	Very Good	Good	Excellent
LX Sedan 4D	FB2F5	18605	10300	10800	11800	14150
Manual, 5-Spd w/Overdrive	E		(550)	(550)	(680)	(680)

CIVIC—4-Cyl. VTEC—Equipment Schedule 6
W.B. 103.2", 105.1" (Sed); 1.8 Liter.

Body Type	VIN	List	Good	Very Good	Good	Excellent
DX Sedan 4D	FB2E2	16555	8450	8900	9850	11900
DX Coupe 2D	FG3A2	16355	8250	8700	9750	11850
LX Coupe 2D	FG3A5	18405	9550	10050	11050	13250
EX Coupe 2D	FG3B8	21255	11100	11650	12700	15100
Automatic, 5-Spd			475	475	590	590

CIVIC—4-Cyl. VTEC—Equipment Schedule 6
W.B. 103.2", 105.1" (Sed); 1.8 Liter, 2.4 Liter.

Body Type	VIN	List	Good	Very Good	Good	Excellent
HF Sedan 4D	FB2F6	20205	10800	11300	12300	14650
EX Sedan 4D	FB2F8	21255	11350	11900	12900	15300
EX-L Sedan 4D	FB2F9	22705	12300	12900	13850	16350
EX-L Coupe 2D	FG3B9	22705	12150	12700	13650	16100
Si Coupe 2D	FG4A5	22955	13350	13900	15000	17450
Si Sedan 4D	FB6E5	23155	13550	14100	15200	17650

CIVIC—4-Cyl. Hybrid—Equipment Schedule 6
W.B. 105.1"; 1.3 Liter.

Body Type	VIN	List	Good	Very Good	Good	Excellent
Sedan 4D	FB4F2	24800	12000	12500	13550	15850

CIVIC—4-Cyl. NGV—Equipment Schedule 6
W.B. 106.3"; 1.8 Liter.

Body Type	VIN	List	Good	Very Good	Good	Excellent
Sedan 4D	FB5F5	26925	13050	13600	14600	17000

ACCORD—4-Cyl. VTEC—Equipment Schedule 6
W.B. 107.9", 110.2" (Sed); 2.4 Liter.

Body Type	VIN	List	Good	Very Good	Good	Excellent
LX Sedan 4D	CP2F3	23050	11400	12000	12900	15250
LX-P Sedan 4D	CP2F4	24050	11750	12300	13250	15600
LX-S Coupe 2D	CS1B3	24650	11500	12000	13000	15250
SE Sedan 4D	CP2F6	24800	12150	12700	13700	16150
EX Sedan 4D	CP2F7	25975	12750	13350	14300	16900
EX Coupe 2D	CS1B7	26325	12500	13050	14100	16500
EX-L Sedan 4D	CP2F8	28425	13150	13750	14850	17550
EX-L Coupe 2D	CS1B8	28425	13300	13850	15050	17650
Manual, 5-Spd			(575)	(575)	(660)	(660)
V6, 3.5 Liter	2		800	800	920	920

2013 HONDA — (1,2,5orJ)(9,HorK)(B,G,MorX)ZF1C4–D–#

CR-Z—4-Cyl. i-VTEC Hybrid—Equipment Schedule 6
W.B. 95.9"; 1.5 Liter.

Body Type	VIN	List	Good	Very Good	Good	Excellent
Coupe 2D	ZF1C4	20765	10950	11450	12450	14650
EX Coupe 2D	ZF1C6	22445	11550	12050	13200	15500

FIT—4-Cyl. VTEC—Equipment Schedule 6
W.B. 98.4"; 1.5 Liter.

Body Type	VIN	List	Good	Very Good	Good	Excellent
Hatchback 4D	GE8G3	16115	10500	11000	11700	13550
Sport Hatchback 4D	GE8G5	17850	11300	11800	12550	14550
Automatic, 5-Spd	G		500	500	580	580

FIT EV—AC Electric—Equipment Schedule 6
W.B. 98.4".

Body Type	VIN	List	Good	Very Good	Good	Excellent
Hatchback 4D	ZA2H4	37415				

INSIGHT—4-Cyl. Hybrid—Equipment Schedule 3
W.B. 100.4"; 1.3 Liter.

Body Type	VIN	List	Good	Very Good	Good	Excellent
Hatchback 4D	ZE2H3	19290	9450	9850	11100	13300
LX Hatchback 4D	ZE2H5	21065	10350	10750	12050	14400
EX Hatchback 4D	ZE2H7	22755	11750	12200	13500	15950

CIVIC—4-Cyl.—Equipment Schedule 6
W.B. 105.1"; 1.8 Liter.

Body Type	VIN	List	Good	Very Good	Good	Excellent
LX Sedan 4D	FB2F5	19755	12200	12800	13750	16150
LX Coupe 2D	FG3B5	19555	12000	12550	13450	15800
EX Coupe 2D	FG3B8	21605	13350	13950	14950	17450
Manual, 5-Spd	E		(550)	(550)	(655)	(655)

CIVIC—4-Cyl.—Equipment Schedule 6
W.B. 103.2", 105.1" (Sed); 1.8 Liter.

Body Type	VIN	List	Good	Very Good	Good	Excellent
HF Sedan 4D	FB2F6	20555	12550	13150	14050	16450
EX Sedan 4D	FB2F8	21605	13450	14050	15050	17550
EX-L Sedan 4D	FB2F9	23055	14450	15100	16000	18550
EX-L Coupe 2D	FG3B9	23055	14250	14900	15800	18350
Si Sedan 4D	FB6E5	23505	15000	15550	16650	19200
Si Coupe 2D	FB6E5	23305	14600	15150	16250	18800

CIVIC—4-Cyl. Hybrid—Equipment Schedule 6
W.B. 105.1"; 1.3 Liter.

Body Type	VIN	List	Good	Very Good	Good	Excellent
Sedan 4D	FB4F2	25150	14650	15200	16200	18500

2013 HONDA

Body Type	VIN	List	Trade-In Good	Very Good	Pvt-Party Good	Retail Excellent
CIVIC—4-Cyl. NGV—Equipment Schedule 6						
W.B. 106.3"; 1.8 Liter.						
Sedan 4D	FB5F5	27255	**15900**	**16450**	**17450**	**19900**
ACCORD—4-Cyl.—Equipment Schedule 4						
W.B. 107.3", 109.3" (Sed); 2.4 Liter.						
LX Sedan 4D	CR2F3	23270	**13950**	**14600**	**15800**	**18650**
Sport Sedan 4D	CR2F5	24980	**15250**	**15950**	**17250**	**20400**
LX-S Coupe 2D	CT1B3	24990	**14050**	**14600**	**15850**	**18450**
EX Sedan 4D	CR2F7	26195	**15800**	**16500**	**17800**	**21100**
EX Coupe 2D	CT1B7	26665	**15650**	**16250**	**17550**	**20400**
EX-L Sedan 4D	CR2F8	28785	**16850**	**17600**	**18900**	**22300**
EX-L Coupe 2D	CT2B8	28860	**16700**	**17350**	**18650**	**21700**
Touring Sedan 4D	CR3F9	34220	**20400**	**21300**	**22700**	**26700**
Manual, 6-Spd			**(600)**	**(600)**	**(710)**	**(710)**
V6, i-VTEC, 3.5 Liter			**875**	**875**	**1025**	**1025**

2014 HONDA — (1,2,5orJ)(9,HorK)(B,G,MorX)ZF1C4-E-#

Body Type	VIN	List	Trade-In Good	Very Good	Pvt-Party Good	Retail Excellent
CR-Z—4-Cyl. i-VTEC Hybrid—Equipment Schedule 6						
W.B. 95.9"; 1.5 Liter.						
Coupe 2D	ZF1C4	20785	**13700**	**14250**	**15300**	**17700**
EX Coupe 2D	ZF1C6	22630	**14750**	**15350**	**16400**	**18950**
INSIGHT—4-Cyl. Hybrid—Equipment Schedule 3						
W.B. 100.4"; 1.3 Liter.						
Hatchback 4D	ZE2H3	19515	**12500**	**13000**	**14150**	**16450**
LX Hatchback 4D	ZE2H5	21290	**13400**	**13900**	**15050**	**17300**
EX Hatchback 4D	ZE2H7	22980	**14550**	**15100**	**16250**	**18650**
CIVIC—4-Cyl.—Equipment Schedule 6						
W.B. 103.2", 105.1" (Sed); 1.8 Liter.						
LX Sedan 4D	FB2F5	19980	**13500**	**14100**	**15100**	**17550**
LX Coupe 2D	FG3B5	19780	**13350**	**13950**	**14950**	**17400**
HF Sedan 4D	FB2F6	20730	**14250**	**14900**	**15750**	**18250**
EX Sedan 4D	FB2F8	21880	**15150**	**15800**	**16650**	**19250**
EX Coupe 2D	FG3B8	21880	**15150**	**15800**	**16650**	**19250**
EX-L Sedan 4D	FB2F9	23530	**16150**	**16850**	**17600**	**20200**
EX-L Coupe 2D	FG3B9	23330	**15850**	**16550**	**17350**	**19950**
Manual, 5-Spd			**(550)**	**(550)**	**(645)**	**(645)**
CIVIC—4-Cyl. i-VTEC—Equipment Schedule 6						
W.B. 103.2", 105.1" (Sed); 2.4 Liter.						
Si Sedan 4D	FB6E5	23780	**16550**	**17150**	**18200**	**20900**
Si Coupe 2D	FG4A5	23580	**16200**	**16800**	**17850**	**20500**
CIVIC—4-Cyl. Hybrid—Equipment Schedule 6						
W.B. 105.1"; 1.5 Liter.						
Sedan 4D	FB4F2	25425	**16900**	**17500**	**18300**	**20700**
CIVIC—4-Cyl. Natural Gas—Equipment Schedule 5						
W.B. 105.1"; 1.8 Liter.						
Sedan 4D	FB5F5	27430	**18450**	**19100**	**19900**	**22400**
ACCORD—4-Cyl.—Equipment Schedule 3						
W.B. 107.3", 109.3" (Sed); 2.4 Liter.						
LX Sedan 4D	CR2F3	23545	**15100**	**15750**	**16900**	**19800**
LX-S Coupe 2D	CT1B3	25265	**15300**	**15850**	**17250**	**20100**
Sport Sedan 4D	CR2F5	25305	**16800**	**17500**	**18800**	**22200**
EX Sedan 4D	CR2F7	26470	**17150**	**17900**	**19250**	**22700**
EX Coupe 2D	CT1B7	26940	**17000**	**17600**	**19050**	**22200**
EX-L Sedan 4D	CR2F8	29060	**18000**	**18750**	**20100**	**23600**
EX-L Coupe 2D	CT1B8	29135	**18250**	**18900**	**20400**	**23800**
Manual, 6-Spd			**(625)**	**(625)**	**(720)**	**(720)**
V6, PZEV, 3.5 Liter			**950**	**950**	**1110**	**1110**
ACCORD—4-Cyl. VTEC Hybrid—Equipment Schedule 3						
W.B. 109.3"; 2.0 Liter.						
Sedan 4D	CR6F3	29945	**19500**	**20300**	**21000**	**24100**
EX-L Sedan 4D	CR6F5	32695	**20500**	**21300**	**22000**	**25100**
Touring Sedan 4D	CR6F7	35695	**22000**	**22900**	**23500**	**26700**
ACCORD—4-Cyl. i-VTEC Plug-In Hybrid—Equipment Schedule 3						
W.B. 109.3"; 2.0 Liter.						
Sedan 4D	CR5F7	40570	**22700**	**23600**	**24000**	**27000**
ACCORD—V6—Equipment Schedule 3						
W.B. 109.3"; 3.5 Liter.						
Touring Sedan 4D	CR3F9	34270	**21500**	**22400**	**23700**	**27800**

Body Type	VIN	List	Trade-In Good	Trade-In Very Good	Pvt-Party Good	Retail Excellent

HYUNDAI

2000 HYUNDAI — KMH(CF35G)–Y–#

ACCENT—4-Cyl.—Equipment Schedule 6
W.B. 96.1"; 1.5 Liter.

Body Type	VIN	List	Good	Very Good	Good	Excellent
L Hatchback 2D	CF35G	9434	425	500	950	1600
GS Hatchback 2D	CG35G	10784	500	575	1025	1750
GL Sedan 4D	CG45G	10884	500	575	1075	1850

ELANTRA—4-Cyl.—Equipment Schedule 5
W.B. 100.4"; 2.0 Liter.

GLS Sedan 4D	JF34F	12934	500	575	1150	2025
GLS Wagon 4D	JW34F	13684	675	750	1400	2400

TIBURON—4-Cyl.—Equipment Schedule 5
W.B. 97.4"; 2.0 Liter.

Coupe 2D	JG24F	15184	550	625	1225	2150

SONATA—4-Cyl.—Equipment Schedule 5
W.B. 106.3"; 2.4 Liter.

Sedan 4D	WF14S	15934	650	750	1375	2450

SONATA—V6—Equipment Schedule 5
W.B. 106.3"; 2.5 Liter.

GLS Sedan 4D	WF34V	17934	800	925	1600	2850

2001 HYUNDAI — KMH(CF35G)–1–#

ACCENT—4-Cyl.—Equipment Schedule 6
W.B. 96.1"; 1.5 Liter, 1.6 Liter.

L Hatchback 2D	CF35G	10184	450	550	1025	1725
GS Hatchback 2D	CH35C	10584	550	625	1125	1900
GL Sedan 4D	CG45C	11084	525	600	1125	1925

ELANTRA—4-Cyl.—Equipment Schedule 5
W.B. 102.7"; 2.0 Liter.

GLS Sedan 4D	JF35D	13734	500	575	1200	2075
GT Hatchback 4D	JF35D	15234	775	850	1600	2775

TIBURON—4-Cyl.—Equipment Schedule 5
W.B. 97.4"; 2.0 Liter.

Coupe 2D	JG25D	15734	800	900	1650	2900

SONATA—4-Cyl.—Equipment Schedule 5
W.B. 106.3"; 2.4 Liter.

Sedan 4D	WF15S	15934	750	850	1475	2625

SONATA—V6—Equipment Schedule 5
W.B. 106.3"; 2.5 Liter.

GLS Sedan 4D	WF35V	17934	950	1075	1800	3175

XG300—V6—Equipment Schedule 3
W.B. 108.3"; 3.0 Liter.

Sedan 4D	FU45D	23934	625	700	1225	2050
L Sedan 4D	FU45D	25434	825	925	1475	2475

2002 HYUNDAI — KMH(CF35G)–2–#

ACCENT—4-Cyl.—Equipment Schedule 6
W.B. 96.1"; 1.5 Liter, 1.6 Liter.

L Hatchback 2D	CF35G	10244	500	575	1100	1900
GS Hatchback 2D	CH35C	10744	575	650	1200	2075
GL Sedan 4D	CG45C	11144	575	650	1225	2150

ELANTRA—4-Cyl.—Equipment Schedule 5
W.B. 102.7"; 2.0 Liter.

GLS Sedan 4D	DN45D	13794	625	700	1400	2475
GT Hatchback 4D	DN55D	15294	875	975	1775	3125

SONATA—4-Cyl.—Equipment Schedule 5
W.B. 106.3"; 2.4 Liter.

Sedan 4D	WF15S	16494	950	1100	1725	2975
V6, 2.7 Liter	H		150	150	200	200

SONATA—V6—Equipment Schedule 5
W.B. 106.3"; 2.7 Liter.

GLS Sedan 4D	WF35H	17994	1200	1375	2125	3700
LX Sedan 4D	WF35H	19319	1475	1675	2450	4225

XG350—V6—Equipment Schedule 3
W.B. 108.3"; 3.5 Liter.

Sedan 4D	FU45E	24494	825	925	1600	2750
L Sedan 4D	FU45E	26094	1025	1150	1875	3200

Body Type	VIN	List	Trade-In Good	Very Good	Pvt-Party Good	Retail Excellent

2003 HYUNDAI — KMH(CF35C)-3-#

ACCENT—4-Cyl.—Equipment Schedule 6
W.B. 96.1"; 1.6 Liter.

Body Type	VIN	List	Good	Very Good	Good	Excellent
Hatchback 2D	CF35C	10745	525	625	1175	2025
GL Hatchback 2D	CG35C	11144	725	825	1375	2350
GL Sedan 4D	CG45C	11544	700	775	1350	2300
GT Hatchback 2D	CG45C	11144	775	900	1425	2400

ELANTRA—4-Cyl.—Equipment Schedule 5
W.B. 102.7"; 2.0 Liter.

GLS Sedan 4D	DN45D	13794	1025	1125	1925	3275
GT Sedan 4D	DN55D	15444	1225	1350	2150	3625
GT Hatchback 4D	DN55D	15444	1225	1350	2150	3650

TIBURON—4-Cyl.—Equipment Schedule 3
W.B. 99.6"; 2.0 Liter.

Coupe 2D	HM65D	16494	1525	1725	2400	3925
Manual, 5-Spd			(225)	(225)	(300)	(300)

TIBURON—V6—Equipment Schedule 3
W.B. 99.6"; 2.7 Liter.

GT Coupe 2D	HN65F	19244	1575	1775	2325	3725
Manual, 5-Spd			(225)	(225)	(300)	(300)

SONATA—4-Cyl.—Equipment Schedule 5
W.B. 106.3"; 2.4 Liter.

Sedan 4D	WF15S	16494	1125	1300	2050	3525
V6, 2.7 Liter	H		200	200	265	265

SONATA—V6—Equipment Schedule 5
W.B. 106.3"; 2.7 Liter.

GLS Sedan 4D	WF35H	18094	1425	1625	2650	4725
LX Sedan 4D	WF35H	19319	1750	2000	2950	5050

XG350—V6—Equipment Schedule 3
W.B. 106.3"; 3.5 Liter.

Sedan 4D	FU45E	24494	1150	1275	1875	3075
L Sedan 4D	FU45E	26094	1350	1500	2175	3575

2004 HYUNDAI — KMH(CF35C)-4-#

ACCENT—4-Cyl.—Equipment Schedule 6
W.B. 96.1"; 1.6 Liter.

Hatchback 2D	CF35C	11289	700	800	1325	2250
GL Hatchback 2D	CG35C	11439	800	900	1450	2450
GL Sedan 4D	CG45C	11839	925	1050	1625	2725
GT Hatchback 2D	CG45C	11939	1000	1125	1725	2875

ELANTRA—4-Cyl.—Equipment Schedule 5
W.B. 102.7"; 2.0 Liter.

GLS Sedan 4D	DN45D	14639	1150	1275	2150	3700
GT Sedan 4D	DN55D	16189	1475	1625	2350	3850
GT Hatchback 4D	DN55D	16189	1475	1625	2400	3950

TIBURON—4-Cyl.—Equipment Schedule 3
W.B. 99.6"; 2.0 Liter.

Coupe 2D	HM65D	18439	2050	2300	2975	4575
Manual, 5-Spd			(275)	(275)	(365)	(365)

TIBURON—V6—Equipment Schedule 3
W.B. 99.6"; 2.7 Liter.

GT Coupe 2D	HN65F	19639	2250	2500	3300	5150
GT Special Ed Cpe 2D	HN65F	20987	2600	2900	3850	5975
Manual, 5-Spd			(275)	(275)	(365)	(365)

SONATA—4-Cyl.—Equipment Schedule 5
W.B. 106.3"; 2.4 Liter.

Sedan 4D	WF15S	17339	1175	1350	2125	3700
V6, 2.7 Liter	H		250	250	335	335

SONATA—V6—Equipment Schedule 5
W.B. 106.3"; 2.7 Liter.

GLS Sedan 4D	WF35H	19339	1700	1925	2975	5175
LX Sedan 4D	WF35H	20339	2050	2325	3425	5700

XG350—V6—Equipment Schedule 3
W.B. 108.3"; 3.5 Liter.

Sedan 4D	FU45E	24589	1450	1600	2250	3650
L Sedan 4D	FU45E	26189	1650	1800	2550	4125

2005 HYUNDAI — KMH(CG35C)-5-#

ACCENT—4-Cyl.—Equipment Schedule 6
W.B. 96.1"; 1.6 Liter.

GLS Hatchback 2D	CG35C	11344	1050	1175	2075	3500

2005 HYUNDAI

Body Type	VIN	List	Trade-In Good	Very Good	Pvt-Party Good	Retail Excellent
GLS Sedan 4D	CG45C	11844	1350	1525	2450	4125
GT Hatchback 2D	CG35C	11939	1425	1600	2425	3975
ELANTRA—4-Cyl.—Equipment Schedule 5						
W.B. 102.7"; 2.0 Liter.						
GLS Sedan 4D	DN46D	14644	1725	1900	2875	4500
GLS Hatchback 4D	DN56D	14944	1825	2000	3000	4650
GT Sedan 4D	DN46D	16194	2025	2225	3150	4800
GT Hatchback 4D	DN56D	16194	2025	2225	3175	4850
TIBURON—4-Cyl.—Equipment Schedule 3						
W.B. 99.6"; 2.0 Liter.						
GS Coupe 2D	HM65D	17494	2075	2350	3150	4775
Manual, 5-Spd.			(325)	(325)	(435)	(435)
TIBURON—V6—Equipment Schedule 3						
W.B. 99.6"; 2.7 Liter.						
GT Coupe 2D	HN65F	19494	2225	2525	3400	5175
SE Coupe 2D	HN65F	20594	2550	2900	3900	5975
Manual, 5-Spd.			(325)	(325)	(435)	(435)
SONATA—4-Cyl.—Equipment Schedule 5						
W.B. 106.3"; 2.4 Liter.						
GL Sedan 4D	WF25S	17394	1925	2200	3025	4725
V6, 2.7 Liter	H		300	300	400	400
SONATA—V6—Equipment Schedule 5						
W.B. 106.3"; 2.7 Liter.						
GLS Sedan 4D	WF35H	19394	2400	2725	3625	5550
LX Sedan 4D	WF35H	20394	2925	3325	4275	6475
XG350—V6—Equipment Schedule 3						
W.B. 108.3"; 3.5 Liter.						
Sedan 4D	FU45E	24994	1575	1750	2650	4100
L Sedan 4D	FU45E	26594	1825	2025	2975	4600

2006 HYUNDAI — KMH(CN46C)-6-#

Body Type	VIN	List	Trade-In Good	Very Good	Pvt-Party Good	Retail Excellent
ACCENT—4-Cyl.—Equipment Schedule 6						
W.B. 98.4"; 1.6 Liter.						
GLS Sedan 4D	CN46C	13845	2025	2300	3300	5050
Manual, 5-Spd.			(275)	(275)	(365)	(365)
ELANTRA—4-Cyl.—Equipment Schedule 5						
W.B. 102.7"; 2.0 Liter.						
GLS Sedan 4D	DN46D	15095	2050	2275	3400	5175
GLS Hatchback 4D	DN56D	15495	2100	2325	3500	5325
Limited Sedan 4D	DN46D	16045	2200	2450	3600	5450
GT Hatchback 4D	DN56D	16415	2375	2625	3750	5600
TIBURON—4-Cyl.—Equipment Schedule 3						
W.B. 99.6"; 2.0 Liter.						
GS Coupe 2D	HM65D	17595	2475	2800	3650	5275
Manual, 5-Spd.			(375)	(375)	(500)	(500)
TIBURON—V6—Equipment Schedule 3						
W.B. 99.6"; 2.7 Liter.						
GT Coupe 2D	HN65F	19995	2925	3275	4175	6025
GT Limited Coupe 2D	HN65F	21995	3350	3725	4750	6825
SE Coupe 2D	HN65F	21595	3325	3675	4575	6600
Manual, 5-Spd.			(375)	(375)	(500)	(500)
SONATA—4-Cyl.—Equipment Schedule 5						
W.B. 107.4"; 2.4 Liter.						
GL Sedan 4D	ET46C	19395	3150	3550	4275	6100
GLS Sedan 4D	EU46C	19995	3550	4000	4725	6725
V6, 3.3 Liter	F		350	350	465	465
SONATA—V6—Equipment Schedule 5						
W.B. 107.4"; 3.3 Liter.						
LX Sedan 4D	EU46F	23495	3975	4425	5250	7450
AZERA—V6—Equipment Schedule 3						
W.B. 109.4"; 3.8 Liter.						
SE Sedan 4D	FC46F	24995	3450	3800	4550	6325
Limited Sedan 4D	FC46F	27495	4175	4575	5375	7400
Premium Pkg			275	275	365	365
Ultimate Pkg			275	275	365	365

2007 HYUNDAI — KMH(CM36C)-7-#

Body Type	VIN	List	Trade-In Good	Very Good	Pvt-Party Good	Retail Excellent
ACCENT—4-Cyl.—Equipment Schedule 6						
W.B. 98.4"; 1.6 Liter.						
GS Hatchback 2D	CM36C	11995	2150	2400	3175	4725
GLS Sedan 4D	CN46C	14145	2725	3050	3875	5675
SE Hatchback 2D	CN36C	15495	2900	3250	4225	6150

Body Type	VIN	List	Trade-In Good	Trade-In Very Good	Pvt-Party Good	Retail Excellent
Manual, 5-Spd			**(300)**	**(300)**	**(400)**	**(400)**
ELANTRA—4-Cyl.—Equipment Schedule 5						
W.B. 104.3"; 2.0 Liter.						
GLS Sedan 4D	DU46D	16495	**3300**	**3600**	**4675**	**6675**
SE Sedan 4D	DU46D	17295	**3450**	**3750**	**4825**	**6800**
Limited Sedan 4D	DU46D	18295	**3750**	**4050**	**5125**	**7175**
Manual, 5-Spd			**(400)**	**(400)**	**(535)**	**(535)**
TIBURON—4-Cyl.—Equipment Schedule 3						
W.B. 99.6"; 2.0 Liter.						
GS Coupe 2D	HM65D	18295	**2975**	**3325**	**4200**	**5950**
Manual, 5-Spd			**(400)**	**(400)**	**(535)**	**(535)**
TIBURON—V6—Equipment Schedule 3						
W.B. 99.6"; 2.7 Liter.						
GT Coupe 2D	HN66F	20995	**3525**	**3900**	**4825**	**6750**
GT Limited Coupe 2D	HN66F	22395	**4225**	**4650**	**5600**	**7725**
SE Coupe 2D	HN66F	22595	**3625**	**4000**	**5000**	**7025**
Manual, 5-Spd			**(400)**	**(400)**	**(535)**	**(535)**
SONATA—4-Cyl.—Equipment Schedule 5						
W.B. 107.4"; 2.4 Liter.						
GLS Sedan 4D	ET46C	18895	**3800**	**4225**	**5050**	**7050**
Manual, 5-Spd			**(400)**	**(400)**	**(535)**	**(535)**
SONATA—V6—Equipment Schedule 5						
W.B. 107.4"; 3.3 Liter.						
SE Sedan 4D	EU46F	21595	**4275**	**4725**	**5575**	**7775**
Limited Sedan 4D	EU46F	23595	**4750**	**5225**	**6175**	**8625**
AZERA—V6—Equipment Schedule 3						
W.B. 109.4"; 3.3 Liter, 3.8 Liter.						
GLS Sedan 4D	FC46D	24895	**4500**	**4900**	**5575**	**7400**
SE Sedan 4D	FC46F	25195	**4675**	**5075**	**5750**	**7600**
Limited Sedan 4D	FC46F	27795	**4875**	**5300**	**6050**	**8050**
Premium Pkg			**300**	**300**	**400**	**400**
Ultimate Pkg			**275**	**275**	**375**	**375**

2008 HYUNDAI — (KMHor5NP)(CM36C)-8-#

Body Type	VIN	List	Trade-In Good	Trade-In Very Good	Pvt-Party Good	Retail Excellent
ACCENT—4-Cyl.—Equipment Schedule 6						
W.B. 98.4"; 1.6 Liter.						
GS Hatchback 2D	CM36C	12395	**2650**	**2950**	**3650**	**5175**
GLS Sedan 4D	CN46C	14545	**3225**	**3550**	**4325**	**6050**
SE Hatchback 4D	CN36C	15995	**3475**	**3825**	**4750**	**6600**
Manual, 5-Spd w/Overdrive			**(350)**	**(350)**	**(470)**	**(470)**
ELANTRA—4-Cyl.—Equipment Schedule 3						
W.B. 104.3"; 2.0 Liter.						
GLS Sedan 4D	DU46D	15145	**4150**	**4475**	**5500**	**7475**
SE Sedan 4D	DU46D	17845	**4525**	**4875**	**5875**	**7900**
Manual, 5-Spd w/Overdrive			**(425)**	**(425)**	**(555)**	**(555)**
TIBURON—4-Cyl.—Equipment Schedule 3						
W.B. 99.6"; 2.0 Liter.						
GS Coupe 2D	HM65D	18595	**4125**	**4475**	**5325**	**7125**
Manual, 5-Spd			**(425)**	**(425)**	**(555)**	**(555)**
TIBURON—V6—Equipment Schedule 3						
W.B. 99.6"; 2.7 Liter.						
GT Coupe 2D	HN66F	21495	**4575**	**4950**	**5875**	**7925**
GT Limited Coupe 2D	HN66F	22995	**5350**	**5775**	**6850**	**9075**
SE Coupe 2D	HN66F	22845	**5025**	**5425**	**6400**	**8575**
Manual, 5-Spd			**(425)**	**(425)**	**(555)**	**(555)**
Manual, 6-Spd			**0**	**0**	**0**	**0**
SONATA—4-Cyl.—Equipment Schedule 5						
W.B. 107.4"; 2.4 Liter.						
GLS Sedan 4D	ET46C	19545	**4475**	**4900**	**5675**	**7625**
Manual, 5-Spd			**(425)**	**(425)**	**(555)**	**(555)**
V6, 3.3 Liter	F		**475**	**475**	**645**	**645**
SONATA—V6—Equipment Schedule 5						
W.B. 107.4"; 3.3 Liter.						
SE Sedan 4D	EU46F	22745	**5500**	**5975**	**6800**	**9050**
Manual, 5-Spd			**(425)**	**(425)**	**(555)**	**(555)**
4-Cyl, 2.4 Liter	C		**(425)**	**(425)**	**(550)**	**(550)**
SONATA—V6—Equipment Schedule 5						
W.B. 107.4"; 3.3 Liter.						
Limited Sedan 4D	EU46F	24695	**5775**	**6275**	**7350**	**9800**
4-Cyl, 2.4 Liter	C		**(425)**	**(425)**	**(550)**	**(550)**
AZERA—V6—Equipment Schedule 3						
W.B. 109.4"; 3.3 Liter, 3.8 Liter.						
GLS Sedan 4D	FC46D	25295	**5000**	**5400**	**6125**	**7800**

Body Type	VIN	List	Trade-In Good	Very Good	Pvt-Party Good	Retail Excellent
Limited Sedan 4D	FC46F	29245	6150	6600	7325	9275
Ultimate Pkg			275	275	375	375

2009 HYUNDAI — (KMHor5NP)(CM36C)–9–#

ACCENT—4-Cyl.—Equipment Schedule 6
W.B. 98.4"; 1.6 Liter.

Body Type	VIN	List	Trade-In Good	Very Good	Pvt-Party Good	Retail Excellent
GS Hatchback 2D	CM36C	12745	3575	3875	4775	6500
GLS Sedan 4D	CN46C	14595	4025	4350	5300	7200
SE Hatchback 2D	CN36C	16545	4475	4825	5825	7875
Manual, 5-Spd w/Overdrive			(375)	(375)	(500)	(500)
ELANTRA—4-Cyl.—Equipment Schedule 5 W.B. 104.3", 106.3"(Wag); 2.0 Liter.						
GLS Sedan 4D	DU46D	15795	5250	5600	6625	8725
SE Sedan 4D	DU46D	18495	5675	6050	7200	9325
Touring Wagon 4D	DC86E	19295	6975	7400	8575	10950
Manual, 5-Spd w/Overdrive			(450)	(450)	(600)	(600)
SONATA—4-Cyl.—Equipment Schedule 5 W.B. 107.4"; 2.4 Liter.						
GLS Sedan 4D	ET46C	20195	5725	6175	7100	9125
Manual, 5-Spd w/Overdrive			(450)	(450)	(600)	(600)
V6, 3.3 Liter	F		525	525	690	690
SONATA—V6—Equipment Schedule 5 W.B. 107.4"; 3.3 Liter.						
SE Sedan 4D	EU46F	22745	6675	7150	8200	10550
Manual, 5-Spd w/Overdrive			(450)	(450)	(600)	(600)
4-Cyl, 2.4 Liter	C		(475)	(475)	(625)	(625)
SONATA—V6—Equipment Schedule 5 W.B. 107.4"; 3.3 Liter.						
Limited Sedan 4D	EU46F	27245	7425	7950	9200	11950
4-Cyl, 2.4 Liter	C		(475)	(475)	(625)	(625)
AZERA—V6—Equipment Schedule 3 W.B. 109.4"; 3.3 Liter, 3.8 Liter.						
GLS Sedan 4D	FC46D	25295	6575	7025	7825	9750
Limited Sedan 4D	FC46F	29245	7350	7800	8750	10900
Ultimate Pkg			300	300	385	385
Premium Pkg			350	350	460	460
GENESIS—V6—Equipment Schedule 3 W.B. 115.6"; 3.8 Liter.						
3.8 Sedan 4D	GB46E	33000	10400	10950	11700	14050
Technology Pkg			1150	1150	1420	1420
GENESIS—V8—Equipment Schedule 3 W.B. 115.6"; 4.6 Liter.						
4.6 Sedan 4D	GC46F	38000	11650	12250	13150	15800
Technology Pkg			1150	1150	1425	1425

2010 HYUNDAI — (KMHor5NP)(CM3AC)–A–#

ACCENT—4-Cyl.—Equipment Schedule 6
W.B. 98.4"; 1.6 Liter.

Body Type	VIN	List	Trade-In Good	Very Good	Pvt-Party Good	Retail Excellent
Blue Hatchback 2D	CM3AC	10690	3050	3325	4025	5450
ACCENT—4-Cyl.—Equipment Schedule 6 W.B. 98.4"; 1.6 Liter.						
GS Hatchback 2D	CM3AC	13715	4500	4825	5800	7700
GLS Sedan 4D	CN46C	15365	4725	5075	6050	8025
SE Hatchback 2D	CN3AC	17715	5675	6075	7275	9500
Manual, 5-Spd w/Overdrive			(475)	(475)	(625)	(625)
ELANTRA—4-Cyl.—Equipment Schedule 5 W.B. 104.3"; 2.0 Liter.						
Blue Sedan 4D	DU4AD	14865	5325	5675	6875	8900
GLS Sedan 4D	DU4AD	17615	6125	6500	7625	9700
SE Sedan 4D	DU4AD	18565	6700	7100	8150	10250
ELANTRA—4-Cyl.—Equipment Schedule 5 W.B. 106.3"; 2.0 Liter.						
GLS Touring Wagon	DB8AE	17915	6400	6800	7875	9975
SE Touring Wagon 4D	DC8AE	20515	7700	8150	9175	11350
Manual, 5-Spd w/Overdrive			(500)	(500)	(655)	(655)
SONATA—4-Cyl.—Equipment Schedule 5 W.B. 107.4"; 3.3 Liter.						
GLS Sedan 4D	ET4AC	20620	6625	7050	7900	9850
Manual, 5-Spd w/Overdrive			(500)	(500)	(630)	(630)
SONATA—V6—Equipment Schedule 5 W.B. 107.4"; 3.3 Liter.						
SE Sedan 4D	EU4AF	24770	8175	8675	9700	12100

Body Type	VIN	List	Trade-In Good	Very Good	Pvt-Party Good	Retail Excellent
Limited Sedan 4D	EU4AF	27270	**8850**	**9375**	**10600**	**13300**
4-Cyl, 2.4 Liter			**(575)**	**(575)**	**(755)**	**(755)**

AZERA—V6—Equipment Schedule 3
W.B. 109.4"; 3.3 Liter, 3.8 Liter.

Body Type	VIN	List	Trade-In Good	Very Good	Pvt-Party Good	Retail Excellent
GLS Sedan 4D	FC4DD	25745	**7800**	**8250**	**9075**	**10950**
Limited Sedan 4D	FC4DF	30345	**9625**	**10100**	**11050**	**13300**
Premium Pkg			**400**	**400**	**505**	**505**

GENESIS—4-Cyl. Turbo—Equipment Schedule 3
W.B. 111.0"; 2.0 Liter.

Body Type	VIN	List	Trade-In Good	Very Good	Pvt-Party Good	Retail Excellent
2.0T Coupe 2D	HT6KD	22750	**8900**	**9400**	**10300**	**12500**
2.0T R-Spec Coupe 2D	HT6KD	24500	**9150**	**9625**	**10500**	**12800**
2.0T Premium Coupe	HT6KD	25000	**9100**	**9600**	**10550**	**12800**
2.0T Track Coupe 2D	HT6KD	27500	**10200**	**10700**	**11650**	**14050**

GENESIS—V6—Equipment Schedule 3
W.B. 111.0", 115.6" (Sed); 3.8 Liter.

Body Type	VIN	List	Trade-In Good	Very Good	Pvt-Party Good	Retail Excellent
3.8 Sedan 4D	GC4DE	33800	**11850**	**12400**	**13500**	**16150**
3.8 Coupe 2D	HU2KH	25750	**10150**	**10700**	**11750**	**14350**
3.8 Grand Touring	HU6KH	29250	**10300**	**10850**	**11950**	**14550**
3.8 Track Coupe 2D	HU6KH	31250	**10400**	**10950**	**12050**	**14700**
Premium Pkg			**1000**	**1000**	**1205**	**1205**
Technology Pkg			**1225**	**1225**	**1465**	**1465**

GENESIS—V8—Equipment Schedule 3
W.B. 115.6"; 4.6 Liter.

Body Type	VIN	List	Trade-In Good	Very Good	Pvt-Party Good	Retail Excellent
4.6 Sedan 4D	GC4DF	40300	**12900**	**13500**	**14800**	**17750**
Technology Pkg			**1225**	**1225**	**1470**	**1470**

2011 HYUNDAI — 5N(MorP)orKM(8orH)(CM3AC)-B-#

ACCENT—4-Cyl.—Equipment Schedule 6
W.B. 98.4"; 1.6 Liter.

Body Type	VIN	List	Trade-In Good	Very Good	Pvt-Party Good	Retail Excellent
GL Hatchback 2D	CM3AC	10705	**3700**	**4025**	**4700**	**6050**

ACCENT—4-Cyl.—Equipment Schedule 6
W.B. 98.4"; 1.6 Liter.

Body Type	VIN	List	Trade-In Good	Very Good	Pvt-Party Good	Retail Excellent
GS Hatchback 2D	CM3AC	14415	**5425**	**5775**	**6875**	**8800**
GLS Sedan 4D	CN4AC	15415	**5525**	**5875**	**6950**	**8850**
SE Hatchback 2D	CN3AC	16865	**6925**	**7350**	**8450**	**10650**
Manual, 5-Spd w/Overdrive			**(500)**	**(500)**	**(665)**	**(665)**

ELANTRA—4-Cyl.—Equipment Schedule 5
W.B. 106.3"; 1.8 Liter.

Body Type	VIN	List	Trade-In Good	Very Good	Pvt-Party Good	Retail Excellent
GLS Sedan 4D	DH4AE	17800	**8175**	**8625**	**9675**	**11800**
Limited Sedan 4D	DH4AE	20700	**9200**	**9675**	**10700**	**12950**

ELANTRA—4-Cyl.—Equipment Schedule 5
W.B. 106.3"; 2.0 Liter.

Body Type	VIN	List	Trade-In Good	Very Good	Pvt-Party Good	Retail Excellent
GLS Touring Wag 4D	DB8AE	17915	**8200**	**8650**	**9700**	**11850**
Touring SE Wagon 4D	DC8AE	21015	**9300**	**9800**	**10800**	**13050**
Manual, 5-Spd w/Overdrive			**(500)**	**(500)**	**(630)**	**(630)**

SONATA—4-Cyl.—Equipment Schedule 5
W.B. 110.0"; 2.4 Liter.

Body Type	VIN	List	Trade-In Good	Very Good	Pvt-Party Good	Retail Excellent
GLS Sedan 4D	EB4AC	20915	**9450**	**9950**	**11000**	**13400**
Manual, 6-Spd w/Overdrive			**(500)**	**(500)**	**(625)**	**(625)**

SONATA—4-Cyl.—Equipment Schedule 5
W.B. 110.0"; 2.4 Liter.

Body Type	VIN	List	Trade-In Good	Very Good	Pvt-Party Good	Retail Excellent
SE Sedan 4D	EC4AC	23315	**10250**	**10750**	**11900**	**14500**
Limited Sedan 4D	EC4AC	26015	**11100**	**11650**	**12950**	**15800**
4-Cyl, Turbo, 2.0 Liter	B		**1250**	**1250**	**1575**	**1575**

SONATA—4-Cyl. Hybrid—Equipment Schedule 5
W.B. 110.0"; 2.4 Liter.

Body Type	VIN	List	Trade-In Good	Very Good	Pvt-Party Good	Retail Excellent
Sedan 4D	EC4AA	26545	**10950**	**11500**	**12800**	**15650**

AZERA—V6—Equipment Schedule 3
W.B. 109.4"; 3.3 Liter, 3.8 Liter.

Body Type	VIN	List	Trade-In Good	Very Good	Pvt-Party Good	Retail Excellent
GLS Sedan 4D	FC4DD	26270	**10200**	**10650**	**11500**	**13500**
Limited Sedan 4D	FC4DF	30870	**11850**	**12400**	**13250**	**15550**
Premium Pkg			**450**	**450**	**540**	**540**

GENESIS—4-Cyl. Turbo—Equipment Schedule 3
W.B. 111.0"; 2.0 Liter.

Body Type	VIN	List	Trade-In Good	Very Good	Pvt-Party Good	Retail Excellent
2.0T Coupe 2D	HT6KD	23050	**11200**	**11700**	**12550**	**14850**
2.0T R-Spec Coupe 2D	HT6KD	25300	**11250**	**11750**	**12750**	**15150**
2.0T Premium Cpe 2D	HT6KD	27550	**11400**	**11950**	**13000**	**15350**

GENESIS—V6—Equipment Schedule 3
W.B. 111.0", 115.6" (Sed); 3.8 Liter.

Body Type	VIN	List	Trade-In Good	Very Good	Pvt-Party Good	Retail Excellent
3.8 Sedan 4D	GC4DE	33800	**13200**	**13800**	**15000**	**18000**
3.8 R-Spec Coupe 2D	HU6KH	27550	**12100**	**12650**	**13650**	**16150**
3.8 Grand Touring	HU6KH	30550	**12950**	**13500**	**14600**	**17400**
3.8 Track Coupe 2D	HU6KH	31550	**12950**	**13550**	**14750**	**17500**

Body Type	VIN	List	Trade-In Good	Very Good	Pvt-Party Good	Retail Excellent
Premium Pkg	----	----	**1050**	**1050**	**1290**	**1290**
Technology Pkg	----	----	**1275**	**1275**	**1565**	**1565**
GENESIS—V8—Equipment Schedule 3						
W.B. 115.6"; 4.6 Liter.						
4.6 Sedan 4D	GC4DF	43800	**14400**	**15000**	**16400**	**19500**
Technology Pkg	----	----	**1275**	**1275**	**1610**	**1610**
EQUUS—V8—Equipment Schedule 3						
W.B. 119.9"; 4.6 Liter.						
Signature Sedan 4D	GH4JF	58900	**20600**	**21500**	**22200**	**25500**
Ultimate Sedan 4D	GH4JF	65400	**22800**	**23700**	**24400**	**27900**

2012 HYUNDAI — 5NPorKMH(CT4AE)–C–#

Body Type	VIN	List	Trade-In Good	Very Good	Pvt-Party Good	Retail Excellent
ACCENT—4-Cyl.—Equipment Schedule 6						
W.B. 98.4"; 1.6 Liter.						
GLS Sedan 4D	CT4AE	15955	**7525**	**7950**	**9025**	**11150**
GS Hatchback 4D	CT5AE	16555	**7525**	**7950**	**9050**	**11200**
Manual, 6-Spd w/Overdrive	----	----	**(550)**	**(550)**	**(720)**	**(720)**
ACCENT—4-Cyl.—Equipment Schedule 6						
W.B. 98.4"; 1.6 Liter.						
SE Hatchback 4D	CU5AE	16555	**7925**	**8350**	**9475**	**11700**
Auto, 6-Spd w/Overdrive	----	----	**475**	**475**	**620**	**620**
VELOSTER—4-Cyl.—Equipment Schedule 4						
W.B. 104.3"; 1.6 Liter.						
Coupe 3D	TC6AD	19310	**11050**	**11600**	**12600**	**14950**
Style Pkg	----	----	**250**	**250**	**310**	**310**
Tech Pkg	----	----	**450**	**450**	**540**	**540**
ELANTRA—4-Cyl.—Equipment Schedule 5						
W.B. 106.3"; 1.8 Liter, 2.0 Liter.						
GLS Sedan 4D	DH4AE	18195	**9625**	**10100**	**11150**	**13400**
Touring GLS Wagon	DB8AE	17945	**9150**	**9625**	**10650**	**12850**
Touring SE Wagon 4D	DC8AE	21045	**10300**	**10850**	**11800**	**14100**
Manual, 5-Spd w/Overdrive	----	----	**(525)**	**(525)**	**(655)**	**(655)**
Manual, 6-Spd w/Overdrive	----	----	**(525)**	**(525)**	**(670)**	**(670)**
ELANTRA—4-Cyl.—Equipment Schedule 5						
W.B. 106.3"; 1.8 Liter.						
Limited Sedan 4D	DH4AE	21195	**11300**	**11850**	**12850**	**15250**
SONATA—4-Cyl.—Equipment Schedule 5						
W.B. 110.0"; 2.4 Liter.						
GLS Sedan 4D	EB4AC	21455	**10250**	**10750**	**11850**	**14250**
Manual, 6-Spd w/Overdrive	----	----	**(525)**	**(525)**	**(650)**	**(650)**
SONATA—4-Cyl.—Equipment Schedule 5						
W.B. 110.0"; 2.4 Liter.						
SE Sedan 4D	EC4AC	23855	**10950**	**11450**	**12650**	**15200**
Limited Sedan 4D	EC4AC	27105	**12900**	**13500**	**14800**	**17750**
4-Cyl, Turbo, 2.0 Liter	B		**1300**	**1300**	**1625**	**1625**
SONATA—4-Cyl. Hybrid—Equipment Schedule 5						
W.B. 110.0"; 2.4 Liter.						
Sedan 4D	EC4A4	26625	**11800**	**12300**	**13600**	**16350**
AZERA—V6—Equipment Schedule 3						
W.B. 112.0"; 3.3 Liter.						
Sedan 4D	FH4DG	32875	**15050**	**15600**	**16800**	**19650**
GENESIS—4-Cyl. Turbo—Equipment Schedule 3						
W.B. 111.0"; 2.0 Liter.						
2.0T Coupe 2D	HT6KD	23100	**12200**	**12700**	**13650**	**16000**
2.0T R-Spec Coupe 2D	HT6KD	25350	**12400**	**12900**	**13900**	**16300**
2.0T Premium Cpe 2D	HT6KD	27600	**13000**	**13500**	**14450**	**16850**
GENESIS—V6—Equipment Schedule 3						
W.B. 111.0", 115.6" (Sed); 3.8 Liter.						
3.8 Sedan 4D	GC4DG	35050	**14550**	**15100**	**16350**	**19100**
3.8 R-Spec Coupe 2D	HU6KH	27600	**13000**	**13500**	**14650**	**17200**
3.8 Grand Touring	HU6KH	30600	**14650**	**15250**	**16350**	**19150**
3.8 Track Coupe 2D	HU6KH	31600	**14650**	**15200**	**16400**	**19250**
Premium Pkg	----	----	**1125**	**1125**	**1340**	**1340**
Technology Pkg	----	----	**1350**	**1350**	**1625**	**1625**
GENESIS—V8—Equipment Schedule 3						
W.B. 115.6"; 4.6 Liter, 5.0 Liter.						
4.6 Sedan 4D	GC4DF	45350	**16200**	**16850**	**18350**	**21700**
5.0 Sedan 4D	GC4DH	46350	**19600**	**20300**	**22100**	**26200**
5.0 R-Spec Sedan 4D	GC4DH	47350	**20500**	**21300**	**23100**	**27300**
EQUUS—V8—Equipment Schedule 3						
W.B. 119.9"; 5.0 Liter.						
Signature Sedan 4D	GH4JH	59650	**23900**	**24900**	**25700**	**29300**
Ultimate Sedan 4D	GH4JH	66650	**26100**	**27100**	**27900**	**31800**

Body Type	VIN	List	Trade-In Good	Very Good	Pvt-Party Good	Retail Excellent

2013 HYUNDAI — 5NPorKMH(CT4AE)-D-#

ACCENT—4-Cyl.—Equipment Schedule 6
W.B. 98.4"; 1.6 Liter.

Body Type	VIN	List	Good	Very Good	Good	Excellent
GLS Sedan 4D	CT4AE	15320	**8350**	**8775**	**9975**	**12300**
GS Hatchback 4D	CT5AE	15570	**8600**	**9050**	**10200**	**12550**
SE Hatchback 4D	CU5AE	16870	**9375**	**9850**	**11050**	**13500**
Auto, 6-Spd w/Overdrive			**500**	**500**	**660**	**660**

VELOSTER—4-Cyl.—Equipment Schedule 4
W.B. 104.3"; 1.6 Liter.

Coupe 3D	TC6AD	19475	**11750**	**12300**	**13350**	**15800**
RE:MIX Coupe 3D	TC6AD	21925	**11900**	**12500**	**13500**	**16000**
Style Pkg			**275**	**275**	**330**	**330**
Tech Pkg			**450**	**450**	**560**	**560**

VELOSTER—4-Cyl. Turbo—Equipment Schedule 4
W.B. 104.3"; 1.6 Liter.

Coupe 3D	TC6AE	23725	**13150**	**13750**	**14800**	**17350**

ELANTRA—4-Cyl.—Equipment Schedule 5
W.B. 106.3"; 1.8 Liter.

GLS Sedan 4D	DH4AE	18470	**10650**	**11150**	**12150**	**14500**
GS Coupe 2D	DH6AE	19220	**11100**	**11600**	**12550**	**14900**
SE Coupe 2D	DH6AE	21520	**12700**	**13250**	**14200**	**16650**
GT Hatchback 4D	D35LE	20170	**11900**	**12450**	**13450**	**15900**
Manual, 6-Spd			**(550)**	**(550)**	**(680)**	**(680)**

ELANTRA—4-Cyl.—Equipment Schedule 5
W.B. 106.3"; 1.8 Liter.

Limited Sedan 4D	DH4AE	21720	**12900**	**13500**	**14400**	**16850**

SONATA—4-Cyl.—Equipment Schedule 5
W.B. 110.0"; 2.4 Liter.

GLS Sedan 4D	EB4AC	21670	**11300**	**11800**	**12900**	**15300**

SONATA—4-Cyl.—Equipment Schedule 5
W.B. 110.0"; 2.4 Liter.

SE Sedan 4D	EC4AC	24120	**12100**	**12600**	**13750**	**16300**
Limited Sedan 4D	EC4AC	26620	**13750**	**14300**	**15750**	**18800**
4-Cyl, Turbo, 2.0 Liter	B		**1375**	**1375**	**1635**	**1635**

SONATA—4-Cyl. Hybrid—Equipment Schedule 5
W.B. 110.0"; 2.4 Liter.

Sedan 4D	EC4A4	26445	**12650**	**13200**	**14400**	**17100**
Limited Sedan 4D	EC4A4	31345	**15050**	**15650**	**17200**	**20500**

AZERA—V6—Equipment Schedule 3
W.B. 112.0"; 3.3 Liter.

Sedan 4D	FG4JG	33125	**17100**	**17700**	**18750**	**21500**
Technology Pkg			**1425**	**1425**	**1640**	**1640**

GENESIS—4-Cyl. Turbo—Equipment Schedule 3
W.B. 111.0"; 2.0 Liter.

2.0T Coupe 2D	HT6KD	25125	**13750**	**14250**	**15300**	**17750**
2.0T R-Spec Coupe 2D	HT6KD	27375	**14250**	**14750**	**15850**	**18450**
2.0T Premium Cpe 2D	HT6KD	29625	**14050**	**14550**	**15600**	**18050**

GENESIS—V6—Equipment Schedule 3
W.B. 111.0", 115.6" (Sed); 3.8 Liter.

3.8 Sedan 4D	GC4DD	35075	**15300**	**15900**	**17250**	**20200**
3.8 R-Spec Coupe 2D	HU6KJ	29625	**15900**	**16500**	**17500**	**20200**
3.8 Grand Touring 2D	HU6KJ	32875	**16250**	**16850**	**17900**	**20700**
3.8 Track Coupe 2D	HU6KJ	33875	**17100**	**17700**	**18750**	**21600**
Premium Pkg			**1175**	**1175**	**1415**	**1415**
Technology Pkg			**1425**	**1425**	**1715**	**1715**

GENESIS—V8—Equipment Schedule 3
W.B. 115.6"; 5.0 Liter.

5.0 R-Spec Sedan 4D	GC4DH	47675	**22200**	**23000**	**24800**	**29200**

EQUUS—V8—Equipment Schedule 3
W.B. 119.9"; 5.0 Liter.

Signature Sedan 4D	GH4JH	60150	**27100**	**28100**	**29100**	**33100**
Ultimate Sedan 4D	GH4JH	67150	**29600**	**30700**	**31700**	**36000**

2014 HYUNDAI — 5NPorKMH(CT4AE)-E-#

ACCENT—4-Cyl.—Equipment Schedule 6
W.B. 101.2"; 1.6 Liter.

GLS Sedan 4D	CT4AE	15455	**9375**	**9850**	**10850**	**13050**
GS Hatchback 4D	CT5AE	15705	**9675**	**10150**	**11150**	**13350**
SE Hatchback 4D	CU5AE	17205	**11000**	**11500**	**12500**	**14850**
Auto, 6-Spd w/Overdrive			**525**	**525**	**655**	**655**

2014 HYUNDAI

Body	Type	VIN	List	Trade-In Good	Very Good	Pvt-Party Good	Retail Excellent
VELOSTER—4-Cyl.—Equipment Schedule 4							
W.B. 104.3"; 1.6 Liter.							
Coupe 3D		TC6AD	19860	12950	13550	14500	17000
RE:FLEX Coupe 3D		TC6AD	22460	14600	15250	16150	18700
VELOSTER—4-Cyl. Turbo—Equipment Schedule 4							
W.B. 104.3"; 1.6 Liter.							
R-spec Coupe 3D		TC6AE	22110	14200	14850	15750	18300
Coupe 3D		TC6AE	24110	15350	16050	17000	19700
ELANTRA—4-Cyl.—Equipment Schedule 5							
W.B. 104.3" (GT), 106.3"; 1.8 Liter, 2.0 Liter.							
SE Sedan 4D		DH4AE	19010	11950	12500	13550	16000
Sport Sedan 4D		DH4AH	23510	15700	16400	17250	19900
GT Hatchback 4D		D35LH	20560	13200	13800	14700	17200
Manual, 6-Spd				(575)	(575)	(705)	(705)
ELANTRA—4-Cyl.—Equipment Schedule 5							
W.B. 106.3"; 1.8 Liter, 2.0 Liter.							
Coupe 2D		DH6AH	20410	13100	13700	14600	17050
Limited Sedan 4D		DH4AE	22460	14050	14650	15600	18150
SONATA—4-Cyl.—Equipment Schedule 5							
W.B. 110.0"; 2.4 Liter.							
GLS Sedan 4D		EB4AC	22145	12450	13000	14100	16700
SONATA—4-Cyl.—Equipment Schedule 5							
W.B. 110.0"; 2.4 Liter.							
SE Sedan 4D		EC4A	24995	13650	14200	15400	18050
Limited Sedan 4D		EC4AC	27695	15600	16200	17350	20200
4-Cyl, Turbo, 2.0 Liter		B		1425	1425	1680	1680
SONATA—4-Cyl. Hybrid—Equipment Schedule 5							
W.B. 110.0"; 2.4 Liter.							
Sedan 4D		EC4A4	26810	15050	15650	16850	19700
Limited Sedan 4D		EC4A4	31345	22000	22800	23400	26700
AZERA—V6—Equipment Schedule 3							
W.B. 112.0"; 3.3 Liter.							
Sedan 4D		FG4JG	31895	17200	17800	18900	21600
Limited Sedan 4D		FH4JG	35645	19500	20200	21200	24100
GENESIS—4-Cyl. Turbo—Equipment Schedule 3							
W.B. 111.0"; 2.0 Liter.							
2.0T Coupe 2D		HT6KD	27245	17500	18150	18950	21600
2.0T R-Spec Coupe 2D		HT6KD	28095	18100	18750	19600	22400
2.0T Premium Cpe 2D		HT6KD	30195	20200	20900	21500	24300
GENESIS—V6—Equipment Schedule 3							
W.B. 111.0"; 3.8 Liter.							
3.8 R-Spec Coupe 2D		HU6KJ	30245	20000	20700	21500	24400
3.8 Grand Touring 2D		HU6KJ	33045	22400	23100	23800	26900
3.8 Ultimate Cpe 2D		HU6KJ	34295	23600	24300	25000	28200
GENESIS—V6—Equipment Schedule 3							
W.B. 115.6"; 3.8 Liter.							
3.8 Sedan 4D		GC4DD	36120	19200	19900	21000	24100
Adaptive Cruise Control				500	500	585	585
Premium Pkg				1250	1250	1455	1455
Technology Pkg				1500	1500	1760	1760
GENESIS—V8—Equipment Schedule 3							
W.B. 115.6"; 5.0 Liter.							
5.0 R-Spec Sedan 4D		GC4DH	48320	24400	25300	27000	31400
Adaptive Cruise Control				(500)	(500)	(585)	(585)
EQUUS—V8—Equipment Schedule 3							
W.B. 119.9"; 5.0 Liter.							
Signature Sedan 4D		GH4JH	61920	35900	37100	37600	42000
Ultimate Sedan 4D		GH4JH	68920	38400	39700	40200	44900

INFINITI

2000 INFINITI — JNK(CP11A)-Y-#

Body	Type	VIN	List	Trade-In Good	Very Good	Pvt-Party Good	Retail Excellent
G20—4-Cyl.—Equipment Schedule 1							
W.B. 102.4"; 2.0 Liter.							
Sedan 4D		CP11A	24220	1325	1475	2125	3575
Touring				100	100	135	135
Manual, 5-Spd				(200)	(200)	(255)	(255)
I30—V6—Equipment Schedule 1							
W.B. 108.3"; 3.0 Liter.							
Sedan 4D		CA21A	29990	1475	1650	2175	3525
Touring				100	100	135	135

2000 INFINITI

Body Type	VIN	List	Trade-In Good	Very Good	Pvt-Party Good	Retail Excellent
Q45—V8—Equipment Schedule 1						
W.B. 111.4"; 4.1 Liter.						
Sedan 4D	BY31A	49420	**2200**	**2450**	**3150**	**4875**
Touring		....	**100**	**100**	**135**	**135**
Anniversary Ed		....	**175**	**175**	**250**	**250**

2001 INFINITI — JNK(CP11A)-1-#

Body Type	VIN	List	Trade-In Good	Very Good	Pvt-Party Good	Retail Excellent
G20—4-Cyl.—Equipment Schedule 1						
W.B. 102.4"; 2.0 Liter.						
Sedan 4D	CP11A	24220	**1575**	**1775**	**2375**	**3850**
Touring		....	**100**	**100**	**135**	**135**
Manual, 5-Spd		....	**(225)**	**(225)**	**(300)**	**(300)**
I30—V6—Equipment Schedule 1						
W.B. 108.3"; 3.0 Liter.						
Sedan 4D	CA31A	29990	**1650**	**1850**	**2475**	**3925**
Touring		....	**100**	**100**	**135**	**135**
Q45—V8—Equipment Schedule 1						
W.B. 111.4"; 4.1 Liter.						
Sedan 4D	BY31A	49420	**2800**	**3150**	**3750**	**5525**
Touring		....	**100**	**100**	**135**	**135**

2002 INFINITI — JNK(CP11A)-2-#

Body Type	VIN	List	Trade-In Good	Very Good	Pvt-Party Good	Retail Excellent
G20—4-Cyl.—Equipment Schedule 1						
W.B. 102.4"; 2.0 Liter.						
Sedan 4D	CP11A	24340	**1825**	**2050**	**2750**	**4375**
Sport Pkg		....	**125**	**125**	**165**	**165**
Manual, 5-Spd		....	**(275)**	**(275)**	**(370)**	**(370)**
I35—V6—Equipment Schedule 1						
W.B. 108.3"; 3.5 Liter.						
Sedan 4D	DA31A	29295	**2100**	**2350**	**2950**	**4525**
Sport Pkg		....	**150**	**150**	**200**	**200**
Q45—V8—Equipment Schedule 1						
W.B. 113.0"; 4.5 Liter.						
Sedan 4D	BF01A	51045	**3575**	**3950**	**4475**	**6350**
Sport Pkg		....	**150**	**150**	**200**	**200**
Premium Pkg		....	**625**	**625**	**815**	**815**

2003 INFINITI — JNK(CV51E)-3-#

Body Type	VIN	List	Trade-In Good	Very Good	Pvt-Party Good	Retail Excellent
G35—V6—Equipment Schedule 1						
W.B. 112.2"; 3.5 Liter.						
Sedan 4D	CV51E	29495	**3350**	**3675**	**4375**	**6250**
Sport Coupe 2D	CV54E	32945	**4650**	**5075**	**5800**	**8050**
I35—V6—Equipment Schedule 1						
W.B. 108.3"; 3.5 Liter.						
Sedan 4D	DA31A	30995	**2600**	**2900**	**3475**	**5125**
Sport Pkg		....	**200**	**200**	**265**	**265**
M45—V8—Equipment Schedule 1						
W.B. 110.2"; 4.5 Liter.						
Sedan 4D	AY41E	43845	**3500**	**3825**	**5000**	**7125**
Q45—V8—Equipment Schedule 1						
W.B. 113.0"; 4.5 Liter.						
Sedan 4D	BF01A	52545	**4325**	**4750**	**5275**	**7175**
Premium Sedan 4D	BF01A	62145	**6025**	**6550**	**7300**	**9825**

2004 INFINITI — JNK(CV51E)-4-#

Body Type	VIN	List	Trade-In Good	Very Good	Pvt-Party Good	Retail Excellent
G35—V6—Equipment Schedule 1						
W.B. 112.2"; 3.5 Liter.						
Sedan 4D	CV51E	30690	**3875**	**4225**	**5000**	**6975**
Coupe 2D	CV54E	32140	**5500**	**5975**	**6750**	**9050**
AWD	F		**600**	**600**	**785**	**785**
I35—V6—Equipment Schedule 1						
W.B. 108.3"; 3.5 Liter.						
Sedan 4D	DA31A	31190	**3200**	**3550**	**4200**	**6125**
M45—V8—Equipment Schedule 1						
W.B. 110.2"; 4.5 Liter.						
Sedan 4D	AY41E	44840	**4500**	**4850**	**6050**	**8325**
Q45—V8—Equipment Schedule 1						
W.B. 113.0"; 4.5 Liter.						
Sedan 4D	BF01A	52990	**5175**	**5650**	**6325**	**8450**
Premium Sedan 4D	BF01A	62190	**7125**	**7725**	**8525**	**11300**
Journey Pkg		....	**750**	**750**	**945**	**945**

2005 INFINITI

Body Type	VIN	List	Trade-In Good	Trade-In Very Good	Pvt-Party Good	Retail Excellent

2005 INFINITI — JNK(CV51E)-5-#

G35—V6—Equipment Schedule 1
W.B. 112.2"; 3.5 Liter.

Sedan 4D	CV51E	31310	5475	5900	6950	9250
x AWD Sedan 4D	CV51F	34260	5525	5950	7025	9350
Coupe 2D	CV54E	31310	6650	7200	7975	10400

Q45—V8—Equipment Schedule 1
W.B. 113.0"; 4.5 Liter.

Sedan 4D	BF01A	56810	5350	5825	6750	9050
Premium Pkg			825	825	1035	1035

2006 INFINITI — JNK(CV51E)-6-#

G35—V6—Equipment Schedule 1
W.B. 112.2"; 3.5 Liter.

Sedan 4D	CV51E	32150	6675	7125	8100	10500
x AWD Sedan 4D	CV51F	34710	6750	7200	8200	10650
Coupe 2D	CV54E	33900	7950	8550	9325	11900

M35—V6—Equipment Schedule 1
W.B. 114.2"; 3.5 Liter.

Sedan 4D	AY01E	41250	7725	8200	9725	12400
x AWD Sedan 4D	AY01F	44040	8475	8975	10550	13400
Sport Sedan 4D	AY01E	44050	8125	8600	10150	12950
Premium Pkg			475	475	635	635

M45—V8—Equipment Schedule 1
W.B. 114.2"; 4.5 Liter.

Sedan 4D	BY01E	47560	8675	9200	11150	14250
Sport Sedan 4D	BY01E	50360	9950	10500	12550	15950
Premium Pkg			600	600	795	795

Q45—V8—Equipment Schedule 1
W.B. 113.0"; 4.5 Liter.

Sport Sedan 4D	BF01A	58750	6550	7075	8225	11000
Premium Pkg			875	875	1110	1110

2007 INFINITI — JNK(BV61E)-7-#

G35—V6—Equipment Schedule 1
W.B. 112.2"; 3.5 Liter.

Sedan 4D	BV61E	34500	8975	9500	10300	12800
Journey Sedan 4D	BV61E	34950	9075	9625	10450	12950
Sport Sedan 4D	BV61E	36500	9250	9800	10750	13350
x AWD Sedan 4D	BV61F	36800	9075	9600	10500	13050
Coupe 2D	CV54E	34150	8800	9400	10150	12750

M35—V6—Equipment Schedule 1
W.B. 114.2"; 3.5 Liter.

Sedan 4D	AY01E	42150	9450	10000	11550	14500
x AWD Sedan 4D	AY01F	45265	10100	10650	12350	15450
Sport Sedan 4D	AY01E	44950	9875	10400	12100	15150
Premium Pkg			500	500	665	665

M45—V8—Equipment Schedule 1
W.B. 114.2"; 4.5 Liter.

Sedan 4D	BY01E	49800	10700	11250	13000	16250
Sport Sedan 4D	BY01E	51200	11950	12550	14500	18000
Premium Pkg			625	625	850	850

2008 INFINITI — JNK(BV61E)-8-#

G35—V6—Equipment Schedule 1
W.B. 112.2"; 3.5 Liter.

Sedan 4D	BV61E	32315	10600	11150	12050	14650
Journey Sedan 4D	BV61E	32765	10750	11300	12200	14850
Sport Sedan 4D	BV61E	33115	10950	11550	12550	15250
x AWD Sedan 4D	BV61F	34815	10750	11300	12250	14900

G37—V6—Equipment Schedule 1
W.B. 112.2"; 3.7 Liter.

Coupe 2D	CV64E	34965	11150	11800	12550	15200
Journey Coupe 2D	CV64E	35715	11450	12150	12900	15650
Sport Coupe 2D	CV64E	36265	11700	12400	13100	15900

M35—V6—Equipment Schedule 1
W.B. 114.2"; 3.5 Liter.

Sedan 4D	AY01E	43765	11400	12000	13350	16200
x AWD Sedan 4D	AY01F	45515	11700	12300	13700	16650
Premium Pkg			525	525	665	665

Body Type	VIN	List	Trade-In Good	Very Good	Pvt-Party Good	Retail Excellent
M45—V8—Equipment Schedule 1						
W.B. 114.2"; 4.5 Liter.						
Sedan 4D	BY01E	50065	**12700**	**13350**	**14750**	**17850**
x AWD Sedan 4D	BY01F	52565	**14000**	**14650**	**16250**	**19650**
Premium Pkg			**525**	**525**	**665**	**665**

2009 INFINITI — JNK(CV61E)-9-#

Body Type	VIN	List	Good	Very Good	Good	Excellent
G37—V6—Equipment Schedule 1						
W.B. 112.2"; 3.7 Liter.						
Sedan 4D	CV61E	34115	**12150**	**12700**	**13750**	**16400**
Coupe 2D	CV64E	36765	**13100**	**13750**	**14550**	**17250**
Convertible 2D	CV66E	44715	**15600**	**16350**	**17100**	**20200**
Journey Sedan 4D	CV61E	34565	**12350**	**12950**	**13950**	**16650**
Journey Coupe 2D	CV64E	37515	**13500**	**14200**	**14950**	**17700**
Sport Sedan 4D	CV61E	35115	**12850**	**13450**	**14450**	**17250**
Sport Coupe 2D	CV64E	37865	**13950**	**14650**	**15400**	**18200**
Sport Convertible 2D	CV66E	44765	**16250**	**17050**	**17800**	**21100**
x AWD Sedan 4D	CV61F	36615	**12300**	**12900**	**13900**	**16650**
x AWD Coupe 2D	CV64F	39565	**13400**	**14050**	**14850**	**17650**
M35—V6—Equipment Schedule 1						
W.B. 114.2"; 3.5 Liter.						
Sedan 4D	CY01E	46615	**12950**	**13600**	**15050**	**18150**
x AWD Sedan 4D	CY01F	48765	**13350**	**14000**	**15450**	**18550**
Premium Pkg			**550**	**550**	**690**	**690**
M45—V8—Equipment Schedule 1						
W.B. 114.2"; 4.5 Liter.						
Sedan 4D	BY01E	52965	**14950**	**15650**	**17200**	**20600**
x AWD Sedan 4D	BY01F	56765	**16200**	**16950**	**18650**	**22400**
Premium Pkg			**550**	**550**	**690**	**690**

2010 INFINITI — JNK(CV6AE)-A-#

Body Type	VIN	List	Good	Very Good	Good	Excellent
G37—V6—Equipment Schedule 1						
W.B. 112.2"; 3.7 Liter.						
Sedan 4D	CV6AE	34115	**14250**	**14850**	**16000**	**18750**
Coupe 2D	CV6EE	36915	**15050**	**15750**	**16600**	**19450**
Sport Sedan 4D	CV6AE	37865	**15350**	**16000**	**17100**	**20000**
Sport Coupe 2D	CV6EE	41265	**16150**	**16900**	**17750**	**20800**
Sport Convertible 2D	CV6FE	47815	**19500**	**20300**	**21100**	**24600**
Anniversary Ed Sed	CV6AE	44650	**16500**	**17350**	**18550**	**21800**
Anniversary Ed Cpe	CV6EE	51415	**20600**	**21500**	**22300**	**25900**
Anniversary Ed Conv	CV6FE	55765	**22500**	**23400**	**24200**	**28200**
AWD	F		**0**	**0**	**0**	**0**
G37—V6—Equipment Schedule 1						
W.B. 112.2"; 3.7 Liter.						
Convertible 2D	CV6FE	45215	**18500**	**19300**	**20200**	**23500**
Journey Sedan 4D	CV6AE	36315	**14350**	**14950**	**16100**	**18950**
Journey Coupe 2D	CV6EE	39365	**15550**	**16250**	**17150**	**20000**
x AWD Sedan 4D	CV6AF	37915	**14400**	**15000**	**16150**	**19000**
x AWD Coupe 2D	CV6EF	41015	**15550**	**16250**	**17200**	**20200**
Intelligent Cruise Ctrl			**400**	**400**	**475**	**475**
Premium Pkg			**575**	**575**	**690**	**690**
Sport Pkg			**575**	**575**	**690**	**690**
M35—V6—Equipment Schedule 1						
W.B. 114.2"; 3.5 Liter.						
Sedan 4D	CY0AP	46665	**15750**	**16450**	**17700**	**20800**
x AWD Sedan 4D	CY0AR	48815	**16100**	**16850**	**18100**	**21300**
M45—V8—Equipment Schedule 1						
W.B. 114.2"; 4.5 Liter.						
Sedan 4D	BY0AP	53015	**17700**	**18450**	**19800**	**23300**
x AWD Sedan 4D	BY0AR	56815	**19000**	**19800**	**21200**	**24900**
Premium Pkg			**575**	**575**	**700**	**700**

2011 INFINITI — JN1(DV6AE)-B-#

Body Type	VIN	List	Good	Very Good	Good	Excellent
G25—V6—Equipment Schedule 1						
W.B. 112.2"; 2.5 Liter.						
Sedan 4D	DV6AE	31825	**13650**	**14200**	**15250**	**17700**
Journey Sedan 4D	DV6AE	34225	**14150**	**14700**	**15800**	**18350**
x AWD Sedan 4D	DV6AF	35825	**14650**	**15250**	**16350**	**18950**
G37—V6—Equipment Schedule 1						
W.B. 112.2"; 3.7 Liter.						
Coupe 2D	CV6EE	36925	**17200**	**17900**	**18850**	**21800**
Sport Appearance Ed	CV6AE	40075	**17200**	**17850**	**19050**	**22100**

2011 INFINITI

Body Type	VIN	List	Trade-In Good	Very Good	Pvt-Party Good	Retail Excellent
Sport Sedan 4D	CV6AE	40325	17900	18550	19750	22800
Sport Coupe 2D	CV6EE	41275	18500	19250	20200	23300
Sport Convertible 2D	CV6FE	49825	22500	23300	24300	28000
Limited Ed Sedan 4D	CV6AE	44275	19050	19800	21000	24300
x AWD Sport Appear	CV6AF	41675	17800	18450	19700	22800
G37—V6—Equipment Schedule 1						
W.B. 112.2"; 3.7 Liter.						
Convertible 2D	CV6FE	45375	21400	22200	23100	26700
Journey Sedan 4D	CV6AE	36925	16550	17200	18300	21200
Journey Coupe 2D	CV6EE	39525	17900	18650	19550	22600
x AWD Sedan 4D	CV6AF	38525	16750	17400	18550	21500
x AWD Coupe 2D	CV6EF	41025	17900	18650	19550	22600
Intelligent Cruise Ctrl			425	425	500	500
Premium Pkg			600	600	710	710
Sport Pkg			625	625	740	740
G IPL—V6—Equipment Schedule 1						
W.B. 112.2"; 3.7 Liter.						
Coupe 2D	CV6EE	50725	22900	23700	24700	28500
M37—V6—Equipment Schedule 1						
W.B. 112.2"; 3.7 Liter.						
Sedan 4D	BY1AP	47115	20600	21400	22500	26200
x AWD Sedan 4D	BY1AR	49265	21500	22500	23500	27200
Premium Pkg			600	600	705	705
Technology Pkg			1275	1275	1515	1515
Sport Pkg			625	625	735	735
Sport Touring Pkg			900	900	1060	1060
Deluxe Touring Pkg			900	900	1060	1060
M56—V8—Equipment Schedule 1						
W.B. 114.2"; 5.6 Liter.						
Sedan 4D	AY1AP	58415	23000	23900	25000	29000
x AWD Sedan 4D	AY1AR	62215	24200	25200	26400	30600
Premium Pkg			600	600	700	700
Technology Pkg			1275	1275	1500	1500
Sport Pkg			625	625	730	730
Sport Touring Pkg			900	900	1050	1050
Deluxe Touring Pkg			900	900	1050	1050

2012 INFINITI — (3orJ)N1(DV6AE)–C–#

Body Type	VIN	List	Trade-In Good	Very Good	Pvt-Party Good	Retail Excellent
G25—V6—Equipment Schedule 1						
W.B. 112.2"; 2.5 Liter.						
Sedan 4D	DV6AE	33295	15450	16000	17000	19450
Journey Sedan 4D	DV6AE	35695	16500	17100	18150	20700
x AWD Sedan 4D	DV6AF	37295	16700	17300	18350	21000
G37—V6—Equipment Schedule 1						
W.B. 112.2"; 3.7 Liter.						
Coupe 2D	CV6AE	38495	19500	20300	21200	24200
Sport Appearance 4D	CV6AE	40245	19450	20200	21200	24200
Sport Sedan 4D	CV6AE	41495	20200	20900	21900	25000
Sport Coupe 2D	CV6EE	44695	21300	22100	23000	26200
Sport Convertible 2D	CV6FE	51745	25100	26000	26900	30600
Limited Ed Sedan 4D	CV6AE	45445	21800	22600	23700	27100
G37—V6—Equipment Schedule 1						
W.B. 112.2"; 3.7 Liter.						
Convertible 2D	CV6FE	47295	24200	25100	26000	29600
Journey Sedan 4D	CV6AE	37095	18950	19650	20700	23600
Journey Coupe 2D	CV6EE	39945	20200	20900	21800	24900
x AWD Sedan 4D	CV6AF	38695	19150	19850	20900	23900
x AWD Coupe 2D	CV6EF	41595	20400	21100	22000	25200
Intelligent Speed Ctrl			450	450	520	520
Premium Pkg			650	650	750	750
Sport Pkg			700	700	805	805
G IPL—V6—Equipment Schedule 1						
W.B. 112.2"; 3.7 Liter.						
Coupe 2D	CV6EE	52145	25300	26100	27100	30900
M35—V6 Hybrid—Equipment Schedule 1						
W.B. 114.2"; 3.5 Liter.						
Sedan 4D	EY1AP	54575	24300	25300	26200	30200
Premium Pkg			650	650	735	735
Deluxe Touring Pkg			925	925	1045	1045
Technology Pkg			1350	1350	1535	1535
M37—V6—Equipment Schedule 1						
W.B. 114.2"; 3.7 Liter.						
Sedan 4D	BY1AP	48575	23500	24500	25400	29200

2012 INFINITI

Body Type	VIN	List	Trade-In Good	Very Good	Pvt-Party Good	Retail Excellent
x AWD Sedan 4D	BY1AF	50725	24200	25200	26100	30000
Premium Pkg			650	650	735	735
Technology Pkg			1350	1350	1540	1540
Sport Pkg			700	700	795	795
Sport Touring Pkg			925	925	1050	1050
Deluxe Touring Pkg			925	925	1050	1050
M56—V8—Equipment Schedule 1						
W.B. 114.2"; 5.6 Liter.						
Sedan 4D	AY1AP	59975	27900	29000	29800	34100
x AWD Sedan 4D	AY1AF	63775	29100	30200	31200	35600
Technology Pkg			1350	1350	1525	1525
Sport Pkg			700	700	785	785
Sport Touring Pkg			925	925	1040	1040
Deluxe Touring Pkg			925	925	1040	1040

2013 INFINITI — (3orJ)N1(CV6FE)–D–#

Body Type	VIN	List	Trade-In Good	Very Good	Pvt-Party Good	Retail Excellent
G37—V6—Equipment Schedule 1						
W.B. 112.2"; 3.7 Liter.						
Sport Sedan 4D	CV6AP	42395	22400	23100	24100	27200
Sport Coupe 2D	CV6EK	46405	24100	24900	25700	29000
Sport Convertible 2D	CV6FE	52895	29200	30100	31000	34900
G37—V6—Equipment Schedule 1						
W.B. 112.2"; 3.7 Liter.						
Convertible 2D	CV6FE	48095	27800	28700	29500	33200
Journey Sedan 4D	CV6AP	37795	20400	21100	22100	24900
Journey Coupe 2D	CV6EK	41305	22300	23100	23900	27000
x AWD Sedan 4D	CV6AR	39395	21000	21700	22700	25600
x AWD Coupe 2D	CV6EL	42955	22800	23600	24400	27600
Intelligent Cruise Control			475	475	540	540
Premium Pkg			700	700	795	795
Sport Pkg			800	800	905	905
G IPL—V6—Equipment Schedule 1						
W.B. 112.2"; 3.7 Liter.						
Coupe 2D	CV6EK	53295	28300	29300	30100	34000
Convertible 2D	CV6FE	61495	32900	33900	34600	38900
M35—V6 Hybrid—Equipment Schedule 1						
W.B. 114.2"; 3.5 Liter.						
Sedan 4D	EY1AP	55655	28900	30100	30900	35200
Premium Pkg			700	700	775	775
Technology Pkg			1425	1425	1580	1580
Touring Pkg			950	950	1050	1050
M37—V6—Equipment Schedule 1						
W.B. 114.2"; 3.7 Liter.						
Sedan 4D	BY1AP	49605	28100	29200	30000	34200
x AWD Sedan 4D	BY1AR	51755	28800	30000	30700	35000
Premium Pkg			700	700	775	775
Sport Pkg			800	800	890	890
Technology Pkg			1425	1425	1585	1585
Touring Pkg			950	950	1055	1055
M56—V8—Equipment Schedule 1						
W.B. 114.2"; 5.6 Liter.						
Sedan 4D	AY1AP	62105	32500	33800	34400	39000
x AWD Sedan 4D	AY1AR	64605	33800	35100	35700	40500
Sport Pkg			800	800	885	885
Technology Pkg			1425	1425	1575	1575
Touring Pkg			950	950	1050	1050

2014 INFINITI — (3orJ)N1(AV7AP)–E–#

Body Type	VIN	List	Trade-In Good	Very Good	Pvt-Party Good	Retail Excellent
Q50—V6—Equipment Schedule 1						
W.B. 112.2"; 3.7 Liter.						
3.7 Sedan 4D		37605	25400	26200	27000	30200
3.7 Premium Sed		40455	26700	27500	28300	31700
S 3.7 Sedan 4D		44105	28400	29300	30100	33600
Technology Pkg			750	750	850	850
Deluxe Touring Pkg			575	575	640	640
AWD			1500	1500	1675	1675
Q50—V6 Hybrid—Equipment Schedule 1						
W.B. 112.2"; 3.5 Liter.						
Premium Sedan 4D	AV7AP	44605	27600	28500	29200	32600
S Sedan 4D		47255	29400	30400	31100	34800
AWD			1500	1500	1670	1670

2014 INFINITI

Body Type	VIN	List	Trade-In Good	Very Good	Pvt-Party Good	Retail Excellent
Q60—V6—Equipment Schedule 1						
W.B. 112.2"; 3.7 Liter.						
Journey Coupe 2D	CV6EK	41305	25500	26400	27100	30400
Convertible 2D	CV6FE	48805	32000	33000	33600	37500
S Coupe 2D	CV6EK	46405	28900	29800	30500	34100
S Convertible 2D	CV6FE	53655	33500	34500	35100	39200
IPL Convertible 2D	CV6FE	62355	36500	37700	38200	42600
Intelligent Cruise Control			500	500	560	560
Q60 AWD—V6—Equipment Schedule 1						
W.B. 112.2"; 3.7 Liter.						
Coupe 2D	CV6EK	42955	26700	27600	28200	31700
Intelligent Cruise Control			500	500	560	560
Q70—V6—Equipment Schedule 1						
W.B. 114.2"; 3.7 Liter.						
3.7 Sedan 4D	BY1AP	50405	32900	34100	34900	39700
Intelligent Cruise Control			500	500	545	545
Deluxe Touring Pkg			975	975	1065	1065
Premium Pkg			750	750	820	820
Sport Pkg			900	900	985	985
Technology Pkg			1500	1500	1640	1640
AWD	R		1500	1500	1640	1640
Q70—V6 Hybrid—Equipment Schedule 1						
W.B. 114.2"; 3.5 Liter.						
Sedan 4D	EY1AP	56455	33700	35000	35700	40500
Intelligent Cruise Control			500	500	545	545
Deluxe Touring Pkg			975	975	1065	1065
Premium Pkg			750	750	820	820
Technology Pkg			1500	1500	1635	1635
Q70—V8—Equipment Schedule 1						
W.B. 114.2"; 5.6 Liter.						
5.6 Sedan 4D	AY1AP	64205	36600	37900	38400	43400
AWD	R		1500	1500	1635	1635

JAGUAR

2000 JAGUAR — SAJ(DorJ)(A01C)-Y-#

Body Type	VIN	List	Good	Very Good	Good	Excellent
S-TYPE—V6—Equipment Schedule 1						
W.B. 114.5"; 3.0 Liter.						
Sedan 4D	A01C	44980	1150	1300	1725	2725
Sport Pkg			125	125	165	165
S-TYPE—V8—Equipment Schedule 1						
W.B. 114.5"; 4.0 Liter.						
Sedan 4D	A01D	48580	1650	1850	2350	3650
Sport Pkg			125	125	165	165
XJ8—V8—Equipment Schedule 1						
W.B. 113.0", 117.9" (L & Vanden Plas); 4.0 Liter.						
Sedan 4D	A14C	56245	700	800	1400	2400
L Sedan 4D	A23C	61295	975	1100	1700	2875
Vanden Plas Sedan 4D	A24C	65345	1625	1800	2625	4275
XJR—V8 Supercharged—Equipment Schedule 1						
W.B. 113.0"; 4.0 Liter.						
Sedan 4D	A15B	69145	2200	2450	3350	5350
XJ8—V8 Supercharged—Equipment Schedule 1						
W.B. 117.9"; 4.0 Liter.						
Vanden Plas Sedan 4D	A14B	81245	4000	4375	5850	8725
XK8—V8—Equipment Schedule 2						
W.B. 101.9"; 4.0 Liter.						
Coupe 2D	A41C	66795	1875	2050	2950	4625
Convertible 2D	A42C	71795	2625	2875	3825	5800
XKR—V8 Supercharged—Equipment Schedule 2						
W.B. 101.9"; 4.0 Liter.						
Coupe 2D	A41B	77395	1775	1925	2450	3575
Convertible 2D	A42B	82395	3000	3275	3775	5250

2001 JAGUAR — SAJD(A01C)-1-#

Body Type	VIN	List	Good	Very Good	Good	Excellent
S-TYPE—V6—Equipment Schedule 1						
W.B. 114.5"; 3.0 Liter.						
Sedan 4D	A01C	46250	1725	1925	2375	3550
Sport Pkg			125	125	175	175
S-TYPE—V8—Equipment Schedule 1						
W.B. 114.5"; 4.0 Liter.						

2001 JAGUAR

Body Type	VIN	List	Trade-In Good	Trade-In Very Good	Pvt-Party Good	Retail Excellent
Sedan 4D	A01D	49950	2200	2450	2975	4425
Sport Pkg			125	125	175	175
XJ8—V8—Equipment Schedule 1						
W.B. 113.0", 117.9" (L & Vanden Plas); 4.0 Liter.						
Sedan 4D	A14C	56950	700	800	1475	2550
L Sedan 4D	A23C	62950	975	1100	1775	3025
Vanden Plas Sedan 4D	A24C	68250	1725	1950	2825	4600
XJR—V8 Supercharged—Equipment Schedule 1						
W.B. 113.0". 4.0 Liter.						
Sedan 4D	A15B	69930	2250	2500	3475	5575
XJ8—V8 Supercharged—Equipment Schedule 1						
W.B. 117.9". 4.0 Liter.						
Vanden Plas Sedan 4D	A25B	83950	4775	5200	6275	8725
XK8—V8—Equipment Schedule 2						
W.B. 101.9". 4.0 Liter.						
Coupe 2D	A41C	69750	2025	2225	3150	4875
Convertible 2D	A42C	74750	2775	3050	4025	6025
XKR—V8 Supercharged—Equipment Schedule 2						
W.B. 101.9". 4.0 Liter.						
Coupe 2D	A41B	80750	2750	3025	3475	4825
Convertible 2D	A42B	85750	3800	4125	4750	6400

2002 JAGUAR — SAJ-(A51D)-2-#

Body Type	VIN	List	Trade-In Good	Trade-In Very Good	Pvt-Party Good	Retail Excellent
X-TYPE AWD—V6—Equipment Schedule 2						
W.B. 106.7"; 2.5 Liter, 3.0 Liter.						
2.5L Sedan 4D	A51D	34370	1275	1450	2225	3700
2.5L Sport Sedan 4D	A53D	36370	1300	1475	2250	3825
3.0L Sedan 4D	A51C	39095	1425	1625	2500	4225
3.0L Sport Sedan 4D	A53C	41095	1700	1925	2850	4725
Manual, 5-Spd			(300)	(300)	(395)	(395)
S-TYPE—V6—Equipment Schedule 1						
W.B. 114.5". 3.0 Liter.						
Sedan 4D	A01C	46320	1725	1925	2375	3550
Sport			600	600	795	795
Manual, 5-Spd			(300)	(300)	(395)	(395)
S-TYPE—V8—Equipment Schedule 1						
W.B. 114.5". 4.0 Liter.						
Sedan 4D	A01D	49975	2225	2475	3050	4550
Sport			600	600	795	795
XJ8—V8—Equipment Schedule 1						
W.B. 113.0". 4.0 Liter.						
Sedan 4D	A14C	56975	875	975	1600	2725
XJ SPORT—V8—Equipment Schedule 1						
W.B. 113.0". 4.0 Liter.						
Sedan 4D	A14C	59975	1275	1425	2050	3400
VANDEN PLAS—V8—Equipment Schedule 1						
W.B. 117.9". 4.0 Liter.						
Sedan 4D	A24C	68975	1925	2150	2950	4650
XJR—V8 Supercharged—Equipment Schedule 1						
W.B. 113.0". 4.0 Liter.						
Sedan 4D	A15B	72475	2875	3225	4150	6375
100 Sedan 4D	A15B		4175	4600	5875	8775
XJ SUPER—V8 Supercharged—Equipment Schedule 1						
W.B. 117.9". 4.0 Liter.						
Sedan 4D	A25B	79975	6925	7475	8425	11350
XK8—V8—Equipment Schedule 2						
W.B. 101.9". 4.0 Liter.						
Coupe 2D	A41C	69975	2300	2525	3400	5125
Convertible 2D	A42C	74975	3650	3975	5025	7175
XKR—V8 Supercharged—Equipment Schedule 2						
W.B. 101.9". 4.0 Liter.						
Coupe 2D	A41B	82975	2850	3125	3775	5275
Convertible 2D	A42B	87975	4100	4425	5125	6925
100 Coupe 2D	A41B	84000	****	****	****	18100
100 Convertible 2D	A42B		****	****	****	17450

2003 JAGUAR — SAJ-(A51D)-3-#

Body Type	VIN	List	Trade-In Good	Trade-In Very Good	Pvt-Party Good	Retail Excellent
X-TYPE AWD—V6—Equipment Schedule 2						
W.B. 106.7"; 2.5 Liter, 3.0 Liter.						
2.5L Sedan 4D	A51D	29950	1575	1775	2525	4100
3.0L Sedan 4D	A51C	36950	1725	1950	2825	4625
Sport Pkg			525	525	685	685

Body Type	VIN	List	Trade-In Good	Very Good	Pvt-Party Good	Retail Excellent
Manual, 5-Spd			(325)	(325)	(445)	(445)
S-TYPE—V6—Equipment Schedule 1						
W.B. 114.5"; 3.0 Liter.						
Sedan 4D	A01T	44975	1725	1925	2400	3600
Sport Pkg			675	675	885	885
Manual, 5-Spd			(325)	(325)	(445)	(445)
V8, 4.2 Liter	U		450	450	600	600
S-TYPE R—V8 Supercharged—Equipment Schedule 1						
W.B. 114.5"; 4.2 Liter.						
Sedan 4D	A03V	62400	3875	4275	5075	7225
XJ8—V8—Equipment Schedule 1						
W.B. 113.0"; 4.0 Liter.						
Sedan 4D	A14C	56975	1825	2025	2675	4125
XJ SPORT—V8—Equipment Schedule 1						
W.B. 113.0"; 4.0 Liter.						
Sedan 4D	A12C	59975	2225	2475	3200	4875
VANDEN PLAS—V8—Equipment Schedule 1						
W.B. 117.9"; 4.0 Liter.						
Sedan 4D	A24C	68975	2500	2775	3675	5675
XJR—V8 Supercharged—Equipment Schedule 1						
W.B. 113.0"; 4.0 Liter.						
Sedan 4D	A15B	72475	3950	4325	5475	8075
XJ SUPER—V8 Supercharged—Equipment Schedule 1						
W.B. 117.9"; 4.0 Liter.						
Sedan 4D	A25B	79975	8925	9600	10450	13750
XK8—V8—Equipment Schedule 2						
W.B. 101.9"; 4.2 Liter.						
Coupe 2D	A41C	69975	3225	3500	4350	6100
Convertible 2D	A42C	74975	4825	5175	5900	7850
XKR—V8 Supercharged—Equipment Schedule 2						
W.B. 101.9"; 4.2 Liter.						
Coupe 2D	A41B	81975	3200	3500	4250	5900
Convertible 2D	A42B	86975	4575	4925	5700	7675
Handling Pkg			1250	1250	1640	1640

2004 JAGUAR — SAJ-(WA51D)-4-#

Body Type	VIN	List	Trade-In Good	Very Good	Pvt-Party Good	Retail Excellent
X-TYPE AWD—V6—Equipment Schedule 1						
W.B. 106.7"; 2.5 Liter, 3.0 Liter.						
2.5L Sedan 4D	WA51D	30520	1775	1975	2750	4350
3.0L Sedan 4D	WA51C	33995	2025	2275	3075	4850
Sport Pkg			575	575	755	755
Manual, 5-Spd			(375)	(375)	(490)	(490)
S-TYPE—V6—Equipment Schedule 1						
W.B. 114.5"; 3.0 Liter.						
Sedan 4D	WA01T	44995	1825	2025	2550	3775
Sport Pkg			725	725	980	980
Manual, 5-Spd			(375)	(375)	(490)	(490)
V8, 4.2 Liter			475	475	635	635
S-TYPE R—V8 Supercharged—Equipment Schedule 1						
W.B. 114.5"; 4.2 Liter.						
Sedan 4D	WA03V	63120	4275	4700	5725	8250
XJ8—V8—Equipment Schedule 1						
W.B. 119.4"; 4.2 Liter.						
Sedan 4D	WA71C	59995	1900	2100	2750	4175
VANDEN PLAS—V8—Equipment Schedule 1						
W.B. 119.4"; 4.2 Liter.						
Sedan 4D	WA74C	68995	3125	3475	4350	6325
XJR—V8 Supercharged—Equipment Schedule 1						
W.B. 119.4"; 4.2 Liter.						
Sedan 4D	WA73B	74995	4475	4900	5800	8150
XK8—V8—Equipment Schedule 2						
W.B. 101.9"; 4.2 Liter.						
Coupe 2D	WA41C	69995	3925	4225	5025	6825
Convertible 2D	WA42C	74995	5575	5950	6725	8875
XKR—V8 Supercharged—Equipment Schedule 2						
W.B. 101.9"; 4.2 Liter.						
Coupe 2D	WA41B	82995	3725	4025	4700	6325
Convertible 2D	WA42B	87995	6150	6550	7500	9700
Handling Pkg			1350	1350	1655	1655

2005 JAGUAR

Body Type	VIN	List	Trade-In Good	Very Good	Pvt-Party Good	Retail Excellent

2005 JAGUAR — SAJD(WA51D)-5-#

X-TYPE AWD—V6—Equipment Schedule 2
W.B. 106.7"; 2.5 Liter, 3.0 Liter.

2.5L Sedan 4D	WA51D	32245	**2025**	**2275**	**3200**	**4925**
3.0L Sedan 4D	WA51C	34995	**2025**	**2275**	**3300**	**5200**
3.0L Wagon 4D	WA54C	36995	**3625**	**4025**	**5475**	**8300**
Sport Pkg		------	625	625	825	825
VDP Edition		------	1025	1025	1375	1375
Manual, 5-Spd		------	(400)	(400)	(540)	(540)

S-TYPE—V6—Equipment Schedule 1
W.B. 114.5"; 3.0 Liter.

Sedan 4D	WA01T	45995	**2725**	**3050**	**3900**	**5750**
Sport Pkg		------	800	800	1075	1075
VDP Edition		------	900	900	1200	1200
V8, 4.2 Liter		------	500	500	665	665

S-TYPE R—V8 Supercharged—Equipment Schedule 1
W.B. 114.5"; 4.2 Liter.

Sedan 4D	WA03V	58995	**6500**	**7050**	**8775**	**12400**

XJ8—V8—Equipment Schedule 1
W.B. 119.4", 124.4" (L); 4.2 Liter.

Sedan 4D	WA71C	61495	**4275**	**4675**	**5525**	**7600**
L Sedan 4D	WA79C	63495	**5175**	**5650**	**6700**	**9075**

VANDEN PLAS—V8—Equipment Schedule 1
W.B. 124.4"; 4.2 Liter.

Sedan 4D	WA82C	70995	**6300**	**6825**	**8075**	**11000**

XJR—V8 Supercharged—Equipment Schedule 1
W.B. 119.4"; 4.2 Liter.

Sedan 4D	WA73B	75995	**8950**	**9625**	**11050**	**14750**

XJ SUPER—V8 Supercharged—Equipment Schedule 1
W.B. 124.4"; 4.2 Liter.

Sedan 4D	WA82B	89995	**10800**	**11550**	**12500**	**16000**

XK8—V8—Equipment Schedule 2
W.B. 101.9"; 4.2 Liter.

Coupe 2D	DA41C	70495	**5025**	**5375**	**6475**	**8525**
Convertible 2D	DA42C	75495	**6550**	**6975**	**8075**	**10450**

XKR—V8 Supercharged—Equipment Schedule 2
W.B. 101.9"; 4.2 Liter.

Coupe 2D	DA41B	82995	**5950**	**6350**	**7700**	**10150**
Convertible 2D	DA42B	87995	**8400**	**8900**	**10350**	**13400**
Handling Pkg		------	1425	1425	1805	1805

2006 JAGUAR — SAJ-(WA51A)-6-#

X-TYPE AWD—V6—Equipment Schedule 2
W.B. 106.7"; 3.0 Liter.

3.0L Sedan 4D	WA51A	32995	**2625**	**2950**	**3750**	**5500**
3.0L Wagon 4D	WA54A	36995	**4350**	**4775**	**5925**	**8475**
Sport Pkg		------	675	675	895	895
VDP Edition		------	1125	1125	1500	1500

S-TYPE—V6—Equipment Schedule 1
W.B. 114.5"; 3.0 Liter.

Sedan 4D	WA01A	45995	**3275**	**3625**	**4425**	**6300**
VDP Edition		------	975	975	1305	1305
V8, 4.2 Liter	B	------	600	600	800	800

S-TYPE R—V8 Supercharged—Equipment Schedule 1
W.B. 114.5"; 4.2 Liter.

Sedan 4D	WA03C	63995	**7050**	**7650**	**9300**	**12850**

XJ8—V8—Equipment Schedule 1
W.B. 119.4", 124.4" (L); 4.2 Liter.

Sedan 4D	WA71B	62495	**5325**	**5775**	**6825**	**9050**
L Sedan 4D	WA79B	64995	**7700**	**8300**	**9400**	**12300**

VANDEN PLAS—V8—Equipment Schedule 1
W.B. 124.4"; 4.2 Liter.

Sedan 4D	WA82B	74995	**8500**	**9125**	**10300**	**13450**

XJR—V8 Supercharged—Equipment Schedule 1
W.B. 119.4"; 4.2 Liter.

Sedan 4D	WA73C	79995	**10200**	**10900**	**12150**	**15750**

XJ SUPER—V8 Supercharged—Equipment Schedule 1
W.B. 124.4"; 4.2 Liter.

Sedan 4D	WA82C	91995	**12450**	**13200**	**14100**	**17650**
Portfolio Sedan 4D	WA86C	115995	**22900**	**24100**	**24900**	**30700**

2006 JAGUAR

Body Type	VIN	List	Trade-In Good	Very Good	Pvt-Party Good	Retail Excellent
XK8—V8—Equipment Schedule 2						
W.B. 101.9"; 4.2 Liter.						
Coupe 2D	DA41C	70495	6750	7150	8250	10600
Convertible 2D	DA42C	75495	8275	8775	9975	12650
XKR—V8 Supercharged—Equipment Schedule 2						
W.B. 101.9"; 4.2 Liter.						
Coupe 2D	DA41B	82995	7150	7600	9000	11400
Convertible 2D	DA42B	87995	9700	10250	11650	14550
Handling Pkg			1525	1525	1910	1910

2007 JAGUAR — SAJ-(WA51A)-7-#

Body Type	VIN	List	Trade-In Good	Very Good	Pvt-Party Good	Retail Excellent
X-TYPE AWD—V6—Equipment Schedule 2						
W.B. 106.7"; 3.0 Liter.						
3.0L Sedan 4D	WA51A	34995	4125	4525	5350	7300
3.0L Wagon 4D	WA54A	39995	5850	6350	7500	10100
Luxury Pkg			400	400	520	520
S-TYPE—V6—Equipment Schedule 1						
W.B. 114.5"; 3.0 Liter.						
Sedan 4D	WA01A	49000	4700	5100	5925	7950
V8, 4.2 Liter	B		700	700	935	935
S-TYPE R—V8 Supercharged—Equipment Schedule 1						
W.B. 114.5"; 4.2 Liter.						
Sedan 4D	WA03C	64000	9600	10300	11800	15450
XJ8—V8—Equipment Schedule 1						
W.B. 119.4", 124.4" (L); 4.2 Liter.						
Sedan 4D	WA71B	64250	7500	8050	8925	11400
L Sedan 4D	WA79B	67750	9775	10450	11450	14500
VANDEN PLAS—V8—Equipment Schedule 1						
W.B. 124.4"; 4.2 Liter.						
Sedan 4D	WA82B	75500	10450	11150	12350	15600
XJR—V8 Supercharged—Equipment Schedule 1						
W.B. 119.4"; 4.2 Liter.						
Sedan 4D	WA73C	81500	12250	13000	14100	17650
XJ SUPER—V8 Supercharged—Equipment Schedule 1						
W.B. 124.4"; 4.2 Liter.						
Sedan 4D	WA82C	92000	14800	15650	16600	20500
XK—V8—Equipment Schedule 2						
W.B. 108.3"; 4.2 Liter.						
Coupe 2D	WA43B	75500	11450	12050	13400	16450
Convertible 2D	WA44B	81500	13450	14100	15550	19050
Luxury Pkg			1125	1125	1375	1375
XKR—V8 Supercharged—Equipment Schedule 2						
W.B. 108.3"; 4.2 Liter.						
Coupe 2D	WA43C	86500	13850	14550	15300	18150
Convertible 2D	WA44C	92500	15850	16600	17400	20700
Luxury Pkg			1125	1125	1280	1280

2008 JAGUAR — SAJ-(WA51A)-8-#

Body Type	VIN	List	Trade-In Good	Very Good	Pvt-Party Good	Retail Excellent
X-TYPE AWD—V6—Equipment Schedule 2						
W.B. 106.7"; 3.0 Liter.						
3.0L Sedan 4D	WA51A	35725	4975	5350	6375	8375
3.0L Wagon 4D	WA54A	39995	6700	7175	8250	10700
Luxury Pkg			400	400	545	545
S-TYPE—V6—Equipment Schedule 1						
W.B. 114.5"; 3.0 Liter.						
Sedan 4D	WA01A	50000	9100	9725	10600	13300
V8, 4.2 Liter	B		800	800	940	940
S-TYPE R—V8 Supercharged—Equipment Schedule 1						
W.B. 114.5"; 4.2 Liter.						
Sedan 4D	WA03C	66000	13850	14750	15900	19750
Luxury Pkg			400	400	455	455
XJ8—V8—Equipment Schedule 1						
W.B. 119.4", 124.4" (L); 4.2 Liter.						
Sedan 4D	WA71B	65500	10850	11500	12400	15150
L Sedan 4D	WA79B	69000	13100	13850	14900	18200
VANDEN PLAS—V8—Equipment Schedule 1						
W.B. 124.4"; 4.2 Liter.						
Sedan 4D	WA82B	77750	13900	14700	15750	19250
XJR—V8 Supercharged—Equipment Schedule 1						
W.B. 119.4"; 4.2 Liter.						
Sedan 4D	WA73C	85250	17400	18350	19400	23600

DEDUCT FOR RECONDITIONING

0415

2008 JAGUAR

Body Type	VIN	List	Trade-In Good	Very Good	Pvt-Party Good	Retail Excellent
XJ SUPER—V8 Supercharged—Equipment Schedule 1						
W.B. 124.4"; 4.2 Liter.						
Sedan 4D	WA82C	95750	**17200**	**18100**	**19100**	**23100**
XK—V8—Equipment Schedule 2						
W.B. 108.3"; 4.2 Liter.						
Coupe 2D	WA43B	76500	**14950**	**15650**	**16950**	**20300**
Convertible 2D	WA44B	82500	**18150**	**18950**	**20400**	**24400**
Luxury Pkg			**1200**	**1200**	**1435**	**1435**
XKR—V8 Supercharged—Equipment Schedule 2						
W.B. 108.3"; 4.2 Liter.						
Coupe 2D	WA43C	87700	**19050**	**19900**	**20500**	**23700**
Portfolio Coupe 2D	WA45C	99700	**21500**	**22400**	**23200**	**27000**
Convertible 2D	WA44C	93700	**20700**	**21500**	**22100**	**25600**
Portfolio Conv 2D	WA46C	104800	**22200**	**23100**	**23900**	**27800**
Luxury Pkg			**1200**	**1200**	**1360**	**1360**

2009 JAGUAR — SAJ-(WA05B)-9-#

Body Type	VIN	List	Trade-In Good	Very Good	Pvt-Party Good	Retail Excellent
XF—V8—Equipment Schedule 1						
W.B. 114.5"; 4.2 Liter.						
Luxury Sedan 4D	WA05B	49975	**13300**	**14000**	**15200**	**18500**
Prem Luxury Sed 4D	WA06B	55975	**13750**	**14450**	**15650**	**19000**
XF—V8 Supercharged—Equipment Schedule 1						
W.B. 114.5"; 4.2 Liter.						
Sedan 4D	WA07C	62975	**16450**	**17250**	**18600**	**22600**
XJ8—V8—Equipment Schedule 1						
W.B. 119.4", 124.4" (L); 4.2 Liter.						
Sedan 4D	WA71B	66475	**12350**	**13000**	**14450**	**17850**
L Sedan 4D	WA79B	69975	**14650**	**15400**	**17050**	**21000**
VANDEN PLAS—V8—Equipment Schedule 1						
W.B. 124.4"; 4.2 Liter.						
Sedan 4D	WA82B	76850	**16700**	**17500**	**19000**	**23200**
XJR—V8 Supercharged—Equipment Schedule 1						
W.B. 119.4"; 4.2 Liter.						
Sedan 4D	WA73C	84350	**18900**	**19800**	**21500**	**26200**
XJ SUPER—V8 Supercharged—Equipment Schedule 1						
W.B. 124.4"; 4.2 Liter.						
Sedan 4D	WA82C	94850	**19350**	**20300**	**20700**	**24000**
Portfolio Sedan 4D	WA86C	105000	**31400**	**32800**	**32800**	**37700**
XK—V8—Equipment Schedule 2						
W.B. 108.3"; 4.2 Liter.						
Coupe 2D	WA43B	77775	**17850**	**18600**	**19800**	**23200**
Convertible 2D	WA44B	83775	**21100**	**21900**	**23100**	**26900**
Luxury Pkg			**1275**	**1275**	**1545**	**1545**
XKR—V8 Supercharged—Equipment Schedule 2						
W.B. 108.3"; 4.2 Liter.						
Coupe 2D	WA43C	88175	**19150**	**19900**	**20800**	**24100**
Convertible 2D	WA44C	94175	**21100**	**22000**	**22900**	**26500**
Portfolio Coupe 2D	WA45C	95975	**21800**	**22700**	**23800**	**27600**
Portfolio Conv 2D	WA46C	101975	**22600**	**23500**	**24700**	**28600**
Luxury Pkg			**1275**	**1275**	**1445**	**1445**

2010 JAGUAR — SAJ-(WA0FA)-A-#

Body Type	VIN	List	Trade-In Good	Very Good	Pvt-Party Good	Retail Excellent
XF—V8—Equipment Schedule 1						
W.B. 114.5"; 4.2 Liter, 5.0 Liter (Premium).						
Sports Sedan 4D	WA0FA	52000	**16850**	**17600**	**19000**	**22700**
Premium Sedan 4D	WA0GB	57000	**18100**	**18900**	**20200**	**24100**
XF—V8 Supercharged—Equipment Schedule 1						
W.B. 114.5"; 5.0 Liter.						
Sports Sedan 4D	WA0HE	68000	**20800**	**21700**	**23200**	**27600**
XFR—V8 Supercharged—Equipment Schedule 1						
W.B. 114.5"; 5.0 Liter.						
Sports Sedan 4D	WA0JC	80000	**27800**	**28900**	**30600**	**36400**
XK—V8—Equipment Schedule 2						
W.B. 108.3"; 5.0 Liter.						
Coupe 2D	WA4DB	83000	**24600**	**25500**	**26200**	**29600**
Convertible 2D	WA4EB	89000	**28700**	**29700**	**30800**	**35100**
XKR—V8 Supercharged—Equipment Schedule 2						
W.B. 108.3"; 5.0 Liter.						
Coupe 2D	WA4DC	96000	**25900**	**26800**	**28000**	**32300**
Convertible 2D	WA4EC	102000	**27000**	**28000**	**29300**	**33800**

2011 JAGUAR

Body Type	VIN	List	Trade-In Good	Very Good	Pvt-Party Good	Retail Excellent

2011 JAGUAR — SAJ–(WA0FB)–B–#

XF—V8—Equipment Schedule 1
W.B. 114.5"; 5.0 Liter.
Sports Sedan 4D	WA0FB	53000	20000	20800	22400	26500
Premium Sedan 4D	WA0GB	57000	21900	22800	24300	28600

XF—V8 Supercharged—Equipment Schedule 1
W.B. 114.5"; 5.0 Liter.
Sports Sedan 4D	WA0HE	68000	24600	25500	27200	32000

XFR—V8 Supercharged—Equipment Schedule 1
W.B. 114.5"; 5.0 Liter.
Sports Sedan 4D	WA0JC	80000	31800	32900	35000	41100

XJ—V8—Equipment Schedule 2
W.B. 119.4", 124.3" (XJL); 5.0 Liter.
XJ Sedan 4D	WA1CB	72500	28100	29100	30200	34700
XJL Sedan 4D	WA2CB	79500	29300	30400	31500	36300
Luxury Pkg			1425	1425	1630	1630

XJ—V8 Supercharged—Equipment Schedule 2
W.B. 119.4", 124.3" (XJL); 5.0 Liter.
XJ Sedan 4D	WA1GE	87500	34400	35600	36800	42300
XJL Sedan 4D	WA2GE	90500	35300	36500	37700	43500

XJ SUPERSPORT—V8 Supercharged—Equipment Schedule 2
W.B. 119.4", 124.3" (XJL); 5.0 Liter.
XJ Sedan 4D	WA1JC	110000	45100	46700	47400	54000
XJL Sedan 4D	WA2JC	113000	49300	51000	51900	59000

XK—V8—Equipment Schedule 2
W.B. 108.3"; 5.0 Liter.
Coupe 2D	WA4FB	83000	28100	29000	29800	33400
Convertible 2D	WA4GB	89000	34500	35700	36200	40400

XKR—V8 Supercharged—Equipment Schedule 2
W.B. 108.3"; 5.0 Liter.
Coupe 2D	WA4DC	96000	34800	36000	36500	40700
Convertible 2D	WA4EC	102000	37100	38300	38800	43200

XKR175—V8 Supercharged—Equipment Schedule 2
W.B. 108.3"; 5.0 Liter.
75th Anniv Coupe	WA4DC	105500	39200	40500	41200	46200

2012 JAGUAR — SAJ–(WA0FB)–C–#

XF—V8—Equipment Schedule 1
W.B. 114.5"; 5.0 Liter.
Sedan 4D	WA0FB	53875	23500	24300	25800	29800
Portfolio Sedan 4D	WA0GB	59875	28000	28900	30300	34900

XF—V8 Supercharged—Equipment Schedule 1
W.B. 114.5"; 5.0 Liter.
Sedan 4D	WA0HE	68975	30900	31900	33500	38500

XFR—V8 Supercharged—Equipment Schedule 1
W.B. 114.5"; 5.0 Liter.
Sedan 4D	WA0JC	82875	38900	40200	41900	48200

XJ—V8—Equipment Schedule 2
W.B. 119.4", 124.3" (XJL); 5.0 Liter.
XJ Sedan 4D	WA1CB	74575	30200	31300	32000	36200
XJL Portfolio Sedan	WA2GB	81575	34800	35900	36600	41300

XJ—V8 Supercharged—Equipment Schedule 2
W.B. 119.4", 124.3" (XJL); 5.0 Liter.
XJ Sedan 4D	WA1GE	89475	38700	40000	40600	45700
XJL Sedan 4D	WA2GE	92475	41700	43000	43600	49000

XJ SUPERSPORT—V8 Supercharged—Equipment Schedule 2
W.B. 119.4", 124.3" (XJL); 5.0 Liter.
XJ Sedan 4D	WA1JC	110475	50100	51700	52400	58800
XJL Sedan 4D	WA2JC	118575	54700	56400	57100	64000

XK—V8—Equipment Schedule 2
W.B. 108.3"; 5.0 Liter.
Coupe 2D	WA4FB	85375	36700	37900	38400	42600
Convertible 2D	WA4GB	91375	43200	44500	44900	49700

XKR—V8 Supercharged—Equipment Schedule 2
W.B. 108.3"; 5.0 Liter.
Coupe 2D	WA4DC	98375	40900	42200	42800	47700
Convertible 2D	WA4EC	104375	43900	45300	45800	50900

XKR-S—V8 Supercharged—Equipment Schedule 2
W.B. 108.3"; 5.0 Liter.
Coupe 2D	WA4HA	132875	60000	61800	62700	69900
Convertible 2D	WA4JA	138875	63000	64900	65700	73200

2013 JAGUAR

Body Type	VIN	List	Trade-In Good	Trade-In Very Good	Pvt-Party Good	Retail Excellent

2013 JAGUAR — SAJ-(WA0E7)-D-#

XF—V6 Supercharged—Equipment Schedule 1
W.B. 114.5"; 3.0 Liter.

Body Type	VIN	List	Good	Very Good	Good	Excellent
Sedan 4D	WA0E7	50875	**28800**	**29700**	**30700**	**34700**
AWD	J		1300	1300	1445	1445
4-Cyl, Turbo, 2.0 Liter	S		(1300)	(1300)	(1445)	(1445)

XF—V8 Supercharged—Equipment Schedule 1
W.B. 114.5"; 5.0 Liter.

Sedan 4D	WA0HE	68975	**41200**	**42400**	**43500**	**48900**

XFR—V8 Supercharged—Equipment Schedule 1
W.B. 114.5"; 5.0 Liter.

Sedan 4D	WA0JC	84075	**48000**	**49500**	**50600**	**56900**

XFR-S—V8 Supercharged—Equipment Schedule 1
W.B. 114.5"; 5.0 Liter.

Sedan 4D	WA0KZ	99895				

XJ—V6 Supercharged—Equipment Schedule 2
W.B. 119.4"; 3.0 Liter.

XJ Sedan 4D	WA1C7	74075	**37700**	**38900**	**40100**	**45400**
AWD	J		1300	1300	1425	1425

XJ—V8—Equipment Schedule 2
W.B. 124.3"; 5.0 Liter.

XJL Portfolio Sedan	WA2GB	82075	**42400**	**43800**	**44300**	**49600**
AWD	J		1300	1300	1420	1420
V6, Supercharged, 3.0L	D		975	975	1060	1060

XJ—V8 Supercharged—Equipment Schedule 2
W.B. 119.4", 124.3" (XJL); 5.0 Liter.

XJ Sedan 4D	WA1GE	90475	**46200**	**47700**	**48800**	**55200**
XJL Sedan 4D	WA2GE	93475	**48400**	**49900**	**51200**	**57700**

XJ SUPERSPORT—V8 Supercharged—Equipment Schedule 2
W.B. 119.4", 124.3" (XJL); 5.0 Liter.

XJ Sedan 4D	WA1JC	113075	**57100**	**58800**	**59600**	**66600**
XJL Sedan 4D	WA2JC	119575	**61700**	**63600**	**64200**	**71700**
XJL Ultimate Sedan	WA2KC	155875	**100100**	**103000**	**100900**	**109800**

XK—V8—Equipment Schedule 2
W.B. 108.3"; 5.0 Liter.

Coupe 2D	WA4FB	85375	**44200**	**45500**	**47500**	**54100**
Convertible 2D	WA4GB	91375	**46500**	**47800**	**49900**	**56800**
Touring Coupe 2D	WA4DB	79875	**45100**	**46500**	**48600**	**55500**
Touring Conv 2D	WA4EB	85875	**48800**	**50300**	**52800**	**60100**

XKR—V8 Supercharged—Equipment Schedule 2
W.B. 108.3"; 5.0 Liter.

Coupe 2D	WA4DC	98375	**46300**	**47600**	**48400**	**53400**
Convertible 2D	WA4EC	104375	**49300**	**50700**	**51300**	**56600**

XKR-S—V8 Supercharged—Equipment Schedule 2
W.B. 108.3"; 5.0 Liter.

Coupe 2D	WA4HA	132875	**66000**	**67900**	**68100**	**75000**
Convertible 2D	WA4JA	138875	**68700**	**70600**	**70800**	**77900**

2014 JAGUAR — SAJ-(WA6E7)-E-#

F-TYPE—V6 Supercharged—Equipment Schedule 2
W.B. 103.2"; 3.0 Liter.

Convertible 2D	WA6E7	69895	**52000**	**53600**	**54300**	**59900**
S Convertible 2D	WA6FC	81895	**58000**	**59700**	**60000**	**65900**

F-TYPE AWD—V8 Supercharged—Equipment Schedule 2
W.B. 103.2"; 5.0 Liter.

S Convertible 2D	WA6GL	92895	**68100**	**70100**	**69700**	**76100**

XF—V6 Supercharged—Equipment Schedule 1
W.B. 114.5"; 3.0 Liter.

Sedan 4D	WA0EX	51395	**34000**	**35100**	**35900**	**40100**
Adaptive Cruise Control			500	500	545	545
AWD	J		1425	1425	1560	1560
4-Cyl, Turbo, 2.0 Liter	S		(1400)	(1400)	(1530)	(1530)

XF—V8 Supercharged—Equipment Schedule 1
W.B. 114.5"; 5.0 Liter.

Sedan 4D	WA0HP	68995	**46600**	**48000**	**48700**	**54200**

XFR—V8 Supercharged—Equipment Schedule 1
W.B. 114.5"; 5.0 Liter.

Sedan 4D	WA0JH	84095	**53100**	**54600**	**55800**	**62300**

XJ—V6 Supercharged—Equipment Schedule 2
W.B. 119.4"; 3.0 Liter.

XJ Sedan 4D	WA1CZ	75095	**50700**	**52300**	**52800**	**58800**

2014 JAGUAR

Body Type	VIN	List	Trade-In Good	Very Good	Pvt-Party Good	Retail Excellent
XJL Portfolio Sedan	WA2GZ	82095	55500	57200	57900	64700
Adaptive Cruise Control			500	500	540	540
Portfolio Pkg			1300	1300	1400	1400
AWD	J		1425	1425	1535	1535

XJ—V8 Supercharged—Equipment Schedule 2
W.B. 119.4", 124.3" (XJL, XJR LWB); 5.0 Liter.

XJ Sedan 4D	WA1GT	91495	59300	61100	61600	68600
XJL Sedan 4D	WA2GT	94495	61800	63600	64100	71400
XJR Sedan 4D	WA1EK	116895				
XJR LWB Sedan 4D	WA2EK	119495				
Adaptive Cruise Control			500	500	540	540

XK—V8—Equipment Schedule 2
W.B. 108.3"; 5.0 Liter.

Coupe 2D	WA4FB	85395	59800	61500	63000	70500
Convertible 2D	WA4GB	91395	62100	63900	65200	72800
Touring Coupe 2D	WA4DB	79895	60700	62500	64000	71500
Touring Conv 2D	WA4EB	85895	64800	66600	68100	76100
Adaptive Cruise Control			500	500	535	535
Portfolio Pkg			1300	1300	1385	1385

XKR—V8 Supercharged—Equipment Schedule 2
W.B. 108.3"; 5.0 Liter.

Coupe 2D	WA4DC	98395	64300	66200	66200	72500
Convertible 2D	WA4EC	104395	67300	69200	68600	74600
Adaptive Cruise Control			500	500	530	530
Black Pkg			775	775	825	825
Dynamic & Black Pack			1950	1950	2075	2075
Dynamic Pkg			1000	1000	1065	1065
Portfolio Pkg			1300	1300	1385	1385

XKR-S—V8 Supercharged—Equipment Schedule 2
W.B. 108.3"; 5.0 Liter.

Coupe 2D	WA4HC	132895	84000	86400	85500	93000
Convertible 2D	WA4JC	138895	86700	89100	88100	95900
GT Coupe 2D	WA4HA	174895				
Bright Pack			875	875	920	920

KIA

2000 KIA — KNA(FA121)-Y-#

SEPHIA—4-Cyl.—Equipment Schedule 6
W.B. 100.8"; 1.8 Liter.

Sedan 4D	FA121	11605	425	500	1100	1950
LS Sedan 4D	FA121	12345	550	650	1300	2325

SPECTRA—4-Cyl.—Equipment Schedule 6
W.B. 100.8"; 1.8 Liter.

GS Sedan 4D	FB161	11245	425	500	1025	1800
GSX Sedan 4D	FB161	13445	600	675	1300	2275

2001 KIA — KNA(DC123)-1-#

RIO—4-Cyl.—Equipment Schedule 6
W.B. 94.9"; 1.5 Liter.

Sedan 4D	DC123	11755	425	500	1075	1925

SEPHIA—4-Cyl.—Equipment Schedule 6
W.B. 100.8"; 1.8 Liter.

Sedan 4D	FB121	11945	500	575	1275	2300
LS Sedan 4D	FB121	12645	675	775	1525	2775

SPECTRA—4-Cyl.—Equipment Schedule 6
W.B. 100.8"; 1.8 Liter.

GS Hatchback 4D	FB161	12345	425	500	1050	1825
GSX Hatchback 4D	FB161	13445	625	725	1325	2300

OPTIMA—4-Cyl.—Equipment Schedule 5
W.B. 106.3"; 2.4 Liter.

LX Sedan 4D	GD126	16599	725	825	1425	2475
SE Sedan 4D	GD126	18899	1225	1375	2100	3575
V6, 2.5 Liter	4		100	100	135	135

2002 KIA — KNA(DC123)-2-#

RIO—4-Cyl.—Equipment Schedule 6
W.B. 94.9"; 1.5 Liter.

Sedan 4D	DC123	12120	600	675	1425	2625
Cinco Wagon 4D	DC163	10465	450	525	1350	2600

Body Type	VIN	List	Trade-In Good	Very Good	Pvt-Party Good	Retail Excellent
SPECTRA—4-Cyl.—Equipment Schedule 6						
W.B. 100.8"; 1.8 Liter.						
Sedan 4D	FB121	12450	**450**	**525**	**1025**	**1775**
GS Hatchback 4D	FB161	12850	**650**	**750**	**1325**	**2275**
LS Sedan 4D	FB121	13090	**700**	**800**	**1375**	**2350**
GSX Hatchback 4D	FB161	14090	**825**	**950**	**1550**	**2650**
OPTIMA—4-Cyl.—Equipment Schedule 5						
W.B. 106.3"; 2.4 Liter.						
LX Sedan 4D	GD126	16244	**1075**	**1200**	**1875**	**3125**
SE Sedan 4D	GD126	17894	**1675**	**1875**	**2650**	**4375**
V6, 2.7 Liter	8		**175**	**175**	**235**	**235**

2003 KIA — KNA(DC125)-3-#

Body Type	VIN	List	Trade-In Good	Very Good	Pvt-Party Good	Retail Excellent
RIO—4-Cyl.—Equipment Schedule 6						
W.B. 94.9"; 1.6 Liter.						
Sedan 4D	DC125	12780	**800**	**925**	**1875**	**3475**
Cinco Wagon 4D	DC165	10620	**650**	**750**	**1725**	**3275**
SPECTRA—4-Cyl.—Equipment Schedule 6						
W.B. 100.8"; 1.8 Liter.						
Sedan 4D	FB121	12715	**575**	**650**	**1300**	**2275**
GS Hatchback 4D	FB161	13140	**700**	**800**	**1450**	**2525**
LS Sedan 4D	FB121	13320	**800**	**900**	**1550**	**2700**
GSX Hatchback 4D	FB161	14360	**1000**	**1125**	**1875**	**3250**
OPTIMA—4-Cyl.—Equipment Schedule 5						
W.B. 106.3"; 2.4 Liter.						
LX Sedan 4D	GD126	16915	**1525**	**1675**	**2350**	**3850**
SE Sedan 4D	GD126	18590	**1975**	**2200**	**3100**	**4950**
V6, 2.7 Liter	8		**250**	**250**	**335**	**335**

2004 KIA — KNA(DC125)-4-#

Body Type	VIN	List	Trade-In Good	Very Good	Pvt-Party Good	Retail Excellent
RIO—4-Cyl.—Equipment Schedule 6						
W.B. 94.9"; 1.6 Liter.						
Sedan 4D	DC125	12930	**925**	**1050**	**2075**	**3800**
Cinco Wagon 4D	DC165	11155	**775**	**875**	**1900**	**3575**
SPECTRA—4-Cyl.—Equipment Schedule 6						
W.B. 100.8", 102.8" (LX & EX); 1.8 Liter, 2.0 Liter.						
Sedan 4D	FB121	13320	**950**	**1050**	**1600**	**2625**
GS Hatchback 4D	FB161	13580	**1150**	**1275**	**1825**	**3000**
LS Sedan 4D	FB121	13590	**1000**	**1125**	**1700**	**2825**
LX Sedan 4D	FB121	14120	**1150**	**1275**	**1825**	**3000**
EX Sedan 4D	FB121	14290	**1300**	**1450**	**2025**	**3275**
GSX Hatchback 4D	FB161	14630	**1450**	**1600**	**2200**	**3550**
OPTIMA—4-Cyl.—Equipment Schedule 5						
W.B. 106.3"; 2.4 Liter.						
LX Sedan 4D	GD126	16960	**1725**	**1925**	**2675**	**4200**
EX Sedan 4D	GD126	18635	**2350**	**2600**	**3575**	**5600**
V6, 2.7 Liter	8		**300**	**300**	**400**	**400**
AMANTI—V6—Equipment Schedule 3						
W.B. 110.2"; 3.5 Liter.						
Sedan 4D	LD124	25535	**1550**	**1725**	**2525**	**4075**

2005 KIA — KNA(DC125)-5-#

Body Type	VIN	List	Trade-In Good	Very Good	Pvt-Party Good	Retail Excellent
RIO—4-Cyl.—Equipment Schedule 6						
W.B. 94.9"; 1.6 Liter.						
Sedan 4D	DC125	13835	**1025**	**1175**	**2275**	**4000**
Cinco Wagon 4D	DC165	11155	**950**	**1075**	**2175**	**3850**
SPECTRA—4-Cyl.—Equipment Schedule 5						
W.B. 102.8"; 2.0 Liter.						
LX Sedan 4D	FE121	14135	**1375**	**1525**	**2150**	**3325**
EX Sedan 4D	FE121	15265	**1625**	**1825**	**2550**	**3900**
SX Sedan 4D	FE121	16510	**1725**	**1925**	**2675**	**4075**
SPECTRA5—4-Cyl.—Equipment Schedule 6						
W.B. 102.8"; 2.0 Liter.						
Hatchback 4D	FE161	16510	**1825**	**2025**	**2800**	**4250**
OPTIMA—4-Cyl.—Equipment Schedule 5						
W.B. 106.3"; 2.4 Liter.						
LX Sedan 4D	GD126	17740	**1950**	**2175**	**3125**	**4800**
EX Sedan 4D	GD126	19190	**2725**	**3050**	**4250**	**6550**
V6, 2.7 Liter	8		**350**	**350**	**465**	**465**
AMANTI—V6—Equipment Schedule 3						
W.B. 110.2"; 3.5 Liter.						
Sedan 4D	LD124	25840	**1750**	**1950**	**3050**	**4775**

Body Type	VIN	List	Trade-In Good	Very Good	Pvt-Party Good	Retail Excellent
2006 KIA — KNA(DE123)-6-#						
RIO—4-Cyl.—Equipment Schedule 6						
W.B. 98.4"; 1.6 Liter.						
Sedan 4D	DE123	11110	**1350**	**1525**	**2525**	**4150**
RIO—4-Cyl.—Equipment Schedule 6						
W.B. 98.4"; 1.6 Liter.						
LX Sedan 4D	DE123	14125	**2000**	**2250**	**3125**	**4775**
Manual, 5-Spd			**(275)**	**(275)**	**(365)**	**(365)**
RIO5—4-Cyl.—Equipment Schedule 6						
W.B. 98.4"; 1.6 Liter.						
SX Hatchback 4D	DE163	14040	**1850**	**2075**	**3050**	**4775**
SPECTRA—4-Cyl.—Equipment Schedule 6						
W.B. 102.8"; 2.0 Liter.						
LX Sedan 4D	FE121	13475	**1450**	**1650**	**2525**	**3825**
SPECTRA—4-Cyl.—Equipment Schedule 6						
W.B. 102.8"; 2.0 Liter.						
EX Sedan 4D	FE121	15840	**1950**	**2200**	**3150**	**4700**
SX Sedan 4D	FE121	17140	**2275**	**2550**	**3550**	**5250**
Manual, 5-Spd			**(275)**	**(275)**	**(365)**	**(365)**
SPECTRA5—4-Cyl.—Equipment Schedule 6						
W.B. 102.8"; 2.0 Liter.						
Hatchback 4D	FE161	17140	**2375**	**2675**	**3650**	**5425**
Manual, 5-Spd			**(275)**	**(275)**	**(365)**	**(365)**
OPTIMA—4-Cyl.—Equipment Schedule 5						
W.B. 106.3"; 2.4 Liter.						
LX Sedan 4D	GD126	18040	**3100**	**3425**	**4300**	**6175**
EX Sedan 4D	GD126	19490	**3825**	**4175**	**5325**	**7575**
V6, 2.7 Liter	8		**400**	**400**	**535**	**535**
OPTIMA (2006.5)—4-Cyl.—Equipment Schedule 5						
W.B. 107.1"; 2.4 Liter.						
LX Sedan 4D	GE123	18250	**2800**	**3075**	**3950**	**5525**
V6, 2.7 Liter	4		**400**	**400**	**535**	**535**
OPTIMA (2006.5)—V6—Equipment Schedule 5						
W.B. 107.1"; 2.7 Liter.						
EX Sedan 4D	GE124	21000	**3725**	**4050**	**4875**	**6750**
4-Cyl, 2.4 Liter	3		**(450)**	**(450)**	**(615)**	**(615)**
AMANTI—V6—Equipment Schedule 3						
W.B. 110.2"; 3.5 Liter.						
Sedan 4D	LD124	28435	**2625**	**2925**	**3850**	**5550**
2007 KIA — KNA(DE123)-7-#						
RIO—4-Cyl.—Equipment Schedule 6						
W.B. 98.4"; 1.6 Liter.						
Sedan 4D	DE123	11350	**1775**	**1975**	**2875**	**4500**
RIO—4-Cyl.—Equipment Schedule 6						
W.B. 98.4"; 1.6 Liter.						
LX Sedan 4D	DE123	14925	**2625**	**2900**	**3775**	**5600**
SX Sedan 4D	DE123	14290	**2550**	**2825**	**3725**	**5525**
Manual, 5-Spd			**(300)**	**(300)**	**(400)**	**(400)**
RIO5—4-Cyl.—Equipment Schedule 6						
W.B. 98.4"; 1.6 Liter.						
SX Hatchback 4D	DE163	14330	**2525**	**2800**	**3700**	**5500**
Automatic			**300**	**300**	**400**	**400**
SPECTRA—4-Cyl.—Equipment Schedule 6						
W.B. 102.8"; 2.0 Liter.						
LX Sedan 4D	FE121	13495	**1875**	**2075**	**2850**	**4225**
SPECTRA—4-Cyl.—Equipment Schedule 6						
W.B. 102.8"; 2.0 Liter.						
EX Sedan 4D	FE121	16495	**2525**	**2800**	**3775**	**5500**
SX Sedan 4D	FE121	17595	**2975**	**3275**	**4325**	**6225**
Manual, 5-Spd			**(300)**	**(300)**	**(400)**	**(400)**
SPECTRA5—4-Cyl.—Equipment Schedule 6						
W.B. 102.8"; 2.0 Liter.						
SX Hatchback 4D	FE161	17595	**3175**	**3500**	**4575**	**6575**
Manual, 5-Spd			**(300)**	**(300)**	**(400)**	**(400)**
RONDO—V6—Equipment Schedule 4						
W.B. 106.3"; 2.7 Liter.						
LX Wagon 4D	FG526	19495	**3175**	**3500**	**4450**	**6225**
EX Wagon 4D	FG526	20795	**3575**	**3925**	**4925**	**6875**
4-Cyl, 2.4 Liter	5		**(250)**	**(250)**	**(320)**	**(320)**

Body Type	VIN	List	Trade-In Good	Very Good	Pvt-Party Good	Retail Excellent
OPTIMA—4-Cyl.—Equipment Schedule 5						
W.B. 107.1"; 2.4 Liter.						
LX Sedan 4D	GE123	18250	**3400**	**3700**	**4725**	**6575**
Manual, 5-Spd			**(400)**	**(400)**	**(535)**	**(535)**
V6, 2.7 Liter	4		**450**	**450**	**600**	**600**
OPTIMA—4-Cyl.—Equipment Schedule 5						
W.B. 107.1"; 2.4 Liter.						
EX Sedan 4D	GE123	19995	**4125**	**4475**	**5575**	**7700**
V6, 2.7 Liter	4		**450**	**450**	**600**	**600**
AMANTI—V6—Equipment Schedule 3						
W.B. 110.2"; 3.8 Liter.						
Sedan 4D	LD125	26175	**3600**	**3925**	**4900**	**6825**

2008 KIA — KNA(DE123)-8-#

Body Type	VIN	List	Trade-In Good	Very Good	Pvt-Party Good	Retail Excellent
RIO—4-Cyl.—Equipment Schedule 6						
W.B. 98.4"; 1.6 Liter.						
Sedan 4D	DE123	11515	**2200**	**2425**	**3200**	**4625**
RIO—4-Cyl.—Equipment Schedule 6						
W.B. 98.4"; 1.6 Liter.						
LX Sedan 4D	DE123	14390	**3075**	**3375**	**4250**	**6050**
SX Sedan 4D	DE123	14725	**3300**	**3625**	**4475**	**6325**
Manual, 5-Spd w/Overdrive			**(350)**	**(350)**	**(470)**	**(470)**
RIO5—4-Cyl.—Equipment Schedule 6						
W.B. 98.4"; 1.6 Liter.						
LX Hatchback 4D	DE163	15090	**3300**	**3625**	**4425**	**6175**
Manual, 5-Spd w/Overdrive			**(350)**	**(350)**	**(470)**	**(470)**
RIO5—4-Cyl.—Equipment Schedule 6						
W.B. 98.4"; 1.6 Liter.						
SX Hatchback 4D	DE163	14495	**3225**	**3550**	**4375**	**6200**
Automatic, 4-Spd w/OD			**300**	**300**	**400**	**400**
SPECTRA—4-Cyl.—Equipment Schedule 6						
W.B. 102.8"; 2.0 Liter.						
LX Sedan 4D	FE121	14520	**2575**	**2850**	**3625**	**5100**
EX Sedan 4D	FE121	16520	**3125**	**3425**	**4275**	**5950**
SX Sedan 4D	FE121	17620	**3475**	**3775**	**4775**	**6625**
Manual, 5-Spd w/Overdrive			**(350)**	**(350)**	**(470)**	**(470)**
SPECTRA5—4-Cyl.—Equipment Schedule 6						
W.B. 102.8"; 2.0 Liter.						
SX Hatchback 4D	FE161	17620	**3675**	**3975**	**5025**	**6925**
Manual, 5-Spd w/Overdrive			**(350)**	**(350)**	**(470)**	**(470)**
RONDO—V6—Equipment Schedule 4						
W.B. 106.3"; 2.7 Liter.						
LX Wagon 4D	FG526	19495	**3875**	**4200**	**5350**	**7425**
EX Wagon 4D	FG526	20795	**4375**	**4725**	**5900**	**8100**
4-Cyl, 2.4 Liter	5		**(275)**	**(275)**	**(350)**	**(350)**
OPTIMA—4-Cyl.—Equipment Schedule 5						
W.B. 107.1"; 2.4 Liter.						
LX Sedan 4D	GE123	18390	**4275**	**4600**	**5650**	**7575**
EX Sedan 4D	GE123	20135	**5000**	**5350**	**6475**	**8650**
Manual, 5-Spd w/Overdrive			**(425)**	**(425)**	**(555)**	**(555)**
V6, 2.7 Liter	4		**500**	**500**	**665**	**665**
AMANTI—V6—Equipment Schedule 3						
W.B. 110.2"; 3.8 Liter.						
Sedan 4D	LD125	26195	**5075**	**5475**	**6525**	**8500**

2009 KIA — KNA(DE123)-9-#

Body Type	VIN	List	Trade-In Good	Very Good	Pvt-Party Good	Retail Excellent
RIO—4-Cyl.—Equipment Schedule 6						
W.B. 98.4"; 1.6 Liter.						
Sedan 4D	DE123	12145	**2800**	**3075**	**3700**	**5050**
RIO—4-Cyl.—Equipment Schedule 6						
W.B. 98.4"; 1.6 Liter.						
LX Sedan 4D	DE223	14825	**3700**	**4025**	**5000**	**6825**
SX Sedan 4D	DE223	15390	**3900**	**4250**	**5225**	**7100**
Manual, 5-Spd w/Overdrive			**(375)**	**(375)**	**(500)**	**(500)**
RIO5—4-Cyl.—Equipment Schedule 6						
W.B. 98.4"; 1.6 Liter.						
SX Hatchback 4D	DE163	14930	**3650**	**3975**	**4950**	**6750**
Automatic, 4-Spd w/OD			**350**	**350**	**465**	**465**
RIO5—4-Cyl.—Equipment Schedule 6						
W.B. 98.4"; 1.6 Liter.						
LX Hatchback 4D	DE243	15525	**3750**	**4075**	**5000**	**6775**
Manual, 5-Spd w/Overdrive			**(375)**	**(375)**	**(500)**	**(500)**

2009 KIA

Body Type	VIN	List	Trade-In Good	Very Good	Pvt-Party Good	Retail Excellent
SPECTRA—4-Cyl.—Equipment Schedule 6						
W.B. 102.8"; 2.0 Liter.						
LX Sedan 4D	FE221	14850	3650	3950	4725	6200
EX Sedan 4D	FE221	16750	4100	4425	5300	6975
SX Sedan 4D	FE221	17750	4600	4925	5850	7675
Manual, 5-Spd w/Overdrive			(375)	(375)	(500)	(500)
SPECTRA5—4-Cyl.—Equipment Schedule 6						
W.B. 102.8"; 2.0 Liter.						
SX Hatchback 4D	FE241	17995	4800	5150	6075	7950
Manual, 5-Spd w/Overdrive			(375)	(375)	(500)	(500)
RONDO—V6—Equipment Schedule 4						
W.B. 106.3"; 2.7 Liter.						
LX Wagon 4D	FG526	20145	5275	5650	6675	8750
EX Wagon 4D	FG526	22945	5850	6225	7475	9700
4-Cyl, 2.4 Liter	5		(275)	(275)	(380)	(380)
OPTIMA—4-Cyl.—Equipment Schedule 5						
W.B. 107.1"; 2.4 Liter.						
LX Sedan 4D	GE123	19625	5600	5950	7150	9175
EX Sedan 4D	GE123	21365	6150	6525	7925	10250
SX Sedan 4D	GE123	21815	7000	7400	9025	11700
Manual, 5-Spd w/Overdrive			(450)	(450)	(600)	(600)
V6, 2.7 Liter	4		575	575	765	765
AMANTI—V6—Equipment Schedule 3						
W.B. 110.2"; 3.8 Liter.						
Sedan 4D	LD225	26795	5900	6275	7300	9250

2010 KIA — KN(AorD)(DF4A3)–A–#

Body Type	VIN	List	Trade-In Good	Very Good	Pvt-Party Good	Retail Excellent
RIO—4-Cyl.—Equipment Schedule 6						
W.B. 98.4"; 1.6 Liter.						
Sedan 4D	DF4A3	12390	3375	3650	4300	5700
RIO—4-Cyl.—Equipment Schedule 6						
W.B. 98.4"; 1.6 Liter.						
LX Sedan 4D	DH4A3	16790	4850	5200	6125	8025
SX Sedan 4D	DH4A3	16490	5050	5400	6425	8450
Manual, 5-Spd w/Overdrive			(475)	(475)	(625)	(625)
RIO5—4-Cyl.—Equipment Schedule 6						
W.B. 98.4"; 1.6 Liter.						
LX Hatchback 4D	DG5A3	14590	4450	4775	5750	7575
Automatic, 4-Spd w/OD			400	400	535	535
RIO5—4-Cyl.—Equipment Schedule 6						
W.B. 98.4"; 1.6 Liter.						
SX Hatchback 4D	DH5A3	16790	5100	5475	6625	8625
Manual, 5-Spd w/Overdrive			(475)	(475)	(625)	(625)
SOUL—4-Cyl.—Equipment Schedule 6						
W.B. 100.4"; 2.0 Liter.						
Wagon 4D	JT2A1	13995	6025	6400	7525	9500
+ Wagon 4D	JT2A2	15645	7425	7850	9000	11200
Sport Wagon 4D	JT2A2	17645	7875	8325	9475	11750
! Wagon 4D	JT2A2	17645	7875	8325	9475	11750
Automatic, 4-Spd w/OD			400	400	530	530
FORTE—4-Cyl.—Equipment Schedule 6						
W.B. 104.3"; 2.0 Liter, 2.4 Liter (SX).						
LX Sedan 4D	FT1A2	15390	5575	5975	6950	8875
EX Sedan 4D	FU4A2	17490	6375	6800	7825	9925
Koup EX Coupe 2D	FU6A2	18290	7650	8125	9225	11600
SX Sedan 4D	FW4A3	18890	7950	8450	9550	12000
Koup SX Coupe 2D	FW6A3	19390	8350	8850	9925	12400
OPTIMA—4-Cyl.—Equipment Schedule 5						
W.B. 107.1"; 2.4 Liter.						
LX Sedan 4D	GG4A3	19890	6675	7050	8125	10050
EX Sedan 4D	GH4A3	21690	7750	8150	9550	11900
SX Sedan 4D	GH4A3	22490	8600	9025	10500	13000
Manual, 5-Spd w/Overdrive			(500)	(500)	(620)	(620)
V6, 2.7 Liter	4		650	650	845	845
RONDO—4-Cyl.—Equipment Schedule 4						
W.B. 106.3"; 2.4 Liter.						
LX Wagon 4D	HG8C8	19890	6750	7150	8325	10500

2011 KIA — KN(AorD)(DF4A3)–B–#

Body Type	VIN	List	Trade-In Good	Very Good	Pvt-Party Good	Retail Excellent
RIO—4-Cyl.—Equipment Schedule 6						
W.B. 98.4"; 1.6 Liter.						
Sedan 4D	DF4A3	12990	4750	5075	5875	7475

Body Type	VIN	List	Trade-In Good	Very Good	Pvt-Party Good	Retail Excellent
LX Sedan 4D	DG4A3	15690	**6025**	**6425**	**7475**	**9475**
SX Sedan 4D	DH4A3	16790	**7325**	**7775**	**8875**	**11050**
RIO5—4-Cyl.—Equipment Schedule 6						
W.B. 98.4"; 1.6 Liter.						
LX Hatchback 4D	DG5A3	16090	**6125**	**6525**	**7550**	**9525**
SX Hatchback 4D	DH5A3	17090	**7850**	**8300**	**9400**	**11700**
SOUL—4-Cyl.—Equipment Schedule 6						
W.B. 100.4"; 1.6 Liter, 2.0 Liter.						
Wagon 4D	JT2A1	13995	**7000**	**7375**	**8500**	**10500**
Sport Wagon 4D	JT2A2	19190	**9000**	**9425**	**10600**	**12850**
! Wagon 4D	JT2A2	19190	**9000**	**9425**	**10600**	**12850**
SOUL—4-Cyl.—Equipment Schedule 6						
W.B. 100.4"; 2.0 Liter.						
+ Wagon 4D	JT2A2	16190	**8550**	**8950**	**10100**	**12300**
Automatic, 4-Spd w/OD			**450**	**450**	**580**	**580**
FORTE—4-Cyl.—Equipment Schedule 6						
W.B. 104.3"; 2.0 Liter, 2.4 Liter (SX).						
LX Sedan 4D	FT4A2	16690	**6600**	**7000**	**8025**	**10050**
Koup EX Coupe 2D	FT6A2	18690	**8475**	**8925**	**10100**	**12500**
Koup SX Coupe 2D	FW6A3	20090	**9225**	**9700**	**10850**	**13350**
SX Hatchback 4D	FW5A3	20090	**9225**	**9700**	**10850**	**13300**
Manual, 6-Spd w/Overdrive			**(500)**	**(500)**	**(665)**	**(665)**
FORTE—6-Cyl.—Equipment Schedule 6						
W.B. 104.3"; 2.0 Liter, 2.4 Liter (SX).						
EX Hatchback 4D	FU5A2	17590	**6925**	**7350**	**8500**	**10700**
EX Sedan 4D	FU4A2	18090	**7425**	**7850**	**8975**	**11150**
SX Sedan 4D	FW4A3	19590	**8875**	**9350**	**10550**	**13050**
OPTIMA—4-Cyl.—Equipment Schedule 5						
W.B. 110.0"; 2.4 Liter.						
LX Sedan 4D	GM4A7	21190	**9800**	**10250**	**11150**	**13100**
EX Sedan 4D	GN4A7	23190	**11300**	**11800**	**12850**	**15100**
Manual, 6-Spd w/Overdrive			**(500)**	**(500)**	**(585)**	**(585)**
4-Cyl, Turbo, 2.0 Liter	6		**1500**	**1500**	**1765**	**1765**
OPTIMA—4-Cyl. Turbo—Equipment Schedule 5						
W.B. 110.0"; 2.0 Liter.						
SX Sedan 4D	GR4A6	26690	**12800**	**13300**	**14550**	**17050**

2012 KIA — 5XXorKN(AorD)(JT2A5)-C-#

Body Type	VIN	List	Trade-In Good	Very Good	Pvt-Party Good	Retail Excellent
SOUL—4-Cyl.—Equipment Schedule 6						
W.B. 100.4"; 1.6 Liter, 2.0 Liter.						
Wagon 4D	JT2A5	14650	**8250**	**8650**	**9800**	**11850**
+ Wagon 4D	JT2A6	17050	**9425**	**9850**	**11050**	**13200**
Automatic, 6-Spd			**475**	**475**	**610**	**610**
SOUL—4-Cyl.—Equipment Schedule 6						
W.B. 100.4"; 2.0 Liter.						
! Wagon 4D	JT2A6	20350	**9925**	**10350**	**11650**	**13950**
RIO—4-Cyl.—Equipment Schedule 6						
W.B. 101.2"; 1.6 Liter.						
LX Sedan 4D	DM4A3	15450	**7400**	**7825**	**8875**	**10900**
Manual, 6-Spd.			**(550)**	**(550)**	**(715)**	**(715)**
RIO—4-Cyl.—Equipment Schedule 6						
W.B. 101.2"; 1.6 Liter.						
LX Hatchback 4D	DM5A3	14350	**6925**	**7325**	**8375**	**10400**
Automatic, 6-Spd w/OD			**475**	**475**	**625**	**625**
RIO—4-Cyl.—Equipment Schedule 6						
W.B. 101.2"; 1.6 Liter, 2.0 Liter.						
EX Sedan 4D	DN4A3	17050	**8550**	**9000**	**10000**	**12200**
EX Hatchback 4D	DN5A3	17250	**8750**	**9225**	**10200**	**12400**
SX Sedan 4D	DN4A3	18250	**9600**	**10100**	**11100**	**13400**
SX Hatchback 4D	DN5A3	18450	**9650**	**10150**	**11200**	**13550**
FORTE—4-Cyl.—Equipment Schedule 6						
W.B. 104.3"; 2.0 Liter, 2.4 Liter (SX).						
LX Sedan 4D	FT4A2	16950	**7525**	**7925**	**9050**	**11100**
Koup EX Coupe 2D	FT6A2	18950	**9125**	**9575**	**10750**	**13150**
Koup SX Coupe 2D	FW6A3	20350	**9700**	**10200**	**11450**	**13950**
Manual, 6-Spd w/Overdrive			**(550)**	**(550)**	**(725)**	**(725)**
FORTE—4-Cyl.—Equipment Schedule 6						
W.B. 104.3"; 2.0 Liter, 2.4 Liter (SX).						
EX Hatchback 4D	FU5A2	18850	**9025**	**9475**	**10650**	**13000**
EX Sedan 4D	FU4A2	18350	**8575**	**9000**	**10150**	**12450**
SX Hatchback 4D	FW5A3	20350	**9900**	**10400**	**11600**	**14050**
SX Sedan 4D	FW4A3	19850	**9450**	**9925**	**11200**	**13650**

2012 KIA

Body Type	VIN	List	Trade-In Good	Very Good	Pvt-Party Good	Retail Excellent
OPTIMA—4-Cyl.—Equipment Schedule 5						
W.B. 110.0"; 2.4 Liter.						
LX Sedan 4D	GM4A7	21750	11100	11600	12700	14900
EX Sedan 4D	GN4A7	23950	12450	12950	14250	16750
4-Cyl, Turbo, 2.0 Liter	6		1600	1600	1915	1915
OPTIMA—4-Cyl. Turbo—Equipment Schedule 5						
W.B. 110.0"; 2.0 Liter.						
SX Sedan 4D	GR4A6	27250	15450	16050	17450	20300
OPTIMA—4-Cyl. Hybrid—Equipment Schedule 5						
W.B. 110.0"; 2.4 Liter.						
Sedan 4D	GM4AD	26450	12950	13450	14650	17100

2013 KIA — 5XXorKN(AorD)(JT2A5)–D–#

Body Type	VIN	List	Trade-In Good	Very Good	Pvt-Party Good	Retail Excellent
SOUL—4-Cyl.—Equipment Schedule 6						
W.B. 100.4"; 1.6 Liter, 2.0 Liter.						
Wagon 4D	JT2A5	15175	9175	9575	10850	12950
+ Wagon 4D	JT2A6	17475	10400	10850	12100	14400
Automatic, 6-Spd			500	500	615	615
SOUL—4-Cyl.—Equipment Schedule 6						
W.B. 100.4"; 2.0 Liter.						
! Wagon 4D	JT2A6	20675	10950	11400	12650	14950
RIO—4-Cyl.—Equipment Schedule 6						
W.B. 101.2"; 1.6 Liter.						
LX Sedan 4D	DM4A3	14350	7850	8275	9325	11400
LX Hatchback 4D	DM5A3	14550	8050	8475	9525	11600
Automatic, 6-Spd			500	500	640	640
RIO—4-Cyl.—Equipment Schedule 6						
W.B. 101.2"; 1.6 Liter.						
EX Sedan 4D	DN4A3	17250	9400	9875	10950	13200
EX Hatchback 4D	DN5A3	17450	9600	10050	11150	13450
SX Sedan 4D	DN4A3	18450	10400	10900	11950	14300
SX Hatchback 4D	DN5A3	18650	10600	11100	12100	14500
FORTE—4-Cyl.—Equipment Schedule 6						
W.B. 104.3"; 2.0 Liter, 2.4 Liter (SX).						
LX Sedan 4D	FT4A2	17175	8325	8725	9800	11850
EX Sedan 4D	FT4A2	18575	9750	10200	11400	13750
EX Hatchback 4D	FU5A2	19075	10300	10750	12000	14450
SX Sedan 4D	FW4A3	20075	11200	11700	12900	15450
SX Hatchback 4D	FW5A3	20575	11350	11850	13100	15650
Koup SX Coupe 2D	FW6A3	19575	10800	11300	12500	15050
FORTE—4-Cyl.—Equipment Schedule 6						
W.B. 104.3"; 2.0 Liter						
Koup EX Coupe 2D	FU6A2	18175	9650	10100	11350	13750
Manual, 6-Spd w/OD			(550)	(550)	(700)	(700)
OPTIMA—4-Cyl.—Equipment Schedule 5						
W.B. 110.0"; 2.4 Liter.						
LX Sedan 4D	GM4A7	21975	11800	12250	13550	15850
EX Sedan 4D	GN4A7	24275	13500	14000	15450	18050
OPTIMA—4-Cyl. Hybrid—Equipment Schedule 5						
W.B. 110.0"; 2.4 Liter.						
LX Sedan 4D	GM4AD	26675	13250	13750	15250	17900
EX Sedan 4D	GN4AD	32725	16850	17450	18850	22000
OPTIMA—4-Cyl. Turbo—Equipment Schedule 5						
W.B. 110.0"; 2.0 Liter.						
SX Sedan 4D	GR4A6	27575	18450	19150	20200	23000
Limited Sedan 4D		35275	19850	20600	21800	24800

2014 KIA — 5XXorKN(AorD)(DM4A3)–E–#

Body Type	VIN	List	Trade-In Good	Very Good	Pvt-Party Good	Retail Excellent
RIO—4-Cyl.—Equipment Schedule 6						
W.B. 101.2"; 1.6 Liter.						
LX Sedan 4D	DM4A3	14600	9325	9800	10850	13100
LX Hatchback 4D	DM5A3	14700	9425	9900	10900	13100
Automatic, 6-Spd			525	525	655	655
RIO—4-Cyl.—Equipment Schedule 6						
W.B. 101.2"; 1.6 Liter.						
EX Sedan 4D	DN4A3	17500	11800	12350	13300	15700
EX Hatchback 4D	DN5A3	17700	12000	12550	13500	15950
SX Sedan 4D	DN4A3	18600	12400	12950	13900	16400
SX Hatchback 4D	DN5A3	18790	12600	13150	14050	16550
SOUL—4-Cyl.—Equipment Schedule 6						
W.B. 101.2"; 1.6 Liter.						
Wagon 4D	JN3A2	15495	10550	11000	12200	14350

2014 KIA

Body Type	VIN	List	Trade-In Good	Very Good	Pvt-Party Good	Retail Excellent
Automatic, 6-Spd			525	525	650	650
SOUL—4-Cyl.—Equipment Schedule 6						
W.B. 101.2"; 2.0 Liter.						
+ Wagon 4D	JP3A5	18995	12200	12650	13800	16050
Primo Pkg			375	375	465	465
SOUL—4-Cyl.—Equipment Schedule 6						
W.B. 101.2"; 2.0 Liter.						
! Wagon 4D	JX3A5	21095	13800	14350	15500	17950
The Whole Shabang			275	275	335	335
FORTE—4-Cyl.—Equipment Schedule 6						
W.B. 106.3"; 1.8 Liter.						
LX Sedan 4D	FK4A6	18200	10300	10750	11800	14000
Koup EX Coupe 2D	FX6A8	20400	11600	12100	13300	15850
Manual, 6-Spd			(550)	(550)	(665)	(665)
FORTE—4-Cyl.—Equipment Schedule 6						
W.B. 106.3"; 2.0 Liter.						
EX Sedan 4D	FX4A8	20200	11500	12000	13100	15550
EX Hatchback 4D	FX5A8	20500	12050	12550	13750	16300
FORTE—4-Cyl. Turbo—Equipment Schedule 6						
W.B. 106.3"; 1.6 Liter.						
Koup SX Coupe 2D	FZ6A3	22400	12700	13250	14350	16950
SX Hatchback 4D	FZ5A3	22700	13100	13650	14900	17600
Manual, 6-Spd			(550)	(550)	(670)	(670)
OPTIMA—4-Cyl.—Equipment Schedule 5						
W.B. 110.0"; 2.4 Liter.						
LX Sedan 4D	GM4A7	22300	13000	13500	15000	17600
EX Sedan 4D	GN4A7	24700	14950	15500	16900	19550
SX Sedan 4D	GR4A7	26050	16350	16950	18000	20500
OPTIMA—4-Cyl. Hybrid—Equipment Schedule 5						
W.B. 110.0"; 2.4 Liter.						
LX Sedan 4D	GM4AD	26795	14050	14600	15950	18450
EX Sedan 4D	GN4AD	32795	19550	20300	21500	24500
OPTIMA—4-Cyl. Turbo—Equipment Schedule 5						
W.B. 110.0"; 2.0 Liter.						
SX Sedan 4D	GR4A6	28000	19450	20100	21400	24500
Limited Sedan 4D		37100	21500	22200	23300	26400
CADENZA—V6 GDI—Equipment Schedule 3						
W.B. 112.0"; 3.3 Liter.						
Premium Sedan 4D	LN4D7	35900	17050	17650	19350	22900
Adv. Smart Cruise Ctrl			500	500	610	610
CADENZA—V6 GDI—Equipment Schedule 3						
W.B. 112.0"; 3.3 Liter.						
Limited Sedan 4D		43200	19800	20500	21900	25300

LAMBORGHINI

2006 LAMBORGHINI — ZHW(GU12T)-6-#

GALLARDO—V10—Equipment Schedule 2
W.B. 100.8"; 5.0 Liter.

Coupe 2D	GU12T	171300	****	****	****	95900
SE Coupe 2D	GU12T	194670	****	****	****	120500
Spyder Roadster 2D	GU22T	196300	****	****	****	118100

MURCIELAGO—V12—Equipment Schedule 2
W.B. 104.9"; 6.2 Liter.

Coupe 2D	BU16S	289300	****	****	****	157500
Roadster 2D	BU26S	320500	****	****	****	169000

2007 LAMBORGHINI — ZHW(GU12T)-7-#

GALLARDO—V10—Equipment Schedule 2
W.B. 100.8"; 5.0 Liter.

Coupe 2D	GU12T	180550	****	****	****	104200
Spyder Roadster 2D	GU22T	199000	****	****	****	126400

MURCIELAGO—V12—Equipment Schedule 2
W.B. 104.9"; 6.2 Liter.

Coupe 2D	BU37S	313100	****	****	****	188600
Roadster 2D	BU47S	347000	****	****	****	200000

2008 LAMBORGHINI — ZHW(GU12T)-8-#

GALLARDO—V10—Equipment Schedule 2
W.B. 100.8"; 5.0 Liter.

Coupe 2D	GU12T	196300	****	****	****	113000

2008 LAMBORGHINI

Body Type	VIN	List	Trade-In Good	Very Good	Pvt-Party Good	Retail Excellent
Coupe 2D	GU43T	234440	****	****	****	140900
Spyder Roadster 2D	GU22T	227760	****	****	****	134600
MURCIELAGO—V12—Equipment Schedule 2						
W.B. 104.9"; 6.2 Liter.						
Coupe 2D	BU37S	347800	****	****	****	215000
Roadster 2D	BU47S	380600	****	****	****	226100

2009 LAMBORGHINI — ZHW(GU54T)-9-#

GALLARDO AWD—V10—Equipment Schedule 2
W.B. 100.7"; 5.2 Liter.

Body Type	VIN	List	Good	Very Good	Good	Excellent
LP 560-4 Coupe 2D	GU54T	205100	****	****	****	163500
LP 560-4 Roadster 2D	GU22T	223000	****	****	****	184700
MURCIELAGO AWD—V12—Equipment Schedule 2						
W.B. 104.9"; 6.5 Liter.						
Coupe 2D	BU47S	389800	****	****	****	253000
LP 640 Coupe 2D	BU37S	361400	****	****	****	242000

2010 LAMBORGHINI — ZHW(GU5BZ)-A-#

GALLARDO LP 550-2—V10—Equipment Schedule 2
W.B. 100.8"; 5.2 Liter.

Body Type	VIN	List	Good	Very Good	Good	Excellent
Valentino Balboni Cpe	GU5BZ	222795	****	****	****	174200
GALLARDO LP 560-4 AWD—V10—Equipment Schedule 2						
W.B. 100.7"; 5.2 Liter.						
Coupe 2D	GU54T	206095	****	****	****	175800
Roadster 2D	GU6AU	223995	****	****	****	200100
MURCIELAGO AWD—V12—Equipment Schedule 2						
W.B. 104.9"; 6.5 Liter.						
LP 640-4 Coupe 2D	BU37S	361395	****	****	****	268200
LP 640-4 Conv 2D	BU4AN	389795	****	****	****	279000
LP 650-4 Conv 2D	BU4AN	423695	****	****	****	297300
SuperVeloce Coupe	BU8AH	456395	****	****	****	355400

2011 LAMBORGHINI — ZHW(GU5BZ)-B-#

GALLARDO—V10—Equipment Schedule 2
W.B. 100.8"; 5.2 Liter.

Body Type	VIN	List	Good	Very Good	Good	Excellent
LP 550-2 Bicolore 2D	GU5BZ	199095	****	****	****	174800
GALLARDO AWD—V10—Equipment Schedule 2						
W.B. 100.7" (560-4 Cpe), 100.8"; 5.2 Liter.						
LP 560-4 Coupe 2D	GU54T	210095	****	****	****	184600
LP 560-4 Spyder 2D	GU6AU	235795	****	****	****	203600
LP 570-4 Superleggera	GU7AJ	245695	****	****	****	223600
LP 570-4 Performante	GU8AJ	232300	****	****	****	232300

2012 LAMBORGHINI — ZHW(GU5BZ)-C-#

GALLARDO—V10—Equipment Schedule 2
W.B. 100.8"; 5.2 Liter.

Body Type	VIN	List	Good	Very Good	Good	Excellent
LP 550-2 Coupe 2D	GU5BZ	193895	****	****	****	193200
LP 550-2 Bicolore 2D	GU5BZ	196995	****	****	****	186800
GALLARDO AWD—V10—Equipment Schedule 2						
W.B. 100.7" (560-4 Cpe), 100.8"; 5.2 Liter.						
LP 560-4 Coupe 2D	GU5AU	207995	****	****	****	196600
LP 560-4 Spyder 2D	GU6AU	231395	****	****	****	210600
LP 570-4 Superleggera	GU7AJ	243595	****	****	****	235600
LP 570-4 Performante	GU8AJ	253095	****	****	****	244300
AVENTADOR AWD—V12—Equipment Schedule 2						
W.B.106.3"; 6.5 Liter.						
LP 700-4 Coupe 2D	UC1ZD	389995	****	****	****	455600

2013 LAMBORGHINI — ZHW(GU5BZ)-D-#

GALLARDO—V10—Equipment Schedule 2
W.B. 100.8"; 5.2 Liter.

Body Type	VIN	List	Good	Very Good	Good	Excellent
LP 550-2 Coupe 2D	GU5BZ	196995	****	****	****	204000
LP 550-2 Spyder 2D	GU6BZ	214595	****	****	****	261600
GALLARDO AWD—V10—Equipment Schedule 2						
W.B. 100.8"; 5.2 Liter.						
LP 560-4 Coupe 2D	GU5AU	207995	****	****	****	208200
LP 560-4 Spyder 2D	GU6AU	230495	****	****	****	222300
LP 570-4 Superleggera	GU7AJ	246295	****	****	****	247300
LP 570-4 Performante	GU8AJ	256695	****	****	****	256000
AVENTADOR AWD—V12—Equipment Schedule 2						
W.B. 106.3"; 6.5 Liter.						

Body Type	VIN	List	Trade-In Good	Very Good	Pvt-Party Good	Retail Excellent
LP 700-4 Coupe 2D	UC1ZD	404195	****	****	****	489000
LP 700-4 Roadster 2D	UR1ZD	448295	****	****	****	494000

LEXUS

2000 LEXUS — JT8(BF28G)-Y-#

ES 300—V6—Equipment Schedule 1
W.B. 105.1"; 3.0 Liter.

Sedan 4D	BF28G	34785	2200	2425	2950	4375
Platinum Series			125	125	180	180

GS 300—6-Cyl.—Equipment Schedule 1
W.B. 110.2"; 3.0 Liter.

Sedan 4D	BD68S	40880	2100	2325	2975	4525
Platinum Series			125	125	180	180

GS 400—V8—Equipment Schedule 1
W.B. 110.2"; 4.0 Liter.

Sedan 4D	BH68X	47520	3625	4000	4825	7125
Platinum Series			125	125	180	180

SC 300—6-Cyl.—Equipment Schedule 1
W.B. 105.9"; 3.0 Liter.

Sport Coupe 2D	CD32Z	47140	3675	3975	4675	6475
Traction Control			100	100	135	135

SC 400—V8—Equipment Schedule 1
W.B. 105.9"; 4.0 Liter.

Sport Coupe 2D	CH32Y	57530	4400	4750	5675	7825
Traction Control			100	100	135	135

LS 400—V8—Equipment Schedule 1
W.B. 112.2"; 4.0 Liter.

Sedan 4D	BH28F	55420	3975	4325	4875	6650
Platinum Series			125	125	170	170

2001 LEXUS — JT(8orH)(BF28G)-1-#

ES 300—V6—Equipment Schedule 1
W.B. 105.1"; 3.0 Liter.

Sedan 4D	BF28G	34935	2550	2825	3375	5000
Coach Edition			150	150	200	200

IS 300—6-Cyl.—Equipment Schedule 1
W.B. 105.1"; 3.0 Liter.

Sedan 4D	BD182	34055	3325	3700	4275	6175

GS 300—6-Cyl.—Equipment Schedule 1
W.B. 110.2"; 3.0 Liter.

Sedan 4D	BD68S	41780	2750	3075	3625	5325

GS 430—V8—Equipment Schedule 1
W.B. 110.2"; 4.3 Liter.

Sedan 4D	BN68X	50580	4175	4600	5450	7825

LS 430—V8—Equipment Schedule 1
W.B. 115.2"; 4.3 Liter.

Sedan 4D	BN30F	54550	5300	5700	6525	8800
Dynamic Cruise Control			200	200	265	265
Ultra Luxury Pkg			1300	1300	1735	1735

2002 LEXUS — JT(8orH)(BF30G)-2-#

ES 300—V6—Equipment Schedule 1
W.B. 107.1"; 3.0 Liter.

Sedan 4D	BF30G	33640	3550	3900	4425	6250

IS 300—6-Cyl.—Equipment Schedule 1
W.B. 105.1"; 3.0 Liter.

Sedan 4D	BD192	33655	3975	4400	5025	7050
Sport Cross H'Back 4D	ED192	35195	4075	4500	5150	7225
Manual, 5-Spd			(300)	(300)	(395)	(395)

GS 300—6-Cyl.—Equipment Schedule 1
W.B. 110.2"; 3.0 Liter.

Sedan 4D	BD69S	41840	3350	3700	4325	6250
SportDesign			325	325	425	425

GS 430—V8—Equipment Schedule 1
W.B. 110.2"; 4.3 Liter.

Sedan 4D	BL69S	48980	4725	5175	6100	8700

LS 430—V8—Equipment Schedule 1
W.B. 115.2"; 4.3 Liter.

Sedan 4D	BN30F	56080	5550	5950	6775	9075
Dynamic Cruise Control			225	225	300	300

2002 LEXUS

Body Type	VIN	List	Trade-In Good	Very Good	Pvt-Party Good	Retail Excellent
Ultra Luxury Pkg			1450	1450	1935	1935
SC 430—V8—Equipment Schedule 1						
W.B. 103.1"; 4.3 Liter.						
Convertible 2D	FN48Y	59030	6500	6925	8325	11250

2003 LEXUS — JT(8orH)(BF30G)-3-#

Body Type	VIN	List	Trade-In Good	Very Good	Pvt-Party Good	Retail Excellent
ES 300—V6—Equipment Schedule 1						
W.B. 107.1"; 3.0 Liter.						
Sedan 4D	BF30G	33780	4275	4675	5250	7200
IS 300—6-Cyl.—Equipment Schedule 1						
W.B. 105.1"; 3.0 Liter.						
Sedan 4D	BD192	32485	5000	5450	6050	8250
Sport Cross H'Back 4D	ED192	32525	5100	5550	6150	8400
SportDesign			575	575	760	760
Manual, 5-Spd			(325)	(325)	(445)	(445)
GS 300—6-Cyl.—Equipment Schedule 1						
W.B. 110.2"; 3.0 Liter.						
Sedan 4D	BD69S	40960	3950	4350	5075	7175
SportDesign			350	350	465	465
GS 430—V8—Equipment Schedule 1						
W.B. 110.2"; 4.3 Liter.						
Sedan 4D	BL69S	48400	5450	5925	6800	9475
LS 430—V8—Equipment Schedule 1						
W.B. 115.2"; 4.3 Liter.						
Sedan 4D	BN30F	56600	6700	7150	8150	10700
Dynamic Cruise Control			250	250	325	325
Ultra Luxury Pkg			1575	1575	2065	2065
SC 430—V8—Equipment Schedule 1						
W.B. 103.1"; 4.3 Liter.						
Convertible 2D	FN48Y	62600	7250	7700	9150	12200

2004 LEXUS — JT(8orH)(BA30G)-4-#

Body Type	VIN	List	Trade-In Good	Very Good	Pvt-Party Good	Retail Excellent
ES 330—V6—Equipment Schedule 1						
W.B. 107.1"; 3.3 Liter.						
Sedan 4D	BA30G	32350	5475	5925	6450	8600
IS 300—6-Cyl.—Equipment Schedule 1						
W.B. 105.1"; 3.0 Liter.						
Sedan 4D	BD192	32815	5875	6400	7150	9550
Sport Cross H'Back 4D	ED192	32855	5975	6500	7250	9700
SportDesign			625	625	820	820
Manual, 5-Spd			(375)	(375)	(490)	(490)
GS 300—6-Cyl.—Equipment Schedule 1						
W.B. 110.2"; 3.0 Liter.						
Sedan 4D	BD68S	41010	4925	5375	6025	8250
GS 430—V8—Equipment Schedule 1						
W.B. 110.2"; 4.3 Liter.						
Sedan 4D	BL69S	48450	6250	6775	7825	10700
LS 430—V8—Equipment Schedule 1						
W.B. 115.2"; 4.3 Liter.						
Sedan 4D	BN30F	55750	9675	10250	11700	15300
Dynamic Cruise Control			275	275	365	365
Ultra Luxury Pkg			1675	1675	2235	2235
SC 430—V8—Equipment Schedule 1						
W.B. 103.1"; 4.3 Liter.						
Convertible 2D	FN48Y	63200	9075	9600	11000	14300

2005 LEXUS — JT(8orH)(BA30G)-5-#

Body Type	VIN	List	Trade-In Good	Very Good	Pvt-Party Good	Retail Excellent
ES 330—V6—Equipment Schedule 1						
W.B. 107.1"; 3.3 Liter.						
Sedan 4D	BA30G	32600	6275	6750	7550	9825
IS 300—6-Cyl.—Equipment Schedule 1						
W.B. 105.1"; 3.0 Liter.						
Sedan 4D	BD192	34315	7075	7650	8475	11100
Sport Cross H'Back 4D	ED192	34355	7175	7750	8600	11250
Manual, 5-Spd			(400)	(400)	(540)	(540)
GS 300—6-Cyl.—Equipment Schedule 1						
W.B. 110.2"; 3.0 Liter.						
Sedan 4D	BD69S	41160	5850	6325	7425	10050
GS 430—V8—Equipment Schedule 1						
W.B. 110.2"; 4.3 Liter.						
Sedan 4D	BL69S	48600	7250	7825	9200	12450

Body Type	VIN	List	Trade-In Good	Very Good	Pvt-Party Good	Retail Excellent
LS 430—V8—Equipment Schedule 1						
W.B. 115.2"; 4.3 Liter.						
Sedan 4D	BN36F	56300	10850	11450	12950	16550
Dynamic Cruise Control		------	300	300	390	390
Ultra Luxury Pkg		------	1775	1775	2300	2300
SC 430—V8—Equipment Schedule 1						
W.B. 103.1"; 4.3 Liter.						
Convertible 2D	FN48Y	63800	9650	10200	11750	15150

2006 LEXUS — JT(8orH)(BA30G)-6-#

Body Type	VIN	List	Trade-In Good	Very Good	Pvt-Party Good	Retail Excellent
ES 330—V6—Equipment Schedule 1						
W.B. 107.1"; 3.3 Liter.						
Sedan 4D	BA30G	32950	7250	7775	8600	11000
IS 250—V6—Equipment Schedule 1						
W.B. 107.5"; 2.5 Liter.						
Sedan 4D	BK262	31750	8450	9075	9850	12550
Adaptive Cruise Control		------	325	325	420	420
Luxury Pkg		------	700	700	905	905
Sport Pkg		------	675	675	880	880
AWD		------	1025	1025	1325	1325
IS 350—V6—Equipment Schedule 1						
W.B. 107.5"; 3.5 Liter.						
Sedan 4D	BE262	36030	9850	10550	11650	14800
Adaptive Cruise Control		------	325	325	420	420
Luxury Pkg		------	700	700	900	900
Sport Pkg		------	675	675	880	880
GS 300 AWD—V6—Equipment Schedule 1						
W.B. 112.2"; 3.0 Liter.						
Sedan 4D	CH96S	45545	9650	10350	11450	14600
Adaptive Cruise Control		------	325	325	415	415
RWD	B	------	(575)	(575)	(740)	(740)
GS 430—V8—Equipment Schedule 1						
W.B. 112.2"; 4.3 Liter.						
Sedan 4D	BN96S	53025	11100	11900	13000	16450
Adaptive Cruise Control		------	325	325	410	410
LS 430—V8—Equipment Schedule 1						
W.B. 115.2"; 4.3 Liter.						
Sedan 4D	BN36F	57175	11350	11950	13500	16950
Dynamic Cruise Control		------	325	325	400	400
Ultra Luxury Pkg		------	1850	1850	2275	2275
SC 430—V8—Equipment Schedule 1						
W.B. 103.1"; 4.3 Liter.						
Convertible 2D	FN48Y	66005	11250	11900	13500	17000
Pebble Beach Special Ed		------	300	300	395	395

2007 LEXUS — JT(8orH)(BK262)-7-#

Body Type	VIN	List	Trade-In Good	Very Good	Pvt-Party Good	Retail Excellent
IS 250—V6—Equipment Schedule 1						
W.B. 107.5"; 2.5 Liter.						
Sedan 4D	BK262	32015	9825	10500	11300	14050
Adaptive Cruise Control		------	350	350	440	440
Luxury Pkg		------	750	750	950	950
AWD		------	1100	1100	1390	1390
IS 350—V6—Equipment Schedule 1						
W.B. 107.5"; 3.5 Liter.						
Sedan 4D	BE262	36295	11350	12100	13050	16200
Adaptive Cruise Control		------	350	350	440	440
Luxury Pkg		------	750	750	945	945
Sport Pkg		------	725	725	925	925
ES 350—V6—Equipment Schedule 1						
W.B. 109.3"; 3.5 Liter.						
Sedan 4D	BJ46G	35145	9200	9800	10650	13300
Premium Pkg		------	250	250	315	315
Premium Plus Pkg		------	500	500	625	625
Ultra Luxury Pkg		------	1950	1950	2445	2445
GS 350 AWD—V6—Equipment Schedule 1						
W.B. 112.2"; 3.5 Liter.						
Sedan 4D	CE96S	46865	11300	12050	13000	16150
Adaptive Cruise Control		------	350	350	430	430
RWD	B	------	(625)	(625)	(770)	(770)
GS 430—V8—Equipment Schedule 1						
W.B. 112.2"; 4.3 Liter.						
Sedan 4D	BN96S	53070	12800	13600	14550	18000

Body Type	VIN	List	Trade-In Good	Very Good	Pvt-Party Good	Retail Excellent
Adaptive Cruise Control			350	350	425	425
GS 450h—V6 Hybrid—Equipment Schedule 1						
W.B. 112.2''; 3.5 Liter.						
Sedan 4D	BC96S	55595	12900	13700	14650	18200
Adaptive Cruise Control			350	350	430	430
LS 460—V8—Equipment Schedule 1						
W.B. 116.9'', 121.7'' (L); 4.6 Liter.						
Sedan 4D	BL46F	61715	16350	17150	17850	21100
L Sedan 4D	GL46F	71715	19050	19950	20700	24400
Executive Pkg			2400	2400	2810	2810
Luxury Pkg			375	375	445	445
Touring			450	450	525	525
SC 430—V8—Equipment Schedule 1						
W.B. 103.1''; 4.3 Liter.						
Convertible 2D	FN45Y	66150	14450	15200	16550	20300
Pebble Beach Special Ed			325	325	405	405

2008 LEXUS — JT(8orH)(BK262)-8-#

Body Type	VIN	List	Trade-In Good	Very Good	Pvt-Party Good	Retail Excellent
IS 250—V6—Equipment Schedule 1						
W.B. 107.5''; 2.5 Liter.						
Sedan 4D	BK262	32390	11400	12050	12850	15650
Adaptive Cruise Control			375	375	460	460
Luxury Plus Pkg			800	800	980	980
AWD			1175	1175	1440	1440
IS 350—V6—Equipment Schedule 1						
W.B. 107.5''; 3.5 Liter.						
Sedan 4D	BE262	36670	13050	13800	14800	18050
Adaptive Cruise Control			375	375	465	465
Luxury Plus Pkg			800	800	990	990
Sport Pkg			800	800	975	975
IS F—V8—Equipment Schedule 1						
W.B. 107.5''; 5.0 Liter.						
Sedan 4D	BP262	56765	22600	23800	23800	27800
ES 350—V6—Equipment Schedule 1						
W.B. 109.3''; 3.5 Liter.						
Sedan 4D	BJ46G	34485	10550	11150	11900	14550
Dynamic Radar Cruise Ctrl			375	375	465	465
Pebble Beach Edition			350	350	425	425
Premium Pkg			275	275	330	330
Premium Plus Pkg			525	525	665	665
Ultra Luxury Pkg			2025	2025	2500	2500
GS 350 AWD—V6—Equipment Schedule 1						
W.B. 112.2''; 3.5 Liter.						
Sedan 4D	CE96S	47375	14550	15350	16100	19350
Adaptive Cruise Control			375	375	435	435
RWD	B		(675)	(675)	(790)	(790)
GS 450h—V6 Hybrid—Equipment Schedule 1						
W.B. 112.2''; 3.5 Liter.						
Sedan 4D	BC96S	55665	16800	17700	18550	22300
Adaptive Cruise Control			375	375	440	440
GS 460—V8—Equipment Schedule 1						
W.B. 112.2''; 4.6 Liter.						
Sedan 4D	BN96S	53385	16700	17600	18400	22100
Adaptive Cruise Control			375	375	440	440
LS 460—V8—Equipment Schedule 1						
W.B. 116.9'', 121.7'' (L); 4.6 Liter.						
Sedan 4D	BL46F	62265	18300	19100	19850	23100
L Sedan 4D	GL46F	72265	20800	21700	22400	26100
Executive Pkg			2525	2525	2910	2910
Luxury Pkg			400	400	465	465
Touring			475	475	555	555
Rear Seat Upgrade Pkg			825	825	950	950
LS 600h AWD—V8 Hybrid—Equipment Schedule 1						
W.B. 121.7''; 5.0 Liter.						
L Sedan 4D	DU46F	104765	26200	27200	28200	33000
Executive Pkg			2525	2525	2940	2940
SC 430—V8—Equipment Schedule 1						
W.B. 103.1''; 4.3 Liter.						
Convertible 2D	FN45Y	66220	18800	19650	20800	24700
Pebble Beach Special Ed			350	350	410	410

2009 LEXUS

Body Type	VIN	List	Trade-In Good	Very Good	Pvt-Party Good	Retail Excellent

2009 LEXUS — JT(8orH)(BK262)-9-#

IS 250—V6—Equipment Schedule 1
W.B. 107.5"; 2.5 Liter.
Sedan 4D	BK262	33200	13150	13800	14750	17550
Luxury Plus Pkg			850	850	1025	1025
AWD	C		1250	1250	1505	1505

IS 350—V6—Equipment Schedule 1
W.B. 107.5"; 3.5 Liter.
Sedan 4D	BE262	37430	16000	16800	17750	21200
Luxury Plus Pkg			850	850	1025	1025
Sport Pkg			850	850	1015	1015

IS F—V8—Equipment Schedule 1
W.B. 107.5"; 5.0 Liter.
| Sedan 4D | BP262 | 57435 | 27200 | 28400 | 28400 | 32600 |

ES 350—V6—Equipment Schedule 1
W.B. 109.3"; 3.5 Liter.
| Sedan 4D | BJ46G | 35145 | 12550 | 13200 | 14050 | 16850 |
| Ultra Luxury Pkg | | | 2100 | 2100 | 2520 | 2520 |

GS 350 AWD—V6—Equipment Schedule 1
W.B. 112.2"; 3.5 Liter.
| Sedan 4D | CE96S | 47675 | 16650 | 17500 | 18250 | 21500 |
| RWD | B | | (725) | (725) | (820) | (820) |

GS 450h—V6 Hybrid—Equipment Schedule 1
W.B. 112.2"; 3.5 Liter.
| Sedan 4D | BC96S | 57225 | 18950 | 19850 | 20600 | 24300 |

GS 460—V8—Equipment Schedule 1
W.B. 112.2"; 4.6 Liter.
| Sedan 4D | BN96S | 54145 | 19000 | 19900 | 20600 | 24200 |

LS 460—V8—Equipment Schedule 1
W.B. 116.9", 121.7" (L); 4.6 Liter.
Sedan 4D	BL46F	64500	19900	20700	21600	25000
L Sedan 4D	GL46F	74410	23100	24000	25000	29000
Luxury Pkg			425	425	500	500
Touring			500	500	595	595
AWD	C		1550	1550	1785	1785

LS 600h—V8 Hybrid—Equipment Schedule 1
W.B. 121.7"; 5.0 Liter.
| L Sedan 4D | DU46F | 106710 | 28700 | 29800 | 31300 | 36600 |
| Executive Seating | | | 2650 | 2650 | 3145 | 3145 |

SC 430—V8—Equipment Schedule 1
W.B. 103.1"; 4.3 Liter.
| Convertible 2D | FN45Y | 67630 | 25300 | 26400 | 27100 | 31400 |
| Pebble Beach Special Ed | | | 350 | 350 | 415 | 415 |

2010 LEXUS — JTH(BB1BA)-A-#

HS 250h—4-Cyl. Hybrid—Equipment Schedule 1
W.B. 106.3"; 2.4 Liter.
| Sedan 4D | BB1BA | 35075 | 14300 | 14950 | 15950 | 18850 |
| Premium Sedan 4D | BB1BA | 37845 | 15050 | 15700 | 16700 | 19600 |

IS 250—V6—Equipment Schedule 1
W.B. 107.5"; 2.5 Liter.
Sedan 4D	BF5C2	33890	15200	15900	16750	19550
Convertible 2D	FF2C2	40535	18550	19350	20200	23600
Luxury Plus Pkg			900	900	1065	1065
AWD	C		1325	1325	1570	1570

IS 350—V6—Equipment Schedule 1
W.B. 107.5"; 3.5 Liter.
Sedan 4D	BE5C2	38170	18550	19350	20200	23600
Convertible 2D	FE2C2	44815	20600	21500	22300	26000
Luxury Plus Value Edition			900	900	1060	1060

IS F—V8—Equipment Schedule 1
W.B. 107.5"; 5.0 Liter.
| Sedan 4D | BP5C2 | 58635 | 30800 | 32000 | 32300 | 36700 |

ES 350—V6—Equipment Schedule 1
W.B. 109.3"; 3.5 Liter.
| Sedan 4D | BK1EG | 35675 | 15400 | 16100 | 17050 | 20000 |
| Ultra Luxury Pkg | | | 2175 | 2175 | 2575 | 2575 |

GS 350 AWD—V6—Equipment Schedule 1
W.B. 112.2"; 3.5 Liter.
| Sedan 4D | CE1KB | 47825 | 18950 | 19750 | 20600 | 24100 |
| RWD | B | | (750) | (750) | (865) | (865) |

Body Type	VIN	List	Trade-In Good	Very Good	Pvt-Party Good	Retail Excellent
GS 450h—V6 Hybrid—Equipment Schedule 1						
W.B. 112.2"; 3.5 Liter.						
Sedan 4D	BC1KS	57425	21700	22600	23500	27400
GS 460—V8—Equipment Schedule 1						
W.B. 112.2"; 4.6 Liter.						
Sedan 4D	BL1KS	54345	21800	22800	23600	27500
LS 460—V8—Equipment Schedule 1						
W.B. 116.9", 121.7" (L); 4.6 Liter.						
Sedan 4D	BL5EF	65555	26300	27300	28400	32600
L Sedan 4D	GL5EF	71100	29600	30700	31900	36600
Sport Pkg			2275	2275	2580	2580
Luxury Pkg			450	450	515	515
AWD	C		1625	1625	1850	1850
LS 600h—V8 Hybrid—Equipment Schedule 1						
W.B. 121.7"; 5.0 Liter.						
L Sedan 4D	DU1EF	109675	42900	44300	45800	52600
SC 430—V8—Equipment Schedule 1						
W.B. 103.1"; 4.3 Liter.						
Convertible 2D	FN2EY	68380	27300	28500	29200	33700

2011 LEXUS — JTH(KD5BH)-B-#

Body Type	VIN	List	Trade-In Good	Very Good	Pvt-Party Good	Retail Excellent
CT 200h—4-Cyl. Hybrid—Equipment Schedule 1						
W.B. 102.4"; 1.8 Liter.						
Hatchback 4D	KD5BH	29995	17150	17850	18550	21300
Premium H'Back 4D	KD5BH	31775	18550	19300	20000	22900
HS 250h—4-Cyl. Hybrid—Equipment Schedule 1						
W.B. 106.3"; 2.4 Liter.						
Sedan 4D	BB1BA	35975	17050	17750	18700	21700
Premium Sedan 4D	BB1BA	38745	18200	18900	19800	22800
Touring Pkg			525	525	605	605
Technology Pkg			650	650	760	760
IS 250—V6—Equipment Schedule 1						
W.B. 107.5"; 2.5 Liter.						
Sedan 4D	BF5C2	34190	17700	18450	19200	22000
Luxury Plus Value Edition			950	950	1100	1100
F-Sport Pkg			950	950	1095	1095
AWD			1400	1400	1625	1625
IS 250C—V6—Equipment Schedule 1						
W.B. 107.5"; 2.5 Liter.						
Convertible 2D	FF2C2	41935	22500	23300	24100	27600
Luxury Pkg			950	950	1100	1100
IS 350—V6—Equipment Schedule 1						
W.B. 107.5"; 3.5 Liter.						
Sedan 4D	BE5C2	39445	21100	21900	22700	26000
Luxury Plus Value Edition			950	950	1100	1100
F-Sport Pkg			950	950	1095	1095
AWD			1400	1400	1620	1620
IS 350C—V6—Equipment Schedule 1						
W.B. 107.5"; 3.5 Liter.						
Convertible 2D	FE2C2	46215	25100	26000	26900	30800
Luxury Pkg			950	950	1100	1100
IS F—V8—Equipment Schedule 1						
W.B. 107.5"; 5.0 Liter.						
Sedan 4D	BP5C2	59335	34500	35700	36000	40600
ES 350—V6—Equipment Schedule 1						
W.B. 109.3"; 3.5 Liter.						
Sedan 4D	BK1EG	36400	17400	18150	19100	22100
Ultra Luxury Pkg			2300	2300	2680	2680
GS 350 AWD—V6—Equipment Schedule 1						
W.B. 112.2"; 3.5 Liter.						
Sedan 4D	CE1KS	48825	21100	22000	22800	26300
RWD	B		(800)	(800)	(900)	(900)
GS 450h—V6 Hybrid—Equipment Schedule 1						
W.B. 112.2"; 3.5 Liter.						
Sedan 4D	BC1KS	58825	23900	24800	25700	29500
GS 460—V8—Equipment Schedule 1						
W.B. 112.2"; 4.6 Liter.						
Sedan 4D	BL1KS	55345	24000	24900	25800	29600
LS 460—V8—Equipment Schedule 1						
W.B. 116.9", 121.7" (L); 4.6 Liter.						
Sedan 4D	BL5EF	66255	29500	30500	31700	36100
L Sedan 4D	GL5EF	71800	32500	33600	35000	39800
Sport Pkg			2425	2425	2715	2715

2011 LEXUS

Body Type	VIN	List	Trade-In Good	Very Good	Pvt-Party Good	Retail Excellent
Luxury Pkg			475	475	535	535
AWD	C		1725	1725	1935	1935
LS 600h—V8 Hybrid—Equipment Schedule 1						
W.B. 121.7"; 5.0 Liter.						
L Sedan 4D	DU5EF	110875	47500	49000	50900	58100

2012 LEXUS — JTH(KD5BH)–C–#

CT 200h—4-Cyl. Hybrid—Equipment Schedule 1
W.B. 102.4"; 1.8 Liter.

Body Type	VIN	List	Good	Very Good	Pvt-Party Good	Retail Excellent
Hatchback 4D	KD5BH	29995	18200	18900	19650	22300
Premium H'Back 4D	KD5BH	32125	19200	19900	20700	23500
Dynamic Cruise Control			450	450	515	515
F Sport Pkg			1500	1500	1710	1710
F Sport Special Edition			425	425	500	500
HS 250h—4-Cyl. Hybrid—Equipment Schedule 1						
W.B. 106.3"; 2.4 Liter.						
Sedan 4D	BB1BA	37905	19400	20100	20900	23800
Premium Sedan 4D	BB1BA	40675	20600	21300	22100	25200
Touring Pkg			550	550	625	625
Technology Pkg			675	675	790	790
IS 250—V6—Equipment Schedule 1						
W.B. 107.5"; 2.5 Liter.						
Sedan 4D	BF5C2	35640	19550	20300	21100	24000
Luxury Plus Value Edition			1000	1000	1150	1150
F-Sport Pkg			1000	1000	1150	1150
AWD			1500	1500	1725	1725
IS 250C—V6—Equipment Schedule 1						
W.B. 107.5"; 2.5 Liter.						
Convertible 2D	FF2C2	43235	25800	26700	27600	31300
Luxury Pkg			1000	1000	1145	1145
IS 350—V6—Equipment Schedule 1						
W.B. 107.5"; 3.5 Liter.						
Sedan 4D	BE5C2	40895	22900	23800	24500	27900
Luxury Plus Value Edition			1000	1000	1145	1145
F-Sport Pkg			1000	1000	1145	1145
AWD			1500	1500	1715	1715
IS 350C—V6—Equipment Schedule 1						
W.B. 107.5"; 3.5 Liter.						
Convertible 2D	FE2C2	47515	28600	29600	30500	34700
Luxury Pkg			1000	1000	1145	1145
IS F—V8—Equipment Schedule 1						
W.B. 107.5"; 5.0 Liter.						
Sedan 4D	BP5C2	62175	38200	39500	40000	44800
ES 350—V6—Equipment Schedule 1						
W.B. 109.3"; 3.5 Liter.						
Sedan 4D	BK1EG	37600	20800	21700	22400	25600
Ultra Luxury Pkg			2350	2350	2680	2680
LS 460—V8—Equipment Schedule 1						
W.B. 116.9", 121.7" (L); 4.6 Liter.						
Sedan 4D	BL5EF	68005	35100	36300	37300	41900
L Sedan 4D	GL5EF	73650	38200	39400	40500	45500
Sport Special Ed 4D	BL5EF	77875	39500	40700	41900	47200
Sport Pkg			2575	2575	2830	2830
Luxury Pkg			500	500	550	550
AWD	C		1825	1825	2005	2005
LS 600h—V8 Hybrid—Equipment Schedule 1						
W.B. 121.7"; 5.0 Liter.						
L Sedan 4D	DU5EF	113125	53100	54800	56300	63300
LFA—V10—Equipment Schedule 1						
W.B. 102.6"; 4.8 Liter.						
Coupe 2D	HX8BH	377400	****	****	****	374300

2013 LEXUS — JTH(KD5BH)–D–#

CT 200h—4-Cyl. Hybrid—Equipment Schedule 1
W.B. 102.4"; 1.8 Liter.

Body Type	VIN	List	Good	Very Good	Pvt-Party Good	Retail Excellent
Hatchback 4D	KD5BH	32745	21200	22000	22700	25700
IS 250—V6—Equipment Schedule 1						
W.B. 107.5"; 2.5 Liter.						
Sedan 4D	BF5C2	35960	22100	22800	23600	26700
Luxury Plus Value Edition			1050	1050	1195	1195
F Sport Pkg			1000	1000	1135	1135
AWD	C		1600	1600	1820	1820

Body Type	VIN	List	Trade-In Good	Very Good	Pvt-Party Good	Retail Excellent
IS 250C—V6—Equipment Schedule 1						
W.B. 107.5"; 2.5 Liter.						
Convertible 2D	FF2C2	43405	29600	30600	31500	35500
Luxury Pkg			1050	1050	1190	1190
IS 350—V6—Equipment Schedule 1						
W.B. 107.5"; 3.5 Liter.						
Sedan 4D	BE5C2	41215	26400	27300	28100	31800
Luxury Plus Value Edition			1050	1050	1190	1190
F Sport Pkg			1000	1000	1135	1135
AWD	C		1600	1600	1815	1815
IS 350C—V6—Equipment Schedule 1						
W.B. 107.5"; 3.5 Liter.						
Convertible 2D	FE2C2	47685	31700	32700	33600	37800
Luxury Pkg			1050	1050	1190	1190
IS F—V8—Equipment Schedule 1						
W.B. 107.5"; 5.0 Liter.						
Sedan 4D	BP5C2	62495	42000	43300	43800	48900
ES 300h—4-Cyl. Hybrid—Equipment Schedule 1						
W.B. 111.0"; 2.5 Liter.						
Sedan 4D	BW7GG	39745	29100	30100	30700	34300
ES 350—V6—Equipment Schedule 1						
W.B. 111.0"; 3.5 Liter.						
Sedan 4D	BK7GG	36995	26000	26900	27500	30800
Ultra Luxury Pkg			2425	2425	2695	2695
GS 350—V6—Equipment Schedule 1						
W.B. 112.2"; 3.5 Liter.						
Sedan 4D	BE1BL	47775	30200	31200	32500	37100
Luxury Pkg			2000	2000	2345	2345
Premium Pkg			1100	1100	1290	1290
F Sport Pkg			1600	1600	1875	1875
AWD	C		900	900	1055	1055
GS 450h—V6 Hybrid—Equipment Schedule 1						
W.B. 112.2"; 3.5 Liter.						
Sedan 4D	BS1BL	59825	34700	35800	37000	42100
Luxury Pkg			2000	2000	2330	2330
LS 460—V8—Equipment Schedule 1						
W.B. 116.9", 121.7" (L); 4.6 Liter.						
Sedan 4D	BL1EF	72885	47400	48800	49800	55300
L Sedan 4D	GL1EF	79185	52700	54300	55200	61200
Ultra Luxury Pkg			700	700	745	745
AWD	C		1900	1900	2035	2035
LS 600h—V8 Hybrid—Equipment Schedule 1						
W.B. 121.7"; 5.0 Liter.						
L Sedan 4D	DU1EF	120805	70200	72300	72900	80800
2014 LEXUS — JTH(KD5BH)-E-#						
CT 200h—4-Cyl. Hybrid—Equipment Schedule 1						
W.B. 102.4"; 1.8 Liter.						
Hatchback 4D	KD5BH	32960	23700	24500	25200	28200
Dynamic Cruise Control			500	500	555	555
F Sport Pkg			1700	1700	1890	1890
IS 250—V6—Equipment Schedule 1						
W.B. 110.2"; 2.5 Liter.						
Sedan 4D	BF1D2	36845	27700	28700	29100	32400
Dynamic Cruise Control			500	500	550	550
Luxury Pkg			1100	1100	1215	1215
F-Sport Pkg			1000	1000	1105	1105
AWD	C		1600	1600	1765	1765
IS 250C—V6—Equipment Schedule 1						
W.B. 107.5"; 2.5 Liter.						
Convertible 2D	FF2C2	43620	33800	34900	35400	39500
Dynamic Cruise Control			500	500	555	555
Luxury Pkg			1100	1100	1220	1220
F-Sport Pkg			1000	1000	1110	1110
IS 350—V6—Equipment Schedule 1						
W.B. 110.2"; 3.5 Liter.						
Sedan 4D	BE1D2	40360	31600	32600	33100	36900
Dynamic Cruise Control			500	500	555	555
Luxury Pkg			1100	1100	1215	1215
F-Sport Pkg			1000	1000	1105	1105
AWD	C		1600	1600	1770	1770
IS 350C—V6—Equipment Schedule 1						
W.B. 107.5"; 3.5 Liter.						

2014 LEXUS

Body Type	VIN	List	Trade-In Good	Very Good	Pvt-Party Good	Retail Excellent
Convertible 2D	FE2C2	47900	37200	38400	38900	43300
Dynamic Cruise Control			500	500	555	555
Luxury Pkg			1100	1100	1220	1220
F-Sport Pkg			1000	1000	1110	1110
ES 300h—4-Cyl. Hybrid—Equipment Schedule 1						
W.B. 111.0"; 2.5 Liter.						
Sedan 4D	BK1GG	40260	30500	31500	31900	35600
Dynamic Radar Cruise Ctrl			500	500	550	550
Ultra Luxury Pkg			2525	2525	2785	2785
ES 350—V6—Equipment Schedule 1						
W.B. 111.0"; 3.5 Liter.						
Sedan 4D	BW1GG	37380	28500	29500	30000	33400
Dynamic Radar Cruise Ctrl			500	500	550	550
Ultra Luxury Pkg			2525	2525	2790	2790
GS 350—V6—Equipment Schedule 1						
W.B. 112.2"; 3.5 Liter.						
Sedan 4D	BE1BL	48610	36500	37700	38500	43400
Adaptive Cruise Control			500	500	570	570
Luxury Pkg			2200	2200	2515	2515
Premium Pkg			1200	1200	1370	1370
F Sport Pkg			1700	1700	1940	1940
AWD	C		1000	1000	1140	1140
GS 450h—V6 Hybrid—Equipment Schedule 1						
W.B. 112.2"; 3.5 Liter.						
Sedan 4D	BS1BL	60510	41000	42300	43100	48400
Adaptive Cruise Control			500	500	570	570
Luxury Pkg			2200	2200	2505	2505
Premium Pkg			1200	1200	1365	1365
LS 460—V8—Equipment Schedule 1						
W.B. 116.9", 121.7" (L); 4.6 Liter.						
Sedan 4D	BL5EF	73050	53900	55500	56900	63700
L Sedan 4D	GL5EF	79350	59200	61000	62400	69700
Dynamic Cruise Control			500	500	530	530
Ultra Luxury Pkg			750	750	800	800
F Sport Pkg			1700	1700	1810	1810
Executive Class Seating			3000	3000	3190	3190
AWD	C		2000	2000	2130	2130
LS 600h—V8 Hybrid—Equipment Schedule 1						
W.B. 121.7"; 5.0 Liter.						
L Sedan 4D	DU1EF	120970	76700	78900	79200	87300
Dynamic Cruise Control			500	500	530	530
Ultra Luxury Pkg			750	750	795	795
Executive Class Seating			3000	3000	3190	3190

LINCOLN

2000 LINCOLN — 1LN(HM81W)-Y-#

TOWN CAR—V8—Equipment Schedule 2
W.B. 117.7", 123.7" (L Pkg); 4.6 Liter.

Body Type	VIN	List	Good	Very Good	Good	Excellent
Executive Sedan 4D	HM81W	39300	1075	1225	1725	2825
Signature Sedan 4D	HM82W	41300	1250	1425	1950	3175
Cartier Sedan 4D	HM83W	43800	1325	1500	2100	3475
L Pkg			825	825	1115	1115
Touring			75	75	100	100
CONTINENTAL—V8—Equipment Schedule 2						
W.B. 117.7"; 4.6 Liter.						
Sedan 4D	HM97V	39550	1600	1775	2625	4425
LS—V6—Equipment Schedule 2						
W.B. 114.5"; 3.0 Liter.						
Sedan 4D	HM86S	31450	1175	1325	1850	3000
Sport Pkg			75	75	100	100
Manual, 5-Spd			(225)	(225)	(300)	(300)
LS—V8—Equipment Schedule 2						
W.B. 114.5"; 3.9 Liter.						
Sedan 4D	HM87A	35225	1850	2075	2850	4525
Sport Pkg			75	75	100	100

2001 LINCOLN — 1LN(HM81W)-1-#

TOWN CAR—V8—Equipment Schedule 2
W.B. 117.7", 123.7" (L); 4.6 Liter.

Body Type	VIN	List	Good	Very Good	Good	Excellent
Executive Sedan 4D	HM81W	39865	1100	1250	1775	2950

2001 LINCOLN

Body Type	VIN	List	Trade-In Good	Very Good	Pvt-Party Good	Retail Excellent
Executive L Sed 4D	HM84W	44225	2225	2475	3375	5425
Signature Sedan 4D	HM82W	42035	1300	1450	2025	3350
Signature Touring 4D	HM82W	42745	1350	1525	2100	3475
Cartier Sedan 4D	HM83W	44620	1575	1775	2400	3925
Cartier L Sedan 4D	HM85W	49230	3000	3350	4425	7000
CONTINENTAL—V8—Equipment Schedule 2						
W.B. 109.0"; 4.6 Liter.						
Sedan 4D	HM97V	40100	1775	2000	2950	4850
LS—V6—Equipment Schedule 2						
W.B. 114.5"; 3.0 Liter.						
Sedan 4D	HM86S	32250	1525	1700	2200	3500
Sport Pkg		-------	75	75	105	105
Manual, 5-Spd		-------	(225)	(225)	(300)	(300)
LS—V8—Equipment Schedule 2						
W.B. 114.5"; 3.9 Liter.						
Sedan 4D	HM87A	36280	2150	2425	3175	4925
Sport Pkg		-------	75	75	105	105

2002 LINCOLN — 1LN(HM81W)-2-#

Body Type	VIN	List	Trade-In Good	Very Good	Pvt-Party Good	Retail Excellent
TOWN CAR—V8—Equipment Schedule 2						
W.B. 117.7", 123.7" (L); 4.6 Liter.						
Executive Sedan 4D	HM81W	40540	1200	1350	1900	3125
Executive L Sed 4D	HM84W	44260	2650	2950	3975	6275
Signature Sedan 4D	HM82W	42710	1475	1650	2375	3875
Signature Touring 4D	HM82W	43420	1525	1725	2450	3975
Cartier Sedan 4D	HM83W	45095	1925	2150	2975	4800
Cartier L Sedan 4D	HM85W	49605	3400	3775	4975	7800
CONTINENTAL—V8—Equipment Schedule 2						
W.B. 109.0"; 4.6 Liter.						
Sedan 4D	HM97V	38555	2050	2275	3175	5050
LS—V6—Equipment Schedule 2						
W.B. 114.5"; 3.0 Liter.						
Sedan 4D	HM86S	33455	1675	1875	2425	3800
LSE		-------	900	900	1200	1200
Manual, 5-Spd		-------	(275)	(275)	(370)	(370)
LS—V8—Equipment Schedule 2						
W.B. 114.5"; 3.9 Liter.						
Sedan 4D	HM87A	37630	2475	2750	3525	5375
LSE		-------	900	900	1200	1200

2003 LINCOLN — 1LN(HM81W)-3-#

Body Type	VIN	List	Trade-In Good	Very Good	Pvt-Party Good	Retail Excellent
TOWN CAR—V8—Equipment Schedule 2						
W.B. 117.7", 123.7" (L); 4.6 Liter.						
Executive Sedan 4D	HM81W	41140	1400	1575	2200	3600
Executive L Sed 4D	HM84W	45115	3250	3625	4575	6975
Signature Sedan 4D	HM82W	43600	1650	1850	2625	4250
Cartier Sedan 4D	HM83W	46110	2200	2450	3325	5275
Cartier L Sedan 4D	HM85W	51570	4250	4700	5950	8925
Limited Edition		-------	350	350	460	460
LS—V6—Equipment Schedule 2						
W.B. 114.5"; 3.0 Liter.						
Sedan 4D	HM86S	40695	2300	2575	3275	4975
V6, 3.0 Liter	S		(750)	(750)	(1015)	(1015)

2004 LINCOLN — 1LN(HM81W)-4-#

Body Type	VIN	List	Trade-In Good	Very Good	Pvt-Party Good	Retail Excellent
TOWN CAR—V8—Equipment Schedule 2						
W.B. 117.7", 123.7" (L); 4.6 Liter.						
Executive Sedan 4D	HM81W	42810	2125	2350	3025	4650
Executive L Sed 4D	HM84W	45790	4125	4525	5750	8600
Signature Sedan 4D	HM81W	41815	2300	2550	3350	5175
Ultimate Sedan 4D	HM83W	44925	3125	3475	4425	6750
Ultimate L Sedan 4D	HM85W	50470	5250	5750	7375	10900
LS—V6—Equipment Schedule 2						
W.B. 114.5"; 3.0 Liter.						
Sedan 4D	HM86S	32495	2325	2600	3300	4975
LS—V8—Equipment Schedule 2						
W.B. 114.5"; 3.9 Liter.						
Sport Sedan 4D	HM87A	40095	3325	3700	4600	6850
LSE		-------	1100	1100	1465	1465

2005 LINCOLN

Body Type	VIN	List	Trade-In Good	Very Good	Pvt-Party Good	Retail Excellent

2005 LINCOLN — 1LN(ForH)(M86S)-5-#

LS—V6—Equipment Schedule 2
W.B. 114.5"; 3.0 Liter.

Sedan 4D	M86S	32965	2200	2450	3425	5225

LS—V8—Equipment Schedule 2
W.B. 114.5"; 3.9 Liter.

Sport Sedan 4D	M87A	40515	3325	3675	4725	6975
LSE			1200	1200	1600	1600

TOWN CAR—V8—Equipment Schedule 2
W.B. 117.7", 123.7" (L); 4.6 Liter.

Signature Sedan 4D	M81W	42470	2725	3050	4050	6150
Signature Ltd Sed 4D	M83W	45310	3375	3725	5025	7500
Executive L Sedan 4D	M84W	46445	4850	5300	6625	9600
Signature L Sedan 4D	M85W	50915	5800	6300	8000	11500
Limited Edition			225	225	310	310

2006 LINCOLN — (1or3)LN(ForH)(M261)-6-#

ZEPHYR—V6—Equipment Schedule 2
W.B. 107.4"; 3.0 Liter.

Sedan 4D	M261	29660	4400	4750	5825	8125

LS—V8—Equipment Schedule 2
W.B. 114.5"; 3.9 Liter.

Sedan 4D	M87A	39945	3250	3600	4400	6300

TOWN CAR—V8—Equipment Schedule 2
W.B. 117.7", 123.7" (L); 4.6 Liter.

Signature Sedan 4D	M81W	42875	3450	3800	4825	6900
Signature Ltd Sedan	M82W	45740	4300	4700	5800	8225
Designer Sedan 4D	M83W	46735	5150	5575	6775	9525
Executive L Sedan 4D	M84W	46990	5825	6325	7750	10800
Signature L Sedan 4D	M85W	51345	8375	9000	10700	14650

2007 LINCOLN — (1or3)LN-(M26T)-7-#

MKZ—V6—Equipment Schedule 2
W.B. 107.4"; 3.5 Liter.

Sedan 4D	M26T	29890	5250	5650	6750	9000
AWD	8		1025	1025	1370	1370

TOWN CAR—V8—Equipment Schedule 2
W.B. 117.7", 123.7" (L); 4.6 Liter.

Signature Sedan 4D	M81W	42985	4750	5150	5800	7675
Signature Ltd Sedan	M82W	45850	5250	5700	6625	8750
Designer Sedan 4D	M83W	48110	6400	6900	7800	10150
Executive L Sedan 4D	M84W	47160	8375	8975	9925	12800
Signature L Sedan 4D	M85W	51455	9800	10500	11650	15000

2008 LINCOLN — (1or3)LN-(M26T)-8-#

MKZ—V6—Equipment Schedule 2
W.B. 107.4"; 3.5 Liter.

Sedan 4D	M26T	30915	6575	7000	7950	10150
AWD			1100	1100	1455	1455

TOWN CAR—V8—Equipment Schedule 2
W.B. 117.7", 123.7" (L); 4.6 Liter.

Signature Ltd Sed 4D	M82W	45910	6900	7375	8325	10650
Signature L Sedan 4D	M85W	51515	10950	11600	12800	16100

2009 LINCOLN — (1or3)LN-(M26T)-9-#

MKZ—V6—Equipment Schedule 2
W.B. 107.4"; 3.5 Liter.

Sedan 4D	M26T	32535	8050	8525	9525	11850
AWD			1150	1150	1505	1505

MKS—V6—Equipment Schedule 2
W.B. 112.9"; 3.7 Liter.

Sedan 4D	M93R	38465	10150	10750	12100	15100
AWD			2100	2100	2745	2745

TOWN CAR—V8—Equipment Schedule 2
W.B. 117.7", 123.7" (L); 4.6 Liter.

Signature Ltd Sedan	M82W	46760	8700	9200	10300	12850
Signature L Sedan 4D	M85W	52430	12550	13200	14500	17850

Body Type	VIN	List	Trade-In Good	Very Good	Pvt-Party Good	Retail Excellent

2010 LINCOLN — (1or3)LN-(L2GC)-A-#

MKZ—V6—Equipment Schedule 2
W.B. 107.4"; 3.5 Liter.

Body Type	VIN	List	Good	Very Good	Good	Excellent
Sedan 4D	L2GC	34965	9700	10200	11250	13700
AWD	J		1225	1225	1550	1550

MKS—V6—Equipment Schedule 2
W.B. 112.9"; 3.7 Liter.

Sedan 4D	L9DR	41695	11600	12150	13700	16950
AWD	E		2225	2225	2840	2840

MKS—V6 EcoBoost Twin Turbo—Equipment Schedule 2
W.B. 112.9"; 3.5 Liter.

Sedan 4D	L9FT	48985	15550	16250	18200	22300

TOWN CAR—V8—Equipment Schedule 2
W.B. 117.7", 123.7" (L); 4.6 Liter.

Signature Ltd Sedan	L8CV	47470	11700	12300	13750	16900
Signature L Sedan 4D	L8FV	53140	16450	17150	18950	23100

2011 LINCOLN — (1or3)LN-(L2GC)-B-#

MKZ—V6—Equipment Schedule 2
W.B. 107.4"; 3.5 Liter.

Sedan 4D	L2GC	35180	11100	11650	12650	15150
AWD	J		1300	1300	1615	1615

MKZ—4-Cyl. Hybrid—Equipment Schedule 2
W.B. 107.4"; 2.5 Liter.

Sedan 4D	L2L3	35180	12000	12600	13850	16800

MKS—V6—Equipment Schedule 2
W.B. 112.9"; 3.7 Liter.

Sedan 4D	L9DR	42095	13100	13650	15350	18600
AWD	E		2325	2325	2950	2950

MKS—V6 EcoBoost Twin Turbo—Equipment Schedule 2
W.B. 112.9"; 3.5 Liter.

Sedan 4D	L9FT	48985	17150	17850	19750	23900

TOWN CAR—V8—Equipment Schedule 2
W.B. 117.7", 123.7" (L); 4.6 Liter.

Signature L/D Sedan	L8CV	47870	16700	17400	18700	21900
Signature L Sedan	L8FV	53540	21200	22000	23300	27200

2012 LINCOLN — (1,2or3)LN-(L2GC)-C-#

MKZ—V6—Equipment Schedule 2
W.B. 107.4"; 3.5 Liter.

Sedan 4D	L2GC	35630	13200	13800	14800	17450
AWD	J		1375	1375	1655	1655

MKZ—4-Cyl. Hybrid—Equipment Schedule 2
W.B. 107.4"; 2.5 Liter.

Sedan 4D	L2L3	35630	14650	15300	16550	19650

MKS—V6—Equipment Schedule 2
W.B. 112.9"; 3.7 Liter.

Sedan 4D	L9DR	42375	14950	15550	17250	20600
AWD	E		2450	2450	3075	3075

MKS AWD—V6 EcoBoost Twin Turbo—Equipment Schedule 2
W.B. 112.9"; 3.5 Liter.

Sedan 4D	L9FT	49265	19000	19700	21600	25700

2013 LINCOLN — (1,2or3)LN-(L2G9)-D-#

MKZ—4-Cyl. EcoBoost—Equipment Schedule 2
W.B. 112.2"; 2.0 Liter.

Sedan 4D	L2G9	36800	19100	19900	20900	24100
AWD	J		1425	1425	1680	1680
V6, 3.7 Liter	K		550	550	645	645

MKZ—4-Cyl. Hybrid—Equipment Schedule 2
W.B. 107.4"; 2.0 Liter.

Sedan 4D	L2LU	36800	21200	22100	23000	26500

MKS—V6—Equipment Schedule 2
W.B. 112.9"; 3.7 Liter.

Sedan 4D	L9DK	43685	18350	19000	20800	24500
AWD	E		2575	2575	3165	3165

MKS AWD—V6 EcoBoost Twin Turbo—Equipment Schedule 2
W.B. 112.9"; 3.5 Liter.

Sedan 4D	L9FT	50675	22400	23200	25100	29600

2014 LINCOLN

Body Type	VIN	List	Trade-In Good	Very Good	Pvt-Party Good	Retail Excellent

2014 LINCOLN — (1,2or3)LN-(L2G9)-E-#

MKZ—4-Cyl. EcoBoost—Equipment Schedule 2
W.B. 112.2"; 2.0 Liter.

Sedan 4D	L2G9	36820	20900	21700	22500	25700
AWD	J		1500	1500	1730	1730
V6, 3.7 Liter	K		650	650	750	750

MKZ—4-Cyl. Hybrid—Equipment Schedule 2
W.B. 112.2"; 2.0 Liter.

Sedan 4D	L2LU	36820	23400	24300	25000	28600

MKS—V6—Equipment Schedule 2
W.B. 112.9"; 3.7 Liter.

Sedan 4D	L9DK	41320	20300	21100	22200	25400
AWD	E		2700	2700	3095	3095

MKS AWD—V6 EcoBoost Twin Turbo—Equipment Schedule 2
W.B. 112.9"; 3.5 Liter.

Sedan 4D	L9FT	48310	24300	25200	26300	30100

LOTUS

2005 LOTUS — SCC(PC111)-5-#

ELISE—4-Cyl.—Equipment Schedule 1
W.B. 90.5"; 1.8 Liter.

Coupe 2D	PC111	43915	****	****	****	18150
Sport Pkg			****	****	****	400
Touring Pkg			****	****	****	565

2006 LOTUS — SCC(PC111)-6-#

ELISE—4-Cyl.—Equipment Schedule 1
W.B. 90.5"; 1.8 Liter.

Coupe 2D	PC111	43915	****	****	****	21400
Sport Pkg			****	****	****	420
Touring Pkg			****	****	****	600
Track Pkg			****	****	****	1425

EXIGE—4-Cyl.—Equipment Schedule 1
W.B. 90.5"; 1.8 Liter.

Coupe 2D	PC111	51915	****	****	****	27000
Touring Pkg			****	****	****	600
Track Pkg			****	****	****	1415

2007 LOTUS — SCC(PC111)-7-#

ELISE—4-Cyl.—Equipment Schedule 2
W.B. 90.5"; 1.8 Liter.

Coupe 2D	PC111	44915	****	****	****	24900
Track Pkg			****	****	****	1465

EXIGE S—4-Cyl. Supercharged—Equipment Schedule 1
W.B. 90.5"; 1.8 Liter.

Coupe 2D	VC111	60815	****	****	****	33200
Track Pkg			****	****	****	1450

2008 LOTUS — SCC(PC111)-8-#

ELISE—4-Cyl.—Equipment Schedule 2
W.B. 90.5"; 1.8 Liter.

Coupe 2D	PC111	47195	****	****	****	28500
Sport Pkg			****	****	****	495
Touring Pkg			****	****	****	680

ELISE—4-Cyl. Supercharged—Equipment Schedule 2
W.B. 90.5"; 1.8 Liter.

SC Coupe 2D	ZC111	55425	****	****	****	33100
Sport Pkg			****	****	****	490
Touring Pkg			****	****	****	680

EXIGE S—4-Cyl. Supercharged—Equipment Schedule 1
W.B. 90.5"; 1.8 Liter.

Coupe 2D	VC111	61925	****	****	****	37000
240 Coupe 2D	WC111	65815	****	****	****	38600
Touring Pkg			****	****	****	680
Track Pkg			****	****	****	1495

2009 LOTUS

Body Type	VIN	List	Trade-In Good	Very Good	Pvt-Party Good	Retail Excellent

2009 LOTUS — SCC(PC111)-9-#

ELISE—4-Cyl.—Equipment Schedule 2
W.B. 90.5"; 1.8 Liter.

Coupe 2D	PC111	48175	****	****	****	**33800**
Sport Pkg			****	****	****	**540**
Touring Pkg			****	****	****	**720**

ELISE—4-Cyl. Supercharged—Equipment Schedule 2
W.B. 90.5"; 1.8 Liter.

SC Coupe 2D	ZC111	55915	****	****	****	**38500**
Sport Pkg			****	****	****	**540**
Touring Pkg			****	****	****	**720**

EXIGE—4-Cyl. Supercharged—Equipment Schedule 1
W.B. 90.5"; 1.8 Liter.

S240 Coupe 2D	AC111	66615	****	****	****	**43800**
S260 Coupe 2D	AC111	75920	****	****	****	**49800**
Touring Pkg			****	****	****	**720**
Track Pkg			****	****	****	**1540**

2010 LOTUS — SCC(LHCPC)-A-#

ELISE—4-Cyl.—Equipment Schedule 2
W.B. 90.5"; 1.8 Liter.

Coupe 2D	LHCPC	48375	****	****	****	**38300**
Sport Pkg			****	****	****	**590**
Touring Pkg			****	****	****	**720**

ELISE—4-Cyl. Supercharged—Equipment Schedule 2
W.B. 90.5"; 1.8 Liter.

SC Coupe 2D	LHCZC	56115	****	****	****	**42700**
Sport Pkg			****	****	****	**590**
Touring Pkg			****	****	****	**720**

EXIGE—4-Cyl. Supercharged—Equipment Schedule 1
W.B. 90.5"; 1.8 Liter.

S240 Coupe 2D	LHHWC	66815	****	****	****	**49100**
Touring Pkg			****	****	****	**715**
Track Pkg			****	****	****	**1535**

EVORA—V6—Equipment Schedule 2
W.B. 101.4"; 3.5 Liter.

Coupe 2D	LMDTU	74165	****	****	****	**59800**
Premium Pkg			****	****	****	**775**
Sport Pkg			****	****	****	**590**
Technology Pkg			****	****	****	**1245**

2011 LOTUS — SCC(LHCPC)-B-#

ELISE—4-Cyl.—Equipment Schedule 2
W.B. 90.5"; 1.6 Liter.

Coupe 2D	LHCPC	48375	****	****	****	**42100**
Sport Pkg			****	****	****	**665**
Touring Pkg			****	****	****	**745**

ELISE—4-Cyl. Supercharged—Equipment Schedule 2
W.B. 90.5"; 1.8 Liter.

SC Coupe 2D	LHCZC	56115	****	****	****	**45000**
Sport Pkg			****	****	****	**660**
Touring Pkg			****	****	****	**740**

EXIGE—4-Cyl. Supercharged—Equipment Schedule 1
W.B. 90.5"; 1.8 Liter.

S240 Coupe 2D	LHHAC	66815	****	****	****	**49400**
S260 Sport Coupe 2D	LHHAC	76075	****	****	****	**54400**
Touring Pkg			****	****	****	**740**
Track Pkg			****	****	****	**1585**

EVORA—V6—Equipment Schedule 2
W.B. 101.4"; 3.5 Liter.

Coupe 2D	LMDTC	65175	****	****	****	**59900**
Sport Pkg			****	****	****	**655**
Technology Pkg			****	****	****	**1350**

2012 LOTUS — SCC(LMDTC)-C-#

EVORA—V6—Equipment Schedule 2
W.B. 101.4"; 3.5 Liter.

Coupe 2D	LMDTC	67275	****	****	****	**61400**
Sport Pkg			****	****	****	**735**
Technology Pkg			****	****	****	**1420**

2013 LOTUS

Body Type	VIN	List	Trade-In Good	Very Good	Pvt-Party Good	Retail Excellent

2013 LOTUS — SCC(LMDTC)-D-#

EVORA—V6—Equipment Schedule 2
W.B. 101.4"; 3.5 Liter.

Body Type	VIN	List	Good	Very Good	Good	Excellent
Coupe 2D	LMDTC	68285	****	****	****	**63800**
Sport Pkg			****	****	****	**835**
Tech Pkg			****	****	****	**1495**

EVORA—V6 Supercharged—Equipment Schedule 2
W.B. 101.4"; 3.5 Liter.

Body Type	VIN	List	Good	Very Good	Good	Excellent
S Coupe 2D	LMDSC	78585	****	****	****	**66900**
Sport Pkg			****	****	****	**835**
Tech Pkg			****	****	****	**1495**

2014 LOTUS — SCC(LMDTC)-E-#

EVORA—V6—Equipment Schedule 2
W.B. 101.4"; 3.5 Liter.

Body Type	VIN	List
Coupe 2D	LMDTC	70235

EVORA—V6 Supercharged—Equipment Schedule 2
W.B. 101.4"; 3.5 Liter.

Body Type	VIN	List
S Coupe 2D	LMDSC	80235
Technology Pkg		

MASERATI

2005 MASERATI — ZAM(BC38A)-5-#

COUPE—V8—Equipment Schedule 1
W.B. 104.7"; 4.2 Liter.

Body Type	VIN	List	Good	Very Good	Good	Excellent
Cambiocorsa Coupe	BC38A	88227	11350	11950	12600	15100
GT Coupe 2D	BC38A	99522	10350	10900	11700	14150

2006 MASERATI — ZAM(BC38A)-6-#

GT—V8—Equipment Schedule 1
W.B. 104.7"; 4.2 Liter.

Body Type	VIN	List	Good	Very Good	Good	Excellent
GT Coupe 2D	BC38A	81250	12600	13250	14750	18400

CAMBIOCORSA—V8—Equipment Schedule 1
W.B. 104.7"; 4.2 Liter.

Body Type	VIN	List	Good	Very Good	Good	Excellent
Coupe 2D	BC38A	88927	13600	14300	15550	19050

GRANSPORT—V8—Equipment Schedule 1
W.B. 104.7"; 4.2 Liter.

Body Type	VIN	List	Good	Very Good	Good	Excellent
Coupe 2D	EC38A	100222	18600	19500	20900	25400
LE Coupe 2D	EC38A	105472	19300	20200	21700	26600
Spyder Convertible 2D	EB18A	101250	20800	21800	23200	28400

QUATTROPORTE—V8—Equipment Schedule 1
W.B. 120.6"; 4.2 Liter.

Body Type	VIN	List	Good	Very Good	Good	Excellent
Sedan 4D	CE39A	105050	12500	13200	14400	17650
Executive GT Sed 4D	CE39A	117250	13300	14000	15550	19400

2007 MASERATI — ZAM(FE39A)-7-#

QUATTROPORTE—V8—Equipment Schedule 2
W.B. 120.6"; 4.2 Liter.

Body Type	VIN	List	Good	Very Good	Good	Excellent
DuoSelect Sedan 4D	FE39A	111950	16650	17450	18350	21900
Sedan 4D	CE39A	113600	15000	15750	16800	20200
DuoSelect Exec GT	FE39A	121950	20300	21200	22400	26800
Executive GT Sed 4D	CE39A	123750	19300	20200	21500	25900
DuoSelect Sport GT	FE39A	120650	17250	18050	19150	23000
Sport GT Sedan 4D	CE39A	122450	18650	19500	20700	24900

2008 MASERATI — ZAM(GJ45A)-8-#

GRANTURISMO—V8—Equipment Schedule 2
W.B. 115.8"; 4.2 Liter.

Body Type	VIN	List	Good	Very Good	Good	Excellent
Coupe 2D	GJ45A	113450	30700	31900	33600	40000

QUATTROPORTE—V8—Equipment Schedule 2
W.B. 120.6"; 4.2 Liter.

Body Type	VIN	List	Good	Very Good	Good	Excellent
Sedan 4D	CE39A	119000	18750	19600	20700	24400
Executive GT Sed 4D	FE39A	129150	24000	24900	26200	31000

2009 MASERATI — ZAM(GJ45A)-9-#

GRANTURISMO—V8—Equipment Schedule 2
W.B. 115.8"; 4.2 Liter, 4.7 Liter.

2009 MASERATI

Body Type	VIN	List	Trade-In Good	Trade-In Very Good	Pvt-Party Good	Retail Excellent
Coupe 2D	GJ45A	121100	36300	37600	38100	43300
S Coupe 2D	HJ45A	125600	42300	43800	44100	50000

QUATTROPORTE—V8—Equipment Schedule 2
W.B. 120.6"; 4.2 Liter.

Sedan 4D	FK39A	124150	27300	28400	29900	34900
S Sedan 4D	JK39A	130150	29400	30400	32100	37600
Sport GT S Sedan 4D	FE39A	138100	32800	34000	35700	41700

2010 MASERATI — ZAM(45GLA)–A–#

GRANTURISMO—V8—Equipment Schedule 2
W.B. 115.8"; 4.2 Liter, 4.7 Liter.

Coupe 2D	45GLA	121900	41000	42400	42800	48100
S Coupe 2D	45KLA	125900	48400	50000	50500	56500
Convertible 2D	45KMA	139700	57100	59000	59000	65600

QUATTROPORTE—V8—Equipment Schedule 2
W.B. 120.6"; 4.2 Liter, 4.7 Liter.

Sedan 4D	39FKA	124150	32600	33800	36000	42200
S Sedan 4D	39JKA	130650	34600	35800	37700	43800
Sport GT S Sedan 4D	39KKA	138600	38100	39400	41800	48900

2011 MASERATI — ZAM(45GLA)–B–#

GRANTURISMO—V8—Equipment Schedule 2
W.B. 115.8"; 4.2 Liter, 4.7 Liter.

Coupe 2D	45GLA	122800	46100	47600	48100	53700
S Coupe 2D	45KLA	126400	50200	53700	53800	59400
Convertible 2D	45KMA	140200	60000	61900	62000	68700

QUATTROPORTE—V8—Equipment Schedule 2
W.B. 120.6"; 4.2 Liter, 4.7 Liter.

Sedan 4D	39FKA	125150	40700	42100	43100	48700
S Sedan 4D	39JKA	131150	42700	44100	45200	51100
Sport GT S Sedan 4D	39KKA	139100	46200	47700	48800	55200

2012 MASERATI — ZAM(45KLA)–C–#

GRANTURISMO—V8—Equipment Schedule 2
W.B. 115.8"; 4.7 Liter.

S Coupe 2D	45KLA	126500	67300	69300	69500	76700
MC Coupe 2D	45MLA	143400	76700	78900	79500	88300
Convertible 2D	45KMA	140800	74900	77100	77100	85100
Sport Convertible 2D	45MMA	146300	80400	82700	83500	93000

QUATTROPORTE—V8—Equipment Schedule 2
W.B. 120.6"; 4.7 Liter.

S Sedan 4D	39JKA	131150	51100	52700	55300	63300
Sport GT S Sedan 4D	39KKA	139100	54600	56300	59200	67900

2013 MASERATI — ZAM(45VLA)–D–#

GRANTURISMO—V8—Equipment Schedule 2
W.B. 115.8"; 4.7 Liter.

Sport Coupe 2D	45VLA	129800	71500	73500	73700	81200
Sport Convertible 2D	45VMA	146800	84500	86900	87600	97100
Convertible 2D	45MMA	142100	80500	82800	83100	91700
MC Coupe 2D	45VLA	146900	80800	83100	83900	93100

QUATTROPORTE—V8—Equipment Schedule 2
W.B. 120.6"; 4.7 Liter.

S Sedan 4D	39NKA	132150	58000	59700	62200	70700
Sport GT S Sedan 4D	39MKA	140100	61500	63300	65900	74800

MAYBACH

2005 MAYBACH — WDB(VF78J)–5–#

57—V12 Twin Turbo—Equipment Schedule 1
W.B. 133.5"; 5.5 Liter.

Sedan 4D	VF78J	327250	****	****	****	90700

62—V12 Twin Turbo—Equipment Schedule 1
W.B. 150.7"; 5.5 Liter.

Sedan 4D	VG78J	377750	****	****	****	126200

2006 MAYBACH — WDB(VF78J)–6–#

57—V12 Twin Turbo—Equipment Schedule 1
W.B. 133.5"; 5.5 Liter, 6.0 Liter.

2006 MAYBACH

Body Type	VIN	List	Trade-In Good	Very Good	Pvt-Party Good	Retail Excellent
Sedan 4D	VF78J	335250	****	****	****	126500
S Sedan 4D	VF79J	369750	****	****	****	147000
62—V12 Twin Turbo—Equipment Schedule 1						
W.B. 150.7"; 5.5 Liter.						
Sedan 4D	VG78J	385250	****	****	****	166300

2007 MAYBACH — WDB(VF78J)-7-#

57—V12 Twin Turbo—Equipment Schedule 1
W.B. 133.5"; 5.5 Liter, 6.0 Liter.

Body Type	VIN	List	Good	Very Good	Good	Excellent
Sedan 4D	VF78J	338250	****	****	****	166200
S Sedan 4D	VF79J	377750	****	****	****	186000
62—V12 Twin Turbo—Equipment Schedule 1						
W.B. 133.5", 150.7"; 5.5 Liter, 6.0 Liter.						
Sedan 4D	VG78J	389250	****	****	****	204600
S Sedan 4D	VG79J	428750	****	****	****	223100

2008 MAYBACH — WDB(VF78J)-8-#

57—V12 Twin Turbo—Equipment Schedule 1
W.B. 133.5", 150.7"; 5.5 Liter, 6.0 Liter.

Body Type	VIN	List	Good	Very Good	Good	Excellent
Sedan 4D	VF78J	343250	****	****	****	195700
S Sedan 4D	VF79J	382750	****	****	****	215100
62—V12 Twin Turbo—Equipment Schedule 1						
W.B. 133.5", 150.7"; 5.5 Liter, 6.0 Liter.						
Sedan 4D	VG78J	394250	****	****	****	246800
S Sedan 4D	VG79J	433750	****	****	****	269100

2009 MAYBACH — WDB(VF78J)-9-#

57—V12 Twin Turbo—Equipment Schedule 1
W.B. 133.5", 150.7"; 5.5 Liter, 6.0 Liter.

Body Type	VIN	List	Good	Very Good	Good	Excellent
Sedan 4D	VF78J	360250	****	****	****	237000
S Sedan 4D	VF79J	400250	****	****	****	256100
62—V12 Twin Turbo—Equipment Schedule 1						
W.B. 150.7"; 5.5 Liter, 6.0 Liter.						
Sedan 4D	VG78J	411750	****	****	****	292600
S Sedan 4D	VG79J	451250	****	****	****	314500
LANDAULET—V12 Twin Turbo—Equipment Schedule 1						
Sedan 4D		1382750				

2010 MAYBACH — WDB(VF7JB)-A-#

57—V12 Twin Turbo—Equipment Schedule 1
W.B. 133.5", 150.7"; 5.5 Liter, 6.0 Liter.

Body Type	VIN	List	Good	Very Good	Good	Excellent
Sedan 4D	VF7JB	368750	****	****	****	322000
S Sedan 4D	VF7KB	408250	****	****	****	340700
Zeppelin Sedan 4D	VG7KB	458250	****	****	****	408600
62—V12 Twin Turbo—Equipment Schedule 1						
W.B. 150.7"; 5.5 Liter, 6.0 Liter.						
Sedan 4D	VG7JB	454750	****	****	****	376600
S Sedan 4D		494250	****	****	****	406400
Zeppelin Sedan 4D	VG7KB	509250	****	****	****	464100
LANDAULET—V12 Twin Turbo—Equipment Schedule 1						
W.B. 150.7"; 6.0 Liter.						
Sedan 4D	VG7KB	1382750				

2011 MAYBACH — WDB(VF7JB)-B-#

57—V12 Twin Turbo—Equipment Schedule 1
W.B. 133.5", 150.7"; 5.5 Liter, 6.0 Liter.

Body Type	VIN	List	Good	Very Good	Good	Excellent
Sedan 4D	VF7JB	375250	****	****	****	359900
S Sedan 4D	VF7HB	414750	****	****	****	378400
62—V12 Twin Turbo—Equipment Schedule 1						
W.B. 150.7"; 5.5 Liter, 6.0 Liter.						
Sedan 4D	VG7JB	430750	****	****	****	413500
S Sedan 4D	VG7HB	470250	****	****	****	443000
LANDAULET—V12 Twin Turbo—Equipment Schedule 1						
W.B. 150.7"; 6.0 Liter.						
Sedan 4D	VG7HB	1382750				

2012 MAYBACH — WDB(VF7JB)-C-#

57—V12 Twin Turbo—Equipment Schedule 1
W.B. 133.5", 150.7"; 5.5 Liter, 6.0 Liter.

Body Type	VIN	List	Good	Very Good	Good	Excellent
Sedan 4D	VF7JB	379050	****	****	****	395800

Body Type	VIN	List	Trade-In Good	Very Good	Pvt-Party Good	Retail Excellent
S Sedan 4D	VF7HB	418950	****	****	****	414000
62—V12 Twin Turbo—Equipment Schedule 1						
W.B. 150.7"; 5.5 Liter, 6.0 Liter.						
Sedan 4D	VG7JB	430450	****	****	****	448900
S Sedan 4D	VG7HB	470350	****	****	****	477900
LANDAULET—V12 Twin Turbo—Equipment Schedule 1						
W.B. 150.7"; 6.0 Liter.						
Sedan 4D	VG7HB	1382750				

MAZDA

2000 MAZDA — (Jor1)(M1orYV)(BJ222)–Y–#

PROTEGE'—4-Cyl.—Equipment Schedule 6
W.B. 102.8"; 1.6 Liter, 1.8 Liter.

Body Type	VIN	List	Good	Very Good	Good	Excellent
DX Sedan 4D	BJ222	13995	525	600	1200	2075
LX Sedan 4D	BJ222	14840	725	825	1500	2625
ES Sedan 4D	BJ221	15490	875	1000	1700	2925
626—4-Cyl.—Equipment Schedule 4						
W.B. 105.1"; 2.0 Liter.						
LX Sedan 4D	GF22C	19695	1475	1675	2275	3750
ES Sedan 4D	GF22C	21095	1750	1975	2775	4525
Manual, 5-Spd			(175)	(175)	(235)	(235)
V6, 2.5 Liter	D		100	100	135	135
MX-5 MIATA—4-Cyl.—Equipment Schedule 6						
W.B. 89.2"; 1.8 Liter.						
Convertible 2D	NB353	22595	1925	2125	2800	4250
LS Convertible 2D	NB353	25115	2375	2625	3425	5175
Special Ed Conv 2D	NB353	25505	2475	2725	3550	5400
Hard Top			300	300	400	400
MILLENIA—V6—Equipment Schedule 2						
W.B. 108.3"; 2.5 Liter.						
Sedan 4D	TA221	25445	875	1000	1550	2600
MILLENIA—V6 Supercharged—Equipment Schedule 2						
W.B. 108.3"; 2.3 Liter.						
S Sedan 4D	TA221	30445	1125	1275	1900	3150
Millennium Edition			100	100	135	135

2001 MAZDA — (Jor1)(M1orYV)(BJ222)–1–#

PROTEGE'—4-Cyl.—Equipment Schedule 6
W.B. 102.8"; 1.6 Liter, 2.0 Liter.

Body Type	VIN	List	Good	Very Good	Good	Excellent
DX Sedan 4D	BJ222	14095	550	650	1225	2125
LX Sedan 4D	BJ222	14895	775	900	1550	2675
ES Sedan 4D	BJ225	16015	950	1075	1800	3075
MP3 Sedan 4D	BJ227	18500	1100	1225	1675	2625
626—4-Cyl.—Equipment Schedule 4						
W.B. 105.1"; 2.0 Liter.						
LX Sedan 4D	GF22C	20015	1650	1875	2475	4000
ES Sedan 4D	GF22C	21415	2000	2250	3000	4725
Manual, 5-Spd			(200)	(200)	(265)	(265)
V6, 2.5 Liter	D		100	100	135	135
MX-5 MIATA—4-Cyl.—Equipment Schedule 6						
W.B. 89.2"; 1.8 Liter.						
Convertible 2D	NB353	21660	2100	2325	2975	4475
LS Convertible 2D	NB353	24410	2625	2925	3575	5275
SE Convertible 2D	NB353	26195	2725	3025	3800	5675
Hard Top			300	300	400	400
MILLENIA—V6—Equipment Schedule 2						
W.B. 108.3"; 2.5 Liter.						
Sedan 4D	TA221	28505	1125	1250	1825	2975
MILLENIA—V6 Supercharged—Equipment Schedule 2						
W.B. 108.3"; 2.3 Liter.						
S Sedan 4D	TA221	31505	1375	1550	2150	3500

2002 MAZDA — (Jor1)(M1orYV)(BJ222)–2–#

PROTEGE'—4-Cyl.—Equipment Schedule 6
W.B. 102.8"; 2.0 Liter.

Body Type	VIN	List	Good	Very Good	Good	Excellent
DX Sedan 4D	BJ222	14530	650	750	1625	2950
LX Sedan 4D	BJ222	15335	825	950	1850	3325
ES Sedan 4D	BJ221	16060	1100	1250	2200	3900

PROTEGE'5—4-Cyl.—Equipment Schedule 6
W.B. 102.8"; 2.0 Liter.

Body Type	VIN	List	Trade-In Good	Very Good	Pvt-Party Good	Retail Excellent
Hatchback 4D	BJ245	16815	1400	1575	2750	4850
626—4-Cyl.—Equipment Schedule 4						
W.B. 105.1"; 2.0 Liter.						
LX Sedan 4D	GF22C	20015	1900	2150	2925	4675
ES Sedan 4D	GF22C	22915	2675	3000	3950	6175
Manual, 5-Spd			(200)	(200)	(265)	(265)
V6, 2.5 Liter	D		150	150	200	200
MX-5 MIATA—4-Cyl.—Equipment Schedule 6						
W.B. 89.2"; 1.8 Liter.						
Convertible 2D	NB353	21660	2350	2600	3225	4725
LS Convertible 2D	NB353	24410	2850	3150	3800	5475
SE Convertible 2D	NB353	26275	3050	3350	4075	5925
Hard Top			350	350	465	465
MILLENIA—V6—Equipment Schedule 2						
W.B. 108.3"; 2.5 Liter.						
Sedan 4D	TA221	28505	1250	1400	1975	3225
MILLENIA—V6 Supercharged—Equipment Schedule 2						
W.B. 108.3"; 2.3 Liter.						
S Sedan 4D	TA222	31505	1500	1675	2300	3725

2003 MAZDA — (Jor1)(M1orYV)(BJ225)-3-#

PROTEGE'—4-Cyl.—Equipment Schedule 6						
W.B. 102.8"; 2.0 Liter.						
DX Sedan 4D	BJ225	14690	825	925	1725	3050
LX Sedan 4D	BJ225	15575	1050	1175	1950	3350
ES Sedan 4D	BJ225	16300	1350	1500	2325	3950
PROTEGE'5—4-Cyl.—Equipment Schedule 6						
W.B. 102.8"; 2.0 Liter.						
Hatchback 4D	BJ245	17055	1700	1900	2950	4900
PROTEGE'—4-Cyl. Turbo—Equipment Schedule 6						
W.B. 102.8"; 2.0 Liter.						
Mazdaspeed Sedan 4D	BJ227	20500	2500	2775	3300	4800
6—4-Cyl.—Equipment Schedule 4						
W.B. 105.3"; 2.3 Liter.						
i Sedan 4D	FP80C	19900	1625	1850	2700	4450
Sport Pkg			225	225	295	295
Manual, 5-Spd			(250)	(250)	(335)	(335)
6—V6—Equipment Schedule 4						
W.B. 105.3"; 3.0 Liter.						
s Sedan 4D	FP80D	22520	2000	2250	3200	5200
Sport Pkg			225	225	295	295
Manual, 5-Spd			(250)	(250)	(335)	(335)
MX-5 MIATA—4-Cyl.—Equipment Schedule 6						
W.B. 89.2"; 1.8 Liter.						
Club Sport Conv 2D	NB353	20000	****	****	****	9550
Convertible 2D	NB353	22125	2775	3075	3600	5150
Shinsen Conv 2D	NB353	23625	3350	3675	4200	5875
LS Convertible 2D	NB353	24905	3350	3650	4350	6100
SE Convertible 2D	NB353	26550	3750	4075	4825	6775
Hard Top			375	375	500	500

2004 MAZDA — (Jor1)(M1orYV)(BK12F)-4-#

MAZDA3—4-Cyl.—Equipment Schedule 6						
W.B. 103.9"; 2.0 Liter, 2.3 Liter.						
i Sedan 4D	BK12F	15100	2725	3000	3775	5675
s Sedan 4D	BK123	17825	3175	3525	4300	6375
s Hatchback 4D	BK143	18315	3350	3700	4475	6550
MAZDA6—4-Cyl.—Equipment Schedule 4						
W.B. 105.3"; 2.3 Liter.						
i Sedan 4D	FP80C	20120	2275	2525	3250	5025
i Hatchback 4D	FP84C	22165	2725	3050	3875	5950
Sport Pkg			250	250	315	315
Manual, 5-Spd			(300)	(300)	(400)	(400)
MAZDA6—V6—Equipment Schedule 4						
W.B. 105.3"; 3.0 Liter.						
s Sedan 4D	FP80D	22765	2725	3050	3825	5850
s Hatchback 4D	FP84D	24315	3150	3500	4400	6700
s Wagon 4D	FP82D	23645	2950	3300	4050	6150
Sport Pkg			250	250	315	315
Manual, 5-Spd			(300)	(300)	(400)	(400)
MX-5 MIATA—4-Cyl.—Equipment Schedule 6						
W.B. 89.2"; 1.8 Liter.						

Body Type	VIN	List	Trade-In Good	Very Good	Pvt-Party Good	Retail Excellent
Convertible 2D	NB353	22388	3175	3475	4050	5675
LS Convertible 2D	NB353	25193	3750	4100	4875	6825
Hard Top			400	400	535	535
MX-5 MIATA—4-Cyl. Turbo—Equipment Schedule 6						
W.B. 89.2"; 1.8 Liter.						
Mazdaspeed Conv.	NB354	26020	4050	4400	5225	7250
RX-8—Rotary—Equipment Schedule 3						
W.B. 106.4"; 1.3 Liter.						
Coupe 4D	FE173	25700	2275	2500	3400	5300
Sport Pkg			325	325	435	435
Touring			475	475	645	645
Grand Touring Pkg			650	650	865	865

2005 MAZDA — (Jor1)(M1orYV)—(K12F)-5-#

	VIN	List	Trade-In Good	Very Good	Pvt-Party Good	Retail Excellent
MAZDA3—4-Cyl.—Equipment Schedule 6						
W.B. 103.9"; 2.0 Liter, 2.3 Liter.						
i Sedan 4D	K12F	15100	2775	3100	4000	5900
s Sedan 4D	K123	18035	3300	3650	4575	6600
s Hatchback 4D	K143	18525	3400	3750	4675	6750
sp Sedan 4D	K323	20130	3450	3825	4875	7025
sp Hatchback 4D	K343	20130	3450	3825	4875	7025
MAZDA6—4-Cyl.—Equipment Schedule 4						
W.B. 105.3"; 2.3 Liter.						
i Sedan 4D	P80C	20590	2575	2875	3725	5625
i Sport Sedan 4D	P80C	23090	3175	3550	4325	6300
i Sport Hatchback 4D	P84C	23620	3425	3800	4600	6700
i Grand Touring Sedan	P80C	24940	3700	4100	5075	7325
Manual, 5-Spd.			(350)	(350)	(465)	(465)
MAZDA6—V6—Equipment Schedule 4						
W.B. 105.3"; 3.0 Liter.						
s Sedan 4D	P80D	24990	3300	3675	4475	6500
s Hatchback 4D	P84D	25690	3550	3950	4900	7100
s Base Sport Wagon	P82D	24590	3450	3825	4675	6850
s Sport Wagon 4D	P82D	25720	3700	4100	5075	7325
s Grand Touring Sedan	P80D	26870	4100	4525	5550	7975
s Grand Touring Wagon	P82D	27540	4300	4750	5775	8300
Manual, 5-Spd.			(350)	(350)	(465)	(465)
MX-5 MIATA—4-Cyl.—Equipment Schedule 6						
W.B. 89.2"; 1.8 Liter.						
Convertible 2D	B353	22643	3450	3775	4500	6200
LS Convertible 2D	B353	25448	4175	4525	5475	7475
Hard Top			425	425	565	565
MX-5 MIATA—4-Cyl. Turbo—Equipment Schedule 6						
W.B. 89.2"; 1.8 Liter.						
Mazdaspeed Conv 2D	B354	26325	4725	5100	6050	8225
RX-8—Rotary—Equipment Schedule 3						
W.B. 106.4"; 1.3 Liter.						
Coupe 4D	E173	26120	2425	2675	3675	5550
Shinka Special Ed 4D	E173	32220	3450	3800	5050	7450
Sport Pkg			350	350	465	465
Touring			525	525	705	705
Grand Touring Pkg			700	700	935	935

2006 MAZDA — (Jor1)(M1orYV)—(K12F)-6-#

	VIN	List	Trade-In Good	Very Good	Pvt-Party Good	Retail Excellent
MAZDA3—4-Cyl.—Equipment Schedule 6						
W.B. 103.9"; 2.0 Liter, 2.3 Liter.						
i Sedan 4D	K12F	15170	3225	3575	4550	6475
i Touring Sedan 4D	K12F	17450	3675	4025	4850	6850
s Sedan 4D	K123	18390	3775	4150	5125	7200
s Hatchback 4D	K143	18880	3875	4250	5250	7350
s Touring Sedan 4D	K123	19125	3975	4350	5350	7500
s Touring Hatchback 4D	K143	19125	3975	4350	5350	7500
s Grand Touring Sedan	K123	20675	4075	4450	5475	7650
s Grand Touring H'Bck	K143	20675	4075	4450	5475	7650
Manual, 5-Spd.			(275)	(275)	(365)	(365)
MAZDA6—4-Cyl.—Equipment Schedule 4						
W.B. 105.3"; 2.3 Liter.						
i Sedan 4D	P80C	20570	2850	3200	4125	6025
i Sport Sedan 4D	P80C	23270	3325	3700	4650	6750
i Sport Hatchback 4D	P84C	23670	3800	4200	5225	7500
i Grand Touring Sedan	P80C	25270	4425	4850	5950	8500
i Grand Sport Sedan 4D	P80C	25770	4750	5200	6325	9000

2006 MAZDA

Body Type	VIN	List	Trade-In Good	Very Good	Pvt-Party Good	Retail Excellent
Manual, 5-Spd			(400)	(400)	(535)	(535)
MAZDA6—V6—Equipment Schedule 4						
W.B. 105.3"; 3.0 Liter.						
s Sedan 4D	P80D	24520	3450	3825	4800	6950
s Wagon 4D	P82D	25520	3850	4250	5275	7600
s Sport Sedan 4D	P80D	25420	3900	4300	5350	7675
s Sport Hatchback 4D	P84D	26020	4125	4550	5600	8025
s Sport Wagon 4D	P82D	26120	4300	4725	5800	8300
s Grand Sport Sedan	P80D	27820	4750	5200	6325	9000
s Grand Touring Wagon	P82D	27720	4875	5325	6475	9200
s Grand Sport Sedan	P80D	28620	4950	5425	6550	9300
s Grand Sport H'Back	P84D	29220	4875	5325	6475	9200
s Grand Sport Wag 4D	P82D	29420	5225	5700	6875	9750
Manual, 5-Spd			(400)	(400)	(535)	(535)
MAZDASPEED6 AWD—4-Cyl. Turbo—Equipment Schedule 4						
W.B. 105.3"; 2.3 Liter.						
Sport Sedan 4D	G12L	28555	4325	4725	5525	7450
Grand Touring Sed 4D	G12L	30485	4925	5325	6200	8325
MX-5 MIATA—4-Cyl.—Equipment Schedule 6						
W.B. 91.7"; 2.0 Liter.						
Club Spec Conv 2D	C25F	20995	4450	4825	5550	7300
Convertible 2D	C25F	21995	4675	5050	5800	7650
Touring Convertible 2D	C25F	22995	5175	5575	6375	8375
Sport Convertible 2D	C25F	23495	5625	6025	6850	9000
Grand Touring Conv	C25F	24995	5575	6000	7000	9125
3rd Generation Ltd Cnv	C25F	27260	7725	8225	9450	12350
Hard Top			450	450	590	590
RX-8—Rotary—Equipment Schedule 3						
W.B. 106.4"; 1.3 Liter.						
Coupe 4D	E173	26995	3250	3550	4600	6750
Shinka Spcl Ed 4D	E173	33880	4325	4700	6025	8650
Sport Pkg			375	375	515	515
Touring			575	575	760	760
Grand Touring Pkg			750	750	1000	1000

2007 MAZDA — (Jor1)(M1orYV)-(K12F)-7-#

Body Type	VIN	List	Trade-In Good	Very Good	Pvt-Party Good	Retail Excellent
MAZDA3—4-Cyl.—Equipment Schedule 6						
W.B. 103.9"; 2.0 Liter, 2.3 Liter.						
i Sport Sedan 4D	K12F	15255	3700	4050	5050	7050
i Touring Sedan 4D	K12F	17615	3925	4275	5250	7275
s Sport Sedan 4D	K123	18600	5025	5425	6350	8525
s Sport Hatchback 4D	K143	19090	5050	5450	6400	8650
s Touring Sedan 4D	K123	19835	5125	5525	6475	8725
s Touring Hatchback 4D	K143	19835	5150	5550	6500	8750
s Grand Touring Sedan	K123	21305	5225	5650	6575	8825
s Grand Touring H'Bck	K143	21305	5225	5650	6575	8825
Manual, 5-Spd			(300)	(300)	(400)	(400)
MAZDASPEED3—4-Cyl. Turbo—Equipment Schedule 6						
W.B. 103.9"; 2.3 Liter.						
Sport Hatchback 4D	K14L	22800	5775	6250	7500	10000
Grand Touring H'Back	K14L	24515	7125	7650	8875	11650
MAZDA6—4-Cyl.—Equipment Schedule 4						
W.B. 105.3"; 2.3 Liter.						
i Sport Sedan 4D	P80C	20425	3200	3550	4575	6625
i Sport Value Ed Sedan	P80C	20925	3400	3750	4800	6950
i Spt Value Ed H'Back	P84C	21925	4250	4650	5800	8275
i Touring Sedan 4D	P80C	23015	3900	4275	5375	7725
i Touring Hatchback 4D	P84C	24015	5000	5450	6650	9425
i Grand Touring Sedan	P80C	24585	4825	5250	6450	9125
i Grand Touring H'Back	P84C	25335	5075	5525	6725	9525
Manual, 5-Spd			(425)	(425)	(565)	(565)
MAZDA6—V6—Equipment Schedule 4						
W.B. 105.3"; 3.0 Liter.						
s Sport Value Sedan 4D	P80D	23635	3900	4275	5375	7725
s Spt Value Ed H'Back	P84D	24635	4700	5125	6325	8975
s Spt Value Ed Wagon	P82D	24685	4350	4750	5900	8425
s Touring Sedan 4D	P80D	25725	4825	5250	6450	9125
s Touring H'Back 4D	P84D	26725	5325	5800	7225	10150
s Touring Wagon 4D	P82D	26775	5675	6175	7725	10800
s Grand Touring Sedan	P80D	27595	5350	5825	7250	10200
s Grand Touring H'Back	P84D	28345	5700	6200	7675	10700
s Grand Touring Wagon	P82D	28395	5825	6350	7900	11050
Manual, 5-Spd			(425)	(425)	(565)	(565)

Body Type	VIN	List	Trade-In Good	Very Good	Pvt-Party Good	Retail Excellent
MAZDASPEED6 AWD—4-Cyl. Turbo—Equipment Schedule 4						
W.B. 105.3"; 2.3 Liter.						
Sport Sedan 4D	G12L	28590	5475	5900	6850	8975
Grand Touring Sedan	G12L	30520	6100	6550	7625	9975
MX-5 MIATA—4-Cyl.—Equipment Schedule 6						
W.B. 91.7"; 2.0 Liter.						
SV Convertible 2D	C25F	20995	5150	5525	6225	8025
Sport Conv Hard Top	C26F	24945	6525	6950	8050	10400
MX-5 MIATA—4-Cyl.—Equipment Schedule 6						
W.B. 91.7"; 2.0 Liter.						
Sport Convertible 2D	C25F	21995	5375	5775	6650	8550
Touring Convertible 2D	C25F	23800	5775	6175	7150	9150
Grand Touring Conv	C25F	25060	6450	6875	7850	10050
Touring Conv Hard Top	C26F	24789	6625	7050	8075	10300
Grand Touring HT 2D	C26F	28055	8025	8525	9625	12300
RX-8—Rotary—Equipment Schedule 3						
W.B. 106.4"; 1.3 Liter.						
Sport Coupe 4D	E173	27030	4075	4425	5275	7150
Touring Coupe 4D	E173	30930	5125	5550	6600	8825
Grand Touring Coupe	E173	32365	6900	7400	8425	10950
Performance Pkg			425	425	555	555

2008 MAZDA — (Jor1)(M1orYV)–(K12F)–8–#

Body Type	VIN	List	Trade-In Good	Very Good	Pvt-Party Good	Retail Excellent
MAZDA3—4-Cyl.—Equipment Schedule 6						
W.B. 103.9"; 2.0 Liter, 2.3 Liter.						
i Sport Sedan 4D	K12F	15390	4575	4950	6025	8175
i Touring Sedan 4D	K12F	17750	5125	5525	6425	8425
i Touring Value Sed 4D	K12F	17230	5025	5400	6325	8300
s Sport Sedan 4D	K123	18980	5950	6400	7450	9625
s Sport Hatchback 4D	K143	19470	6175	6625	7700	9950
s Touring Sedan 4D	K123	19970	6400	6850	7900	10200
s Touring Hatchback 4D	K143	19970	6525	7000	8025	10300
s Grand Touring Sedan	K123	21440	7325	7820	8800	11150
s Grand Touring H'Bck	K143	21440	6850	7325	8325	10650
Manual, 5-Spd w/Overdrive			(350)	(350)	(470)	(470)
MAZDASPEED3—4-Cyl. Turbo—Equipment Schedule 6						
W.B. 103.9"; 2.3 Liter.						
Sport Hatchback 4D	K14L	22935	7500	8000	9075	11550
Grand Touring H'Back	K14L	24650	8300	8850	9825	12350
MAZDA6—4-Cyl.—Equipment Schedule 4						
W.B. 105.3"; 2.3 Liter.						
i Sport Sedan 4D	P80C	19585	4000	4375	5250	7150
i Sport Value Sedan 4D	P80C	21245	4675	5075	6100	8375
i Spt Value Ed H'Back	P84C	22245	5250	5675	6975	9500
i Touring Sedan 4D	P80C	22835	4850	5275	6300	8600
i Touring Hatchback 4D	P84C	23835	5625	6075	7400	10050
i Grand Touring Sedan	P80C	24685	6150	6625	7950	10700
i Grand Touring H'Back	P84C	25435	6475	6975	8300	11150
MAZDA6—V6—Equipment Schedule 4						
W.B. 105.3"; 3.0 Liter.						
s Sport Value Sedan 4D	P80D	23755	5250	5675	6950	9450
s Spt Value Ed H'Back	P84D	24755	6150	6625	7950	10700
s Touring Sedan 4D	P80D	25445	5825	6275	7600	10300
s Touring H'Back 4D	P84D	26445	6475	6975	8300	11150
s Grand Touring Sedan	P80D	27595	7800	8350	9950	13350
s Grand Touring H'Back	P84D	28345	7700	8250	9850	13250
Manual, 5-Spd w/Overdrive			(450)	(450)	(600)	(600)
MX-5 MIATA—4-Cyl.—Equipment Schedule 6						
W.B. 91.7"; 2.0 Liter.						
SV Convertible 2D	C25F	21180	5350	5700	6650	8450
MX-5 MIATA—4-Cyl.—Equipment Schedule 6						
W.B. 91.7"; 2.0 Liter.						
Sport Convertible 2D	C25F	22180	6250	6650	7550	9450
Touring Convertible 2D	C25F	24225	6250	6625	7625	9625
Grand Touring Conv	C25F	25485	7125	7550	8500	10650
Special Ed Conv 2D	C26F	27225	7800	8250	9275	11550
Power Hard Top			1125	1125	1400	1400
RX-8—Rotary—Equipment Schedule 3						
W.B. 106.4"; 1.3 Liter.						
Sport Coupe 4D	E173	27030	5175	5550	6350	8225
Touring Coupe 4D	E173	30930	7225	7700	8775	11200
Grand Touring Coupe	E173	32365	8475	9000	10150	12850
40th Anniv Coupe 4D	E173	32705	8525	9050	10200	12900

Body Type	VIN	List	Trade-In Good	Very Good	Pvt-Party Good	Retail Excellent
Performance Pkg			450	450	595	595

2009 MAZDA — (Jor1)(M1orYV)–(K12F)–9–#

MAZDA3—4-Cyl.—Equipment Schedule 6
W.B. 103.9"; 2.0 Liter, 2.3 Liter.

i Sport Sedan 4D	K12F	16060	5675	6050	7250	9425
i Touring Value Sed 4D	K12F	18465	6550	6950	7975	10050
s Sport Sedan 4D	K123	19455	6825	7250	8325	10550
s Sport Hatchback 4D	K143	19945	7650	8100	9175	11500
s Touring Sedan 4D	K123	20445	7750	8200	9275	11600
s Touring Hatchback 4D	K143	20445	8000	8475	9525	11850
s Grand Touring Sedan	K123	22215	8200	8675	9700	12050
s Grand Touring H'Bck	K143	22215	8250	8725	9750	12100
Manual, 5-Spd w/Overdrive			(375)	(375)	(500)	(500)

MAZDASPEED3—4-Cyl. Turbo—Equipment Schedule 6
W.B. 103.9"; 2.3 Liter.

Sport Hatchback 4D	K14L	23410	8925	9425	10400	12750
Grand Touring H'Back	K14L	25125	9675	10200	11150	13550

MAZDA6—4-Cyl.—Equipment Schedule 4
W.B. 109.8"; 2.5 Liter.

i Sport Value Sedan 4D	P80A	19220	5775	6200	7150	9200
i Sport Sedan 4D	P81A	21820	6175	6625	7550	9650
i Touring Sedan 4D	P82A	23275	6900	7375	8350	10650
i Grand Touring Sedan	P82A	26480	8025	8575	9650	12300

MAZDA6—V6—Equipment Schedule 4
W.B. 109.8"; 3.7 Liter.

s Sport Sedan 4D	P81B	24800	7475	8000	9050	11500
s Touring Sedan 4D	P82B	25745	8550	9125	10200	12950
s Grand Touring Sedan	P82B	28930	9400	10000	11300	14350

MX-5 MIATA—4-Cyl.—Equipment Schedule 6
W.B. 91.7"; 2.0 Liter.

SV Convertible 2D	C25F	22420	7200	7600	8450	10350

MX-5 MIATA—4-Cyl.—Equipment Schedule 6
W.B. 91.7"; 2.0 Liter.

Sport Convertible 2D	C25F	23420	7800	8225	9125	11100
Touring Convertible 2D	C25F	25760	8300	8725	9675	11800
Grand Touring Conv	C25F	27020	8600	9050	10050	12250
Power Hard Top			1200	1200	1455	1455

RX-8—Rotary—Equipment Schedule 3
W.B. 106.4"; 1.3 Liter.

Sport Coupe 4D	E174	27085	6225	6625	7525	9425
Touring Coupe 4D	E17M	29210	8425	8900	9925	12300
Grand Touring Coupe	E17M	32350	9075	9575	10600	13100
R3 Coupe 4D	E174	32580	9325	9850	10900	13450

2010 MAZDA — (Jor1)(M1orYV)–(L1SF)–A–#

MAZDA3—4-Cyl.—Equipment Schedule 6
W.B. 103.9"; 2.0 Liter.

i SV Sedan 4D	L1SF	16045	6075	6450	7425	9250

MAZDA3—4-Cyl.—Equipment Schedule 6
W.B. 103.9"; 2.0 Liter, 2.5 Liter.

i Sport Sedan 4D	L1SF	17495	7000	7400	8575	10800
i Touring Sedan 4D	L1SF	19020	7575	8000	9075	11250
s Sport Sedan 4D	L1S5	20210	8850	9300	10450	12900
s Sport Hatchback 4D	L1H5	21090	9050	9525	10550	12900
s Grand Touring Sedan 4D	L1S5	22970	9675	10200	11300	13800
s Grand Touring H'Bck	L1H5	23550	9875	10400	11500	14050
Manual, 5-Spd w/Overdrive			(475)	(475)	(615)	(615)

MAZDASPEED—4-Cyl. Turbo—Equipment Schedule 6
W.B. 103.0"; 2.3 Liter.

Sport Hatchback 4D	L1H3	24090	11450	12000	13000	15500

MAZDA6—4-Cyl.—Equipment Schedule 4
W.B. 109.8"; 2.5 Liter.

i Sport Value Sedan 4D	Z8BH	19200	6725	7150	8125	10250
i Sport Sedan 4D	Z8BH	21070	6875	7300	8300	10450
i Touring Sedan 4D	Z8CH	22550	8025	8525	9600	12050
i Touring Plus Sedan 4D	Z8CH	24500	8625	9150	10250	12800
i Grand Touring Sed 4D	Z8CH	26685	8950	9500	10700	13350

MAZDA6—V6—Equipment Schedule 4
W.B. 109.8"; 3.7 Liter.

s Touring Plus Sedan 4D	Z8CB	27200	9400	9950	11200	14000
s Grand Touring Sed 4D	Z8CB	29140	10400	11000	12500	15800

2010 MAZDA

Body Type	VIN	List	Trade-In Good	Very Good	Pvt-Party Good	Retail Excellent
MX-5 MIATA—4-Cyl.—Equipment Schedule 6						
W.B. 91.7'; 2.0 Liter.						
Sport Convertible 2D	C2EF	23560	10150	10600	11550	13650
Touring Convertible 2D	C2EF	25900	10650	11150	12050	14250
Grand Touring Conv 2D	C2EF	27160	10900	11400	12450	14850
Power Hard Top		———	1275	1275	1500	1500
RX-8—Rotary—Equipment Schedule 3						
W.B. 106.3'; 1.3 Liter.						
Sport Coupe 4D	E1CP	27245	8700	9175	9975	11950
Grand Touring Coupe	E1TM	33410	11350	11950	12850	15300
R3 Coupe 4D	E1CP	32740	11700	12300	13100	15400

2011 MAZDA — 1YVorJM1–(E1HY)–B–#

Body Type	VIN	List	Trade-In Good	Very Good	Pvt-Party Good	Retail Excellent
MAZDA2—4-Cyl.—Equipment Schedule 6						
W.B. 98.0'; 1.5 Liter.						
Sport Hatchback 4D	E1HY	14730	6175	6575	7600	9575
Touring Hatchback 4D	E1HY	16185	6825	7225	8200	10200
Automatic, 4-Spd			450	450	600	600
MAZDA3—4-Cyl.—Equipment Schedule 6						
W.B. 103.9'; 2.0 Liter.						
i SV Sedan 4D	L1TF	16200	6850	7225	8475	10600
MAZDA3—4-Cyl.—Equipment Schedule 6						
W.B. 103.9'; 2.0 Liter, 2.5 Liter.						
i Sport Sedan 4D	L1UF	18350	8075	8500	9700	11900
i Touring Sedan 4D	L1VF	19745	8725	9150	10400	12750
s Sport Sedan 4D	L1U5	21140	9775	10250	11450	13850
s Sport Hatchback 4D	L1K5	21640	10150	10650	11850	14250
s Grand Touring Sedan	L1W5	24105	11050	11550	12700	15200
s Grand Touring H'Back	L1M5	24605	11200	11700	12900	15450
Manual, 5-Spd w/Overdrive		———	(500)	(500)	(635)	(635)
MAZDASPEED3—4-Cyl. Turbo—Equipment Schedule 6						
W.B. 103.9'; 2.3 Liter.						
Sport Hatchback 4D	L1K3	24090	12550	13100	14050	16550
MAZDA6—4-Cyl.—Equipment Schedule 4						
W.B. 109.8'; 2.5 Liter.						
i Sport Sedan 4D	Z8BH	21785	8650	9150	10250	12650
i Touring Sedan 4D	Z8CH	23430	9100	9625	10850	13350
i Touring Plus Sedan 4D	Z8CH	25035	9850	10400	11600	14300
i Grand Touring Sed 4D	Z8CH	27615	10250	10800	12050	14850
MAZDA6—V6—Equipment Schedule 4						
W.B. 109.8'; 3.7 Liter.						
s Touring Plus Sedan 4D	Z8CB	27875	11200	11750	13050	16000
s Grand Touring Sed 4D	Z8CB	30115	12050	12700	14150	17500
MX-5 MIATA—4-Cyl.—Equipment Schedule 6						
W.B. 91.7'; 2.0 Liter.						
Sport Convertible 2D	C2JF	23710	10850	11300	12250	14400
Touring Convertible 2D	C2LF	26050	11950	12450	13400	15600
Grand Touring Conv 2D	C2NF	27310	12500	13000	14050	16400
Special Ed Conv 2D	C1SF	31720	14300	14900	16000	18600
Power Hard Top		———	1375	1375	1560	1560
RX-8—Rotary—Equipment Schedule 6						
W.B. 106.3'; 1.3 Liter.						
Sport Coupe 4D	E1RP	27590	11250	11800	12450	14450
R3 Coupe 4D	E1T4	33085	14100	15050	16200	19100
Grand Touring Coupe	E1SP	33755	14000	14650	15500	17950

2012 MAZDA — 1YVorJM1–(E1HY)–C–#

Body Type	VIN	List	Trade-In Good	Very Good	Pvt-Party Good	Retail Excellent
MAZDA2—4-Cyl.—Equipment Schedule 6						
W.B. 98.0'; 1.5 Liter.						
Sport Hatchback 4D	E1HY	15165	7275	7700	8775	10850
Touring Hatchback 4D	E1HY	16650	7750	8200	9300	11500
Automatic, 4-Spd			475	475	615	615
MAZDA3—4-Cyl.—Equipment Schedule 6						
W.B. 103.9'; 2.0 Liter.						
i SV Sedan 4D	L1TF	16595	7950	8350	9600	11800
MAZDA3—4-Cyl.—Equipment Schedule 6						
W.B. 103.9'; 2.0 Liter, 2.5 Liter.						
i Sport Sedan 4D	L1UF	18350	9150	9575	10800	13100
i Touring Sedan 4D	L1VF	19745	9475	9900	11150	13500
i Touring Hatchback 4D	L1L7	20595	10550	11050	12250	14650
i Grand Touring Sedan	L1W7	23095	11750	12250	13450	15950
i Grand Touring H'Back	L1M7	23595	12650	13200	14300	16800

2012 MAZDA

Body Type	VIN	List	Trade-In Good	Trade-In Very Good	Pvt-Party Good	Retail Excellent
s Grand Touring Sed 4D	L1W5	23865	12900	13450	14550	17100
s Grand Touring H'Back	L1M5	24365	13200	13750	14850	17400
Manual, 5-Spd			(475)	(475)	(590)	(590)
Manual, 6-Spd SKYACTIV			0	0	0	0
MAZDA3—4-Cyl.—Equipment Schedule 6						
W.B. 103.9"; 2.5 Liter.						
s Touring Sedan 4D	L1V5	21495	11000	11500	12650	15100
s Touring Hatchback 4D	L1L5	21995	11200	11700	12800	15200
Auto 5-Spd w/Manual Mode			475	475	585	585
MAZDASPEED3—4-Cyl. Turbo—Equipment Schedule 6						
W.B. 103.9"; 2.3 Liter.						
Touring Hatchback 4D	L1L3	24495	13750	14300	15350	17800
MAZDA6—4-Cyl.—Equipment Schedule 4						
W.B. 109.8"; 2.5 Liter.						
i Sport Sedan 4D	Z8BH	22035	9375	9850	11000	13450
i Touring Sedan 4D	Z8DH	23680	10100	10650	11850	14450
i Touring Plus Sedan	Z8EH	25285	11400	11950	13300	16150
i Grand Touring Sedan	Z8CH	27865	12150	12750	14100	17150
MAZDA6—V6—Equipment Schedule 4						
W.B. 109.8"; 3.7 Liter.						
s Touring Plus Sedan	Z8EB	28125	12650	13250	14600	17750
s Grand Touring Sedan	Z8CB	30365	13250	13900	15500	18850
MX-5 MIATA—4-Cyl.—Equipment Schedule 6						
W.B. 91.7"; 2.0 Liter.						
Sport Convertible 2D	C2JF	23985	11700	12200	13200	15300
Touring Convertible 2D	C2LF	26345	13250	13750	14850	17150
Grand Touring Conv 2D	C2NF	27615	14050	14600	15700	18100
Special Ed Conv 2D	C2SF	32020	16350	16950	18050	20700
Power Hard Top			1450	1450	1630	1630

2013 MAZDA — 1YVorJM1-(DE1KY)-D-#

Body Type	VIN	List	Trade-In Good	Trade-In Very Good	Pvt-Party Good	Retail Excellent
MAZDA2—4-Cyl.—Equipment Schedule 6						
W.B. 98.0"; 1.5 Liter.						
Sport Hatchback 4D	DE1KY	15515	8100	8525	9750	12050
Touring Hatchback 4D	DE1LY	17005	8425	8850	10150	12550
Automatic, 4-Spd			500	500	655	655
MAZDA3—4-Cyl.—Equipment Schedule 6						
W.B. 103.9"; 2.0 Liter.						
i SV Sedan 4D	BL1TF	17495	9025	9425	10750	13050
i Touring Hatchback	BL1L7	20795	11700	12150	13450	15950
Auto, 5-Spd w/Manual Mode			500	500	640	640
MAZDA3—4-Cyl.—Equipment Schedule 6						
W.B. 103.9"; 2.0 Liter, 2.5 Liter.						
i Sport Sedan 4D	BL1U7	20020	10350	10800	12050	14400
i Touring Sedan 4D	BL1V7	21145	11800	12250	13550	16050
i Grand Touring HBk	BL1M7	24095	13500	14050	15300	17900
i Grand Touring Sedan	BL1W7	23595	13150	13650	14850	17400
s Grand Touring Sed	BL1W5	25945	14500	15050	16250	18900
s Grand Touring HBk	BL1M5	26445	14900	15500	16650	19300
MAZDASPEED3—4-Cyl. Turbo—Equipment Schedule 6						
W.B. 103.9"; 2.3 Liter.						
Touring Hatchback 4D	BL1L3	24995	16150	16750	17700	20300
MAZDA6—4-Cyl.—Equipment Schedule 4						
W.B. 109.8"; 2.5 Liter.						
i Sport Sedan 4D	Z8BH	22520	10650	11150	12300	14800
i Touring Sedan 4D	Z8DH	24165	11450	12000	13250	15950
i Touring Plus Sedan	Z8EH	25965	12600	13150	14450	17400
i Grand Touring Sedan	Z8CH	28545	13350	13950	15400	18550
MAZDA6—V6—Equipment Schedule 4						
W.B. 109.8"; 3.7 Liter.						
s Grand Touring Sedan	Z8CB	30785	14450	15100	16600	20000
MX-5 MIATA—4-Cyl.—Equipment Schedule 6						
W.B. 91.7"; 2.0 Liter.						
Sport Convertible 2D	NC2JF	25595	13150	13650	14600	16750
Club Convertible 2D	NG2LF	27500	15250	15800	16850	19150
Grand Touring Conv	NC2NF	28145	15950	16550	17600	20000
Power Hard Top			1525	1525	1705	1705

2014 MAZDA — 1YVorJM1-(DE1KY)-E-#

Body Type	VIN	List	Trade-In Good	Trade-In Very Good	Pvt-Party Good	Retail Excellent
MAZDA2—4-Cyl.—Equipment Schedule 6						
W.B. 98.0"; 1.5 Liter.						
Sport Hatchback 4D	DE1KY	15515	9525	10000	11000	13250

2014 MAZDA

Body Type	VIN	List	Trade-In Good	Very Good	Pvt-Party Good	Retail Excellent
Touring Hatchback 4D	DE1LY	17005	10150	10650	11650	13950
Automatic, 4-Spd			525	525	660	660
MAZDA3—4-Cyl.—Equipment Schedule 6						
W.B. 106.3"; 2.0 Liter.						
i SV Sedan 4D	BM1T7	17740	11500	11950	13200	15650
i Sport Hatchback 4D	BM1K7	19740	12800	13350	14500	17000
i Touring Hatchback	BM1L7	20890	14150	14700	15900	18450
Auto, 6-Spd SKYACTIV			525	525	640	640
MAZDA3—4-Cyl.—Equipment Schedule 6						
W.B. 106.3"; 2.0 Liter.						
i Sport Sedan 4D	BM1U7	20290	13000	13550	14700	17200
i Touring Sedan 4D	BM1V7	21440	14900	15450	16600	19200
i Grand Touring Sed	BM1W7	24590	15900	16500	17550	20200
i Grand Touring HBk	BM1M7	25090	16350	16950	18000	20700
MAZDA3—4-Cyl.—Equipment Schedule 6						
W.B. 106.3"; 2.5 Liter.						
s Touring Sedan 4D	BM1V3	25390	16500	17150	18150	20800
s Grand Touring Sed	BM1W3	26790	18300	18950	19850	22600
s Touring Hatchback	BM1L3	25890	16900	17550	18450	21000
s Grand Touring HBk	BM1M3	27290	18750	19400	20300	23100
MAZDA6—4-Cyl.—Equipment Schedule 4						
W.B. 111.4"; 2.5 Liter.						
i Sport Sedan 4D	GJ1U6	23290	14600	15250	16300	19100
i Touring Sedan 4D	GJ1V6	25290	15550	16250	17300	20300
MAZDA6—4-Cyl.—Equipment Schedule 4						
W.B. 111.4"; 2.5 Liter.						
i Grand Touring Sedan	GJ1W6	30290	18200	18950	20100	23500
MX-5 MIATA—4-Cyl.—Equipment Schedule 6						
W.B. 91.7"; 2.0 Liter.						
Sport Convertible 2D	NC2JF	25595	15500	16100	17050	19250
Club Convertible 2D	NC2MF	27700	17150	17750	18700	21100
Grand Touring Conv	NC2NF	28345	18750	19400	20300	22900
Power Hard Top			1600	1600	1775	1775

McLAREN

2012 McLaren

MP4-12C—V8 Twin Turbo—Equipment Schedule 2
W.B. 105.1"; 3.8 Liter.

Body Type	VIN	List	Good	Very Good	Good	Excellent
Coupe 2D	11AAA	231400	****	****	****	227800

2013 McLaren

MP4-12C—V8 Twin Turbo—Equipment Schedule 2
W.B. 105.1"; 3.8 Liter.

Body Type	VIN	List	Good	Very Good	Good	Excellent
Coupe 2D	11BAA	241800	****	****	****	238300

MERCEDES-BENZ

2000 MERCEDES-BENZ — WDB(KK47F)-Y-#

Body Type	VIN	List	Good	Very Good	Good	Excellent
SLK-CLASS—4-Cyl. Supercharged—Equipment Schedule 1						
W.B. 94.5"; 2.3 Liter.						
SLK230 Roadster 2D	KK47F	42495	2600	2825	3500	5050
Sport Pkg			475	475	635	635
designo Edition			425	425	565	565
Manual, 5-Spd			(250)	(250)	(325)	(325)
C-CLASS—4-Cyl. Supercharged—Equipment Schedule 1						
W.B. 105.9"; 2.3 Liter.						
C230 Sedan 4D	HA24G	34820	1475	1650	2300	3700
Sport Pkg			200	200	265	265
C-CLASS—V6—Equipment Schedule 1						
W.B. 105.9"; 2.8 Liter.						
C280 Sedan 4D	HA29G	39020	1600	1775	2550	4075
Sport Pkg			200	200	265	265
C-CLASS—V8—Equipment Schedule 1						
W.B. 105.9"; 4.3 Liter.						
C43 Sedan 4D	HA33G	53595	3400	3725	4225	5950
CLK-CLASS—V6—Equipment Schedule 1						
W.B. 105.9"; 3.2 Liter.						
CLK320 Coupe 2D	LJ65G	43505	1875	2050	2675	3975

Body Type	VIN	List	Trade-In Good	Trade-In Very Good	Pvt-Party Good	Retail Excellent
CLK320 Cabriolet 2D	LK65G	48695	2050	2225	2950	4400
designo Edition		-----	425	425	565	565
CLK-CLASS—V8—Equipment Schedule 1						
W.B. 105.9"; 4.3 Liter.						
CLK430 Coupe 2D	LJ70G	51005	2275	2475	3200	4725
CLK430 Cabriolet 2D	LK70G	56195	2375	2600	3400	5100
designo Edition		-----	425	425	565	565
E-CLASS—V6—Equipment Schedule 1						
W.B. 111.5"; 3.2 Liter.						
E320 Sedan 4D	JF65G	48825	1575	1750	2200	3425
E320 AWD Sedan 4D	JF82G	51625	1500	1675	2100	3300
E320 Wagon 4D	JH65F	49675	1575	1750	2350	3700
E320 AWD Wagon 4D	JH82F	52475	1850	2050	2600	3975
designo Edition		-----	425	425	565	565
E-CLASS—V8—Equipment Schedule 1						
W.B. 111.5"; 4.3 Liter. 5.5 Liter.						
E430 Sedan 4D	JF70G	54175	2275	2525	3175	4800
E430 AWD Sedan 4D	JF83G	56975	2825	3125	3750	5575
E55 Sedan 4D	JF74G	71395	3500	3800	4225	5700
Sport Pkg (E430)		-----	475	475	635	635
designo Edition		-----	425	425	565	565
CL-CLASS—V8—Equipment Schedule 1						
W.B. 113.6"; 5.0 Liter.						
CL500 Coupe 2D	PJ75J	87145	1675	1825	2550	3925
S-CLASS—V8—Equipment Schedule 1						
W.B. 121.5"; 4.3 Liter. 5.0 Liter.						
S430 Sedan 4D	NG70J	70295	1925	2100	2650	3975
S500 Sedan 4D	NG75J	79445	2000	2200	2875	4275
Sport Pkg		-----	700	700	935	935
designo Edition		-----	425	425	565	565
DISTRONIC Cruise Control		-----	175	175	235	235
SL-CLASS—V8—Equipment Schedule 1						
W.B. 99.0"; 5.0 Liter.						
SL500 Roadster 2D	FA68F	84195	3400	3700	4525	6500
Sport Pkg		-----	700	700	935	935
designo Edition		-----	425	425	565	565
Panorama Roof		-----	575	575	765	765
SL-CLASS—V12—Equipment Schedule 1						
W.B. 99.0"; 6.0 Liter.						
SL600 Roadster 2D	FA76F	132145	4500	4875	5950	8400
Sport Pkg		-----	700	700	935	935
designo Edition		-----	425	425	565	565
Panorama Roof		-----	575	575	765	765

2001 MERCEDES-BENZ — WDB(KK49F)-1-#

Body Type	VIN	List	Trade-In Good	Trade-In Very Good	Pvt-Party Good	Retail Excellent
SLK-CLASS—4-Cyl. Supercharged—Equipment Schedule 1						
W.B. 94.5"; 2.3 Liter.						
SLK230 Roadster 2D	KK49F	40495	2700	2950	3675	5325
Sport Pkg		-----	550	550	735	735
designo Edition		-----	475	475	625	625
Manual, 6-Spd		-----	(275)	(275)	(375)	(375)
SLK-CLASS—V6—Equipment Schedule 1						
W.B. 94.5"; 3.2 Liter.						
SLK320 Roadster 2D	KK65F	45495	2850	3125	3850	5550
Sport Pkg		-----	550	550	735	735
designo Edition		-----	475	475	625	625
Manual, 6-Spd		-----	(275)	(275)	(375)	(375)
C-CLASS—V6—Equipment Schedule 1						
W.B. 106.9"; 2.6 Liter. 3.2 Liter.						
C240 Sedan 4D	RF61G	34610	2000	2200	2900	4425
C320 Sedan 4D	RF64G	40310	2175	2400	3125	4750
Sport Pkg		-----	200	200	265	265
Manual, 6-Spd		-----	(275)	(275)	(375)	(375)
CLK-CLASS—V6—Equipment Schedule 1						
W.B. 105.9"; 3.2 Liter.						
CLK320 Coupe 2D	LJ65G	42595	2075	2275	2950	4350
CLK320 Cabriolet 2D	LK65G	49545	2325	2550	3325	4925
designo Edition		-----	475	475	625	625
CLK-CLASS—V8—Equipment Schedule 1						
W.B. 105.9"; 4.3 Liter. 5.5 Liter.						
CLK430 Coupe 2D	LJ70G	50295	2500	2725	3475	5075
CLK430 Cabriolet 2D	LK70G	57145	2700	2975	3850	5725
CLK55 Coupe 2D	LJ74G	68045	3525	3850	4750	6875

2001 MERCEDES-BENZ

Body Type	VIN	List	Trade-In Good	Very Good	Pvt-Party Good	Retail Excellent
designo Edition			475	475	625	625

E-CLASS—V6—Equipment Schedule 1
W.B. 111.5"; 3.2 Liter.

Body Type	VIN	List	Good	Very Good	Good	Excellent
E320 Sedan 4D	JF65F	48495	1775	1975	2525	3825
E320 AWD Sedan 4D	JF82F	51345	1650	1825	2350	3600
E320 Wagon 4D	JH65F	49295	1900	2100	2675	4025
E320 AWD Wagon 4D	JH82F	52145	2200	2425	3000	4500
designo Edition (ex AWD)			475	475	625	625
Sport Pkg (ex AWD)			550	550	735	735

E-CLASS—V8—Equipment Schedule 1
W.B. 111.5"; 4.3 Liter, 5.5 Liter.

Body Type	VIN	List	Good	Very Good	Good	Excellent
E430 Sedan 4D	JF70F	53845	2400	2650	3275	4875
E430 AWD Sedan 4D	JF83G	56695	3000	3325	3975	5850
E55 Sedan 4D	JF744	70945	3600	3900	4575	6275
designo Edition			475	475	625	625
Sport Pkg (E430 RWD)			550	550	735	735

CL-CLASS—V8—Equipment Schedule 1
W.B. 113.6"; 5.0 Liter, 5.5 Liter.

Body Type	VIN	List	Good	Very Good	Good	Excellent
CL500 Coupe 2D	PJ73J	89145	2175	2375	3100	4575
CL55 Coupe 2D	PJ73J	100145	6300	6725	8300	11550
DISTRONIC Cruise Control			200	200	260	260
Sport Pkg (CL500)			800	800	1035	1035
designo Edition			475	475	610	610

CL-CLASS—V12—Equipment Schedule 1
W.B. 113.6"; 5.8 Liter.

Body Type	VIN	List	Good	Very Good	Good	Excellent
CL600 Coupe 2D	PJ78J	119145	5075	5475	6975	9825
DISTRONIC Cruise Control			200	200	250	250
Sport Pkg			800	800	1005	1005
designo Edition			475	475	590	590

S-CLASS—V8—Equipment Schedule 1
W.B. 121.5"; 4.3 Liter, 5.0 Liter, 5.5 Liter.

Body Type	VIN	List	Good	Very Good	Good	Excellent
S430 Sedan 4D	NG70J	71445	2225	2425	3150	4650
S500 Sedan 4D	NG75J	80595	2375	2600	3325	4900
S55 Sedan 4D	NG73J	98645	3725	4075	4725	6525
DISTRONIC Cruise Control			200	200	265	265
Sport Pkg (S430,S500)			800	800	1065	1065
designo Edition			475	475	625	625

S-CLASS—V12—Equipment Schedule 1
W.B. 121.5"; 6.0 Liter.

Body Type	VIN	List	Good	Very Good	Good	Excellent
S600 Sedan 4D	NG78J	115985	3325	3625	4575	6550
DISTRONIC Cruise Control			200	200	260	260
Sport Pkg			800	800	1045	1045
designo Edition			475	475	615	615

SL-CLASS—V8—Equipment Schedule 1
W.B. 99.0"; 5.0 Liter.

Body Type	VIN	List	Good	Very Good	Good	Excellent
SL500 Roadster 2D	FA68F	84445	4175	4500	5425	7550
designo Edition			475	475	625	625
Panorama Roof			650	650	865	865

SL-CLASS—V12—Equipment Schedule 1
W.B. 99.0"; 6.0 Liter.

Body Type	VIN	List	Good	Very Good	Good	Excellent
SL600 Roadster 2D	FA76F	129595	5475	5475	7125	9775
designo Edition			475	475	625	625
Panorama Roof			650	650	865	865

2002 MERCEDES-BENZ — WDB(KK49F)-2-#

SLK-CLASS—4-Cyl. Supercharged—Equipment Schedule 1
W.B. 94.5"; 2.3 Liter.

Body Type	VIN	List	Good	Very Good	Good	Excellent
SLK230 Roadster 2D	KK49F	41345	3200	3500	4150	5850
Sport Pkg			625	625	835	835
designo Edition			525	525	685	685
Manual, 6-Spd			(325)	(325)	(430)	(430)

SLK-CLASS—V6—Equipment Schedule 1
W.B. 94.5"; 3.2 Liter.

Body Type	VIN	List	Good	Very Good	Good	Excellent
SLK320 Roadster 2D	KK65F	46745	3625	3950	4825	6750
Sport Pkg			625	625	835	835
designo Edition			525	525	685	685
Manual, 6-Spd			(325)	(325)	(430)	(430)

SLK-CLASS—V6 Supercharged—Equipment Schedule 1
W.B. 94.5"; 3.2 Liter.

Body Type	VIN	List	Good	Very Good	Good	Excellent
SLK32 Roadster 2D	KK66F	55545	5600	6000	6975	9300
designo Edition			525	525	685	685

C-CLASS—4-Cyl. Supercharged—Equipment Schedule 1
W.B. 106.9"; 2.3 Liter.

2002 MERCEDES-BENZ

Body Type	VIN	List	Trade-In Good	Very Good	Pvt-Party Good	Retail Excellent
C230 Sport Coupe 2D	RN47J	29490	1850	2050	2700	4100
Manual, 6-Spd			(325)	(325)	(430)	(430)
C-CLASS—V6—Equipment Schedule 1						
W.B. 106.9"; 2.6 Liter, 3.2 Liter.						
C240 Sedan 4D	RF61J	33680	2475	2725	3425	5100
C320 Sedan 4D	RF64J	38780	2725	3025	3725	5500
C320 Wagon 4D	RH64J	40280	2800	3100	3825	5625
Sport Pkg			250	250	335	335
Manual, 6-Spd			(325)	(325)	(430)	(430)
C-CLASS—V6 Supercharged—Equipment Schedule 1						
W.B. 106.9"; 3.2 Liter.						
C32 Sedan 4D	RF65J	50545	4025	4375	4950	6775
CLK-CLASS—V6—Equipment Schedule 1						
W.B. 105.9"; 3.2 Liter.						
CLK320 Coupe 2D	LJ65G	44565	2350	2575	3300	4800
CLK320 Cabriolet 2D	LK65G	50245	2725	2975	3775	5525
Sport Pkg			625	625	835	835
designo Edition			525	525	685	685
CLK-CLASS—V8—Equipment Schedule 1						
W.B. 105.9"; 4.3 Liter, 5.5 Liter.						
CLK430 Coupe 2D	LJ70G	52265	2800	3075	3850	5550
CLK430 Cabriolet 2D	LK70G	57945	3125	3400	4350	6350
CLK55 Coupe 2D	LJ74G	69095	4475	4850	5675	7925
CLK55 Cabriolet 2D	LK74G	79645	4025	4375	5325	7575
designo Edition			525	525	685	685
E-CLASS—V6—Equipment Schedule 1						
W.B. 111.5"; 3.2 Liter.						
E320 Sedan 4D	JF65J	50280	2100	2325	2900	4350
E320 AWD Sedan 4D	JF82J	53130	2000	2200	2800	4200
E320 Wagon 4D	JH65J	51080	2175	2400	3000	4500
E320 AWD Wagon 4D	JH82J	53130	2725	3025	3625	5325
Sport Pkg (ex AWD)			625	625	835	835
designo Edition (ex AWD)			525	525	685	685
E-CLASS—V8—Equipment Schedule 1						
W.B. 111.5"; 4.3 Liter, 5.5 Liter.						
E430 Sedan 4D	JF70J	55680	2750	3050	3675	5400
E430 AWD Sedan 4D	JF83J	58530	3250	3575	4250	6175
E55 Sedan 4D	JF74J	71995	4075	4400	5175	7025
Sport Pkg (E430 RWD)			625	625	835	835
designo Edition			525	525	685	685
CL-CLASS—V8—Equipment Schedule 1						
W.B. 113.6"; 5.0 Liter, 5.5 Liter.						
CL500 Coupe 2D	PJ75J	92395	2625	2875	3500	5025
CL55 Coupe 2D	PJ73J	105145	7225	7700	9175	12350
DISTRONIC Cruise Control			225	225	285	285
Sport Pkg (CL500)			925	925	1165	1165
designo Edition			525	525	650	650
CL-CLASS—V12—Equipment Schedule 1						
W.B. 113.6"; 5.8 Liter.						
CL600 Coupe 2D	PJ78J	120895	5125	5525	7000	9850
DISTRONIC Cruise Control			225	225	285	285
Sport Pkg			925	925	1170	1170
designo Edition			525	525	650	650
S-CLASS—V8—Equipment Schedule 1						
W.B. 121.5"; 4.3 Liter, 5.0 Liter, 5.5 Liter.						
S430 Sedan 4D	NG72J	72495	2825	3075	3750	5350
S500 Sedan 4D	NG75J	81845	2925	3200	3850	5500
S55 Sedan 4D	NG73J	101145	5875	6350	6925	9025
DISTRONIC Cruise Control			225	225	300	300
Sport Pkg			925	925	1235	1235
designo Edition			525	525	685	685
S-CLASS—V12—Equipment Schedule 1						
W.B. 121.5"; 5.8 Liter.						
S600 Sedan 4D	NG78J	117545	3675	3975	5025	7150
DISTRONIC Cruise Control			225	225	300	300
Sport Pkg			925	925	1230	1230
designo Edition			525	525	685	685
SL-CLASS—V8—Equipment Schedule 1						
W.B. 99.0"; 5.0 Liter.						
SL500 Roadster 2D	FA68F	85445	4800	5175	6075	8325
Sport Pkg			925	925	1235	1235
Panorama Roof			725	725	965	965
Silver Arrow Edition			550	550	735	735

EQUIPMENT & MILEAGE PAGE 9 TO 23

Body Type	VIN	List	Trade-In Good	Very Good	Pvt-Party Good	Retail Excellent
SL-CLASS—V12—Equipment Schedule 1						
W.B. 99.0"; 6.0 Liter.						
SL600 Roadster 2D	FA76F	132195	**6500**	**6950**	**8200**	**11050**
Panorama Roof			**725**	**725**	**960**	**960**
Silver Arrow Edition			**550**	**550**	**730**	**730**
2003 MERCEDES-BENZ — WDB(KK49F)-3-#						
SLK-CLASS—4-Cyl. Supercharged—Equipment Schedule 1						
W.B. 94.5"; 2.3 Liter.						
SLK230 Roadster 2D	KK49F	40265	**3400**	**3700**	**4750**	**6825**
Sport Pkg			**625**	**625**	**835**	**835**
designo Edition			**550**	**550**	**745**	**745**
Manual, 6-Spd			**(350)**	**(350)**	**(480)**	**(480)**
SLK-CLASS—V6—Equipment Schedule 1						
W.B. 94.5"; 3.2 Liter.						
SLK320 Roadster 2D	KK65F	45715	**4175**	**4500**	**5625**	**7950**
Sport Pkg			**625**	**625**	**835**	**835**
designo Edition			**550**	**550**	**745**	**745**
Manual, 6-Spd			**(350)**	**(350)**	**(480)**	**(480)**
SLK-CLASS—V6 Supercharged—Equipment Schedule 1						
W.B. 94.5"; 3.2 Liter.						
SLK32 Roadster 2D	KK66F	56115	**6775**	**7225**	**8275**	**10850**
designo Edition			**550**	**550**	**745**	**745**
C-CLASS—4-Cyl. Supercharged—Equipment Schedule 1						
W.B. 106.9"; 1.8 Liter.						
C230 Sport Sedan 4D	RF40J	30310	**2950**	**3250**	**3875**	**5600**
C230 Sport Coupe 2D	RN40J	28270	**2425**	**2650**	**3225**	**4650**
Manual, 6-Spd			**(350)**	**(350)**	**(480)**	**(480)**
C-CLASS—V6—Equipment Schedule 1						
W.B. 106.9"; 2.6 Liter, 3.2 Liter.						
C240 Sedan 4D	RF61J	32165	**3000**	**3300**	**3950**	**5675**
C240 4MATIC Sed 4D	RF81J	33965	**3250**	**3550**	**4250**	**6075**
C240 Wagon 4D	RH61J	33545	**3125**	**3425**	**4100**	**5875**
C240 4MATIC Wag 4D	RH81J	35445	**3425**	**3750**	**4575**	**6525**
C320 Sedan 4D	RF64J	38790	**3400**	**3725**	**4550**	**6500**
C320 Sport Sedan 4D	RF64J	38790	**3650**	**3975**	**4875**	**6950**
C320 4MATIC Sed 4D	RF84J	40590	**3825**	**4175**	**5075**	**7225**
C320 4MATIC Spt Sed	RF84J	35920	**3800**	**4150**	**5050**	**7175**
C320 Coupe 2D	RN64J	30620	**2600**	**2850**	**3400**	**4875**
C320 Wagon 4D	RH64J	38840	**3600**	**3925**	**4775**	**6800**
C320 4MATIC Wag 4D	RH84J	40640	**3825**	**4175**	**5050**	**7175**
DISTRONIC Cruise Control			**250**	**250**	**335**	**335**
Manual, 6-Spd			**(350)**	**(350)**	**(480)**	**(480)**
C-CLASS—V6 Supercharged—Equipment Schedule 1						
W.B. 106.9"; 3.2 Liter.						
C32 Sedan 4D	RF65J	52065	**4850**	**5250**	**5900**	**7975**
CLK-CLASS—V6—Equipment Schedule 1						
W.B. 105.9", 106.9" (Coupe); 3.2 Liter.						
CLK320 Coupe 2D	TJ65J	44565	**3425**	**3700**	**4400**	**6100**
CLK320 Cabriolet 2D	LK65G	50615	**3300**	**3575**	**4550**	**6500**
DISTRONIC Cruise Control			**250**	**250**	**335**	**335**
Sport Pkg (Cabriolet)			**625**	**625**	**835**	**835**
designo Edition			**550**	**550**	**745**	**745**
CLK-CLASS—V8—Equipment Schedule 1						
W.B. 105.9", 106.9" (Coupe); 4.3 Liter, 5.0 Liter, 5.5 Liter.						
CLK430 Cabriolet 2D	LK70G	58315	**3725**	**4025**	**5125**	**7350**
CLK500 Coupe 2D	TJ75J	52865	**3850**	**4150**	**5025**	**6925**
CLK55 Coupe 2D	TJ76H	69470	**5400**	**5825**	**6850**	**9325**
DISTRONIC Cruise Control			**250**	**250**	**335**	**335**
designo Edition			**550**	**550**	**745**	**745**
E-CLASS—V6—Equipment Schedule 1						
W.B. 111.5", 112.4" (Sed); 3.2 Liter.						
E320 Sedan 4D	UF65J	49165	**3450**	**3800**	**4600**	**6600**
E320 Wagon 4D	JH65J	55415	**4050**	**4450**	**5300**	**7525**
E320 4MATIC Wag 4D	JH82J	55415	**4200**	**4600**	**5450**	**7750**
DISTRONIC Cruise Control			**250**	**250**	**335**	**335**
Sport Pkg (Sedan)			**625**	**625**	**835**	**835**
E-CLASS—V8—Equipment Schedule 1						
W.B. 112.4"; 5.0 Liter.						
E500 Sedan 4D	UF70J	57065	**3450**	**3800**	**4600**	**6575**
DISTRONIC Cruise Control			**250**	**250**	**335**	**335**
Sport Pkg			**625**	**625**	**835**	**835**

Body Type	VIN	List	Trade-In Good	Very Good	Pvt-Party Good	Retail Excellent
E-CLASS—V8 Supercharged—Equipment Schedule 1						
W.B. 112.4"; 5.5 Liter.						
E55 Sedan 4D	UF72J	76720	7175	7650	8825	11700
DISTRONIC Cruise Control			250	250	335	335
CL-CLASS—V8—Equipment Schedule 1						
W.B. 113.6"; 5.0 Liter.						
CL500 Coupe 2D	PJ75J	93315	3250	3550	4225	5800
DISTRONIC Cruise Control			250	250	295	295
Sport Pkg			1050	1050	1230	1230
designo Edition			550	550	655	655
CL-CLASS—V8 Supercharged—Equipment Schedule 1						
W.B. 113.6"; 5.5 Liter.						
CL55 Coupe 2D	PJ74J	115265	8000	8500	9875	13100
DISTRONIC Cruise Control			250	250	285	285
designo Edition			550	550	645	645
CL-CLASS—V12 Twin Turbo—Equipment Schedule 1						
W.B. 113.6"; 5.5 Liter.						
CL600 Coupe 2D	PJ76J	127265	5900	6300	7675	10500
DISTRONIC Cruise Control			250	250	300	300
Sport Pkg			1050	1050	1255	1255
designo Edition			550	550	670	670
S-CLASS—V8—Equipment Schedule 1						
W.B. 121.5"; 4.3 Liter, 5.0 Liter.						
S430 Sedan 4D	NG70J	73265	3375	3675	4275	5900
S430 4MATIC Sed 4D	NG83J	76165	4150	4500	5300	7200
S500 Sedan 4D	NG75J	82665	3550	3825	4450	6100
S500 4MATIC Sed 4D	NG84J	85565	4850	5200	6075	8250
DISTRONIC Cruise Control			250	250	335	335
Sport Pkg			1050	1050	1400	1400
designo Edition			550	550	745	745
S-CLASS—V8 Supercharged—Equipment Schedule 1						
W.B. 121.5"; 5.5 Liter.						
S55 Sedan 4D	NG74J	107165	6050	6500	7300	9650
DISTRONIC Cruise Control			250	250	305	305
designo Edition			550	550	680	680
S-CLASS—V12—Equipment Schedule 1						
W.B. 121.5"; 5.8 Liter.						
S600 Sedan 4D	NG76J	121205	4450	4800	5875	8000
DISTRONIC Cruise Control			250	250	320	320
Sport Pkg			1050	1050	1340	1340
designo Edition			550	550	715	715
SL-CLASS—V8—Equipment Schedule 1						
W.B. 100.8"; 5.0 Liter.						
SL500 Roadster 2D	SK75F	87655	7050	7500	8650	11450
DISTRONIC Cruise Control			250	250	320	320
Sport Pkg			1050	1050	1350	1350
designo Edition			550	550	720	720
Launch Edition			1425	1425	1830	1830
SL-CLASS—V8 Supercharged—Equipment Schedule 1						
W.B. 100.8"; 5.5 Liter.						
SL55 Roadster 2D	SK74F	114915	10900	11550	12400	15550
DISTRONIC Cruise Control			250	250	290	290
designo Edition			550	550	655	655

2004 MERCEDES-BENZ — WDB(KK49F)-4-#

Body Type	VIN	List	Trade-In Good	Very Good	Pvt-Party Good	Retail Excellent
SLK-CLASS—4-Cyl. Supercharged—Equipment Schedule 1						
W.B. 94.5"; 2.3 Liter.						
SLK230 Roadster 2D	KK49F	40320	4425	4775	5800	8000
SLK230 Special Ed	KK49F	41920	5125	5500	6775	9275
Sport Pkg			625	625	835	835
designo Edition			600	600	805	805
Manual, 6-Spd			(400)	(400)	(535)	(535)
SLK-CLASS—V6—Equipment Schedule 1						
W.B. 94.5"; 3.2 Liter.						
SLK320 Roadster 2D	KK65F	47330	5075	5450	6525	8950
SLK320 Special Ed	KK65F	47370	5425	5800	7125	9725
Sport Pkg			625	625	835	835
designo Edition			600	600	805	805
Manual, 6-Spd			(400)	(400)	(535)	(535)
SLK-CLASS—V6 Supercharged—Equipment Schedule 1						
W.B. 94.5"; 3.2 Liter.						
SLK32 Roadster 2D	KK66F	56170	8850	9375	10500	13450
designo Edition			600	600	785	785

2004 MERCEDES-BENZ

Body Type	VIN	List	Trade-In Good	Very Good	Pvt-Party Good	Retail Excellent
C-CLASS—4-Cyl. Supercharged—Equipment Schedule 1						
W.B. 106.9"; 1.8 Liter.						
C230 Sport Sedan 4D	RF40J	33180	**3625**	**3950**	**4750**	**6675**
C230 Sport Coupe 2D	RN47J	30090	**3050**	**3350**	**3925**	**5575**
Manual, 6-Spd			**(400)**	**(400)**	**(535)**	**(535)**
C-CLASS—V6—Equipment Schedule 1						
W.B. 106.9"; 2.6 Liter, 3.2 Liter.						
C240 Sedan 4D	RF61J	33920	**3525**	**3825**	**4625**	**6500**
C240 4MATIC Sed 4D	RF81J	35120	**3775**	**4100**	**4925**	**6900**
C240 Wagon 4D	RH61J	35290	**3725**	**4050**	**4850**	**6825**
C240 4MATIC Wag 4D	RH81J	36490	**4050**	**4375**	**5225**	**7325**
C320 Sedan 4D	RF64J	39270	**4050**	**4375**	**5225**	**7325**
C320 Sport Sedan 4D	RF64J	38070	**4300**	**4650**	**5525**	**7700**
C320 4MATIC Sed 4D	RF84J	40470	**4575**	**4925**	**5850**	**8125**
C320 Sport Coupe 2D	RN64J	29610	**3100**	**3400**	**4000**	**5650**
C320 Wagon 4D	RH64J	40640	**4575**	**4925**	**5850**	**8125**
C320 4MATIC Wag 4D	RH84J	41840	**4900**	**5275**	**6225**	**8625**
DISTRONIC Cruise Control			**275**	**275**	**365**	**365**
Manual, 6-Spd			**(400)**	**(400)**	**(535)**	**(535)**
C-CLASS—V6 Supercharged—Equipment Schedule 1						
W.B. 106.9"; 3.2 Liter.						
C32 Sedan 4D	RF65J	53120	**6125**	**6575**	**7375**	**9725**
CLK-CLASS—V6—Equipment Schedule 1						
W.B. 106.9"; 3.2 Liter.						
CLK320 Coupe 2D	TJ65J	46480	**4250**	**4550**	**5375**	**7275**
CLK320 Cabriolet 2D	LK65G	52120	**4875**	**5225**	**6150**	**8325**
DISTRONIC Cruise Control			**275**	**275**	**365**	**365**
designo Edition			**600**	**600**	**805**	**805**
CLK-CLASS—V8—Equipment Schedule 1						
W.B. 106.9"; 5.0 Liter, 5.5 Liter.						
CLK500 Coupe 2D	TJ75J	54520	**4800**	**5125**	**6025**	**8100**
CLK500 Cabriolet 2D	TK75G	61570	**5175**	**5550**	**6700**	**9050**
CLK55 Coupe 2D	TJ76H	70620	**6700**	**7175**	**8100**	**10700**
CLK55 Cabriolet 2D	LJ74G	80220	**7375**	**7875**	**8825**	**11550**
DISTRONIC Cruise Control			**275**	**275**	**365**	**365**
designo Edition			**600**	**600**	**805**	**805**
E-CLASS—V6—Equipment Schedule 1						
W.B. 112.4"; 3.2 Liter.						
E320 Sedan 4D	UF65J	49410	**4200**	**4575**	**5250**	**7250**
E320 4MATIC Sed 4D	UF82J	51910	**4450**	**4850**	**5525**	**7600**
E320 Wagon 4D	UH65J	51910	**5200**	**5650**	**6400**	**8750**
E320 4MATIC Wag 4D	UH82J	54410	**6375**	**6900**	**7850**	**10650**
DISTRONIC Cruise Control			**275**	**275**	**365**	**365**
Appearance Pkg			**625**	**625**	**835**	**835**
Sport Pkg			**625**	**625**	**835**	**835**
designo Edition			**600**	**600**	**805**	**805**
E-CLASS—V8—Equipment Schedule 1						
W.B. 112.4"; 5.0 Liter.						
E500 Sedan 4D	UF70J	58510	**4200**	**4575**	**5200**	**7175**
E500 4MATIC Sed 4D	UF83J	60545	**5800**	**6275**	**7225**	**9825**
E500 4MATIC Wag 4D	UH83J	63210	**7125**	**7650**	**8725**	**11750**
DISTRONIC Cruise Control			**275**	**275**	**365**	**365**
Appearance Pkg			**625**	**625**	**835**	**835**
Sport Pkg			**625**	**625**	**835**	**835**
designo Edition			**600**	**600**	**805**	**805**
E-CLASS—V8 Supercharged—Equipment Schedule 1						
W.B. 112.4"; 5.5 Liter.						
E55 Sedan 4D	UF76J	80070	**8375**	**8875**	**10100**	**13100**
DISTRONIC Cruise Control			**275**	**275**	**365**	**365**
designo Edition			**600**	**600**	**805**	**805**
CL-CLASS—V8—Equipment Schedule 1						
W.B. 113.6"; 5.0 Liter.						
CL500 Coupe 2D	PJ75J	94520	**4325**	**4650**	**5200**	**6825**
DISTRONIC Cruise Control			**275**	**275**	**325**	**325**
Sport Pkg			**1175**	**1175**	**1385**	**1385**
designo Edition			**600**	**600**	**710**	**710**
CL-CLASS—V8 Supercharged—Equipment Schedule 1						
W.B. 113.6"; 5.5 Liter.						
CL55 Coupe 2D	PJ74J	119520	**9000**	**9525**	**10800**	**13950**
DISTRONIC Cruise Control			**275**	**275**	**325**	**325**
designo Edition			**600**	**600**	**710**	**710**
CL-CLASS—V12 Twin Turbo—Equipment Schedule 1						
W.B. 113.6"; 5.5 Liter.						

2004 MERCEDES-BENZ

Body Type	VIN	List	Trade-In Good	Very Good	Pvt-Party Good	Retail Excellent
CL600 Coupe 2D	PJ76J	129320	6850	7300	8725	11700
DISTRONIC Cruise Control			275	275	335	335
Sport Pkg			1175	1175	1440	1440
designo Edition			600	600	740	740
S-CLASS—V8—Equipment Schedule 1						
W.B. 121.5"; 4.3 Liter, 5.0 Liter.						
S430 Sedan 4D	NG70J	74320	4050	4350	5075	6850
S430 4MATIC Sed 4D	NG83J	78220	5775	6175	7050	9375
S500 Sedan 4D	NG75J	83770	4325	4650	5375	7175
S500 4MATIC Sed 4D	NG84J	86970	5825	6225	7125	9500
DISTRONIC Cruise Control			275	275	365	365
Sport Pkg			1175	1175	1560	1560
designo Edition			600	600	805	805
S-CLASS—V8 Supercharged—Equipment Schedule 1						
W.B. 121.5"; 5.5 Liter.						
S55 Sedan 4D	NG74J	111870	6775	7250	8225	10800
DISTRONIC Cruise Control			275	275	325	325
designo Edition			600	600	715	715
S-CLASS—V12 Twin Turbo—Equipment Schedule 1						
W.B. 121.5"; 5.5 Liter.						
S600 Sedan 4D	NG76J	124260	5550	5925	6950	9200
DISTRONIC Cruise Control			275	275	365	365
Sport Pkg			1175	1175	1565	1565
designo Edition			600	600	805	805
SL-CLASS—V8—Equipment Schedule 1						
W.B. 100.8"; 5.0 Liter.						
SL500 Roadster 2D	SK75F	89800	9275	9825	10850	13850
DISTRONIC Cruise Control			275	275	350	350
Sport Pkg			1175	1175	1495	1495
designo Edition			600	600	770	770
SL-CLASS—V8 Supercharged—Equipment Schedule 1						
W.B. 100.8"; 5.5 Liter.						
SL55 Roadster 2D	SK74F	121450	12450	13150	13950	17200
DISTRONIC Cruise Control			275	275	320	320
designo Edition			600	600	700	700
SL-CLASS—V12 Twin Turbo—Equipment Schedule 1						
W.B. 100.8"; 5.5 Liter.						
SL600 Roadster 2D	SK76F	128550	13100	13850	15050	19000
DISTRONIC Cruise Control			275	275	340	340
Sport Pkg			1175	1175	1465	1465
designo Edition			600	600	755	755

2005 MERCEDES-BENZ — WDBorWDD(WK56F)-5-#

Body Type	VIN	List	Trade-In Good	Very Good	Pvt-Party Good	Retail Excellent
SLK-CLASS—V6—Equipment Schedule 1						
W.B. 95.7"; 3.5 Liter.						
SLK350 Roadster 2D	WK56F	47610	7625	8100	9350	12050
Sport Pkg			625	625	825	825
designo Edition			650	650	855	855
Manual, 6-Spd			(425)	(425)	(560)	(560)
SLK-CLASS—V8—Equipment Schedule 1						
W.B. 95.7"; 5.5 Liter.						
SLK55 Roadster 2D	WK73F	61220	12050	12700	13950	17350
designo Edition			650	650	795	795
C-CLASS—4-Cyl. Supercharged—Equipment Schedule 1						
W.B. 106.9"; 1.8 Liter.						
C230 Sport Sedan 4D	RF40J	34650	4525	4875	5800	7875
C230 Sport Coupe 2D	RN40J	30850	3850	4175	5050	6900
Manual, 6-Spd			(425)	(425)	(565)	(565)
C-CLASS—V6—Equipment Schedule 1						
W.B. 106.9"; 2.6 Liter, 3.2 Liter.						
C240 Sedan 4D	RF61J	36660	4625	5000	5900	8025
C240 4MATIC Sedan	RF81J	37860	4850	5225	6150	8350
C240 Wagon 4D	RH61J	38030	4900	5275	6225	8425
C240 4MATIC Wagon	RH81J	39230	5150	5550	6500	8800
C320 Sedan 4D	RF64J	41960	5150	5550	6500	8800
C320 4MATIC Sedan	RF84J	43160	5475	5900	7075	9525
C320 Sport Sedan 4D	RF64J	39460	5175	5575	6725	9075
C320 Sport Coupe 2D	RN64J	33250	3950	4275	5150	7050
Manual, 6-Spd			(425)	(425)	(565)	(565)
C-CLASS—V8—Equipment Schedule 1						
W.B. 106.9"; 5.5 Liter.						
C55 Sedan 4D	RF76J	54620	7200	7700	8775	11450

0415

2005 MERCEDES-BENZ

Body Type	VIN	List	Trade-In Good	Very Good	Pvt-Party Good	Retail Excellent
CLK-CLASS—V6—Equipment Schedule 1						
W.B. 106.9"; 3.2 Liter.						
CLK320 Coupe 2D	TJ65G	47410	4900	5250	6350	8325
CLK320 Cabriolet 2D	TK65G	53420	5800	6200	7525	9975
designo Edition			650	650	865	865
CLK-CLASS—V8—Equipment Schedule 1						
W.B. 106.9"; 5.0 Liter, 5.5 Liter.						
CLK500 Coupe 2D	TJ75G	55910	5525	5900	7075	9300
CLK500 Cabriolet 2D	TK75G	61920	6400	6825	8150	10750
CLK55 Coupe 2D	TJ76G	71620	8175	8725	9825	12750
CLK55 Cabriolet 2D	TK76G	82870	8225	8775	9825	12650
designo Edition			650	650	865	865
E-CLASS—6-Cyl. Turbo Diesel—Equipment Schedule 1						
W.B. 112.4"; 3.2 Liter.						
E320 CDI Sedan 4D	UF26J	52855	9850	10550	11550	14950
designo Edition			650	650	835	835
E-CLASS—V6—Equipment Schedule 1						
W.B. 112.4"; 3.2 Liter.						
E320 Sedan 4D	UF65J	52280	5650	6100	7000	9300
E320 4MATIC Sedan	UF82J	54770	5850	6325	7275	9675
E320 Wagon 4D	UH65J	54400	6525	7025	8000	10600
E320 4MATIC Wagon	UH82J	56900	8425	9025	10000	13050
Appearance Pkg			625	625	815	815
Sport Pkg			625	625	815	815
designo Edition			650	650	845	845
E-CLASS—V8—Equipment Schedule 1						
W.B. 112.4"; 5.0 Liter.						
E500 Sedan 4D	UF70J	60480	6100	6575	7525	10000
E500 4MATIC Sedan	UF83J	61420	8625	9225	10400	13700
E500 4MATIC Wagon	UH83J	63950	9100	9750	10950	14400
Appearance Pkg			625	625	810	810
Sport Pkg			625	625	810	810
designo Edition			650	650	845	845
E-CLASS—V8 Supercharged—Equipment Schedule 1						
W.B. 112.4"; 5.5 Liter.						
E55 Sedan 4D	UF76J	81920	9700	10250	11500	14600
E55 Wagon 4D	UF86J	83220	12500	13150	14750	18550
DISTRONIC Cruise Control			300	300	385	385
designo Edition			650	650	835	835
CL-CLASS—V8—Equipment Schedule 1						
W.B. 113.6"; 5.0 Liter.						
CL500 Coupe 2D	PJ75J	94620	6200	6625	7450	9425
DISTRONIC Cruise Control			300	300	360	360
Sport Pkg			1300	1300	1565	1565
designo Edition			650	650	780	780
CL-CLASS—V8 Supercharged—Equipment Schedule 1						
W.B. 113.6"; 5.5 Liter.						
CL55 Coupe 2D	PJ74J	119620	11000	11600	12800	16000
DISTRONIC Cruise Control			300	300	360	360
designo Edition			650	650	780	780
CL-CLASS—V12 Twin Turbo—Equipment Schedule 1						
W.B. 113.6"; 5.5 Liter, 6.0 Liter.						
CL600 Coupe 2D	PJ76J	128620	8875	9400	10600	13400
CL65 Coupe 2D	PJ79J	178220	23400	24700	26100	32500
DISTRONIC Cruise Control			300	300	365	365
Sport Pkg			1300	1300	1585	1585
designo Edition			650	650	790	790
S-CLASS—V8—Equipment Schedule 1						
W.B. 121.5"; 4.3 Liter, 5.0 Liter.						
S430 Sedan 4D	NG70J	76020	5925	6325	7475	9750
S430 4MATIC Sedan	NG83J	76020	7825	8300	9625	12450
S500 Sedan 4D	NG75J	84620	6625	7050	8300	10750
S500 4MATIC Sedan	NG84J	84620	8000	8500	9925	12850
DISTRONIC Cruise Control			300	300	380	380
Sport Pkg			1300	1300	1640	1640
designo Edition			650	650	820	820
S-CLASS—V8 Supercharged—Equipment Schedule 1						
W.B. 121.5"; 5.5 Liter.						
S55 Sedan 4D	NG74J	112620	8125	8675	9900	12950
DISTRONIC Cruise Control			300	300	355	355
designo Edition			650	650	765	765
S-CLASS—V12 Twin Turbo—Equipment Schedule 1						
W.B. 121.5"; 5.5 Liter.						

Body Type	VIN	List	Trade-In Good	Very Good	Pvt-Party Good	Retail Excellent
S600 Sedan 4D	NG76J	125470	6475	6900	8225	10750
DISTRONIC Cruise Control			300	300	400	400
Sport Pkg			1300	1300	1735	1735
designo Edition			650	650	865	865
SL-CLASS—V8—Equipment Schedule 1						
W.B. 100.8"; 5.0 Liter.						
SL500 Roadster 2D	SK75F	91920	10850	11500	12700	15950
DISTRONIC Cruise Control			300	300	375	375
Sport Pkg			1300	1300	1625	1625
designo Edition			650	650	810	810
SL-CLASS—V8 Supercharged—Equipment Schedule 1						
W.B. 100.8"; 5.5 Liter.						
SL55 Roadster 2D	SK74F	120120	14050	14750	15700	19050
DISTRONIC Cruise Control			300	300	345	345
designo Edition			650	650	745	745
SL-CLASS—V12 Twin Turbo—Equipment Schedule 1						
W.B. 100.8"; 5.5 Liter, 6.0 Liter.						
SL600 Roadster 2D	SK76F	125620	17950	18850	20400	25300
SL65 Roadster 2D	SK79F	182720	23500	24600	25500	30600
DISTRONIC Cruise Control			300	300	370	370
Sport Pkg (SL600)			1300	1300	1600	1600
designo Edition			650	650	800	800
SLR-CLASS—V8 Supercharged—Equipment Schedule 1						
W.B. 106.3"; 5.5 Liter.						
McLaren Coupe 2D	AJ76F	455750	****	****	****	184100

Body Type	VIN	List	Trade-In Good	Very Good	Pvt-Party Good	Retail Excellent
SLK-CLASS—V6—Equipment Schedule 1						
W.B. 95.7"; 3.0 Liter, 3.5 Liter.						
SLK280 Roadster 2D	WK54F	45085	7325	7775	9125	11800
SLK350 Roadster 2D	WK56F	49135	8250	8750	10350	13300
Sport Pkg			625	625	830	830
designo Edition			700	700	930	930
Manual, 6-Spd			(450)	(450)	(595)	(595)
SLK-CLASS—V8—Equipment Schedule 1						
W.B. 95.7"; 5.5 Liter.						
SLK55 Roadster 2D	WK73F	63575	12450	13100	14500	17950
designo Edition			700	700	865	865
C-CLASS—V6—Equipment Schedule 1						
W.B. 106.9"; 2.5 Liter, 3.0 Liter, 3.5 Liter.						
C230 Sport Sedan 4D	RF52J	33155	5250	5650	6875	9175
C280 Sedan 4D	RF54J	35515	5350	5775	7000	9325
C280 4MATIC Sedan	RF92J	37315	5600	6025	7200	9625
C350 Sedan 4D	RF56J	40715	6000	6425	7650	10200
C350 4MATIC Sedan	RF87J	42515	6550	7000	8250	10950
Manual, 6-Spd			(450)	(450)	(600)	(600)
C-CLASS—V8—Equipment Schedule 1						
W.B. 106.9"; 5.5 Liter.						
C55 Sedan 4D	RF76J	56225	8300	8825	10200	13100
CLK-CLASS—V6—Equipment Schedule 1						
W.B. 106.9"; 3.5 Liter.						
CLK350 Coupe 2D	TJ56J	49025	6150	6550	7725	10050
CLK350 Cabriolet 2D	TK56G	55975	7400	7875	9175	11850
KEYLESS-GO			200	200	255	255
designo Edition			700	700	935	935
CLK-CLASS—V8—Equipment Schedule 1						
W.B. 106.9"; 5.0 Liter, 5.5 Liter.						
CLK500 Coupe 2D	TJ57J	57325	6825	7275	8550	11050
CLK500 Cabriolet 2D	TK75G	64275	8575	9075	10400	13300
CLK55 Cabriolet 2D	TK76G	84275	11800	12500	13550	16800
KEYLESS-GO			200	200	255	255
designo Edition			700	700	935	935
E-CLASS—6-Cyl. Turbo Diesel—Equipment Schedule 1						
W.B. 112.4"; 3.2 Liter.						
E320 CDI Sedan 4D	UF26J	54845	9975	10650	12050	15600
KEYLESS-GO			200	200	245	245
designo Edition			700	700	905	905
E-CLASS—V6—Equipment Schedule 1						
W.B. 112.4"; 3.5 Liter.						
E350 Sedan 4D	UF56J	52325	6725	7225	8000	10350
E350 4MATIC Sedan	UF87J	54825	7775	8325	9275	11950
E350 Wagon 4D	UH56J	54505	7750	8325	9250	11950
E350 4MATIC Wagon	UH87J	57005	8725	9325	10400	13350

2006 MERCEDES-BENZ

Body Type	VIN	List	Trade-In Good	Very Good	Pvt-Party Good	Retail Excellent
KEYLESS-GO	------	------	200	200	240	240
Appearance Pkg	------	------	625	625	790	790
Sport Pkg	------	------	625	625	790	790
designo Edition	------	------	700	700	880	880
E-CLASS—V8—Equipment Schedule 1						
W.B. 112.4"; 5.0 Liter.						
E500 Sedan 4D	UF70J	60675	8550	9125	10050	12950
E500 4MATIC Sedan	UF83J	64475	9275	9900	11050	14150
E500 4MATIC Wagon	UH83J	65505	10050	10750	11950	15300
KEYLESS-GO	------	------	200	200	240	240
Appearance Pkg	------	------	625	625	790	790
Sport Pkg	------	------	625	625	790	790
designo Edition	------	------	700	700	885	885
E-CLASS—V8 Supercharged—Equipment Schedule 1						
W.B. 112.4"; 5.5 Liter.						
E55 Sedan 4D	UF76J	84275	11200	11800	13250	16550
E55 Wagon 4D	UH76J	83375	14200	14900	16400	20400
KEYLESS-GO	------	------	200	200	230	230
Adaptive Cruise Control	------	------	325	325	390	390
designo Edition	------	------	700	700	845	845
CL-CLASS—V8—Equipment Schedule 1						
W.B. 113.6"; 5.0 Liter.						
CL500 Coupe 2D	PJ75J	97275	8500	9000	10000	12500
Adaptive Cruise Control	------	------	325	325	395	395
designo Edition	------	------	700	700	855	855
CL-CLASS—V8 Supercharged—Equipment Schedule 1						
W.B. 113.6"; 5.5 Liter.						
CL55 Coupe 2D	PJ74J	122975	13250	13900	15500	19350
Adaptive Cruise Control	------	------	325	325	400	400
designo Edition	------	------	700	700	860	860
CL-CLASS—V12 Twin Turbo—Equipment Schedule 1						
W.B. 113.6"; 6.0 Liter.						
CL600 Coupe 2D	PJ76J	132875	11050	11650	13150	16450
CL65 Coupe 2D	PJ79J	182975	26700	28100	27800	32600
Adaptive Cruise Control	------	------	325	325	400	400
designo Edition	------	------	700	700	860	860
CLS-CLASS—V8—Equipment Schedule 1						
W.B. 112.4"; 5.0 Liter.						
CLS500 Coupe 4D	DJ75X	66975	10900	11500	12900	16000
Adaptive Cruise Control	------	------	325	325	400	400
Sport Pkg	------	------	1425	1425	1760	1760
designo Edition	------	------	700	700	865	865
CLS-CLASS—V8 Supercharged—Equipment Schedule 1						
W.B. 112.4"; 5.5 Liter.						
CLS55 Coupe 2D	DJ76X	89075	14250	15050	15550	18650
Adaptive Cruise Control	------	------	325	325	370	370
designo Edition	------	------	700	700	800	800
S-CLASS—V6—Equipment Schedule 1						
W.B. 121.5"; 3.7 Liter.						
S350 Sedan 4D	NF67J	65675	6775	7200	8250	10450
KEYLESS-GO	------	------	200	200	235	235
Adaptive Cruise Control	------	------	325	325	400	400
S-CLASS—V8—Equipment Schedule 1						
W.B. 121.5"; 4.3 Liter, 5.0 Liter.						
S430 Sedan 4D	NG70J	78025	7550	8025	9175	11650
S430 4MATIC Sedan	NG83J	79025	9200	9725	11250	14200
S500 Sedan 4D	NG75J	87825	8625	9125	10550	13300
S500 4MATIC Sedan	NG84J	88125	10050	10600	12050	15150
KEYLESS-GO	------	------	200	200	235	235
Adaptive Cruise Control	------	------	325	325	400	400
Sport Pkg	------	------	1425	1425	1760	1760
designo Edition	------	------	700	700	860	860
S-CLASS—V8 Supercharged—Equipment Schedule 1						
W.B. 121.5"; 5.5 Liter.						
S55 Sedan 4D	NG74J	116625	9875	10500	11700	14750
Adaptive Cruise Control	------	------	325	325	370	370
designo Edition	------	------	700	700	795	795
S-CLASS—V12 Twin Turbo—Equipment Schedule 1						
W.B. 121.5"; 5.5 Liter, 6.0 Liter.						
S600 Sedan 4D	NG76J	131725	7775	8250	9900	12800
S65 Sedan 4D	NG79J	169775	19800	20800	23400	29600
Adaptive Cruise Control	------	------	325	325	375	375
Sport Pkg (S600)	------	------	1425	1425	1645	1645

2006 MERCEDES-BENZ

Body Type	VIN	List	Trade-In Good	Very Good	Pvt-Party Good	Retail Excellent
designo Edition			700	700	810	810
SL-CLASS—V8—Equipment Schedule 1						
W.B. 100.8"; 5.0 Liter.						
SL500 Roadster 2D	SK75F	94675	12450	13100	14450	18000
KEYLESS-GO			200	200	240	240
Adaptive Cruise Control			325	325	405	405
Sport Pkg			1425	1425	1775	1775
designo Edition			700	700	870	870
SL-CLASS—V8 Supercharged—Equipment Schedule 1						
W.B. 100.8"; 5.5 Liter.						
SL55 Roadster 2D	SK74F	127875	17300	18150	18850	22400
KEYLESS-GO			200	200	215	215
Adaptive Cruise Control			325	325	365	365
Performance Pkg			3275	3275	3685	3685
designo Edition			700	700	785	785
SL-CLASS—V12 Twin Turbo—Equipment Schedule 1						
W.B. 100.8"; 5.5 Liter, 6.0 Liter.						
SL600 Roadster 2D	SK76F	134275	20100	21000	22500	27500
SL65 Roadster 2D	SK79F	188375	26800	28000	28700	34000
Adaptive Cruise Control			325	325	400	400
Sport Pkg (SL600)			1425	1425	1750	1750
designo Edition			700	700	860	860
SLR-CLASS—V8 Supercharged—Equipment Schedule 1						
W.B. 106.3"; 5.5 Liter.						
McLaren Coupe 2D	AJ76F	455750	****	****	****	227600

2007 MERCEDES-BENZ — WDBorWDD(WK54F)-7-#

Body Type	VIN	List	Trade-In Good	Very Good	Pvt-Party Good	Retail Excellent
SLK-CLASS—V6—Equipment Schedule 1						
W.B. 95.7"; 3.0 Liter, 3.5 Liter.						
SLK280 Roadster 2D	WK54F	45555	9500	9950	11300	14100
SLK350 Roadster 2D	WK56F	49605	10400	10950	12400	15500
AMG Sport Pkg			625	625	790	790
designo Edition			750	750	945	945
Manual, 6-Spd			(475)	(475)	(600)	(600)
SLK-CLASS—V8—Equipment Schedule 1						
W.B. 95.7"; 5.5 Liter.						
SLK55 Roadster 2D	WK73F	64575	16150	16900	18100	21900
designo Edition			750	750	890	890
Performance Pkg			3475	3475	4145	4145
C-CLASS—V6—Equipment Schedule 1						
W.B. 106.9"; 2.5 Liter, 3.0 Liter, 3.5 Liter.						
C230 Sport Sedan 4D	RF52J	34205	6500	6950	8100	10500
C280 Sedan 4D	RF54J	35965	6600	7050	8200	10650
C280 4MATIC Sedan	RF92J	37765	7000	7475	8650	11200
C350 Sedan 4D	RF56J	41165	7700	8200	9400	12150
C350 4MATIC Sedan	RF87J	42965	8300	8825	10050	12950
Manual, 6-Spd			(475)	(475)	(635)	(635)
CLK-CLASS—V6—Equipment Schedule 1						
W.B. 106.9"; 3.5 Liter.						
CLK350 Coupe 2D	TJ56J	49505	7700	8175	11650	11650
CLK350 Cabriolet 2D	TK56F	54975	9050	9575	10850	13650
KEYLESS-GO			200	200	265	265
designo Edition			750	750	990	990
CLK-CLASS—V8—Equipment Schedule 1						
W.B. 106.9"; 5.5 Liter, 6.3 Liter.						
CLK550 Coupe 2D	TJ72H	58205	9325	9875	11100	13850
CLK550 Cabriolet 2D	TK72F	63675	10450	11000	12450	15500
CLK63 Cabriolet 2D	TK77G	92575	15050	15800	16600	20000
KEYLESS-GO			200	200	260	260
designo Edition			750	750	980	980
E-CLASS—V6 Turbo Diesel—Equipment Schedule 1						
W.B. 112.4"; 3.0 Liter.						
E320 BlueTEC Sed	UF22X	52325	11400	12100	13000	16150
KEYLESS-GO			200	200	245	245
P1 Pkg			300	300	365	365
P2 Pkg			300	300	355	355
designo Edition			750	750	915	915
E-CLASS—V6—Equipment Schedule 1						
W.B. 112.4"; 3.5 Liter.						
E350 Sedan 4D	UF56X	51325	8325	8900	9625	12050
E350 4MATIC Sedan	UF87X	56475	9250	9850	10750	13400
E350 4MATIC Wagon	UH87X	53825	11900	12650	13600	16900
KEYLESS-GO			200	200	245	245

Body Type	VIN	List	Trade-In Good	Very Good	Pvt-Party Good	Retail Excellent
P1 Pkg			300	300	370	370
P2 Pkg			300	300	355	355
Sport Pkg (Sedan)			625	625	770	770
designo Edition			750	750	925	925
E-CLASS—V8—Equipment Schedule 1						
W.B. 112.4"; 5.5 Liter, 6.3 Liter.						
E550 Sedan 4D	UF72X	59775	9850	10500	11350	14150
E550 4MATIC Sedan	UF90X	62275	11500	12200	13250	16500
E63 Sedan 4D	UF77X	85375	14400	15100	16450	20100
E63 Wagon 4D	UH77X	86175	17950	18800	20200	24600
KEYLESS-GO			200	200	245	245
P1 Pkg			300	300	365	365
P2 Pkg			300	300	355	355
AMG Sport Pkg (E550)			625	625	765	765
designo Edition			750	750	915	915
CL-CLASS—V8—Equipment Schedule 1						
W.B. 116.3"; 5.5 Liter.						
CL550 Coupe 2D	EJ71X	100675	17450	18300	18950	22300
Adaptive Cruise Control			350	350	385	385
P1 Pkg			300	300	330	330
P2 Pkg			300	300	320	320
AMG Sport Pkg			625	625	685	685
designo Edition			750	750	825	825
CL-CLASS—V12 Twin Turbo—Equipment Schedule 1						
W.B. 116.3"; 5.5 Liter.						
CL600 Coupe 2D	EJ76X	144975	20200	21100	21900	25800
Adaptive Cruise Control			350	350	385	385
designo Edition			750	750	825	825
CLS-CLASS—V8—Equipment Schedule 1						
W.B. 112.4"; 5.5 Liter, 6.3 Liter.						
CLS550 Coupe 4D	DJ72X	68975	13200	13850	15300	18850
CLS63 Coupe 4D	DJ77X	92975	17150	18050	18400	21800
Adaptive Cruise Control			350	350	430	430
AMG Sport Pkg (CLS550)			1550	1550	1910	1910
designo Edition			750	750	925	925
S-CLASS—V8—Equipment Schedule 1						
W.B. 124.6"; 5.5 Liter.						
S550 Sedan 4D	NG71X	87175	15450	16200	17650	21600
S550 4MATIC Sedan	NG86X	89525	17000	17800	19400	23800
KEYLESS-GO			200	200	245	245
Adaptive Cruise Control			350	350	430	430
P1 Pkg			300	300	370	370
P2 Pkg			300	300	360	360
P3 Pkg			500	500	615	615
AMG Sport Pkg			1550	1550	1915	1915
designo Edition			750	750	925	925
S-CLASS—V12 Twin Turbo—Equipment Schedule 1						
W.B. 124.6"; 5.5 Liter, 6.0 Liter.						
S600 Sedan 4D	NG76X	143675	18500	19350	20800	25300
S65 Sedan 4D	NG79X	184875	30100	31400	33200	40100
Adaptive Cruise Control			350	350	395	395
designo Edition			750	750	845	845
SL-CLASS—V8—Equipment Schedule 1						
W.B. 100.8"; 5.5 Liter.						
SL550 Roadster 2D	SK71F	97275	16050	16800	18200	22200
KEYLESS-GO			200	200	245	245
Adaptive Cruise Control			350	350	430	430
Premium Pkg I			300	300	370	370
Premium Pkg II			300	300	360	360
AMG Sport Pkg			1550	1550	1915	1915
designo Edition			750	750	925	925
SL-CLASS—V8 Supercharged—Equipment Schedule 1						
W.B. 100.8"; 5.5 Liter.						
SL55 Roadster 2D	SK72F	132175	19600	20500	21200	24900
KEYLESS-GO			200	200	225	225
Adaptive Cruise Control			350	350	395	395
designo Edition			750	750	850	850
Performance Pkg			3475	3475	3940	3940
SL-CLASS—V12 Twin Turbo—Equipment Schedule 1						
W.B. 100.8"; 5.5 Liter, 6.0 Liter.						
SL600 Roadster 2D	SK77F	135375	21700	22700	24300	29400
SL65 Roadster 2D	SK79F	189375	31800	33100	33600	39200
Adaptive Cruise Control			350	350	430	430

2007 MERCEDES-BENZ

Body Type	VIN	List	Trade-In Good	Very Good	Pvt-Party Good	Retail Excellent
AMG Sport Pkg (SL600)			1550	1550	1895	1895
designo Edition			750	750	915	915
SLR-CLASS—V8 Supercharged—Equipment Schedule 1						
W.B. 106.3"; 5.5 Liter.						
McLaren 722 Edition	AJ76F	485750	****	****	****	256700

2008 MERCEDES-BENZ — WDBorWDD(WK54F)–8–#

Body Type	VIN	List	Trade-In Good	Very Good	Pvt-Party Good	Retail Excellent
SLK-CLASS—V6—Equipment Schedule 1						
W.B. 95.7"; 3.5 Liter.						
SLK280 Roadster 2D	WK54F	46115	10750	11300	12500	15350
SLK280 Edition Rdstr	WK54F	51100	11300	11850	13200	16150
SLK350 Roadster 2D	WK56F	49975	12400	13000	14350	17500
SLK350 Edition Rdstr	WK56F	56800	17200	17950	19500	23500
AMG Sport Pkg			1650	1650	2045	2045
designo Edition			800	800	990	990
Manual, 6-Spd w/Overdrive			(425)	(425)	(515)	(515)
SLK-CLASS—V8—Equipment Schedule 1						
W.B. 95.7"; 5.5 Liter.						
SLK55 Roadster 2D	WK73F	65025	20600	21500	22600	26600
Performance Pkg			3700	3700	4265	4265
C-CLASS—V6—Equipment Schedule 1						
W.B. 108.7"; 3.0 Liter, 3.5 Liter.						
C300 Sport Sed 4D	GF54X	34915	10750	11300	12350	15000
C300 Sport 4MATIC	GF81X	36715	11200	11800	12850	15650
C300 Luxury Sedan 4D	GF54X	35175	10400	10950	11900	14500
C300 Luxury 4MATIC	GF81X	35925	10850	11400	12450	15200
C350 Sport Sedan 4D	GF56X	38775	12100	12750	13750	16750
Multimedia Pkg			250	250	295	295
P1 Pkg			300	300	375	375
P2 Pkg			300	300	385	385
Manual, 6-Spd Overdrive			(425)	(425)	(515)	(515)
C-CLASS—V8—Equipment Schedule 1						
W.B. 108.7"; 6.3 Liter.						
C63 AMG Sedan 4D	GF77X	54625	20800	21700	22300	26000
P1 Pkg			300	300	340	340
P2 Pkg			300	300	350	350
CLK-CLASS—V6—Equipment Schedule 1						
W.B. 106.9"; 3.5 Liter.						
CLK350 Coupe 2D	TJ56H	47275	9750	10300	11250	13700
CLK350 Cabriolet 2D	TK56F	55325	11150	11700	12650	15800
KEYLESS-GO			200	200	250	250
P1 Pkg			300	300	375	375
P2 Pkg			300	300	385	385
P3 Pkg			500	500	625	625
designo Edition			800	800	1000	1000
CLK-CLASS—V8—Equipment Schedule 1						
W.B. 106.9"; 5.5 Liter, 6.3 Liter.						
CLK550 Coupe 2D	TJ72H	56975	11750	12350	13450	16350
CLK550 Cabriolet 2D	TK72F	64025	13100	13700	15050	18200
CLK63 Cabriolet 2D	TK77G	90325	18200	19050	19850	23500
KEYLESS-GO			200	200	250	250
P1 Pkg			300	300	375	375
P2 Pkg			300	300	385	385
P3 Pkg			500	500	620	620
designo Edition			800	800	995	995
CLK-CLASS—V8—Equipment Schedule 1						
W.B. 106.9"; 6.3 Liter.						
CLK63 Black Series	TJ77H	135825	33700	35100	35300	40800
E-CLASS—V6 Turbo Diesel—Equipment Schedule 1						
W.B. 112.4"; 3.0 Liter.						
E320 BlueTEC Sedan	UF22X	52675	13700	14450	15200	18250
KEYLESS-GO			200	200	230	230
P1 Pkg			300	300	350	350
P2 Pkg			300	300	360	360
designo Edition			800	800	930	930
E-CLASS—V6—Equipment Schedule 1						
W.B. 112.4"; 3.5 Liter.						
E350 Sedan 4D	UF56X	51675	10400	11000	11650	14100
E350 4MATIC Sedan	UF87X	53175	10900	11550	12150	14650
E350 4MATIC Wagon	UH87X	56475	13900	14650	15450	18600
KEYLESS-GO			200	200	235	235
P1 Pkg			300	300	350	350
P2 Pkg			300	300	365	365

2008 MERCEDES-BENZ

Body	Type	VIN	List	Trade-In Good	Very Good	Pvt-Party Good	Retail Excellent
	AMG Sport Pkg (Sedan)			625	625	735	735
	designo Edition			800	800	940	940
E-CLASS—V8—Equipment Schedule 1							
W.B. 112.4"; 5.5 Liter, 6.3 Liter.							
E550 Sedan 4D		UF72X	61875	12050	12750	13450	16250
E550 4MATIC Sedan		UF90X	63375	16900	17800	18550	22200
E63 Sedan 4D		UF77X	85775	17300	18050	19400	23200
E63 Wagon 4D		UH77X	86575	20300	21200	22500	26800
	KEYLESS-GO			200	200	235	235
	P1 Pkg			300	300	350	350
	P2 Pkg			300	300	365	365
	AMG Sport Pkg			625	625	735	735
	designo Edition			800	800	940	940
	Performance Pkg			3700	3700	4430	4430
CL-CLASS—V8—Equipment Schedule 1							
W.B. 116.3"; 5.5 Liter.							
CL550 Coupe 2D		EJ71X	104425	21100	22000	22700	26400
	Adaptive Cruise Control			375	375	420	420
	Premium Pkg 1			300	300	335	335
	Premium Pkg 2			300	300	345	345
	AMG Sport Pkg			1650	1650	1845	1845
	designo Edition			800	800	895	895
	Performance Pkg			3700	3700	4170	4170
CL-CLASS—V8—Equipment Schedule 1							
W.B. 116.3"; 6.2 Liter.							
CL63 Coupe 2D		EJ77X	138325	26500	27500	28600	33500
	Adaptive Cruise Control			375	375	425	425
	Premium Pkg 2			300	300	350	350
	designo Edition			800	800	905	905
	Performance Pkg			3700	3700	4170	4170
CL-CLASS—V12 Twin Turbo—Equipment Schedule 1							
W.B. 116.3"; 5.5 Liter.							
CL600 Coupe 2D		EJ76X	148225	27200	28300	29400	34300
	DISTRONIC Cruise Control			375	375	425	425
	designo Edition			800	800	905	905
CL-CLASS—V12 Twin Turbo—Equipment Schedule 1							
W.B. 116.3"; 6.0 Liter.							
CL65 Coupe 2D		EJ79X	197775	62100	64600	63300	72000
	designo Edition			800	800	870	870
CLS-CLASS—V8—Equipment Schedule 1							
W.B. 112.4"; 5.5 Liter, 6.3 Liter.							
CLS550 Coupe 4D		DJ72X	70075	16100	16800	18100	21700
CLS63 Coupe 4D		DJ77X	96975	20300	21200	22000	26000
	KEYLESS-GO			200	200	240	240
	Adaptive Cruise Control			375	375	450	450
	designo Edition			800	800	960	960
	P1 Pkg			300	300	340	340
	P2 Pkg			300	300	375	375
	AMG Sport Pkg (CLS550)			1650	1650	1985	1985
	Performance Pkg			3700	3700	4200	4200
S-CLASS—V8—Equipment Schedule 1							
W.B. 124.6"; 5.5 Liter.							
S550 Sedan 4D		NG71X	88775	19800	20600	21600	25400
S550 4MATIC Sedan		NG86X	91775	21300	22200	23200	27200
	Adaptive Cruise Control			375	375	440	440
	Premium Pkg 1			300	300	350	350
	Premium Pkg 2			300	300	365	365
	Premium Pkg 3			500	500	585	585
	AMG Sport Pkg			1650	1650	1940	1940
	designo Edition			800	800	940	940
	Performance Pkg			3700	3700	4505	4505
S-CLASS—V8—Equipment Schedule 1							
W.B. 124.6"; 6.3 Liter.							
S63 Sedan 4D		NG77X	127775	23600	24700	26100	31300
	Adaptive Cruise Control			375	375	455	455
	Premium Pkg 3			500	500	610	610
	Performance Pkg			3700	3700	4505	4505
S-CLASS—V12 Twin Turbo—Equipment Schedule 1							
W.B. 124.6"; 5.5 Liter, 6.0 Liter.							
S600 Sedan 4D		NG76X	147975	23400	24400	25600	30100
S65 Sedan 4D		NG79X	186575	35300	36600	38300	45200
	designo Edition			800	800	875	875

2008 MERCEDES-BENZ

Body Type	VIN	List	Trade-In Good	Very Good	Pvt-Party Good	Retail Excellent
SL-CLASS—V8—Equipment Schedule 1						
W.B. 100.8"; 5.5 Liter.						
SL550 Roadster 2D	SK71F	97425	20000	20900	22400	26900
KEYLESS-GO		------	200	200	245	245
Adaptive Cruise Control		------	375	375	460	460
Premium Pkg 1		------	300	300	365	365
AMG Sport Pkg		------	1650	1650	2020	2020
designo Edition		------	800	800	980	980
SL-CLASS—V8 Supercharged—Equipment Schedule 1						
W.B. 100.8"; 5.5 Liter.						
SL55 Roadster 2D	SK72F	132725	23800	24800	25200	29000
KEYLESS-GO		------	200	200	225	225
Adaptive Cruise Control		------	375	375	425	425
Premium Pkg 1		------	300	300	340	340
designo Edition		------	800	800	905	905
Performance Pkg		------	3700	3700	4170	4170
SL-CLASS—V12 Twin Turbo—Equipment Schedule 1						
W.B. 100.8"; 5.5 Liter, 6.0 Liter.						
SL600 Roadster 2D	SK77F	134025	25500	26600	28200	33500
SL65 Roadster 2D	SK79F	188025	36600	38000	38300	43900
Adaptive Cruise Control		------	375	375	450	450
AMG Sport Pkg (SL600)		------	1650	1650	1990	1990
designo Edition		------	800	800	965	965
SLR-CLASS—V8 Supercharged—Equipment Schedule 1						
W.B. 106.3"; 5.5 Liter.						
McLaren Roadster 2D	AK76F	500750	****	****	****	267800

2009 MERCEDES-BENZ — WDBorWDD(WK54F)-9-#

Body Type	VIN	List	Trade-In Good	Very Good	Pvt-Party Good	Retail Excellent
SLK-CLASS—V6—Equipment Schedule 1						
W.B. 95.7"; 3.0 Liter, 3.5 Liter.						
SLK300 Roadster 2D	WK54F	47285	12850	13450	14850	17800
SLK350 Roadster 2D	WK56F	50825	15300	15950	17400	20800
Multimedia Pkg		------	250	250	300	300
Premium Pkg 1		------	350	350	420	420
AMG Sport Pkg		------	700	700	845	845
Manual, 6-Spd w/Overdrive		------	(450)	(450)	(535)	(535)
SLK-CLASS—V8—Equipment Schedule 1						
W.B. 95.7"; 5.5 Liter.						
SLK55 Roadster 2D	WK73F	65175	24400	25300	26400	30500
Multimedia Pkg		------	250	250	285	285
Performance Pkg		------	3900	3900	4435	4435
C-CLASS—V6—Equipment Schedule 1						
W.B. 108.7"; 3.0 Liter.						
C300 Sport Sedan 4D	GF54X	32975	12350	12900	13950	16650
C300 Sport 4MATIC	GF81X	35715	12800	13400	14600	17450
C300 Luxury Sedan 4D	GF54X	36275	12150	12700	13750	16400
C300 Luxury 4MATIC	GF81X	35975	12600	13200	14350	17150
Multimedia Pkg		------	250	250	305	305
Premium Pkg 1		------	350	350	425	425
Premium Pkg 2		------	325	325	405	405
Manual, 6-Spd Overdrive		------	(450)	(450)	(540)	(540)
C-CLASS—V6—Equipment Schedule 1						
W.B. 108.7"; 3.5 Liter.						
C350 Sport Sedan 4D	GF56X	39075	14050	14700	15900	18950
Multimedia Pkg		------	250	250	305	305
Premium Pkg 2		------	325	325	400	400
C-CLASS—V8—Equipment Schedule 1						
W.B. 108.7"; 6.3 Liter.						
C63 Sedan 4D	GF77X	55975	24900	25900	26500	30400
Multimedia Pkg		------	250	250	280	280
Premium Pkg 2		------	325	325	370	370
Performance Pkg		------	1325	1325	1480	1480
CLK-CLASS—V6—Equipment Schedule 1						
W.B. 106.9"; 3.5 Liter.						
CLK350 Coupe 2D	TJ56H	47675	11700	12300	13300	15900
CLK350 Cabriolet 2D	TK56F	55975	14050	14650	15950	18950
KEYLESS-GO		------	200	200	245	245
Premium Pkg 1		------	350	350	430	430
Premium Pkg 2		------	325	325	405	405
AMG Sport Pkg		------	700	700	860	860
designo Edition		------	825	825	1010	1010
CLK-CLASS—V8—Equipment Schedule 1						
W.B. 106.9"; 5.5 Liter.						

2009 MERCEDES-BENZ

Body Type	VIN	List	Trade-In Good	Very Good	Pvt-Party Good	Retail Excellent
CLK550 Coupe 2D	TJ72H	57375	14100	14800	15900	18950
CLK550 Cabriolet 2D	TK72F	65375	16100	16800	18050	21300
KEYLESS-GO			200	200	245	245
Premium Pkg 1			350	350	425	425
Premium Pkg 2			325	325	405	405
designo Edition			825	825	1005	1005
E-CLASS—V6 Turbo Diesel—Equipment Schedule 1						
W.B. 112.4"; 3.0 Liter.						
E320 BlueTEC Sedan	UF22X	53775	16950	17800	18750	22300
KEYLESS-GO			200	200	235	235
Premium Pkg 1			350	350	410	410
Premium Pkg 2			325	325	390	390
designo Edition			825	825	970	970
E-CLASS—V6—Equipment Schedule 1						
W.B. 112.4"; 3.5 Liter.						
E350 Sedan 4D	UF56X	52775	13350	14050	15050	18000
E350 4MATIC Sedan	UF87X	52775	14000	14700	15600	18600
E350 4MATIC Wagon	UH87X	56825	17750	18600	19550	23300
KEYLESS-GO			200	200	235	235
Premium Pkg 1			350	350	415	415
Premium Pkg 2			325	325	390	390
AMG Sport Pkg (Sedan)			700	700	825	825
designo Edition			825	825	975	975
E-CLASS—V8—Equipment Schedule 1						
W.B. 112.4"; 5.5 Liter, 6.3 Liter.						
E550 Sedan 4D	UF72X	61275	18450	19300	20300	24200
E550 4MATIC Sedan	UF90X	64475	21100	22100	23100	27400
E63 Sedan 4D	UF77X	86875	23000	23900	25000	29000
E63 Wagon 4D	UH77X	87675	25900	26900	28000	32500
KEYLESS-GO			200	200	235	235
Adaptive Cruise Control			375	375	430	430
Premium Pkg 1			350	350	410	410
Premium Pkg 2			325	325	385	385
AMG Sport Pkg			700	700	820	820
designo Edition			825	825	970	970
Performance Pkg			3900	3900	4480	4480
CL-CLASS—V8—Equipment Schedule 1						
W.B. 116.3"; 5.5 Liter, 6.3 Liter.						
CL550 4MATIC Coupe	EJ71X	105975	25700	26700	27400	31500
CL63 Coupe 2D	EJ77X	140575	34500	35800	36500	41700
DISTRONIC PLUS			375	375	430	430
Premium Pkg 2			325	325	380	380
designo Edition			825	825	945	945
AMG Sport Pkg			1700	1700	1950	1950
Performance Pkg			3900	3900	4460	4460
CL-CLASS—V12 Twin Turbo—Equipment Schedule 1						
W.B. 116.3"; 5.5 Liter, 6.0 Liter.						
CL600 Coupe 2D	EJ76X	149775	40400	41900	42600	48600
CL65 Coupe 2D	EJ79X	200575	75600	78300	76500	85500
Adaptive Cruise Control			375	375	430	430
designo Edition			825	825	945	945
CLS-CLASS—V8—Equipment Schedule 1						
W.B. 112.4"; 5.5 Liter, 6.3 Liter.						
CLS550 Coupe 4D	DJ72X	69775	19600	20400	22200	26500
CLS63 Coupe 4D	DJ77X	95375	22000	22900	24100	28500
KEYLESS-GO			200	200	235	235
Adaptive Cruise Control			375	375	440	440
P1 Pkg			350	350	410	410
AMG Sport Pkg (CLS550)			1700	1700	2005	2005
designo Edition			825	825	970	970
Performance Pkg			3900	3900	4635	4635
S-CLASS—V8—Equipment Schedule 1						
W.B. 124.6"; 5.5 Liter.						
S550 Sedan 4D	NG71X	89125	23400	24300	25300	29400
S550 4MATIC Sedan	NG86X	92125	24900	25800	26900	31100
Premium Pkg 2			325	325	385	385
AMG Sport Pkg			1700	1700	1980	1980
designo Edition			825	825	960	960
S-CLASS—V8—Equipment Schedule 1						
W.B. 124.6"; 6.3 Liter.						
S63 Sedan 4D	NG77X	129225	27900	29100	30400	35800
DISTRONIC PLUS			375	375	445	445
designo Edition			825	825	985	985

2009 MERCEDES-BENZ

Body Type	VIN	List	Trade-In Good	Very Good	Pvt-Party Good	Retail Excellent
Performance Pkg			3900	3900	4655	4655
S-CLASS—V12 Twin Turbo—Equipment Schedule 1						
W.B. 124.6"; 5.5 Liter, 6.0 Liter.						
S600 Sedan 4D	NG76X	148325	38100	39500	44100	48000
S65 Sedan 4D	NG79X	195825	52200	54000	55300	63400
designo Edition			825	825	895	895
SL-CLASS—V8—Equipment Schedule 1						
W.B. 100.8"; 5.5 Liter, 6.3 Liter.						
SL550 Roadster 2D	SK71F	96775	28000	29100	30400	35400
SL63 Roadster 2D	SK70F	132875	33700	35000	35600	40600
KEYLESS-GO			200	200	235	235
Adaptive Cruise Control			375	375	440	440
Premium Pkg 1			350	350	410	410
designo Edition			825	825	965	965
SL-CLASS—V12 Twin Turbo—Equipment Schedule 1						
W.B. 100.8"; 5.5 Liter, 6.0 Liter.						
SL600 Roadster 2D	SK77F	136975	38500	39900	41200	47600
SL65 Roadster 2D	SK79F	191575	55400	57300	57900	65700
KEYLESS-GO			200	200	230	230
Adaptive Cruise Control			375	375	430	430
designo Edition			825	825	950	950
SLR-CLASS—V8 Supercharged—Equipment Schedule 1						
W.B. 106.3"; 5.5 Liter.						
McLaren Roadster 2D	AK76F	500750	****	****	****	312300

2010 MERCEDES-BENZ — WDBorWDD(WK5EA)-A-#

Body Type	VIN	List	Trade-In Good	Very Good	Pvt-Party Good	Retail Excellent
SLK-CLASS—V6—Equipment Schedule 1						
W.B. 95.7"; 3.0 Liter, 3.5 Liter.						
SLK300 Roadster 2D	WK5EA	47775	16650	17300	18650	21800
SLK350 Roadster 2D	WK5JA	52775	19100	19800	21200	24700
Multimedia Pkg			275	275	320	320
Premium Pkg I			400	400	465	465
AMG Sport Pkg			775	775	900	900
Manual, 6-Spd w/Overdrive			(475)	(475)	(545)	(545)
SLK-CLASS—V8—Equipment Schedule 1						
W.B. 95.7"; 5.5 Liter.						
SLK55 Roadster 2D	WK7DA	68525	31000	32100	32900	37300
Performance Pkg			3900	3900	4330	4330
C-CLASS—V6—Equipment Schedule 1						
W.B. 108.7"; 3.0 Liter, 3.5 Liter.						
C300 Sport Sedan 4D	GF5EB	34475	13950	14550	15650	18350
C300 Sport 4MATIC	GF8BB	37975	14600	15200	16300	19150
C300 Luxury Sedan 4D	GF5EB	36175	13650	14250	15350	18050
C300 Luxury 4MATIC	GF8BB	38175	14300	14900	16000	18750
KEYLESS-GO			200	200	240	240
Multimedia Pkg			275	275	330	330
Premium Pkg 1			400	400	475	475
Premium Pkg 2			350	350	415	415
Manual, 6-Spd Overdrive			(475)	(475)	(560)	(560)
C-CLASS—V6—Equipment Schedule 1						
W.B. 108.7"; 3.5 Liter.						
C350 Sport Sedan 4D	GF5GB	40625	16350	17050	18200	21300
KEYLESS-GO			200	200	240	240
Multimedia Pkg			275	275	325	325
Premium 2 Pkg			350	350	415	415
C-CLASS—V8—Equipment Schedule 1						
W.B. 108.7"; 6.3 Liter.						
C63 Sedan 4D	GF7HB	60325	28600	29600	30300	34400
KEYLESS-GO			200	200	220	220
Multimedia Pkg			275	275	305	305
Premium Pkg 2			350	350	390	390
Performance Pkg			1375	1375	1545	1545
E-CLASS—V6—Equipment Schedule 1						
W.B. 108.7", 113.1" (Sed); 3.5 Liter.						
E350 Sedan 4D	HF5GB	49475	17800	18600	19550	22900
E350 4MATIC Sedan	HF8HB	51975	18500	19300	20300	23700
E350 Coupe 2D	KJ5GB	48925	18700	19500	20500	24000
KEYLESS-GO			200	200	230	230
DISTRONIC Cruise Control			400	400	460	460
Driver Assistance Pkg			575	575	660	660
AMG Sport Pkg (Sedan)			775	775	890	890
E-CLASS—V8—Equipment Schedule 1						
W.B. 108.7", 113.1" (Sed); 5.5 Liter.						

Body Type	VIN	List	Trade-In Good	Very Good	Pvt-Party Good	Retail Excellent
E550 Sedan 4D	HF7CB	57175	21400	22300	23300	27200
E550 4MATIC Sedan	HF9AB	59675	24000	25000	26000	30400
E550 Coupe 2D	KJ7CB	55525	21000	21900	22800	26700
E63 Sedan 4D	HF7HB	88325	29800	30800	31600	35800
KEYLESS-GO			200	200	230	230
DISTRONIC Cruise Control			400	400	460	460
Driver Assistance Pkg			575	575	660	660
Premium Pkg 1			400	400	460	460
Premium Pkg 2			350	350	400	400
AMG Sport Pkg (E550)			775	775	890	890
Performance Pkg			3900	3900	4270	4270

CL-CLASS—V8—Equipment Schedule 1
W.B. 116.3"; 5.5 Liter.

Body Type	VIN	List	Trade-In Good	Very Good	Pvt-Party Good	Retail Excellent
CL550 4MATIC Coupe	EJ8GB	112575	30300	31300	32300	36800
DISTRONIC Cruise Control			400	400	450	450
designo Edition			850	850	960	960
Premium Pkg 2			350	350	395	395

CL-CLASS—V8—Equipment Schedule 1
W.B. 116.3"; 6.3 Liter.

Body Type	VIN	List	Trade-In Good	Very Good	Pvt-Party Good	Retail Excellent
CL63 Coupe 2D	EJ7HB	148675	44400	45900	47100	53800
DISTRONIC Cruise Control			400	400	455	455
Premium Pkg 2			350	350	400	400
designo Edition			850	850	970	970
Performance Pkg			3900	3900	4440	4440

CL-CLASS—V12—Equipment Schedule 1
W.B. 116.3"; 5.5 Liter, 6.0 Liter.

Body Type	VIN	List	Trade-In Good	Very Good	Pvt-Party Good	Retail Excellent
CL600 Coupe 2D	EJ7GB	158275	47300	48900	50100	57100
CL65 Coupe 2D	EJ7KB	211045	94000	97100	96400	104500
designo Edition			850	850	915	915

CLS-CLASS—V8—Equipment Schedule 1
W.B. 112.4"; 5.5 Liter, 6.3 Liter.

Body Type	VIN	List	Trade-In Good	Very Good	Pvt-Party Good	Retail Excellent
CLS550 Coupe 4D	DJ7CB	74575	22900	23800	24900	28700
CLS63 Coupe 4D	DJ7HB	101425	27200	28200	29000	33200
KEYLESS-GO			200	200	225	225
Adaptive Cruise Control			400	400	455	455
Sport Pkg Plus One			1750	1750	1990	1990
AMG Sport Pkg (CLS550)			1750	1750	1990	1990
Premium Pkg 1			400	400	450	450
designo Edition			850	850	965	965
Performance Pkg			3900	3900	4410	4410

S-CLASS—V6 Hybrid—Equipment Schedule 1
W.B. 124.6"; 3.5 Liter.

Body Type	VIN	List	Trade-In Good	Very Good	Pvt-Party Good	Retail Excellent
S400 Sedan 4D	NG9FB	88825	26400	27400	28600	32800
KEYLESS-GO			200	200	230	230
DISTRONIC PLUS			400	400	465	465
Driver Assistance Pkg			575	575	670	670
Premium Pkg 1			400	400	465	465
Premium Pkg 2			350	350	405	405
Sport Pkg Plus One			775	775	900	900
AMG Sport Pkg			1750	1750	2035	2035
designo Edition			850	850	985	985

S-CLASS—V8—Equipment Schedule 1
W.B. 124.6"; 5.5 Liter, 6.3 Liter.

Body Type	VIN	List	Trade-In Good	Very Good	Pvt-Party Good	Retail Excellent
S550 Sedan 4D	NG7BB	93475	29100	30200	31500	36200
S550 4MATIC Sedan	NG8GB	96475	30500	31600	32900	37800
KEYLESS-GO			200	200	230	230
DISTRONIC PLUS			400	400	465	465
Driver Assistance Pkg			575	575	670	670
Premium Pkg 2			350	350	405	405
Sport Pkg Plus One			775	775	900	900
AMG Sport Pkg			1750	1750	2035	2035
designo Edition			850	850	990	990

S-CLASS—V8—Equipment Schedule 1
W.B. 124.6"; 6.3 Liter.

Body Type	VIN	List	Trade-In Good	Very Good	Pvt-Party Good	Retail Excellent
S63 Sedan 4D	NG7HB	137425	36200	37500	38700	44600
KEYLESS-GO			200	200	230	230
DISTRONIC PLUS			400	400	460	460
Driver Assistance Pkg			575	575	660	660
designo Edition			850	850	980	980
Performance Pkg			3900	3900	4495	4495

S-CLASS—V12 Twin Turbo—Equipment Schedule 1
W.B. 124.6"; 5.5 Liter.

Body Type	VIN	List	Trade-In Good	Very Good	Pvt-Party Good	Retail Excellent
S600 Sedan 4D	NG7GB	153575	40400	41800	43500	50300

Body Type	VIN	List	Trade-In Good	Very Good	Pvt-Party Good	Retail Excellent
KEYLESS-GO			200	200	220	220
designo Edition			850	850	940	940
S-CLASS—V12 Twin Turbo—Equipment Schedule 1						
W.B. 124.6"; 6.0 Liter.						
S65 Sedan 4D	NG7KB	205025	54500	56300	57700	65700
designo Edition			850	850	935	935

2011 MERCEDES-BENZ — WDBorWDD(WK5EA)-B-#

SLK-CLASS—V6—Equipment Schedule 1
W.B. 95.7"; 3.0 Liter, 3.5 Liter.

Body Type	VIN	List	Good	Very Good	Good	Excellent
SLK300 Roadster 2D	WK5EA	48525	19750	20500	21700	25000
SLK350 Roadster 2D	WK5JA	54175	22800	23600	24800	28500
Multimedia Pkg			300	300	340	340
Sport Pkg			850	850	970	970
Premium Pkg 1			850	850	980	980
Manual, 6-Spd w/Overdrive	E		(500)	(500)	(570)	(570)

C-CLASS—V6—Equipment Schedule 1
W.B. 108.7"; 3.0 Liter.

Body Type	VIN	List	Good	Very Good	Good	Excellent
C300 Sport Sed 4D	GF5EB	34865	16600	17250	18300	21100
C300 Luxury Sedan 4D	GF5EB	36775	16300	16950	17950	20700
C300 Sport 4MATIC	GF8BB	38365	17150	17850	18900	21800
C300 Luxury 4MATIC	GF8BB	38775	16900	17550	18600	21500
KEYLESS-GO			200	200	235	235
Multimedia Pkg			300	300	350	350
Premium Pkg 1			450	450	525	525
Manual, 6-Spd Overdrive			(500)	(500)	(580)	(580)

C-CLASS—V6—Equipment Schedule 1
W.B. 108.7"; 3.5 Liter.

Body Type	VIN	List	Good	Very Good	Good	Excellent
C350 Sport Sedan 4D	GF5GB	40865	19200	19900	21000	24200
KEYLESS-GO			200	200	235	235
Multimedia Pkg			300	300	350	350

C-CLASS—V8—Equipment Schedule 1
W.B. 108.7"; 6.3 Liter.

Body Type	VIN	List	Good	Very Good	Good	Excellent
C63 AMG Sedan 4D	GF7HB	61175	32400	33500	34100	38300
KEYLESS-GO			200	200	225	225
Multimedia Pkg			300	300	335	335

E-CLASS—V6—Equipment Schedule 1
W.B. 108.7", 113.2" (Sed); 3.5 Liter.

Body Type	VIN	List	Good	Very Good	Good	Excellent
E350 Sedan 4D	HF5GB	50275	22800	23700	24400	27900
E350 4MATIC Sedan	HF8HB	52775	23300	24200	24900	28500
E350 Coupe 2D	KJ5GB	49725	23500	24400	25200	28800
E350 Convertible 2D	KK5GF	57725	28700	29800	30600	34900
E350 4MATIC Wagon	HH8HB	57075	26500	27500	28200	32200
KEYLESS-GO			200	200	225	225
DISTRONIC Cruise Control			425	425	480	480
Driver Assistance Pkg			600	600	680	680
Premium Pkg 1			450	450	510	510
Premium Pkg 2			375	375	420	420
AMG Sport Pkg			850	850	965	965

E-CLASS—V6 Turbo Diesel—Equipment Schedule 1
W.B. 113.2"; 3.0 Liter.

Body Type	VIN	List	Good	Very Good	Good	Excellent
E350 BlueTEC Sed 4D	HF2EB	51775	24900	25900	26700	30500
KEYLESS-GO			200	200	225	225
DISTRONIC Cruise Control			425	425	480	480
Driver Assistance Pkg			600	600	680	680
Premium Pkg 1			450	450	510	510
Premium Pkg 2			375	375	420	420
AMG Sport Pkg			850	850	965	965

E-CLASS—V8—Equipment Schedule 1
W.B. 108.7", 113.2" (Sed); 5.5 Liter, 6.3 Liter

Body Type	VIN	List	Good	Very Good	Good	Excellent
E550 Sedan 4D	HF7CB	57975	26200	27300	28000	32000
E550 4MATIC Sedan	HF9AB	60475	28800	30000	30700	35100
E550 Coupe 2D	KJ7CB	56325	25800	26900	27600	31600
E550 Convertible 2D	KK7CF	65675	34900	36200	37000	42100
E63 AMG Sedan 4D	HF7HB	88475	35900	37000	37700	42200
KEYLESS-GO			200	200	225	225
DISTRONIC Cruise Control			425	425	480	480
Premium Pkg 1			450	450	510	510
Premium Pkg 2			375	375	420	420
AMG Sport Pkg			850	850	965	965
Performance Pkg			3900	3900	4270	4270

CL-CLASS—V8 Twin Turbo—Equipment Schedule 1
W.B. 116.3"; 4.6 Liter, 5.5 Liter.

2011 MERCEDES-BENZ

Body Type	VIN	List	Trade-In Good	Very Good	Pvt-Party Good	Retail Excellent
CL550 4MATIC Cpe	EJ9EB	114025	42200	43600	44600	50300
CL63 Coupe 2D	EJ7EB	151125	57300	59100	60300	67800
DISTRONIC PLUS			425	425	480	480
Premium Pkg 2			375	375	420	420
Performance Pkg			3900	3900	4415	4415
designo Edition			875	875	990	990

CL-CLASS—V12 Twin Turbo—Equipment Schedule 1
W.B. 116.3"; 5.5 Liter, 6.0 Liter.

Body Type	VIN	List	Trade-In Good	Very Good	Pvt-Party Good	Retail Excellent
CL600 Coupe 2D	EJ7GB	157875	58900	60800	62300	70400
CL65 Coupe 2D	EJ7KB	210175	115800	119300	116300	126800
designo Edition			875	875	995	995

CLS-CLASS—V8 Twin Turbo—Equipment Schedule 1
W.B. 112.4"; 5.5 Liter, 6.3 Liter.

Body Type	VIN	List	Trade-In Good	Very Good	Pvt-Party Good	Retail Excellent
CLS550 Coupe 4D	DJ7CB	76175	27400	28400	29800	34200
CLS63 AMG Coupe 4D	DJ7HB	102525	30700	31700	33300	38400
KEYLESS-GO			200	200	230	230
Adaptive Cruise Control			425	425	490	490
Premium Pkg 1			450	450	520	520

S-CLASS—V6 Hybrid—Equipment Schedule 1
W.B. 124.6"; 3.5 Liter.

Body Type	VIN	List	Trade-In Good	Very Good	Pvt-Party Good	Retail Excellent
S400 Sedan 4D	NG9FB	91875	29400	30400	32000	36800
Bang & Olufsen BeoSound			2625	2625	3055	3055
KEYLESS-GO			200	200	235	235
DISTRONIC PLUS			425	425	495	495
Driver Assistance Pkg			600	600	700	700
Premium Pkg 2			375	375	430	430
Sport Pkg Plus One			850	850	990	990
Sport Pkg			1800	1800	2095	2095

S-CLASS—V8 Twin Turbo—Equipment Schedule 1
W.B. 124.6"; 5.5 Liter, 6.3 Liter.

Body Type	VIN	List	Trade-In Good	Very Good	Pvt-Party Good	Retail Excellent
S550 Sedan 4D	NG7BB	94525	32200	33300	35000	40100
S550 4MATIC Sedan	NG8GB	97525	33700	34800	36500	41800
S63 Sedan 4D	NG7EB	137875	49300	50900	52300	59200
Bang & Olufsen BeoSound			2625	2625	3055	3055
DISTRONIC PLUS			425	425	495	495
KEYLESS-GO			200	200	235	235
Driver Assistance Pkg			600	600	700	700
Sport Pkg Plus One			850	850	990	990
Premium Pkg 2			375	375	430	430
AMG Sport Pkg			1800	1800	2100	2100
Performance Pkg			3900	3900	4420	4420

S-CLASS—V12 Twin Turbo—Equipment Schedule 1
W.B. 124.6"; 5.5 Liter, 6.0 Liter.

Body Type	VIN	List	Trade-In Good	Very Good	Pvt-Party Good	Retail Excellent
S600 Sedan 4D	NG7GB	158925	64200	66200	66900	74700
S65 Sedan 4D	NG7KB	211975	78600	81100	81000	89900
DISTRONIC PLUS			425	425	460	460

SL-CLASS—V8—Equipment Schedule 1
W.B. 100.8"; 5.5 Liter, 6.3 Liter.

Body Type	VIN	List	Trade-In Good	Very Good	Pvt-Party Good	Retail Excellent
SL550 Roadster	SK7BA	104775	41900	43300	44100	49600
SL63 AMG Roadster	SK7AA	142525	47300	48800	49200	54600
KEYLESS-GO			200	200	225	225
Adaptive Cruise Control			425	425	475	475
designo Edition			875	875	980	980
Premium Pkg 1			875	875	975	975
Performance Pkg			3900	3900	4250	4250

SL-CLASS—V12 Twin Turbo—Equipment Schedule 1
W.B. 100.8"; 6.0 Liter.

Body Type	VIN	List	Trade-In Good	Very Good	Pvt-Party Good	Retail Excellent
SL65 Roadster 2D	SK7KA	202225	83100	85700	84900	93500
Adaptive Cruise Control			425	425	460	460

SLS-CLASS—V8—Equipment Schedule 1
W.B. 105.5"; 6.3 Liter.

Body Type	VIN	List	Trade-In Good	Very Good	Pvt-Party Good	Retail Excellent
AMG Coupe 2D	RJ7HA	187450	****	****	****	175100
Bang & Olufsen Sound			****	****	****	2645
Ceramic Brakes			****	****	****	3840

2012 MERCEDES-BENZ — WDBorWDD(PK4HA)-C-#

SLK-CLASS—4-Cyl. Turbo—Equipment Schedule 1
W.B. 95.7"; 1.8 Liter.

Body Type	VIN	List	Trade-In Good	Very Good	Pvt-Party Good	Retail Excellent
SLK250 Roadster 2D	PK4HA	43375	25200	26000	27100	30600
KEYLESS-GO			200	200	220	220
DISTRONIC PLUS			450	450	500	500
Multimedia Pkg			325	325	360	360
Premium Pkg 1			900	900	1000	1000

2012 MERCEDES-BENZ

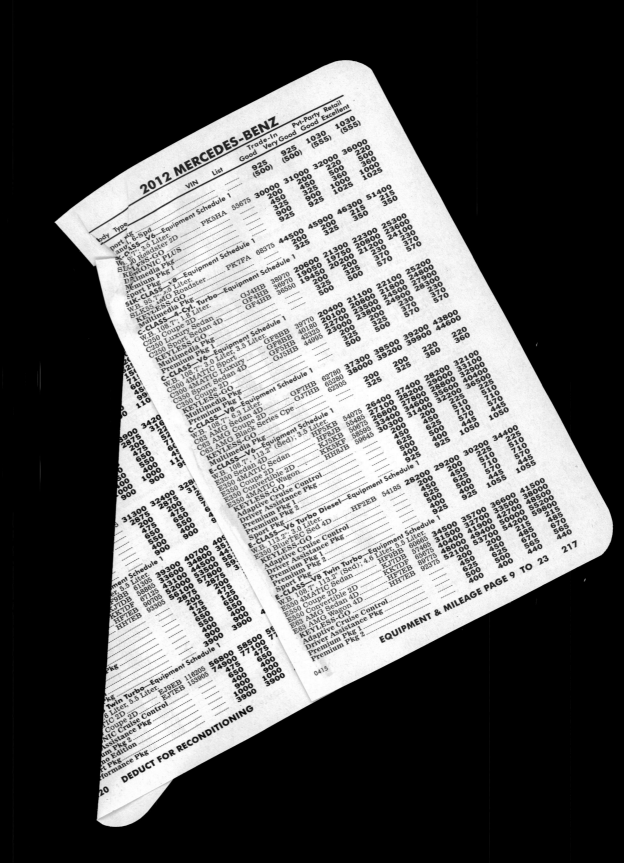

Body Type	VIN	List	Trade-In Good	Very Good	Pvt-Party Retail Good	Retail Excellent
			925 (500)	925 (500)	1030 (555)	1030 (555)
Sport Pkg						
SS-Spd						
C-CLASS—V6						
C-77; 3.3 Liter						
SLK 350 Roadster 2D	PK5HA	55675	30000	31000	32000	36000
KEYLESS-GO			200	200	220	220
AIRMATIC PLUS			450	450	360	360
Multimedia Pkg			325	900	1000	1025
Premium Pkg I			925	4590	46300	51400
SLK-CLASS—V8—Equipment Schedule 1	PK7FA	68375	44500	45900	46300	51400
3.9 Liter			200	200	215	215
SLK55 AMG Roadster			325	325	350	350
W.B. 95.7"; 5.4 Liter						
KEYLESS-GO						
Multimedia Pkg				44500	45900	25300
C-CLASS—4-Cyl. Turbo—Equipment Schedule 1			23000	22300	23600	
108.7"; 1.8 Liter			200	200	230	230
C250 Coupe 2D	PK7FA	68375	44500	21300	20800	24100
C250 Luxury Sedan			19750	20200	21200	370
C250 Sport Sedan 4D			325	200	370	570
KEYLESS-GO				500	570	
Multimedia Pkg	GJ4HB	38970	20600	21300	22100	25200
Premium Pkg I	GF4HB	36970	19050	20200	21400	24900
C-CLASS—V6—Equipment Schedule 1	GF4HB	36650	19650	20100	24500	28300
108.7"; 3.0 Liter, 3.5 Liter			200	325	370	570
C300 4MATIC Sport			500	500	570	
C300 4MATIC Luxury			20400	21100	22100	25200
C350 Sport Sedan 4D			20100	20800	24500	27900
C350 Coupe 2D	GF8BB	39770	22700	23800	24900	28300
C350 Coupe 2D	GF8BB	40180	23000	200	325	370
KEYLESS-GO	GF9HB	42525	500	500	570	
Multimedia Pkg	GJ5HB	44995	38500	39200	43800	44600
Premium Pkg I			23000	200	220	220
C-CLASS—V8			125	325	360	360
W.B. 108.7"; 6.3 Liter			500	500	570	
C63 AMG Sedan 4D	GF7HB	62780	37300	28000	28200	32100
C63 AMG Coupe 2D	GJ7HB	65280	38000	27100	28200	510
C63 AMG Black Series Cpe		62035		200	325	525
KEYLESS-GO			26400	27400	28800	36500
Multimedia Pkg			26100	27200	28600	225
E-CLASS—V6	GF7HB	54073	27600	28700	32225	710
W.B. 108.7"; 3.5 Liter		55485	26800	31400	450	445
E350 Sedan 4D	HF5KB	50875	30300	31400	450	1050
E350 4MATIC Sedan	KK5KB			625	570	710
E350 Coupe 2D	KK5KF	59645		400	1050	1055
E350 Convertible 2D	HH8JB			925		
E350 4MATIC Wagon			29200	30200	30400	34400
KEYLESS-GO			200	200	225	
Adaptive Cruise Control			450	450	570	710
Driver Assistance Pkg			500	500	443	1055
Premium Pkg 1			625	925	1055	
Premium Pkg 2			625			
Sport Pkg			500		41500	
E-CLASS—V6 Turbo Diesel—Equipment Schedule 1	HF2EB	54185	28200	29200	36600	38000
W.B. 113.2"; 3.0 Liter			625	500	42700	49500
E350 BlueTEC Sed 4D			35700	35500	485	
KEYLESS-GO			625	500	485	565
Adaptive Cruise Control	HF7DB	57465	34500	34400	41900	485
Driver Assistance Pkg	HF7DB	60665	40400	41900	54200	485
Premium Pkg 1	KK7DB	65675	48100	53200	625	565
Premium Pkg 2			450	200	625	565
E-CLASS—V8 Twin Turbo—Equipment Schedule 1	HF7EB	89775	48100	53200	485	565
W.B. 108.7"; 113.2" (Sed); 4.6 Liter, 5.5 Liter	HHTEB	92375	450	625	485	440
E550 Sedan 4D			400	500	625	440
E550 4MATIC Sedan				400	440	
E550 Coupe 2D						
E550 Convertible 2D						
E550 AMG Wagon 4D						
E63 AMG Sedan 4D						
KEYLESS-GO						
Adaptive Cruise Control						
Driver Assistance Pkg						
Premium Pkg 1						
Premium Pkg 2						

0415

DEDUCT FOR RECONDITIONING

Body Type	VIN	List	Trade-In Good	Very Good	Pvt Party Good	Retail Excellent
Performance Pkg			3900	3900	419.	415
CL-CLASS—V8 Twin Turbo—Equipment Schedule 1						
W.B. 116.3"; 4.6 Liter, 5.5 Liter.						
CL550 Coupe 2D	EJ9EB	115850	48200	49700	5130	
CL63 Coupe 2D	EJ7EB	153250	62100	64000	653	
DISTRONIC PLUS			450	450		
Driver Assistance Pkg			625	625		
Premium Pkg 2			400	400		
designo Edition			900	900		
Performance Pkg			3900	3900		
CL-CLASS—V12 Twin Turbo—Equipment Schedule 1						
W.B. 116.3"; 5.5 Liter, 6.0 Liter.						
CL600 Coupe 2D	EJ7EB	163050	64100	660		
CL65 Coupe 2D	EJ7KB	214850	134300	138		
designo Edition			900			
CLS-CLASS—V8 Twin Turbo—Equipment Schedule 1						
W.B. 113.2"; 4.6 Liter.						
CLS550 Coupe 4D	LJ7DB	72175	39200			
CLS550 4MATIC Cpe	LJ9BB	74675	41600			
KEYLESS-GO			20			
DISTRONIC PLUS			4			
Driver Assistance Pkg						
Premium Pkg 1						
designo Edition						
CLS-CLASS—V8—Equipment Schedule 1						
W.B. 113.2"; 5.5 Liter.						
CLS63 AMG Sedan 4D	LJ7EB	9577				
DISTRONIC PLUS						
Driver Assistance Pkg						
Premium Pkg 1						
designo Edition						
Performance Pkg						
S-CLASS—V6 Hybrid—Equipment Sc						
W.B. 124.6"; 3.5 Liter.						
S400 Sedan 4D	NG9F					
Bang & Olufsen BeoSound						
KEYLESS-GO						
DISTRONIC PLUS						
Driver Assistance Pkg						
designo Edition						
Premium Pkg 2						
Sport Pkg						
S-CLASS—V6 Turbo Dies						
W.B. 124.6"; 3.0 Liter.						
S350 BlueTec 4MATIC						
KEYLESS-GO						
DISTRONIC PLUS						
Driver Assistance Pkg						
designo Edition						
Premium Pkg 2						
Sport Pkg Plus One						
Sport Pkg						
S-CLASS—V8 Twin Turbo—Equi						
W.B. 124.6"; 5.5 Liter.						
S550 Sedan 4D	NG7DB					
S550 4MATIC Sedan	NG9EB	99				
Bang & Olufsen BeoSound						
KEYLESS-GO			45			
DISTRONIC PLUS			625	5		
Driver Assistance Pkg			900			
designo Edition			400	400		
Premium Pkg 2			925	925		
Sport Pkg Plus One			1850	1850	211	
Sport Pkg						
S-CLASS—V8 Twin Turbo—Equipment Schedule 1						
W.B. 124.6"; 6.3 Liter.						
S63 Sedan 4D	NG7EB	141050	55700	57500	58700	65
DISTRONIC PLUS			450	450	505	
Driver Assistance Pkg			625	625	700	
designo Edition			900	900	1005	
Performance Pkg			3900	3900	4360	
S-CLASS—V12 Twin Turbo—Equipment Schedule 1						
W.B. 124.6"; 5.5 Liter.						

Body Type	VIN	List	Trade-In Good	Very Good	Pvt-Party Good	Retail
Sport Pkg						
E-CLASS—V6—Equipment Schedule 1						
W.B. 108.7", 113.2"; 3.5 Liter.						
E350 Sedan 4D	HF5KB	53635				
E350 4MATIC Sed 4D	HF8KB	54405				
E350 Coupe 2D	KK5KB	52025				
E350 4MATIC Wagon	KK8KF	54525				
E350 4convertible Coupe	HH0JB	59975				
E350 4MATIC Sedan		58605				
Bang & Olufsen Sound						
KEYLESS-GO						
Appearance Pkg						
DISTRONIC PLUS						
Driver Assistance Pkg						
Premium Pkg 2						
designo Edition						
Sport Pkg Plus 2						
E-CLASS—V6 Turbo Diesel—Equipment Schedule 1						
W.B. 113.2"; 3.0 Liter.						
E350 BlueTec Sed 4D	HF2EB	54725				
KEYLESS-GO						
DISTRONIC PLUS						
Driver Assistance Pkg						
Premium Pkg 1						
Sport Pkg Plus 1						
designo Edition						
E-CLASS—V6 Hybrid—Equipment Schedule						
W.B. 113.2"; 3.5 Liter.						
E400 Sedan 4D	HF9FB	5832				
Bang & Olufsen Sound						
KEYLESS-GO						
DISTRONIC PLUS						
Driver Assistance Pkg						
Premium Pkg 1						
designo Edition						
E-CLASS—V8 Twin Turbo—Equip						
W.B. 108.7", 113.2" (Sed); 4.6 Li						
E550 Sedan 4D						
E550 4MATIC Sed 4D						
E550 Coupe 2D						
E550 Convertible 2D						
E63 AMG Sedan 4D						
Bang & Olufsen Sound						
KEYLESS-GO						
DISTRONIC PLUS						
Appearance Pkg						
Driver Assistance						
Premium Pkg 2						
designo Edition						
Performance Pkg						
CL-CLASS—V8 T						
W.B. 116.3"; 4.6						
CL550 Coupe						
CL63 AMG						
DISTRO						
Driver						
desig						

EQUIPMENT & MIL

2013 MERCEDES-BENZ

Body Type	VIN	List	Trade-In Good	Very Good	Pvt-Party Good	Retail Excellent

CL-CLASS—V12 Twin Turbo—Equipment Schedule 1
W.B. 116.3"; 5.5 Liter, 6.0 Liter.

CL600 Coupe 2D	EJ7GB	161205	73800	76000	76700	85000
CL65 AMG Coupe 2D	EJ7KB	214105	138700	142600	139300	150700
designo Edition			900	900	975	975

CLS-CLASS—V8 Twin Turbo—Equipment Schedule 1
W.B. 113.1"; 4.6 Liter, 5.5 Liter.

CLS550 Coupe 4D	LJ7DB	72905	44000	45300	46600	52400
CLS550 4MATIC Cpe	LJ9BB	75405	46100	47500	49300	55500
CLS63 AMG Coupe 4D	LJ7EB	96805	57000	58700	59200	65400
Bang & Olufsen Sound			2875	2875	3035	3035
KEYLESS-GO			200	200	210	210
DISTRONIC PLUS			475	475	500	500
Driver Assistance Pkg			650	650	685	685
Premium Pkg 1			550	550	580	580
designo Edition			900	900	950	950
Performance Pkg			3900	3900	4215	4215

S-CLASS—V6 Hybrid—Equipment Schedule 1
W.B. 124.6"; 3.5 Liter.

S400 Sedan 4D	NG9FB	93225	47200	48600	49900	56000
Bang & Olufsen BeoSound			2875	2875	3015	3015
DISTRONIC PLUS			475	475	500	500
Driver Assistance Pkg			650	650	680	680
Sport Pkg Plus One			1000	1000	1050	1050
Sport Pkg			1900	1900	1995	1995
designo Edition			900	900	945	945

S-CLASS BlueTEC—V6 Turbo Diesel—Equipment Schedule 1
W.B. 124.6"; 3.0 Liter.

S350 4MATIC 4D	NG8DB	93905	49100	50600	52100	58500
Bang & Olufsen BeoSound			2875	2875	3015	3015
DISTRONIC PLUS			475	475	500	500
Driver Assistance Pkg			650	650	680	680
Sport Pkg Plus One			1000	1000	1050	1050
Sport Pkg			1900	1900	1995	1995
designo Edition			900	900	945	945

S-CLASS—V8 Twin Turbo—Equipment Schedule 1
W.B. 124.6"; 4.6 Liter.

S550 Sedan 4D	NG7DB	95905	47400	48800	50200	56200
S550 4MATIC Sedan	NG9EB	98905	48900	50300	51800	57900
Bang & Olufsen BeoSound			2875	2875	3005	3005
DISTRONIC PLUS			475	475	495	495
Driver Assistance Pkg			650	650	680	680
Sport Pkg Plus One			1000	1000	1045	1045
Sport Pkg			1900	1900	1990	1990
designo Edition			900	900	940	940

S-CLASS—V8 Twin Turbo—Equipment Schedule 1
W.B. 124.6"; 5.5 Liter.

S63 Sedan 4D	NG7EB	140905	63000	64800	66400	74500
Bang & Olufsen BeoSound			2875	2875	3140	3140
DISTRONIC PLUS			475	475	520	520
Driver Assistance Pkg			650	650	710	710
designo Edition			900	900	985	985
Performance Pkg			3900	3900	4265	4265

S-CLASS—V12 Twin Turbo—Equipment Schedule 1
W.B. 124.6"; 5.5 Liter.

S600 Sedan 4D	NG7GB	163805	79800	82100	82600	91300
DISTRONIC PLUS			475	475	520	520
designo Edition			900	900	985	985

S-CLASS—V12 Twin Turbo—Equipment Schedule 1
W.B. 124.6"; 6.0 Liter.

| S65 Sedan 4D | NG7KB | 215005 | 93800 | 96400 | 96400 | 105800 |
| designo Edition | | | 900 | 900 | 980 | 980 |

SL-CLASS—V8 Twin Turbo—Equipment Schedule 1
W.B. 101.8"; 4.6 Liter, 5.5 Liter.

SL550 Roadster	JK7DA	106405	63000	64900	65300	72000
SL63 AMG Roadster	JK7EA	146705	88700	91300	89400	96500
KEYLESS-GO			200	200	220	220
Bang & Olufsen BeoSound			2875	2875	3140	3140
Adaptive Cruise Control			475	475	520	520
Driver Assistance Pkg			650	650	710	710
Premium Pkg			950	950	1010	1010
designo Edition			900	900	950	950

2013 MERCEDES-BENZ

Body Type	VIN	List	Trade-In Good	Very Good	Pvt-Party Good	Retail Excellent
SL-CLASS—V12 Twin Turbo—Equipment Schedule 1						
W.B. 101.8"; 6.0 Liter.						
SL65 AMG Roadster	JK7KA	214445	**117000**	**120300**	**118100**	**127900**
designo Edition			900	900	955	955
Premium Pkg			950	950	1015	1015
SLS-CLASS—V8 Twin Turbo—Equipment Schedule 1						
W.B. 105.5"; 6.3 Liter.						
AMG GT Coupe 2D	RJ7JA	202505	****	****	****	**190500**
AMG GT Convertible	RK7JA	209005	****	****	****	**195800**
Bang & Olufsen Sound			****	****	****	2900
Ceramic Brakes			****	****	****	4040

2014 MERCEDES-BENZ — WDBorWDD(PK4HA)-E-#

Body Type	VIN	List	Trade-In Good	Very Good	Pvt-Party Good	Retail Excellent
SLK-CLASS—4-Cyl. Turbo—Equipment Schedule 1						
W.B. 95.7"; 1.8 Liter.						
SLK250 Roadster 2D	PK4HA	44450	**33600**	**34700**	**35300**	**39200**
KEYLESS-GO			200	200	215	215
DISTRONIC PLUS			500	500	540	540
Driver Assistance Pkg			675	675	730	730
Premium Pkg 1			900	900	975	975
Multimedia Pkg			375	375	405	405
Sport Pkg			1050	1050	1140	1140
designo Edition			900	900	975	975
B-CLASS—Electric Drive—Equipment Schedule 1						
W.B. 106.3".						
Hatchback 4D	VP9AB	42375	**31500**	**31500**	**34300**	**36900**
Multimedia Pkg			375	375	425	425
Premium Pkg			575	575	650	650
CLA-CLASS—4-Cyl. Turbo—Equipment Schedule 1						
W.B. 106.3"; 2.0 Liter.						
CLA250 Coupe 4D	SJ4EB	30825	**25400**	**26200**	**26900**	**30200**
CLA250 4MATIC 4D	SJ4GB	32825	**27100**	**28000**	**28500**	**31900**
CLA45 AMG 4MATIC	SJ5CB	48375	**47400**	**49100**	**48000**	**52600**
Driver Assistance Pkg			675	675	745	745
Multimedia Pkg			375	375	415	415
Premium Pkg			575	575	635	635
Sport Pkg			1050	1050	1160	1160
C-CLASS—4-Cyl. Turbo—Equipment Schedule 1						
W.B. 108.7"; 1.8 Liter.						
C250 Sport Sedan 4D	GF4HB	36725	**22400**	**23200**	**24100**	**27200**
C250 Luxury Sedan	GF4HB	37175	**22200**	**23000**	**24000**	**27100**
C250 Coupe 2D	GJ4HB	39125	**25600**	**26700**	**27600**	**30900**
KEYLESS-GO			200	200	225	225
DISTRONIC PLUS			500	500	565	565
Multimedia Pkg			375	375	425	425
Premium Pkg 1			575	575	650	650
Sport Pkg			1050	1050	1185	1185
C-CLASS—V6—Equipment Schedule 1						
W.B. 108.7"; 3.5 Liter.						
C300 4MATIC Sport	GF8AB	40325	**25000**	**25800**	**26800**	**30100**
C300 4MATIC Luxury	GF8AB	40775	**24700**	**25500**	**26500**	**29800**
C350 Sport Sedan 4D	GF5HB	43025	**28200**	**29100**	**30100**	**33800**
C350 Coupe 2D	GJ5HB	44775	**29100**	**30100**	**31100**	**35000**
C350 4MATIC Cpe 2D	GJ8JB	46775	**30300**	**31300**	**32300**	**36300**
KEYLESS-GO			200	200	225	225
Full Leather			525	525	590	590
DISTRONIC PLUS			500	500	560	560
Driver Assistance Pkg			675	675	760	760
Multimedia Pkg			375	375	420	420
Premium Pkg 1			575	575	650	650
Sport Pkg			1050	1050	1180	1180
C-CLASS—V8—Equipment Schedule 1						
W.B. 108.9"; 6.3 Liter.						
C63 AMG Sedan 4D	GF7HB	62875	**46100**	**46300**	**48800**	**52300**
C63 AMG Coupe 2D	GJ7HB	65375	**49200**	**49400**	**52000**	**55600**
C63 AMG Ed 507 Sed	GF7HB	72625				
C63 AMG Ed 507 Cpe	GJ7HB	75125				
KEYLESS-GO			200	200	220	220
DISTRONIC PLUS			500	500	550	550
Driver Assistance Pkg			675	675	740	740
Multimedia Pkg			375	375	410	410
E-CLASS—BlueTEC—4-Cyl. Turbo Diesel—Equipment Schedule 1						
W.B. 113.2"; 2.1 Liter.						

0415

2014 MERCEDES-BENZ

Body	Type	VIN	List	Trade-In Good	Trade-In Very Good	Pvt-Party Good	Retail Excellent
E250 Sedan 4D		HF0EB	52305	38800	40100	40100	44200
E250 4MATIC Sedan		HF9HB	54805	40000	41400	41200	45400
KEYLESS-GO				200	200	215	215
Bang & Olufsen Sound		....	3000	3000	3245	3245
Premium Pkg		....	575	575	620	620
Sport Pkg		....	1050	1050	1135	1135
designo Edition		....	900	900	975	975

E-CLASS—V6—Equipment Schedule 1
W.B. 108.7"; 113.2" (Sed); 3.5 Liter.

E350 Sedan 4D		HF5KB	52805	35400	36600	37100	41400
E350 4MATIC Sedan		HF8JB	55405	36700	38000	38400	42800
E350 Coupe 2D		KJ5KB	53105	36400	37600	37600	41500
E350 4MATIC 2D		KJ8JB	55605	37900	39200	39100	43200
E350 Cabriolet 2D		KK5KF	61105	43100	44500	44300	48800
E350 4MATIC Wagon		HH8JB	59505	46300	47900	47600	52500
KEYLESS-GO				200	200	220	220
Bang & Olufsen Sound		....	3000	3000	3270	3270
DISTRONIC PLUS		....	500	500	545	545
Driver Assistance Pkg		....	675	675	735	735
Premium Pkg 1		....	575	575	625	625
Sport Pkg		....	1050	1050	1145	1145
designo Edition		....	900	900	980	980

E-CLASS—V6 Hybrid—Equipment Schedule 1
W.B. 113.2"; 3.5 Liter.

E400 Sedan 4D		HF9FB	57605	37100	38400	38400	42500
KEYLESS-GO				200	200	220	220
Bang & Olufsen Sound		....	3000	3000	3280	3280
DISTRONIC PLUS		....	500	500	545	545
Premium Pkg		....	575	575	630	630

E-CLASS—V8 Twin Turbo—Equipment Schedule 1
W.B. 108.7", 113.2" (Sed); 4.6 Liter, 5.5 Liter.

E550 4MATIC Sedan		HF9BB	62305	45400	46900	46700	51500
E550 Coupe 2D		KJ7DB	59905	39600	41000	40900	45100
E550 Cabriolet 2D		KK7DF	68205	49500	51200	51100	56300
E63 AMG 4MATIC Sed		HF9CB	93675	61900	63700	64900	72200
KEYLESS-GO				200	200	220	220
Bang & Olufsen Sound		....	3000	3000	3270	3270
DISTRONIC PLUS		....	500	500	545	545
designo Edition		....	900	900	960	960
Sport Pkg		....	1050	1050	1145	1145
Premium Pkg		....	575	575	625	625
Driver Assistance Pkg		....	675	675	735	735

CLS-CLASS—V8 Twin Turbo—Equipment Schedule 1
W.B. 113.1"; 4.6 Liter, 5.5 Liter.

CLS550 Coupe 4D		LJ7DB	73025	50200	51700	52900	58900
CLS550 4MATIC Cpe		LJ9BB	75525	52700	54300	55600	62000
CLS63 AMG 4MATIC		LJ9CB	100425				
CLS63 AMG S 4MATIC		LJ7GB	107425				
KEYLESS-GO				200	200	210	210
Bang & Olufsen Sound		....	3000	3000	3165	3165
DISTRONIC PLUS		....	500	500	525	525
Driver Assistance Pkg		....	675	675	710	710
designo Edition		....	900	900	950	950
Premium Pkg 1		....	575	575	605	605
Performance Pkg		....				

S-CLASS—V8 Twin Turbo—Equipment Schedule 1
W.B. 124.6"; 4.6 Liter, 5.5 Liter.

S550 Sedan 4D		UG8CB	93825	74100	76200	75600	82400
S550 4MATIC Sedan		UG8FB	96825	76900	79100	78300	85300
S63 AMG Sedan 4D		UG7JB	140425	100100	103000	102500	112100
DISTRONIC PLUS		....	500	500	515	515
Driver Assistance Pkg		....	675	675	700	700
designo Edition		....	900	900	930	930
Sport Pkg Plus One		....	1050	1050	1090	1090
Sport Pkg		....	1950	1950	2020	2020
Premium 1 Pkg		....	575	575	595	595

SL-CLASS—V8 Twin Turbo—Equipment Schedule 1
W.B. 101.8"; 4.6 Liter.

SL550 Roadster 2D		JK7DA	107605	72600	74700	75200	82900
Bang & Olufsen BeoSound		....	3000	3000	3285	3285
DISTRONIC PLUS		....	500	500	545	545
Driver Assistance Pkg		....	675	675	740	740
designo Edition		....	900	900	985	985

Body Type	VIN	List	Trade-In Good	Very Good	Pvt-Party Good	Retail Excellent

MERCURY

2000 MERCURY — (1,2or3)(MEorZW)–(M653)–Y–#

MYSTIQUE—4-Cyl.—Equipment Schedule 5
W.B. 106.5"; 2.0 Liter.
| GS Sedan 4D | M653 | 17495 | 800 | 900 | 1525 | 2625 |

MYSTIQUE—V6—Equipment Schedule 5
W.B. 106.5"; 2.5 Liter.
| LS Sedan 4D | M66L | 18795 | 1075 | 1200 | 1875 | 3175 |

SABLE—V6—Equipment Schedule 4
W.B. 108.5"; 3.0 Liter.
GS Sedan 4D	M50U	19395	700	800	1400	2425
GS Wagon 4D	M58U	21195	950	1075	1725	2950
LS Sedan 4D	M53U	20495	875	975	1600	2750
V6, 24V, 3.0 Liter	S		100	100	135	135

SABLE—V6 24V—Equipment Schedule 4
W.B. 108.5"; 3.0 Liter.
| LS Premium Sedan 4D | M55S | 21795 | 1025 | 1175 | 1825 | 3125 |
| LS Premium Wagon 4D | M59S | 22895 | 1125 | 1275 | 1975 | 3350 |

COUGAR—V6—Equipment Schedule 4
W.B. 106.4"; 2.5 Liter.
Coupe 2D	T61L	18880	700	800	1275	2125
Manual, 5-Spd			(125)	(125)	(160)	(160)
4-Cyl, 2.0 Liter	3		(200)	(200)	(250)	(250)

GRAND MARQUIS—V8—Equipment Schedule 4
W.B. 114.7"; 4.6 Liter.
| GS Sedan 4D | M74W | 23020 | 600 | 700 | 1350 | 2425 |
| LS Sedan 4D | M75W | 24920 | 825 | 950 | 1675 | 2925 |

2001 MERCURY — (1or2)(MEorZW)–(M50U)–1–#

SABLE—V6—Equipment Schedule 4
W.B. 108.5"; 3.0 Liter.
GS Sedan 4D	M50U	19785	800	900	1500	2600
GS Wagon 4D	M58U	21585	1125	1250	1925	3275
LS Sedan 4D	M53U	20885	1050	1175	1825	3100
V6, 24V, 3.0 Liter	S		100	100	135	135

SABLE—V6 24V—Equipment Schedule 4
W.B. 108.5"; 3.0 Liter.
| LS Premium Sedan 4D | M55S | 22185 | 1200 | 1350 | 2025 | 3450 |
| LS Premium Wagon 4D | M59S | 23285 | 1225 | 1375 | 2050 | 3500 |

COUGAR—V6—Equipment Schedule 4
W.B. 106.4"; 2.5 Liter.
Coupe 2D	T61L	18545	800	900	1425	2375
C2 Coupe 2D	T61L	20660	1125	1250	1825	2975
Zn Coupe 2D	T61L	21645	1225	1350	1950	3200
Manual, 5-Spd			(175)	(175)	(235)	(235)
4-Cyl, 2.0 Liter	3		(225)	(225)	(285)	(285)

GRAND MARQUIS—V8—Equipment Schedule 4
W.B. 114.7"; 4.6 Liter.
| GS Sedan 4D | M74W | 23460 | 650 | 750 | 1400 | 2500 |
| LS Sedan 4D | M75W | 25360 | 900 | 1025 | 1700 | 2975 |

2002 MERCURY — (1or2)(MEorZW)–(M50U)–2–#

SABLE—V6—Equipment Schedule 4
W.B. 108.5"; 3.0 Liter.
| GS Sedan 4D | M50U | 20255 | 900 | 1025 | 1625 | 2750 |
| GS Wagon 4D | M58U | 21665 | 1275 | 1425 | 2100 | 3550 |

SABLE—V6 24V—Equipment Schedule 4
W.B. 108.5"; 3.0 Liter.
| LS Premium Sedan 4D | M55S | 22680 | 1350 | 1500 | 2225 | 3725 |
| LS Premium Wagon 4D | M59S | 23845 | 1375 | 1550 | 2250 | 3775 |

COUGAR—V6—Equipment Schedule 4
W.B. 106.4"; 2.5 Liter.
Coupe 2D	T61L	18490	1000	1125	1625	2600
Sport Coupe 2D	T61L	18990	1150	1275	1800	2875
C2 Coupe 2D	T61L	19505	1250	1375	1925	3100
Xr Coupe 2D	T61L	19940	1300	1450	1975	3150
Manual, 5-Spd			(175)	(175)	(240)	(240)
4-Cyl, 2.0 Liter	3		(250)	(250)	(325)	(325)
35th Anniversary			50	50	65	65

2002 MERCURY

Body Type	VIN	List	Trade-In Good	Very Good	Pvt-Party Good	Retail Excellent
GRAND MARQUIS—V8—Equipment Schedule 4						
W.B. 114.7"; 4.6 Liter.						
GS Sedan 4D	M74W	24325	875	1000	1650	2875
LS Sedan 4D	M75W	27800	1175	1325	2025	3475
LSE Sedan 4D	M75W	29305	1400	1575	2325	3925

2003 MERCURY — (1or2)ME—(M50U)-3-#

SABLE—V6—Equipment Schedule 4						
W.B. 108.5"; 3.0 Liter.						
GS Sedan 4D	M50U	20770	1325	1500	2300	3900
GS Wagon 4D	M58U	22180	1650	1850	2850	4750
SABLE—V6 24V—Equipment Schedule 4						
W.B. 108.5"; 3.0 Liter.						
LS Premium Sedan 4D	M55S	23145	1700	1900	2850	4800
LS Premium Wagon 4D	M59S	24310	1675	1875	2925	4925
GRAND MARQUIS—V8—Equipment Schedule 4						
W.B. 114.7"; 4.6 Liter.						
GS Sedan 4D	M74W	24875	1275	1425	2150	3675
LS Sedan 4D	M75W	28605	1475	1675	2525	4250
LSE Sedan 4D	M75W	30110	1775	2000	2900	4800
Limited Edition			350	350	475	475
MARAUDER—V8—Equipment Schedule 2						
W.B. 114.7"; 4.6 Liter.						
Sedan 4D	M75V	34495	3525	3925	4750	7150

2004 MERCURY — (1or2)ME—(M50U)-4-#

SABLE—V6—Equipment Schedule 4						
W.B. 108.5"; 3.0 Liter.						
GS Sedan 4D	M50U	21595	1525	1700	2500	4175
GS Wagon 4D	M58U	22595	1875	2075	3075	5050
SABLE—V6 24V—Equipment Schedule 4						
W.B. 108.5"; 3.0 Liter.						
LS Premium Sedan 4D	M55S	23895	1950	2175	3225	5275
LS Premium Wagon 4D	M59S	24795	1950	2175	3250	5350
GRAND MARQUIS—V8—Equipment Schedule 4						
W.B. 114.7"; 4.6 Liter.						
GS Sedan 4D	M74W	24695	1650	1875	2650	4275
LS Sedan 4D	M75W	29595	1950	2200	3100	5025
Limited Edition			375	375	510	510
MARAUDER—V8—Equipment Schedule 2						
W.B. 114.7"; 4.6 Liter.						
Sedan 4D	M79V	34495	5450	6000	7100	10100

2005 MERCURY — (1or2)ME—(M50U)-5-#

SABLE—V6—Equipment Schedule 4						
W.B. 108.5"; 3.0 Liter.						
GS Sedan 4D	M50U	21525	1825	2050	3200	5175
SABLE—V6 24V—Equipment Schedule 4						
W.B. 108.5"; 3.0 Liter.						
LS Sedan 4D	M55S	24490	2000	2225	3425	5500
LS Wagon 4D	M59S	25800	2100	2350	3550	5675
MONTEGO—V6—Equipment Schedule 4						
W.B. 112.9"; 3.0 Liter.						
Luxury Sedan 4D	M401	24995	2325	2600	3550	5400
Premier Sedan 4D	M421	27195	2550	2850	3725	5575
AWD			500	500	665	665
GRAND MARQUIS—V8—Equipment Schedule 4						
W.B. 114.7"; 4.6 Liter.						
GS Sedan 4D	M74W	25095	2050	2300	3150	4800
LS Sedan 4D	M75W	30150	2575	2900	3700	5500
LSE Sedan 4D	M75W	30620	2725	3050	3875	5750

2006 MERCURY — (1,2or3)ME—(M07Z)-6-#

MILAN—4-Cyl.—Equipment Schedule 4						
W.B. 107.4"; 2.3 Liter.						
Sedan 4D	M07Z	19820	3075	3375	4425	6375
Premier Sedan 4D	M08Z	21715	3450	3775	4875	6975
Manual, 5-Spd			(400)	(400)	(535)	(535)
V6, 3.0 Liter	1		575	575	770	770
MONTEGO—V6—Equipment Schedule 4						
W.B. 112.9"; 3.0 Liter.						
Luxury Sedan 4D	M401	25130	2850	3200	4100	5900

2006 MERCURY

Body Type	VIN	List	Trade-In Good	Very Good	Pvt-Party Good	Retail Excellent
Premier Sedan 4D	M421	27580	3250	3600	4575	6600
AWD			550	550	720	720
GRAND MARQUIS—V8—Equipment Schedule 4						
W.B. 114.7"; 4.6 Liter.						
GS Sedan 4D	M74W	25555	2975	3300	4000	5725
LS Sedan 4D	M75V	30840	3300	3675	4375	6250
Limited Edition			450	450	590	590

2007 MERCURY—(1,2or3)ME-(M07Z)-7-#

Body Type	VIN	List	Trade-In Good	Very Good	Pvt-Party Good	Retail Excellent
MILAN—4-Cyl.—Equipment Schedule 4						
W.B. 107.4"; 2.3 Liter.						
Sedan 4D	M07Z	22465	3750	4100	5175	7250
Premier Sedan 4D	M08Z	23995	4100	4475	5575	7775
AWD			775	775	1025	1025
Manual, 5-Spd			(425)	(425)	(565)	(565)
V6, 3.0 Liter	1		625	625	815	815
MONTEGO—V6—Equipment Schedule 4						
W.B. 112.9"; 3.0 Liter.						
Sedan 4D	M401	24220	3925	4300	5225	7300
Premier Sedan 4D	M421	27995	4125	4500	5600	7950
AWD			575	575	775	775
GRAND MARQUIS—V8—Equipment Schedule 4						
W.B. 114.6"; 4.6 Liter.						
GS Sedan 4D	M74V	25660	3700	4075	4800	6600
LS Sedan 4D	M75V	30320	4075	4475	5225	7175
Palm Beach Edition			375	375	510	510

2008 MERCURY — (1,2or3)ME-(M07Z)-8-#

Body Type	VIN	List	Trade-In Good	Very Good	Pvt-Party Good	Retail Excellent
MILAN—4-Cyl.—Equipment Schedule 4						
W.B. 107.4"; 2.3 Liter.						
Sedan 4D	M07Z	20325	4600	4950	5950	7975
Premier Sedan 4D	M08Z	22020	5225	5600	6625	8850
AWD			825	825	1100	1100
Manual, 5-Spd w/Overdrive			(450)	(450)	(600)	(600)
V6, 3.0 Liter	1		650	650	860	860
SABLE—V6—Equipment Schedule 4						
W.B. 112.9"; 3.5 Liter.						
Sedan 4D	M40W	24290	5000	5375	6350	8500
Premier Sedan 4D	M42W	28080	5225	5625	6650	8925
AWD			1250	1250	1675	1675
GRAND MARQUIS—V8—Equipment Schedule 4						
W.B. 114.6"; 4.6 Liter.						
GS Sedan 4D	M74V	25830	4875	5275	5875	7675
LS Sedan 4D	M75V	28720	5075	5500	6200	8175
Palm Beach Edition			400	400	535	535

2009 MERCURY — (1,2or3)ME-(M07Z)-9-#

Body Type	VIN	List	Trade-In Good	Very Good	Pvt-Party Good	Retail Excellent
MILAN—4-Cyl.—Equipment Schedule 4						
W.B. 107.4"; 2.3 Liter.						
Sedan 4D	M07Z	20910	5675	6050	7225	9375
Premier Sedan 4D	M08Z	23160	6550	6975	8200	10550
AWD			875	875	1175	1175
Manual, 5-Spd w/Overdrive			(500)	(500)	(665)	(665)
V6, 3.0 Liter			675	675	905	905
SABLE—V6—Equipment Schedule 4						
W.B. 112.9"; 3.5 Liter.						
Sedan 4D	M40W	25250	7175	7625	8675	10950
Premier Sedan 4D	M42W	29510	7275	7725	8850	11250
AWD			1350	1350	1795	1795
GRAND MARQUIS—V8—Equipment Schedule 4						
W.B. 114.6"; 4.6 Liter.						
LS Sedan 4D	M75V	29585	7400	7900	8800	11050

2010 MERCURY — (2or3)ME-(M0HA)-A-#

Body Type	VIN	List	Trade-In Good	Very Good	Pvt-Party Good	Retail Excellent
MILAN—4-Cyl.—Equipment Schedule 4						
W.B. 107.4"; 2.5 Liter.						
Sedan 4D	M0HA	21905	7125	7525	8775	11100
MILAN—4-Cyl. Hybrid—Equipment Schedule 4						
W.B. 107.4"; 2.5 Liter.						
Sedan 4D	M0L3	28225	10350	10850	11800	14150
MILAN—V6 Flex Fuel—Equipment Schedule 4						
W.B. 107.4"; 3.0 Liter.						

0415

Body Type	VIN	List	Trade-In Good	Very Good	Pvt-Party Good	Retail Excellent
Premier Sedan 4D	M0JA	26675	7800	8250	9600	12150
AWD	C		1000	1000	1335	1335
4-Cyl, 2.5 Liter	A		(625)	(625)	(845)	(845)
GRAND MARQUIS—V8—Equipment Schedule 4						
W.B. 114.6"; 4.6 Liter.						
LS Sedan 4D	M7FV	30285	9675	10250	11150	13650

2011 MERCURY — (2or3)ME–(M0HA)–B–#

MILAN—4-Cyl.—Equipment Schedule 4						
W.B. 107.4"; 2.5 Liter.						
Sedan 4D	M0HA	22750	8550	9000	10400	13000
MILAN—4-Cyl. Hybrid—Equipment Schedule 4						
W.B. 107.4"; 2.5 Liter.						
Sedan 4D	M0L3	29070	11600	12150	13100	15500
MILAN—V6 Flex Fuel—Equipment Schedule 4						
W.B. 107.4"; 3.0 Liter.						
Premier Sedan 4D	M0JA	25890	9275	9750	11300	14050
AWD	C		675	675	860	860
4-Cyl, 2.5 Liter	A		(675)	(675)	(875)	(875)
GRAND MARQUIS—V8—Equipment Schedule 4						
W.B. 114.6"; 4.6 Liter.						
LS Sedan 4D	M7FV	30810	11850	12450	13500	16250

MINI

2002 MINI — (WMW(RC334)–2–#

COOPER—4-Cyl.—Equipment Schedule 3						
W.B. 97.1"; 1.6 Liter.						
Hatchback 2D	RC334	16850	1975	2200	3050	4800
Sport Pkg			225	225	305	305
COOPER—4-Cyl. Supercharged—Equipment Schedule 3						
W.B. 97.1"; 1.6 Liter.						
S Hatchback 2D	RE334	19850	1950	2125	3025	4675
Sport Pkg			225	225	305	305
John Cooper Works			1300	1300	1735	1735

2003 MINI — WMW(RC334)–3–#

COOPER—4-Cyl.—Equipment Schedule 3						
W.B. 97.1"; 1.6 Liter.						
Hatchback 2D	RC334	18575	2500	2775	3525	5325
Sport Pkg			250	250	335	335
COOPER—4-Cyl. Supercharged—Equipment Schedule 3						
W.B. 97.1"; 1.6 Liter.						
S Hatchback 2D	RE334	20325	2900	3175	4025	5875
Sport Pkg			250	250	335	335
John Cooper Works			1425	1425	1885	1885

2004 MINI — WMW(RC334)–4–#

COOPER—4-Cyl.—Equipment Schedule 3						
W.B. 97.1"; 1.6 Liter.						
Hatchback 2D	RC334	18299	2825	3125	3875	5750
Sport Pkg			275	275	355	355
COOPER—4-Cyl. Supercharged—Equipment Schedule 3						
W.B. 97.1"; 1.6 Liter.						
S Hatchback 2D	RE334	19999	3375	3650	4425	6250
Sport Pkg			275	275	355	355
MC40 Pkg			1250	1250	1665	1665
John Cooper Works			1525	1525	2040	2040

2005 MINI — WMW(RC334)–5–#

COOPER—4-Cyl.—Equipment Schedule 3						
W.B. 97.1"; 1.6 Liter.						
Hatchback 2D	RC334	18299	2975	3300	4175	6050
Sport Pkg			275	275	380	380
COOPER CONVERTIBLE—4-Cyl.—Equipment Schedule 3						
W.B. 97.1"; 1.6 Liter.						
Convertible 2D	RF334	22800	3225	3575	4550	6625
Sport Pkg			275	275	380	380
COOPER—4-Cyl. Supercharged—Equipment Schedule 3						
W.B. 97.1"; 1.6 Liter.						

Body Type	VIN	List	Trade-In Good	Very Good	Pvt-Party Good	Retail Excellent
S Hatchback 2D	RE334	20449	3500	3775	4800	6650
Sport Pkg			275	275	380	380
John Cooper Works			1650	1650	2195	2195
COOPER CONVERTIBLE—4-Cyl. Supercharged—Equipment Schedule 3						
W.B. 97.1"; 1.6 Liter.						
S Convertible 2D	RH334	24950	3975	4300	5550	7775
Sport Pkg			275	275	380	380
John Cooper Works			1650	1650	2195	2195

2006 MINI — WMW(RC335)-6-#

Body Type	VIN	List	Trade-In Good	Very Good	Pvt-Party Good	Retail Excellent
COOPER—4-Cyl.—Equipment Schedule 3						
W.B. 97.1"; 1.6 Liter.						
Hatchback 2D	RC335	18800	3475	3825	4750	6700
Sport Pkg			300	300	405	405
Checkmate Pkg			450	450	590	590
COOPER CONVERTIBLE—4-Cyl.—Equipment Schedule 3						
W.B. 97.1"; 1.6 Liter.						
Convertible 2D	RF335	23300	3775	4150	5175	7275
Sport Pkg			300	300	405	405
COOPER—4-Cyl. Supercharged—Equipment Schedule 3						
W.B. 97.1"; 1.6 Liter.						
S Hatchback 2D	RE335	22500	3900	4200	5225	7075
S GP Hatchback 2D	RE935	31150	****	****	****	15850
Sport Pkg			300	300	405	405
Checkmate Pkg			450	450	590	590
John Cooper Works (ex GP)			1750	1750	2345	2345
COOPER CONVERTIBLE—4-Cyl. Supercharged—Equipment Schedule 3						
W.B. 97.1"; 1.6 Liter.						
S Convertible 2D	RH335	26800	4625	4950	6100	8300
Sport Pkg			300	300	405	405
John Cooper Works			1750	1750	2345	2345

2007 MINI — WMW(MF335)-7-#

Body Type	VIN	List	Trade-In Good	Very Good	Pvt-Party Good	Retail Excellent
COOPER—4-Cyl.—Equipment Schedule 3						
W.B. 97.1"; 1.6 Liter.						
Hatchback 2D	MF335	20050	4200	4575	5500	7475
Sport Pkg			325	325	435	435
COOPER—4-Cyl. Turbo—Equipment Schedule 3						
W.B. 97.1"; 1.6 Liter.						
S Hatchback 2D	MF735	23200	4925	5275	6250	8225
Sport Pkg			325	325	435	435
COOPER CONVERTIBLE—4-Cyl.—Equipment Schedule 3						
W.B. 97.1"; 1.6 Liter.						
Convertible 2D	RF335	23900	4525	4900	5900	8025
Sport Pkg			325	325	435	435
COOPER CONVERTIBLE—4-Cyl. Turbo—Equipment Schedule 3						
W.B. 97.1"; 1.6 Liter.						
S Convertible 2D	RH335	27400	5450	5825	7375	9875
Sport Pkg			325	325	435	435
John Cooper Works			1875	1875	2500	2500

2008 MINI — WMW(MF335)-8-#

Body Type	VIN	List	Trade-In Good	Very Good	Pvt-Party Good	Retail Excellent
COOPER—4-Cyl.—Equipment Schedule 3						
W.B. 97.1"; 1.6 Liter.						
Hatchback 2D	MF335	19950	5250	5650	6525	8550
Sport Pkg			350	350	465	465
John Cooper Works			2000	2000	2665	2665
COOPER—4-Cyl. Turbo—Equipment Schedule 3						
W.B. 97.1"; 1.6 Liter.						
S Hatchback 2D	MF735	23100	5875	6250	7300	9225
Sport Pkg			350	350	465	465
John Cooper Works			2000	2000	2665	2665
COOPER CONVERTIBLE—4-Cyl.—Equipment Schedule 3						
W.B. 97.1"; 1.6 Liter.						
Convertible 2D	RF335	23850	5350	5750	6875	9025
Sport Pkg			350	350	465	465
COOPER CONVERTIBLE—4-Cyl. Turbo—Equipment Schedule 3						
W.B. 97.1"; 1.6 Liter.						
S Convertible 2D	RH335	27300	6625	7025	8250	10500
Sport Pkg			350	350	465	465
John Cooper Works			2000	2000	2665	2665

2008 MINI

Body Type	VIN	List	Trade-In Good	Very Good	Pvt-Party Good	Retail Excellent
COOPER CLUBMAN—4-Cyl.—Equipment Schedule 3						
W.B. 100.4"; 1.6 Liter						
Hatchback 2D	ML335	21850	**6500**	**6900**	**8025**	**10200**
Sport Pkg		------	350	350	465	465
John Cooper Works		------	2000	2000	2665	2665
COOPER CLUBMAN—4-Cyl. Turbo—Equipment Schedule 3						
W.B. 100.4"; 1.6 Liter						
S Hatchback 2D	MM335	25350	**6250**	**6625**	**7625**	**9500**
Sport Pkg		------	350	350	450	450
John Cooper Works		------	2000	2000	2560	2560

2009 MINI — WMW(MF335)-9-#

Body Type	VIN	List	Trade-In Good	Very Good	Pvt-Party Good	Retail Excellent
COOPER HARDTOP—4-Cyl.—Equipment Schedule 3						
W.B. 97.1" 1.6 Liter						
Hatchback 2D	MF335	20450	**6175**	**6575**	**7600**	**9650**
Sport Pkg		------	400	400	535	535
COOPER HARDTOP—4-Cyl. Turbo—Equipment Schedule 3						
W.B. 97.1"; 1.6 Liter						
S Hatchback 2D	MF735	22600	**6975**	**7350**	**8375**	**10350**
Sport Pkg		------	400	400	520	520
COOPER CONVERTIBLE—4-Cyl.—Equipment Schedule 3						
W.B. 97.1" 1.6 Liter						
Convertible 2D	MR335	25800	**7075**	**7500**	**8525**	**10750**
Sport Pkg		------	400	400	530	530
COOPER CONVERTIBLE—4-Cyl. Turbo—Equipment Schedule 3						
W.B. 97.1"; 1.6 Liter						
S Convertible 2D	MS335	27450	**8150**	**8575**	**9675**	**11850**
Sport Pkg		------	400	400	510	510
COOPER CLUBMAN—4-Cyl.—Equipment Schedule 3						
W.B. 100.4". 1.6 Liter						
Hatchback 2D	ML335	22100	**6925**	**7325**	**8475**	**10600**
Sport Pkg		------	400	400	520	520
COOPER CLUBMAN—4-Cyl. Turbo—Equipment Schedule 3						
W.B. 100.4"; 1.6 Liter						
S Hatchback 2D	MM335	25600	**7675**	**8075**	**9225**	**11350**
Sport Pkg		------	400	400	500	500
JOHN COOPER WORKS HARDTOP—4-Cyl. Turbo—Equipment Schedule 3						
W.B. 97.1"; 1.6 Liter						
Hatchback 2D	MF935	29200	**9950**	**10400**	**11650**	**14150**
JOHN COOPER WORKS CONVERTIBLE—4-Cyl. Turbo—Equip Sch 3						
W.B. 97.1"; 1.6 Liter						
Convertible 2D	MS935	34950	**13100**	**13700**	**15300**	**18550**
JOHN COOPER WORKS CLUBMAN—4-Cyl. Turbo—Equipment Sch 3						
W.B. 100.4"; 1.6 Liter						
Hatchback 2D	MM935	31450	**9500**	**9975**	**11150**	**13500**

2010 MINI — WMW(MF3C5)-A-#

Body Type	VIN	List	Trade-In Good	Very Good	Pvt-Party Good	Retail Excellent
COOPER HARDTOP—4-Cyl.—Equipment Schedule 3						
W.B. 97.1"; 1.6 Liter						
Hatchback 2D	MF3C5	19950	**7325**	**7750**	**8825**	**10950**
Sport Pkg		------	450	450	590	590
Camden Pkg		------	875	875	1150	1150
Mayfair Pkg		------	700	700	920	920
COOPER HARDTOP—4-Cyl. Turbo—Equipment Schedule 3						
W.B. 97.1"; 1.6 Liter						
S Hatchback 2D	MF7C5	23000	**8650**	**9075**	**10100**	**12150**
Sport Pkg		------	450	450	565	565
Camden Pkg		------	875	875	1095	1095
Mayfair Pkg		------	700	700	875	875
COOPER CONVERTIBLE—4-Cyl.—Equipment Schedule 3						
W.B. 97.1"; 1.6 Liter						
Convertible 2D	MR3C5	26200	**8900**	**9350**	**10400**	**12700**
Sport Pkg		------	450	450	570	570
COOPER CONVERTIBLE—4-Cyl. Turbo—Equipment Schedule 3						
W.B. 97.1"; 1.6 Liter						
S Convertible 2D	MS3C5	27850	**10900**	**11400**	**12550**	**14900**
Sport Pkg		------	450	450	545	545
COOPER CLUBMAN—4-Cyl.—Equipment Schedule 3						
W.B. 100.3"; 1.6 Liter						
Hatchback 2D	ML3C5	22400	**8275**	**8700**	**9875**	**12000**
Sport Pkg		------	450	450	565	565

Body Type	VIN	List	Trade-In Good	Very Good	Pvt-Party Good	Retail Excellent
COOPER CLUBMAN—4-Cyl. Turbo—Equipment Schedule 3						
W.B. 100.3"; 1.6 Liter.						
S Hatchback 2D	MM3C5	26000	9625	10100	11200	13400
Sport Pkg			450	450	540	540
JOHN COOPER WORKS HARDTOP—4-Cyl. Turbo—Equipment Schedule 3						
W.B. 97.1"; 1.6 Liter.						
Hatchback 2D	MF9C5	29500	12250	12750	14000	16600
JOHN COOPER WORKS CONVERTIBLE—4-Cyl. Turbo—Equip Sch 3						
W.B. 97.1"; 1.6 Liter.						
Convertible 2D	MS9C5	34700	15300	15900	17450	20600
JOHN COOPER WORKS CLUBMAN—4-Cyl. Turbo—Equipment Sch 3						
W.B. 100.3"; 1.6 Liter.						
Hatchback 2D	MM9C5	31700	12200	12750	13950	16600
2011 MINI — WMW(SU3C5)-B-#						
COOPER HARDTOP—4-Cyl.—Equipment Schedule 3						
W.B. 97.1"; 1.6 Liter.						
Hatchback 2D	SU3C5	21350	9275	9700	10850	13100
Sport Pkg			500	500	625	625
COOPER HARDTOP—4-Cyl. Turbo—Equipment Schedule 3						
W.B. 97.1"; 1.6 Liter.						
S Hatchback 2D	SV3C5	23700	10800	11250	12350	14500
Sport Pkg			500	500	600	600
COOPER CONVERTIBLE—4-Cyl.—Equipment Schedule 3						
W.B. 97.1"; 1.6 Liter.						
Convertible 2D	ZN3C5	26800	11550	12050	13250	15800
Sport Pkg			500	500	610	610
COOPER CONVERTIBLE—4-Cyl. Turbo—Equipment Schedule 3						
W.B. 97.1"; 1.6 Liter.						
S Convertible 2D	ZP3C5	28550	12950	13450	14800	17300
Sport Pkg			500	500	610	610
COOPER CLUBMAN—4-Cyl.—Equipment Schedule 3						
W.B. 100.3"; 1.6 Liter.						
Hatchback 2D	ZF3C5	23050	10200	10650	11850	14100
Sport Pkg			500	500	605	605
COOPER CLUBMAN—4-Cyl. Turbo—Equipment Schedule 3						
W.B. 100.3"; 1.6 Liter.						
S Hatchback 2D	ZG3C5	26750	11700	12200	13400	15800
Sport Pkg			500	500	590	590
COOPER COUNTRYMAN—4-Cyl.—Equipment Schedule 3						
W.B. 102.2"; 1.6 Liter.						
Hatchback 4D	ZB3C5	22350	13450	14050	15050	17400
Sport Pkg			500	500	580	580
COOPER COUNTRYMAN—4-Cyl. Turbo—Equipment Schedule 3						
W.B. 102.2"; 1.6 Liter.						
S Hatchback 4D	ZC3C5	25950	14600	15200	16150	18600
Sport Pkg			500	500	575	575
COOPER COUNTRYMAN AWD—4-Cyl. Turbo—Equipment Sch 3						
W.B. 102.2"; 1.6 Liter.						
S ALL4 Hatchback 4D	ZC5C5	27650	16250	16900	17800	20300
Sport Pkg			500	500	570	570
JOHN COOPER WORKS HARDTOP—4-Cyl. Turbo—Equipment Schedule 3						
W.B. 97.1"; 1.6 Liter.						
Hatchback 2D	SV9C5	29800	14900	15500	16750	19450
JOHN COOPER WORKS CONVERTIBLE—4-Cyl. Turbo—Equip Sch 3						
W.B. 97.1"; 1.6 Liter.						
Convertible 2D	ZP9C5	35000	16900	17550	18950	22000
JOHN COOPER WORKS CLUBMAN—4-Cyl. Turbo—Equipment Sch 3						
W.B. 100.3"; 1.6 Liter.						
Hatchback 2D	ZG9C5	32000	15600	16200	17700	20900
2012 MINI — WMW(SU3C5)-C-#						
COOPER HARDTOP—4-Cyl.—Equipment Schedule 3						
W.B. 97.1"; 1.6 Liter.						
Hatchback 2D	SU3C5	21450	11700	12200	13300	15650
Sport Pkg			550	550	660	660
COOPER HARDTOP—4-Cyl. Turbo—Equipment Schedule 3						
W.B. 97.1"; 1.6 Liter.						
S Hatchback 2D	SV3C5	23800	13050	13550	14700	16950
Sport Pkg			550	550	645	645
COOPER COUPE—4-Cyl.—Equipment Schedule 3						
W.B. 97.1"; 1.6 Liter.						

Body Type	VIN	List	Trade-In Good	Very Good	Pvt-Party Good	Retail Excellent
Coupe 2D	SX1C5	22000	**10900**	**11350**	**12350**	**14450**
Sport Pkg			550	550	640	640
COOPER COUPE—4-Cyl. Turbo—Equipment Schedule 3						
W.B. 97.1"; 1.6 Liter.						
S Coupe 2D	SX3C5	25300	**13050**	**13550**	**14550**	**16800**
Sport Pkg			550	550	635	635
COOPER ROADSTER—4-Cyl.—Equipment Schedule 3						
W.B. 97.1"; 1.6 Liter.						
Roadster 2D	SY1C5	25050	**13150**	**13700**	**14900**	**17250**
Sport Pkg			550	550	645	645
COOPER ROADSTER—4-Cyl. Turbo—Equipment Schedule 3						
W.B. 97.1"; 1.6 Liter.						
S Roadster 2D	SY3C5	28050	**14700**	**15300**	**16550**	**19200**
Sport Pkg			550	550	640	640
COOPER CONVERTIBLE—4-Cyl.—Equipment Schedule 3						
W.B. 97.1"; 1.6 Liter.						
Convertible 2D	ZN3C5	26900	**13350**	**13900**	**15150**	**17800**
Sport Pkg			550	550	655	655
COOPER CONVERTIBLE—4-Cyl. Turbo—Equipment Schedule 3						
W.B. 97.1"; 1.6 Liter.						
S Convertible 2D	ZP3C5	28650	**15850**	**16450**	**17650**	**20300**
Sport Pkg			550	550	630	630
COOPER CLUBMAN—4-Cyl.—Equipment Schedule 3						
W.B. 100.3"; 1.6 Liter.						
Hatchback 2D	ZF3C5	23150	**11800**	**12250**	**13450**	**15750**
Sport Pkg			550	550	650	650
COOPER CLUBMAN—4-Cyl. Turbo—Equipment Schedule 3						
W.B. 100.3"; 1.6 Liter.						
S Hatchback 2D	ZG3C5	26850	**14550**	**15150**	**16400**	**19100**
Sport Pkg			550	550	640	640
COOPER COUNTRYMAN—4-Cyl.—Equipment Schedule 3						
W.B. 102.2"; 1.6 Liter.						
Hatchback 4D	ZB3C5	22450	**14400**	**14950**	**16050**	**18500**
Sport Pkg			550	550	635	635
COOPER COUNTRYMAN—4-Cyl. Turbo—Equipment Schedule 3						
W.B. 102.2"; 1.6 Liter.						
S Hatchback 4D	ZC3C5	26050	**16300**	**16900**	**17950**	**20500**
Sport Pkg			550	550	625	625
COOPER COUNTRYMAN AWD—4-Cyl. Turbo—Equipment Sch 3						
W.B. 102.2"; 1.6 Liter.						
S ALL4 Hatchback 4D	ZC5C5	27750	**17550**	**18200**	**19300**	**22100**
Sport Pkg			550	550	620	620
JOHN COOPER WORKS HARDTOP—4-Cyl. Turbo—Equipment Schedule 3						
W.B. 97.1"; 1.6 Liter.						
Hatchback 2D	SV9C5	30600	**17800**	**18450**	**19550**	**22300**
JOHN COOPER WORKS COUPE—4-Cyl. Turbo—Equipment Schedule 3						
W.B. 97.1"; 1.6 Liter.						
Coupe 2D	SX5C5	31900	**17450**	**18100**	**19300**	**22100**
JOHN COOPER WORKS ROADSTER—4-Cyl. Turbo—Equipment Schedule 3						
W.B. 97.1"; 1.6 Liter.						
Roadster 2D	SY5C5	35200	**19500**	**20200**	**21500**	**24700**
JOHN COOPER WORKS CONVERTIBLE—4-Cyl. Turbo—Equipment Sch 3						
W.B. 97.1"; 1.6 Liter.						
Convertible 2D	ZP9C5	35800	**20700**	**21400**	**22700**	**26100**
JOHN COOPER WORKS CLUBMAN—4-Cyl. Turbo—Equipment Sch 3						
W.B. 100.3"; 1.6 Liter.						
Hatchback 2D	ZG9C5	32100	**18500**	**19200**	**20600**	**24000**

2013 MINI — WMW(SU3C5)-D-#

Body Type	VIN	List	Trade-In Good	Very Good	Pvt-Party Good	Retail Excellent
COOPER HARDTOP—4-Cyl.—Equipment Schedule 3						
W.B. 97.1"; 1.6 Liter.						
Hatchback 2D	SU3C5	20400	**12050**	**12550**	**13700**	**16050**
Sport Pkg			600	600	720	720
COOPER HARDTOP—4-Cyl. Turbo—Equipment Schedule 3						
W.B. 97.1"; 1.6 Liter.						
S Hatchback 2D	SV3C5	24000	**15200**	**15800**	**16850**	**19150**
Sport Pkg			600	600	690	690
COOPER COUPE—4-Cyl.—Equipment Schedule 3						
W.B. 97.1"; 1.6 Liter.						
Coupe 2D	SX1C5	22150	**11950**	**12400**	**13600**	**15800**
Sport Pkg			600	600	700	700
COOPER COUPE—4-Cyl. Turbo—Equipment Schedule 3						
W.B. 97.1"; 1.6 Liter.						

2013 MINI

Body Type	VIN	List	Trade-In Good	Very Good	Pvt-Party Good	Retail Excellent
S Coupe 2D	SX3C5	25450	**14250**	**14800**	**15950**	**18350**
Sport Pkg			**600**	**600**	**685**	**685**
COOPER PACEMAN—4-Cyl.—Equipment Schedule 3						
W.B. 102.2"; 1.6 Liter.						
Hatchback 2D	SS1C5	24600	**13750**	**14250**	**15600**	**18150**
COOPER PACEMAN—4-Cyl. Turbo—Equipment Schedule 3						
W.B. 102.2"; 1.6 Liter.						
S Hatchback 2D	SS5C5	28200	**16200**	**16800**	**18000**	**20600**
Sport Pkg			**600**	**600**	**685**	**685**
COOPER PACEMAN AWD—4-Cyl. Turbo—Equipment Schedule 3						
W.B. 102.2"; 1.6 Liter.						
S ALL4 Hatchback 2D	SS7C5	29900	**17350**	**17950**	**19100**	**21800**
Sport Pkg			**600**	**600**	**680**	**680**
COOPER PACEMAN JOHN COOPER WORKS AWD—4-Cyl. Turbo—Sch 3						
W.B. 102.2"; 1.6 Liter.						
ALL4 Hatchback 2D	SS9C5	36900	**23400**	**24200**	**25200**	**28500**
COOPER CONVERTIBLE—4-Cyl.—Equipment Schedule 3						
Convertible 2D	ZN3C5	25850	**14750**	**15350**	**16550**	**19200**
Sport Pkg			**600**	**600**	**705**	**705**
COOPER CONVERTIBLE—4-Cyl. Turbo—Equipment Schedule 3						
W.B. 97.1"; 1.6 Liter.						
S Convertible 2D	ZP3C5	28850	**18050**	**18650**	**19850**	**22600**
Sport Pkg			**600**	**600**	**680**	**680**
COOPER ROADSTER—4-Cyl.—Equipment Schedule 3						
W.B. 97.1"; 1.6 Liter.						
Roadster 2D	SY1C5	26250	**15250**	**15800**	**16900**	**19350**
Sport Pkg			**600**	**600**	**695**	**695**
COOPER ROADSTER—4-Cyl. Turbo—Equipment Schedule 3						
W.B. 97.1"; 1.6 Liter.						
S Roadster 2D	SY3C5	29250	**16850**	**17450**	**18650**	**21400**
Sport Pkg			**600**	**600**	**690**	**690**
COOPER CLUBMAN—4-Cyl.—Equipment Schedule 3						
W.B. 100.3"; 1.6 Liter.						
Hatchback 2D	ZF3C5	22100	**12550**	**13050**	**14250**	**16600**
Sport Pkg			**600**	**600**	**705**	**705**
COOPER CLUBMAN—4-Cyl. Turbo—Equipment Schedule 3						
W.B. 100.3"; 1.6 Liter.						
S Hatchback 2D	ZG3C5	25800	**15250**	**15850**	**17200**	**20100**
Sport Pkg			**600**	**600**	**695**	**695**
COOPER CLUBVAN—4-Cyl.—Equipment Schedule 3						
W.B. 100.3"; 1.6 Liter.						
Hatchback 2D	ZF3C5	25995				
Sport Pkg						
COOPER COUNTRYMAN—4-Cyl.—Equipment Schedule 3						
W.B. 102.2"; 1.6 Liter.						
Hatchback 4D	ZB3C5	22700	**15500**	**16050**	**17150**	**19600**
Sport Pkg			**600**	**600**	**685**	**685**
COOPER COUNTRYMAN—4-Cyl. Turbo—Equipment Schedule 3						
W.B. 102.2"; 1.6 Liter.						
Hatchback 4D	ZC3C5	26300	**17650**	**18300**	**19350**	**22000**
Sport Pkg			**600**	**600**	**675**	**675**
COOPER COUNTRYMAN AWD—4-Cyl. Turbo—Equipment Sch 3						
W.B. 102.2"; 1.6 Liter.						
ALL4 Hatchback 4D	ZC5C5	28000	**18850**	**19500**	**20600**	**23500**
Sport Pkg			**600**	**600**	**675**	**675**
JOHN COOPER WORKS HARDTOP—4-Cyl. Turbo—Equipment Schedule 3						
W.B. 97.1"; 1.6 Liter.						
Hatchback 2D	SU9C5	30800	**20600**	**21300**	**22300**	**25100**
JOHN COOPER WORKS COUPE—4-Cyl. Turbo—Equipment Schedule 3						
W.B. 97.1"; 1.6 Liter.						
John Cooper Works	SX9C5	32050	**18750**	**19450**	**20700**	**23700**
JOHN COOPER WORKS CONVERTIBLE—4-Cyl. Turbo—Equipment Sch 3						
W.B. 97.1"; 1.6 Liter.						
Convertible 2D	MR9C5	36000	**24100**	**24900**	**26100**	**29600**
JOHN COOPER WORKS ROADSTER—4-Cyl. Turbo—Equipment Schedule 3						
W.B. 97.1"; 1.6 Liter.						
Roadster 2D	SY9C5	36400	**21800**	**22600**	**23800**	**27100**
JOHN COOPER WORKS CLUBMAN—4-Cyl. Turbo—Equipment Sch 3						
W.B. 100.3"; 1.6 Liter.						
Hatchback 2D	MH9C5	33000	**20300**	**21100**	**22600**	**26100**
JOHN COOPER WORKS COUNTRYMAN AWD—4-Cyl. Turbo—Equip Sch 3						
W.B. 100.3"; 1.6 Liter.						
ALL4 Hatchback 4D	XD135	35550	**24400**	**25200**	**26300**	**29800**

2014 MINI

Body Type	VIN	List	Trade-In Good	Very Good	Pvt-Party Good	Retail Excellent

2014 MINI — WMW(XM5C5)-E-#

COOPER COUPE—4-Cyl.—Equipment Schedule 3
W.B. 97.1"; 1.6 Liter.

Body Type	VIN	List	Good	Very Good	Good	Excellent
Coupe 2D	SX1C5	22245	14500	15050	16250	18600
Sport Pkg			650	650	745	745
Recaro Seats			475	475	535	535

COOPER COUPE—4-Cyl. Turbo—Equipment Schedule 3
W.B. 97.1"; 1.6 Liter.

S Coupe 2D	SX3C5	25545	17650	18250	19300	21800
Sport Pkg			650	650	730	730
Recaro Seats			475	475	525	525

COOPER PACEMAN—4-Cyl.—Equipment Schedule 3
W.B. 102.2"; 1.6 Liter.

Hatchback 2D	SS1C5	24095	14700	15250	16550	19150
Sport Pkg			650	650	760	760

COOPER PACEMAN—4-Cyl. Turbo—Equipment Schedule 3
W.B. 102.2"; 1.6 Liter.

S Hatchback 2D	SS5C5	27695	18450	19100	20200	23000
Sport Pkg			650	650	735	735

COOPER PACEMAN AWD—4-Cyl. Turbo—Equipment Schedule 3
W.B. 102.2"; 1.6 Liter.

ALL4 Hatchback 4D	SS7C5	29395	19850	20500	21600	24500
Sport Pkg			650	650	730	730

COOPER CONVERTIBLE—4-Cyl.—Equipment Schedule 3
W.B. 97.1"; 1.6 Liter.

Convertible 2D	ZN3C5	25945	19250	19950	20900	23800
Sport Pkg			650	650	735	735

COOPER CONVERTIBLE—4-Cyl. Turbo—Equipment Schedule 3
W.B. 97.1"; 1.6 Liter.

S Convertible 2D	ZP3C5	28945	20800	21500	22600	25400
Sport Pkg			650	650	725	725

COOPER ROADSTER—4-Cyl.—Equipment Schedule 3
W.B. 97.1"; 1.6 Liter.

Roadster 2D	SY1C5	27595	16500	17100	18300	20900
Sport Pkg			650	650	755	755

COOPER ROADSTER—4-Cyl. Turbo—Equipment Schedule 3
W.B. 97.1"; 1.6 Liter.

Cooper S Roadster 2D		29345				

COOPER CLUBMAN—4-Cyl.—Equipment Schedule 3
W.B. 100.3"; 1.6 Liter.

Hatchback 2D	ZF3C5	23445	15550	16100	17250	19750
Sport Pkg			650	650	745	745
Recaro Seats			475	475	535	535

COOPER CLUBMAN—4-Cyl. Turbo—Equipment Schedule 3
W.B. 100.3"; 1.6 Liter.

S Hatchback 2D	ZG3C5	27145	18000	18650	19900	22900
Sport Pkg			650	650	740	740
Recaro Seats			475	475	535	535

COOPER COUNTRYMAN—4-Cyl.—Equipment Schedule 3
W.B. 102.2"; 1.6 Liter.

Hatchback 4D	ZB3C5	24145	17200	17800	18800	21300
Sport Pkg			650	650	740	740

COOPER COUNTRYMAN—4-Cyl. Turbo—Equipment Schedule 3
W.B. 102.2"; 1.6 Liter.

S Hatchback 4D	ZC3C5	27745	20100	20800	21700	24400
Sport Pkg			650	650	730	730

COOPER COUNTRYMAN AWD—4-Cyl. Turbo—Equipment Sch 3
W.B. 102.2"; 1.6 Liter.

ALL4 Hatchback 4D	ZC5C5	29445	21800	22500	23400	26400
Sport Pkg			650	650	725	725

JOHN COOPER WORKS COUPE—4-Cyl. Turbo—Equipment Schedule 3
W.B. 97.1"; 1.6 Liter.

Coupe 2D	SX9C5	32145	23200	24000	25100	28300
Recaro Seats			475	475	520	520

JOHN COOPER WORKS PACEMAN AWD—4-Cyl. Turbo—Equip Sch 3
W.B. 102.2"; 1.6 Liter.

ALL4 Hatchback 4D	SS9C5	36395	26400	27200	28200	31700

JOHN COOPER WORKS CONVERTIBLE—4-Cyl. Turbo—Equipment Sch 3
W.B. 97.1"; 1.6 Liter.

Convertible 2D	MR9C5	36095	26300	27100	28300	31800

JOHN COOPER WORKS ROADSTER—4-Cyl. Turbo—Equipment Sch 3
W.B. 97.1"; 1.6 Liter.

Body Type	VIN	List	Trade-In Good	Very Good	Pvt-Party Good	Retail Excellent
Roadster 2D	SY9C5	37745	27600	28500	27700	29300
JOHN COOPER WORKS CLUBMAN—4-Cyl. Turbo—Equipment Sch 3						
W.B. 100.3"; 1.6 Liter.						
Hatchback 2D	MH9C5	34345	24800	25600	26900	30700
Recaro Seats			475	475	525	525
JOHN COOPER WORKS COUNTRYMAN AWD—4-Cyl. Turbo—Equip Sch 3						
W.B. 100.3"; 1.6 Liter.						
ALL4 Hatchback 4D	XD1C5	36995	26900	27800	28800	32300

MITSUBISHI

2000 MITSUBISHI — (J,4or6)(A3orMM)A(Y26A)-Y-#

Body Type	VIN	List	Trade-In Good	Very Good	Pvt-Party Good	Retail Excellent
MIRAGE—4-Cyl.—Equipment Schedule 6						
W.B. 95.1", 98.4" (Sed); 1.5 Liter, 1.8 Liter.						
DE Sedan 4D	Y26A	14412	600	675	1250	2125
DE Coupe 2D	Y11A	13062	475	550	1050	1800
LS Sedan 4D	Y36C	17372	725	800	1425	2400
LS Coupe 2D	Y31C	15032	700	800	1375	2300
ECLIPSE—4-Cyl.—Equipment Schedule 4						
W.B. 100.8"; 2.4 Liter.						
RS Coupe 2D	C34G	18932	700	800	1275	2075
GS Coupe 2D	C44G	20482	825	950	1475	2425
Automatic			125	125	165	165
ECLIPSE—V6—Equipment Schedule 4						
W.B. 100.8"; 3.0 Liter.						
GT Coupe 2D	C84L	21622	1025	1125	1700	2775
Traction Control			100	100	135	135
Automatic			125	125	165	165
GALANT—4-Cyl.—Equipment Schedule 4						
W.B. 103.7"; 2.4 Liter.						
DE Sedan 4D	A36G	17792	500	575	1200	2075
ES Sedan 4D	A46G	18692	525	625	1225	2150
V6, 3.0 Liter	L		100	100	135	135
GALANT—V6—Equipment Schedule 4						
W.B. 103.7"; 3.0 Liter.						
LS Sedan 4D	A56L	24092	1200	1350	2250	3900
GTZ Sedan 4D	A46L	24192	1325	1500	2425	4225
DIAMANTE—V6—Equipment Schedule 4						
W.B. 107.1"; 3.5 Liter.						
ES Sedan 4D	P57P	25467	825	925	1625	2800
LS Sedan 4D	P67P	28367	1075	1200	1975	3400

2001 MITSUBISHI -(J,4or6)(A3orMM)A(Y11A)-1-#

Body Type	VIN	List	Trade-In Good	Very Good	Pvt-Party Good	Retail Excellent
MIRAGE—4-Cyl.—Equipment Schedule 6						
W.B. 95.1", 98.4" (Sed); 1.5 Liter, 1.8 Liter.						
DE Coupe 2D	Y11A	13277	500	575	1075	1825
ES Sedan 4D	Y26C	14417	725	800	1400	2375
LS Sedan 4D	Y36C	14997	800	900	1500	2500
LS Coupe 2D	Y31C	15237	850	950	1525	2500
ECLIPSE—4-Cyl.—Equipment Schedule 4						
W.B. 100.8"; 2.4 Liter.						
RS Coupe 2D	C31G	18507	750	825	1325	2200
GS Coupe 2D	C41G	19317	875	975	1475	2425
GS Spyder Conv 2D	E35G	23927	1300	1450	2000	3275
Automatic			125	125	165	165
ECLIPSE—V6—Equipment Schedule 4						
W.B. 100.8"; 3.0 Liter.						
GT Coupe 2D	C81H	21467	1175	1300	1850	2975
GT Spyder Conv 2D	E55H	26927	1625	1800	2550	4075
Traction Control			100	100	150	150
Automatic			125	125	165	165
GALANT—4-Cyl.—Equipment Schedule 4						
W.B. 103.7"; 2.4 Liter.						
DE Sedan 4D	A36G	18077	500	600	1200	2075
ES Sedan 4D	A46G	18927	525	625	1225	2150
V6, 3.0 Liter	H		100	100	135	135
GALANT—V6—Equipment Schedule 4						
W.B. 103.7"; 3.0 Liter.						
LS Sedan 4D	A56H	24427	1250	1400	2300	3975
GTZ Sedan 4D	A46H	24527	1450	1625	2625	4550

2001 MITSUBISHI

Body Type	VIN	List	Trade-In Good	Very Good	Pvt-Party Good	Retail Excellent
DIAMANTE—V6—Equipment Schedule 4						
W.B. 107.1"; 3.5 Liter.						
ES Sedan 4D	P57P	25907	875	975	1650	2800
LS Sedan 4D	P67P	28927	1175	1325	2050	3475

2002 MITSUBISHI—(J,4or6)(A3orMM)A(Y11A)-2-#

Body Type	VIN	List	Trade-In Good	Very Good	Pvt-Party Good	Retail Excellent
MIRAGE—4-Cyl.—Equipment Schedule 6						
W.B. 95.1"; 1.5 Liter, 1.8 Liter.						
DE Coupe 2D	Y11A	13362	525	600	1100	1850
LS Coupe 2D	Y31C	15332	1050	1150	1800	3000
LANCER—4-Cyl.—Equipment Schedule 6						
W.B. 102.4"; 2.0 Liter.						
ES Sedan 4D	J26E	15242	1125	1225	2000	3400
LS Sedan 4D	J36E	16442	1150	1250	2025	3450
OZ Rally Sedan 4D	J86E	16832	1250	1375	2175	3675
ECLIPSE—4-Cyl.—Equipment Schedule 4						
W.B. 100.8"; 2.4 Liter.						
RS Coupe 2D	C31G	18642	750	850	1350	2225
GS Coupe 2D	C41G	19512	975	1075	1625	2675
GS Spyder Conv 2D	E35G	24172	1350	1500	2075	3375
Automatic			125	125	165	165
ECLIPSE—V6—Equipment Schedule 4						
W.B. 100.8"; 3.0 Liter.						
GT Coupe 2D	C81H	21702	1400	1525	2150	3475
GT Spyder Conv 2D	E55H	27152	2050	2275	3200	5100
Automatic			125	125	165	165
Traction Control			125	125	165	165
GALANT—4-Cyl.—Equipment Schedule 4						
W.B. 103.7"; 2.4 Liter.						
DE Sedan 4D	A36G	18262	525	600	1200	2100
ES Sedan 4D	A46G	19072	550	625	1250	2175
LS Sedan 4D	A46G	21672	1300	1450	2325	4025
V6, 3.0 Liter	L		175	175	235	235
GALANT—V6—Equipment Schedule 4						
W.B. 103.7"; 3.0 Liter.						
GTZ Sedan 4D	A46H	24712	1575	1750	2725	4650
DIAMANTE—V6—Equipment Schedule 4						
W.B. 107.1"; 3.5 Liter.						
ES Sedan 4D	P57P	26247	975	1100	1775	3025
VR-X Sedan 4D	P67P	27557	1250	1400	2150	3625
LS Sedan 4D	P67P	29007	1325	1475	2250	3775

2003 MITSUBISHI — (J,4or6)(A3orMM)A(J26E)-3-#

Body Type	VIN	List	Trade-In Good	Very Good	Pvt-Party Good	Retail Excellent
LANCER—4-Cyl.—Equipment Schedule 6						
W.B. 102.4"; 2.0 Liter.						
ES Sedan 4D	J26E	15387	1575	1725	2575	4250
LS Sedan 4D	J36E	16617	1600	1750	2600	4300
OZ Rally Sedan 4D	J86E	17117	1825	2000	3050	4975
LANCER AWD—4-Cyl. Turbo—Equipment Schedule 4						
W.B. 103.3"; 2.0 Liter.						
Evolution Sedan 4D	H86F	29582	7525	8100	9150	12300
ECLIPSE—4-Cyl.—Equipment Schedule 4						
W.B. 100.8"; 2.4 Liter.						
RS Coupe 2D	C34G	18717	1125	1275	1725	2700
GS Coupe 2D	C44G	19617	1275	1425	1950	3100
GS Spyder Conv 2D	E45G	24397	1775	1950	2525	3950
Automatic			150	150	200	200
ECLIPSE—V6—Equipment Schedule 4						
W.B. 100.8"; 3.0 Liter.						
GT Coupe 2D	C84H	21807	1550	1700	2300	3625
GT Spyder Conv 2D	E85H	27592	2350	2575	3425	5225
GTS Coupe 2D	C74H	24777	2400	2625	3450	5225
GTS Spyder Conv 2D	E75H	30242	2900	3200	4075	6125
Automatic			150	150	200	200
Traction Control			125	125	180	180
GALANT—4-Cyl.—Equipment Schedule 4						
W.B. 103.7"; 2.4 Liter.						
DE Sedan 4D	A36G	18347	550	650	1325	2375
ES Sedan 4D	A46G	19157	575	675	1325	2350
LS Sedan 4D	A46G	21757	1325	1500	2375	4050
V6, 3.0 Liter	H		250	250	335	335

EQUIPMENT & MILEAGE PAGE 9 TO 23   235

Body Type	VIN	List	Trade-In Good	Very Good	Pvt-Party Good	Retail Excellent
GALANT—V6—Equipment Schedule 4						
W.B. 103.7"; 3.0 Liter.						
GTZ Sedan 4D	A46H	25047	**1700**	**1900**	**2875**	**4850**
DIAMANTE—V6—Equipment Schedule 4						
W.B. 107.1"; 3.5 Liter.						
ES Sedan 4D	P57P	26557	**1325**	**1475**	**2125**	**3475**
VR-X Sedan 4D	P87P	27677	**1625**	**1800**	**2525**	**4075**
LS Sedan 4D	P67P	29027	**1700**	**1900**	**2625**	**4225**

2004 MITSUBISHI — (J,4or6)(A3)A(J26E)-4-#

Body Type	VIN	List	Trade-In Good	Very Good	Pvt-Party Good	Retail Excellent
LANCER—4-Cyl.—Equipment Schedule 6						
W.B. 102.4"; 2.0 Liter, 2.4 Liter.						
ES Sedan 4D	J26E	14972	**1825**	**2000**	**2900**	**4600**
LS Sedan 4D	J36E	16572	**2050**	**2250**	**3200**	**5050**
LS Wagon 4D	D29F	17172	**2050**	**2250**	**3200**	**5050**
OZ Rally Sedan 4D	J86E	17172	**2225**	**2425**	**3450**	**5425**
Ralliart Sedan 4D	J66F	18572	**2000**	**2200**	**2850**	**4275**
Ralliart Wagon 4D	D69F	19772	**2475**	**2725**	**3425**	**5100**
LANCER AWD—4-Cyl. Turbo—Equipment Schedule 4						
W.B. 103.3"; 2.0 Liter.						
Evolution RS Sedan 4D	H36D	27374	**6950**	**7475**	**8500**	**11450**
Evolution Sedan 4D	H86D	30574	**8000**	**8575**	**9600**	**12800**
ECLIPSE—4-Cyl.—Equipment Schedule 4						
W.B. 100.8"; 2.4 Liter.						
RS Coupe 2D	C34G	18892	**1300**	**1425**	**1900**	**3000**
GS Coupe 2D	C44G	19892	**1925**	**2125**	**2650**	**4050**
GS Spyder Conv 2D	E45G	24892	**2200**	**2450**	**3075**	**4650**
Automatic			**175**	**175**	**235**	**235**
ECLIPSE—V6—Equipment Schedule 4						
W.B. 100.8"; 3.0 Liter.						
GT Coupe 2D	C84H	22092	**1775**	**1950**	**2650**	**4075**
GT Spyder Conv 2D	E85H	28144	**2725**	**3000**	**3850**	**5775**
GTS Coupe 2D	C74H	25092	**2975**	**3275**	**4150**	**6150**
GTS Spyder Conv 2D	E75H	30794	**3425**	**3750**	**4900**	**7225**
Automatic			**175**	**175**	**235**	**235**
GALANT—4-Cyl.—Equipment Schedule 4						
W.B. 108.3"; 2.4 Liter.						
DE Sedan 4D	A36G	18592	**1525**	**1700**	**2325**	**3700**
ES Sedan 4D	A46G	19592	**1750**	**1950**	**2600**	**4100**
V6, 3.8 Liter	S		**300**	**300**	**400**	**400**
GALANT—V6—Equipment Schedule 4						
W.B. 108.3"; 3.8 Liter.						
LS Sedan 4D	A46H	21592	**2700**	**3000**	**3925**	**6000**
GTS Sedan 4D	A46H	26292	**2900**	**3225**	**4175**	**6375**
DIAMANTE—V6—Equipment Schedule 4						
W.B. 107.2"; 3.5 Liter.						
ES Sedan 4D	P57P	25594	**1750**	**1950**	**2675**	**4225**
VR-X Sedan 4D	P87P	27414	**2125**	**2350**	**3175**	**4925**
LS Sedan 4D	P67P	28214	**2175**	**2400**	**3250**	**5050**

2005 MITSUBISHI — (J,4or6)(A3)A(J26E)-5-#

Body Type	VIN	List	Trade-In Good	Very Good	Pvt-Party Good	Retail Excellent
LANCER—4-Cyl.—Equipment Schedule 6						
W.B. 102.4"; 2.0 Liter, 2.4 Liter.						
ES Sedan 4D	J26E	15474	**1825**	**2000**	**3025**	**4725**
OZ Rally Sedan 4D	J86E	17874	**2375**	**2600**	**3725**	**5725**
Ralliart Sedan 4D	J66F	18774	**2175**	**2400**	**3300**	**4925**
LANCER AWD—4-Cyl. Turbo—Equipment Schedule 4						
W.B. 103.3"; 2.0 Liter.						
Evolution RS Sedan 4D	H36D	28774	**9225**	**9875**	**10900**	**14100**
Evolution VIII Sedan	H76D	31574	**10550**	**11250**	**12150**	**15550**
Evolution MR Ed Sedan	H86D	35574	**11700**	**12450**	**13450**	**17150**
ECLIPSE—4-Cyl.—Equipment Schedule 4						
W.B. 100.8"; 2.4 Liter.						
GS Coupe 2D	C44G	20044	**1950**	**2150**	**3125**	**4850**
GS Spyder Conv 2D	E45G	25494	**2475**	**2750**	**3725**	**5625**
Automatic			**200**	**200**	**265**	**265**
ECLIPSE—V6—Equipment Schedule 4						
W.B. 100.8"; 3.0 Liter.						
GT Coupe 2D	C84H	23494	**2250**	**2500**	**3425**	**5125**
GT Spyder Conv 2D	E55H	28494	**3275**	**3575**	**4650**	**6675**
GTS Coupe 2D	C74H	25244	**3275**	**3575**	**4675**	**6725**
GTS Spyder Conv 2D	E75H	31094	**3775**	**4100**	**5200**	**7400**

2005 MITSUBISHI

Body Type	VIN	List	Trade-In Good	Trade-In Very Good	Pvt-Party Good	Retail Excellent
Automatic			**200**	**200**	**265**	**265**
GALANT—4-Cyl.—Equipment Schedule 4						
W.B. 108.3"; 2.4 Liter.						
DE Sedan 4D	B26F	19594	**1875**	**2100**	**2775**	**4100**
ES Sedan 4D	B46F	20494	**2175**	**2425**	**3125**	**4575**
SE Sedan 4D	B46F	21594	**2675**	**3000**	**3700**	**5350**
GALANT—V6—Equipment Schedule 4						
W.B. 108.3"; 3.8 Liter.						
LS Sedan 4D	B46S	23094	**3375**	**3750**	**4700**	**6700**
GTS Sedan 4D	B76S	27094	**3875**	**4275**	**5250**	**7400**

2006 MITSUBISHI — (J,4or6)(A3)A(J26E)-6-#

Body Type	VIN	List	Trade-In Good	Trade-In Very Good	Pvt-Party Good	Retail Excellent
LANCER—4-Cyl.—Equipment Schedule 6						
W.B. 102.4"; 2.0 Liter, 2.4 Liter.						
ES Sedan 4D	J26E	16104	**2050**	**2275**	**3350**	**5050**
SE Sedan 4D	J26E	16704	**2125**	**2350**	**3500**	**5300**
OZ Rally Sedan 4D	J86E	18404	**2925**	**3225**	**4350**	**6325**
Ralliart Sedan 4D	J66F	19574	**2775**	**3050**	**4000**	**5825**
LANCER AWD—4-Cyl. Turbo—Equipment Schedule 4						
W.B. 103.3"; 2.0 Liter.						
Evolution RS Sedan 4D	H36C	29274	**10700**	**11400**	**12500**	**15850**
Evolution IX Sedan 4D	H86C	31994	**12400**	**13200**	**14150**	**17800**
Evolution MR Sedan 4D	H86C	35784	**13750**	**14600**	**15600**	**19550**
ECLIPSE—4-Cyl.—Equipment Schedule 4						
W.B. 101.4"; 2.4 Liter.						
GS Coupe 2D	K24F	20924	**3425**	**3775**	**4525**	**6400**
ECLIPSE—V6—Equipment Schedule 4						
W.B. 101.4"; 3.8 Liter.						
GT Coupe 2D	K34T	25224	**3375**	**3675**	**4650**	**6525**
Special Edition	4		**875**	**875**	**1165**	**1165**
GALANT—4-Cyl.—Equipment Schedule 4						
W.B. 108.3"; 2.4 Liter.						
DE Sedan 4D	B26F	19994	**2000**	**2250**	**3025**	**4375**
ES Sedan 4D	B46F	20894	**2600**	**2925**	**3725**	**5275**
SE Sedan 4D	B36F	22594	**3125**	**3475**	**4325**	**6050**
GALANT—V6—Equipment Schedule 4						
W.B. 108.3"; 3.8 Liter.						
LS Sedan 4D	B46S	23594	**4025**	**4425**	**5350**	**7400**
GTS Sedan 4D	B76S	27594	**4475**	**4900**	**5850**	**8075**

2007 MITSUBISHI — (Jor4)(A3)A(J26E)-7-#

Body Type	VIN	List	Trade-In Good	Trade-In Very Good	Pvt-Party Good	Retail Excellent
LANCER—4-Cyl.—Equipment Schedule 6						
W.B. 102.4"; 2.0 Liter.						
ES Sedan 4D	J26E	16104	**2525**	**2800**	**3800**	**5600**
Manual, 5-Spd w/Overdrive			**(325)**	**(325)**	**(440)**	**(440)**
ECLIPSE—4-Cyl.—Equipment Schedule 4						
W.B. 101.4"; 2.4 Liter.						
GS Coupe 2D	K24F	21224	**3925**	**4300**	**5150**	**7100**
GS Spyder Conv 2D	L25F	26914	**4275**	**4675**	**5650**	**7825**
SE Coupe 2D	K64F	23024	**4325**	**4725**	**5650**	**7800**
ECLIPSE—V6—Equipment Schedule 4						
W.B. 101.4"; 3.8 Liter.						
GT Coupe 2D	K34T	24924	**4275**	**4625**	**5600**	**7650**
GT Spyder Conv 2D	L35T	29794	**4675**	**5050**	**6175**	**8250**
GALANT—4-Cyl.—Equipment Schedule 4						
W.B. 108.3"; 2.4 Liter.						
DE Sedan 4D	B26F	20524	**2625**	**2925**	**3775**	**5350**
ES Sedan 4D	B36F	21624	**3250**	**3575**	**4450**	**6225**
SE Sedan 4D	B36F	23324	**4150**	**4525**	**5450**	**7450**
GALANT—V6—Equipment Schedule 4						
W.B. 108.3"; 3.8 Liter.						
GTS Sedan 4D	B56S	25624	**5075**	**5500**	**6550**	**8975**
Ralliart Sedan 4D	B76T	27624	**5675**	**6150**	**7400**	**10050**

2008 MITSUBISHI — (1,4orJ)A3-(U16U)-8-#

Body Type	VIN	List	Trade-In Good	Trade-In Very Good	Pvt-Party Good	Retail Excellent
LANCER—4-Cyl.—Equipment Schedule 6						
W.B. 103.7"; 2.0 Liter.						
DE Sedan 4D	U16U	15515	**3925**	**4225**	**5175**	**7025**
ES Sedan 4D	U26U	17515	**4775**	**5125**	**6075**	**8075**
GTS Sedan 4D	U86U	19115	**6175**	**6575**	**7825**	**10300**
Manual, 5-Spd w/Overdrive			**(350)**	**(350)**	**(470)**	**(470)**

2008 MITSUBISHI

Body Type	VIN	List	Trade-In Good	Very Good	Pvt-Party Good	Retail Excellent
LANCER—4-Cyl. Turbo—Equipment Schedule 4						
W.B. 104.3"; 2.0 Liter.						
Evolution GSR Sedan	W86V	33615	15600	16400	17050	20400
Evolution MR Sedan	W56V	38940	19500	20500	21200	25400
ECLIPSE—4-Cyl.—Equipment Schedule 4						
W.B. 101.4"; 2.4 Liter.						
GS Coupe 2D	K24F	21624	4750	5150	5950	7875
GS Spyder Conv 2D	L25F	27324	5275	5700	6825	9075
SE Coupe 2D	K64F	25424	5325	5750	6875	9175
V6, 3.8 Liter (SE)	T		1800	1800	2400	2400
ECLIPSE—V6—Equipment Schedule 4						
W.B. 101.4"; 3.8 Liter.						
GT Coupe 2D	K34T	25124	5300	5700	6700	8675
GT Spyder Conv 2D	L35T	30224	6600	7050	7700	9525
GALANT—4-Cyl.—Equipment Schedule 4						
W.B. 108.3"; 2.4 Liter.						
DE Sedan 4D	B26F	20624	3350	3675	4500	6150
ES Sedan 4D	B36F	21724	4050	4400	5325	7225
GALANT—V6—Equipment Schedule 4						
W.B. 108.3"; 3.8 Liter.						
Ralliart Sedan 4D	B76T	27774	7350	7900	9350	12350

2009 MITSUBISHI — (1,4orJ)A3-(K24F)-9-#

Body Type	VIN	List	Trade-In Good	Very Good	Pvt-Party Good	Retail Excellent
ECLIPSE—4-Cyl.—Equipment Schedule 4						
W.B. 101.4"; 2.4 Liter.						
GS Coupe 2D	K24F	20749	6300	6775	7550	9550
GS Spyder Conv 2D	L25F	26449	7425	7925	8975	11400
ECLIPSE—V6—Equipment Schedule 4						
W.B. 101.4"; 3.8 Liter.						
GT Coupe 2D	K34T	25799	8275	8775	9850	12350
GT Spyder Conv 2D	L35T	29649	9750	10300	11450	14200
LANCER—4-Cyl.—Equipment Schedule 6						
W.B. 103.7"; 2.0 Liter, 2.4 Liter.						
DE Sedan 4D	U16U	15540	4750	5075	6000	7850
ES Sedan 4D	U26U	17740	5425	5800	6900	8900
GTS Sedan 4D	U86U	19640	7375	7825	8925	11200
Manual, 5-Spd w/Overdrive			(375)	(375)	(500)	(500)
LANCER AWD—4-Cyl. Turbo—Equipment Schedule 4						
W.B. 103.7"; 2.0 Liter.						
Ralliart Sedan 4D	V66V	27165	9575	10100	11100	13650
GALANT—4-Cyl.—Equipment Schedule 4						
W.B. 108.3"; 2.4 Liter.						
ES Sedan 4D	B36F	21724	5675	6100	7150	9225
Sport Ed Sedan 4D	B36F	23124	6525	7000	8125	10500
GALANT—V6—Equipment Schedule 4						
W.B. 108.3"; 3.8 Liter.						
Sport Sedan 4D	B46T	25124	8225	8775	10300	13400
Ralliart Sedan 4D	B76T	27924	8650	9225	10850	14150

2010 MITSUBISHI — (4orJ)A3-(K2DF)-A-#

Body Type	VIN	List	Trade-In Good	Very Good	Pvt-Party Good	Retail Excellent
ECLIPSE—4-Cyl.—Equipment Schedule 4						
W.B. 101.4"; 2.4 Liter.						
GS Coupe 2D	K2DF	22419	6950	7450	8225	10200
GS Sport Coupe 2D	K5DF	25763	7650	8175	9100	11300
GS Spyder Conv 2D	L2EF	28519	8450	9025	9975	12400
ECLIPSE—V6—Equipment Schedule 4						
W.B. 101.4"; 3.8 Liter.						
GT Coupe 2D	K3DT	30128	10200	10700	11700	14250
GT Spyder Conv 2D	L3ET	33548	11200	11800	12850	15550
LANCER—4-Cyl.—Equipment Schedule 6						
W.B. 103.7"; 2.0 Liter, 2.4 Liter.						
DE Sedan 4D	U1FU	16410	6075	6450	7475	9400
ES Sedan 4D	U2FU	18610	6700	7100	8125	10150
GTS Sedan 4D	U8FW	20710	8975	9475	10450	12800
GTS Sportback 4D	X8HW	20925	9025	9525	10550	12900
Manual, 5-Spd w/Overdrive			(475)	(475)	(625)	(625)
LANCER AWD—4-Cyl. Turbo—Equipment Schedule 4						
W.B. 103.7"; 2.0 Liter.						
Ralliart Sedan 4D	V6FV	27910	12800	13450	14250	16750
Ralliart Sportback 4D	Y6HV	28310	13000	13600	14400	16850
Evolution GSR Sedan	W8FV	34310	18500	19350	20300	23700
Evolution SE Sedan	W6FV	36535	19650	20500	21500	25300

Body Type	VIN	List	Trade-In Good	Very Good	Pvt-Party Good	Retail Excellent
Evolution MR Sedan	W5FV	39710	21400	22300	23200	26900
Evolution MR Touring	W5FV	41710	22700	23700	24500	28500
GALANT—4-Cyl.—Equipment Schedule 4						
W.B. 108.3"; 2.4 Liter.						
FE Sedan 4D	B2FF	22260	5925	6350	7500	9700
ES Sedan 4D	B3FF	22319	6425	6875	8075	10400
SE Sedan 4D	B3FF	24719	7625	8125	9550	12300

2011 MITSUBISHI — (4orJ)A3–(K5DF)–B–#

Body Type	VIN	List	Trade-In Good	Very Good	Pvt-Party Good	Retail Excellent
ECLIPSE—4-Cyl.—Equipment Schedule 4						
W.B. 101.4"; 2.4 Liter.						
GS Coupe 2D	K5DF	20744	8325	8875	9650	11700
ECLIPSE—4-Cyl.—Equipment Schedule 4						
W.B. 101.4"; 2.4 Liter.						
GS Sport Coupe	K5DF	25673	8900	9475	10350	12650
GS Spyder Conv 2D	L5EF	28744	9550	10150	11050	13450
ECLIPSE—V6—Equipment Schedule 4						
W.B. 101.4"; 3.8 Liter.						
GT Coupe 2D	K3DT	30153	10900	11450	12500	14950
GT Spyder Conv 2D	L3ET	33573	12450	13050	14050	16750
LANCER—4-Cyl.—Equipment Schedule 4						
W.B. 103.7"; 2.0 Liter.						
DE Sedan 4D	U1FU	15740	6725	7125	8125	10100
ES Sportback 4D	X2HU	18455	7950	8375	9425	11550
LANCER—4-Cyl.—Equipment Schedule 6						
W.B. 103.7"; 2.0 Liter, 2.4 Liter.						
ES Sedan 4D	U2FU	17155	7600	8025	9100	11200
GTS Sedan 4D	U8FW	21055	9775	10300	11400	13850
GTS Sportback 4D	X8HW	21455	10000	10500	11600	14100
Manual, 5-Spd w/Overdrive			(500)	(500)	(650)	(650)
LANCER AWD—4-Cyl. Turbo—Equipment Schedule 4						
W.B. 103.7"; 2.0 Liter.						
Ralliart Sedan 4D	V6FV	28240	13700	14350	15150	17700
Ralliart Sportback 4D	Y6HV	28640	14000	14650	15500	18100
Evolution GSR Sedan	W8FV	34335	19250	20100	21000	24200
Evolution MR Sedan	W5FV	39735	22200	23100	24000	27600
GALANT—4-Cyl.—Equipment Schedule 4						
W.B. 108.3"; 2.4 Liter.						
FE Sedan 4D	B2FF	22903	7350	7825	8925	11150
ES Sedan 4D	B3FF	22344	7575	8050	9200	11500
SE Sedan 4D	B3FF	24744	8775	9325	10600	13250

2012 MITSUBISHI — (4orJ)A3–(K2DF)–C–#

Body Type	VIN	List	Trade-In Good	Very Good	Pvt-Party Good	Retail Excellent
ECLIPSE—4-Cyl.—Equipment Schedule 4						
W.B. 101.4"; 2.4 Liter.						
GS Coupe 2D	K2DF	21259	9050	9625	10550	12800
ECLIPSE—4-Cyl.—Equipment Schedule 4						
W.B. 101.4"; 2.4 Liter.						
GS Sport Coupe 2D	K5DF	25688	10100	10700	11800	14450
GS Spyder Conv 2D	L5EF	26574	10650	11250	12450	15200
GS Sport Spyder Conv	L5EF	28759	11100	11750	12950	15850
SE Coupe 2D	K5DF	25703	10550	11150	12300	15000
SE Spyder Conv 2D	L5EF	29074	11600	12250	13400	16250
ECLIPSE—V6—Equipment Schedule 4						
W.B. 101.4"; 3.8 Liter.						
GT Coupe 2D	K3DT	30168	12700	13300	14300	16950
GT Spyder Conv 2D	L3ET	33588	14150	14800	16000	18950
LANCER—4-Cyl.—Equipment Schedule 4						
W.B. 103.7"; 2.0 Liter, 2.4 Liter.						
DE Sedan 4D	U1FU	16490	7775	8200	9250	11300
ES Sportback 4D	X2HU	19190	9175	9650	10650	12800
GT Sportback 4D	X8HW	22140	11050	11600	12700	15200
LANCER—4-Cyl.—Equipment Schedule 6						
W.B. 103.7"; 2.0 Liter.						
ES Sedan 4D	U2FU	18690	8575	9050	10050	12200
GT Sedan 4D	U8FW	20640	9875	10350	11450	13800
Manual, 5-Spd.			(500)	(500)	(625)	(625)
LANCER AWD—4-Cyl.—Equipment Schedule 6						
W.B. 103.7"; 2.4 Liter.						
SE Sedan 4D	V2FW	20990	10150	10650	11650	13950
LANCER AWD—4-Cyl. Turbo—Equipment Schedule 4						
W.B. 103.7", 104.3"; 2.0 Liter.						

Body Type	VIN	List	Trade-In Good	Very Good	Pvt-Party Good	Retail Excellent
Ralliart Sedan 4D	V6FV	28790	15450	16150	16850	19400
Evolution GSR Sedan	W8FV	35290	22000	22800	23600	26900
Evolution MR Sedan	W5FV	38490	24900	25800	26700	30300
GALANT—4-Cyl.—Equipment Schedule 4						
W.B. 108.3"; 2.4 Liter.						
FE Sedan 4D	B2FF	22903	8100	8600	9700	11950
ES Sedan 4D	B3FF	22694	8500	9025	10150	12450
SE Sedan 4D	B3FF	25094	9725	10250	11550	14200

2013 MITSUBISHI — (4orJ)A3-(U1FU)-D-#

Body Type	VIN	List	Trade-In Good	Very Good	Pvt-Party Good	Retail Excellent
LANCER—4-Cyl.—Equipment Schedule 6						
W.B. 103.7"; 2.0 Liter.						
DE Sedan 4D	U1FU	16790	8400	8850	10000	12250
LANCER—4-Cyl.—Equipment Schedule 6						
W.B. 103.7"; 2.0 Liter, 2.4 Liter.						
ES Sedan 4D	U2FU	17890	9200	9675	10900	13300
GT Sedan 4D	U8FW	20790	11200	11700	12900	15450
Manual, 5-Spd			(500)	(500)	(640)	(640)
LANCER—4-Cyl.—Equipment Schedule 6						
W.B. 103.7"; 2.0 Liter, 2.4 Liter.						
ES Hatchback 4D	X2HU	19290	10050	10550	11750	14250
GT Hatchback 4D	X8HW	22290	12050	12600	13750	16350
LANCER AWD—4-Cyl.—Equipment Schedule 6						
W.B. 103.7"; 2.4 Liter.						
SE Sedan 4D	V2FW	21090	11500	12050	13150	15700
LANCER AWD—4-Cyl. Turbo—Equipment Schedule 4						
W.B. 103.7", 104.3"; 2.0 Liter.						
Ralliart Sedan 4D	V6FV	28890	17750	18500	19200	21900
Evolution GSR Sedan	W8FV	35490	23900	24800	25700	29100
Evolution MR Sedan	W5FV	38690	26800	27800	28900	32400

2014 MITSUBISHI — (4orJ)A3-(A3HJ)-E-#

Body Type	VIN	List	Trade-In Good	Very Good	Pvt-Party Good	Retail Excellent
MIRAGE—3-Cyl.—Equipment Schedule 6						
W.B. 96.5"; 1.2 Liter.						
DE Hatchback 4D	A3HJ	13790	7700	8100	9125	11150
ES Hatchback 4D	A4HJ	14990	8325	8775	9750	11750
i-MiEV—AC Electric—Equipment Schedule 4						
W.B. 100.4".						
ES Hatchback 4D	215H4	23845	13250	13800	14700	16850
LANCER—4-Cyl.—Equipment Schedule 6						
W.B. 103.7"; 2.0 Liter, 2.4 Liter.						
ES Sedan 4D	U2FU	18890	10450	10950	12100	14600
GT Sedan 4D	U8FW	22240	12550	13150	14350	16950
Manual, 5-Spd			(525)	(525)	(660)	(660)
LANCER AWD—4-Cyl.—Equipment Schedule 6						
W.B. 103.7"; 2.4 Liter.						
SE Sedan 4D	V2FW	21490	12350	12900	14100	16650
LANCER—4-Cyl.—Equipment Schedule 6						
W.B. 103.7"; 2.0 Liter, 2.4 Liter.						
ES Hatchback 4D	X2HU	19390	11200	11750	12950	15500
GT Hatchback 4D	X8HW	22740	13050	13650	14800	17450
LANCER AWD—4-Cyl. Turbo—Equipment Schedule 4						
W.B. 103.7", 104.3" (Evolution); 2.0 Liter.						
Ralliart Sedan 4D	V6FV	29190	19400	20200	20800	23600
Evolution GSR Sedan	W8FV	35790				
Evolution MR Sedan	W5FV	38990				

NISSAN

2000 NISSAN — (1N4,JN1or3N1)(CB51D)-Y-#

Body Type	VIN	List	Trade-In Good	Very Good	Pvt-Party Good	Retail Excellent
SENTRA—4-Cyl.—Equipment Schedule 6						
W.B. 99.8"; 1.8 Liter, 2.0 Liter.						
XE Sedan 4D	CB51D	12169	600	675	1300	2250
GXE Sedan 4D	CB51D	14019	725	825	1500	2600
CA Sedan 4D	DB51D	15319	800	900	1600	2775
SE Sedan 4D	BB51D	15419	950	1050	1825	3125
ALTIMA—4-Cyl.—Equipment Schedule 4						
W.B. 103.1"; 2.4 Liter.						
XE Sedan 4D	DL01D	18459	925	1025	1650	2800
GXE Sedan 4D	DL01D	18659	975	1100	1725	2900
SE Sedan 4D	DL01D	19960	1275	1425	2125	3550

2000 NISSAN

Body Type	VIN	List	Trade-In Good	Very Good	Pvt-Party Good	Retail Excellent
GLE Sedan 4D	DL01D	20910	1500	1675	2400	4025
Manual, 5-Spd			(175)	(175)	(235)	(235)
MAXIMA—V6—Equipment Schedule 4						
W.B. 108.3"; 3.0 Liter.						
GXE Sedan 4D	CA31A	23269	1275	1425	2125	3575
SE Sedan 4D	CA31A	24669	1400	1550	2300	3850
GLE Sedan 4D	CA31A	26769	1600	1775	2550	4275
Manual, 5-Spd			(175)	(175)	(235)	(235)

2001 NISSAN — (1N4,JN1or3N1)(CB51D)-1-#

SENTRA—4-Cyl.—Equipment Schedule 6
W.B. 99.8"; 1.8 Liter, 2.0 Liter.

Body Type	VIN	List	Good	Very Good	Good	Excellent
XE Sedan 4D	CB51D	13368	625	700	1350	2300
GXE Sedan 4D	CB51D	14019	800	900	1625	2800
CA Sedan 4D	DB51D	15319	1075	1200	2000	3425
SE Sedan 4D	BB51D	15419	1175	1300	2150	3650
ALTIMA—4-Cyl.—Equipment Schedule 4						
W.B. 103.1"; 2.4 Liter.						
XE Sedan 4D	DL01D	18459	1250	1400	2025	3300
GXE Sedan 4D	DL01D	18659	1300	1475	2075	3400
SE Sedan 4D	DL01D	19960	1750	1950	2650	4275
GLE Sedan 4D	DL01D	20190	1900	2125	2975	4725
LE Pkg			75	75	85	85
Manual, 5-Spd			(200)	(200)	(265)	(265)
MAXIMA—V6—Equipment Schedule 4						
W.B. 108.3"; 3.0 Liter.						
GXE Sedan 4D	CA31D	23469	1325	1475	2250	3825
SE Sedan 4D	CA31D	24869	1525	1700	2525	4250
SE 20th Anniv Sed 4D	CA31A	28169	1800	2000	3000	4975
GLE Sedan 4D	CA31D	26969	1725	1925	2800	4650
Manual, 5-Spd			(200)	(200)	(265)	(265)

2002 NISSAN — (1N4,JN1or3N1)(CB51D)-2-#

SENTRA—4-Cyl.—Equipment Schedule 6
W.B. 99.8"; 1.8 Liter, 2.5 Liter.

Body Type	VIN	List	Good	Very Good	Good	Excellent
XE Sedan 4D	CB51D	13588	875	950	1625	2775
GXE Sedan 4D	CB51D	14289	1150	1250	2000	3350
CA Sedan 4D	DB51D	15439	1525	1675	2375	3850
SE-R Sedan 4D	AB51A	16539	1525	1675	2175	3350
SE-R Spec V Sedan 4D	AB51A	17539	1750	1925	2650	4125
ALTIMA—4-Cyl.—Equipment Schedule 4						
W.B. 110.2"; 2.5 Liter.						
2.5 Sedan 4D	AL11D	17869	1600	1775	2450	3975
2.5 S Sedan 4D	AL11D	19389	1800	2000	2700	4350
2.5 SL Sedan 4D	AL11D	23239	2300	2550	3475	5475
Manual, 5-Spd			(200)	(200)	(265)	(265)
ALTIMA—V6—Equipment Schedule 4						
W.B. 110.2"; 3.5 Liter.						
3.5 SE Sedan 4D	BL11D	23689	2550	2825	3800	5950
Manual, 5-Spd			(200)	(200)	(265)	(265)
MAXIMA—V6—Equipment Schedule 4						
W.B. 108.3"; 3.5 Liter.						
GXE Sedan 4D	CA31D	25239	1625	1825	2550	4175
SE Sedan 4D	CA31D	25989	1925	2150	3025	4825
GLE Sedan 4D	CA31D	27639	2150	2400	3325	5275

2003 NISSAN — (1N4,JN1or3N1)(CB51D)-3-#

SENTRA—4-Cyl.—Equipment Schedule 6
W.B. 99.8"; 1.8 Liter, 2.5 Liter.

Body Type	VIN	List	Good	Very Good	Good	Excellent
XE Sedan 4D	CB51D	13888	1200	1325	2075	3475
GXE Sedan 4D	CB51D	14639	1500	1650	2450	4075
Limited Sedan 4D	AB51D	17139	1950	2150	3000	4700
SE-R Sedan 4D	AB51D	16739	1725	1900	2650	4175
SE-R Spec V Sed 4D	AB51D	17739	1925	2125	2950	4600
ALTIMA—4-Cyl.—Equipment Schedule 4						
W.B. 110.2"; 2.5 Liter.						
2.5 Sedan 4D	AL11D	17689	1850	2075	2800	4400
2.5 S Sedan 4D	AL11D	19539	2125	2375	3175	4925
2.5 SL Sedan 4D	AL11D	23539	2725	3050	3925	6000
Manual, 5-Spd			(250)	(250)	(335)	(335)
ALTIMA—V6—Equipment Schedule 4						
W.B. 110.2"; 3.5 Liter.						

Body Type	VIN	List	Trade-In Good	Very Good	Pvt-Party Good	Retail Excellent
3.5 SE Sedan 4D	BL11D	23689	**3050**	**3400**	**4325**	**6575**
Manual, 5-Spd			**(250)**	**(250)**	**(335)**	**(335)**
MAXIMA—V6—Equipment Schedule 4						
W.B. 108.3"; 3.5 Liter.						
GXE Sedan 4D	DA31D	25439	**2225**	**2475**	**3225**	**4950**
SE Sedan 4D	DA31D	26189	**2500**	**2800**	**3575**	**5425**
GLE Sedan 4D	DA31D	28089	**2600**	**2900**	**3750**	**5750**
350Z—V6—Equipment Schedule 3						
W.B. 104.3"; 3.5 Liter.						
Coupe 2D	AZ34D	26809	**3850**	**4175**	**5050**	**7175**
Enthusiast Coupe 2D	AZ34D	29759	**4450**	**4800**	**5675**	**7900**
Performance Cpe 2D	AZ34D	30969	**4650**	**5025**	**5900**	**8200**
Touring Coupe 2D	AZ34D	32129	**4650**	**5025**	**5875**	**8150**
Track Coupe 2D	AZ34D	34619	**4875**	**5275**	**6300**	**8700**

Body Type	VIN	List	Trade-In Good	Very Good	Pvt-Party Good	Retail Excellent
SENTRA—4-Cyl.—Equipment Schedule 6						
W.B. 99.8"; 1.8 Liter.						
Sedan 4D	CB51D	13760	**1700**	**1875**	**2775**	**4475**
S Sedan 4D	CB51D	14740	**1875**	**2050**	**3000**	**4800**
SE-R Sedan 4D	AB51D	17640	**2075**	**2300**	**3175**	**4975**
SE-R Spec V Sed 4D	AB51D	17840	**2225**	**2425**	**3325**	**5150**
4-Cyl, 2.5 Liter	A		**125**	**125**	**180**	**180**
ALTIMA—4-Cyl.—Equipment Schedule 4						
W.B. 110.2"; 2.5 Liter.						
2.5 Sedan 4D	AL11D	17890	**2200**	**2450**	**3200**	**4900**
2.5 S Sedan 4D	AL11D	19740	**2500**	**2775**	**3575**	**5425**
2.5 SL Sedan 4D	AL11D	23740	**3500**	**3850**	**4825**	**7175**
Manual, 5-Spd			**(300)**	**(300)**	**(400)**	**(400)**
ALTIMA—V6—Equipment Schedule 4						
W.B. 110.2"; 3.5 Liter.						
3.5 SE Sedan 4D	BL11D	23790	**3650**	**4025**	**5000**	**7425**
Manual, 5-Spd			**(300)**	**(300)**	**(400)**	**(400)**
MAXIMA—V6—Equipment Schedule 4						
W.B. 111.2"; 3.5 Liter.						
SE Sedan 4D	BA41E	27510	**3150**	**3475**	**4350**	**6475**
SL Sedan 4D	BA41E	29440	**3250**	**3600**	**4525**	**6725**
350Z—V6—Equipment Schedule 3						
W.B. 104.3"; 3.5 Liter.						
Coupe 2D	AZ34D	26910	**4325**	**4675**	**5525**	**7700**
Enthusiast Coupe 2D	AZ34D	29860	**4850**	**5225**	**6225**	**8475**
Enthusiast Roadster	AZ36A	35580	**5550**	**5975**	**6950**	**9375**
Performance Cpe 2D	AZ34D	31070	**5050**	**5450**	**6450**	**8775**
Track Coupe 2D	AZ34D	34720	**5950**	**6400**	**7400**	**9975**
Touring Coupe 2D	AZ34D	33820	**5050**	**5450**	**6450**	**8775**
Touring Roadster 2D	AZ36A	37950	**5750**	**6175**	**7050**	**9375**

Body Type	VIN	List	Trade-In Good	Very Good	Pvt-Party Good	Retail Excellent
SENTRA—4-Cyl.—Equipment Schedule 6						
W.B. 99.8"; 1.8 Liter, 2.5 Liter.						
Sedan 4D	CB51D	14280	**2100**	**2325**	**3350**	**5175**
S Sedan 4D	CB51D	16280	**2425**	**2675**	**3675**	**5525**
SE-R Sedan 4D	AB51D	18180	**2650**	**2925**	**3825**	**5625**
SE-R Spec V Sed 4D	AB51D	18380	**2850**	**3125**	**4125**	**6125**
Special Edition			**25**	**25**	**35**	**35**
ALTIMA—4-Cyl.—Equipment Schedule 4						
W.B. 110.2"; 2.5 Liter.						
2.5 Sedan 4D	AL11D	17760	**2900**	**3225**	**4075**	**5900**
2.5 S Sedan 4D	AL11D	20110	**3350**	**3700**	**4600**	**6600**
SL			**475**	**475**	**615**	**615**
Manual, 5-Spd			**(350)**	**(350)**	**(465)**	**(465)**
ALTIMA—V6—Equipment Schedule 4						
W.B. 110.2"; 3.5 Liter.						
3.5 SE Sedan 4D	BL11D	24310	**3950**	**4350**	**5475**	**7800**
3.5 SL Sedan 4D	BL11D	27460	**4550**	**4975**	**6175**	**8775**
3.5 SE-R Sedan 4D	BL11D	29760	**5275**	**5725**	**7225**	**10200**
Manual, 5-Spd			**(350)**	**(350)**	**(465)**	**(465)**
MAXIMA—V6—Equipment Schedule 4						
W.B. 111.2"; 3.5 Liter.						
SE Sedan 4D	BA41E	28080	**3500**	**3850**	**4950**	**7125**
SL Sedan 4D	BA41E	29910	**3675**	**4025**	**5175**	**7450**

2005 NISSAN

Body Type	VIN	List	Trade-In Good	Very Good	Pvt-Party Good	Retail Excellent
350Z—V6—Equipment Schedule 3						
W.B. 104.3"; 3.5 Liter.						
Coupe 2D	AZ35D	27060	5100	5500	6600	8850
Enthusiast Coupe 2D	AZ34D	30010	5900	6325	7325	9650
Enthusiast Roadster	AZ36A	36030	6500	6975	8000	10450
Performance Cpe 2D	AZ34D	31210	6100	6550	7550	9950
Touring Coupe 2D	AZ34D	32360	6325	6775	7825	10250
Touring Roadster 2D	AZ36A	38430	7000	7500	8425	10850
Track Coupe 2D	AZ34D	34860	7500	8000	8925	11450
35th Anniv Coupe 2D	AZ34D	37660	8725	9300	10400	13350
Grand Touring Rdstr	AZ36D	39300	7500	8000	8875	11350

2006 NISSAN — (1N4,JN1or3N1)(CB51D)-6-#

Body Type	VIN	List	Trade-In Good	Very Good	Pvt-Party Good	Retail Excellent
SENTRA—4-Cyl.—Equipment Schedule 6						
W.B. 99.8"; 1.8 Liter, 2.5 Liter.						
Sedan 4D	CB51D	14615	2550	2825	3950	5850
S Sedan 4D	CB51D	16615	2800	3075	4250	6250
Manual, 5-Spd			(275)	(275)	(365)	(365)
SENTRA—4-Cyl.—Equipment Schedule 6						
W.B. 99.8"; 1.8 Liter, 2.5 Liter.						
SE-R Sedan 4D	AB51D	18580	3400	3700	4700	6600
SE-R Spec V Sed 4D	AB51D	18780	3700	4025	5000	7000
Special Edition			50	50	55	55
ALTIMA—4-Cyl.—Equipment Schedule 4						
W.B. 110.2"; 2.5 Liter.						
2.5 Sedan 4D	AL11D	18230	3175	3525	4375	6150
SL			500	500	665	665
ALTIMA—4-Cyl.—Equipment Schedule 4						
W.B. 110.2"; 2.5 Liter.						
2.5 S Sedan 4D	AL11D	20580	3900	4275	5225	7250
SL			500	500	665	665
Manual, 5-Spd			(400)	(400)	(535)	(535)
ALTIMA—V6—Equipment Schedule 4						
W.B. 110.2"; 3.5 Liter.						
3.5 SE Sedan 4D	BL11D	24730	4975	5400	6450	8875
3.5 SL Sedan 4D	BL11D	27880	5375	5850	7225	9925
3.5 SE-R Sedan 4D	BL11D	30130	6225	6750	8200	11250
Manual, 5-Spd			(400)	(400)	(535)	(535)
Manual, 6-Spd			0	0	0	0
MAXIMA—V6—Equipment Schedule 4						
W.B. 111.2"; 3.5 Liter.						
SE Sedan 4D	BA41E	28515	4325	4700	5700	7925
SL Sedan 4D	BA41E	30580	4725	5125	6150	8500
350Z—V6—Equipment Schedule 3						
W.B. 104.3"; 3.5 Liter.						
Coupe 2D	AZ34D	28030	5900	6350	7375	9675
Enthusiast Coupe 2D	AZ34D	30730	6625	7075	8100	10450
Enthusiast Roadster	AZ36A	35665	7375	7850	8875	11400
Touring Coupe 2D	AZ34D	33330	7225	7700	8725	11250
Touring Roadster 2D	AZ36A	39285	7825	8325	9200	11650
Track Coupe 2D	AZ34D	34930	8450	9000	9925	12550
Grand Touring Coupe	AZ34D	37465	8175	8725	9850	12550
Grand Touring Rdstr	AZ36D	41615	8175	8725	9650	12150

2007 NISSAN—(1N4,JN1or3N1)(BC11E)-7-#

Body Type	VIN	List	Trade-In Good	Very Good	Pvt-Party Good	Retail Excellent
VERSA—4-Cyl.—Equipment Schedule 6						
W.B. 102.4"; 1.8 Liter.						
S Sedan 4D	BC11E	13975	3200	3550	4425	6275
S Hatchback 4D	BC13E	13975	3350	3700	4600	6525
SL Sedan 4D	BC11E	16175	3925	4300	5250	7400
SL Hatchback 4D	BC13E	16175	3850	4225	5175	7275
Manual, 6-Spd			(350)	(350)	(465)	(465)
SENTRA—4-Cyl.—Equipment Schedule 6						
W.B. 105.7"; 2.0 Liter.						
Sedan 4D	AB61E	16175	3925	4275	5425	7625
S Sedan 4D	AB61E	17075	4025	4375	5550	7800
Manual, 6-Spd			(350)	(350)	(465)	(465)
SENTRA—4-Cyl.—Equipment Schedule 6						
W.B. 105.7"; 2.0 Liter, 2.5 Liter.						
SL Sedan 4D	AB61E	19015	4325	4675	5900	8250
SE-R Sedan 4D	BB61E	20015	4700	5075	6350	7950
SE-R Spec V Sedan	CB61E	20515	5150	5525	6550	8650

Body Type	VIN	List	Trade-In Good	Very Good	Pvt-Party Good	Retail Excellent
ALTIMA—4-Cyl.—Equipment Schedule 4						
W.B. 109.3"; 2.5 Liter.						
2.5 Sedan 4D	AL21E	18565	5250	5675	6425	8450
2.5 S Sedan 4D	AL21E	20925	5550	6000	6750	8875
SL			600	600	800	800
ALTIMA—4-Cyl. Hybrid—Equipment Schedule 4						
W.B. 109.3"; 2.5 Liter.						
Sedan 4D	CL21E	25015	6100	6575	7575	9925
ALTIMA—V6—Equipment Schedule 4						
W.B. 109.3"; 3.5 Liter.						
3.5 SE Sedan 4D	BL21E	25125	7325	7875	9225	12200
3.5 SL Sedan 4D	BL21E	29015	8375	8950	10400	13750
MAXIMA—V6—Equipment Schedule 4						
W.B. 111.2"; 3.5 Liter.						
SE Sedan 4D	BA41E	28665	5425	5850	6925	9175
SL Sedan 4D	BA41E	30915	5800	6250	7400	9775
Driver's Preferred Pkg			325	325	435	435
350Z—V6—Equipment Schedule 3						
W.B. 104.3"; 3.5 Liter.						
Coupe 2D	BZ34D	28515	6650	7100	8175	10500
Enthusiast Coupe 2D	BZ34D	30600	7500	8000	9050	11550
Enthusiast Roadster	BZ36A	37175	8400	8925	9875	12450
Touring Coupe 2D	BZ34D	33200	8500	9025	9975	12550
Touring Roadster 2D	BZ36A	39525	8800	9350	10150	12650
Grand Touring Coupe	BZ34A	37725	9275	9850	10950	13750
Grand Touring Rdstr	BZ36A	41875	9275	9850	10750	13250
NISMO Coupe 2D	BZ34D	38695	****	****	****	15450
2008 NISSAN — (1N4,JN1or3N1)(BC11E)-8-#						
VERSA—4-Cyl.—Equipment Schedule 6						
W.B. 102.4"; 1.8 Liter.						
S Sedan 4D	BC11E	14170	3800	4150	5000	6875
S Hatchback 4D	BC13E	14270	3925	4275	5175	7100
SL Sedan 4D	BC11E	16120	4400	4800	5700	7725
SL Hatchback 4D	BC13E	16470	4500	4900	5800	7875
Manual, 6-Spd w/Overdrive			(375)	(375)	(500)	(500)
SENTRA—4-Cyl.—Equipment Schedule 6						
W.B. 105.7"; 2.0 Liter.						
S Sedan 4D	AB61E	17730	4850	5225	6250	8375
Manual, 6-Spd			(400)	(400)	(525)	(525)
SENTRA—4-Cyl.—Equipment Schedule 6						
W.B. 105.7"; 2.0 Liter, 2.5 Liter.						
Sedan 4D	AB61E	16375	4650	5000	6025	8100
SL Sedan 4D	AB61E	19305	5300	5675	6675	8825
SE-R Sedan 4D	BB61E	20305	5325	5700	6800	8950
SE-R Spec V Sedan	CB61E	20305	6300	6700	7700	9900
ALTIMA—4-Cyl.—Equipment Schedule 4						
W.B. 105.3", 109.3" (Sed); 2.5 Liter.						
2.5 Sedan 4D	AL21E	18855	6100	6525	7525	9725
2.5 S Sedan 4D	AL21E	21625	6575	7025	8050	10350
2.5 S Coupe 2D	AL24E	21650	7525	8025	9250	11900
SL			700	700	935	935
ALTIMA—4-Cyl. Hybrid—Equipment Schedule 4						
W.B. 109.3"; 2.5 Liter.						
Sedan 4D	CL21E	25695	7900	8425	9650	12400
ALTIMA—V6—Equipment Schedule 4						
W.B. 105.3", 109.3" (Sed); 3.5 Liter.						
3.5 SE Sedan 4D	BL21E	25630	8650	9200	10450	13400
3.5 SE Coupe 2D	BL24E	26050	9725	10350	11800	15150
3.5 SL Sedan 4D	BL21E	28905	9425	10000	11500	14750
MAXIMA—V6—Equipment Schedule 4						
W.B. 111.2"; 3.5 Liter.						
SE Sedan 4D	BA41E	28755	6550	7000	7925	10100
SL Sedan 4D	BA41E	31005	7325	7800	8800	11250
350Z—V6—Equipment Schedule 3						
W.B. 104.3"; 3.5 Liter.						
Coupe 2D	BZ34D	28605	8075	8550	9575	11900
Enthusiast Coupe 2D	BZ34D	31305	8875	9375	10300	12700
Enthusiast Roadster	BZ36A	37940	9700	10250	11250	13800
Touring Coupe 2D	BZ34D	33935	9800	10350	11250	13700
Touring Roadster 2D	BZ36A	40290	10100	10650	11550	14000
Grand Touring Cpe 2D	BZ34D	38400	10600	11200	12250	15000
Grand Touring Rdstr	BZ36A	42640	10700	11300	12100	14600

Body Type	VIN	List	Trade-In Good	Very Good	Pvt-Party Good	Retail Excellent
NISMO Coupe 2D	BZ34D	38775	****	****	****	**16800**

2009 NISSAN — (1N4,JN1or3N1)(AZ28R)–9–#

CUBE—4-Cyl.—Equipment Schedule 6
W.B. 99.6"; 1.8 Liter.

Body Type	VIN	List	Trade-In Good	Very Good	Pvt-Party Good	Retail Excellent
Wagon 4D	AZ28R	14770	5625	6000	6975	8900
SL Sport Wagon 4D	AZ28R	17570	7000	7425	8400	10550
Krom Sport Wagon	AZ28R	20150	8250	8725	9675	12000

CUBE—4-Cyl.—Equipment Schedule 6
W.B. 99.6"; 1.8 Liter.

S Sport Wagon 4D	AZ28T	16410	6150	6550	7550	9625
Manual, 6-Spd			(425)	(425)	(565)	(565)

VERSA—4-Cyl.—Equipment Schedule 6
W.B. 102.4"; 1.6 Liter.

Sedan 4D	CC11E	11685	3400	3725	4475	5975
Automatic, 4-Spd w/OD			350	350	465	465

VERSA—4-Cyl.—Equipment Schedule 6
W.B. 102.4"; 1.8 Liter.

S Sedan 4D	BC11E	14685	4450	4825	5725	7625
S Hatchback 4D	BC13E	14685	4450	4825	5725	7625
Manual, 6-Spd w/Overdrive			(400)	(400)	(535)	(535)

VERSA—4-Cyl.—Equipment Schedule 6
W.B. 102.4"; 1.8 Liter.

SL Sedan 4D	BC11E	16650	4925	5325	6250	8300
SL Hatchback 4D	BC13E	16870	5025	6375	6375	8425
SL FE Plus Hatchback	BC13E	17050	5175	5575	6550	8650

SENTRA—4-Cyl.—Equipment Schedule 6
W.B. 105.7"; 2.0 Liter.

Sedan 4D	AB61E	17425	5650	6025	7175	9300
S Sedan 4D	AB61E	18455	5800	6175	7325	9500
Manual, 6-Spd			(425)	(425)	(565)	(565)

SENTRA—4-Cyl.—Equipment Schedule 6
W.B. 105.7"; 2.0 Liter, 2.5 Liter.

FE Plus Sedan 4D	AB61E	18000	5750	6125	7250	9400
S FE Plus Sedan 4D	AB61E	19030	6000	6400	7550	9750
SR FE Plus Sedan 4D	AB61E	18480	5975	6375	7450	9550
SL Sedan 4D	AB61E	20355	6350	6750	7875	10100
SL FE Plus Sedan 4D	AB61E	20930	6550	6950	8150	10500
SE-R Sedan 4D	BB61E	21355	6925	7350	8400	10650
SE-R Spec V Sedan	CB61E	21855	7375	7825	8975	11350

ALTIMA—4-Cyl.—Equipment Schedule 4
W.B. 105.3", 109.3" (Sed); 2.5 Liter.

2.5 Sedan 4D	AL21E	20595	7175	7625	8650	10900
2.5 S Sedan 4D	AL21E	22235	7500	7975	9100	11450
2.5 S Coupe 2D	AL24E	22945	8900	9425	10600	13300
SL			800	800	1050	1050

ALTIMA—4-Cyl. Hybrid—Equipment Schedule 4
W.B. 109.3"; 2.5 Liter.

Sedan 4D	CL21E	27345	9250	9775	11100	13900

ALTIMA—V6—Equipment Schedule 4
W.B. 105.3", 109.3" (Sed); 3.5 Liter.

3.5 SE Sedan 4D	BL21E	26375	10050	10600	11950	14950
3.5 SE Coupe 2D	BL24E	27585	11050	11600	13150	16500
3.5 SL Sedan 4D	BL21E	30075	10800	11400	12850	16100

MAXIMA—V6—Equipment Schedule 4
W.B. 109.3"; 3.5 Liter.

S Sedan 4D	BA41E	29985	10900	11500	12400	15000
SV Sedan 4D	BA41E	32685	11200	11800	12800	15500

350Z—V6—Equipment Schedule 3
W.B. 104.3"; 3.5 Liter.

Enthusiast Roadster	BZ36A	38565	14050	14700	15550	18250
Touring Roadster 2D	BZ36A	40915	14250	14900	15700	18350
Grand Touring Rdstr	BZ36A	43265	15150	15850	16550	19250

370Z—V6—Equipment Schedule 4
W.B. 100.4"; 3.7 Liter.

Coupe 2D	AZ44E	30650	12400	12950	13800	16300
Touring Coupe 2D	AZ44E	35180	14150	14800	15600	18250
NISMO Coupe 2D	AZ44E	39850	****	****	****	21200
Sport Pkg			1100	1100	1245	1245

LEAF—AC Electric—Equipment Schedule 3
W.B. 106.3".

S Hatchback 4D	AZ0CP	29650	13300	13900	14700	16950
SV Hatchback 4D	AZ0CP	32670	13900	14500	15250	17550

Body Type	VIN	List	Trade-In Good	Trade-In Very Good	Pvt-Party Good	Retail Excellent
SL Hatchback 4D	AZ0CP	35690	14950	15600	16300	18700
GT-R AWD—V6 Turbo—Equipment Schedule 2						
W.B. 109.5"; 3.8 Liter.						
Coupe 2D	AR54M	77840	41200	42700	42900	48500
Premium Coupe 2D	AR54F	80090	42000	43500	43700	49400

2010 NISSAN — (1,3orJ)N(1,4or6)(AZ2KT)–A–#

Body Type	VIN	List	Trade-In Good	Trade-In Very Good	Pvt-Party Good	Retail Excellent
CUBE—4-Cyl.—Equipment Schedule 6						
W.B. 99.6"; 1.8 Liter.						
S Sport Wagon 4D	AZ2KT	16750	6950	7350	8375	10450
Manual, 6-Spd w/Overdrive			(475)	(475)	(625)	(625)
CUBE—4-Cyl.—Equipment Schedule 6						
W.B. 99.6"; 1.8 Liter.						
Wagon 4D	AZ2KR	14710	6125	6500	7500	9450
SL Sport Wagon 4D	AZ2KR	17850	7825	8275	9275	11450
Krom Sport Wagon	AZ2KR	20840	9025	9525	10450	12800
VERSA—4-Cyl.—Equipment Schedule 6						
W.B. 102.4"; 1.6 Liter.						
Sedan 4D	CC1AE	11710	4600	4950	5675	7300
Automatic, 4-Spd w/OD			400	400	535	535
VERSA—4-Cyl.—Equipment Schedule 6						
W.B. 102.4"; 1.8 Liter.						
S Sedan 4D	BC1AE	14820	5450	5850	6825	8700
S Hatchback 4D	BC1CE	14870	5500	5900	6900	8850
Manual, 6-Spd w/Overdrive			(475)	(475)	(625)	(625)
VERSA—4-Cyl.—Equipment Schedule 6						
W.B. 102.4"; 1.8 Liter.						
SL Sedan 4D	BC1AE	16820	6350	6775	7775	9850
SL Hatchback 4D	BC1CE	17250	6800	7250	8275	10500
SENTRA—4-Cyl.—Equipment Schedule 6						
W.B. 105.7"; 2.0 Liter.						
Sedan 4D	AB6AP	17320	6525	6950	8025	10150
Manual, 6-Spd w/Overdrive			(475)	(475)	(625)	(625)
SENTRA—4-Cyl.—Equipment Schedule 6						
W.B. 105.7"; 2.0 Liter, 2.5 Liter.						
S Sedan 4D	AB6AP	17880	6775	7200	8250	10400
SR Sedan 4D	AB6AP	17880	6775	7200	8250	10400
SL Sedan 4D	AB6AP	19280	7900	8350	9450	11750
SE-R Sedan 4D	BB6AP	20300	8450	8925	10050	12500
SE-R Spec V Sedan	CB6AP	20800	8750	9250	10400	12850
ALTIMA—4-Cyl.—Equipment Schedule 4						
W.B. 105.3", 109.3" (Sed); 2.5 Liter.						
2.5 Sedan 4D	AL2AP	20620	8475	8925	10050	12350
2.5 S Sedan 4D	AL2AP	22560	8775	9250	10350	12700
2.5 S Coupe 2D	AL2EP	23660	10050	10600	11850	14550
SL			900	900	1145	1145
ALTIMA—4-Cyl. Hybrid—Equipment Schedule 4						
W.B. 109.3"; 2.5 Liter.						
Sedan 4D	CL2AP	27500	10450	11000	12250	15000
Premium Pkg			1000	1000	1270	1270
ALTIMA—V6—Equipment Schedule 4						
W.B. 105.3", 109.3" (Sed); 3.5 Liter.						
3.5 SR Sedan 4D	BL2AP	25240	11300	11900	13300	16300
3.5 SR Coupe 2D	BL2EP	27990	11950	12550	14100	17350
Premium Pkg			1000	1000	1275	1275
MAXIMA—V6—Equipment Schedule 4						
W.B. 109.3"; 3.5 Liter.						
S Sedan 4D	AA5AE	31180	12250	12800	13850	16500
SV Sedan 4D	AA5AE	33900	12600	13200	14200	16950
370Z—V6—Equipment Schedule 4						
W.B. 100.4"; 3.7 Liter.						
Coupe 2D	AZ4EE	30710	14550	15200	16100	18650
Roadster 2D	AZ4FH	37690	17050	17750	18550	21300
Touring Coupe 2D	AZ4EE	35380	16450	17100	17900	20600
Touring Roadster 2D	AZ4FH	42540	17750	18500	19150	21900
NISMO Coupe 2D	AZ4EE	39910	****	****	****	23600
Sport Pkg			1200	1200	1340	1340
GT-R AWD—V6 Twin Turbo—Equipment Schedule 2						
W.B. 109.4"; 3.8 Liter.						
Coupe 2D	AR5EF	81790	47300	48900	49300	55600
Premium Coupe 2D	AR5EF	84040	47700	49400	49900	56100

Body Type	VIN	List	Trade-In Good	Very Good	Pvt-Party Good	Retail Excellent

2011 NISSAN — (1,3orJ)N(1or4)(AZ2KT)–B–#

CUBE—4-Cyl.—Equipment Schedule 6
W.B. 99.6"; 1.8 Liter.

Body Type	VIN	List	Good	Very Good	Good	Excellent
S Sport Wagon 4D	AZ2KT	17430	**7875**	**8300**	**9325**	**11400**
Manual, 6-Spd w/Overdrive			**(500)**	**(500)**	**(640)**	**(640)**

CUBE—4-Cyl.—Equipment Schedule 6
W.B. 99.6"; 1.8 Liter.

Wagon 4D	AZ2KR	15040	**6825**	**7225**	**8200**	**10100**
SL Sport Wagon 4D	AZ2KR	18500	**8925**	**9400**	**10400**	**12600**
S Krom Sport Wagon	AZ2KR	21940	**9975**	**10500**	**11500**	**13850**

VERSA—4-Cyl.—Equipment Schedule 6
W.B. 102.4"; 1.6 Liter.

Sedan 4D	CC1AP	11990	**5175**	**5525**	**6500**	**8225**
Automatic, 4-Spd w/OD			**450**	**450**	**600**	**600**

VERSA—4-Cyl.—Equipment Schedule 6
W.B. 102.4"; 1.8 Liter.

S Sedan 4D	BC1AP	15350	**6175**	**6575**	**7500**	**9350**
S Hatchback 4D	BC1CP	15300	**6075**	**6475**	**7550**	**9575**
Manual, 6-Spd w/Overdrive			**(500)**	**(500)**	**(665)**	**(665)**

VERSA—4-Cyl.—Equipment Schedule 6
W.B. 102.4"; 1.8 Liter.

SL Sedan 4D	BC1AP	17220	**7350**	**7775**	**8950**	**11250**
SL Hatchback 4D	BC1CP	17650	**8300**	**8750**	**9875**	**12250**

SENTRA—4-Cyl.—Equipment Schedule 6
W.B. 105.7"; 2.0 Liter.

Sedan 4D	AB6AP	17104	**7750**	**8175**	**9275**	**11450**
Manual, 6-Spd w/Overdrive			**(500)**	**(500)**	**(655)**	**(655)**

SENTRA—4-Cyl.—Equipment Schedule 6
W.B. 105.7"; 2.0 Liter, 2.5 Liter.

S Sedan 4D	AB6AP	18200	**7950**	**8375**	**9450**	**11650**
SR Sedan 4D	AB6AP	18200	**8050**	**8475**	**9575**	**11800**
SL Sedan 4D	AB6AP	19600	**9000**	**9475**	**10500**	**12850**
SE-R Sedan 4D	BB6AP	20330	**9425**	**9925**	**11050**	**13450**
SE-R Spec V Sedan	CB6AP	20830	**9725**	**10250**	**11350**	**13800**

ALTIMA—4-Cyl.—Equipment Schedule 4
W.B. 105.3", 109.3" (Sed); 2.5 Liter.

2.5 Sedan 4D	AL2AP	20650	**9225**	**9675**	**10900**	**13300**
2.5 S Sedan 4D	AL2AP	22810	**9725**	**10200**	**11500**	**13950**
2.5 S Coupe 2D	AL2EP	24190	**10800**	**11300**	**12700**	**15450**
SL			**900**	**900**	**1140**	**1140**

ALTIMA—4-Cyl. Hybrid—Equipment Schedule 4
W.B. 109.3"; 2.5 Liter.

Sedan 4D	CL2AP	27530	**11350**	**11900**	**13300**	**16200**
Premium Pkg			**1050**	**1050**	**1335**	**1335**

ALTIMA—V6—Equipment Schedule 4
W.B. 105.3", 109.3" (Sed); 3.5 Liter.

3.5 SR Sedan 4D	BL2AP	25490	**12250**	**12800**	**14350**	**17450**
3.5 SR Coupe 2D	BL2EP	28520	**13250**	**13800**	**15550**	**18900**
Premium Pkg			**1050**	**1050**	**1340**	**1340**

MAXIMA—V6—Equipment Schedule 4
W.B. 109.3"; 3.5 Liter.

S Sedan 4D	AA5AP	31560	**14050**	**14650**	**15850**	**18750**
SV Sedan 4D	AA5AP	34280	**14200**	**14800**	**16000**	**18900**

370Z—V6—Equipment Schedule 4
W.B. 100.4"; 3.7 Liter.

Coupe 2D	AZ4EH	31360	**15900**	**16550**	**17600**	**20300**
Roadster 2D	AZ4FH	38270	**18450**	**19150**	**20100**	**23000**
Touring Coupe 2D	AZ4EH	36030	**17650**	**18350**	**19300**	**22100**
Touring Roadster 2D	AZ4FH	43150	**19350**	**20100**	**20900**	**23800**
NISMO Coupe 2D	AZ4EH	40740	********	********	********	**25400**
Sport Pkg			**1275**	**1275**	**1435**	**1435**

LEAF—AC Electric—Equipment Schedule 3
W.B. 106.3".

SV Hatchback 4D	AZ0CP	33600	**9025**	**9500**	**10250**	**12150**
SL Hatchback 4D	AZ0CP	34540	**9325**	**9800**	**10500**	**12450**
Quick Charge Port			**550**	**550**	**645**	**645**

GT-R AWD—V6 Twin Turbo—Equipment Schedule 2
W.B. 109.4"; 3.8 Liter.

Premium Coupe 2D	AR5EF	85060	**49400**	**51000**	**51700**	**57800**

Body Type	VIN	List	Trade-In Good	Very Good	Pvt-Party Good	Retail Excellent

2012 NISSAN — (1,3orJ)N(1,3or4)(AZ2KT)–C–#

CUBE—4-Cyl.—Equipment Schedule 6
W.B. 99.6"; 1.8 Liter.

Body Type	VIN	List	Good	Very Good	Good	Excellent
S Sport Wagon 4D	AZ2KT	18200	**9275**	**9750**	**10800**	**13050**
Manual, 6-Spd.	-------		**(550)**	**(550)**	**(690)**	**(690)**

CUBE—4-Cyl.—Equipment Schedule 6
W.B. 99.6"; 1.8 Liter.

Body Type	VIN	List	Good	Very Good	Good	Excellent
Wagon 4D	AZ2KT	15760	**7775**	**8200**	**9250**	**11300**
SL Sport Wagon 4D	AZ2KT	19300	**10100**	**10650**	**11650**	**13900**

VERSA—4-Cyl.—Equipment Schedule 6
W.B. 102.4"; 1.6 Liter.

Body Type	VIN	List	Good	Very Good	Good	Excellent
S Sedan 4D	CN7AP	11750	**7250**	**7650**	**8600**	**10550**
Automatic, CVT			**475**	**475**	**610**	**610**

VERSA—4-Cyl.—Equipment Schedule 6
W.B. 102.4"; 1.8 Liter.

Body Type	VIN	List	Good	Very Good	Good	Excellent
S Hatchback 4D	BC1CP	16260	**8400**	**8850**	**9925**	**12200**
Manual, 6-Spd.	-------		**(550)**	**(550)**	**(710)**	**(710)**

VERSA—4-Cyl.—Equipment Schedule 6
W.B. 102.4"; 1.6 Liter, 1.8 Liter.

Body Type	VIN	List	Good	Very Good	Good	Excellent
SV Sedan 4D	CN7AP	15320	**8100**	**8525**	**9600**	**11800**
SL Sedan 4D	CN7AP	16320	**9100**	**9575**	**10700**	**13100**
SL Hatchback 4D	BC1CP	19150	**10050**	**10550**	**11600**	**14100**

SENTRA—4-Cyl.—Equipment Schedule 6
W.B. 105.7"; 2.0 Liter.

Body Type	VIN	List	Good	Very Good	Good	Excellent
Sedan 4D	AB6AP	18210	**9150**	**9600**	**10650**	**12950**
Manual, 6-Spd.	-------		**(550)**	**(550)**	**(710)**	**(710)**

SENTRA—4-Cyl.—Equipment Schedule 6
W.B. 105.7"; 2.0 Liter, 2.5 Liter.

Body Type	VIN	List	Good	Very Good	Good	Excellent
S Sedan 4D	AB6AP	18740	**9225**	**9700**	**10800**	**13050**
SR Sedan 4D	AB6AP	18740	**9225**	**9700**	**10800**	**13000**
SL Sedan 4D	AB6AP	20140	**10450**	**11000**	**12000**	**14350**
SE-R Sedan 4D	BB6AP	20870	**11450**	**12050**	**13250**	**15950**
SE-R Spec V Sedan 4D	CB6AP	21370	**11800**	**12400**	**13600**	**16400**

ALTIMA—4-Cyl.—Equipment Schedule 4
W.B. 105.3", 109.3" (Sed); 2.5 Liter.

Body Type	VIN	List	Good	Very Good	Good	Excellent
2.5 Sedan 4D	AL2AP	21170	**10300**	**10750**	**12100**	**14600**
2.5 S Sedan 4D	AL2AP	23330	**10700**	**11150**	**12550**	**15150**
2.5 S Coupe 2D	AL2EP	24860	**11850**	**12350**	**13900**	**16750**
SL			**900**	**900**	**1130**	**1130**

ALTIMA—V6—Equipment Schedule 4
W.B. 105.3", 109.3" (Sed); 3.5 Liter.

Body Type	VIN	List	Good	Very Good	Good	Excellent
3.5 SR Sedan 4D	BL2AP	26190	**13000**	**13550**	**15300**	**18500**
3.5 SR Coupe 2D	BL2EP	29190	**14350**	**14950**	**16800**	**20300**
Premium Pkg			**1125**	**1125**	**1410**	**1410**

MAXIMA—V6—Equipment Schedule 4
W.B. 109.3"; 3.5 Liter.

Body Type	VIN	List	Good	Very Good	Good	Excellent
S Sedan 4D	AA5AP	32510	**14800**	**15400**	**16700**	**19600**
SV Sedan 4D	AA5AP	35210	**15400**	**16000**	**17350**	**20400**
Premium Pkg			**1000**	**1000**	**1195**	**1195**
Sport Pkg			**325**	**325**	**390**	**390**

370Z—V6—Equipment Schedule 4
W.B. 100.4"; 3.7 Liter.

Body Type	VIN	List	Good	Very Good	Good	Excellent
Coupe 2D	AZ4EH	32210	**16850**	**17450**	**18600**	**21300**
Roadster 2D	AZ4FH	40260	**19800**	**20500**	**21500**	**24300**
Touring Coupe 2D	AZ4EH	36910	**18500**	**19200**	**20200**	**23000**
Touring Roadster 2D	AZ4FH	44280	**20600**	**21300**	**22200**	**25100**
NISMO Coupe 2D	AZ4EH	41590	**21700**	**22400**	**23400**	**26400**
Sport Pkg			**1350**	**1350**	**1520**	**1520**

LEAF—AC Electric—Equipment Schedule 3
W.B. 106.3".

Body Type	VIN	List	Good	Very Good	Good	Excellent
SV Hatchback 4D	AZ0CP	36050	**10750**	**11300**	**12500**	**14050**
SL Hatchback 4D	AZ0CP	38100	**11200**	**11750**	**12500**	**14550**

GT-R AWD—V6 Twin Turbo—Equipment Schedule 2
W.B. 109.4"; 3.8 Liter.

Body Type	VIN	List	Good	Very Good	Good	Excellent
Premium Coupe 2D	AR5EF	90950	**57500**	**59300**	**59500**	**65900**
Black Edition Coupe	AR5EF	96100	**60700**	**62700**	**62700**	**69300**

2013 NISSAN — (1,3orJ)N(1,3or4)(AZ2KT)–D–#

CUBE—4-Cyl.—Equipment Schedule 6
W.B. 99.6"; 1.8 Liter.

Body Type	VIN	List	Good	Very Good	Good	Excellent
S Wagon 4D	AZ2KT	18550	**10350**	**10850**	**11900**	**14250**

Body Type	VIN	List	Trade-In Good	Very Good	Pvt-Party Good	Retail Excellent
Manual, 6-Spd			**(550)**	**(550)**	**(680)**	**(680)**
CUBE—4-Cyl.—Equipment Schedule 6						
W.B. 99.6"; 1.8 Liter.						
SL Wagon 4D	AZ2KT	19650	**11150**	**11650**	**12750**	**15100**
VERSA—4-Cyl.—Equipment Schedule 6						
W.B. 102.4"; 1.6 Liter, 1.8 Liter.						
S Sedan 4D	CN7AP	12770	**8075**	**8500**	**9475**	**11500**
S Plus Sedan 4D	CN7AP	14470	**8550**	**9000**	**10050**	**12200**
SV Sedan 4D	CN7AP	15770	**8750**	**9200**	**10300**	**12600**
SL Sedan 4D	CN7AP	17700	**9600**	**10050**	**11250**	**13650**
SENTRA—4-Cyl.—Equipment Schedule 6						
W.B. 106.3"; 1.8 Liter.						
FE+ S Sedan 4D	AB7AP	18440	**10550**	**11100**	**12000**	**14150**
FE+ SV Sedan 4D	AB7AP	18600	**10650**	**11150**	**12050**	**14250**
SV Sedan 4D	AB7AP	18750	**10800**	**11300**	**12200**	**14400**
SR Sedan 4D	AB7AP	19650	**11350**	**11900**	**12900**	**15200**
SL Sedan 4D	AB7AP	20540	**12250**	**12800**	**13700**	**16100**
SENTRA—4-Cyl.—Equipment Schedule 6						
W.B. 106.3"; 1.8 Liter.						
S Sedan 4D	AB7AP	18040	**10450**	**11000**	**11900**	**14050**
Manual, 6-Spd			**(550)**	**(550)**	**(680)**	**(680)**
ALTIMA—4-Cyl.—Equipment Schedule 4						
W.B. 105.3", 109.3" (Sed); 2.5 Liter.						
2.5 Sedan 4D	AL3AP	22280	**11950**	**12450**	**13650**	**16100**
2.5 S Sedan 4D	AL3AP	23280	**12350**	**12850**	**14100**	**16650**
2.5 S Coupe 2D	AL2EP	25760	**13050**	**13550**	**15050**	**17850**
2.5 SV Sedan 4D	AL3AP	24880	**13050**	**13600**	**14950**	**17700**
2.5 SL Sedan 4D	AL3AP	28830	**15000**	**15600**	**17300**	**20600**
Premium Pkg			**1175**	**1175**	**1410**	**1410**
ALTIMA—V6—Equipment Schedule 4						
W.B. 105.3", 109.3" (Sed); 3.5 Liter.						
3.5 S Sedan 4D	BL3AP	26140	**14300**	**14850**	**16550**	**19700**
3.5 SV Sedan 4D	BL3AP	28560	**14700**	**15250**	**16950**	**20200**
3.5 SL Sedan 4D	BL3AP	30860	**15850**	**16450**	**18100**	**21500**
MAXIMA—V6—Equipment Schedule 4						
W.B. 109.3"; 3.5 Liter.						
S Sedan 4D	AA5AP	33560	**15300**	**15900**	**17450**	**20600**
SV Sedan 4D	AA5AP	35860	**16550**	**17200**	**18900**	**22400**
Premium Pkg			**1100**	**1100**	**1310**	**1310**
Sport Pkg			**350**	**350**	**415**	**415**
370Z—V6—Equipment Schedule 4						
W.B. 100.4"; 3.7 Liter.						
Coupe 2D	AZ4EH	33900	**19150**	**19850**	**21000**	**24000**
Roadster 2D	AZ4FH	42250	**22100**	**22900**	**23900**	**27100**
Touring Coupe 2D	AZ4EH	38600	**20900**	**21600**	**22700**	**25700**
Touring Roadster 2D	AZ4FH	44950	**22900**	**23700**	**24700**	**27900**
NISMO Coupe 2D	AZ4EH	43800	**24000**	**24800**	**25800**	**29100**
Sport Pkg			**1425**	**1425**	**1600**	**1600**
LEAF—AC Electric—Equipment Schedule 3						
W.B. 106.3".						
S Hatchback 4D	AZ0CP	29650	**13300**	**13900**	**14700**	**16950**
SV Hatchback 4D	AZ0CP	32670	**13900**	**14500**	**15250**	**17550**
SL Hatchback 4D	AZ0CP	35690	**14950**	**15600**	**16300**	**18700**
Quick Charge Port			**600**	**600**	**685**	**685**
GT-R AWD—V6 Twin Turbo—Equipment Schedule 2						
W.B. 109.4"; 3.8 Liter.						
Premium Coupe 2D	AR5EF	97820	**60700**	**62700**	**62100**	**67900**
Black Edition Coupe	AR5EF	107320	**64000**	**66100**	**65300**	**71400**

2014 NISSAN — (1,3orJ)N(1,3or4)(AZ2KR)–E–#

Body Type	VIN	List	Trade-In Good	Very Good	Pvt-Party Good	Retail Excellent
CUBE—4-Cyl.—Equipment Schedule 6						
W.B. 99.6"; 1.8 Liter.						
S Wagon 4D	AZ2KR	18570	**11050**	**11600**	**12600**	**14950**
Manual, 6-Spd			**(550)**	**(550)**	**(670)**	**(670)**
CUBE—4-Cyl.—Equipment Schedule 6						
W.B. 99.6"; 1.8 Liter.						
SL Wagon 4D	AZ2KR	19670	**12000**	**12550**	**13550**	**15950**
VERSA—4-Cyl.—Equipment Schedule 6						
W.B. 102.4"; 1.6 Liter.						
S Sedan 4D	CN7AP	12780	**8625**	**9075**	**10000**	**12050**
Automatic, 4-Spd			**525**	**525**	**655**	**655**
VERSA—4-Cyl.—Equipment Schedule 6						
W.B. 102.4"; 1.6 Liter.						

Body Type	VIN	List	Trade-In Good	Very Good	Pvt-Party Good	Retail Excellent
S Plus Sedan 4D	CN7AP	14580	8950	9400	10400	12600
SV Sedan 4D	CN7AP	16030	9200	9650	10800	13100
SL Sedan 4D	CN7AP	17680	10400	10900	11950	14350
Note S Hatchback 4D	CE2CP	14800	9000	9450	10500	12700
Note S Plus H'Back 4D	CE2CP	16050	9400	9875	11000	13300
Note SV Hatchback 4D	CE2CP	16800	9700	10150	11300	13700
SENTRA—4-Cyl.—Equipment Schedule 6						
W.B. 106.3"; 1.8 Liter.						
S Sedan 4D	AB7AP	17600	11250	11800	12700	14950
Manual, 6-Spd			(550)	(550)	(670)	(670)
SENTRA—4-Cyl.—Equipment Schedule 6						
W.B. 106.3"; 1.8 Liter.						
FE+ Sedan 4D	AB7AP	18000	11450	12000	12900	15150
FE+ SV Sedan 4D	AB7AP	18700	12050	12600	13500	15800
SR Sedan 4D	AB7AP	19500	12600	13200	14100	16500
SV Sedan 4D	AB7AP	18300	11750	12300	13200	15450
SL Sedan 4D	AB7AP	20400	13050	13650	14500	16950
ALTIMA—4-Cyl.—Equipment Schedule 4						
W.B. 109.3"; 2.5 Liter.						
2.5 Sedan 4D	AL3AP	22670	12850	13400	14800	17450
2.5 S Sedan 4D	AL3AP	23190	13450	14000	15450	18200
2.5 SV Sedan 4D	AL3AP	24990	14050	14600	16100	18950
2.5 SL Sedan 4D	AL3AP	28570	16500	17100	18650	22000
ALTIMA—V6—Equipment Schedule 4						
W.B. 109.3"; 3.5 Liter.						
3.5 S Sedan 4D	BL3AP	26970	16000	16600	18100	21300
3.5 SV Sedan 4D	BL3AP	29170	16600	17200	19100	22800
3.5 SL Sedan 4D	BL3AP	31470	17500	18150	19900	23500
MAXIMA—V6—Equipment Schedule 4						
W.B. 109.3"; 3.5 Liter.						
S Sedan 4D	AA5AP	31810	16000	16550	18100	21300
SV Sedan 4D	AA5AP	34900	18200	18850	20600	24400
Premium Pkg			1200	1200	1455	1455
Sport Pkg			375	375	455	455
370Z—V6—Equipment Schedule 4						
W.B. 100.4"; 3.7 Liter.						
Coupe 2D	AZ4EH	30800	21900	22700	23800	27000
Roadster 2D	AZ4FH	42280	24900	25700	26700	30100
Touring Coupe 2D	AZ4EH	36080	23600	24400	25400	28600
Touring Roadster 2D	AZ4FH	46280	25700	26500	27400	30800
NISMO Coupe 2D	AZ4EH	43830	26800	27700	28600	32000
Sport Pkg			1500	1500	1680	1680
LEAF—AC Electric—Equipment Schedule 3						
W.B. 106.3".						
S Hatchback 4D	AZ0CP	29830	17050	17800	18350	20900
SV Hatchback 4D	AZ0CP	32850	19750	20600	20900	23600
SL Hatchback 4D	AZ0CP	35870	20500	21400	21700	24400
Quick Charge Port			625	625	705	705
GT-R AWD—V6 Twin Turbo—Equipment Schedule 2						
W.B. 109.4"; 3.8 Liter.						
Premium Coupe 2D	AR5EF	100590	65100	67200	66300	72300
Black Edition Coupe	AR5EF	110330	68700	70900	69800	76000
Track Edition Coupe	AR5EF	116710				
Special Edition Pkg			2475	2475	2615	2615

OLDSMOBILE

2000 OLDSMOBILE — (1or2)G3(NK52T)-Y-#

Body Type	VIN	List	Trade-In Good	Very Good	Pvt-Party Good	Retail Excellent
ALERO—4-Cyl.—Equipment Schedule 5						
W.B. 107.0"; 2.4 Liter.						
GX Sedan 4D	NK52T	16995	525	600	1150	2000
GX Coupe 2D	NK12T	16995	525	600	1150	2000
GL Sedan 4D	NL52T	18185	725	825	1450	2500
GL Coupe 2D	NL12T	18185	675	775	1375	2375
V6, 3.4 Liter	E		125	125	155	155
ALERO—V6—Equipment Schedule 4						
W.B. 107.0"; 3.4 Liter.						
GLS Sedan 4D	NF52E	21900	1075	1200	1950	3375
GLS Coupe 2D	NF12E	21900	1025	1150	1900	3275
INTRIGUE—V6—Equipment Schedule 4						
W.B. 109.0"; 3.5 Liter.						

2000 OLDSMOBILE

Body Type	VIN	List	Trade-In Good	Very Good	Pvt-Party Good	Retail Excellent
GX Sedan 4D	WH52H	22650	800	900	1525	2650
GL Sedan 4D	WS52H	24280	925	1050	1700	2900
GLS Sedan 4D	WX52H	26280	1250	1400	2125	3625
Sterling Edition			25	25	50	50

2001 OLDSMOBILE — 1G3(NK52T)-1-#

ALERO—4-Cyl.—Equipment Schedule 5
W.B. 107.0"; 2.4 Liter.

Body Type	VIN	List	Trade-In Good	Very Good	Pvt-Party Good	Retail Excellent
GX Sedan 4D	NK52T	17785	650	725	1325	2300
GX Coupe 2D	NK12T	17785	675	750	1375	2375
GL Sedan 4D	NL52T	19195	775	875	1500	2600
GL Coupe 2D	NL12T	19195	725	800	1425	2450
V6, 3.4 Liter	E		125	125	175	175

ALERO—V6—Equipment Schedule 4
W.B. 107.0"; 3.4 Liter.

Body Type	VIN	List	Trade-In Good	Very Good	Pvt-Party Good	Retail Excellent
GLS Sedan 4D	NF52E	22540	1175	1300	2050	3500
GLS Coupe 2D	NF12E	22765	1100	1225	1950	3325

INTRIGUE—V6—Equipment Schedule 4
W.B. 109.0"; 3.5 Liter.

Body Type	VIN	List	Trade-In Good	Very Good	Pvt-Party Good	Retail Excellent
GX Sedan 4D	WH52H	22995	1075	1200	1850	3125
GL Sedan 4D	WS52H	24750	1375	1550	2225	3750
GLS Sedan 4D	WX52H	27115	1700	1900	2650	4400

AURORA—V6—Equipment Schedule 2
W.B. 112.2"; 3.5 Liter.

Body Type	VIN	List	Trade-In Good	Very Good	Pvt-Party Good	Retail Excellent
Sedan 4D	GR64H	31579	1725	1925	2500	3825

AURORA—V8—Equipment Schedule 2
W.B. 112.2"; 4.0 Liter.

Body Type	VIN	List	Trade-In Good	Very Good	Pvt-Party Good	Retail Excellent
Sedan 4D	GS64C	35314	2425	2700	3400	5175

2002 OLDSMOBILE — 1G3(NK52T)-2-#

ALERO—4-Cyl.—Equipment Schedule 5
W.B. 107.0"; 2.2 Liter.

Body Type	VIN	List	Trade-In Good	Very Good	Pvt-Party Good	Retail Excellent
GX Sedan 4D	NK52T	18055	775	875	1525	2625
GX Coupe 2D	NK12T	18055	775	875	1525	2625
GL Sedan 4D	NL52T	20040	875	975	1650	2850
GL Coupe 2D	NL12T	20265	800	900	1550	2675
V6, 3.4 Liter	E		150	150	195	195

ALERO—V6—Equipment Schedule 4
W.B. 107.0"; 3.4 Liter.

Body Type	VIN	List	Trade-In Good	Very Good	Pvt-Party Good	Retail Excellent
GLS Sedan 4D	NF52E	22675	1300	1450	2250	3825
GLS Coupe 2D	NF12E	22900	1200	1325	2100	3600

INTRIGUE—V6—Equipment Schedule 4
W.B. 109.0"; 3.5 Liter.

Body Type	VIN	List	Trade-In Good	Very Good	Pvt-Party Good	Retail Excellent
GX Sedan 4D	WH52H	23427	1500	1675	2400	4000
GL Sedan 4D	WS52H	25012	1700	1900	2775	4550
GLS Sedan 4D	WX52H	28502	2025	2250	3200	5225

AURORA—V6—Equipment Schedule 2
W.B. 112.2"; 3.5 Liter.

Body Type	VIN	List	Trade-In Good	Very Good	Pvt-Party Good	Retail Excellent
Sedan 4D	GR64H	31665	2175	2425	3075	4650

AURORA—V8—Equipment Schedule 2
W.B. 112.2"; 4.0 Liter.

Body Type	VIN	List	Trade-In Good	Very Good	Pvt-Party Good	Retail Excellent
Sedan 4D	GS64C	35660	2825	3150	3900	5850

2003 OLDSMOBILE — 1G3(NK52F)-3-#

ALERO—4-Cyl.—Equipment Schedule 5
W.B. 107.0"; 2.2 Liter.

Body Type	VIN	List	Trade-In Good	Very Good	Pvt-Party Good	Retail Excellent
GX Sedan 4D	NK52F	18335	900	1025	1675	2825
GX Coupe 2D	NK12F	18335	875	1000	1625	2750
GL Sedan 4D	NL52F	20175	975	1100	1775	2975
GL Coupe 2D	NL12F	20175	975	1100	1775	2975
V6, 3.4 Liter	E		150	150	215	215

ALERO—V6—Equipment Schedule 4
W.B. 107.0"; 3.4 Liter.

Body Type	VIN	List	Trade-In Good	Very Good	Pvt-Party Good	Retail Excellent
GLS Sedan 4D	NF52E	22755	1625	1825	2650	4400
GLS Coupe 2D	NF12E	23005	1475	1650	2450	4075

AURORA—V8—Equipment Schedule 2
W.B. 112.2"; 4.0 Liter.

Body Type	VIN	List	Trade-In Good	Very Good	Pvt-Party Good	Retail Excellent
Sedan 4D	GS64C	34775	3325	3675	4400	6425

2004 OLDSMOBILE — 1G3(NK52F)-4-#

ALERO—4-Cyl.—Equipment Schedule 5
W.B. 107.0"; 2.2 Liter.

2004 OLDSMOBILE

Body Type	VIN	List	Trade-In Good	Very Good	Pvt-Party Good	Retail Excellent
GX Sedan 4D	NK52F	18825	1050	1175	1875	3125
GX Coupe 2D	NK12F	18825	950	1075	1725	2900
GL Sedan 4D	NL52F	20775	1250	1400	2125	3525
GL Coupe 2D	NL12F	20775	1250	1400	2125	3525
V6, 3.4 Liter	E		175	175	235	235
ALERO—V6—Equipment Schedule 4						
W.B. 107.0"; 3.4 Liter.						
GLS Sedan 4D	NF52E	23425	1825	2025	3000	4900
GLS Coupe 2D	NF12E	23675	1675	1850	2800	4575

PLYMOUTH

2000 PLYMOUTH — (1or3)P3(EorH)(S46C)-Y-#

NEON—4-Cyl.—Equipment Schedule 6
W.B. 105.0"; 2.0 Liter.

Highline Sedan 4D	S46C	13890	600	700	1175	1975
LX Sedan 4D	S46C	14680	875	1000	1600	2725
BREEZE—4-Cyl.—Equipment Schedule 6						
W.B. 108.0"; 2.0 Liter, 2.4 Liter.						
Sedan 4D	J46C	17525	500	575	1275	2300
PROWLER—V6—Equipment Schedule 1						
W.B. 113.3"; 3.5 Liter.						
Roadster 2D	W65G	43500	10050	10600	11050	13500

2001 PLYMOUTH — 1P3(EorH)(S46C)-1-#

NEON—4-Cyl.—Equipment Schedule 6
W.B. 105.0"; 2.0 Liter.

Highline Sedan 4D	S46C	14275	625	725	1225	2075
LX Sedan 4D	S46C	15095	900	1025	1650	2800

PONTIAC

2000 PONTIAC — (1,2,3or4)G2(JB524)-Y-#

SUNFIRE—4-Cyl.—Equipment Schedule 5
W.B. 104.1"; 2.2 Liter, 2.4 Liter.

SE Sedan 4D	JB524	15120	525	600	1125	1975
SE Coupe 2D	JB124	15020	475	550	1050	1850
GT Coupe 2D	JD12T	17530	800	900	1550	2700
GT Convertible 2D	JD32T	22120	1125	1275	2025	3550
GRAND AM—4-Cyl.—Equipment Schedule 5						
W.B. 107.0"; 2.4 Liter.						
SE Coupe 2D	NE12T	17240	700	800	1400	2400
V6, 3.4 Liter	E		125	125	165	165
GRAND AM—V6—Equipment Schedule 5						
W.B. 107.0"; 3.4 Liter.						
SE Sedan 4D	NE52T	17540	875	1000	1625	2775
4-Cyl, 2.4 Liter	T		(125)	(125)	(160)	(160)
GRAND AM—V6—Equipment Schedule 5						
W.B. 107.0"; 3.4 Liter.						
GT Sedan 4D	NW52E	20385	1175	1325	2025	3400
GT Coupe 2D	NW12E	20085	1125	1275	1950	3300
FIREBIRD—V6—Equipment Schedule 4						
W.B. 101.1"; 3.8 Liter.						
Coupe 2D	FS22K	20535	1500	1650	2000	2975
Convertible 2D	FS32K	26440	2500	2750	3300	4825
T-Bar Roof			225	225	300	300
Manual, 5-Spd			(175)	(175)	(235)	(235)
FIREBIRD—V8—Equipment Schedule 4						
W.B. 101.1"; 5.7 Liter.						
Formula Coupe 2D	FV22G	24055	2650	2900	3500	5075
Trans Am Coupe 2D	FV22G	27165	3200	3525	4150	6000
Trans Am Conv 2D	FV32G	31235	4175	4550	5500	7875
T-Bar Roof			225	225	300	300
Ram Air Handling Pkg			450	450	595	595
GRAND PRIX—V6—Equipment Schedule 4						
W.B. 110.5"; 3.8 Liter.						
SE Sedan 4D	WJ52K	20610	650	750	1425	2475
GT Sedan 4D	WP52K	22105	950	1075	1825	3150
GT Coupe 2D	WP12K	21955	875	1000	1725	2975

2000 PONTIAC

Body Type	VIN	List	Trade-In Good	Very Good	Pvt-Party Good	Retail Excellent
V6, 3.1 Liter	J		(200)	(200)	(250)	(250)
GRAND PRIX—V6 Supercharged—Equipment Schedule 4						
W.B. 110.5"; 3.8 Liter.						
GTP Sedan 4D	WR521	24870	1400	1575	2425	4150
GTP Coupe 2D	WR121	24720	1350	1525	2375	4050
BONNEVILLE—V6—Equipment Schedule 4						
W.B. 112.2"; 3.8 Liter.						
SE Sedan 4D	HX52K	24295	775	875	1500	2575
SLE Sedan 4D	HY52K	27995	1150	1300	2000	3400
SSEi Sedan 4D	HZ52K	32250	1475	1650	2450	4125
V6, Supercharged, 3.8L	1		150	150	200	200

2001 PONTIAC — (1,2or3)G(2or7)(JB524)-1-#

Body Type	VIN	List	Trade-In Good	Very Good	Pvt-Party Good	Retail Excellent
SUNFIRE—4-Cyl.—Equipment Schedule 5						
W.B. 104.1"; 2.2 Liter, 2.4 Liter.						
SE Sedan 4D	JB524	15650	575	675	1275	2275
SE Coupe 2D	JB124	15395	525	600	1225	2150
GT Coupe 2D	JD12T	17625	850	975	1625	2850
GRAND AM—4-Cyl.—Equipment Schedule 5						
W.B. 107.0"; 2.4 Liter.						
SE Coupe 2D	NE12T	17500	950	1075	1725	2875
V6, 3.4 Liter	E		125	125	165	165
GRAND AM—V6—Equipment Schedule 5						
W.B. 107.0"; 3.4 Liter.						
SE Sedan 4D	NE52E	17800	1150	1300	1975	3300
4-Cyl, 2.4 Liter	T		(125)	(125)	(180)	(180)
GRAND AM—V6—Equipment Schedule 5						
W.B. 107.0"; 3.4 Liter.						
GT Sedan 4D	NW52E	21110	1575	1775	2525	4150
GT Coupe 2D	NW12E	20810	1550	1750	2500	4100
FIREBIRD—V6—Equipment Schedule 5						
W.B. 101.1"; 3.8 Liter.						
Coupe 2D	FS22K	20810	1750	1925	2325	3400
Convertible 2D	FS32K	26735	2975	3275	3800	5425
T-Bar Roof			225	225	300	300
Manual, 5-Spd			(150)	(150)	(200)	(200)
75th Anniversary			275	275	375	375
FIREBIRD—V8—Equipment Schedule 5						
W.B. 101.1"; 5.7 Liter.						
Formula Coupe 2D	FV22G	24480	3250	3550	4125	5875
Trans Am Coupe 2D	FV22G	27590	3875	4225	5025	7100
Trans Am Conv 2D	FV32G	31660	5075	5500	6475	9075
T-Bar Roof			225	225	300	300
Ram Air Handling Pkg			500	500	665	665
75th Anniversary			275	275	375	375
NHRA Pkg			150	150	190	190
GRAND PRIX—V6—Equipment Schedule 4						
W.B. 110.5"; 3.1 Liter, 3.8 Liter.						
SE Sedan 4D	WJ52J	21135	700	800	1500	2650
GT Sedan 4D	WP52K	22615	1100	1250	2050	3525
GT Coupe 2D	WP12K	22465	1025	1150	1950	3375
Special Edition			75	75	100	100
GRAND PRIX—V6 Supercharged—Equipment Schedule 4						
W.B. 110.5"; 3.8 Liter.						
GTP Sedan 4D	WR521	24870	1500	1675	2625	4500
GTP Coupe 2D	WR121	25935	1550	1725	2650	4525
Special Edition			75	75	100	100
BONNEVILLE—V6—Equipment Schedule 4						
W.B. 112.2"; 3.8 Liter.						
SE Sedan 4D	HX52K	25730	875	1000	1675	2875
SLE Sedan 4D	HY52K	28700	1300	1475	2250	3800
BONNEVILLE—V6 Supercharged—Equipment Schedule 4						
W.B. 112.2"; 3.8 Liter.						
SSEi Sedan 4D	HZ521	33070	1700	1900	2725	4500

2002 PONTIAC — (1or2)G2(JB524)-2-#

Body Type	VIN	List	Trade-In Good	Very Good	Pvt-Party Good	Retail Excellent
SUNFIRE—4-Cyl.—Equipment Schedule 5						
W.B. 104.1"; 2.2 Liter, 2.4 Liter.						
SE Sedan 4D	JB524	16545	700	800	1425	2500
SE Coupe 2D	JB124	16045	675	775	1375	2425
GT Coupe 2D	JD12T	18205	950	1075	1575	3075

Body Type	VIN	List	Trade-In Good	Trade-In Very Good	Pvt-Party Good	Retail Excellent
GRAND AM—4-Cyl.—Equipment Schedule 5						
W.B. 107.0"; 2.2 Liter.						
SE Coupe 2D	NE12T	18210	1325	1475	2150	3550
V6, 3.4 Liter	E		150	150	200	200
GRAND AM—V6—Equipment Schedule 5						
W.B. 107.0"; 3.4 Liter.						
SE Sedan 4D	NE52E	20385	1550	1725	2450	4000
4-Cyl, 2.2 Liter	F		(175)	(175)	(230)	(230)
GRAND AM—V6—Equipment Schedule 5						
W.B. 107.0"; 3.4 Liter.						
GT Sedan 4D	NW52E	21425	1850	2075	2975	4775
GT Coupe 2D	NW12E	21275	1800	2025	2900	4675
FIREBIRD—V6—Equipment Schedule 4						
W.B. 101.1"; 3.8 Liter.						
Coupe 2D	FS22K	21105	2175	2375	2775	3950
Convertible 2D	FS32K	27205	3575	3900	4425	6150
T-Bar Roof			225	225	300	300
GT Pkg			150	150	205	205
Manual, 5-Spd			(200)	(200)	(265)	(265)
FIREBIRD—V8—Equipment Schedule 4						
W.B. 101.1"; 5.7 Liter.						
Formula Coupe 2D	FV22G	26235	3825	4175	4850	6725
Trans Am Coupe 2D	FV22G	28265	4775	5175	5950	8225
Trans Am Conv 2D	FV32G	32335	5800	6250	7375	10150
T-Bar Roof			225	225	300	300
Collector Edition			300	300	415	415
NHRA Pkg			150	150	205	205
Ram Air Handling Pkg			575	575	760	760
GRAND PRIX—V6—Equipment Schedule 4						
W.B. 110.5"; 3.1 Liter, 3.8 Liter.						
SE Sedan 4D	WJ52J	21575	900	1000	1750	3025
GT Sedan 4D	WP52K	23695	1250	1400	2300	4000
GT Coupe 2D	WP12K	23545	1175	1325	2200	3825
GRAND PRIX—V6 Supercharged—Equipment Schedule 4						
W.B. 110.5"; 3.8 Liter.						
GTP Sedan 4D	WR521	26415	1575	1775	2750	4675
GTP Coupe 2D	WR121	26235	1575	1775	2850	4850
BONNEVILLE—V6—Equipment Schedule 4						
W.B. 112.2"; 3.8 Liter.						
SE Sedan 4D	HX52K	26355	1125	1250	1900	3175
SLE Sedan 4D	HY52K	29545	1625	1800	2525	4125
BONNEVILLE—V6 Supercharged—Equipment Schedule 4						
W.B. 112.2"; 3.8 Liter.						
SSEi Sedan 4D	HZ521	33605	2025	2250	3250	5250

2003 PONTIAC — (1or5)G2orY2(JB12F)-3-#

Body Type	VIN	List	Trade-In Good	Trade-In Very Good	Pvt-Party Good	Retail Excellent
SUNFIRE—4-Cyl.—Equipment Schedule 5						
W.B. 104.1"; 2.2 Liter.						
Coupe 2D	JB12F	15435	950	1100	1750	2975
VIBE—4-Cyl.—Equipment Schedule 6						
W.B. 102.4"; 1.8 Liter.						
Sport Wagon 4D	SL628	17700	2575	2850	3575	5425
GT Sport Wagon	SN62L	19900	2750	3075	3750	5650
AWD	M		600	600	800	800
GRAND AM—V6—Equipment Schedule 5						
W.B. 107.0"; 3.4 Liter.						
SE Sedan 4D	NE52E	20620	1750	1950	2875	4650
4-Cyl, 2.2 Liter	F		(200)	(200)	(255)	(255)
GRAND AM—V6—Equipment Schedule 5						
W.B. 107.0"; 3.4 Liter.						
GT Sedan 4D	NW52E	21640	2250	2500	3575	5750
GT Coupe 2D	NW12E	21640	2200	2450	3525	5650
GRAND PRIX—V6—Equipment Schedule 4						
W.B. 110.5"; 3.1 Liter, 3.8 Liter.						
SE Sedan 4D	WK52J	22140	1000	1125	1875	3225
GT Sedan 4D	WP52K	23990	1550	1725	2675	4450
GRAND PRIX—V6 Supercharged—Equipment Schedule 4						
W.B. 110.5"; 3.8 Liter.						
GTP Sedan 4D	WR521	26800	1925	2150	3175	5200
BONNEVILLE—V6—Equipment Schedule 4						
W.B. 112.2"; 3.8 Liter.						
SE Sedan 4D	HX52K	26665	1550	1725	2350	3750
SLE Sedan 4D	HY52K	29855	1925	2125	2950	4650

0415

2003 PONTIAC

Body Type	VIN	List	Trade-In Good	Very Good	Pvt-Party Good	Retail Excellent
BONNEVILLE—V6 Supercharged—Equipment Schedule 4						
W.B. 112.2"; 3.8 Liter.						
SSEi Sedan 4D	HZ541	34085	**2500**	**2775**	**3775**	**5900**

2004 PONTIAC — (1,2,5or6)G2orY2(JB12F)-4-#

SUNFIRE—4-Cyl.—Equipment Schedule 5						
W.B. 104.1"; 2.2 Liter.						
Coupe 2D	JB12F	16695	**1150**	**1300**	**2025**	**3475**
VIBE—4-Cyl.—Equipment Schedule 6						
W.B. 102.4" 1.8 Liter.						
Sport Wagon 4D	SL628	17895	**2950**	**3300**	**3925**	**5800**
GT Sport Wagon	SN62L	19995	**3300**	**3675**	**4250**	**6175**
AWD	M		**650**	**650**	**865**	**865**
GRAND AM—V6—Equipment Schedule 5						
W.B. 107.0"; 3.4 Liter.						
SE Sedan 4D	NE52E	21210	**2175**	**2400**	**3375**	**5325**
4-Cyl, 2.2 Liter	F		**(200)**	**(200)**	**(275)**	**(275)**
GRAND AM—V6—Equipment Schedule 5						
W.B. 107.0"; 3.4 Liter.						
GT Sedan 4D	NW52E	22450	**2875**	**3175**	**4225**	**6525**
GT Coupe 2D	NW12E	22450	**2775**	**3075**	**4100**	**6350**
GRAND PRIX—V6—Equipment Schedule 4						
W.B. 110.5"; 3.8 Liter.						
GT Sedan 4D	WP522	22395	**2425**	**2700**	**3675**	**5750**
GRAND PRIX—V6 Supercharged—Equipment Schedule 4						
W.B. 110.5"; 3.8 Liter.						
GTP Sedan 4D	WR524	26495	**2675**	**2950**	**4050**	**6325**
BONNEVILLE—V6—Equipment Schedule 4						
W.B. 112.2"; 3.8 Liter.						
SE Sedan 4D	HX52K	27570	**1850**	**2075**	**2850**	**4475**
SLE Sedan 4D	HY52K	30420	**2475**	**2750**	**3625**	**5600**
BONNEVILLE—V8—Equipment Schedule 4						
W.B. 112.2"; 4.6 Liter.						
GXP Sedan 4D	HZ54Y	35995	**2975**	**3325**	**4525**	**7075**
GTO—V8—Equipment Schedule 2						
W.B. 109.8"; 5.7 Liter.						
Coupe 2D	VX13G	33495	**4900**	**5300**	**6275**	**8725**

2005 PONTIAC — (1,2,3,5or6)G2orY2(JB12F)-5-#

SUNFIRE—4-Cyl.—Equipment Schedule 5						
W.B. 104.1"; 2.2 Liter.						
Coupe 2D	JB12F	15650	**1150**	**1325**	**2125**	**3525**
VIBE—4-Cyl.—Equipment Schedule 6						
W.B. 102.4"; 1.8 Liter.						
Sport Wagon 4D	SL628	18325	**3125**	**3475**	**4250**	**6175**
GT Sport Wagon	SN62L	20535	**3625**	**4025**	**4825**	**6800**
AWD	M		**700**	**700**	**935**	**935**
GRAND AM—V6—Equipment Schedule 5						
W.B. 107.0"; 3.4 Liter.						
SE Sedan 4D	NE52E	21210	**2500**	**2800**	**3925**	**6050**
4-Cyl, 2.2 Liter	F		**(225)**	**(225)**	**(300)**	**(300)**
GRAND AM—V6—Equipment Schedule 5						
W.B. 107.0"; 3.4 Liter.						
GT Coupe 2D	NW12E	22990	**3075**	**3400**	**4800**	**7275**
GRAND PRIX—V6—Equipment Schedule 4						
W.B. 110.5"; 3.8 Liter.						
Sedan 4D	WP522	23560	**2750**	**3075**	**4175**	**6300**
GT Sedan 4D	WS522	25460	**3150**	**3500**	**4800**	**7300**
GRAND PRIX—V6 Supercharged—Equipment Schedule 4						
W.B. 110.5"; 3.8 Liter.						
GTP Sedan 4D	WR524	27220	**3950**	**4350**	**5750**	**8450**
GRAND PRIX—V6—Equipment Schedule 4						
W.B. 110.5"; 5.3 Liter.						
GXP Sedan 4D	WC52C	29995	**3850**	**4225**	**5825**	**8750**
G6—V6—Equipment Schedule 4						
W.B. 112.3"; 3.5 Liter.						
Sedan 4D	ZG528	21700	**2800**	**3125**	**3900**	**5625**
GT Sedan 4D	ZH528	23925	**3150**	**3500**	**4550**	**6550**
BONNEVILLE—V6—Equipment Schedule 4						
W.B. 112.2"; 3.8 Liter.						
SE Sedan 4D	HX52K	28650	**1850**	**2075**	**3075**	**4800**
SLE Sedan 4D	HY52K	31035	**2550**	**2850**	**3875**	**5875**

2005 PONTIAC

Body Type	VIN	List	Trade-In Good	Very Good	Pvt-Party Good	Retail Excellent
BONNEVILLE—V8—Equipment Schedule 4						
W.B. 112.2"; 4.6 Liter.						
GXP Sedan 4D	HZ54Y	36120	3125	3475	4800	7325
GTO—V8—Equipment Schedule 2						
W.B. 109.8"; 6.0 Liter.						
Coupe 2D	VX12U	34295	6225	6675	8075	10950

2006 PONTIAC — (1,2,3,5or6)G2orY2(SL658)-6-#

Body Type	VIN	List	Trade-In Good	Very Good	Pvt-Party Good	Retail Excellent
VIBE—4-Cyl.—Equipment Schedule 6						
W.B. 102.4"; 1.8 Liter.						
Sport Wagon 4D	SL658	17840	3625	4000	4875	6850
Manual, 5-Spd			(275)	(275)	(365)	(365)
AWD	M		750	750	1000	1000
VIBE—4-Cyl.—Equipment Schedule 6						
W.B. 102.4"; 1.8 Liter.						
GT Sport Wagon 4D	SN65L	21015	4950	5400	6175	8350
AWD	M		750	750	1000	1000
SOLSTICE—4-Cyl.—Equipment Schedule 6						
W.B. 95.1"; 2.4 Liter.						
Convertible 2D	MB35B	19995	3775	4125	5000	6950
GRAND PRIX—V6—Equipment Schedule 4						
W.B. 110.5"; 3.8 Liter.						
Sedan 4D	WP552	22990	3075	3400	4550	6625
GRAND PRIX—V6 Supercharged—Equipment Schedule 4						
W.B. 110.5"; 3.8 Liter.						
GT Sedan 4D	WR554	26745	4050	4425	5600	7925
GRAND PRIX—V8—Equipment Schedule 4						
W.B. 110.5"; 5.3 Liter.						
GXP Sedan 4D	WC55C	29395	4775	5175	6625	9475
G6—4-Cyl.—Equipment Schedule 4						
W.B. 112.3"; 2.4 Liter.						
Sedan 4D	ZG558	20655	3100	3425	4325	6125
V6, 3.5 Liter	8		375	375	500	500
G6—V6—Equipment Schedule 4						
W.B. 112.3"; 3.5 Liter, 3.9 Liter.						
GT Sedan 4D	ZH558	23180	3650	4000	5000	7025
GT Coupe 2D	ZH158	22955	4175	4550	5650	7900
GT Hard Top Conv 2D	ZH358	28490	6100	6600	8450	11900
GTP Sedan 4D	ZM551	24835	4650	5050	6250	8775
GTP Coupe 2D	ZM151	24610	4750	5150	6375	8950
GTP Hard Top Conv	ZM351	29990	7425	7975	10000	13950
GTO—V8—Equipment Schedule 2						
W.B. 109.8"; 6.0 Liter.						
Coupe 2D	VX12U	32995	7200	7675	9025	11900

2007 PONTIAC — (1,2,3,5or6)G2orY2(SL658)-7-#

Body Type	VIN	List	Trade-In Good	Very Good	Pvt-Party Good	Retail Excellent
VIBE—4-Cyl.—Equipment Schedule 6						
W.B. 102.4"; 1.8 Liter.						
Sport Wagon 4D	SL658	17995	4400	4775	5625	7650
Manual, 5-Spd			(300)	(300)	(400)	(400)
SOLSTICE—4-Cyl.—Equipment Schedule 6						
W.B. 95.1"; 2.4 Liter.						
Convertible 2D	MB35B	22955	4325	4700	5600	7600
Automatic			300	300	400	400
SOLSTICE—4-Cyl. Turbo—Equipment Schedule 6						
W.B. 95.1"; 2.0 Liter.						
GXP Convertible 2D	MG35X	27955	4950	5350	6350	8600
Automatic			300	300	400	400
GRAND PRIX—V6—Equipment Schedule 4						
W.B. 110.5"; 3.8 Liter.						
Sedan 4D	WP552	22315	3675	4025	5050	7025
GRAND PRIX—V6 Supercharged—Equipment Schedule 4						
W.B. 110.5"; 3.8 Liter.						
GT Sedan 4D	WR554	25235	4525	4925	5975	8200
GRAND PRIX—V8—Equipment Schedule 4						
W.B. 110.5"; 5.3 Liter.						
GXP Sedan 4D	WC55C	29315	5600	6050	7425	10150
G5—4-Cyl.—Equipment Schedule 4						
W.B. 103.5"; 2.2 Liter, 2.4 Liter.						
Coupe 2D	AL15F	15845	2925	3275	4225	6075
GT Coupe 2D	AN15B	18645	3725	4100	5150	7325

2007 PONTIAC

Body Type	VIN	List	Trade-In Good	Very Good	Pvt-Party Good	Retail Excellent
G6—4-Cyl.—Equipment Schedule 4						
W.B. 112.3"; 2.4 Liter.						
Sedan 4D	ZG55B	19265	3475	3800	4650	6400
Sport Pkg			250	250	325	325
G6—V6—Equipment Schedule 4						
W.B. 112.3"; 3.5 Liter, 3.6 Liter, 3.9 Liter.						
GT Sedan 4D	ZH55N	22615	4225	4600	5525	7575
GT Coupe 2D	ZH15N	22415	4525	4900	5875	8000
GT Hard Top Conv 2D	ZH35N	29215	6700	7225	8775	11900
GTP Sedan 4D	ZM557	25115	5175	5600	6825	9225
GTP Coupe 2D	ZM157	24915	5175	5600	6825	9225
Sport Pkg			200	200	275	275

2008 PONTIAC—(1,2,3or6G2,5Y2orKL2)(SL658)—8—#

Body Type	VIN	List	Trade-In Good	Very Good	Pvt-Party Good	Retail Excellent
VIBE—4-Cyl.—Equipment Schedule 6						
W.B. 102.4"; 1.8 Liter.						
Sport Wagon 4D	SL658	18195	5200	5600	6425	8425
Manual, 5-Spd w/Overdrive	P		(350)	(350)	(470)	(470)
SOLSTICE—4-Cyl.—Equipment Schedule 6						
W.B. 95.1"; 2.4 Liter.						
Convertible 2D	MB35B	22295	5125	5525	6425	8450
Automatic, 5-Spd			300	300	400	400
SOLSTICE—4-Cyl. Turbo—Equipment Schedule 6						
W.B. 95.1"; 2.0 Liter.						
GXP Convertible 2D	MG35X	27895	6250	6675	7900	10350
Automatic, 5-Spd			300	300	400	400
GRAND PRIX—V6—Equipment Schedule 4						
W.B. 110.5"; 3.8 Liter.						
Sedan 4D	WP552	22500	4725	5075	6125	8250
GRAND PRIX—V8—Equipment Schedule 4						
W.B. 110.5"; 5.3 Liter.						
GXP Sedan 4D	WC55C	29500	6325	6750	8175	10900
G5—4-Cyl.—Equipment Schedule 4						
W.B. 103.5"; 2.2 Liter, 2.4 Liter.						
Coupe 2D	AL15F	16450	3500	3850	4850	6750
GT Coupe 2D	AS15B	20560	4475	4875	5950	8175
G6—4-Cyl.—Equipment Schedule 4						
W.B. 112.3"; 2.4 Liter.						
Sedan 4D	ZG55B	19995	4650	5025	6000	8050
Sport Pkg			250	250	345	345
G6—V6—Equipment Schedule 4						
W.B. 112.3"; 3.5 Liter, 3.6 Liter, 3.9 Liter.						
GT Sedan 4D	ZH55N	22995	5050	5425	6450	8625
GT Coupe 2D	ZH15N	22995	5325	5725	6975	9275
GT Hard Top Conv 2D	ZH35N	29995	7550	8050	9875	13250
GXP Sedan 4D	ZM557	27310	6325	6750	8325	11150
GXP Coupe 2D	ZM157	27105	6650	7100	8625	11500
Sport Pkg			225	225	295	295
G8—V6—Equipment Schedule 4						
W.B. 114.8"; 3.6 Liter.						
Sedan 4D	EC557	27595	8725	9225	10300	12850
G8—V8—Equipment Schedule 4						
W.B. 114.8"; 6.0 Liter.						
GT Sedan 4D	ER55Y	29995	10650	11250	12450	15400

2009 PONTIAC—(1,2,3or6G2,5Y2orKL2)(SP678)—9—#

Body Type	VIN	List	Trade-In Good	Very Good	Pvt-Party Good	Retail Excellent
VIBE—4-Cyl.—Equipment Schedule 6						
W.B. 102.4"; 1.8 Liter, 2.4 Liter.						
Sport Wagon 4D	SP678	16745	6200	6600	7600	9600
GT Sport Wagon 4D	SR670	20945	7700	8175	9100	11300
Manual, 5-Spd w/Overdrive	L		(375)	(375)	(495)	(495)
AWD	M		1400	1400	1835	1835
SOLSTICE—4-Cyl.—Equipment Schedule 6						
W.B. 95.1"; 2.4 Liter.						
Coupe 2D	MB25B	26845	7150	7575	8650	10850
Convertible 2D	MB35B	23870	6625	7025	8050	10150
Street Ed Conv 2D	MK35B	30030	8075	8550	9725	12150
Automatic, 5-Spd			350	350	450	450
SOLSTICE—4-Cyl. Turbo—Equipment Schedule 6						
W.B. 95.1"; 2.0 Liter.						
GXP Coupe 2D	MG25X	30995	8425	8925	10100	12600
GXP Convertible 2D	MG35X	29080	7925	8400	9500	11850

Body Type	VIN	List	Trade-In Good	Very Good	Pvt-Party Good	Retail Excellent
Automatic, 5-Spd			350	350	450	450
G3—4-Cyl.—Equipment Schedule 6						
W.B. 97.6"; 1.6 Liter.						
Hatchback 4D	TD62E	14995	3425	3725	4550	6150
Automatic, 4-Spd w/OD			350	350	465	465
G5—4-Cyl.—Equipment Schedule 4						
W.B. 103.5"; 2.2 Liter.						
Coupe 2D	AS15H	17860	4400	4750	5675	7575
GT Coupe 2D	AT15H	21160	5350	5750	6925	9150
G6—4-Cyl.—Equipment Schedule 4						
W.B. 112.3"; 2.4 Liter.						
Sedan 4D	ZG55B	20295	5425	5800	6750	8575
Sport Pkg			275	275	360	360
G6—V6—Equipment Schedule 4						
W.B. 112.3"; 3.5 Liter, 3.6 Liter, 3.9 Liter.						
GT Sedan 4D	ZH55N	24095	6350	6750	7800	9875
GT Coupe 2D	ZH15N	23995	6550	6975	8000	10100
GT Hard Top Conv 2D	ZH35N	31785	8600	9100	10650	13600
GXP Sedan 4D	ZM557	28495	7750	8225	9475	12000
GXP Coupe 2D	ZM157	28395	7900	8375	9650	12200
Sport Pkg			225	225	315	315
G6 (2009.5)—4-Cyl.—Equipment Schedule 4						
W.B. 112.3"; 2.4 Liter.						
Sedan 4D	ZG55B	21835	5700	6075	7075	8975
Coupe 2D	ZJ15B	22890	6400	6825	7800	9825
G6 (2009.5)—V6—Equipment Schedule 4						
W.B. 112.3"; 3.5 Liter, 3.6 Liter, 3.9 Liter.						
GT Sedan 4D	ZK55K	25380	6675	7100	8125	10250
GT Coupe 2D	ZK15K	25280	7200	7650	8775	11050
GT Hard Top Conv 2D	ZH35N	32970	9600	10150	11750	15000
GXP Sedan 4D	ZM557	29730	8150	8625	9975	12650
GXP Coupe 2D	ZM157	29630	8550	9050	10400	13150
G8—V6—Equipment Schedule 4						
W.B. 114.8"; 3.6 Liter.						
Sedan 4D	ER577	27995	10250	10750	11800	14300
G8—V8—Equipment Schedule 4						
W.B. 114.8"; 6.0 Liter, 6.2 Liter.						
GT Sedan 4D	EC57Y	31360	12450	13050	14300	17200
GXP Sedan 4D	EP57W	39995	18400	19200	20100	23600

2010 PONTIAC — (1,5orK)(G,LorY)2(SP6E8)-A-#

Body Type	VIN	List	Trade-In Good	Very Good	Pvt-Party Good	Retail Excellent
VIBE—4-Cyl.—Equipment Schedule 6						
W.B. 102.4"; 1.8 Liter, 2.4 Liter.						
Sport Wagon 4D	SP6E8	17585	7025	7450	8625	10800
Manual, 5-Spd w/Overdrive	N		(475)	(475)	(610)	(610)
AWD	M		1475	1475	1910	1910
VIBE—4-Cyl.—Equipment Schedule 4						
W.B. 102.4"; 2.4 Liter.						
GT Sport Wagon 4D	SR6E0	22560	8775	9250	10350	12700
Manual, 5-Spd w/Overdrive	N		(475)	(475)	(605)	(605)
G3—4-Cyl.—Equipment Schedule 6						
W.B. 97.6"; 1.6 Liter.						
Hatchback 4D	TD62E	14995	4525	4875	5700	7425
Automatic, 4-Spd w/OD			400	400	535	535
G6—4-Cyl.—Equipment Schedule 6						
W.B. 112.3"; 2.4 Liter.						
Sedan 4D	ZA5EB	21995	7550	7975	9125	11350

PORSCHE

2000 PORSCHE — WPO(CA298)-Y-#

Body Type	VIN	List	Trade-In Good	Very Good	Pvt-Party Good	Retail Excellent
BOXSTER—6-Cyl.—Equipment Schedule 1						
W.B. 95.2"; 2.7 Liter, 3.2 Liter.						
Cabriolet 2D	CA298	44745	3225	3525	4350	6150
S Cabriolet 2D	CB298	53245	4275	4600	5675	8025
Full Leather			100	100	135	135
Hard Top			300	300	400	400
Aero Kit			1100	1100	1465	1465
Sport Design			325	325	430	430
Sport Touring Pkg			775	775	1035	1035
Automatic w/Tiptronic			300	300	400	400

2000 PORSCHE

Body Type	VIN	List	Trade-In Good	Very Good	Pvt-Party Good	Retail Excellent
911 CARRERA—6-Cyl.—Equipment Schedule 1						
W.B. 92.6"; 3.4 Liter.						
Coupe 2D	AA299	71375	5775	6175	7075	9225
Cabriolet 2D	CA299	80755	6575	7025	8100	10600
Full Leather			100	100	115	115
Hard Top (Cabriolet)			300	300	355	355
Aero Kit			1100	1100	1295	1295
Automatic w/Tiptronic			300	300	355	355
911 CARRERA 4 AWD—6-Cyl.—Equipment Schedule 1						
W.B. 92.6"; 3.4 Liter.						
Coupe 2D	AA299	76805	7150	7625	8725	11400
Cabriolet 2D	CA299	86185	7950	8450	9600	12450
Full Leather			100	100	115	115
Hard Top			300	300	355	355
Aero Kit			1100	1100	1295	1295
Millennium Pkg			2575	2575	3045	3045
Automatic w/Tiptronic			300	300	355	355

2001 PORSCHE — WPO(CA298)-1-#

Body Type	VIN	List	Trade-In Good	Very Good	Pvt-Party Good	Retail Excellent
BOXSTER—6-Cyl.—Equipment Schedule 1						
W.B. 95.2"; 2.7 Liter, 3.2 Liter.						
Cabriolet 2D	CA298	42865	3300	3600	4450	6325
S Cabriolet 2D	CB298	50965	4350	4700	5825	8275
Full Leather			100	100	135	135
Hard Top			300	300	400	400
Aero Kit			1200	1200	1600	1600
Sport Design			375	375	485	485
Sport Touring Pkg			900	900	1200	1200
Automatic w/Tiptronic			300	300	400	400
911 CARRERA—6-Cyl.—Equipment Schedule 1						
W.B. 92.6"; 3.4 Liter.						
Coupe 2D	AA299	70275	6900	7350	8050	10150
Cabriolet 2D	CA299	79775	7900	8400	9150	11500
Full Leather			100	100	105	105
Hard Top (Cabriolet)			300	300	320	320
Aero Kit			1200	1200	1295	1295
Automatic w/Tiptronic			300	300	325	325
911 CARRERA 4 AWD—6-Cyl.—Equipment Schedule 1						
W.B. 92.6"; 3.4 Liter.						
Coupe 2D	AA299	75320	8275	8800	9625	12100
Cabriolet 2D	CA299	84820	8825	9375	10250	12800
Full Leather			100	100	105	105
Hard Top (Cabriolet)			300	300	320	320
Aero Kit			1200	1200	1290	1290
Automatic w/Tiptronic			300	300	325	325
911 TURBO AWD—6-Cyl. Turbo—Equipment Schedule 1						
W.B. 92.5"; 3.6 Liter.						
Coupe 2D	AB299	111765	13850	14600	15400	18750
Full Leather			100	100	110	110
Aero Kit			1200	1200	1310	1310
Automatic w/Tiptronic			300	300	325	325

2002 PORSCHE — WPO(CA298)-2-#

Body Type	VIN	List	Trade-In Good	Very Good	Pvt-Party Good	Retail Excellent
BOXSTER—6-Cyl.—Equipment Schedule 1						
W.B. 95.2"; 2.7 Liter, 3.2 Liter.						
Cabriolet 2D	CA298	43365	3650	3950	4975	7100
S Cabriolet 2D	CB298	52365	4850	5200	6600	9425
Full Leather			100	100	135	135
Hard Top			350	350	465	465
Aero Kit			1300	1300	1735	1735
Sport Design			400	400	545	545
Sport Touring Pkg			1075	1075	1435	1435
Automatic w/Tiptronic			350	350	465	465
911 CARRERA—6-Cyl.—Equipment Schedule 1						
W.B. 92.6"; 3.6 Liter.						
Coupe 2D	AA299	73450	7875	8375	9150	11400
Targa 2D	AA299	75965	10550	11200	12100	15050
Cabriolet 2D	CA299	83150	8650	9175	10050	12550
Full Leather			100	100	105	105
Hard Top (Cabriolet)			350	350	375	375
Aero Kit			1300	1300	1390	1390
Automatic w/Tiptronic			350	350	375	375

2002 PORSCHE

Body Type	VIN	List	Trade-In Good	Very Good	Pvt-Party Good	Retail Excellent
911 CARRERA 4 AWD—6-Cyl.—Equipment Schedule 1						
W.B. 92.5" (4S), 92.6"; 3.6 Liter.						
4S Coupe 2D	AA299	80965	9650	10250	11050	13750
Cabriolet 2D	CA299	88750	9850	10450	11400	14150
Full Leather		-----	100	100	105	105
Hard Top		-----	350	350	375	375
Aero Kit		-----	1300	1300	1385	1385
Automatic w/Tiptronic		-----	350	350	375	375
911 TURBO AWD—6-Cyl. Turbo—Equipment Schedule 1						
W.B. 92.6"; 3.6 Liter.						
Coupe 2D	AB299	115765	14250	15050	15850	19200
Full Leather		-----	100	100	110	110
Aero Kit		-----	1300	1300	1415	1415
Automatic w/Tiptronic		-----	350	350	380	380
911 TURBO—6-Cyl. Turbo—Equipment Schedule 1						
W.B. 92.6"; 3.6 Liter.						
GT2 Coupe 2D	AB299	180665	****	****	****	59700

2003 PORSCHE — WPO(CA298)-3-#

Body Type	VIN	List	Trade-In Good	Very Good	Pvt-Party Good	Retail Excellent
BOXSTER—6-Cyl.—Equipment Schedule 1						
W.B. 95.1"; 2.7 Liter, 3.2 Liter.						
Cabriolet 2D	CA298	45485	4800	5175	6325	8625
S Cabriolet 2D	CB298	54485	6800	7250	8825	12000
Full Leather		-----	100	100	135	135
Hard Top		-----	375	375	500	500
Aero Kit		-----	1400	1400	1865	1865
Sport Design		-----	450	450	605	605
Automatic w/Tiptronic		-----	400	400	535	535
911 CARRERA—6-Cyl.—Equipment Schedule 1						
W.B. 92.6"; 3.6 Liter.						
Coupe 2D	AA299	72435	10550	11150	11900	14550
Targa 2D	BA299	79835	12350	13050	13850	16850
Cabriolet 2D	CA299	82235	11350	12000	12800	15650
Full Leather		-----	100	100	105	105
Hard Top (Cabriolet)		-----	375	375	395	395
Aero Kit		-----	1400	1400	1475	1475
Automatic w/Tiptronic		-----	400	400	420	420
911 CARRERA 4 AWD—6-Cyl.—Equipment Schedule 1						
W.B. 92.6"; 3.6 Liter.						
4S Coupe 2D	AA299	82565	12800	13500	14350	17450
Cabriolet 2D	CA299	87835	12600	13300	14150	17300
Full Leather		-----	100	100	105	105
Hard Top		-----	375	375	395	395
Aero Kit		-----	1400	1400	1470	1470
Automatic w/Tiptronic		-----	400	400	420	420
911 TURBO AWD—6-Cyl. Turbo—Equipment Schedule 1						
W.B. 92.6"; 3.6 Liter.						
Coupe 2D	AB299	118265	15150	16000	16700	20100
Full Leather		-----	100	100	110	110
Aero Kit		-----	1400	1400	1515	1515
Automatic w/Tiptronic		-----	400	400	430	430
911 TURBO—6-Cyl. Turbo—Equipment Schedule 1						
W.B. 92.6"; 3.6 Liter.						
GT2 Coupe 2D	AB299	183765	****	****	****	65600

2004 PORSCHE — WPO(CA298)-4-#

Body Type	VIN	List	Trade-In Good	Very Good	Pvt-Party Good	Retail Excellent
BOXSTER—6-Cyl.—Equipment Schedule 1						
W.B. 95.1"; 2.7 Liter, 3.2 Liter.						
Cabriolet 2D	CA298	45485	5600	6000	7175	9625
S Cabriolet 2D	CB298	54485	8075	8550	10050	13350
Full Leather		-----	100	100	135	135
Hard Top		-----	400	400	535	535
Aero Kit		-----	1500	1500	2000	2000
Sport Design		-----	500	500	665	665
Special Edition		-----	800	800	1065	1065
Automatic w/Tiptronic		-----	450	450	600	600
911 CARRERA—6-Cyl.—Equipment Schedule 1						
W.B. 92.6"; 3.6 Liter.						
Coupe 2D	AA299	72435	12000	12650	13100	15500
Targa 2D	BA299	79835	14100	14900	15300	18050
Cabriolet 2D	CA299	82235	14300	15100	15500	18350
40th Anniversary		-----	3225	3225	3360	3360

2004 PORSCHE

Body Type	VIN	List	Trade-In Good	Very Good	Pvt-Party Good	Retail Excellent
Full Leather		------	100	100	105	105
Hard Top (Cabriolet)		------	400	400	415	415
Aero Kit		------	1500	1500	1570	1570
Automatic w/Tiptronic		------	450	450	470	470
911 CARRERA 4 AWD—6-Cyl.—Equipment Schedule 1						
W.B. 92.5"; 3.6 Liter.						
Cabriolet 2D	CA299	86285	15800	16650	17000	20100
4S Coupe 2D	AA299	84165	15300	16100	16550	19550
4S Cabriolet 2D	CA299	93965	17750	18650	19000	22300
Full Leather		------	100	100	105	105
Hard Top (Cabriolet)		------	400	400	415	415
Aero Kit		------	1500	1500	1560	1560
Automatic w/Tiptronic		------	450	450	470	470
911 TURBO AWD—6-Cyl. Turbo—Equipment Schedule 1						
W.B. 92.5"; 3.6 Liter.						
Coupe 2D	AB299	120465	17200	18100	18650	22200
Cabriolet 2D	CB299	130265	19200	20200	20700	24500
Full Leather		------	100	100	105	105
Aero Kit		------	1500	1500	1610	1610
Power Kit X-50		------	1500	1500	1610	1610
Automatic w/Tiptronic		------	450	450	485	485
911 GT2 TURBO—6-Cyl. Turbo—Equipment Schedule 1						
W.B. 92.7"; 3.6 Liter.						
Coupe 2D	AB299	193765	****	****	****	76300
911 GT3—6-Cyl.—Equipment Schedule 1						
W.B. 92.7"; 3.6 Liter.						
Coupe 2D	AC299	101965	31200	32700	33100	39000
CARRERA GT—V10—Equipment Schedule 1						
W.B. 107.5"; 5.7 Liter.						
Roadster 2D	CA298	446165	****	****	****	280900

2005 PORSCHE — WPO(CA298)-5-#

Body Type	VIN	List	Trade-In Good	Very Good	Pvt-Party Good	Retail Excellent
BOXSTER—6-Cyl.—Equipment Schedule 1						
W.B. 95.1"; 2.7 Liter, 3.2 Liter.						
Cabriolet 2D	CA298	44595	8425	8925	10200	13100
S Cabriolet 2D	CB298	53895	10350	10900	12500	16000
Full Leather		------	125	125	165	165
Hard Top		------	425	425	555	555
Aero Kit		------	1575	1575	2065	2065
Sport Pkg		------	500	500	655	655
Automatic w/Tiptronic		------	500	500	655	655
911 CARRERA—6-Cyl.—Equipment Schedule 1						
W.B. 92.5" (S), 92.6"; 3.6 Liter, 3.8 Liter.						
Coupe 2D	AA299	73165	16350	17200	17950	21300
Targa 2D	BA299	79865	18900	19850	20700	24600
Cabriolet 2D	CA299	82965	18200	19100	20000	23900
S Coupe 2D	AB299	79895	19150	20100	21000	25000
S Cabriolet 2D	CB299	89695	20500	21500	22300	26600
Full Leather		------	125	125	140	140
Hard Top (Cabriolet)		------	425	425	480	480
Aero Kit		------	1575	1575	1770	1770
Automatic w/Tiptronic		------	500	500	560	560
911 CARRERA 4 AWD—6-Cyl.—Equipment Schedule 1						
W.B. 92.5"; 3.6 Liter.						
4S Coupe 2D	AA299	84195	19000	19950	20800	24800
4S Cabriolet 2D	CA299	93995	21600	22600	23500	28000
Full Leather		------	125	125	140	140
Hard Top (Cabriolet)		------	425	425	480	480
Aero Kit		------	1575	1575	1780	1780
Automatic w/Tiptronic		------	500	500	565	565
911 TURBO AWD—6-Cyl. Turbo—Equipment Schedule 1						
W.B. 92.5"; 3.6 Liter.						
Cabriolet 2D	CB299	130295	28900	30300	30500	35500
S Coupe 2D	AB299	133495	29200	30600	31000	36300
S Cabriolet 2D	CB299	143295	30700	32200	32500	37900
Full Leather		------	125	125	130	130
Aero Kit		------	1575	1575	1655	1655
Power Kit X-50		------	1575	1575	1655	1655
Automatic w/Tiptronic		------	500	500	525	525
911 GT2—6-Cyl. Turbo—Equipment Schedule 1						
W.B. 92.5"; 3.6 Liter.						
Coupe 2D	AB299	193795	****	****	****	85600

Body Type	VIN	List	Trade-In Good	Very Good	Pvt-Party Good	Retail Excellent

911 GT3—6-Cyl.—Equipment Schedule 1
W.B. 92.5"; 3.6 Liter.
Coupe 2D AC299 101995 **35900 37500 37800 44200**

CARRERA GT—V10—Equipment Schedule 1
W.B. 107.5"; 5.7 Liter.
Roadster 2D .... CA298 448400 ****** **** **** 332400**

2006 PORSCHE — WPO(CA298)-6-#

BOXSTER—6-Cyl.—Equipment Schedule 1
W.B. 95.1"; 2.7 Liter, 3.2 Liter.
Cabriolet 2D	CA298	45795	9100	9625	11150	14100
S Cabriolet 2D	CB298	55495	12050	12700	14300	17950
Full Leather			150	150	195	195
Hard Top			450	450	580	580
Aero Kit			1650	1650	2135	2135
Sport Pkg			500	500	645	645
Automatic w/Tiptronic			550	550	710	710

CAYMAN—6-Cyl.—Equipment Schedule 1
W.B. 95.1"; 3.4 Liter.
S Coupe 2D	AB298	59695	14750	15500	16550	20100
Full Leather			150	150	180	180
Automatic w/Tiptronic			550	550	660	660

911 CARRERA—6-Cyl.—Equipment Schedule 1
W.B. 92.5"; 3.6 Liter, 3.8 Liter.
Coupe 2D	AA299	73615	18600	19500	20300	24100
Cabriolet 2D	CA299	83715	19600	20600	21600	25600
S Coupe 2D	AB299	83715	20700	21700	22600	26900
S Cabriolet 2D	CB299	93745	22600	23600	24600	29100
Full Leather			150	150	170	170
Hard Top (Cabriolet)			450	450	510	510
Aero Kit			1650	1650	1865	1865
Automatic w/Tiptronic			550	550	620	620

911 CARRERA 4 AWD—6-Cyl.—Equipment Schedule 1
W.B. 92.5"; 3.6 Liter, 3.8 Liter.
Coupe 2D	AA299	79415	18800	19750	20700	24600
Cabriolet 2D	CA299	89445	19750	20700	21700	25900
4S Coupe 2D	AB299	89415	19550	20500	21500	25700
4S Cabriolet 2D	CB299	99445	23700	24900	25900	30900
Full Leather			150	150	170	170
Hard Top (Cabriolet)			450	450	510	510
Aero Kit			1650	1650	1870	1870
Automatic w/Tiptronic			550	550	625	625

2007 PORSCHE — WPO(CA298)-7-#

BOXSTER—6-Cyl.—Equipment Schedule 1
W.B. 95.1"; 2.7 Liter, 3.4 Liter.
Cabriolet 2D	CA298	46395	10850	11400	12800	15850
S Cabriolet 2D	CB298	56295	14950	15650	17100	20900
Full Leather			175	175	220	220
Hard Top			475	475	595	595
Aero Kit			1725	1725	2160	2160
Sport Pkg			500	500	625	625
Automatic w/Tiptronic			575	575	720	720

CAYMAN—6-Cyl.—Equipment Schedule 1
W.B. 95.1"; 2.7 Liter, 3.4 Liter.
Coupe 2D	AA298	54955	13550	14250	15500	18900
S Coupe 2D	AB298	64455	17100	17900	19150	23200
Full Leather			175	175	215	215
Automatic w/Tiptronic			575	575	705	705

911 CARRERA—6-Cyl.—Equipment Schedule 1
W.B. 92.5"; 3.6 Liter.
Coupe 2D	AA299	73195	20900	21800	22800	26900
Cabriolet 2D	CA299	83395	22600	23700	24700	29300
Full Leather			175	175	200	200
Hard Top (Cabriolet)			475	475	545	545
Aero Kit			1725	1725	1965	1965
PASM Sport Suspension			700	700	795	795
Automatic w/Tiptronic			575	575	655	655

911 CARRERA—6-Cyl.—Equipment Schedule 1
W.B. 92.5"; 3.8 Liter.
| S Coupe 2D | AB299 | 83395 | 24600 | 25700 | 26600 | 31300 |
| S Cabriolet 2D | CB299 | 93595 | 25800 | 27000 | 28000 | 33000 |

2007 PORSCHE

Body Type	VIN	List	Trade-In Good	Very Good	Pvt-Party Good	Retail Excellent
Full Leather		-------	175	175	200	200
Hard Top		-------	475	475	540	540
Aero Kit		-------	1725	1725	1965	1965
Automatic w/Tiptronic		-------	575	575	655	655

911 CARRERA 4 AWD—6-Cyl.—Equipment Schedule 1
W.B. 92.5"; 3.6 Liter.

Body Type	VIN	List	Trade-In Good	Very Good	Pvt-Party Good	Retail Excellent
Coupe 2D	AA299	78995	22200	23200	24200	28500
Cabriolet 2D	CA299	89195	24700	25800	26800	31500
Full Leather		-------	175	175	200	200
Hard Top (Cabriolet)		-------	475	475	540	540
Aero Kit		-------	1725	1725	1965	1965
PASM Sport Suspension		-------	700	700	795	795
Automatic w/Tiptronic		-------	575	575	655	655

911 CARRERA 4 AWD—6-Cyl.—Equipment Schedule 1
W.B. 92.5"; 3.8 Liter.

Body Type	VIN	List	Trade-In Good	Very Good	Pvt-Party Good	Retail Excellent
4S Coupe 2D	AB299	89195	25000	26100	27100	31900
4S Cabriolet 2D	CB299	99395	28100	29400	30500	35900
Full Leather		-------	175	175	200	200
Hard Top		-------	475	475	540	540
Aero Kit		-------	1725	1725	1965	1965
Automatic w/Tiptronic		-------	575	575	655	655

911 TARGA AWD—6-Cyl.—Equipment Schedule 1
W.B. 92.5"; 3.6 Liter.

Body Type	VIN	List	Trade-In Good	Very Good	Pvt-Party Good	Retail Excellent
4 Coupe 2D	BA299	86495	25600	26800	27700	32600
Full Leather		-------	175	175	200	200
PASM Sport Suspension		-------	700	700	795	795
Automatic w/Tiptronic		-------	575	575	655	655

911 TARGA AWD—6-Cyl.—Equipment Schedule 1
W.B. 92.5"; 3.8 Liter.

Body Type	VIN	List	Trade-In Good	Very Good	Pvt-Party Good	Retail Excellent
4S Coupe 2D	BB299	96695	27900	29200	30200	35500
Full Leather		-------	175	175	200	200
Automatic w/Tiptronic		-------	575	575	650	650

911 GT3—6-Cyl.—Equipment Schedule 1
W.B. 92.7"; 3.6 Liter.

Body Type	VIN	List	Trade-In Good	Very Good	Pvt-Party Good	Retail Excellent
Coupe 2D	AC299	106795	45500	47400	47100	54000
Full Leather		-------	175	175	195	195

911 TURBO AWD—6-Cyl. Turbo—Equipment Schedule 1
W.B. 92.5"; 3.6 Liter.

Body Type	VIN	List	Trade-In Good	Very Good	Pvt-Party Good	Retail Excellent
Coupe 2D	AD299	123695	37000	38600	39000	45100
Full Leather		-------	175	175	195	195
Automatic w/Tiptronic		-------	575	575	650	650

2008 PORSCHE — WPO(CA298)-8-#

BOXSTER—6-Cyl.—Equipment Schedule 1
W.B. 95.1"; 2.7 Liter, 3.4 Liter.

Body Type	VIN	List	Trade-In Good	Very Good	Pvt-Party Good	Retail Excellent
Cabriolet 2D	CA298	46660	14600	15250	16650	20100
Limited Edition Cab	CA298	50760	18650	19500	21000	25200
S Cabriolet 2D	CB298	56560	19300	20200	21600	25800
S Limited Edition	CB298	60760	21000	21900	23500	28300
Full Leather		-------	200	200	240	240
Hard Top		-------	500	500	600	600
Aero Kit		-------	1800	1800	2155	2155
Sport Pkg		-------	500	500	600	600
Automatic w/Tiptronic		-------	600	600	715	715

CAYMAN—6-Cyl.—Equipment Schedule 1
W.B. 95.1"; 2.7 Liter, 3.4 Liter.

Body Type	VIN	List	Trade-In Good	Very Good	Pvt-Party Good	Retail Excellent
Coupe 2D	AA298	53470	15700	16400	17650	21100
S Coupe 2D	AB298	63170	19900	20800	22000	26200
S Design Ed 1 Cpe 2D	AB298	70760	22800	23800	25100	29800
Full Leather		-------	200	200	240	240
Automatic w/Tiptronic		-------	600	600	720	720

911 CARRERA—6-Cyl.—Equipment Schedule 1
W.B. 92.5"; 3.6 Liter.

Body Type	VIN	List	Trade-In Good	Very Good	Pvt-Party Good	Retail Excellent
Coupe 2D	AA299	74360	24400	25500	26000	29900
Cabriolet 2D	CA299	84660	28100	29300	29900	34400
Full Leather		-------	200	200	215	215
Hard Top (Cabriolet)		-------	500	500	545	545
Aero Kit		-------	1800	1800	1960	1960
PASM Sport Suspension		-------	725	725	790	790
Automatic w/Tiptronic		-------	600	600	655	655

911 CARRERA—6-Cyl.—Equipment Schedule 1
W.B. 92.5"; 3.8 Liter.

Body Type	VIN	List	Trade-In Good	Very Good	Pvt-Party Good	Retail Excellent
S Coupe 2D	AB299	84660	30300	31500	32100	36800

Body Type	VIN	List	Trade-In Good	Very Good	Pvt-Party Good	Retail Excellent
S Cabriolet 2D	CB299	94960	31500	32800	33300	38300
Full Leather		------	200	200	220	220
Hard Top (Cabriolet)		------	500	500	545	545
Power Kit X51		------	1800	1800	1965	1965
Automatic w/Tiptronic		------	600	600	655	655
911 CARRERA 4 AWD—6-Cyl.—Equipment Schedule 1						
W.B. 92.5"; 3.6 Liter.						
Coupe 2D	AA299	80260	25100	26200	26800	30900
Full Leather		------	200	200	220	220
Aero Kit		------	1800	1800	1970	1970
PASM Sport Suspension		------	725	725	795	795
Automatic w/Tiptronic		------	600	600	655	655
911 CARRERA 4 AWD—6-Cyl.—Equipment Schedule 1						
W.B. 92.5"; 3.6 Liter, 3.8 Liter.						
Cabriolet 2D	CA299	90560	29400	30700	31300	35900
4S Coupe 2D	AB299	90560	31500	32800	33300	38100
4S Cabriolet 2D	CB299	100860	35500	37000	37400	42800
Full Leather		------	200	200	220	220
Hard Top (Cabriolet)		------	500	500	545	545
Aero Kit		------	1800	1800	1955	1955
Power Kit X51		------	1800	1800	1955	1955
Automatic w/Tiptronic		------	600	600	655	655
911 TARGA AWD—6-Cyl.—Equipment Schedule 1						
W.B. 92.5"; 3.6 Liter.						
4 Coupe 2D	BA299	87860	29300	30500	31200	35800
Full Leather		------	200	200	220	220
PASM Sport Suspension		------	725	725	795	795
Automatic w/Tiptronic		------	600	600	655	655
911 TARGA AWD—6-Cyl.—Equipment Schedule 1						
W.B. 92.5"; 3.8 Liter.						
4S Coupe 2D	BB299	98160	30700	32000	32500	37400
Full Leather		------	200	200	220	220
Power Kit X51		------	1800	1800	1965	1965
Automatic w/Tiptronic		------	600	600	655	655
911 TURBO AWD—6-Cyl. Turbo—Equipment Schedule 1						
W.B. 92.5"; 3.6 Liter.						
Coupe 2D	AD299	127060	40400	42100	42400	48500
Cabriolet 2D	CD299	137360	43100	44900	45100	51600
Full Leather		------	200	200	225	225
Automatic w/Tiptronic		------	600	600	670	670
911 GT2—6-Cyl. Twin Turbo—Equipment Schedule 1						
W.B. 92.5"; 3.6 Liter.						
Coupe 2D	AD299	192560	****	****	****	105400
911 GT3—6-Cyl.—Equipment Schedule 1						
W.B. 92.5"; 3.6 Liter.						
Coupe 2D	AC299	108360	55000	57200	56800	64200

2009 PORSCHE — WPO(CA298)-9-#

Body Type	VIN	List	Trade-In Good	Very Good	Pvt-Party Good	Retail Excellent
BOXSTER—6-Cyl.—Equipment Schedule 1						
W.B. 95.1"; 2.9 Liter, 3.4 Liter.						
Cabriolet 2D	CA298	50880	17650	18350	19700	23300
S Cabriolet 2D	CB298	60980	23300	24200	25500	29900
Full Leather		------	250	250	290	290
Hard Top		------	550	550	645	645
Aero Kit		------	1925	1925	2250	2250
Sport Pkg		------	575	575	670	670
Automatic, PDK		------	700	700	820	820
CAYMAN—6-Cyl.—Equipment Schedule 1						
W.B. 95.1"; 2.9 Liter, 3.4 Liter.						
Coupe 2D	AA298	51160	19650	20400	21600	25200
S Coupe 2D	AB298	64570	25800	26800	28100	32700
Full Leather		------	250	250	290	290
Automatic, PDK		------	700	700	815	815
911 CARRERA—6-Cyl.—Equipment Schedule 1						
W.B. 92.5"; 3.6 Liter.						
Coupe 2D	AA299	80540	29700	30900	31700	36200
Full Leather		------	250	250	275	275
Aero Kit		------	1925	1925	2130	2130
PASM Sport Suspension		------	750	750	830	830
Automatic, PDK		------	700	700	775	775
911 CARRERA—6-Cyl.—Equipment Schedule 1						
W.B. 92.5"; 3.8 Liter.						
S Coupe 2D	AB299	91140	37700	39100	39800	45400

2009 PORSCHE

Body Type	VIN	List	Trade-In Good	Very Good	Pvt-Party Good	Retail Excellent
Full Leather			250	250	275	275
Aero Kit			1925	1925	2125	2125
PASM Sport Suspension			750	750	830	830
Automatic, PDK			700	700	775	775
911 CARRERA—6-Cyl.—Equipment Schedule 1						
W.B. 92.5"; 3.6 Liter.						
Cabriolet 2D	CA299	91140	35100	36500	37200	42400
Full Leather			250	250	275	275
Hard Top			550	550	610	610
Aero Kit			1925	1925	2130	2130
Automatic, PDK			700	700	775	775
911 CARRERA—6-Cyl.—Equipment Schedule 1						
W.B. 92.5"; 3.8 Liter.						
S Cabriolet 2D	CB299	101740	39400	40900	41500	47300
Full Leather			250	250	275	275
Aero Kit			1925	1925	2125	2125
Automatic, PDK			700	700	770	770
911 CARRERA 4 AWD—6-Cyl.—Equipment Schedule 1						
W.B. 92.5"; 3.6 Liter, 3.8 Liter.						
Coupe 2D	AA299	91140	32700	34000	34700	39700
4S Coupe 2D	AB299	97240	38400	39900	40500	46200
Full Leather			250	250	275	275
Aero Kit			1925	1925	2130	2130
PASM Sport Suspension			750	750	830	830
Automatic, PDK			700	700	775	775
911 CARRERA 4 AWD—6-Cyl.—Equipment Schedule 1						
W.B. 92.5"; 3.6 Liter, 3.8 Liter.						
Cabriolet 2D	CA299	97240	37000	38500	39100	44600
4S Cabriolet 2D	CB299	107840	42900	44500	45000	51300
Full Leather			250	250	275	275
Hard Top			550	550	605	605
Aero Kit			1925	1925	2125	2125
Automatic, PDK			700	700	770	770
911 TARGA AWD—6-Cyl.—Equipment Schedule 1						
W.B. 92.5"; 3.8 Liter.						
4S Coupe 2D	BB299	105040	39400	41000	41600	47500
Full Leather			250	250	275	275
Automatic, PDK			700	700	775	775
911 TURBO AWD—6-Cyl. Turbo—Equipment Schedule 1						
W.B. 92.5"; 3.6 Liter.						
Coupe 2D	AD299	130980	42600	44200	44800	51100
Full Leather			250	250	275	275
Automatic w/Tiptronic			700	700	775	775
911 TURBO AWD—6-Cyl. Turbo—Equipment Schedule 1						
W.B. 92.5"; 3.6 Liter.						
Cabriolet 2D	CD299	143580	49400	51300	52100	59400
Full Leather			250	250	275	275
Automatic w/Tiptronic			700	700	775	775
911 GT2—6-Cyl. Twin Turbo—Equipment Schedule 1						
W.B. 92.5"; 3.6 Liter.						
Coupe 2D	AD299	194950	****	****	****	117300

2010 PORSCHE — WPO(CA2A8)—A-#

Body Type	VIN	List	Trade-In Good	Very Good	Pvt-Party Good	Retail Excellent
BOXSTER—6-Cyl.—Equipment Schedule 1						
W.B. 95.1"; 2.9 Liter, 3.4 Liter						
Cabriolet 2D	CA2A8	48550	22100	22900	24000	27700
S Cabriolet 2D	CB2A8	58950	27000	28000	29300	33700
Full Leather			300	300	340	340
Hard Top			575	575	645	645
SportDesign			650	650	740	740
Automatic, PDK			800	800	915	915
CAYMAN—6-Cyl.—Equipment Schedule 1						
W.B. 95.1"; 2.9 Liter, 3.4 Liter.						
Coupe 2D	AA2A8	52350	22300	23200	24300	28000
S Coupe 2D	AB2A8	65870	29100	30100	31500	36300
Full Leather			300	300	345	345
Automatic, PDK			800	800	920	920
911 CARRERA—6-Cyl.—Equipment Schedule 1						
W.B. 92.5"; 3.6 Liter.						
Coupe 2D	AA2A9	78750	32600	33900	34700	39500
Cabriolet 2D	CA2A9	89750	37800	39200	40000	45400
Full Leather			300	300	340	340
Hard Top			575	575	650	650

0415 **EQUIPMENT & MILEAGE PAGE 9 TO 23** 265

2010 PORSCHE

Body Type	VIN	List	Trade-In Good	Very Good	Pvt-Party Good	Retail Excellent
Aero Kit			2050	2050	2325	2325
Active Sport Suspension			775	775	880	880
PASM Sport Suspension			775	775	880	880
Automatic, PDK			800	800	905	905
911 CARRERA—6-Cyl.—Equipment Schedule 1						
W.B. 92.5"; 3.8 Liter.						
S Coupe 2D	AB2A9	89750	40400	41900	42600	48300
Full Leather			300	300	340	340
Aero Kit			2050	2050	2320	2320
PASM Sport Suspension			775	775	875	875
Power Kit X51			2050	2050	2320	2320
Automatic, PDK			800	800	905	905
911 CARRERA—6-Cyl.—Equipment Schedule 1						
W.B. 92.5"; 3.8 Liter.						
S Cabriolet 2D	CB2A9	100750	44800	46400	47000	53300
Full Leather			300	300	340	340
Hard Top			575	575	650	650
Powerkit X51			2050	2050	2310	2310
Automatic, PDK			800	800	900	900
911 CARRERA 4 AWD—6-Cyl.—Equipment Schedule 1						
W.B. 92.5"; 3.6 Liter, 3.8 Liter.						
Coupe 2D	AA2A9	85050	35200	36600	37300	42500
4S Coupe 2D	AB2A9	96050	41600	43100	43800	49700
Full Leather			300	300	340	340
Aero Kit			2050	2050	2325	2325
Powerkit X51			2050	2050	2315	2315
PASM Sport Suspension			775	775	880	880
Automatic, PDK			800	800	905	905
911 CARRERA 4 AWD—6-Cyl.—Equipment Schedule 1						
W.B. 92.5"; 3.6 Liter, 3.8 Liter.						
Cabriolet 2D	CA2A9	96050	40300	41800	42600	48300
4S Cabriolet 2D	CB2A9	107050	45500	47200	47700	53800
Full Leather			300	300	340	340
Hard Top			575	575	650	650
Powerkit X51			2050	2050	2320	2320
Automatic, PDK			800	800	905	905
911 TARGA AWD—6-Cyl.—Equipment Schedule 1						
W.B. 92.5"; 3.6 Liter.						
4 Coupe 2D	BA2A9	93050	39600	41000	41800	47400
Full Leather			300	300	340	340
PASM Sport Suspension			775	775	875	875
Automatic, PDK			800	800	905	905
911 TARGA AWD—6-Cyl.—Equipment Schedule 1						
W.B. 92.5"; 3.8 Liter.						
4S Coupe 2D	BB2A9	104050	42100	43700	44400	50400
Full Leather			300	300	340	340
Powerkit X51			2050	2050	2315	2315
Automatic, PDK			800	800	905	905
911 TURBO AWD—6-Cyl. Turbo—Equipment Schedule 1						
W.B. 92.5"; 3.6 Liter.						
Coupe 2D	AD2A9	133750	57500	59600	60200	68000
Cabriolet 2D	CD2A8	144750	64700	67000	67400	75900
Full Leather			300	300	330	330
Automatic, PDK			800	800	885	885
911 GT3—6-Cyl.—Equipment Schedule 1						
W.B. 92.7"; 3.8 Liter.						
Coupe 2D	AC2A9	113150	83200	86000	85100	94800
RS Coupe 2D	AC2A9	133750	94800	98100	96900	108000
PANAMERA—V8—Equipment Schedule 1						
W.B. 115.0"; 4.8 Liter.						
S Sedan 4D	AB2A7	90775	41200	42600	42600	47800
PANAMERA AWD—V8—Equipment Schedule 1						
W.B. 115.0"; 4.8 Liter.						
4S Sedan 4D	AB2A7	94775	42200	43700	43600	48900
PANAMERA AWD—V8 Twin Turbo—Equipment Schedule 1						
W.B. 115.0"; 4.8 Liter.						
Sedan 4D	AC2A7	133575	57200	59200	59400	66800

2011 PORSCHE — WPO(CA2A8)–B–#

Body Type	VIN	List	Trade-In Good	Very Good	Pvt-Party Good	Retail Excellent
BOXSTER—6-Cyl.—Equipment Schedule 1						
W.B. 95.1"; 2.9 Liter, 3.4 Liter.						
Convertible 2D	CA2A8	49050	24500	25400	26600	30400
S Convertible 2D	CB2A8	59550	30800	31800	33000	37500

Body Type	VIN	List	Trade-In Good	Very Good	Pvt-Party Good	Retail Excellent
Spyder Convertible 2D	CB2A8	64510	36900	38100	39300	44500
Full Leather			350	350	395	395
Hard Top			600	600	680	680
SportDesign Pkg			725	725	820	820
Automatic, PDK			875	875	990	990
CAYMAN—6-Cyl.—Equipment Schedule 1						
W.B. 95.1"; 2.9 Liter, 3.4 Liter.						
Coupe 2D	AA2A8	54400	26500	27400	28700	32900
S Coupe 2D	AB2A8	66470	34600	35800	37000	42100
Full Leather			350	350	395	395
Automatic, PDK			875	875	985	985
911 CARRERA—6-Cyl.—Equipment Schedule 1						
W.B. 92.5"; 3.6 Liter.						
Coupe 2D	AA2A9	78750	36900	38300	38800	43600
Cabriolet 2D	CA2A9	89750	42900	44400	44800	50200
Full Leather			350	350	385	385
Hard Top			600	600	655	655
Aero Kit			2175	2175	2395	2395
PASM Sport Suspension			800	800	880	880
Automatic, PDK			875	875	990	990
911 CARRERA—6-Cyl.—Equipment Schedule 1						
W.B. 92.5"; 3.8 Liter.						
S Coupe 2D	AB2A9	91450	45900	47500	48200	53900
Full Leather			350	350	385	385
Aero Kit			2175	2175	2385	2385
Powerkit			2175	2175	2385	2385
PASM Sport Suspension			800	800	875	875
Automatic, PDK			875	875	960	960
911 CARRERA—6-Cyl.—Equipment Schedule 1						
W.B. 92.5"; 3.8 Liter.						
S Cabriolet 2D	CB2A9	102450	48800	50500	51100	57200
Full Leather			350	350	385	385
Hard Top			600	600	655	655
Powerkit			2175	2175	2385	2385
Automatic, PDK			875	875	960	960
911 CARRERA 4 AWD—6-Cyl.—Equipment Schedule 1						
W.B. 92.5"; 3.6 Liter, 3.8 Liter.						
Coupe 2D	AA2A9	85050	40000	41400	41900	47100
Cabriolet 2D	CA2A9	96050	45200	46800	47100	52800
4S Coupe 2D	AB2A9	97750	46200	47800	48200	54000
Full Leather			350	350	385	385
Hard Top			600	600	655	655
Aero Kit			2175	2175	2385	2385
Powerkit			2175	2175	2385	2385
PASM Sport Suspension			800	800	880	880
Automatic, PDK			875	875	960	960
911 CARRERA 4 AWD—6-Cyl.—Equipment Schedule 1						
W.B. 92.5"; 3.8 Liter.						
4S Cabriolet 2D	CB2A9	108750	50500	52300	52800	59100
Full Leather			350	350	385	385
Hard Top			600	600	655	655
Powerkit			2175	2175	2380	2380
Automatic, PDK			875	875	960	960
911 TARGA AWD—6-Cyl.—Equipment Schedule 1						
W.B. 92.5"; 3.6 Liter.						
4 Coupe 2D	BA2A9	93050	43900	45400	45900	51400
Full Leather			350	350	385	385
PASM Sport Suspension			800	800	880	880
Automatic, PDK			875	875	960	960
911 TARGA AWD—6-Cyl.—Equipment Schedule 1						
W.B. 92.5"; 3.8 Liter.						
4S Coupe 2D	BB2A9	105750	46500	48100	48800	54600
Full Leather			350	350	385	385
Powerkit			2175	2175	2385	2385
Automatic, PDK			875	875	960	960
911 TURBO AWD—6-Cyl. Twin Turbo—Equipment Schedule 1						
W.B. 92.5"; 3.8 Liter.						
Coupe 2D	AD2A9	136450	65900	68100	68300	76400
Full Leather			350	350	385	385
Aero Kit			2175	2175	2405	2405
Automatic, PDK			875	875	965	965
911 TURBO AWD—6-Cyl. Twin Turbo—Equipment Schedule 1						
W.B. 92.5"; 3.8 Liter.						

2011 PORSCHE

Body Type	VIN	List	Trade-In Good	Very Good	Pvt-Party Good	Retail Excellent
Convertible 2D	CD2A9	147750	76500	79100	78800	87700
Full Leather			350	350	385	385
Hard Top			600	600	660	660
Automatic, PDK			875	875	965	965
911 TURBO S AWD—6-Cyl. Twin Turbo—Equipment Schedule 1						
W.B. 92.5"; 3.8 Liter.						
Coupe 2D	AD2A9	161650	77800	80400	80200	89300
Convertible 2D	CD2A9	173050	84300	87100	86400	95800
Full Leather			350	350	385	385
Aero Kit			2175	2175	2400	2400
911 GT3—6-Cyl.—Equipment Schedule 1						
W.B. 92.7"; 3.8 Liter, 4.0 Liter.						
Coupe 2D	AC2A9	116650	98700	102000	101100	111900
RS Coupe 2D	AC2A9	136450	110300	114000	112900	125000
RS 4.0 Coupe 2D	AC2A9	185950	136300	140800	138800	153500
Full Leather			350	350	385	385
911 GTS—6-Cyl.—Equipment Schedule 1						
W.B. 92.5"; 3.8 Liter.						
Coupe 2D	AB2A9	104050	51700	53500	54100	60600
Aero Kit			2175	2175	2385	2385
PASM Sport Suspension			800	800	875	875
911 GTS—6-Cyl.—Equipment Schedule 1						
W.B. 92.5"; 3.8 Liter.						
Convertible 2D	CB2A9	113850	55600	57500	58000	64900
Hard Top			600	600	655	655
Aero Kit			2175	2175	2380	2380
911 SPEEDSTER—6-Cyl.—Equipment Schedule 1						
W.B. 92.5"; 3.8 Liter.						
Convertible 2D	CB2A9	204950	152700	157700	153500	167900
911 GT2 RS—6-Cyl. Twin Turbo—Equipment Schedule 1						
W.B. 92.7"; 3.6 Liter.						
Coupe 2D	AE2A9	245950	****	****	****	187500
PANAMERA—V6—Equipment Schedule 1						
W.B. 115.0"; 3.6 Liter.						
Sedan 4D	AA2A7	75375	39400	40700	41200	46100
Automatic, PDK			875	875	950	950
PANAMERA AWD—V6—Equipment Schedule 1						
W.B. 115.0"; 3.6 Liter.						
4 Sedan 4D	AA2A7	79875	41900	43300	43600	48700
PANAMERA—V8—Equipment Schedule 1						
W.B. 115.0"; 4.8 Liter.						
S Sedan 4D	AB2A7	90775	45600	47100	47500	53100
Automatic, PDK			875	875	955	955
PANAMERA AWD—V8—Equipment Schedule 1						
W.B. 115.0"; 4.8 Liter.						
4S Sedan 4D	AB2A7	95675	46900	48400	49200	55000
PANAMERA AWD—V8 Twin Turbo—Equipment Schedule 1						
W.B. 115.0"; 4.8 Liter.						
Turbo Sedan 4D	AC2A7	136275	61600	63600	63900	71300

2012 PORSCHE — WPO(CA2A8)–C–#

Body Type	VIN	List	Trade-In Good	Very Good	Pvt-Party Good	Retail Excellent
BOXSTER—6-Cyl.—Equipment Schedule 1						
W.B. 95.1"; 2.9 Liter, 3.4 Liter.						
Convertible 2D	CA2A8	49050	27300	28200	29300	33100
S Convertible 2D	CB2A8	59550	34800	35900	37000	41700
Spyder Convertible 2D	CB2A8	62750	39100	40300	41200	46100
S Black Ed Conv 2D	CB2A8	63450	36100	37300	38300	43000
Full Leather			400	400	445	445
Hard Top			625	625	700	700
SportDesign Pkg			800	800	895	895
Auto, 7-Spd w/PDK MM			950	950	1060	1060
CAYMAN—6-Cyl.—Equipment Schedule 1						
W.B. 95.1"; 2.9 Liter, 3.4 Liter.						
Coupe 2D	AA2A8	56270	31800	32800	33900	38200
S Coupe 2D	AB2A8	70670	39900	41100	42200	47400
R Coupe 2D	AB2A8	70910	43800	45100	46400	52300
S Black Ed Coupe 2D	AB2A8	72110	41700	43000	44100	49600
Full Leather			400	400	445	445
Auto, 7-Spd w/PDK			950	950	1060	1060
911 CARRERA—6-Cyl.—Equipment Schedule 1						
W.B. 92.5"; 3.6 Liter.						
997 Coupe 2D	AA2A9	79950	45100	46700	47700	53600
Cabriolet 2D	AB2A9	91050	53600	55400	55900	62300

Body Type	VIN	List	Trade-In Good	Very Good	Pvt-Party Good	Retail Excellent
Full Leather			400	400	445	445
Sport Chrono Pkg Plus			400	400	445	445
Aero Kit			2300	2300	2550	2550
PASM Sport Suspension			825	825	915	915
Ceramic Brakes			3900	3900	4320	4320
Auto, 7-Spd PDK Manual			950	950	1050	1050
911 CARRERA—6-Cyl.—Equipment Schedule 1						
W.B. 92.5"; 3.4 Liter.						
991 Coupe 2D	AA2A9	83050	47600	49200	50100	56200
Full Leather			400	400	440	440
Premium Pkg			800	800	885	885
Premium Plus Pkg			2600	2600	2890	2890
Sport Chrono Pkg			575	575	635	635
Porsche Torque Vectoring			650	650	730	730
Ceramic Brakes			3900	3900	4315	4315
911 CARRERA BLACK EDITION—6-Cyl.—Equipment Schedule 1						
W.B. 92.5"; 3.6 Liter.						
Coupe 2D	AA2A9	82250	50700	52400	52900	58900
Convertible 2D	CA2A9	92250	50800	52600	53200	59300
Full Leather			400	400	440	440
Hard Top			625	625	690	690
Sport Chrono Pkg Plus			400	400	440	440
PASM Sport Suspension			825	825	910	910
Ceramic Brakes			3900	3900	4300	4300
Auto, 7-Spd PDK Manual			950	950	1045	1045
911 CARRERA 4 AWD—6-Cyl.—Equipment Schedule 1						
W.B. 92.5"; 3.6 Liter, 3.8 Liter.						
Coupe 2D	AA2A9	86350	53400	55200	55700	61900
Cabriolet 2D	CA2A9	97450	55100	57000	57200	63400
4S Coupe 2D	AB2A9	99250	59000	61000	61300	68300
GTS Coupe 2D	AB2A9	111150	63100	65200	65500	72800
Full Leather			400	400	440	440
Aero Kit			2300	2300	2535	2535
25 Yrs Exclusive Pkg			925	925	1025	1025
Powerkit			2300	2300	2530	2530
Sport Chrono Pkg Plus			400	400	440	440
PASM Sport Suspension			825	825	910	910
Ceramic Brakes			3900	3900	4300	4300
Auto, 7-Spd PDK Manual			950	950	1045	1045
911 CARRERA 4 AWD—6-Cyl.—Equipment Schedule 1						
W.B. 92.5"; 3.8 Liter.						
4S Cabriolet 2D	CB2A9	110350	60600	62700	63100	70400
GTS Convertible 2D	CB2A9	121050	67800	70100	70100	77800
Full Leather			400	400	440	440
Hard Top			625	625	685	685
25 Yrs Exclusive Pkg			925	925	1030	1030
Sport Chrono Pkg Plus			400	400	440	440
Powerkit			2300	2300	2540	2540
Ceramic Brakes			3900	3900	4310	4310
Auto, 7-Spd PDK Manual			950	950	1050	1050
911 CARRERA S—6-Cyl.—Equipment Schedule 1						
W.B. 92.5"; 3.8 Liter.						
997 Coupe 2D	AB2A9	92850	56900	58800	59100	65600
Cabriolet 2D	CB2A9	103950	59000	60900	61500	68700
Full Leather			400	400	440	440
Powerkit			2300	2300	2535	2535
Sport Chrono Pkg Plus			400	400	440	440
Ceramic Brakes			3900	3900	4300	4300
Auto, 7-Spd PDK Manual			950	950	1050	1050
911 CARRERA S—6-Cyl.—Equipment Schedule 1						
W.B. 92.5"; 3.8 Liter.						
991 Coupe 2D	AB2A9	97350	57900	59800	60300	67300
Full Leather			400	400	435	435
Premium Pkg			800	800	875	875
Premium Plus Pkg			2600	2600	2850	2850
Sport Chrono Pkg			575	575	625	625
PASM Sport Suspension			825	825	900	900
Ceramic Brakes			3900	3900	4255	4255
Auto, 7-Spd PDK Manual			950	950	1035	1035
911 TARGA AWD—6-Cyl.—Equipment Schedule 1						
W.B. 92.5"; 3.6 Liter.						
4 Coupe 2D	BA2A9	94450	54600	56400	56900	63300
Full Leather			400	400	440	440

2012 PORSCHE

Body Type	VIN	List	Trade-In Good	Very Good	Pvt-Party Good	Retail Excellent
25 Yrs Exclusive Pkg			925	925	1030	1030
PASM Sport Suspension			825	825	910	910
Sport Chrono Pkg Plus			400	400	440	440
Ceramic Brakes			3900	3900	4310	4310
Auto, 7-Spd PDK Manual			950	950	1050	1050
911 TARGA AWD—6-Cyl.—Equipment Schedule 1						
W.B. 92.5"; 3.8 Liter.						
4S Coupe 2D	BB2A9	107350	57500	59500	59900	66800
Full Leather			400	400	440	440
25 Yrs Exclusive Pkg			925	925	1030	1030
Powerkit			2300	2300	2540	2540
Sport Chrono Pkg Plus			400	400	440	440
Ceramic Brakes			3900	3900	4305	4305
Auto, 7-Spd PDK Manual			950	950	1050	1050
911 TURBO AWD—6-Cyl. Twin Turbo—Equipment Schedule 1						
W.B. 92.5"; 3.8 Liter.						
Coupe 2D	AD2A9	138450	76100	78600	78400	86800
Cabriolet 2D	CD2A9	149950	86700	89600	88700	98000
Full Leather			400	400	440	440
25 Yrs Exclusive Pkg			925	925	1030	1030
Sport Chrono Pkg			575	575	635	635
Hard Top			625	625	680	680
Ceramic Brakes			3900	3900	4300	4300
Auto, 7-Spd PDK Manual			950	950	1045	1045
911 TURBO S AWD—6-Cyl. Twin Turbo—Equipment Schedule 1						
W.B. 92.5"; 3.8 Liter.						
Coupe 2D	AD2A9	161650	88100	91000	90100	99600
Convertible 2D	CD2A9	173050	94500	97600	96300	106100
Aero Kit			2300	2300	2510	2510
Hard Top			625	625	680	680
25 Yrs Exclusive Pkg			925	925	1020	1020
911 GT3—6-Cyl.—Equipment Schedule 1						
W.B. 92.7"; 3.8 Liter, 4.0 Liter.						
Coupe 2D	AB2A9	116650	****	****	****	126800
RS Coupe 2D	AB2A9	136450	****	****	****	141900
RS 4.0 Coupe 2D	AC2A9	185950	****	****	****	168400
Sport Chrono Pkg Plus			****	****	****	435
Ceramic Brakes			****	****	****	4230
911 CARRERA GTS—6-Cyl.—Equipment Schedule 1						
W.B. 92.5"; 3.8 Liter.						
Coupe 2D	AB2A9	104050	63600	65800	65600	72600
Convertible 2D	CB2A9	113850	67500	69800	69500	76800
Hard Top			625	625	685	685
25 Yrs Exclusive Pkg			925	925	1030	1030
Sport Chrono Pkg Plus			400	400	440	440
Ceramic Brakes			3900	3900	4300	4300
911 SPEEDSTER—6-Cyl.—Equipment Schedule 1						
W.B. 92.5"; 3.8 Liter.						
Convertible 2D	CB2A9	204950	****	****	****	178900
911 GT2 RS—6-Cyl. Twin Turbo—Equipment Schedule 1						
W.B. 92.7"; 3.6 Liter.						
Coupe 2D	AA2A9	245950	****	****	****	202400
Sport Chrono Pkg Plus			****	****	****	435
PANAMERA—V6—Equipment Schedule 1						
W.B. 114.9"; 3.6 Liter.						
Sedan 4D	AA2A7	76175	44800	46200	46700	52000
Adaptive Cruise Control			450	450	485	485
PANAMERA—V6 Hybrid—Equipment Schedule 1						
W.B. 114.9"; 3.0 Liter.						
S Sedan 4D	AD2A7	95975	50600	52200	53500	60000
Adaptive Cruise Control			450	450	490	490
PANAMERA AWD—V6—Equipment Schedule 1						
W.B. 114.9"; 3.6 Liter.						
4 Sedan 4D	AA2A7	80775	47700	49200	50000	55500
Adaptive Cruise Control			450	450	485	485
PANAMERA—V8—Equipment Schedule 1						
W.B. 114.9"; 4.8 Liter.						
S Sedan 4D	AB2A7	91275	53200	54800	55500	61700
Adaptive Cruise Control			450	450	485	485
PANAMERA AWD—V8—Equipment Schedule 1						
W.B. 114.9"; 4.8 Liter.						
4S Sedan 4D	AB2A7	96175	54300	56000	56800	63200
Adaptive Cruise Control			450	450	485	485

2012 PORSCHE

Body Type	VIN	List	Trade-In Good	Very Good	Pvt-Party Good	Retail Excellent
PANAMERA AWD—V8 Twin Turbo—Equipment Schedule 1						
W.B. 115.0"; 4.8 Liter.						
Turbo Sedan 4D	AC2A7	137675	69600	71700	72100	79900
Turbo S Sedan 4D	AC2A7	174175	85000	87600	86300	94300
Adaptive Cruise Control			450	450	485	485

2013 PORSCHE — WPO(CA2A8)–D–#

Body Type	VIN	List	Trade-In Good	Very Good	Pvt-Party Good	Retail Excellent
BOXSTER—6-Cyl.—Equipment Schedule 1						
W.B. 95.1"; 2.7 Liter, 3.4 Liter.						
Convertible 2D	CA2A8	50450	36600	37700	38500	42900
S Convertible 2D	CB2A8	61850	46500	47900	48500	53700
Full Leather			450	450	490	490
Auto, 7-Spd w/PDK Manual			1025	1025	1120	1120
911 CARRERA—6-Cyl.—Equipment Schedule 1						
W.B. 92.5", 96.5" (Cab); 3.4 Liter.						
Coupe 2D	AA2A9	83050	55800	57700	58000	64300
Cabriolet 2D	CA2A9	94650	66300	68500	68100	75000
Full Leather			450	450	480	480
Premium Pkg			800	800	860	860
Premium Plus Pkg			2700	2700	2900	2900
SportDesign Pkg			1425	1425	1530	1530
PASM Sport Suspension			850	850	910	910
Ceramic Brakes			4000	4000	4290	4290
Auto, 7-Spd PDK Manual			1025	1025	1100	1100
911 CARRERA 4 AWD—6-Cyl.—Equipment Schedule 1						
W.B. 92.5"; 3.6 Liter, 3.8 Liter.						
Coupe 2D	AA2A9	86350	61200	63200	63100	69700
Cabriolet 2D	CA2A9	97450	68400	70700	70200	77200
4S Coupe 2D	AB2A9	99250	74400	76800	76100	83600
Full Leather			450	450	480	480
25 Years Exclusive Pkg			1000	1000	1070	1070
PASM Sport Suspension			850	850	910	910
Ceramic Brakes			4000	4000	4280	4280
Auto, 7-Spd PDK Manual			1025	1025	1095	1095
911 CARRERA 4 AWD—6-Cyl.—Equipment Schedule 1						
W.B. 92.5"; 3.8 Liter.						
4S Cabriolet 2D	CB2A9	110350	78000	80600	79800	87800
Full Leather			450	450	480	480
25 Yrs Exclusive Pkg			1000	1000	1065	1065
Powerkit			2400	2400	2560	2560
SportDesign			1425	1425	1520	1520
Ceramic Brakes			4000	4000	4270	4270
Auto, 7-Spd PDK Manual			1025	1025	1095	1095
911 CARRERA S—6-Cyl.—Equipment Schedule 1						
W.B. 92.5", 96.5" (Cab); 3.8 Liter.						
Coupe 2D	AB2A9	97350	66600	68800	68800	76000
Cabriolet 2D	CB2A9	108950	74000	76400	75900	83700
Full Leather			450	450	485	485
Premium Pkg			800	800	865	865
Premium Plus Pkg			2700	2700	2920	2920
SportDesign Pkg			1425	1425	1540	1540
PASM Sport Suspension			850	850	920	920
Ceramic Brakes			4000	4000	4320	4320
Auto, 7-Spd PDK Manual			1025	1025	1105	1105
911 TURBO AWD—6-Cyl. Twin Turbo—Equipment Schedule 1						
W.B. 92.5"; 3.8 Liter.						
Coupe 2D	AD2A9	138450	90500	93400	92200	101200
Cabriolet 2D	CD2A9	149950	100500	103800	102500	112200
Full Leather			450	450	485	485
Hard Top			650	650	700	700
Ceramic Brakes			4000	4000	4315	4315
Auto, 7-Spd PDK Manual			1025	1025	1105	1105
911 TURBO S AWD—6-Cyl. Twin Turbo—Equipment Schedule 1						
W.B. 92.5"; 3.8 Liter.						
Coupe 2D	AD2A9	161650	102000	105200	104000	114000
Cabriolet 2D	CD2A9	173050	110400	113900	112100	122500
Hard Top			650	650	700	700
PANAMERA—V6—Equipment Schedule 1						
W.B. 114.9"; 3.6 Liter.						
Sedan 4D		76825	51500	53000	54100	60200
Platinum Ed Sedan		81475	54700	56400	57400	63900
PANAMERA—V6 Hybrid—Equipment Schedule 1						
W.B. 114.9"; 3.0 Liter.						

Body Type	VIN	List	Trade-In Good	Very Good	Pvt-Party Good	Retail Excellent
S Sedan 4D	97125	59800	61600	62400	69200
PANAMERA AWD—V6—Equipment Schedule 1						
W.B. 114.9"; 3.6 Liter.						
4 Sedan 4D	81425	54800	56500	57500	64100
4 Platinum Ed Sed	85575	55800	57500	58200	64500
PANAMERA—V8—Equipment Schedule 1						
W.B. 114.9"; 4.8 Liter.						
S Sedan 4D	92325	63900	65800	66000	72700
PANAMERA AWD—V8—Equipment Schedule 1						
W.B. 114.9"; 4.8 Liter.						
4S Sedan 4D	97325	63700	65500	65900	72600
GTS Sedan 4D	111975	80100	82400	81200	88300
PANAMERA AWD—V8 Twin Turbo—Equipment Schedule 1						
W.B. 114.9"; 4.8 Liter.						
Sedan 4D	139625	78900	81100	81100	89200
S Sedan 4D	176275	95100	97800	96100	104400

2014 PORSCHE — WPO(CA2A8)—E–#

Body Type	VIN	List	Trade-In Good	Very Good	Pvt-Party Good	Retail Excellent
BOXSTER—6-Cyl.—Equipment Schedule 1						
W.B. 95.1"; 2.7 Liter, 3.4 Liter.						
Convertible 2D	CA2A8	51350	42200	43500	44000	48600
S Convertible 2D	CB2A8	63050	53200	54800	55300	60800
Full Leather		----	525	525	570	570
Porsche Torque Vectoring		----	675	675	745	745
Premium Pkg		----	800	800	865	865
Sport Chrono Pkg		----	600	600	640	640
Auto, 7-Spd PDK Manual		----	1100	1100	1190	1190
CAYMAN—6-Cyl.—Equipment Schedule 1						
W.B. 97.4"; 2.7 Liter.						
Coupe 2D	AA2A8	53550	45900	47200	47600	52400
S Coupe 2D	AB2A8	65700	56200	57800	58300	64100
Adaptive Cruise Control		----	500	500	540	540
Porsche Torque Vectoring		----	675	675	740	740
Auto, 7-Spd w/PDK MM		----	1100	1100	1185	1185
911 CARRERA—6-Cyl.—Equipment Schedule 1						
W.B. 92.5", 96.5" (Cab); 3.4 Liter.						
Coupe 2D	AA2A9	85250	69200	71400	71200	78600
Cabriolet 2D	CA2A9	97150	84600	87300	85600	93300
50th Anniv Ed Coupe	AB2A9	125050				
Adaptive Cruise Control		----				
Full Leather		----	525	525	555	555
Porsche Torque Vectoring		----	675	675	725	725
Sport Chrono Pkg		----	600	600	625	625
SportDesign Pkg		----	1500	1500	1585	1585
PASM Sport Suspension		----	875	875	925	925
Auto, 7-Spd PDK Manual		----	1100	1100	1165	1165
911 CARRERA 4 AWD—6-Cyl.—Equipment Schedule 1						
W.B. 92.5"; 3.4 Liter, 3.8 Liter.						
Coupe 2D	AA2A9	91980	74900	77400	76300	83500
Cabriolet 2D	CA2A9	103880	87200	90000	88100	95900
4S Coupe 2D	AB2A9	106580	92400	95300	93300	101600
Full Leather		----	525	525	555	555
Adaptive Cruise Control		----	500	500	530	530
Aero Kit		----	2500	2500	2640	2640
PASM Sport Suspension		----	875	875	925	925
Auto, 7-Spd PDK Manual		----	1100	1100	1160	1160
911 CARRERA S—6-Cyl.—Equipment Schedule 1						
W.B. 92.5", 96.5" (Cab); 3.8 Liter.						
Coupe 2D	AB2A9	99850	84600	87400	86000	94100
Cabriolet 2D	CB2A9	111750	92300	95200	93400	102000
Full Leather		----	525	525	555	555
Adaptive Cruise Control		----	500	500	530	530
PASM Sport Suspension		----	875	875	930	930
Aero Kit		----	2500	2500	2655	2655
Auto, 7-Spd PDK Manual		----	1100	1100	1170	1170
911 TURBO AWD—6-Cyl. Twin Turbo—Equipment Schedule 1						
W.B. 92.5"; 3.8 Liter.						
Coupe 2D	AD2A9	149250	139000	143300	139000	150200
Adaptive Cruise Control		----	500	500	525	525
911 TURBO S AWD—6-Cyl. Twin Turbo—Equipment Schedule 1						
W.B. 92.5"; 3.8 Liter.						
Coupe 2D	AD2A9	182050	148000	152600	147900	160000
Adaptive Cruise Control		----	500	500	525	525

Body Type	VIN	List	Trade-In Good	Very Good	Pvt-Party Good	Retail Excellent
PANAMERA—V6—Equipment Schedule 1						
W.B. 114.9"; 3.6 Liter.						
Sedan 4D	79075		60300	62000	62500	69000
Adaptive Cruise Control			500	500	535	535
PANAMERA—V6 Twin Turbo—Equipment Schedule 1						
W.B. 114.9"; 3.6 Liter.						
S Sedan 4D	94175		72700	74800	74400	81400
Adaptive Cruise Control			500	500	530	530

ROLLS ROYCE

2005 ROLLS ROYCE — SCA(1S684)-5-#

PHANTOM—V12—Equipment Schedule 2
W.B. 140.6"; 6.8 Liter.

Body Type	VIN	List	Good	Very Good	Good	Excellent
Sedan 4D	1S684	328750	****	****	****	115100

2006 ROLLS ROYCE — SCA(1S684) - 6-#

PHANTOM—V12—Equipment Schedule 2
2.B. 140.6"; 6.8 Liter.

Sedan 4D	1S684	329750	****	****	****	147900

2007 ROLLS ROYCE — SCA(1S685)-7-#

PHANTOM—V12—Equipment Schedule 2
W.B. 140.6", 150.4" (Ext); 6.8 Liter.

Sedan 4D	1S685	335350	****	****	****	180100
Extended Sedan 4D	1L685	387500	****	****	****	224900

2008 ROLLS ROYCE — SCA(1S685)-8-#

PHANTOM—V12—Equipment Schedule 2
W.B. 130.7"; 140.6" (Sed); 150.4" (Ext); 6.8 Liter.

Sedan 4D	1S685	345000	****	****	****	203300
Extended Sedan 4D	1L685	408000	****	****	****	248100
Drophead Coupe 2D	2D685	412000	****	****	****	281000

2009 ROLLS ROYCE — SCA(1S685)-9-#

PHANTOM—V12—Equipment Schedule 2
W.B. 130.7", 140.6" (Sed); 150.4" (Ext); 6.8 Liter.

Sedan 4D	1S685	382000	****	****	****	231200
Extended Sedan 4D	1L685	452000	****	****	****	281200
Coupe 2D	3C675	402000	****	****	****	262000
Drophead Coupe 2D	2D685	436000	****	****	****	305800

2010 ROLLS ROYCE — SCA(664S5)-A-#

GHOST—V12 Twin Turbo—Equipment Schedule 2
W.B. 129.7"; 6.6 Liter.

Sedan 4D	664S5	247000	****	****	****	205000

PHANTOM—V12—Equipment Schedule 2
W.B. 130.7", 140.6" (Sed); 150.4" (Ext); 6.8 Liter.

Sedan 4D	681S5	382000	****	****	****	272200
Extended Sedan 4D	681L5	452000	****	****	****	321000
Coupe 2D	683C5	410000	****	****	****	302300
Drophead Coupe 2D	682D5	445000	****	****	****	345100

2011 ROLLS ROYCE — SCA(664S5)-B-#

GHOST—V12 Twin Turbo—Equipment Schedule 2
W.B. 129.7"; 6.6 Liter.

Sedan 4D	664S5	250200	****	****	****	240900

PHANTOM—V12—Equipment Schedule 2
W.B. 130.7", 140.6" (Sed); 150.4" (Ext); 6.8 Liter.

Sedan 4D	681S5	385000	****	****	****	305200
Extended Sedan 4D	681L5	455000	****	****	****	352900
Coupe 2D	673C5	413000	****	****	****	336600
Drophead Conv 2D	682D5	452000	****	****	****	378600

2012 ROLLS ROYCE — SCA(664S5)-C-#

GHOST—V12 Twin Turbo—Equipment Schedule 2
W.B. 129.7", 136.4" (Ext); 6.6 Liter.

Sedan 4D	664S5	253700	****	****	****	263600
Extended Sedan 4D	664L5	292000	****	****	****	282700

Body Type	VIN	List	Trade-In Good	Very Good	Pvt-Party Good	Retail Excellent
PHANTOM—V12—Equipment Schedule 2						
W.B. 130.7", 140.6" (Sed), 150.4" (Ext); 6.8 Liter.						
Sedan 4D	681S5	385000	****	****	****	341500
Extended Sedan 4D	681L5	455000	****	****	****	392100
Coupe 2D	683C5	413000	****	****	****	373800
Drophead Conv 2D	682D5	452000	****	****	****	417600

2013 ROLLS ROYCE—SCA(664S5)–D–#

Body Type	VIN	List	Trade-In Good	Very Good	Pvt-Party Good	Retail Excellent
GHOST—V12 Twin Turbo—Equipment Schedule 2						
W.B. 129.7", 136.4" (Ext); 6.6 Liter.						
Sedan 4D	664S5	260750	****	****	****	277600
Extended Sedan 4D	664L5	298000	****	****	****	296800
PHANTOM—V12—Equipment Schedule 2						
W.B. 130.7", 140.6" (Sed), 150.4" (Ext); 6.8 Liter.						
Sedan 4D	681S5	403970	****	****	****	356600
Extended Sedan 4D	681L5	475295	****	****	****	405800
Coupe 2D	683C5	434295	****	****	****	388900
Drophead Conv 2D	682D5	474900	****	****	****	431700

SRT

2013 SRT — (1,2or3)C3–(DEAZ)–D–#

Body Type	VIN	List	Trade-In Good	Very Good	Pvt-Party Good	Retail Excellent
VIPER—V10—Equipment Schedule 2						
W.B. 98.8"; 8.4 Liter.						
Coupe 2D	DEAZ	104990	57100	58900	59100	65300
GTS Coupe 2D	DEBZ	124990	75300	77600	77200	85000
Grand Touring Pkg			1000	1000	1055	1055
Track Package			1500	1500	1585	1585

SAAB

2000 SAAB — YS3(DD35H)–Y–#

Body Type	VIN	List	Trade-In Good	Very Good	Pvt-Party Good	Retail Excellent
9-3—4-Cyl. Turbo—Equipment Schedule 3						
W.B. 102.6"; 2.0 Liter.						
Hatchback 2D	DD35H	27675	400	450	1000	1750
Hatchback 4D	DD55H	28175	400	450	1000	1750
Convertible 2D	DD75H	41225	725	825	1400	2350
Automatic	8		125	125	165	165
9-3—4-Cyl. HO Turbo—Equipment Schedule 2						
W.B. 102.6"; 2.0 Liter, 2.3 Liter.						
SE Hatchback 4D	DF55K	33670	575	650	1225	2100
SE Convertible 2D	DF75K	44770	775	875	1450	2450
Viggen Hatchback 2D	DP35K	38325	1750	1925	2675	4250
Viggen Hatchback 4D	DP55G	38325	1525	1675	2300	3675
Viggen Convertible 2D	DP75G	45570	2000	2200	3025	4725
Automatic	8		125	125	165	165
9-5—4-Cyl. Turbo—Equipment Schedule 2						
W.B. 106.4", 106.6" (Wagon); 2.3 Liter.						
Sedan 4D	ED48E	35300	650	750	1275	2150
Wagon 4D	ED58E	35300	675	775	1325	2275
Gary Fisher Edition			300	300	400	400
Manual, 5-Spd	5		(200)	(200)	(255)	(255)
9-5—4-Cyl. HO Turbo—Equipment Schedule 2						
W.B. 106.4", 106.6" (Wagon); 2.3 Liter.						
Aero Sedan 4D	EH48G	41550	1575	1750	2525	4225
Aero Wagon 4D	EH58G	44145	1825	2025	3000	4950
Manual, 5-Spd	5		(200)	(200)	(255)	(255)
9-5—V6 Turbo—Equipment Schedule 2						
W.B. 106.4", 106.6" (Wagon); 3.0 Liter.						
SE Sedan 4D	EF48Z	38325	850	975	1575	2650
SE Wagon 4D	EF58Z	38325	1025	1175	1800	3025

2001 SAAB — YS3(DD35H)–1–#

Body Type	VIN	List	Trade-In Good	Very Good	Pvt-Party Good	Retail Excellent
9-3—4-Cyl. Turbo—Equipment Schedule 3						
W.B. 102.6"; 2.0 Liter.						
Hatchback 2D	DD35H	27070	450	500	1100	1900
Hatchback 4D	DD55H	27570	450	500	1100	1900
Automatic			125	125	165	165

2001 SAAB

Body Type	VIN	List	Trade-In Good	Very Good	Pvt-Party Good	Retail Excellent
9-3—4-Cyl. HO Turbo—Equipment Schedule 3						
W.B. 102.6"; 2.0 Liter, 2.3 Liter.						
SE Hatchback 4D	DF55K	33170	675	750	1375	2350
SE Convertible 2D	DF75K	40570	975	1075	1700	2850
Viggen Hatchback 2D	DP35G	38570	2175	2400	3150	4850
Viggen Hatchback 4D	DP55G	38570	1850	2025	2750	4250
Viggen Convertible 2D	DP75G	45570	2450	2700	3500	5350
Automatic			125	125	165	165
9-5—4-Cyl. Turbo—Equipment Schedule 2						
W.B. 106.4"; 2.3 Liter.						
Sedan 4D	ED48E	34570	700	800	1350	2275
Wagon 4D	ED58E	35270	750	850	1500	2575
Manual, 5-Spd			(225)	(225)	(300)	(300)
9-5—4-Cyl. HO Turbo—Equipment Schedule 2						
W.B. 106.4"; 2.3 Liter.						
Aero Sedan 4D	EH48G	40750	1625	1825	2700	4550
Aero Wagon 4D	EH58G	41450	1900	2125	3225	5325
Manual, 5-Spd			(225)	(225)	(300)	(300)
9-5—V6 Turbo—Equipment Schedule 2						
W.B. 106.4"; 3.0 Liter.						
SE Sedan 4D	EF48Z	39225	875	1000	1700	2950
SE Wagon 4D	EF58Z	39925	1125	1250	2000	3425
2002 SAAB — YS3(DF55K)-2-#						
9-3—4-Cyl. Turbo—Equipment Schedule 3						
W.B. 102.6"; 2.0 Liter.						
SE Hatchback 4D	DF55K	29820	775	850	1575	2725
SE Convertible 2D	DF75K	41820	1200	1325	2050	3400
Automatic			125	125	165	165
9-3—4-Cyl. HO Turbo—Equipment Schedule 3						
W.B. 102.6"; 2.3 Liter.						
Viggen Hatchback 2D	DP35G	38720	2650	2900	3725	5600
Viggen Hatchback 4D	DP55G	38720	2250	2475	3225	4900
Viggen Convertible 2D	DP75G	45620	2950	3250	4100	6125
9-5—4-Cyl. Turbo—Equipment Schedule 2						
W.B. 106.4"; 2.3 Liter.						
Linear Sedan 4D	EB49E	35820	725	800	1375	2350
Linear Wagon 4D	EB59E	36520	750	850	1550	2675
Manual, 5-Spd	5		(275)	(275)	(370)	(370)
9-5—4-Cyl. HO Turbo—Equipment Schedule 2						
W.B. 106.4"; 2.3 Liter.						
Aero Sedan 4D	EH49G	40475	1625	1800	2800	4675
Aero Wagon 4D	EH59G	41175	1950	2175	3275	5425
Manual, 5-Spd	5		(275)	(275)	(370)	(370)
9-5—V6 Turbo—Equipment Schedule 2						
W.B. 106.4"; 3.0 Liter.						
Arc Sedan 4D	ED49Z	39275	900	1000	1750	3050
Arc Wagon 4D	ED59Z	39975	1150	1275	2075	3550
2003 SAAB — YS3(FB49S)-3-#						
9-3—4-Cyl. Turbo—Equipment Schedule 3						
W.B. 105.3"; 2.0 Liter.						
Linear Sedan 4D	FB49S	27725	1300	1450	2075	3375
9-3—4-Cyl. HO Turbo—Equipment Schedule 3						
W.B. 102.6", 105.3" (Sed); 2.0 Liter.						
Arc Sedan 4D	FD49Y	31820	1525	1700	2425	3950
Vector Sedan 4D	FF46Y	33120	1650	1825	2650	4225
SE Convertible 2D	DF75K	40620	1650	1825	2650	4200
9-5—4-Cyl. Turbo—Equipment Schedule 2						
W.B. 106.4"; 2.3 Liter.						
Linear Sedan 4D	EB49E	35920	775	875	1475	2475
Linear Wagon 4D	EB59E	36620	825	925	1625	2800
Manual, 5-Spd			(275)	(275)	(365)	(365)
9-5—4-Cyl. HO Turbo—Equipment Schedule 2						
W.B. 106.4"; 2.3 Liter.						
Aero Sedan 4D	EH49G	40575	1875	2100	3100	5075
Aero Wagon 4D	EH59G	41275	2350	2625	3775	6075
Manual, 5-Spd			(275)	(275)	(365)	(365)
9-5—V6 Turbo—Equipment Schedule 2						
W.B. 106.4"; 3.0 Liter.						
Arc Sedan 4D	ED49Z	39275	1025	1150	1875	3200
Arc Wagon 4D	ED59Z	39975	1350	1500	2275	3775

2004 SAAB

Body Type	VIN	List	Trade-In Good	Very Good	Pvt-Party Good	Retail Excellent

2004 SAAB — YS3(FB45S)-4-#

9-3—4-Cyl. Turbo—Equipment Schedule 3
W.B. 105.3"; 2.0 Liter.

| Linear Sedan 4D | FB49S | 28015 | 1550 | 1725 | 2475 | 3925 |

9-3—4-Cyl. HO Turbo—Equipment Schedule 3
W.B. 105.3"; 2.0 Liter.

Arc Sedan 4D	FD49Y	32110	1825	2025	2825	4425
Arc Convertible 2D	FD79Y	41920	2750	3050	4050	6200
Aero Sedan 4D	FH49Y	34710	2200	2425	3325	5150
Aero Convertible 2D	FH79Y	44525	3100	3400	4400	6650

9-5—4-Cyl. Turbo—Equipment Schedule 2
W.B. 106.4"; 2.3 Liter.

Linear Wagon 4D	EB59E	34225	1450	1625	2175	3475
Arc Sedan 4D	ED49G	36455	1600	1775	2450	3875
Arc Wagon 4D	ED59G	37165	1875	2075	2750	4250
Manual, 5-Spd.			(325)	(325)	(435)	(435)

9-5—4-Cyl. HO Turbo—Equipment Schedule 2
W.B. 106.4"; 2.3 Liter.

Aero Sedan 4D	EH49G	41490	2800	3125	4000	6075
Aero Wagon 4D	EH59G	42195	3075	3400	4350	6550
Manual, 5-Spd.			(325)	(325)	(435)	(435)

2005 SAAB — (YS3orJF4)(GG616)-5-#

9-2X AWD—4-Cyl.—Equipment Schedule 3
W.B. 99.4"; 2.5 Liter.

| Linear Wagon 4D | GG616 | 24935 | 3100 | 3400 | 4525 | 6775 |

9-2X AWD—4-Cyl. Turbo—Equipment Schedule 3
W.B. 99.4"; 2.0 Liter.

| Aero Wagon 4D | GG226 | 28895 | 4500 | 4900 | 5950 | 8300 |

9-3—4-Cyl. Turbo—Equipment Schedule 3
W.B. 105.3"; 2.0 Liter.

| Linear Sedan 4D | FB49S | 28920 | 1975 | 2200 | 3025 | 4525 |
| Linear Convertible 2D | FB79S | 39170 | 3025 | 3325 | 4350 | 6375 |

9-3—4-Cyl. HO Turbo—Equipment Schedule 3
W.B. 105.3"; 2.0 Liter.

Arc Sedan 4D	FD49Y	32320	2350	2600	3525	5225
Arc Convertible 2D	FD79Y	42170	3250	3575	4775	6950
Aero Sedan 4D	FH49Y	34200	2725	3025	4000	5900
Aero Convertible 2D	FH79Y	44670	3600	3950	5175	7475

9-5—4-Cyl. Turbo—Equipment Schedule 2
W.B. 106.4"; 2.3 Liter.

Linear Wagon 4D	EB59E	34620	1550	1725	2425	3700
Arc Sedan 4D	ED49A	36970	1525	1725	2550	3925
Arc Wagon 4D	ED59A	37770	1875	2100	2950	4475
Manual, 5-Spd.			(375)	(375)	(500)	(500)

9-5—4-Cyl. HO Turbo—Equipment Schedule 2
W.B. 106.4"; 2.3 Liter.

Aero Sedan 4D	EH49G	42020	3000	3325	4325	6400
Aero Wagon 4D	EH59G	42820	3375	3750	4950	7275
Manual, 5-Spd.			(375)	(375)	(500)	(500)

2006 SAAB — (YS3orJF4)(GG616)-6-#

9-2X AWD—4-Cyl.—Equipment Schedule 3
W.B. 99.4"; 2.5 Liter.

| 2.5i Wagon 4D | GG616 | 24960 | 3475 | 3800 | 5000 | 7350 |

9-2X AWD—4-Cyl. Turbo—Equipment Schedule 3
W.B. 99.4"; 2.0 Liter.

| Aero Wagon 4D | GG726 | 28920 | 4975 | 5400 | 6500 | 8975 |

9-3—4-Cyl. Turbo—Equipment Schedule 3
W.B. 105.3"; 2.0 Liter.

2.0T Sedan 4D	FD49Y	27970	2450	2700	3575	5150
2.0T Convertible 2D	FD79Y	38570	3750	4075	5100	7175
2.0T SportCombi Wag	FD59Y	28970	2800	3075	4025	5775

9-3—6-Cyl. Turbo—Equipment Schedule 3
W.B. 105.3"; 2.8 Liter.

Aero Sedan 4D	FH41U	33970	3375	3675	4700	6675
Aero Convertible 2D	FH71U	43970	4450	4800	5875	8150
Aero SportCombi Wag	FH51U	34970	3800	4125	5225	7400
20th Anniversary			825	825	1110	1110

9-5—4-Cyl. Turbo—Equipment Schedule 2
W.B. 106.4"; 2.3 Liter.

2006 SAAB

Body Type	VIN	List	Trade-In Good	Very Good	Pvt-Party Good	Retail Excellent
2.3T Sedan 4D	ED45G	36170	2525	2825	3600	5100
2.3T SportCombi Wag	ED56G	37170	3525	3875	4750	6600
Manual, 5-Spd			(425)	(425)	(565)	(565)

2007 SAAB — (YS3orJF4)(FD49Y)-7-#

9-3—4-Cyl. Turbo—Equipment Schedule 3
W.B. 105.3"; 2.0 Liter.

2.0T Sedan 4D	FD49Y	27995	3325	3650	4525	6200
2.0T Convertible 2D	FD79Y	38595	4625	5000	5850	7850
2.0T SportCombi Wag	FD59Y	28995	4050	4400	5225	7025

9-3—V6 Turbo—Equipment Schedule 3
W.B. 105.3"; 2.8 Liter.

Aero Sedan 4D	FH41U	34295	4525	4900	5775	7750
Aero Convertible 2D	FH716	44195	5225	5625	6800	9050
Aero SportCombi Wag	FH51U	35195	5050	5425	6350	8475
4-Cyl. Turbo, 2.0L (Wag)	Y		(1225)	(1225)	(1635)	(1635)

9-5—4-Cyl. Turbo—Equipment Schedule 2
W.B. 106.4"; 2.3 Liter.

2.3T Sedan 4D	ED45G	36465	3600	3950	4775	6500
2.3T Aero Sedan 4D	EH49G	36535	4275	4650	5525	7475
2.3T SportCombi Wag	ED55G	37465	4550	4950	5875	8000
2.3T Aero SportCombi	EH59G	37535	5000	5425	6400	8675
Manual, 5-Spd			(475)	(475)	(620)	(620)

2008 SAAB — (YS3orJF4)(FB49Y)-8-#

9-3—4-Cyl. Turbo—Equipment Schedule 3
W.B. 105.3"; 2.0 Liter.

2.0T Sedan 4D	FB49Y	29735	4575	4925	5750	7575
2.0T Convertible 2D	FB79Y	41060	6650	7100	8200	10600
2.0T SportCombi Wag	FB59Y	30980	5325	5700	6525	8475

9-3—V6 Turbo—Equipment Schedule 3
W.B. 105.3"; 2.8 Liter.

Aero Sedan 4D	FH41U	36715	5900	6325	7325	9475
Aero Convertible 2D	FH71U	47015	8675	9175	10350	13200
Aero SportCombi Wag	FH51U	37615	6875	7325	8450	10950
XWD	2,7		1525	1525	2015	2015

9-3 AWD—V6 Turbo—Equipment Schedule 3
W.B. 105.3"; 2.8 Liter.

Turbo X Sedan 4D	FM42R	43860	7975	8450	9750	12550
Turbo X SportCombi	FM57U	44660	8225	8725	9900	12650

9-5—4-Cyl. Turbo—Equipment Schedule 2
W.B. 106.4"; 2.3 Liter.

2.3T Sedan 4D	ED49G	37205	5175	5550	6275	8100
2.3T Aero Sedan 4D	EH49G	38300	5375	5800	6725	8675
2.3T SportCombi Wag	ED59G	38455	5900	6325	7275	9350
2.3T Aero SportCombi	EH59G	39550	6250	6700	7700	9900
Manual, 5-Spd w/Overdrive	5		(500)	(500)	(630)	(630)

2009 SAAB — (YS3)(FB49Y)-9-#

9-3—4-Cyl. Turbo—Equipment Schedule 3
W.B. 105.3"; 2.0 Liter.

2.0T Sedan 4D	FB49Y	31535	5800	6175	7200	9175
2.0T Convertible 2D	FB79Y	44280	8950	9450	10650	13300
2.0T SportCombi Wag	FB59Y	32390	6550	6975	8000	10100
XWD			1600	1600	2145	2145

9-3 AWD—V6 Turbo—Equipment Schedule 3
W.B. 105.3"; 2.8 Liter.

Aero Sedan 4D	FH42R	44010	8750	9250	10450	13050
Aero SportCombi Wag	FH52R	45290	9050	9550	10750	13450

9-3—V6 Turbo—Equipment Schedule 3
W.B. 105.3"; 2.8 Liter.

Aero Convertible 2D	FH71R	51735	10700	11250	12500	15500

9-5—4-Cyl. Turbo—Equipment Schedule 2
W.B. 106.4"; 2.3 Liter.

2.3T Sedan 4D	ED49G	39285	10250	10850	11850	14450
2.3T SportCombi Wag	ED59G	40555	11100	11700	12800	15650
Aero Sedan 4D	EH49G	40305	10650	11250	12250	14950
Aero SportCombi Wag	EH59G	41670	11450	12050	13200	16100
Griffin Sedan 4D	EB49G	42775	11150	11750	12950	15900
Griffin SptCombi Wag	EB59G	44045	11500	12100	13350	16450
Manual, 5-Spd w/Overdrive	5		(550)	(550)	(625)	(625)

2010 SAAB

Body Type	VIN	List	Trade-In Good	Very Good	Pvt-Party Good	Retail Excellent

2010 SAAB — (YS3)(FA4CY)–A–#

9-3—4-Cyl. Turbo—Equipment Schedule 3
W.B. 105.3"; 2.0 Liter.

2.0T Sport Sedan 4D	FA4CY	31075	6950	7375	8425	10500
2.0T Convertible 2D	FE7CY	42165	10850	11400	12650	15450
2.0T SportCombi Wag	FA5CY	32505	7950	8400	9475	11700
Aero Sport Sedan 4D	FC4CY	37515	10600	11150	12350	15100
Aero Convertible 2D	FG7CY	47255	13150	13800	15100	18250
Aero SportCombi Wag	FC5CY	39195	10900	11450	12700	15550
XWD	B,N		1700	1700	2230	2230

9-3X AWD—4-Cyl. Turbo—Equipment Schedule 3
W.B. 105.3"; 2.0 Liter.

SportCombi Wagon	FD5BY	37800	10300	10800	11950	14600

9-5 AWD—V6 Turbo—Equipment Schedule 2
W.B. 111.7"; 2.8 Liter.

Aero Sedan 4D	ER4BJ	49990	12650	13250	14600	17650

2011 SAAB — (YS3)(FA4CY)–B–#

9-3—4-Cyl. Turbo—Equipment Schedule 3
W.B. 105.3"; 2.0 Liter.

2.0T Sport Sedan 4D	FA4CY	31075	8525	8975	10050	12300
2.0T Convertible 2D	FE7CY	42165	12300	12900	14150	17100
2.0T SportCombi Wag	FA5CY	32505	10150	10700	11800	14300
Aero Sport Sedan 4D	FC4CY	36165	12300	12900	14150	17100
Aero Convertible 2D	FG7CY	45905	14750	15450	16700	19950
Aero SportCombi Wag	FC5CY	37845	12650	13250	14500	17450

9-3X AWD—4-Cyl. Turbo—Equipment Schedule 3
W.B. 105.3"; 2.0 Liter.

SportCombi Wagon	FD5BY	37800	11850	12450	13700	16650
Turbo4 XWD Sedan	FA4BZ	33220	10550	11100	12200	14800
Aero XWD Sport Sed	FC4NY	38940	12900	13550	14700	17700
Auto, 6-Spd w/Sentronic	B		275	275	335	335

9-5—4-Cyl. Turbo—Equipment Schedule 3
W.B. 111.7"; 2.0 Liter.

Turbo4 Sedan 4D	GN4AR	39350	13750	14300	15550	18300
Turbo4 Premium 4D	GN4AR	44260	13900	14500	15700	18550

9-5 AWD—V6 Turbo—Equipment Schedule 3
W.B. 111.7"; 2.8 Liter.

Turbo6 Sedan 4D	GN4BJ	48855	14900	15550	16850	19900
Aero Sedan 4D	GR4BJ	51390	15200	15850	17150	20200

SATURN

2000 SATURN — 1G8(JorZ)(F528)–Y–#

SATURN—4-Cyl.—Equipment Schedule 6
W.B. 102.4"; 1.9 Liter.

SL Sedan 4D	F528	12085	475	550	1175	2125
SL1 Sedan 4D	G528	12885	475	550	1175	2125
SL2 Sedan 4D	J527	13335	525	625	1225	2300
SC1 Coupe 3D	N128	12975	450	525	1175	2100
SC2 Coupe 3D	R127	15885	625	725	1425	2550
SW2 Wagon 4D	J827	14730	575	675	1350	2450

SATURN L-SERIES—4-Cyl.—Equipment Schedule 3
W.B. 106.5"; 2.2 Liter.

LS Sedan 4D	R52F	16700	350	400	825	1375
LS1 Sedan 4D	T52F	18150	400	450	975	1675
LW1 Wagon 4D	U82F	19375	475	525	1075	1850
Manual, 5-Spd			(175)	(175)	(235)	(235)

SATURN L-SERIES—V6—Equipment Schedule 3
W.B. 106.5"; 3.0 Liter.

LS2 Sedan 4D	W52R	20575	700	800	1475	2550
LW2 Wagon 4D	W82R	21800	900	1025	1750	3000

2001 SATURN — 1G8(JorZ)(F528)–1–#

SATURN—4-Cyl.—Equipment Schedule 6
W.B. 102.4"; 1.9 Liter.

SL Sedan 4D	F528	11995	525	625	1225	2150
SL1 Sedan 4D	G528	12910	525	625	1225	2200
SL2 Sedan 4D	J527	13360	625	725	1375	2450

2001 SATURN

Body Type	VIN	List	Trade-In Good	Trade-In Very Good	Pvt-Party Good	Retail Excellent
SC1 Coupe 3D	N128	13960	650	750	1425	2525
SC2 Coupe 3D	R127	16110	800	925	1650	2925
SW2 Wagon 4D	J827	14755	775	900	1625	2875
SATURN L-SERIES—4-Cyl.—Equipment Schedule 3						
W.B. 106.5"; 2.2 Liter.						
L100 Sedan 4D	R52F	16245	400	450	950	1625
L200 Sedan 4D	T52F	18210	525	600	1175	2000
LW200 Wagon 4D	U82F	19335	650	750	1350	2300
Manual, 5-Spd			(200)	(200)	(265)	(265)
SATURN L-SERIES—V6—Equipment Schedule 3						
W.B. 106.5"; 3.0 Liter.						
L300 Sedan 4D	W52R	19995	1025	1150	1925	3300
LW300 Wagon 4D	W82R	21860	1250	1400	2225	3800

2002 SATURN — 1G8(JorZ)(F528)-2-#

Body Type	VIN	List	Trade-In Good	Trade-In Very Good	Pvt-Party Good	Retail Excellent
SATURN—4-Cyl.—Equipment Schedule 3						
W.B. 102.4"; 1.9 Liter.						
SL Sedan 4D	F528	11995	575	650	1250	2200
SL1 Sedan 4D	G528	13275	625	725	1275	2225
SL2 Sedan 4D	J527	13800	800	900	1525	2650
SC1 Coupe 3D	N128	14325	825	950	1575	2725
SC2 Coupe 3D	R127	16545	975	1100	1775	3075
SATURN L-SERIES—4-Cyl.—Equipment Schedule 3						
W.B. 106.5"; 2.2 Liter.						
L100 Sedan 4D	R52F	16870	475	550	1075	1850
L200 Sedan 4D	T52F	19070	800	900	1525	2625
LW200 Wagon 4D	U82F	20515	900	1000	1675	2850
Manual, 5-Spd			(200)	(200)	(265)	(265)
SATURN L-SERIES—V6—Equipment Schedule 3						
W.B. 106.5"; 3.0 Liter.						
L300 Sedan 4D	W52R	20920	1300	1450	2200	3725
LW300 Wagon 4D	W82R	22850	1525	1700	2500	4200

2003 SATURN — 1G8(AG54F)-3-#

Body Type	VIN	List	Trade-In Good	Trade-In Very Good	Pvt-Party Good	Retail Excellent
ION—4-Cyl.—Equipment Schedule 6						
W.B. 103.2"; 2.2 Liter.						
1 Sedan 4D	AG54F	12895	875	1000	1650	2825
2 Sedan 4D	AJ54F	14895	1050	1200	1875	3200
3 Sedan 4D	AL52F	16595	1325	1500	2225	3750
2 Quad Coupe 4D	AN12F	15395	1150	1300	2000	3400
3 Quad Coupe 4D	AW12F	16895	1425	1600	2350	3950
SATURN L-SERIES—4-Cyl.—Equipment Schedule 3						
W.B. 106.5"; 2.2 Liter.						
L200 Sedan 4D	JT54F	19040	1000	1125	1825	3075
LW200 Wagon 4D	JU84F	20850	1100	1225	1950	3275
Manual, 5-Spd			(250)	(250)	(335)	(335)
SATURN L-SERIES—V6—Equipment Schedule 3						
W.B. 106.5"; 3.0 Liter.						
L300 Sedan 4D	JW54F	21255	1600	1775	2575	4275
LW300 Wagon 4D	JW84R	23185	1775	1975	2925	4775

2004 SATURN — 1G8(AG54F)-4-#

Body Type	VIN	List	Trade-In Good	Trade-In Very Good	Pvt-Party Good	Retail Excellent
ION—4-Cyl.—Equipment Schedule 6						
W.B. 103.2"; 2.2 Liter.						
1 Sedan 4D	AG54F	11975	1200	1375	2025	3375
2 Sedan 4D	AJ52F	15200	1475	1650	2350	3900
3 Sedan 4D	AL52F	16725	1700	1900	2650	4350
2 Quad Coupe 4D	AN12F	15750	1575	1750	2500	4175
3 Quad Coupe 4D	AW12F	17250	1700	1900	2675	4450
ION—4-Cyl. Supercharged—Equipment Schedule 6						
W.B. 103.5"; 2.0 Liter.						
Red Line Quad Cpe 4D	AY12P	20950	1975	2225	2875	4450
SATURN L-SERIES—4-Cyl.—Equipment Schedule 3						
W.B. 106.5"; 2.2 Liter.						
L300 Sedan 4D	JC54F	16995	1350	1500	2225	3675
L300 Wagon 4D	JC84F	19045	1525	1700	2425	3975
SATURN L-SERIES—V6—Equipment Schedule 3						
W.B. 106.5"; 3.0 Liter.						
L300 Sedan 4D	JD54R	21410	2075	2300	3200	5025
L300 Wagon 4D	JD84R	23560	2325	2575	3500	5475

2005 SATURN

Body Type	VIN	List	Trade-In Good	Very Good	Pvt-Party Good	Retail Excellent

2005 SATURN — 1G8(AG52F)-5-#

ION—4-Cyl.—Equipment Schedule 6
W.B. 103.2"; 2.2 Liter.

1 Sedan 4D	AG52F	12975	1175	1325	2125	3550
2 Sedan 4D	AJ52F	15845	1525	1700	2550	4125
3 Sedan 4D	AL52F	17370	1850	2100	3025	4750
2 Quad Coupe 4D	AN12F	16395	1625	1850	2700	4275
3 Quad Coupe 4D	AW12F	18145	2025	2300	3200	4975

ION—4-Cyl. Supercharged—Equipment Schedule 6
W.B. 103.2"; 2.0 Liter.

Red Line Quad Cpe 4D	AY12P	21450	2675	3025	3700	5375

SATURN L-SERIES—V6—Equipment Schedule 3
W.B. 106.5"; 3.0 Liter.

L300 Sedan 4D	JD54R	21995	2325	2575	3650	5625

2006 SATURN — 1G8(AJ55F)-6-#

ION—4-Cyl.—Equipment Schedule 6
W.B. 103.2"; 2.2 Liter, 2.4 Liter.

2 Sedan 4D	AJ55F	13390	1750	1975	2950	4675
3 Sedan 4D	AL55F	15790	2250	2525	3725	5775
2 Quad Coupe 4D	AN15F	13825	1850	2075	3200	5050
3 Quad Coupe 4D	AW15F	17090	2550	2875	4025	6150
Manual, 5-Spd	M		(275)	(275)	(365)	(365)

ION—4-Cyl. Supercharged—Equipment Schedule 6
W.B. 103.2"; 2.0 Liter.

Red Line Quad Cpe 4D	AY15P	19990	3200	3550	4125	5775

2007 SATURN — 1G8(AJ55F)-7-#

ION—4-Cyl.—Equipment Schedule 6
W.B. 103.2"; 2.2 Liter, 2.4 Liter.

2 Sedan 4D	AJ55F	13495	2325	2575	3475	5225
3 Sedan 4D	AL55F	15915	2950	3275	4400	6475
2 Quad Coupe 4D	AN15F	14495	2675	2975	3900	5825
3 Quad Coupe 4D	AW15F	17215	3150	3500	4625	6825
Manual, 5-Spd	M		(300)	(300)	(400)	(400)

ION—4-Cyl. Supercharged—Equipment Schedule 6
W.B. 103.2"; 2.0 Liter.

Red Line Quad Cpe 4D	AY15P	20420	4100	4500	5350	7375

AURA—V6—Equipment Schedule 4
W.B. 112.3"; 3.5 Liter, 3.6 Liter.

XE Sedan 4D	ZS57N	20595	3575	3925	5000	7125
XR Sedan 4D	ZV577	24595	4200	4575	5775	8200
Panorama Roof			300	300	415	415

SKY—4-Cyl.—Equipment Schedule 3
W.B. 95.1"; 2.4 Liter.

Roadster 2D	MB35B	24540	4425	4800	5700	7700

SKY—4-Cyl. Turbo—Equipment Schedule 3
W.B. 95.1"; 2.0 Liter.

Red Line Roadster 2D	MG35X	29745	4725	5100	6350	8600

2008 SATURN — 1G8(AR671)-8-#

ASTRA—4-Cyl.—Equipment Schedule 4
W.B. 102.9"; 1.8 Liter.

XE Hatchback 4D	AR671	17718	3725	4100	4700	6375
XR Hatchback 2D	AT271	18870	4000	4375	5125	6925
XR Hatchback 4D	AT671	19115	4125	4500	5275	7100

AURA—4-Cyl. Hybrid—Equipment Schedule 4
W.B. 112.3"; 2.4 Liter.

Green Line Sedan 4D	ZR575	22790	5800	6250	7850	10850

AURA—V6—Equipment Schedule 4
W.B. 112.3"; 3.5 Liter, 3.6 Liter.

XE Sedan 4D	ZS57N	21495	4575	4950	6100	8425
XR Sedan 4D	ZV577	25495	5325	5750	7025	9700
4-Cyl, 2.4 Liter	B		(250)	(250)	(340)	(340)

SKY—4-Cyl.—Equipment Schedule 3
W.B. 95.1"; 2.4 Liter.

Roadster 2D	MC35B	26520	5800	6200	7225	9350

SKY—4-Cyl. Turbo—Equipment Schedule 3
W.B. 95.1"; 2.0 Liter.

Red Line Roadster 2D	MG35X	30700	6800	7250	8300	10700

280   DEDUCT FOR RECONDITIONING

0415

2009 SATURN

Body Type	VIN	List	Trade-In Good	Very Good	Pvt-Party Good	Retail Excellent

2009 SATURN — 1G8(ZR575)-9-#

AURA—4-Cyl. Hybrid—Equipment Schedule 4
W.B. 112.3"; 2.4 Liter.

Body Type	VIN	List	Good	Very Good	Good	Excellent
Sedan 4D	ZR575	25580	6700	7175	8650	11550

AURA—4-Cyl.—Equipment Schedule 4
W.B. 112.3"; 2.4 Liter.

XE Sedan 4D	ZS57B	21995	5325	5750	6825	9125

AURA—V6—Equipment Schedule 4
W.B. 112.3"; 3.6 Liter.

XR Sedan 4D	ZV577	26595	6225	6700	8050	10700
4-Cyl, 2.4 Liter	B		(275)	(275)	(380)	(380)

SKY—4-Cyl.—Equipment Schedule 3
W.B. 95.1"; 2.4 Liter.

Roadster 2D	MN35B	27780	7150	7575	8625	10800

SKY—4-Cyl. Turbo—Equipment Schedule 3
W.B. 95.1"; 2.0 Liter.

Red Line Roadster 2D	MG35X	32090	8600	9075	10150	12600

SCION

2004 SCION — JT(KorL)(KT624)-4-#

xA—4-Cyl.—Equipment Schedule 6
W.B. 93.3"; 1.5 Liter.

Hatchback 4D	KT624	13765	2250	2500	3125	4675

xB—4-Cyl.—Equipment Schedule 6
W.B. 98.4"; 1.5 Liter.

Sport Wagon 4D	KT324	13765	2925	3275	3875	5775

2005 SCION — JT(KorL)(KT624)-5-#

xA—4-Cyl.—Equipment Schedule 6
W.B. 93.3"; 1.5 Liter.

Hatchback 4D	KT624	13795	3150	3450	4175	5900
Release Series 1.0			450	450	600	600
Release Series 2.0			275	275	375	375

xB—4-Cyl.—Equipment Schedule 6
W.B. 98.4"; 1.5 Liter.

Sport Wagon 4D	KT334	14995	3550	3950	4775	6750
Release Series 2.0			350	350	465	465

tC—4-Cyl.—Equipment Schedule 4
W.B. 106.3"; 2.4 Liter.

Hatchback Coupe 2D	DE177	17265	3750	4075	5000	6950

2006 SCION — JT(KorL)(KT624)-6-#

xA—4-Cyl.—Equipment Schedule 6
W.B. 93.3"; 1.5 Liter.

Hatchback 4D	KT624	14110	3475	3800	4650	6450
Release Series 2.0			300	300	400	400
Release Series 3.0			650	650	865	865
Manual, 5-Spd			(275)	(275)	(365)	(365)

xB—4-Cyl.—Equipment Schedule 6
W.B. 98.4"; 1.5 Liter.

Sport Wagon 4D	KT324	15260	4125	4550	5325	7325
Release Series 2.0			375	375	500	500
Release Series 3.0			650	650	865	865
Manual, 5-Spd	3		(275)	(275)	(365)	(365)

tC—4-Cyl.—Equipment Schedule 4
W.B. 106.3"; 2.4 Liter.

Hatchback Coupe 2D	DE177	17580	4250	4600	5550	7600
Release Series 2.0			650	650	865	865
Special Edition			800	800	1065	1065

2007 SCION — JT(KorL)(DE177)-7-#

tC—4-Cyl.—Equipment Schedule 4
W.B. 106.3"; 2.4 Liter.

Spec H'Back Coupe 2D	DE177	16340	4625	5000	5900	7950
Hatchback Coupe 2D	DE177	17820	4975	5350	6250	8350
Release Series 3.0			700	700	935	935

2008 SCION

Body Type	VIN	List	Trade-In Good	Very Good	Pvt-Party Good	Retail Excellent

2008 SCION — JT(KorL)(KU104)-8-#

xD—4-Cyl.—Equipment Schedule 4
W.B. 96.9"; 1.8 Liter.
| Hatchback 4D | KU104 | 15970 | 5400 | 5800 | 6800 | 8800 |
| Release Series 1.0 | | | 700 | 700 | 940 | 940 |

xB—4-Cyl.—Equipment Schedule 6
W.B. 102.4"; 2.4 Liter.
| Sport Wagon 4D | KE50E | 17270 | 6050 | 6525 | 7425 | 9625 |
| Manual, 5-Spd w/Overdrive | | | (350) | (350) | (470) | (470) |

tC—4-Cyl.—Equipment Schedule 4
W.B. 106.3"; 2.4 Liter.
Spec H'Back Coupe 2D	DE167	16720	5300	5675	6700	8725
Hatchback Coupe 2D	DE167	18470	5650	6050	7050	9125
Release Series 4.0			600	600	800	800

2009 SCION — JT(KorL)(KU104)-9-#

xD—4-Cyl.—Equipment Schedule 4
W.B. 96.9"; 1.8 Liter.
| Hatchback 4D | KU104 | 16145 | 6425 | 6850 | 7800 | 9800 |
| Release Series 2.0 | | | 725 | 725 | 935 | 935 |

xB—4-Cyl.—Equipment Schedule 6
W.B. 102.4"; 2.4 Liter.
| Sport Wagon 4D | KE50E | 17320 | 7000 | 7500 | 8375 | 10550 |
| Manual, 5-Spd w/Overdrive | | | (375) | (375) | (495) | (495) |

tC—4-Cyl.—Equipment Schedule 4
W.B. 106.3"; 2.4 Liter.
| Hatchback Coupe 2D | DE167 | 18470 | 6200 | 6600 | 7600 | 9600 |
| Release Series 5.0 | | | 600 | 600 | 800 | 800 |

2010 SCION — JT(KorL)(KU4B4)-A-#

xD—4-Cyl.—Equipment Schedule 4
W.B. 96.9"; 1.8 Liter.
| Hatchback 4D | KU4B4 | 16295 | 7450 | 7875 | 8875 | 10900 |

xB—4-Cyl.—Equipment Schedule 6
W.B. 102.4"; 2.4 Liter.
| Sport Wagon 4D | ZE4FE | 17395 | 8125 | 8625 | 9475 | 11650 |
| Manual, 5-Spd w/Overdrive | | | (475) | (475) | (605) | (605) |

xB—4-Cyl.—Equipment Schedule 6
W.B. 102.4"; 2.4 Liter.
| Release Series 7.0 2D | ZE4FE | 18990 | 8575 | 9075 | 10000 | 12350 |
| Automatic, 4-Spd w/OD | | | 400 | 400 | 505 | 505 |

tC—4-Cyl.—Equipment Schedule 4
W.B. 106.3"; 2.4 Liter.
| Hatchback Coupe 2D | DE3B7 | 18520 | 7425 | 7850 | 8825 | 10900 |
| Release Series 6.0 2D | DE3B7 | 19290 | 8250 | 8700 | 9700 | 11950 |

2011 SCION — JT(KorL)(KU4B4)-B-#

xD—4-Cyl.—Equipment Schedule 4
W.B. 96.9"; 1.8 Liter.
| Hatchback 4D | KU4B4 | 16420 | 8475 | 8925 | 9925 | 12000 |
| Release Series 3.0 4D | KU4B4 | 18425 | 9375 | 9850 | 10900 | 13050 |

xB—4-Cyl.—Equipment Schedule 6
W.B. 102.4"; 2.4 Liter.
| Sport Wagon 4D | ZE4FE | 17680 | 9325 | 9850 | 10750 | 12950 |
| Manual, 5-Spd w/Overdrive | | | (500) | (500) | (625) | (625) |

xB—4-Cyl.—Equipment Schedule 6
W.B. 102.4"; 2.4 Liter.
| Release Series 8.0 Wag | ZE4FE | 19125 | 10050 | 10600 | 11450 | 13800 |
| Automatic, 4-Spd w/OD | | | 450 | 450 | 555 | 555 |

tC—4-Cyl.—Equipment Schedule 4
W.B. 102.4"; 2.4 Liter.
| Hatchback Coupe 2D | JF5C7 | 19995 | 9025 | 9500 | 10500 | 12700 |

2012 SCION — JT(K,LorN)(JJ1B0)-C-#

iQ—4-Cyl.—Equipment Schedule 4
W.B. 78.7"; 1.3 Liter.
| Hatchback 2D | JJ1B0 | 15995 | 7725 | 8150 | 8875 | 10550 |

xD—4-Cyl.—Equipment Schedule 4
W.B. 96.9"; 1.8 Liter.
| Hatchback 4D | KU4B4 | 16875 | 9600 | 10050 | 11150 | 13250 |

282   DEDUCT FOR RECONDITIONING

0415

2012 SCION

Body Type	VIN	List	Trade-In Good	Very Good	Pvt-Party Good	Retail Excellent
Release Series 4.0 4D	KU4B4	17780	10500	11000	12000	14200
xB—4-Cyl.—Equipment Schedule 6						
W.B. 102.4"; 2.4 Liter.						
Sport Wagon 4D	ZE4FE	17980	10300	10850	11700	13900
tC—4-Cyl.—Equipment Schedule 4						
W.B. 106.3"; 2.4 Liter.						
Hatchback Coupe 2D	JF5C7	20295	11000	11550	12450	14700
Release Series 7.0 2D	JF5C7	22625	11750	12300	13250	15700

2013 SCION — JT(K,LorN)(JJXB0)-D-#

Body Type	VIN	List	Trade-In Good	Very Good	Pvt-Party Good	Retail Excellent
iQ—4-Cyl.—Equipment Schedule 4						
W.B. 78.7"; 1.3 Liter.						
Hatchback 2D	JJXB0	16140	8200	8650	9425	11250
xD—4-Cyl.—Equipment Schedule 4						
W.B. 96.9"; 1.8 Liter.						
Hatchback 4D	KUPB4	17275	10500	11000	12050	14150
10 Series H'Back 4D	KUPB4	19710	12050	12600	13600	15850
xB—4-Cyl.—Equipment Schedule 6						
W.B. 102.4"; 2.4 Liter.						
Sport Wagon 4D	ZE4FE	18675	11650	12200	13050	15350
10 Series Spt Wagon	ZE4FE	20915	12850	13450	14300	16650
tC—4-Cyl.—Equipment Schedule 4						
W.B. 106.3"; 2.5 Liter.						
Hatchback Coupe 2D	JF5C7	20455	11750	12300	13200	15500
Release Series 8.0 2D	JF5C7	23595	13000	13550	14450	16850
FR-S—4-Cyl.—Equipment Schedule 4						
W.B. 101.2"; 2.0 Liter.						
Coupe 2D	ZNAA1	24930	16000	16650	17550	20100

2014 SCION — JT(K,LorN)(JJXB0)-E-#

Body Type	VIN	List	Trade-In Good	Very Good	Pvt-Party Good	Retail Excellent
iQ—4-Cyl.—Equipment Schedule 4						
W.B. 78.7"; 1.3 Liter.						
Hatchback 2D	JJXB0	16420	9175	9625	10450	12350
10 Series H'Back 2D	JJXB0	18605	10950	11450	12200	14250
xD—4-Cyl.—Equipment Schedule 4						
W.B. 96.9"; 1.8 Liter.						
Hatchback 4D	KUPB4	17475	11450	11950	13000	15250
xB—4-Cyl.—Equipment Schedule 6						
W.B. 102.4"; 2.4 Liter.						
Sport Wagon 4D	ZE4FE	18675	13650	14250	15150	17550
10 Series Sport Wagon	ZE4FE	20915	14650	15300	16050	18550
tC—4-Cyl.—Equipment Schedule 4						
W.B. 106.3"; 2.5 Liter.						
Hatchback Coupe 2D	JF5C7	20965	12900	13500	14450	16850
Monogram Series 2D	JF5C7	23155	14150	14750	15650	18100
10 Series H'Back 2D	JF5C7	23195	14700	15350	16150	18650
FR-S—4-Cyl.—Equipment Schedule 4						
W.B. 101.2"; 2.0 Liter.						
Coupe 2D	ZNAA1	26555	17550	18250	19100	21700
Monogram Series 2D	ZNAA1	29255	19750	20500	21200	23900

SMART

2009 SMART — WME(EJ31X)-9-#

Body Type	VIN	List	Trade-In Good	Very Good	Pvt-Party Good	Retail Excellent
FORTWO—3-Cyl.—Equipment Schedule 3						
W.B. 73.5"; 1.0 Liter.						
Pure Hatchback 2D	EJ31X	12635	3075	3350	4000	5350
Passion Hatchback 2D	EJ31X	14635	3575	3875	4550	6000
Passion Conv 4D	EK31X	17635	4050	4375	5225	6850
BRABUS H'Back 2D	EJ31X	18635	4650	4975	5900	7750
BRABUS Conv 2D	EK31X	21635	5425	5800	6750	8775

2010 SMART — WME(EJ3BA)-A-#

Body Type	VIN	List	Trade-In Good	Very Good	Pvt-Party Good	Retail Excellent
FORTWO—3-Cyl.—Equipment Schedule 3						
W.B. 73.5"; 1.0 Liter.						
Pure Coupe 2D	EJ3BA	12635	4150	4450	5175	6650
Passion Coupe 2D	EJ3BA	14635	4675	5000	5775	7375
Passion Conv 2D	EK4BA	17635	5575	5950	6900	8700

Body Type	VIN	List	Trade-In Good	Very Good	Pvt-Party Good	Retail Excellent

2011 SMART — WME(EJ3BA)-B-#

FORTWO—3-Cyl.—Equipment Schedule 3
W.B. 73.5"; 1.0 Liter.

Body Type	VIN	List	Good	Very Good	Good	Excellent
Pure Coupe 2D	EJ3BA	13240	4250	4550	5350	6875
Passion Coupe 2D	EJ3BA	15440	5100	5425	6300	8000
Passion Conv 2D	EK3BA	18440	6125	6500	7525	9400

2012 SMART — WME(EJ3BA)-C-#

FORTWO—3-Cyl.—Equipment Schedule 3
W.B. 73.5"; 1.0 Liter.

Body Type	VIN	List	Good	Very Good	Good	Excellent
Pure Coupe 2D	EJ3BA	13240	5100	5425	6200	7800
Passion Coupe 2D	EJ3BA	15440	5775	6125	7150	8925
Passion Conv 2D	EK3BA	18440	7275	7700	8625	10550

2013 SMART — WME(EJ3BA)-D-#

FORTWO—3-Cyl.—Equipment Schedule 3
W.B. 73.5"; 1.0 Liter.

Body Type	VIN	List	Good	Very Good	Good	Excellent
Pure Coupe 2D	EJ3BA	13240	6625	7000	7925	9675
Passion Hatchback 2D	EJ3BA	15640	7200	7600	8525	10400
Passion Conv 2D	EK3BA	18640	9000	9450	10350	12350

2014 SMART — WME(EJ3BA)-E-#

FORTWO—3-Cyl.—Equipment Schedule 3
W.B. 73.5"; 1.0 Liter.

Body Type	VIN	List	Good	Very Good	Good	Excellent
Pure Coupe 2D	EJ3BA	15200	8175	8600	9600	11600
Passion Conv 2D	EK3BA	18640	10900	11450	12250	14400

FORTWO—Electric Drive—Equipment Schedule 3
W.B. 73.5".

Body Type	VIN	List	Good	Very Good	Good	Excellent
Coupe 2D	EJ9AA	25750	12700	13250	14350	16900
Convertible 2D	EK9AA	28750	14200	14800	15900	18650

SUBARU

2000 SUBARU — JF1or4S3(GC435)-Y-#

IMPREZA AWD—4-Cyl.—Equipment Schedule 5
W.B. 99.2"; 2.2 Liter, 2.5 Liter.

Body Type	VIN	List	Good	Very Good	Good	Excellent
L Sedan 4D	GC435	17190	900	1025	1525	2500
L Coupe 2D	GM435	17190	900	1025	1500	2450
L Sport Wagon 4D	GF435	17590	1100	1250	1800	2975
Outback Sport Wag 4D	GF485	19390	1350	1550	2225	3750
2.5RS Sedan 4D	GC675	20590	1450	1650	2300	3825
2.5RS Coupe 2D	GM675	20590	1400	1575	2225	3725

LEGACY AWD—4-Cyl.—Equipment Schedule 4
W.B. 104.3"; 2.5 Liter.

Body Type	VIN	List	Good	Very Good	Good	Excellent
Brighton Wagon 4D	BH625	19690	1325	1500	2050	3350
L Sedan 4D	BE635	20490	1125	1275	1800	2975
L Wagon 4D	BH635	21190	1475	1675	2225	3625
GT Sedan 4D	BE645	24990	1800	2025	2725	4350
GT Limited Sedan 4D	BE656	25590	2050	2300	3050	4825
GT Wagon 4D	BH645	24990	2125	2400	3150	4975
Dual Moon Roofs			(75)	(75)	(105)	(105)
Manual, 5-Spd (Sedan)			(175)	(175)	(235)	(235)

OUTBACK AWD—4-Cyl.—Equipment Schedule 4
W.B. 104.3"; 2.5 Liter.

Body Type	VIN	List	Good	Very Good	Good	Excellent
Wagon 4D	BH666	23990	1100	1250	2075	3675
Limited Sedan 4D	BE686	26390	1200	1350	2225	3925
Limited Wagon 4D	BH686	27390	1300	1450	2350	4150
Dual Moon Roofs			(75)	(75)	(105)	(105)

2001 SUBARU — JF1or4S3(GC435)-1-#

IMPREZA AWD—4-Cyl.—Equipment Schedule 5
W.B. 99.2"; 2.2 Liter, 2.5 Liter.

Body Type	VIN	List	Good	Very Good	Good	Excellent
L Sedan 4D	GC435	17290	1025	1175	1675	2725
L Coupe 2D	GM435	17290	1025	1175	1625	2625
L Sport Wagon 4D	GF435	17690	1175	1350	1850	3025
Outback Sport Wag 4D	GF485	19490	1600	1825	2550	4125
2.5RS Sedan 4D	GC675	20790	1650	1875	2575	4125
2.5RS Coupe 2D	GM675	20790	1650	1875	2575	4125

2001 SUBARU

Body Type	VIN	List	Trade-In Good	Very Good	Pvt-Party Good	Retail Excellent
LEGACY AWD—4-Cyl.—Equipment Schedule 4						
W.B. 104.3"; 2.5 Liter.						
L Sedan 4D	BE635	20590	1375	1550	2100	3450
L Wagon 4D	BH635	21290	1700	1900	2600	4175
GT Sedan 4D	BE645	24190	2175	2450	3200	5050
GT Limited Sedan 4D	BE656	25690	2450	2750	3550	5550
GT Wagon 4D	BH645	25090	2550	2850	3675	5725
Dual Moon Roofs		......	75	75	115	115
Manual, 5-Spd (Sedan)		......	(200)	(200)	(265)	(265)
OUTBACK AWD—4-Cyl.—Equipment Schedule 4						
W.B. 104.3"; 2.5 Liter.						
Wagon 4D	BH665	24190	1475	1650	2500	4200
Limited Sedan 4D	BE686	26490	1625	1825	2700	4500
Limited Wagon 4D	BH686	27590	1700	1900	2800	4650
Dual Moon Roofs		......	(75)	(75)	(115)	(115)
OUTBACK AWD—H6—Equipment Schedule 4						
W.B. 104.3"; 3.0 Liter.						
L.L. Bean Wagon 4D	BH806	29990	2050	2300	3275	5375
VDC Wagon 4D	BH896	32390	2950	3300	4500	7225
Dual Moon Roofs		......	(75)	(75)	(115)	(115)

2002 SUBARU — JF1or4S3(GG655)-2-#

Body Type	VIN	List	Trade-In Good	Very Good	Pvt-Party Good	Retail Excellent
IMPREZA AWD—4-Cyl.—Equipment Schedule 5						
W.B. 99.4"; 2.5 Liter.						
2.5TS Sport Wagon 4D	GG655	18820	1700	1925	2650	4225
Outback Sport Wag 4D	GF485	20320	2250	2550	3350	5250
2.5RS Sedan 4D	GC675	20320	1925	2175	2925	4625
IMPREZA AWD—4-Cyl. Turbo—Equipment Schedule 4						
W.B. 99.4"; 2.0 liter.						
WRX Sedan 4D	GD295	25520	3225	3550	4350	6375
WRX Sport Wagon 4D	GG295	25020	3025	3325	4100	6050
LEGACY AWD—4-Cyl.—Equipment Schedule 4						
W.B. 104.3"; 2.5 Liter.						
L Sedan 4D	BE635	20620	1675	1900	2550	4025
L Wagon 4D	BH635	21320	2100	2375	3075	4775
GT Sedan 4D	BE645	24220	2725	3075	3825	5850
GT Limited Sedan 4D	BE656	26020	3000	3375	4175	6325
GT Wagon 4D	BH645	25120	2975	3350	4125	6275
Dual Moon Roofs		......	100	100	125	125
Manual, 5-Spd (Sedan)		......	(200)	(200)	(265)	(265)
OUTBACK AWD—4-Cyl.—Equipment Schedule 4						
W.B. 104.3"; 2.5 Liter.						
Wagon 4D	BH665	24220	2125	2375	3250	5175
Limited Sedan 4D	BE686	26520	2375	2650	3575	5650
Limited Wagon 4D	BH686	27620	2450	2750	3675	5800
Dual Moon Roofs		......	(100)	(100)	(125)	(125)
OUTBACK AWD—H6—Equipment Schedule 4						
W.B. 104.3"; 3.0 Liter.						
Sedan 4D	BE896	28520	2425	2725	3625	5750
L.L. Bean Wagon 4D	BH806	30020	2825	3175	4150	6500
VDC Sedan 4D	BE806	30920	3175	3550	4600	7175
VDC Wagon 4D	BH896	32420	3500	3900	5200	8025
Dual Moon Roofs		......	100	100	125	125

2003 SUBARU — JF1or4S3(GG655)-3-#

Body Type	VIN	List	Trade-In Good	Very Good	Pvt-Party Good	Retail Excellent
IMPREZA AWD—4-Cyl.—Equipment Schedule 5						
W.B. 99.4"; 2.5 Liter.						
2.5TS Sport Wagon 4D	GG655	18920	1950	2200	2925	4600
Outbk "Sport" Spt Wg	GG685	20120	2525	2850	3650	5600
2.5RS Sedan 4D	GD675	20420	2175	2450	3225	5000
IMPREZA AWD—4-Cyl. Turbo—Equipment Schedule 4						
W.B. 99.4"; 2.0 liter.						
WRX Sedan 4D	GD296	25720	4200	4575	5425	7575
WRX Sport Wagon 4D	GG296	25220	3975	4350	5150	7225
LEGACY AWD—4-Cyl.—Equipment Schedule 4						
W.B. 104.3"; 2.5 Liter.						
L Sedan 4D	BE635	20820	2125	2375	3025	4600
L Wagon 4D	BH635	21520	2500	2800	3475	5225
L Special Ed Sed 4D	BE635	21320	2275	2550	3200	4850
L Special Ed Wag 4D	BH635	22420	2750	3075	3750	5625
GT Sedan 4D	BE646	26320	3225	3600	4325	6400
GT Wagon 4D	BH646	27220	3650	4050	4975	7325

2003 SUBARU

Body Type	VIN	List	Trade-In Good	Trade-In Very Good	Pvt-Party Good	Retail Excellent
Dual Moon Roofs	------	------	(100)	(100)	(135)	(135)
Manual, 5-Spd (Sedan)	------	------	(250)	(250)	(335)	(335)
OUTBACK AWD—4-Cyl.—Equipment Schedule 4						
W.B. 104.3"; 2.5 Liter.						
Wagon 4D	BH675	24370	2800	3125	3900	5900
Limited Sedan 4D	BE686	26820	3075	3425	4225	6375
Limited Wagon 4D	BH686	27920	3200	3550	4400	6600
Dual Moon Roofs	------	------	(100)	(100)	(135)	(135)
OUTBACK AWD—H6—Equipment Schedule 4						
W.B. 104.3"; 3.0 Liter.						
Sedan 4D	BE896	29020	3125	3475	4300	6450
Wagon 4D	BH896	27520	2700	3025	3800	5750
L.L. Bean Wagon 4D	BH806	30520	3475	3875	4875	7275
VDC Sedan 4D	BE896	31420	3875	4300	5350	7950
VDC Wagon 4D	BH896	32000	4400	4850	5975	8825

2004 SUBARU — JF1or4S3(GG655)-4-#

Body Type	VIN	List	Trade-In Good	Trade-In Very Good	Pvt-Party Good	Retail Excellent
IMPREZA AWD—4-Cyl.—Equipment Schedule 5						
W.B. 99.4"; 2.5 Liter.						
2.5TS Sport Wagon 4D	GG655	19245	2325	2600	3350	5100
Outback Sport Wag	GG655	20445	3125	3500	4300	6425
2.5RS Sedan 4D	GD675	20745	2625	2950	3700	5600
IMPREZA AWD—4-Cyl. Turbo—Equipment Schedule 4						
W.B. 99.4"; 2.0 Liter.						
WRX Sedan 4D	GD296	26045	5325	5750	6725	9075
WRX Sport Wagon 4D	GG296	25545	5200	5600	6375	8650
IMPREZA AWD—4-Cyl. HO Turbo—Equipment Schedule 4						
W.B. 100.0"; 2.5 Liter.						
WRX STi Sedan 4D	GD706	31545	10200	10850	11950	15550
LEGACY AWD—4-Cyl.—Equipment Schedule 4						
W.B. 104.3"; 2.5 Liter.						
L Sedan 4D	BE635	21245	2575	2875	3500	5175
L Wagon 4D	BH635	21945	3125	3500	3950	5650
GT Sedan 4D	BE646	26645	3925	4325	5175	7475
GT Wagon 4D	BH646	27545	4325	4750	5650	8100
Dual Moon Roofs	------	------	(100)	(100)	(135)	(135)
Manual, 5-Spd	------	------	(300)	(300)	(400)	(400)
OUTBACK AWD—4-Cyl.—Equipment Schedule 4						
W.B. 104.3"; 2.5 Liter.						
Wagon 4D	BH675	24695	3325	3675	4425	6400
Limited Sedan 4D	BE686	27145	3650	4025	4800	6900
Limited Wagon 4D	BH686	28245	3850	4225	5025	7200
Dual Moon Roofs	------	------	(100)	(100)	(135)	(135)
OUTBACK AWD—H6—Equipment Schedule 4						
W.B. 104.3"; 3.0 Liter.						
Sedan 4D	BE896	29345	3750	4125	4900	7050
35th Anniv Wagon 4D	BH815	27645	3225	3575	4300	6225
L.L. Bean Wagon 4D	BH806	30845	4300	4725	5550	7900
VDC Sedan 4D	BE896	31545	4750	5200	6075	8625
VDC Wagon 4D	BH896	33045	5100	5575	6675	9425

2005 SUBARU — (JFor4S)(1,3or4)(GD296)-5-#

Body Type	VIN	List	Trade-In Good	Trade-In Very Good	Pvt-Party Good	Retail Excellent
IMPREZA AWD—4-Cyl.—Equipment Schedule 5						
W.B. 99.4"; 2.5 Liter.						
2.5RS Sedan 4D	GD675	19470	3400	3775	4475	6350
2.5RS Sport Wagon 4D	GG675	19470	3575	3975	4825	6825
Outback Sport Wag	GG685	20370	4875	5375	6175	8475
Outback Spt Spcl Ed	GG685	20320	4775	5250	6075	8375
IMPREZA AWD—4-Cyl. Turbo—Equipment Schedule 4						
W.B. 99.4"; 2.0 Liter.						
WRX Sedan 4D	GD296	25370	7175	7675	8625	11100
WRX Sport Wagon 4D	GG296	24870	6825	7300	8250	10650
IMPREZA AWD—4-Cyl. HO Turbo—Equipment Schedule 4						
W.B. 99.4"; 2.5 Liter.						
WRX STi Sedan 4D	GD706	32770	12300	13050	14000	17600
LEGACY AWD—4-Cyl.—Equipment Schedule 4						
W.B. 105.1"; 2.5 Liter.						
2.5i Sedan 4D	BL616	22870	3475	3850	4775	6850
2.5i Wagon 4D	BP616	23870	3800	4200	5175	7400
2.5i Limited Sedan 4D	BL626	26120	4500	4925	6075	8700
2.5i Limited Wagon 4D	BP626	27320	4650	5100	6175	8750
Dual Moon Roofs	------	------	(125)	(125)	(165)	(165)

286   DEDUCT FOR RECONDITIONING   0415

Body Type	VIN	List	Trade-In Good	Very Good	Pvt-Party Good	Retail Excellent
Manual, 5-Spd			(350)	(350)	(465)	(465)

LEGACY AWD—4-Cyl. Turbo—Equipment Schedule 4
W.B. 105.1"; 2.5 Liter.

Body Type	VIN	List	Good	Very Good	Good	Excellent
2.5GT Sedan 4D	BL686	27870	4750	5200	6275	8900
2.5GT Wagon 4D	BP686	28870	4950	5400	6550	9300
2.5GT Limited Sed 4D	BL676	30370	6600	7175	8425	11600
2.5GT Limited Wag 4D	BP676	31570	7850	8500	10000	13750
Dual Moon Roofs			(125)	(125)	(165)	(165)
Manual, 5-Spd			(350)	(350)	(465)	(465)

OUTBACK AWD—4-Cyl.—Equipment Schedule 4
W.B. 105.1"; 2.5 Liter.

Body Type	VIN	List	Good	Very Good	Good	Excellent
2.5i Wagon 4D	BP61C	25870	4175	4575	5275	7225
2.5i Limited Wagon	BP62C	28670	4750	5175	5975	8175
Dual Moon Roofs			(125)	(125)	(165)	(165)

OUTBACK AWD—4-Cyl. Turbo—Equipment Schedule 4
W.B. 105.1"; 2.5 Liter.

Body Type	VIN	List	Good	Very Good	Good	Excellent
2.5XT Wagon 4D	BP68C	29870	4800	5250	6225	8525
2.5XT Limited Wagon	BP67C	32570	5450	5950	6950	9475
Dual Moon Roofs			(125)	(125)	(165)	(165)

OUTBACK AWD—H6—Equipment Schedule 4
W.B. 105.1"; 3.0 Liter.

Body Type	VIN	List	Good	Very Good	Good	Excellent
3.0R Sedan 4D	BL84C	31670	6700	7275	8575	11700
3.0R L.L. Bean Wagon	BP86C	32870	7150	7750	9075	12350
3.0R VDC Ltd Wagon	BP85C	34070	8400	9050	10550	14400
Dual Moon Roofs			(125)	(125)	(165)	(165)

2006 SUBARU — (JFor4S)(1,3or4)(GD676)–6–#

IMPREZA AWD—4-Cyl.—Equipment Schedule 5
W.B. 99.4"; 2.5 Liter.

Body Type	VIN	List	Good	Very Good	Good	Excellent
2.5i Sedan 4D	GD676	19720	3900	4325	5125	7100
2.5i Sport Wagon	GG676	19720	4175	4625	5450	7525
Outback Sport Wagon	GG686	20620	5425	5950	6925	9250

IMPREZA AWD—4-Cyl. Turbo—Equipment Schedule 4
W.B. 99.4"; 2.5 Liter.

Body Type	VIN	List	Good	Very Good	Good	Excellent
WRX TR Sedan 4D	GD796	24620	7225	7700	8700	11150
WRX Sedan 4D	GD796	25620	8475	9000	9950	12600
WRX Sport Wagon 4D	GG796	25120	8075	8600	9600	12250
WRX Limited Sedan	GD796	29120	9600	10200	11400	14500
WRX Limited Spt Wag	GG796	28620	9600	10200	11400	14500

IMPREZA AWD—4-Cyl. HO Turbo—Equipment Schedule 4
W.B. 100.0"; 2.5 Liter.

Body Type	VIN	List	Good	Very Good	Good	Excellent
WRX STi Sedan 4D	GD706	33620	13600	14350	15450	19200

LEGACY AWD—4-Cyl.—Equipment Schedule 4
W.B. 105.1"; 2.5 Liter.

Body Type	VIN	List	Good	Very Good	Good	Excellent
i Sedan 4D	BL616	23520	4150	4550	5350	7375
i Wagon 4D	BP616	24520	4450	4875	5600	7575
i Limited Sedan 4D	BL626	26120	5425	5925	6925	9275
i Limited Wagon 4D	BP626	27320	5775	6300	7300	9725
Manual, 5-Spd			(400)	(400)	(535)	(535)

LEGACY AWD—4-Cyl. Turbo—Equipment Schedule 4
W.B. 105.1"; 2.5 Liter.

Body Type	VIN	List	Good	Very Good	Good	Excellent
GT Limited Sed 4D	BL676	30620	8825	9500	10850	14350
GT Limited Wag 4D	BP676	31820	9625	10350	11550	15100
Manual, 5-Spd			(400)	(400)	(530)	(530)

OUTBACK AWD—4-Cyl.—Equipment Schedule 4
W.B. 105.1"; 2.5 Liter.

Body Type	VIN	List	Good	Very Good	Good	Excellent
2.5i Wagon 4D	BP61C	26420	4825	5275	6100	8050
2.5i Limited Sedan 4D	BL62C	28020	5200	5675	6500	8575
2.5i Limited Wagon	BP62C	29220	6450	6975	7800	10250

OUTBACK AWD—4-Cyl. Turbo—Equipment Schedule 4
W.B. 105.1"; 2.5 Liter.

Body Type	VIN	List	Good	Very Good	Good	Excellent
2.5XT Wagon 4D	BP68C	30420	6625	7150	7975	10450
2.5XT Limited Wagon	BP67C	32820	7525	8125	9050	11800

OUTBACK AWD—H6—Equipment Schedule 4
W.B. 105.1"; 3.0 Liter.

Body Type	VIN	List	Good	Very Good	Good	Excellent
3.0R Wagon 4D	BP84C	29620	7100	7675	8575	11200
3.0R L.L. Bean Sed 4D	BL86C	31920	8400	9050	10250	13500
3.0R L.L. Bean Wagon	BP86C	33120	8800	9450	10650	14000
3.0R VDC Ltd Wagon	BP85C	36320	9850	10550	11800	15450

Body Type	VIN	List	Trade-In Good	Very Good	Pvt-Party Good	Retail Excellent

2007 SUBARU — (JFor4S)(1,3or4)(GD616)–7–#

IMPREZA AWD—4-Cyl.—Equipment Schedule 5
W.B. 99.4"; 2.5 Liter.

Body Type	VIN	List	Good	Very Good	Good	Excellent
2.5i Sedan 4D	GD616	19420	**4725**	**5175**	**5925**	**7950**
2.5i Sport Wagon	GG616	19420	**4925**	**5375**	**6175**	**8300**
Outback Sport Wagon	GG626	20620	**6050**	**6575**	**7475**	**9825**
Manual, 5-Spd			**(400)**	**(400)**	**(535)**	**(535)**

IMPREZA AWD—4-Cyl. Turbo—Equipment Schedule 4
W.B. 99.4"; 2.5 Liter.

WRX TR Sedan 4D	GD756	24620	**8750**	**9275**	**10250**	**12900**
WRX Sedan 4D	GD746	25620	**10000**	**10600**	**11550**	**14300**
WRX Sport Wagon 4D	GG746	25120	**9700**	**10250**	**11300**	**14200**
WRX Limited Sedan	GD746	29120	**11300**	**11950**	**13100**	**16350**
WRX Limited Spt Wag	GG746	28620	**11350**	**12000**	**13150**	**16400**

IMPREZA AWD—4-Cyl. HO Turbo—Equipment Schedule 4
W.B. 99.4"; 2.5 Liter.

WRX STi Sedan 4D	GD766	34120	**15350**	**16150**	**17100**	**20800**
WRX STi Limited Sed	GD776	34120	**15850**	**16650**	**17700**	**21600**

LEGACY AWD—4-Cyl.—Equipment Schedule 4
W.B. 105.1"; 2.5 Liter.

i Sedan 4D	BL616	22120	**4925**	**5350**	**6175**	**8325**
i Wagon 4D	BP616	23620	**5025**	**5475**	**6500**	**8725**
i Limited Sedan 4D	BL626	24720	**6400**	**6925**	**8050**	**10700**
i Limited Wagon 4D	BP626	25920	**6725**	**7275**	**8425**	**11150**
Manual, 5-Spd			**(425)**	**(425)**	**(565)**	**(565)**

LEGACY AWD—4-Cyl. Turbo—Equipment Schedule 4
W.B. 105.1"; 2.5 Liter.

GT Limited Sedan 4D	BL676	30120	**9775**	**10450**	**11800**	**15450**
GT Limited Wagon 4D	BP676	31520	**10850**	**11600**	**12900**	**16700**
GT spec.B Sedan 4D	BL696	34620	**11350**	**12150**	**13700**	**17800**
Manual, 5-Spd			**(425)**	**(425)**	**(565)**	**(565)**

OUTBACK AWD—4-Cyl.—Equipment Schedule 4
W.B. 105.1"; 2.5 Liter.

2.5i Basic Wagon 4D	BP61C	23620	**5300**	**5750**	**6575**	**8550**
2.5i Wagon 4D	BP61C	25220	**5850**	**6325**	**7175**	**9300**
2.5i Limited Sedan 4D	BL62C	27020	**6725**	**7250**	**8100**	**10500**
2.5i Limited Wagon 4D	BP62C	28020	**7850**	**8425**	**9325**	**12000**

OUTBACK AWD—4-Cyl. Turbo—Equipment Schedule 4
W.B. 105.1"; 2.5 Liter.

2.5XT Limited Wagon	BP63C	32820	**8925**	**9575**	**10550**	**13550**

OUTBACK AWD—H6 HO—Equipment Schedule 4
W.B. 105.1"; 3.0 Liter.

3.0R L.L. Bean Sedan	BL86C	30920	**10000**	**10700**	**11800**	**15150**
3.0R L.L. Bean Wagon	BP86C	32120	**10000**	**10700**	**11800**	**15150**

2008 SUBARU — (JFor4S)(1,3or4)(GE616)–8–#

IMPREZA AWD—4-Cyl.—Equipment Schedule 5
W.B. 103.1"; 2.5 Liter.

2.5i Sedan 4D	GE616	18640	**5600**	**6050**	**7025**	**9175**
2.5i Premium Sedan	GE616	20140	**6850**	**7350**	**8200**	**10450**
2.5i Sport Wagon	GH616	19140	**6600**	**7100**	**7975**	**10200**
2.5i Premium Wagon	GH616	20640	**7050**	**7575**	**8375**	**10650**
Outback Sport Wagon	GH636	21640	**8200**	**8775**	**9600**	**12050**
Manual, 5-Spd w/Overdrive			**(425)**	**(425)**	**(555)**	**(555)**

IMPREZA AWD—4-Cyl. Turbo—Equipment Schedule 4
W.B. 103.1", 103.3" (STI); 2.5 Liter.

WRX Sedan 4D	GE756	25995	**11300**	**11900**	**12700**	**15300**
WRX Premium Sedan	GE756	27095	**11700**	**12350**	**13200**	**15900**
WRX Sport Wagon 4D	GH746	26495	**11500**	**12100**	**13000**	**15650**
WRX Premium Wagon	GH756	27595	**12000**	**12650**	**13500**	**16250**
WRX STI Sport Wagon	GR796	35640	**17650**	**18500**	**19350**	**23000**

LEGACY AWD—4-Cyl.—Equipment Schedule 4
W.B. 105.1"; 2.5 Liter.

2.5i Sedan 4D	BL616	22140	**5700**	**6125**	**7000**	**9025**
2.5i Limited Sedan 4D	BL626	24740	**7950**	**8475**	**9600**	**12300**
Manual, 5-Spd w/Overdrive			**(450)**	**(450)**	**(580)**	**(580)**

LEGACY AWD—4-Cyl. Turbo—Equipment Schedule 4
W.B. 105.1"; 2.5 Liter.

2.5GT Limited Sedan	BL676	30440	**10800**	**11500**	**12750**	**16150**
2.5GT spec.B Sedan	BL696	34640	**12450**	**13200**	**14450**	**18200**
Manual, 5-Spd HD w/OD			**(450)**	**(450)**	**(570)**	**(570)**

2008 SUBARU

Body Type	VIN	List	Trade-In Good	Very Good	Pvt-Party Good	Retail Excellent
LEGACY AWD—6-Cyl.—Equipment Schedule 4						
W.B. 105.1"; 3.0 Liter.						
3.0R Limited Sedan 4D	BL856	31940	**11300**	**12000**	**13200**	**16650**
OUTBACK AWD—4-Cyl.—Equipment Schedule 4						
W.B. 105.1"; 2.5 Liter.						
Basic Wagon 4D	BP60C	23640	**6925**	**7400**	**8200**	**10350**
2.5i Wagon 4D	BP61C	25240	**7400**	**7925**	**8775**	**11050**
2.5i Limited Wagon 4D	BP62C	28040	**9700**	**10300**	**11300**	**14100**
OUTBACK AWD—4-Cyl. Turbo—Equipment Schedule 4						
W.B. 105.1"; 2.5 Liter.						
2.5XT Limited Wag	BP63C	32840	**10650**	**11300**	**12300**	**15300**
OUTBACK AWD—H6—Equipment Schedule 4						
W.B. 105.1"; 3.0 Liter.						
3.0R L.L. Bean Wagon	BP86C	32140	**11250**	**11950**	**13000**	**16200**

2009 SUBARU — (JFor4S)(1,3or4)(GE616)-9-#

Body Type	VIN	List	Trade-In Good	Very Good	Pvt-Party Good	Retail Excellent
IMPREZA AWD—4-Cyl.—Equipment Schedule 5						
W.B. 103.1"; 2.5 Liter.						
2.5i Sedan 4D	GE616	19160	**6950**	**7425**	**8350**	**10550**
2.5i Premium Sedan	GE606	21160	**8100**	**8625**	**9550**	**11900**
2.5i Sport Wagon	GH616	19660	**8000**	**8525**	**9400**	**11650**
2.5i Premium Wagon	GH606	21660	**8300**	**8825**	**9725**	**12050**
Outback Sport Wagon	GH636	21660	**9350**	**9900**	**10800**	**13250**
Manual, 5-Spd w/Overdrive			**(450)**	**(450)**	**(600)**	**(600)**
IMPREZA AWD—4-Cyl. Turbo—Equipment Schedule 4						
W.B. 103.1", 103.3" (STI); 2.5 Liter.						
WRX Sedan 4D	GE766	25660	**12650**	**13250**	**14150**	**16800**
WRX Premium Sedan	GE766	28160	**13100**	**13700**	**14750**	**17450**
WRX Sport Wagon	GH766	26160	**12950**	**13550**	**14550**	**17250**
WRX Premium Wagon	GH766	28660	**13430**	**14000**	**15050**	**17800**
2.5GT Sedan 4D	GE746	27660	**12750**	**13450**	**14250**	**17250**
2.5GT Sport Wagon	GH746	28160	**12900**	**13600**	**14400**	**17400**
WRX STI Sport Wag	GR896	35660	**19450**	**20300**	**21200**	**24800**
LEGACY AWD—4-Cyl.—Equipment Schedule 4						
W.B. 105.1"; 2.5 Liter.						
2.5i Sedan 4D	BL606	22460	**7200**	**7675**	**8525**	**10550**
2.5i Limited Sedan 4D	BL626	25660	**9325**	**9850**	**10900**	**13450**
Manual, 5-Spd w/Overdrive			**(500)**	**(500)**	**(620)**	**(620)**
LEGACY AWD—4-Cyl. Turbo—Equipment Schedule 4						
W.B. 105.1"; 2.5 Liter.						
2.5GT Limited Sedan	BL676	31060	**11900**	**12500**	**13750**	**16950**
2.5GT spec.B Sedan	BL696	35260	**13500**	**14200**	**15600**	**19150**
Manual, 5-Spd HD w/OD			**(500)**	**(500)**	**(625)**	**(625)**
LEGACY AWD—6-Cyl.—Equipment Schedule 4						
W.B. 105.1"; 3.0 Liter.						
3.0R Sedan 4D	BL846	27260	**10650**	**11200**	**12300**	**15150**
3.0R Limited Sedan 4D	BL856	30560	**12350**	**13000**	**14200**	**17450**
OUTBACK AWD—4-Cyl.—Equipment Schedule 4						
W.B. 105.1"; 2.5 Liter.						
2.5i Wagon 4D	BP60C	23960	**9750**	**10300**	**11100**	**13350**
2.5i Limited Wagon 4D	BP66C	28960	**11650**	**12300**	**13150**	**15850**
OUTBACK AWD—4-Cyl. Turbo—Equipment Schedule 4						
W.B. 105.1"; 2.5 Liter.						
2.5XT Limited Wagon	BP63C	33460	**12450**	**13100**	**14050**	**16950**
OUTBACK AWD—H6—Equipment Schedule 4						
W.B. 105.1"; 3.0 Liter.						
3.0R Limited Wagon	BP85C	32760	**12750**	**13400**	**14450**	**17450**

2010 SUBARU — (JFor4S)(1,3or4)(GE6A6)-A-#

Body Type	VIN	List	Trade-In Good	Very Good	Pvt-Party Good	Retail Excellent
IMPREZA AWD—4-Cyl.—Equipment Schedule 5						
W.B. 103.1"; 2.5 Liter.						
2.5i Sedan 4D	GE6A6	18190	**8275**	**8725**	**9700**	**11900**
2.5i Premium Sedan	GE6A6	19190	**8975**	**9450**	**10400**	**12650**
2.5i Sport Wagon	GH6A6	18690	**8775**	**9250**	**10200**	**12400**
2.5i Premium Wagon	GH6A6	19690	**9625**	**10100**	**11050**	**13400**
Outback Sport Wagon	GH6D6	20690	**10300**	**10850**	**11800**	**14200**
Manual, 5-Spd w/Overdrive			**(500)**	**(500)**	**(630)**	**(630)**
IMPREZA AWD—4-Cyl. Turbo—Equipment Schedule 4						
W.B. 103.1", 103.3" (STI); 2.5 Liter.						
WRX Sedan 4D	GE7G6	25690	**14500**	**15100**	**16100**	**18800**
WRX Premium Sedan	GE7G6	28190	**15350**	**16000**	**17000**	**19800**
WRX Limited Sedan	GE7G6	29190	**16950**	**17650**	**18700**	**21800**

2010 SUBARU

Body Type	VIN	List	Trade-In Good	Very Good	Pvt-Party Good	Retail Excellent
WRX Sport Wagon	GH7G6	26190	14900	15500	16500	19200
WRX Premium Wagon	GH7G6	28690	15550	16250	17250	20100
WRX Limited Wagon	GH7G6	29690	17550	18300	19350	22500
2.5GT Sedan 4D	GE7E6	27690	13700	14350	15250	18100
2.5GT Sport Wagon	GH7E6	28190	13900	14550	15550	18500
WRX STI Sport Wagon	GR8H6	35690	21900	22800	23700	27300
WRX STI Spec Ed Wag	GR8H6	33690	22200	23100	23900	27400

LEGACY AWD—4-Cyl.—Equipment Schedule 4
W.B. 108.3"; 2.5 Liter.

Body Type	VIN	List	Good	Very Good	Good	Excellent
2.5i Sedan 4D	BMAA6	21690	9275	9750	10700	12900
2.5i Premium Sedan	BMAB6	22690	9775	10300	11250	13550
2.5i Limited Sedan 4D	BMCJ6	25660	12000	12550	13700	16500

LEGACY AWD—4-Cyl. Turbo—Equipment Schedule 4
W.B. 108.3"; 2.5 Liter.

Body Type	VIN	List	Good	Very Good	Good	Excellent
2.5GT Premium Sedan	BMFC6	28660	15600	16300	17700	21200
2.5GT Limited Sedan	BMFJ6	30660	16500	17250	18750	22600

LEGACY AWD—6-Cyl.—Equipment Schedule 4
W.B. 108.3"; 3.6 Liter.

Body Type	VIN	List	Good	Very Good	Good	Excellent
3.6R Sedan 4D	BMDA6	25660	11900	12450	13600	16400
3.6R Premium Sedan	BMDC6	26660	12900	13550	14750	17750
3.6R Limited Sed 4D	BMDJ6	28660	14600	15250	16650	20100

OUTBACK AWD—4-Cyl.—Equipment Schedule 4
W.B. 107.9"; 2.5 Liter.

Body Type	VIN	List	Good	Very Good	Good	Excellent
2.5i Wagon 4D	BRCAC	24690	11150	11700	12550	14850
2.5i Premium Wagon	BRCBC	26290	12850	13450	14500	17150
2.5i Limited Wagon	BRCJC	28690	14800	15500	16600	19700

OUTBACK AWD—6-Cyl.—Equipment Schedule 4
W.B. 107.9"; 3.6 Liter.

Body Type	VIN	List	Good	Very Good	Good	Excellent
3.6R Wagon 4D	BRDAC	28690	14350	15000	16100	19100
3.6R Premium Wagon	BRECC	29690	15400	16100	17300	20600
3.6R Limited Wagon	BRDJC	31690	16350	17050	18200	21600

2011 SUBARU — (JF0r4S)(1,3or4)(GE6A6)-B-#

IMPREZA AWD—4-Cyl.—Equipment Schedule 5
W.B. 103.1"; 2.5 Liter.

Body Type	VIN	List	Good	Very Good	Good	Excellent
2.5i Sedan 4D	GE6A6	18220	9775	10250	11250	13500
2.5i Premium Sedan	GE8B6	19220	10550	11050	12000	14350
2.5i Sport Wagon	GH6A6	18720	10250	10750	11750	14050
2.5i Premium Wagon	GH8B6	19720	11200	11700	12700	15050
Outback Sport Wagon	GH6D6	20720	11850	12400	13350	15850
Manual, 5-Spd w/Overdrive			(500)	(500)	(625)	(625)

IMPREZA AWD—4-Cyl. Turbo—Equipment Schedule 4
W.B. 103.3"; 2.5 Liter.

Body Type	VIN	List	Good	Very Good	Good	Excellent
WRX Sedan 4D	GV7F6	26220	16550	17200	18100	20700
WRX Premium Sedan	GV7F6	28720	17800	18450	19350	22100
WRX Limited Sedan	GV7F6	29720	19000	19750	20700	23700
WRX Sport Wagon	GR7E6	29720	17100	17750	18650	21300
WRX Premium Wagon	GR7E6	28720	17950	18600	19550	22400
WRX Limited Wagon	GR7E6	29720	19650	20400	21300	24300
WRX STI Sedan 4D	GV8J6	34720	23800	24600	25400	28800
WRX STI Limited Sed	GV8J6	38070	24100	25000	25800	29300
WRX STI Sport Wagon	GR8H6	36720	24300	25100	25900	29300

LEGACY AWD—4-Cyl.—Equipment Schedule 4
W.B. 108.3"; 2.5 Liter.

Body Type	VIN	List	Good	Very Good	Good	Excellent
2.5i Sedan 4D	BMAA6	21720	10950	11450	12350	14600
2.5i Premium Sedan	BMAB6	22720	11400	11950	12950	15300
2.5i Limited Sedan 4D	BMCJ6	26020	12900	13450	14650	17300

LEGACY AWD—4-Cyl. Turbo—Equipment Schedule 4
W.B. 108.3"; 2.5 Liter.

Body Type	VIN	List	Good	Very Good	Good	Excellent
2.5GT Limited Sedan	BMFK6	32120	18100	18800	20200	23900

LEGACY AWD—6-Cyl.—Equipment Schedule 4
W.B. 108.3"; 3.6 Liter.

Body Type	VIN	List	Good	Very Good	Good	Excellent
3.6R Sedan 4D	BMDA6	25720	12900	13450	14650	17300
3.6R Premium Sedan	BMDC6	26720	14100	14700	15900	18750
3.6R Limited Sedan	BMDJ6	29020	16200	16850	18200	21500

OUTBACK AWD—4-Cyl.—Equipment Schedule 4
W.B. 107.9"; 2.5 Liter.

Body Type	VIN	List	Good	Very Good	Good	Excellent
2.5i Wagon 4D	BRAAC	24920	13100	13650	14650	17100
2.5i Premium Wagon	BRCBC	26220	14900	15550	16650	19450
2.5i Limited Wagon	BRCJC	29220	16500	17150	18350	21400

OUTBACK AWD—6-Cyl.—Equipment Schedule 4
W.B. 107.9"; 3.6 Liter.

Body Type	VIN	List	Good	Very Good	Good	Excellent
3.6R Wagon 4D	BRDAC	28920	16350	17000	18300	21500

2011 SUBARU

Body Type	VIN	List	Trade-In Good	Very Good	Pvt-Party Good	Retail Excellent
3.6R Premium Wagon	BRDCC	29920	17600	18300	19550	22800
3.6R Limited Wagon	BRDJC	32220	18250	19000	20200	23500

2012 SUBARU — JF1or4S3(GJAA6)-C-#

IMPREZA AWD—4-Cyl.—Equipment Schedule 5
W.B. 104.1"; 2.0 Liter.

2.0i Sedan 4D	GJAA6	18245	11350	11800	12850	15200
2.0i Wagon 4D	GPAA6	18745	11500	12000	13000	15350
2.0i Premium Wagon	GPAB6	20045	12750	13300	14250	16700
2.0i Sport Prem Wag	GPAL6	21045	13200	13700	14700	17150
Manual, 5-Spd			(525)	(525)	(640)	(640)

IMPREZA AWD—4-Cyl.—Equipment Schedule 5
W.B. 104.1"; 2.0 Liter.

2.0i Premium Sedan	GJAB6	19545	12350	12850	13850	16250
2.0i Limited Sedan	GJAG6	22345	13900	14400	15350	17850
2.0i Limited Wagon	GPAG6	22845	14450	15000	15850	18350
2.0i Sport Ltd Wagon	GPAR6	23345	14700	15250	16150	18650

IMPREZA AWD—4-Cyl. Turbo—Equipment Schedule 4
W.B. 103.3"; 2.5 Liter.

WRX Sedan 4D	GV7E6	26345	18350	19000	19800	22300
WRX Premium Sedan	GV7F6	28845	19500	20200	21000	23700
WRX Limited Sed	GV7F6	29845	20800	21500	22400	25300
WRX Sport Wagon	GR7E6	26345	19200	19900	20800	23400
WRX Premium Wagon	GR7E6	28845	19700	20400	21300	24000
WRX Limited Wagon	GR7E6	29845	21400	22100	23000	25900
WRX STI Sedan 4D	GV8J6	34845	25800	26700	27400	30700
WRX STI Limited Sed	GV8J6	38195	27000	27900	28700	32200
WRX STI Sport Wagon	GR8H6	36845	26300	27200	27900	31200

LEGACY AWD—4-Cyl.—Equipment Schedule 4
W.B. 108.3"; 2.5 Liter.

2.5i Sedan 4D	BMAA6	21745	11750	12250	13250	15500
2.5i Premium Sedan	BMAB6	23045	12550	13050	14050	16450
2.5i Limited Sedan 4D	BMAK6	26345	14550	15100	16250	18950

LEGACY AWD—4-Cyl. Turbo—Equipment Schedule 4
W.B. 108.3"; 2.5 Liter.

2.5GT Sedan 4D	BMFL6	32345	19750	20500	21900	25600

LEGACY AWD—6-Cyl.—Equipment Schedule 4
W.B. 108.3"; 3.6 Liter.

3.6R Sedan 4D	BMEA6	25845	14100	14650	15800	18450
3.6R Premium Sedan	BMEC6	27045	15650	16200	17450	20300
3.6R Limited Sedan	BMEJ6	29345	17500	18100	19400	22600

OUTBACK AWD—4-Cyl.—Equipment Schedule 4
W.B. 107.9"; 2.5 Liter.

2.5i Wagon 4D	BRCAC	24070	14900	15500	16600	19200
2.5i Premium Wagon	BRCBC	25570	16300	16900	18050	20900
2.5i Limited Wagon	BRCJC	29470	18150	18800	20000	23200

OUTBACK AWD—6-Cyl.—Equipment Schedule 4
W.B. 107.9"; 3.6 Liter.

3.6R Wagon 4D	BREAC	29070	18050	18700	19950	23100
3.6R Premium Wagon	BRECC	30270	19300	20000	21300	24600
3.6R Limited Wagon	BREJC	32470	19900	20600	21800	25200

2013 SUBARU — JF1or4S3(ZCAB1)-D-#

BRZ—4-Cyl.—Equipment Schedule 4
W.B. 101.2"; 2.0 Liter.

Premium Coupe 2D	ZCAB1	27365	14750	15350	16350	18850
Limited Coupe 2D	ZCAC1	29365	15650	16250	17250	19850

IMPREZA AWD—4-Cyl.—Equipment Schedule 5
W.B. 104.1"; 2.0 Liter.

2.0i Sedan 4D	GJAA6	19665	12700	13200	14250	16700
2.0i Premium Sedan	GJAB6	21065	13400	13900	14950	17400
2.0i Wagon 4D	GPAA6	20165	13050	13550	14650	17100
2.0i Premium Wagon	GPAB6	21565	14100	14600	15650	18200
2.0i Sport Prem Wag	GPAL6	22565	14800	15300	16300	18800
Manual, 5-Spd			(550)	(550)	(660)	(660)

IMPREZA AWD—4-Cyl.—Equipment Schedule 5
W.B. 104.1"; 2.0 Liter.

2.0i Limited Sedan	GJAG6	22565	15000	15500	16500	19000
2.0i Limited Wagon	GPAG6	23265	15150	15700	16600	19150
2.0i Sport Ltd Wagon	GPAR6	23765	15600	16150	17050	19600

IMPREZA AWD—4-Cyl. Turbo—Equipment Schedule 5
W.B. 103.3"; 2.5 Liter.

2013 SUBARU

Body Type	VIN	List	Trade-In Good	Very Good	Pvt-Party Good	Retail Excellent
WRX Sedan 4D	GV7E6	26565	19900	20600	21500	24200
WRX Premium Sedan	GV7F6	29065	21200	22000	22800	25600
WRX Limited Sed	GJ7F6	30065	22400	23200	24000	27000
WRX STI Sedan 4D	GV8J6	35065	27300	28200	28900	32200
WRX STI Limited Sed	GJ8J6	38415	28700	29600	30500	34000
WRX Sport Wagon	GR7E6	26565	20800	21500	22400	25200
WRX Premium Wagon	GR7E6	29065	21300	22000	22900	25700
WRX Limited Wagon	GR7E6	30065	22900	23700	24500	27500
WRX STI Sport Wagon	GR8H6	37065	27800	28700	29400	32800

LEGACY AWD—4-Cyl.—Equipment Schedule 4
W.B. 108.3"; 2.5 Liter.

Body Type	VIN	List	Trade-In Good	Very Good	Pvt-Party Good	Retail Excellent
2.5i Sedan 4D	BMAA6	21070	12900	13400	14650	17100
2.5i Premium Sedan	BMCB6	23270	13850	14350	15650	18250
2.5i Sport Sedan 4D		25270	15350	15950	17250	20100
2.5i Limited Sedan 4D	BMCJ6	26670	16600	17200	18450	21400

LEGACY AWD—6-Cyl.—Equipment Schedule 4
W.B. 108.3"; 3.6 Liter.

Body Type	VIN	List	Trade-In Good	Very Good	Pvt-Party Good	Retail Excellent
3.6R Sedan 4D	BMDA6	26170	16150	16750	18000	20900
3.6R Limited Sedan	BMDJ6	29670	19650	20300	21300	24300

OUTBACK AWD—4-Cyl.—Equipment Schedule 4
W.B. 107.9"; 2.5 Liter.

Body Type	VIN	List	Trade-In Good	Very Good	Pvt-Party Good	Retail Excellent
2.5i Wagon 4D	BRCAC	25290	16150	16700	17800	20400
2.5i Premium Wagon	BRCBC	26790	17950	18550	19750	22600
2.5i Limited Wagon	BRCJC	29890	20300	21000	22100	25300

OUTBACK AWD—6-Cyl.—Equipment Schedule 4
W.B. 107.9"; 3.6 Liter.

Body Type	VIN	List	Trade-In Good	Very Good	Pvt-Party Good	Retail Excellent
3.6R Wagon 4D	BRDAC	29290	19950	20600	21800	25000
3.6R Limited Wagon	BRDJC	32890	22300	23000	24200	27500

2014 SUBARU — JF1or4S3(ZCAB)–E–#

BRZ—4-Cyl.—Equipment Schedule 4
W.B. 101.2"; 2.0 Liter.

Body Type	VIN	List	Trade-In Good	Very Good	Pvt-Party Good	Retail Excellent
Premium Coupe 2D	ZCAB	26390	16650	17300	18250	20900
Limited Coupe 2D	ZCAC	29490	18150	18850	19700	22500

IMPREZA AWD—4-Cyl.—Equipment Schedule 4
W.B. 104.1"; 2.0 Liter.

Body Type	VIN	List	Trade-In Good	Very Good	Pvt-Party Good	Retail Excellent
2.0i Sedan 4D	GJAA6	19690	14000	14500	15600	18100
2.0i Wagon 4D	GPAA6	20190	14650	15200	16200	18750
2.0i Premium Sedan	GJAB6	21090	15050	15600	16600	19150
2.0i Premium Wagon	GPAB6	21590	15600	16150	17100	19700
2.0i Sport Prem Wag	GPAL6	22590	16350	16950	17850	20500
Manual, 5-Spd			(575)	(575)	(675)	(675)

IMPREZA AWD—4-Cyl.—Equipment Schedule 4
W.B. 104.1"; 2.0 Liter.

Body Type	VIN	List	Trade-In Good	Very Good	Pvt-Party Good	Retail Excellent
2.0i Limited Sedan	GJAG6	22990	16650	17250	18150	20800
2.0i Limited Wagon	GPAG6	23490	16850	17450	18350	21000
2.0i Sport Ltd Wagon	GPAR6	23990	17350	17950	18800	21500

LEGACY AWD—4-Cyl.—Equipment Schedule 4
W.B. 108.3"; 2.5 Liter.

Body Type	VIN	List	Trade-In Good	Very Good	Pvt-Party Good	Retail Excellent
2.5i Sedan 4D	BMAA6	22090	14900	15450	16550	19100
2.5i Premium Sedan	BMBC6	24090	16350	16900	18000	20700
2.5i Sport Sedan 4D	BMBG6	25490	17550	18150	19150	21900
2.5i Limited Sedan 4D	BMBK6	26690	18200	18850	19900	22700
Adaptive Cruise Control			500	500	535	535

LEGACY AWD—6-Cyl.—Equipment Schedule 4
W.B. 108.3"; 3.6 Liter.

Body Type	VIN	List	Trade-In Good	Very Good	Pvt-Party Good	Retail Excellent
3.6R Limited Sedan	BMDK6	29690	21400	22100	23000	26000
Adaptive Cruise Control			500	500	540	540

OUTBACK AWD—4-Cyl.—Equipment Schedule 4
W.B. 107.9"; 2.5 Liter.

Body Type	VIN	List	Trade-In Good	Very Good	Pvt-Party Good	Retail Excellent
2.5i Wagon 4D	BRCA	25320	18350	19000	20100	22900
2.5i Premium Wagon	BRCC	27620	19950	20600	21600	24500
2.5i Limited Wagon	ARCK	29920	22000	22800	23500	26300

OUTBACK AWD—6-Cyl.—Equipment Schedule 4
W.B. 107.9"; 3.6 Liter.

Body Type	VIN	List	Trade-In Good	Very Good	Pvt-Party Good	Retail Excellent
3.6R Limited Wagon	BRDK	32920	24700	25500	26200	29100

Body Type	VIN	List	Trade-In Good	Trade-In Very Good	Pvt-Party Good	Retail Excellent

SUZUKI

2000 SUZUKI — (JSor2S)3(AB21H)-Y-#

SWIFT—4-Cyl.—Equipment Schedule 6
W.B. 93.1"; 1.3 Liter.

Body Type	VIN	List	Good	Very Good	Good	Excellent
GA Hatchback 2D	AB21H	9499	625	725	1325	2325
GL Hatchback 2D	AB21H	10499	600	700	1250	2200

ESTEEM—4-Cyl.—Equipment Schedule 6
W.B. 97.6"; 1.6 Liter, 1.8 Liter.

GL Sedan 4D	GB31S	13349	575	675	1275	2225
GL Wagon 4D	GB31W	13849	675	775	1425	2500
GLX Sedan 4D	GB31S	14349	750	850	1550	2700
GLX Wagon 4D	GB31W	14849	825	950	1650	2875

2001 SUZUKI — (JSor2S)2(AB21H)-1-#

SWIFT—4-Cyl.—Equipment Schedule 6
W.B. 93.1"; 1.3 Liter.

GA Hatchback 2D	AB21H	9729	675	775	1450	2600
GL Hatchback 2D	AB21H	10729	650	750	1350	2375

ESTEEM—4-Cyl.—Equipment Schedule 6
W.B. 97.6"; 1.8 Liter.

GL Sedan 4D	GB41S	13679	600	700	1325	2300
GL Wagon 4D	GB41W	14179	725	825	1525	2650
GLX Sedan 4D	GB41S	14479	800	900	1625	2825
GLX Wagon 4D	GB41W	14979	850	975	1700	2975

2002 SUZUKI — JS2(RA41S)-2-#

AERIO—4-Cyl.—Equipment Schedule 6
W.B. 97.6"; 2.0 Liter.

S Sedan 4D	RA41S	14999	650	750	1525	2750
GS Sedan 4D	RA41S	14999	750	850	1575	2750
SX Wagon 4D	RC41H	15999	925	1050	1925	3400

ESTEEM—4-Cyl.—Equipment Schedule 6
W.B. 97.6"; 1.8 Liter.

GL Sedan 4D	GB41S	13799	700	800	1425	2475
GL Wagon 4D	GB41W	14299	800	900	1575	2725
GLX Sedan 4D	GB41S	14799	900	1025	1725	2950
GLX Wagon 4D	GB41W	15299	1000	1125	1875	3200

2003 SUZUKI — JS2(RA41S)-3-#

AERIO—4-Cyl.—Equipment Schedule 6
W.B. 97.6"; 2.0 Liter.

S Sedan 4D	RA41S	14019	900	1000	1850	3300
GS Sedan 4D	RA41S	15294	900	1025	1825	3175
SX Wagon 4D	RC41H	15519	1175	1300	2250	3925
AWD	B		250	250	345	345

2004 SUZUKI — JS2orKL5(RA61S)-4-#

AERIO—4-Cyl.—Equipment Schedule 6
W.B. 97.6"; 2.3 Liter.

S Sedan 4D	RA61S	14299	1175	1300	2200	3800
LX Sedan 4D	RA61S	15999	1300	1450	2400	4175
SX Wagon 4D	RC61H	16299	1475	1625	2600	4475
AWD	B		275	275	360	360

FORENZA—4-Cyl.—Equipment Schedule 3
W.B. 102.4"; 2.0 Liter.

S Sedan 4D	JD52Z	13799	975	1100	1650	2700
LX Sedan 4D	JJ52Z	15699	1125	1250	1800	2900
EX Sedan 4D	JJ52Z	16499	1225	1375	1975	3200
Manual, 5-Spd			(300)	(300)	(400)	(400)

VERONA—6-Cyl.—Equipment Schedule 3
W.B. 106.3"; 2.5 Liter.

S Sedan 4D	VJ52L	16999	800	900	1500	2525
LX Sedan 4D	VJ52L	18299	1125	1250	1925	3225
EX Sedan 4D	VM52L	19999	1200	1325	2025	3375

Body Type	VIN	List	Trade-In Good	Very Good	Pvt-Party Good	Retail Excellent

2005 SUZUKI — JS2orKL5(RA62S)–5–#

AERIO—4-Cyl.—Equipment Schedule 6
W.B. 97.6"; 2.3 Liter.

Body Type	VIN	List	Good	Very Good	Good	Excellent
S Sedan 4D	RA62S	14894	1275	1425	2450	4150
LX Sedan 4D	RA61S	16594	1400	1575	2725	4575
SX Wagon 4D	RC61H	16894	1600	1775	3000	4975
AWD	B,D		275	275	365	365

FORENZA—4-Cyl.—Equipment Schedule 3
W.B. 102.4"; 2.0 Liter.

S Sedan 4D	JD56Z	14794	950	1075	1800	2925
S Wagon 4D	JD86Z	15294	1050	1175	1875	3000
LX Sedan 4D	JJ56Z	16694	1100	1250	1975	3175
LX Wagon 4D	JJ86Z	17194	1275	1425	2150	3400
EX Sedan 4D	JJ56Z	17494	1375	1525	2250	3525
EX Wagon 4D	JJ86Z	17994	1475	1650	2350	3700
Manual, 5-Spd			(350)	(350)	(465)	(465)

RENO—4-Cyl.—Equipment Schedule 4
W.B. 102.4"; 2.0 Liter.

S Hatchback 4D	JD66Z	14794	1025	1175	1700	2600
LX Hatchback 4D	JD66Z	16694	1875	2100	2875	4375
EX Hatchback 4D	JJ66Z	17494	1975	2225	3000	4550
Manual, 5-Spd			(350)	(350)	(465)	(465)

VERONA—6-Cyl.—Equipment Schedule 3
W.B. 106.3"; 2.5 Liter.

S Sedan 4D	VJ56L	17994	875	1000	1800	2950
LX Sedan 4D	VJ56L	19794	1375	1550	2425	3925
EX Sedan 4D	VM56L	20994	1500	1675	2700	4325

2006 SUZUKI — JS2orKL5(RA62S)–6–#

AERIO—4-Cyl.—Equipment Schedule 6
W.B. 97.6"; 2.3 Liter.

Sedan 4D	RA62S	15479	1475	1650	2675	4325
SX Wagon 4D	RC61H	15979	2000	2225	3275	5100
Manual, 5-Spd			(275)	(275)	(365)	(365)

AERIO—4-Cyl.—Equipment Schedule 6
W.B. 97.6"; 2.3 Liter.

Premium Sedan 4D	RA61S	15679	1725	1900	2925	4575
SX Premium Wagon	RA61H	15879	1950	2150	3200	4975
Automatic			275	275	365	365
AWD	B		275	275	380	380

FORENZA—4-Cyl.—Equipment Schedule 3
W.B. 102.4"; 2.0 Liter.

Sedan 4D	JD56Z	15179	1075	1200	1975	3125
Premium Sedan 4D	JJ56Z	16579	1725	1925	2975	4575
Wagon 4D	JD86Z	15879	1275	1425	2225	3500
Premium Wagon 4D	JJ86Z	17279	1825	2050	3100	4750
Manual, 5-Spd			(400)	(400)	(535)	(535)

RENO—4-Cyl.—Equipment Schedule 4
W.B. 102.4"; 2.0 Liter.

Hatchback 4D	JD66Z	14679	1100	1250	1975	3100
Convenience H'Back	JD66Z	15729	1650	1875	2825	4400
Premium Hatchback	JD66Z	16879	2125	2375	3450	5275
Manual, 5-Spd			(400)	(400)	(535)	(535)

VERONA—6-Cyl.—Equipment Schedule 3
W.B. 106.3"; 2.5 Liter.

Sedan 4D	VJ56L	18879	1050	1175	2300	3875
Luxury Sedan 4D	VM56L	20879	1500	1675	2850	4725

2007 SUZUKI — JS2orKL5(RA62S)–7–#

AERIO—4-Cyl.—Equipment Schedule 6
W.B. 97.6"; 2.3 Liter.

Sedan 4D	RA62S	16594	1675	1850	2900	4575
Manual, 5-Spd			(300)	(300)	(400)	(400)

AERIO—4-Cyl.—Equipment Schedule 6
W.B. 97.6"; 2.3 Liter.

Premium Sedan 4D	RA61S	16824	2325	2575	3750	5750
AWD	B		300	300	390	390

SX4—4-Cyl.—Equipment Schedule 4
W.B. 98.4"; 2.0 Liter.

Hatchback 4D	YB413	16594	2475	2825	3650	5325
Sport H'Back Sed 4D	YB417	17994	2875	3250	4100	5925

294   DEDUCT FOR RECONDITIONING

0415

2007 SUZUKI

Body Type	VIN	List	Trade-In Good	Very Good	Pvt-Party Good	Retail Excellent
Manual, 5-Spd			(425)	(425)	(565)	(565)
FORENZA—4-Cyl.—Equipment Schedule 3						
W.B. 102.4"; 2.0 Liter.						
Sedan 4D	JD56Z	15594	1400	1550	2250	3425
Wagon 4D	JD86Z	16294	1650	1825	2575	3850
Manual, 5-Spd			(425)	(425)	(565)	(565)
RENO—4-Cyl.—Equipment Schedule 4						
W.B. 102.4"; 2.0 Liter.						
Hatchback 4D	JD66Z	15094	1400	1575	2275	3475
Manual, 5-Spd			(425)	(425)	(565)	(565)

2008 SUZUKI — JS2orKL5(YC414)-8-#

Body Type	VIN	List	Trade-In Good	Very Good	Pvt-Party Good	Retail Excellent
SX4—4-Cyl.—Equipment Schedule 4						
W.B. 98.4"; 2.0 Liter.						
Sedan 4D	YC414	15395	1750	1950	2700	3975
Sport Sedan 4D	YC415	16495	3175	3525	4300	6050
Sport Road Trip Sed	YC417	17099	4050	4450	5450	7575
Road Trip Ed H'Back	YA417	17099	4125	4525	5550	7700
Manual, 5-Spd w/Overdrive			(450)	(450)	(600)	(600)
SX4 AWD—4-Cyl.—Equipment Schedule 4						
W.B. 98.4"; 2.0 Liter.						
Hatchback 4D	YB413	16995	3550	3925	4850	6775
FWD			(1125)	(1125)	(1515)	(1515)
Manual, 5-Spd w/Overdrive			(450)	(450)	(600)	(600)
FORENZA—4-Cyl.—Equipment Schedule 3						
W.B. 102.4"; 2.0 Liter.						
Sedan 4D	JD56Z	15974	1750	1925	2725	4125
Wagon 4D	JD86Z	16874	1850	2025	2950	4400
Manual, 5-Spd w/Overdrive			(450)	(450)	(600)	(600)
RENO—4-Cyl.—Equipment Schedule 4						
W.B. 102.4"; 2.0 Liter.						
Hatchback 4D	JD66Z	15324	1850	2050	2800	4125
Manual, 5-Spd w/Overdrive			(450)	(450)	(600)	(600)

2009 SUZUKI — JS2orKL5(YC411)-9-#

Body Type	VIN	List	Trade-In Good	Very Good	Pvt-Party Good	Retail Excellent
SX4—4-Cyl.—Equipment Schedule 4						
W.B. 98.4"; 2.0 Liter.						
Sedan 4D	YC411	13959	2600	2850	3550	4925
LE Sedan 4D	YC412	16899	3400	3725	4600	6250
Sport Sedan 4D	YC414	17499	3700	4050	4975	6775
Manual, 5-Spd w/Overdrive			(500)	(500)	(665)	(665)
SX4 AWD—4-Cyl.—Equipment Schedule 4						
W.B. 98.4"; 2.0 Liter.						
Hatchback 4D	YB413	18234	4575	4975	5900	7900
FWD			(1025)	(1025)	(1380)	(1380)
Manual, 5-Spd w/Overdrive			(500)	(500)	(665)	(665)

2010 SUZUKI — JS2(YC5A1)-A-#

Body Type	VIN	List	Trade-In Good	Very Good	Pvt-Party Good	Retail Excellent
SX4—4-Cyl.—Equipment Schedule 4						
W.B. 98.4"; 2.0 Liter.						
Sedan 4D	YC5A1	14094	2825	3075	3925	5425
Sportback 4D	YA5A9	19834	5100	5450	6550	8650
LE Sedan 4D	YC5A2	15684	3750	4075	5000	6675
Sport S Sedan 4D	YC5A4	17984	4300	4625	5625	7500
Sport SE Sedan 4D	YC5A4	18434	4600	4950	5950	7875
Sport GTS Sedan 4D	YC5A9	19584	5050	5425	6550	8700
SX4 AWD—4-Cyl.—Equipment Schedule 4						
W.B. 98.4"; 2.0 Liter.						
Hatchback 4D	YB5A3	18684	4700	5050	6100	8100
FWD	A		(1100)	(1100)	(1470)	(1470)
KIZASHI—4-Cyl.—Equipment Schedule 4						
W.B. 106.3"; 2.4 Liter.						
S Sedan 4D	RE9A1	21234	4200	4500	5300	6800
SE Sedan 4D	RE9A3	22234	5250	5600	6650	8450
GTS Sedan 4D	RE9A5	24334	6750	7150	8300	10400
SLS Sedan 4D	RE9A7	26234	8000	8425	9775	12300
AWD	F		1475	1475	1965	1965

2011 SUZUKI — JS2(YC5A1)-B-#

Body Type	VIN	List	Trade-In Good	Very Good	Pvt-Party Good	Retail Excellent
SX4—4-Cyl.—Equipment Schedule 4						
W.B. 98.4"; 2.0 Liter.						
Sedan 4D	YC5A1	14244	3950	4250	5200	6825

2011 SUZUKI

Body Type	VIN	List	Trade-In Good	Very Good	Pvt-Party Good	Retail Excellent
LE Sedan 4D	YC5A2	15940	5175	5525	6425	8225
LE Annv Ed Sedan 4D	YC5A2	17744	6225	6625	7775	9875
Sport S Sedan 4D	YC5A4	17124	5075	5425	6575	8475
Sport SE Sedan 4D	YC5A4	18494	5725	6075	7275	9300
Sport GTS Sedan 4D	YC5A9	19644	6800	7225	8425	10650
Sportback 4D	YA5A5	19894	6000	6375	7550	9625
SX4 AWD—4-Cyl.—Equipment Schedule 4						
W.B. 98.4"; 2.0 Liter.						
Hatchback 4D	YB5A3	17744	5250	5600	6800	8825
Premium H'Back 4D	YB5A3	19344	6375	6775	7950	10100
KIZASHI—4-Cyl.—Equipment Schedule 4						
W.B. 106.3"; 2.4 Liter.						
S Sedan 4D	RE9A1	21644	5175	5475	6350	7950
SE Sedan 4D	RE9A3	22644	6800	7175	8325	10350
Sport GTS Sedan 4D	RE9A6	24744	8125	8525	9850	12150
Sport SLS Sedan 4D	RE9A7	26544	9150	9575	11050	13650
AWD	F		1550	1550	2050	2050

2012 SUZUKI — JS2(YC5A1)–C–#

Body Type	VIN	List	Trade-In Good	Very Good	Pvt-Party Good	Retail Excellent
SX4—4-Cyl.—Equipment Schedule 4						
W.B. 98.4"; 2.0 Liter.						
Sedan 4D	YC5A1	14464	4425	4725	5800	7575
LE Sedan 4D	YC5A3	18314	5825	6175	7400	9400
Sport SE Sedan 4D	YC5A5	18964	6525	6900	8150	10300
Sportback 4D	YA5A5	18764	6475	6850	8100	10250
Technology H'Back 4D	YA5A5	19264	6600	6975	8400	10750
SX4 AWD—4-Cyl.—Equipment Schedule 4						
W.B. 98.4"; 2.0 Liter.						
Hatchback 4D	YB5A3	17764	6050	6400	7600	9625
Premium H'Back 4D	YB5A3	19640	7050	7425	8775	11050
Technology Value 4D	YB5A3	20414	8150	8550	9975	12500
KIZASHI—4-Cyl.—Equipment Schedule 4						
W.B. 106.3"; 2.4 Liter.						
S Sedan 4D	RE9A1	21764	6175	6500	7650	9450
SE Sedan 4D	RE9A3	23064	7825	8225	9575	11750
Sport GTS Sedan 4D	RE9A6	25164	9025	9425	10850	13250
Sport SLS Sedan 4D	RE9A8	28363	10000	10450	12050	14700
AWD	F		1650	1650	2115	2115

2013 SUZUKI — JS2(YC5A3)–D–#

Body Type	VIN	List	Trade-In Good	Very Good	Pvt-Party Good	Retail Excellent
SX4—4-Cyl.—Equipment Schedule 4						
W.B. 98.4"; 2.0 Liter.						
LE Sedan 4D	YC5A3	16640	6425	6775	8000	10050
LE Popular Sedan 4D	YC5A3	18644	7650	8025	9300	11500
Sport SE Sedan 4D	YC5A5	19594	8350	8750	10000	12300
SX4 AWD—4-Cyl.—Equipment Schedule 4						
W.B. 98.4"; 2.0 Liter.						
Hatchback 4D	YB5A3	17794	7000	7350	8625	10750
FWD	A		(1300)	(1300)	(1735)	(1735)
SX4 AWD—4-Cyl.—Equipment Schedule 4						
W.B. 98.4"; 2.0 Liter.						
Premium H'Back 4D	YB5A3	19970	8950	9350	10700	13200
Technology Value 4D	YB5A4	21244	9375	9825	11200	13700
KIZASHI—4-Cyl.—Equipment Schedule 4						
W.B. 106.3"; 2.4 Liter.						
Sedan 4D	RE9A1	20794	7800	8175	9750	12150
SE Sedan 4D	RE9A3	22544	9350	9750	11000	13150
Sport GTS Sedan 4D	RE9A6	26594	10550	11000	12800	15800
AWD	F		1725	1725	2030	2030
KIZASHI AWD—4-Cyl.—Equipment Schedule 4						
W.B. 106.3"; 2.4 Liter.						
Sport SLS Sedan 4D	RF9A8	29794	11450	11900	13900	17150

TESLA

2013 TESLA

Body Type	VIN	List	Trade-In Good	Very Good	Pvt-Party Good	Retail Excellent
MODEL S—AC Electric—Equipment Schedule 2						
W.B. 116.5".						
Sedan 4D	SA-A	68570	72900	75400	72700	78600
Performance Sedan 4D	SA-A	93570	81900	84600	81200	87600
Signature Sedan 4D	SA-D	96570	82900	85700	82100	88600

2013 TESLA

Body Type	VIN	List	Trade-In Good	Very Good	Pvt-Party Good	Retail Excellent
Signature Performance	SA-D	106570	88300	91300	87300	94100

2014 TESLA

MODEL S—AC Electric—Equipment Schedule 2
W.B. 116.5".

Sedan 4D	SA	71070	76400	79000	76000	82100
Performance Sedan 4D	SA	94570	85300	88200	84500	91100

TOYOTA

2000 TOYOTA—(J,1,2or4)(NorT)(X,1,2or5)(BT123)–Y–#

ECHO—4-Cyl.—Equipment Schedule 6
W.B. 93.3"; 1.5 Liter.

Sedan 4D	BT123	11945	1250	1400	2125	3600
Coupe 2D	AT123	11645	1100	1250	1950	3275

COROLLA—4-Cyl.—Equipment Schedule 6
W.B. 97.0"; 1.8 Liter.

VE Sedan 4D	BR12E	13603	725	825	1525	2675
CE Sedan 4D	BR12E	14653	875	975	1625	2750
LE Sedan 4D	BR12E	15523	1125	1250	2000	3375

CAMRY—4-Cyl.—Equipment Schedule 4
W.B. 105.2"; 2.2 Liter.

CE Sedan 4D	BG22K	19820	1350	1500	2225	3700
LE Sedan 4D	BG22K	20743	1475	1650	2400	3975
XLE Sedan 4D	BG22K	24423	1600	1775	2575	4250
Manual, 5-Spd			(175)	(175)	(235)	(235)
V6, 3.0 Liter	F		75	75	100	100

SOLARA—4-Cyl.—Equipment Schedule 4
W.B. 105.1"; 2.2 Liter.

SE Coupe 2D	CG22P	20193	1575	1775	2450	3925
SE Convertible 2D	FG22P	25523	2350	2650	3425	5325
Manual, 5-Spd			(175)	(175)	(235)	(235)
V6, 3.0 Liter	F		75	75	100	100

SOLARA—V6—Equipment Schedule 4
W.B. 105.1"; 3.0 Liter.

SLE Coupe 2D	CF22P	26293	2400	2700	3475	5425
SLE Convertible 2D	FF22P	30943	3025	3375	4225	6475

MR2 SPYDER—4-Cyl.—Equipment Schedule 4
W.B. 96.5"; 1.8 Liter.

Convertible 2D	FG320	23553	2375	2625	3250	4900

CELICA—4-Cyl.—Equipment Schedule 4
W.B. 102.3"; 1.8 Liter.

GT Liftback 2D	DR32T	17970	1700	1875	2550	4000
GT-S Liftback 2D	DY32T	21620	2175	2400	3175	4950
Automatic			125	125	165	165

AVALON—V6—Equipment Schedule 4
W.B. 107.1"; 3.0 Liter.

XL Sedan 4D	BF28B	25650	1675	1850	2650	4250
XLS Sedan 4D	BF28B	30210	2000	2200	3075	4850

2001 TOYOTA—(J,1,2or4)(NorT)(D,X,1or2)(BT123)–1–#

ECHO—4-Cyl.—Equipment Schedule 6
W.B. 93.3"; 1.5 Liter.

Sedan 4D	BT123	11930	1525	1700	2425	4025
Coupe 2D	AT123	11400	1350	1500	2200	3650

COROLLA—4-Cyl.—Equipment Schedule 6
W.B. 97.0"; 1.8 Liter.

CE Sedan 4D	BR12E	13753	1050	1175	1800	2950
S Sedan 4D	BR12E	14343	1225	1350	2025	3300
LE Sedan 4D	BR12E	14863	1275	1425	2125	3525

PRIUS—4-Cyl. Hybrid—Equipment Schedule 3
W.B. 100.4"; 1.5 Liter.

Sedan 4D	BK12U	20450	1125	1275	2100	3700

CAMRY—4-Cyl.—Equipment Schedule 4
W.B. 105.1"; 2.2 Liter.

CE Sedan 4D	BG22K	19733	1725	1900	2650	4300
LE Sedan 4D	BG22K	20895	1675	1850	2700	4350
XLE Sedan 4D	BG22K	24575	1950	2150	3075	4900
Manual, 5-Spd			(200)	(200)	(265)	(265)
V6, 3.0 Liter	F		75	75	100	100

Body Type	VIN	List	Trade-In Good	Very Good	Pvt-Party Good	Retail Excellent
SOLARA—4-Cyl.—Equipment Schedule 4						
W.B. 105.1"; 2.2 Liter.						
SE Coupe 2D	CG22P	20245	1700	1900	2600	4150
SE Convertible 2D	FG22P	25575	2575	2875	3700	5750
Manual, 5-Spd.			(200)	(200)	(265)	(265)
V6, 3.0 Liter	F		75	75	100	100
SOLARA—V6—Equipment Schedule 4						
W.B. 105.1"; 3.0 Liter.						
SLE Coupe 2D	CF22P	25645	2575	2875	3700	5750
SLE Convertible 2D	FF22P	30995	3200	3575	4575	6950
MR2 SPYDER—4-Cyl.—Equipment Schedule 4						
W.B. 96.5"; 1.8 Liter.						
Convertible 2D	FG320	24065	2700	2975	3575	5250
CELICA—4-Cyl.—Equipment Schedule 4						
W.B. 102.3"; 1.8 Liter.						
GT Liftback 2D	DR32T	18285	2000	2225	2825	4325
GT-S Liftback 2D	DY32T	21935	2475	2725	3450	5250
Automatic			125	125	165	165
AVALON—V6—Equipment Schedule 4						
W.B. 107.1"; 3.0 Liter.						
XL Sedan 4D	BF28B	26325	1925	2125	2950	4625
XLS Sedan 4D	BF28B	30885	2250	2475	3350	5225

Body Type	VIN	List	Trade-In Good	Very Good	Pvt-Party Good	Retail Excellent
ECHO—4-Cyl.—Equipment Schedule 6						
W.B. 93.3"; 1.5 Liter.						
Sedan 4D	BT123	12265	1700	1900	2725	4400
Coupe 2D	AT123	11675	1575	1750	2450	3975
COROLLA—4-Cyl.—Equipment Schedule 4						
W.B. 97.0"; 1.8 Liter.						
CE Sedan 4D	BR12E	13533	1325	1475	2100	3425
S Sedan 4D	BR12E	14073	1500	1650	2325	3750
LE Sedan 4D	BR12E	14443	1550	1700	2575	4175
PRIUS—4-Cyl. Hybrid—Equipment Schedule 3						
W.B. 100.4"; 1.5 Liter.						
Sedan 4D	BK12U	20480	1525	1725	2575	4300
CAMRY—4-Cyl.—Equipment Schedule 4						
W.B. 107.1"; 2.4 Liter.						
LE Sedan 4D	BE32K	20285	2375	2600	3650	5750
SE Sedan 4D	BE32K	21625	2500	2750	3825	6000
XLE Sedan 4D	BF32K	25890	3025	3325	4450	6850
Manual, 5-Spd.			(200)	(200)	(265)	(265)
V6, 3.0 Liter	F		125	125	165	165
SOLARA—4-Cyl.—Equipment Schedule 4						
W.B. 105.1"; 2.4 Liter.						
SE Coupe 2D	CE22P	20650	1800	2025	2800	4475
SE Convertible 2D	FE22P	25980	3100	3450	4375	6725
Manual, 5-Spd.			(200)	(200)	(265)	(265)
V6, 3.0 Liter	F		125	125	165	165
SOLARA—V6—Equipment Schedule 4						
W.B. 105.1"; 3.0 Liter.						
SLE Coupe 2D	CF22P	25160	2875	3225	4125	6350
SLE Convertible 2D	FF22P	31010	3600	3975	5150	7825
MR2 SPYDER—4-Cyl.—Equipment Schedule 4						
W.B. 96.5"; 1.8 Liter.						
Convertible 2D	FR320	25000	3475	3825	4425	6325
CELICA—4-Cyl.—Equipment Schedule 4						
W.B. 102.4"; 1.8 Liter.						
GT Liftback 2D	DR32T	18390	2375	2625	3225	4825
GT-S Liftback 2D	DY32T	22040	3000	3325	4025	5950
Automatic			125	125	165	165
AVALON—V6—Equipment Schedule 4						
W.B. 107.1"; 3.0 Liter.						
XL Sedan 4D	BF28B	26330	2300	2525	3275	4950
XLS Sedan 4D	BF28B	30890	2800	3100	3875	5775

Body Type	VIN	List	Trade-In Good	Very Good	Pvt-Party Good	Retail Excellent
ECHO—4-Cyl.—Equipment Schedule 6						
W.B. 93.3"; 1.5 Liter.						
Sedan 4D	BT123	12375	1975	2225	2975	4650
Coupe 2D	AT123	11785	1775	2000	2700	4250

Body Type	VIN	List	Trade-In Good	Very Good	Pvt-Party Good	Retail Excellent
COROLLA—4-Cyl.—Equipment Schedule 6						
W.B. 102.4"; 1.8 Liter.						
CE Sedan 4D	BR32E	14055	2725	3000	3675	5400
S Sedan 4D	BR32E	15000	2850	3125	3825	5600
LE Sedan 4D	BR32E	15165	3100	3400	4100	6000
Sport Pkg			75	75	105	105
TRD Pkg			150	150	200	200
PRIUS—4-Cyl. Hybrid—Equipment Schedule 3						
W.B. 100.4"; 1.5 Liter.						
Sedan 4D	BK12U	20730	1925	2150	3075	5000
MATRIX—4-Cyl.—Equipment Schedule 6						
W.B. 102.4"; 1.8 Liter.						
Sport Wagon 4D	KR32E	15985	2875	3225	3875	5750
XR Sport Wagon 4D	KR32E	17495	3350	3725	4525	6650
XRS Sport Wagon 4D	KY32E	19235	3250	3625	4400	6450
TRD Pkg			275	275	380	380
4WD			600	600	800	800
CAMRY—4-Cyl.—Equipment Schedule 4						
W.B. 107.1"; 2.4 Liter.						
LE Sedan 4D	BE30K	20285	3175	3475	4300	6325
SE Sedan 4D	BE30K	21625	3450	3775	4650	6800
Manual, 5-Spd			(250)	(250)	(335)	(335)
V6, 3.0 Liter	F		175	175	235	235
CAMRY—V6—Equipment Schedule 4						
W.B. 107.1"; 3.0 Liter.						
XLE Sedan 4D	BF30K	25920	3875	4225	5300	7725
4-Cyl, 2.4 Liter	E		(175)	(175)	(235)	(235)
SOLARA—4-Cyl.—Equipment Schedule 4						
W.B. 105.1"; 2.4 Liter.						
SE Coupe 2D	CE22P	20650	2300	2575	3225	4850
SE Convertible 2D	FE22P	25980	3450	3825	4725	6950
Manual, 5-Spd			(250)	(250)	(335)	(335)
V6, 3.0 Liter	F		175	175	235	235
SOLARA—V6—Equipment Schedule 4						
W.B. 105.1"; 3.0 Liter.						
SLE Coupe 2D	CF22P	25160	3550	3925	4825	7050
SLE Convertible 2D	FF22P	31010	4350	4800	5775	8400
MR2 SPYDER—4-Cyl.—Equipment Schedule 4						
W.B. 96.5"; 1.8 Liter.						
Convertible 2D	FR320	25055	4250	4650	5350	7450
CELICA—4-Cyl.—Equipment Schedule 4						
W.B. 102.4"; 1.8 Liter.						
GT Liftback 2D	DR32T	18610	2800	3125	3700	5400
GT-S Liftback 2D	DY32T	22455	3475	3825	4500	6525
Automatic			150	150	200	200
AVALON—V6—Equipment Schedule 4						
W.B. 107.1"; 3.0 Liter.						
XL Sedan 4D	BF28B	26330	3100	3400	4075	5875
XLS Sedan 4D	BF28B	27150	3425	3750	4600	6625

2004 TOYOTA—(J,1,2or4)(NorT)D,Xor1(BT123)—4-#

Body Type	VIN	List	Trade-In Good	Very Good	Pvt-Party Good	Retail Excellent
ECHO—4-Cyl.—Equipment Schedule 6						
W.B. 93.3"; 1.5 Liter.						
Sedan 4D	BT123	12215	2225	2475	3225	4950
Coupe 2D	AT123	11685	2000	2225	2950	4525
COROLLA—4-Cyl.—Equipment Schedule 6						
W.B. 102.4"; 1.8 Liter.						
CE Sedan 4D	BR32E	14085	3000	3300	3925	5625
S Sedan 4D	BR32E	15030	3300	3600	4325	6125
LE Sedan 4D	BR32E	15295	3425	3725	4575	6525
PRIUS—4-Cyl. Hybrid—Equipment Schedule 3						
W.B. 106.3"; 1.5 Liter.						
Hatchback Sedan 4D	KB20U	20510	3375	3725	4600	6725
MATRIX—4-Cyl.—Equipment Schedule 6						
W.B. 102.4"; 1.8 Liter.						
Sport Wagon 4D	KR32E	15985	3350	3725	4475	6450
XR Sport Wagon 4D	KR32E	17495	3850	4250	5050	7250
XRS Sport Wagon 4D	KY32E	19265	3950	4350	5175	7400
Sport Pkg			300	300	410	410
4WD	L		650	650	865	865
CAMRY—4-Cyl.—Equipment Schedule 4						
W.B. 107.1"; 2.4 Liter.						
Sedan 4D	BE32K	19390	3550	3875	4700	6650

Body Type	VIN	List	Trade-In Good	Very Good	Pvt-Party Good	Retail Excellent
LE Sedan 4D	BE32K	20390	3825	4150	5000	7075
SE Sedan 4D	BE32K	21220	4150	4500	5400	7600
Manual, 5-Spd.			(300)	(300)	(400)	(400)
V6, 3.0 Liter	F,A		225	225	300	300
CAMRY—V6—Equipment Schedule 4						
W.B. 107.1"; 3.0 Liter.						
XLE Sedan 4D	BF32K	25920	4950	5350	6375	8950
4-Cyl., 2.4 Liter			(200)	(200)	(265)	(265)
SOLARA—4-Cyl.—Equipment Schedule 4						
W.B. 107.2"; 2.4 Liter.						
SE Coupe 2D	CE38P	20465	2750	3050	3725	5550
SE Sport Coupe 2D	CE38P	21960	3350	3700	4475	6575
Manual, 5-Spd.			(300)	(300)	(400)	(400)
V6, 3.3 Liter	A		225	225	300	300
SOLARA—V6—Equipment Schedule 4						
W.B. 107.2"; 3.3 Liter.						
SLE Coupe 2D	CA389	26510	4450	4875	5875	8500
4-Cyl., 2.4 Liter	E		(200)	(200)	(265)	(265)
SOLARA—V6—Equipment Schedule 4						
W.B 107.1"; 3.3 Liter.						
SE Convertible 2D	FA22P	26465	4075	4475	5450	7900
SLE Convertible 2D	FA22P	29965	5075	5550	6625	9525
MR2 SPYDER—4-Cyl.—Equipment Schedule 4						
W.B. 96.5"; 1.8 Liter.						
Convertible 2D	FR320	25410	5150	5575	6350	8750
CELICA—4-Cyl.—Equipment Schedule 4						
W.B. 102.4"; 1.8 Liter.						
GT Liftback 2D	DR32T	17905	3625	3975	4775	6775
GT-S Liftback 2D	DY32T	22570	4500	4900	5800	8200
Automatic			175	175	235	235
AVALON—V6—Equipment Schedule 4						
W.B. 107.1"; 3.0 Liter.						
XL Sedan 4D	BF28B	26560	3550	3875	4675	6625
XLS Sedan 4D	BF28B	31020	4075	4425	5275	7425

2005 TOYOTA—(J,1,2or4)(NorT)D,Xor1(BT123)–5–#

Body Type	VIN	List	Trade-In Good	Very Good	Pvt-Party Good	Retail Excellent
ECHO—4-Cyl.—Equipment Schedule 6						
W.B. 93.3"; 1.5 Liter.						
Sedan 4D	BT123	12620	2525	2800	3700	5475
Coupe 2D	AT123	12090	2225	2475	3300	4925
COROLLA—4-Cyl.—Equipment Schedule 6						
W.B. 102.4"; 1.8 Liter.						
CE Sedan 4D	BR32E	14220	3625	3975	4875	6775
S Sedan 4D	BR32E	15265	3825	4175	5100	7100
LE Sedan 4D	BR32E	15430	4175	4550	5475	7575
XRS Sedan 4D	BY32E	17995	4500	4875	5875	8100
PRIUS—4-Cyl. Hybrid—Equipment Schedule 3						
W.B. 106.3"; 1.5 Liter.						
Hatchback Sedan 4D	KB22U	21515	4425	4850	5725	7975
MATRIX—4-Cyl.—Equipment Schedule 6						
W.B. 102.4"; 1.8 Liter.						
Sport Wagon 4D	KR32E	16105	3675	4050	4875	6875
XR Sport Wagon 4D	KR32E	17615	4050	4450	5400	7675
XRS Sport Wagon 4D	KY32E	19290	4300	4725	5600	7825
4WD	L		700	700	935	935
CAMRY—4-Cyl.—Equipment Schedule 4						
W.B. 107.1"; 2.4 Liter.						
Sedan 4D	BE32K	19415	4375	4725	5550	7550
LE Sedan 4D	BE32K	20515	4825	5200	6050	8200
SE Sedan 4D	BE32K	21345	5400	5800	6900	9275
Manual, 5-Spd.			(350)	(350)	(465)	(465)
V6, 3.0 Liter	F,A		275	275	365	365
CAMRY—V6—Equipment Schedule 4						
W.B. 107.1"; 3.0 Liter.						
XLE Sedan 4D	BF32K	25945	6100	6550	7700	10350
4-Cyl., 2.4 Liter	E		(275)	(275)	(365)	(365)
SOLARA—4-Cyl.—Equipment Schedule 4						
W.B. 107.1"; 2.4 Liter.						
SE Coupe 2D	CE38P	20590	3100	3450	4075	5750
SE Sport Coupe 2D	CE38P	22085	3625	3975	4900	6950
Manual, 5-Spd.			(350)	(350)	(465)	(465)
V6, 3.3 Liter	A		275	275	365	365

2005 TOYOTA

Body Type	VIN	List	Trade-In Good	Very Good	Pvt-Party Good	Retail Excellent
SOLARA—V6—Equipment Schedule 4						
W.B. 107.1"; 3.3 Liter.						
SLE Coupe 2D	CA38P	26635	**4800**	**5250**	**6400**	**8925**
4-Cyl, 2.4 Liter	E		**(275)**	**(275)**	**(365)**	**(365)**
SOLARA—V6—Equipment Schedule 4						
W.B. 107.1"; 3.3 Liter.						
SE Convertible 2D	FA38P	26920	**4500**	**4900**	**5900**	**8250**
SLE Convertible 2D	FA38P	30190	**5475**	**5950**	**7225**	**10050**
MR2 SPYDER—4-Cyl.—Equipment Schedule 4						
W.B. 96.5"; 1.8 Liter.						
Convertible 2D	FR320	26685	**5450**	**5900**	**6775**	**9000**
CELICA—4-Cyl.—Equipment Schedule 4						
W.B. 102.4"; 1.8 Liter.						
GT Liftback 2D	DR32T	19830	**3975**	**4350**	**5200**	**7200**
GT-S Liftback 2D	DY32T	23575	**5050**	**5475**	**6450**	**8875**
Automatic			**200**	**200**	**265**	**265**
AVALON—V6—Equipment Schedule 4						
W.B. 111.0"; 3.5 Liter.						
XL Sedan 4D	BK36B	26890	**5075**	**5475**	**6400**	**8500**
Touring Sedan 4D	BK36B	29140	**6275**	**6725**	**7550**	**9800**
XLS Sedan 4D	BK36B	31340	**6075**	**6525**	**7475**	**9850**
Limited Sedan 4D	BK36B	34080	**6450**	**6900**	**7900**	**10400**

2006 TOYOTA—(1,2,4orJ)(NorT)(1,DorX)(BR32E)—6-#

Body Type	VIN	List	Trade-In Good	Very Good	Pvt-Party Good	Retail Excellent
COROLLA—4-Cyl.—Equipment Schedule 6						
W.B. 102.4"; 1.8 Liter.						
CE Sedan 4D	BR32E	14545	**4075**	**4425**	**5300**	**7250**
S Sedan 4D	BR32E	15590	**4375**	**4725**	**5650**	**7700**
LE Sedan 4D	BR32E	15755	**4675**	**5050**	**5975**	**8125**
XRS Sedan 4D	BY32E	18320	**5300**	**5700**	**6675**	**9000**
PRIUS—4-Cyl. Hybrid—Equipment Schedule 3						
W.B. 106.3"; 1.5 Liter.						
Hatchback Sedan 4D	KB22U	22305	**5150**	**5600**	**6400**	**8650**
Package #5			**250**	**250**	**330**	**330**
MATRIX—4-Cyl.—Equipment Schedule 6						
W.B. 102.4"; 1.8 Liter.						
Sport Wagon 4D	KR32E	16450	**4225**	**4625**	**5450**	**7525**
XR Sport Wagon 4D	KR32E	17960	**4725**	**5150**	**6025**	**8275**
Manual, 5-Spd			**(275)**	**(275)**	**(365)**	**(365)**
4WD	L		**750**	**750**	**1000**	**1000**
MATRIX—4-Cyl.—Equipment Schedule 6						
W.B. 102.4"; 1.8 Liter.						
XRS Sport Wagon 4D	KY32E	19640	**4875**	**5325**	**6200**	**8500**
4WD	L		**750**	**750**	**1000**	**1000**
CAMRY—4-Cyl.—Equipment Schedule 4						
W.B. 107.1"; 2.4 Liter.						
Sedan 4D	BE32K	18985	**4950**	**5325**	**6125**	**8175**
LE Sedan 4D	BE32K	20915	**5350**	**5750**	**6550**	**8700**
SE Sedan 4D	BE32K	21745	**6150**	**6600**	**7725**	**10200**
Manual, 5-Spd			**(400)**	**(400)**	**(535)**	**(535)**
V6, 3.0 Liter	FA		**325**	**325**	**435**	**435**
CAMRY—V6—Equipment Schedule 4						
W.B. 107.1"; 3.0 Liter.						
XLE Sedan 4D	BF32K	26425	**7075**	**7575**	**8800**	**11600**
4-Cyl, 2.4 Liter	E		**(325)**	**(325)**	**(430)**	**(430)**
SOLARA—4-Cyl.—Equipment Schedule 4						
W.B. 107.1"; 2.4 Liter.						
SE Coupe 2D	CE38P	20900	**3600**	**3950**	**4600**	**6225**
SE Sport Coupe 2D	CE38P	22395	**4300**	**4700**	**5400**	**7325**
Manual, 5-Spd			**(400)**	**(400)**	**(535)**	**(535)**
V6, 3.3 Liter	A		**325**	**325**	**435**	**435**
SOLARA—V6—Equipment Schedule 4						
W.B. 107.1"; 3.3 Liter.						
SLE Coupe 2D	CA38P	26875	**5625**	**6100**	**7150**	**9600**
4-Cyl, 2.4 Liter	E		**(325)**	**(325)**	**(435)**	**(435)**
SOLARA—V6—Equipment Schedule 4						
W.B. 107.1"; 3.3 Liter.						
SE Convertible 2D	FA38P	27480	**5050**	**5500**	**6525**	**8750**
SLE Convertible 2D	FA38P	30750	**6775**	**7325**	**8575**	**11600**
AVALON—V6—Equipment Schedule 4						
W.B. 111.0"; 3.5 Liter.						
XL Sedan 4D	BK36B	27165	**5525**	**5950**	**6900**	**8975**
Touring Sedan 4D	BK36B	29415	**6425**	**6875**	**7725**	**10000**

Body Type	VIN	List	Trade-In Good	Very Good	Pvt-Party Good	Retail Excellent
XLS Sedan 4D	BK36B	31615	6975	7450	8375	10850
Limited Sedan 4D	BK36B	34355	7550	8050	9050	11650

2007 TOYOTA—(1,2,4orJ)(NorT)(1,DorX)(JT923)—7—#

YARIS—4-Cyl.—Equipment Schedule 6
W.B. 96.9", 100.4" (Sedan); 1.5 Liter.
Hatchback 2D	JT923	12430	3600	3900	4900	6700
Sedan 4D	BT923	13130	3725	4025	5100	7000
S Sedan 4D	BT923	14630	4675	5025	5950	7850
Manual, 5-Spd			(300)	(300)	(400)	(400)

COROLLA—4-Cyl.—Equipment Schedule 6
W.B. 102.4"; 1.8 Liter.
CE Sedan 4D	BR32E	14785	4600	4975	5850	7850
S Sedan 4D	BR32E	15830	5000	5375	6300	8400
LE Sedan 4D	BR32E	15995	5050	5425	6375	8525
Manual, 5-Spd			(350)	(350)	(465)	(465)

PRIUS—4-Cyl. Hybrid—Equipment Schedule 3
W.B. 106.3"; 1.5 Liter.
Hatchback Sedan 4D	KB20U	22755	5700	6150	7100	9375
Touring H'Back 4D	KB20U	23650	6475	6975	7875	10200
Package #5			275	275	360	360
Package #6			275	275	360	360

MATRIX—4-Cyl.—Equipment Schedule 6
W.B. 102.4"; 1.8 Liter.
Sport Wagon 4D	KR30E	16640	4800	5200	6025	8125
XR Sport Wagon 4D	KR30E	18150	5525	5975	7025	9425
Manual, 5-Spd			(300)	(300)	(400)	(400)

CAMRY—4-Cyl.—Equipment Schedule 4
W.B. 109.3"; 2.4 Liter.
CE Sedan 4D	BE46K	19900	5975	6400	7325	9500
LE Sedan 4D	BE46K	21355	6475	6950	7925	10200
SE Sedan 4D	BE46K	22520	7775	8300	9375	12050
XLE Sedan 4D	BE46K	25280	8525	9075	10200	13100
Manual, 5-Spd			(425)	(425)	(545)	(545)
V6, 3.5 Liter	K		375	375	480	480

CAMRY—4-Cyl. Hybrid—Equipment Schedule 4
W.B. 109.3"; 2.4 Liter.
Sedan 4D	BB46K	26480	6625	7150	8275	10900

SOLARA—4-Cyl.—Equipment Schedule 4
W.B. 107.1"; 2.4 Liter.
SE Coupe 2D	CE30P	21340	4325	4700	5350	7075
Sport Coupe 2D	CE30P	23610	4975	5375	6050	7950
Manual, 5-Spd			(425)	(425)	(555)	(555)
V6, 3.3 Liter	A		375	375	490	490

SOLARA—V6—Equipment Schedule 4
W.B. 107.1"; 3.3 Liter.
SLE Coupe 2D	CA309	27565	7025	7550	8450	10950
4-Cyl, 2.4 Liter	E		(350)	(350)	(460)	(460)

SOLARA—V6—Equipment Schedule 4
W.B. 107.1"; 3.3 Liter.
SE Convertible 2D	FA38P	27770	6425	6925	7775	10050
Sport Convertible 2D	FA38P	30040	7525	8075	9000	11600
SLE Convertible 2D	FA38P	31040	8175	8750	9725	12550

AVALON—V6—Equipment Schedule 4
W.B. 111.0"; 3.5 Liter.
XL Sedan 4D	BK36B	27455	6425	6875	7750	9900
Touring Sedan 4D	BK36B	29705	7300	7800	8650	10950
XLS Sedan 4D	BK36B	31905	8050	8575	9475	12050
Limited Sedan 4D	BK36B	34645	8950	9500	10350	13100

2008 TOYOTA—(1,2,4orJ)(NorT)(1,DorX)(JT923)—8—#

YARIS—4-Cyl.—Equipment Schedule 6
W.B. 96.9", 100.4" (Sedan); 1.5 Liter.
Hatchback 2D	JT923	12860	4225	4550	5575	7425
Sedan 4D	BT923	13560	4875	5225	6175	8075
S Hatchback 2D	JT923	14535	4975	5325	6300	8250
S Sedan 4D	BT923	15060	5175	5525	6500	8450
Manual, 5-Spd w/Overdrive			(350)	(350)	(470)	(470)

COROLLA—4-Cyl.—Equipment Schedule 6
W.B. 102.4"; 1.8 Liter.
CE Sedan 4D	BR32E	15065	5075	5450	6475	8450
S Sedan 4D	BR32E	16110	5500	5900	6950	9075

Body Type	VIN	List	Trade-In Good	Very Good	Pvt-Party Good	Retail Excellent
LE Sedan 4D	BR32E	16275	5625	6025	7075	9200
Manual, 5-Spd w/Overdrive			(350)	(350)	(470)	(470)
PRIUS—4-Cyl. Hybrid—Equipment Schedule 3						
W.B. 106.3"; 1.5 Liter.						
Standard H'Back Sed	KB20U	21610	6025	6475	7475	9700
Hatchback Sedan 4D	KB20U	22985	6750	7225	8150	10450
Touring H'Back 4D	KB20U	23880	7575	8075	9025	11400
Package #4			200	200	265	265
Package #5			300	300	390	390
Package #6			300	300	390	390
MATRIX—4-Cyl.—Equipment Schedule 6						
W.B. 102.4"; 1.8 Liter.						
Sport Wagon 4D	KR30E	16970	5325	5725	6750	8825
XR Sport Wagon 4D	KR30E	18480	6600	7075	8150	10600
Manual, 5-Spd			(300)	(300)	(400)	(400)
CAMRY—4-Cyl.—Equipment Schedule 4						
W.B. 109.3"; 2.4 Liter.						
Sedan 4D	BE46K	20280	6825	7275	8150	10300
LE Sedan 4D	BE46K	21735	7375	7850	8725	11000
SE Sedan 4D	BE46K	22900	8725	9250	10100	12550
XLE Sedan 4D	BE46K	25660	9375	9925	10900	13550
Manual, 5-Spd w/Overdrive			(450)	(450)	(565)	(565)
V6, 3.5 Liter	K		400	400	500	500
CAMRY—4-Cyl. Hybrid—Equipment Schedule 4						
W.B. 109.3"; 2.4 Liter.						
Sedan 4D	BB46K	25860	7650	8150	9125	11600
SOLARA—4-Cyl.—Equipment Schedule 4						
W.B. 107.1"; 2.4 Liter.						
SE Coupe 2D	CE30P	21420	5100	5500	6375	8200
SE Sport Coupe 2D	CE30P	23690	6225	6650	7500	9500
Manual, 5-Spd w/Overdrive			(450)	(450)	(585)	(585)
V6, 3.3 Liter	A		400	400	520	520
SOLARA—V6—Equipment Schedule 4						
W.B. 107.1"; 3.3 Liter.						
SLE Coupe 2D	CA30P	27565	8100	8625	9575	12050
4-Cyl, 2.4 Liter	E		(525)	(525)	(675)	(675)
SOLARA—V6—Equipment Schedule 4						
W.B. 107.1"; 3.3 Liter.						
SE Convertible 2D	FA38P	27850	7525	8025	9000	11350
Sport Convertible 2D	FA38P	30120	8550	9100	10100	12650
SLE Convertible 2D	FA38P	31120	9050	9600	10650	13400
AVALON—V6—Equipment Schedule 4						
W.B. 111.0"; 3.5 Liter.						
XL Sedan 4D	BK36B	27735	7625	8100	8875	10950
Touring Sedan 4D	BK36B	29985	8825	9350	10100	12450
XLS Sedan 4D	BK36B	32035	8975	9500	10400	12900
Limited Sedan 4D	BK36B	35075	9725	10250	11200	13800

2009 TOYOTA—(1,2,4orJ)(NorT)(1,DorX)(JT903)-9-#

Body Type	VIN	List	Trade-In Good	Very Good	Pvt-Party Good	Retail Excellent
YARIS—4-Cyl.—Equipment Schedule 6						
W.B. 96.9", 100.4" (Sedan); 1.5 Liter.						
Hatchback 2D	JT903	12955	4825	5150	6175	8075
Sedan 4D	BT903	14515	5400	5775	6950	8950
S Hatchback 2D	JT903	15575	5500	5875	7000	9000
S Sedan 4D	BT903	16630	6050	6425	7550	9600
Manual, 5-Spd w/Overdrive			(375)	(375)	(500)	(500)
YARIS—4-Cyl.—Equipment Schedule 6						
W.B. 96.9", 100.4" (Sedan); 1.5 Liter.						
Hatchback 4D	KT903	14025	5475	5825	6825	8800
S Hatchback 4D	KT903	15875	5675	6050	7200	9200
COROLLA—4-Cyl.—Equipment Schedule 6						
W.B. 102.4"; 1.8 Liter, 2.4 Liter.						
Sedan 4D	BU40E	15910	6475	6875	7850	9900
S Sedan 4D	BU40E	16980	6950	7375	8350	10500
XRS Sedan 4D	BE40E	19420	8850	9350	10550	13250
Manual, 5-Spd w/Overdrive			(375)	(375)	(500)	(500)
COROLLA—4-Cyl.—Equipment Schedule 6						
W.B. 102.4"; 1.8 Liter.						
LE Sedan 4D	BU40E	17310	7075	7500	8550	10750
XLE Sedan 4D	BU40E	18210	8450	8950	10100	12650
PRIUS—4-Cyl. Hybrid—Equipment Schedule 3						
W.B. 106.3"; 1.5 Liter.						
Standard H'Back Sed	KB20U	22750	7425	7875	8850	11000

Body Type	VIN	List	Trade-In Good	Very Good	Pvt-Party Good	Retail Excellent
Hatchback Sedan 4D	KB20U	24035	8275	8750	9700	11950
Touring H'Back 4D	KB20U	24930	9225	9750	10700	13100
Package #2			100	100	130	130
Package #3			100	100	130	130
Package #4			150	150	195	195
Package #5			325	325	405	405
Package #6			325	325	405	405
MATRIX—4-Cyl.—Equipment Schedule 6						
W.B. 102.4"; 1.8 Liter, 2.4 Liter.						
Sport Wagon 4D	KU40E	17850	6475	6875	7825	9850
XRS Sport Wagon 4D	GE40E	21320	8500	9000	9975	12350
Manual, 5-Spd w/Overdrive			(375)	(375)	(495)	(495)
MATRIX—4-Cyl.—Equipment Schedule 6						
W.B. 102.4"; 2.4 Liter.						
S Sport Wagon 4D	KE40E	18920	7150	7575	8700	10950
4WD			1125	1125	1495	1495
Automatic, 5-Spd			350	350	465	465
CAMRY—4-Cyl.—Equipment Schedule 4						
W.B. 109.3"; 2.4 Liter.						
Sedan 4D	BE46K	20430	7975	8450	9375	11600
LE Sedan 4D	BE46K	21885	8425	8900	9850	12150
SE Sedan 4D	BE46K	23050	9675	10200	11250	13800
XLE Sedan 4D	BE46K	25810	10250	10800	11900	14650
Manual, 5-Spd w/Overdrive			(500)	(500)	(615)	(615)
V6, 3.5 Liter	K		475	475	580	580
CAMRY—4-Cyl. Hybrid—Equipment Schedule 4						
W.B. 109.3"; 2.4 Liter.						
Sedan 4D	BB46K	26010	10000	10550	11500	14000
AVALON—V6—Equipment Schedule 4						
W.B. 111.0"; 3.5 Liter.						
XL Sedan 4D	BK36B	28505	8200	8700	9525	11650
XLS Sedan 4D	BK36B	32805	10650	11200	12100	14700
Limited Sedan 4D	BK36B	35845	11450	12050	13000	15750

2010 TOYOTA—(2,4orJ)T(1,DorN)(JT4K3)-A-#

Body Type	VIN	List	Trade-In Good	Very Good	Pvt-Party Good	Retail Excellent
YARIS—4-Cyl.—Equipment Schedule 6						
W.B. 96.9", 100.4" (Sed); 1.5 Liter.						
Hatchback 2D	JT4K3	13905	5350	5700	6850	8775
Hatchback 4D	KT4K3	14205	5750	6125	7225	9175
Sedan 4D	BT4K3	14665	6025	6400	7500	9475
Manual, 5-Spd w/Overdrive			(475)	(475)	(625)	(625)
COROLLA—4-Cyl.—Equipment Schedule 6						
W.B. 102.4"; 1.8 Liter, 2.4 Liter.						
Sedan 4D	BU4EE	16070	7550	8000	9000	11100
S Sedan 4D	BU4EE	17140	8150	8625	9650	11900
XRS Sedan 4D	BE4EE	19580	9875	10400	11600	14250
Manual, 5-Spd w/Overdrive			(475)	(475)	(615)	(615)
COROLLA—4-Cyl.—Equipment Schedule 6						
W.B. 102.4"; 1.8 Liter.						
LE Sedan 4D	BU4EE	17470	8000	8475	9475	11700
XLE Sedan 4D	BU4EE	18370	9350	9850	10950	13450
PRIUS—4-Cyl. Hybrid—Equipment Schedule 3						
W.B. 106.3"; 1.8 Liter.						
I Hatchback 4D	KN3DU	22150	10550	11050	12000	14350
II Hatchback 4D	KN3DU	23150	10850	11400	12250	14550
III Hatchback 4D	KN3DU	24550	11500	12050	12950	15350
IV Hatchback 4D	KN3DU	27350	12850	13450	14250	16700
V Hatchback 4D	KN3DU	28820	13500	14100	14950	17450
MATRIX—4-Cyl.—Equipment Schedule 6						
W.B. 102.4"; 1.8 Liter, 2.4 Liter.						
Sport Wagon 4D	KU4EE	18110	7425	7850	9050	11300
XRS Sport Wagon 4D	ME4EE	21520	8775	9250	10450	12900
Manual, 5-Spd w/Overdrive			(475)	(475)	(610)	(610)
MATRIX—4-Cyl.—Equipment Schedule 6						
W.B. 102.4"; 2.4 Liter.						
S Sport Wagon 4D	KE4EE	19210	7875	8325	9425	11650
4WD			1200	1200	1520	1520
Automatic, 5-Spd			400	400	505	505
CAMRY—4-Cyl.—Equipment Schedule 4						
W.B. 109.3"; 2.5 Liter.						
Sedan 4D	BF3EK	21195	9175	9675	10700	13100
LE Sedan 4D	BF3EK	22650	9625	10150	11200	13650
SE Sedan 4D	BF3EK	23915	10550	11100	12150	14850

Body Type	VIN	List	Trade-In Good	Very Good	Pvt-Party Good	Retail Excellent
XLE Sedan 4D	BF3EK	26675	**11250**	**11800**	**12950**	**15750**
V6, 3.5 Liter	K		550	550	665	665
CAMRY—4-Cyl. Hybrid—Equipment Schedule 4						
W.B. 109.3"; 2.4 Liter.						
Sedan 4D	BB3EK	26900	**11700**	**12250**	**13400**	**15950**
AVALON—V6—Equipment Schedule 4						
W.B. 111.0"; 3.5 Liter.						
XL Sedan 4D	BK36B	28695	**10200**	**10750**	**11600**	**13900**
XLS Sedan 4D	BK36B	32995	**12550**	**13150**	**14200**	**17000**
Limited Sedan 4D	BK36B	36035	**13400**	**14050**	**15100**	**18000**

Body Type	VIN	List	Trade-In Good	Very Good	Pvt-Party Good	Retail Excellent
YARIS—4-Cyl.—Equipment Schedule 6						
W.B. 96.9", 100.4" (Sed); 1.5 Liter.						
Hatchback 2D	JT4KE	14415	**6275**	**6675**	**7800**	**9800**
Hatchback 4D	KT4K3	14017	**6125**	**6525**	**7675**	**9650**
Sedan 4D	BT4KE	15175	**6550**	**6950**	**8050**	**10050**
Manual, 5-Spd w/Overdrive			**(500)**	**(500)**	**(665)**	**(665)**
COROLLA—4-Cyl.—Equipment Schedule 6						
W.B. 102.4"; 1.8 Liter.						
Sedan 4D	BU4EE	16360	**8525**	**9000**	**9975**	**12100**
S Sedan 4D	BU4EE	18230	**9625**	**10100**	**11150**	**13450**
Manual, 5-Spd w/Overdrive			**(500)**	**(500)**	**(630)**	**(630)**
COROLLA—4-Cyl.—Equipment Schedule 6						
W.B. 102.4"; 1.8 Liter.						
LE Sedan 4D	BU4EE	18060	**8875**	**9350**	**10300**	**12450**
PRIUS—4-Cyl. Hybrid—Equipment Schedule 3						
W.B. 106.3"; 1.8 Liter.						
One Hatchback 4D	KN3DU	22410	**11800**	**12350**	**13300**	**15650**
Two Hatchback 4D	KN3DU	23810	**12150**	**12700**	**13600**	**15900**
Three Hatchback 4D	KN3DU	24810	**13250**	**13800**	**14800**	**17200**
Four Hatchback 4D	KN3DU	27610	**14600**	**15200**	**16100**	**18550**
Five Hatchback 4D	KN3DU	29080	**15800**	**16450**	**17250**	**19800**
MATRIX—4-Cyl.—Equipment Schedule 6						
W.B. 102.4"; 1.8 Liter.						
Sport Wagon 4D	KU4EE	20145	**9350**	**9800**	**10850**	**13000**
Manual, 5-Spd w/Overdrive			**(500)**	**(500)**	**(600)**	**(600)**
MATRIX—4-Cyl.—Equipment Schedule 6						
W.B. 102.4"; 2.4 Liter.						
S Sport Wagon 4D	KE4EE	20025	**9450**	**9900**	**10950**	**13100**
4WD	L		1400	1400	1685	1685
Automatic, 4-Spd			450	450	540	540
CAMRY—4-Cyl.—Equipment Schedule 4						
W.B. 109.3"; 2.5 Liter.						
Sedan 4D	BF3EK	21405	**10400**	**10900**	**11850**	**14200**
LE Sedan 4D	BF3EK	22860	**10650**	**11200**	**12100**	**14500**
SE Sedan 4D	BF3EK	24125	**11650**	**12250**	**13300**	**15900**
XLE Sedan 4D	BF3EK	26885	**12300**	**12900**	**14000**	**16800**
V6, 3.5 Liter	K		600	600	710	710
CAMRY—4-Cyl. Hybrid—Equipment Schedule 4						
W.B. 109.3"; 2.4 Liter.						
Sedan 4D	BB3EK	27160	**13400**	**14000**	**15100**	**17700**
AVALON—V6—Equipment Schedule 4						
W.B. 111.0"; 3.5 Liter.						
Sedan 4D	BK3DB	33005	**15750**	**16500**	**17300**	**20200**
Limited Sedan 4D	BK3DB	36245	**16850**	**17600**	**18400**	**21500**

Body Type	VIN	List	Trade-In Good	Very Good	Pvt-Party Good	Retail Excellent
YARIS—4-Cyl.—Equipment Schedule 6						
W.B. 98.8"; 1.5 Liter.						
L Hatchback 2D	JT4D3	15600	**7625**	**8050**	**9300**	**11500**
SE Hatchback 4D	KT4D3	17960	**9200**	**9700**	**10950**	**13350**
Manual, 5-Spd			**(500)**	**(500)**	**(650)**	**(650)**
YARIS—4-Cyl.—Equipment Schedule 6						
W.B. 98.8"; 1.5 Liter.						
L Hatchback 4D	KT4D3	15900	**7875**	**8325**	**9475**	**11600**
LE Hatchback 2D	JT4D3	16385	**8425**	**8875**	**10050**	**12250**
LE Hatchback 4D	KT4D3	16860	**8675**	**9150**	**10300**	**12600**
Sedan 4D	BT4K3	16120	**8075**	**8525**	**9700**	**11900**
COROLLA—4-Cyl.—Equipment Schedule 6						
W.B. 102.4"; 1.8 Liter.						
L Sedan 4D	BU4EE	16890	**9225**	**9700**	**10650**	**12800**

2012 TOYOTA

Body Type	VIN	List	Trade-In Good	Very Good	Pvt-Party Good	Retail Excellent
S Sedan 4D	BU4EE	18750	10300	10800	11800	14050
Manual, 5-Spd			(550)	(550)	(690)	(690)
COROLLA—4-Cyl.—Equipment Schedule 6						
W.B. 102.4"; 1.8 Liter.						
LE Sedan 4D	BU4EE	18670	9700	10200	11200	13350
PRIUS C—4-Cyl. Hybrid—Equipment Schedule 3						
W.B. 100.4"; 1.5 Liter.						
One Hatchback 4D	KDTB3	19710	11300	11750	12850	15050
Two Hatchback 4D	KDTB3	20660	11850	12350	13400	15650
Three Hatchback 4D	KDTB3	22395	12450	13000	14000	16250
Four Hatchback 4D	KDTB3	23565	13350	13900	14950	17250
PRIUS—4-Cyl. Hybrid—Equipment Schedule 3						
W.B. 106.3"; 1.8 Liter.						
One Hatchback 4D	KN3DU	23775	13250	13800	14800	17250
Two Hatchback 4D	KN3DU	24760	13550	14100	15200	17650
Three Hatchback 4D	KN3DU	26325	14300	14850	15900	18400
Four Hatchback 4D	KN3DU	28995	15850	16450	17400	19950
Five Hatchback 4D	KN3DU	30565	17950	18600	19500	22300
PRIUS PLUG-IN—4-Cyl. Hybrid—Equipment Schedule 3						
W.B. 106.3"; 1.8 Liter.						
Hatchback 4D	KN3DP	32760	16100	16700	17450	19800
Advanced H'Back 4D	KN3DP	40285	22200	22800	23500	26400
PRIUS V—4-Cyl. Hybrid—Equipment Schedule 3						
W.B. 109.4"; 1.8 Liter.						
Two Wagon 4D	ZN3EU	27160	14800	15400	16250	18600
Three Wagon 4D	ZN3EU	29225	15200	15800	16700	19100
Five Wagon 4D	ZN3EU	30750	16300	16900	17800	20300
Technology Pkg			1350	1350	1550	1550
MATRIX—4-Cyl.—Equipment Schedule 6						
W.B. 102.4"; 1.8 Liter.						
Sport Wagon 4D	KU4EE	20445	11200	11700	12750	14900
Manual, 5-Spd			(475)	(475)	(570)	(570)
MATRIX—4-Cyl.—Equipment Schedule 6						
W.B. 102.4"; 2.4 Liter.						
S Sport Wagon 4D	KE4EE	20325	11050	11500	12450	14600
AWD	L		1525	1525	1835	1835
Automatic, 4-Spd			550	550	660	660
CAMRY—4-Cyl.—Equipment Schedule 4						
W.B. 109.3"; 2.5 Liter.						
L Sedan 4D	BF1FK	22715	11550	12150	13150	15600
LE Sedan 4D	BF1FK	23260	11850	12400	13400	15900
SE Sedan 4D	BF1FK	23760	13100	13750	14750	17500
XLE Sedan 4D	BF1FK	25485	14450	15100	16250	19200
V6, 3.5 Liter	K		650	650	780	780
CAMRY—4-Cyl. Hybrid—Equipment Schedule 4						
W.B. 109.3"; 2.5 Liter.						
LE Sedan 4D	BD1FK	26660	15400	16000	17050	19550
XLE Sedan 4D	BD1FK	28160	17400	18050	19150	22100
AVALON—V6—Equipment Schedule 4						
W.B. 111.0"; 3.5 Liter.						
Sedan 4D	BK3DB	33955	16450	17150	18000	20800
Limited Sedan 4D	BK3DB	37195	18700	18600	19400	22400

2013 TOYOTA—(2,4,5orJ)T(1,4,DorF)(KTLD3)–D–#

Body Type	VIN	List	Trade-In Good	Very Good	Pvt-Party Good	Retail Excellent
YARIS—4-Cyl.—Equipment Schedule 6						
W.B. 98.8"; 1.5 Liter.						
SE Hatchback 4D	KTLD3	18075	9925	10450	11900	14600
L Hatchback 2D	JTLD3	15890	8525	9000	10300	12700
Manual, 5-Spd			(500)	(500)	(640)	(640)
YARIS—4-Cyl.—Equipment Schedule 6						
W.B. 98.8"; 1.5 Liter.						
L Hatchback 4D	KTLD3	16190	8775	9250	10450	12700
LE Hatchback 2D	JTLD3	16750	9025	9500	10950	13450
LE Hatchback 4D	KTLD3	17225	9275	9750	11250	13850
COROLLA—4-Cyl.—Equipment Schedule 6						
W.B. 102.4"; 1.8 Liter.						
L Sedan 4D	BU4EE	17855	10300	10800	11750	13950
S Sedan 4D	BU4EE	19855	11600	12200	13100	15450
Manual, 5-Spd			(500)	(500)	(615)	(615)
COROLLA—4-Cyl.—Equipment Schedule 6						
W.B. 102.4"; 1.8 Liter.						
LE Sedan 4D	BU4EE	18975	10950	11500	12400	14650

2013 TOYOTA

Body Type	VIN	List	Trade-In Good	Very Good	Pvt-Party Good	Retail Excellent
PRIUS C—4-Cyl. Hybrid—Equipment Schedule 3						
W.B. 100.4"; 1.5 Liter.						
One Hatchback 4D	KDTB3	19840	12300	12750	13900	16150
Two Hatchback 4D	KDTB3	20790	13050	13550	14750	17050
Three Hatchback 4D	KDTB3	24120	13950	14500	15600	17950
Four Hatchback 4D	KDTB3	24120	14750	15300	16350	18750
PRIUS—4-Cyl. Hybrid—Equipment Schedule 3						
W.B. 106.3"; 1.8 Liter.						
One Hatchback 4D	KN3DU	23975	14150	14700	15850	18250
Two Hatchback 4D	KN3DU	24960	14750	15300	16400	18850
Three Hatchback 4D	KN3DU	26525	15250	15850	16950	19450
Persona Spcl Ed 4D	KN3DU	27890	16700	17300	18350	21000
Four Hatchback 4D	KN3DU	29195	17350	17900	19000	21700
Five Hatchback 4D	KN3DU	30765	18950	19650	20600	23400
PRIUS PLUG-IN—4-Cyl. Hybrid—Equipment Schedule 3						
W.B. 106.3"; 1.8 Liter.						
Hatchback 4D	KN3DP	32760	17500	18100	18950	21400
Advanced Hatchback 4D	KN3DP	40285	22800	23500	24300	27300
PRIUS V—4-Cyl. Hybrid—Equipment Schedule 3						
W.B. 109.4"; 1.8 Liter.						
Two Wagon 4D	ZN3EU	27410	16550	17150	18000	20400
Three Wagon 4D	ZN3EU	28175	16950	17550	18450	20900
Five Wagon 4D	ZN3EU	31055	18250	18900	19750	22300
Technology Pkg			1400	1400	1585	1585
MATRIX—4-Cyl.—Equipment Schedule 6						
W.B. 102.4"; 1.8 Liter.						
L Sport Wagon 4D	KU4EE	20910	13050	13550	14550	16800
Manual, 5-Spd			(500)	(500)	(580)	(580)
MATRIX—4-Cyl.—Equipment Schedule 6						
W.B. 102.4"; 2.4 Liter.						
S Sport Wagon 4D	KE4EE	21060	13200	13700	14700	17000
Automatic, 4-Spd			500	500	580	580
AWD	L		1675	1675	1940	1940
CAMRY—4-Cyl.—Equipment Schedule 4						
W.B. 109.3"; 2.5 Liter.						
L Sedan 4D	BF1FK	22995	12700	13250	14300	16900
LE Sedan 4D	BF1FK	23440	13050	13650	14750	17400
CAMRY—4-Cyl.—Equipment Schedule 4						
W.B. 109.3"; 2.5 Liter.						
SE Sedan 4D	BF1FK	24160	13900	14500	15800	18700
XLE Sedan 4D	BF1FK	25615	15750	16450	17600	20600
V6, 3.5 Liter	K		700	700	840	840
CAMRY—4-Cyl. Hybrid—Equipment Schedule 4						
W.B. 109.3"; 2.5 Liter.						
LE Sedan 4D	BD1FK	26900	16700	17300	18300	20900
XLE Sedan 4D	BD1FK	28430	18150	18800	20000	22900
AVALON—4-Cyl. Hybrid—Equipment Schedule 4						
W.B. 111.0"; 2.5 Liter.						
XLE Premium Sedan	BD1EB	36350	22100	23000	23800	27200
XLE Touring Sedan	BD1EB	38045	22600	23500	24300	27800
Limited Sedan 4D	BD1EB	42195	22900	23900	24700	28500
AVALON—V6—Equipment Schedule 4						
W.B. 111.0"; 3.5 Liter.						
XLE Sedan 4D	BK1EB	31785	18000	18800	19700	22700
XLE Premium Sedan	BK1EB	33990	18850	19650	20400	23500
XLE Touring Sedan	BK1EB	36295	19700	20500	21400	24600
Limited Sedan 4D	BK1EB	40445	21100	21900	22700	26100
Dynamic Cruise Control			475	475	535	535

2014 TOYOTA—(2,4,5orJ)T(1,4,DorF)(KTUD3)—E—#

Body Type	VIN	List	Trade-In Good	Very Good	Pvt-Party Good	Retail Excellent
YARIS—4-Cyl.—Equipment Schedule 6						
W.B. 98.8"; 1.5 Liter.						
L Hatchback 4D	KTUD3	16265	9625	10100	11300	13600
LE Hatchback 2D	JTUD3	16825	9725	10250	11600	14100
LE Hatchback 4D	KTUD3	17300	10050	10600	11900	14450
YARIS—4-Cyl.—Equipment Schedule 6						
W.B. 98.8"; 1.5 Liter.						
L Hatchback 2D	JTUD3	15965	9375	9875	11150	13600
SE Hatchback 4D	KTUD3	18150	10750	11300	12600	15200
Manual, 5-Spd			(525)	(525)	(660)	(660)
COROLLA—4-Cyl.—Equipment Schedule 6						
W.B. 106.3"; 1.8 Liter.						
L Sedan 4D	BURHE	18195	11450	12000	13000	15300

2014 TOYOTA

Body Type	VIN	List	Trade-In Good	Very Good	Pvt-Party Good	Retail Excellent
LE Sedan 4D	BURHE	19095	12250	12800	13700	16050
LE Eco Sedan 4D	BPRHE	19495	12600	13200	14100	16500
LE Plus Sedan 4D	BURHE	19495	12600	13200	14150	16600
LE Eco Plus Sedan 4D	BPRHE	20195	13050	13650	14600	17050
LE Premium Sedan	BURHE	20195	13050	13650	14650	17150
LE Eco Premium 4D	20895	13650	14300	15200	17600
S Sedan 4D	BURHE	19795	12800	13350	14350	16700
S Premium Sedan 4D	BURHE	21195	13950	14600	15550	18050

COROLLA—4-Cyl.—Equipment Schedule 6
W.B. 102.4"; 1.8 Liter.

| S Plus Sedan 4D | BURHE | 20495 | 13300 | 13900 | 14900 | 17350 |
| Manual, 6-Spd | | | (525) | (525) | (625) | (625) |

PRIUS C—4-Cyl. Hybrid—Equipment Schedule 3
W.B. 100.4"; 1.5 Liter.

One Hatchback 4D	KDTB3	19890	13550	14050	15250	17650
Two Hatchback 4D	KDTB3	20840	14350	14900	16000	18450
Three Hatchback 4D	KDTB3	22575	15350	15900	17000	19450
Four Hatchback 4D	KDTB3	24170	16300	16850	17900	20400

PRIUS—4-Cyl. Hybrid—Equipment Schedule 3
W.B. 106.3"; 1.8 Liter.

One Hatchback 4D	KN3DU	24025	15200	15750	16850	19300
Two Hatchback 4D	KN3DU	25010	15950	16500	17550	20000
Three Hatchback 4D	KN3DU	26575	16300	16900	17950	20500
Four Hatchback 4D	KN3DU	29245	18600	19250	20200	22900
Five Hatchback 4D	KN3DU	30815	19950	20600	21600	24400

PRIUS V—4-Cyl. Hybrid—Equipment Schedule 3
W.B. 109.4"; 1.8 Liter.

Two Wagon 4D	ZN3EU	27560	18550	19200	20100	22700
Three Wagon 4D	ZN3EU	28325	18950	19600	20500	23100
Five Wagon 4D	ZN3EU	31205	20300	21000	21800	24500
Dynamic Cruise Control			500	500	560	560

PRIUS PLUG-IN—4-Cyl. Hybrid—Equipment Schedule 6
W.B. 106.3".

| Hatchback 4D | KN3DP | 30800 | 22400 | 23200 | 23700 | 26400 |
| Advanced Hatchback | KN3DP | 35715 | 27600 | 28500 | 28800 | 31800 |

CAMRY—4-Cyl.—Equipment Schedule 6
W.B. 109.3"; 2.5 Liter.

| L Sedan 4D | BF1FK | 23045 | 12850 | 13450 | 14750 | 17450 |
| LE Sedan 4D | BF1FK | 23490 | 13350 | 14000 | 15200 | 17950 |

CAMRY—4-Cyl.—Equipment Schedule 6
W.B. 109.3"; 2.5 Liter.

SE Sedan 4D	BF1FK	24210	14150	14800	15950	18750
SE Sport Sedan 4D	BF1FK	25900	15150	15800	16950	19850
XLE Sedan 4D	BF1FK	26620	16300	17000	18050	21000
V6, 3.5 Liter	K		750	750	895	895

CAMRY—4-Cyl. Hybrid—Equipment Schedule 4
W.B. 109.3"; 2.5 Liter.

LE Sedan 4D	BD1FK	26950	18750	19400	20300	22900
XLE Sedan 4D	BD1FK	29435	20700	21400	22100	24800
SE Sedan 4D	BD1FK	28755	19700	20400	21300	24100

AVALON—4-Cyl. Hybrid—Equipment Schedule 4
W.B. 111.0"; 2.5 Liter.

XLE Premium Sedan	BD1EB	36365	23500	24500	25200	28800
XLE Touring Sedan	BD1EB	37560	24000	25000	25700	29400
Limited Sedan 4D	BD1EB	42210	24400	25300	26200	30000

AVALON—V6—Equipment Schedule 4
W.B. 111.0"; 3.5 Liter.

XLE Sedan 4D	BK1EB	32150	19350	20200	21000	24100
XLE Premium Sedan	BK1EB	34005	20800	21700	22400	25500
XLE Touring Sedan	BK1EB	35810	21700	22600	23300	26600
Limited Sedan 4D	BK1EB	40460	22800	23800	24400	27900
Dynamic Cruise Control			500	500	560	560

VOLKSWAGEN

2000 VOLKSWAGEN — (3orW)VW(BC21J)-Y-#

GOLF—4-Cyl.—Equipment Schedule 6
W.B. 98.9"; 2.0 Liter.

| GL Hatchback 2D | BC21J | 15425 | 600 | 675 | 1225 | 2075 |
| GLS Hatchback 4D | GC21J | 16875 | 950 | 1075 | 1700 | 2850 |

2000 VOLKSWAGEN

Body Type	VIN	List	Trade-In Good	Very Good	Pvt-Party Good	Retail Excellent
GOLF—4-Cyl. Turbo—Equipment Schedule 6						
W.B. 98.9"; 1.8 Liter.						
GLS Hatchback 4D	GH21J	18425	**1150**	**1275**	**1950**	**3275**
GOLF—4-Cyl. Turbo Diesel—Equipment Schedule 6						
W.B. 98.9"; 1.9 Liter.						
GL TDI H'Back 2D	BF21J	16720	**1775**	**1950**	**2925**	**4775**
GLS TDI H'Back 4D	GF21J	17295	**2300**	**2525**	**3625**	**5800**
GTI—4-Cyl.—Equipment Schedule 6						
W.B. 98.9"; 2.0 Liter.						
GLS Hatchback 2D	DC21J	18200	**1000**	**1150**	**1775**	**3025**
GTI—4-Cyl. Turbo—Equipment Schedule 6						
W.B. 98.9"; 1.8 Liter.						
GLS Hatchback 2D	DH21J	19750	**1250**	**1425**	**2100**	**3525**
GTI—V6—Equipment Schedule 6						
W.B. 98.9"; 2.8 Liter.						
GLX Hatchback 2D	DE21J	23145	**1700**	**1925**	**2750**	**4600**
NEW BEETLE—4-Cyl.—Equipment Schedule 6						
W.B. 98.9"; 2.0 Liter.						
GL Hatchback 2D	BC21C	16425	**1225**	**1350**	**2150**	**3675**
GLS Hatchback 2D	CC21C	17375	**1075**	**1200**	**1950**	**3300**
NEW BEETLE—4-Cyl. Turbo—Equipment Schedule 6						
W.B. 98.9"; 1.8 Liter.						
GLS Hatchback 2D	CD21C	19525	**1175**	**1300**	**2075**	**3525**
GLX Hatchback 2D	DD21C	21600	**1175**	**1300**	**2175**	**3725**
NEW BEETLE—4-Cyl. Turbo Diesel—Equipment Schedule 6						
W.B. 98.9"; 1.9 Liter.						
GLS TDI H'Back 2D	CF21C	18425	**1325**	**1475**	**2225**	**3725**
JETTA—4-Cyl.—Equipment Schedule 6						
W.B. 98.9"; 2.0 Liter.						
GL Sedan 4D	RC29M	17225	**750**	**825**	**1425**	**2425**
GLS Sedan 4D	SC29M	18175	**875**	**975**	**1600**	**2700**
JETTA—4-Cyl. Turbo—Equipment Schedule 6						
W.B. 98.9"; 1.8 Liter.						
GLS Sedan 4D	SD29M	19725	**625**	**700**	**1275**	**2175**
JETTA—4-Cyl. Turbo Diesel—Equipment Schedule 6						
W.B. 98.9"; 1.9 Liter.						
GL TDI Sedan 4D	RF29M	18520	**1600**	**1775**	**2500**	**3950**
GLS TDI Sedan 4D	SF29M	19225	**1875**	**2075**	**2850**	**4475**
JETTA—V6—Equipment Schedule 6						
W.B. 98.9"; 2.8 Liter.						
GLS Sedan 4D	SE29M	20475	**900**	**1000**	**1650**	**2775**
GLX Sedan 4D	TE29M	24695	**1100**	**1225**	**1900**	**3175**
CABRIO—4-Cyl.—Equipment Schedule 3						
W.B. 97.4"; 2.0 Liter.						
GL Convertible 2D	CC21V	22015	**675**	**750**	**1375**	**2375**
GLS Convertible 2D	DC21V	24700	**875**	**975**	**1675**	**2850**
Manual, 5-Spd			**(100)**	**(100)**	**(135)**	**(135)**
PASSAT—4-Cyl. Turbo—Equipment Schedule 4						
W.B. 106.4"; 1.8 Liter.						
GLS Sedan 4D	MA23B	22800	**1075**	**1225**	**1625**	**2600**
GLS Wagon 4D	NA23B	23600	**1275**	**1450**	**1875**	**2975**
Manual, 5-Spd			**(175)**	**(175)**	**(235)**	**(235)**
V6, 2.8 Liter	D		**100**	**100**	**135**	**135**
PASSAT—V6—Equipment Schedule 4						
W.B. 106.4"; 2.8 Liter.						
GLX Sedan 4D	PD23B	29255	**2125**	**2400**	**3025**	**4725**
GLX Wagon 4D	VD23B	30055	**2100**	**2375**	**3000**	**4650**
Manual, 5-Spd			**(175)**	**(175)**	**(235)**	**(235)**
PASSAT 4MOTION AWD—V6—Equipment Schedule 4						
W.B. 106.4"; 2.8 Liter.						
GLS Sedan 4D	TH23B	27050	**2275**	**2575**	**3225**	**5000**
GLS Wagon 4D	RH23B	27850	**2325**	**2625**	**3300**	**5100**
GLX Sedan 4D	UH23B	30905	**2525**	**2850**	**3550**	**5475**
GLX Wagon 4D	WH23B	31705	**2550**	**2875**	**3575**	**5525**

2001 VOLKSWAGEN — (3orW)VW(BK21J)–1–#

Body Type	VIN	List	Trade-In Good	Very Good	Pvt-Party Good	Retail Excellent
GOLF—4-Cyl.—Equipment Schedule 6						
W.B. 98.9"; 2.0 Liter.						
GL Hatchback 2D	BK21J	15425	**850**	**975**	**1500**	**2475**
GLS Hatchback 4D	GK21J	16875	**1150**	**1300**	**1900**	**3100**
GOLF—4-Cyl. Turbo—Equipment Schedule 6						
W.B. 98.9"; 1.8 Liter.						
GLS Hatchback 4D	GC21J	18425	**1300**	**1475**	**2075**	**3400**

2001 VOLKSWAGEN

Body Type	VIN	List	Trade-In Good	Very Good	Pvt-Party Good	Retail Excellent
GOLF—4-Cyl. Turbo Diesel—Equipment Schedule 6						
W.B. 98.9"; 1.9 Liter.						
GL TDI H'Back 2D	BP21J	16720	2100	2325	3275	5225
GLS TDI H'Back 4D	GP21J	17925	2650	2950	3975	6225
GTI—4-Cyl. Turbo—Equipment Schedule 6						
W.B. 98.9"; 1.8 Liter.						
GLS Hatchback 2D	DC21J	19800	1350	1500	2175	3625
GTI—V6—Equipment Schedule 6						
W.B. 98.9"; 2.8 Liter.						
GLX Hatchback 2D	PG21J	23425	1775	1975	2825	4625
NEW BEETLE—4-Cyl.—Equipment Schedule 6						
W.B. 98.7"; 2.0 Liter.						
GL Hatchback 2D	BK21C	17325	1400	1550	2350	3950
GLS Hatchback 2D	CK21C	17375	1250	1375	2250	3850
NEW BEETLE—4-Cyl. Turbo—Equipment Schedule 6						
W.B. 98.7"; 1.8 Liter.						
GLS Hatchback 2D	CD21C	19550	1375	1525	2425	4125
Sport Hatchback 2D	ED21C	21175	1425	1575	2500	4275
GLX Hatchback 2D	DD21C	21775	1550	1700	2625	4450
NEW BEETLE—4-Cyl. Turbo Diesel—Equipment Schedule 6						
W.B. 98.7"; 1.9 Liter.						
GLS TDI H'Back 2D	CP21C	18425	1500	1650	2475	4025
JETTA—4-Cyl.—Equipment Schedule 6						
W.B. 98.9", 99.0" (Wag); 2.0 Liter.						
GL Sedan 4D	RK29M	18125	800	900	1525	2550
GLS Sedan 4D	SK29M	19075	1000	1125	1775	2975
GLS Wagon 4D	SK21J	19150	875	975	1625	2725
JETTA—4-Cyl. Turbo—Equipment Schedule 6						
W.B. 98.9"; 1.8 Liter.						
GLS Sedan 4D	SD29M	19725	925	1050	1700	2825
Wolfsburg Edition			25	25	35	35
JETTA—4-Cyl. Turbo Diesel—Equipment Schedule 6						
W.B. 98.9"; 1.9 Liter.						
GL TDI Sedan 4D	RP29M	18520	2025	2225	2875	4350
GLS TDI Sedan 4D	SP29M	19225	2425	2650	3375	5050
JETTA—V6—Equipment Schedule 6						
W.B. 98.9", 99.0" (Wag); 2.8 Liter.						
GLS Sedan 4D	SG29M	20475	1075	1200	1875	3125
GLS Wagon 4D	SG21J	21325	1275	1425	2125	3525
GLX Sedan 4D	TG29M	24825	1275	1425	2125	3525
GLX Wagon 4D	TG21J	25950	1375	1525	2250	3725
CABRIO—4-Cyl.—Equipment Schedule 3						
W.B. 97.4"; 2.0 Liter.						
GL Convertible 2D	BC21V	21625	750	850	1425	2400
GLS Convertible 2D	CC21V	22000	1000	1100	1750	2925
GLX Convertible 2D	DC21V	23700	1200	1325	2025	3350
Manual, 5-Spd			(175)	(175)	(235)	(235)
PASSAT—4-Cyl. Turbo—Equipment Schedule 4						
W.B. 106.4"; 1.8 Liter.						
GLS Sedan 4D	AD23B	23050	1200	1350	1800	2900
GLS Wagon 4D	HD23B	23850	1750	1975	2525	3950
Manual, 5-Spd			(200)	(200)	(265)	(265)
V6, 2.8 Liter	H		100	100	135	135
NEW PASSAT—4-Cyl. Turbo—Equipment Schedule 4						
W.B. 106.4"; 1.8 Liter.						
GLS Sedan 4D	PD23B	23375	1275	1450	2025	3350
GLS Wagon 4D	VD23B	24175	1400	1600	2175	3575
Manual, 5-Spd			(200)	(200)	(265)	(265)
V6, 2.8 Liter	H		100	100	135	135
PASSAT—V6—Equipment Schedule 4						
W.B. 106.4"; 2.8 Liter.						
GLX Sedan 4D	BH23B	29810	2375	2675	3275	5025
GLX Wagon 4D	JH23B	30610	2375	2675	3275	5025
Manual, 5-Spd			(200)	(200)	(265)	(265)
NEW PASSAT—V6—Equipment Schedule 4						
W.B. 106.4"; 2.8 Liter.						
GLX Sedan 4D	RD23B	30375	1800	2025	2800	4500
GLX Wagon 4D	WD23B	31175	2275	2575	3425	5425
Manual, 5-Spd			(200)	(200)	(265)	(265)
PASSAT 4MOTION AWD—V6—Equipment Schedule 4						
W.B. 106.4"; 2.8 Liter.						
GLS Sedan 4D	DH23B	27400	2475	2775	3375	5150
GLS Wagon 4D	KH23B	28200	2625	2950	3625	5525

2001 VOLKSWAGEN

Body Type	VIN	List	Trade-In Good	Trade-In Very Good	Pvt-Party Good	Retail Excellent
GLX Sedan 4D	EH23B	31560	2975	3350	4025	6075
GLX Wagon 4D	LH23B	32360	3025	3400	4075	6175
NEW PASSAT 4MOTION AWD—V6—Equipment Schedule 4						
W.B. 106.4"; 2.8 Liter.						
GLS Sedan 4D	SH23B	27625	1800	2025	2800	4500
GLS Wagon 4D	XH23B	28425	2100	2375	3200	5075
GLX Sedan 4D	TH23B	32125	2425	2725	3625	5725
GLX Wagon 4D	YH23B	32925	2725	3075	4025	6300

2002 VOLKSWAGEN–(3,9orW)(BorV)W(BK21J)–2–#

Body Type	VIN	List	Trade-In Good	Trade-In Very Good	Pvt-Party Good	Retail Excellent
GOLF—4-Cyl.—Equipment Schedule 6						
W.B. 98.9"; 2.0 Liter.						
GL Hatchback 2D	BK21J	15600	1050	1200	1825	3050
GL Hatchback 4D	FK21J	15800	1250	1400	2075	3450
GLS Hatchback 4D	GK21J	17150	1450	1625	2350	3850
GOLF—4-Cyl. Turbo Diesel—Equipment Schedule 6						
W.B. 98.9"; 1.9 Liter.						
GL TDI H'Back 2D	BP21J	16895	2300	2525	3425	5300
GL TDI H'Back 4D	FP21J	17095	2450	2700	3575	5500
GLS TDI H'Back 4D	GP21J	18200	2925	3225	4175	6325
GTI—4-Cyl. Turbo—Equipment Schedule 6						
W.B. 98.9"; 1.8 Liter.						
Hatchback 2D	DE61J	19460	1750	1975	2525	4000
337 Edition H'Back 2D	DE61J	22775	2075	2325	3100	4925
GTI VR6—V6—Equipment Schedule 6						
W.B. 98.9"; 2.8 Liter.						
Hatchback 2D	DH61J	20845	2025	2275	3050	4825
NEW BEETLE—4-Cyl.—Equipment Schedule 6						
W.B. 98.7"; 2.0 Liter.						
GL Hatchback 2D	BK21C	17325	1475	1625	2425	4025
GLS Hatchback 2D	CK21C	17400	1575	1725	2500	4150
NEW BEETLE—4-Cyl. Turbo—Equipment Schedule 6						
W.B. 98.7"; 1.8 Liter.						
GLS Hatchback 2D	CD21C	19750	1725	1875	2700	4450
Sport Hatchback 2D	ED21C	20800	1775	1925	2800	4650
GLX Hatchback 2D	DD21C	22050	1775	1975	2900	4750
S Hatchback 2D	FE21C	23905	1775	1975	2900	4750
NEW BEETLE—4-Cyl. Turbo Diesel—Equipment Schedule 6						
W.B. 98.7"; 1.9 Liter.						
GLS TDI H'Back 2D	CP21C	18450	1950	2150	3000	4725
JETTA—4-Cyl.—Equipment Schedule 6						
W.B. 98.9", 99.0" (Wag): 2.0 Liter.						
GL Sedan 4D	RK69M	18275	1075	1175	1875	3125
GL Wagon 4D	RK61J	19075	1075	1175	1875	3125
GLS Sedan 4D	SK69M	19325	1125	1300	2000	3325
GLS Wagon 4D	SK21J	19250	1125	1250	1925	3225
JETTA—4-Cyl. Turbo—Equipment Schedule 6						
W.B. 98.9", 99.0" (Wag): 1.8 Liter.						
GLS Sedan 4D	SE69M	20100	1075	1175	1875	3125
GLS Wagon 4D	SE21J	20900	1275	1400	2100	3500
JETTA—4-Cyl. Turbo Diesel—Equipment Schedule 6						
W.B. 98.9", 99.0" (Wag): 1.9 Liter.						
GL TDI Sedan 4D	RP69M	18695	2125	2350	3075	4675
GL TDI Wagon 4D	RP69M	19495	2300	2550	3275	4975
GLS TDI Sedan 4D	SP69M	19500	2650	2950	3725	5575
GLS TDI Wagon 4D	SP69M	20300	3150	3475	4325	6425
JETTA—V6—Equipment Schedule 6						
W.B. 98.9", 99.0" (Wag): 2.8 Liter.						
GLS Sedan 4D	SH69M	20750	1225	1350	2050	3425
GLS Wagon 4D	SH61J	21550	1425	1575	2300	3800
GLI Sedan 4D	VH69M	23500	1625	1775	2575	4200
GLX Sedan 4D	TH69M	25250	1625	1775	2575	4200
GLX Wagon 4D	TH61J	26050	1725	1900	2700	4375
CABRIO—4-Cyl.—Equipment Schedule 3						
W.B. 97.4"; 2.0 Liter.						
GL Convertible 2D	BC21V	21025	950	1050	1625	2675
GLS Convertible 2D	CC21V	22025	1200	1325	1950	3200
GLX Convertible 2D	DC21V	23725	1425	1575	2250	3650
Manual, 5-Spd.			(175)	(175)	(240)	(240)
PASSAT—4-Cyl. Turbo—Equipment Schedule 4						
W.B. 106.4"; 1.8 Liter.						
GLS Sedan 4D	PD63B	23375	1550	1725	2425	3975
GLS Wagon 4D	VD63B	24175	1600	1800	2575	4225

Body	Type	VIN	List	Trade-In Good	Very Good	Pvt-Party Good	Retail Excellent
Manual, 5-Spd				**(200)**	**(200)**	**(265)**	**(265)**
V6, 2.8 Liter		H		**150**	**150**	**200**	**200**

PASSAT—V6—Equipment Schedule 4
W.B. 106.4"; 2.8 Liter.

GLX Sedan 4D		RH63B	30375	**2125**	**2375**	**3300**	**5300**
GLX Wagon 4D		WH63B	31175	**2700**	**3025**	**4075**	**6475**
Manual, 5-Spd				**(200)**	**(200)**	**(265)**	**(265)**

PASSAT 4MOTION AWD—V6—Equipment Schedule 4
W.B. 106.4"; 2.8 Liter.

GLS Sedan 4D		SH63B	27625	**2350**	**2625**	**3600**	**5775**
GLS Wagon 4D		XH63B	28425	**2450**	**2725**	**3750**	**5975**
GLX Sedan 4D		TH63B	32125	**2875**	**3225**	**4300**	**6825**
GLX Wagon 4D		YH63B	32925	**3200**	**3575**	**4750**	**7475**

PASSAT 4MOTION AWD—W8—Equipment Schedule 4
W.B. 106.4"; 4.0 Liter.

Sedan 4D		UH63B	38450	**3275**	**3650**	**4450**	**6700**
Wagon 4D		ZH63B	39250	**3375**	**3775**	**4525**	**6800**

2003 VOLKSWAGEN — (3,9orW)(BorV)W(BK21J)-3-#

GOLF—4-Cyl.—Equipment Schedule 6
W.B. 98.9"; 2.0 Liter.

GL Hatchback 2D		BK21J	15870	**1275**	**1425**	**2150**	**3600**
GL Hatchback 4D		FK21J	16070	**1375**	**1525**	**2250**	**3775**
GLS Hatchback 4D		GK21J	18095	**1625**	**1825**	**2725**	**4450**

GOLF—4-Cyl. Turbo Diesel—Equipment Schedule 6
W.B. 98.9"; 1.9 Liter.

GL TDI H'Back 2D		BP21J	17295	**2775**	**3050**	**3975**	**6025**
GL TDI H'Back 4D		FP21J	17495	**2825**	**3100**	**3925**	**5850**
GLS TDI H'Back 4D		GP21J	19285	**3350**	**3675**	**4675**	**6850**

GTI—4-Cyl. Turbo—Equipment Schedule 6
W.B. 98.9"; 1.8 Liter.

Hatchback 2D		DE61J	19640	**2150**	**2400**	**2975**	**4500**
20th Anniv H'Back 2D		D61J	23800	**2700**	**3000**	**3700**	**5600**

GTI VR6—V6—Equipment Schedule 6
W.B. 98.9"; 2.8 Liter.

Hatchback 2D		DH61J	22570	**2700**	**3000**	**3700**	**5600**

NEW BEETLE—4-Cyl.—Equipment Schedule 6
W.B. 98.7", 98.8" (Conv); 2.0 Liter.

GL Hatchback 2D		BK21C	16525	**1525**	**1675**	**2475**	**4075**
GL Convertible 2D		BK21Y	22200	**2075**	**2275**	**3225**	**5100**
GLS Hatchback 2D		CK21C	18390	**1750**	**1925**	**2800**	**4475**
GLS Convertible 2D		CK21Y	22425	**1900**	**2075**	**2975**	**4750**
4-Cyl, Turbo, 1.8 Liter				**150**	**150**	**195**	**195**

NEW BEETLE—4-Cyl. Turbo—Equipment Schedule 6
W.B. 98.7", 98.8" (Conv); 1.8 Liter.

GLX Hatchback 2D		DE21C	22215	**1950**	**2125**	**3100**	**4950**
GLX Convertible 2D		DD21Y	26125	**2175**	**2375**	**3350**	**5300**
S Hatchback 2D		FE21C	24115	**2100**	**2300**	**3250**	**5125**

NEW BEETLE—4-Cyl. Turbo Diesel—Equipment Schedule 6
W.B. 98.7"; 1.9 Liter.

GL TDI H'Back 2D		BP21C	17770	**1925**	**2100**	**2875**	**4425**
GLS TDI H'Back 2D		CP21C	19570	**2500**	**2725**	**3550**	**5375**

JETTA—4-Cyl.—Equipment Schedule 6
W.B. 98.9", 99.0" (Wag); 2.0 Liter.

GL Sedan 4D		RK69M	18550	**1475**	**1625**	**2275**	**3700**
GL Wagon 4D		RK61J	19350	**1450**	**1575**	**2250**	**3650**
GLS Sedan 4D		SK66M	20240	**1575**	**1725**	**2400**	**3900**
GLS Wagon 4D		SK61J	20165	**1575**	**1725**	**2400**	**3900**
4-Cyl, Turbo, 1.8 Liter		E		**325**	**325**	**425**	**425**

JETTA—4-Cyl. Turbo—Equipment Schedule 6
W.B. 98.9", 99.0" (Wag); 1.8 Liter.

Wolfsburg Sedan 4D		PE69M	20075	**1500**	**1650**	**2325**	**3750**

JETTA—4-Cyl. Turbo Diesel—Equipment Schedule 6
W.B. 98.9", 99.0" (Wag); 1.9 Liter.

GL TDI Sedan 4D		RP69M	19065	**2650**	**2900**	**3600**	**5325**
GL TDI Wagon 4D		RP61J	19865	**2750**	**3025**	**3725**	**5500**
GLS TDI Sedan 4D		SP69M	20545	**3100**	**3400**	**4125**	**6050**
GLS TDI Wagon 4D		SP61J	21345	**3425**	**3750**	**4675**	**6800**

JETTA—V6—Equipment Schedule 6
W.B. 98.9"; 2.8 Liter.

GLI Sedan 4D		VH69M	23525	**2100**	**2325**	**3225**	**5050**
GLX Sedan 4D		TH69M	27515	**2350**	**2600**	**3550**	**5550**

2003 VOLKSWAGEN

Body Type	VIN	List	Trade-In Good	Very Good	Pvt-Party Good	Retail Excellent
PASSAT—4-Cyl. Turbo—Equipment Schedule 4						
W.B. 106.4"; 1.8 Liter.						
GL Sedan 4D	MD63B	23400	1050	1175	1775	2925
GL Wagon 4D	ND63B	24200	1225	1375	1975	3250
GLS Sedan 4D	PD63B	24535	1600	1800	2575	4150
GLS Wagon 4D	VD63B	27835	1725	1925	2725	4375
Manual, 5-Spd			(250)	(250)	(335)	(335)
V6, 2.8 Liter	H		200	200	265	265
PASSAT—V6—Equipment Schedule 4						
W.B. 106.4"; 2.8 Liter.						
GLX Sedan 4D	RH63B	30400	2275	2550	3475	5500
GLX Wagon 4D	WH63B	31200	2825	3175	4200	6575
Manual, 5-Spd			(250)	(250)	(335)	(335)
PASSAT 4MOTION AWD—V6—Equipment Schedule 4						
W.B. 106.4"; 2.8 Liter.						
GLX Sedan 4D	TH63B	32150	3025	3375	4450	6950
GLX Wagon 4D	YH63B	32950	3375	3750	4925	7650
PASSAT 4MOTION AWD—W8—Equipment Schedule 4						
W.B. 106.4"; 4.0 Liter.						
Sedan 4D	UK63B	38475	3850	4275	5350	8050
Wagon 4D	ZK63B	39275	4050	4500	5600	8400

2004 VOLKSWAGEN–(W,3or9)(VorB)W(BK21J)–4–#

Body Type	VIN	List	Trade-In Good	Very Good	Pvt-Party Good	Retail Excellent
GOLF—4-Cyl.—Equipment Schedule 6						
W.B. 98.9"; 2.0 Liter.						
GL Hatchback 2D	BK21J	16155	1400	1575	2375	3900
GL Hatchback 4D	FK21J	16355	1550	1750	2525	4075
GLS Hatchback 4D	GK21J	18715	1825	2050	2925	4650
GOLF—4-Cyl. Turbo Diesel—Equipment Schedule 6						
W.B. 98.9"; 1.9 Liter.						
GL TDI H'Back 4D	FP21J	17775	3075	3375	4350	6375
GLS TDI H'Back 4D	GP21J	19895	3625	3950	5000	7250
GTI—4-Cyl. Turbo—Equipment Schedule 6						
W.B. 98.9"; 1.8 Liter.						
Hatchback 2D	DE61J	19825	2650	2925	3600	5350
GTI VR6—V6—Equipment Schedule 6						
W.B. 98.9"; 2.8 Liter.						
Hatchback 2D	DH61J	22645	3400	3750	4500	6600
R32 AWD—V6—Equipment Schedule 3						
W.B. 99.1"; 3.2 Liter.						
Hatchback 2D	KG61J	29675	7800	8450	8975	11700
NEW BEETLE—4-Cyl.—Equipment Schedule 6						
W.B. 98.7", 98.8" (Conv); 2.0 Liter.						
GL Hatchback 2D	BK21C	17780	1725	1900	2775	4425
GL Convertible 2D	BK21Y	22650	2250	2475	3500	5475
GLS Hatchback 2D	CK21C	19095	1975	2175	3100	4875
GLS Convertible 2D	CK21Y	23215	2200	2400	3350	5200
4-Cyl, Turbo, 1.8 Liter	D		150	150	215	215
NEW BEETLE—4-Cyl. Turbo—Equipment Schedule 6						
W.B. 98.7"; 1.8 Liter.						
S Hatchback 2D	FE21C	24425	3100	3400	4275	6325
NEW BEETLE—4-Cyl. Turbo Diesel—Equipment Schedule 6						
W.B. 98.7"; 1.9 Liter.						
GL TDI H'Back 2D	BP21C	18205	2200	2425	3225	4900
GLS TDI H'Back 2D	CP21C	20335	2825	3125	3950	5850
JETTA—4-Cyl.—Equipment Schedule 6						
W.B. 98.9", 99.0" (Wag); 2.0 Liter.						
GL Sedan 4D	RK29M	18880	1675	1825	2550	4000
GL Wagon 4D	RK61J	19880	1750	1925	2725	4325
GLS Sedan 4D	SK29M	20910	1975	2150	3025	4725
GLS Wagon 4D	SK21J	21035	1800	1975	2800	4425
4-Cyl, Turbo, 1.8 Liter	E		350	350	475	475
JETTA—4-Cyl. Turbo—Equipment Schedule 6						
W.B. 98.9"; 1.8 Liter.						
GLI Sedan 4D	VH69M	23785	2750	3025	4000	6125
V6, 2.8 Liter	H		100	100	140	140
JETTA—4-Cyl. Turbo Diesel—Equipment Schedule 6						
W.B. 98.9", 99.0" (Wag); 1.9 Liter.						
GL TDI Sedan 4D	RP29M	19245	2950	3225	3875	5600
GL TDI Wagon 4D	RP21J	20245	3050	3325	3975	5750
GLS TDI Sedan 4D	SP69M	21055	3275	3575	4250	6125
GLS TDI Wagon 4D	SP61J	22055	3650	3975	4850	6900

2004 VOLKSWAGEN

Body Type	VIN	List	Trade-In Good	Very Good	Pvt-Party Good	Retail Excellent
PASSAT—4-Cyl. Turbo—Equipment Schedule 4						
W.B. 106.4"; 1.8 Liter.						
GL Sedan 4D	MD63B	23430	1200	1350	1925	3150
GL Wagon 4D	ND63B	24430	1450	1625	2250	3625
GLS Sedan 4D	PD63B	25030	1925	2150	2925	4625
GLS Wagon 4D	VD63B	26030	2075	2300	3125	4900
Manual, 5-Spd			(300)	(300)	(400)	(400)
PASSAT 4MOTION AWD—4-Cyl. Turbo—Equipment Schedule 4						
W.B. 106.4"; 1.8 Liter.						
GLS Sedan 4D	PD63B	26780	2950	3275	4250	6550
GLS Wagon 4D	VD63B	27780	3250	3625	4800	7325
Manual, 5-Spd			(300)	(300)	(400)	(400)
PASSAT—4-Cyl. Turbo Diesel—Equipment Schedule 4						
W.B. 106.4"; 2.0 Liter.						
GL TDI Sedan 4D	ME63B	23635	3725	4125	4625	6425
GL TDI Wagon 4D	NE63B	24635	3825	4250	4725	6575
GLS TDI Sedan 4D	PE63B	25235	4900	5400	5925	8175
GLS TDI Wagon 4D	VE63B	26235	5050	5550	6100	8400
Manual, 5-Spd			(300)	(300)	(400)	(400)
PASSAT—V6—Equipment Schedule 4						
W.B. 106.4"; 2.8 Liter.						
GLX Sedan 4D	RH63B	31430	2800	3125	4075	6275
GLX Wagon 4D	WH63B	32430	3475	3850	5100	7750
Manual, 5-Spd			(300)	(300)	(400)	(400)
PASSAT 4MOTION AWD—V6—Equipment Schedule 4						
W.B. 106.4"; 2.8 Liter.						
GLX Sedan 4D	TH63B	33180	3600	4000	5250	7975
GLX Wagon 4D	YH63B	34180	4000	4425	5775	8725
PASSAT 4MOTION AWD—W8—Equipment Schedule 4						
W.B. 106.4"; 4.0 Liter.						
Sedan 4D	UK63B	39235	4825	5300	6050	8550
Wagon 4D	ZK63B	40235	5025	5525	6325	8925
Sport Pkg			175	175	225	225
PHAETON AWD—V8—Equipment Schedule 1						
W.B. 118.1"; 4.2 Liter.						
Sedan 4D	AF63D	65215	4600	4950	5550	7300
4-Passenger Seating			275	275	340	340
W12, 6.0 Liter	H		2000	2000	2510	2510

2005 VOLKSWAGEN—(W,3or9)(VorB)W(BL61J)-5-#

Body Type	VIN	List	Trade-In Good	Very Good	Pvt-Party Good	Retail Excellent
GOLF—4-Cyl.—Equipment Schedule 6						
W.B. 98.9"; 2.0 Liter.						
GL Hatchback 2D	BL61J	15830	1475	1650	2575	4050
GL Hatchback 4D	FL61J	16030	1525	1700	2675	4225
GLS Hatchback 4D	GL61J	18390	1925	2150	3100	4775
GOLF—4-Cyl. Turbo Diesel—Equipment Schedule 6						
W.B. 98.9"; 1.9 Liter.						
GL TDI H'Back 4D	FR61J	17450	3300	3600	4700	6775
GLS TDI H'Back 4D	GR61J	19580	4000	4325	5350	7475
GTI—4-Cyl. Turbo—Equipment Schedule 6						
W.B. 98.9"; 1.8 Liter.						
Hatchback 2D	DE61J	19510	2950	3275	4150	6100
GTI VR6—V6—Equipment Schedule 6						
W.B. 98.9"; 2.8 Liter.						
Hatchback 2D	DH61J	22330	3650	4025	5100	7350
NEW BEETLE—4-Cyl.—Equipment Schedule 6						
W.B. 98.7", 98.8" (Conv); 2.0 Liter.						
GL Hatchback 2D	BK31C	18220	2050	2250	3200	4875
GL Convertible 2D	BM31Y	22940	2700	2975	4025	6050
GLS Hatchback 2D	CK31C	19945	2350	2575	3550	5350
GLS Convertible 2D	CM31Y	23615	2500	2750	3750	5600
Bi-Color H'Back 2D	CK31C	21360	2550	2800	3800	5700
Dark Flint Ed Conv	CM31Y	26405	2550	2800	3800	5700
4-Cyl, Turbo, 1.8 Liter	D		175	175	230	230
NEW BEETLE—4-Cyl. Turbo Diesel—Equipment Schedule 6						
W.B. 98.7"; 1.9 Liter.						
GLS TDI H'Back 2D	CR31C	20585	2850	3125	4100	6025
JETTA—4-Cyl.—Equipment Schedule 6						
W.B. 98.9", 99.0" (Wag); 2.0 Liter.						
GL Sedan 4D	RK69M	19130	1825	2000	2875	4375
GL Wagon 4D	RL61J	20130	2050	2250	3125	4725
GLS Sedan 4D	SK69M	21170	2300	2525	3450	5150
GLS Wagon 4D	SL61J	21295	2150	2375	3250	4900

Body Type	VIN	List	Trade-In Good	Very Good	Pvt-Party Good	Retail Excellent
4-Cyl, Turbo, 1.8 Liter .... E			400	400	520	520
JETTA—4-Cyl. Turbo—Equipment Schedule 6						
W.B. 98.9", 99.0" (Wag); 1.8 Liter.						
GLI Sedan 4D SE69M	24645		3200	3500	4550	6650
JETTA—4-Cyl. Turbo Diesel—Equipment Schedule 6						
W.B. 98.9", 99.0" (Wag); 1.9 Liter.						
GL TDI Wagon 4D RR61J	20505		3150	3450	4225	5975
GLS TDI Sedan 4D SR69M	21315		3350	3650	4450	6250
GLS TDI Wagon 4D SR61J	22315		3725	4050	5000	7000
NEW JETTA—5-Cyl.—Equipment Schedule 6						
W.B. 101.5"; 2.5 Liter.						
Value Edition Sed 4D PF71K	18515		2450	2700	3575	5250
2.5 Sedan 4D SF71K	21005		2950	3250	4125	5950
Package #1			200	200	255	255
Package #2			400	400	525	525
NEW JETTA—4-Cyl. Turbo Diesel—Equipment Schedule 6						
W.B. 101.5"; 1.9 Liter.						
TDI Sedan 4D RT71K	22000		3625	3975	4975	7025
Package #1			200	200	255	255
Package #2			400	400	525	525
PASSAT—4-Cyl. Turbo—Equipment Schedule 4						
W.B. 106.4"; 1.8 Liter.						
GL Sedan 4D MD63B	23760		1450	1625	2275	3525
GL Wagon 4D ND63B	24760		1675	1875	2625	4025
GLS Sedan 4D AD63B	26030		2200	2450	3275	4900
GLS Wagon 4D CD63B	27030		2350	2625	3450	5150
Manual, 5-Spd			(350)	(350)	(465)	(465)
PASSAT 4MOTION AWD—4-Cyl. Turbo—Equipment Schedule 4						
W.B. 106.4"; 1.8 Liter.						
GLS Sedan 4D BD63B	27780		3300	3675	4725	6925
GLS Wagon 4D DD63B	28780		3800	4200	5325	7750
Manual, 5-Spd			(350)	(350)	(465)	(465)
PASSAT—4-Cyl. Turbo Diesel—Equipment Schedule 4						
W.B. 106.4"; 2.0 Liter.						
GL TDI Sedan 4D ME63B	23935		4175	4625	5150	6950
GL TDI Wagon 4D NE63B	24935		4275	4725	5250	7100
GLS TDI Sedan 4D AE63B	26235		5250	5775	6525	8750
GLS TDI Wagon 4D CE63B	27235		5550	6100	6850	9175
PASSAT—V6—Equipment Schedule 4						
W.B. 106.4"; 2.8 Liter.						
GLX Sedan 4D RU63B	31440		3325	3700	4775	6975
GLX Wagon 4D WU63B	32440		4250	4675	5875	8500
Manual, 5-Spd			(350)	(350)	(465)	(465)
PASSAT 4MOTION AWD—V6—Equipment Schedule 4						
W.B. 106.4"; 2.8 Liter.						
GLX Sedan 4D TU63B	33190		4300	4725	5925	8575
GLX Wagon 4D YU63B	34190		4800	5250	6550	9425
PHAETON—V8—Equipment Schedule 1						
W.B. 118.1"; 4.2 Liter.						
Sedan 4D AF93D	68865		4550	4900	5775	7650
4-Passenger Seating			300	300	400	400
W12, 6.0 Liter .... H			2325	2325	3110	3110

2006 VOLKSWAGEN—(W,3or9)(VorB)W(BR71K)-6-#

Body Type	VIN	List	Trade-In Good	Very Good	Pvt-Party Good	Retail Excellent
RABBIT—5-Cyl.—Equipment Schedule 6						
W.B. 101.5"; 2.5 Liter.						
Hatchback 2D BR71K	16695		2825	3150	3850	5450
Hatchback 4D DR71K	18695		3300	3625	4500	6325
Manual, 5-Spd .... A			(275)	(275)	(365)	(365)
GOLF—4-Cyl.—Equipment Schedule 6						
W.B. 98.9"; 2.0 Liter.						
GL Hatchback 4D FL61J	16645		1950	2175	3150	4675
GLS Hatchback 4D GL61J	19005		2700	3000	3875	5675
GOLF—4-Cyl. Turbo Diesel—Equipment Schedule 6						
W.B. 98.9"; 1.9 Liter.						
GLS TDI H'Back 4D GR61J	20195		5125	5525	6650	8875
GTI—4-Cyl. Turbo—Equipment Schedule 6						
W.B. 98.9", 101.5"; 1.8 Liter, 2.0 Liter.						
1.8T Hatchback 2D DE61J	20955		3475	3825	4800	6800
2.0T Hatchback 2D EV71K	22620		4425	4825	5850	8200
Package #2			750	750	985	985
NEW BEETLE—5-Cyl.—Equipment Schedule 6						
W.B. 98.7", 98.8" (Conv); 2.5 Liter.						

2006 VOLKSWAGEN

Body Type	VIN	List	Trade-In Good	Very Good	Pvt-Party Good	Retail Excellent
2.5 Hatchback 2D	PF31C	18870	2625	2900	4050	6025
2.5 Convertible 2D	PF31Y	23610	3475	3800	4875	6975
Package #1			200	200	270	270
Package #2			425	425	550	550
Manual, 5-Spd			(275)	(275)	(365)	(365)
NEW BEETLE—4-Cyl. Turbo Diesel—Equipment Schedule 6						
W.B. 98.7"; 1.9 Liter.						
TDI Hatchback 2D	PR31C	19005	3050	3350	4425	6350
Package #1	R		200	200	270	270
Package #2	S		425	425	550	550
JETTA—5-Cyl.—Equipment Schedule 6						
W.B. 101.5"; 2.5 Liter.						
2.5 Value Ed Sedan	PF71K	15990	3025	3325	4300	6125
2.5 Sedan 4D	RF71K	21980	3350	3675	4650	6575
Package #1	S		200	200	270	270
Package #2	D		425	425	550	550
Manual, 5-Spd			(275)	(275)	(365)	(365)
JETTA—4-Cyl. Turbo—Equipment Schedule 6						
W.B. 101.5"; 2.0 Liter.						
2.0T Sedan 4D	AJ71K	25080	3975	4325	5350	7475
Package #1	K		200	200	270	270
Package #2	M		425	425	550	550
Package #3	N		600	600	795	795
Manual, 6-Spd			(300)	(300)	(400)	(400)
Manual, 6-Spd			(300)	(300)	(400)	(400)
JETTA—4-Cyl. Turbo—Equipment Schedule 6						
W.B. 101.5"; 2.0 Liter.						
GLI Sedan 4D	TJ71K	24405	3775	4100	5200	7375
Package #1	K		200	200	270	270
Package #2	M		425	425	550	550
JETTA—4-Cyl. Turbo Diesel—Equipment Schedule 6						
W.B. 101.5"; 1.9 Liter.						
TDI Sedan 4D	RT71K	22980	5250	5650	6475	8600
TDI Special Ed Sedan	FT71K	22980	5975	6425	7500	9950
Package #1			200	200	270	270
Package #2			425	425	550	550
Manual, 5-Spd			(275)	(275)	(365)	(365)
PASSAT—4-Cyl. Turbo—Equipment Schedule 4						
W.B. 106.7"; 2.0 Liter.						
2.0T Value Ed Sedan	AK73C	24640	3025	3375	4050	5725
2.0T Sedan 4D	AK73C	25590	3325	3700	4350	6075
Luxury Pkg			725	725	980	980
PASSAT—V6—Equipment Schedule 4						
W.B. 106.7"; 3.6 Liter.						
3.6 Sedan 4D	AU73C	30565	4625	5075	6125	8550
Luxury Pkg			725	725	980	980
PASSAT 4MOTION AWD—V6—Equipment Schedule 4						
W.B. 106.4"; 3.6 Liter.						
3.6 Sedan 4D	BU73C	32515	5500	6000	7325	10100
Luxury Pkg			725	725	980	980
PHAETON—V8—Equipment Schedule 1						
W.B. 118.1"; 4.2 Liter.						
Sedan 4D	AF03D	68655	6425	6825	7700	9675
4-Passenger Seating			375	375	455	455
W12, 6.0 Liter	K		2675	2675	3305	3305

2007 VOLKSWAGEN–(W,3or9)(VorB)W(BR71K)–7–#

Body Type	VIN	List	Trade-In Good	Very Good	Pvt-Party Good	Retail Excellent
RABBIT—5-Cyl.—Equipment Schedule 6						
W.B. 101.5"; 2.5 Liter.						
Hatchback 2D	BR71K	16705	3550	3875	4800	6600
Hatchback 4D	DR71K	18825	4050	4400	5375	7400
Manual, 5-Spd	A		(300)	(300)	(400)	(400)
GTI—4-Cyl. Turbo—Equipment Schedule 6						
W.B. 101.5"; 2.0 Liter.						
2.0T Hatchback 2D	EV71K	22730	5200	5625	6700	9025
Package #2			775	775	1040	1040
Automatic DSG w/Tiptronic			300	300	400	400
GTI—4-Cyl. Turbo—Equipment Schedule 6						
W.B. 101.5"; 2.0 Liter.						
2.0T Hatchback 4D	HV71K	24305	5775	6250	7275	9600
Package #2			775	775	1040	1040
Manual, 6-Spd	G		(350)	(350)	(465)	(465)

2007 VOLKSWAGEN

Body Type	VIN	List	Trade-In Good	Very Good	Pvt-Party Good	Retail Excellent
EOS—4-Cyl. Turbo—Equipment Schedule 3						
W.B. 101.5"; 2.0 Liter.						
Hardtop Conv 2D	AA71F	28620	4650	5125	5750	7725
2.0T Hardtop Conv 2D	DA71F	31825	4775	5250	5900	7950
EOS—V6—Equipment Schedule 3						
W.B. 101.5"; 3.2 Liter.						
3.2L Hardtop Conv 2D	DB71F	37480	6275	6850	7475	9675
NEW BEETLE—5-Cyl.—Equipment Schedule 6						
W.B. 98.7"; 98.8" (Conv); 2.5 Liter.						
2.5 Hatchback 2D	PW31C	18885	3175	3475	4500	6400
2.5 Convertible 2D	PF31Y	23825	3975	4300	5400	7550
Package #1			200	200	280	280
Package #2			425	425	575	575
Triple White Ed (Conv)			400	400	540	540
Manual, 5-Spd			(300)	(300)	(400)	(400)
JETTA—5-Cyl.—Equipment Schedule 6						
W.B. 101.5"; 2.5 Liter.						
Sedan 4D	GF71K	19690	3700	4025	4950	6825
2.5 Sedan 4D	PF71K	19695	3975	4300	5275	7275
Wolfsburg Ed Sedan	EF71K	21175	4800	5150	6125	8300
Package #1			200	200	280	280
Package #2			425	425	575	575
Manual, 5-Spd			(300)	(300)	(400)	(400)
JETTA—4-Cyl. Turbo—Equipment Schedule 6						
W.B. 101.5"; 2.0 Liter.						
2.0T Sedan 4D	AJ71K	23695	4900	5275	6225	8400
Package #1			200	200	280	280
Package #2			425	425	575	575
Manual, 6-Spd			(350)	(350)	(465)	(465)
JETTA—4-Cyl. Turbo—Equipment Schedule 6						
W.B. 101.5"; 2.0 Liter.						
GLI Sedan 4D	TJ71K	24620	5925	6350	7375	9700
Package #1			200	200	280	280
Package #2			425	425	575	575
Automatic w/Tiptronic			300	300	400	400
PASSAT—4-Cyl. Turbo—Equipment Schedule 4						
W.B. 106.7"; 2.0 Liter.						
Sedan 4D	JK73C	24665	2750	3075	3850	5425
Wagon 4D	XK73C	26085	3800	4175	4850	6550
2.0T Sedan 4D	AK73C	25665	3975	4350	5075	6850
2.0T Value Ed Wag 4D	LK73C	25855	3975	4350	5125	6925
2.0T Wagon 4D	LK73C	26805	4050	4425	5100	6850
2.0T Wolfsburg Ed Sed	AK73C	27630	4775	5200	6075	8225
Luxury Pkg			775	775	1050	1050
Sport Pkg			825	825	1110	1110
PASSAT—V6—Equipment Schedule 4						
W.B. 106.7"; 3.6 Liter.						
3.6 Sedan 4D	AU73C	30590	6550	7075	8100	10750
3.6 Wagon 4D	LU73C	31790	8275	8900	10200	13550
Luxury Pkg			775	775	1050	1050
Sport Pkg			825	825	1110	1110
PASSAT 4MOTION AWD—V6—Equipment Schedule 4						
W.B. 106.7"; 3.6 Liter.						
3.6 Sedan 4D	BU73C	32540	7325	7900	9000	11850
3.6 Wagon 4D	MU73C	33740	8800	9450	10800	14200
Luxury Pkg			775	775	1050	1050
Sport Pkg			825	825	1110	1110

2008 VOLKSWAGEN—(W,3or9)(VorB)W(BA71K)-8-#

Body Type	VIN	List	Trade-In Good	Very Good	Pvt-Party Good	Retail Excellent
RABBIT—5-Cyl.—Equipment Schedule 6						
W.B. 101.5"; 2.5 Liter.						
Hatchback 2D	BA71K	17205	4300	4650	5625	7600
Hatchback 4D	DA71K	19200	4775	5150	6200	8375
Manual, 5-Spd w/Overdrive	A		(350)	(350)	(470)	(470)
GTI—4-Cyl. Turbo—Equipment Schedule 6						
W.B. 101.5"; 2.0 Liter.						
2.0T Hatchback 2D	EV71K	24445	5975	6400	7425	9650
Automatic, 6-Spd	F		300	300	400	400
4-Cyl, PZEV, 2.0 Liter	D		0	0	0	0
GTI—4-Cyl. Turbo—Equipment Schedule 6						
W.B. 101.5"; 2.0 Liter.						
2.0T Hatchback 4D	HV71K	24945	7100	7600	8725	11250
Manual, 6-Spd w/OD	G		(375)	(375)	(495)	(495)

2008 VOLKSWAGEN

Body Type	VIN	List	Trade-In Good	Very Good	Pvt-Party Good	Retail Excellent
4-Cyl, PZEV, 2.0 Liter	D		0	0	0	0
EOS—4-Cyl. Turbo—Equipment Schedule 3						
W.B. 101.5"; 2.0 Liter.						
Hardtop Conv 2D	AA71F	30630	5650	6125	6725	8550
Komfort HT Conv 2D	BA71F	32280	5750	6250	6875	8750
LUX Hardtop Conv 2D	FA71F	35630	7200	7800	8425	10600
EOS—V6—Equipment Schedule 3						
W.B. 101.5"; 3.2 Liter.						
VR6 Hardtop Conv 2D	DB71F	38630	7400	7975	8650	10900
NEW BEETLE—5-Cyl.—Equipment Schedule 6						
W.B. 98.8"; 2.5 Liter.						
S Hatchback 2D	PW31C	19080	3925	4250	5275	7200
S Convertible 2D	PF31Y	24840	5375	5775	6900	9050
Package #1			225	225	295	295
Manual, 5-Spd w/Overdrive			(350)	(350)	(470)	(470)
NEW BEETLE—5-Cyl.—Equipment Schedule 6						
W.B. 98.8"; 2.5 Liter.						
SE Hatchback 2D	RW31C	21080	5250	5625	6625	8775
SE Convertible 2D	RF31Y	26265	5850	6275	7325	9525
Triple White Pkg			125	125	175	175
GLI—4-Cyl. Turbo—Equipment Schedule 4						
W.B. 101.5"; 2.0 Liter.						
2.0T Sedan 4D	BJ71K	25945	8225	8725	9650	12050
JETTA—5-Cyl.—Equipment Schedule 6						
W.B. 101.5"; 2.5 Liter.						
S Sedan 4D	JM71K	18705	4125	4450	5400	7275
SE Sedan 4D	RM71K	21475	5275	5650	6575	8675
Manual, 5-Spd w/Overdrive			(350)	(350)	(470)	(470)
JETTA—4-Cyl. Turbo—Equipment Schedule 6						
W.B. 101.5"; 2.5 Liter.						
SEL Sedan 4D	RM71K	23465	6050	6450	7550	9825
JETTA—4-Cyl. Turbo—Equipment Schedule 6						
W.B. 101.5"; 2.0 Liter.						
Wolfsburg Ed Sedan	RJ71A	22600	6450	6875	7925	10200
Manual, 6-Spd w/Overdrive			(375)	(375)	(500)	(500)
R32—V6—Equipment Schedule 3						
W.B. 101.5"; 3.2 Liter.						
Hatchback 2D	KC71K	33630	11000	11650	12300	14950
PASSAT—4-Cyl. Turbo—Equipment Schedule 4						
W.B. 106.7"; 2.0 Liter.						
Sedan 4D	JK73C	25630	3450	3750	4275	5550
Wagon 4D	XK73C	26830	4300	4675	5275	6775
Komfort Sedan 4D	AK73C	28430	5275	5675	6325	7925
Komfort Wagon 4D	LK73C	29630	7075	7575	8375	10450
LUX Sedan 4D	EK73C	30630	6325	6775	7450	9325
LUX Wagon 4D	TK73C	31830	8700	9275	10100	12550
PASSAT—V6—Equipment Schedule 4						
W.B. 106.7"; 3.6 Liter.						
VR6 Sedan 4D	CU73C	36630	7575	8100	9075	11500
PASSAT 4MOTION AWD—V6—Equipment Schedule 4						
W.B. 106.7"; 3.6 Liter.						
VR6 Sedan 4D	DU73C	38580	8475	9025	9950	12500
VR6 Wagon 4D	RU73C	39780	9950	10550	11750	14850

2009 VOLKSWAGEN—(W,3or9)(VorB)W(AA71K)-9-#

Body Type	VIN	List	Trade-In Good	Very Good	Pvt-Party Good	Retail Excellent
RABBIT—5-Cyl.—Equipment Schedule 6						
W.B. 101.5"; 2.5 Liter.						
S Hatchback 2D	AA71K	16540	5150	5525	6475	8250
Auto, 6-Spd w/Overdrive			350	350	465	465
RABBIT—5-Cyl.—Equipment Schedule 6						
W.B. 101.5"; 2.5 Liter.						
S Hatchback 4D	CA71K	19640	6225	6625	7675	9750
GTI—4-Cyl. Turbo—Equipment Schedule 6						
W.B. 101.5"; 2.0 Liter.						
2.0T Hatchback 2D	EV71K	24740	7450	7900	8925	11150
Automatic, 6-Spd	F		350	350	440	440
4-Cyl, PZEV, 2.0 Liter	D		0	0	0	0
GTI—4-Cyl. Turbo—Equipment Schedule 6						
W.B. 101.5"; 2.0 Liter.						
2.0T Hatchback 4D	HV71K	25340	8800	9325	10450	13050
Manual, 6-Spd	G		(400)	(400)	(505)	(505)
4-Cyl, PZEV, 2.0 Liter	D		0	0	0	0

Body Type	VIN	List	Trade-In Good	Very Good	Pvt-Party Good	Retail Excellent
EOS—4-Cyl. Turbo—Equipment Schedule 3						
W.B. 101.5"; 2.0 Liter.						
Komfort HT Conv 2D	BA71F	32580	7725	8275	9250	11700
LUX Hardtop Conv 2D	FA71F	35890	9225	9825	10900	13650
NEW BEETLE—5-Cyl.—Equipment Schedule 6						
W.B. 98.8"; 2.5 Liter.						
Hatchback 2D	PW31C	19740	5100	5450	6375	8300
Manual, 5-Spd w/Overdrive			(375)	(375)	(500)	(500)
NEW BEETLE—5-Cyl.—Equipment Schedule 6						
W.B. 98.8"; 2.5 Liter.						
Convertible 2D	PF31Y	26240	7500	7950	9025	11350
GLI—4-Cyl. Turbo—Equipment Schedule 4						
W.B. 101.5"; 2.0 Liter.						
2.0T Sedan 4D	BJ71K	26340	9250	9775	10700	13150
JETTA—5-Cyl.—Equipment Schedule 6						
W.B. 101.5"; 2.5 Liter.						
S Sedan 4D	JM71K	19090	5050	5400	6350	8325
S Sportwagen 4D	KM71K	20749	6025	6425	7525	9700
SE Sedan 4D	RM71K	21670	6075	6475	7575	9750
California Edition			800	800	1065	1065
Panorama Roof			525	525	690	690
Manual, 5-Spd w/Overdrive			(375)	(375)	(500)	(500)
JETTA—5-Cyl.—Equipment Schedule 6						
W.B. 101.5"; 2.5 Liter.						
SE Sportwagen 4D	PM71K	21999	6600	7025	8075	10250
Panorama Roof			525	525	690	690
Automatic, 6-Spd w/OD			350	350	465	465
JETTA—5-Cyl.—Equipment Schedule 6						
W.B. 101.5"; 2.5 Liter.						
SEL Sedan 4D	RM71K	23440	7075	7525	8625	10900
JETTA—4-Cyl. Turbo—Equipment Schedule 6						
W.B. 101.5"; 2.0 Liter.						
Wolfsburg Ed Sedan	RJ71K	23095	7100	7525	8575	10850
Manual, 6-Spd w/Overdrive			(400)	(400)	(535)	(535)
JETTA—4-Cyl. Turbo—Equipment Schedule 6						
W.B. 101.5"; 2.0 Liter.						
SEL Sportwagen 4D	PJ71K	26640	8500	9000	9975	12350
Panorama Roof			525	525	670	670
Automatic, 6-Spd DSG			350	350	455	455
JETTA—4-Cyl. Turbo Diesel—Equipment Schedule 6						
W.B. 101.5"; 2.0 Liter.						
TDI Sedan 4D	AL71K	23740	8325	8800	9725	11950
Loyal Ed Sedan 4D	CL71K	23140	7975	8450	9450	11750
TDI Sportwagen 4D	PL71K	25340	10600	11200	12000	14500
Panorama Roof			525	525	645	645
Manual, 6-Spd w/Overdrive			(400)	(400)	(520)	(520)
PASSAT—4-Cyl. Turbo—Equipment Schedule 4						
W.B. 106.7"; 2.0 Liter.						
Komfort Sedan 4D	AK73C	28990	6850	7300	8200	10250
Komfort Wagon 4D	LK73C	30380	8125	8600	9675	12100
CC—4-Cyl. Turbo—Equipment Schedule 4						
W.B. 106.7"; 2.0 Liter.						
Sport Sedan 4D	ML73C	28580	8000	8475	9325	11450
Luxury Sedan 4D	HL73C	32680	9200	9725	10600	12950
CC—V6—Equipment Schedule 4						
W.B. 106.7"; 3.6 Liter.						
VR6 Sport Sedan 4D	EU73C	38990	9975	10550	11500	14000
CC 4MOTION AWD—V6—Equipment Schedule 4						
W.B. 106.7"; 3.6 Liter.						
VR6 Sedan 4D	GU73C	39990	10600	11150	12150	14800
2010 VOLKSWAGEN — (Wor3)VW(AA7AJ)–A–#						
GOLF—5-Cyl.—Equipment Schedule 6						
W.B. 101.5"; 2.5 Liter.						
Hatchback 2D	AA7AJ	18190	7000	7400	8300	10200
Automatic, 6-Spd w/OD			400	400	500	500
GOLF—5-Cyl.—Equipment Schedule 6						
W.B. 101.5"; 2.5 Liter.						
Hatchback 4D	DB7AJ	19890	7500	7925	8975	11050
GOLF—4-Cyl. Turbo Diesel—Equipment Schedule 6						
W.B. 101.5"; 2.0 Liter.						
TDI Hatchback 2D	MM7AJ	22889	10450	11000	11750	14050
TDI Hatchback 4D	NM7AJ	23489	11000	11550	12500	14950

Body Type	VIN	List	Trade-In Good	Very Good	Pvt-Party Good	Retail Excellent
Automatic, 6-Spd DSG			**400**	**400**	**490**	**490**
GTI—4-Cyl. Turbo—Equipment Schedule 6						
W.B. 101.5"; 2.0 Liter.						
2.0T Hatchback 2D	EV71K	24239	**10150**	**10650**	**11650**	**14050**
Automatic, 6-Spd	F		**400**	**400**	**480**	**480**
GTI—4-Cyl. Turbo—Equipment Schedule 6						
W.B. 101.5"; 2.0 Liter.						
2.0T Hatchback 4D	HD7AJ	25690	**10950**	**11500**	**12600**	**15200**
Manual, 6-Spd	G		**(475)**	**(475)**	**(560)**	**(560)**
EOS—4-Cyl. Turbo—Equipment Schedule 3						
W.B. 101.5"; 2.0 Liter.						
Komfort HT Conv 2D	BA7AH	33840	**10250**	**10850**	**12050**	**14950**
LUX Hardtop Conv 2D	FA7AH	36240	**11750**	**12350**	**13700**	**16950**
NEW BEETLE—5-Cyl.—Equipment Schedule 6						
W.B. 98.8"; 2.5 Liter.						
Hatchback 2D	PW31C	20340	**5950**	**6325**	**7375**	**9325**
Manual, 5-Spd			**(400)**	**(400)**	**(535)**	**(535)**
NEW BEETLE—5-Cyl.—Equipment Schedule 6						
W.B. 98.8"; 2.5 Liter.						
Final Edition H'Back	PW3AG	21140	**7025**	**7450**	**8525**	**10700**
Red Rock Ed H'Back	PW3AG	21140	**6450**	**6850**	**7950**	**10050**
Convertible 2D	PF31Y	27140	**9300**	**9800**	**10850**	**13300**
Final Edition Conv	RW3AL	28140	**10400**	**10950**	**11950**	**14500**
JETTA—5-Cyl.—Equipment Schedule 6						
W.B. 101.5"; 2.5 Liter.						
S Sedan 4D	JXA8J	19405	**6000**	**6375**	**7450**	**9475**
S Sportwagen 4D	KX8AJ	21065	**7350**	**7775**	**8900**	**11100**
Limited Ed Sedan 4D	JXA8J	20145	**7100**	**7525**	**8700**	**10950**
SE Sedan 4D	RX8AJ	22195	**7450**	**7900**	**8975**	**11200**
Panorama Roof			**550**	**550**	**725**	**725**
Manual, 5-Spd w/Overdrive			**(475)**	**(475)**	**(625)**	**(625)**
JETTA—5-Cyl.—Equipment Schedule 6						
W.B. 101.5"; 2.5 Liter.						
SE Sportwagen 4D	PX8AJ	23990	**8300**	**8775**	**9775**	**12050**
SEL Sedan 4D	RX8AJ	24205	**8400**	**8875**	**9975**	**12350**
Panorama Roof			**550**	**550**	**710**	**710**
JETTA—4-Cyl. Turbo—Equipment Schedule 6						
W.B. 101.5"; 2.0 Liter.						
Wolfsburg Ed Sedan	RJ8AJ	23800	**8450**	**8925**	**10050**	**12450**
Manual, 6-Spd w/Overdrive			**(475)**	**(475)**	**(615)**	**(615)**
JETTA—4-Cyl. Turbo Diesel—Equipment Schedule 6						
W.B. 101.5"; 2.0 Liter.						
TDI Sedan 4D	AL8AJ	24460	**9975**	**10500**	**11400**	**13700**
TDI Cup Ed Sedan	AL8AJ	26140	**12300**	**12900**	**13700**	**16250**
TDI Sportwagen 4D	PL8AJ	26110	**11950**	**12550**	**13400**	**15950**
Panorama Roof			**550**	**550**	**660**	**660**
Manual, 6-Spd w/Overdrive			**(475)**	**(475)**	**(585)**	**(585)**
PASSAT—4-Cyl. Turbo—Equipment Schedule 4						
W.B. 106.7"; 2.0 Liter.						
Komfort Sedan 4D	JK7AN	27695	**8500**	**8950**	**9900**	**12050**
Komfort Wagon 4D	XK7AN	29095	**9625**	**10100**	**11150**	**13550**
CC—4-Cyl. Turbo—Equipment Schedule 4						
W.B. 106.7"; 2.0 Liter.						
Sport Sedan 4D	ML7AN	29400	**9275**	**9775**	**10850**	**13150**
Luxury Sedan 4D	HL7AN	33630	**11000**	**11550**	**12600**	**15250**
R-Line Pkg			**400**	**400**	**495**	**495**
CC—V6—Equipment Schedule 4						
W.B. 106.7"; 3.6 Liter.						
VR6 Sport Sedan 4D	EU7AN	39815	**12050**	**12600**	**13850**	**16750**
CC 4MOTION AWD—V6—Equipment Schedule 4						
W.B. 106.7"; 3.6 Liter.						
VR6 Sedan 4D	GU7AN	40865	**13700**	**14300**	**15650**	**18800**
2011 VOLKSWAGEN — (Wor3)VW(AA7AJ)-B-#						
GOLF—5-Cyl.—Equipment Schedule 6						
W.B. 101.5"; 2.5 Liter.						
Hatchback 2D	AA7AJ	19030	**8075**	**8500**	**9500**	**11500**
Automatic, 6-Spd w/OD			**450**	**450**	**560**	**560**
GOLF—5-Cyl.—Equipment Schedule 6						
W.B. 101.5"; 2.5 Liter.						
Hatchback 4D	DA7AJ	20750	**8750**	**9175**	**10250**	**12400**
GOLF—4-Cyl. Turbo Diesel—Equipment Schedule 6						
W.B. 101.5"; 2.0 Liter.						

2011 VOLKSWAGEN

Body Type	VIN	List	Trade-In Good	Very Good	Pvt-Party Good	Retail Excellent
TDI Hatchback 2D	MM7AJ	23580	**12050**	**12600**	**13400**	**15700**
TDI Hatchback 4D	NM7AJ	24205	**12700**	**13300**	**14250**	**16800**
Automatic, 6-Spd DSG			**450**	**450**	**535**	**535**
GTI—4-Cyl. Turbo—Equipment Schedule 6						
W.B. 101.5"; 2.0 Liter.						
2.0T Hatchback 2D	FV7AJ	24460	**11850**	**12350**	**13400**	**15750**
Automatic, 6-Spd	F		**450**	**450**	**525**	**525**
GTI—4-Cyl. Turbo—Equipment Schedule 6						
W.B. 101.5"; 2.0 Liter.						
2.0T Hatchback 4D	HV7AJ	26160	**12700**	**13250**	**14350**	**16950**
Manual, 6-Spd	G		**(500)**	**(500)**	**(585)**	**(585)**
EOS—4-Cyl. Turbo—Equipment Schedule 3						
W.B. 101.5"; 2.0 Liter.						
Komfort HT Conv 2D	AD7AH	34810	**12600**	**13200**	**14450**	**17300**
LUX Hardtop Conv 2D	FD7AH	36870	**14150**	**14800**	**16000**	**19100**
JETTA—4-Cyl.—Equipment Schedule 6						
W.B. 104.4"; 2.0 Liter.						
Sedan 4D	2K8AJ	16865	**6575**	**6975**	**8125**	**10250**
S Sedan 4D	1K8AJ	17865	**7075**	**7475**	**8550**	**10650**
Manual, 5-Spd w/Overdrive	1		**(500)**	**(500)**	**(665)**	**(665)**
JETTA—5-Cyl.—Equipment Schedule 6						
W.B. 101.5"; 2.5 Liter.						
S SportWagen 4D	KX8AJ	20595	**9600**	**10100**	**11150**	**13500**
Manual, 5-Spd w/Overdrive	K		**(500)**	**(500)**	**(630)**	**(630)**
JETTA—5-Cyl.—Equipment Schedule 6						
W.B. 101.5"; 2.5 Liter.						
SE SportWagen 4D	PX8AJ	24225	**11250**	**11800**	**12750**	**15200**
Panorama Moon Roof			**575**	**575**	**700**	**700**
JETTA—5-Cyl.—Equipment Schedule 6						
W.B. 101.5"; 2.5 Liter.						
SE Sedan 4D	DX8AJ	20065	**8200**	**8650**	**9775**	**12050**
SEL Sedan 4D	LX8AJ	23265	**10500**	**11050**	**12050**	**14500**
Manual, 5-Spd w/Overdrive	B		**(500)**	**(500)**	**(655)**	**(655)**
JETTA—4-Cyl. Turbo Diesel—Equipment Schedule 6						
W.B. 101.5"; 2.0 Liter.						
TDI Sedan 4D	LL8AJ	24865	**12000**	**12600**	**13500**	**16000**
TDI SportWagen 4D	PL8AJ	26600	**14000**	**14650**	**15550**	**18200**
Panorama Moon Roof			**575**	**575**	**680**	**680**
Manual, 6-Spd w/Overdrive	3		**(500)**	**(500)**	**(610)**	**(610)**
CC—4-Cyl. Turbo—Equipment Schedule 4						
W.B. 106.7"; 2.0 Liter.						
Sport Sedan 4D	MN7AN	30120	**10250**	**10750**	**11800**	**14150**
Luxury Sedan 4D	HN7AN	31995	**11850**	**12350**	**13450**	**15900**
R-Line Sedan 4D	MN7AN	32040	**10500**	**11000**	**12100**	**14450**
Lux Plus Sedan 4D	HN7AN	34395	**11900**	**12450**	**13600**	**16200**
Lux Limited Sedan 4D	HN7AN	35195	**12050**	**12600**	**13750**	**16350**
CC 4MOTION AWD—V6—Equipment Schedule 4						
W.B. 106.7"; 3.6 Liter.						
VR6 Sedan 4D	GU7AN	40810	**15250**	**15850**	**17300**	**20500**

2012 VOLKSWAGEN — (1,3orW)VW(AA7AJ)-C-#

Body Type	VIN	List	Good	Very Good	Good	Excellent
GOLF—5-Cyl.—Equipment Schedule 6						
W.B. 101.5"; 2.5 Liter.						
2.5L Hatchback 2D	AA7AJ	18765	**8825**	**9250**	**10350**	**12500**
Automatic, 6-Spd			**475**	**475**	**595**	**595**
GOLF—5-Cyl.—Equipment Schedule 6						
W.B. 101.5"; 2.5 Liter.						
2.5L Hatchback 4D	DA7AJ	20565	**9500**	**9925**	**11200**	**13550**
GOLF AWD—4-Cyl. Turbo—Equipment Schedule 6						
W.B. 101.5"; 2.0 Liter.						
R Hatchback 2D	RF7AU	34760	**21700**	**22500**	**23300**	**26400**
R Hatchback 4D	PF7AU	36860	**22400**	**23200**	**24000**	**27200**
GOLF—4-Cyl. Turbo Diesel—Equipment Schedule 6						
W.B. 101.5"; 2.0 Liter.						
TDI Hatchback 2D	MM7AJ	24765	**12650**	**13250**	**14350**	**16950**
TDI Hatchback 4D	DM7AJ	25465	**13650**	**14300**	**15350**	**18000**
Automatic, 6-Spd DSG			**475**	**475**	**560**	**560**
BEETLE—5-Cyl.—Equipment Schedule 6						
W.B. 99.9"; 2.5 Liter.						
Hatchback 2D	AX7AT	19765	**9450**	**9925**	**10950**	**13200**
2.5L Hatchback 2D	HX7AT	20565	**9800**	**10300**	**11350**	**13600**
BEETLE—4-Cyl. Turbo—Equipment Schedule 6						
W.B. 99.9"; 2.0 Liter.						

2012 VOLKSWAGEN

Body Type	VIN	List	Trade-In Good	Very Good	Pvt-Party Good	Retail Excellent
2.0T Hatchback 2D	487AT	24165	**11800**	**12350**	**13350**	**15750**
2.0T Launch Ed 2D	V87AT	25720	**12700**	**13300**	**14200**	**16650**
GTI—4-Cyl. Turbo—Equipment Schedule 6						
W.B. 101.5"; 2.0 Liter.						
2.0T Hatchback 2D	EV7AJ	24465	**13150**	**13650**	**14850**	**17300**
Automatic, 6-Spd	F		**475**	**475**	**540**	**540**
GTI—4-Cyl. Turbo—Equipment Schedule 6						
W.B. 101.5"; 2.0 Liter.						
2.0T Hatchback 4D	HV7AJ	26165	**13900**	**14450**	**15600**	**18100**
Manual, 6-Spd w/OD	G		**(550)**	**(550)**	**(625)**	**(625)**
EOS—4-Cyl. Turbo—Equipment Schedule 3						
W.B. 101.5"; 2.0 Liter.						
Komfort HT Conv 2D	BW7AH	34765	**14750**	**15400**	**16600**	**19650**
LUX Hardtop Conv	FW7AH	38020	**16250**	**16950**	**18000**	**21100**
Executive HT Conv	FW7AH	41175	**18250**	**19000**	**20100**	**23600**
JETTA—4-Cyl.—Equipment Schedule 6						
W.B. 104.4"; 2.0 Liter.						
2.0L Sedan 4D	1K8AJ	16135	**7900**	**8350**	**9475**	**11650**
2.0L S Sedan 4D	1K7AJ	17265	**8300**	**8750**	**9850**	**12050**
Manual, 5-Spd	1		**(500)**	**(500)**	**(660)**	**(660)**
JETTA—4-Cyl. Turbo—Equipment Schedule 6						
W.B. 104.4"; 2.0 Liter.						
2.0T GLI Sedan 4D	567AJ	24515	**12850**	**13450**	**14500**	**17000**
2.0T GLI Autobahn Sed	567AJ	26565	**14650**	**15300**	**16250**	**18900**
Manual, 6-Spd	5		**(500)**	**(500)**	**(600)**	**(600)**
JETTA—4-Cyl. Turbo Diesel—Equipment Schedule 6						
W.B. 104.4"; 2.0 Liter.						
2.0L TDI Sedan 4D	3L7AJ	23295	**12750**	**13350**	**14400**	**16950**
Manual, 6-Spd	3		**(500)**	**(500)**	**(605)**	**(605)**
JETTA—5-Cyl.—Equipment Schedule 6						
W.B. 104.4"; 2.5 Liter.						
2.5L SE Sedan 4D	DX7AJ	20365	**9600**	**10100**	**11250**	**13600**
Manual, 5-Spd	B		**(500)**	**(500)**	**(635)**	**(635)**
JETTA—5-Cyl.—Equipment Schedule 6						
W.B. 104.4"; 2.5 Liter.						
2.5L SEL Sedan 4D	GX7AJ	23965	**12000**	**12600**	**13600**	**16050**
Manual, 5-Spd	G		**(500)**	**(500)**	**(610)**	**(610)**
JETTA—5-Cyl.—Equipment Schedule 6						
W.B. 104.4"; 2.5 Liter.						
2.5L SEL Premium Sed	LX7AJ	25575	**14000**	**14650**	**15650**	**18350**
JETTA SPORTWAGEN—5-Cyl.—Equipment Schedule 6						
W.B. 101.5"; 2.5 Liter.						
2.5L S SportWagen 4D	KX7AJ	22065	**10950**	**11450**	**12500**	**14900**
Manual, 5-Spd	K		**(500)**	**(500)**	**(615)**	**(615)**
JETTA SPORTWAGEN—5-Cyl.—Equipment Schedule 6						
W.B. 101.5"; 2.5 Liter.						
2.5L SE SportWagen	PX7AJ	24980	**13150**	**13750**	**14700**	**17200**
Panorama Moon Roof			**600**	**600**	**715**	**715**
JETTA SPORTWAGEN—4-Cyl. Turbo Diesel—Equipment Schedule 6						
W.B. 101.5"; 2.0 Liter.						
2.0L TDI SportWagen	ML7AJ	27410	**15350**	**16050**	**16950**	**19650**
Panorama Moon Roof			**600**	**600**	**700**	**700**
Manual, 6-Spd	M		**(500)**	**(500)**	**(585)**	**(585)**
PASSAT—5-Cyl.—Equipment Schedule 4						
W.B. 110.4"; 2.5 Liter.						
S Sedan 4D	AH7A3	23460	**9125**	**9550**	**10450**	**12350**
SE Sedan 4D	BH7A3	25595	**11150**	**11600**	**12700**	**14900**
SEL Sedan 4D	CH7A3	29165	**13300**	**13850**	**15000**	**17550**
SEL Premium Sed 4D	CH7A3	30665	**14650**	**15250**	**16450**	**19250**
PASSAT—4-Cyl. Turbo Diesel—Equipment Schedule 4						
W.B. 110.4"; 2.0 Liter.						
TDI SE Sedan 4D	BN7A3	28665	**15350**	**15900**	**17250**	**20200**
TDI SEL Premium Sed	CN7A3	32965	**16900**	**17550**	**18900**	**22100**
PASSAT—V6—Equipment Schedule 4						
W.B. 110.4"; 3.6 Liter.						
SE Sedan 4D	BM7A3	29765	**13850**	**14400**	**15650**	**18350**
SEL Premium Sed 4D	CM7A3	33720	**15200**	**15800**	**17100**	**20000**
CC—4-Cyl. Turbo—Equipment Schedule 4						
W.B. 106.7"; 2.0 Liter.						
Sport Sedan 4D	MN7AN	30435	**12400**	**12900**	**14100**	**16750**
Luxury Sedan 4D	HN7AN	32240	**13300**	**13850**	**15200**	**17900**
R-Line Sedan 4D	HN7AN	32280	**13050**	**13550**	**14750**	**17400**
Lux Plus Sedan 4D	HN7AN	34685	**14150**	**14700**	**16050**	**18850**

2012 VOLKSWAGEN

Body Type	VIN	List	Trade-In Good	Very Good	Pvt-Party Good	Retail Excellent
Lux Limited Sedan 4D	HN7AN	35485	13500	14050	15450	18250

CC 4MOTION AWD—V6—Equipment Schedule 4
W.B. 106.7"; 3.6 Liter.

| VR6 Sedan 4D | GU7AN | 41210 | 17400 | 18050 | 19600 | 23100 |

2013 VOLKSWAGEN — (1,3orW)VW(AB7AJ)–D–#

GOLF—5-Cyl.—Equipment Schedule 6
W.B. 101.5"; 2.5 Liter.

| 2.5L Hatchback 2D | AB7AJ | 18790 | 9425 | 9850 | 11100 | 13400 |
| Automatic, 6-Spd DSG | | | 500 | 500 | 625 | 625 |

GOLF—5-Cyl.—Equipment Schedule 6
W.B. 101.5"; 2.5 Liter.

| 2.5L Hatchback 4D | DB7AJ | 20590 | 10400 | 10850 | 12150 | 14600 |

GOLF AWD—4-Cyl. Turbo—Equipment Schedule 6
W.B. 101.5"; 2.0 Liter.

| R Hatchback 2D | RF7AJ | 34990 | 23600 | 24400 | 25300 | 28400 |
| R Hatchback 4D | PF7AJ | 35385 | 23900 | 24700 | 25600 | 28700 |

GOLF—4-Cyl. Turbo Diesel—Equipment Schedule 6
W.B. 101.5"; 2.0 Liter.

TDI Hatchback 2D	MM7AJ	25030	14650	15300	16350	19050
TDI Hatchback 4D	NM7AJ	25730	15550	16250	17150	19900
Automatic, 6-Spd DSG			500	500	580	580

BEETLE—5-Cyl.—Equipment Schedule 6
W.B. 99.9"; 2.5 Liter.

2.5L Entry Hatchback	FX7AT	19790	10950	11450	12400	14650
2.5L Hatchback 2D	HX7AT	20590	11350	11900	12900	15300
2.5L Fender Ed H'Bck	HX7AT	25235	14400	15050	15950	18500
2.5L Convertible 2D	5X7AT	25790	14850	15550	16400	18950
2.5L 50's Ed Conv 2D	5P7AT	26890	15350	16050	16900	19550
2.5L 70's Ed Conv 2D	5P7AT	29390	17050	17800	18600	21400

BEETLE—4-Cyl. Turbo—Equipment Schedule 6
W.B. 99.9"; 2.0 Liter.

Hatchback 2D	467AT	24190	13400	14050	15000	17600
Convertible 2D	867AT	28590	16600	17300	18150	20900
Fender Ed H'Back 2D	467AT	28925	16900	17650	18400	21200
R-Line H'Back 2D	467AT	30940				
60's Ed Convertible 2D	7A7AT	33190	19550	20400	21000	23900

BEETLE—4-Cyl. Turbo Diesel—Equipment Schedule 6
W.B. 99.9"; 2.0 Liter.

| TDI Hatchback 2D | RL7AT | 24090 | 14000 | 14650 | 15550 | 18100 |
| TDI Convertible 2D | 6L7AT | 28690 | 16150 | 16850 | 17600 | 20200 |

GTI—4-Cyl. Turbo—Equipment Schedule 6
W.B. 101.5"; 2.0 Liter.

Hatchback Sedan 4D	HV7AJ	25390	15400	15950	17250	20000
Wolfsburg Ed H'Back	GV7AJ	25890	15550	16150	17400	20200
Driver's Ed H'Back 4D	GV7AJ	30490	16700	17300	18850	22000
Autobahn HBack 4D	HV7AJ	31390	17550	18200	19750	23000

GTI—4-Cyl. Turbo—Equipment Schedule 6
W.B. 101.5"; 2.0 Liter.

Hatchback Coupe 2D	FV7AJ	24790	14850	15400	16650	19250
Autobahn HBack 2D	FV7AJ	30790	17050	17700	19200	22440
Automatic, 6-Spd	F		500	500	570	570

EOS—4-Cyl. Turbo—Equipment Schedule 3
W.B. 101.5"; 2.0 Liter.

Komfort Conv 2D	BW8AH	35175	17650	18300	19250	22200
Sport Conv 2D	BW8AH	37325	18350	19050	20000	23200
Lux Conv 2D	FW8AH	40025	19200	19900	20900	24100
Executive Conv 2D	FW8AH	41770	21000	21800	22800	26400

JETTA—4-Cyl.—Equipment Schedule 6
W.B. 104.4"; 2.0 Liter.

2.0L Sedan 4D	2K7AJ	17440	9275	9725	10850	13100
2.0L S Sedan 4D	2K7AJ	18570	9975	10500	11550	13900
Manual, 5-Spd	1		(500)	(500)	(640)	(640)

JETTA—4-Cyl. Turbo—Equipment Schedule 6
W.B. 104.4"; 2.0 Liter.

2.0T GLI Sedan 4D	467AJ	25840	14300	14950	15950	18600
2.0T GLI Autobahn 4D	467AJ	28090	15700	16400	17300	20000
Manual, 6-Spd	5		(500)	(500)	(590)	(590)

JETTA—4-Cyl. Turbo Diesel—Equipment Schedule 6
W.B. 104.4"; 2.0 Liter.

| 2.0L TDI Sedan 4D | LL7AJ | 24885 | 14750 | 15400 | 16350 | 19000 |
| Manual, 6-Spd | 3 | | (500) | (500) | (595) | (595) |

2013 VOLKSWAGEN

Body Type	VIN	List	Trade-In Good	Very Good	Pvt-Party Good	Retail Excellent
JETTA—4-Cyl. Turbo Hybrid—Equipment Schedule 6						
W.B. 104.4"; 1.4 Liter.						
Sedan 4D	637AJ	25790	13650	14300	15400	18050
SE Sedan 4D	637AJ	27785	13900	14550	15600	18300
SEL Sedan 4D	637AJ	30120	14350	15000	16100	18850
SEL Premium Sedan 4D	637AJ	31975	15800	16500	17500	20300
JETTA—5-Cyl.—Equipment Schedule 6						
W.B. 104.4"; 2.5 Liter.						
2.5L SE Sedan 4D	DX7AJ	20890	10700	11200	12300	14700
2.5L SEL Sedan 4D	LX7AJ	24790	13150	13800	14800	17350
Manual, 5-Spd	B		(500)	(500)	(625)	(625)
JETTA SPORTWAGEN—5-Cyl.—Equipment Schedule 6						
W.B. 101.5"; 2.5 Liter.						
2.5L S SportWagen 4D	PX7AJ	22290	11850	12400	13450	15900
2.5L SE SportWagen	PX7AJ	25005	13900	14550	15500	18000
JETTA SPORTWAGEN—4-Cyl. Turbo Diesel—Equipment Schedule 6						
W.B. 101.5"; 2.0 Liter.						
2.0L TDI SportWagen	PL7AJ	27435	17150	17900	18700	21600
PASSAT—5-Cyl.—Equipment Schedule 4						
W.B. 110.4"; 2.5 Liter.						
2.5L S Sedan 4D	AH7A3	23740	10250	10700	12000	14350
Wolfsburg Ed Sedan	AH783	24290	11000	11450	12700	15150
2.5L SE Sedan 4D	BH7A3	25840	12350	12850	14000	16450
2.5L SEL Sedan 4D	CH7A3	29720	14750	15300	16650	19550
2.5L SEL Premium 4D	CH7A3	31220	15750	16300	17500	20300
PASSAT—4-Cyl. Turbo Diesel—Equipment Schedule 4						
W.B. 110.4"; 2.0 Liter.						
TDI SE Sedan 4D	BN7A3	29020	16850	17450	18800	21900
TDI SEL Premium Sed	CN7A3	33710	18250	18850	20300	23600
PASSAT—V6—Equipment Schedule 4						
W.B. 110.4"; 3.6 Liter.						
SE Sedan 4D	BM7A3	30030	15350	15900	17250	20200
SEL Premium Sed 4D	CM7A3	34320	15850	16400	17850	20900
CC—4-Cyl. Turbo—Equipment Schedule 4						
W.B. 106.7"; 2.0 Liter.						
Sport Sedan 4D	BN7AN	32890	14650	15200	16650	19600
Sport Plus Sedan 4D	BN7AN	33820	14900	15450	17000	20000
R-Line Sedan 4D	BN7AN	34120	14350	14900	16450	19450
Luxury Sedan 4D	RN7AN	36460	17600	18250	19750	23100
CC—V6—Equipment Schedule 4						
W.B. 106.7"; 3.6 Liter.						
VR6 Lux Sedan 4D	HU7AN	38550	18600	19250	20900	24400
CC 4MOTION AWD—V6—Equipment Schedule 4						
W.B. 106.7"; 3.6 Liter.						
VR6 Sedan 4D	GU7AN	42240	21500	22300	23700	27500

2014 VOLKSWAGEN — (1,3orW)VW(DB7AJ)−E−#

Body Type	VIN	List	Trade-In Good	Very Good	Pvt-Party Good	Retail Excellent
GOLF—5-Cyl.—Equipment Schedule 6						
W.B. 101.5"; 2.5 Liter.						
2.5L Hatchback 4D	DB7AJ	20815	12750	13250	14300	16650
GOLF—4-Cyl. Turbo Diesel—Equipment Schedule 6						
W.B. 101.5"; 2.0 Liter.						
TDI Hatchback 4D	NM7AJ	26020	17150	17900	18700	21500
BEETLE—4-Cyl. Turbo—Equipment Schedule 6						
W.B. 100.0"; 1.8 Liter.						
1.8T Hatchback 2D	H07AT	21115	12400	12950	13950	16350
Auto, 6-Spd Tiptronic	J		525	525	640	640
BEETLE—4-Cyl. Turbo—Equipment Schedule 6						
W.B. 100.0"; 1.8 Liter.						
1.8T Convertible 2D	507AT	25990	16300	17000	17650	20300
BEETLE—5-Cyl.—Equipment Schedule 6						
W.B. 100.0"; 2.5 Liter.						
2.5L Hatchback 2D	HX7AT	20815	12100	12700	13650	16050
2.5L Convertible 2D	5X7AT	25815	16100	16800	17650	20400
Auto, 6-Spd Tiptronic	J		525	525	630	630
BEETLE—4-Cyl. Turbo—Equipment Schedule 6						
W.B. 100.0"; 2.0 Liter.						
R-Line H'Back 2D	4S7AT	25615	16000	16700	17450	20100
R-Line Conv 2D	8S7AT	29815	18250	19000	19600	22400
GSR Hatchback 2D	4S7AT	30815	19050	19850	20400	23100
Auto, 6-Spd Tiptronic	V		525	525	615	615
BEETLE—4-Cyl. Turbo Diesel—Equipment Schedule 6						
W.B. 100.0"; 2.0 Liter.						

2014 VOLKSWAGEN

Body Type	VIN	List	Trade-In Good	Very Good	Pvt-Party Good	Retail Excellent
TDI Hatchback 2D	RL7AT	25015	17050	17750	18500	21200
TDI Convertible 2D	6L7AT	29315	20400	21300	21700	24600
Auto, 6-Spd Tiptronic	J		525	525	600	600
GTI—4-Cyl. Turbo—Equipment Schedule 6						
W.B. 101.5"; 2.0 Liter.						
Wolfsburg H'Back 2D	GD7AJ	25915	16750	17350	18600	21500
Driver's Ed H'Back 2D	GD7AJ	30515	18450	19100	20600	23900
Auto, 6-Spd Tiptronic	H		525	525	600	600
EOS—4-Cyl. Turbo—Equipment Schedule 3						
W.B. 101.5"; 2.0 Liter.						
Komfort Conv 2D	BW8AH	36060	22400	23200	23900	27100
Executive Conv 2D	FW8AH	42560	25900	26800	27500	31300
Sport Conv 2D	BW8AH	38790	23100	23900	24700	28000
JETTA—4-Cyl.—Equipment Schedule 6						
W.B. 104.4"; 2.0 Liter.						
2.0L Base Sedan 4D	1K5AJ	16515	9475	9950	11100	13400
JETTA—4-Cyl.—Equipment Schedule 6						
W.B. 104.4"; 2.0 Liter.						
2.0L S Sedan 4D	2K5AJ	18815	10400	10900	12100	14500
Manual, 5-Spd	1		(525)	(525)	(660)	(660)
JETTA—4-Cyl. Turbo—Equipment Schedule 6						
W.B. 104.4"; 1.8 Liter.						
1.8T SE Sedan 4D	D05AJ	20815	11550	12100	13200	15650
Manual, 5-Spd	B		(525)	(525)	(645)	(645)
JETTA—4-Cyl. Turbo—Equipment Schedule 6						
W.B. 104.4"; 1.8 Liter.						
1.8T SEL Sedan 4D	L05AJ	26410	15850	16500	17400	20100
2.0T GLI Ed 30 Sed 4D	4S5AJ	29375	18350	19150	19800	22600
JETTA—4-Cyl. Turbo—Equipment Schedule 6						
W.B. 2.0 Liter.						
2.0T GLI Sedan 4D	4S5AJ	26175	15850	16500	17400	20100
2.0T GLI Autobahn 4D	4S5AJ	28415	17600	18350	19050	21800
Manual, 6-Spd	5		(525)	(525)	(615)	(615)
JETTA—4-Cyl. Turbo Diesel—Equipment Schedule 6						
W.B. 104.4"; 2.0 Liter.						
2.0L TDI Value Ed 4D	LL5AJ	23215	15700	16400	17300	20000
JETTA—4-Cyl. Turbo Diesel—Equipment Schedule 6						
W.B. 104.4"; 2.0 Liter.						
2.0L TDI Sedan 4D	LL5AJ	25115	17000	17750	18600	21400
Manual, 6-Spd	3		(525)	(525)	(615)	(615)
JETTA—4-Cyl. Turbo Hybrid—Equipment Schedule 6						
W.B. 104.4"; 2.0 Liter.						
Sedan 4D	635AJ	26380	17550	18300	19150	22100
SE Sedan 4D	635AJ	28080	18150	18900	19700	22700
SEL Sedan 4D	635AJ	30665	19550	20300	21100	24200
SEL Premium Sedan 4D	635AJ	32265	21000	21900	22500	25700
JETTA SPORTWAGEN—5-Cyl.—Equipment Schedule 6						
W.B. 101.5"; 2.5 Liter.						
2.5L S SportWagen 4D	PX7AJ	22715	13100	13700	14750	17300
2.5L SE SportWagen 4D	PX7AJ	25415	14400	15000	16000	18600
Manual, 5-Spd	K		(525)	(525)	(630)	(630)
JETTA SPORTWAGEN—4-Cyl. Turbo Diesel—Equipment Sch 6						
W.B. 101.5"; 2.0 Liter.						
2.0L TDI SportWagen	PL7AJ	28170	19650	20500	21200	24200
Manual, 6-Spd	M		(525)	(525)	(600)	(600)
PASSAT—4-Cyl. Turbo—Equipment Schedule 4						
W.B. 110.4"; 1.8 Liter.						
1.8T S Sedan 4D	AS7A3	22915	11750	12200	13650	16300
1.8T Wolfsburg Ed 4D	AS7A3	24815	13450	13950	15450	18250
1.8T SE Sedan 4D	BS7A3	26695	14850	15400	16850	19850
1.8T Sport Sedan 4D	BS7A3	28495	15450	16000	17550	20700
1.8T SEL Premium Sed	CS7A3	32115	18200	18850	20600	24300
PASSAT—5-Cyl.—Equipment Schedule 4						
W.B. 110.4"; 2.5 Liter.						
2.5L S Sedan 4D	AH7A3	22765	11250	11700	12950	15400
2.5L Wolfsburg Ed Sed	AH7A3	24315	12950	13450	14950	17650
2.5L SE Sedan 4D	BS7A3	25865	13450	13950	15550	18400
PASSAT—4-Cyl. Turbo Diesel—Equipment Schedule 4						
W.B. 110.4"; 2.0 Liter.						
TDI SE Sedan 4D	BN7A3	29495	17850	18450	19900	23200
TDI SEL Premium 4D	CN7A3	34215	19750	20400	22100	25800
PASSAT—V6—Equipment Schedule 4						
W.B. 110.4"; 3.6 Liter.						

Body Type	VIN	List	Trade-In Good	Trade-In Very Good	Pvt-Party Good	Retail Excellent
SE Sedan 4D	BM7A3	30485	16050	16650	18250	21500
SEL Premium Sed 4D	CM7A3	35085	18950	19600	21300	25000
CC—4-Cyl. Turbo—Equipment Schedule 4						
W.B. 106.7"; 2.0 Liter.						
2.0T Sport Sedan 4D	BN7AN	34460	18650	19300	20800	24200
2.0T R-Line Sed 4D	BN7AN	35695	19000	19650	21100	24600
2.0T Executive Sedan	RN7AN	37860	21400	22100	23500	27200
CC 4MOTION AWD—V6—Equipment Schedule 4						
W.B. 106.7"; 3.6 Liter.						
3.6 VR6 Exec Sedan	GU7AN	43310	24800	25600	26800	30500

VOLVO

2000 VOLVO — YV1(VS252)-Y-#

40 SERIES—4-Cyl. Turbo—Equipment Schedule 3
W.B. 100.3"; 1.9 Liter.

Body Type	VIN	List	Good	Very Good	Good	Excellent
S40 Sedan 4D	VS252	23475	900	1000	1725	3025
V40 Wagon 4D	VW252	24475	1300	1450	2300	3975
70 SERIES—5-Cyl.—Equipment Schedule 3						
W.B. 104.9"; 2.4 Liter.						
S70 Sedan 4D	LS61J	29075	950	1075	1675	2825
S70 SE Sedan 4D	LS61J	30075	975	1100	1675	2825
V70 Wagon 4D	LW61J	30375	1075	1200	1775	2975
V70 SE Wagon 4D	LW61J	31575	1225	1400	1975	3275
Manual, 5-Spd	4		(125)	(125)	(165)	(165)
70 SERIES—5-Cyl. Turbo—Equipment Schedule 1						
W.B. 104.5", 104.9" (C70, S70 & V70 ex. AWD); 2.3 Liter, 2.4 Liter.						
C70 LT Coupe 2D	NK56D	36475	925	1075	1750	3050
C70 LT Convertible 2D	NC56D	45675	850	975	1650	2925
C70 HT Coupe 2D	NK53D	40075	1325	1525	2300	4025
C70 HT Conv 2D	NC53D	47075	1350	1550	2250	3850
S70 GLT Sedan 4D	LS56D	34675	1675	1875	2650	4325
S70 GLT SE Sedan 4D	LS56D	33075	1875	2100	2900	4725
V70 GLT Wagon 4D	LW56D	35975	1825	2050	2850	4625
S70 T-5 Sedan 4D	LS53D	37275	1875	2100	2925	4750
S70 AWD Sedan 4D	LT56D	36575	2225	2475	3375	5450
V70 XC AWD Wag 4D	LZ56D	39075	2275	2550	3475	5575
V70 XC AWD SE Wag	LZ56D	37575	2100	2375	3275	5300
V70 R AWD Wagon 4D	LV60D	42075	3075	3425	4500	7125
80 SERIES—6-Cyl.—Equipment Schedule 1						
W.B. 109.9"; 2.9 Liter.						
S80 2.9 Sedan 4D	TS94D	37775	1150	1325	1875	3125
80 SERIES—6-Cyl. Turbo—Equipment Schedule 1						
W.B. 109.9"; 2.8 Liter.						
S80 T6 Sedan 4D	TS90D	42275	1825	2050	2950	4875

2001 VOLVO — YV1(VS295)-1-#

40 SERIES—4-Cyl. Turbo—Equipment Schedule 3
W.B. 100.9"; 1.9 Liter.

Body Type	VIN	List	Good	Very Good	Good	Excellent
S40 Sedan 4D	VS295	24075	1075	1225	1825	3050
S40 SE Sedan 4D	VS295	28025	1275	1425	2150	3625
V40 Wagon 4D	VW295	25075	1575	1750	2525	4225
V40 SE Wagon 4D	VW295	29025	1675	1875	2800	4625
60 SERIES—5-Cyl.—Equipment Schedule 3						
W.B. 106.9"; 2.4 Liter.						
S60 2.4 Sedan 4D	RS61N	27075	675	775	1400	2425
60 SERIES—5-Cyl. Turbo—Equipment Schedule 3						
W.B. 106.9"; 2.3 Liter, 2.4 Liter.						
S60 2.4T Sedan 4D	RS58D	30375	900	1025	1675	2900
S60 T5 Sedan 4D	RS53D	33675	1300	1475	2225	3850
70 SERIES—5-Cyl.—Equipment Schedule 1						
W.B. 108.5"; 2.4 Liter.						
V70 Wagon 4D	SW61N	31075	1075	1225	1800	2975
70 SERIES—5-Cyl. Turbo—Equipment Schedule 1						
W.B. 104.9", 108.5" (V70 ex XC), 108.8" (XC); 2.3 Liter, 2.4 Liter.						
C70 LT Convertible 2D	NC56D	44075	875	1000	1675	2975
C70 HT Coupe 2D	NK53D	38475	1375	1575	2350	4050
C70 HT Conv 2D	NC53D	47075	1425	1625	2325	3950
V70 2.4T Wagon 4D	SW58D	35375	1825	2050	2900	4725
V70 T5 Wagon 4D	SW53D	36675	1950	2200	3075	4975
V70 XC AWD Wag 4D	SZ58D	37975	2300	2575	3525	5625

2001 VOLVO

Body Type	VIN	List	Trade-In Good	Very Good	Pvt-Party Good	Retail Excellent
80 SERIES—6-Cyl.—Equipment Schedule 1						
W.B. 109.9"; 2.9 Liter.						
S80 2.9 Sedan 4D	TS94D	38675	**1175**	**1325**	**2000**	**3400**
80 SERIES—6-Cyl. Turbo—Equipment Schedule 1						
W.B. 109.9"; 2.8 Liter.						
S80 T6A Sedan 4D	TS90D	42675	**2000**	**2250**	**3075**	**4950**
S80 T6 Executive 4D	TS90D	48075	**2125**	**2400**	**3275**	**5300**

2002 VOLVO — YV1(VS295)-2-#

Body Type	VIN	List	Trade-In Good	Very Good	Pvt-Party Good	Retail Excellent
40 SERIES—4-Cyl. Turbo—Equipment Schedule 3						
W.B. 100.9"; 1.9 Liter.						
S40 Sedan 4D	VS295	24525	**1175**	**1325**	**1900**	**3100**
V40 Wagon 4D	VW295	25525	**1800**	**2000**	**2725**	**4300**
60 SERIES—5-Cyl.—Equipment Schedule 3						
W.B. 106.9"; 2.4 Liter.						
S60 2.4 Sedan 4D	RS61N	27750	**875**	**1000**	**1725**	**3025**
60 SERIES—5-Cyl. Turbo—Equipment Schedule 3						
W.B. 106.9"; 2.3 Liter, 2.4 Liter.						
S60 2.4T Sedan 4D	RS58D	32250	**1175**	**1350**	**2100**	**3600**
S60 T5 Sedan 4D	RS53D	35850	**1550**	**1775**	**2675**	**4525**
S60 2.4T AWD Sed 4D	RH58D	34000	**1525**	**1725**	**2625**	**4425**
70 SERIES—5-Cyl.—Equipment Schedule 3						
W.B. 108.5"; 2.4 Liter.						
V70 Wagon 4D	SW61R	31650	**1125**	**1250**	**1875**	**3100**
70 SERIES—5-Cyl. Turbo—Equipment Schedule 1						
W.B. 104.9", 108.5" (V70 ex XC), 108.8" (XC); 2.3 Liter, 2.4 Liter.						
C70 LT Convertible 2D	NC56D	44750	**950**	**1100**	**1775**	**3100**
C70 HT Coupe 2D	NK53D	38150	**1475**	**1675**	**2400**	**4100**
C70 HT Convertible	NC53D	46750	**1500**	**1700**	**2375**	**4000**
V70 2.4T Wagon 4D	SW58D	36150	**2050**	**2275**	**3100**	**4900**
V70 2.4T AWD Wag 4D	SJ58D	37900	**2375**	**2650**	**3525**	**5550**
V70 T5 Wagon 4D	SW53D	38350	**2150**	**2400**	**3225**	**5100**
V70 XC AWD Wag 4D	SZ58D	38425	**2475**	**2750**	**3650**	**5725**
80 SERIES—6-Cyl.—Equipment Schedule 1						
W.B. 109.9"; 2.9 Liter.						
S80 2.9 Sedan 4D	TS94D	38775	**1475**	**1650**	**2250**	**3700**
80 SERIES—6-Cyl. Turbo—Equipment Schedule 1						
W.B. 109.9"; 2.9 Liter.						
S80 T6 Sedan 4D	TS90D	42775	**2325**	**2600**	**3375**	**5350**
S80 T6 Executive 4D	TS90D	50575	**2600**	**2925**	**3725**	**5825**

2003 VOLVO — YV1(VS275)-3-#

Body Type	VIN	List	Trade-In Good	Very Good	Pvt-Party Good	Retail Excellent
40 SERIES—4-Cyl. Turbo—Equipment Schedule 3						
W.B. 100.9"; 1.9 Liter.						
S40 Sedan 4D	VS275	24560	**1350**	**1500**	**2075**	**3350**
V40 Wagon 4D	VW275	25560	**1875**	**2075**	**2825**	**4425**
60 SERIES—5-Cyl.—Equipment Schedule 3						
W.B. 107.0"; 2.4 Liter.						
S60 2.4 Sedan 4D	RS61T	28230	**1400**	**1575**	**2100**	**3375**
60 SERIES—5-Cyl. Turbo—Equipment Schedule 3						
W.B. 107.0"; 2.3 Liter, 2.4 Liter, 2.5 Liter.						
S60 2.4T Sedan 4D	RS58D	31085	**1825**	**2050**	**2725**	**4300**
S60 2.5T AWD Sed 4D	RH59H	32835	**2200**	**2450**	**3200**	**5000**
S60 T5 Sedan 4D	RS53D	34685	**2200**	**2450**	**3100**	**4775**
70 SERIES—5-Cyl.—Equipment Schedule 3						
W.B. 108.5"; 2.4 Liter.						
V70 Wagon 4D	SW61T	29530	**1400**	**1550**	**2050**	**3300**
70 SERIES—5-Cyl. Turbo—Equipment Schedule 1						
W.B. 104.9", 108.5" (V70), 108.8" (XC70); 2.3 Liter, 2.4 Liter, 2.5 Liter.						
C70 LT Convertible 2D	NC63D	44785	**1400**	**1575**	**2250**	**3800**
C70 HT Conv 2D	NC62D	47785	**1925**	**2200**	**3025**	**4950**
V70 2.4T Wagon 4D	SW58D	31530	**2350**	**2625**	**3400**	**5275**
V70 2.5T AWD Wag 4D	SJ59H	33280	**2850**	**3200**	**3950**	**6000**
V70 T5 Wagon 4D	SW53D	35730	**2375**	**2650**	**3450**	**5325**
XC70 AWD Wagon 4D	SZ59H	34530	**2950**	**3300**	**4075**	**6150**
80 SERIES—6-Cyl.—Equipment Schedule 1						
W.B. 109.9"; 2.9 Liter.						
S80 2.9 Sedan 4D	TS92D	39110	**1650**	**1850**	**2450**	**4000**
80 SERIES—6-Cyl. Turbo—Equipment Schedule 1						
W.B. 109.9"; 2.9 Liter.						
S80 T6 Sedan 4D	TS91D	44595	**2600**	**2900**	**3700**	**5775**

Body Type	VIN	List	Trade-In Good	Trade-In Very Good	Pvt-Party Good	Retail Excellent
S80 T6 Elite Sedan 4D	TS91Z	48880	2875	3200	4025	6200

2004 VOLVO — YV1(VS275)-4-#

40 SERIES—4-Cyl. Turbo—Equipment Schedule 3
W.B. 101.0"; 1.9 Liter.

S40 Sedan 4D	VS275	25385	1500	1675	2400	3900
S40 LSE Sedan 4D	VS275	29530	1600	1775	2625	4250
V40 Wagon 4D	VW275	26885	2150	2400	3325	5225
V40 LSE Wagon 4D	VW275	30530	2275	2525	3575	5675

40 SERIES—5-Cyl.—Equipment Schedule 3
W.B. 103.9"; 2.4 Liter.

S40 2.4i Sedan 4D	MS382	27170	2075	2300	3075	4800

40 SERIES—5-Cyl. Turbo—Equipment Schedule 3
W.B. 103.9"; 2.5 Liter.

S40 T5 Sedan 4D	MS682	29970	2375	2625	3575	5625

60 SERIES—5-Cyl.—Equipment Schedule 3
W.B. 106.9" 2.4 Liter.

S60 2.4 Sedan 4D	RS61T	28645	1550	1750	2200	3425

60 SERIES—5-Cyl. Turbo—Equipment Schedule 3
W.B. 106.9", 107.0" (R); 2.3 Liter,2.5 Liter.

S60 2.5T Sedan 4D	RS59V	30295	2075	2325	2875	4350
S60 T5 Sedan 4D	RS53D	34845	2225	2475	3175	4875
S60 R AWD Sedan 4D	RH52Y	38810	3675	4075	4925	7225
AWD (2.5T)			700	700	935	935

70 SERIES—5-Cyl.—Equipment Schedule 3
W.B. 108.5"; 2.4 Liter.

V70 Wagon 4D	SW61T	30145	1675	1875	2475	3850

70 SERIES—5-Cyl. Turbo—Equipment Schedule 1
W.B. 104.9", 108.5" (V70), 108.8" (XC70); 2.3L, 2.4L, 2.5L.

C70 LT Convertible 2D	NC63D	40565	1875	2125	2775	4400
C70 HT Conv 2D	NC62D	43565	2475	2800	3500	5425
V70 2.5T Wagon 4D	SW59V	35070	2875	3200	4025	6125
V70 T5 Wagon 4D	SW53D	38145	2775	3100	3900	5950
V70 R AWD Wagon 4D	SJ52Y	40600	4200	4625	5775	8525
XC70 AWD Wagon 4D	SZ59H	38145	3300	3650	4625	6900
AWD (2.5T)			700	700	935	935

80 SERIES—6-Cyl.—Equipment Schedule 1
W.B. 109.9"; 2.9 Liter.

S80 2.9 Sedan 4D	TS92D	39725	2375	2675	3275	4975

80 SERIES—5-Cyl. Turbo—Equipment Schedule 1
W.B. 109.9"; 2.5 Liter.

S80 2.5T Sedan 4D	TR59V	38630	2175	2425	3025	4625

80 SERIES—6-Cyl. Twin Turbo—Equipment Schedule 1
W.B. 109.9"; 2.9 Liter.

S80 T6 Sedan 4D	TS91Z	45210	3400	3775	4375	6400
S80 T6 Premier Sed 4D	TS91Z	49200	3575	3975	4600	6700

2005 VOLVO — YV1(MS392)-5-#

40 SERIES—5-Cyl.—Equipment Schedule 3
W.B. 103.9"; 2.4 Liter.

S40 2.4i Sedan 4D	MS392	25145	2600	2925	3850	5750

40 SERIES—5-Cyl. Turbo—Equipment Schedule 3
W.B. 103.9"; 2.5 Liter.

S40 T5 Sedan 4D	MS682	27945	3300	3650	4725	6975
AWD	H		550	550	735	735

50 SERIES—5-Cyl.—Equipment Schedule 3
W.B. 103.9"; 2.4 Liter.

V50 2.4i Sport Wagon	MW382	28640	2900	3250	4050	5975

50 SERIES—5-Cyl. Turbo—Equipment Schedule 3
W.B. 103.9"; 2.5 Liter.

V50 T5 Sport Wagon	MW682	29145	3775	4175	5200	7525
AWD			550	550	735	735

60 SERIES—5-Cyl.—Equipment Schedule 3
W.B. 106.9"; 2.4 Liter.

S60 2.4 Sedan 4D	RS612	28920	2475	2775	3525	5225

60 SERIES—5-Cyl. Turbo—Equipment Schedule 3
W.B. 106.9"; 2.4 Liter, 2.5 Liter.

S60 2.5T Sedan 4D	RS592	30420	2825	3175	4000	5925
S60 T5 Sedan 4D	RS547	35170	3300	3675	4625	6850
S60 R AWD Sedan 4D	RH527	39185	4675	5150	6325	9125
AWD (2.5T)			725	725	965	965

2005 VOLVO

Body Type	VIN	List	Trade-In Good	Very Good	Pvt-Party Good	Retail Excellent
70 SERIES—5-Cyl.—Equipment Schedule 3						
W.B. 108.5"; 2.4 Liter.						
V70 Wagon 4D	SW612	30445	3100	3450	4250	6175
70 SERIES—5-Cyl. Turbo—Equipment Schedule 1						
W.B. 108.5", 108.8" (XC70); 2.4 Liter, 2.5 Liter.						
V70 2.5T Wagon 4D	SW592	36895	4750	5200	6275	8850
V70 T5 Wagon 4D	SW547	39345	4700	5125	6225	8850
V70 R AWD Wagon 4D	SJ527	40685	6200	6725	8175	11450
XC70 AWD Wagon 4D	SZ592	38145	4875	5325	6475	9150
80 SERIES—5-Cyl. Turbo—Equipment Schedule 1						
W.B. 109.9"; 2.5 Liter.						
S80 2.5T Sedan 4D	TS592	39185	3275	3650	4575	6775
AWD			625	625	825	825
80 SERIES—6-Cyl. Twin Turbo—Equipment Schedule 1						
W.B. 109.9"; 2.9 Liter.						
S80 T6 Sedan 4D	TS911	45210	4775	5250	6225	8775
S80 T6 Premier Sed 4D	TR911	49200	4800	5275	6450	9250

2006 VOLVO — YV1(MS382)-6-#

Body Type	VIN	List	Trade-In Good	Very Good	Pvt-Party Good	Retail Excellent
40 SERIES—5-Cyl.—Equipment Schedule 3						
W.B. 103.9"; 2.4 Liter.						
S40 2.4i Sedan 4D	MS382	25650	3275	3625	4525	6550
40 SERIES—5-Cyl. Turbo—Equipment Schedule 3						
W.B. 103.9"; 2.5 Liter.						
S40 T5 Sedan 4D	MS682	28510	3700	4075	5200	7475
AWD	H		575	575	765	765
50 SERIES—5-Cyl.—Equipment Schedule 3						
W.B. 103.9"; 2.4 Liter.						
V50 2.4i Sport Wagon	MW382	26900	3500	3875	4650	6550
50 SERIES—5-Cyl. Turbo—Equipment Schedule 3						
W.B. 103.9"; 2.5 Liter.						
V50 T5 Sport Wag	MW682	29735	4650	5100	5975	8300
AWD	J		575	575	765	765
60 SERIES—5-Cyl. Turbo—Equipment Schedule 3						
W.B. 106.9"; 2.4 Liter, 2.5 Liter.						
S60 2.5T Sedan 4D	RS592	30965	3025	3400	4325	6250
S60 T5 Sedan 4D	RS547	33940	3675	4075	5150	7450
S60 R AWD Sedan 4D	RH527	39865	5000	5500	6825	9575
AWD (2.5T)			750	750	1000	1000
70 SERIES—5-Cyl.—Equipment Schedule 3						
W.B. 108.5"; 2.4 Liter.						
V70 2.4 Wagon 4D	SW612	31140	3750	4100	5000	7000
70 SERIES—5-Cyl. Turbo—Equipment Schedule 1						
W.B. 103.9" (C70), 108.5" (V70), 108.8" (XC70); 2.5 Liter.						
C70 T5 Convertible 2D	MC682	40655	5025	5575	6825	9650
V70 2.5T Wagon 4D	SW592	36445	5100	5550	6800	9375
V70 R AWD Wagon 4D	SJ527	41490	7325	7900	9325	12700
XC70 AWD Wagon 4D	SZ592	39390	5825	6300	7625	10550
XC70 Ocean Race Wag	SZ592	41430	6350	6875	8725	12400
80 SERIES—5-Cyl. Turbo—Equipment Schedule 1						
W.B. 109.9"; 2.5 Liter.						
S80 2.5T Sedan 4D	TS592	38280	4250	4675	5725	8150
AWD			675	675	885	885

2007 VOLVO — YV1(MS382)-7-#

Body Type	VIN	List	Trade-In Good	Very Good	Pvt-Party Good	Retail Excellent
40 SERIES—5-Cyl.—Equipment Schedule 3						
W.B. 103.9"; 2.4 Liter.						
S40 2.4i Sedan 4D	MS382	26185	4050	4425	5575	7875
40 SERIES—5-Cyl. Turbo—Equipment Schedule 3						
W.B. 103.9"; 2.5 Liter.						
S40 T5 Sedan 4D	MS682	30335	4575	5000	6375	8925
AWD	H		600	600	800	800
50 SERIES—5-Cyl.—Equipment Schedule 3						
W.B. 103.9"; 2.4 Liter.						
V50 2.4i Sport Wagon	MW382	27385	4500	4950	5775	7775
50 SERIES—5-Cyl. Turbo—Equipment Schedule 3						
W.B. 103.9"; 2.5 Liter.						
V50 T5 Sport Wag 4D	MW682	30285	5625	6125	7050	9450
AWD	J		600	600	800	800
60 SERIES—5-Cyl. Turbo—Equipment Schedule 3						
W.B. 106.9"; 2.4 Liter, 2.5 Liter.						
S60 2.5T Sedan 4D	RS592	31580	4225	4625	5425	7400

2007 VOLVO

Body Type	VIN	List	Trade-In Good	Very Good	Pvt-Party Good	Retail Excellent
S60 T5 Sedan 4D	RS547	34680	4725	5175	6250	8550
S60 R AWD Sedan 4D	RH527	40930	6500	7050	8200	11000
AWD (2.5T)			775	775	1020	1020
70 SERIES—5-Cyl.—Equipment Schedule 3						
W.B. 108.5"; 2.4 Liter.						
V70 2.4 Wagon 4D	SW612	31740	4800	5200	6250	8325
70 SERIES—5-Cyl. Turbo—Equipment Schedule 1						
W.B. 103.9" (C70), 108.5" (V70), 108.8" (XC70); 2.5 Liter.						
C70 T5 Convertible 2D	MC682	41035	6075	6650	7850	10800
V70 2.5T Wagon 4D	SW932	37210	7175	7700	8875	11700
V70 R AWD Wagon 4D	SJ527	42885	9100	9750	11150	14650
XC70 AWD Wagon 4D	SZ592	40110	7075	7600	8900	11900
80 SERIES—6-Cyl.—Equipment Schedule 1						
W.B. 111.6"; 3.2 Liter.						
S80 Sedan 4D	AS982	39400	4975	5425	6600	9000
Sport Pkg			275	275	360	360
AWD			700	700	940	940

2008 VOLVO — YV1(MK672)-8-#

Body Type	VIN	List	Trade-In Good	Very Good	Pvt-Party Good	Retail Excellent
30 SERIES—5-Cyl. Turbo—Equipment Schedule 3						
W.B. 103.9"; 2.5 Liter.						
C30 T5 1.0 H'Back 2D	MK672	23695	5800	6250	6750	8425
C30 T5 2.0 H'Back 2D	MK672	26445	7100	7625	8075	10000
C30 T5 2.0 R-Design	MK672	26445	8050	8625	9025	11050
40 SERIES—5-Cyl.—Equipment Schedule 3						
W.B. 103.9"; 2.4 Liter.						
S40 2.4i Sedan 4D	MS382	26360	5375	5825	7000	9375
40 SERIES—5-Cyl. Turbo—Equipment Schedule 3						
W.B. 103.9"; 2.5 Liter.						
S40 T5 Sedan 4D	MS672	29260	6175	6650	7875	10450
AWD			650	650	865	865
50 SERIES—5-Cyl.—Equipment Schedule 3						
W.B. 103.9"; 2.4 Liter.						
V50 2.4i Sport Wagon	MW382	27560	5925	6400	7500	9950
50 SERIES—5-Cyl. Turbo—Equipment Schedule 3						
W.B. 103.9"; 2.5 Liter.						
V50 T5 Sport Wag 4D	MW672	30460	8525	9125	10400	13600
AWD			650	650	865	865
60 SERIES—5-Cyl. Turbo—Equipment Schedule 3						
W.B. 106.9"; 2.4 Liter, 2.5 Liter.						
S60 2.5T Sedan 4D	RS592	31630	5100	5500	6375	8500
S60 T5 Sedan 4D	RS547	34730	5800	6275	7375	9775
AWD			800	800	1065	1065
70 SERIES—5-Cyl. Turbo—Equipment Schedule 1						
W.B. 103.9"; 2.5 Liter.						
C70 T5 Convertible 2D	MC672	41235	8100	8725	9750	12650
70 SERIES—6-Cyl.—Equipment Schedule 3						
W.B. 110.8"; 3.2 Liter.						
V70 3.2 Wagon 4D	SW612	33210	9075	9650	10400	12900
70 SERIES AWD—6-Cyl.—Equipment Schedule 1						
W.B. 110.8"; 3.2 Liter.						
XC70 3.2 AWD Wagon	BZ982	37520	11750	12450	13500	16800
80 SERIES—6-Cyl.—Equipment Schedule 1						
W.B. 111.6"; 3.2 Liter.						
S80 Sedan 4D	AS982	39450	6100	6600	7425	9575
Sport Pkg			275	275	365	365
AWD			750	750	965	965
V8, 4.4 Liter			3000	3000	3870	3870
80 SERIES AWD—6-Cyl. Turbo—Equipment Schedule 1						
W.B. 111.6"; 3.0 Liter.						
S80 T6 Sedan 4D	AH992	42790	8175	8750	9575	12150
Sport Pkg			275	275	360	360

2009 VOLVO — YV1(MK672)-9-#

Body Type	VIN	List	Trade-In Good	Very Good	Pvt-Party Good	Retail Excellent
30 SERIES—5-Cyl. Turbo—Equipment Schedule 3						
W.B. 103.9"; 2.5 Liter.						
C30 T5 H'Back 2D	MK672	24625	8100	8625	9400	11650
C30 T5 R-Design 2D	MK672	26775	9025	9600	10500	13050
40 SERIES—5-Cyl.—Equipment Schedule 3						
W.B. 103.9"; 2.4 Liter.						
S40 2.4i Sedan 4D	MS382	29375	7425	7950	8950	11300

330   **DEDUCT FOR RECONDITIONING**   0415

2009 VOLVO

Body Type	VIN	List	Trade-In Good	Very Good	Pvt-Party Good	Retail Excellent
40 SERIES—5-Cyl. Turbo—Equipment Schedule 3						
W.B. 103.9"; 2.5 Liter.						
S40 T5 R-Design Sedan	MS672	33175	**8225**	**8800**	**9800**	**12350**
AWD	H		**675**	**675**	**885**	**885**
50 SERIES—5-Cyl.—Equipment Schedule 3						
W.B. 103.9"; 2.4 Liter.						
V50 2.4i Sport Wagon	MW382	30595	**7800**	**8350**	**9425**	**12050**
50 SERIES AWD—5-Cyl. Turbo—Equipment Schedule 3						
W.B. 103.9"; 2.5 Liter.						
V50 T5 Sport Wagon	MJ672	36295	**10800**	**11450**	**12750**	**16200**
60 SERIES—5-Cyl. Turbo—Equipment Schedule 3						
W.B. 106.9"; 2.4 Liter, 2.5 Liter.						
S60 2.5T SE Sed 4D	RS592	31775	**6800**	**7275**	**8175**	**10400**
S60 2.5T Sedan 4D	RS592	33625	**7400**	**7900**	**8950**	**11400**
S60 T5 Sedan 4D	RS547	37225	**8350**	**8900**	**10000**	**12750**
AWD			**875**	**875**	**1125**	**1125**
70 SERIES—5-Cyl. Turbo—Equipment Schedule 1						
W.B. 103.9"; 2.5 Liter.						
C70 T5 Convertible 2D	MC672	41845	**11600**	**12350**	**13150**	**16100**
70 SERIES—6-Cyl.—Equipment Schedule 3						
W.B. 110.9"; 3.2 Liter.						
V70 3.2 Wagon 4D	SW612	33695	**10400**	**10950**	**11700**	**14100**
70 SERIES AWD—6-Cyl.—Equipment Schedule 1						
W.B. 110.8"; 3.0 Liter, 3.2 Liter.						
XC70 3.2 Wagon 4D	BZ982	38045	**12850**	**13550**	**14500**	**17450**
XC70 T6 Wagon 4D	BZ992	40295	**14650**	**15400**	**16350**	**19600**
80 SERIES—6-Cyl.—Equipment Schedule 1						
W.B. 111.6"; 3.2 Liter.						
S80 3.2 Sedan 4D	AS982	40425	**7950**	**8475**	**9300**	**11550**
80 SERIES AWD—6-Cyl. Turbo—Equipment Schedule 1						
W.B. 111.6"; 3.0 Liter.						
S80 T6 Sedan 4D	AH992	42875	**10050**	**10650**	**11550**	**14300**
80 SERIES AWD—V8—Equipment Schedule 1						
W.B. 111.6"; 4.4 Liter.						
S80 Sedan 4D	AH852	52675	**14550**	**15400**	**16450**	**20100**

2010 VOLVO — YV(1or4)(672MK)–A–#

Body Type	VIN	List	Trade-In Good	Very Good	Pvt-Party Good	Retail Excellent
30 SERIES—5-Cyl. Turbo—Equipment Schedule 3						
W.B. 103.9"; 2.5 Liter.						
C30 T5 H'Back 2D	672MK	24950	**9150**	**9700**	**10700**	**13200**
C30 T5 R-Design 2D	672MK	27150	**10600**	**11200**	**12250**	**15100**
40 SERIES—5-Cyl. Turbo—Equipment Schedule 3						
W.B. 103.9"; 2.4 Liter.						
S40 2.4i Sedan 4D	382MS	28300	**8950**	**9550**	**10400**	**12700**
40 SERIES—5-Cyl. Turbo—Equipment Schedule 3						
W.B. 103.9"; 2.5 Liter.						
S40 T5 R-Design 4D	672MS	32000	**9600**	**10200**	**11050**	**13500**
AWD	H		**700**	**700**	**850**	**850**
50 SERIES—5-Cyl. Turbo—Equipment Schedule 3						
W.B. 103.9"; 2.4 Liter.						
V50 2.4i Sport Wagon	382MW	29550	**9600**	**10150**	**11450**	**14350**
50 SERIES AWD—5-Cyl. Turbo—Equipment Schedule 3						
W.B. 103.9"; 2.5 Liter.						
V50 T5 R-Design Wag	672MJ	33900	**13500**	**14200**	**15850**	**19700**
70 SERIES—5-Cyl. Turbo—Equipment Schedule 1						
W.B. 103.9"; 2.5 Liter.						
C70 T5 Convertible 2D	672MC	42100	**12900**	**13600**	**14250**	**16800**
70 SERIES—6-Cyl.—Equipment Schedule 3						
W.B. 110.8"; 3.2 Liter.						
V70 3.2 Wagon 4D	982BW	34400	**14050**	**14700**	**15650**	**18350**
V70 R-Design Wagon	960BW	38850	**18000**	**18800**	**19800**	**23200**
70 SERIES AWD—6-Cyl.—Equipment Schedule 1						
W.B. 110.8"; 3.0 Liter, 3.2 Liter.						
XC70 3.2 Wagon 4D	962BZ	38800	**16700**	**17450**	**18500**	**21700**
XC70 T6 Wagon 4D	992BZ	43650	**18500**	**19300**	**20300**	**23800**
80 SERIES—6-Cyl.—Equipment Schedule 1						
W.B. 111.6"; 3.2 Liter.						
S80 Sedan 4D	960AS	40050	**10650**	**11250**	**12150**	**14800**
80 SERIES AWD—6-Cyl. Turbo—Equipment Schedule 1						
W.B. 111.6"; 3.0 Liter.						
S80 T6 Sedan 4D	992AH	43800	**12550**	**13250**	**14350**	**17450**
80 SERIES AWD—V8—Equipment Schedule 1						
W.B. 111.6"; 4.4 Liter.						

2010 VOLVO

Body Type	VIN	List	Trade-In Good	Very Good	Pvt-Party Good	Retail Excellent
S80 Sedan 4D	852AH	51800	**17250**	**18150**	**19050**	**22800**

2011 VOLVO — YV(1or4)(672MK)–B–#

30 SERIES—5-Cyl. Turbo—Equipment Schedule 3
W.B. 103.9"; 2.5 Liter.

C30 T5 H'Back 2D	672MK	25450	**11450**	**12000**	**13200**	**16000**
C30 R-Design 2D	672MK	27800	**12750**	**13400**	**14700**	**17850**

40 SERIES—5-Cyl. Turbo—Equipment Schedule 3
W.B. 103.9"; 2.5 Liter.

S40 T5 Sedan 4D	672MS	28600	**11050**	**11700**	**12650**	**15300**
S40 T5 R-Design 4D	672MS	32000	**12300**	**13000**	**13950**	**16750**

50 SERIES—5-Cyl. Turbo—Equipment Schedule 3
W.B. 103.9"; 2.5 Liter.

V50 T5 Sport Wagon	672MW	29850	**14650**	**15350**	**17250**	**21400**
V50 R-Design Wagon	672MW	33700	**16700**	**17450**	**19450**	**24100**

60 SERIES AWD—6-Cyl. Turbo—Equipment Schedule 3
W.B. 109.3"; 3.0 Liter.

S60 T6 Sedan 4D	902FH	38550	**15250**	**15950**	**17050**	**20300**

70 SERIES—5-Cyl. Turbo—Equipment Schedule 1
W.B. 103.9"; 2.5 Liter.

C70 T5 Convertible 2D	672MC	40800	**16600**	**17400**	**17950**	**20700**

70 SERIES—6-Cyl.—Equipment Schedule 1
W.B. 110.8"; 3.2 Liter.

XC70 3.2 Wagon 4D	952BL	32850	**20100**	**20800**	**21900**	**25400**

70 SERIES AWD—6-Cyl. Turbo—Equipment Schedule 1
W.B. 110.8"; 3.0 Liter.

XC70 T6 Wagon 4D	902BZ	38850	**23500**	**24400**	**25300**	**29200**

80 SERIES—6-Cyl.—Equipment Schedule 1
W.B. 111.6"; 3.2 Liter.

S80 Sedan 4D	952AS	37800	**13350**	**14000**	**14950**	**17800**

80 SERIES AWD—6-Cyl. Turbo—Equipment Schedule 1
W.B. 111.6"; 3.0 Liter.

S80 T6 Sedan 4D	902AH	41550	**16850**	**17650**	**18500**	**21800**

2012 VOLVO — YV(1or4)(672MK)–C–#

30 SERIES—5-Cyl. Turbo—Equipment Schedule 3
W.B. 103.9"; 2.5 Liter.

C30 T5 H'Back 2D	672MK	25575	**13000**	**13600**	**14850**	**17750**
C30 R-Design 2D	672MK	27975	**14950**	**15650**	**16850**	**20100**

60 SERIES—5-Cyl. Turbo—Equipment Schedule 3
W.B. 109.3"; 2.5 Liter.

S60 T5 Sedan 4D	622FS	32300	**13350**	**14000**	**15500**	**18800**

60 SERIES AWD—6-Cyl. Turbo—Equipment Schedule 3
W.B. 109.3"; 3.0 Liter.

S60 T6 Sedan 4D	902FH	38550	**18500**	**19300**	**21100**	**25400**
S60 T6 R-Design 4D	902FH	43150	**22500**	**23400**	**25200**	**30200**

70 SERIES—5-Cyl. Turbo—Equipment Schedule 1
W.B. 103.9"; 2.5 Liter.

C70 T5 Convertible 2D	672MC	40825	**19650**	**20400**	**20800**	**23500**

70 SERIES—6-Cyl.—Equipment Schedule 1
W.B. 110.8"; 3.2 Liter.

XC70 3.2 Wagon 4D	952BL	36375	**22200**	**23000**	**23900**	**27200**

70 SERIES AWD—6-Cyl. Turbo—Equipment Schedule 1
W.B. 110.8"; 3.0 Liter.

XC70 T6 Wagon 4D	902BZ	39475	**25500**	**26400**	**27200**	**30800**

80 SERIES—6-Cyl.—Equipment Schedule 1
W.B. 111.6"; 3.2 Liter.

S80 Sedan 4D	952AS	38425	**15500**	**16200**	**17400**	**20600**

80 SERIES AWD—6-Cyl. Turbo—Equipment Schedule 1
W.B. 111.6"; 3.0 Liter.

S80 T6 Sedan 4D	902AH	42175	**18950**	**19800**	**20800**	**24400**

2013 VOLVO — YV(1or4)(672MK)–D–#

30 SERIES—5-Cyl. Turbo—Equipment Schedule 3
W.B. 103.9"; 2.5 Liter.

C30 T5 H'Back 2D	672MK	26395	**16300**	**17000**	**17650**	**20300**
C30 T5 Premier 2D	672MK	27995	**18300**	**19050**	**20000**	**23400**
C30 T5 Premier Plus	672MK	29095	**19000**	**19800**	**20500**	**23700**
C30 T5 Platinum 2D	672MK	31395	**20900**	**21800**	**22400**	**25700**
C30 T5 R-Design 2D	672MK	28745	**18400**	**19150**	**19800**	**22700**
C30 T5 R-Dsgn Prmr	672MK	30345	**20800**	**21700**	**22400**	**25700**
C30 T5 R-Dsgn Prmr +	672MK	31445	**21100**	**22000**	**22500**	**25700**

DEDUCT FOR RECONDITIONING 0415

2013 VOLVO

Body Type	VIN	List	Trade-In Good	Trade-In Very Good	Pvt-Party Good	Retail Excellent
C30 T5 R Platinum	672MK	33745	**21800**	**22700**	**23300**	**26700**

S60—5-Cyl. Turbo—Equipment Schedule 3
W.B. 109.3"; 2.5 Liter.

T5 Sedan 4D	612FS	32645	**15450**	**16150**	**17450**	**20800**
T5 Premier Sedan	612FS	34845	**16400**	**17100**	**18400**	**21800**
T5 Premier Plus Sedan	612FS	35995	**16900**	**17650**	**19000**	**22500**
T5 Platinum Sedan 4D	612FS	38695	**18600**	**19400**	**20800**	**24700**
Adaptive Cruise Control			475	475	505	505
AWD	H		1100	1100	1165	1165

S60 AWD—6-Cyl. Turbo—Equipment Schedule 3
W.B. 109.3"; 3.0 Liter.

T6 Sedan 4D	902FH	41345	**20600**	**21400**	**22900**	**27000**
T6 Premier Plus 4D	902FH	42495	**21000**	**21800**	**23400**	**27700**
T6 Platinum Sedan	902FH	45195	**23300**	**24200**	**25900**	**30700**
T6 R-Design Sedan 4D	902FH	44795	**23100**	**24000**	**25900**	**30800**
T6 R-Design Platinum	902FH	47495	**24000**	**25000**	**26700**	**31600**
Adaptive Cruise Control			475	475	505	505

70 SERIES—5-Cyl. Turbo—Equipment Schedule 1
W.B. 103.9"; 2.5 Liter.

C70 T5 Convertible 2D	672MC	41885	**25400**	**26300**	**26700**	**30100**
C70 T5 Premier + Conv	672MC	43085	**25200**	**26100**	**26600**	**30100**
C70 T5 Platinum Conv	672MC	45685	**27500**	**28500**	**29000**	**32700**

70 SERIES AWD—6-Cyl. Turbo—Equipment Schedule 1
W.B. 110.8"; 3.2 Liter.

XC70 3.2 Wagon 4D	952BZ	36345	**23800**	**24600**	**26700**	**31400**
XC70 3.2 Premier Wag	952BZ	39595	**25300**	**26100**	**28200**	**33000**
XC70 Premier Plus Wag	952BZ	41495	**26800**	**27600**	**29900**	**35000**
XC70 Platinum Wag 4D	952BZ	44195	**30000**	**30900**	**33400**	**39100**
Adaptive Cruise Control			475	475	525	525
FWD	L		(1200)	(1200)	(1320)	(1320)

70 SERIES AWD—6-Cyl. Turbo—Equipment Schedule 1
W.B. 110.8"; 3.0 Liter.

XC70 T6 Wagon 4D	902BZ	40995	**28900**	**29800**	**31800**	**37000**
XC70 T6 Premier Plus	902BZ	42995	**27300**	**28200**	**30600**	**36100**
XC70 T6 Platinum Wag	902BZ	45695	**29200**	**30100**	**32700**	**38400**

80 SERIES—6-Cyl.—Equipment Schedule 1
W.B. 111.6"; 3.2 Liter.

S80 Sedan 4D	952AS	39845	**20600**	**21400**	**22800**	**26900**
S80 Premier Plus Sed	952AS	40995	**21200**	**22100**	**23600**	**28000**
S80 Platinum Sed	952AS	43695	**22700**	**23600**	**25100**	**29600**
Adaptive Cruise Control			475	475	535	535

80 SERIES AWD—6-Cyl. Turbo—Equipment Schedule 1
W.B. 111.6"; 3.0 Liter.

S80 T6 Sedan 4D	902AH	43845	**23700**	**24600**	**26100**	**30700**
S80 T6 Premier Plus	902AH	44995	**24000**	**24900**	**26500**	**31400**
S80 T6 Platinum Sed	902AH	47695	**26300**	**27300**	**28700**	**33500**
Adaptive Cruise Control			475	475	525	525

2014 VOLVO — YV(1or4)(612FS)-E-#

S60—5-Cyl. Turbo—Equipment Schedule 3
W.B. 109.3"; 2.5 Liter.

T5 Sedan 4D	612FS	33315	**19400**	**20200**	**21300**	**24800**
T5 Premier Sedan 4D	612FS	35815	**20400**	**21200**	**22200**	**25800**
T5 Premier Plus Sedan	612FS	36465	**20900**	**21800**	**22800**	**26500**
T5 Platinum Sedan	612FS	39165	**22600**	**23500**	**24600**	**28700**
Adaptive Cruise Control			500	500	535	535
AWD	H		1300	1300	1385	1385

S60 AWD—6-Cyl. Turbo—Equipment Schedule 3
W.B. 109.3"; 3.0 Liter.

T6 Sedan	902FH	40165	**24500**	**25500**	**26700**	**31000**
T6 Premier Plus 4D	902FH	40815	**24900**	**25900**	**27200**	**31700**
T6 Platinum Sedan	902FH	43515	**27300**	**28400**	**29700**	**34700**
T6 R-Design Sedan	902FH	43615	**27100**	**28100**	**29500**	**34400**
T6 R-Design Platinum	902FH	46615	**28000**	**29100**	**30500**	**35600**
Adaptive Cruise Control			500	500	530	530

S80—6-Cyl.—Equipment Schedule 1
W.B. 111.6"; 3.2 Liter.

3.2 Sedan 4D	952AS	40815	**23800**	**24700**	**25900**	**30200**
3.2 Premier Plus Sedan	952AS	42315	**24400**	**25400**	**26700**	**31300**
3.2 Platinum Sedan	952AS	45015	**25900**	**26900**	**28200**	**32800**

S80 AWD—6-Cyl. Turbo—Equipment Schedule 1
W.B. 111.6"; 3.0 Liter.

T6 Sedan 4D	902AH	44865	**25500**	**26500**	**27800**	**32500**

Body Type	VIN	List	Trade-In Good	Trade-In Very Good	Pvt-Party Good	Retail Excellent
T6 Premier Plus Sed.............	902AH	46365	27200	28300	29600	34600
T6 Platinum Sedan 4D	902AH	49065	29500	30600	31800	36800

Body Type	VIN	List	Trade-In Good	Very Good	Pvt-Party Good	Retail Excellent

Truck & Van Section

ACURA

2000 ACURA — No Production

2001 ACURA — 2HN(YD182)-1-#

MDX 4WD—V6—Truck Equipment Schedule T3

	VIN	List	Good	Very Good	Good	Excellent
Sport Utility 4D	YD182	34850	2050	2325	3125	4750
Touring Spt Util 4D	YD186	37450	2650	3000	3850	5750

2002 ACURA — 2HN(YD182)-2-#

MDX 4WD—V6—Truck Equipment Schedule T3

	VIN	List	Good	Very Good	Good	Excellent
Sport Utility 4D	YD182	35180	2850	3225	3925	5650
Touring Spt Util 4D	YD186	37780	3550	3950	4825	6875

2003 ACURA — 2HN(YD182)-3-#

MDX 4WD—V6—Truck Equipment Schedule T3

	VIN	List	Good	Very Good	Good	Excellent
Sport Utility 4D	YD182	36200	3575	3975	4850	6850
Touring Spt Util 4D	YD186	38800	4375	4825	5725	8050

2004 ACURA — 2NH(YD182)-4-#

MDX 4WD—V6—Truck Equipment Schedule T3

	VIN	List	Good	Very Good	Good	Excellent
Sport Utility 4D	YD182	36945	4325	4750	5650	7850
Touring Spt Util 4D	YD186	39545	5100	5600	6675	9200

2005 ACURA — 2HN(YD182)-5-#

MDX 4WD—V6—Truck Equipment Schedule T3

	VIN	List	Good	Very Good	Good	Excellent
Sport Utility 4D	YD182	37270	5625	6125	7125	9600
Touring Spt Util 4D	YD186	40095	6800	7375	8525	11500

2006 ACURA — 2HN(YD182)-6-#

MDX 4WD—V6—Truck Equipment Schedule T3

	VIN	List	Good	Very Good	Good	Excellent
Sport Utility 4D	YD182	37740	7075	7650	8575	11150
Touring Spt Util 4D	YD186	40565	8475	9125	10100	13150

2007 ACURA — 2HN(TB182)-7-#

RDX SH-AWD—4-Cyl. Turbo—Truck Equipment Schedule T3

	VIN	List	Good	Very Good	Good	Excellent
Sport Utility 4D	TB182	33610	9550	10100	10950	13400
Technology Pkg			350	350	405	405

MDX AWD—V6 VTEC—Truck Equipment Schedule T3

	VIN	List	Good	Very Good	Good	Excellent
Sport Utility 4D	YD282	40665	12700	13500	14050	17050
Sport Pkg			350	350	400	400
Technology Pkg			800	800	950	950

2008 ACURA — 2HNor5J8(TB182)-8-#

RDX AWD—4-Cyl. Turbo—Truck Equipment Schedule T3

	VIN	List	Good	Very Good	Good	Excellent
Sport Utility 4D	TB182	33910	10550	11100	11950	14400
Technology Pkg			350	350	430	430

MDX AWD—V6 VTEC—Truck Equipment Schedule T3

	VIN	List	Good	Very Good	Good	Excellent
Sport Utility 4D	YD282	40910	14150	15000	15800	19050
Sport Pkg			350	350	425	425
Technology Pkg			875	875	1025	1025

2009 ACURA — 2HNor5J8(TB182)-9-#

RDX AWD—4-Cyl. Turbo—Truck Equipment Schedule T3

	VIN	List	Good	Very Good	Good	Excellent
Sport Utility 4D	TB182	34455	13350	14000	15100	17800
Technology Pkg			375	375	440	440

MDX AWD—V6 VTEC—Truck Equipment Schedule T3

	VIN	List	Good	Very Good	Good	Excellent
Sport Utility 4D	YD282	41550	17700	18600	19350	22700
Sport Pkg			375	375	440	440
Technology Pkg			925	925	1065	1065

TRUCKS & VANS

Body Type	VIN	List	Trade-In Good	Very Good	Pvt-Party Good	Retail Excellent
2010 ACURA — 2HNor5J8(TB1H2)–A–#						
RDX AWD—4-Cyl. Turbo—Truck Equipment Schedule T3						
Sport Utility 4D	TB1H2	35330	16000	16700	17650	20400
Technology Pkg			400	400	455	455
FWD	2		(1100)	(1100)	(1255)	(1255)
MDX AWD—V6 VTEC—Truck Equipment Schedule T3						
Sport Utility 4D	YD282	43040	20500	21300	22100	25500
Advance Pkg			1175	1175	1335	1335
Technology Pkg			975	975	1110	1110
ZDX AWD—V6 VTEC—Truck Equipment Schedule T3						
Sport Utility 4D	YB1H2	46305	22600	23500	23900	27000
Advance Pkg			1175	1175	1275	1275
Technology Pkg			400	400	435	435
2011 ACURA — 2HNor5J8(TB1H2)–B–#						
RDX AWD—4-Cyl. Turbo—Truck Equipment Schedule T3						
Sport Utility 4D	TB1H2	35480	17900	18600	19650	22400
Technology Pkg			425	425	470	470
FWD	2		(1100)	(1100)	(1235)	(1235)
MDX AWD—V6 VTEC—Truck Equipment Schedule T3						
Sport Utility 4D	YD2H2	43440	23300	24200	24900	28200
Advance Pkg			1250	1250	1375	1375
Technology Pkg			1025	1025	1140	1140
ZDX AWD—V6 VTEC—Truck Equipment Schedule T3						
Sport Utility 4D	YB1H2	46505	24200	25100	25600	28500
Advance Pkg			1250	1250	1335	1335
Technology Pkg			425	425	450	450
2012 ACURA — 2HNor5J8(TB2H2)–C–#						
RDX—4-Cyl. Turbo—Truck Equipment Schedule T3						
Sport Utility 4D	TB2H2	33780	19150	19850	20900	23600
Technology Pkg			450	450	495	495
RDX SH-AWD—4-Cyl. Turbo—Truck Equipment Schedule T3						
Sport Utility 4D	TB1H2	35780	21100	21800	22800	25800
Technology Pkg			450	450	490	490
MDX AWD—V6 VTEC—Truck Equipment Schedule T3						
Sport Utility 4D	YD2H2	43815	26400	27300	28000	31500
Advance Pkg			1300	1300	1435	1435
Technology Pkg			1075	1075	1195	1195
ZDX AWD—V6 VTEC—Truck Equipment Schedule T3						
Sport Utility 4D	YB1H2	46905	25800	26700	27700	31300
Advance Pkg			1300	1300	1445	1445
Technology Pkg			450	450	485	485
2013 ACURA — 2HNor5J8(TB4H3)–D–#						
RDX AWD—4-Cyl. Turbo—Truck Equipment Schedule T3						
Sport Utility 4D	TB4H3	36615	25100	25900	27100	30600
Technology Pkg			450	450	510	510
FWD	3		(800)	(800)	(885)	(885)
MDX AWD—V6 VTEC—Truck Equipment Schedule T3						
Sport Utility 4D	YD2H2	44175	30800	31800	32300	35900
Advance Pkg			1375	1375	1490	1490
Technology Pkg			1150	1150	1240	1240
ZDX AWD—V6 VTEC—Truck Equipment Schedule T3						
Sport Utility 4D	YB1H6	51815	26900	27700	28700	32100
2014 ACURA — 2HNor5J8(TB4H3)–E–#						
RDX AWD—4-Cyl. Turbo—Truck Equipment Schedule T3						
Sport Utility 4D	TB4H3	36815	27700	28600	29500	33000
Technology Pkg			475	475	520	520
FWD	3		(800)	(800)	(870)	(870)
MDX AWD—V6 VTEC—Truck Equipment Schedule T3						
Sport Utility 4D	YD4H2	45185	37800	38900	39100	42900
Advance Pkg			1425	1425	1535	1535
Technology Pkg			1200	1200	1280	1280

Body Type	VIN	List	Trade-In Good	Very Good	Pvt-Party Good	Retail Excellent

AUDI

2009 AUDI — WA1(KF98R)-9-#

Q5 QUATTRO AWD—V6—Truck Equipment Schedule T3

Body Type	VIN	List	Good	Very Good	Good	Excellent
3.2 Premium Utility	KF98R	38025	15250	16000	16700	19550
S-Line Pkg	E		700	700	795	795

Q7 QUATTRO AWD—V6—Truck Equipment Schedule T3

3.6 Sport Utility 4D	AY74L	44325	16450	17200	18150	21000
3.6 Premium Utility	AY74L	47725	18850	19650	20600	23900
Premium Plus Pkg			750	750	870	870
Prestige Pkg			1525	1525	1740	1740

Q7 QUATTRO AWD—V6 Turbo Diesel—Truck Equipment Sch T3

3.0 TDI Sport Util	AM74L	51725	22900	23900	24900	28800
Premium Plus Pkg			750	750	865	865
Prestige Pkg			1525	1525	1735	1735

Q7 QUATTRO AWD—V8—Truck Equipment Schedule T3

4.2 Premium Utility	BV74L	60045	22600	23600	24500	28300
Bang & Olufsen Sound			2375	2375	2695	2695
S-Line Pkg	E		700	700	795	795
Adaptive Cruise Control			375	375	425	425

2010 AUDI — WA1(CKAFP)-A-#

Q5 QUATTRO AWD—V6—Truck Equipment Schedule T3

3.2 Premium Util	CKAFP	38175	19900	20700	21400	24700
Bang & Olufsen Sound			350	350	395	395
Premium Plus Pkg			800	800	905	905
S-Line Pkg	M,W		800	800	905	905

Q7 QUATTRO AWD—V6—Truck Equipment Schedule T3

3.6 Premium Util	CYAFE	47725	24800	25800	26700	30400
Premium Plus Pkg			800	800	910	910
Prestige Pkg			1600	1600	1820	1820
S-Line Pkg	M,W		800	800	910	910

Q7 QUATTRO AWD—V6 Turbo Diesel—Truck Equipment Schedule T3

3.0 TDI Premium	CMAFE	51725	28500	29600	30500	34700
Bang & Olufsen Sound			2500	2500	2825	2825
Premium Plus Pkg			800	800	905	905
Prestige Pkg			1600	1600	1815	1815
S-Line Pkg	M,W		800	800	905	905

Q7 QUATTRO AWD—V8—Truck Equipment Schedule T3

4.2 Premium Util	DVAFE	61825	28700	29800	30700	34900
Bang & Olufsen Sound			2500	2500	2830	2830
S-Line Pkg	D		800	800	910	910
Adaptive Cruise Control			400	400	455	455

2011 AUDI — WA1(CFBFP)-B-#

Q5 QUATTRO AWD—4-Cyl. Turbo—Truck Equipment Schedule T3

2.0T Premium Util	CFBFP	36075	21900	22800	23600	26900
Bang & Olufsen Sound			350	350	395	395
Premium Plus Pkg			850	850	940	940

Q5 QUATTRO AWD—V6—Truck Equipment Schedule T3

3.2 Premium Util	CKBFP	43375	25500	26400	27500	31600
Bang & Olufsen Sound			350	350	400	400
Prestige Pkg			1675	1675	1905	1905
S-Line Pkg			900	900	1020	1020

Q7 QUATTRO AWD—V6 Turbo Diesel—Truck Equipment Schedule T3

3.0 TDI Premium	CMAFE	51775	32900	34100	35000	39600
Bang & Olufsen Sound			2625	2625	2970	2970
Premium Plus Pkg			850	850	950	950

Q7 QUATTRO AWD—V6 Supercharged—Truck Equipment Schedule T3

3.0 Premium Util	CGAFE	46575	28300	29400	30200	34200
3.0 Prestige Utility	VGAFE	59775	34300	35500	36500	41300
Bang & Olufsen Sound			2625	2625	2980	2980
Premium Plus Pkg			850	850	955	955
S-Line Pkg			900	900	1025	1025

2012 AUDI — WA1(CFAFP)-C-#

Q5 QUATTRO AWD—4-Cyl. Turbo—Truck Equipment Schedule T3

| 2.0T Premium SUV | CFAFP | 36475 | 25200 | 26100 | 26800 | 30300 |
| Bang & Olufsen Sound | | | 350 | 350 | 395 | 395 |

TRUCKS & VANS

Body Type	VIN	List	Trade-In Good	Very Good	Pvt-Party Good	Retail Excellent
Premium Plus Pkg			875	875	965	965
Q5 QUATTRO AWD—V6—Truck Equipment Schedule T3						
3.2 Premium Plus	DKAFP	43875	29000	30000	30900	34800
Bang & Olufsen Sound			350	350	395	395
Prestige Pkg			1750	1750	1935	1935
S-Line Pkg			1000	1000	1100	1100
Q7 QUATTRO AWD—V6 Turbo Diesel—Truck Equipment Schedule T3						
3.0 TDI Premium	CMAFE	52325	36200	37400	38200	42800
Bang & Olufsen Sound			2750	2750	3080	3080
Premium Plus Pkg			875	875	985	985
Prestige Pkg			1750	1750	1975	1975
S-Line Pkg			1000	1000	1120	1120
Q7 QUATTRO AWD—V6 Supercharged—Truck Equipment Schedule T3						
3.0 Premium Util	AGAFE	47125	31400	32500	33300	37400
3.0T S-Line Prstg	DGAFE	60825	39500	40900	41700	46800
Bang & Olufsen Sound			2750	2750	3085	3085
Premium Plus Pkg			875	875	990	990
S-Line Pkg			1000	1000	1125	1125

2013 AUDI — WA1(CFAFP)-D-#

Body Type	VIN	List	Trade-In Good	Very Good	Pvt-Party Good	Retail Excellent
Q5 QUATTRO AWD—4-Cyl. Turbo—Truck Equipment Schedule T3						
2.0T Premium SUV	CFAFP	36795	26500	27400	28100	31500
2.0T Premium Plus	LFAFP	41095	29800	30800	31500	35100
Bang & Olufsen Sound			375	375	400	400
Q5 QUATTRO AWD—4-Cyl. Turbo Hybrid—Truck Equipment Schedule T3						
Prestige SUV 4D	C8AFP	51795	34700	35900	36300	40300
Q5 QUATTRO AWD—V6 Turbo—Truck Equipment Schedule T3						
3.0TPremiumPlus	DGAFP	44795	33100	34200	34600	38500
3.0T Prestige SUV	WGAFP	52295	35700	36800	37200	41300
Bang & Olufsen Sound			375	375	400	400
S-Line Pkg			1000	1000	1085	1085
Q7 QUATTRO AWD—V6 Supercharged—Truck Equipment Schedule T3						
3.0T Premium Util	CGAFE	47695	32500	33600	34900	39600
3.0T Premium +	LGAFE	54045	37300	38600	39800	45000
3.0TSLinePrestige	DGAFE	61445	42800	44200	45200	50700
Bang & Olufsen Sound			2875	2875	3245	3245
S-Line Pkg			1000	1000	1130	1130
Q7 QUATTRO AWD—V6 Turbo Diesel—Truck Equipment Schedule T3						
3.0 TDI Premium	CMAFE	52895	37400	38700	39800	44900
3.0 TDI Prem Plus	LMAFE	59245	41400	42800	43800	49300
3.0 TDI Prestige	VMAFE	65445	46300	47900	48600	54300
Bang & Olufsen Sound			2875	2875	3225	3225
S-Line Pkg			1000	1000	1120	1120

2014 AUDI — WA1(CFAFP)-E-#

Body Type	VIN	List	Trade-In Good	Very Good	Pvt-Party Good	Retail Excellent
Q5 QUATTRO AWD—4-Cyl. Turbo—Truck Equipment Schedule T3						
2.0T Premium	CFAFP	38195	29100	30000	30800	34500
2.0T Premium Plus	LFAFP	42095	32300	33300	33900	37700
Bang & Olufsen Sound			375	375	405	405
Q5 QUATTRO AWD—4-Cyl. Turbo Hybrid—Truck Equipment Schedule T3						
Prestige Sport Util	CCAFP	52195	37600	38800	38900	43000
Q5 QUATTRO AWD—V6 Supercharged—Truck Equipment Schedule T3						
3.0TPremiumPlus	DGAFP	45295	35300	36400	36700	40700
3.0T Prestige 4D	WGAFP	52795	38600	39800	40000	44100
Bang & Olufsen Sound			375	375	400	400
S-Line Pkg			1000	1000	1070	1070
Q5 QUATTRO AWD—V6 Turbo Diesel—Truck Equipment Schedule T3						
TDI PremiumPlus	CMAFP	47395	36900	38000	38300	42300
TDI Prestige 4D	VMAFP	54895	40800	42100	42500	47300
Bang & Olufsen Sound			375	375	400	400
Q7 QUATTRO AWD—V6 Supercharged—Truck Equipment Schedule T3						
3.0T Premium 4D	CGAFE	48595	38800	40200	41100	46100
3.0T Premium +	LGAFE	54595	44600	46100	46800	52400
3.0TS-Line Prstg	DGAFE	61795	49600	51300	52100	58000
Bang & Olufsen Sound			3000	3000	3340	3340
S-Line Pkg			1000	1000	1110	1110
Q7 QUATTRO AWD—V6 Turbo Diesel—Truck Equipment Schedule T3						
TDI Premium 4D	CMAFE	53795	43700	45200	45900	51300
TDI Premium +	LMAFE	59795	48200	49900	50800	56700
TDI Prestige 4D	VMAFE	65795	53200	55000	55500	61600
Bang & Olufsen Sound			3000	3000	3320	3320
Sensing Cruise Control			500	500	555	555

Body Type	VIN	List	Trade-In Good	Trade-In Very Good	Pvt-Party Good	Retail Excellent
S-Line Pkg			1000	1000	1105	1105
SQ5 QUATTRO AWD—V6 Supercharged—Truck Equipment Schedule T3						
Premium Plus 4D	CGAFP	52795	40100	41600	41400	46000
Bang & Olufsen Sound			375	375	400	400
SQ5 QUATTRO AWD—V6 Supercharged—Truck Equipment Schedule T3						
Prestige Sport Util	VGAFP	60295	44600	46200	45700	50500

BMW

2000 BMW — WBA(FB335)–Y–#

Body Type	VIN	List	Good	Very Good	Good	Excellent
X5 AWD—V8—Truck Equipment Schedule T3						
4.4i Sport Utility 4D	FB335	49970	2025	2250	3200	4700
Sport Pkg			150	150	200	200

2001 BMW — WBA(FA535)–1–#

Body Type	VIN	List	Good	Very Good	Good	Excellent
X5 AWD—6-Cyl.—Truck Equipment Schedule T3						
3.0i Sport Utility 4D	FA535	42195	2550	2825	3675	5225
Sport Pkg			150	150	215	215
X5 AWD—V8—Truck Equipment Schedule T3						
4.4i Sport Utility 4D	FB335	49970	2850	3150	4050	5750
Sport Pkg			150	150	215	215

2002 BMW — 5UX(FA535)–2–#

Body Type	VIN	List	Good	Very Good	Good	Excellent
X5 AWD—6-Cyl.—Truck Equipment Schedule T3						
3.0i Sport Util 4D	FA535	42270	3200	3500	4525	6250
Sport Pkg			175	175	225	225
X5 AWD—V8—Truck Equipment Schedule T3						
4.4i Sport Util 4D	FB335	50045	3500	3800	4875	6750
4.6is Sport Util 4D	FB935	66845	4700	5050	6275	8550
Sport Pkg			175	175	225	225

2003 BMW — 5UX(FA535)–3–#

Body Type	VIN	List	Good	Very Good	Good	Excellent
X5 AWD—6-Cyl.—Truck Equipment Schedule T3						
3.0i Sport Util 4D	FA535	42920	3650	3950	5050	6925
Sport Pkg			175	175	240	240
X5 AWD—V8—Truck Equipment Schedule T3						
4.4i Sport Util 4D	FB335	50645	3950	4275	5400	7425
4.6is Sport Util 4D	FB935	67495	6500	6950	8500	11300
Sport Pkg			175	175	240	240

2004 BMW — WBXor5UX(PA734)–4–#

Body Type	VIN	List	Good	Very Good	Good	Excellent
X3 AWD—6-Cyl.—Truck Equipment Schedule T3						
2.5i Sport Utility 4D	PA734	33740	4275	4625	5575	7450
3.0i Sport Utility 4D	PA934	38270	4875	5250	6275	8325
Sport Pkg			200	200	255	255
Premium Pkg			700	700	940	940
X5 AWD—6-Cyl.—Truck Equipment Schedule T3						
3.0i Sport Utility 4D	FA135	40995	4725	5100	6150	8200
Sport Pkg			200	200	255	255
X5 AWD—V8—Truck Equipment Schedule T3						
4.4i Sport Util 4D	FB535	52195	5050	5450	6750	9025
4.8is Sport Util 4D	FA935	70495	7300	7775	9225	12050
Sport Pkg			200	200	255	255

2005 BMW — WBXor5UX(PA734)–5–#

Body Type	VIN	List	Good	Very Good	Good	Excellent
X3 AWD—6-Cyl.—Truck Equipment Schedule T3						
2.5i Sport Utility 4D	PA734	34715	4700	5050	5925	7725
3.0i Sport Utility 4D	PA934	38445	5050	5425	6525	8475
Sport Pkg			200	200	265	265
Premium Pkg			775	775	1010	1010
X5 AWD—6-Cyl.—Truck Equipment Schedule T3						
3.0i Sport Utility 4D	FA135	45120	5500	5900	7125	9350
Sport Pkg			200	200	265	265
X5 AWD—V8—Truck Equipment Schedule T3						
4.4i Sport Utility 4D	FB535	53495	6300	6725	8025	10500
4.8is Sport Util 4D	FA935	70795	7850	8350	9775	12650
Sport Pkg			200	200	265	265

Body Type	VIN	List	Trade-In Good	Trade-In Very Good	Pvt-Party Good	Retail Excellent

2006 BMW — WBXor5UX(PA934)-6-#

X3 AWD—6-Cyl.—Truck Equipment Schedule T3
3.0i Sport Utility 4D	PA934	38945	6800	7225	8575	11100
Sport Pkg			200	200	265	265
Premium Pkg			825	825	1095	1095

X5 AWD—6-Cyl.—Truck Equipment Schedule T3
| 3.0i Sport Util 4D | FA135 | 45920 | 6625 | 7050 | 8325 | 10700 |
| Sport Pkg | | | 200 | 200 | 265 | 265 |

X5 AWD—V8—Truck Equipment Schedule T3
4.4i Sport Utility 4D	FB535	54295	7425	7875	9250	11850
4.8is Sport Util 4D	FA935	71795	8300	8800	10450	13350
Sport Pkg			200	200	265	265

2007 BMW — WBXor5UX(PC934)-7-#

X3 AWD—6-Cyl.—Truck Equipment Schedule T3
3.0si Sport Util 4D	PC934	41145	8650	9150	10450	13100
Sport Pkg			200	200	260	260
Premium Pkg			875	875	1150	1150

X5 AWD—6-Cyl.—Truck Equipment Schedule T3
3.0si Sport Util 4D	FE435	48045	11950	12550	13700	16500
Sport Pkg			200	200	240	240
Third Row Seat			375	375	445	445

X5 AWD—V8—Truck Equipment Schedule T3
4.8i Sport Utility 4D	FE834	55195	12950	13600	14800	17900
Sport Pkg			200	200	240	240
Third Row Seat			375	375	450	450

2008 BMW — WBXor5UX(PC934)-8-#

X3 AWD—6-Cyl.—Truck Equipment Schedule T3
3.0si Sport Util 4D	PC934	40225	10600	11150	12400	15150
Sport Pkg			200	200	250	250
Premium Pkg			950	950	1175	1175

X5 AWD—6-Cyl.—Truck Equipment Schedule T3
3.0si Sport Util 4D	FE435	46675	13550	14200	15150	17850
Sport Pkg			200	200	235	235
Third Row Seat			400	400	470	470

X5 AWD—V8—Truck Equipment Schedule T3
4.8i Sport Utility 4D	FE835	55275	15050	15700	16750	19750
Sport Pkg			200	200	235	235
Third Row Seat			400	400	470	470

X6 AWD—V6 Twin Turbo—Truck Equipment Schedule T3
| 35i Sport Utility 4D | FG435 | 53275 | 22100 | 23000 | 23400 | 26800 |
| Sport Pkg | | | 200 | 200 | 220 | 220 |

X6 AWD—V8 Twin Turbo—Truck Equipment Schedule T3
| 50i Sport Utility 4D | FG835 | 63775 | 23300 | 24200 | 24800 | 28400 |
| Sport Pkg | | | 200 | 200 | 220 | 220 |

2009 BMW — WBXor5UX(PC934)-9-#

X3 AWD—6-Cyl.—Truck Equipment Schedule T3
3.0i Sport Utility 4D	PC934	41975	12750	13350	14800	17650
Sport Pkg			250	250	305	305
Premium Pkg			1000	1000	1220	1220

X5 AWD—6-Cyl.—Truck Equipment Schedule T3
30i Sport Utility 4D	FE435	49775	16650	17350	18300	21200
Sport Pkg			250	250	290	290
Third Row Seat			475	475	545	545

X5 AWD—6-Cyl. Turbo Diesel—Truck Equipment Sch T3
35d Sport Utility 4D	FF035	53475	18800	19550	20600	23800
Sport Pkg			250	250	285	285
Third Row Seat			475	475	545	545

X5 AWD—V8—Truck Equipment Schedule T3
48i Sport Utility 4D	FE835	57025	19000	19750	20800	24000
Sport Pkg			250	250	285	285
Third Row Seat			475	475	545	545

X6 AWD—V6 Twin Turbo—Truck Equipment Schedule T3
| 35i Sport Utility 4D | FG435 | 56725 | 25100 | 26000 | 26700 | 30500 |
| Sport Pkg | | | 250 | 250 | 280 | 280 |

X6 AWD—V8 Twin Turbo—Truck Equipment Schedule T3
| 50i Sport Utility 4D | FG835 | 67475 | 26300 | 27400 | 28100 | 32100 |
| Sport Pkg | | | 250 | 250 | 280 | 280 |

Body Type	VIN	List	Trade-In Good	Trade-In Very Good	Pvt-Party Good	Retail Excellent
2010 BMW — (Wor5)(B,UorY)(MorX)(PC9C4)–A–#						
X3 AWD—6-Cyl.—Truck Equipment Schedule T3						
3.0i Spt Utility 4D	PC9C4	39575	16250	16900	17800	20300
Sport Pkg			275	275	310	310
Premium Pkg			1000	1000	1125	1125
X5 AWD—6-Cyl.—Truck Equipment Schedule T3						
xDrive30i Spt Util	FE4C	48475	19700	20500	21500	24500
Sport Activity Pkg			275	275	315	315
M Sport Pkg			1100	1100	1260	1260
Third Row Seat			550	550	630	630
X5 AWD—6-Cyl. Turbo Diesel—Truck Equipment Schedule T3						
xDrive35d Spt Util	FF0C	52175	22200	23000	23900	27300
Sport Activity Pkg			275	275	315	315
Third Row Seat			550	550	625	625
X5 AWD—V8—Truck Equipment Schedule T3						
xDrive48i Spt Util	FE8C	57175	22700	23500	24500	28000
Sport Activity Pkg			275	275	315	315
M Sport Pkg			1100	1100	1260	1260
Third Row Seat			550	550	630	630
X5 M AWD—V8 Twin Turbo—Truck Equipment Schedule T3						
Sport Utility 4D	GY0C5	86375	34800	36200	36400	41200
X6 AWD—V6 Twin Turbo—Truck Equipment Schedule T3						
35i Sport Utility 4D	FG4C5	57375	27800	28800	29500	33300
Sport Pkg			275	275	305	305
X6 AWD—V8 Twin Turbo—Truck Equipment Schedule T3						
50i Sport Utility 4D	FG8C5	68075	29500	30600	31400	35400
Sport Pkg			275	275	305	305
X6 M AWD—V8 Twin Turbo—Truck Equipment Schedule T3						
Sport Utility 4D	GZ0C5	89875	37900	39200	40100	45500
X6 AWD—V8 Twin Turbo ActiveHybrid—Truck Equipment Sch T3						
Sport Utility 4D	FH0C5	89775	32000	33100	33800	38200
Adaptive Cruise Control			(400)	(400)	(445)	(445)
2011 BMW — 5(UXorYM)(WX5C5)–B–#						
X3 AWD—6-Cyl.—Truck Equipment Schedule T3						
xDrive28i Spt Utl	WX5C5	39075	22100	22900	23900	27100
Sport Pkg			300	300	335	335
Premium Pkg			1000	1000	1115	1115
X3 AWD—6-Cyl. Twin Turbo—Truck Equipment Schedule T3						
xDrive35i Spt Util	WX7C5	43375	25100	26000	27100	30700
Sport Pkg			300	300	335	335
Premium Pkg			1000	1000	1115	1115
X5 AWD—6-Cyl. Turbo—Truck Equipment Schedule T3						
35i Sport Utility 4D	ZV4C5	48125	24600	25500	26500	29900
35i Premium SUV	ZV4C5	52475	26000	27000	27900	31500
35i Sport Activity	ZV4C5	54975	26200	27200	28200	31900
M Sport Pkg			1125	1125	1265	1265
Third Row Seat			600	600	670	670
X5 AWD—6-Cyl. Twin Turbo Diesel—Truck Equipment Schedule T3						
35d Sport Util 4D	ZW0C5	53625	26000	27800	28800	32500
Premium Pkg			850	850	945	945
Sport Activity Pkg			300	300	335	335
Third Row Seat			600	600	675	675
X5 AWD—V8 Twin Turbo—Truck Equipment Schedule T3						
50i Sport Utility 4D	ZV8C5	59275	27400	28400	29300	33100
Sport Activity Pkg			300	300	335	335
M Sport Pkg			1125	1125	1260	1260
Third Row Seat			600	600	670	670
X5 M AWD—V8 Twin Turbo—Truck Equipment Schedule T3						
xDrive Sport Utl	GY0C5	86575	39100	40700	40600	45600
X6 AWD—V6 Twin Turbo—Truck Equipment Schedule T3						
35i Sport Utility 4D	FG2C5	57375	31100	32100	33100	37400
Sport Pkg			300	300	335	335
Active Cruise Control			425	425	475	475
X6 AWD—V8 Twin Turbo—Truck Equipment Schedule T3						
50i Sport Utility 4D	FG8C5	68075	33100	34200	35200	39700
Sport Pkg			300	300	335	335
Active Cruise Control			425	425	475	475
X6 M AWD—V8 Twin Turbo—Truck Equipment Schedule T3						
Sport Utility 4D	GZ0C5	98075	44800	46200	46900	52600

TRUCKS & VANS

Body Type	VIN	List	Trade-In Good	Very Good	Pvt-Party Good	Retail Excellent
X6 AWD—V8 Twin Turbo ActiveHybrid—Truck Equipment Sch T3						
Sport Utility 4D	FH0C5	89775	35300	36500	37500	42400

2012 BMW — 5(UXorYM)(WX5C5)—C-#

Body Type	VIN	List	Trade-In Good	Very Good	Pvt-Party Good	Retail Excellent
X3 AWD—6-Cyl.—Truck Equipment Schedule T3						
xDrive28i Spt Util	WX5C5	37725	23900	24700	25500	28500
Sport Activity Pkg			325	325	355	355
Premium Pkg			1000	1000	1090	1090
X3 AWD—6-Cyl. Twin Turbo—Truck Equipment Schedule T3						
xDrive35i Spt Util	WX7C5	43275	26500	27400	28200	31600
Sport Activity Pkg			325	325	355	355
Premium Pkg			1000	1000	1100	1100
X5 AWD—6-Cyl. Turbo—Truck Equipment Schedule T3						
35i Sport Utility 4D	ZV4C5	48075	30800	31800	32600	36300
35i Premium Utility	ZV4C5	55675	32800	33800	34600	38500
35i Sport Activity	ZV4C5	58175	33000	34000	34800	38800
Sport Pkg			325	325	360	360
M Sport Pkg			1150	1150	1270	1270
Third Row Seat			650	650	720	720
X5 AWD—6-Cyl. Twin Turbo Diesel—Truck Equipment Schedule T3						
35d Sport Utility	ZW0C5	57175	33600	34600	35500	39600
Premium Pkg			875	875	975	975
Sport Activity Pkg			325	325	360	360
Third Row Seat			650	650	720	720
X5 AWD—V8 Twin Turbo—Truck Equipment Schedule T3						
50i Sport Utility 4D	ZV8C5	64675	35200	36300	37100	41400
Sport Activity Pkg			325	325	360	360
Premium Pkg			875	875	975	975
M Sport Pkg			1150	1150	1275	1275
Third Row Seat			650	650	720	720
X5 M AWD—V8 Twin Turbo—Truck Equipment Schedule T3						
Sport Utility 4D	GY0C5	88145	46500	48300	47600	52800
X6 AWD—V6 Twin Turbo—Truck Equipment Schedule T3						
35i Sport Utility 4D	FG2C5	59775	38100	39300	40200	44900
Sport Pkg			325	325	360	360
Active Cruise Control			450	450	495	495
X6 AWD—V8 Twin Turbo—Truck Equipment Schedule T3						
50i Sport Utility 4D	FG8C5	70375	41300	42600	43600	48700
Sport Pkg			325	325	360	360
Active Cruise Control			450	450	500	500
X6 M AWD—V8 Twin Turbo—Truck Equipment Schedule T3						
Sport Utility 4D	GZ0C5	91195	47800	49300	49900	55600

2013 BMW — 5(UXorYM)(VM1C5)—D-#

Body Type	VIN	List	Trade-In Good	Very Good	Pvt-Party Good	Retail Excellent
X1—4-Cyl. Twin Turbo—Truck Equipment Schedule T3						
sDrive28i Spt Util	VM1C5	32995	20200	20900	21800	24500
Premium Pkg			1000	1000	1095	1095
M Sport Pkg			1175	1175	1290	1290
Ultimate Pkg			2650	2650	2910	2910
X1 AWD—4-Cyl. Twin Turbo—Truck Equipment Schedule T3						
xDrive28i Spt Util	VL1C5	34695	22300	23000	24100	27200
Premium Pkg			1000	1000	1115	1115
M Sport Pkg			1175	1175	1310	1310
Ultimate Pkg			2650	2650	2950	2950
X1 AWD—6-Cyl. Twin Turbo—Truck Equipment Schedule T3						
xDrive35i Spt Util	VM5C5	40795	26300	27100	28200	31600
Premium Pkg			1000	1000	1105	1105
M Sport Pkg			1175	1175	1295	1295
Ultimate Pkg			2650	2650	2925	2925
X3 AWD—4-Cyl. Turbo—Truck Equipment Schedule T3						
xDrive28i Spt Util	WX9C5	39395	25200	26000	26900	30000
Sport Activity Pkg			350	350	385	385
Premium Pkg			1000	1000	1095	1095
M Sport Pkg			1175	1175	1290	1290
X3 AWD—6-Cyl. Twin Turbo—Truck Equipment Schedule T3						
xDrive35i Spt Util	WX7C5	44495	31200	32200	33100	36800
Sport Activity Pkg			350	350	385	385
Premium Pkg			1000	1000	1095	1095
M Sport Pkg			1175	1175	1285	1285
X5 AWD—6-Cyl. Twin Turbo—Truck Equipment Schedule T3						
35i Sport Utility 4D	ZV4C5	48395	34100	35200	36000	40100
35i Premium Utility	ZV4C5	56095	39200	40400	41300	45900

2013 BMW

Body Type	VIN	List	Trade-In Good	Very Good	Pvt-Party Good	Retail Excellent
35i Sport Activity	ZV4C5	58595	40000	41200	42000	46700
Third Row Seat			700	700	775	775
X5 AWD—6-Cyl. Twin Turbo Diesel—Truck Equipment Schedule T3						
35d Sport Utility	ZW0C5	57595	40200	41400	42200	46900
Sport Activity Pkg			350	350	385	385
Premium Pkg			925	925	1015	1015
X5 AWD—V8 Twin Turbo—Truck Equipment Schedule T3						
50i Sport Utility 4D	ZV8C5	65095	42000	43300	44000	48800
Sport Activity Pkg			350	350	385	385
Premium Pkg			925	925	1015	1015
M Sport Pkg			1175	1175	1295	1295
X5 M AWD—V8 Twin Turbo—Truck Equipment Schedule T3						
Sport Utility 4D	GY0C5	89745	56600	58800	57700	63500
X6 AWD—6-Cyl. Twin Turbo—Truck Equipment Schedule T3						
xDrive35i Spt Util	FG2C5	60695	42500	43800	44300	48800
Premium Pkg			925	925	995	995
Active Cruise Control			475	475	515	515
X6 AWD—V8 Twin Turbo—Truck Equipment Schedule T3						
xDrive 50i Spt Util	FG8C5	71295	48200	49600	50200	55300
Premium Pkg			925	925	995	995
Active Cruise Control			475	475	510	510
X6 M AWD—V8 Twin Turbo—Truck Equipment Schedule T3						
Sport Utility 4D	GZ0C5	93795	59100	60800	61700	68400

2014 BMW — 5(UXorYM)(VM1C5)-E-#

Body Type	VIN	List	Trade-In Good	Very Good	Pvt-Party Good	Retail Excellent
X1—4-Cyl. Twin Turbo—Truck Equipment Schedule T3						
sDrive28i Spt Util	VM1C5	33145	22700	23400	24300	27100
Premium Pkg			650	650	710	710
M Sport Line			1200	1200	1315	1315
Ultimate Pkg			2675	2675	2930	2930
X1 AWD—4-Cyl. Twin Turbo—Truck Equipment Schedule T3						
xDrive28i Spt Util	VL1C5	34845	24300	25100	26100	29200
Premium Pkg			1000	1000	1095	1095
M Sport Line			1200	1200	1315	1315
Ultimate Pkg			2675	2675	2935	2935
X1 AWD—6-Cyl. Twin Turbo—Truck Equipment Schedule T3						
xDrive35i Spt Util	VM5C5	40945	27700	28600	29300	32500
Premium Pkg			1000	1000	1080	1080
M Sport Line			1200	1200	1295	1295
Ultimate Pkg			2675	2675	2885	2885
X3 AWD—4-Cyl. Twin Turbo—Truck Equipment Schedule T3						
xDrive28i Spt Util	WX9C5	41945	32800	33900	34200	37500
Premium Pkg			1000	1000	1055	1055
M Sport Pkg			1200	1200	1270	1270
X3 AWD—6-Cyl. Twin Turbo—Truck Equipment Schedule T3						
xDrive35i Spt Util	WX7C5	47045	36000	37100	37400	41100
Premium Pkg			1000	1000	1060	1060
M Sport Pkg			1200	1200	1275	1275
X5 AWD—6-Cyl. Twin Turbo—Truck Equipment Schedule T3						
sDrive 35i Spt Util	KR2C5	55175	47400	48800	48700	53100
xDrive 35i Spt Util	KR0C5	57475	48700	50100	50200	54700
Bang & Olufsen Sound			3000	3000	3220	3220
Third Row Seat			750	750	805	805
Premium Pkg			950	950	1030	1030
M Sport Line			1200	1200	1290	1290
X5 AWD—6-Cyl. Twin Turbo Diesel—Truck Equipment Schedule T3						
xDrive 35d Spt Util	KS4C5	58975	52100	53600	53400	58000
Bang & Olufsen Sound			3000	3000	3200	3200
Premium Pkg			950	950	1025	1025
M Sport Line			1200	1200	1280	1280
X5 AWD—V8 Twin Turbo—Truck Equipment Schedule T3						
xDrive 50i Spt Util	KR6C5	69125	57800	59500	59200	64300
Bang & Olufsen Sound			3000	3000	3200	3200
M Sport Line			1200	1200	1280	1280
X6 AWD—6-Cyl. Twin Turbo—Truck Equipment Schedule T3						
xDrive35i Spt Util	FG2C5	60695	47800	49200	49200	53500
Premium Pkg			950	950	1010	1010
Active Cruise Control			500	500	525	525
X6 AWD—V8 Twin Turbo—Truck Equipment Schedule T3						
xDrive 50i Spt Util	FG8C5	71295	54500	56200	55900	60700
Premium Pkg			950	950	1010	1010
X6 M AWD—V8 Twin Turbo—Truck Equipment Schedule T3						
Sport Utility 4D	GZ0C5	93795	73500	75600	75600	82900

Body Type	VIN	List	Trade-In Good	Very Good	Pvt-Party Good	Retail Excellent

BUICK

2002 BUICK — 3G5–(A03E)–2–#

RENDEZVOUS—V6—Truck Equipment Schedule T3
CX Sport Utility 4D	A03E	26279	750	875	1625	2650
Third Row Seat			175	175	250	250
AWD	B		400	400	520	520

RENDEZVOUS AWD—V6—Truck Equipment Schedule T3
CXL Sport Utility 4D	B03E	31502	1050	1225	2125	3550
Third Row Seat			175	175	250	250

2003 BUICK — 3G5–(A03E)–3–#

RENDEZVOUS—V6—Truck Equipment Schedule T3
CX Sport Utility 4D	A03E	26975	1075	1225	2100	3450
CXL Sport Utility 4D	B03E	30200	1375	1575	2650	4350
Third Row Seat			200	200	265	265
AWD	B		425	425	555	555

2004 BUICK — (3G5or5GA)–(A03E)–4–#

RENDEZVOUS—V6—Truck Equipment Schedule T3
CX Sport Utility 4D	A03E	26545	1375	1575	2575	4125
CXL Sport Utility 4D	A03E	31410	1850	2100	3125	4900
Third Row Seat			200	200	280	280
AWD	B		450	450	595	595
V6, 3.6 Liter	7		300	300	390	390

RENDEZVOUS AWD—V6—Truck Equipment Schedule T3
Ultra Sport Utility 4D	B037	39695	2225	2525	3650	5700
Third Row Seat			200	200	280	280

RAINIER AWD—6-Cyl.—Truck Equipment Schedule T1
CXL Sport Utility 4D	T13S	37895	2875	3225	4325	6525
2WD	S		(900)	(900)	(1190)	(1190)
V8, 5.3 Liter	P		200	200	265	265

2005 BUICK — (3G5or5GA)–(A04E)–5–#

RENDEZVOUS—V6—Truck Equipment Schedule T3
CX Sport Utility 4D	A04E	27270	2250	2525	3475	5225
CXL Sport Utility 4D	A03E	31600	2800	3125	4150	6150
Ultra Sport Util 4D	A03E	36840	3125	3475	4525	6700
Third Row Seat			225	225	300	300
AWD	B		475	475	630	630
V6, 3.6 Liter	7		325	325	420	420

TERRAZA—V6—Truck Equipment Schedule T3
CX Minivan 4D	V23L	28825	3225	3600	4725	7025
CXL Minivan 4D	V33L	31885	3650	4050	5250	7725
AWD	X		500	500	650	650

RAINIER AWD—6-Cyl.—Truck Equipment Schedule T1
CXL Sport Utility 4D	T13S	37590	3750	4150	5375	7800
2WD	S		(975)	(975)	(1300)	(1300)
V8, 5.3 Liter	M		225	225	300	300

2006 BUICK — (3G5or5GA)–(A03L)–6–#

RENDEZVOUS—V6—Truck Equipment Schedule T3
CX Sport Utility 4D	A03L	27305	3100	3450	4525	6525
CXL Sport Utility 4D	A03L	30955	3675	4050	5175	7375
Third Row Seat			225	225	315	315
AWD	B		500	500	665	665
V6, 3.6 Liter	7		325	325	445	445

TERRAZA—V6—Truck Equipment Schedule T3
CX Minivan 4D	V23L	28530	3950	4375	5625	8150
CXL Minivan 4D	V33L	31930	4525	4975	6325	9125
AWD	X		525	525	690	690

RAINIER AWD—6-Cyl.—Truck Equipment Schedule T1
CXL Sport Utility 4D	T13S	35785	4850	5300	6425	8925
2WD	S		(1050)	(1050)	(1410)	(1410)
V8, 5.3 Liter	M		250	250	335	335

TRUCKS & VANS

Body Type	VIN	List	Trade-In Good	Very Good	Pvt-Party Good	Retail Excellent
2007 BUICK — (3G5or5GA)–(A03L)–7–#						
RENDEZVOUS—V6—Truck Equipment Schedule T3						
CX Sport Utility 4D	A03L	25795	3875	4250	5300	7375
CXL Sport Utility 4D	A03L	29370	4625	5050	6100	8325
Third Row Seat			250	250	335	335
TERRAZA—V6—Truck Equipment Schedule T3						
CX Minivan 4D	V231	27275	4975	5425	6750	9575
CX Plus Minivan 4D	V231	28615	4925	5375	6900	9775
CXL Minivan 4D	V331	31395	5825	6325	7950	11150
RAINIER AWD—6-Cyl.—Truck Equipment Schedule T1						
CXL Sport Utility 4D	T13S	34140	5900	6400	7600	10200
2WD	S		(1150)	(1150)	(1520)	(1520)
V8, 5.3 Liter	M		275	275	365	365
2008 BUICK — (3G5or5GA)–(R137)–8–#						
ENCLAVE—V6—Truck Equipment Schedule T3						
CX Sport Utility 4D	R137	34760	9675	10200	11400	13900
CXL Sport Utility 4D	R237	36990	11700	12250	13650	16600
AWD	V		725	725	900	900
2009 BUICK — (3G5or5GA)–(R13D)–9–#						
ENCLAVE—V6—Truck Equipment Schedule T3						
CX Sport Utility 4D	R13D	37805	10750	11250	12550	15050
CXL Sport Utility 4D	R23D	40115	13350	13950	15400	18400
AWD	V		750	750	930	930
2010 BUICK — (3G5or5GA)–(RAED)–A–#						
ENCLAVE—V6—Truck Equipment Schedule T3						
CX Sport Utility	RAED	35993	13750	14350	15550	18150
CXL Sport Utility	RBED	39105	15850	16500	17850	20900
AWD	V		800	800	935	935
2011 BUICK — (5GA)–(RAED)–B–#						
ENCLAVE—V6—Truck Equipment Schedule T3						
CX Sport Utility	RAED	36290	15000	15600	16750	19300
CXL Sport Utility	RBED	39405	18550	19250	20400	23400
AWD	V		825	825	960	960
2012 BUICK — (5GA)–(RAED)–C–#						
ENCLAVE—V6—Truck Equipment Schedule T3						
Sport Utility 4D	RAED	37410	17900	18550	19750	22600
Convenience Util	RBED	38330	18700	19400	20600	23500
Leather Spt Util	RCED	40525	21600	22400	23600	26800
Premium Spt Util	RDED	43890	23300	24100	25200	28500
AWD	V		875	875	985	985
2013 BUICK — (5GA)–(JARB)–D–#						
ENCORE—4-Cyl. Turbo—Truck Equipment Schedule T1						
Sport Utility 4D	JARB	24950	13650	14150	15200	17450
Convenience Util	JBRB	25760	14850	15400	16500	18850
Leather Sport Util	JCRB	27460	15700	16300	17400	19950
Premium Sport Util	JDRB	28940	17800	18400	19500	22300
AWD	E		950	950	1060	1060
ENCLAVE—V6—Truck Equipment Schedule T3						
Convenience 4D	RBED	39270	21200	21900	23400	26800
Leather Sport Util	RCED	43285	23600	24400	25900	29600
Premium Sport Util	RDED	46450	27200	28100	29700	33900
AWD	V		950	950	1085	1085
2014 BUICK — (5GA)–(JAEB)–E–#						
ENCORE—4-Cyl. Turbo—Truck Equipment Schedule T1						
Sport Utility 4D	JAEB	25085	15000	15550	16950	19700
Convenience 4D	JBEB	26710	16050	16600	17800	20500
Leather Sport Util	JCEB	28410	16800	17350	18450	21100
Premium Sport Util	JDEB	29890	19600	20300	21200	23900
AWD	E		1025	1025	1180	1180
ENCLAVE—V6—Truck Equipment Schedule T1						
Convenience 4D	RAKD	39665	24300	24700	26400	30300
Leather Sport Util	RBKD	43680	27900	28800	30500	34800

Body Type	VIN	List	Trade-In Good	Very Good	Pvt-Party Good	Retail Excellent
Premium Sport Util	RCKD	47240	**31200**	**32200**	**34000**	**38700**
AWD	V		**1025**	**1025**	**1175**	**1175**

CADILLAC

2000 CADILLAC — 1GY–(K13R)–Y–#

ESCALADE AWD—V8—Truck Equipment Schedule T3
| Sport Utility 4D | K13R | 46875 | **1350** | **1500** | **2450** | **3850** |

2001 CADILLAC — No Production

2002 CADILLAC — (1or3)GY–(K63N)–2–#

ESCALADE AWD—V8—Truck Equipment Schedule T3
Sport Utility 4D	K63N	51980	**3925**	**4275**	**5650**	**8000**
2WD	C		(450)	(450)	(600)	(600)
V8, 5.3 Liter	T		(200)	(200)	(260)	(260)

ESCALADE EXT AWD—V8—Truck Equipment Schedule T3
| Sport Util Pickup 4D | K13N | 49990 | **3775** | **4100** | **5450** | **7725** |

2003 CADILLAC — (1or3)GY–(K63N)–3–#

ESCALADE AWD—V8—Truck Equipment Schedule T3
Sport Utility 4D	K63N	53975	**5200**	**5575**	**6900**	**9450**
2WD	C		(500)	(500)	(665)	(665)
V8, 5.3 Liter	T		(225)	(225)	(285)	(285)

ESCALADE EXT AWD—V8—Truck Equipment Schedule T3
| Sport Util Pickup 4D | K63N | 51215 | **5000** | **5375** | **6675** | **9150** |

ESCALADE ESV AWD—V8—Truck Equipment Schedule T3
| Sport Utility 4D | K66N | 56160 | **5425** | **5825** | **7375** | **10050** |

2004 CADILLAC — (1or3)GY–(E637)–4–#

SRX AWD—V6—Truck Equipment Schedule T3
Sport Utility 4D	E637	40935	**3250**	**3575**	**4500**	**6375**
Third Row Seat			700	700	920	920
Luxury Performance			1100	1100	1465	1465
2WD			(450)	(450)	(600)	(600)
V8, 4.6 Liter	A		250	250	320	320

ESCALADE AWD—V8—Truck Equipment Schedule T3
Sport Utility 4D	K63N	55695	**5925**	**6325**	**7850**	**10550**
2WD	C		(550)	(550)	(735)	(735)
V8, 5.3 Liter	T		(225)	(225)	(315)	(315)

ESCALADE EXT AWD—V8—Truck Equipment Schedule T3
| Sport Util Pickup 4D | K63N | 52975 | **5675** | **6075** | **7575** | **10200** |

ESCALADE ESV AWD—V8—Truck Equipment Schedule T3
| Sport Utility 4D | K66N | 58095 | **6525** | **6950** | **8600** | **11500** |
| Platinum Utility 4D | K66N | 69730 | **8450** | **8975** | **10800** | **14250** |

2005 CADILLAC — (1or3)GY–(E637)–5–#

SRX AWD—V6—Truck Equipment Schedule T3
Sport Utility 4D	E637	41895	**3800**	**4150**	**5250**	**7350**
Third Row Seat			725	725	950	950
Luxury Performance			1200	1200	1595	1595
2WD			(500)	(500)	(660)	(660)
V8, 4.6 Liter	A		275	275	350	350

ESCALADE AWD—V8—Truck Equipment Schedule T3
Sport Utility 4D	K63N	56615	**7950**	**8425**	**9825**	**12700**
2WD	C		(600)	(600)	(800)	(800)
V8, 5.3 Liter	T		(250)	(250)	(345)	(345)

ESCALADE EXT AWD—V8—Truck Equipment Schedule T3
| Sport Util Pickup 4D | K62N | 53895 | **7700** | **8175** | **9550** | **12350** |

ESCALADE ESV AWD—V8—Truck Equipment Schedule T3
| Sport Utility 4D | K66N | 59015 | **8775** | **9300** | **10800** | **13850** |
| Platinum Sport Util | K66N | 70385 | **10700** | **11300** | **12950** | **16500** |

2006 CADILLAC — (1or3)GY–(E637)–6–#

SRX AWD—V6—Truck Equipment Schedule T3
Sport Utility 4D	E637	39390	**4525**	**4900**	**6125**	**8275**
Third Row Seat			725	725	980	980
2WD			(550)	(550)	(720)	(720)
V8, 4.6 Liter	A		275	275	380	380

TRUCKS & VANS

Body Type	VIN	List	Trade-In Good	Trade-In Very Good	Pvt-Party Good	Retail Excellent
ESCALADE AWD—V8—Truck Equipment Schedule T3						
Sport Utility 4D	K63N	57280	9450	10000	11600	14700
2WD	C		(650)	(650)	(850)	(850)
ESCALADE EXT AWD—V8—Truck Equipment Schedule T3						
Sport Util Pickup 4D	K62N	54210	9250	9800	11400	14400
ESCALADE ESV AWD—V8—Truck Equipment Schedule T3						
Sport Utility 4D	K66N	59680	10350	10950	12550	15850
Platinum Sport Util	K66N	71050	12300	12950	14600	18200

2007 CADILLAC — (1or3)GY–(E637)–7–#

Body Type	VIN	List	Trade-In Good	Trade-In Very Good	Pvt-Party Good	Retail Excellent
SRX AWD—V6—Truck Equipment Schedule T3						
Sport Utility 4D	E637	39595	6525	6975	8125	10550
Third Row Seat			750	750	1005	1005
2WD			(575)	(575)	(775)	(775)
V8, 4.6 Liter	A		300	300	410	410
ESCALADE AWD—V8—Truck Equipment Schedule T3						
Sport Utility 4D	K638	57675	17950	18800	20000	24100
2WD	C		(700)	(700)	(850)	(850)
ESCALADE EXT AWD—V8—Truck Equipment Schedule T3						
Sport Util Pickup 4D	K628	54605	17750	18600	19800	23800
ESCALADE ESV AWD—V8—Truck Equipment Schedule T3						
Sport Utility 4D	K668	60075	18450	19300	20600	24800

2008 CADILLAC — (1or3)GY–(E437)–8–#

Body Type	VIN	List	Trade-In Good	Trade-In Very Good	Pvt-Party Good	Retail Excellent
SRX AWD—V6—Truck Equipment Schedule T3						
Sport Utility 4D	E437	41480	8525	9050	10050	12500
Third Row Seat			775	775	955	955
2WD	2,6		(700)	(700)	(855)	(855)
V8, 4.6 Liter	A		450	450	555	555
ESCALADE AWD—V8—Truck Equipment Schedule T3						
Sport Utility 4D	K638	58195	20500	21400	22400	26300
2WD	C		(750)	(750)	(880)	(880)
ESCALADE EXT AWD—V8—Truck Equipment Schedule T3						
Sport Util Pickup 4D	K628	55115	20200	21000	22100	25900
Luxury Collection			575	575	675	675
ESCALADE ESV AWD—V8—Truck Equipment Schedule T3						
Sport Utility 4D	K668	60610	21200	22100	23100	27100
Luxury Collection			575	575	675	675
Platinum Edition			1650	1650	1945	1945
2WD	C		(750)	(750)	(885)	(885)

2009 CADILLAC — (1or3)GY–(E437)–9–#

Body Type	VIN	List	Trade-In Good	Trade-In Very Good	Pvt-Party Good	Retail Excellent
SRX AWD—V6—Truck Equipment Schedule T3						
Sport Utility 4D	E437	41480	9975	10550	11650	14300
Third Row Seat			800	800	970	970
2WD	2,6		(725)	(725)	(895)	(895)
V8, 4.6 Liter	A		450	450	545	545
ESCALADE AWD—V8—Truck Equipment Schedule T3						
Sport Utility 4D	K132	63305	23100	24000	25100	29000
2WD	C		(875)	(875)	(1010)	(1010)
ESCALADE AWD—V8 Hybrid—Truck Equipment Schedule T3						
Sport Utility 4D	K435	74325	25100	26100	27200	31400
2WD	C		(875)	(875)	(1015)	(1015)
ESCALADE EXT AWD—V8—Truck Equipment Schedule T3						
Sport Util Pickup 4D	K628	59690	22800	23700	24700	28500
Luxury Collection			600	600	695	695
ESCALADE ESV AWD—V8—Truck Equipment Schedule T3						
Sport Utility 4D	K668	65835	24500	25500	26600	30800
Luxury Collection			600	600	695	695
Platinum Edition			1700	1700	1965	1965
2WD	C		(875)	(875)	(1010)	(1010)

2010 CADILLAC — (1or3)GY–(NBEY)–A–#

Body Type	VIN	List	Trade-In Good	Trade-In Very Good	Pvt-Party Good	Retail Excellent
SRX—V6—Truck Equipment Schedule T3						
Sport Utility 4D	NBEY	34155	15700	16450	17900	21600
Performance Pkg			725	725	880	880
AWD	E		725	725	880	880
V6, Turbo, 2.8 Liter	4		2000	2000	2425	2425
ESCALADE AWD—V8 Flex Fuel—Truck Equipment Schedule T3						
Sport Utility 4D	KAEF	65995	27500	28500	29600	33800
2WD	C		(1000)	(1000)	(1140)	(1140)

TRUCKS & VANS

TRUCKS & VANS

Body Type	VIN	List	Trade-In Good	Very Good	Pvt-Party Good	Retail Excellent
ESCALADE AWD—V8 Hybrid—Truck Equipment Schedule T3						
Sport Utility 4D	KEEJ	76925	29700	30700	31800	36100
2WD	C		(1000)	(1000)	(1135)	(1135)
ESCALADE EXT AWD—V8—Truck Equipment Schedule T3						
Sport Util Pickup 4D	K628	62370	27000	28000	29000	33100
Luxury Pkg			625	625	710	710
Premium Pkg			1250	1250	1420	1420
ESCALADE ESV AWD—V8 Flex Fuel—Truck Equipment Schedule T3						
Sport Utility 4D	KKEF	68550	30200	31200	32200	36600
Luxury Pkg			625	625	705	705
Platinum Edition			1750	1750	1975	1975
2WD			(1000)	(1000)	(1130)	(1130)

2011 CADILLAC — (1or3)(GGorGY)-(NBEY)-B-#

Body Type	VIN	List	Trade-In Good	Very Good	Pvt-Party Good	Retail Excellent
SRX—V6—Truck Equipment Schedule T3						
Sport Utility 4D	NBEY	34705	18200	19050	20100	23400
Luxury Collection			650	650	755	755
Performance Pkg			750	750	870	870
Premium Collection			1300	1300	1505	1505
AWD	E		800	800	925	925
V6, Turbo, 2.8 Liter	6		2100	2100	2435	2435
ESCALADE AWD—V8 Flex Fuel—Truck Equipment Schedule T3						
Sport Utility 4D	4AEF	65995	32100	33200	33900	38000
2WD	3		(1100)	(1100)	(1225)	(1225)
ESCALADE AWD—V8 Hybrid—Truck Equipment Schedule T3						
Sport Utility 4D	4EEJ	76925	35000	36100	36900	41400
2WD	3		(1100)	(1100)	(1230)	(1230)
ESCALADE EXT AWD—V8 Flex Fuel—Truck Equipment Schedule T3						
Sport Util Pickup 4D	4LEF	62835	31600	32600	33400	37300
Luxury Pkg			650	650	720	720
Premium Pkg			1300	1300	1445	1445
ESCALADE ESV AWD—V8 Flex Fuel—Truck Equipment Schedule T3						
Sport Utility 4D	4GEF	69215	34500	35600	36400	40900
Luxury Pkg			650	650	725	725
Platinum Edition			1800	1800	2010	2010
2WD	3		(1100)	(1100)	(1230)	(1230)

2012 CADILLAC — (1or3)GYor3GG-(NGE3)-C-#

Body Type	VIN	List	Trade-In Good	Very Good	Pvt-Party Good	Retail Excellent
SRX—V6—Truck Equipment Schedule T3						
Sport Utility 4D	NGE3	36860	19500	20300	21600	25300
Luxury Collection			675	675	785	785
Performance Pkg			775	775	900	900
AWD	D,E,F,H		875	875	1015	1015
ESCALADE AWD—V8 Flex Fuel—Truck Equipment Schedule T3						
Sport Utility 4D	4AEF	66670	35200	36300	37300	41800
2WD	3		(1200)	(1200)	(1335)	(1335)
ESCALADE AWD—V8 Hybrid—Truck Equipment Schedule T3						
Sport Utility 4D	4EEJ	77350	41400	42700	43600	48700
2WD	2		(1200)	(1200)	(1330)	(1330)
ESCALADE EXT AWD—V8 Flex Fuel—Truck Equipment Schedule T3						
Sport Util Pickup 4D	4LEF	64010	34700	35800	36700	41100
Luxury Pkg			675	675	750	750
Premium Pkg			1350	1350	1500	1500
ESCALADE ESV AWD—V8 Flex Fuel—Truck Equipment Schedule T3						
Sport Utility 4D	4GEF	69270	39000	40200	41200	46200
Luxury Pkg			675	675	750	750
Platinum Edition			1850	1850	2060	2060
2WD	3		(1200)	(1200)	(1335)	(1335)

2013 CADILLAC — (1or3)GYor3GG-(NAE3)-D-#

Body Type	VIN	List	Trade-In Good	Very Good	Pvt-Party Good	Retail Excellent
SRX—V6 Flex Fuel—Truck Equipment Schedule T3						
Sport Utility 4D	NAE3	38050	20400	21300	22500	26300
Luxury Collection	NCE3	43425	22400	23300	24700	28800
Performance 4D	NDE3	45800	26200	27200	28500	33000
Premium Collection	NEE3	48640	28300	29400	30600	35400
AWD	G		950	950	1095	1095
ESCALADE AWD—V8 Flex Fuel—Truck Equipment Schedule T3						
Sport Utility 4D	4AEF	66715	37000	38200	39100	43600
Luxury Spt Util 4D	4BEF	70940	39600	40800	41700	46500
Premium Spt Util 4D	4CEF	75220	42600	43900	44800	49800
Platinum Ed 4D	4DEF	83490	48100	49500	50600	56100
2WD	3		(1300)	(1300)	(1435)	(1435)

Body Type	VIN	List	Trade-In Good	Trade-In Very Good	Pvt-Party Good	Retail Excellent
ESCALADE AWD—V8 Hybrid—Truck Equipment Schedule T3						
Sport Utility 4D	4EEJ	77395	43700	45000	45900	51000
Platinum Spt Util 4D	4FEJ	86840	50100	51600	52500	58100
2WD	3	......	(1300)	(1300)	(1430)	(1430)
ESCALADE EXT AWD—V8 Flex Fuel—Truck Equipment Schedule T3						
Sport Util Pickup 4D	4LEF	64055	36200	37400	38300	42700
Luxury Sport Util	4MEF	68245	37900	39100	40000	44600
Premium Sport Util	4NEF	70635	39400	40600	41500	46300
ESCALADE ESV AWD—V8 Flex Fuel—Truck Equipment Schedule T3						
Sport Utility 4D	4GEF	69315	41500	42700	43700	48600
Luxury Spt Util 4D	4HEF	73540	41900	43100	44100	49000
Premium Spt Util 4D	4JEF	78420	45300	46700	47600	52900
Platinum Sport Util	4KEF	86000	49600	51100	52000	57600
2WD	3	......	(1300)	(1300)	(1430)	(1430)

Body Type	VIN	List	Trade-In Good	Trade-In Very Good	Pvt-Party Good	Retail Excellent
SRX—V6 Flex Fuel—Truck Equipment Schedule T3						
Sport Utility 4D	NAE3	38430	24700	25700	26800	30900
Luxury Sport Utility	NBE3	43805	29000	30200	31300	35900
Performance 4D	NCE3	46180	30200	31300	32500	37400
Premium Sport Utility	NDE3	49070	32500	33700	34700	39600
AWD	E	......	1025	1025	1145	1145
ESCALADE AWD—V8 Flex Fuel—Truck Equipment Schedule T3						
Sport Utility 4D	4AEF	67290	43000	44300	44800	49500
Luxury Spt Util 4D	4BEF	71515	45600	47000	47400	52300
Premium Spt Util 4D	4CEF	75795	48300	49800	50500	55600
Platinum Ed Spt Util	4DEF	84065	54500	56100	56500	61900
2WD	3	......	(1400)	(1400)	(1525)	(1525)
ESCALADE ESV AWD—V8 Flex Fuel—Truck Equipment Schedule T3						
Sport Utility 4D	4GEF	69890	47300	48700	49000	53900
Luxury Spt Util 4D	4HEF	74115	47300	48800	49500	54500
Premium Spt Util 4D	4JEF	78995	51200	52700	53200	58400
Platinum Sport Util	4KEF	86665	55400	57000	57400	63000
2WD	3	......	(1500)	(1500)	(1620)	(1620)

CHEVROLET/GMC

Body Type	VIN	List	Trade-In Good	Trade-In Very Good	Pvt-Party Good	Retail Excellent
TRACKER 4WD—4-Cyl.—Truck Equipment Schedule T2						
Sport Util Conv 2D	J186	15425	550	650	1575	2700
Sport Utility 4D	J13C	16650	950	1100	2150	3725
2WD	E	......	(275)	(275)	(365)	(365)
BLAZER/JIMMY 4WD—V6—Truck Equipment Schedule T1						
Sport Utility 2D	T18W	23495	500	600	1475	2575
Sport Utility 4D	T13W	26995	800	925	1900	3250
2WD	S	......	(550)	(550)	(750)	(750)
ENVOY 4WD—V6—Truck Equipment Schedule T3						
Sport Utility 4D	T13W	34695	1675	1925	3050	4925
TAHOE 4WD—V8 4.8L Engine (New)—Truck Equipment Schedule T1						
Sport Utility 4D	K13V	29441	1600	1800	3150	5300
Third Row Seat		......	200	200	265	265
2WD	C	......	(350)	(350)	(465)	(465)
V8, 5.3 Liter	T	......	75	75	100	100
TAHOE 4WD—V8 5.7L Engine—Truck Equipment Schedule T1						
Sport Utility 4D	K13R	39544	1375	1550	2825	4775
2WD	C	......	(350)	(350)	(465)	(465)
YUKON 4WD—V8 (New)—Truck Equipment Schedule T1						
SLE Sport Utility 4D	K13V	35835	1900	2125	3600	6000
Third Row Seat		......	200	200	265	265
2WD	C	......	(350)	(350)	(465)	(465)
V8, 5.3 Liter	T	......	75	75	100	100
YUKON DENALI 4WD—V8—Truck Equipment Schedule T3						
Sport Utility 4D	K13R	44185	2075	2350	3350	5250
SUBURBAN 4WD—V8—Truck Equipment Schedule T1						
K1500 Sport Utility	K16T	29362	1450	1625	3100	5325
K2500 Sport Utility	K26U	31330	1575	1775	3275	5625
Third Row Seat		......	200	200	265	265
2WD	C	......	(550)	(550)	(750)	(750)
YUKON XL 4WD—V8—Truck Equipment Schedule T1						
1500 Sport Utility	K13T	38081	1875	2100	3775	6425
2500 Sport Utility	K23U	39683	1975	2200	3925	6675

Body Type	VIN	List	Trade-In Good	Very Good	Pvt-Party Good	Retail Excellent
Third Row Seat	C		200	200	265	265
2WD			(550)	(550)	(750)	(750)
VENTURE—V6—Truck Equipment Schedule T2						
Cargo Minivan 4D	U05E	22330	800	950	1575	2550
VENTURE—V6—Truck Equipment Schedule T1						
Minivan 4D	U05E	21230	475	575	1200	2025
Extended Minivan	X09E	24930	575	700	1325	2225
ASTRO/SAFARI—V6—Truck Equipment Schedule T2						
Cargo/SL Cargo	M19W	20635	1100	1275	2025	3375
Dutch Doors			50	50	65	65
AWD	L		250	250	335	335
ASTRO/SAFARI—V6—Truck Equipment Schedule T1						
Minivan/SL Minivan	M19W	21982	875	1025	1750	2900
Dutch Doors			50	50	65	65
AWD	L		250	250	335	335
EXPRESS/SAVANA—V8—Truck Equipment Schedule T1						
1500 Passenger Van	G15M	24240	1525	1725	2500	4100
2500 Passenger Van	G25R	26245	1600	1825	2600	4250
3500 Passenger Van	G35R	26534	1725	1950	2775	4525
5-Passenger Seating	9		(200)	(200)	(265)	(265)
155" WB			50	50	65	65
V6, 4.3 Liter	W		(200)	(200)	(265)	(265)
V8, 5.7 Liter (1500)	R		150	150	200	200
V8, 454/7.4 Liter	J		100	100	135	135
V8, Turbo Dsl, 6.5L	F		100	100	120	120
EXPRESS/SAVANA—V6—Truck Equipment Schedule T1						
1500 Cargo Van	G15W	21910	1000	1150	1750	2975
2500 Cargo Van	G25W	22360	1050	1200	1800	3075
155" WB			50	50	65	65
V8, 5.0 Liter	M		100	100	135	135
V8, 5.7 Liter	R		150	150	200	200
V8, Turbo Diesel, 6.5L	F		125	125	180	180
EXPRESS/SAVANA—V8—Truck Equipment Schedule T1						
3500 Cargo Van	G35R	23894	1100	1250	1875	3175
155" WB			50	50	65	65
V8, 454/7.4 Liter	J		200	200	265	265
V8, Turbo Diesel, 6.5L	F		125	125	180	180
S10/SONOMA PICKUP—4-Cyl.—Truck Equipment Schedule T2						
Short Bed	S144	12610	1225	1350	2100	3575
Long Bed	S144	12661	1050	1150	1850	3150
Extended Cab	S194	15309	1775	1975	3075	5125
Third Door			100	100	145	145
4WD	T		400	400	535	535
V6, 4.3 Liter	W		200	200	265	265
SILVERADO/SIERRA REGULAR CAB—V8 (New)—Truck Schedule T1						
1500 Short Bed	C14V	18510	1775	2000	2700	4300
1500 Long Bed	C14V	18810	1725	1950	2600	4175
2500 Long Bed	C24T	21950	2050	2250	2875	4325
2500 HD Long Bed	C24T	23074	2300	2525	3200	4775
4WD	K		650	650	865	865
V6, 4.3 Liter	W		(350)	(350)	(465)	(465)
V8, 5.3 Liter (1500)	T		75	75	100	100
V8, 6.0 Liter	U		150	150	200	200
SILVERADO/SIERRA EXTENDED CAB—V8 (New)—Truck Schedule T1						
1500 Short Bed	C19V	22884	3000	3375	4125	6275
1500 Long Bed	C19V	23184	2700	3025	3775	5825
2500 Short Bed	C29T	24400	3425	3750	4625	6825
Fourth Door			125	125	165	165
4WD	K		650	650	865	865
V6, 4.3 Liter	W		(350)	(350)	(465)	(465)
V8, 5.3 Liter (1500)	T		75	75	100	100
V8, 6.0 Liter	U		150	150	200	200
SILVERADO/SIERRA EXTENDED CAB—V8 (New)—Truck Schedule T1						
2500 HD Short Bed	C29U	28324	3550	3900	4950	7275
2500 HD Long Bed	C29U	25524	3475	3800	4675	6900
Fourth Door			125	125	165	165
4WD	K		650	650	865	865
REGULAR CAB PICKUP—V8—Truck Equipment Schedule T1						
2500 HD Long Bed	C24R	21837	1950	2175	3075	5000
3500 Long Bed	C34R	22435	2000	2250	3125	5100
4WD	K		650	650	865	865
V8, 454/7.4 Liter	J		150	150	200	200
V8, Turbo Diesel, 6.5L	F		275	275	365	365

TRUCKS & VANS (side tab)

Body Type	VIN	List	Trade-In Good	Trade-In Very Good	Pvt-Party Good	Retail Excellent
EXTENDED CAB PICKUP 4WD—V8—Truck Equipment Schedule T1						
2500 HD Short Bed	K29R	26547	3025	3375	4600	7375
V8, 454/7.4 Liter	J		150	150	200	200
V8, Turbo Diesel, 6.5L	F		275	275	365	365
EXTENDED CAB PICKUP—V8—Truck Equipment Schedule T1						
2500 HD Long Bed	C29R	23441	2725	3075	4175	6725
3500 Long Bed	C39R	25861	2700	3025	4150	6675
4WD	K		650	650	865	865
V8, 454/7.4 Liter	J		150	150	200	200
V8, Turbo Diesel, 6.5L	F		275	275	365	365
CREW CAB PICKUP—V8—Truck Equipment Schedule T1						
2500 Short Bed	C23R	24826	2875	3225	4375	7050
3500 Short Bed	C33R	27045	3600	4000	5425	8650
3500 Long Bed	C33R	25565	3325	3700	5025	8050
4WD	K		650	650	865	865
V8, 454/7.4 Liter	J		150	150	200	200
V8, Turbo Diesel, 6.5L	F		275	275	365	365

2001 CHEVY/GMC—(1,2or3)(CorG)(A,B,CorN)—J18C-1-#

Body Type	VIN	List	Trade-In Good	Trade-In Very Good	Pvt-Party Good	Retail Excellent
TRACKER 4WD—4-Cyl.—Truck Equipment Schedule T2						
Sport Util Conv 2D	J18C	16760	875	1000	1925	3225
Sport Utility 4D	J13C	17380	1300	1475	2500	4200
ZR2 Spt Utl Conv 2D	J78C	18835	1350	1525	2575	4325
2WD	E		(300)	(300)	(400)	(400)
TRACKER 4WD—V6—Truck Equipment Schedule T2						
ZR2 Sport Utility 4D	J734	21200	1775	2025	2950	4550
LT Sport Utility 4D	J634	21880	2175	2475	3450	5275
2WD	E		(300)	(300)	(400)	(400)
BLAZER/JIMMY 4WD—V6—Truck Equipment Schedule T1						
Sport Utility 2D	T18W	23745	650	775	1675	2850
Sport Utility 4D	T13W	27345	975	1150	2125	3550
2WD	S		(650)	(650)	(860)	(860)
TAHOE 4WD—V8—Truck Equipment Schedule T1						
Sport Utility 4D	K13V	31021	2325	2600	3725	5775
Third Row Seat			200	200	265	265
2WD	C		(400)	(400)	(535)	(535)
V8, 5.3 Liter	T		75	75	100	100
YUKON 4WD—V8—Truck Equipment Schedule T1						
SLE Sport Utility 4D	K13V	36128	2700	3025	4200	6475
Third Row Seat			200	200	265	265
2WD	C		(400)	(400)	(535)	(535)
V8, 5.3 Liter	T,Z		75	75	100	100
YUKON DENALI AWD—V8—Truck Equipment Schedule T3						
Sport Utility 4D	K13U	46680	2700	3050	4000	6025
SUBURBAN 4WD—V8—Truck Equipment Schedule T1						
K1500 Sport Utility	K16T	29602	1975	2225	3600	5850
K2500 Sport Utility	K26U	31545	2100	2350	3750	6100
Third Row Seat			200	200	265	265
2WD	C		(650)	(650)	(860)	(860)
V8, 8.1 Liter	G		175	175	240	240
YUKON XL 4WD—V8—Truck Equipment Schedule T1						
1500 Sport Utility	K13T	36287	2550	2850	4375	7050
2500 Sport Utility	K23U	37659	2675	3000	4550	7300
2WD	C		(650)	(650)	(860)	(860)
V8, 8.1 Liter	G		175	175	240	240
YUKON XL DENALI AWD—V8—Truck Equipment Schedule T3						
1500 Sport Utility 4D	K16U	48185	2550	2900	3725	5575
VENTURE—V6—Truck Equipment Schedule T1						
Minivan 4D	U05E	21605	700	825	1475	2475
Extended Minivan	X09E	26085	800	925	1600	2675
ASTRO/SAFARI—V6—Truck Equipment Schedule T2						
Cargo/SL Cargo	M19W	21238	1350	1550	2275	3750
Dutch Doors			50	50	65	65
AWD	L		250	250	335	335
ASTRO/SAFARI—V6—Truck Equipment Schedule T2						
Minivan 3D	M19W	23886	1250	1425	2150	3550
Dutch Doors			50	50	65	65
AWD	L		250	250	335	335
EXPRESS/SAVANA VAN—V8—Truck Equipment Schedule T1						
1500 Passenger Van	G15M	24730	1900	2150	2850	4475
2500 Passenger Van	G25M	26735	2000	2275	2975	4675
3500 Passenger Van	G35R	27024	2125	2400	3150	4950
155" WB			50	50	65	65

TRUCKS & VANS

TRUCKS & VANS

Body Type	VIN	List	Trade-In Good	Very Good	Pvt-Party Good	Retail Excellent
V6, 4.3 Liter	W		(200)	(200)	(265)	(265)
V8, 5.7 Liter (1500)	R		150	150	200	200
V8, 8.1 Liter	G		100	100	135	135
V8, Turbo Dsl, 6.5L	F		100	100	135	135
EXPRESS/SAVANA VAN—V8—Truck Equipment Schedule T1						
1500 Cargo Van	G15M	22520	1325	1500	2200	3725
2500 Cargo Van	G25M	22650	1375	1575	2275	3825
3500 Cargo Van	G35R	24929	1425	1625	2350	3950
155" WB			50	50	65	65
V6, 4.3 Liter	W		(200)	(200)	(265)	(265)
V8, 5.7 Liter (ex 3500)	R		150	150	200	200
V8, 8.1 Liter	G		200	200	265	265
V8, Turbo Diesel, 6.5L	F		150	150	200	200
S10/SONOMA PICKUP—4-Cyl. Flex Fuel—Truck Equip Schedule T2						
Short Bed	S145	12859	1550	1700	2350	3825
Long Bed	S145	13210	1350	1475	2100	3400
Extended Cab	S195	16203	2125	2350	3300	5250
Third Door			125	125	165	165
4WD	T		400	400	535	535
V6, 4.3 Liter	T		200	200	265	265
S10/SONOMA CREW CAB 4WD—V6—Truck Equip Schedule T1						
LS/SLS Short Bed	T13W	25369	3525	3875	5225	8125
SILVERADO/SIERRA REGULAR CAB—V8—Truck Equip Schedule T1						
1500 Short Bed	C14V	19185	1975	2225	2950	4675
1500 Long Bed	C14V	19485	1850	2075	2775	4400
2500 Long Bed	C24U	23689	2475	2725	3225	4675
2500 HD Long Bed	C24U	24109	2725	3000	3550	5100
3500 Long Bed	C34U	25361	2725	3000	3550	5100
4WD	K		750	750	1000	1000
V6, 4.3 Liter	W		(350)	(350)	(465)	(465)
V8, 5.3 Liter	T		75	75	100	100
V8, 8.1 Liter	G		175	175	240	240
V8, Turbo Diesel, 6.6L	1		2525	2525	3370	3370
SILVERADO/SIERRA EXTENDED CAB—V8—Truck Equip Schedule T1						
1500 Short Bed	C19V	23589	3150	3525	4375	6675
1500 Long Bed	C19V	23889	2925	3300	4100	6275
2500 HD Short Bed	C29U	26614	4000	4350	5225	7450
2500 HD Long Bed	C29U	26859	3825	4175	5025	7150
3500 Long Bed	C39U	28141	3900	4250	5125	7300
4WD	K		750	750	1000	1000
V6, 4.3 Liter	W		(350)	(350)	(465)	(465)
V8, 5.3 Liter	T		75	75	100	100
V8, 8.1 Liter	G		175	175	240	240
V8, Turbo Diesel, 6.6L	1		2525	2525	3370	3370
SILVERADO/SIERRA EXTENDED CAB 4WD—V8—Truck Equip Sch T1						
2500 Short Bed	K29U	29039	3800	4150	5000	7125
SIERRA EXTENDED CAB PICKUP AWD—V8—Truck Equip Schedule T1						
1500 C3 Short Bed	C1UU	38995	5450	6025	7500	11050
SILVERADO/SIERRA CREW CAB—V8—Truck Equipment Schedule T1						
1500 HD Short Bed	C13U	28912	3675	4100	5150	7775
2500 HD Short Bed	C23U	27984	4275	4650	5575	7925
2500 HD Long Bed	C23U	28284	4200	4575	5475	7800
3500 Long Bed	C33U	30766	4325	4700	5625	8000
4WD	K		750	750	1000	1000
V8, 8.1 Liter	G		175	175	240	240
V8, Turbo Diesel, 6.6L	1		2525	2525	3370	3370

2002 CHEVY/GMC—(1,2or3)(CorG)(A,B,CorN)—(J18C)—2—#

Body Type	VIN	List	Trade-In Good	Very Good	Pvt-Party Good	Retail Excellent
TRACKER 4WD—4-Cyl.—Truck Equipment Schedule T2						
Sport Util Conv 2D	J18C	17415	1275	1450	2425	3950
Sport Utility 4D	J13C	18105	1750	1975	3175	5125
ZR2 Spt Utl Conv 2D	J78C	19395	1800	2050	3275	5250
2WD	E		(375)	(375)	(500)	(500)
V6, 2.5 Liter	4		250	250	345	345
TRACKER 4WD—V6—Truck Equipment Schedule T2						
ZR2 Sport Utility 4D	J734	21845	2400	2700	3675	5525
LT Sport Utility 4D	J634	22270	2775	3125	4150	6175
2WD	E		(375)	(375)	(500)	(500)
BLAZER 4WD—V6—Truck Equipment Schedule T1						
Sport Utility 2D	T18W	23895	925	1075	1950	3200
Sport Utility 4D	T13W	26130	1325	1500	2450	4025
2WD			(725)	(725)	(970)	(970)

2002 CHEVROLET/GMC

Body Type	VIN	List	Trade-In Good	Very Good	Pvt-Party Good	Retail Excellent
TRAILBLAZER 4WD—6-Cyl.—Truck Equipment Schedule T1						
Sport Utility 4D	T1S3	28130	1500	1700	2550	4075
Ext Spt Util 4D	T16S	33610	1475	1675	2700	4300
2WD	S		(450)	(450)	(600)	(600)
ENVOY 4WD—6-Cyl.—Truck Equipment Schedule T1						
Sport Utility 4D	T13S	31770	1950	2225	3275	5125
2WD	S		(450)	(450)	(600)	(600)
ENVOY XL 4WD—6-Cyl.—Truck Equipment Schedule T1						
Sport Utility 4D	T16S	33820	1950	2200	3300	5200
2WD	S		(450)	(450)	(600)	(600)
TAHOE 4WD—V8—Truck Equipment Schedule T1						
Sport Utility 4D	K13V	36345	2950	3275	4275	6325
Third Row Seat			250	250	335	335
2WD	C		(450)	(450)	(600)	(600)
V8, 5.3 Liter	T,Z		125	125	165	165
YUKON 4WD—V8—Truck Equipment Schedule T1						
Sport Utility 4D	K13V	37000	3350	3700	4925	7225
Third Row Seat			250	250	335	335
2WD	C		(450)	(450)	(600)	(600)
V8, 5.3 Liter	T,Z		125	125	165	165
YUKON DENALI 4WD—V8—Truck Equipment Schedule T3						
Sport Utility 4D	K63V	47355	3325	3725	4750	6950
SUBURBAN 4WD—V8—Truck Equipment Schedule T1						
K1500 Sport Utility	K16T	39219	2550	2875	4250	6700
K2500 Sport Utility	K26U	40916	2700	3025	4450	6975
2WD	C		(725)	(725)	(970)	(970)
V8, 8.1 Liter	G		200	200	260	260
YUKON XL 4WD—V8—Truck Equipment Schedule T1						
1500 Sport Utility	K13T	37047	3125	3475	5000	7775
2500 Sport Utility	K23T	38419	3125	3475	5175	8025
2WD	C		(725)	(725)	(970)	(970)
V8, 8.1 Liter	G		200	200	260	260
YUKON XL DENALI AWD—V8—Truck Equipment Schedule T3						
1500 Sport Utility 4D	K66U	48890	3200	3625	4575	6625
VENTURE—V6—Truck Equipment Schedule T2						
Cargo Minivan 4D	U05E	24697	1150	1325	2050	3350
VENTURE—V6—Truck Equipment Schedule T1						
Minivan 4D	U03E	22035	875	1025	1700	2800
Ext Minivan 4D	X03E	26255	1100	1275	1975	3250
5-Passenger Seating			(250)	(250)	(335)	(335)
AWD			300	300	400	400
ASTRO/SAFARI—V6—Truck Equipment Schedule T2						
Cargo/SL Cargo	M19W	21768	1550	1775	2600	4150
Dutch Doors			75	75	100	100
AWD	L		300	300	400	400
ASTRO/SAFARI—V6—Truck Equipment Schedule T1						
Minivan 3D	M19X	24416	1525	1750	2575	4100
Dutch Doors			75	75	100	100
AWD	L		300	300	400	400
EXPRESS/SAVANA VAN—V8—Truck Equipment Schedule T1						
1500 Passenger Van	G15M	25287	2825	3175	3950	6050
2500 Passenger Van	G25R	27292	2900	3250	4050	6200
3500 Passenger Van	G35R	27581	3075	3450	4275	6525
155" WB			75	75	100	100
V6, 4.3 Liter	W		(250)	(250)	(335)	(335)
V8, 5.7 Liter (1500)	R		175	175	235	235
V8, 8.1 Liter			125	125	165	165
V8, Turbo Dsl, 6.5L	F		125	125	165	165
EXPRESS/SAVANA VAN—V8—Truck Equipment Schedule T1						
1500 Cargo Van	G15M	22948	1825	2050	2950	4850
2500 Cargo Van	G25M	23078	1900	2125	3050	5025
3500 Cargo Van	G35R	25357	1975	2200	3150	5200
155" WB			75	75	100	100
V6, 4.3 Liter	W		(250)	(250)	(335)	(335)
V8, 5.7 Liter (ex 3500)	R		175	175	235	235
V8, 8.1 Liter			250	250	335	335
V8, Turbo Diesel, 6.5L	F		200	200	265	265
S10/SONOMA PICKUP—4-Cyl. Flex Fuel—Truck Equipment Sch T2						
Short Bed	S145	14327	2000	2200	3025	4700
Long Bed	S145	15772	1675	1850	2475	3925
Extended Cab	S195	16309	2550	2800	3750	5800
4WD	T		550	550	735	735
V6, 4.3 Liter	W		250	250	335	335

2002 CHEVROLET/GMC

Body Type	VIN	List	Trade-In Good	Very Good	Pvt-Party Good	Retail Excellent
S10/SONOMA CREW CAB PICKUP 4WD—V6—Truck Equipment Sch T1						
LS/SLS Short Bed	T13W	24584	4025	4400	5900	8950
AVALANCHE 4WD—V8—Truck Equipment Schedule T1						
1500 Spt Util Pickup	C13T	33965	3950	4350	5650	8525
2500 Spt Util Pickup	C23G	35865	5025	5500	6975	10350
2WD			(725)	(725)	(970)	(970)
North Face Edition			450	450	585	585
SILVERADO/SIERRA REGULAR CAB—V8—Truck Equipment Schedule T1						
1500 Short Bed	C14V	20028	2225	2475	3250	5100
1500 Long Bed	C14V	20028	2025	2250	3000	4750
2500 Long Bed	C24U	24182	3150	3450	3925	5475
2500 HD Long Bed	C24U	24672	3500	3825	4350	6050
3500 Long Bed	C34U	29017	3550	3875	4400	6150
4WD	K		900	900	1200	1200
V6, 4.3 Liter	W,X		(375)	(375)	(500)	(500)
V8, 5.3 Liter	T		125	125	165	165
V8, 8.1 Liter	G		200	200	260	260
V8, Turbo Diesel, 6.6L	1		2700	2700	3600	3600
SILVERADO/SIERRA EXTENDED CAB—V8—Truck Equipment Schedule T1						
1500 Short Bed	C19V	23952	3475	3875	4850	7300
1500 Long Bed	C19V	25052	3175	3550	4500	6825
2500 HD Short Bed	K29U	27177	4950	5350	6225	8625
2500 HD Long Bed	C29U	27452	4800	5200	6050	8375
3500 Long Bed	C39U	28734	4925	5325	6200	8575
Quadrasteer			350	350	460	460
4WD	K		900	900	1200	1200
V6, 4.3 Liter	W,X		(375)	(375)	(500)	(500)
V8, 5.3 Liter	T		125	125	165	165
V8, 8.1 Liter	G		200	200	260	260
V8, Turbo Diesel, 6.6L	1		2700	2700	3600	3600
SILVERADO/SIERRA EXTENDED CAB 4WD—V8—Truck Equipment Sch T1						
2500 Short Bed	K29U	29407	4650	5050	5875	8150
SIERRA DENALI EXT CAB PICKUP 4WD—V8—Truck Equipment Schedule T3						
1500 Short Bed	K69U	44105	8700	9300	10300	13550
SILVERADO/SIERRA CREW CAB PICKUP—V8—Truck Equipment Sch T1						
1500 HD Short Bed	C13U	29425	4325	4775	5850	8675
2500 HD Short Bed	C23U	28577	5275	5700	6600	9150
2500 HD Long Bed	C23U	28877	5200	5625	6525	9025
3500 Long Bed	C33U	30159	5350	5775	6700	9275
4WD	K		900	900	1200	1200
V8, 8.1 Liter	G		200	200	260	260
V8, Turbo Diesel, 6.6L	1		2700	2700	3600	3600

2003 CHEVY/GMC—(1,2or3)(CorG)(A,B,CorN)—(J18C)—3—#

Body Type	VIN	List	Trade-In Good	Very Good	Pvt-Party Good	Retail Excellent
TRACKER 4WD—4-Cyl.—Truck Equipment Schedule T2						
Sport Utl Conv 2D	J18C	17815	1750	1975	2975	4625
Sport Utility 4D	J13C	18505	2375	2675	3825	5875
ZR2 Spt Utl Conv 2D	J78C	19675	2400	2700	3850	5925
2WD	E		(450)	(450)	(600)	(600)
V6, 2.5 Liter	4		275	275	375	375
TRACKER 4WD—V6—Truck Equipment Schedule T2						
ZR2 Sport Utility 4D	J734	22125	2950	3300	4225	6150
LT Sport Utility 4D	J634	22550	3275	3650	4775	6925
2WD	E		(450)	(450)	(600)	(600)
BLAZER—V6—Truck Equipment Schedule T1						
Xtreme Sport Utl 2D	T18X	24170	875	1000	1925	3200
BLAZER 4WD—V6—Truck Equipment Schedule T1						
LS Sport Utility 2D	T18X	24705	1225	1375	2350	3900
LS Sport Utility 4D	T13X	26585	1575	1800	2950	4775
2WD	S		(800)	(800)	(1080)	(1080)
TRAILBLAZER 4WD—6-Cyl.—Truck Equipment Schedule T1						
LS Sport Utility 4D	T13S	28800	1700	1950	3000	4775
LS Extended Spt Utl	T16S	33510	2100	2375	3550	5550
LT Sport Utility 4D	T13S	32345	2025	2300	3450	5450
LT Extended Spt Utl	T16S	34295	2300	2600	3800	5900
LTZ Sport Utility 4D	T13S	36195	2325	2650	3825	6000
2WD	S		(800)	(800)	(1080)	(1080)
V8, 5.3 Liter	P		175	175	235	235
ENVOY 4WD—6-Cyl.—Truck Equipment Schedule T1						
SLE Sport Utility 4D	T13S	31495	2325	2650	3825	6000
SLT Sport Utility 4D	T13S	36345	2275	2575	3750	5900
2WD	S		(800)	(800)	(1080)	(1080)

354 **DEDUCT FOR RECONDITIONING**   0415

2003 CHEVROLET/GMC

Body Type	VIN	List	Trade-In Good	Very Good	Pvt-Party Good	Retail Excellent
ENVOY XL 4WD—6-Cyl.—Truck Equipment Schedule T1						
SLE Sport Utility 4D	T16S	33795	2650	3000	4250	6550
SLT Sport Utility 4D	T16S	38145	2800	3150	4450	6825
2WD	S		(800)	(800)	(1080)	(1080)
V8, 5.3 Liter	P		175	175	235	235
TAHOE 4WD—V8—Truck Equipment Schedule T1						
LS Sport Utility 4D	K13V	37387	3375	3725	4725	6725
LT Sport Utility 4D	K13V	41380	3925	4300	5375	7600
Third Row Seat			275	275	365	365
2WD	C		(500)	(500)	(665)	(665)
V8, 5.3 Liter	C		175	175	235	235
YUKON—V8—Truck Equipment Schedule T1						
SLE Sport Utility 4D	C13V	35027	3250	3575	4425	6325
Third Row Seat			275	275	365	365
4WD	K		500	500	660	660
V8, 5.3 Liter	T		175	175	235	235
YUKON 4WD—V8—Truck Equipment Schedule T1						
SLT Sport Utility 4D	K13V	40300	4625	5050	6200	8725
Third Row Seat			275	275	365	365
2WD	C		(500)	(500)	(665)	(665)
V8, 5.3 Liter	T		175	175	235	235
YUKON DENALI 4WD—V8—Truck Equipment Schedule T3						
Sport Utility 4D	K63U	48195	4675	5150	6150	8675
SUBURBAN 4WD—V8—Truck Equipment Schedule T1						
K1500 LS Sport Util	K16T	43875	3200	3550	4675	6775
K1500 LT Sport Util	K16T	40630	4000	4400	5625	8075
K2500 LS Sport Util	K26U	45575	4100	4500	5725	8225
K2500 LT Sport Util	K26U	42230	4925	5375	6725	9600
Quadrasteer			375	375	510	510
2WD	C		(800)	(800)	(1080)	(1080)
V8, 8.1 Liter	G		200	200	280	280
YUKON XL—V8—Truck Equipment Schedule T1						
1500 SLE Sport Util	C16T	37967	3000	3350	4425	6425
4WD	K		800	800	1060	1060
YUKON XL 4WD—V8—Truck Equipment Schedule T1						
1500 SLT Sport Util	K16Z	43590	4825	5250	6600	9400
2500 SLE Sport Util	K26U	42875	4150	4550	5800	8325
2500 SLT Sport Util	K26U	46165	4900	5350	6900	9850
Quadrasteer			375	375	510	510
2WD	C		(800)	(800)	(1080)	(1080)
V8, 8.1 Liter	G		200	200	280	280
YUKON XL DENALI AWD—V8—Truck Equipment Schedule T3						
1500 Sport Utility 4D	K16U	50859	4175	4625	5650	7975
VENTURE—V6—Truck Equipment Schedule T2						
Cargo Minivan 4D	U03E	22925	1500	1700	2525	4025
VENTURE—V6—Truck Equipment Schedule T1						
Minivan 4D	U03E	23139	1325	1500	2200	3550
Ext Minivan 4D	X03E	24509	1400	1600	2300	3700
LS Minivan 4D	U13E	25845	1675	1900	2750	4350
LS Ext Minivan	X03E	26845	1725	1950	2825	4450
LT Ext Minivan	X03E	29745	2125	2400	3350	5225
WarnerBros Ext	X13E	31995	2225	2500	3475	5400
5-Passenger Seating			(275)	(275)	(365)	(365)
AWD	V		350	350	465	465
ASTRO/SAFARI—V6—Truck Equipment Schedule T2						
Cargo/SL Cargo 3D	M19X	21952	2075	2350	3250	5025
Dutch Doors			100	100	135	135
AWD	L		350	350	465	465
ASTRO/SAFARI—V6—Truck Equipment Schedule T1						
Minivan 3D	M19X	23801	2050	2325	3225	4975
LS Minivan 3D	M19X	25390	2150	2450	3350	5150
LT Minivan 3D	M19X	29291	2350	2675	3600	5525
Dutch Doors			100	100	135	135
AWD	L		350	350	465	465
EXPRESS/SAVANA VAN—V8—Truck Equipment Schedule T1						
1500 Passenger	G15T	27005	3425	3825	4875	7325
1500 LS Passenger	G15T	28240	3550	3950	5025	7550
2500 Passenger	G25U	28000	3475	3875	4925	7400
2500 Extended	G29U	28995	3675	4100	5200	7775
2500 LS Passenger	G25U	30740	3750	4175	5275	7900
2500 LS Extended	G29U	31590	3900	4325	5475	8175
3500 Passenger	G35U	28504	3775	4200	5325	7950
3500 Extended	G39U	29499	3875	4300	5450	8125

TRUCKS & VANS

Body Type	VIN	List	Trade-In Good	Trade-In Very Good	Pvt-Party Good	Retail Excellent
3500 LS Passenger	G35U	31244	4025	4475	5625	8400
3500 LS Extended	G39U	32094	4100	4550	5725	8525
AWD	H		350	350	465	465
V6, 4.3 Liter	X		(275)	(275)	(365)	(365)
EXPRESS VAN—V6—Truck Equipment Schedule T1						
1500 Cargo Van	G15X	23185	2550	2850	3600	5575
AWD	H		425	425	550	550
V8, 5.3 Liter	T		275	275	355	355
EXPRESS VAN—V8—Truck Equipment Schedule T1						
1500 Cargo Van	G15X	23265	2900	3250	4075	6275
AWD	H		425	425	550	550
V6, 4.3 Liter	X		(275)	(275)	(365)	(365)
EXPRESS/SAVANA VAN—V8—Truck Equipment Schedule T1						
2500 Cargo Van	G25V	23415	2975	3325	4175	6425
2500 Ext Cargo	G29V	24695	3050	3400	4275	6575
3500 Cargo Van	G35U	25969	3075	3425	4300	6625
3500 Ext Cargo	G39U	27249	3500	3875	4875	7450
V6, 4.3 Liter	X		(275)	(275)	(365)	(365)
V8, 5.3 Liter (ex 1500)	T		150	150	200	200
V8, 6.0 Liter (ex 3500)	U		275	275	365	365
S10/SONOMA REGULAR CAB PICKUP—4-Cyl.—Truck Equip Sch T2						
2D 6'	S14H	14771	1425	1550	2075	3275
2D 7 1/3'	S14H	16216	1500	1650	2175	3400
LS/SLS 2D 6'	S14H	16495	1625	1800	2450	3800
LS/SLS 2D 7 1/3'	S14H	17945	1700	1875	2550	3925
S10/SONOMA EXTENDED CAB PICKUP—4-Cyl.—Truck Equip Sch T2						
3D 6'	S19H	16593	2000	2200	2900	4450
4WD	T		650	650	865	865
V6, 4.3 Liter	X		275	275	365	365
S10/SONOMA CREW CAB PICKUP 4WD—V6—Truck Equipment Sch T2						
LS/SLS 4D 4 1/2'	T13X	24404	3850	4175	5375	7925
SSR REGULAR CAB PICKUP—V8—Truck Equipment Schedule T3						
LS Convertible 2D	S14P	41995	9875	10500	10950	13750
AVALANCHE 4WD—V8—Truck Equipment Schedule T1						
1500 Spt Util Pickup	K13T	35139	5125	5600	6825	9875
2500 Spt Util Pickup	K23G	37039	6200	6750	8325	11950
2WD	C		(800)	(800)	(1080)	(1080)
North Face Edition			475	475	620	620
SILVERADO REGULAR CAB PICKUP—V8—Truck Equipment Sch T1						
1500 2D 6 1/2'	C14X	20031	2475	2750	3325	4950
1500 LS/SLE 2D 6 1/2'	C14X	23584	2675	2975	3550	5275
4WD	K		1100	1100	1465	1465
V8, 4.8 Liter	V		350	350	455	455
V8, 5.3 Liter	T		550	550	735	735
SIERRA REGULAR CAB PICKUP—V8—Truck Equipment Sch T1						
1500 2D 6 1/2'	C14V	20726	2725	3050	3625	5350
4WD	K		1100	1100	1465	1465
V6, 4.3 Liter	X		(400)	(400)	(535)	(535)
V8, 5.3 Liter	T		175	175	235	235
SILVERADO/SIERRA REGULAR CAB PICKUP—V8—Truck Equipment Sch T1						
1500 2D 8'	C14V	21026	2350	2625	3175	4750
1500 LS/SLE 2D 8'	C14V	24310	2800	3150	3700	5475
2500 Work Trk 8'	C24U	24810	2900	3175	3725	5300
2500 HD Wrk Trk 8'	C24U	25060	3150	3450	4175	5875
2500 HD 2D 8'	C24U	23627	3500	3825	4575	6400
2500 HD 2D 8'	C24U	23877	3950	4300	5100	7100
2500 LS/SLE 2D 8'	C24U	27460	3975	4325	5100	7125
2500 HD LS/SLE 8'	C24U	27710	4125	4475	5275	7350
4WD	K		1100	1100	1465	1465
V6, 4.3 Liter	X		(400)	(400)	(535)	(535)
V8, 5.3 Liter	T		175	175	235	235
V8, 8.1 Liter	G		200	200	280	280
V8, Turbo Diesel, 6.6L	1		3000	3000	4015	4015
SILVERADO/SIERRA REGULAR CAB 4WD—V8 Turbo Diesel—Truck Sch T1						
3500 2D 8'	K341	29317	7625	8175	9600	13050
3500 LS/SLE 2D 8'	K341	31960	8275	8850	10350	14050
V8, 6.0 Liter	X		(3700)	(3700)	(4935)	(4935)
V8, 8.1 Liter	G		(3000)	(3000)	(4000)	(4000)
SILVERADO/SIERRA EXTENDED CAB PICKUP—V8—Truck Equip Sch T1						
1500 Work Trk 6 1/2'	C19V	24110	3500	3875	4525	6575
1500 4D 6 1/2'	C19V	24465	3800	4225	5000	7250
1500 4D 8'	C19V	25565	3500	3900	4650	6775
1500 LS/SLE 4D 6 1/2'	C19V	27265	4325	4775	5625	8075

Body Type	VIN	List	Trade-In Good	Very Good	Pvt-Party Good	Retail Excellent
1500 LS/SLE 4D 8'	C19V	27565	4225	4675	5500	7900
1500 LT/SLT 4D 6 1/2'	C19V	32475	4725	5200	6075	8700
1500 LT/SLT 4D 8'	C19V	32775	4350	4800	5650	8100
2500 HD 4D 6 1/2'	C29U	26257	5275	5700	6825	9400
2500 HD 4D 8'	C29U	26532	5475	5900	7050	9700
2500HD LS/SLE 8'	C29U	30560	5775	6225	7375	10150
2500HD LT/SLT 8'	C29U	34743	6000	6450	7650	10500
Quadrasteer			375	375	510	510
4WD	K		1100	1100	1465	1465
V6, 4.3 Liter	X		(400)	(400)	(535)	(535)
V8, 5.3 Liter	T		175	175	235	235
V8, 8.1 Liter	G		200	200	280	280
V8, Turbo Diesel, 6.6L	1		3000	3000	4015	4015
SILVERADO/SIERRA EXTENDED CAB PICKUP 4WD—V8—Truck Sch T1						
2500 4D 6 1/2'	K29U	29822	5025	5425	6525	9000
2500 LS/SLE 6 1/2'	K29U	32765	5800	6250	7425	10200
2500 LT/SLT 6 1/2'	K29U	37285	5800	6250	7425	10200
SILVERADO/SIERRA EXTENDED CAB PICKUP 4WD—V8—Truck Equip T1						
2500HD LS/SLE 6 1/2	K29U	30260	7325	7850	9250	12600
2500HD LT/SLT 6 1/2	K29U	34443	7425	7950	9375	12750
3500 LS/SLE 4D 8'	K39U	31510	7650	8200	9625	13100
2WD	C		(1200)	(1200)	(1585)	(1585)
V8, 8.1 Liter	G		200	200	280	280
V8, Turbo Diesel, 6.6L	1		3000	3000	4015	4015
SILVERADO/SIERRA EXTENDED CAB PICKUP 4WD—V8 Turbo Diesel—Truck Sch T1						
3500 4D 8'	K231	28909	10600	11300	13100	17750
3500 LT/SLT 8'	K391	35310	11600	12300	14300	19350
2WD	C		(1200)	(1200)	(1585)	(1585)
V8, 6.0 Liter	U		(3700)	(3700)	(4935)	(4935)
V8, 8.1 Liter	G		(3000)	(3000)	(4000)	(4000)
SILVERADO SS EXTENDED CAB PICKUP AWD—V8—Truck Equip Sch T3						
1500 4D 6 1/2'	K19U	39995	9050	9850	11250	15650
SIERRA DENALI EXTENDED CAB PICKUP AWD—V8—Truck Equip Sch T3						
1500 4D 6 1/2'	K19U	44995	8150	8725	9925	13250
SILVERADO/SIERRA CREW CAB PICKUP 4WD—V8 Turbo Diesel—Truck Equip T1						
2500HD LT/SLT 6 1/2	K231	46435	11350	12050	13900	18650
2WD	C		(1200)	(1200)	(1585)	(1585)
V8, 6.0 Liter	U		(3700)	(3700)	(4935)	(4935)
V8, 8.1 Liter	G		(3000)	(3000)	(4000)	(4000)
SILVERADO CREW CAB PICKUP 4WD—V8—Truck Equip Schedule T1						
1500HD LS 6 1/2	K13U	33860	7125	7775	9075	12800
1500HD LT 6 1/2	K13U	38140	7350	8025	9425	13250
Quadrasteer			375	375	510	510
2WD	S		(800)	(800)	(1080)	(1080)
SIERRA CREW CAB PICKUP—V8—Truck Equip Schedule T1						
1500 HD SLE 6 1/2'	C13U	30442	5725	6275	7450	10550
4WD	K		1100	1100	1465	1465
SIERRA CREW CAB PICKUP 4WD—V8—Truck Equip Schedule T1						
1500 HD SLT 6 1/2'	K13U	33348	7800	8500	9925	13950
2WD	C		(1200)	(1200)	(1585)	(1585)
SILVERADO/SIERRA CREW CAB PICKUP 4WD—V8—Truck Equip Sch T1						
2500 HD 4D 6 1/2	K23U	32640	7125	7650	9025	12300
2500HD LS/SLE 6 1/2	K23U	34629	7550	8100	9500	12950
3500 4D 8'	K33U	31620	7175	7700	9100	12400
2WD	C		(1200)	(1200)	(1585)	(1585)
V8, 8.1 Liter	G		200	200	280	280
V8, Turbo Diesel, 6.6L	1		3000	3000	4015	4015
SILVERADO/SIERRA CREW CAB PICKUP—V8—Truck Equip Schedule T1						
2500 HD 4D 8'	C23U	29577	5775	6225	7375	10150
2500HD LS/SLE 8'	C23U	32410	6200	6675	7875	10800
2500HD LT/SLT 8'	C23U	36831	6375	6850	8075	11050
4WD	K		1100	1100	1465	1465
V8, 8.1 Liter	G		200	200	280	280
V8, Turbo Diesel, 6.6L	1		3000	3000	4015	4015
SILVERADO/SIERRA CREW CAB 4WD—V8 Turbo Diesel—Truck Equip T1						
3500 LS/SLE 4D 8'	K331	33372	11750	12450	14450	19550
3500 LT/SLT 4D 8'	K331	37410	11900	12600	14600	19750
2WD	C		(1200)	(1200)	(1585)	(1585)
V8, 6.0 Liter	U		(3700)	(3700)	(4935)	(4935)
V8, 8.1 Liter	G		(3000)	(3000)	(4000)	(4000)

TRUCKS & VANS

Body Type	VIN	List	Trade-In Good	Very Good	Pvt-Party Good	Retail Excellent

2004 CHEVY/GMC—(1,2or3)(CorG)(A,B,CorN)—(J134)—4-#

TRACKER 4WD—V6—Truck Equipment Schedule T2
Sport Utility 4D	J1354	21355	3100	3450	4550	6725
ZR2 Sport Utility 4D	J734	22705	3500	3875	5000	7200
LT Sport Utility 4D	J634	23105	4000	4400	5625	8050
2WD	E		(525)	(525)	(700)	(700)

BLAZER—V6—Truck Equipment Schedule T1
| Xtreme Spt Util 2D | S18X | 24940 | 1425 | 1600 | 2500 | 4000 |

BLAZER 4WD—V6—Truck Equipment Schedule T1
LS Sport Utility 2D	T18X	25395	1650	1875	2925	4600
LS Sport Utility 4D	T13X	27345	2175	2450	3600	5575
2WD	S		(900)	(900)	(1190)	(1190)

TRAILBLAZER 4WD—6-Cyl.—Truck Equipment Schedule T1
LS Sport Utility 4D	T13S	30045	2150	2425	3450	5275
LT Sport Utility 4D	T13S	32855	2675	3025	4075	6175
LS Ext Sport Util	T16S	32595	2900	3275	4275	6275
LT Ext Sport Util	T16S	34805	3100	3450	4500	6625
2WD	S		(900)	(900)	(1190)	(1190)
V8, 5.3 Liter	P		200	200	265	265

ENVOY 4WD—6-Cyl.—Truck Equipment Schedule T1
SLE Sport Utility 4D	T13S	34655	2975	3350	4450	6700
SLT Sport Utility 4D	T13S	36905	3000	3375	4500	6750
2WD	S		(900)	(900)	(1190)	(1190)

ENVOY XL 4WD—6-Cyl.—Truck Equipment Schedule T1
SLE Sport Utility 4D	T16S	36455	3525	3900	5025	7350
SLT Sport Utility 4D	T16S	38705	3625	4025	5325	7750
2WD	S		(900)	(900)	(1190)	(1190)
V8, 5.3 Liter	P		200	200	265	265

ENVOY XUV 4WD—6-Cyl.—Truck Equipment Schedule T1
SLE Sport Utility 4D	T12S	34150	2750	3075	3925	5700
2WD	S		(900)	(900)	(1190)	(1190)
V8, 5.3 Liter	P		200	200	265	265

ENVOY XUV 4WD—V8—Truck Equipment Schedule T1
SLT Sport Utiltiy 4D	T12P	40215	3475	3850	5000	7200
2WD	S		(900)	(900)	(1190)	(1190)
6-Cyl, 4.2 Liter	S		(225)	(225)	(290)	(290)

TAHOE 4WD—V8—Truck Equipment Schedule T1
LS Sport Utility 4D	K13V	38425	4550	4975	6075	8475
LT Sport Utility 4D	K13V	44600	5100	5550	6900	9575
Third Row Seat			300	300	400	400
2WD	C		(550)	(550)	(735)	(735)
V8, 5.3 Liter	T		200	200	265	265

YUKON—V8—Truck Equipment Schedule T1
SLE Sport Utility 4D	C13V	35725	4250	4650	5750	8025
Third Row Seat			300	300	400	400
4WD	K		550	550	735	735
V8, 5.3 Liter	T		200	200	265	265

YUKON 4WD—V8—Truck Equipment Schedule T1
SLT Sport Utility 4D	K13V	41315	5800	6275	7675	10650
Third Row Seat			300	300	400	400
2WD	C		(550)	(550)	(735)	(735)
V8, 5.3 Liter	T		200	200	265	265

YUKON DENALI AWD—V8—Truck Equipment Schedule T3
| Sport Utility 4D | K13U | 50125 | 5625 | 6150 | 7400 | 10250 |

SUBURBAN 4WD—V8—Truck Equipment Schedule T1
K1500 LS Sport Util	K16T	45870	4100	4475	5650	8025
K1500 LT Sport Util	K16T	53070	4900	5325	6575	9250
K2500 LS Sport Util	K26U	42600	4825	5250	6700	9450
K2500 LT Sport Util	K26U	47570	6025	6525	8075	11300
Quadrasteer			425	425	555	555
2WD	C		(900)	(900)	(1190)	(1190)
V8, 8.1 Liter	G		225	225	295	295

YUKON XL—V8—Truck Equipment Schedule T1
| 1500 SLE Sport Util | C16T | 38775 | 3700 | 4050 | 5175 | 7400 |
| 4WD | K | | 875 | 875 | 1175 | 1175 |

YUKON XL 4WD—V8—Truck Equipment Schedule T1
1500 SLT Sport Util	K16Z	44765	5550	6025	7525	10550
2500 SLE Sport Util	K26U	43210	4875	5300	6750	9500
2500 SLT Sport Util	K26U	46500	5875	6350	7900	11050
Quadrasteer			425	425	555	555
2WD	C		(900)	(900)	(1190)	(1190)
V8, 8.1 Liter	G		225	225	295	295

Body Type	VIN	List	Trade-In Good	Very Good	Pvt-Party Good	Retail Excellent
YUKON XL DENALI AWD—V8—Truck Equipment Schedule T3						
1500 Sport Utility 4D	K16U	51775	5625	6175	7300	10000
VENTURE—V6—Truck Equipment Schedule T2						
Cargo Minivan 4D	U03E	23120	1775	2000	2875	4525
VENTURE—V6—Truck Equipment Schedule T1						
Minivan 4D	U03E	21995	1650	1850	2725	4275
LS Minivan 4D	U13E	26040	2100	2350	3300	5150
Ext Minivan 4D	X03E	23570	1725	1950	2825	4425
LS Ext Minivan 4D	X03E	27390	2225	2500	3475	5375
LT Ext Minivan 4D	X13E	31290	2500	2800	3825	5875
5-Passenger Seating			(300)	(300)	(400)	(400)
AWD	V		400	400	535	535
ASTRO/SAFARI—V6—Truck Equipment Schedule T2						
Cargo 3D	M19X	22965	2800	3175	4125	6200
Dutch Doors			100	100	135	135
AWD	L		400	400	535	535
ASTRO/SAFARI—V6—Truck Equipment Schedule T1						
Minivan 3D	M19X	24395	2725	3075	4025	6075
LS/SLE Minivan	M19X	25970	2875	3250	4200	6325
LT/SLT Minivan	M19X	29870	3100	3500	4500	6725
Dutch Doors			100	100	135	135
AWD	L		400	400	535	535
EXPRESS/SAVANA VAN—V8—Truck Equipment Schedule T1						
1500 Passenger	G15T	27280	4300	4750	5700	8225
1500 LS Passenger	G15T	28905	4450	4925	5875	8475
2500 Passenger	G25U	28685	4375	4850	5800	8350
2500 LS Passenger	G25U	31805	4650	5125	6125	8800
3500 Passenger	G35U	29089	4700	5200	6200	8900
3500 LS Passenger	G35U	32209	4975	5475	6525	9350
3500 Extended	G39U	30409	4825	5325	6325	9100
3500 LS Extended	G39U	33004	5100	5625	6650	9550
AWD	H		450	450	585	585
V6, 4.3 Liter	X		(300)	(300)	(400)	(400)
EXPRESS VAN—V6—Truck Equipment Schedule T1						
1500 Cargo Van	G15X	23575	3400	3800	4675	7075
AWD	H		450	450	585	585
V8, 5.3 Liter	T		300	300	395	395
SAVANA VAN—V8—Truck Equipment Schedule T1						
1500 Cargo Van	G15T	23185	3775	4200	5150	7775
AWD	H		450	450	585	585
V6, 4.3 Liter	X		(300)	(300)	(400)	(400)
EXPRESS/SAVANA VAN—V8—Truck Equipment Schedule T1						
2500 Cargo Van	G25V	23965	3800	4225	5350	8050
2500 Extended	G29V	25100	3900	4350	5475	8250
3500 Cargo Van	G35U	27194	3925	4375	5500	8275
3500 Extended	G30U	28414	4450	4925	6125	9125
AWD	H		450	450	585	585
V6, 4.3 Liter	X		(300)	(300)	(400)	(400)
V8, 5.3 Liter (2500)	T		175	175	235	235
V8, 6.0 Liter (2500)	U		300	300	400	400
S10/SONOMA CREW CAB PICKUP 4WD—V6—Truck Equipment Sch T1						
LS/SLS 4D 4 1/2'	T13X	25095	4975	5375	6275	8725
COLORADO/CANYON REGULAR CAB PICKUP—4-Cyl.—Truck Equip Sch T2						
Base/SL 2D 6'	S148	17295	2825	3150	3750	5475
LS/SLE 2D 6'	S148	18135	3225	3575	4200	6100
4WD	T		800	800	1055	1055
5-Cyl, 3.5 Liter	6		150	150	205	205
COLORADO/CANYON EXT CAB PICKUP—4-Cyl.—Truck Equip Sch T2						
LS 4D 6'	S198	21235	4800	5275	6175	8800
SL 4D 6'	S198	22210	4075	4500	5325	7650
4WD	T		800	800	1040	1040
5-Cyl, 3.5 Liter	6		150	150	200	200
COLORADO/CANYON EXT CAB PICKUP—5-Cyl.—Truck Equip Sch T2						
Base 4D 6'	S196	20640	3575	3925	4900	7200
SLE 4D 6'	S196	24555	4975	5450	6375	9075
4WD	T		800	800	1065	1065
4-Cyl, 2.8 Liter	8		(150)	(150)	(195)	(195)
COLORADO/CANYON CREW CAB PICKUP—5-Cyl.—Truck Equip Sch T2						
LS/SLE 4D 5'	S136	23505	5500	6000	7225	10250
4WD	T		800	800	1035	1035
4-Cyl, 2.8 Liter	8		(150)	(150)	(190)	(190)
SSR REGULAR CAB PICKUP—V8—Truck Equipment Schedule T3						
Convertible 2D	S14P	41995	11700	12450	13100	16550

TRUCKS & VANS

Body Type	VIN	List	Trade-In Good	Trade-In Very Good	Pvt-Party Good	Retail Excellent
AVALANCHE 4WD—V8—Truck Equipment Schedule T1						
1500 Spt Util Pickup	K12T	36100	6475	7025	8175	11250
2500 Spt Util Pickup	K22G	37935	8050	8700	10100	13850
2WD	C		(900)	(900)	(1190)	(1190)
SILVERADO REGULAR CAB PICKUP—V6—Truck Equipment Sch T1						
1500 2D 6 1/2'	C14X	21905	3075	3425	3925	5650
4WD	K		1200	1200	1600	1600
V8, 4.8 Liter	V		375	375	500	500
V8, 5.3 Liter			575	575	775	775
SIERRA REGULAR CAB PICKUP—V8—Truck Equipment Sch T1						
1500 2D 6 1/2'	C14V	23400	3350	3725	4225	6050
4WD	K		1200	1200	1600	1600
V6, 4.3 Liter	X		(425)	(425)	(565)	(565)
V8, 5.3 Liter	T		200	200	265	265
SILVERADO/SIERRA REGULAR CAB PICKUP—V8—Truck Equipment Sch T1						
1500 Work Trk 6 1/2'	C14V	21185	1900	2100	2575	3850
1500 Work Truck 8'	C14V	21385	1650	1825	2250	3475
1500 2D 8'	C14V	23700	2900	3225	3725	5375
1500 LS/SLE 2D 6 1/2'	C14V	25585	3500	3875	4400	6275
1500 LS/SLE 2D 8'	C14V	25885	3250	3600	4100	5900
1500 Wrk Trk 2D 8'	C24U	25465	4475	4825	5400	7200
2500 2D 8'	C24U	26660	5450	5850	6475	8600
2500 LS/SLE 2D 8'	C24U	28215	5600	6025	6850	9075
2500 HD Work Trk 8'	C24U	25940	4825	5200	5775	7700
2500 HD 2D 8'	C24U	26910	5800	6225	7075	9375
2500 HD LS/SLE 8'	C24U	28690	6225	6675	7525	9975
4WD	K		1200	1200	1600	1600
V6, 4.3 Liter	X		(425)	(425)	(565)	(565)
V8, 5.3 Liter	T		200	200	265	265
V8, 8.1 Liter	G		225	225	270	270
V8, 6.6L Turbo Dsl	1,2		3325	3325	4045	4045
SILVERADO/SIERRA REGULAR CAB 4WD—V8—Truck Equipment Sch T1						
3500 Wrk Trk 2D 8'	K34U	29595	5050	5450	6025	8025
V8, 8.1 Liter	G		225	225	270	270
V8, 6.6L Turbo Dsl	1,2		3325	3325	4045	4045
SILVERADO/SIERRA REGULAR CAB 4WD—V8 Turbo Diesel—Truck Equipment Sch T1						
3500 2D 8'	K341,2	30940	9950	10600	11850	15600
3500 LS/SLE 2D 8'	K341,2	31845	10450	11100	12400	16300
V8, 6.0 Liter	U		(4000)	(4000)	(4875)	(4875)
V8, 8.1 Liter	G		(3450)	(3450)	(4205)	(4205)
SILVERADO REGULAR CAB PICKUP 4WD—V8—Truck Equipment Sch T1						
1500 Z71 2D 6 1/2'	K14V	30235	5050	5525	6300	8800
1500 Z71 2D 8'	K14V	30535	4850	5325	6075	8500
V8, 5.3 Liter	T		200	200	265	265
SILVERADO/SIERRA EXT CAB PICKUP—V8—Truck Equipment Schedule T1						
1500 Work Trk 6 1/2'	C19V	25090	3900	4300	5000	7075
1500 Work Truck 8'	C19V	25740	3450	3825	4325	6200
1500 4D 6 1/2'	C19V	26260	4625	5075	5825	8175
1500 4D 8'	C19V	26815	4225	4650	5375	7575
1500 LS/SLE 4D 6 1/2'	C19V	28145	4900	5375	6125	8575
1500 LS/SLE 4D 8'	C19V	28995	4775	5250	5975	8400
2500 HD Wk Trk 6 1/2	C29U	28590	7050	7550	8475	11200
2500 HD Wrk Trk 8'	C29U	28890	6850	7325	8250	10900
2500 HD 4D 6 1/2'	C29U	29160	7600	8125	9175	12100
2500 HD 4D 8'	C29U	29460	7925	8475	9550	12600
2500 HD LS/SLE 8'	C29U	31540	8250	8800	9900	13050
2500HD LT/SLT 6 1/2	K29U	35423	10450	11100	12400	16300
2500 HD LT/SLT 8'	C29U	35723	8400	8975	10050	13250
3500 Wrk Trk 4D 8'	C39U	30150	6825	7300	8200	10850
4WD	K		1200	1200	1600	1600
V6, 4.3 Liter	X		(425)	(425)	(565)	(565)
V8, 5.3 Liter	T		200	200	265	265
V8, 6.0 Liter	N		400	400	520	520
V8, 8.1 Liter	G		225	225	270	270
V8, 6.6L Turbo Dsl	1,2		3325	3325	4040	4040
SILVERADO/SIERRA EXT CAB 4WD PICKUP—V8—Truck Equipment Sch T1						
2500 Wrk Trk 6 1/2'	K29U	30820	6425	6900	7775	10250
2500 4D 6 1/2	K29U	31615	7375	7900	8925	11800
2500 LS/SLE 6 1/2	K29U	33520	7850	8400	9450	12450
2500 LT/SLT 6 1/2	K29U	38040	8150	8700	9775	12900
2500HD LS/SLE 6 1/2	K31240	31240	10150	10800	12100	15900
3500 LS/SLE 4D 1/2	K39U	32490	10850	11500	12850	16900
2WD	C		(1525)	(1525)	(1850)	(1850)

Body Type	VIN	List	Trade-In Good	Very Good	Pvt-Party Good	Retail Excellent
V8, 8.1 Liter	G		225	225	270	270
V8, 6.6L Turbo Dsl	1,2		3325	3325	4040	4040
SILVERADO/SIERRA EXT CAB 4WD—V8 Turbo Diesel—Truck Equip Sch T1						
3500 4D 8'	K391,2	30400	13550	14350	16100	21100
3500 LT/SLT 4D 8'	K391,2	36290	15000	15900	17750	23300
2WD	C		(1525)	(1525)	(1855)	(1855)
V8, 6.0 Liter	C		(4000)	(4000)	(4865)	(4865)
V8, 8.1 Liter	G		(3450)	(3450)	(4195)	(4195)
SILVERADO/SIERRA EXT CAB PICKUP—V8—Truck Equipment Schedule T1						
1500 LT/SLT 4D 6 1/2'	C19T	33455	5625	6150	7125	9925
1500 LT/SLT 4D 8'	C19T	33755	5325	5825	6600	9225
4WD	K		1200	1200	1600	1600
V8, 6.0 Liter	K		400	400	520	520
SILVERADO EXTENDED CAB PICKUP 4WD—V8—Truck Equipment Sch T1						
1500 Z71 4D 6 1/2'	K19V	32202	6225	6800	7800	10800
V8, 5.3 Liter	T		200	200	265	265
SILVERADO EXTENDED CAB PICKUP 4WD—V8—Truck Equipment Sch T1						
1500 Z71 4D 8'	K19T	33402	6025	6575	7575	10500
SILVERADO SS EXT CAB PICKUP AWD—V8—Truck Equipment Schedule T3						
1500 4D 6 1/2'	K19N	40195	10100	10900	12250	16650
SIERRA DENALI EXT CAB PICKUP AWD—V8—Truck Equip Schedule T3						
1500 4D 6 1/2'	K69U	41995	9375	9975	11300	14950
SILVERADO/SIERRA CREW CAB PICKUP—V8—Truck Equipment Sch T1						
1500 LS/SLE 4D 5 3/4'	C13T	31020	6200	6775	7800	10800
1500 LT/SLT 4D 5 3/4'	C13T	35023	6725	7325	8375	11550
2500 LS/SLE 4D 6 1/2'	C23U	31540	9000	9600	10750	14150
2500 LT/SLT 4D 6 1/2'	C23U	36386	9250	9850	11000	14500
2500HD Wk Trk 6 1/2'	C23U	30590	7400	7925	8950	11800
2500 HD Wrk Trk 8'	C23U	30890	7300	7825	8825	11650
2500 HD 4D 8'	C23U	31160	8700	9275	10400	13700
2500 HD LS/SLE 8'	C23U	33390	9000	9600	10750	14150
2500 HD LT/SLT 8'	C23U	37811	9250	9850	11000	14500
3500 Work Truck 8'	C33U	32150	7525	8050	9075	12000
Quadrasteer			425	425	555	555
4WD	K		1200	1200	1600	1600
V8, 8.1 Liter	G		225	225	270	270
V8, 6.6L Turbo Dsl	1,2		3325	3325	4040	4040
SIERRA CREW CAB PICKUP—V8—Truck Equipment Sch T1						
3500 4D 8'	C33U	31710	8900	9500	10650	14000
4WD			1200	1200	1460	1460
V8, Turbo Diesel, 6.6L	1,2		3325	3325	4050	4050
V8, 8.1 Liter	G		225	225	270	270
SILVERADO CREW CAB PICKUP 4WD—V8—Truck Equipment Sch T1						
3500 4D 8'	K33U	31710	10550	11200	12500	16450
2WD	C		(1525)	(1525)	(1855)	(1855)
V8, 6.6L Turbo Dsl	1,2		3325	3325	4040	4040
V8, 8.1 Liter	G		225	225	270	270
SILVERADO/SIERRA CREW CAB 4WD—V8—Truck Equipment Sch T1						
2500 HD 4D 6 1/2'	K23U	34210	10550	11200	12500	16450
2500HD LS/SLE 6 1/2'	K23U	35735	10750	11400	12750	16750
2WD	C		(1525)	(1525)	(1855)	(1855)
V8, 8.1 Liter	G		225	225	270	270
V8, 6.6L Turbo Dsl	1,2		3325	3325	4040	4040
SILVERADO/SIERRA CREW CAB 4WD—V8 Turbo Diesel—Truck Sch T1						
2500HD LT/SLT 6'	K231,2	47618	14850	15700	17300	22500
3500 LS/SLE 4D 8'	K331,2	34352	15000	15900	17750	23300
3500 LT/SLT 4D 8'	K331,2	38390	15300	16200	18100	23700
2WD	C		(1525)	(1525)	(1855)	(1855)
V8, 6.0 Liter	U		(4000)	(4000)	(4870)	(4870)
V8, 8.1 Liter	G		(3450)	(3450)	(4200)	(4200)
SILVERADO CREW CAB PICKUP 4WD—V8—Truck Equipment Sch T1						
1500 Z71 4D 5 3/4'	K13T	35049	6675	7275	8325	11500

Body Type	VIN	List	Trade-In Good	Very Good	Pvt-Party Good	Retail Excellent
BLAZER—V6—Truck Equipment Schedule T1						
Xtreme Spt Util 2D	S18X	24940	2150	2425	3425	5175
BLAZER 4WD—V6—Truck Equipment Schedule T1						
LS Sport Utility 2D	T18X	25850	2500	2825	3850	5775
LS Sport Utility 4D	T13X	28025	3200	3550	4725	6950
2WD	S		(975)	(975)	(1300)	(1300)
EQUINOX—V6—Truck Equipment Schedule T1						
LS Sport Utility 4D	L13F	21660	2400	2725	3700	5550
LT Sport Utility 4D	L63F	23600	2975	3325	4350	6450

SEE BACK PAGES FOR TRUCK EQUIPMENT

TRUCKS & VANS

2005 CHEVROLET/GMC

Body Type	VIN	List	Trade-In Good	Very Good	Pvt-Party Good	Retail Excellent
AWD		2,7	550	550	735	735
TRAILBLAZER 4WD—6-Cyl.—Truck Equipment Schedule T1						
LS Sport Utility 4D	T13S	30655	2800	3150	4125	6075
LT Sport Utility 4D	T13S	33305	3350	3725	4800	7025
LS Ext Sport Util	T16S	32775	3525	3900	4900	6900
LT Ext Sport Util	T16S	34955	3775	4150	5200	7300
2WD	S		(975)	(975)	(1300)	(1300)
V8, 5.3 Liter	S		225	225	300	300
ENVOY 4WD—6-Cyl.—Truck Equipment Schedule T1						
SLE Sport Utility 4D	T13S	32685	3550	3925	5150	7500
SLT Sport Utility 4D	T13S	37025	4000	4400	5675	8200
2WD	S		(975)	(975)	(1300)	(1300)
ENVOY DENALI 4WD—V8—Truck Equipment Schedule T3						
Sport Utility 4D	T63M	39640	4875	5350	6625	9100
2WD	S		(975)	(975)	(1300)	(1300)
ENVOY XL 4WD—6-Cyl.—Truck Equipment Schedule T1						
SLE Sport Utility 4D	T16S	34355	4200	4600	5700	7975
SLT Sport Utility 4D	T16S	38675	4575	5000	6150	8575
2WD	S		(975)	(975)	(1300)	(1300)
V8, 5.3 Liter	M		225	225	300	300
ENVOY XL DENALI 4WD—V8—Truck Equipment Schedule T3						
Sport Utility 4D	T16M	40920	5475	5950	7125	9650
2WD	S		(975)	(975)	(1300)	(1300)
ENVOY XUV 4WD—6-Cyl.—Truck Equipment Schedule T1						
SLE Sport Utility 4D	T12S	34440	3875	4275	5475	7800
2WD	S		(975)	(975)	(1300)	(1300)
V8, 5.3 Liter	M		225	225	300	300
ENVOY XUV 4WD—V8—Truck Equipment Schedule T1						
SLT Sport Utility 4D	T12M	39975	4725	5150	6600	9250
2WD	S		(975)	(975)	(1300)	(1300)
6-Cyl, 4.2 Liter	S		(225)	(225)	(315)	(315)
TAHOE 4WD—V8—Truck Equipment Schedule T1						
LS Sport Utility 4D	K13V	39185	5600	6075	7275	9825
LT Sport Utility 4D	K13V	45155	6775	7300	8550	11450
Third Row Seat			325	325	435	435
2WD	C		(600)	(600)	(800)	(800)
V8, 5.3 Liter	T		225	225	300	300
YUKON—V8—Truck Equipment Schedule T1						
SLE Sport Utility 4D	C13V	36310	5600	6075	7225	9725
Third Row Seat			325	325	435	435
4WD	K		600	600	800	800
V8, 5.3 Liter	T		225	225	300	300
YUKON 4WD—V8—Truck Equipment Schedule T1						
SLT Sport Utility 4D	K13V	42075	7625	8175	9525	12700
Third Row Seat			325	325	435	435
2WD	C		(600)	(600)	(800)	(800)
V8, 5.3 Liter	T		225	225	300	300
YUKON DENALI AWD—V8—Truck Equipment Schedule T3						
Sport Utility 4D	K63U	50885	7900	8550	9625	12750
SUBURBAN 4WD—V8—Truck Equipment Schedule T1						
K1500 LS Sport Util	K16Z	42415	4900	5325	6600	9075
K1500 LT Sport Util	K16Z	48005	5900	6375	7725	10500
K2500 LS Sport Util	K26U	43690	6000	6475	7825	10650
K2500 LT Sport Util	K26U	48890	7175	7725	9225	12500
Quadrasteer			450	450	605	605
2WD	C		(975)	(975)	(1300)	(1300)
V8, 8.1 Liter	G		225	225	315	315
YUKON XL—V8—Truck Equipment Schedule T1						
1500 SLE Sport Util	C16Z	39360	4350	4725	5800	8025
Quadrasteer			450	450	605	605
4WD	K		975	975	1285	1285
YUKON XL 4WD—V8—Truck Equipment Schedule T1						
1500 SLT Sport Util	K16Z	46295	6700	7225	8700	11800
2500 SLE Sport Util	K26U	43560	6050	6525	7900	10750
2500 SLT Sport Util	K26U	47370	7300	7850	9375	12700
Quadrasteer			450	450	605	605
2WD	C		(975)	(975)	(1300)	(1300)
V8, 8.1 Liter	G		225	225	315	315
YUKON XL DENALI AWD—V8—Truck Equipment Schedule T3						
1500 Sport Utility 4D	K66U	52355	7450	8100	9225	12300
VENTURE—V6—Truck Equipment Schedule T2						
Cargo Minivan 4D	V13E	23880	2225	2500	3375	5100

TRUCKS & VANS

362   DEDUCT FOR RECONDITIONING

0415

Body Type	VIN	List	Trade-In Good	Trade-In Very Good	Pvt-Party Good	Retail Excellent
VENTURE—V6—Truck Equipment Schedule T1						
Ext Minivan 4D	V03E	24080	2025	2275	3125	4750
LS Ext Minivan	V23E	27550	2600	2925	3825	5750
LT Ext Minivan	V33E	31475	2975	3325	4300	6400
5-Passenger Seating			(325)	(325)	(435)	(435)
ASTRO/SAFARI—V6—Truck Equipment Schedule T2						
Cargo 3D	M19X	23540	3450	3850	4925	7200
Dutch Doors			100	100	135	135
AWD	L		450	450	600	600
ASTRO/SAFARI—V6—Truck Equipment Schedule T1						
Minivan 3D	M19X	25040	3400	3800	4875	7125
LS Minivan 3D	M19X	28535	3675	4100	5200	7575
LT Minivan 3D	M19X	30185	3950	4375	5550	8050
Dutch Doors			100	100	135	135
AWD	L		450	450	600	600
UPLANDER—V6—Truck Equipment Schedule T2						
Cargo Minivan 4D	V13L	21415	2050	2300	3225	4975
UPLANDER—V6—Truck Equipment Schedule T1						
Extended Minivan	V03L	24350	1900	2150	3000	4600
LS Extended	V23L	26955	2050	2325	3175	4875
LT Extended	V33L	29385	2575	2925	3825	5750
AWD	X		375	375	510	510
EXPRESS/SAVANA VAN—V8—Truck Equipment Schedule T1						
1500 Passenger	G15T	26305	4975	5475	6825	9600
1500 LS Passenger	G15T	26690	5225	5750	7075	9900
2500 Passenger	G25V	29405	5200	5725	7100	9950
2500 LS Passenger	G25V	29540	5250	5775	7150	10050
3500 Passenger	G35U	30009	5400	6000	7400	10350
3500 LS Passenger	G35U	30624	5550	6100	7500	10500
3500 Extended	G39U	31594	5525	6075	7500	10500
3500 LS Extended	G39U	31594	5675	6225	7650	10700
V6, 4.3 Liter	X		(325)	(325)	(435)	(435)
EXPRESS VAN—V6—Truck Equipment Schedule T1						
1500 Cargo Van	G15X	23980	3875	4300	5350	7650
AWD	H		475	475	620	620
V8, 5.3 Liter	T		325	325	430	430
SAVANA VAN—V8—Truck Equipment Schedule T1						
1500 Cargo Van	G15X	23575	4275	4725	5825	8275
AWD	H		475	475	620	620
V6, 4.3 Liter	X		(325)	(325)	(435)	(435)
EXPRESS/SAVANA VAN—V8—Truck Equipment Schedule T1						
2500 Cargo Van	G25T	24275	4550	5025	6150	8725
3500 Cargo Van	G35U	26809	4700	5175	6325	8950
V8, 6.0 Liter	U		325	325	435	435
EXPRESS/SAVANA VAN—V8—Truck Equipment Schedule T1						
2500 Extended	G29T	25415	4650	5125	6250	8875
3500 Extended	G39V	28014	4850	5325	6500	9200
V6, 4.3 Liter	X		(325)	(325)	(435)	(435)
V8, 6.0 Liter	U		325	325	435	435
COLORADO/CANYON REGULAR CAB PICKUP—4-Cyl.—Truck Equip Sch T2						
Base/SL 2D 6'	S148	17425	2650	2975	3850	5625
LS 2D 6'	S148	18425	3075	3425	4400	6425
4WD	T		900	900	1200	1200
5-Cyl, 3.5 Liter	6		175	175	215	215
CANYON REGULAR CAB PICKUP—5-Cyl.—Truck Equip Sch T2						
SLE 2D 6'	S146	19870	3175	3550	4550	6550
4WD	T		900	900	1200	1200
4-Cyl, 2.8 Liter	8		(150)	(150)	(210)	(210)
COLORADO EXTENDED CAB PICKUP—4-Cyl.—Truck Equipment Sch T2						
LS 4D 6'	S198	21545	4775	5225	6475	9200
4WD	T		900	900	1200	1200
5-Cyl, 3.5 Liter	6		175	175	215	215
COLORADO EXTENDED CAB PICKUP—5-Cyl.—Truck Equipment Sch T2						
Base 4D 6'	S196	20770	3950	4350	5525	7925
4WD	T		900	900	1200	1200
4-Cyl, 2.8 Liter	8		(150)	(150)	(210)	(210)
CANYON EXTENDED CAB PICKUP—4-Cyl.—Truck Equipment Sch T2						
SL 4D 6'	S198	20100	3925	4325	5500	7875
4WD	T		900	900	1200	1200
5-Cyl, 3.5 Liter	6		175	175	215	215
CANYON EXTENDED CAB PICKUP—5-Cyl.—Truck Equipment Sch T2						
SLE 4D 6'	S196	22990	4950	5425	6650	9400
4WD	T		900	900	1200	1200

Body Type	VIN	List	Trade-In Good	Very Good	Pvt-Party Good	Retail Excellent
4-Cyl, 2.8 Liter	8		(150)	(150)	(210)	(210)
COLORADO/CANYON CREW CAB PICKUP—5-Cyl.—Truck Equip Sch T2						
LS/SLE 4D 5'	S136	23915	5700	6225	7775	10950
4WD	T		900	900	1200	1200
4-Cyl, 2.8 Liter	8		(150)	(150)	(210)	(210)
SSR REGULAR CAB PICKUP—V8—Truck Equipment Schedule T3						
Convertible 2D	S14H	43055	12850	13650	14400	17950
AVALANCHE 4WD—V8—Truck Equipment Schedule T1						
1500 LS Util Pickup	K12Z	37765	8150	8800	10000	13200
1500 LT Util Pickup	K12Z	41805	8950	9650	10800	14150
2500 LS Util Pickup	K22G	39175	10250	11000	12350	16150
2500 LT Util Pickup	K22G	43215	10600	11400	12650	16500
2WD	C		(975)	(975)	(1300)	(1300)
SILVERADO/SIERRA REGULAR CAB PICKUP—V6—Truck Equipment Sch T1						
1500 2D 6 1/2'	C14X	22555	3175	3550	4400	6175
4WD	K		1300	1300	1735	1735
V8, 4.8 Liter	V		425	425	550	550
V8, 5.3 Liter	T		650	650	855	855
V8, FFV, 5.3 Liter	F		600	600	785	785
SILVERADO/SIERRA REGULAR CAB PICKUP—V8—Truck Equipment Sch T1						
1500 Work Trk 6 1/2'	C14V	21830	2300	2600	3275	4700
1500 Work Truck 8'	C14V	21930	2000	2250	2975	4300
1500 2D 8'	C14V	23935	3200	3575	4300	6025
1500 LS/SLE 2D 6 1/2'	C14V	26585	3775	4200	5075	7050
1500 LS/SLE 2D 8'	C14V	26585	3500	3900	4775	6650
2500 HD Wrk Trk 8'	C24U	26585	4925	5325	6300	8425
2500 HD 2D 8'	C24U	27700	6225	6675	7825	10350
2500 HD LS/SLE 8'	C24U	29100	6775	7250	8600	11350
4WD	K		1300	1300	1735	1735
V6, 4.3 Liter	X		(450)	(450)	(600)	(600)
V8, 5.3 Liter	T		225	225	300	300
V8, 8.1 Liter	G		225	225	270	270
V8, 6.6L Turbo Dsl	2		3625	3625	4185	4185
SILVERADO REGULAR CAB PICKUP 4WD—V8—Truck Equipment Sch T1						
1500 Z71 2D 6 1/2'	K14V	30570	5650	6175	7325	10000
1500 Z71 2D 8'	K14V	30870	5450	5950	7100	9700
V8, 5.3 Liter	T		225	225	300	300
SILVERADO/SIERRA REGULAR CAB PICKUP 4WD—V8—Truck Equip Sch T1						
3500 Work Truck 8'	K34U	30855	5075	5475	6625	8825
V8, 8.1 Liter	G		225	225	270	270
V8, 6.6L Turbo Dsl	2		3625	3625	4200	4200
SILVERADO/SIERRA REGULAR 4WD—V8 Turbo Diesel—Sch T1						
3500 2D 8'	K342	31730	10550	11200	12800	16650
3500 LS/SLE 2D 8'	K342	32510	11150	11850	13600	17750
V8, 6.0 Liter	U		(4400)	(4400)	(5020)	(5020)
V8, 8.1 Liter	G		(3700)	(3700)	(4225)	(4225)
SILVERADO/SIERRA EXTENDED CAB—V8 Hybrid—Truck Equipment Sch T1						
1500 LS/SLE 6 1/2'	C19T	28845	10200	11000	12450	16700
4WD	K		1300	1300	1735	1735
SILVERADO/SIERRA EXTENDED CAB—V8—Truck Equip Sch T1						
1500 Work Trk 6 1/2'	C19V	25790	4500	4975	5925	8200
1500 Work Truck 8'	C19V	24790	3750	4175	5050	7000
1500 4D 6 1/2'	C19V	27295	5025	5500	6625	9100
1500 4D 8'	C19V	28295	4725	5200	6125	8450
1500 LS/SLE 4D 6 1/2'	C19V	28845	5375	5875	7025	9600
1500 LS/SLE 4D 8'	C19V	30045	5175	5675	6800	9300
1500 LT/SLT 4D 6 1/2'	C19T	33985	6400	6975	8175	11100
1500 LT/SLT 4D 8'	C19T	34285	5750	6275	7450	10150
2500HD Wk Trk 6 1/2'	C29U	29050	7125	7625	8975	11850
2500 HD Wrk Trk 8'	C29U	29350	7225	7725	9100	12000
2500 HD 4D 6 1/2'	C29U	30000	8750	9325	10850	14250
2500 HD 4D 8'	C29U	30300	8650	9225	10750	14100
2500 HD LS/SLE 8'	C29U	32000	9350	9950	11500	15100
2500 HD LT/SLT 8'	C29U	37280	9600	10200	11800	15450
3500 Work Truck 8'	C39U	30610	7425	7925	9300	12250
Quadrasteer			450	450	605	605
4WD	K		1300	1300	1735	1735
V6, 4.3 Liter	X		(450)	(450)	(600)	(600)
V8, 5.3L (ex LT/SLT)	T		225	225	300	300
V8, 8.1 Liter	G		225	225	270	270
V8, 6.6L Turbo Dsl	2		3625	3625	4155	4155
SILVERADO/SIERRA EXTENDED CAB PICKUP 4WD—V8—Truck Sch T1						
2500HD LS/SLE 6 1/2'	K29U	31700	11650	12350	14150	18450

TRUCKS & VANS

Body Type	VIN	List	Trade-In Good	Very Good	Pvt-Party Good	Retail Excellent
2500HD LT/SLT 6 1/2	K29U	36980	12000	12750	14450	18800
3500 LS/SLE 4D 8'	K39U	32950	12650	13400	15350	20000
2WD	C		(1675)	(1675)	(1920)	(1920)
V8, 8.1 Liter	G		225	225	270	270
V8, 6.6L Turbo Dsl			3625	3625	4150	4150
SILVERADO/SIERRA EXTENDED CAB 4WD—V8 Turbo Diesel—Truck Sch T1						
3500 4D 8'	K392	31240	15800	16700	18850	24500
3500 LT/SLT 4D 8'	K392	37845	17150	18100	20300	26400
2WD	C		(1675)	(1675)	(1920)	(1920)
V8, 6.0 Liter	U		(4400)	(4400)	(5020)	(5020)
V8, 8.1 Liter	G		(3700)	(3700)	(4220)	(4220)
SILVERADO EXTENDED CAB PICKUP 4WD—V8—Truck Equipment Sch T1						
1500 Z71 4D 6 1/2	K19V	32485	7000	7625	8925	12150
1500 Z71 4D 8'	K19V	33685	6875	7475	8700	11850
V8, 5.3 Liter	T		225	225	300	300
SILVERADO SS EXT CAB PICKUP—V8—Truck Equipment Schedule T1						
1500 4D 6 1/2	C19N	36440	11150	12050	13600	18150
AWD	K		1300	1300	1735	1735
SILVERADO/SIERRA CREW CAB PICKUP—V8—Truck Equip Schedule T1						
1500 LS/SLE 4D 5 3/4'	C13T	30875	6850	7450	8675	11800
1500 LT/SLT 4D 5 3/4'	C13T	35555	7275	7900	9225	12550
2500HD Wrk Trk 6 1/2	C23U	31150	8900	9500	11000	14450
2500 HD Wrk Trk 8'	C23U	31450	8700	9275	10800	14150
2500 HD 4D 8'	C23U	32400	10150	10800	12400	16200
2500 HD LS/SLE 8'	C23U	33950	10450	11100	12750	16650
2500 HD LT/SLT 8'	C23U	38370	10950	11600	13300	17350
3500 Work Truck 8'	C33U	32710	8900	9500	11000	14450
Quadrasteer			450	450	605	605
4WD	K		1300	1300	1735	1735
V8, 8.1 Liter			225	225	270	270
V8, 6.6L Turbo Dsl	2		3625	3625	4145	4145
SILVERADO/SIERRA CREW CAB PICKUP 4WD—V8—Truck Equip Sch T1						
1500HD LS/SLE 6 1/2	K13U	35795	10600	11450	13000	17500
1500HD LT/SLT 6 1/2	K13U	40035	10850	11750	13400	18000
2500 HD 4D 6 1/2	K23U	35015	12450	13200	15050	19600
2500HD LS/SLE 6 1/2	K23U	36395	12550	13300	15250	19900
3500 4D 8'	K33U	33340	12450	13200	15050	19600
2WD	C		(1675)	(1675)	(2245)	(2245)
V8, 6.6L Turbo Dsl	2		3625	3625	4150	4150
V8, 8.1 Liter			225	225	270	270
SILVERADO/SIERRA CREW CAB 4WD—V8 Turbo Diesel—Truck Sch T1						
2500HD LS/SLE 6 1/2	K232	48580	17150	18100	20100	25800
3500 LS/SLE 4D 8'	K332	34910	16850	17800	20000	26000
3500 LT/SLT 4D 8'	K332	38950	18050	19050	21400	27700
2WD	C		(1675)	(1675)	(1945)	(1945)
V8, 6.0 Liter	U		(4400)	(4400)	(5080)	(5080)
V8, 8.1 Liter	G		(3700)	(3700)	(4270)	(4270)
SILVERADO CREW CAB PICKUP 4WD—V8—Truck Equipment Sch T1						
1500 Z71 4D 5 3/4'	K13T	35385	7175	7800	9125	12400
SIERRA DENALI CREW CAB PICKUP AWD—V8—Truck Equip Schedule T3						
1500 4D 5 3/4'	K63N	42585	12050	12800	14550	18850

2006 CHEVY/GMC—(1,2or3)(CorG)(A,B,CorN)-(L13F)-6-#

Body Type	VIN	List	Trade-In Good	Very Good	Pvt-Party Good	Retail Excellent
EQUINOX—V6—Truck Equipment Schedule T1						
LS Sport Utility 4D	L13F	22345	3300	3650	4750	6800
LT Sport Utility 4D	L63F	22990	3775	4150	5300	7550
AWD	7		575	575	780	780
TRAILBLAZER 4WD—6-Cyl.—Truck Equipment Schedule T1						
LS Sport Utility 4D	T13S	27240	3850	4250	5250	7350
LT Sport Utility 4D	T13S	29535	4450	4875	5950	8275
LS Ext Sport Util	T16S	28840	4475	4875	5950	8200
LT Ext Sport Util	T16S	30940	4775	5200	6325	8675
2WD	S		(1050)	(1050)	(1410)	(1410)
V8, 5.3 Liter			250	250	335	335
TRAILBLAZER 4WD—V8—Truck Equipment Schedule T1						
SS Sport Utility 4D	T13H	33505	8325	8950	10300	13650
2WD	S		(1050)	(1050)	(1410)	(1410)
ENVOY 4WD—6-Cyl.—Truck Equipment Schedule T1						
SLE Sport Utility 4D	T13S	31550	4750	5200	6300	8750
SLT Sport Utility 4D	T13S	32585	5000	5475	6875	9525
2WD	S		(1050)	(1050)	(1410)	(1410)
ENVOY DENALI 4WD—V8—Truck Equipment Schedule T3						
Sport Utility 4D	T63M	39395	6425	6925	8275	11200

TRUCKS & VANS

Body Type	VIN	List	Trade-In Good	Very Good	Pvt-Party Good	Retail Excellent
2WD	S	------	(1050)	(1050)	(1410)	(1410)
ENVOY XL 4WD—6-Cyl.—Truck Equipment Schedule T1						
SLE Sport Utility 4D	T16S	32880	4950	5400	6875	9475
SLT Sport Utility 4D	T16S	33870	5225	5700	7175	9875
2WD	S	------	(1050)	(1050)	(1410)	(1410)
V8, 5.3 Liter	M	------	250	250	335	335
ENVOY XL DENALI 4WD—V8—Truck Equipment Schedule T3						
Sport Utility 4D	T66M	40825	7350	7925	9100	11900
2WD	S	------	(1050)	(1050)	(1410)	(1410)
TAHOE 4WD—V8—Truck Equipment Schedule T1						
LS Sport Utility 4D	K13V	40750	5950	6400	7625	10200
LT Sport Utility 4D	K13V	45625	7650	8200	9625	12800
Third Row Seat			350	350	465	465
2WD	C	------	(650)	(650)	(865)	(865)
V8, 5.3 Liter	T	------	250	250	335	335
YUKON—V8—Truck Equipment Schedule T1						
SLE Sport Utility 4D	C13V	37280	6250	6725	8000	10700
Third Row Seat			350	350	465	465
4WD	K	------	650	650	865	865
V8, 5.3 Liter	T	------	250	250	335	335
YUKON 4WD—V8—Truck Equipment Schedule T1						
SL Sport Utility 4D	K13V	37640	6625	7125	8400	11250
SLT Sport Utility 4D	K13V	42210	8550	9150	10600	14050
Third Row Seat			350	350	465	465
2WD	C	------	(1050)	(1050)	(1410)	(1410)
V8, 5.3 Liter	T	------	250	250	335	335
YUKON DENALI AWD—V8—Truck Equipment Schedule T3						
Sport Utility 4D	K63U	51160	9700	10450	11750	15250
SUBURBAN 4WD—V8—Truck Equipment Schedule T1						
K1500 LS Sport Util	K16Z	42440	6250	6750	8150	11050
K1500 LT Sport Util	K16Z	47935	7275	7800	9400	12700
K1500 LTZ Spt Utl	K16Z	53400	9525	10250	11200	14350
K2500 LS Sport Util	K26U	48820	7425	7950	9550	12900
K2500 LT Sport Util	K26U	44920	8575	9150	10800	14450
2WD	C	------	(1050)	(1050)	(1410)	(1410)
V8, 8.1 Liter	G	------	250	250	335	335
YUKON XL—V8—Truck Equipment Schedule T1						
1500 SLE Sport Util	C16Z	40330	5850	6325	7750	10600
4WD	K	------	1050	1050	1395	1395
YUKON XL 4WD—V8—Truck Equipment Schedule T1						
1500 SL Sport Util	K16Z	40413	6300	6800	8250	11250
1500 SLT Sport Util	K16Z	46820	8325	8900	10550	14150
2500 SLE Sport Util	K26U	44105	7525	8050	9675	13050
2500 SLT Sport Util	K26U	47395	8625	9250	11050	14850
2WD	C	------	(1050)	(1050)	(1410)	(1410)
V8, 8.1 Liter	G	------	250	250	335	335
YUKON XL DENALI AWD—V8—Truck Equipment Schedule T3						
1500 Sport Utility 4D	K66U	52810	9800	10550	11750	15200
UPLANDER—V6—Truck Equipment Schedule T2						
Cargo Minivan 4D	V13L	21640	2725	3050	3975	5925
UPLANDER—V6—Truck Equipment Schedule T1						
LS Minivan 4D	U23L	21990	1800	2050	3025	4625
LS Extended 4D	V23L	24575	2175	2450	3475	5250
LT Extended 4D	V33L	28385	3000	3350	4475	6600
AWD	X	------	425	425	560	560
EXPRESS/SAVANA VAN—V8—Truck Equipment Schedule T1						
1500 LS Passenger	G15T	26770	5750	6300	7400	9975
1500 LT Passenger	G15T	28580	6050	6600	7750	10400
2500 LS Passenger	G25V	28625	5925	6475	7600	10200
2500 LT Passenger	G25V	30435	6250	6825	7975	10700
3500 LS Passenger	G35U	30704	6375	6950	8200	11000
3500 LS Extended	G39U	29574	6900	7525	8800	11800
3500 LT Passenger	G35U	32119	6800	7425	8675	11650
3500 LT Extended	G39U	29914	7350	8000	9300	12450
AWD	H	------	500	500	660	660
V6, 4.3 Liter	X	------	(350)	(350)	(465)	(465)
EXPRESS VAN—V6—Truck Equipment Schedule T1						
1500 Cargo Van	G15X	22660	4825	5300	6275	8675
AWD	H	------	500	500	660	660
V8, 5.3 Liter	T	------	350	350	465	465
SAVANA VAN—V8—Truck Equipment Schedule T1						
1500 Cargo Van	G15T	23980	5175	5675	6875	9450
AWD	H	------	500	500	660	660

0415

Body Type	VIN	List	Trade-In Good	Trade-In Very Good	Pvt-Party Good	Retail Excellent
V6, 4.3 Liter	X		(350)	(350)	(465)	(465)

EXPRESS/SAVANA VAN—V8—Truck Equipment Schedule T1

2500 Cargo Van	G25V	25750	5550	6075	7300	10050
2500 Extended	G29V	24175	5725	6275	7500	10300
3500 Cargo Van	G35V	27434	5775	6325	7550	10350
3500 Extended	G39V	26729	6250	6825	8100	11100
V8, 6.0 Liter	U		350	350	465	465
V8, 6.6L Turbo Dsl	2		3950	3950	5265	5265

COLORADO/CANYON REGULAR CAB PICKUP—4-Cyl.—Truck Equip Sch T1

Work Truck 2D 6'	S148	17085	2300	2600	3500	5050
LS/SL 2D 6'	S148	17085	2950	3275	4275	6075
LT 2D 6'	S148	18715	3450	3825	4825	6775
4WD	T		1000	1000	1335	1335
5-Cyl, 3.5 Liter	6		175	175	230	230

CANYON REGULAR CAB PICKUP—5-Cyl.—Truck Equipment Sch T1

SLE 2D 6'	S146	20410	3625	4000	4975	6975
4WD	T		1000	1000	1335	1335
4-Cyl, 2.8 Liter	8		(175)	(175)	(225)	(225)

CANYON EXTENDED CAB PICKUP—4-Cyl.—Truck Equipment Sch T1

Work Truck 4D 6'	S198	19460	3825	4200	5250	7350
4WD	T		1000	1000	1335	1335
5-Cyl, 3.5 Liter	6		175	175	230	230

COLORADO/CANYON EXTENDED CAB PICKUP—4-Cyl.—Truck Sch T1

LS/SL 4D 6'	S198	19460	4375	4775	5925	8325
4WD	T		1000	1000	1335	1335
5-Cyl, 3.5 Liter	6		175	175	230	230

COLORADO/CANYON EXTENDED CAB PICKUP—5-Cyl.—Truck Sch T1

LT/SLE 4D 6'	S196	22090	5325	5800	7125	9825
4WD	T		1000	1000	1335	1335
4-Cyl, 2.8 Liter	8		(175)	(175)	(225)	(225)

COLORADO/CANYON CREW CAB PICKUP—5-Cyl.—Truck Equip Sch T1

LT/SLE 4D 5 1/4'	S136	23900	6500	7025	8525	11700
4WD	T		1000	1000	1335	1335
4-Cyl, 2.8 Liter	8		(175)	(175)	(225)	(225)

CANYON CREW CAB PICKUP—5-Cyl.—Truck Equipment Sch T2

SLT 4D 5'	S136	26810	6600	7125	8650	11850
4WD	T		1000	1000	1335	1335

SSR REGULAR CAB PICKUP—V8—Truck Equipment Schedule T3

Convertible 2D	S14H	39990	15650	16500	17350	21300

AVALANCHE 4WD—V8—Truck Equipment Schedule T1

1500 LS Util Pickup	K12Z	37885	8925	9575	10850	14050
1500 LT Util Pickup	K12Z	41730	9525	10200	11400	14700
2500 LS Util Pickup	K22G	39295	10800	11550	13100	17000
2500 LT Util Pickup	K22G	43140	11050	11800	13250	17000
2WD	C		(1050)	(1050)	(1410)	(1410)

SILVERADO REGULAR CAB PICKUP—V6—Truck Equipment Sch T1

1500 LS/SL 2D 6 1/2'	C14X	23345	4075	4500	5325	7250
4WD	K		1600	1600	2135	2135
V8, 4.8 Liter	V		450	450	600	600
V8, 5.3 Liter	T		700	700	935	935
V8, FFV, 5.3 Liter	Z		650	650	855	855

SILVERADO/SIERRA REGULAR CAB PICKUP—V8—Truck Equipment Sch T1

1500 Work Trk 6 1/2'	C14V	18755	2675	3000	3775	5250
1500 Work Truck 8'	C14V	19030	2500	2800	3450	4825
1500 LS/SL 2D 8'	C14V	23875	4175	4600	5425	7400
1500 LT/SLE 6 1/2'	C14V	23875	4350	4775	5625	7650
1500 LT/SLE 8'	C14V	24165	4250	4675	5500	7500
2500 HD Wrk Trk 8'	C24U	23795	5400	5800	6825	8900
2500 HD LS/SL 8'	C24U	27295	6850	7325	8575	11200
3500 Wrk Trk 2D 8'	C34U	24060	5675	6100	7200	9375
3500 SL 8'	C34U	30275	7050	7525	8775	11400
3500 LT/SLE 2D 8'	C34U	26355	7400	7900	9100	11750
4WD	K		1600	1600	2135	2135
V6, 4.3 Liter	X		(450)	(450)	(600)	(600)
V8, 5.3 Liter	T		250	250	335	335
V8, 8.1 Liter	G		250	250	295	295
V8, 6.6L Turbo Dsl	2,D		3950	3950	4655	4655

SILVERADO/SIERRA REGULAR CAB PICKUP 4WD—V8—Truck Equip Sch T1

2500 HD LT/SLE 8'	K24U	25455	9225	9800	11250	14450
2WD	C		(2075)	(2075)	(2425)	(2425)
V8, 8.1 Liter	G		250	250	295	295
V8, 6.6L Turbo Dsl	2,D		3950	3950	4635	4635

TRUCKS & VANS

Body Type	VIN	List	Trade-In Good	Very Good	Pvt-Party Good	Retail Excellent
SILVERADO REGULAR CAB PICKUP—V8 Turbo Diesel—Truck Equip Sch T1						
3500 LS 2D 8'	C342,D	30275	11150	11850	13600	17500
4WD	K		1600	1600	1875	1875
V8, 6.0 Liter	U		(4700)	(4700)	(5510)	(5510)
V8, 8.1 Liter	G		(4100)	(4100)	(4810)	(4810)
SILVERADO/SIERRA EXTENDED CAB PICKUP—V8—Truck Equip Sch T1						
1500 LT/SLE 4D 8'	C19T	27660	6750	7350	8550	11450
4WD	K		1600	1600	2135	2135
SILVERADO EXTENDED CAB—V8 Hybrid—Truck Equip Sch T1						
1500 LT 4D 6 1/2'	C19T	26485	11050	11900	13400	17750
4WD	K		1600	1600	2135	2135
SIERRA EXTENDED CAB 4WD—V8 Hybrid—Truck Equip Sch T1						
1500 SLE 4D 6 1/2'	K19T	26485	13200	14150	15700	20400
2WD	C		(2075)	(2075)	(2750)	(2750)
SILVERADO/SIERRA EXTENDED CAB PICKUP—V8—Truck Equip Sch T1						
1500 Work Trk 6 1/2'	C19V	22935	4950	5425	6300	8500
1500 Work Truck 8'	C19V	25040	4375	4800	5650	7675
1500 LS 4D 6 1/2'	C19V	27195	6800	7400	8600	11500
1500 LS/SL 4D 8'	C19V	28125	6425	7000	8175	10950
1500 LT/SLE 4D 6 1/2'	C19V	26485	7300	7925	9150	12250
4WD	K		1600	1600	2135	2135
V8, 5.3 Liter	T,B,Z		250	250	335	,335
SILVERADO/SIERRA EXTENDED CAB PICKUP—V8—Truck Equip Sch T1						
1500 SLT 4D 5 3/4'	C19T	30130	7475	8100	9350	12500
1500 SLT 4D 5 3/4'	C19T	31200	9375	10100	11400	15000
1500 SLT 4D 8'	C19T	31840	7325	7950	9175	12250
2500HD Wk Trk 6 1/2'	C29U	26485	8300	8825	10100	13000
2500HD Work Trk 8'	C29U	26780	8200	8725	10000	12950
2500 HD LS 4D 6 1/2'	C29U	29570	9975	10600	12050	15450
2500 HD LS/SL 4D 8'	C29U	29860	9875	10500	11900	15300
2500 HD SLT 8'	C29U	33400	11250	11900	13450	17200
3500 Work Truck 8'	C39U	27350	8400	8950	10200	13150
4WD	K		1600	1600	1875	1875
V8, 6.6L Turbo Dsl	2,D		3950	3950	4630	4630
V8, 8.1 Liter	G		250	250	295	295
SIERRA EXTENDED CAB PICKUP—V8 Turbo Diesel—Truck Equip Sch T1						
3500 SL 4D 8'	C392,D	32790	14250	15050	16850	21500
4WD	K		1600	1600	1865	1865
V8, 6.0 Liter	U		(4700)	(4700)	(5485)	(5485)
V8, 8.1 Liter	G		(4100)	(4100)	(4785)	(4785)
SIERRA EXTENDED CAB PICKUP 4WD—V8—Truck Equip Sch T1						
1500 SL 4D 6 1/2'	K19V	27195	9475	10200	11350	14800
2WD	C		(2075)	(2075)	(2700)	(2700)
V6, 4.3 Liter	X		(450)	(450)	(590)	(590)
V8, 5.3 Liter	T		250	250	325	325
SIERRA EXTENDED CAB PICKUP 4WD—V8—Truck Equip Sch T1						
1500 SLT 4D 6 1/2'	K19B	31350	10400	11200	12750	16900
2WD	C		(2075)	(2075)	(2750)	(2750)
V8, HO, 6.0 Liter	N		450	450	605	605
SILVERADO/SIERRA EXTENDED CAB PICKUP 4WD—V8—Truck Sch T1						
2500 HD LS 6 1/2'	K29N	29570	12150	12900	14550	18600
2500HD LT/SLE 6 1/2'	K29N	29200	12800	13550	15400	19750
2500 HD SLT 6 1/2'	K29U	33110	13650	14450	16200	20700
3500 LS 4D 8'	K39U	28000	12000	12750	14400	18400
2WD	C		(2075)	(2075)	(2415)	(2415)
V8, 8.1 Liter	G		250	250	290	290
V8, 6.6L Turbo Dsl	2,D		3950	3950	4625	4625
SIERRA EXTENDED CAB—V8 Turbo Diesel—Truck Equipment Sch T1						
3500 SL 4D 8'	C392,D	32790	14250	15050	16850	21500
4WD	K		1600	1600	1865	1865
V8, 6.0 Liter	U		(4700)	(4700)	(5485)	(5485)
V8, 8.1 Liter	G		(4100)	(4100)	(4785)	(4785)
SILVERADO/SIERRA EXTENDED CAB 4WD—V8 Turbo Diesel—Truck Sch T1						
3500 LT/SLE 4D 8'	K392,D	29900	17200	18150	20100	25600
2WD	C		(2075)	(2075)	(2410)	(2410)
V8, 6.0 Liter	U		(4700)	(4700)	(5485)	(5485)
V8, 8.1 Liter	G		(4100)	(4100)	(4785)	(4785)
SILVERADO SS EXTENDED CAB PICKUP—V8—Truck Equip Schedule T3						
1500 4D 6 1/2'	C19N	36625	12600	13550	15150	19800
SILVERADO/SIERRA CREW CAB PICKUP—Truck Equip Schedule T2						
1500 LS/SL 4D 5 3/4'	C13V	27990	8875	9575	10950	14550
1500 LT/SLE 4D 5 3/4'	C13T	29040	9175	9900	11250	14950
1500 HD SLE 6 1/2'	C13U	32855	10050	10800	12400	16200

Body Type	VIN	List	Trade-In Good	Very Good	Pvt-Party Good	Retail Excellent
2500 HD Wk Tk 6 1/2'	C23U	28480	9875	10500	11900	15300
2500 HD Wk Trk 8'	C23U	28770	9775	10350	11850	15200
2500 HD LS/SL 8'	C23U	31830	11300	12000	13650	17450
2500 HD LT/SLE 8'	C23U	31415	12450	13200	14800	18800
2500 HD SLT 8'	C23U	35475	12850	13600	15300	19550
4WD	K		1600	1600	2135	2135
V8, HO, 6.0 Liter	N		450	450	605	605
V8, 8.1 Liter	G		250	250	295	295
V8, 6.6L Turbo Dsl	2,D		3950	3950	4630	4630
SILVERADO/SIERRA CREW CAB PICKUP 4WD—V8—Truck Equip Sch T1						
1500 SLT 4D 5 3/4'	K13T	33215	12100	12950	14450	18950
1500 SLT LT 6 1/2'	K13U	36305	12250	13150	14350	18600
1500 SLT LT 8'	K13U	34205	13150	14100	15900	20900
2500HD LS/SL 6 1/2'	K23U	34485	13850	14650	16450	21000
2WD	C		(2075)	(2075)	(2410)	(2410)
V8, 8.1 Liter	G		250	250	290	290
V8, 6.6L Turbo Dsl	2,D		3950	3950	4615	4615
SILVERADO CREW CAB 4WD—V8 Turbo Diesel—Truck Equip Sch T1						
3500 LS 4D 8'	K332,D	35005	18600	19600	21600	27500
2WD	C		(2075)	(2075)	(2405)	(2405)
V8, 6.0 Liter	U		(4700)	(4700)	(5475)	(5475)
V8, 8.1 Liter	G		(4100)	(4100)	(4780)	(4780)
SIERRA CREW CAB—V8 Turbo Diesel—Truck Equipment Sch T1						
3500 SL 4D 8'	C332,D	35005	16200	17100	19050	24200
3500 SLE 4D 8'	C332,D	32515	16600	17500	19450	24700
4WD	K		1600	1600	1865	1865
V8, 6.0 Liter	U		(4700)	(4700)	(5475)	(5475)
V8, 8.1 Liter	G		(4100)	(4100)	(4775)	(4775)
SILVERADO/SIERRA CREW CAB 4WD—V8 Turbo Diesel—Truck Equip Sch T1						
2500HD LT/SLE 6'	K232,D	43415	18800	19800	21600	27200
2500 HD SLT 6 1/2'	K232,D	48050	19600	20600	22700	28800
3500 LT 4D 8'	K332,D	32015	18600	19600	21600	27500
3500 SLT 4D 8'	K332,D	35885	19700	20700	22800	29000
2WD	C		(2075)	(2075)	(2405)	(2405)
V8, 6.0 Liter	U		(4700)	(4700)	(5475)	(5475)
V8, 8.1 Liter	G		(4100)	(4100)	(4780)	(4780)
SIERRA DENALI CREW CAB PICKUP AWD—V8—Truck Equip Schedule T3						
1500 4D 5 3/4'	K63N	42610	13700	14450	16000	20200

2007 CHEVY/GMC—(1,2or3)(CorG)(A,B,CorN)—(L13F)—7—#

Body Type	VIN	List	Trade-In Good	Very Good	Pvt-Party Good	Retail Excellent
EQUINOX—V6—Truck Equipment Schedule T1						
LS Sport Utility 4D	L13F	22680	4175	4550	5625	7800
LT Sport Utility 4D	L63F	23655	4825	5250	6375	8775
AWD	2,7		625	625	825	825
TRAILBLAZER 4WD—6-Cyl.—Truck Equipment Schedule T1						
LS Sport Utility 4D	T13S	27735	4975	5400	6375	8600
LT Sport Utility 4D	T13S	30945	5400	5875	7050	9500
2WD	S		(1150)	(1150)	(1520)	(1520)
V8, 5.3 Liter	M		275	275	365	365
TRAILBLAZER AWD—V8—Truck Equipment Schedule T1						
SS Sport Utility 4D	T13H	34015	9950	10650	11850	15100
2WD	S		(1150)	(1150)	(1460)	(1460)
ENVOY 4WD—6-Cyl.—Truck Equipment Schedule T1						
SLE Sport Utility 4D	T13S	29330	5800	6300	7525	10100
SLT Sport Utility 4D	T13S	33695	6400	6925	8275	11050
2WD	S		(1150)	(1150)	(1520)	(1520)
ENVOY DENALI 4WD—V8—Truck Equipment Schedule T3						
Sport Utility 4D	T63M	37570	7700	8250	9450	12300
2WD	S		(1150)	(1150)	(1500)	(1500)
ACADIA—V6—Truck Equipment Schedule T1						
SLE Sport Utility 4D	R13T	29990	8000	8575	9650	12400
AWD	V		675	675	900	900
ACADIA AWD—V6—Truck Equipment Schedule T1						
SLT Sport Utiltiy 4D	V23T	35960	9875	10550	11950	15450
2WD	R		(650)	(650)	(860)	(860)
TAHOE—V8—Truck Equipment Schedule T1						
LS Sport Utility 4D	C13C	34755	11300	12000	13000	16200
Third Row Seat			375	375	470	470
4WD	K		1125	1125	1420	1420
V8, 5.3 Liter	J		275	275	345	345
TAHOE 4WD—V8—Truck Equipment Schedule T1						
LT Sport Utility 4D	K130	40120	14000	14800	15950	19900
LTZ Sport Utility 4D	K130	48980	15750	16750	17550	21700

TRUCKS & VANS

Body Type	VIN	List	Trade-In Good	Very Good	Pvt-Party Good	Retail Excellent
Third Row Seat	C	......	375	375	470	470
2WD		......	(1150)	(1150)	(1435)	(1435)
YUKON—V8—Truck Equipment Schedule T1						
SLE Sport Utility 4D	C130	34690	12000	12750	14000	17600
Third Row Seat		......	375	375	480	480
4WD	K	......	1125	1125	1455	1455
V8, 4.8 Liter	C	......	(300)	(300)	(370)	(370)
YUKON 4WD—V8—Truck Equipment Schedule T1						
SLT Sport Utility 4D	K130	41670	15050	15950	17050	21100
Third Row Seat		......	375	375	465	465
2WD	C	......	(1150)	(1150)	(1415)	(1415)
V8, 4.8 Liter	C	......	(300)	(300)	(360)	(360)
YUKON DENALI AWD—V8—Truck Equipment Schedule T3						
Sport Utility 4D	K638	48370	16300	17350	18200	22500
SUBURBAN 4WD—V8—Truck Equipment Schedule T1						
K1500 LS Sport Util	K163	39790	11900	12650	13900	17500
K1500 LT Sport Util	K163	43540	13500	14300	15600	19550
K1500 LTZ Sport Utl	K163	48455	14450	15400	16250	20200
K2500 LS Sport Util	K26K	41715	13600	14400	15700	19650
K2500 LT Sport Util	K26K	39705	14800	15700	17050	21300
2WD	C	......	(1150)	(1150)	(1470)	(1470)
V8, 6.0 Liter	Y	......	475	475	625	625
YUKON XL 4WD—V8—Truck Equipment Schedule T1						
1500 SLE Sport Util	K163	37790	12400	13150	14450	18150
1500 SLT Sport Util	K163	44170	14500	15400	16700	20900
2500 SLE Sport Util	K26K	41765	13300	14100	15400	19350
2500 SLT Sport Util	K26K	45345	15550	16450	17800	22200
2WD	C	......	(1150)	(1150)	(1470)	(1470)
V8, 6.0 Liter	Y	......	475	475	625	625
YUKON XL DENALI AWD—V8—Truck Equipment Schedule T3						
1500 Sport Utility 4D	K168	50870	15300	16300	17250	21500
UPLANDER—V6—Truck Equipment Schedule T2						
Cargo Minivan 4D	V131	22670	2900	3225	4450	6575
UPLANDER—V6—Truck Equipment Schedule T1						
LS Minivan 4D	U231	20770	2700	3000	3900	5725
LS Extended Minivan	V231	23845	3175	3525	4625	6700
LT Extended Minivan	V331	27970	4400	4825	6050	8625
EXPRESS/SAVANA VAN—V8—Truck Equipment Schedule T1						
1500 LS Passenger	G15T	26460	6575	7125	8150	10650
1500 LT Passenger	G15Z	27955	6875	7450	8475	11050
2500 LS Passenger	G25V	27265	6775	7325	8350	10900
2500 LT Passenger	G25V	29075	7075	7650	8675	11300
3500 LS Passenger	G35U	29299	7475	8075	9125	11850
3500 LS Extended	G39U	31529	8775	9475	10600	13750
3500 LT Passenger	G35U	30714	8525	9200	10350	13400
3500 LT Extended	G39U	31869	9175	9900	11050	14300
AWD	H	......	525	525	660	660
EXPRESS VAN—V6—Truck Equipment Schedule T1						
1500 Cargo Van	G15X	23130	6325	6875	8075	10850
AWD	H	......	525	525	695	695
V8, 5.3 Liter	T	......	375	375	500	500
SAVANA VAN—V8—Truck Equipment Schedule T1						
1500 Cargo Van	G15T	22720	6800	7375	8650	11650
AWD	H	......	525	525	695	695
V6, 4.3 Liter	X	......	(375)	(375)	(500)	(500)
EXPRESS/SAVANA VAN—V8—Truck Equipment Schedule T1						
2500 Cargo Van	G25V	23495	7300	7900	9225	12400
2500 Extended	G29V	24595	7500	8100	9425	12650
3500 Cargo Van	G35V	26095	7650	8275	9600	12900
3500 Extended	G39V	27674	8000	8650	10000	13400
3500 Van Cab-Ch	G31Z	24773	7525	8125	9875	13500
V8, 6.0 Liter	U	......	375	375	500	500
V8, 6.6L Turbo Dsl	2,6	......	4100	4100	5465	5465
COLORADO/CANYON REGULAR CAB PICKUP—4-Cyl.—Truck Equip Sch T1						
Work Truck 2D 6'	S149	17455	3425	3750	4675	6475
LS/SL 2D 6'	S149	19455	3850	4200	5150	7100
LT/SLE 2D 6'	S149	21085	4350	4725	5725	7850
4WD	T	......	1100	1100	1460	1460
5-Cyl, 3.7 Liter	E	......	175	175	240	240
CANYON REGULAR CAB PICKUP—5-Cyl.—Truck Equipment Sch T1						
SLE 2D 6'	S14E	19135	4475	4875	5875	8025
4WD	T	......	1100	1100	1465	1465
4-Cyl, 2.9 Liter	9	......	(175)	(175)	(225)	(225)

2007 CHEVROLET/GMC

Body Type	VIN	List	Trade-In Good	Very Good	Pvt-Party Good	Retail Excellent
CANYON EXTENDED CAB PICKUP—4-Cyl.—Truck Equipment Sch T1						
Work Truck 4D 6'	S199	19455	4850	5275	6500	8850
4WD	T		1100	1100	1460	1460
5-Cyl, 3.7 Liter	E		175	175	240	240
COLORADO/CANYON EXTENDED CAB PICKUP—4-Cyl.—Truck Equip Sch T1						
LS/SL 4D 6'	S199	19455	5325	5775	7025	9550
4WD	T		1100	1100	1460	1460
5-Cyl, 3.7 Liter	E		175	175	240	240
COLORADO/CANYON EXTENDED CAB PICKUP—5-Cyl.—Truck Equip Sch T1						
LT/SLE 4D 6'	S19E	22085	6650	7175	8625	11600
4WD	T		1100	1100	1435	1435
4-Cyl, 2.9 Liter	9		(175)	(175)	(220)	(220)
COLORADO/CANYON CREW CAB PICKUP—5-Cyl.—Truck Equip Sch T2						
LT/SLE 4D 5 1/4'	S13E	23360	7700	8275	9800	13150
4WD	T		1100	1100	1450	1450
4-Cyl, 2.9 Liter	9		(175)	(175)	(225)	(225)
CANYON CREW CAB PICKUP—5-Cyl.—Truck Equipment Sch T2						
SLT 4D 5'	S13E	25720	9225	9875	11350	14900
4WD	T		1100	1100	1390	1390
AVALANCHE—V8—Truck Equipment Schedule T1						
LS Spt Util Pickup	K123	36610	12750	13600	14600	18150
LT Spt Util Pickup	K123	36940	13450	14300	15350	19050
LTZ Spt Util Pickup	K123	43670	14950	15850	16950	21000
2WD	C		(1150)	(1150)	(1445)	(1445)
SILVERADO CLASSIC REGULAR CAB—V6—Truck Equipment Sch T1						
1500 LS 2D 6 1/2'	C14X	22070	3700	4050	4750	6325
4WD	K		2000	2000	2665	2665
V8, 4.8 Liter	V		450	450	600	600
V8, 5.3 Liter	T		775	775	1025	1025
SILVERADO/SIERRA CLASSIC REGULAR CAB—V8—Truck Equipment Sch T1						
1500 Work Trk 6 1/2'	C14V	19350	3425	3775	4425	5900
1500 Work Truck 8'	C14V	19625	3100	3450	3975	5300
1500 SL 2D 6 1/2'	C14V	23015	4625	5025	5800	7675
1500 LS/SL 2D 8'	C14V	23455	3625	3975	4675	6225
1500 LT/SLE 2D 6 1/2'	C14V	24250	5125	5550	6250	8200
1500 LT/SLE 2D 8'	C14V	24540	5025	5450	6150	8050
2500 HD Wrk Trk 8'	C24V	24220	5125	5500	6675	8700
2500 HD LT/SLE 8'	C24U	25880	7150	7600	8900	11500
3500 Work Truck 8'	C34U	25355	5525	5925	7125	9250
3500 LS/SL 2D 8'	C34U	25410	6800	7250	8450	10950
3500 LT/SLE 2D 8'	C34U	27185	7300	7825	9100	11750
4WD	K		2000	2000	2665	2665
V6, 4.3 Liter	X		(450)	(450)	(600)	(600)
V8, 5.3 Liter	T		275	275	365	365
V8, 8.1 Liter	G		275	275	325	325
V8, 6.6L Turbo Dsl	D		4100	4100	4870	4870
SIERRA CLASSIC REGULAR CAB 4WD—V8—Truck Equipment Sch T1						
2500 HD SL 2D 8'	K24U	24915	9050	9600	11100	14250
2WD	C		(2250)	(2250)	(2650)	(2650)
V8, 8.1 Liter	G		275	275	325	325
V8, 6.6L Turbo Dsl	D		4100	4100	4845	4845
SILVERADO CLASSIC REGULAR CAB—V8 Turbo Diesel—Truck Sch T1						
2500 HD LS 2D 8'	C24D	33240	10850	11450	13150	16800
4WD	K		2000	2000	2355	2355
V8, 6.0 Liter	U		(4900)	(4900)	(5770)	(5770)
V8, 8.1 Liter	G		(4225)	(4225)	(4975)	(4975)
SILVERADO CLASSIC REGULAR CAB—V8—Truck Equipment Sch T1						
3500 LT 2D 8'	C34U	26780	7350	7825	9100	11750
4WD	K		2000	2000	2370	2370
V8, 8.1 Liter	G		275	275	325	325
SILVERADO/SIERRA CLASSIC EXTENDED CAB—V8—Truck Equip Sch T1						
1500 LT/SLE 4D 5 3/4'	C19T	27830	8000	8625	9650	12500
1500 LT/SLE 4D 8'	C19T	28035	7000	7550	8575	11150
1500 SLT 4D 5 3/4'	C19T	31575	8700	9350	10400	13450
1500 SLT 4D 8'	C19T	32015	7800	8400	9450	12250
4WD	K		2000	2000	2635	2635
SILVERADO/SIERRA CLASSIC EXTENDED 4WD—V8 Hybrid—Truck Sch T1						
1500 LT/SLE 6 1/2'	K19T	33105	14300	15300	16700	21400
2WD	C		(2250)	(2250)	(2905)	(2905)
SILVERADO/SIERRA CLASSIC EXTENDED CAB—V8—Truck Equip Sch T1						
1500 Work Trk 6 1/2'	C19V	23310	5450	5925	7025	9375
1500 Work Truck 8'	C19V	25415	5200	5650	6325	8275
1500 LS 4D 6 1/2'	C19V	25785	6800	7350	8375	10900

TRUCKS & VANS

Body Type	VIN	List	Trade-In Good	Very Good	Pvt-Party Good	Retail Excellent
1500 LS/SL 4D 8'	C19V	26815	6300	6825	7775	10150
1500 LT/SLE 4D 6 1/2'	C19V	26860	7100	7675	8700	11300
2500HD WkTrk 6 1/2'	C29U	26910	8500	9000	10350	13300
2500HD Wrk Trk 8'	C29U	27205	8300	8800	10150	13050
2500 HD LS 6 1/2'	C29U	28310	9900	10500	12050	15400
2500 HD LS/SL 4D 8'	C29U	28605	9800	10400	11900	15250
2500 HD SLE 6 1/2'	C29U	30125	10400	11000	12550	16050
2500 HD LT/SLE 8'	C29U	28825	9950	10550	12100	15450
2500 HD SLT 6 1/2'	C29U	33485	11200	11850	13600	17300
2500 HD SLT 4D 8'	C29U	33775	11000	11600	13350	17000
3500 Work Truck 8'	C39U	27775	8500	9000	10350	13300
3500 LS/SL 4D 8'	C39U	29520	10000	10600	12150	15550
3500 SLE 4D 8'	C39V	30825	10500	11100	12900	16700
4WD	K		2000	2000	2635	2635
V6, 4.3 Liter	X		(450)	(450)	(595)	(595)
V8, 5.3 Liter	T		275	275	365	365
V8, 8.1 Liter	G		275	275	325	325
V8, 6.6L Turbo Dsl	D		4100	4100	4845	4845
SILVERADO CLASSIC EXTENDED CAB—V8 Turbo Diesel—Truck Sch T1						
3500 LT 4D 8'	C39D	38080	15050	15850	17750	22500
4WD	K		2000	2000	2340	2340
V8, 6.0 Liter	U		(4900)	(4900)	(5740)	(5740)
V8, 8.1 Liter	G		(4225)	(4225)	(4950)	(4950)
SILVERADO CLASSIC EXTENDED CAB 4WD—V8—Truck Equip Sch T1						
2500 HD LT 6 1/2'	K29U	28530	13050	13750	15550	19750
2WD	C		(2250)	(2250)	(2635)	(2635)
V8, 8.1 Liter	G		275	275	320	320
V8, 6.6L Turbo Dsl	D		4100	4100	4815	4815
SILVERADO CLASSIC EXTENDED CAB 4WD—V8—Truck Equipment Sch T1						
1500 SL 4D 6 1/2'	K19V	25785	9550	10250	11350	14650
1500 SLT 4D 6 1/2'	K19Z	31725	11200	12000	13250	17000
2500 HD SL 4D 6 1/2'	K29U	28310	12550	13250	15050	19150
2WD	C		(2250)	(2250)	(2955)	(2955)
V6, 4.3 Liter	X		(450)	(450)	(590)	(590)
V8, 5.3 Liter	T,B		275	275	360	360
V8, 6.6L Turbo Dsl	D		4100	4100	4825	4825
V8, 8.1 Liter	G		275	275	325	325
SILVERADO SS CLASSIC EXTENDED CAB—V8—Truck Equip Sch T3						
1500 4D 6 1/2'	C19N	34180	13250	14150	15550	19850
SILVERADO/SIERRA CLASSIC CREW CAB—V8—Truck Equip Schedule T1						
1500 LS/SL 4D 5 3/4'	C13V	25695	8500	9150	10200	13200
1500 LT 4D 5 3/4'	C13Z	29415	8700	9350	10400	13450
1500 SLT 4D 5 3/4'	C13Z	33590	9550	10250	11350	14650
4WD	K		2000	2000	2630	2630
V8, 6.0 Liter	N		475	475	640	640
SIERRA CLASSIC CREW CAB—V8—Truck Equipment Schedule T1						
1500 SLE 4D 8'	C19J	28205	9350	10050	11150	14400
4WD	K		2000	2000	2625	2625
SILVERADO/SIERRA CLASSIC CREW CAB—V8—Truck Equip Schedule T1						
1500 HD LT 6 1/2'	C13Z	34180	9550	10250	11350	14650
1500 HD SLT 6 1/2'	C13U	34580	10650	11450	12650	16300
2500HD WrkTrk 6 1/2'	C23U	28905	9750	10350	11850	15200
2500HD Wrk Trk 8'	C23U	29195	9650	10250	11750	15050
2500 HD LS/SL 4D 8'	C23U	30595	11200	11850	13600	17300
2500HD LT/SLE 8'	C23U	30745	11750	12450	14200	18050
2500 HD SLT 4D 8'	C23U	35850	12750	13450	15250	19350
3500 Work Truck 8'	C33U	30015	9950	10550	12100	15450
3500 SLE 4D/DR 8'	C33U	32940	11950	12650	14400	18300
3500 SLT 4D 8'	C33U	36260	12950	13650	15500	19650
4WD	K		2000	2000	2360	2360
V8, 8.1 Liter	G		275	275	325	325
V8, 6.6L Turbo Dsl	D		4100	4100	4835	4835
SIERRA CLASSIC CREW CAB 4WD—V8—Truck Equip Schedule T1						
2500 SLE 4D 5 3/4'	K13Z	29915	11350	12150	13450	17250
1500 HD SLE 6 1/2'	K13U	30545	12250	13100	14350	18400
2500 HD SL 4D 6 1/2'	K23U	30295	14200	14950	16850	21400
2WD	C		(2250)	(2250)	(2945)	(2945)
V8, 8.1 Liter	G		275	275	320	320
V8, 6.6L Turbo Dsl	D		4100	4100	4815	4815
SIERRA CLASSIC CREW CAB 4WD—V8 Turbo Diesel—Truck Sch T1						
2500 HD SLE 6 1/2'	K23D	32045	19300	20300	22400	28200
3500 SL 4D 8'	K33D	31515	20900	21900	24100	30400
2WD	C		(2250)	(2250)	(2625)	(2625)

2007 CHEVROLET/GMC

Body Type	VIN	List	Trade-In Good	Very Good	Pvt-Party Good	Retail Excellent
V8, 6.0 Liter	U		(4900)	(4900)	(5735)	(5735)
V8, 8.1 Liter	G		(4225)	(4225)	(4945)	(4945)
SILVERADO CLASSIC CREW CAB—V8 Turbo Diesel—Truck Sch T1						
2500 HD LS 6 1/2'	C23D	37525	16000	16850	18850	23800
3500 LS 4D 8'	C33D	38745	16000	16850	18850	23800
4WD			2000	2000	2345	2345
V8, 6.0 Liter	U		(4900)	(4900)	(5750)	(5750)
V8, 8.1 Liter	G		(4225)	(4225)	(4955)	(4955)
SILVERADO/SIERRA CLASSIC CREW CAB 4WD—V8 Turbo Diesel—Sch T1						
2500 HD LT 6 1/2'	K23D	39590	19300	20300	22400	28200
2500 HD SLT 6 1/2'	K23D	35560	20300	21300	23500	29600
3500 LT 4D 8'	K33D	42975	19300	20300	22400	28200
2WD	C		(2250)	(2250)	(2620)	(2620)
V8, 6.0 Liter	U		(4900)	(4900)	(5730)	(5730)
V8, 8.1 Liter	G		(4225)	(4225)	(4940)	(4940)
SIERRA DENALI CLASSIC CREW CAB AWD—V8—Truck Equip Sch T3						
1500 4D 5 3/4'	K63N	40025	15650	16450	17950	22300
SILVERADO/SIERRA REGULAR CAB—V8—Truck Equipment Schedule T1						
1500 Work Trk 6 1/2'	C140	19360	4925	5350	6075	8000
4WD	K		2000	2000	2665	2665
V6, 4.3 Liter	X		(450)	(450)	(600)	(600)
V8, 5.3 Liter	J		275	275	365	365
SILVERADO REGULAR CAB—V6—Truck Equipment Schedule T1						
1500 Work Truck 8'	C14X	19055	3850	4225	4900	6525
4WD	K		2000	2000	2665	2665
V8, 4.8 Liter	X		450	450	600	600
V8, 5.3 Liter	J		775	775	1025	1025
SIERRA REGULAR CAB—V8—Truck Equipment Schedule T1						
1500 Work Truck 8'	C14C	20525	4475	4875	5575	7375
4WD	K		2000	2000	2665	2665
V6, 4.3 Liter	X		(450)	(450)	(600)	(600)
V8, 5.3 Liter	J		275	275	365	365
SILVERADO/SIERRA REGULAR CAB—V8—Truck Equipment Schedule T1						
2500 HD Work Trk 8'	C24K	25443	5475	5875	7075	9200
2500 HD LT/SLE 8'	C24U	24575	8600	9125	10450	13450
3500 HD Wrk Trk 8'	C34K	25665	5675	6075	7275	9450
3500 SLE 2D 8'	C34K	28060	8750	9275	10650	13650
4WD	K		2000	2000	2645	2645
V8, 6.6L Turbo Dsl			4100	4100	4850	4850
SILVERADO REGULAR CAB 4WD—V8 Turbo Diesel—Truck Equip Sch T1						
3500 HD LT 8'	K346	28060	15900	16750	18750	23700
2WD	C		(2250)	(2250)	(2630)	(2630)
V8, 6.0 Liter	K		(4900)	(4900)	(5755)	(5755)
SILVERADO EXTENDED CAB PICKUP—V6—Truck Equipment Sch T1						
1500 Work Truck 6'	C19X	23900	6500	7025	7975	10350
4WD	K		2000	2000	2650	2650
V8, 4.8 Liter	X		(300)	(300)	(385)	(385)
V8, 5.3 Liter	J		500	500	650	650
SIERRA EXTENDED CAB PICKUP—V8—Truck Equipment Sch T1						
1500 Work Truck 6'	C19C	24500	7000	7550	8575	11150
4WD	K		2000	2000	2640	2640
V6, 4.3 Liter	X		(450)	(450)	(595)	(595)
V8, 5.3 Liter	J		275	275	365	365
SILVERADO/SIERRA EXTENDED CAB PICKUP—V8—Truck Equip Sch T1						
1500 Work Truck 5 3/4'	C190	23605	7200	7775	8775	11400
1500 Work Truck 8'	C190	25245	7300	7875	8900	11550
1500 LT/SLE 4D 8'	C19J	28205	9350	10050	11150	14400
1500 LTZ/SLT 5 3/4'	C19J	32105	10450	11200	12350	15900
1500 LTZ/SLT 4D 8'	C19J	32695	9850	10550	11700	15050
4WD	K		2000	2000	2650	2650
V6, 4.3 Liter	X		(450)	(450)	(595)	(595)
V8, 6.0 Liter	Y		475	475	635	635
V6, 4.3 Liter	X		(450)	(450)	(595)	(595)
SILVERADO EXTENDED CAB PICKUP 4WD—V8—Truck Sch T1						
1500 LTZ/SLT 6 1/2'	K19J	35500	12950	13800	15200	19450
2WD	C		(2250)	(2250)	(2870)	(2870)
V8, 6.0 Liter	Y		475	475	620	620
SILVERADO EXTENDED CAB PICKUP—V8—Truck Equip Sch T1						
1500 LT/SLE 4D 5 3/4'	C19C	26565	9650	10350	11500	14800
1500 LT/SLE 4D 6 1/2'	C19C	26860	9050	9700	10850	14000
4WD	K		2000	2000	2630	2630
V8, 5.3 Liter	J		275	275	360	360
V8, 6.0 Liter	Y		475	475	635	635

Body Type	VIN	List	Trade-In Good	Very Good	Pvt-Party Good	Retail Excellent
SILVERADO/SIERRA EXTENDED CAB PICKUP—V8—Truck Equip Sch T1						
2500 HD Work Trk 6'	C29K	27475	9750	10350	11850	15200
2500 HD Work Trk 8'	C29K	27770	9650	10250	11750	15050
3500 HD Wrk Trk 8'	C39K	28785	10050	10650	12200	15600
3500 HD LTZ/SLT 8'	C39K	36045	13200	13950	15750	19950
4WD	K		2000	2000	2630	2630
V8, 6.6L Turbo Dsl	6		4100	4100	4835	4835
SILVERADO/SIERRA EXTENDED CAB PICKUP 4WD—V8—Truck Sch T1						
2500HD LT/SLE 6 1/2'	K29K	30470	14950	15750	17650	22400
2500 HD LT/SLE 8'	K29K	30765	14700	15450	17400	22100
2500 HD LTZ/SLT 6'	K29K	35395	15850	16650	18600	23600
2500 HD LTZ/SLT 8'	K29K	35690	15650	16450	18400	23300
2WD	C		(2250)	(2250)	(2630)	(2630)
V8, 6.6L Turbo Dsl	6		4100	4100	4805	4805
SILVERADO/SIERRA EXTENDED CAB 4WD—V8 Turbo Diesel—Truck Sch T1						
3500 HD LT/SLE 8'	K396	31790	19700	20700	22900	28600
2WD	C		(2250)	(2250)	(2625)	(2625)
V8, 6.0 Liter	K		(4900)	(4900)	(5740)	(5740)
SILVERADO/SIERRA CREW CAB PICKUP—V8—Truck Equip Schedule T1						
1500 Wrk Trk 5 3/4'	C133	27600	9250	9925	11050	14250
1500 LT/SLE 5 3/4'	C13C	29415	11450	12250	13500	17300
2500 HD LT/SLE 8'	C23K	32840	14300	15100	16950	21500
2500 HD LTZ/SLT 8'	C23K	37680	15050	15850	17750	22500
4WD	K		2000	2000	2620	2620
V8, 5.3 Liter	J,M		275	275	360	360
V8, 6.0 Liter	Y		475	475	635	635
V8, 6.6L Turbo Dsl	6		4100	4100	4795	4795
SIERRA CREW CAB PICKUP—V8—Truck Equip Schedule T1						
2500 HD Work Trk 6'	C23K	28025	11900	12600	14350	18250
2500 HD Work Trk 8'	C23K	29045	11750	12450	14200	18050
3500 Work Truck 8'	C33K	29975	12300	13000	14750	18750
4WD	K		2000	2000	2355	2355
V8, 6.6L Turbo Dsl	6		4100	4100	4830	4830
SILVERADO/SIERRA CREW CAB 4WD—V8—Truck Equip Sch T1						
1500 LTZ/SLT 5 3/4'	K13M	33520	14800	15800	17250	22100
2WD	C		(2250)	(2250)	(2885)	(2885)
V8, 6.0 Liter	Y		475	475	635	635
SILVERADO/SIERRA CREW CAB 4WD—V8 Turbo Diesel—Truck Sch T1						
3500 HD LT/SLE 8'	K336	32380	22000	23100	25300	31700
3500 HD LTZ/SLT 8'	K336	37010	23000	24100	26400	33100
2WD	C		(2250)	(2250)	(2615)	(2615)
V8, 6.0 Liter	K		(4900)	(4900)	(5715)	(5715)
SILVERADO CREW CAB PICKUP—V8—Truck Equipment Sch T1						
2500 HD Work Trk 6'	C23K	31850	11900	12600	14350	18250
4WD	K		2000	2000	2355	2355
V8, 6.6L Turbo Dsl	6		4100	4100	4830	4830
SILVERADO CREW CAB—V8 Turbo Diesel—Truck Equip Sch T1						
2500 HD Work Trk 8'	C236	37440	16400	17250	19250	24300
3500 HD Wrk Trk 8'	C336	29975	16900	17800	19800	25000
4WD	K		2000	2000	2340	2340
V8, 6.0 Liter	K		(4900)	(4900)	(5735)	(5735)
SILVERADO/SIERRA CREW CAB 4WD—V8 Turbo Diesel—Truck Sch T1						
2500 HD LT/SLE 6'	K236	44040	21600	22700	24600	30700
2500 HD LTZ/SLT 8'	K236	48880	22600	23700	26100	32800
2WD	C		(2250)	(2250)	(2620)	(2620)
V8, 6.0 Liter	K		(4900)	(4900)	(5730)	(5730)
SIERRA DENALI CREW CAB PICKUP AWD—V8—Truck Equip Schedule T3						
1500 4D 5 3/4'	K638	42095	20100	21100	22700	28000
2WD	C		(700)	(700)	(810)	(810)

2008 CHEVY/GMC–(1,2or3)(CorG)(A,B,CorN)–(L13F)–8–#

Body Type	VIN	List	Trade-In Good	Very Good	Pvt-Party Good	Retail Excellent
EQUINOX—V6—Truck Equipment Schedule T1						
LS Sport Utility 4D	L13F	22995	5075	5475	6350	8300
LT Sport Utility 4D	L33F	23855	5675	6100	7225	9425
AWD	2,4,6,8,0		650	650	860	860
EQUINOX AWD—V6—Truck Equipment Schedule T1						
LTZ Sport Utility 4D	L63F	29295	8200	8750	10100	13100
Sport SUV 4D	L037	29595	8600	9150	10600	13700
FWD	7		(675)	(675)	(885)	(885)
TRAILBLAZER 4WD—6-Cyl.—Truck Equipment Schedule T1						
LS Sport Utility 4D	T13S	29650	6000	6450	7625	9950
LT Sport Utility 4D	T13S	28415	6500	6975	8225	10750
2WD	S		(1225)	(1225)	(1630)	(1630)

Body Type	VIN	List	Trade-In Good	Very Good	Pvt-Party Good	Retail Excellent
V8, 5.3 Liter	M		300	300	400	400
TRAILBLAZER AWD—V8—Truck Equipment Schedule T1						
SS Sport Utility 4D	T33H	33990	12650	13400	14650	18000
2WD	S		(1225)	(1225)	(1475)	(1475)
ENVOY 4WD—6-Cyl.—Truck Equipment Schedule T1						
SLE Sport Utility 4D	T23S	29850	6950	7425	8800	11500
SLT Sport Utility 4D	T13S	33795	7650	8175	9575	12500
2WD	S		(1225)	(1225)	(1630)	(1630)
ENVOY DENALI 4WD—V8—Truck Equipment Schedule T3						
Sport Utility 4D	T43M	36730	10250	10900	12050	15050
2WD	S		(1225)	(1225)	(1505)	(1505)
ACADIA—V6—Truck Equipment Schedule T1						
SLE Sport Utility 4D	R137	29845	9100	9675	10700	13250
AWD			725	725	900	900
ACADIA AWD—V6—Truck Equipment Schedule T1						
SLT Sport Utility 4D	V237	36310	11500	12200	13350	16550
2WD	R		(700)	(700)	(865)	(865)
TAHOE—V8—Truck Equipment Schedule T1						
LS Sport Utility 4D	C13C	34995	12650	13350	14250	17250
Third Row Seat			400	400	485	485
4WD	K		1225	1225	1480	1480
V8, FFV, 5.3L	0		300	300	365	365
TAHOE 4WD—V8—Truck Equipment Schedule T1						
LT Sport Utility 4D	K130	40650	16200	17050	18000	21700
LTZ Sport Utility 4D	K130	48230	17850	18850	19250	22900
Third Row Seat			400	400	485	485
2WD	C		(1225)	(1225)	(1480)	(1480)
V8, 6.2 Liter	8		500	500	580	580
TAHOE 4WD—V8 Hybrid—Truck Equipment Schedule T1						
Sport Utility 4D	K135	53295	17050	17950	19100	23200
Third Row Seat			400	400	490	490
2WD	C		(1225)	(1225)	(1500)	(1500)
YUKON—V8—Truck Equipment Schedule T1						
SLE Sport Utility 4D	C230	36490	13600	14400	15400	18650
Third Row Seat			400	400	490	490
4WD	K		1225	1225	1480	1480
V8, 4.8 Liter	C		(300)	(300)	(380)	(380)
YUKON 4WD—V8—Truck Equipment Schedule T1						
SLT Sport Utility 4D	K330	42700	16950	17850	18950	23000
Third Row Seat			400	400	490	490
2WD	C		(1225)	(1225)	(1495)	(1495)
YUKON 4WD—V8 Hybrid—Truck Equipment Schedule T1						
Sport Utility 4D	K135	53755	17150	18050	19200	23300
Third Row Seat			400	400	490	490
2WD	C		(1225)	(1225)	(1500)	(1500)
YUKON DENALI AWD—V8—Truck Equipment Schedule T3						
Sport Utility 4D	K038	49420	18450	19450	19900	23700
2WD	C		(1225)	(1225)	(1420)	(1420)
SUBURBAN 4WD—V8—Truck Equipment Schedule T1						
K1500 LS Sport Utl	K163	41080	13750	14500	15650	19050
K1500 LT Spt Util	K263	42005	15450	16300	17400	21200
K1500 LTZ Spt Util	K363	49320	17750	18750	19350	23200
K2500 LS Sport Utl	K46K	43375	15650	16500	17650	21500
K2500 LT Sport Utl	K26K	40575	16900	17800	18950	23000
2WD	C		(1225)	(1225)	(1505)	(1505)
V8, 6.0 Liter	Y		525	525	635	635
YUKON XL 4WD—V8—Truck Equipment Schedule T1						
1500 SLE Sport Util	K263	38990	14350	15150	16250	19750
1500 SLT Sport Util	K363	45215	16650	17500	18600	22600
2500 SLE Sport Util	K56K	43190	15250	16050	17200	21000
2500 SLT Sport Util	K66K	46585	17400	18300	19450	23600
2WD	C		(1225)	(1225)	(1500)	(1500)
V8, 6.0 Liter	C		525	525	630	630
YUKON XL DENALI AWD—V8—Truck Equipment Schedule T3						
1500 Sport Utility 4D	K068	51980	18650	19700	20300	24400
2WD	C		(1225)	(1225)	(1445)	(1445)
UPLANDER—V6—Truck Equipment Schedule T2						
Cargo Minivan 4D	V131	23385	3925	4275	5575	7950
UPLANDER—V6—Truck Equipment Schedule T1						
LS Minivan 4D	U231	21870	3650	4000	4925	6775
LS Extended Minivan	V231	24540	4250	4625	5650	7750
LT Extended Minivan	V331	29540	5425	5850	7000	9500

TRUCKS & VANS

Body Type	VIN	List	Trade-In Good	Very Good	Pvt-Party Good	Retail Excellent
EXPRESS/SAVANA VAN—V8—Truck Equipment Schedule T1						
1500 LS Passenger	G154	26710	7725	8300	9375	11950
1500 LT Passenger	G154	28560	8125	8700	9800	12500
2500 LS Passenger	G25K	28195	7975	8550	9650	12300
2500 LT Passenger	G25K	30045	8325	8925	10050	12800
3500 LS Passenger	G35K	29914	8625	9225	10400	13250
3500 LS Extended	G39K	32429	9525	10150	11400	14450
3500 LT Passenger	G35K	31369	9425	10050	11300	14350
3500 LT Extended	G39K	32799	10250	10900	12150	15400
AWD	H		550	550	680	680
EXPRESS VAN—V6—Truck Equipment Schedule T1						
1500 Cargo Van	G15X	24650	8125	8700	9850	12700
AWD	H		550	550	690	690
V8, 5.3 Liter	4		525	525	665	665
SAVANA VAN—V8—Truck Equipment Schedule T1						
1500 Cargo	G154	23130	8675	9300	10450	13500
AWD	H		550	550	690	690
V6, 4.3 Liter	X		(400)	(400)	(505)	(505)
EXPRESS/SAVANA VAN—V8—Truck Equipment Schedule T1						
2500 Cargo Van	G25C	24205	9100	9750	11000	14150
2500 Extended	G29C	25240	9700	10400	11650	15000
3500 Cargo Van	G35C	26809	9900	10600	11900	15250
3500 Extended	G39C	27784	10000	10700	12000	15400
V8, 6.0 Liter	K		400	400	505	505
V8, 6.6L Turbo Dsl	C		4250	4250	5370	5370
COLORADO/CANYON REGULAR CAB PICKUP—4-Cyl.—Truck Equip Sch T1						
Work Truck 2D 6'	S149	16290	3675	4000	4925	6625
LT 2D 6'	S349	17530	4875	5250	6275	8375
4WD	T		1300	1300	1660	1660
5-Cyl, 3.7 Liter	E		200	200	240	240
COLORADO/CANYON REGULAR CAB PICKUP—4-Cyl.—Truck Equip Sch T1						
LS/SL 2D 6'	S249	16565	4475	4825	5825	7750
4WD	T		1300	1300	1695	1695
5-Cyl, 3.7 Liter	E		200	200	245	245
CANYON REGULAR CAB PICKUP—5-Cyl.—Truck Equipment Sch T1						
SLE 2D 6'	S34E	18335	5000	5375	6625	8800
4WD	T		1300	1300	1645	1645
4-Cyl, 2.9 Liter	9		(175)	(175)	(225)	(225)
CANYON EXTENDED CAB PICKUP—4-Cyl.—Truck Equipment Sch T1						
Work Truck 4D 6'	S199	18365	6000	6425	7750	10200
4WD	T		1300	1300	1640	1640
5-Cyl, 3.7 Liter	E		200	200	240	240
COLORADO/CANYON EXTENDED CAB PICKUP—4-Cyl.—Truck Equip T1						
LS/SL 4D 6'	S299	18855	6200	6650	7975	10500
4WD	T		1300	1300	1640	1640
5-Cyl, 3.7 Liter	E		200	200	240	240
COLORADO EXTENDED CAB PICKUP—5-Cyl.—Truck Equipment Sch T2						
LT 4D 6'	S39E	21990	7300	7800	9300	12250
4WD	T		1300	1300	1650	1650
4-Cyl, 2.9 Liter	9		(175)	(175)	(230)	(230)
CANYON EXTENDED CAB PICKUP—5-Cyl.—Truck Equipment Sch T2						
SLE 4D 6'	S39E	20760	7300	7800	9300	12250
4WD	T		1300	1300	1660	1660
4-Cyl, 2.9 Liter	9		(175)	(175)	(230)	(230)
COLORADO/CANYON CREW CAB PICKUP—5-Cyl.—Truck Equip Sch T2						
LT/SLE 4D 5 1/4'	S33E	22600	9050	9625	11350	14850
4WD	T		1300	1300	1635	1635
4-Cyl, 2.9 Liter	9		(175)	(175)	(225)	(225)
CANYON CREW CAB PICKUP—5-Cyl.—Truck Equipment Sch T2						
SLT 4D 5'	S53E	27240	9875	10500	12150	15750
4WD	T		1300	1300	1625	1625
AVALANCHE 4WD—V8—Truck Equipment Schedule T1						
LS Spt Util Pickup	K123	37385	15050	15900	16800	20200
LT Spt Util Pickup	K223	37465	16450	17350	18300	22100
LTZ Spt Util Pickup	K333	38255	18450	19450	20400	24600
2WD	C		(1225)	(1225)	(1435)	(1435)
SILVERADO/SIERRA REGULAR CAB PICKUP—V8—Truck Equipment Sch T1						
1500 Work Trk 6 1/2'	C140	19540	6075	6525	7500	9600
4WD	K		2200	2200	2845	2845
V6, 4.3 Liter	X		(450)	(450)	(580)	(580)
V8, 5.3 Liter	J		300	300	390	390
SILVERADO REGULAR CAB PICKUP—V6—Truck Equipment Sch T1						
1500 Work Truck 8'	C14X	18380	4950	5350	6100	7900

TRUCKS & VANS

Body Type	VIN	List	Trade-In Good	Trade-In Very Good	Pvt-Party Good	Retail Excellent
4WD	K		2200	2200	2865	2865
V8, 4.8 Liter	C		450	450	585	585
V8, 5.3 Liter	J		875	875	1135	1135
SIERRA REGULAR CAB PICKUP—V8—Truck Equipment Sch T1						
1500 Work Truck 8'	C14C	18485	5425	5850	6800	8750
4WD	K		2200	2200	2850	2850
V6, 4.3 Liter	X		(450)	(450)	(585)	(585)
V8, 5.3 Liter	J		300	300	390	390
SILVERADO/SIERRA REGULAR CAB PICKUP—V8—Truck Equipment Sch T1						
1500 LT/SLE 2D 6 1/2'	C24C	24955	8325	8900	10000	12700
1500 LT/SLE 2D 8'	C24C	27880	7825	8375	9450	12000
2500 HD Wrk Trk 8'	C54K	24755	6825	7250	8325	10400
2500 HD LT/SLE 8'	C54K	28400	9300	9825	11050	13650
3500 HD Wrk Trk 8'	C74K	24975	6925	7350	8450	10550
3500 SLE 2D 8'	C84K	28340	9450	9975	11200	13850
4WD	K		2200	2200	2825	2825
V6, 4.3 Liter	X		(450)	(450)	(580)	(580)
V8, 5.3 Liter	J		300	300	385	385
V8, 6.6L Turbo Dsl	6		4250	4250	4950	4950
SILVERADO REGULAR CAB 4WD—V8 Turbo Diesel—Truck Equip Sch T1						
3500 HD LT 8'	K846	28340	17100	17900	19550	23900
2WD	C		(2450)	(2450)	(2830)	(2830)
V8, 6.0 Liter	K		(5100)	(5100)	(5880)	(5880)
SILVERADO/SIERRA EXTENDED CAB PICKUP—V8—Truck Equip Sch T1						
1500 Work Truck 4D 8'	C190	29810	8275	8825	9950	12600
1500 LT/SLE 4D 8'	C290	28125	10600	11300	12550	15800
1500 LTZ/SLT 5 3/4'	C390	32135	12200	12950	14350	18050
1500 LTZ/SLT 4D 8'	C390	32725	11550	12300	13650	17200
4WD	K		2200	2200	2815	2815
V8, 6.0 Liter	Y		525	525	660	660
SILVERADO/SIERRA EXTENDED CAB PICKUP 4WD—V8—Truck Sch T1						
1500 LTZ/SLT 6 1/2'	K39J	35530	14950	15800	17400	21800
2WD	C		(2450)	(2450)	(3060)	(3060)
V8, 6.0 Liter	Y		525	525	645	645
SILVERADO EXTENDED CAB PICKUP—V6—Truck Equipment Sch T1						
1500 Work Trk 6 1/2'	C19X	23325	7675	8200	9300	11800
4WD	K		2200	2200	2820	2820
V8, 4.8 Liter	C		450	450	575	575
V8, 5.3 Liter	J		875	875	1115	1115
SIERRA EXTENDED CAB PICKUP—V8—Truck Equipment Sch T1						
1500 Work Trk 6 1/2'	C19C	23430	8375	8950	10050	12750
4WD	K		2200	2200	2820	2820
V6, 4.3 Liter	X		(450)	(450)	(575)	(575)
V8, 5.3 Liter	J		300	300	385	385
SILVERADO/SIERRA EXTENDED CAB PICKUP—V8—Truck Equip Sch T1						
1500 Work Trk 5 3/4'	C19C	23975	8575	9150	10250	13000
1500 LS/SL 4D 6 1/2'	C19C	24425	9975	10600	11850	14950
1500 LT/SLE 4D 5 3/4'	C29C	26935	10900	11600	12850	16200
1500 LT/SLE 4D 6 1/2'	C29C	30035	10700	11400	12600	15900
2500HD Wk Trk 6 1/2'	C49K	28050	11100	11700	13000	16000
2500 HD Wrk Trk 8'	C49K	29180	11000	11550	12900	15900
3500 HD Wrk Trk 8'	C79K	29675	11300	11900	13250	16350
3500 HD LTZ/SLT 8'	C99K	36885	14550	15250	16800	20600
4WD	K		2200	2200	2805	2805
V6, 4.3 Liter	X		(450)	(450)	(575)	(575)
V8, 5.3 Liter	J		300	300	380	380
V8, 6.0 Liter	Y		525	525	660	660
V8, 6.6L Turbo Dsl	6		4250	4250	4910	4910
SILVERADO/SIERRA EXTENDED CAB PICKUP 4WD—V8—Truck Sch T1						
2500HD LT/SLE 6 1/2'	K59K	30750	16200	17000	18550	22700
2500 HD LT/SLE 8'	K59K	31045	15900	16700	18250	22300
2500 HD LTZ/SLT 6'	K69K	35425	17300	18100	19750	24100
2500 HD LTZ/SLT 8'	K69K	35720	17100	17900	19550	23900
2WD	C		(2450)	(2450)	(2835)	(2835)
V8, 6.6L Turbo Dsl	6		4250	4250	4910	4910
SILVERADO/SIERRA EXTENDED CAB 4WD—V8 Turbo Diesel—Truck Sch T1						
3500 HD LT/SLE 8'	K896	40005	21300	22300	24100	29400
2WD	C		(2450)	(2450)	(2835)	(2835)
V8, 6.0 Liter	K		(5100)	(5100)	(5890)	(5890)
SILVERADO CREW CAB PICKUP—V8—Truck Equipment Schedule T1						
1500 Work Trk 5 3/4'	C130	31220	10950	11650	12950	16300
4WD	K		2200	2200	2800	2800
V8, 4.8 Liter	C		(300)	(300)	(395)	(395)

TRUCKS & VANS

Body Type	VIN	List	Trade-In Good	Very Good	Pvt-Party Good	Retail Excellent
SIERRA CREW CAB PICKUP—V8—Truck Equipment Schedule T1						
1500 Work Trck 5 3/4'	C13C	28195	10650	11350	12550	15850
4WD			2200	2200	2810	2810
V8, 5.3 Liter	J		300	300	385	385
SILVERADO/SIERRA CREW CAB PICKUP—V8—Truck Equipment Sch T1						
1500 LS/SL 5 3/4'	C13C	30015	12250	13000	14350	18100
4WD			2200	2200	2795	2795
SILVERADO/SIERRA CREW CAB PICKUP—V8—Truck Equipment Sch T1						
1500 LT/SLE 5 3/4'	C23C	29785	13150	13950	15450	19400
2500 HD Wk Tk 6 1/2'	C23K	32280	13350	14000	15500	19050
2500 HD LT/SLE 8'	C23K	33120	16000	16800	18350	22400
2500HD LTZ/SLT 8'	C23K	37710	16800	17600	19200	23500
4WD	K		2200	2200	2795	2795
V8, 6.0 Liter	C		525	525	655	655
V8, 6.6L Turbo Dsl	6		4250	4250	4910	4910
SILVERADO/SIERRA CREW CAB PICKUP 4WD—V8—Truck Equip Sch T1						
1500 LTZ/SLT 5 3/4'	K33M	39620	18750	19800	21300	26400
2WD	C		(2450)	(2450)	(3045)	(3045)
V8, 6.0 Liter	Y		525	525	640	640
SILVERADO CREW CAB—V8 Turbo Diesel—Truck Equip Schedule T1						
2500 HD Work Trk 8'	C436	40970	18000	18850	20500	25000
3500 HD Work Trk 8'	C736	39830	18650	19550	21200	25900
4WD	K		2200	2200	2540	2540
V8, 6.0 Liter	C		(5100)	(5100)	(5895)	(5895)
SILVERADO/SIERRA CREW CAB 4WD—V8 Turbo Diesel—Truck Sch T1						
2500HD LT/SLE 6 1/2'	K536	44320	23800	24800	26500	32000
2WD	C		(2450)	(2450)	(2825)	(2825)
V8, 6.0 Liter	C		(5100)	(5100)	(5870)	(5870)
SIERRA CREW CAB PICKUP—V8—Truck Equipment Schedule T1						
3500 Work Truck 8'	C73K	31435	14050	14750	16250	19950
4WD	K		2200	2200	2545	2545
V8, 6.6L Turbo Dsl	6		4250	4250	4920	4920
SILVERADO/SIERRA CREW CAB 4WD—V8 Turbo Diesel—Truck Sch T1						
2500HD LTZ/SLT 6'	K636	48910	24900	26000	27900	33900
3500 HD LT/SLE 8'	K836	43735	24100	25100	27000	32900
3500 HD LTZ/SLT 8'	K936	47455	25100	26200	28100	34200
2WD	C		(2450)	(2450)	(2825)	(2825)
V8, 6.0 Liter	C		(5100)	(5100)	(5860)	(5860)
SIERRA DENALI CREW CAB PICKUP AWD—V8—Truck Equip Schedule T3						
1500 4D 5 3/4'	K658	42120	22800	23800	25200	30300
2WD	C		(750)	(750)	(860)	(860)

Body Type	VIN	List	Trade-In Good	Very Good	Pvt-Party Good	Retail Excellent
EQUINOX—V6—Truck Equipment Schedule T1						
LS Sport Utility 4D	L13F	24250	6725	7175	8200	10250
LT Sport Utility 4D	L33F	25170	7525	7975	9150	11450
AWD	2,4,6,8,0		700	700	875	875
EQUINOX AWD—V6—Truck Equipment Schedule T1						
LTZ Sport Utility 4D	L83F	30700	9400	9950	11250	14050
Sport SUV 4D	L037	31005	10050	10600	11950	14850
FWD	7		(725)	(725)	(905)	(905)
TRAILBLAZER 4WD—6-Cyl.—Truck Equipment Schedule T1						
LT Sport Utility 4D	T33S	31165	8475	9000	10300	13000
2WD	S		(1300)	(1300)	(1695)	(1695)
TRAILBLAZER AWD—V8—Truck Equipment Schedule T1						
SS Sport Utility 4D	T33S	39165	16050	16850	18050	21700
2WD	S		(1300)	(1300)	(1560)	(1560)
ENVOY 4WD—6-Cyl.—Truck Equipment Schedule T1						
SLE Sport Utility 4D	T33S	32550	8975	9525	10850	13700
SLT Sport Utility 4D	T43S	36360	9625	10200	11650	14650
2WD	S		(1300)	(1300)	(1690)	(1690)
ENVOY DENALI 4WD—V8—Truck Equipment Schedule T3						
Sport Utility 4D	T53M	38460	13600	14250	15600	18850
2WD	S		(1300)	(1300)	(1590)	(1590)
ACADIA—V6—Truck Equipment Schedule T1						
SLE Sport Utility 4D	R137	31685	10450	11000	12000	14500
AWD	V		750	750	895	895
ACADIA AWD—V6—Truck Equipment Schedule T1						
SLT Sport Utility 4D	V23D	38085	13000	13700	14900	17900
2WD	R		(725)	(725)	(875)	(875)
TRAVERSE—V6—Truck Equipment Schedule T1						
LS Sport Utility 4D	R13D	28900	9250	9775	11000	13600
AWD	V		1300	1300	1645	1645

TRUCKS & VANS

Body Type	VIN	List	Trade-In Good	Very Good	Pvt-Party Good	Retail Excellent
TRAVERSE AWD—V6—Truck Equipment Schedule T1						
LT Sport Utility 4D	V23D	33545	11650	12300	13600	16750
LTZ Sport Utility 4D	V33D	41810	14200	14950	16550	20400
2WD	R		(1300)	(1300)	(1645)	(1645)
TAHOE—V8—Truck Equipment Schedule T1						
LS XFE Sport Util	C133	39115	14750	15500	16650	19950
LT XFE Sport Util	C233	40465	15450	16200	17400	20900
TAHOE—V8—Truck Equipment Schedule T1						
LS Sport Utility 4D	C13C	37915	13750	14450	15650	18850
Third Row Seat			475	475	570	570
4WD	K		1300	1300	1565	1565
V8, 5.3 Liter	0		325	325	390	390
TAHOE 4WD—V8—Truck Equipment Schedule T1						
LT Sport Utility 4D	K230	43115	18200	19100	20300	24200
LTZ Sport Utility 4D	K320	52350	22300	23400	24000	28100
Third Row Seat			475	475	565	565
2WD	C		(1300)	(1300)	(1560)	(1560)
V8, 6.2 Liter	2		525	525	610	610
TAHOE 4WD—V8 Hybrid—Truck Equipment Schedule T1						
Sport Utility 4D	K135	54210	19600	20500	21800	26000
Third Row Seat			475	475	570	570
2WD	C		(1300)	(1300)	(1565)	(1565)
YUKON—V8—Truck Equipment Schedule T1						
SLE XFE Sport Util	C23C	39855	16250	17050	18150	21700
SLT XFE Sport Util	C330	44295	17400	18250	19450	23200
YUKON—V8—Truck Equipment Schedule T1						
SLE Sport Utility 4D	C260	38405	15350	16100	17300	20800
Third Row Seat			475	475	570	570
4WD	K		1300	1300	1555	1555
V8, 4.8 Liter	C		(325)	(325)	(395)	(395)
YUKON 4WD—V8—Truck Equipment Schedule T1						
SLT Sport Utility 4D	K360	45700	19400	20300	21500	25700
Third Row Seat			475	475	570	570
2WD	C		(1300)	(1300)	(1565)	(1565)
YUKON 4WD—V8 Hybrid—Truck Equipment Schedule T1						
Sport Utility 4D	K135	54680	19700	20600	21900	26100
Third Row Seat			475	475	570	570
2WD	C		(1300)	(1300)	(1570)	(1570)
YUKON DENALI AWD—V8—Truck Equipment Schedule T3						
Sport Utility 4D	K032	52880	22900	24000	24600	28800
2WD	C		(1300)	(1300)	(1520)	(1520)
YUKON DENALI 4WD—V8 Hybrid—Truck Equipment Schedule T3						
Sport Utility 4D	K035	54080	25800	27000	27600	32300
2WD	C		(1300)	(1300)	(1515)	(1515)
SUBURBAN 4WD—V8—Truck Equipment Schedule T1						
K1500 LS Sport Util	K163	44165	16050	16850	18100	21800
K1500 LT Sport Util	K263	45175	18250	19100	20400	24400
K1500 LTZ Sport Util	K363	54410	22800	23900	24700	29100
K2500 LS Sport Util	K46K	45770	18550	19450	20700	24800
K2500 LT Sport Util	K56K	46065	19800	20800	22000	26300
2WD	C		(1300)	(1300)	(1590)	(1590)
V8, 6.0 Liter	Y		550	550	665	665
YUKON XL 4WD—V8—Truck Equipment Schedule T1						
1500 SLE Sport Util	K263	40855	16750	17550	18800	22600
1500 SLT Sport Util	K363	47780	19200	20100	21400	25600
2500 SLE Sport Util	K56K	46435	17850	18700	19950	24000
2500 SLT Sport Util	K66K	50490	20300	21300	22500	26900
2WD	C		(1300)	(1300)	(1585)	(1585)
V8, 6.0 Liter	Y		550	550	665	665
YUKON XL DENALI AWD—V8—Truck Equipment Schedule T3						
1500 Sport Utility 4D	K168	55605	23400	24500	25400	29900
2WD	C		(1300)	(1300)	(1525)	(1525)
EXPRESS/SAVANA VAN—V8—Truck Equipment Schedule T1						
1500 LS Passenger	G154	28760	8625	9150	10250	12750
1500 LT Passenger	G154	31305	9375	9925	11100	13800
2500 LS Passenger	G25K	29865	8875	9400	10550	13150
2500 LT Passenger	G25K	32410	9675	10250	11450	14200
3500 LS Passenger	G35K	32160	9875	10450	11650	14450
3500 LT Passenger	G35K	34310	11050	11650	13000	16100
3500 LS Extended	G39K	34725	11100	11750	13050	16200
3500 LT Extended	G39K	35095	11750	12450	13750	17050
AWD	H		575	575	695	695

0415   **SEE BACK PAGES FOR TRUCK EQUIPMENT**   379

TRUCKS & VANS

Body Type	VIN	List	Trade-In Good	Very Good	Pvt-Party Good	Retail Excellent
EXPRESS VAN—V6—Truck Equipment Schedule T1						
1500 Cargo Van	G15X	25635	9625	10250	11450	14350
AWD	H		575	575	705	705
V8, 5.3 Liter	4		575	575	690	690
SAVANA VAN—V8—Truck Equipment Schedule T1						
1500 Cargo Van	G154	26340	10250	10900	12150	15200
AWD	H		575	575	705	705
V6, 4.3 Liter	X		(475)	(475)	(580)	(580)
EXPRESS/SAVANA VAN—V8—Truck Equipment Schedule T1						
2500 Cargo Van	G25C	25520	10850	11500	12800	16050
2500 Extended	G29C	28075	11200	11850	13150	16500
3500 Cargo Van	G35C	28940	11150	11800	13100	16450
3500 Extended	G39C	30520	11550	12250	13550	16950
V8, 6.0L	K		450	450	550	550
V8, 6.6L Turbo Dsl	6		4475	4475	5480	5480
COLORADO/CANYON REGULAR CAB PICKUP—4-Cyl.—Truck Equip Sch T1						
Work Truck 2D 6'	S149	18455	5475	5875	7100	9150
LT/SLE 2D 6'	S349	19125	5600	6000	7225	9300
4WD	T		1500	1500	1800	1800
5-Cyl, 3.7 Liter	E		200	200	240	240
CANYON REGULAR CAB PICKUP—5-Cyl.—Truck Equip Sch T1						
SLE 2D 6'	S34E	20195	5925	6325	7550	9700
4WD	T		1500	1500	1795	1795
4-Cyl, 2.9 Liter	9		(200)	(200)	(225)	(225)
COLORADO/CANYON EXTENDED CAB PICKUP—4-Cyl.—Truck Sch T1						
Work Truck 4D 6'	S199	23545	7600	8050	9450	12050
4WD	T		1500	1500	1780	1780
5-Cyl, 3.7 Liter	E		200	200	235	235
COLORADO/CANYON EXTENDED CAB—5-Cyl.—Truck Equip Sch T1						
LT/SLE 4D 6'	S39E	24000	8100	8575	9975	12700
4WD	T		1500	1500	1815	1815
4-Cyl, 2.9 Liter	9		(200)	(200)	(230)	(230)
V8, 5.3 Liter	L		650	650	785	785
CANYON EXTENDED CAB PICKUP—5-Cyl.—Truck Equip Schedule T2						
SLT 4D 6'	S59E	21255	9525	10050	11600	14700
4WD	T		1500	1500	1770	1770
V8, 5.3 Liter	L		750	750	900	900
COLORADO/CANYON CREW CAB PICKUP—5-Cyl.—Truck Equip Sch T2						
LT/SLE 4D 5 1/4'	S32E	25850	10850	11550	13250	16700
4WD	T		1500	1500	1765	1765
4-Cyl, 2.9 Liter	9		(200)	(200)	(225)	(225)
V8, 5.3 Liter	L		650	650	765	765
CANYON CREW CAB PICKUP—5-Cyl.—Truck Equipment Schedule T2						
SLT 4D 5'	S53E	24200	11150	11750	13450	16900
4WD	T		1500	1500	1760	1760
V8, 5.3 Liter	L		750	750	895	895
AVALANCHE 4WD—V8—Truck Equipment Schedule T1						
LS Spt Util Pickup	K120	39125	16550	17350	18350	21800
LT Spt Util Pickup	K220	39125	18450	19300	20300	24100
LTZ Spt Util Pickup	K320	46495	21000	22000	23000	27200
2WD	C		(1300)	(1300)	(1485)	(1485)
SILVERADO/SIERRA REGULAR CAB PICKUP—V8—Truck Equipment Sch T1						
1500 Work Trk 6 1/2'	C140	19620	7975	8475	9450	11650
4WD	K		2600	2600	3180	3180
V6, 4.3 Liter	X		(525)	(525)	(640)	(640)
V8, 5.3 Liter	J		325	325	395	395
SILVERADO REGULAR CAB PICKUP—V6—Truck Equipment Sch T1						
1500 Work Truck 8'	C14X	19410	6800	7250	8150	10100
4WD	K		2600	2600	3190	3190
V8, 4.8 Liter	C		525	525	645	645
V8, 5.3 Liter	J		925	925	1140	1140
SIERRA REGULAR CAB PICKUP—V8—Truck Equipment Sch T1						
1500 Work Truck 8'	C14C	21685	7425	7900	8875	10950
4WD	K		2600	2600	3190	3190
V6, 4.3 Liter	X		(525)	(525)	(645)	(645)
V8, 5.3 Liter	J		325	325	400	400
SILVERADO/SIERRA REGULAR CAB PICKUP—V8—Truck Equipment Sch T1						
1500 LT/SLE 6 1/2'	C24C	26135	10200	10800	11900	14600
1500 LT/SLE 8'	C24C	27220	9475	10000	11100	13650
2500 HD Work Trk 8'	C44K	25890	8950	9425	10700	13100
2500 HD LT/SLE 8'	C54K	25890	11250	11800	13250	16150
3500 Work Truck 8'	C74K	26110	9050	9525	10800	13200
3500 SLE 2D 8'	C84K	26135	11350	11900	13350	16250

Body Type	VIN	List	Trade-In Good	Very Good	Pvt-Party Good	Retail Excellent
4WD	K		2600	2600	3180	3180
V6, 4.3 Liter	X		(525)	(525)	(640)	(640)
V8, 5.3 Liter	J		325	325	395	395
V8, 6.6L Turbo Dsl	6		4475	4475	5005	5005
SILVERADO REGULAR CAB 4WD—V8 Turbo Diesel—Truck Equip Sch T1						
3500 LT 2D 8'	K846	38220	19450	20300	22200	26800
2WD	C		(2650)	(2650)	(2945)	(2945)
V8, 6.0 Liter	K		(5300)	(5300)	(5890)	(5890)
SILVERADO EXTENDED CAB PICKUP—V6—Truck Equip Sch T1						
1500 Work Trk 6 1/2'	C19X	40200	9525	10050	11150	13700
4WD	K		2600	2600	3180	3180
V8, 4.8 Liter	C		525	525	640	640
V8, 5.3 Liter	J		925	925	1140	1140
SIERRA EXTENDED CAB PICKUP—V8—Truck Equipment Sch T1						
1500 Work Trk 6 1/2'	C19C	26710	9775	10350	11450	14050
4WD	K		2600	2600	3180	3180
V6, 4.3 Liter	X		(525)	(525)	(640)	(640)
V8, 5.3 Liter	J		325	325	395	395
SILVERADO/SIERRA EXTENDED CAB PICKUP—V8—Truck Equip Sch T1						
1500 Work Trk 4D 8'	C19J	28835	10100	10700	11800	14500
1500 LT/SLE 4D 8'	C29J	30710	12550	13250	14500	17750
1500 LTZ/SLT 6 1/2'	C39J	34055	14350	15100	16500	20200
1500 LTZ/SLT 4D 8'	C39J	34655	12800	13500	14750	18050
4WD	K		2600	2600	3175	3175
V8, 6.0 Liter	Y		550	550	670	670
SILVERADO/SIERRA EXTENDED CAB PICKUP 4WD—V8—Truck Sch T1						
1500 LTZ/SLT 6 1/2'	K39J	37505	16700	17550	19000	23200
2WD	C		(2650)	(2650)	(3200)	(3200)
V8, 6.0 Liter	C		550	550	665	665
SILVERADO/SIERRA EXTENDED CAB PICKUP—V8—Truck Equip Sch T1						
1500 Work Trk 5 3/4'	C19C	25080	10450	11050	12150	14900
1500 LS/SL 4D 6 1/2'	C19C	29780	12350	13050	14250	17450
1500 LT/SLE 4D 5 3/4'	C29C	28150	12850	13550	14800	18100
1500 LT/SLE 4D 6 1/2'	C29C	28795	12600	13300	14550	17800
2500HD WrkTrk 6 1/2'	C49K	29190	13850	14500	16100	19550
2500 HD Work Trk 8'	C49K	29235	13550	14200	15750	19150
3500 Work Truck 8'	C79K	30270	14150	14800	16400	19850
3500 LTZ/SLT 4D 8'	C99R	37640	17500	18250	20000	24200
4WD	K		2600	2600	3165	3165
V6, 4.3 Liter	X		(525)	(525)	(640)	(640)
V8, 5.3 Liter	J		325	325	395	395
V8, 6.0 Liter	Y		550	550	670	670
V8, 6.6L Turbo Dsl	6		4475	4475	4975	4975
SILVERADO/SIERRA EXTENDED CAB PICKUP 4WD—V8—Truck Sch T1						
2500HD LT/SLE 6 1/2'	K59K	32000	19350	20200	22000	26600
2500 HD LT/SLE 8'	K59K	32045	19150	20000	21900	26400
2500HD LTZ/SLT 6 '	K69K	37235	20500	21300	23200	28000
2500HD LTZ/SLT 8'	K69K	37280	20300	21100	23000	27800
2WD	C		(2650)	(2650)	(2950)	(2950)
V8, 6.6L Turbo Dsl	6		4475	4475	4975	4975
SILVERADO/SIERRA EXTENDED CAB 4WD—V8 Turbo Diesel—Truck Sch T1						
3500 LT/SLE 4D 8'	K89K	44165	24600	25600	27700	33400
2WD	C		(2650)	(2650)	(2940)	(2940)
V8, 6.0 Liter	K		(5300)	(5300)	(5875)	(5875)
SILVERADO/SIERRA CREW CAB PICKUP—V8—Truck Equipment Sch T1						
1500 Wrk Trck 5 3/4'	C13C	30030	12850	13550	14800	18100
1500 XFE 5 3/4'	C233	33080	14850	15600	17050	20800
1500 LS/SL 5 3/4'	C13C	29685	15050	15800	17200	21000
1500 LT/SLE 5 3/4'	C23C	32120	15350	16150	17550	21400
2500 HD Work Truck 6	C43R	34790	16300	17050	18750	22700
2500 HD LT/SLE 8'	C53K	34155	18650	19500	21300	25700
2500 HD LTZ/SLT 8'	C63K	39300	19750	20600	22500	27100
4WD	K		2600	2600	3165	3165
V8, 6.0 Liter	Y		550	550	670	670
V8, 6.6L Turbo Dsl	6		4475	4475	4985	4985
SIERRA CREW CAB PICKUP—V8—Truck Equipment Sch T1						
2500 Work Truck 8'	C43R	32385	16000	16750	18400	22300
3500 Work Truck 8'	C73K	33640	17000	17750	19500	23600
4WD	K		2600	2600	2885	2885
V8, Turbo Diesel, 6.6L	6		4475	4475	4965	4965
SILVERADO/SIERRA CREW CAB PICKUP 4WD—V8—Truck Equip Sch T1						
1500 LTZ/SLT 5 3/4'	K33M	41650	20700	21700	23300	28400
2WD	C		(2650)	(2650)	(3165)	(3165)

Body Type	VIN	List	Trade-In Good	Very Good	Pvt-Party Good	Retail Excellent
V8, 6.0 Liter	Y		550	550	655	655
SILVERADO/SIERRA CREW CAB 4WD—V8 Turbo Diesel—Truck Sch T1						
2500 HD LT/SLE 6'	K536	50800	26800	27900	29800	35700
2500 HD LTZ/SLT 6'	K636	47650	28100	29300	31500	37900
3500 HD LT/SLE 8'	K836	45230	27500	28700	30700	36900
3500 HD LTZ/SLT 8'	K936	50165	28600	29800	32100	38700
2WD	C		(2650)	(2650)	(2945)	(2945)
V8, 6.0 Liter	K		(5300)	(5300)	(5885)	(5885)
SILVERADO CREW CAB PICKUP—V8 Turbo Diesel—Truck Equip Sch T1						
2500 HD Work Trk 8'	C436	39080	21000	21900	23600	28200
3500 HD Work Trk 8'	C736	40025	22000	23000	24900	30100
4WD	K		2600	2600	2890	2890
SILVERADO CREW CAB PICKUP—V8 Hybrid—Truck Equip Sch T1			(5300)	(5300)	(5890)	(5890)
1500 4D 5 3/4'	C135	38995	16450	17300	18750	22900
4WD	K		2600	2600	3165	3165
SIERRA CREW CAB PICKUP 4WD—V8 Hybrid—Truck Equip Sch T1						
1500 4D 5 3/4'	K135	38995	19450	20400	21900	26700
2WD	C		(2650)	(2650)	(3195)	(3195)
SIERRA DENALI CREW CAB PICKUP AWD—V8—Truck Equip Schedule T3						
1500 4D 5 3/4'	K032	43665	24800	25800	27100	31800
2WD	C		(875)	(875)	(965)	(965)

Body Type	VIN	List	Trade-In Good	Very Good	Pvt-Party Good	Retail Excellent
EQUINOX—4-Cyl.—Truck Equipment Schedule T1						
LS Sport Utility 4D	LBEW	23185	9400	9900	11050	13400
AWD	C,E,N,G		725	725	875	875
EQUINOX—4-Cyl.—Truck Equipment Schedule T1						
LT Sport Utility 4D	LDEW	24105	10350	10900	12100	14650
AWD	E,N		725	725	875	875
V6, 3.0 Liter	Y		850	850	1015	1015
EQUINOX AWD—V6—Truck Equipment Schedule T1						
LTZ Sport Utility	LGEY	32040	12700	13350	14800	17800
FWD	F		(775)	(775)	(920)	(920)
4-Cyl, 2.4 Liter	W		(700)	(700)	(845)	(845)
TERRAIN—4-Cyl.—Truck Equipment Schedule T1						
SLE Sport Util 4D	LBEW	24995	11100	11650	12600	15050
SLT Sport Util 4D	LFEW	28195	12300	12900	14000	16650
AWD	C,E,G		725	725	840	840
V6, 3.0 Liter	Y		475	475	550	550
ACADIA—V6—Truck Equipment Schedule T1						
SL Sport Utility 4D	RKED	32515	11800	12350	13500	16200
SLE Sport Util 4D	RLED	35090	12850	13450	14550	17300
AWD	V		800	800	925	925
ACADIA AWD—V6—Truck Equipment Schedule T1						
SLT Sport Util 4D	VMED	41360	15900	16600	17850	21200
2WD	R		(775)	(775)	(900)	(900)
TRAVERSE—V6—Truck Equipment Schedule T1						
LS Sport Utility 4D	REED	29999	10800	11350	12700	15500
AWD	V		1375	1375	1730	1730
TRAVERSE AWD—V6—Truck Equipment Schedule T1						
LT Sport Utility 4D	VFED	34520	13500	14150	15700	18950
LTZ Sport Utility	VHED	40760	15800	16550	18300	22200
2WD	R		(1375)	(1375)	(1720)	(1720)
TAHOE—V8—Truck Equipment Schedule T1						
LS Sport Utility 4D	CAE3,0	38230	17150	17900	18950	22200
Third Row Seat			550	550	640	640
4WD	K		1375	1375	1615	1615
TAHOE 4WD—V8—Truck Equipment Schedule T1						
LT Sport Utility 4D	KBE0	45930	22000	22900	24000	28000
LTZ Sport Utility 4D	KCE0	54565	26200	27200	27900	32100
Third Row Seat			550	550	640	640
2WD	C		(1375)	(1375)	(1610)	(1610)
TAHOE 4WD—V8 Hybrid—Truck Equipment Schedule T1						
Sport Utility 4D	KDDJ	54475	23300	24300	25500	29800
Third Row Seat			550	550	640	640
2WD	C		(1375)	(1375)	(1610)	(1610)
YUKON—V8—Truck Equipment Schedule T1						
SLE Sport Utility 4D	CAE0,3	38970	18500	19350	20400	23900
Third Row Seat			550	550	640	640
4WD	K		1375	1375	1610	1610
YUKON 4WD—V8—Truck Equipment Schedule T1						
SLT Sport Utility	KCE0	47615	23100	24100	25200	29400

Body Type	VIN	List	Trade-In Good	Very Good	Pvt-Party Good	Retail Excellent
Third Row Seat			550	550	640	640
2WD	C		(1375)	(1375)	(1615)	(1615)
YUKON 4WD—V8 Hybrid—Truck Equipment Schedule T1						
Sport Utility 4D	KFDJ	54945	24600	25600	26800	31200
Third Row Seat			550	550	635	635
2WD	C		(1375)	(1375)	(1605)	(1605)
YUKON DENALI AWD—V8—Truck Equipment Schedule T3						
Sport Utility 4D	KEEF	56945	26600	27600	28400	32700
Third Row Seat			550	550	625	625
2WD	C		(1375)	(1375)	(1580)	(1580)
YUKON DENALI AWD—V8 Hybrid—Truck Equipment Schedule T3						
Sport Utility 4D	KGEJ	62295	29500	30700	31400	36100
Third Row Seat			550	550	625	625
2WD	C		(1375)	(1375)	(1580)	(1580)
SUBURBAN 4WD—V8—Truck Equipment Schedule T1						
K1500 LS Sport Util	KHE0	44430	18650	19500	20700	24400
K1500 LT Sport Util	KJE0	47940	20900	21800	23000	27100
Third Row Seat			550	550	660	660
2WD	C		(1375)	(1375)	(1665)	(1665)
SUBURBAN 4WD—V8—Truck Equipment Schedule T1						
K1500 LTZ Spt Util	KKE0	56575	25200	26300	27100	31300
K1500 75th Dmnd	KKE3	58740	26200	27300	28000	32400
K2500 LS Spt Util	KLEG	46035	21200	22200	23300	27400
2WD	C		(1375)	(1375)	(1590)	(1590)
SUBURBAN 4WD—V8—Truck Equipment Schedule T1						
K2500 LT Spt Utl	KMEG	49530	22900	23900	25100	29400
2WD	C		(1375)	(1375)	(1655)	(1655)
YUKON XL 4WD—V8—Truck Equipment Schedule T1						
1500 SLE Sport Util	KHE0	43030	19250	20100	21400	25200
1500 SLT Sport Util	KKE0	47615	21900	22900	24100	28300
2500 SLE Sport Util	KNEG	46900	20700	21600	22800	26800
2500 SLT Sport Util	KREG	51305	23400	24400	25600	30000
Third Row Seat			550	550	660	660
2WD	C		(1375)	(1375)	(1670)	(1670)
V8, Flex Fuel, 6.0	2		550	550	660	660
YUKON XL DENALI AWD—V8—Truck Equipment Schedule T3						
1500 Sport Util	KMEF	59700	26600	27700	28500	33000
Third Row Seat			550	550	630	630
2WD	C		(1375)	(1375)	(1595)	(1595)
EXPRESS/SAVANA VAN—V8—Truck Equipment Schedule T1						
1500 LS Passenger	GBD4	29495	9825	10350	11450	13950
1500 LT Passenger	GCD4	31345	10650	11200	12400	15050
2500 LS Passenger	GPDG	31000	10100	10650	11800	14350
2500 LT Passenger	GRDG	32850	10850	11400	12600	15300
3500 LS Passenger	GXDG	33295	11100	11700	12950	15750
3500 LT Passenger	GYDG	34750	12150	12800	14050	17050
3500 LS Extended	GZDG	35165	12800	13450	14750	17900
3500 LT Extended	G1DG	35535	12900	13550	14950	18150
AWD	H		650	650	760	760
EXPRESS VAN—V6—Truck Equipment Schedule T1						
1500 Cargo Van	GADX	25840	11800	12450	13800	17000
AWD	H		650	650	770	770
V8, Flex Fuel, 5.3 Liter	4		550	550	655	655
SAVANA VAN—V8—Truck Equipment Schedule T1						
1500 Cargo Van	GAD4	25635	12450	13150	14450	17800
AWD	H		650	650	770	770
V6, 4.3 Liter	X		(550)	(550)	(650)	(650)
EXPRESS/SAVANA VAN—V8—Truck Equipment Schedule T1						
2500 Cargo Van	GFBA	26755	13050	13750	15250	18750
2500 Extended	GGBA	28615	13350	14050	15550	19150
3500 Cargo Van	GTBA	30075	13400	14100	15600	19150
3500 Extended	GUBA	30960	13750	14450	16000	19650
V8, Flex Fuel, 6.0 Liter	K		475	475	565	565
V8, 6.6L Turbo Dsl	6		5300	5300	6290	6290
EXPRESS/SAVANA VAN—V8 Turbo Diesel—Truck Equipment Schedule T1						
2500 Cargo Van	GFBL	38750	19100	19950	21500	25800
2500 Extended	GGBL	40610	19400	20300	21800	26200
3500 Cargo Van	GTBL	42070	19600	20500	22000	26400
3500 Extended	GUBL	42955	20000	20900	22400	26900
COLORADO/CANYON REGULAR CAB PICKUP—4-Cyl.—Truck Equip Sch T1						
Work Truck 2D 6'	SBD9	18860	7525	7950	9075	11150
LT/SLE 2D 6'	SCD9	19985	8075	8500	9675	11850
4WD	T		1700	1700	1985	1985

TRUCKS & VANS

TRUCKS & VANS

Body Type	VIN	List	Trade-In Good	Very Good	Pvt-Party Good	Retail Excellent
5-Cyl, 3.7 Liter...............	E		200	200	235	235
CANYON REGULAR CAB PICKUP—5-Cyl.—Truck Equipment Sch T1						
SLE 2D 6'...............	SCDE	21055	8675	9125	10300	12600
4WD...............	T		1700	1700	1985	1985
4-Cyl, 2.9 Liter...............	9		(200)	(200)	(235)	(235)
COLORADO/CANYON EXTENDED CAB PICKUP—4-Cyl.—Truck Sch T1						
Work Truck 4D 6'...............	SBD9	24405	10000	10500	11800	14400
4WD...............	T		1700	1700	1980	1980
5-Cyl, 3.7 Liter...............	E		200	200	235	235
COLORADO/CANYON EXTENDED CAB PICKUP—5-Cyl.—Truck Sch T1						
LT/SLE 4D 6'...............	SCDE	24860	11000	11550	12900	15700
4WD...............	T		1700	1700	1975	1975
4-Cyl, 2.9 Liter...............	9		(200)	(200)	(230)	(230)
V8, 5.3 Liter...............	P		700	700	815	815
CANYON EXTENDED CAB PICKUP—5-Cyl.—Truck Equipment Sch T2						
SLT 4D 6'...............	SFDE	26410	12000	12600	14000	17050
4WD...............	T		1700	1700	1975	1975
V8, 5.3 Liter...............	P		850	850	1000	1000
COLORADO/CANYON CREW CAB PICKUP—5-Cyl.—Truck Equip Sch T2						
LT/SLE 4D 5'...............	SCDE	25865	13300	13900	15550	18850
4WD...............	T		1700	1700	1970	1970
4-Cyl, 2.9 Liter...............	9		(200)	(200)	(230)	(230)
V8, 5.3 Liter...............	P		700	700	810	810
CANYON CREW CAB PICKUP—5-Cyl.—Truck Equipment Schedule T2						
SLT 4D 5'...............	SFDE	27960	13950	14600	16200	19650
4WD...............	T		1700	1700	1970	1970
V8, 5.3 Liter...............	P		850	850	1000	1000
AVALANCHE 4WD—V8—Truck Equipment Schedule T1						
LS Spt Util Pickup...............	KEE0	39725	19050	19900	20900	24400
LT Spt Util Pickup...............	KFE0	42830	21800	22700	23800	27800
LTZ Spt Util Pickup...............	KGE0	49815	24500	25600	26700	31200
2WD...............	C		(1375)	(1375)	(1555)	(1555)
SILVERADO REGULAR CAB PICKUP—V6—Truck Equipment Sch T1						
1500 Work Truck 8'...............	CPEX	22235	8675	9150	10100	12150
4WD...............	K		2800	2800	3380	3380
V8, Flex Fuel, 4.8 Liter...............	A		675	675	815	815
V8, Flex Fuel, 5.3 Liter...............	0		1000	1000	1195	1195
SIERRA REGULAR CAB PICKUP—V8—Truck Equipment Schedule T1						
1500 Work Truck 8'...............	CTEA	22235	9425	9925	10950	13150
4WD...............	K		2800	2800	3375	3375
V6, 4.3 Liter...............	X		(600)	(600)	(725)	(725)
V8, Flex Fuel, 5.3 Liter...............	0		350	350	420	420
SILVERADO/SIERRA REGULAR CAB PICKUP—V8—Truck Equipment Sch T1						
1500 Wrk Trk 6 1/2'...............	CPEA	21845	9925	10450	11450	13750
1500 LT/SLE 6 1/2'...............	CSEA	27805	11350	11950	13050	15700
1500 LT/SLE 8'...............	CSEA	27930	10900	11450	12600	15100
2500 HD Wrk Trk 8'...............	CVBG	28460	10300	10800	11900	14200
2500 HD LT/SLE 8'...............	CXBG	31255	12900	13450	14850	17650
3500 Work Truck 8'...............	CZBK	28680	10400	10900	12050	14350
3500 SLE 2D 8'...............	C3BK	31610	13000	13550	14950	17750
4WD...............	K		2800	2800	3360	3360
V6, 4.3 Liter...............	X		(600)	(600)	(720)	(720)
V8, Flex Fuel, 5.3 Liter...............	0		350	350	420	420
V8, 6.6L Turbo Dsl...............	6		5300	5300	5925	5925
SILVERADO REGULAR CAB 4WD—V8 Turbo Diesel—Truck Equip Sch T1						
3500 LT 2D 8'...............	K0B6	39590	21600	22400	24000	28300
2WD...............	C		(2825)	(2825)	(3145)	(3145)
V8, 6.0 Liter...............	G,K		(5500)	(5500)	(6100)	(6100)
SILVERADO/SIERRA EXTENDED CAB—V6—Truck Equipment Sch T1						
1500 Wrk Trk 6 1/2'...............	CPEX	26390	10850	11400	12450	14950
4WD...............	K		2800	2800	3365	3365
V8, Flex Fuel, 4.8 Liter...............	A		675	675	810	810
V8, Flex Fuel, 5.3 Liter...............	0,3		1000	1000	1190	1190
SILVERADO/SIERRA EXTENDED CAB PICKUP—V8—Truck Equip Sch T1						
1500 Work Truck 8'...............	CPE0	31580	11350	11900	13050	15650
1500 LT/SLE 8'...............	CSE0	31230	14050	14700	16050	19200
1500 LTZ/SLT 8'...............	CTE0	36575	14450	15150	16450	19700
4WD...............	K		2800	2800	3360	3360
SILVERADO/SIERRA EXTENDED CAB 4WD—V8—Truck Equip Sch T1						
1500 LTZ/SLT 6 1/2'...............	KTE3	39425	19650	20500	21900	26200
2WD...............	C		(2825)	(2825)	(3360)	(3360)
V8, Flex Fuel, 6.2 Liter...............	2		550	550	650	650

TRUCKS & VANS

Body Type	VIN	List	Trade-In Good	Very Good	Pvt-Party Good	Retail Excellent
SILVERADO/SIERRA EXTENDED CAB PICKUP—V8—Truck Equip Sch T1						
1500 LS/SL 6 1/2'	CREA	29135	13850	14500	15800	18950
1500 LT/SLE 6 1/2'	CSEA	30120	14250	14900	16200	19400
2500 HD WrkTrk 6'	CVBG	30890	15500	16150	17350	20300
2500 HD Wrk Trk 8'	CVBK	30935	15300	15900	17200	20200
3500 Wrk Trk 4D 8'	CZBG	31970	15900	16550	17700	20700
1500 LTZ/SLT 8'	C1BG	39590	19600	20400	22000	26000
4WD	K		2800	2800	3355	3355
V8, 5.3L Flex Fuel	0,3		350	350	420	420
V8, Flex Fuel, 6.2 Liter	2		550	550	660	660
V8, 6.6L Turbo Dsl	6		5300	5300	5880	5880
SILVERADO/SIERRA EXTENDED CAB 4WD—V8—Truck Equip Sch T1						
2500 HD LT/SLE 6'	KXBG	38945	21700	22500	24200	28500
2500 HD LT/SLE 8'	KXBG	38945	21500	22300	24000	28200
2500HD LTZ/SLT 6	KYBG	39185	22900	23800	25400	29900
2500HD LTZ/SLT 8'	KYBG	39230	22700	23600	25200	29700
2WD	C		(2825)	(2825)	(3140)	(3140)
V8, 6.6L Turbo Dsl	6		5300	5300	5875	5875
SILVERADO/SIERRA EXTENDED CAB 4WD—V8 Turbo Diesel—Truck Sch T1						
3500 LT/SLE 8'	K0B6	46065	26900	27900	29700	35000
2WD	C		(2825)	(2825)	(3135)	(3135)
V8, 6.0 Liter	G,K		(5500)	(5500)	(6080)	(6080)
SILVERADO/SIERRA CREW CAB PICKUP—V8—Truck Equipment Sch T1						
1500 XFE 5 3/4'	CSE3	34220	16150	16850	18250	21800
SILVERADO/SIERRA CREW CAB PICKUP 4WD—V8—Truck Equip Sch T1						
1500 LTZ/SLT 5 3/4'	KTE3	43570	22600	23600	25100	29900
2WD	C		(2825)	(2825)	(3365)	(3365)
V8, Flex Fuel, 6.2 Liter	2		550	550	655	655
SILVERADO CREW CAB PICKUP—V8 Hybrid—Truck Equip Sch T1						
1500 4D 5 3/4'	CUEJ	39335	18850	19650	21100	25200
4WD	K		2800	2800	3355	3355
SIERRA CREW CAB PICKUP 4WD—V8 Hybrid—Truck Equip Sch T1						
1500 4D 5 3/4'	KYEJ	39705	21200	22100	23600	28100
2WD	C		(2825)	(2825)	(3385)	(3385)
SILVERADO/SIERRA CREW CAB PICKUP—V8—Truck Equip Sch T1						
1500 Wrk Trk 5 3/4'	CTEA	30370	14000	14650	16000	19150
1500 LS/SL 5 3/4'	CREA	31355	16300	17050	18450	22100
1500 LT/SLE 5 3/4'	CSEA	32460	16900	17650	19050	22800
2500 HD WrkTrk 6'	CVBG	35490	18250	18950	20100	23400
2500 HD LT/SLE 8'	CXBG	36055	20900	21700	23300	27400
2500 HD LTZ/SLT 8'	CYBG	41250	22100	22900	24600	29000
4WD	K		2800	2800	3350	3350
V8, Flex Fuel, 5.3 Liter	0,3		350	350	420	420
V8, Flex Fuel, 6.2 Liter	2		550	550	660	660
V8, 6.6L Turbo Dsl	6		5300	5300	5870	5870
SILVERADO/SIERRA CREW CAB 4WD—V8 Turbo Diesel—Truck Sch T1						
2500 HD LT 6'	KXB6	47550	29200	30300	32000	37400
2500 HD LTZ/SLT 6'	KYB6	52750	30600	31700	33700	39600
2WD	C		(2825)	(2825)	(3135)	(3135)
V8, 6.0 Liter	G		(5500)	(5500)	(6080)	(6080)
SIERRA CREW CAB PICKUP—V8—Truck Equipment Sch T1						
3500 Work Trk 8'	C2B6	33640	18800	19550	21100	25000
4WD	K		2800	2800	3105	3105
V8, 6.6L Turbo Dsl	6		5300	5300	5880	5880
SILVERADO CREW CAB 4WD—V8 Turbo Diesel—Truck Equipment Sch T1						
2500 HD Wrk Trk 8'	CVB6	40780	23300	24200	25200	29000
3500 Work Truck 8'	CZB6	41725	24400	25300	27100	31900
4WD	K		2800	2800	3105	3105
V8, 6.0 Liter	G,K		(5500)	(5500)	(6095)	(6095)
SILVERADO CREW CAB 4WD—V8 Turbo Diesel—Truck Equip Sch T1						
3500 LTZ 4D 8'	K1B6	51120	31400	32500	34500	40600
2WD	C		(2825)	(2825)	(3140)	(3140)
V8, 6.0 Liter	G,K		(5500)	(5500)	(6090)	(6090)
SILVERADO/SIERRA CREW CAB 4WD—V8 Turbo Diesel—Truck Sch T1						
3500 LT/SLE 8'	K0B6	47130	30000	31100	33100	38900
2WD	C		(2825)	(2825)	(3165)	(3165)
V8, 6.0 Liter	G,K		(5500)	(5500)	(6145)	(6145)
SIERRA CREW CAB PICKUP—V8 Turbo Diesel—Truck Sch T1						
3500 SLT 4D 8'	C4B6	42265	28200	29200	31100	36600
4WD	K		2800	2800	3100	3100
V8, 6.0 Liter	G,K		(5500)	(5500)	(6095)	(6095)
SIERRA DENALI CREW CAB PICKUP AWD—V8—Truck Equip Schedule T3						
1500 4D 5 3/4'	KXE2	47430	26100	27100	28200	32400

TRUCKS & VANS

Body Type	VIN	List	Trade-In Good	Very Good	Pvt-Party Good	Retail Excellent
2WD	C	----	(1000)	(1000)	(1095)	(1095)

2011 CHEVY/GMC — (1,2or3)(CorG)(A,B,CorN)–(LBEC)–B

Body Type	VIN	List	Trade-In Good	Very Good	Pvt-Party Good	Retail Excellent
EQUINOX—4-Cyl.—Truck Equipment Schedule T1						
LS Sport Utility 4D	LBEC	23490	10950	11450	12550	14850
AWD	C	----	800	800	930	930
EQUINOX—4-Cyl.—Truck Equipment Schedule T1						
LT Sport Utility 4D	LDEC	24655	11950	12500	13650	16100
AWD	E,N	----	800	800	930	930
V6, Flex Fuel, 3.0 Liter	5	----	950	950	1095	1095
EQUINOX AWD—V6—Truck Equipment Schedule T1						
LTZ Sport Utility 4D	LGE5	32315	14850	15500	16700	19550
FWD	F	----	(1000)	(1000)	(1165)	(1165)
4-Cyl, 2.4 Liter	C	----	(800)	(800)	(920)	(920)
TERRAIN—4-Cyl.—Truck Equipment Schedule T1						
SLE Sport Utility	LMEC	24995	12600	13200	14500	17300
SLT Sport Utility	LUEC	28595	13800	14400	15950	19000
AWD	R	----	800	800	945	945
V6, Flex Fuel, 3.0 Liter	5	----	550	550	650	650
ACADIA—V6—Truck Equipment Schedule T1						
SL Sport Util 4D	RKED	32615	13500	14100	15200	17750
SLE Sport Util 4D	RNED	35240	14300	14900	16050	18800
Denali Sport Util.	RTED	43995	21700	22500	23500	27000
AWD	V	----	825	825	950	950
ACADIA AWD—V6—Truck Equipment Schedule T1						
SLT Sport Utility 4D	VRED	40960	18150	18850	19950	23200
2WD	R	----	(825)	(825)	(940)	(940)
TRAVERSE—V6—Truck Equipment Schedule T1						
LS Sport Utility 4D	REED	29999	12300	12850	14150	16800
AWD	V	----	1475	1475	1760	1760
TRAVERSE AWD—V6—Truck Equipment Schedule T1						
LT Sport Utility 4D	VGED	34640	15550	16200	17700	21000
LTZ Sport Utility	VLED	40750	17900	18600	20300	24000
2WD	R	----	(1475)	(1475)	(1755)	(1755)
TAHOE—V8—Truck Equipment Schedule T1						
LS Sport Util 4D	CAE0	38520	19050	19850	20800	24000
Third Row Seat		----	600	600	685	685
4WD	K	----	1475	1475	1675	1675
TAHOE 4WD—V8—Truck Equipment Schedule T1						
LT Sport Util 4D	KBE0	46220	24000	25000	26000	29800
LTZ Sport Util 4D	KCE0	55110	28000	29100	29900	34100
Third Row Seat		----	600	600	680	680
2WD	C	----	(1475)	(1475)	(1670)	(1670)
TAHOE 4WD—V8 Hybrid—Truck Equipment Schedule T1						
Sport Utility 4D	KDFJ	54490	26300	27300	28400	32700
Third Row Seat		----	600	600	685	685
2WD	C	----	(1475)	(1475)	(1680)	(1680)
YUKON—V8—Truck Equipment Schedule T1						
SLE Sport Utility 4D	2AE0	39485	20500	21300	22300	25600
Third Row Seat		----	600	600	685	685
4WD	2	----	1475	1475	1675	1675
YUKON 4WD—V8—Truck Equipment Schedule T1						
SLT Sport Utility 4D	2CE0	47855	24800	25800	26700	30700
Third Row Seat		----	600	600	680	680
2WD	C	----	(1475)	(1475)	(1670)	(1670)
YUKON 4WD—V8 Hybrid—Truck Equipment Schedule T1						
Sport Utility 4D	2FFJ	54960	27300	28400	29500	34000
Third Row Seat		----	600	600	685	685
2WD	C	----	(1475)	(1475)	(1680)	(1680)
YUKON DENALI AWD—V8—Truck Equipment Schedule T3						
Sport Utility 4D	2EEF	57185	28600	29700	30600	34800
Third Row Seat		----	600	600	675	675
2WD	1	----	(1475)	(1475)	(1655)	(1655)
YUKON DENALI 4WD—V8 Hybrid—Truck Equipment Schedule T3						
Sport Utility 4D	2GEJ	62310	31300	32400	33300	37900
Third Row Seat		----	600	600	675	675
2WD	1	----	(1475)	(1475)	(1655)	(1655)
SUBURBAN 4WD—V8—Truck Equipment Schedule T1						
K1500 LS Sport Util	KHE0	44720	21100	22000	23000	26500
K1500 LT Sport Util	KJE0	48230	23600	24500	25500	29400
K1500 LTZ Spt Utl.	KKE0	57120	29500	30500	31200	35500
K2500 LS Spt Utl	KLEG	46325	23800	24800	25800	29700
K2500 LT Spt Utl	KMEG	49820	26100	27100	28200	32400

TRUCKS & VANS

Body Type	VIN	List	Trade-In Good	Very Good	Pvt-Party Good	Retail Excellent
Third Row Seat	C		600	600	695	695
2WD			(1475)	(1475)	(1705)	(1705)
YUKON XL 4WD—V8—Truck Equipment Schedule T1						
1500 SLE Sport Util	2HE0	46205	21900	22800	23800	27400
1500 SLT Sport Util	2KE0	50365	24500	25500	26500	30500
2500 SLE Sport Util	2NEG	47565	23400	24300	25300	29100
2500 SLT Sport Util	2REG	51695	26500	27500	28600	32900
Third Row Seat			600	600	695	695
2WD	1		(1475)	(1475)	(1700)	(1700)
YUKON XL DENALI AWD—V8—Truck Equipment Schedule T3						
1500 Sport Utility	2MEF	59940	30900	32000	32700	37200
Third Row Seat			600	600	675	675
2WD	1		(1475)	(1475)	(1650)	(1650)
EXPRESS/SAVANA VAN—V8—Truck Equipment Schedule T1						
1500 LS Passenger	GBF4	29690	10900	11400	12500	14900
1500 LT Passenger	GCF4	31540	12200	12750	13900	16500
2500 LS Passenger	GPFA	30200	11150	11650	12800	15250
2500 LT Passenger	GRFA	32050	12440	12950	14200	16850
AWD	H		725	725	835	835
V8, Flex Fuel, 6.0 Liter	G		500	500	560	560
EXPRESS/SAVANA VAN—V8 Flex Fuel—Truck Equipment Sch T1						
3500 LS Passenger	GXFG	33490	12300	12850	14100	16750
3500 LT Passenger	GYFG	34945	13600	14150	15450	18300
3500 LS Extended	GZFG	35360	14100	14700	15950	18900
3500 LT Extended	G1FG	35730	14350	15000	16300	19300
EXPRESS/SAVANA VAN—V8 Turbo Diesel—Truck Equipment Sch T1						
3500 LS Passenger	GXFL	45485	18550	19300	20700	24500
3500 LT Passenger	GYFL	46940	19450	20200	21700	25600
3500 LS Extended	GZFL	47355	19650	20400	21900	25800
3500 LT Extended	G1FL	47725	20300	21100	22500	26500
EXPRESS VAN—V6—Truck Equipment Schedule T1						
1500 Cargo Van	GAFX	26070	13100	13750	15050	18200
AWD	H		725	725	830	830
V8, Flex Fuel, 5.3 Liter	4		675	675	775	775
SAVANA VAN—V8—Truck Equipment Schedule T1						
1500 Cargo Van	7AF4	25840	13800	14450	15800	19100
AWD	8		725	725	830	830
V6, 4.3 Liter	X		(600)	(600)	(690)	(690)
EXPRESS/SAVANA VAN—V8—Truck Equipment Schedule T1						
2500 Cargo Van	GFCB	31275	14700	15400	16800	20200
3500 Cargo Van	GTCB	31445	15650	16400	17800	21400
V8, Flex Fuel, 4.8 Liter	A		(500)	(500)	(565)	(565)
EXPRESS/SAVANA VAN—V8—Truck Equipment Schedule T1						
2500 Extended	GGCA	38880	15250	15950	17350	20900
3500 Extended	GUCA	31185	15850	16600	18000	21600
3500 Van Cab-Ch	G4CA	27210	14700	15350	17100	20700
V8, Flex Fuel, 6.0 Liter	G		500	500	575	575
V8, Turbo Diesel, 6.6L	L		4900	4900	6065	6065
EXPRESS/SAVANA VAN—V8 Turbo Diesel—Truck Equipment Sch T1						
2500 Cargo Van	GFCL	38955	21200	22000	23700	28100
2500 Extended	GGCL	40815	21600	22400	24100	28600
3500 Cargo Van	GTCL	42275	21800	22700	24300	28800
3500 Extended	GUCL	43160	22200	23000	24700	29300
COLORADO/CANYON REGULAR CAB PICKUP—4-Cyl.—Truck Equip Sch T1						
Work Truck 2D 6'	SBF9	18920	9200	9650	10800	12900
LT 2D 6'	SCF9	20045	9900	10350	11550	13800
4WD	T		1900	1900	2190	2190
5-Cyl. 3.7 Liter	E		200	200	230	230
CANYON REGULAR CAB PICKUP—5-Cyl.—Truck Equip Sch T1						
SLE 2D 6'	5MFE	21115	10150	10600	11800	14100
4WD	6		1900	1900	2185	2185
4-Cyl. 2.9 Liter	9		(200)	(200)	(230)	(230)
COLORADO/CANYON EXTENDED CAB PICKUP—4-Cyl.—Truck Equip Sch T1						
Work Truck 4D 6'	SBF9	24465	11550	12050	13350	15900
4WD	T		1900	1900	2190	2190
5-Cyl. 3.7 Liter	E		200	200	230	230
COLORADO/CANYON EXTENDED CAB PICKUP—5-Cyl.—Truck Equip Sch T1						
LT/SLE 4D 6'	SCFE	24920	12800	13350	14700	17450
4WD	9		1900	1900	2185	2185
4-Cyl. 2.9 Liter	9		(200)	(200)	(230)	(230)
V8, 5.3 Liter	P		750	750	860	860
COLORADO/CANYON CREW CAB PICKUP—5-Cyl.—Truck Equip Sch T2						
LT/SLE 4D 5'	SCFE	27240	15000	15650	17200	20400

Body Type	VIN	List	Trade-In Good	Very Good	Pvt-Party Good	Retail Excellent
4WD	T	......	1900	1900	2185	2185
4-Cyl, 2.9 Liter	9	......	(200)	(200)	(230)	(230)
V8, 5.3 Liter	P	......	750	750	860	860
CANYON CREW CAB PICKUP—5-Cyl.—Truck Equipment Schedule T2						
SLT 4D 5'	5NFE	28020	15900	16550	18100	21500
4WD	K	......	1900	1900	2185	2185
V8, 5.3 Liter	P	......	950	950	1105	1105
AVALANCHE 4WD—V8—Truck Equipment Schedule T1						
LS Spt Util Pickup	KFE3	40110	20900	21700	22700	26200
LT Spt Util Pickup	KFE3	43215	23800	24700	25600	29400
LTZ Spt Util Pickup	KGE3	50260	26500	27500	28400	32600
2WD	C	......	(1475)	(1475)	(1630)	(1630)
SILVERADO/SIERRA REGULAR CAB PICKUP—V8—Truck Equipment Sch T1						
1500 Work Trk 6 1/2'	CPEA	23175	11350	11900	13050	15500
1500 Work Truck 8'	CPEA	22235	10300	10750	11800	14050
1500 LT/SLE 6 1/2'	CSEA	27805	12600	13150	14350	16950
1500 LT/SLE 8'	CSEA	27930	12000	12550	13700	16250
2500 HD Wrk Trk 8'	CVCG	28960	10850	11350	12350	14350
2500 LT/SLE 8'	CXCG	32155	14000	14550	15700	18150
3500 Work Truck 8'	CZCG	29800	11200	11700	12700	14700
4WD	K	......	3000	3000	3565	3565
V6, 4.3 Liter	X	......	(675)	(675)	(800)	(800)
V8, Flex Fuel 5.3 Liter	0	......	375	375	445	445
V8, Turbo Diesel, 6.6L	8,L	......	4900	4900	5465	5465
SILVERADO/SIERRA REGULAR CAB 4WD—V8 Turbo Diesel—Truck Sch T1						
3500 LT/SLE 8'	K0C8,L	44335	23100	23900	25200	28900
2WD	C	......	(3025)	(3025)	(3335)	(3335)
V8, 6.0 Liter	C	......	(5700)	(5700)	(6300)	(6300)
SILVERADO/SIERRA EXTENDED CAB PICKUP—V8—Truck Equip Sch T1						
1500 LT/SLE 8'	CSE0	31230	15050	15700	17100	20200
1500 LTZ/SLT 8'	CTE0	36575	16250	16900	18300	21600
4WD	K	......	3000	3000	3560	3560
SILVERADO/SIERRA EXTENDED CAB PICKUP—V6—Truck Equip T1						
1500 Work Trk 6 1/2'	CPEA	26390	12100	12650	13800	16350
4WD	K	......	3000	3000	3565	3565
V8, Flex Fuel, 4.8 Liter	A	......	725	725	850	850
V8, Flex Fuel, 5.3 Liter	0,3	......	1050	1050	1250	1250
SILVERADO/SIERRA EXTENDED CAB PICKUP—V8—Truck Equip Sch T1						
1500 Work Truck 8'	CPE0	31580	12150	12700	13850	16400
4WD	K	......	3000	3000	3565	3565
SILVERADO/SIERRA EXTENDED CAB PICKUP 4WD—V8—Truck Equip T1						
1500 LTZ/SLT 6 1/2'	KTE3	39425	21300	22100	23700	28000
2WD	C	......	(3025)	(3025)	(3535)	(3535)
V8, Flex Fuel, 6.2 Liter	2	......	550	550	645	645
SILVERADO/SIERRA EXTENDED CAB PICKUP—V8—Truck Equip Sch T1						
1500 LS/SL 6 1/2'	CREA	29135	15250	15900	17300	20400
1500 LT/SLE 6 1/2'	CSEA	30120	15650	16300	17700	20900
2500 HD Wrk Trk 6'	CVCG	31140	15950	16600	17800	20700
2500 HD Wrk Trk 8'	CVCG	31335	15750	16400	17650	20500
3500 Work Truck 8'	CZCG	33025	16450	17100	18250	21000
3500 LTZ/SLT 8'	C1CG	40615	20600	21400	22600	25900
4WD	K	......	3000	3000	3555	3555
V8, Flex Fuel, 5.3 Liter	0,3	......	375	375	445	445
V8, Flex Fuel, 6.2 Liter	2	......	550	550	650	650
V8, Turbo Diesel, 6.6L	8	......	4900	4900	5435	5435
SILVERADO/SIERRA EXTENDED CAB PICKUP 4WD—V8—Truck Sch T1						
2500 HD LT/SLE 6'	KXCG	34450	22900	23700	25000	28900
2500 HD LT/SLE 8'	KXCG	34645	22700	23500	24800	28600
2500 HD LTZ/SLT 6'	KYCG	39185	24000	24900	26200	30000
2500 HD LTZ/SLT 8'	KYCG	39380	23800	24700	26000	29800
2WD	C	......	(3025)	(3025)	(3340)	(3340)
V8, Turbo Diesel, 6.6L	8	......	4900	4900	5420	5420
SILVERADO/SIERRA EXTENDED CAB 4WD—V8 Turbo Diesel—Truck Sch T1						
3500 LT/SLE 8'	K0C8,L	47770	28500	29500	30900	35400
2WD	C	......	(3025)	(3025)	(3335)	(3335)
V8, 6.0 Liter	C	......	(5700)	(5700)	(6305)	(6305)
SILVERADO/SIERRA CREW CAB PICKUP—V8—Truck Equipment Sch T1						
1500 XFE 5 3/4'	CSE3	34220	17650	18400	19850	23400
SILVERADO/SIERRA CREW CAB PICKUP 4WD—V8—Truck Equip Sch T1						
1500 LT/SLE 5 3/4'	KTE3	43550	24600	25600	27200	32000
1500 SLT 4D 5 3/4'	2WE3	40120	24800	25800	27500	32400
2WD	C	......	(3025)	(3025)	(3550)	(3550)
V8, Flex Fuel, 6.2 Liter	2	......	550	550	645	645

Body Type	VIN	List	Trade-In Good	Very Good	Pvt-Party Good	Retail Excellent
SILVERADO CREW CAB PICKUP—V8 Hybrid—Truck Equip Sch T1						
1500 4D 5 3/4'	CUEJ	39335	20800	21600	23100	27200
4WD	K		3000	3000	3555	3555
SIERRA CREW CAB PICKUP 4WD—V8 Hybrid—Truck Equip Sch T1						
1500 4D 5 3/4'	2YEJ	46035	23900	24900	26600	31300
2WD	1		(3025)	(3025)	(3575)	(3575)
SILVERADO/SIERRA CREW CAB PICKUP—V8—Truck Equipment Sch T1						
1500 Wrk Trk 5 3/4'	CPEA	33520	15900	16550	17950	21200
1500 LS 4D 5 3/4'	CREA	31355	18650	19400	20900	24600
1500 LT 4D 5 3/4'	CSEA	32460	19450	20200	21700	25600
2500 HD Wrk Trk 6'	CVCG	35995	18700	19400	20600	23700
2500 HD LT/SLE 8'	CXCG	36900	22200	23000	24300	27900
2500 HD LTZ/SLT 8'	CYCG	42100	23900	24800	26100	29900
3500 Work Trk 6 1/2'	CZCG	34560	20600	21400	22600	25900
3500 LT/SLE 6 1/2'	C0CG	37915	23400	24200	25500	29400
3500 LTZ/SLT 6 1/2'	C1CG	42600	24500	25400	26800	30800
4WD	K		3000	3000	3560	3560
V8, Flex Fuel, 5.3 Liter	0,3		375	375	445	445
V8, Flex Fuel, 6.2 Liter	2		550	550	650	650
V8, Turbo Diesel, 6.6L	8		4900	4900	5435	5435
SILVERADO/SIERRA CREW CAB 4WD—V8 Turbo Diesel—Truck Sch T1						
2500 HD LT/SLE 6'	KXC8	48250	30900	32000	33400	38300
2WD	C		(3025)	(3025)	(3340)	(3340)
V8, 6.0 Liter			(5700)	(5700)	(6310)	(6310)
SIERRA CREW CAB PICKUP—V8—Truck Equipment Sch T1						
2500 Work Truck 8'	1ZCG	33235	19000	19750	21100	24400
3500 Work Truck 8'	12CG	34960	19800	20500	21800	25000
4WD	2		3000	3000	3320	3320
V8, 6.6L Turbo Dsl			4900	4900	5425	5425
SILVERADO CREW CAB—V8 Turbo Diesel—Truck Equip Sch T1						
2500 HD Wrk Trk 8'	CVC8,L	41630	23400	24200	25700	29700
3500 Work Truck 8'	CZC8,6	42955	25800	26700	28000	32100
4WD	K		3000	3000	3315	3315
V8, 6.0 Liter			(5700)	(5700)	(6305)	(6305)
SILVERADO CREW CAB PICKUP 4WD—V8 Turbo Diesel—Truck Sch T1						
2500 HD LTZ/SLT 6'	KYC8	53450	32400	33600	35000	40100
3500 LT 4D 8'	K0C8,L	49480	31600	32700	34400	39700
3500 LTZ 4D 8'	KNC8,L	54145	33000	34200	35600	40800
2WD	C		(3025)	(3025)	(3335)	(3335)
V8, 6.0 Liter			(5700)	(5700)	(6305)	(6305)
SIERRA DENALI CREW CAB PICKUP AWD—V8—Truck Equip Schedule T3						
1500 4D 5 3/4'	2XE2	47430	28100	29100	30300	34500
2WD	1		(1100)	(1100)	(1210)	(1210)
SIERRA DENALI CREW CAB PICKUP—V8—Truck Equip Schedule T3						
3500 4D 6 1/2'	16CG	44410	25700	26600	27900	32000
3500 4D 8'	16CG	44595	25500	26400	27700	31800
4WD	2		3000	3000	3320	3320
V8, Turbo Diesel, 6.6L	8		4900	4900	5420	5420
SIERRA DENALI CREW CAB 4WD—V8 Turbo Diesel—Truck Equip Sch T3						
2500 4D 6 1/2'	25C8	55255	33900	35100	36600	41900
2WD	1		(3025)	(3025)	(3340)	(3340)
V8, 6.0 Liter			(5700)	(5700)	(6305)	(6305)

2012 CHEVY/GMC — (1,2or3)(CorG)(A,B,CorN)–(L1EK)–C

Body Type	VIN	List	Trade-In Good	Very Good	Pvt-Party Good	Retail Excellent
CAPTIVA SPORT—4-Cyl.—Truck Equipment Schedule T1						
LS Sport Utility 4D	L1EK	24245	9850	10300	11750	14150
CAPTIVA SPORT—V6—Truck Equipment Sch T1						
LT Sport Utility 4D	L3E5	27395	10450	10900	12400	15050
CAPTIVA SPORT AWD—V6—Truck Equipment Schedule T1						
LTZ Sport Utility 4D	L4E5	32845	12300	12800	14500	17400
EQUINOX—4-Cyl.—Truck Equipment Schedule T1						
LS Sport Utility 4D	LBEK	24260	12350	12850	13900	16150
AWD	C		875	875	1015	1015
EQUINOX—V6—Truck Equipment Schedule T1						
LT Sport Utility 4D	LDEK	25780	13750	14300	15500	18000
AWD	E		875	875	1015	1015
4-Cyl, Flex Fuel, 2.4L	K		(900)	(900)	(1045)	(1045)
EQUINOX AWD—V6—Truck Equipment Sch T1						
LTZ Sport Utility	LGE5	33200	16000	16600	18000	21000
FWD	F		(1075)	(1075)	(1250)	(1250)
TERRAIN—4-Cyl.—Truck Equipment Schedule T1						
SLE Sport Utility	LMEK	26290	13700	14250	15500	18150
SLT Sport Utility	LUEK	29240	15850	16450	17850	20900

TRUCKS & VANS

Body Type	VIN	List	Trade-In Good	Very Good	Pvt-Party Good	Retail Excellent
AWD	R,T		875	875	995	995
V6, Flex Fuel, 3.0 Liter	5		650	650	740	740
ACADIA—V6—Truck Equipment Schedule T1						
SL Sport Utility 4D	RNED	33415	16000	16650	17650	20200
SLE Sport Utility	RPED	35890	16750	17400	18400	21100
Denali Sport Util	RTED	44690	25100	26000	26600	29800
AWD	V		875	875	990	990
ACADIA AWD—V6—Truck Equipment Schedule T1						
SLT Sport Utility	VRED	41640	20200	21000	22000	25200
2WD	R		(875)	(875)	(990)	(990)
TRAVERSE—V6—Truck Equipment Schedule T1						
LS Sport Utility 4D	REED	30240	13800	14350	15900	18750
AWD	V		1550	1550	1850	1850
TRAVERSE AWD—V6—Truck Equipment Schedule T1						
LT Sport Utility 4D	VGED	35340	16900	17550	19100	22300
LTZ Sport Utility	VLED	41615	18150	18800	20600	24400
2WD	V		(1550)	(1550)	(1815)	(1815)
TAHOE—V8—Truck Equipment Schedule T1						
LS Sport Util 4D	CAE0	39400	21800	22700	23500	26800
Third Row Seat			650	650	730	730
4WD	K		1550	1550	1745	1745
TAHOE 4WD—V8—Truck Equipment Schedule T1						
LT Sport Util 4D	KBE0	47400	25900	26900	27900	31800
LTZ Sport Util 4D	KGE0	56720	32400	33500	34100	38000
Third Row Seat			650	650	730	730
2WD	C		(1550)	(1550)	(1745)	(1745)
TAHOE 4WD—V8 Hybrid—Truck Equipment Schedule T1						
Sport Utility 4D	KDFJ	55420	29400	30500	31500	35800
Third Row Seat			650	650	730	730
2WD	C		(1550)	(1550)	(1745)	(1745)
YUKON—V8—Truck Equipment Schedule T1						
SLE Sport Utility 4D	1AE0	40730	22600	23500	24400	27800
Third Row Seat			650	650	730	730
4WD	2		1550	1550	1745	1745
YUKON 4WD—V8—Truck Equipment Schedule T1						
SLT Sport Utility 4D	2CE0	49150	27100	28200	28900	32800
Third Row Seat			650	650	730	730
2WD	1		(1550)	(1550)	(1740)	(1740)
YUKON 4WD—V8 Hybrid—Truck Equipment Schedule T1						
Sport Utility 4D	2FFJ	56005	30400	31500	32500	36800
Third Row Seat			650	650	730	730
2WD	1		(1550)	(1550)	(1745)	(1745)
YUKON DENALI AWD—V8—Truck Equipment Schedule T3						
Sport Utility 4D	2EEF	58730	33000	34100	34600	38700
Third Row Seat			650	650	715	715
2WD	1		(1550)	(1550)	(1710)	(1710)
YUKON DENALI 4WD—V8 Hybrid—Truck Equipment Schedule T3						
Sport Utility 4D	2GFJ	63855	36100	37300	37800	42300
Third Row Seat			650	650	715	715
2WD	1		(1550)	(1550)	(1705)	(1705)
SUBURBAN 4WD—V8—Truck Equipment Schedule T1						
K1500 LS Sport Util	KHE7	42865	23400	24300	25100	28500
K1500 LT Sport Util	KJE7	46625	25100	26000	26900	30600
K1500 LTZ Util	KKE7	55760	32900	34000	34500	38600
K2500 LS Sport Util	KLEG	44475	25600	26500	27400	31200
K2500 LT Spt Utl	KMEG	48215	28000	29000	29900	33900
Third Row Seat			650	650	730	730
2WD	C		(1550)	(1550)	(1740)	(1740)
YUKON XL 4WD—V8—Truck Equipment Schedule T1						
1500 SLE Sport Util	2HE7	47115	24700	25600	26500	30200
1500 SLT Sport Util	2KE7	51295	26100	27000	27900	31700
2500 SLE Sport Util	2NEG	48655	25900	26800	27700	31500
2500 SLT Sport Util	2REG	53035	28100	29100	29900	34000
Third Row Seat			650	650	730	730
2WD	1		(1550)	(1550)	(1740)	(1740)
YUKON XL DENALI AWD—V8—Truck Equipment Schedule T3						
1500 Sport Utility	2MEF	61530	33900	35000	35500	39800
Third Row Seat			650	650	715	715
2WD	1		(1550)	(1550)	(1710)	(1710)
EXPRESS/SAVANA VAN—V8—Truck Equipment Schedule T1						
1500 LS Passenger	GBF4	29920	12650	13150	14400	16950
1500 LT Passenger	GCF4	31770	13850	14400	15650	18400
2500 LS Passenger	GPFA	30710	12800	13350	14550	17100

TRUCKS & VANS

Body Type	VIN	List	Trade-In Good	Trade-In Very Good	Pvt-Party Good	Retail Excellent
2500 LT Passenger	GRFA	32560	14250	14800	16050	18850
AWD	H		800	800	920	920
V8, Flex Fuel, 6.0 Liter	G		525	525	605	605
EXPRESS/SAVANA VAN—V8 Flex Fuel—Truck Equipment Sch T1						
3500 LS Passenger	GXFA	33005	14150	14700	16000	18750
3500 LT Passenger	GYFA	34460	15400	16000	17300	20200
3500 LS Extended	GZFA	34875	16050	16650	17950	21000
3500 LT Extended	G1FA	35245	16600	17250	18550	21700
EXPRESS/SAVANA VAN—V8 Turbo Diesel—Truck Equipment Sch T1						
3500 LS Passenger	GXFL	45935	21000	21700	23100	27000
3500 LT Passenger	GYFL	47400	21900	22600	24100	28100
3500 LS Extended	GZFL	47815	22100	22800	24300	28400
3500 LT Extended	G1FL	48185	22500	23200	24700	28800
EXPRESS VAN—V6—Truck Equipment Schedule T1						
1500 Cargo Van	GAFX	28195	14200	14850	16150	19250
AWD	H		800	800	900	900
V8, Flex Fuel, 5.3 Liter	4		675	675	760	760
SAVANA VAN—V8—Truck Equipment Schedule T1						
1500 Cargo Van	7AF4	27080	14750	15450	16750	19950
AWD	8		800	800	900	900
V6, 4.3 Liter	X		(625)	(625)	(705)	(705)
EXPRESS/SAVANA VAN—V8—Truck Equipment Schedule T1						
2500 Cargo Van	GFCA	27590	15550	16250	17600	20900
2500 Extended	GGCA	29450	16900	17650	19050	22600
3500 Cargo Van	GFCA	30790	17400	18200	19550	23200
3500 Extended	GGCA	31675	18600	19400	20800	24700
V8, Cmprssd NG, 6.0L			800	800	890	890
V8, Flex Fuel, 6.0 Liter	G		525	525	590	590
EXPRESS/SAVANA VAN—V8 Turbo Diesel—Truck Equipment Sch T1						
2500 Cargo Van	GFCL	39535	22300	23000	24500	28700
2500 Extended	GGCL	41395	22700	23500	25000	29200
3500 Cargo Van	GFCL	42735	22900	23700	25200	29500
3500 Extended	GGCL	43620	23400	24200	25800	30100
EXPRESS/SAVANA COMMERCIAL CUTAWAY—V8—Truck Equipment Sch T1						
3500 Van Cab-Ch	G2CA	27840	17600	18200	20000	23800
V8, 6.0 Liter	G		525	525	645	645
COLORADO REGULAR CAB PICKUP—4-Cyl.—Truck Equip Sch T1						
LT 2D 6'	SCF9	21100	11250	11700	12950	15250
4WD	T		2200	2200	2490	2490
5-Cyl, 3.7 Liter	E		200	200	225	225
COLORADO/CANYON REGULAR CAB PICKUP—4-Cyl.—Truck Equip Sch T1						
Work Truck 2D 6'	SBF9	19300	10050	10500	11650	13750
4WD	T		2200	2200	2495	2495
5-Cyl, 3.7 Liter	E		200	200	225	225
CANYON REGULAR CAB PICKUP—5-Cyl.—Truck Equipment Sch T1						
SLE 2D 6'	5MEE	23280	11550	12050	13300	15650
4WD	6		2200	2200	2490	2490
4-Cyl, 2.9 Liter	9		(200)	(200)	(225)	(225)
COLORADO/CANYON EXTENDED CAB—4-Cyl.—Truck Equip Sch T1						
Work Truck 4D 6'	SBF9	24855	12750	13300	14700	17250
4WD	T		2200	2200	2485	2485
5-Cyl, 3.7 Liter	E		200	200	225	225
COLORADO/CANYON EXTENDED CAB PICKUP—5-Cyl.—Truck Equip Sch T1						
LT/SLE 4D 6'	SCFE	25985	14950	15550	17050	19950
4WD	T		2200	2200	2490	2490
4-Cyl, 2.9 Liter	9		(200)	(200)	(225)	(225)
V8, 5.3 Liter	P		800	800	905	905
COLORADO/CANYON CREW CAB PICKUP—5-Cyl.—Truck Equip Sch T1						
LT/SLE 4D 5'	SCFE	27600	16200	16800	18300	21400
4WD	T		2200	2200	2480	2480
4-Cyl, 2.9 Liter	9		(200)	(200)	(225)	(225)
V8, 5.3 Liter	P		800	800	900	900
CANYON CREW CAB PICKUP 4WD—5-Cyl.—Truck Equipment Schedule T1						
SLT 4D 5'	6NFE	32520	18200	18900	20500	23900
V8, 5.3 Liter	P		975	975	1100	1100
AVALANCHE 4WD—V8—Truck Equipment Schedule T1						
LS Spt Util Pickup	KEE7	40720	23200	24000	24800	28100
LT Sport Util Pickup	KFE7	44115	26000	26900	27700	31300
LTZ Spt Util Pickup	KGE7	51175	30500	31500	32200	36300
2WD	C		(1550)	(1550)	(1715)	(1715)
SILVERADO REGULAR CAB PICKUP—V6—Truck Equipment Schedule T1						
1500 Work Truck 8'	CPEX	23330	12800	13350	14600	17200
4WD	K		3200	3200	3820	3820

Body Type	VIN	List	Trade-In Good	Trade-In Very Good	Pvt-Party Good	Retail Excellent
V8, Flex Fuel, 4.8 Liter	A		750	750	905	905
V8, Flex Fuel, 5.3 Liter	0		1150	1150	1370	1370
SIERRA REGULAR CAB PICKUP—V8—Truck Equipment Schedule T1						
1500 Work Truck 8'	1TEA	23330	13050	13550	14950	17650
4WD	2		3200	3200	3815	3815
V6, 4.3 Liter	X		(750)	(750)	(895)	(895)
V8, Flex Fuel, 5.3 Liter	0		400	400	475	475
SILVERADO/SIERRA REGULAR CAB PICKUP—V8—Truck Equipment Sch T1						
1500 Work Trk 6 1/2'	CPEA	22940	13000	13500	14900	17600
1500 LT/SLE 6 1/2'	CSEA	28295	13950	14500	15900	18750
1500 LT/SLE 8'	CSEA	28420	13550	14100	15500	18250
2500 Work Truck 8'	CVCG	29410	13600	14150	15250	17450
2500 LT 8'	CXCG	32255	17350	18000	19150	21900
3500 Work Truck 8'	CZCG	31155	13500	14050	15150	17350
3500 SLE 2D 8'	13CG	33905	16000	16600	17750	20300
4WD	K		3200	3200	3820	3820
V6, 4.3 Liter	X		(750)	(750)	(895)	(895)
V8, Flex Fuel, 5.3 Liter	0		400	400	475	475
V8, Turbo Diesel, 6.6L	8,L		5100	5100	5615	5615
SIERRA REGULAR CAB PICKUP—V8—Truck Equipment Schedule T1						
2500 Work Truck 8'	1ZCG	29795	13600	14150	15250	17450
2500 HD SLE 2D 8'	10CG	32815	17450	18100	19250	22000
3500 Work Truck 8'	12CG	31155	13500	14050	15150	17350
3500 SLE 2D 8'	13CG	33905	16000	16600	17750	20300
4WD	2		3200	3200	3820	3520
V8, 6.6L Turbo Dsl	8,L		5100	5100	5615	5615
SILVERADO REGULAR CAB 4WD—V8 Turbo Diesel—Truck Sch T1						
3500 LT 8'	K0CG	45035	24900	25800	27100	30800
2WD	C		(3200)	(3200)	(3505)	(3505)
V8, Flex Fuel, 6.0 Liter	G		(5900)	(5900)	(6460)	(6460)
SILVERADO/SIERRA EXTENDED CAB PICKUP—V8—Truck Equip Sch T1						
1500 Work Truck 8'	1TE0	29375	13700	14250	15650	18450
1500 LT/SLE 8'	CSE0	32160	16700	17350	18900	22200
1500 LTZ/SLT 8'	CTE0	37350	18250	18900	20500	24100
4WD	2		3200	3200	3820	3820
SILVERADO/SIERRA EXTENDED CAB 4WD—V8—Truck Equip Sch T1						
1500 LTZ/SLT 6 1/2'	KTE7	40200	23400	24300	25600	29500
2WD	C		(3200)	(3200)	(3625)	(3625)
V8, Flex Fuel, 6.2 Liter	2		550	550	625	625
SILVERADO/SIERRA EXTENDED CAB—V6—Truck Equipment Schedule T1						
1500 Work Trk 6 1/2'	CPEX	27335	14600	15150	16600	19550
4WD	K		3200	3200	3615	3615
V8, Flex Fuel, 4.8 Liter	A		750	750	855	855
V8, Flex Fuel, 5.3 Liter	0,7		1150	1150	1300	1300
SILVERADO/SIERRA EXTENDED CAB PICKUP—V8—Truck Equip Sch T1						
1500 LS/SL 6 1/2'	CREA	30525	16700	17350	18900	22200
1500 LT/SLE 6 1/2'	CSEA	31050	17400	18050	19600	23000
2500 HD Wrk Trk 6'	CVCG	31825	17650	18300	19450	22200
2500 HD Wrk Trk 8'	CVCG	32020	17450	18100	19250	22000
3500 Work Truck 8'	CZCG	34230	17450	18100	19250	22000
3500 LTZ/SLT 8'	C1C6	41795	22100	22900	24100	27500
4WD	K		3200	3200	3820	3820
V8, Flex Fuel, 5.3 Liter	0,7		400	400	475	475
V8, Flex Fuel, 6.2 Liter	2		550	550	655	655
V8, Turbo Diesel, 6.6L	8		5100	5100	5610	5610
SILVERADO/SIERRA EXTENDED CAB PICKUP 4WD—V8—Truck Sch T1						
2500 HD LT/SLE 6'	KXCG	34995	24600	25500	26800	30500
2500 HD LT/SLE 8'	KXCG	35190	24400	25300	26500	30200
2500 HD LTZ/SLT 6'	KYCG	40365	25800	26700	28000	31800
2500 HD LTZ/SLT 8'	KYCG	40560	25600	26500	27700	31500
3500 LT 8'	K0CG	48770	30200	31200	32600	37000
2WD	C		(3200)	(3200)	(3505)	(3505)
V8, Turbo Diesel, 6.6L	8		5100	5100	5590	5590
SILVERADO/SIERRA CREW CAB PICKUP—V8—Truck Equipment Sch T1						
1500 Wrk Trk 5 3/4'	CPEA	34465	17700	18350	19900	23400
1500 LS 4D 5 3/4'	CREA	32840	20700	21400	22600	26100
1500 LT 4D 5 3/4'	CSEA	33390	21100	21800	23100	26600
4WD	K		3200	3200	3665	3665
V8, Flex Fuel, 5.3 Liter	0,7		400	400	460	460
V8, Flex Fuel, 6.2 Liter	2		550	550	630	630
SILVERADO CREW CAB PICKUP—V8 Hybrid—Truck Equipment Sch T1						
1500 4D 5 3/4'	CUEJ	40260	22600	23400	24700	28600
4WD	K		3200	3200	3680	3680

Body Type	VIN	List	Trade-In Good	Very Good	Pvt-Party Good	Retail Excellent
SIERRA CREW CAB PICKUP 4WD—V8 Hybrid—Truck Equipment Sch T1						
1500 4D 5 3/4'	2YEJ	40630	25700	26500	28000	32400
2WD	1		(3200)	(3200)	(3660)	(3660)
SILVERADO/SIERRA CREW CAB PICKUP—V8—Truck Equip Sch T1						
1500 XFE 5 3/4'	CSE7	35145	20400	21100	22300	25700
SILVERADO/SIERRA CREW CAB PICKUP—V8—Truck Equip Sch T1						
2500 HD LT/SLE 8'	CXCG	37345	24500	25400	26600	30300
2500 HD LTZ/SLT 8'	CYCG	43230	27200	28200	29400	33400
3500 Work Trk 6 1/2'	CZCG	35865	22200	23000	24200	27600
3500 LT/SLE 6 1/2'	C0CG	38815	25300	26200	27600	31500
3500 LTZ/SLT 6 1/2'	C1CG	43730	26100	27000	28400	32300
4WD	K		3200	3200	3505	3505
V8, 6.6L Turbo Dsl	8,L		5100	5100	5590	5590
SILVERADO/SIERRA CREW CAB PICKUP 4WD—V8—Truck Equip Sch T1						
1500 LTZ 4D 5 3/4'	KTE7	43240	26700	27600	28800	33200
2500 SLT 4D 5 3/4'	2WE7	40785	26800	27700	29300	33900
2WD	C		(3200)	(3200)	(3620)	(3620)
V8, Flex Fuel, 6.2 Liter	2		550	550	620	620
SILVERADO/SIERRA CREW CAB 4WD—V8 Turbo Diesel—V8—Truck Sch T1						
2500 HD SLE 6 1/2'	20C8	49650	33100	34200	35600	40400
2500 HD LTZ 6 1/2'	KYC8	53735	35400	36500	37900	43000
2500 HD SLT 6 1/2'	21C8	55435	34600	35700	37100	42100
2WD	C		(3200)	(3200)	(3495)	(3495)
V8, Flex Fuel, 6.0 Liter	G		(4850)	(4850)	(5305)	(5305)
SILVERADO/SIERRA CREW CAB 4WD—V8 Turbo Diesel—Truck Sch T1						
3500 LT/SLE 8'	K0CG	50555	33800	34900	36500	41700
3500 LTZ 8'	K1CG	55275	35200	36300	37700	42800
2WD	C		(3200)	(3200)	(3545)	(3545)
V8, Flex Fuel, 6.0 Liter	G		(5900)	(5900)	(6535)	(6535)
SILVERADO/SIERRA CREW CAB—V8—Truck Equipment Sch T1						
2500 HD Wrk Trk 6'	CVCG	34030	19950	20700	21900	25000
3500 Work Truck 8'	CZCG	44455	27300	28200	29500	33500
4WD	K		3200	3200	3515	3515
V8, Turbo Diesel, 6.6L	8		5100	5100	5605	5605
SIERRA CREW CAB PICKUP—V8—Truck Equipment Sch T1						
2500 Work Truck 8'	1ZC8	34020	21000	21800	23000	26200
4WD	K		3200	3200	3515	3515
V8, 6.6L Turbo Dsl			5100	5100	5600	5600
SILVERADO/SIERRA CREW CAB—V8 Turbo Diesel—Truck Equip Sch T1						
2500 HD Wrk Trk 8'	CVC8,L	42620	25000	25900	27200	30900
3500 SLT Pickup 8'	14CG	52825	31700	32700	34100	38700
4WD	K		3200	3200	3500	3500
V8, Flex Fuel, 6.0 Liter	G		(5900)	(5900)	(6465)	(6465)
SILVERADO CREW CAB 4WD—V8 Turbo Diesel—Truck Equip Sch T1						
2500 HD LT 6 1/2'	KXC8	48695	32600	33700	35100	39800
2WD	C		(3200)	(3200)	(3500)	(3500)
V8, Flex Fuel, 6.0 Liter	G		(4850)	(4850)	(5320)	(5320)
SIERRA DENALI CREW CAB PICKUP AWD—V8—Truck Equip Schedule T3						
1500 4D 5 3/4'	2XE2	49605	30500	31500	32800	37200
2WD	1		(1500)	(1500)	(1675)	(1675)

2013 CHEVY/GMC — (1,2or3)(CorG)(A,B,CorN)–(L1EK)–D

Body Type	VIN	List	Trade-In Good	Very Good	Pvt-Party Good	Retail Excellent
CAPTIVA SPORT—4-Cyl. Flex Fuel—Truck Equipment Schedule T1						
LS Sport Utility 4D	L1EK	24580	11300	11750	13600	16450
LT Sport Utility 4D	L3EK	26595	12000	12500	14300	17300
LTZ Sport Utility 4D	L4EK	30440	12600	13100	15000	18100
EQUINOX—4-Cyl.—Truck Equipment Schedule T1						
LS Sport Utility 4D	LBEK	24580	13250	13750	15400	18150
AWD	C		950	950	1160	1160
EQUINOX—V6—Truck Equipment Schedule T1						
LT Sport Utility 4D	LDEK	26225	15650	16250	17950	21100
LTZ Sport Utility 4D	LFE3	31340	17600	18200	20200	24000
AWD	E,N		950	950	1130	1130
4-Cyl, 2.4 Liter	K		(1000)	(1000)	(1190)	(1190)
TERRAIN—4-Cyl.—Truck Equipment Schedule T1						
SLE-1 Sport Utility	LMEK	26660	14950	15500	17100	20100
SLE-2 Sport Utility	LSEK	28160	15450	16050	17650	20800
SLT-1 Sport Utility	LUEK	29710	16050	16650	18400	21700
SLT-2 Sport Utility	LEEK	32955	17250	17900	19650	23200
Denali Sport Utility	LYEK	35350	21300	22000	23900	28000
AWD	R		950	950	1125	1125
V6, 3.6 Liter	3		700	700	830	830

TRUCKS & VANS

TRUCKS & VANS

Body Type	VIN	List	Trade-In Good	Very Good	Pvt-Party Good	Retail Excellent
ACADIA—V6—Truck Equipment Schedule T1						
SLE-1 Sport Util	RNED	34875	18350	19000	20200	23300
SLE-2 Sport Util	RPED	36765	19300	20000	21400	24800
AWD	V		950	950	1080	1080
ACADIA AWD—V6—Truck Equipment Schedule T1						
SLT-1 Sport Util	VRED	42605	23600	24400	25900	29800
SLT-2 Sport Util	VSED	44025	24700	25600	27100	31300
Denali Sport Util	VTED	48770	30700	31800	32300	36000
2WD	R		(950)	(950)	(1090)	(1090)
TRAVERSE—V6—Truck Equipment Schedule T1						
LS Sport Utility 4D	RFED	31335	16150	16750	17900	20500
AWD	V		1625	1625	1820	1820
TRAVERSE AWD—V6—Truck Equipment Schedule T1						
LT Sport Utility 4D	VGED	36550	20400	21100	22300	25400
LTZ Sport Utility 4D	VLED	43250	24900	25800	27100	31000
2WD	R		(1625)	(1625)	(1820)	(1820)
TAHOE—V8 Flex Fuel—Truck Equipment Schedule T1						
LS Sport Util 4D	KAE0	44135	22600	23400	24400	27800
4WD	K		1625	1625	1855	1855
TAHOE 4WD—V8 Flex Fuel—Truck Equipment Schedule T1						
Commercial 4D	2BE0	42840				
LT Sport Util 4D	KBB0	48075	26800	27800	28800	32700
LTZ Sport Util 4D	KCX0	57395	32900	33900	34600	38500
Third Row Seat			700	700	795	795
2WD	C		(1625)	(1625)	(1855)	(1855)
TAHOE—V8 Hybrid—Truck Equipment Schedule T1						
Sport Utility 4D	KDEJ	56095	31100	32200	33200	37600
Third Row Seat			700	700	790	790
2WD	C		(1625)	(1625)	(1850)	(1850)
YUKON 4WD—V8 Flex Fuel—Truck Equipment Schedule T1						
Commercial 4D	2BE0	42980				
SLE Sport Utility 4D	2AE0	45440	23600	24500	25600	29100
SLT Sport Utility 4D	2CE0	49770	27800	28800	29800	33900
Third Row Seat			700	700	795	795
2WD	1		(1625)	(1625)	(1855)	(1855)
YUKON 4WD—V8 Hybrid—Truck Equipment Schedule T1						
Sport Utility 4D	2FEJ	56625	31900	33000	34000	38500
Third Row Seat			700	700	790	790
2WD	1		(1625)	(1625)	(1850)	(1850)
YUKON DENALI AWD—V8 Flex Fuel—Truck Equipment Schedule T3						
Sport Utility 4D	2EEF	59350	35800	36900	37500	41600
Third Row Seat			700	700	765	765
2WD	1		(1625)	(1625)	(1780)	(1780)
YUKON DENALI 4WD—V8 Hybrid—Truck Equipment Schedule T3						
Sport Utility 4D	2GEJ	64475	36800	37900	38600	43000
2WD	1		(1625)	(1625)	(1790)	(1790)
SUBURBAN 4WD—V8 Flex Fuel—Truck Equipment Schedule T1						
K1500 Commercial	K5E0	45090				
K1500 LS Sport Util	KHE0	46385	24300	25200	26200	29600
K1500 LT Sport Util	KJE0	50145	26500	27500	28400	32200
K1500 LTZ Utility	KKE0	59435	33600	34600	35600	40000
Third Row Seat			700	700	785	785
2WD	C		(1625)	(1625)	(1840)	(1840)
SUBURBAN 4WD—V8—Truck Equipment Schedule T1						
K2500 Commercial	K5EG	46695				
K2500 LS Spt Util	KLEG	47295	27100	28100	29100	32900
K2500 LT Spt Util	KMEG	51735	29300	30300	31400	35500
2WD	C		(1625)	(1625)	(1840)	(1840)
YUKON XL 4WD—V8 Flex Fuel—Truck Equipment Schedule T1						
1500 Commercial	S2JE7	45145				
1500 SLE Sport Util	S2HE7	47690	25700	26700	27700	31400
1500 SLT Sport Util	S2KE7	51870	27300	28300	29300	33100
Third Row Seat			700	700	785	785
2WD	1		(1625)	(1625)	(1840)	(1840)
YUKON XL DENALI AWD—V8 Flex Fuel—Truck Equipment Schedule T3						
1500 Sport Utility	S2MEF	62105	36800	37900	38600	43300
Third Row Seat			700	700	775	775
2WD	1		(1625)	(1625)	(1810)	(1810)
YUKON XL 4WD—V8—Truck Equipment Schedule T1						
2500 Commercial	W2REG	46765				
2500 SLE Spt Util	W2NRG	49230	27300	28300	29300	33100
2500 SLT Spt Util	W2REG	53610	29600	30700	31700	35800
Third Row Seat			700	700	785	785

Body Type	VIN	List	Trade-In Good	Very Good	Pvt-Party Good	Retail Excellent
2WD	1		(1625)	(1625)	(1840)	(1840)
EXPRESS/SAVANA VAN—V8 Flex Fuel—Truck Equipment Schedule T1						
1500 LS Passenger	GBF4	29965	14600	15150	16450	19250
1500 LT Passenger	GCF4	32270	15600	16150	17500	20500
2500 LS Passenger	GPFA	30860	14700	15250	16550	19350
2500 LT Passenger	GRFA	33165	16200	16800	18100	21200
3500 LS Passenger	GXFA	33155	16100	16700	18050	21100
3500 LT Passenger	GYFA	35065	17250	17850	19250	22400
3500 LS Extended	GZFA	35025	18000	18650	20000	23300
3500 LT Extended	G1FA	35850	18600	19250	20700	24100
AWD	H		875	875	995	995
V8, Flex Fuel, 6.0 Liter	G		550	550	625	625
EXPRESS/SAVANA VAN—V8 Turbo Diesel—Truck Equipment Schedule T1						
3500 LS Passenger	GXFL	46095	22700	23400	24900	29000
3500 LT Passenger	GYFL	48005	23600	24300	25900	30100
3500 LS Extended	GZFL	47965	23700	24500	26100	30300
3500 LT Extended	G1FL	48790	24100	24900	26500	30800
EXPRESS VAN—V6—Truck Equipment Schedule T1						
1500 Cargo Van	GAF4	26315	14900	15550	16750	19700
AWD	H		875	875	995	995
V8, Flex Fuel, 5.3 Liter	4		675	675	770	770
SAVANA VAN—V8—Truck Equipment Schedule T1						
1500 Cargo Van	7AF4	26315	15600	16300	17500	20600
AWD	8		875	875	995	995
V6, 4.3 Liter	X		(650)	(650)	(740)	(740)
EXPRESS/SAVANA VAN—V8 Flex Fuel—Truck Equipment Schedule T1						
2500 Cargo Van	GFCA	27820	16350	17100	18250	21500
2500 Extended	GGCA	29680	17850	18600	19850	23300
3500 Cargo Van	GTCA	31140	18600	19400	20700	24300
3500 Extended	GUCA	32025	19600	20400	21700	25500
V8, CNG, 6.0 Liter	B		825	825	940	940
V8, Flex Fuel, 6.0 Liter	G		550	550	625	625
EXPRESS/SAVANA VAN—V8 Turbo Diesel—Truck Equipment Sch T1						
2500 Cargo Van	GFCL	39765	23400	24100	25600	29600
2500 Extended	GGCL	41625	23800	24600	26000	30000
3500 Cargo Van	GTCL	43085	24000	24800	26200	30300
3500 Extended	GUCL	43970	24400	25400	26800	31000
AVALANCHE 4WD—V8 Flex Fuel—Truck Equipment Schedule T1						
Black Diamond LS	KEE7	40025	24900	25700	26800	30500
Black Diamond LT	KFE7	42670	28100	29000	30100	34200
Black Diamond LTZ	KGE7	48880	32200	33300	34400	38900
2WD	C		(1625)	(1625)	(1785)	(1785)
SIERRA REGULAR CAB PICKUP—V8—Truck Equipment Schedule T1						
1500 Work Truck 8'	1TEA	23980	14000	14500	15850	18450
4WD	2		3300	3300	3740	3740
V6, 4.3 Liter	X		(800)	(800)	(905)	(905)
V8, Flex Fuel, 5.3 Liter	0		400	400	455	455
SILVERADO/SIERRA REGULAR CAB—V8 Flex Fuel—Truck Sch T1						
1500 Work Trk 6 1/2'	CPEX	23590	14800	15350	16700	19400
1500 LT/SLE 6 1/2'	CSEA	28945	15400	15950	17300	20100
1500 LT/SLE 8'	CSEA	29070	15100	15650	16950	19700
2500 Work Truck 8'	CVEG	30295	15250	15800	16900	19250
2500 LT/SLE 2D 8'	CXEG	33475	19650	20400	21600	24500
3500 Work Truck 8'	CZCG	31790	15250	15800	16900	19250
3500 SLE 2D 8'	13CG	34640	18500	19150	20300	23100
4WD	K		3300	3300	3750	3750
V8, Flex Fuel, 5.3 Liter	0		400	400	455	455
V8, Turbo Diesel, 6.6L	8,L		5300	5300	5815	5815
SILVERADO REGULAR CAB PICKUP 4WD—V8 Turbo Diesel—Truck Sch T1						
3500 LT 8'	K0CG	46420	26300	27200	28500	32300
2WD	C		(3300)	(3300)	(3610)	(3610)
V8, Flex Fuel, 6.0 Liter	G		(6100)	(6100)	(6670)	(6670)
SILVERADO/SIERRA EXTENDED CAB PICKUP—V8 Flex Fuel—Truck Sch T1						
1500 Work Truck 8'	CPE0	29775	15850	16400	17500	20100
1500 LS/SL 6 1/2'	CREA	31520	18050	18650	20000	23200
1500 LT/SLE 8'	CSE0	32660	17950	18550	19950	23100
1500 LTZ/SLT 6 1/2'	CTE0	41020	24000	24800	26100	29700
1500 LTZ/SLT 8'	CTE0	37425	19600	20300	21600	25000
4WD			3300	3300	3810	3810
V8, Flex Fuel, 6.2 Liter	2		550	550	620	620
SILVERADO/SIERRA EXTENDED CAB—V8—Truck Equipment Schedule T1						
1500 Work Trk 6 1/2'	CPEX	27735	15650	16200	17300	19900
4WD	K		3300	3300	3735	3735

TRUCKS & VANS

TRUCKS & VANS

Body Type	VIN	List	Trade-In Good	Very Good	Pvt-Party Good	Retail Excellent
V8, Flex Fuel, 4.8 Liter	A	......	400	400	450	450
V8, Flex Fuel, 5.3 Liter	0,7	......	400	400	450	450
SILVERADO/SIERRA EXTENDED CAB—V8 Flex Fuel—Truck Equip Sch T1						
1500 LT/SLE 6 1/2'	CSEA	31550	18650	19300	20500	23500
2500 HD Wrk Trk 6'	CVCG	32325	19250	19950	21100	24000
2500 HD Wrk Trk 8'	CVCG	32520	19050	19750	20900	23800
3500 Work Truck 8'	CZCG	34965	20700	21400	22600	25600
3500 LTZ/SLT 8'	C1CG	42630	24400	25200	26500	30000
4WD	K	......	3300	3300	3795	3795
V8, Flex Fuel, 5.3 Liter	0,7	......	400	400	460	460
V8, Flex Fuel, 6.2 Liter	2	......	550	550	630	630
V8, Turbo Diesel, 6.6L	8,L	......	5300	5300	5820	5820
SILVERADO EXTENDED CAB PICKUP 4WD—V8—Truck Equip Schedule T1						
2500 HD LT/SLE 6'	KXCG	39345	26300	27200	28500	32300
2500 HD LT 8'	KXCG	39540	26100	27000	28300	32100
2500 HD LTZ/SLT 6'	KYCG	44470	28500	29500	30900	35000
2500 HD LTZ 8'	KYCG	44665	28300	29300	30600	34600
3500 LT 8'	K0CG	51660	32500	33500	35000	39500
2WD	C	......	(3300)	(3300)	(3610)	(3610)
V8, Turbo Diesel, 6.6L	8,L	......	5300	5300	5795	5795
SIERRA EXTENDED CAB PICKUP—V8—Truck Equipment Schedule T1						
2500 HD SLE 4D 8'	10CG	36635	23300	24100	25300	28700
2500 SLT 4D 8'	11CG	42040	25300	26100	27400	31000
4WD	2	......	3300	3300	3620	3620
V8, Turbo Diesel, 6.6L	8,L	......	5300	5300	5815	5815
SIERRA EXTENDED CAB PICKUP 4WD—V8 Turbo Diesel—Truck Equip Sch T1						
3500 SLE 4D 8'	23C8	50800	32800	33900	35300	39900
2WD	1	......	(3300)	(3300)	(3605)	(3605)
V8, Flex Fuel, 6.0 Liter	1	......	(6100)	(6100)	(6665)	(6665)
SILVERADO/SIERRA CREW CAB PICKUP—V8 Flex Fuel—Truck Equip Sch T1						
1500 Wrk Trk 5 3/4'	CPEA	31615	19000	19650	21100	24400
1500 LS/SL 4D 5 3/4'	CREA	33290	21000	21700	23100	26700
1500 LT/SLE 5 3/4'	CSEA	34015	21700	22400	23600	26900
4WD	K	......	3300	3300	3745	3745
V8, Flex Fuel, 5.3 Liter	0,7	......	400	400	450	450
V8, Flex Fuel, 6.2 Liter	2	......	550	550	620	620
SILVERADO CREW CAB PICKUP 4WD—V8 Flex Fuel—Truck Equip Sch T1						
1500 LTZ 4D 5 3/4'	CTE0	44380	27400	28300	29500	33700
2WD	C	......	(3300)	(3300)	(3730)	(3730)
V8, Flex Fuel, 6.2 Liter	2	......	550	550	620	620
SILVERADO CREW CAB PICKUP—V8 Hybrid—Truck Equipment Schedule T1						
1500 4D 5 3/4'	CUEJ	40885	23500	24300	25600	29300
4WD	K	......	3300	3300	3725	3725
SIERRA CREW CAB PICKUP 4WD—V8 Hybrid—Truck Equipment Sch T1						
1500 4D 5 3/4'	2YEJ	44705	26600	27400	28900	33100
2WD	1	......	(3300)	(3300)	(3720)	(3720)
SILVERADO/SIERRA CREW CAB PICKUP—V8 Flex Fuel—Truck Equip Sch T1						
1500 XFE 5 3/4'	CSE7	35770	20900	21600	22800	26100
SIERRA CREW CAB PICKUP 4WD—V8 Flex Fuel—Truck Equip Sch T1						
1500 SLT 4D 5 3/4'	2WE7	44085	27500	28400	30100	34700
2WD	1	......	(3300)	(3300)	(3720)	(3720)
V8, Flex Fuel, 6.2 Liter	1	......	550	550	620	620
SIERRA DENALI CREW CAB PICKUP AWD—V8 Flex Fuel—Truck Sch T3						
1500 Denali 4D 5 3/4'	2XE2	49630	32300	33300	34900	39500
2WD	1	......	(1300)	(1300)	(1470)	(1470)
SIERRA CREW CAB PICKUP—V8—Truck Equipment Schedule T1						
2500 Work Truck 8'	1ZCG	34525	21800	22600	23800	27000
Tool Box		......	200	200	220	220
4WD	2	......	3300	3300	3610	3610
V8, Turbo Dsl, 6.6L	L	......	5300	5300	5800	5800
SILVERADO/SIERRA CREW CAB PICKUP—V8—Truck Equip Sch T1						
2500 HD Wrk Trk 6'	CVCG	34330	21300	22100	23300	26500
2500 HD LT/SLE 8'	CXCG	38140	25700	26600	27900	31600
2500 HD LTZ/SLT 8'	CYCG	43860	29100	30100	31400	35500
3500 Work Trk 6 1/2'	CZCG	36600	23700	24500	25800	29200
3500 Work Truck 8'	CZCG	36795	24000	24800	26000	29500
3500 LT/SLE 6 1/2'	C0CG	39650	26400	27300	28700	32600
3500 LTZ/SLT 6 1/2'	C1CG	44440	27200	28100	29500	33600
Tool Box		......	200	200	220	220
4WD	K	......	3300	3300	3615	3615
V8, Turbo Diesel, 6.6L	L,8	......	5300	5300	5805	5805
SILVERADO CREW CAB PICKUP—V8 Turbo Diesel—Truck Equip Sch T1						
2500 HD Wrk Trk 8'	CVC8	42920	27600	28500	29800	33800

Body Type	VIN	List	Trade-In Good	Very Good	Pvt-Party Good	Retail Excellent
Tool Box			200	200	220	220
4WD	K		3300	3300	3615	3615
V8, Flex Fuel, 6.0 Liter	G		(5150)	(5150)	(5635)	(5635)
SILVERADO CREW CAB PICKUP 4WD—V8 Turbo Diesel—Truck Sch T1						
2500 HD LT/SLE 6'	KXC8	49635	33900	35000	36400	41100
2500 HD LTZ/SLT 6'	KYCG	55860	37500	38700	40100	45200
Tool Box			200	200	220	220
2WD	C		(3300)	(3300)	(3605)	(3605)
V8, Flex Fuel, 6.0 Liter	G		(5150)	(5150)	(5615)	(5615)
SILVERADO CREW CAB PICKUP 4WD—V8 Flex Fuel—Truck Equip Sch T1						
3500 LT/SLE 8'	K0CG	51390	35700	36800	38500	43700
3500 LTZ/SLT 8'	K1CG	56180	38200	39400	40800	46100
Tool Box			200	200	220	220
2WD	C		(3300)	(3300)	(3655)	(3655)
V8, Turbo Dsl, 6.6L	C		5300	5300	5800	5800
SIERRA CREW CAB PICKUP 4WD—V8 Turbo Diesel—Truck Equip Sch T1						
2500 HD SLE 4D 6 1/2'	20C8	50750	34400	35500	36900	41700
2500 SLT 4D 6 1/2'	21CG	56360	36200	37300	38800	43800
Tool Box			200	200	220	220
2WD	1		(3300)	(3300)	(3610)	(3610)
V8, Flex Fuel, 6.0 Liter	G		(5150)	(5150)	(5625)	(5625)

2014 CHEVY/GMC — (1,2or3)(CorG)(A,B,CorN)–(L1EK)–E

Body Type	VIN	List	Trade-In Good	Very Good	Pvt-Party Good	Retail Excellent
CAPTIVA SPORT—4-Cyl. Flex Fuel—Truck Equipment Schedule T1						
LS Sport Utility 4D	L1EK	25235	12150	12650	14800	18200
LT Sport Utility 4D	L3EK	26850	12700	13200	15250	18600
LTZ Sport Utility 4D	L4EK	30370	13650	14200	16500	20100
EQUINOX—4-Cyl.—Truck Equipment Schedule T1						
LS Sport Utility 4D	LAEK	25235	14950	15500	16800	19350
AWD	E		1025	1025	1165	1165
EQUINOX—V6—Truck Equipment Schedule T1						
LT Sport Utility 4D	LBE3	26880	17200	17850	19050	21800
LTZ Sport Utility 4D	LHE3	34195	22300	23100	24400	27900
AWD	F,G		1025	1025	1150	1150
4-Cyl, 2.4 Liter	K		(1100)	(1100)	(1235)	(1235)
TERRAIN—4-Cyl.—Truck Equipment Schedule T1						
SLE-1 Sport Utility	LMEK	27390	16700	17350	19150	22600
SLE-2 Sport Utility	LREK	28890	17500	18150	20000	23600
SLT-1 Sport Utility	LSEK	30440	18300	19000	20900	24700
SLT-2 Sport Utility	LTEK	33685	20000	20700	22700	26700
Denali Sport Utility	LUEK	36080	22500	23300	25400	30000
AWD	V		1025	1025	1225	1225
V6, 3.6 Liter	3		750	750	895	895
ACADIA—V6—Truck Equipment Schedule T1						
SLE-1 Sport Util	RNKD	35260	20900	21700	23000	26400
SLE-2 Sport Util	RPKD	37150	22800	23600	24900	28500
AWD	V		1025	1025	1160	1160
ACADIA AWD—V6—Truck Equipment Schedule T1						
SLT-1 Sport Util	VRKD	43315	27300	28200	29500	33600
SLT-2 Sport Util	VSKD	44410	28000	28900	30400	34700
Denali Sport Util	VTKD	49600	32900	34000	34900	39200
2WD	R		(1025)	(1025)	(1155)	(1155)
TRAVERSE—V6—Truck Equipment Schedule T1						
LS Sport Util 4D	RFED	31670	16950	17600	19200	22300
AWD	V		1725	1725	2025	2025
TRAVERSE AWD—V6—Truck Equipment Schedule T1						
LT Sport Utility 4D	VGED	36885	23100	23800	25300	29000
LTZ Sport Utility 4D	VJED	44130	27700	28500	30100	34400
2WD	V		(1725)	(1725)	(1980)	(1980)
TAHOE—V8 Flex Fuel—Truck Equipment Schedule T1						
LS Sport Util 4D	CAE0	42595	25100	26100	27700	32100
Third Row Seat			750	750	885	885
4WD	K		1725	1725	2020	2020
TAHOE 4WD—V8 Flex Fuel—Truck Equipment Schedule T1						
Commercial 4D	K4E0	44300	24200	25100	26800	31000
LT Sport Util 4D	KBE0	49985	29300	30400	32100	37000
LTZ Sport Util 4D	KCE0	58855	36100	37200	38200	42900
Third Row Seat			750	750	880	880
2WD	C		(1725)	(1725)	(2020)	(2020)
YUKON 4WD—V8 Flex Fuel—Truck Equipment Schedule T1						
Commercial 4D	2BE0	44440	24400	25300	27000	31300
SLE Sport Utility 4D	2AE0	47960	26000	27000	28700	33200
SLT Sport Utility 4D	2CE0	51230	30300	31400	33100	38100

Body Type	VIN	List	Trade-In Good	Very Good	Pvt-Party Good	Retail Excellent
2WD	1		(1725)	(1725)	(2015)	(2015)
Third Row Seat			750	750	880	880
YUKON DENALI AWD—V8 Flex Fuel—Truck Equipment Schedule T3						
Sport Utility 4D	2EEF	60810	38600	39800	40800	45700
2WD	1		(1725)	(1725)	(1910)	(1910)
SUBURBAN 4WD—V8 Flex Fuel—Truck Equipment Schedule T1						
1500 Commercial	K5E7	47940	26500	27400	28600	32600
1500 LS Sport Util	KHE7	50295	28700	29700	30800	35000
1500 LT Sport Util	KJE7	53555	31500	32600	33800	38300
1500 LTZ Sport Util	KKE7	62395	38100	39300	40000	44700
2WD	C		(1725)	(1725)	(1950)	(1950)
YUKON XL 4WD—V8 Flex Fuel—Truck Equipment Schedule T1						
1500 SLE Sport Util	2HE7	50210	30200	31200	32400	36800
1500 SLT Sport Util	2KE7	53330	32000	33100	34300	38900
2WD	1		(1725)	(1725)	(1945)	(1945)
YUKON XL DENALI AWD—V8 Flex Fuel—Truck Equipment Sch T1						
1500 Sport Utility	2MEF	63565	40900	42100	42800	47800
2WD	1		(1725)	(1725)	(1895)	(1895)
EXPRESS PASSENGER VAN—V8 Flex Fuel—Truck Equipment Sch T1						
1500 LS Passenger	GBF4	31965	16100	16700	17950	20800
1500 LT Passenger	GCF4	33790	16850	17450	18650	21600
AWD	H		950	950	1090	1090
EXPRESS VAN—V6—Equipment Schedule T1						
1500 Cargo Van	GAFX	27705	17500	18200	19250	22400
AWD	H		950	950	1080	1080
V8, Flex Fuel, 5.3 Liter	C		675	675	770	770
EXPRESS VAN—V8 Flex Fuel—Truck Equipment Schedule T1						
2500 Cargo Van	GFCA	29210	18850	19650	20600	23800
2500 Extended	GGCA	31070	20400	21300	22200	25700
3500 Cargo Van	GTCA	32680	21100	22000	23000	26600
3500 Extended	GUCA	33565	22100	23000	24100	28000
V8, CNG, 6.0 Liter	B		875	875	975	975
V8, Flex Fuel, 6.0 Liter	G		575	575	650	650
EXPRESS VAN—V8 Turbo Diesel—Truck Equipment Schedule T1						
2500 Cargo Van	GFCL	41155	26200	27000	28200	32300
2500 Extended	GGCL	43015	26800	27600	28800	32900
3500 Cargo Van	GTCL	44625	27000	27800	29000	33100
3500 Extended	GUCL	45510	27600	28500	29600	33700
EXPRESS VAN—V8 Flex Fuel—Truck Equipment Schedule T1						
3500 LS Passenger	GXFA	35155	17550	18200	19350	22300
3500 LT Passenger	GYFA	36585	18750	19400	20500	23500
3500 LS Extended	GZFA	37025	19450	20100	21100	24200
3500 LT Extended	G1FA	37370	20100	20800	21800	24900
V8, Flex Fuel, 6.0L	G		575	575	655	655
EXPRESS VAN—V8 Turbo Diesel—Truck Equipment Schedule T1						
3500 LS Passenger	GXFL	48095	24100	24900	26200	30200
3500 LT Passenger	GYFL	49525	25000	25800	27100	31200
3500 LS Extended	GZFL	49965	25200	26000	27300	31300
3500 LT Extended	G1FL	50310	25600	26500	27700	31800
SILVERADO/SIERRA DOUBLE CAB—V6 Flex Fuel EcoTec3—Truck Sch T1						
1500 Work Truck 6'	CPEH	28610	17200	17800	19100	22000
1500 4D 6 1/2'	1TEH	29110	17700	18300	19550	22500
4WD	K		3600	3600	4110	4110
V8, EcoTec3, FF, 5.3L	C		400	400	455	455
SILVERADO DOUBLE CAB 4WD—V8 Flex Fuel EcoTec3—Truck Equip Sch T1						
1500 LT 6 1/2'	KREC	37140	26600	27400	28400	32100
1500 Z71 LT 6 1/2'	KREC	38830	26500	27300	28300	31800
2WD	C		(3600)	(3600)	(3985)	(3985)
V6, EcoTec3, FF, 4.3L	H		(650)	(650)	(720)	(720)
SILVERADO DOUBLE CAB 4WD—V8 Flex Fuel EcoTec3—Truck Equip Sch T1						
1500 LTZ 6 1/2'	KSEC	41020	30000	30900	31900	35800
1500 Z71 LTZ 6 1/2'	KSEC	41800	29800	30700	31500	35200
1500 SLT 6 1/2'	2VEC	41760	30500	31400	32400	36400
2WD	C		(3600)	(3600)	(3965)	(3965)
V8, EcoTec3, FF, 6.2L	C		850	850	935	935
SIERRA DOUBLE CAB 4WD—V8 Flex Fuel EcoTec3—Truck Equip Sch T1						
1500 SLE 6 1/2'	2UEC	39155	27000	27800	28700	32300
2WD	C		(3600)	(3600)	(3970)	(3970)
V6, EcoTec3, 4.3L FF	H		(650)	(650)	(715)	(715)
SILVERADO/SIERRA CREW CAB—V6 Flex Fuel EcoTec3—Truck Equip Sch T1						
1500 Wrk Trk 5 3/4'	CPEH	32710	19550	20200	21500	24800
1500 Wrk Trk 6 1/2'	CPEH	33010	19250	19900	21300	24500
1500 4D 5 3/4 ft	1TEH	33210	19700	20400	21800	25100

Body Type	VIN	List	Trade-In Good	Very Good	Pvt-Party Good	Retail Excellent
1500 4D 6 1/2 ft	1TEH	33510	19550	20200	21600	24900
4WD	2		3600	3600	4115	4115
V8, EcoTec3, FF, 5.3L	C		400	400	455	455
SIERRA CREW CAB 4WD—V6 Flex Fuel EcoTec3—Truck Equipment Sch T1						
1500 SLE 4D 5 3/4'	2UEC	41545	29600	30500	31400	35300
1500 SLE 4D 6 1/2'	2UEC	41845	30300	31200	32200	36100
2WD	1		(3600)	(3600)	(3960)	(3960)
V6, EcoTec3, 4.3L FF	H		(650)	(650)	(715)	(715)
SILVERADO CREW CAB PICKUP—V8 Flex Fuel EcoTec3—Truck Sch T1						
1500 LT 4D 5 3/4'	CREC	36155	22100	22800	24100	27500
1500 LT 4D 6 1/2'	CREC	36455	21800	22500	23400	26300
4WD	K		3600	3600	4065	4065
V6, EcoTec3, FF, 4.3L	H		(650)	(650)	(735)	(735)
SILVERADO CREW CAB 4WD—V8 Flex Fuel EcoTec3—Truck Equip Sch T1						
1500 Z71 LT 5 3/4'	KREC	41420	25500	26300	27300	30800
2WD	C		(3600)	(3600)	(3990)	(3990)
V6, EcoTec3, FF, 4.3L	H		(650)	(650)	(720)	(720)
SILVERADO CREW CAB 4WD—V8 Flex Fuel EcoTec3—Truck Equip Sch T1						
1500 Z71 LT 4D 6'	KREC	41720	25200	26000	27000	30500
2WD	C		(3600)	(3600)	(3995)	(3995)
V6, EcoTec3, FF, 4.3L	H		(650)	(650)	(720)	(720)
SILVERADO CREW CAB 4WD—V8 Flex Fuel EcoTec3—Truck Equip Sch T1						
1500 LTZ 4D 5 3/4'	KSEC	43380	32900	33900	34800	39100
1500 LTZ 4D 6 1/2'	KSEC	43680	32500	33500	34400	38600
1500 SLT 4D 5 3/4'	2VEC	44120	30500	31400	32400	36400
1500 SLT 4D 6 1/2'	2VEC	44420	30700	31600	32600	36600
1500 Z71 LTZ 4D 5'	KSEC	44160	33900	34900	35700	39900
1500 Z71 LTZ 4D 6'	KSEC	44460	33700	34700	35500	39600
1500 HighCountry 5'	KTEC	48475	34300	35400	35800	39800
1500 HighCountry 6'	KTEC	48775	34100	35200	35600	39600
2WD			(3600)	(3600)	(3965)	(3965)
V8, EcoTec3, FF, 6.2L	J		850	850	935	935
SIERRA DENALI CREW CAB 4WD—V8 Flex Fuel EcoTec3—Sch T1						
1500 4D 5 3/4'	2WEC	51060	38500	39700	41000	45900
1500 4D 6 1/2'	2WEC	51360	38300	39500	40700	45600
2WD	1		(1400)	(1400)	(1555)	(1555)
V8 EcoTec3 FF 6.2L	J		550	550	610	610
SILVERADO/SIERRA CREW CAB PICKUP—V8 Flex Fuel—Truck Equip Sch T1						
2500 HD Wrk Trk 6'	CVCG	34590	23000	23800	25000	28300
2500 HD LT/SLE 8'	CXCG	39050	27000	27900	28800	32200
2500 HD LTZ/SLT 8'	CYCG	44770	31800	32800	33600	37400
Tool Box			225	225	245	245
4WD	K		3600	3600	3825	3825
V8, Natural Gas, 6.0L	B		0	0	0	0
V8, Turbo Diesel, 6.6L	8		5500	5500	5845	5845
SIERRA CREW CAB PICKUP 4WD—V8 Turbo Diesel—Truck Equipment Sch T1						
2500 HD SLE 4D 6 1/2'	20C8	49810	35900	37000	38400	43300
2500 SLT 4D 6 1/2'	21C8	55420	41100	42400	43600	48900
2500 Denali 6'	25E8	55735	41900	43200	44600	50200
Tool Box			225	225	245	245
2WD	1		(3600)	(3600)	(3935)	(3935)
V8, Flex Fuel, 6.0 Liter	G		(5425)	(5425)	(5925)	(5925)
V8, Natural Gas, 6.0L	B		0	0	0	0
SILVERADO/SIERRA CREW CAB—V8 Turbo Diesel—Truck Equipment Sch T1						
2500 HD Wrk Trk 8'	CVC8	41980	28700	29700	31000	35100
2500 HD LTZ/SLT 6'	KYC8	54920	40600	41800	42700	47400
Tool Box			225	225	245	245
4WD	K		3600	3600	3945	3945
V8, Flex Fuel, 6.0 Liter	G		(5425)	(5425)	(5940)	(5940)
V8, Natural Gas, 6.0L	B		0	0	0	0
SILVERADO/SIERRA CREW CAB 4WD—V8 Turbo Diesel—Truck Equipment Sch T1						
2500 HD LT/SLE 6'	KXC8	49345	35400	36500	37400	41700
Tool Box			225	225	240	240
2WD	C		(3600)	(3600)	(3825)	(3825)
V8, Flex Fuel, 6.0 Liter	G		(5425)	(5425)	(5755)	(5755)
V8, Natural Gas, 6.0L	B		0	0	0	0

Body Type	VIN	List	Trade-In Good	Very Good	Pvt-Party Good	Retail Excellent

CHRYSLER

2000 CHRYSLER — 1C4-(J253)-Y-#

VOYAGER—V6—Truck Equipment Schedule T1
Minivan 4D	J253	20895	275	350	875	1450
SE Minivan 4D	J453	23840	275	350	875	1450
Grand Minivan 4D	J243	22545	350	425	950	1550
SE Grand Minivan 4D	J443	24835	350	425	950	1550
5-Passenger Seating			(200)	(200)	(265)	(265)
Second Sliding Door			50	50	60	60
4-Cyl, 2.4 Liter	B		(275)	(275)	(355)	(355)

TOWN & COUNTRY—V6—Truck Equipment Schedule T3
LX Minivan	P44R	26950	450	550	1075	1750
LXi Minivan	P54L	31530	575	675	1225	2000
Limited Minivan	P64L	34855	975	1125	1750	2825
Air Conditioning, Rear			100	100	135	135
AWD	T		250	250	335	335

2001 CHRYSLER — 1C(4or8)-(J24G)-1-#

VOYAGER—V6—Truck Equipment Schedule T1
Minivan	J24G	20770	375	475	1000	1575
LX Minivan	J54G	24165	375	475	1000	1575
5-Passenger Seating			(200)	(200)	(265)	(265)
4-Cyl, 2.4 Liter	B		(300)	(300)	(400)	(400)

TOWN & COUNTRY—V6—Truck Equipment Schedule T3
LX Minivan	P44S	26155	650	750	1300	2100
EX Minivan	P54L	26830	750	850	1425	2300
LXi Minivan	P64G	30705	900	1025	1625	2600
Limited Minivan	P64L	35490	1300	1475	2125	3400
Quad Seating			100	100	135	135
Air Conditioning, Rear			100	100	135	135
AWD	T		250	250	335	335

2002 CHRYSLER — 1C(4or8)-(J15B)-2-#

VOYAGER—4-Cyl.—Truck Equipment Schedule T1
eC Minivan	J15B	16995	325	400	900	1425
5-Passenger Seating			(250)	(250)	(335)	(335)

VOYAGER—V6—Truck Equipment Schedule T1
Minivan	J253	19995	475	550	1075	1675
LX Minivan	J453	24060	475	550	1075	1675
5-Passenger Seating			(250)	(250)	(335)	(335)
4-Cyl, 2.4 Liter	B		(375)	(375)	(500)	(500)

TOWN & COUNTRY—V6—Truck Equipment Schedule T3
eL Minivan	P343	24330	425	500	1025	1650
LX Minivan	P443	27065	875	1000	1575	2500
EX Minivan	P74L	26830	1100	1250	1825	2900
LXi Minivan	P543	30970	1150	1300	1900	3000
Limited Minivan	P64L	35990	1625	1825	2475	3900
Quad Seating			125	125	165	165
Air Conditioning, Rear			125	125	165	165
AWD	T		300	300	400	400

2003 CHRYSLER — 1C(4or8)-(J453)-3-#

VOYAGER—V6—Truck Equipment Schedule T1
LX Minivan	J453	24025	475	550	1250	2125
5-Passenger Seating			(275)	(275)	(365)	(365)
4-Cyl, 2.4 Liter	B		(450)	(450)	(600)	(600)

TOWN & COUNTRY—V6—Truck Equipment Schedule T3
eL Minivan	P343	24830	625	725	1450	2425
Minivan	P24R	25975	625	725	1450	2425
LX Minivan	P443	27010	1025	1175	1950	3225
EX Minivan	P74L	27235	1400	1575	2425	3975
LXi Minivan	P54L	34080	1425	1625	2550	4175
Limited Minivan	P64L	36535	2050	2300	3400	5425
Quad Seating			150	150	200	200
Air Conditioning, Rear			150	150	200	200
AWD	T		350	350	465	465

2004 CHRYSLER

Body Type	VIN	List	Trade-In Good	Very Good	Pvt-Party Good	Retail Excellent

2004 CHRYSLER — (1or2)C(4or8)-(P45R)-4-#

TOWN & COUNTRY—V6—Truck Equipment Schedule T3

Minivan	P45R	23520	975	1125	1725	2750
LX Minivan	P44R	27490	1525	1725	2575	4050
EX Minivan	P74L	30110	2050	2300	3250	5075
Touring Minivan	P54L	33245	2150	2425	3400	5275
Limited Minivan	P64L	38380	2850	3200	4325	6625
Quad Seating			150	150	200	200
Air Conditioning, Rear			175	175	235	235
AWD	T		400	400	535	535

PACIFICA—V6—Truck Equipment Schedule T3

Minivan	M684	30410	1625	1825	2725	4150
AWD			450	450	595	595

2005 CHRYSLER — (1or2)C(4or8)-(P45R)-4-#

TOWN & COUNTRY—V6—Truck Equipment Schedule T3

Minivan	P45R	21185	1050	1200	1850	2925
LX Minivan	P44R	25640	1650	1850	2750	4300
Touring Minivan	P54L	27940	2625	2950	3850	5750
Limited Minivan	P64L	35940	3325	3700	4700	6925
Quad Seating			150	150	200	200
Air Conditioning, Rear			200	200	265	265
Signature Series			275	275	370	370

PACIFICA—V6—Truck Equipment Schedule T3

Minivan	M48L	24995	1775	2000	2825	4200
Touring Minivan	M684	28525	2575	2875	3775	5475
AWD	F		475	475	630	630

PACIFICA AWD—V6—Truck Equipment Schedule T3

Limited Minivan	F784	36995	3825	4225	5275	7350

2006 CHRYSLER — (1or2)C(4or8)-(P45R)-6-#

TOWN & COUNTRY—V6—Truck Equipment Schedule T3

Minivan	P45R	21735	1525	1725	2400	3625
LX Minivan	P44R	26100	2325	2600	3475	5100
Touring Minivan	P54L	28590	3350	3700	4650	6675
Limited Minivan	P64L	36465	4475	4900	5975	8425
Quad Seating			150	150	200	200
Signature Series			300	300	400	400

PACIFICA—V6—Truck Equipment Schedule T3

Minivan	M484	25895	2350	2650	3700	5400
Touring Minivan	M684	29095	3325	3675	4700	6625
Signature Series			275	275	370	370
AWD	F		500	500	665	665

PACIFICA AWD—V6—Truck Equipment Schedule T3

Limited Minivan	M784	37415	4600	5025	6150	8500
FWD			(525)	(525)	(695)	(695)

2007 CHRYSLER — (1or2)C(4or8)-(W58N)-7-#

ASPEN 4WD—V8—Truck Equipment Schedule T1

Limited Spt Util 4D	W58N	34265	8150	8725	10250	13550
2WD	X		(1150)	(1150)	(1520)	(1520)
V8, HEMI, 5.7 Liter	2		625	625	835	835

TOWN & COUNTRY—V6—Truck Equipment Schedule T3

Minivan	P45R	21985	1875	2100	2900	4175
LX Minivan	P44R	26350	2725	3050	3850	5425
Touring Minivan	P54L	28790	4250	4650	5575	7650
Limited Minivan	P64L	36860	6125	6625	7950	10750
Quad Seating			150	150	200	200
Signature Series			350	350	465	465

PACIFICA—V6—Truck Equipment Schedule T3

Minivan	M48L	24890	3000	3325	4450	6325
Touring Minivan	M68X	27980	4000	4375	5575	7775
Signature Series			300	300	400	400
AWD	F		525	525	700	700

PACIFICA AWD—V6—Truck Equipment Schedule T3

Limited Minivan	M78X	36205	5350	5800	7325	10000
FWD			(600)	(600)	(795)	(795)

TRUCKS & VANS

0415   **SEE BACK PAGES FOR TRUCK EQUIPMENT**   401

TRUCKS & VANS

Body Type	VIN	List	Trade-In Good	Very Good	Pvt-Party Good	Retail Excellent

2008 CHRYSLER — (1or2)C(4or8)–(W58N)–8–#

ASPEN 4WD—V8—Truck Equipment Schedule T1
Limited Spt Util 4D	W58N	35625	9375	9950	11150	13950
2WD	X	......	(1225)	(1225)	(1595)	(1595)
V8, HEMI, 5.7 Liter	2	......	675	675	865	865

TOWN & COUNTRY—V6—Truck Equipment Schedule T3
LX Minivan	R44H	23190	5025	5400	6325	8425
Touring Minivan	R54P	28430	6800	7275	8600	11300
Limited Minivan	R64X	36400	9150	9725	11200	14600
Quad Seating		......	150	150	200	200

PACIFICA—V6—Truck Equipment Schedule T3
Minivan	M48L	27310	4175	4525	5575	7500
Touring Minivan	M68X	30435	5100	5500	6850	9125
Signature Series		......	350	350	465	465
AWD	F	......	550	550	735	735

PACIFICA AWD—V6—Truck Equipment Schedule T3
| Limited Minivan | M78X | 36925 | 7000 | 7475 | 8925 | 11650 |
| FWD | | ...... | (675) | (675) | (900) | (900) |

2009 CHRYSLER — (1or2)C(4or8)–(W58P)–9–#

ASPEN 4WD—V8—Truck Equipment Schedule T1
Limited Sport Util	W58P	37415	11100	11700	13150	16250
2WD	X	......	(1300)	(1300)	(1695)	(1695)
V8, HEMI, 5.7 Liter	T	......	700	700	910	910

ASPEN 4WD—V8 Hybrid—Truck Equipment Schedule T1
| Limited Sport Util | W18T | 45570 | 14100 | 14800 | 16500 | 20400 |

TOWN & COUNTRY—V6—Truck Equipment Schedule T3
LX Minivan	R44E	26500	6275	6675	7900	10250
Touring Minivan	R541	29665	8325	8825	10250	13150
Limited Minivan	R64X	37300	11550	12150	13950	17700
Quad Seating		......	200	200	265	265

2010 CHRYSLER — (1or2)C(4or8)–(R4DE)–A–#

TOWN & COUNTRY—V6—Truck Equipment Schedule T3
LX Minivan	R4DE	25995	7550	7975	9350	11850
Touring Minivan	R5D1	29245	9100	9575	11100	13950
Limited Minivan	R6DX	35880	13150	13750	15750	19650
Quad Seating		......	250	250	330	330

2011 CHRYSLER — (1or2)C(4or8)–(R5DG)–B–#

TOWN & COUNTRY—V6—Truck Equipment Schedule T3
Touring Minivan	R5DG	30995	11600	12100	13600	16500
Touring-L Minivan	R8DG	32995	13950	14550	16250	19750
Limited Minivan	R6DG	39495	17000	17700	19700	23900

2012 CHRYSLER — (1,2or3)C(4or6)–(C1BG)–C–#

TOWN & COUNTRY—V6—Truck Equipment Schedule T3
Touring Minivan	C1BG	30830	13200	13750	15150	17900
Touring-L Minivan	C1CG	33330	16000	16600	18100	21400
Limited Minivan	C1CG	39495	19150	19850	21600	25500

2013 CHRYSLER — (1,2or3)C(4or6)–(C1BG)–D–#

TOWN & COUNTRY—V6—Truck Equipment Schedule T3
Touring Minivan	C1BG	30990	14750	15300	16500	19150
Touring-L Minivan	C1CG	34290	17500	18100	19450	22600
S Minivan 4D	C1HG	32990	17300	17900	19150	22200
Limited Minivan	C1GG	40990	20900	21600	23000	26600

2014 CHRYSLER — (1,2or3)C(4or6)–(C1BG)–E–#

TOWN & COUNTRY—V6—Truck Equipment Schedule T3
Touring Minivan	C1BG	31760	17100	17700	18800	21500
Touring-L Minivan	C1CG	34990	20300	21000	22200	25400
Touring-L 30th Anv	C1CG	36690				
S Minivan 4D	C1HG	33190	19700	20300	21400	24400
Limited Minivan	C1GG	42290	23500	24200	25500	29100

Body Type	VIN	List	Trade-In Good	Trade-In Very Good	Pvt-Party Good	Retail Excellent

TRUCKS & VANS

DODGE/PLYMOUTH

2000 DODGE/PLYM–(1,2,3or4)B4–(S28N)–Y–#

DURANGO 4WD—V8—Truck Equipment Schedule T1

Body Type	VIN	List	Good	Very Good	Good	Excellent
SLT Sport Utility 4D	S28N	29060	525	650	1575	2775
R/T Sport Utility 4D	S28Z	33810	825	975	2050	3600
Third Row Seat			200	200	265	265
2WD	R		(550)	(550)	(750)	(750)
V8, 5.9 Liter (ex R/T)	Z		100	100	150	150

CARAVAN/VOYAGER—V6—Truck Equipment Schedule T1

Minivan 4D	P243	21905	400	475	1100	1825
SE Minivan 4D	P443	23675	650	750	1400	2325
Grand Minivan 4D	P243	22380	600	700	1325	2200
SE Grand Minivan	P443	24845	350	425	1025	1725
LE Grand Minivan	P54R	27785	950	1075	1800	2975
5-Passenger Seating			(200)	(200)	(265)	(265)
Second Sliding Door			50	50	60	60
AWD	T		250	250	335	335
4-Cyl, 2.4 Liter	B		(275)	(275)	(355)	(355)
V6, 3.8 Liter	L		50	50	65	65

CARAVAN—V6—Truck Equipment Schedule T1

ES Grand Minivan	P54L	29995	1350	1525	2300	3775
Second Sliding Door			50	50	60	60
AWD	T		250	250	335	335

GRAND CARAVAN AWD—V6—Truck Equipment Schedule T1

Sport Minivan 4D	T44L	28670	1025	1175	1925	3175
5-Passenger Seating			(200)	(200)	(265)	(265)

RAM WAGON—V8—Truck Equipment Schedule T1

1500 Passenger Van	B15Y	22245	1300	1475	2150	3625
2500 Passenger Van	B25Y	23670	1425	1625	2325	3925
3500 Maxi Passenger	B35Y	26675	1650	1875	2650	4450
V6, 3.9 Liter	X		50	50	65	65
V8, 5.9 Liter	Z		(200)	(200)	(265)	(265)

RAM VAN—V6—Truck Equipment Schedule T1

1500 Cargo Van	B11X	19575	900	1025	1625	2750
Maxi-Van			50	50	65	65
V8, 5.2 Liter	T,Y		100	100	135	135
V8, 5.9 Liter	Z		200	200	265	265

RAM VAN—V8—Truck Equipment Schedule T1

2500 Cargo Van	B21Y	21075	1200	1350	2050	3475
3500 Cargo Van	B31Y	23260	1500	1700	2450	4175
Maxi-Van			50	50	65	65
V8, 5.9 Liter	Z		50	50	65	65

DAKOTA PICKUP—4-Cyl.—Truck Equipment Schedule T1

Short Bed	L26P	15850	350	425	775	1275
R/T Short Bed	L26Z	20090	600	675	1300	2250
4WD	G		400	400	535	535
V6, 3.9 Liter	X		125	125	165	165
V8, 4.7 Liter	Y		150	150	200	200
V8, 5.9 Liter (ex R/T)	Z		250	250	340	340

DAKOTA PICKUP—V6—Truck Equipment Schedule T1

Club Cab	L22X	19045	1025	1125	1850	3150
R/T Club Cab	L22Z	22340	1325	1475	2250	3850
Quad Cab	L2AX	20290	850	950	1575	2675
4WD	G		400	400	535	535
4-Cyl, 2.5 Liter	P		(100)	(100)	(135)	(135)
V8, 4.7 Liter	N		100	100	135	135
V8, 5.9 Liter (ex R/T)	Z		200	200	265	265

RAM REGULAR CAB PICKUP—V8—Truck Equipment Schedule T1

1500 Short Bed	C16Y	16695	950	1075	1625	2700
1500 Long Bed	C16Y	19980	850	975	1525	2525
2500 Long Bed	C26Z	22570	975	1100	1650	2700
3500 Long Bed	C36Z	24330	1200	1350	1925	3150
Work Special			(250)	(250)	(335)	(335)
4WD	F		650	650	865	865
V6, 3.9 Liter	X		(350)	(350)	(465)	(465)
6-Cyl, Turbo Diesel	6		1475	1475	1965	1965
V8, 5.9 Liter	Z,5		75	75	100	100
V10, 8.0 Liter	W		100	100	135	135

TRUCKS & VANS

Body Type	VIN	List	Trade-In Good	Trade-In Very Good	Pvt-Party Good	Retail Excellent
RAM CLUB CAB PICKUP—V8—Truck Equipment Schedule T1						
1500 Short Bed	C12Y	21890	1475	1650	2375	3950
4WD	F		650	650	865	865
V8, 5.9 Liter	Z		75	75	100	100
RAM QUAD CAB PICKUP—V8—Truck Equipment Schedule T1						
1500 Short Bed	C13Y	22750	1650	1850	2700	4425
1500 Long Bed	C13Y	23030	1550	1725	2475	4100
4WD	F		650	650	865	865
V8, 5.9 Liter	Z		75	75	100	100
RAM QUAD CAB PICKUP 4WD—6-Cyl. Turbo Diesel—Truck Equip Sch T1						
2500 Short Bed	F236	31500	6350	6925	8850	13150
2500 Long Bed	F236	31690	6200	6775	8650	12850
3500 Long Bed	F336	34260	6475	7050	9000	13350
2WD	C		(775)	(775)	(1040)	(1040)
V8, 5.9 Liter	Z,5		(1550)	(1550)	(2070)	(2070)
V10, 8.0 Liter	W		100	100	135	135

2001 DODGE—(1or2)B(4,7or8)—(S28N)—1—#

Body Type	VIN	List	Trade-In Good	Trade-In Very Good	Pvt-Party Good	Retail Excellent
DURANGO 4WD—V8—Truck Equipment Schedule T1						
SLT Sport Utility 4D	S28N	30740	775	925	1800	3025
R/T Sport Utility 4D	S28Z	30990	1300	1500	2500	4200
Third Row Seat			200	200	265	265
2WD	R		(650)	(650)	(860)	(860)
V8, 5.9 Liter (ex R/T)	Z		125	125	165	165
CARAVAN—V6—Truck Equipment Schedule T1						
SE Minivan 4D	P44K	19800	675	775	1475	2475
Sport Minivan 4D	P64K	24165	750	875	1600	2650
SE Grand Minivan	P44K	22440	450	550	1200	2000
Sport Grand 4D	P64K	24915	950	1100	1850	3075
5-Passenger Seating			(200)	(200)	(265)	(265)
AWD	T		250	250	335	335
4-Cyl, 2.4 Liter	B		(300)	(300)	(400)	(400)
V6, 3.8 Liter	L		275	275	360	360
CARAVAN—V6—Truck Equipment Schedule T1						
EX Grand Minivan	P44L	26725	1075	1225	2025	3350
ES Grand Minivan	P54L	29750	1550	1750	2675	4350
5-Passenger Seating			(200)	(200)	(265)	(265)
AWD	T		250	250	335	335
RAM WAGON—V8—Truck Equipment Schedule T1						
1500 Passenger Van	B15Y	22615	1675	1875	2600	4325
2500 Passenger Van	B25Y	24040	1750	1975	2825	4650
3500 Maxi Passenger	B35Y	27055	2000	2250	3175	5200
V6, 3.9 Liter	X		(200)	(200)	(265)	(265)
V8, 5.9 Liter	Z		50	50	65	65
RAM VAN—V6—Truck Equipment Schedule T1						
1500 Cargo Van	B11X	19800	1175	1325	1875	3100
2500 Cargo Van	B21X	21390	1475	1675	2275	3750
Maxi-Van			50	50	65	65
V8, 5.2 Liter	Y		100	100	135	135
V8, 5.9 Liter	Z		200	200	265	265
RAM VAN—V8—Truck Equipment Schedule T1						
3500 Cargo Van	B31Y	23575	1725	1950	2625	4300
Maxi-Van			50	50	65	65
V8, 5.9 Liter	Z		50	50	65	65
DAKOTA PICKUP—4-Cyl.—Truck Equipment Schedule T1						
Short Bed	L26Y	16255	400	450	850	1400
R/T Short Bed	L26Z	20505	625	700	1300	2225
4WD	G		400	400	535	535
V6, 3.9 Liter	X		125	125	165	165
V8, 4.7 Liter	N		150	150	200	200
V8, 5.9 Liter (ex R/T)	Z		275	275	380	380
DAKOTA PICKUP—V6—Truck Equipment Schedule T1						
Club Cab	L22X	19580	1175	1300	2000	3375
R/T Club Cab	L22Z	22885	1500	1675	2400	4025
Quad Cab	L23X	21950	1275	1425	2075	3450
4WD	G		400	400	535	535
4-Cyl, 2.5 Liter	P		(125)	(125)	(165)	(165)
V8, 4.7 Liter	N		100	100	135	135
V8, 5.9 Liter	Z		225	225	300	300
RAM REGULAR CAB PICKUP—V8—Truck Equipment Schedule T1						
1500 Short Bed	C16Y	20145	1100	1225	1825	3025
1500 Long Bed	C16Y	20430	975	1100	1625	2675
2500 Long Bed	C26Z	23475	1175	1325	1850	3025

Body	Type	VIN	List	Trade-In Good	Very Good	Pvt-Party Good	Retail Excellent
3500 Long Bed		C36Z	25360	**1275**	**1450**	**2025**	**3300**
Work Special			....	(250)	(250)	(335)	(335)
4WD		F	....	750	750	1000	1000
V6, 3.9 Liter		X	....	(350)	(350)	(465)	(465)
6-Cyl, Turbo Diesel		6	....	1650	1650	2200	2200
6-Cyl, HO Turbo Dsl		7	....	3150	3150	4195	4195
V8, 5.9 Liter (1500)		5	....	75	75	100	100
V10, 8.0 Liter		W	....	100	100	135	135
RAM CLUB CAB PICKUP—V8—Truck Equipment Schedule T1							
1500 Short Bed		C12Y	21465	**1750**	**1975**	**2800**	**4525**
4WD		F	....	750	750	1000	1000
V8, 5.9 Liter		5	....	75	75	100	100
RAM QUAD CAB PICKUP—V8—Truck Equipment Schedule T1							
1500 Short Bed		C13Y	23375	**2025**	**2275**	**3150**	**5050**
1500 Long Bed		C13Y	23655	**1825**	**2050**	**2900**	**4675**
4WD		F	....	750	750	1000	1000
V8, 5.9 Liter		5	....	75	75	100	100
RAM QUAD CAB PICKUP 4WD—6-Cyl. Turbo Diesel—Truck Equip Sch T1							
2500 Short Bed		F236	33290	**7800**	**8475**	**10660**	**15400**
2500 Long Bed		F236	32580	**7650**	**8325**	**10400**	**15150**
3500 Long Bed		C32Z	35080	**7850**	**8525**	**10650**	**15500**
2WD		C	....	(925)	(925)	(1225)	(1225)
6-Cyl, HO Turbo Dsl		7	....	450	450	610	610
V8, 5.9 Liter		Z	....	(1850)	(1850)	(2460)	(2460)
V10, 8.0 Liter		W	....	100	100	135	135

2002 DODGE — 1B(4,7or8)-(S38N)-2-#

Body	Type	VIN	List	Trade-In Good	Very Good	Pvt-Party Good	Retail Excellent
DURANGO 4WD—V8—Truck Equipment Schedule T1							
Sport Utility 4D		S38N	27595	**1050**	**1225**	**2200**	**3675**
R/T Sport Utility 4D		S78Z	37070	**1675**	**1925**	**3200**	**5250**
Third Row Seat			....	250	250	335	335
2WD		R	....	(725)	(725)	(970)	(970)
V8, 5.9 Liter (ex R/T)		Z	....	125	125	180	180
CARAVAN—4-Cyl.—Truck Equipment Schedule T1							
eC Minivan 4D		P15B	16995	**300**	**375**	**950**	**1600**
5-Passenger Seating			....	(250)	(250)	(335)	(335)
CARAVAN—V6—Truck Equipment Schedule T1							
SE Minivan 4D		P44R	19795	**725**	**850**	**1600**	**2650**
Sport Minivan 4D		P64G	24060	**850**	**1000**	**1750**	**2900**
SE Grand Minivan		P44G	22440	**650**	**775**	**1500**	**2475**
eL Grand Minivan		P34R	24175	**875**	**1025**	**1775**	**2950**
Sport Grand 4D		P64G	24930	**1150**	**1325**	**2150**	**3525**
5-Passenger Seating			....	(250)	(250)	(335)	(335)
AWD		T	....	300	300	400	400
V6, 3.8 Liter		L	....	300	300	410	410
CARAVAN—V6—Truck Equipment Schedule T1							
EX Grand Minivan		P44L	26725	**1275**	**1450**	**2300**	**3800**
ES Grand Minivan		P54L	30135	**1825**	**2075**	**3175**	**5100**
5-Passenger Seating			....	(250)	(250)	(335)	(335)
AWD		T	....	300	300	400	400
RAM WAGON—V8—Truck Equipment Schedule T1							
1500 Passenger Van		B15Y	22035	**2050**	**2300**	**3050**	**4825**
2500 Passenger Van		B25Y	24050	**2175**	**2450**	**3225**	**5100**
3500 Maxi Passenger		B35Y	27055	**2475**	**2775**	**3625**	**5700**
V6, 3.9 Liter		X	....	(250)	(250)	(335)	(335)
V8, 5.9 Liter		5	....	50	50	65	65
RAM VAN—V6—Truck Equipment Schedule T1							
1500 Cargo Van		B11X	20050	**1375**	**1550**	**2275**	**3850**
2500 Cargo Van		B21X	21595	**1675**	**1875**	**2825**	**4725**
Maxi-Van			....	75	75	100	100
V8, 5.2 Liter		Y	....	125	125	165	165
V8, 5.9 Liter		5	....	250	250	335	335
RAM VAN—V8—Truck Equipment Schedule T1							
3500 Cargo Van		B31Y	23780	**1900**	**2125**	**3150**	**5225**
Maxi-Van			....	75	75	100	100
V8, 5.9 Liter		Z	....	50	50	65	65
DAKOTA PICKUP—4-Cyl.—Truck Equipment Schedule T1							
Short Bed		L26T	16370	**425**	**500**	**925**	**1525**
R/T Short Bed		L26Z	21290	**1075**	**1200**	**1700**	**2725**
4WD		G	....	550	550	735	735
V6, 3.9 Liter		X	....	150	150	200	200
V8, 4.7 Liter		N	....	200	200	265	265
V8, 5.9 Liter (ex R/T)		Z	....	325	325	425	425

TRUCKS & VANS

Body Type	VIN	List	Trade-In Good	Very Good	Pvt-Party Good	Retail Excellent
DAKOTA PICKUP—V6—Truck Equipment Schedule T1						
Club Cab	L22X	19695	1700	1875	2425	3850
R/T Club Cab	L22Z	23585	2125	2375	3100	4825
Quad Cab	L23X	21985	1850	2075	2750	4300
4WD	G		550	550	735	735
4-Cyl, 2.5 Liter	P		(150)	(150)	(200)	(200)
V8, 4.7 Liter	N		125	125	165	165
V8, 5.9 Liter (ex R/T)	Z		250	250	335	335
RAM REGULAR CAB PICKUP—V6—Truck Equipment Schedule T1						
1500 Short Bed	C16Y	19620	1425	1575	2025	3150
1500 Long Bed	C16Y	19905	1175	1300	1725	2725
2500 HD Long Bed	C26Z	23490	1225	1375	1875	3000
3500 Long Bed	C36Z	25375	1375	1525	2125	3475
4WD	F		900	900	1200	1200
V6, 3.7 Liter	K		(375)	(375)	(500)	(500)
6-Cyl, Turbo Diesel	6		1875	1875	2500	2500
6-Cyl, HO Turbo Dsl	7		3325	3325	4445	4445
V8, 5.9 Liter (1500)	Z		125	125	165	165
V10, 8.0 Liter	W		125	125	165	165
RAM QUAD CAB PICKUP—V8—Truck Equipment Schedule T1						
1500 Short Bed	C13Y	23840	2650	2950	3650	5450
1500 Long Bed	C13Y	24120	2450	2750	3400	5100
4WD	F		900	900	1200	1200
V8, 5.9 Liter	Z		125	125	165	165
RAM QUAD CAB PICKUP 4WD—6-Cyl. Turbo Diesel—Truck Equip Sch T1						
2500 Short Bed	F236	32595	9275	10050	12100	17200
2500 Long Bed	F236	32785	9025	9775	11750	16700
3500 Long Bed	C33Z	35470	9375	10150	12250	17400
2WD	C		(1050)	(1050)	(1405)	(1405)
6-Cyl, HO Turbo Dsl	7		525	525	700	700
V8, 5.9 Liter	Z		(2125)	(2125)	(2845)	(2845)
V10, 8.0 Liter	W		125	125	165	165

2003 DODGE — (1,2or3)D(3,4,7or8)-(S38N)-3-#

Body Type	VIN	List	Trade-In Good	Very Good	Pvt-Party Good	Retail Excellent
DURANGO 4WD—V8—Truck Equipment Schedule T1						
Sport SUV 4D	S38N	29640	1300	1500	2575	4325
SXT Sport Utility 4D	S38N	30545	1325	1525	2600	4375
SLT Sport Utility 4D	S48N	33565	1425	1650	2850	4750
R/T Sport Utility 4D	S78Z	39240	2250	2550	4000	6475
Third Row Seat			275	275	365	365
2WD	R		(800)	(800)	(1080)	(1080)
V8, 5.9 Liter (ex R/T)	Z		150	150	200	200
CARAVAN—V6—Truck Equipment Schedule T2						
Cargo Minivan	P253	21965	550	650	1325	2200
Grand Cargo Minivan	P253	22850	625	725	1425	2350
CARAVAN—V6—Truck Equipment Schedule T1						
SE Minivan 4D	P25R	21440	950	1100	1850	3050
Sport Minivan 4D	P453	25110	1250	1425	2250	3700
SE Grand Minivan	P24R	22890	1050	1200	2000	3275
eL Grand Minivan	P343	24425	1350	1525	2375	3900
Sport Grand 4D	P44R	28040	1675	1900	2950	4750
5-Passenger Seating			(275)	(275)	(365)	(365)
AWD	T		350	350	465	465
4-Cyl, 2.4 Liter	B		(450)	(450)	(600)	(600)
V6, 3.8 Liter	L		350	350	455	455
CARAVAN—V6—Truck Equipment Schedule T1						
EX Grand Minivan	P74L	26400	1625	1850	2875	4650
ES Grand Minivan	P54L	33335	2300	2575	3850	6125
5-Passenger Seating			(275)	(275)	(365)	(365)
AWD	T		350	350	465	465
RAM VAN—V6—Truck Equipment Schedule T1						
1500 Cargo Van	B11X	20540	1975	2200	3150	5150
1500 Ext Cargo	B11X	21175	2050	2300	3250	5325
2500 Cargo Van	B21X	21640	2075	2325	3300	5375
Maxi-Van			100	100	135	135
V8, 5.2 Liter	Y		150	150	200	200
V8, 5.9 Liter	Z		275	275	365	365
RAM VAN—V8—Truck Equipment Schedule T1						
3500 Cargo Van	B31Y	24415	2375	2650	3775	6125
Maxi-Van			100	100	135	135
V8, 5.9 Liter	Z		50	50	65	65
DAKOTA REGULAR CAB PICKUP—V6—Truck Equipment Sch T1						
2D 6 1/2'	L16X	17680	600	700	1175	1950

406   DEDUCT FOR RECONDITIONING

0415

TRUCKS & VANS

Body Type	VIN	List	Trade-In Good	Very Good	Pvt-Party Good	Retail Excellent
SXT 2D 6 1/2'	L16X	18420	750	850	1350	2200
Sport 2D 6 1/2'	L36X	19000	700	800	1300	2125
SLT 2D 6 1/2'	L46X	19000	800	900	1400	2300
4WD	G		650	650	865	865
V8, 4.7 Liter	N		150	150	200	200
DAKOTA REGULAR CAB PICKUP—V6—Truck Equipment Sch T1						
R/T 2D 6 1/2'	L76Z	22800	1575	1750	2375	3750
DAKOTA CLUB CAB PICKUP—V6—Truck Equipment Schedule T1						
2D 6 1/2'	V12X	19375	1625	1800	2450	3850
SXT 2D 6 1/2'	L12X	20825	1825	2025	2675	4175
Sport 2D 6 1/2'	L32X	20840	1975	2175	2875	4450
SLT 2D 6 1/2'	L42X	20840	2075	2300	3000	4625
4WD	G		650	650	865	865
V8, 4.7 Liter	N		150	150	200	200
V8, 5.9 Liter	Z		275	275	365	365
DAKOTA CLUB CAB PICKUP—V6—Truck Equipment Schedule T1						
R/T 2D 6 1/2'	L72Z	25100	2750	3050	3825	5800
DAKOTA QUAD CAB PICKUP—V6—Truck Equipment Schedule T1						
Sport 4D 5'	L38X	22550	2025	2250	3000	4675
SXT 4D 5'	L18X	23415	2350	2600	3350	5100
SLT 4D 5'	L48X	23025	2450	2700	3475	5275
4WD	G		650	650	865	865
V8, 4.7 Liter	N		150	150	200	200
V8, 5.9 Liter	Z		275	275	365	365
RAM REGULAR CAB PICKUP—V6—Truck Equipment Schedule T1						
1500 ST 2D 6 1/4'	A16X	19635	1575	1750	2200	3400
4WD	U		1100	1100	1465	1465
V8, 4.7 Liter	N		350	350	455	455
V8, 5.9 Liter	Z		475	475	625	625
V8, HEMI, 5.7 Liter	D		950	950	1265	1265
RAM REGULAR CAB PICKUP—V8—Truck Equipment Schedule T1						
1500 ST 2D 8'	A16N	20510	1475	1650	2100	3225
1500 SLT 2D 6 1/4'	A16N	23525	2725	3050	3550	5150
1500 SLT 2D 8'	A16N	23810	2425	2700	3200	4650
1500 Laramie 6 1/4'	U16N	30590	3500	3875	4650	6775
1500 Laramie 2D 8'	A16N	27965	1825	2050	2625	4000
4WD	U		1100	1100	1465	1465
V6, 3.7 Liter	K		(400)	(400)	(535)	(535)
V8, 5.9 Liter	Z		150	150	190	190
V8, HEMI, 5.7 Liter	D		600	600	785	785
RAM REGULAR CAB PICKUP 4WD—V8 HEMI—Truck Equipment Sch T1						
2500 ST 2D 8'	U26D	27460	5625	6150	7375	10400
2500 SLT 2D 8'	U26D	29115	5950	6500	7750	10900
2500 Laramie 2D 8'	U26D	33350	6650	7225	8575	12000
2WD	A		(1200)	(1200)	(1585)	(1585)
V10, 8.0 Liter	W		150	150	200	200
6-Cyl, Turbo Diesel	6		2250	2250	3000	3000
6-Cyl, HO Turbo Dsl	C		3525	3525	4700	4700
RAM REGULAR CAB PICKUP—V8 HEMI—Truck Equipment Schedule T1						
3500 ST 2D 8'	A36D	26140	4575	5025	5925	8425
4WD	U		1100	1100	1465	1465
6-Cyl, Turbo Diesel	6		2250	2250	3000	3000
6-Cyl, HO Turbo Dsl	C		3525	3525	4700	4700
V10, 8.0 Liter	W		150	150	200	200
RAM REGULAR CAB PICKUP—6-Cyl. Turbo Diesel—Truck Sch T1						
3500 ST 2D 8'	A466	27920	7850	8500	10050	14000
3500 Laramie 2D 8'	A466	31450	7850	8500	10050	14000
4WD	U		1100	1100	1465	1465
V8, HEMI, 5.7 Liter	D		(2425)	(2425)	(3235)	(3235)
6-Cyl, HO Turbo Dsl	C		600	600	795	795
V10, 8.0 Liter	W		(2275)	(2275)	(3015)	(3015)
RAM QUAD CAB PICKUP—V8—Truck Equipment Schedule T1						
1500 ST 4D 6 1/4'	A18N	26920	3075	3425	4125	6075
1500 ST 4D 8'	A18N	27275	2800	3125	3800	5625
1500 SLT 4D 6 1/4'	A18N	27325	3475	3850	4775	6950
1500 SLT 4D 8'	A18N	27605	3325	3675	4450	6500
1500 Laramie 4D 8'	A18N	31970	3750	4150	5100	7400
4WD	U		1100	1100	1465	1465
V6, 3.7 Liter	K		(400)	(400)	(535)	(535)
V8, HEMI, 5.7 Liter	D		600	600	785	785
V8, 5.9 Liter	Z		150	150	190	190
RAM QUAD CAB PICKUP 4WD—V8—Truck Equipment Schedule T1						
1500 Laramie 6 1/4'	U18N	34435	5250	5725	7075	10150

Body Type	VIN	List	Trade-In Good	Trade-In Very Good	Pvt-Party Good	Retail Excellent
2WD	A		(1200)	(1200)	(1585)	(1585)
V6, 3.7 Liter	K		(400)	(400)	(535)	(535)
V8, HEMI, 5.7 Liter	D		600	600	785	785
V8, 5.9 Liter	Z		150	150	190	190
RAM QUAD CAB PICKUP 4WD—V8 HEMI—Truck Equipment Sch T1						
2500 ST 4D 6 1/4'	U28D	29715	7050	7650	9025	12650
2500 Laramie 6 1/4'	U28D	36280	8000	8650	10200	14250
3500 ST 4D 8'	U48D	29315	6975	7575	8950	12550
2WD	A		(1200)	(1200)	(1585)	(1585)
6-Cyl, Turbo Diesel	6		2250	2250	3000	3000
6-Cyl, HO Turbo Dsl	C		3525	3525	4700	4700
RAM QUAD CAB PICKUP 4WD—6-Cyl. Turbo Diesel—Truck Equip Sch T1						
3500 SLT 4D 8'	U486	37255	10500	11300	13200	18300
3500 Laramie 4D 8'	U486	41990	10100	10850	12700	17650
2WD	A		(1200)	(1200)	(1585)	(1585)
6-Cyl, HO Turbo Dsl	C		600	600	795	795
V8, HEMI, 5.7 Liter	D		(2425)	(2425)	(3235)	(3235)
V10, 8.0 Liter	W		(2275)	(2275)	(3015)	(3015)
RAM QUAD CAB PICKUP 4WD—V8 Turbo Diesel—Truck Equipment Sch T1						
2500 SLT 4D 6 1/4'	U286	35195	10500	11350	13250	18400
2WD	A		(1200)	(1200)	(1585)	(1585)
V8, HEMI, 5.7 Liter	D		(2425)	(2425)	(3235)	(3235)
V10, 8.0 Liter	W		(2275)	(2275)	(3015)	(3015)
6-Cyl, HO Turbo Dsl	C		600	600	795	795
RAM QUAD CAB PICKUP—V8 HEMI—Truck Equipment Schedule T1						
2500 ST 4D 8'	A28D	26790	5375	5875	7100	10000
2500 SLT 4D 8'	A28D	29345	5850	6375	7650	10750
2500 Laramie 4D 8'	A28D	33405	6575	7150	8500	11900
4WD	U		1100	1100	1465	1465
6-Cyl, Turbo Diesel	6		2250	2250	3000	3000
6-Cyl, HO Turbo Dsl	C		3525	3525	4700	4700
V10, 8.0 Liter	W		150	150	200	200
RAM QUAD CAB PICKUP—6-Cyl. Turbo Diesel—Truck Schedule T1						
3500 ST 4D 6 1/2'	A386	32405	9275	10000	11800	16400
3500 SLT 4D 6 1/2'	A386	34305	10100	10850	12700	17650
3500 Laramie 4D 6 1/2'	A386	38365	10600	11400	13300	18450
4WD	U		1100	1100	1465	1465
6-Cyl, HO Turbo Dsl	C		250	250	335	335

2004 DODGE—(1,3orW)D(2,3,4,5,7or8)—(B38N)—4—#

Body Type	VIN	List	Trade-In Good	Trade-In Very Good	Pvt-Party Good	Retail Excellent
DURANGO 4WD—V8—Truck Equipment Schedule T1						
ST Sport Utility 4D	B38N	29745	2725	3100	4075	6100
SLT Sport Utility 4D	B48N	32160	3075	3475	4525	6725
Limited Sport Utility	B58N	35470	3000	3275	4175	5825
Third Row Seat			300	300	400	400
2WD	D		(900)	(900)	(1190)	(1190)
V6, 3.7 Liter	K		(350)	(350)	(465)	(465)
V8, 5.7 Liter	D		525	525	695	695
CARAVAN CARGO—V6—Truck Equipment Schedule T2						
Minivan	P21R	22585	850	975	1725	2850
Grand Minivan	P23R	23455	875	1000	1775	2950
CARAVAN PASSENGER—4-Cyl.—Truck Equipment Schedule T1						
SE Minivan 4D	P25B	21795	1125	1275	2125	3475
5-Passenger Seating			(300)	(300)	(400)	(400)
CARAVAN PASSENGER—V6—Truck Equipment Schedule T1						
SXT Minivan 4D	P45R	24850	1400	1575	2475	4075
SE Grand Minivan	P24R	24975	1400	1575	2475	4075
5-Passenger Seating			(300)	(300)	(400)	(400)
CARAVAN PASSENGER—V6—Truck Equipment Schedule T1						
EX Grand Minivan	P74L	27225	2050	2300	3525	5650
SXT Grand Minivan	P44L	30335	2050	2300	3525	5650
AWD	T		400	400	535	535
DAKOTA REGULAR CAB PICKUP—V6—Truck Equipment Schedule T1						
Pickup 2D 6 1/2'	L16K	18940	1275	1425	2000	3200
SXT 2D 6 1/2'	L16X	19205	1425	1575	2150	3450
Sport 2D 6 1/2'	L36K	19785	1400	1550	2150	3425
SLT 2D 6 1/2'	L46K	19785	1600	1775	2375	3775
4WD	G		800	800	1065	1065
V8, 4.7 Liter	N		300	300	400	400
DAKOTA CLUB CAB PICKUP—V6—Truck Equipment Schedule T1						
2D 6 1/2'	L12K	21610	2050	2275	2875	4325
SXT 2D 6 1/2'	L22X	21610	2450	2700	3525	5400
Sport 2D 6 1/2'	L32K	21625	2625	2900	3750	5700

Body Type	VIN	List	Trade-In Good	Very Good	Pvt-Party Good	Retail Excellent
SLT 2D 6 1/2'	L42K	21625	**2850**	**3175**	**3925**	**5850**
4WD	G		**800**	**800**	**1065**	**1065**
V8, 4.7 Liter	N		**300**	**300**	**400**	**400**
DAKOTA QUAD CAB PICKUP—V6—Truck Equipment Schedule T1						
Sport 4D 5 1/2'	L38K	23810	**2850**	**3175**	**4050**	**6175**
SXT 4D 5 1/2'	L23X	23810	**3300**	**3650**	**4575**	**6875**
SLT 4D 5 1/2'	L48K	23810	**3400**	**3750**	**4700**	**7050**
4WD	G		**800**	**800**	**1065**	**1065**
V8, 4.7 Liter	N		**300**	**300**	**400**	**400**
RAM REGULAR CAB PICKUP—V6—Truck Equipment Schedule T1						
1500 ST 2D 6 1/4'	A16K	20860	**2025**	**2250**	**2825**	**4200**
4WD	U		**1200**	**1200**	**1600**	**1600**
V8, 4.7 Liter	N		**375**	**375**	**500**	**500**
V8, Flex Fuel, 4.7 Liter			**350**	**350**	**465**	**465**
V8, HEMI, 5.7 Liter	D		**925**	**925**	**1240**	**1240**
RAM REGULAR CAB PICKUP—V8—Truck Equipment Schedule T1						
1500 ST 2D 8'	A16N	22580	**1975**	**2175**	**2750**	**4100**
1500 SLT 2D 6 1/4'	A16N	25400	**3300**	**3650**	**4225**	**6000**
1500 SLT 2D 8'	A16N	25685	**2900**	**3225**	**3750**	**5375**
1500 Laramie 2D 8'	A16N	28620	**2450**	**2700**	**3325**	**4900**
4WD	U		**1200**	**1200**	**1600**	**1600**
V6, 3.7 Liter	K		**(425)**	**(425)**	**(565)**	**(565)**
V8, HEMI, 5.7 Liter	D		**625**	**625**	**840**	**840**
RAM REGULAR CAB PICKUP 4WD—V8—Truck Equipment Schedule T1						
1500 Laramie 6 1/4'	U16N	32010	**4425**	**4850**	**5825**	**8325**
2WD	C		**(1525)**	**(1525)**	**(2035)**	**(2035)**
V8, HEMI, 5.7 Liter	D		**625**	**625**	**840**	**840**
RAM REGULAR CAB PICKUP 4WD—V8 HEMI—Truck Equipment Sch T1						
2500 ST 2D 8'	U26D	28825	**7225**	**7800**	**8725**	**11750**
2500 SLT 2D 8'	U26D	30530	**7600**	**8200**	**9225**	**12400**
2500 Laramie 2D 8'	U26D	34835	**8350**	**9000**	**10050**	**13500**
2WD	C		**(1525)**	**(1525)**	**(1940)**	**(1940)**
6-Cyl, Turbo Diesel	6		**2600**	**2600**	**3310**	**3310**
6-Cyl, HO Turbo Dsl	C		**3725**	**3725**	**4730**	**4730**
RAM REGULAR CAB PICKUP—V8 HEMI—Truck Equipment Schedule T1						
3500 ST 2D 8'	A36D	27975	**5775**	**6275**	**7125**	**9650**
4WD	U		**1200**	**1200**	**1535**	**1535**
6-Cyl, Turbo Diesel	6		**2600**	**2600**	**3330**	**3330**
6-Cyl, HO Turbo Dsl	C		**3725**	**3725**	**4760**	**4760**
RAM REGULAR CAB PICKUP—V8 Turbo Diesel—Truck Equipment Sch T1						
3500 ST 2D 8'	A466	29050	**9125**	**9350**	**11000**	**14700**
3500 Laramie 2D 8'	A466	32680	**9625**	**10350**	**11550**	**15400**
4WD	U		**1200**	**1200**	**1520**	**1520**
V8, HEMI, 5.7 Liter	D		**(2725)**	**(2725)**	**(3445)**	**(3445)**
6-Cyl, HO Turbo Dsl	C		**500**	**500**	**635**	**635**
RAM REGULAR CAB PICKUP—V10—Truck Equipment Schedule T1						
1500 SRT-10 2D 6 1/4'	A16H	47635	**11850**	**12600**	**13650**	**17500**
Manual, 6-Spd			**0**	**0**	**0**	**0**
RAM QUAD CAB PICKUP—V8—Truck Equipment Schedule T1						
1500 ST 4D 6 1/4'	A18N	26455	**3925**	**4300**	**5225**	**7500**
1500 ST 4D 8'	A18N	26735	**3625**	**4000**	**4875**	**7000**
1500 SLT 4D 6 1/4'	A18N	28470	**4400**	**4825**	**5800**	**8275**
1500 SLT 4D 8'	A18N	28750	**4100**	**4500**	**5425**	**7775**
1500 Laramie 8'	A18N	31070	**4700**	**5125**	**6150**	**8775**
4WD	U		**1200**	**1200**	**1600**	**1600**
V6, 3.7 Liter	K		**(425)**	**(425)**	**(565)**	**(565)**
V8, HEMI, 5.7 Liter	D		**625**	**625**	**840**	**840**
RAM QUAD CAB PICKUP 4WD—V8—Truck Equipment Schedule T1						
1500 Laramie 6 1/4'	U18N	35965	**6575**	**7125**	**8600**	**12100**
2WD	C		**(1525)**	**(1525)**	**(2035)**	**(2035)**
V8, HEMI, 5.7 Liter	D		**625**	**625**	**840**	**840**
RAM QUAD CAB PICKUP—V8 HEMI—Truck Equipment Schedule T1						
2500 ST 4D 8'	A28D	28660	**7200**	**7775**	**8800**	**11850**
2500 SLT 4D 8'	A28D	30540	**7650**	**8250**	**9300**	**12500**
2500 Laramie 4D 8'	A28D	33055	**8300**	**8950**	**10000**	**13400**
4WD	U		**1200**	**1200**	**1530**	**1530**
6-Cyl, Turbo Diesel	6		**2600**	**2600**	**3320**	**3320**
6-Cyl, HO Turbo Dsl	C		**3725**	**3725**	**4750**	**4750**
RAM QUAD CAB PICKUP 4WD—V8 HEMI—Truck Equipment Schedule T1						
2500 ST 4D 6 1/4'	U28D	31115	**9125**	**9850**	**11000**	**14700**
2500 Laramie 6 1/4'	U28D	37990	**10150**	**10900**	**12100**	**16150**
3500 SLT 4D 8'	U48D	33860	**9100**	**9800**	**10900**	**14550**
2WD	C		**(1525)**	**(1525)**	**(1930)**	**(1930)**

Body Type	VIN	List	Trade-In Good	Very Good	Pvt-Party Good	Retail Excellent
6-Cyl, Turbo Diesel	6		2600	2600	3295	3295
6-Cyl, HO Turbo Dsl	C		3725	3725	4710	4710
RAM QUAD CAB PICKUP 4WD—6-Cyl. Turbo Diesel—Truck Sch T1						
2500 SLT 4D 6 1/4'	U286	38335	12950	13850	15300	20300
3500 SLT 4D 8'	U486	39660	13000	13950	15500	20600
3500 Laramie 4D 8'	U486	43850	11450	12300	13650	18100
2WD	C		(1525)	(1525)	(1920)	(1920)
6-Cyl, HO Turbo Dsl	C		500	500	630	630
V8, HEMI, 5.7 Liter	D		(2725)	(2725)	(3425)	(3425)
RAM QUAD CAB PICKUP—6-Cyl. Turbo Diesel—Truck Schedule T1						
3500 ST 4D 6 1/4'	A386	35060	11350	12200	13550	18000
4WD	U		1200	1200	1515	1515
6-Cyl, HO Turbo Dsl	C		275	275	345	345
RAM QUAD CAB PICKUP 4WD—6-Cyl. Turbo Diesel—Truck Sch T1						
3500 SLT 4D 6 1/4'	U386	38120	13400	14400	15950	21200
3500 Laramie 6 1/4'	U386	42925	14100	15100	16750	22200
2WD	C		(1525)	(1525)	(1920)	(1920)

Body Type	VIN	List	Trade-In Good	Very Good	Pvt-Party Good	Retail Excellent
DURANGO 4WD—V8—Truck Equipment Schedule T1						
ST Sport Utility 4D	B38N	30610	3625	4025	4925	7025
SXT Sport Utility	B38N	30660	3650	4050	4950	7075
SLT Sport Utility	B48N	33380	3975	4400	5500	7825
Limited Sport Utility	B58N	36560	4250	4600	5700	7675
Third Row Seat			325	325	435	435
2WD	D		(975)	(975)	(1300)	(1300)
V6, 3.7 Liter	K		(400)	(400)	(535)	(535)
V8, HEMI, 5.7 Liter	D		550	550	740	740
CARAVAN CARGO—V6—Truck Equipment Schedule T2						
Minivan	P21R	20185	1025	1175	1900	3050
Grand Minivan	P23R	20185	1050	1175	2000	3275
CARAVAN PASSENGER—V6—Truck Equipment Schedule T1						
Minivan 4D	P25R	18995	1325	1475	2300	3725
SXT Minivan 4D	P45R	22485	1625	1825	2825	4525
Grand Minivan 4D	P24R	22185	1725	1925	2975	4725
SXT Grand Minivan	P44L	27185	2250	2500	3675	5775
5-Passenger Seating			(325)	(325)	(435)	(435)
4-Cyl, 2.4 Liter	B		(600)	(600)	(800)	(800)
DAKOTA CLUB CAB PICKUP—V6—Truck Equipment Schedule T1						
ST 2D 6 1/2'	E22X	21400	1900	2125	3075	4675
SLT 2D 6 1/2'	E42X	23155	2775	3100	4100	6050
4WD	W		900	900	1200	1200
V8, 4.7 Liter	N		325	325	435	435
V8, HO, 4.7 Liter	J		325	325	435	435
DAKOTA CLUB CAB PICKUP 4WD—V8—Truck Equipment Schedule T1						
Laramie 2D 6 1/2'	W52N	28619	4675	5100	6375	9025
2WD	E		(1025)	(1025)	(1365)	(1365)
V6, 3.7 Liter	K		(350)	(350)	(450)	(450)
DAKOTA QUAD CAB PICKUP—V6—Truck Equipment Schedule T1						
ST 4D 5 1/2'	E28K	22800	2725	3050	4175	6275
4WD	W		900	900	1200	1200
V8, 4.7 Liter	N		325	325	435	435
DAKOTA QUAD CAB PICKUP 4WD—V8—Truck Equipment Schedule T1						
SLT 4D 5 1/2'	W48N	28490	4950	5400	6700	9475
Laramie 4D 5 1/2'	W58N	30695	5450	5950	7450	10450
2WD	E		(1025)	(1025)	(1365)	(1365)
V6, 3.7 Liter	K		(350)	(350)	(450)	(450)
RAM REGULAR CAB PICKUP—V6—Truck Equipment Schedule T1						
1500 ST 2D 6 1/4'	A16X	22125	3125	3475	4275	6000
4WD	U		1300	1300	1735	1735
V8, 4.7 Liter	N		425	425	550	550
V8, Flex Fuel, 4.7 Liter	P		375	375	510	510
V8, HEMI, 5.7 Liter	D		1025	1025	1365	1365
RAM REGULAR CAB PICKUP—V8—Truck Equipment Schedule T1						
1500 ST 2D 8'	A16N	23520	3075	3425	4225	5925
1500 SLT 2D 6 1/4'	A16N	25650	3950	4350	5350	7425
1500 SLT 2D 8'	A16N	25935	3500	3875	4850	6750
1500 Laramie 8'	A16N	30085	4000	4400	5400	7500
4WD	U		1300	1300	1735	1735
V6, 3.7 Liter	K		(450)	(450)	(600)	(600)
V8, HEMI, 5.7 Liter	D		675	675	895	895
RAM REGULAR CAB PICKUP 4WD—V8—Truck Equipment Schedule T1						
1500 Laramie 6 1/4'	U16N	33120	6500	7025	8425	11500

Body Type	VIN	List	Trade-In Good	Very Good	Pvt-Party Good	Retail Excellent
2WD	A	......	(1675)	(1675)	(2245)	(2245)
V6, 3.7 Liter	K	......	(450)	(450)	(600)	(600)
V8, HEMI, 5.7 Liter	D	......	675	675	895	895
RAM REGULAR CAB PICKUP 4WD—V8 HEMI—Truck Equipment Sch T1						
2500 ST 2D 8'	S26D	29790	8625	9275	10300	13350
2500 SLT 2D 8'	S26D	31495	9150	9850	10950	14150
2500 Laramie 8'	S26D	34040	9450	10150	11300	14600
Power Wagon		......	4250	4250	4965	4965
2WD	R	......	(1675)	(1675)	(1965)	(1965)
6-Cyl, HO Turbo Dsl	C	......	3900	3900	4565	4565
RAM REGULAR CAB PICKUP—V8 HEMI—Truck Equipment Schedule T1						
3500 ST 2D 8' DR	R36D	28720	7875	8500	9475	12300
4WD	S	......	1300	1300	1520	1520
6-Cyl HO Turbo Dsl	C	......	3900	3900	4580	4580
RAM REGULAR CAB PICKUP—V8 Turbo Diesel—Truck Equip Sch T1						
3500 SLT 2D 8' DR	R46C	29795	12350	13250	14500	18700
3500 Laramie 8' DR	R46C	33425	12900	13800	15200	19600
4WD	S	......	1300	1300	1520	1520
V8, HEMI, 5.7 Liter	D	......	(3000)	(3000)	(3515)	(3515)
RAM REGULAR CAB PICKUP—V10—Truck Equipment Schedule T1						
1500 SRT-10 2D 6 1/4'	A16H	45850	11650	12350	14350	19000
Manual, 6-Spd		......	0	0	0	0
RAM QUAD CAB PICKUP—V8—Truck Equipment Schedule T1						
1500 ST 4D 6 1/4'	A18N	27305	5425	5900	7200	9850
1500 ST 4D 8'	A18N	27660	5075	5525	6800	9300
1500 SLT 4D 6 1/4'	A18N	29395	5950	6450	7775	10600
1500 SLT 4D 8'	A18N	29675	5600	6075	7400	10100
1500 Laramie 8'	A18N	31995	6125	6625	8000	10900
4WD	U	......	1300	1300	1735	1735
V6, 3.7 Liter	K	......	(450)	(450)	(600)	(600)
V8, HEMI, 5.7 Liter	D	......	675	675	895	895
RAM QUAD CAB PICKUP 4WD—V8—Truck Equipment Schedule T1						
1500 Laramie 6 1/4'	U18N	35925	9375	10100	11850	16000
2WD	A	......	(1675)	(1675)	(2245)	(2245)
V6, 3.7 Liter	K	......	(450)	(450)	(600)	(600)
V8, HEMI, 5.7 Liter	D	......	675	675	895	895
RAM QUAD CAB PICKUP—V10—Truck Equipment Schedule T1						
1500 SRT-10 2D 6 1/4'	A18H	50850	13100	13900	15350	19500
RAM QUAD CAB PICKUP—V8 HEMI—Truck Equipment Schedule T1						
2500 ST 4D 8'	R28D	29605	8575	9225	10250	13300
2500 SLT 4D 8'	R28D	31485	9100	9800	10900	14100
2500 Laramie 8'	R28D	35615	9900	10650	11750	15200
4WD	S	......	1300	1300	1520	1520
6-Cyl, HO Turbo Dsl	R	......	3900	3900	4570	4570
RAM QUAD CAB PICKUP 4WD—V8 HEMI—Truck Equipment Schedule T1						
2500 Laramie 6 1/4'	S28D	38765	12100	13000	14200	18350
2500 ST 4D 6 1/4'	S28D	32080	10950	11750	12950	16700
3500 SLT 4D 8'	S48D	34825	10950	11750	12950	16700
2WD	R	......	(1675)	(1675)	(1965)	(1965)
6-Cyl, HO Turbo Dsl	R	......	3900	3900	4560	4560
RAM QUAD CAB PICKUP 4WD—6-Cyl, HO Turbo Diesel—Truck Sch T1						
2500 SLT 4D 6 1/4'	S28C	39345	15800	16850	18350	23600
3500 SLT 4D 8'	S48C	41460	16150	17250	18700	24100
3500 Laramie 8'	S48C	44105	16550	17650	19150	24700
2WD	R	......	(1675)	(1675)	(1960)	(1960)
Power Wagon		......	4250	4250	4950	4950
V8, HEMI, 5.7 Liter	D	......	(3000)	(3000)	(3505)	(3505)
RAM QUAD CAB PICKUP—6-Cyl, HO Turbo Diesel—Truck Schedule T1						
3500 SLT 4D 6 1/4'	R38C	36500	13300	14250	15600	20100
4WD	S	......	1300	1300	1515	1515
RAM QUAD CAB PICKUP 4WD—6-Cyl, HO Turbo Diesel—Truck Sch T1						
3500 SLT 4D 6 1/4'	S38C	39820	16250	17350	18850	24300
3500 Laramie 6 1/4'	S38C	42465	17750	18900	20400	26300
2WD	R	......	(1675)	(1675)	(1960)	(1960)

2006 DODGE — (1,3orW)D(2,3,4,5,7or8)–(B38N)–6–#

Body Type	VIN	List	Trade-In Good	Very Good	Pvt-Party Good	Retail Excellent
DURANGO 4WD—V8—Truck Equipment Schedule T1						
SXT Sport Utility 4D	B38N	31825	4575	5025	6050	8400
SLT Sport Utility 4D	B48N	34275	5000	5525	6575	9100
Limited Sport Utility	B58N	38155	5175	5550	6900	9050
Third Row Seat		......	350	350	465	465
2WD	D	......	(1050)	(1050)	(1410)	(1410)
V6, 3.7 Liter	K	......	(450)	(450)	(600)	(600)

Body Type	VIN	List	Trade-In Good	Very Good	Pvt-Party Good	Retail Excellent
V8, HEMI, 5.7 Liter	2		600	600	790	790
CARAVAN CARGO—V6—Truck Equipment Schedule T2						
Minivan	P21R	20645	1125	1275	2125	3400
Grand Minivan	P23R	21345	1375	1550	2425	3825
CARAVAN PASSENGER—V6—Truck Equipment Schedule T1						
SE Minivan 4D	P25N	19095	1500	1675	2575	4050
SXT Minivan 4D	P45R	23035	2100	2325	3325	5075
Grand Minivan 4D	P24R	23745	2225	2500	3650	5575
SXT Grand Minivan	P44L	27830	2875	3200	4500	6750
5-Passenger Seating			(350)	(350)	(465)	(465)
4-Cyl, 2.4 Liter	B		(650)	(650)	(865)	(865)
DAKOTA CLUB CAB PICKUP—V6—Truck Equipment Schedule T1						
ST 2D 6 1/2'	E22K	21750	1950	2200	3200	4750
SLT 2D 6 1/2'	E42K	23685	3350	3725	4700	6600
4WD	W		1000	1000	1335	1335
V8, 4.7 Liter	N		350	350	465	465
V8, HO, 4.7 Liter	J		350	350	465	465
DAKOTA CLUB CAB PICKUP 4WD—V8—Truck Equipment Schedule T1						
Laramie 2D 6 1/2'	W52N	29450	5450	5925	7300	10000
2WD	E		(1125)	(1125)	(1485)	(1485)
V6, 3.7 Liter	K		(375)	(375)	(490)	(490)
DAKOTA QUAD CAB PICKUP—V6—Truck Equipment Schedule T1						
ST 4D 5 1/2'	E28K	23150	3350	3725	4700	6600
4WD	W		1000	1000	1335	1335
V8, 4.7 Liter	N		350	350	465	465
DAKOTA QUAD CAB PICKUP 4WD—V8—Truck Equipment Schedule T1						
SLT 4D 5 1/2'	W58N	28540	5850	6350	7725	10550
Laramie 4D 5 1/2'	W58N	31015	7425	8000	9500	12900
2WD	E		(1125)	(1125)	(1485)	(1485)
V6, 3.7 Liter	K		(375)	(375)	(490)	(490)
RAM REGULAR CAB PICKUP—V6—Truck Equipment Schedule T1						
1500 ST 2D 6 1/4'	A16K	22795	3575	3925	4825	6625
4WD	U		1600	1600	2135	2135
V8, 4.7 Liter	N		450	450	600	600
V8, Flex Fuel, 4.7 Liter	P		425	425	555	555
V8, HEMI, 5.7 Liter	2		1125	1125	1495	1495
RAM REGULAR CAB PICKUP—V8—Truck Equipment Schedule T1						
1500 ST 2D 8'	A16N	23865	3475	3825	4725	6475
1500 ST 2D 6 1/4'	A16N	26220	4525	4925	5900	8000
1500 SLT 2D 8'	A16N	26505	4075	4450	5400	7350
1500 Laramie 6 1/4'	U16N	34855	7225	7800	9200	12300
1500 Laramie 8'	A16N	30505	4625	5050	6000	8150
4WD	U		1600	1600	2135	2135
V6, 3.7 Liter	K		(450)	(450)	(600)	(600)
V8, HEMI, 5.7 Liter	2		725	725	955	955
RAM REGULAR CAB PICKUP—V8 HEMI—Truck Equipment Schedule T1						
3500 ST 2D 8' DR	L36D	29065	9125	9800	10750	13650
4WD	S,X		1600	1600	1850	1850
6-Cyl, HO Turbo Dsl	C		4100	4100	4740	4740
RAM REGULAR CAB PICKUP 4WD—V8 HEMI—Truck Equipment Schedule T1						
2500 ST 2D 8'	S26D	30460	9700	10400	11450	14500
2500 SLT 2D 8'	S26D	32115	10200	10950	12000	15200
2500 Laramie 2D 8'	S26D	34635	10800	11550	12600	16000
Power Wagon			4450	4450	5145	5145
2WD	R,L		(2075)	(2075)	(2390)	(2390)
6-Cyl, HO Turbo Dsl	C		4100	4100	4750	4750
RAM REGULAR CAB PICKUP—6-Cyl. HO Turbo Diesel—Truck Equipment Sch T1						
3500 SLT 2D 8' DR	L46C	30621	13950	14900	16100	20300
3500 Laramie 8' DR	L46C	31655	14550	15500	16750	21100
4WD	S,X		1600	1600	1845	1845
V8, HEMI, 5.7 Liter	D		(3300)	(3300)	(3805)	(3805)
RAM REGULAR CAB PICKUP—V10—Truck Equipment Schedule T1						
1500 SRT-10 6 1/4'	A16H	48505	13950	14750	15950	19850
Manual, 6-Spd	D		0	0	0	0
RAM QUAD CAB PICKUP—V8—Truck Equipment Schedule T1						
1500 ST 4D 6 1/4'	A18N	27650	6450	6975	8325	11150
1500 ST 4D 8'	A18N	28005	6150	6650	7925	10650
1500 SLT 4D 6 1/4'	A18N	29710	6900	7450	8825	11800
1500 SLT 4D 8'	A18N	29990	6600	7150	8500	11400
1500 Laramie 8'	A18N	33700	7150	7725	9125	12200
4WD	U		1600	1600	2135	2135
V6, 3.7 Liter	K		(450)	(450)	(600)	(600)
V8, HEMI, 5.7 Liter	2		725	725	955	955

Body Type	VIN	List	Trade-In Good	Very Good	Pvt-Party Good	Retail Excellent
RAM QUAD CAB PICKUP 4WD—V8—Truck Equipment Schedule T1						
1500 Laramie 6 1/4'	U18N	37500	10750	11500	13200	17500
2WD	A		(2075)	(2075)	(2750)	(2750)
V8, HEMI, 5.7 Liter	2		725	725	955	955
RAM QUAD CAB PICKUP—V10—Truck Equipment Schedule T1						
1500 SRT-10 6 1/4'	A18H	52710	16050	16900	18150	22500
RAM QUAD CAB PICKUP—V8 HEMI—Truck Equipment Schedule T1						
2500 ST 4D 8'	R28D	30245	10250	11000	12050	15250
2500 SLT 4D 8'	R28D	32220	10750	11500	12550	15900
2500 Laramie 8'	R28D	34825	11300	12100	13300	16850
4WD	S,X		1600	1600	1850	1850
6-Cyl, HO Turbo Dsl	C		4100	4100	4745	4745
RAM QUAD CAB PICKUP 4WD—V8 HEMI—Truck Equipment Schedule T1						
2500 ST 4D 6 1/4'	S28D	38600	12850	13750	14950	18900
2500 Laramie 6 1/4'	S28D	37355	13850	14750	16000	20200
3500 SLT 4D 8'	X48D	35915	12850	13750	14950	18900
2WD	R,L		(2075)	(2075)	(2385)	(2385)
6-Cyl, HO Turbo Dsl	C		4100	4100	4735	4735
RAM QUAD CAB 4WD—6-Cyl. HO Turbo Diesel—Truck Equipment Sch T1						
3500 SLT 4D 8'	X48C	42615	18200	19350	20600	26000
3500 Laramie 8'	X48C	44950	18500	19650	21000	26400
2WD	R,L		(2075)	(2075)	(2380)	(2380)
V8, HEMI, 5.7 Liter	D		(3300)	(3300)	(3805)	(3805)
RAM QUAD CAB 4WD—6-Cyl. HO Turbo Diesel—Truck Equipment Sch T1						
2500 SLT 4D 6 1/4'	S28C	40500	17900	19050	20300	25600
Power Wagon			4450	4450	5135	5135
2WD	R,L		(2075)	(2075)	(2385)	(2385)
V8, HEMI, 5.7 Liter	D		(3300)	(3300)	(3810)	(3810)
RAM QUAD CAB PICKUP—6-Cyl. HO Turbo Diesel—Truck Schedule T1						
3500 ST 4D 6 1/4'	L38C	37065	15500	16500	17750	22400
4WD	S,X		1600	1600	1845	1845
RAM QUAD CAB 4WD—6-Cyl. HO Turbo Diesel—Truck Schedule T1						
3500 SLT 4D 6 1/4'	X38C	41375	18900	20100	21400	27000
3500 Laramie 6 1/4'	X38C	43710	19300	20500	21800	27500
2WD	R,L		(2075)	(2075)	(2380)	(2380)
RAM MEGA CAB PICKUP 4WD—V8 HEMI—Truck Equipment Schedule T1						
1500 SLT 4D 6 1/4'	S19D	35980	12750	13600	15500	20500
1500 Laramie 6 1/4'	S19D	41075	12750	13600	15650	20700
2WD	R		(2075)	(2075)	(2750)	(2750)
RAM MEGA CAB 4WD—6-Cyl. HO Turbo Diesel—Truck Equipment Sch T1						
2500 SLT 4D 6 1/4'	S29C	40500	20700	22000	23300	29400
2500 Laramie 6 1/4'	S29C	42835	20800	22100	23500	29600
2WD	R		(2075)	(2075)	(2380)	(2380)
V8, HEMI, 5.7 Liter	D		(3300)	(3300)	(3800)	(3800)
RAM MEGA CAB 4WD—6-Cyl. HO Turbo Diesel—Truck Schedule T1						
3500 SLT 4D 6 1/4'	X39C	44595	20900	22200	23500	29600
3500 Laramie 6 1/4'	X39C	49690	22300	23700	25100	31600
2WD	R		(2075)	(2075)	(2380)	(2380)

2007 DODGE — (1,2or3)D(2,3,4,5,7or8)–(U28K)–7–#

Body Type	VIN	List	Trade-In Good	Very Good	Pvt-Party Good	Retail Excellent
NITRO 4WD—V6—Truck Equipment Schedule T1						
SXT Sport Utility 4D	U28K	22495	5800	6275	7375	9725
SLT Sport Utility 4D	U58K	24805	6725	7250	8450	11000
R/T Sport Utility 4D	U586	25795	8625	9225	10500	13600
2WD	T		(700)	(700)	(935)	(935)
DURANGO 4WD—V8—Truck Equipment Schedule T1						
SXT Sport Util 4D	B38N	29855	5700	6200	7375	9875
SLT Sport Util 4D	B48N	32675	6100	6625	7825	10450
Limited Sport Util	B58N	36670	6450	6875	8200	10500
Third Row Seat			375	375	500	500
2WD	D		(1150)	(1150)	(1520)	(1520)
V6, 3.7 Liter	K		(500)	(500)	(665)	(665)
V8, HEMI, 5.7 Liter	2		625	625	835	835
CARAVAN CARGO—V6—Truck Equipment Schedule T2						
Minivan	P21R	20845	1925	2150	3125	4800
Grand Minivan	P23R	21545	2050	2275	3300	5050
CARAVAN PASSENGER—V6—Truck Equipment Schedule T1						
Minivan 4D	P25R	19345	2125	2350	3375	5175
SXT Minivan 4D	P45R	23235	2575	2900	4100	6150
Grand Minivan 4D	P24R	23995	2825	3150	4400	6575
SXT Grand Minivan	P44L	28030	3775	4150	5600	8225
5-Passenger Seating			(375)	(375)	(500)	(500)
4-Cyl, 2.4 Liter	B		(700)	(700)	(935)	(935)

TRUCKS & VANS

Body Type	VIN	List	Trade-In Good	Very Good	Pvt-Party Good	Retail Excellent
DAKOTA CLUB CAB PICKUP—V6—Truck Equipment Schedule T1						
ST 2D 6 1/2'	E22K	20840	2800	3125	4025	5650
SLT 2D 6 1/2'	E42K	24630	4775	5200	6225	8475
4WD	W		1100	1100	1465	1465
V8, 4.7 Liter	N		375	375	500	500
V8, HO, 4.7 Liter	N		375	375	500	500
DAKOTA CLUB CAB PICKUP 4WD—V8—Truck Equipment Schedule T1						
Laramie 2D 6 1/2'	W52N	29285	6950	7500	8925	11950
2WD	E		(1625)	(1625)	(2165)	(2165)
V6, 3.7 Liter	K		(400)	(400)	(525)	(525)
DAKOTA QUAD CAB PICKUP—V6—Truck Equipment Schedule T1						
ST 4D 5 1/2'	E28K	23540	4750	5175	6200	8450
4WD	W		1100	1100	1465	1465
V8, 4.7 Liter	N		375	375	500	500
DAKOTA QUAD CAB PICKUP 4WD—V8—Truck Equipment Schedule T1						
SLT 4D 5 1/2'	W48N	29975	7650	8250	9725	13000
2WD	E		(1625)	(1625)	(2165)	(2165)
V6, 3.7 Liter	K		(400)	(400)	(525)	(525)
DAKOTA QUAD CAB PICKUP 4WD—V8—Truck Equipment Schedule T1						
Laramie 4D 5 1/2'	W58N	31070	8350	8975	10500	14000
2WD	E		(1625)	(1625)	(2165)	(2165)
V6, 3.7 Liter	K		(400)	(400)	(525)	(525)
RAM REGULAR CAB PICKUP—V6—Truck Equipment Schedule T1						
1500 ST 2D 6 1/4'	A16K	23375	4275	4650	5675	7700
4WD	U		2000	2000	2665	2665
V8, 4.7 Liter	N		450	450	600	600
V8, Flex Fuel, 4.7 Liter	P		450	450	600	600
V8, HEMI, 5.7 Liter	2		1225	1225	1620	1620
RAM REGULAR CAB PICKUP—V8—Truck Equipment Schedule T1						
1500 ST 2D 6 1/4'	A16N	24225	4075	4450	5425	7400
1500 ST 2D 8'	A16N	26750	5225	5650	6900	9275
1500 SLT 2D 8'	A16N	27035	4725	5125	6350	8575
4WD	U		2000	2000	2665	2665
V6, 3.7 Liter	K		(450)	(450)	(600)	(600)
V8, HEMI, 5.7 Liter	2		750	750	1010	1010
RAM REGULAR CAB PICKUP—V8 HEMI—Truck Equipment Schedule T1						
3500 ST 2D 8' DR	L36D	29425	9975	10650	11800	15000
Power Wagon			4650	4650	5485	5485
4WD	S,X		2000	2000	2370	2370
6-Cyl, HO Trb Dsl 5.9L	C		4300	4300	5095	5095
6-Cyl, Turbo Dsl 6.7L	A		4600	4600	5465	5465
RAM REGULAR CAB 4WD—V8 HEMI—Truck Equipment Schedule T1						
2500 ST 2D 8'	S26D	30820	10600	11300	12550	15900
2500 SLT 2D 8'	S26D	32520	11250	12000	13000	16250
2WD	C		(2250)	(2250)	(2650)	(2650)
6-Cyl, HO Trb Dsl 5.9L	C		4300	4300	5085	5085
6-Cyl, Turbo Dsl 6.7L	A		4600	4600	5455	5455
RAM REGULAR CAB—6-Cyl. Turbo Diesel—Truck Equipment Sch T1						
3500 SLT 2D 8' DR	L46A	30570	14550	15450	16850	21300
4WD	S,X		2000	2000	2360	2360
6-Cyl, HO Trb Dsl 5.9L	C		(250)	(250)	(305)	(305)
V8, HEMI, 5.7 Liter	D		(4225)	(4225)	(4990)	(4990)
RAM QUAD CAB PICKUP—V8—Truck Equipment Schedule T1						
1500 ST 4D 6 1/4'	A18N	28010	7350	7900	9350	12400
1500 ST 4D 8'	A18N	28365	6950	7475	8900	11850
1500 SLT 4D 6 1/4'	A18N	30320	8050	8625	10150	13400
1500 SLT 4D 8'	A18N	30600	7550	8100	9575	12700
4WD	U		2000	2000	2660	2660
V6, 3.7 Liter	K		(450)	(450)	(600)	(600)
V8, HEMI, 5.7 Liter	2		750	750	1005	1005
RAM QUAD CAB PICKUP 4WD—V8 HEMI—Truck Equipment Schedule T1						
1500 Laramie 6 1/4'	U182	37565	12550	13350	15350	20100
2WD	R		(2250)	(2250)	(2930)	(2930)
RAM QUAD CAB PICKUP—V8 HEMI—Truck Equipment Schedule T1						
2500 ST 4D 8'	R28D	30530	10650	11400	12550	15950
2500 SLT 4D 8'	R28D	32530	11200	11950	13150	16650
2500 Laramie 8'	R28D	35010	11900	12700	14050	17750
4WD	S,X		2000	2000	2365	2365
6-Cyl, HO Trb Dsl 5.9L	C		4300	4300	5085	5085
6-Cyl, Turbo Dsl 6.7L	A		4600	4600	5450	5450
RAM QUAD CAB PICKUP 4WD—V8 HEMI—Truck Equipment Schedule T1						
2500 ST 4D 6 1/4'	S28D	37860	13800	14700	16050	20300
2500 Laramie 6 1/4'	S28D	37860	14900	15850	17250	21800

Body Type	VIN	List	Trade-In Good	Trade-In Very Good	Pvt-Party Good	Retail Excellent
3500 ST 4D 8'	X48D	36275	13700	14600	15950	20200
2WD	R		(2250)	(2250)	(2650)	(2650)
6-Cyl, HO Trb Dsl 5.9L	C		4300	4300	5070	5070
6-Cyl, Turbo Dsl 6.7L	A		4600	4600	5450	5450
RAM QUAD CAB 4WD—6-Cyl. Turbo Diesel—Truck Equipment Sch T1						
3500 Laramie 8'	X48A	45014	20200	21400	23000	28800
2WD	R		(2250)	(2250)	(2635)	(2635)
6-Cyl, HO Trb Dsl 5.9L	C		(250)	(250)	(305)	(305)
V8, HEMI, 5.7 Liter	D		(4225)	(4225)	(4975)	(4975)
RAM QUAD CAB PICKUP—6-Cyl. Turbo Diesel—Truck Equipment Sch T1						
3500 ST 4D 6 1/4'	L38A	37425	16300	17300	18750	23600
4WD	S,X		2000	2000	2360	2360
6-Cyl, HO Trb Dsl 5.9L	C		(300)	(300)	(355)	(355)
RAM QUAD CAB 4WD—6-Cyl. Turbo Diesel—Truck Equipment Sch T1						
2500 SLT 4D 6 1/4'	S28A	40985	19400	20500	22100	27800
3500 SLT 4D 6 1/4'	X38A	41810	19900	21100	22600	28400
3500 SLT 4D 8'	X48A	43100	19700	20900	22500	28200
3500 Laramie 6 1/4'	X38A	43315	20400	21600	23200	29100
Power Wagon			4650	4650	5470	5470
2WD	R		(2250)	(2250)	(2635)	(2635)
6-Cyl, HO Trb Dsl 5.9L	C		(250)	(250)	(305)	(305)
V8, HEMI, 5.7 Liter	D		(4225)	(4225)	(4975)	(4975)
RAM MEGA CAB PICKUP 4WD—V8 HEMI—Truck Equipment Schedule T1						
1500 SLT 4D 6 1/4'	S19D	36845	14400	15300	17500	22800
1500 Laramie 6 1/4'	S19D	42050	15100	16050	18250	23800
2WD	D		(2250)	(2250)	(2870)	(2870)
RAM MEGA CAB PICKUP 4WD—6-Cyl. Turbo Diesel—Truck Equip Sch T1						
2500 SLT 4D 6 1/4'	S29A	44120	23100	24400	26100	32800
2WD	R		(2250)	(2250)	(2600)	(2600)
6-Cyl, HO Trb Dsl 5.9L	C		(250)	(250)	(300)	(300)
V8, HEMI, 5.7 Liter	D		(4225)	(4225)	(4905)	(4905)
RAM MEGA CAB 4WD—6-Cyl. HO Turbo Diesel—Truck Equipment Sch T1						
2500 Laramie 6 1/4'	S29C	49090	23300	24600	26400	33100
2WD	A		(2250)	(2250)	(2640)	(2640)
6-Cyl, Turbo Dsl 6.7L	A		250	250	305	305
V8, HEMI, 5.7 Liter	D		(3650)	(3650)	(4300)	(4300)
RAM MEGA CAB 4WD—6-Cyl. HO Turbo Diesel—Truck Schedule T1						
3500 SLT 4D 6 1/4'	X39C	46245	22900	24200	25900	32500
3500 Laramie 6 1/4'	X39C	50515	24000	25400	27100	34000
2WD	L		(2250)	(2250)	(2600)	(2600)
6-Cyl, Turbo Dsl 6.7L	A		200	200	230	230

Body Type	VIN	List	Trade-In Good	Trade-In Very Good	Pvt-Party Good	Retail Excellent
NITRO 4WD—V6—Truck Equipment Schedule T1						
SXT Sport Utility 4D	U28K	21915	6825	7300	8375	10700
SLT Sport Utility 4D	U58K	25325	7775	8275	9500	12100
R/T Sport Utility 4D	U586	28500	9850	10450	11800	14900
2WD			(750)	(750)	(1000)	(1000)
DURANGO 4WD—V8—Truck Equipment Schedule T1						
SXT Sport Utility 4D	B38N	30480	7325	7875	9150	11900
Adventurer Spt Util	B68N	35610	8225	8800	10200	13250
Third Row Seat			400	400	535	535
2WD	D		(1225)	(1225)	(1630)	(1630)
V6, 3.7 Liter	K		(550)	(550)	(735)	(735)
V8, HEMI, 5.7 Liter	2		675	675	885	885
DURANGO 4WD—V8 HEMI—Truck Equipment Schedule T1						
SLT Sport Utility 4D	B482	34800	8225	8800	10150	13200
Limited Sport Util	B582	38870	8725	9200	10500	13000
2WD	D		(1225)	(1225)	(1630)	(1630)
V6, 3.7 Liter	K		(1475)	(1475)	(1975)	(1975)
V8, Flex Fuel, 4.7 Liter	P		(750)	(750)	(1000)	(1000)
CARAVAN CARGO—V6—Truck Equipment Schedule T2						
SE Grand Minivan	N11H	22470	4325	4725	5775	7925
GRAND CARAVAN—V6—Truck Equipment Schedule T1						
SE Minivan	N44H	22470	5250	5700	7050	9575
SXT Minivan	N54P	27535	6425	6925	8400	11350
DAKOTA EXTENDED CAB PICKUP—V6—Truck Equipment Schedule T1						
ST 4D 6 1/2'	E22K	21215	4250	4625	5475	7275
SLT 4D 6 1/2'	E42K	25730	5475	5925	7000	9200
SXT 4D 6 1/2'	E32K	26730	5675	6125	7225	9450
Sport 4D 6 1/2'	E62K	25780	5575	6025	7100	9300
TRX 4D 6 1/2'	E72K	26100	5875	6350	7450	9750
4WD	W		1300	1300	1735	1735

Body Type	VIN	List	Trade-In Good	Very Good	Pvt-Party Good	Retail Excellent
V8, Flex Fuel, 4.7 Liter	N		425	425	565	565
DAKOTA EXTENDED CAB PICKUP 4WD—V8—Truck Equipment Schedule T1						
Laramie 4D 6 1/2'	W52N	33795	8375	8975	10250	13250
2WD	E		(1650)	(1650)	(2200)	(2200)
DAKOTA CREW CAB PICKUP—V6—Truck Equipment Schedule T1						
SXT 4D 5 1/4'	E38K	25420	8125	8700	9975	12900
4WD	W		1300	1300	1735	1735
V8, Flex Fuel, 4.7 Liter	N		425	425	565	565
DAKOTA CREW CAB PICKUP 4WD—V6—Truck Equipment Schedule T1						
ST 4D 5 1/4'	W28K	25730	8825	9425	10800	13900
2WD	E		(1650)	(1650)	(2200)	(2200)
V8, Flex Fuel, 4.7 Liter	N		425	425	565	565
DAKOTA CREW CAB PICKUP—V8 Flex Fuel—Truck Equipment Schedule T1						
SLT 4D 5 1/4'	E48N	27875	8925	9550	10900	14050
4WD	W		1300	1300	1735	1735
V6, 3.7 Liter	K		(425)	(425)	(565)	(565)
DAKOTA CREW CAB 4WD—V8 Flex Fuel—Truck Equipment Sch T1						
TRX 4D 5 1/4'	W78N	31450	10350	11050	12500	16050
Sport 4D 5 1/4'	W68N	31180	10950	11650	13200	16900
2WD	E		(1650)	(1650)	(2200)	(2200)
V6, 3.7 Liter	K		(425)	(425)	(565)	(565)
DAKOTA CREW CAB PICKUP 4WD—V8—Truck Equipment Schedule T1						
Laramie 4D 5 1/4'	W58N	31745	10500	11200	12650	16250
2WD	E		(1650)	(1650)	(2200)	(2200)
RAM REGULAR CAB PICKUP—V6—Truck Equipment Schedule T1						
1500 ST 2D 6 1/4'	A16K	23150	5375	5775	6875	8875
1500 SXT 2D 6 1/4'	A16K	25095	6100	6525	7675	9875
4WD	U		2200	2200	2860	2860
V8, 4.7 Liter	N		625	625	820	820
V8, HEMI, 5.7 Liter	2		1300	1300	1700	1700
RAM REGULAR CAB PICKUP—V8—Truck Equipment Schedule T1						
1500 ST 2D 8'	A16N	24480	5225	5625	6700	8700
1500 SXT 2D 8'	A16N	26425	6175	6600	7750	9975
1500 SLT 2D 6 1/4'	A16N	26570	6950	7425	8600	11050
1500 SLT 2D 8'	A16N	26855	6375	6825	7950	10250
4WD	U		2200	2200	2865	2865
V6, 3.7 Liter	K		(450)	(450)	(585)	(585)
V8, HEMI, 5.7 Liter	2		800	800	1040	1040
RAM REGULAR CAB PICKUP—V8 HEMI—Truck Equipment Schedule T1						
2500 SXT 2D 8'	R26D	29685	9175	9750	10750	13300
3500 ST 2D 8' DR	L36D	29610	10650	11300	12400	15300
4WD	S,X		2200	2200	2600	2600
6-Cyl, Turbo Dsl 6.7L	A		4825	4825	5710	5710
RAM REGULAR CAB PICKUP—6-Cyl. Turbo Diesel—Truck Equip Sch T1						
3500 SLT 2D 8' DR	L46A	31860	16700	17600	19000	23300
4WD	S,X		2200	2200	2600	2600
V8, HEMI, 5.7 Liter	D		(4575)	(4575)	(5405)	(5405)
RAM REGULAR CAB 4WD—V8 HEMI—Truck Equipment Schedule T1						
3500 SXT 2D 8' DR	L46D	31305	14400	14800	16100	19850
2WD	C		(2450)	(2450)	(2900)	(2900)
6-Cyl, Turbo Dsl 6.7L	A		4825	4825	5705	5705
RAM REGULAR CAB 4WD—V8 HEMI—Truck Equipment Schedule T1						
2500 ST 2D 8'	S26D	32130	11600	12300	13450	16600
2500 ST 2D 8'	S26D	34725	12000	12700	13950	17250
Power Wagon			4825	4825	5705	5705
2WD	C		(2450)	(2450)	(2900)	(2900)
6-Cyl, HO Trb Dsl 5.9L	A		4500	4500	5315	5315
6-Cyl, Turbo Dsl 6.7L	A		4825	4825	5705	5705
RAM QUAD CAB PICKUP—V8—Truck Equipment Schedule T1						
1500 ST 2D 6 1/4'	A18N	28365	8975	9550	10900	13900
1500 ST 2D 8'	A18N	29900	8675	9225	10550	13500
1500 SXT 2D 6 1/4'	A18N	30470	9600	10200	11650	14850
1500 SLT 2D 6 1/4'	A18N	32005	9100	9675	11100	14150
1500 SLT 2D 6 1/4'	A18N	30740	9750	10350	11800	15050
1500 SLT 2D 8'	A18N	31410	9300	9900	11300	14400
4WD	U		2200	2200	2820	2820
V6, 3.7 Liter	K		(450)	(450)	(575)	(575)
V8, HEMI, 5.7 Liter	2		800	800	1025	1025
RAM QUAD CAB PICKUP 4WD—V8 HEMI—Truck Equipment Schedule T1						
1500 Laramie 6 1/4'	U182	40680	14600	15400	17300	21900
2WD			(2450)	(2450)	(3120)	(3120)
RAM QUAD CAB PICKUP—V8 HEMI—Truck Equipment Schedule T1						
2500 ST 2D 8'	R28D	30740	12250	13000	14150	17450

2008 DODGE/PLYMOUTH

Body Type	VIN	List	Trade-In Good	Very Good	Pvt-Party Good	Retail Excellent
2500 SXT 4D 8'	R28D	32860	12900	13650	14900	18400
2500 SLT 4D 8'	R28D	34105	12750	13500	14750	18200
2500 Laramie 8'	R28D	37235	13750	14550	15800	19450
3500 SXT 4D 8'	L48D	35295	13050	13800	15100	18600
4WD	S		2200	2200	2595	2595
6-Cyl, Turbo Dsl 6.7L	A		4825	4825	5700	5700

RAM QUAD CAB PICKUP 4WD—V8 HEMI—Truck Equipment Schedule T1
2500 ST 4D 6 1/4'	S282	34840	15550	16400	17750	21800
2500 Laramie 6 1/4'	S282	41575	17000	17900	19300	23700
3500 ST 4D 8'	X48D	36160	15450	16300	17600	21600
2WD	R		(2450)	(2450)	(2890)	(2890)
6-Cyl, Turbo Dsl 6.7L	A		4825	4825	5680	5680
6-Cyl, HO Trb Dsl 5.9L	A		4500	4500	5295	5295

RAM QUAD CAB 4WD—6-Cyl. Turbo Diesel—Equipment Schedule T1
2500 SLT 4D 6 1/4'	S28A	36870	21400	22600	24100	29500
2500 SLT 4D 6 1/4'	S28A	44765	21600	22800	24200	29700
3500 SLT 4D 8'	X48A	45560	22000	23200	24700	30300
3500 Laramie 8'	X48A	48665	22600	23800	25300	31000
Power Wagon	R		4825	4825	5690	5690
2WD	R		(2450)	(2450)	(2895)	(2895)
V8, HEMI, 5.7 Liter	D		(4575)	(4575)	(5390)	(5390)

RAM QUAD CAB PICKUP—6-Cyl. Turbo Diesel—Truck Equipment Sch T1
3500 SXT 4D 6 1/4'	L38A	38105	18400	19400	20800	25500
3500 SXT 4D 6 1/4'	L38A	40565	18750	19800	21200	26000
4WD	X		2200	2200	2585	2585
6-Cyl, HO Trb Dsl 5.9L	X		(300)	(300)	(350)	(350)

RAM QUAD CAB 4WD—6-Cyl. Turbo Diesel—Truck Equipment Sch T1
3500 SLT 4D 6 1/4'	X38A	44645	22200	23400	24900	30500
3500 Laramie 6 1/4'	X38A	48075	22500	23700	25200	30900
2WD	L,R		(2450)	(2450)	(2890)	(2890)

RAM MEGA CAB PICKUP—V8 HEMI—Truck Equipment Schedule T1
| 1500 ST 4D 6 1/4' | A19D | 33695 | 13050 | 13800 | 15600 | 19800 |
| 4WD | S,U | | 2200 | 2200 | 2800 | 2800 |

RAM MEGA CAB PICKUP 4WD—V8 HEMI—Truck Equipment Schedule T1
1500 SLT 4D 6 1/4'	S19D	38665	16150	17050	19000	24000
1500 Laramie 6 1/4'	S19D	42250	17100	18000	20100	25300
2WD	A,R		(2450)	(2450)	(3080)	(3080)

RAM MEGA CAB 4WD—6-Cyl. Turbo Diesel—Truck Equipment Schedule T1
2500 SXT 4D 6 1/4'	S29A	45530	25400	26700	28200	34500
2500 SLT 4D 6 1/4'	S29A	46315	25600	26900	28400	35000
2500 Laramie 6 1/4'	S29A	49630	26000	27400	29000	35500
2WD	R		(2450)	(2450)	(2855)	(2855)
V8, HEMI, 5.7 Liter	D		(4575)	(4575)	(5320)	(5320)

RAM MEGA CAB PICKUP 4WD—6-Cyl. Turbo Diesel—Truck Equip Sch T1
3500 SXT 4D 6 1/4'	X39A	47750	25600	26900	28500	34900
3500 SLT 4D 6 1/4'	X39A	48260	25800	27200	28800	35300
3500 Laramie 6 1/4'	X39C	51400	26300	27700	29300	35900
2WD	L		(2450)	(2450)	(2850)	(2850)

2009 DODGE — (1,3orW)D(2,3,4,5,7or8)–(U28K)–9–#

NITRO 4WD—V6—Truck Equipment Schedule T1
SE Sport Utility 4D	U28K	23795	7800	8250	9575	12100
SLT Sport Utility 4D	U58K	26115	8925	9450	10850	13650
R/T Sport Utility 4D	U58X	29290	11350	11950	13450	16650
2WD	T		(875)	(875)	(1150)	(1150)

JOURNEY—4-Cyl.—Truck Equipment Schedule T1
| SE Sport Utility 4D | G47B | 19985 | 5950 | 6325 | 7675 | 9825 |

JOURNEY—V6—Truck Equipment Schedule T1
| SXT Sport Utility 4D | G57V | 22985 | 6950 | 7350 | 8675 | 11000 |
| AWD | H | | 950 | 950 | 1265 | 1265 |

JOURNEY AWD—V6—Truck Equipment Schedule T1
| R/T Sport Utility 4D | H67V | 26545 | 9650 | 10200 | 11500 | 14200 |
| FWD | G | | (1200) | (1200) | (1560) | (1560) |

DURANGO 4WD—V8—Truck Equipment Schedule T1
SE Sport Utility 4D	B38P	31710	8900	9450	10650	13350
Third Row Seat			475	475	600	600
2WD	D		(1300)	(1300)	(1650)	(1650)
V6, 3.7 Liter	K		(675)	(675)	(850)	(850)

DURANGO 4WD—V8 HEMI—Truck Equipment Schedule T1
SLT Sport Utility 4D	B48T	35835	10500	11100	12450	15550
Limited Sport Utility	B58T	41075	10250	10900	12150	14700
Third Row Seat			475	475	605	605
2WD	D		(1300)	(1300)	(1660)	(1660)

Body Type	VIN	List	Trade-In Good	Very Good	Pvt-Party Good	Retail Excellent
V6, 3.7 Liter	K		(1575)	(1575)	(2020)	(2020)
V8, Flex Fuel, 4.7 Liter	P		(800)	(800)	(1020)	(1020)
DURANGO 4WD—V8 HEMI Hybrid—Truck Equipment Schedule T1						
Limited Sport Utility	B18T	45340	12550	13100	14750	17800
Third Row Seat			475	475	580	580
GRAND CARAVAN—V6—Truck Equipment Schedule T1						
SE Minivan	N44E	24300	6800	7300	8525	11050
SXT Minivan	N541	28595	8175	8725	10100	13050
DAKOTA EXTENDED CAB PICKUP—V6—Truck Equipment Schedule T1						
ST 4D 6 1/2'	E38K	24515	6250	6700	7750	9900
Big Horn/Lone Star	E32K	24090	7250	7775	8900	11350
4WD	W		1500	1500	2000	2000
V8, FFV, 4.7 Liter	P		475	475	635	635
DAKOTA EXTENDED CAB PICKUP 4WD—V6—Truck Equipment Schedule T1						
Laramie 4D 6 1/2'	W52K	29995	9875	10550	11850	15000
2WD	E		(2200)	(2200)	(2905)	(2905)
V8, FFV, 4.7 Liter	P		475	475	625	625
DAKOTA EXTENDED CAB PICKUP 4WD—V6—Truck Equipment Sch T1						
TRX 4D 6 1/2'	W72K	30375	8050	8600	9800	12450
V8, FFV, 4.7 Liter	P		475	475	630	630
DAKOTA CREW CAB PICKUP—V6—Truck Equipment Schedule T1						
Big Horn/Lone Star	E38K	26795	9775	10450	11750	14850
4WD	W		1500	1500	1975	1975
V8, FFV, 4.7 Liter	P		475	475	625	625
DAKOTA CREW CAB PICKUP 4WD—V6—Truck Equipment Schedule T1						
ST 4D 5 1/4'	W32K	27440	10900	11600	13050	16450
2WD	E		(2200)	(2200)	(2895)	(2895)
V8, FFV, 4.7 Liter	P		475	475	625	625
DAKOTA CREW CAB 4WD—V8 Flex Fuel—Truck Equipment Schedule T1						
Laramie 4D 5 1/4'	W58N	32530	12900	13700	15350	19300
2WD	E		(2200)	(2200)	(2860)	(2860)
V6, 3.7 Liter	K		(475)	(475)	(615)	(615)
DAKOTA CREW CAB PICKUP 4WD—V8 Flex Fuel—Truck Equipment Sch T1						
TRX 4D 5 1/4'	W78P	31945	12000	12750	14200	17800
V6, 3.7 Liter	K		(475)	(475)	(625)	(625)
RAM REGULAR CAB PICKUP—V6—Truck Equipment Schedule T1						
1500 ST 2D 6 1/4'	A16K	22170	6375	6800	7750	9650
4WD	V		2600	2600	3190	3190
V8, 4.7 Liter	P		675	675	830	830
V8, HEMI, 5.7 Liter	T		1400	1400	1715	1715
RAM REGULAR CAB PICKUP—V8—Truck Equipment Schedule T1						
1500 ST 2D 8'	B16P	23705	6175	6575	7550	9400
1500 ST 2D 6 1/4'	B16P	26615	8075	8550	9650	11900
1500 SLT 2D 8'	B16P	26915	7475	7950	9000	11150
4WD	V		2600	2600	3205	3205
V6, 3.7 Liter	K		(525)	(525)	(645)	(645)
V8, HEMI, 5.7 Liter	T		875	875	1080	1080
RAM REGULAR CAB PICKUP—V8 HEMI—Truck Equipment Schedule T1						
2500 ST 2D 8'	R26T	31980	10800	11400	12400	14950
4WD	S		2600	2600	2990	2990
6-Cyl, Turbo Dsl 6.7L	L		5050	5050	5805	5805
RAM REGULAR CAB PICKUP 4WD—V8 HEMI—Truck Equipment Schedule T1						
2500 ST 2D 8'	S26T	35185	13250	13950	15100	18200
2500 SLT 2D 8'	S26T	35185	13850	14550	15750	18950
2WD	R,L		(2650)	(2650)	(2985)	(2985)
6-Cyl, Turbo Dsl 6.7L	L		5050	5050	5685	5685
RAM REGULAR CAB PICKUP—6-Cyl. Turbo Diesel—Truck Equip Sch T1						
3500 ST 2D 8' DR	L36L	39034	17800	18650	19900	23900
3500 SLT 2D 8' DR	L36L	41284	18550	19450	20700	24800
4WD	X		2600	2600	2925	2925
RAM REGULAR CAB 4WD—6-Cyl. Turbo Diesel—Truck Equip Sch T1						
3500 SXT 2D 8' DR	L46L	39654	21500	22500	23900	28600
2WD	X		(2650)	(2650)	(2975)	(2975)
RAM QUAD CAB PICKUP—V8—Truck Equipment Schedule T1						
1500 ST 4D 6 1/4'	B18P	27460	10700	11300	12500	15350
1500 SLT 4D 6 1/4'	B18P	30625	11300	11950	13250	16250
4WD	V		2600	2600	3150	3150
V6, 3.7 Liter	K		(525)	(525)	(635)	(635)
V8, HEMI, 5.7 Liter	T		875	875	1060	1060
RAM QUAD CAB PICKUP 4WD—V8 HEMI—Truck Equipment Schedule T1						
1500 Laramie 6 1/4'	V18T	42785	17250	18100	19700	24000
2WD	B		(2650)	(2650)	(3195)	(3195)

Body Type	VIN	List	Trade-In Good	Very Good	Pvt-Party Good	Retail Excellent

RAM QUAD CAB PICKUP—V8 HEMI—Truck Equipment Schedule T1

Body Type	VIN	List	Good	Very Good	Good	Excellent
2500 ST 4D 8'	R28T	33125	14150	14850	16050	19350
2500 SXT 8'	R28T	35155	14750	15500	16650	20000
2500 SLT 4D 8'	R28T	36400	14550	15250	16500	19850
2500 Laramie 8'	R28T	39830	15650	16400	17600	21100
Power Wagon			5025	5025	5645	5645
4WD	S,V		2600	2600	2925	2925
6-Cyl, Turbo Dsl 6.7L	L		5050	5050	5680	5680

RAM QUAD CAB PICKUP 4WD—V8 HEMI—Truck Equipment Schedule T1

Body Type	VIN	List	Good	Very Good	Good	Excellent
2500 ST 4D 6 1/4'	S28T	35000	17500	18350	19600	23500
2500 Laramie 6 1/4'	S28T	42035	18950	19900	21100	25300
2WD	B,R		(2650)	(2650)	(2990)	(2990)
6-Cyl, Turbo Dsl 6.7L	L		5050	5050	5685	5685

RAM QUAD CAB 4WD—6-Cyl. Turbo Diesel—Truck Equipment Sch T1

Body Type	VIN	List	Good	Very Good	Good	Excellent
2500 SLT 4D 6 1/4'	S28L	44925	23800	24900	26300	31400
2500 SXT 4D 6 1/4'	S28L	48165	24000	25100	26500	31700
Power Wagon			5025	5025	5645	5645
2WD	B,R		(2650)	(2650)	(2975)	(2975)
V8, HEMI, 5.7 Liter	T		(4925)	(4925)	(5515)	(5515)

RAM QUAD CAB PICKUP—6-Cyl. Turbo Diesel—Truck Equipment Sch T1

Body Type	VIN	List	Good	Very Good	Good	Excellent
3500 ST 4D 6 1/4'	L38L	41429	20500	21400	22700	27200
3500 SXT 4D 8'	L38L	42334	20900	21900	23200	27800
3500 SXT 4D 8'	L38L	43444	20700	21700	23000	27600
4WD	X		2600	2600	2920	2920

RAM QUAD CAB 4WD—6-Cyl. Turbo Diesel—Truck Equipment Sch T1

Body Type	VIN	List	Good	Very Good	Good	Excellent
2500 SLT 4D 6 1/4'	S28L	44925	23800	24900	26300	31400
3500 ST 4D 8'	X38L	42664	23400	24400	25400	29900
3500 SLT 4D 6 1/4'	X38L	45915	24500	25600	27000	32300
3500 SLT 4D 8'	X38L	46830	24300	25400	26800	32000
3500 Laramie 6 1/4'	X38L	49530	25100	26200	27600	33000
3500 Laramie 8'	X48L	50720	24700	25800	27200	32500
Power Wagon			5025	5025	5645	5645
2WD	B,R		(2650)	(2650)	(2975)	(2975)
V8, HEMI, 5.7 Liter	T		(4925)	(4925)	(5520)	(5520)

RAM CREW CAB PICKUP—V8—Truck Equipment Schedule T1

Body Type	VIN	List	Good	Very Good	Good	Excellent
1500 SLT 4D 5 1/2'	B13P	32780	13200	13900	15350	18800
4WD	V,S		2600	2600	3150	3150
V8, HEMI, 5.7 Liter	T		875	875	1060	1060

RAM CREW CAB PICKUP 4WD—V8—Truck Equipment Schedule T1

Body Type	VIN	List	Good	Very Good	Good	Excellent
1500 ST 4D 5 1/2'	V13P	33040	15950	16750	18300	22300
2WD	B,R		(2650)	(2650)	(3205)	(3205)
V8, HEMI, 5.7 Liter	T		875	875	1055	1055

RAM CREW CAB PICKUP 4WD—V8 HEMI—Truck Equipment Schedule T1

Body Type	VIN	List	Good	Very Good	Good	Excellent
1500 Laramie 5 1/2'	V13T	44935	19350	20300	21900	26700
2WD	B,R		(2650)	(2650)	(3190)	(3190)

RAM MEGA CAB 4WD—6-Cyl. Turbo Diesel—Truck Equipment Schedule T1

Body Type	VIN	List	Good	Very Good	Good	Excellent
2500 SXT 4D 6 1/4'	S29L	47165	27300	28600	29900	35700
2500 Laramie 6 1/4'	S29L	51450	28200	29500	31000	37100
2WD	B,R		(2650)	(2650)	(2975)	(2975)
V8, HEMI, 5.7 Liter	T		(4925)	(4925)	(5515)	(5515)

RAM MEGA CAB 4WD—6-Cyl. Turbo Diesel—Truck Equipment Sch T1

Body Type	VIN	List	Good	Very Good	Good	Excellent
3500 SXT 4D 6 1/4'	X39L	50070	27600	28900	30300	36100
3500 Laramie 6 1/4'	X39L	49530	28500	29800	31400	37500
2WD			(2650)	(2650)	(2980)	(2980)

2010 DODGE—(1,3orW)D(2,3,4,5,7or8)—(U2GK)—A—#

NITRO 4WD—V6—Truck Equipment Schedule T1

Body Type	VIN	List	Good	Very Good	Good	Excellent
SE Sport Util 4D	U2GK	23995	9875	10400	11650	14200
Heat Sport Util	U4GK	23995	10650	11150	12450	15100
SXT Sport Util 4D	U5GK	25640	10850	11400	12750	15450
2WD	T		(1000)	(1000)	(1245)	(1245)
V6, 4.0 Liter	X		1350	1350	1690	1690

NITRO 2WD—V6—Truck Equipment Schedule T1

Body Type	VIN	List	Good	Very Good	Good	Excellent
Detonator Spt Utl	U6GX	28155	12350	12950	14350	17350
Shock Sport Util	U7GX	29155	13050	13700	15200	18400
2WD	T		(1000)	(1000)	(1240)	(1240)

JOURNEY—4-Cyl.—Truck Equipment Schedule T1

Body Type	VIN	List	Good	Very Good	Good	Excellent
SE Sport Utility 4D	G4FB	21165	7400	7800	9175	11400

JOURNEY—V6 HO—Truck Equipment Schedule T1

Body Type	VIN	List	Good	Very Good	Good	Excellent
SXT Sport Utility	G5FV	24465	8400	8850	10250	12600
AWD	H		1000	1000	1285	1285

JOURNEY AWD—V6 HO—Truck Equipment Schedule T1

Body Type	VIN	List	Good	Very Good	Good	Excellent
R/T Sport Utility	H6FV	28870	11000	11550	12850	15500

TRUCKS & VANS

Body Type	VIN	List	Trade-In Good	Trade-In Very Good	Pvt-Party Good	Retail Excellent
FWD	G		**(1100)**	**(1100)**	**(1345)**	**(1345)**
CARAVAN CARGO—V6—Truck Equipment Schedule T2						
Grand Minivan	N1AE	22620	**6475**	**6925**	**7950**	**10100**
GRAND CARAVAN—V6—Truck Equipment Schedule T1						
SE Minivan	N4DE	23995	**8075**	**8600**	**9775**	**12300**
Hero Minivan	N3D1	25675	**8625**	**9175**	**10350**	**13000**
SXT Minivan	N5D1	27300	**9200**	**9775**	**11050**	**13850**
5-Passenger Seating			**(550)**	**(550)**	**(730)**	**(730)**
V6, 4.0 Liter	X		**325**	**325**	**420**	**420**
GRAND CARAVAN—V6—Truck Equipment Schedule T1						
Crew Minivan	N6DX	28795	**9650**	**10250**	**11550**	**14450**
DAKOTA EXTENDED CAB PICKUP—V6—Truck Equipment Sch T1						
ST 4D 6 1/2'	E2BK	23495	**7400**	**7925**	**8875**	**11000**
Big Horn/Lone Star	E3BK	24370	**9000**	**9575**	**10650**	**13150**
4WD	W		**1700**	**1700**	**2155**	**2155**
V8, FFV, 4.7 Liter	P		**550**	**550**	**695**	**695**
DAKOTA CREW CAB PICKUP—V6—Truck Equipment Schedule T1						
Big Horn/Lone Star	E3GK	27065	**11400**	**12100**	**13300**	**16350**
4WD	W		**1700**	**1700**	**2140**	**2140**
V8, FFV, 4.7 Liter	P		**550**	**550**	**690**	**690**
DAKOTA CREW CAB PICKUP 4WD—V6—Truck Equipment Schedule T1						
ST 4D 5 1/4'	W5GK	29075	**12700**	**13450**	**14600**	**17850**
2WD	E		**(2200)**	**(2200)**	**(2740)**	**(2740)**
V8, FFV, 4.7 Liter	P		**550**	**550**	**685**	**685**
DAKOTA CREW CAB 4WD—V8 Flex Fuel—Truck Equipment Sch T1						
Laramie 4D 5 1/4'	W5GP	33795	**14700**	**15600**	**17050**	**20900**
2WD	E		**(2200)**	**(2200)**	**(2770)**	**(2770)**
V6, 3.7 Liter	K		**(550)**	**(550)**	**(690)**	**(690)**
DAKOTA CREW CAB PICKUP 4WD—V8 Flex Fuel—Truck Equipment Sch T1						
TRX 4D 5 1/4'	W7GP	32105	**12750**	**13500**	**14900**	**18300**
RAM REGULAR CAB PICKUP—V6—Truck Equipment Schedule T1						
1500 ST 2D 6 1/3'	B1EK	21510	**7775**	**8225**	**9300**	**11350**
4WD	W		**2800**	**2800**	**3320**	**3320**
V8, Flex Fuel, 4.7 Liter	P		**800**	**800**	**950**	**950**
V8, HEMI, 5.7 Liter	T		**1550**	**1550**	**1835**	**1835**
RAM REGULAR CAB PICKUP—V8—Truck Equipment Schedule T1						
1500 ST 2D 8'	B1EP	21810	**7775**	**7900**	**8975**	**11000**
1500 SLT 2D 6 1/3'	B1EP	25755	**9375**	**9875**	**11050**	**13450**
1500 SLT 2D 8'	B1EP	26055	**8825**	**9300**	**10400**	**12700**
4WD	V		**2800**	**2800**	**3320**	**3320**
V6, 3.7 Liter	K		**(600)**	**(600)**	**(710)**	**(710)**
V8, HEMI, 5.7 Liter	T		**950**	**950**	**1125**	**1125**
RAM REGULAR CAB PICKUP—V8 HEMI—Truck Equipment Schedule T1						
2500 SLT 2D 8'	P2ET	31310	**12650**	**13250**	**14500**	**17250**
4WD	W		**2800**	**2800**	**3235**	**3235**
6-Cyl, Turbo Dsl 6.7L	L		**5275**	**5275**	**6080**	**6080**
RAM REGULAR CAB PICKUP 4WD—V8 HEMI—Truck Equipment Schedule T1						
2500 ST 2D 8'	T2ET	30475	**14950**	**15650**	**16900**	**20000**
2WD	P		**(2825)**	**(2825)**	**(3220)**	**(3220)**
6-Cyl, Turbo Dsl 6.7L	L		**5275**	**5275**	**5980**	**5980**
RAM REGULAR CAB PICKUP—6-Cyl. Turbo Diesel—Truck Equip Sch T1						
3500 ST 2D 8' DR	M4EL	35630	**20200**	**20800**	**22100**	**26100**
3500 SLT 2D 8' DR	M4EL	39270	**20600**	**21500**	**22800**	**26900**
4WD	Y		**2800**	**2800**	**3165**	**3165**
RAM QUAD CAB PICKUP—V8—Truck Equipment Schedule T1						
1500 SLT 4D 6 1/3'	B1GP	29765	**12700**	**13300**	**14650**	**17650**
4WD	V		**2800**	**2800**	**3290**	**3290**
V8, HEMI, 5.7 Liter	T		**950**	**950**	**1115**	**1115**
RAM QUAD CAB PICKUP 4WD—V8—Truck Equipment Schedule T1						
1500 ST 4D 6 1/3'	V1GP	29975	**15400**	**16100**	**17700**	**21300**
2WD	B		**(2825)**	**(2825)**	**(3325)**	**(3325)**
V6, 3.7 Liter	K		**(600)**	**(600)**	**(705)**	**(705)**
V8, HEMI, 5.7 Liter	T		**950**	**950**	**1115**	**1115**
RAM QUAD CAB PICKUP—V8 HEMI—Truck Equipment Schedule T1						
1500 Laramie 6 1/3'	B1GT	37780	**14850**	**15550**	**17100**	**20600**
4WD	V		**2800**	**2800**	**3290**	**3290**
RAM CREW CAB PICKUP—V8—Truck Equipment Schedule T1						
1500 SLT 4D 5 1/2'	B1CT	33230	**16500**	**17200**	**18900**	**22800**
4WD	T,V		**2800**	**2800**	**3300**	**3300**
V8, Flex Fuel, 4.7 Liter	P		**(850)**	**(850)**	**(1000)**	**(1000)**
RAM CREW CAB PICKUP 4WD—V8 HEMI—Truck Equipment Schedule T1						
1500 ST 4D 5 1/2'	V1CT	34880	**19450**	**20300**	**22000**	**26400**
1500 Laramie 5 1/2'	V1CT	45470	**21800**	**22700**	**24600**	**29500**

Body Type	VIN	List	Trade-In Good	Very Good	Pvt-Party Good	Retail Excellent
2WD	B		(2825)	(2825)	(3325)	(3325)
V8, Flex Fuel, 4.7 Liter			(850)	(850)	(995)	(995)
RAM CREW CAB PICKUP 4WD—V8 HEMI—Truck Equipment Schedule T1						
2500 ST 4D 6 1/3'	T2CT	34085	19300	20100	21400	25300
2500 ST 4D 8'	T2CT	31615	15650	16350	17600	20800
2500 SLT 4D 8'	T2CT	36365	16400	17150	18400	21800
2500 Laramie 8'	T2CT	40440	18000	18800	20100	23700
2WD	P		(2825)	(2825)	(3205)	(3205)
6-Cyl, Turbo Dsl 6.7L	L		5275	5275	5955	5955
RAM CREW CAB 4WD—6-Cyl. Turbo Diesel—Truck Equipment Sch T1						
2500 SLT 4D 6 1/3'	T2CL	46245	25900	27000	28400	33500
2500 Laramie 6 1/3'	T2CL	50950	27400	28600	30000	35400
Power Wagon			5225	5225	5910	5910
2WD	P		(2825)	(2825)	(3205)	(3205)
V8, HEMI, 5.7 Liter	X		(5275)	(5275)	(5955)	(5955)
RAM CREW CAB PICKUP—6-Cyl. Turbo Diesel—Truck Equipment Sch T1						
3500 ST 4D 6 1/3'	M3CL	40775	22900	23800	25200	29700
3500 ST 4D 8' DR	M3CL	40975	22700	23600	24800	29100
4WD	Y		2800	2800	3170	3170
RAM CREW CAB 4WD—6-Cyl. Turbo Diesel—Truck Equipment Sch T1						
3500 SLT 4D 6 1/3'	Y3CL	48320	26700	27800	29300	34500
3500 SLT 4D 8' DR	Y3CL	48520	26500	27600	29100	34300
3500 Laramie 6 1/3'	Y3CL	52860	27500	28700	30100	35500
3500 Laramie 8' DR	Y3CL	53060	27100	28300	29700	35000
2WD	P		(2825)	(2825)	(3205)	(3205)
RAM MEGA CAB 4WD—6-Cyl. Turbo Diesel—Truck Equipment Sch T1						
2500 SLT 4D 6 1/3'	S2HL	46945	29200	30400	32000	37700
2WD	P		(2825)	(2825)	(3200)	(3200)
V8, HEMI, 5.7 Liter	T		(5275)	(5275)	(5945)	(5945)
RAM MEGA CAB PICKUP—V8 HEMI—Truck Equipment Schedule T1						
2500 Laramie 6 1/3'	P2HT	40940	21200	22100	23400	27600
4WD	T		2800	2800	3175	3175
6-Cyl, Turbo Dsl 6.7L	L		5275	5275	5965	5965
RAM MEGA CAB PICKUP—6-Cyl. Turbo Diesel—Truck Equipment Sch T1						
3500 Laramie 6 DR	M4HL	48715	27200	28400	29800	35100
4WD	Y		2800	2800	3160	3160
RAM MEGA CAB 4WD—6-Cyl. Turbo Diesel—Truck Equipment Sch T1						
3500 SLT 6 1/3' DR	Y4HL	49020	29800	31000	32600	38400
2WD	M		(2825)	(2825)	(3185)	(3185)

2011 DODGE — 1D4-(U2GK)-B-#

Body Type	VIN	List	Trade-In Good	Very Good	Pvt-Party Good	Retail Excellent
NITRO 4WD—V6—Truck Equipment Schedule T1						
SE Sport Utility 4D	U2GK	24090	10800	11300	12650	15150
Heat Sport Utility	U4GK	24000	12000	12550	13900	16650
SXT Sport Util 4D	U5GK	25735	11700	12200	13650	16350
2WD	T		(1100)	(1100)	(1335)	(1335)
V6, 4.0 Liter			1450	1450	1760	1760
NITRO 4WD—V6—Truck Equipment Schedule T1						
Detonator Spt Util	U6GX	28745	14350	14950	16500	19650
Shock Sport Utility	U7GX	29745	14750	15350	16950	20200
2WD	T		(1100)	(1100)	(1330)	(1330)
JOURNEY—4-Cyl.—Truck Equipment Schedule T1						
Express Sport Util	G4FB	22995	8950	9375	10750	12950
Third Row Seat			400	400	485	485
JOURNEY—V6—Truck Equipment Schedule T1						
Mainstreet Utility	G1FG	23655	9900	10350	11700	14050
Crew Sport Utility	G3FG	29175	11850	12450	13600	16150
Third Row Seat			400	400	485	485
AWD	H		1000	1000	1210	1210
JOURNEY AWD—V6—Truck Equipment Schedule T1						
R/T Sport Utility	G6FG	28995	12850	13450	14750	17450
LUX Sport Utility	G9FG	33490	14750	15400	16700	19700
Third Row Seat			400	400	470	470
FWD	G		(1100)	(1100)	(1295)	(1295)
DURANGO AWD—V6—Truck Equipment Schedule T1						
Express Sport Util	E2GG	32045	15750	16450	17750	20600
Heat Sport Utility	E3GG	33145	16550	17200	18350	21400
2WD	D		(1475)	(1475)	(1725)	(1725)
DURANGO AWD—V6—Truck Equipment Schedule T1						
Crew Sport Utility	E4GG	36045	17250	17950	19100	22300
2WD	D		(1475)	(1475)	(1730)	(1730)
V8, HEMI, 5.7 Liter	T		1800	1800	2120	2120

TRUCKS & VANS

TRUCKS & VANS

Body Type	VIN	List	Trade-In Good	Trade-In Very Good	Pvt-Party Good	Retail Excellent
DURANGO AWD—V8 HEMI—Truck Equipment Schedule T1						
R/T Sport Utility 4D	E6GT	38715	21200	22000	23200	27200
Citadel Sport Utl	E5GT	44645	21900	22600	23700	26900
2WD	D		(1475)	(1475)	(1660)	(1660)
V6, 3.6 Liter	G		(900)	(900)	(1015)	(1015)
CARAVAN CARGO—V6—Truck Equipment Schedule T2						
Grand Minivan	N1AG	23375	7325	7800	8925	11150
GRAND CARAVAN—V6—Truck Equipment Schedule T1						
Express Minivan	N4DG	25830	9325	9875	11100	13750
Mainstreet Minivan	N3DG	26830	9875	10450	11700	14450
Crew Minivan	N5DG	29530	10850	11500	12800	15750
R/T Minivan	N7DG	31430	12600	13300	14700	18050
5-Passenger Seating			(600)	(600)	(775)	(775)

2012 DODGE — (1,2or3)C4–(DCAB)–C–#

Body Type	VIN	List	Trade-In Good	Trade-In Very Good	Pvt-Party Good	Retail Excellent
JOURNEY—4-Cyl.—Truck Equipment Schedule T1						
American Value	DCAB	19795	9125	9550	10950	13150
SE Sport Utility 4D	DCAB	21795	10450	10900	12300	14700
Third Row Seat			425	425	515	515
JOURNEY—V6—Truck Equipment Schedule T1						
SXT Sport Utility	DCBG	25295	12550	13050	14550	17250
Crew Sport Utility	DCDG	29295	14450	15100	16400	19200
R/T Sport Utility	DCEG	30795	15650	16300	17700	20700
Third Row Seat			425	425	515	515
FWD	C		(1200)	(1200)	(1455)	(1455)
4-Cyl, 2.4 Liter	B		(900)	(900)	(1090)	(1090)
DURANGO AWD—V6—Truck Equipment Schedule T1						
SXT Sport Util 4D	DJAG	31845	18700	19400	20400	23500
2WD	H		(1550)	(1550)	(1770)	(1770)
DURANGO AWD—V6—Truck Equipment Schedule T1						
Crew Sport Utility	DJDG	36545	20100	20900	21900	25200
2WD	H		(1550)	(1550)	(1780)	(1780)
V8, HEMI, 5.7 Liter			1100	1100	1260	1260
DURANGO AWD—V8 HEMI—Truck Equipment Schedule T1						
R/T Sport Utility 4D	DJCT	38845	23600	24400	25600	29400
Citadel Sport Util	DJET	43845	24300	25100	26100	29400
2WD	H		(1550)	(1550)	(1735)	(1735)
V6, 3.6 Liter	G		(1000)	(1000)	(1115)	(1115)
GRAND CARAVAN—V6—Truck Equipment Schedule T1						
SE Minivan	DGBG	23830	10050	10650	11950	14700
SXT Minivan	DGCG	27330	11000	11600	13000	15950
Crew Minivan	DGDG	29330	12400	13100	14550	17750
R/T Minivan	DGEG	30830	14200	14950	16550	20100
5-Passenger Seating			(650)	(650)	(840)	(840)

2013 DODGE — (1,2or3)C4–(DCAB)–D–#

Body Type	VIN	List	Trade-In Good	Trade-In Very Good	Pvt-Party Good	Retail Excellent
JOURNEY—4-Cyl.—Truck Equipment Schedule T1						
AVP Sport Utility	DCAB	19990	10350	10800	12150	14400
SE Sport Utility 4D	DCAB	21990	11800	12300	13800	16300
Third Row Seat			450	450	530	530
JOURNEY AWD—V6—Truck Equipment Schedule T1						
SXT Sport Utility	DDBG	27390	14100	14650	16250	19100
Third Row Seat			450	450	530	530
FWD	C		(1300)	(1300)	(1530)	(1530)
4-Cyl, 2.4 Liter	B		(1000)	(1000)	(1175)	(1175)
JOURNEY AWD—V6—Truck Equipment Schedule T1						
Crew Sport Utility	DDDG	30790	15350	15950	17300	20100
R/T Sport Utility	DDEG	31790	16950	17650	18950	21900
Third Row Seat			450	450	525	525
FWD	C		(1300)	(1300)	(1515)	(1515)
DURANGO AWD—V6—Truck Equipment Schedule T1						
SXT Sport Util 4D	DJAG	32190	20800	21500	22500	25600
2WD	H		(1625)	(1625)	(1850)	(1850)
DURANGO AWD—V8 HEMI—Truck Equipment Schedule T1						
Crew Sport Utility	DJDT	38790	23000	23700	24700	28200
Citadel Sport Util	DJET	43190	25700	26500	27600	31100
2WD	H		(1625)	(1625)	(1850)	(1850)
V6, 3.6 Liter	G		(1100)	(1100)	(1245)	(1245)
DURANGO AWD—V8 HEMI—Truck Equipment Schedule T1						
R/T Sport Utility 4D	DJCT	39590	26100	26900	28000	31900
2WD	H		(1625)	(1625)	(1855)	(1855)

Body Type	VIN	List	Trade-In Good	Trade-In Very Good	Pvt-Party Good	Retail Excellent
GRAND CARAVAN—V6 Flex Fuel—Truck Equipment Schedule T1						
AVP Minivan	DGBG	20990	9925	10500	11700	14250
SE Minivan	DGBG	23900	11350	11950	13250	16050
SXT Minivan	DGCG	27490	12550	13200	14500	17550
Crew Minivan	DGDG	29490	13650	14350	15850	19150
R/T Minivan	DGEG	30990	16050	16800	18400	22100

2014 DODGE — (1,2or3)C4–(DCAB)–E–#

Body Type	VIN	List	Good	Very Good	Good	Excellent
JOURNEY—4-Cyl.—Truck Equipment Schedule T1						
AVP Sport Utility	DCAB	20490	11900	12350	13900	16400
SE Sport Utility 4D	DDAG	25890	14950	15500	17050	19750
Third Row Seat			475	475	555	555
JOURNEY AWD—V6—Truck Equipment Schedule T1						
SXT Sport Utility	DDBG	27690	15700	16300	17850	20800
Third Row Seat			475	475	550	550
FWD	C		(1400)	(1400)	(1630)	(1630)
4-Cyl, 2.4 Liter	B		(1100)	(1100)	(1280)	(1280)
JOURNEY AWD—V6—Truck Equipment Schedule T1						
SXT Plus Sport Util 4D		28685	16100	16650	18250	21200
Crossroad Spt Util	DDGB	29390	17900	18550	19950	22800
Third Row Seat			475	475	550	550
FWD	C		(1400)	(1400)	(1625)	(1625)
4-Cyl, 2.4 Liter	B		(1100)	(1100)	(1275)	(1275)
JOURNEY AWD—V6—Truck Equipment Schedule T1						
Limited Sport Util	DDDG	31190	18650	19300	20900	24200
R/T Sport Utility	DDEG	31790	18600	19350	20700	23800
Third Row Seat			475	475	550	550
FWD	C		(1400)	(1400)	(1645)	(1645)
DURANGO AWD—V6 Flex Fuel—Truck Equipment Schedule T1						
SXT Sport Util 4D	DJAG	33190	23000	23800	24800	28400
SXT Plus Sport Util	DJAG	34890	23000	23800	24800	28400
Citadel Sport Util	DJET	44390	30100	31000	32100	35800
2WD	H		(1725)	(1725)	(1940)	(1940)
DURANGO AWD—V8 HEMI—Truck Equipment Schedule T1						
Special Serv Spt Util	DJFT	34290				
Limited Sport Util	DJDT	39390	27200	28100	29200	32700
2WD	H		(1725)	(1725)	(1915)	(1915)
V6, Flex Fuel, 3.6 Liter	G		(1200)	(1200)	(1335)	(1335)
DURANGO AWD—V8 HEMI—Truck Equipment Schedule T1						
R/T Sport Utility 4D	DJCT	42390	28200	29100	30100	34300
2WD	H		(1725)	(1725)	(1935)	(1935)
GRAND CARAVAN—V6 Flex Fuel—Truck Equipment Schedule T1						
AVP Minivan 4D	DGBG	20990	11250	11850	13000	15600
SE Minivan 4D	DGBG	24390	13100	13750	15050	18000
SE 30th Anniv	DGBG	25690	14100	14800	16100	19200
SXT Minivan 4D	DGCG	27690	14850	15600	16950	20200
SXT 30th Anniv	DGCG	28990	16700	17500	18900	22500
R/T Minivan 4D	DGEG	30990	17900	18750	20100	23900

FORD

2000 FORD–(1,2or3)F(B,MorT)–(U70X)–Y–#

Body Type	VIN	List	Good	Very Good	Good	Excellent
EXPLORER SPORT 4WD—V6—Truck Equipment Schedule T1						
Utility 2D	U70X	24690	450	550	1300	2175
2WD	6		(550)	(550)	(750)	(750)
V6, SOHC, 4.0 Liter	E		75	75	115	115
EXPLORER 4WD—V6—Truck Equipment Schedule T1						
XL Sport Utility 4D	U72X	26790	650	775	1575	2650
Eddie Bauer Spt Util	U74P	34470	950	1125	2000	3375
2WD	6		(550)	(550)	(750)	(750)
AWD	8		0	0	0	0
V6, SOHC, 4.0 Liter	E		75	75	115	115
V8, 5.0 Liter	P		100	100	125	125
EXPEDITION 4WD—V8—Truck Equipment Schedule T1						
XLT Sport Utility 4D	U166	33165	775	900	1850	3200
Eddie Bauer Spt Util	U186	40575	1275	1450	2575	4425
Third Row Seat			250	250	320	320
2WD	5,7		(350)	(350)	(465)	(465)
V8, 5.4 Liter	L		75	75	100	100
EXCURSION 4WD—V10—Truck Equipment Schedule T1						
XLT Sport Utility 4D	U41S	38090	2550	2900	3950	6025

TRUCKS & VANS

TRUCKS & VANS

Body Type	VIN	List	Trade-In Good	Trade-In Very Good	Pvt-Party Good	Retail Excellent
Third Row Seat			250	250	320	320
2WD			(350)	(350)	(465)	(465)
V8, 5.4 Liter	L		(250)	(250)	(350)	(350)
V8, Turbo Diesel, 7.3L	F		2425	2425	3235	3235
WINDSTAR—V6—Truck Equipment Schedule T2						
Cargo Minivan	A544	20395	525	625	1350	2350
WINDSTAR—V6—Truck Equipment Schedule T1						
Minivan	A504	23080	400	475	1200	2075
LX Minivan	A514	25045	550	650	1400	2425
SE Minivan	A524	28195	875	1000	1850	3200
SEL Minivan	A534	31095	975	1125	2000	3425
Limited Minivan	A534	33990	1125	1275	2200	3775
Second Sliding Door	0		50	50	60	60
V6, 3.0 Liter	U		(100)	(100)	(120)	(120)
ECONOLINE WAGON—V8—Truck Equipment Schedule T1						
E150 Passenger Van	E11L	23810	1125	1275	1800	2950
E350 Super Duty Van	E31L	25900	1225	1375	1925	3175
E350 Super Duty Ext	S31L	27570	1375	1550	2125	3525
V6, 4.2 Liter	2		(200)	(200)	(265)	(265)
V8, Turbo Diesel, 7.3L	F		1125	1125	1500	1500
V10, 6.8 Liter	S		225	225	300	300
ECONOLINE VAN—V6—Truck Equipment Schedule T1						
E150 Cargo Van	E142	20950	875	975	1625	2750
E250 Cargo Van	E242	22055	925	1025	1700	2900
E250 Extended	E242	22900	1375	1525	2375	4050
V8, 4.6 Liter	W		75	75	100	100
V8, 5.4 Liter	L		100	100	135	135
ECONOLINE VAN—V8—Truck Equipment Schedule T1						
E350 Super Cargo	E34L	24045	1150	1275	2025	3475
E350 Ext SD Cargo	S34L	25475	1475	1625	2525	4325
V8, Turbo Diesel, 7.3L	F		1125	1125	1500	1500
V10, 6.8 Liter	S		225	225	300	300
RANGER PICKUP—4-Cyl.—Truck Equipment Schedule T2						
Short Bed	R10C	11995	650	750	1175	1900
Long Bed	R10C	12465	575	675	1075	1775
Super Cab 2D	R14C	15655	775	875	1375	2275
Super Cab 4D	R14C	16230	1425	1600	2225	3700
4WD	1,5		400	400	535	535
V6, Flex Fuel, 3.0 Liter	V		125	125	165	165
V6, 4.0 Liter	S		150	150	200	200
REGULAR CAB PICKUP—V8—Truck Equipment Schedule T1						
F150 Short Bed	F17W	19510	1400	1575	2250	3775
F150 Long Bed	F17W	19810	1175	1325	1950	3275
4WD	6,8		650	650	865	865
Work Truck			(250)	(250)	(335)	(335)
V6, 4.2 Liter	2		(350)	(350)	(465)	(465)
V8, 5.4 Liter	L		75	75	100	100
REGULAR CAB—V8 Supercharged—Truck Equip Schedule T1						
F150 Lightning	F073	30895	5275	5800	6675	9300
SUPER CAB PICKUP—V8—Truck Equipment Schedule T1						
F150 Short Bed	X17W	22195	2775	3075	4225	6625
F150 Long Bed	X17W	22495	2125	2325	3300	5250
4WD	6,8		650	650	865	865
Work Truck			(250)	(250)	(335)	(335)
V6, 4.2 Liter	2		(350)	(350)	(465)	(465)
V8, 5.4 Liter	L		75	75	100	100
SUPER CAB PICKUP—V8—Truck Equipment Schedule T1						
F150 Harley	X17L	33800	5125	5625	6375	8950
SUPER DUTY REGULAR CAB PICKUP—V8—Truck Equip Schedule T1						
F250 Long Bed	F20L	22450	2075	2300	2950	4500
F350 Long Bed	F30L	23175	2175	2425	3100	4775
4WD	1		650	650	865	865
V8, Turbo Diesel, 7.3L	F		2425	2425	3235	3235
V10, 6.8 Liter	S		250	250	315	315
SUPER DUTY SUPER CAB PICKUP—V8—Truck Equip Schedule T1						
F250 Short Bed	X20L	24620	3075	3425	4300	6575
F250 Long Bed	X20L	24820	2900	3250	4000	6025
F350 Short Bed	X30L	25410	3250	3600	4525	6875
F350 Long Bed	X30L	25610	3150	3500	4375	6675
4WD	1		650	650	865	865
V8, Turbo Diesel, 7.3L	F		2425	2425	3235	3235
V10, 6.8 Liter	S		250	250	315	315

Body Type	VIN	List	Trade-In Good	Very Good	Pvt-Party Good	Retail Excellent
SUPER DUTY CREW CAB PICKUP—V8—Truck Equipment Schedule T1						
F250 Short Bed	W20L	25930	3550	3950	5000	7525
F250 Long Bed	W20L	26130	3525	3900	4850	7300
F350 Short Bed	W30L	26590	3725	4125	5300	8025
F350 Long Bed	W30L	26790	3625	4025	5150	7775
4WD	1		650	650	865	865
V8, Turbo Diesel, 7.3L	F		2425	2425	3235	3235
V10, 6.8 Liter	S		250	250	315	315
2001 FORD — (1or2)F(B,MorT)-(U011)-1-#						
ESCAPE—V6—Truck Equipment Schedule T1						
XLS Sport Utility 4D	U011	19975	675	800	1725	2950
4WD			375	375	510	510
4-Cyl, 2.0 Liter	B		(300)	(300)	(385)	(385)
ESCAPE 4WD—V6—Truck Equipment Schedule T1						
XLT Sport Utility 4D	U041	22815	1250	1425	2400	3975
2WD			(400)	(400)	(535)	(535)
4-Cyl, 2.0 Liter	B		(300)	(300)	(385)	(385)
EXPLORER SPORT 4WD—V6—Truck Equipment Schedule T1						
Sport Utility 2D	U70E	24435	525	625	1375	2275
2WD	6		(650)	(650)	(860)	(860)
EXPLORER 4WD—V6—Truck Equipment Schedule T1						
XLS Sport Utility 4D	U71E	27570	825	950	1700	2750
Eddie Bauer Spt Util	U74E	34590	1175	1350	2150	3500
2WD	6		(650)	(650)	(860)	(860)
AWD	8		0	0	0	0
V8, 5.0 Liter	P		100	100	135	135
EXPLORER SPORT TRAC 4WD—V6—Truck Equipment Sch T1						
Utility Pickup 4D	U77E	25010	2725	3000	4350	6575
2WD	6		(650)	(650)	(860)	(860)
EXPEDITION 4WD—V8—Truck Equipment Schedule T1						
XLT Sport Util 4D	U16W	33405	975	1125	2075	3525
Eddie Bauer Util	U18W	41410	1550	1750	2975	4950
Third Row Seat			275	275	360	360
2WD	5		(400)	(400)	(535)	(535)
V8, 5.4 Liter			75	75	100	100
EXCURSION 4WD—V10—Truck Equipment Schedule T1						
XLT Sport Utility 4D	U41S	38925	3025	3425	4725	7125
Third Row Seat			275	275	360	360
2WD	0,2		(400)	(400)	(535)	(535)
V8, 5.4 Liter			(300)	(300)	(395)	(395)
V8, Turbo Diesel, 7.3L	F		2650	2650	3535	3535
WINDSTAR—V6—Truck Equipment Schedule T2						
Cargo Minivan	A544	20540	700	825	1600	2750
WINDSTAR—V6—Truck Equipment Schedule T1						
LX Minivan	A514	25320	625	750	1500	2600
SE Sport Minivan	A574	27755	1000	1150	2025	3450
SE Minivan	A524	28915	1150	1325	2225	3775
SEL Minivan	A534	31435	1250	1425	2375	4025
Limited Minivan	A584	34085	1375	1575	2525	4300
Second Sliding Door	0		50	50	65	65
ECONOLINE WAGON—V8—Truck Equipment Schedule T1						
E150 Passenger Van	E11W	24060	1675	1875	2425	3875
E350 Super Duty	E31L	26350	1800	2000	2600	4150
E350 Super Duty Ext	S31L	27970	1850	2100	2800	4475
V6, 4.2 Liter	2		(200)	(200)	(265)	(265)
V8, 5.4 Liter (E150)	L		100	100	135	135
V8, Turbo Diesel, 7.3L	F		1125	1125	1500	1500
V10, 6.8 Liter	S		250	250	335	335
ECONOLINE VAN—V6—Truck Equipment Schedule T1						
E150 Cargo Van	E142	21445	1225	1375	2025	3375
E250 Cargo Van	E242	22565	1275	1425	2100	3500
E250 Extended	S242	23410	1725	1925	2900	4825
Crew Van Pkg			150	150	205	205
V8, 4.6 Liter	W		75	75	100	100
V8, 5.4 Liter	L		100	100	135	135
ECONOLINE VAN—V8—Truck Equipment Schedule T1						
E350 Super Cargo	E34L	24995	1525	1700	2475	4125
E350 Ext SD Cargo	S34L	25970	1850	2075	3100	5150
V8, Turbo Diesel, 7.3L	F		1125	1125	1500	1500
V10, 6.8 Liter	S		250	250	335	335
RANGER PICKUP—4-Cyl.—Truck Equipment Schedule T2						
Short Bed	R10C	12400	725	825	1275	2100

TRUCKS & VANS

Body Type	VIN	List	Trade-In Good	Trade-In Very Good	Pvt-Party Good	Retail Excellent
Long Bed	R10C	13515	675	775	1200	2000
Super Cab 2D	R14C	16465	975	1125	1700	2875
Super Cab 4D	R14C	20960	1650	1875	2650	4425
4WD	1,5		400	400	535	535
V6, 3.0 Liter	U		125	125	165	165
V6, 4.0 Liter	E		150	150	200	200
REGULAR CAB PICKUP—V8—Truck Equipment Schedule T1						
F150 Short Bed	F17W	20170	1500	1675	2325	3875
F150 Long Bed	F17W	20470	1300	1450	2050	3375
Work Truck			(250)	(250)	(335)	(335)
4WD	6,8		750	750	1000	1000
V6, 4.2 Liter	2		(350)	(350)	(465)	(465)
V8, 5.4 Liter	L,Z		75	75	100	100
REGULAR CAB PICKUP—V8 Supercharged—Truck Schedule T1						
F150 Lightning	P073	32460	5725	6250	7225	10050
SUPER CAB PICKUP—V8—Truck Equipment Schedule T1						
F150 Short Bed	X17W	22855	1850	2050	3025	4925
F150 Long Bed	X17W	23155	2150	2375	3525	5750
Work Truck			(250)	(250)	(335)	(335)
4WD	6,8		750	750	1000	1000
V6, 4.2 Liter	2		(350)	(350)	(465)	(465)
V8, 5.4 Liter	L,Z		75	75	100	100
SUPERCREW PICKUP—V8—Truck Equipment Schedule T1						
F150 Short Bed 4D	W07W	26940	3325	3650	4950	7650
F150 King Ranch	W07W	31455	4475	4875	6600	10050
4WD	8		750	750	1000	1000
V8, 5.4 Liter	L		75	75	100	100
SUPERCREW PICKUP—V8—Truck Equipment Schedule T1						
F150 Harley	W07L	34495	6925	7550	8475	11600
SUPER DUTY REGULAR CAB—V8—Truck Equipment Schedule T1						
F250 Long Bed	F20L	23155	2100	2350	2975	4550
F350 Long Bed	F30L	23580	2300	2575	3225	4900
4WD	1		750	750	1000	1000
V8, Turbo Diesel, 7.3L	F		2650	2650	3535	3535
V10, 6.8 Liter	S		275	275	355	355
SUPER DUTY SUPER CAB—V8—Truck Equipment Schedule T1						
F250 Short Bed	X20L	25295	3325	3700	4475	6625
F250 Long Bed	X20L	25495	3125	3500	4225	6275
F350 Short Bed	X30L	26085	3450	3825	4725	7000
F350 Long Bed	X30L	26285	3425	3800	4575	6775
4WD	1		750	750	1000	1000
V8, Turbo Diesel, 7.3L	F		2650	2650	3535	3535
V10, 6.8 Liter	S		275	275	355	355
SUPER DUTY CREW CAB—V8—Truck Equipment Schedule T1						
F250 Short Bed	W20L	25295	3925	4325	5300	7775
F250 Long Bed	W20L	26805	3775	4175	5125	7525
F350 Short Bed	W30L	27265	4100	4525	5525	8075
F350 Long Bed	W30L	27465	4025	4425	5425	7950
Platinum Edition			75	75	100	100
4WD	1		750	750	1000	1000
V8, Turbo Diesel, 7.3L	F		2650	2650	3535	3535
V10, 6.8 Liter	S		275	275	355	355

2002 FORD — (1or2)F(B,MorT)–(U011)–2–#

Body Type	VIN	List	Trade-In Good	Trade-In Very Good	Pvt-Party Good	Retail Excellent
ESCAPE—V6—Truck Equipment Schedule T1						
XLS Sport Utility 4D	U011	20465	1175	1325	2150	3450
4WD			450	450	585	585
4-Cyl, 2.0 Liter	B		(325)	(325)	(430)	(430)
ESCAPE 4WD—V6—Truck Equipment Schedule T1						
XLT Sport Utility 4D	U041	23935	2225	2475	3600	5550
2WD			(450)	(450)	(600)	(600)
4-Cyl, 2.0 Liter	B		(325)	(325)	(430)	(430)
EXPLORER SPORT 4WD—V6—Truck Equipment Schedule T1						
Sport Utility 2D	U70E	24785	1150	1325	2125	3425
2WD	6		(725)	(725)	(970)	(970)
EXPLORER 4WD—V6—Truck Equipment Schedule T1						
XLS Sport Utility 4D	U72E	27775	1575	1800	2750	4425
Eddie Bauer Spt Util	U74E	35135	1850	2100	3250	5225
Third Row Seat			250	250	335	335
2WD	6		(725)	(725)	(970)	(970)
V8, 4.6 Liter	W		125	125	165	165
EXPLORER SPORT TRAC 4WD—V6—Truck Equipment Schedule T1						
Utility Pickup 4D	U77E	25410	3425	3750	5175	7625

Body Type	VIN	List	Trade-In Good	Very Good	Pvt-Party Good	Retail Excellent
2WD	6		(725)	(725)	(970)	(970)
EXPEDITION 4WD—V8—Truck Equipment Schedule T1						
XLT Sport Utility	U16W	33810	1275	1450	2375	3900
Eddie Bauer Spt Ut	U18W	41825	1875	2125	3325	5400
Third Row Seat			300	300	400	400
2WD	5,7		(450)	(450)	(600)	(600)
V8, 5.4 Liter	L		125	125	165	165
EXCURSION 4WD—V10—Truck Equipment Schedule T1						
XLT Sport Utility 4D	U41S	38985	4275	4750	5900	8400
Third Row Seat			300	300	400	400
2WD			(450)	(450)	(600)	(600)
V8, 5.4 Liter	L		(325)	(325)	(435)	(435)
V8, Turbo Diesel, 7.3L	F		2875	2875	3835	3835
WINDSTAR—V6—Truck Equipment Schedule T2						
Cargo Minivan	A544	20905	925	1075	1875	3150
WINDSTAR—V6—Truck Equipment Schedule T1						
LX Minivan	A514	22995	750	875	1650	2775
SE Minivan	A524	29280	1375	1575	2475	4125
SEL Minivan	A534	31950	1475	1675	2600	4350
Limited Minivan	A584	34360	1525	1725	2800	4625
Second Sliding Door	0		50	50	65	65
ECONOLINE WAGON—V6—Truck Equipment Schedule T1						
E150 Passenger Van	E112	24660	1825	2050	2750	4350
V8, 4.6 Liter	W		125	125	165	165
V8, 5.4 Liter	L		125	125	165	165
ECONOLINE WAGON—V8—Truck Equipment Schedule T1						
E350 Super Duty	E31L	26950	2025	2275	2975	4650
E350 Super Duty Ext	S31L	28370	2150	2425	3200	5025
V8, Turbo Diesel, 7.3L	F		1300	1300	1735	1735
V10, 6.8 Liter	S		275	275	365	365
ECONOLINE VAN—V6—Truck Equipment Schedule T1						
E150 Cargo Van	E142	21880	1650	1825	2525	4100
E250 Cargo Van	E242	22750	1600	1800	2575	4200
E250 Extended	E242	23960	2150	2400	3350	5375
Crew Van Pkg			175	175	215	215
V8, 4.6 Liter	W		75	75	100	100
V8, 5.4 Liter	L		125	125	165	165
ECONOLINE VAN—V8—Truck Equipment Schedule T1						
E350 Super Cargo	E34L	25230	1900	2125	3000	4825
E350 Ext SD Cargo	E34L	26520	2300	2575	3575	5700
Crew Van Pkg			175	175	215	215
V8, Turbo Diesel, 7.3L	F		1300	1300	1735	1735
V10, 6.8 Liter	S		275	275	365	365
RANGER PICKUP—4-Cyl.—Truck Equipment Schedule T2						
Short Bed	R10C	12725	850	975	1550	2650
Long Bed	R10C	13655	775	875	1450	2475
Super Cab 2D	R14C	16400	1575	1775	2525	4250
Super Cab 4D	R14C	18075	2150	2400	3475	5725
4WD	1,5		550	550	735	735
V6, 3.0 Liter	U		150	150	200	200
V6, Flex Fuel, 3.0 Liter	V		150	150	200	200
V6, 4.0 Liter	E		200	200	265	265
REGULAR CAB PICKUP—V8—Truck Equipment Schedule T1						
F150 Short Bed	F17W	20640	1525	1725	2425	3975
F150 Long Bed	F17W	20940	1325	1500	2125	3525
Work Truck			(300)	(300)	(400)	(400)
4WD	6,8		900	900	1200	1200
V6, 4.2 Liter	2		(375)	(375)	(500)	(500)
V8, 5.4 Liter	L,Z		125	125	165	165
V8, Flex Fuel, 5.4 Liter	M		125	125	165	165
REGULAR CAB PICKUP—V8 Supercharged—Truck Equipment Schedule T1						
F150 Lightning	F073	32490	6300	6875	7975	11100
SUPER CAB PICKUP—V8—Truck Equipment Schedule T1						
F150 Short Bed	X17W	23290	2225	2450	3475	5475
F150 Long Bed	X17W	22840	2250	2475	3625	5850
F150 King Ranch	X17W	29735	3625	3975	5400	8200
Work Truck			(300)	(300)	(400)	(400)
4WD	6,8		900	900	1200	1200
V6, 4.2 Liter	2		(375)	(375)	(500)	(500)
V8, 5.4 Liter	L,Z		125	125	165	165
SUPERCREW PICKUP—V8—Truck Equipment Schedule T1						
F150 Short Bed 4D	W07W	27660	3575	3900	5325	8100
F150 King Ranch 4D	W07W	32135	4975	5375	7100	10600

Body Type	VIN	List	Trade-In Good	Very Good	Pvt-Party Good	Retail Excellent
4WD	8	-----	900	900	1200	1200
V8, 5.4 Liter	L	-----	125	125	165	165
SUPERCREW PICKUP—V8 Supercharged—Truck Equipment Schedule T1						
F150 Harley	W073	36520	7425	8075	8925	11950
SUPER DUTY REGULAR CAB PICKUP—V8—Truck Equipment Schedule T1						
F250 Long Bed	F20L	22725	2100	2350	3025	4650
F350 Long Bed	F30L	23985	2450	2725	3350	5025
4WD	1	-----	900	900	1200	1200
V8, Turbo Diesel, 7.3L	F	-----	2875	2875	3835	3835
V10, 6.8 Liter	S	-----	300	300	390	390
SUPER DUTY SUPER CAB PICKUP—V8—Truck Equipment Schedule T1						
F250 Short Bed	X20L	25715	3500	3875	4675	6750
F250 Long Bed	X20L	25915	3400	3775	4425	6400
F350 Short Bed	X30L	26505	3700	4100	4900	7050
F350 Long Bed	X30L	26705	3575	3950	4750	6850
4WD	1	-----	900	900	1200	1200
V8, Turbo Diesel, 7.3L	F	-----	2875	2875	3835	3835
V10, 6.8 Liter	S	-----	300	300	390	390
SUPER DUTY CREW CAB PICKUP—V8—Truck Equipment Schedule T1						
F250 Short Bed	W20L	27025	4275	4700	5575	7950
F250 Long Bed	W20L	27225	4075	4500	5325	7625
F350 Short Bed	W30L	27685	4475	4925	5800	8250
F350 Long Bed	W30L	27885	4400	4825	5700	8125
4WD	1	-----	900	900	1200	1200
V8, Turbo Diesel, 7.3L	F	-----	2875	2875	3835	3835
V10, 6.8 Liter	S	-----	300	300	390	390

2003 FORD — (1or2)F(B,D,MorT)–(U021)–3–#

Body Type	VIN	List	Trade-In Good	Very Good	Pvt-Party Good	Retail Excellent
ESCAPE—V6—Truck Equipment Schedule T1						
XLS Sport Utility 4D	U021	20925	1375	1550	2325	3675
4WD			500	500	660	660
4-Cyl, 2.0 Liter	B		(350)	(350)	(470)	(470)
ESCAPE 4WD—V6—Truck Equipment Schedule T1						
XLT Sport Utility 4D	U931	25475	2450	2725	3800	5775
Limited Spt Util 4D	U941	27475	2900	3225	4375	6600
2WD	0		(500)	(500)	(665)	(665)
EXPLORER SPORT 4WD—V6—Truck Equipment Schedule T1						
XLS Sport Util 2D	U70E	26055	1450	1650	2500	3900
XLT Spt Util 2D	U70E	27405	1700	1925	2825	4375
2WD	6		(800)	(800)	(1080)	(1080)
EXPLORER 4WD—V6 Flex Fuel—Truck Equipment Schedule T1						
XLS Sport Utility 4D	U72K	29155	1600	1825	2700	4175
XLT Utility 4D	U73K	31695	1875	2125	3050	4700
NBX Sport Utility	U73K	32870	2075	2350	3300	5075
Eddie Bauer 4D	U74K	35970	2625	2975	4000	6100
Limited Spt Util	U75K	36645	2675	3025	4075	6200
Third Row Seat			275	275	365	365
2WD	6		(800)	(800)	(1080)	(1080)
AWD			0	0	0	0
V8, 4.6 Liter	W		150	150	200	200
EXPLORER SPORT TRAC 4WD—V6—Truck Equipment Schedule T1						
XLS Util Pickup 4D	U77E	26285	3175	3550	4675	7025
XLT Sport Pickup	U77K	27880	4150	4500	6150	8900
2WD	6		(800)	(800)	(1080)	(1080)
EXPEDITION—V8—Truck Equipment Schedule T1						
XLT Sport Util 4D	U15W	31295	2075	2325	3200	4825
Third Row Seat			350	350	465	465
4WD	6,8		500	500	660	660
V8, 5.4 Liter	L		175	175	235	235
EXPEDITION 4WD—V8—Truck Equipment Schedule T1						
FX4 Off-Rd Spt Util	U16W	38470	3100	3450	4450	6625
Eddie Bauer Spt Ut	U18W	42055	3350	3750	4925	7275
Third Row Seat			350	350	465	465
2WD	5,7		(500)	(500)	(665)	(665)
V8, 5.4 Liter	L		175	175	235	235
EXCURSION 4WD—V10—Truck Equipment Schedule T1						
XLT Sport Utility 4D	U41S	40340	4725	5200	6325	8875
Eddie Bauer Spt Util	U45S	44405	6300	6875	8275	11450
Limited Spt Util 4D	U43S	45465	6325	6900	8350	11600
Third Row Seat			350	350	465	465
2WD	0,2,4		(500)	(500)	(665)	(665)
V8, 5.4 Liter	L		(350)	(350)	(480)	(480)
V8, Turbo Diesel, 6.0L	P		2725	2725	3620	3620

0415

Body Type	VIN	List	Trade-In Good	Very Good	Pvt-Party Good	Retail Excellent
V8, Turbo Diesel, 7.3L	F		3100	3100	4135	4135
WINDSTAR—V6—Truck Equipment Schedule T2						
Cargo Minivan	A544	21360	1200	1375	2400	4125
WINDSTAR—V6—Truck Equipment Schedule T1						
LX Minivan	A514	23365	1000	1150	2125	3675
SE Minivan	A524	29675	1625	1825	3125	5300
SEL Minivan	A534	32405	1725	1950	3275	5500
Limited Minivan	A584	35110	1875	2100	3500	5900
Second Sliding Door	0		50	50	65	65
ECONOLINE WAGON—V6—Truck Equipment Schedule T1						
E150 XL Passenger	E112	24595	2050	2275	2800	4200
E150 XLT Passenger	E112	27435	2525	2800	3475	5250
E150 Chateau Pass	E112	29600	2925	3275	3850	5675
V8, 4.6 Liter	W		100	100	135	135
V8, 5.4 Liter	M,L		150	150	200	200
ECONOLINE WAGON—V8—Truck Equipment Schedule T1						
E350 XL Super Duty	E31L	27635	2425	2700	3375	5150
E350 XLT Passenger	E31L	30440	3025	3375	3975	5850
E350 Chateau Pass	E31L	32240	3375	3750	4400	6450
E350 XL SD Ext	S31L	29055	3150	3500	4125	6050
E350 XLT Extended	S31L	30910	3300	3675	4300	6300
V8, Turbo Diesel, 7.3L	F		1475	1475	1965	1965
V10, 6.8 Liter	S		350	350	465	465
ECONOLINE VAN—V6—Truck Equipment Schedule T1						
E150 Super Cargo	E142	22420	2400	2675	3525	5475
E250 Super Cargo	E242	23290	2450	2725	3600	5575
E250 Extended SD	E242	24200	3100	3450	4500	6950
Crew Van Pkg			175	175	230	230
V8, 4.6 Liter	W		100	100	135	135
V8, 5.4 Liter	L,M		150	150	200	200
ECONOLINE VAN—V8—Truck Equipment Schedule T1						
E350 Super Cargo	E34L	25770	2925	3250	4250	6575
E350 Extended SD	E34L	26760	3500	3875	5075	7800
Crew Van Pkg			175	175	230	230
V8, Turbo Diesel, 7.3L	F		1475	1475	1965	1965
V10, 6.8 Liter	S		350	350	465	465
RANGER REGULAR CAB PICKUP—4-Cyl.—Truck Equipment Schedule T2						
XL 2D 6'	R10D	14620	1125	1275	1700	2725
XL 2D 7'	R10D	14655	825	925	1350	2150
XLT 2D 6'	R10D	16280	1750	1950	2575	4075
XLT 2D 7'	R10D	17705	1300	1450	1925	3050
4WD	1,5		650	650	865	865
V6, 3.0 Liter	U		175	175	235	235
V6, 4.0 Liter	E		225	225	300	300
RANGER REGULAR CAB PICKUP—V6—Truck Equipment Schedule T2						
Edge Plus 2D 6'	R11U	20450	1750	1950	2575	4075
V6, 4.0 Liter	E		225	225	300	300
RANGER SUPER CAB—4-Cyl.—Truck Equipment Schedule T2						
XLT 4D 6'	R44D	21645	2825	3175	3975	6150
4WD	1,5		650	650	865	865
V6, 3.0 Liter	U		175	175	235	235
V6, Flex Fuel, 3.0 Liter	V		175	175	235	235
V6, 4.0 Liter	E		225	225	300	300
RANGER SUPER CAB—V6—Truck Equipment Schedule T2						
XLT 2D 6'	R14U	20560	2325	2600	3350	5200
4WD	1,5		650	650	865	865
4-Cyl, 2.3 Liter	D		(200)	(200)	(260)	(260)
V6, 4.0 Liter	E		50	50	65	65
RANGER SUPER CAB—V6—Truck Equipment Schedule T2						
XL 2D 6'	R14U	18320	2050	2300	2975	4650
XL 4D 6'	R44U	18905	2225	2500	3200	5000
Edge 2D 6'	R14U	19235	2600	2900	3700	5725
Edge 4D 6'	R44U	21645	2900	3250	4100	6300
Edge Plus 4D 6'	R44U	20990	2525	2825	3600	5575
Tremor 2D 6'	R14U	19775	2325	2600	3350	5200
Tremor Plus 4D 6'	R44U	22075	2100	2350	3050	4750
4WD	1,5		650	650	865	865
V6, 4.0 Liter	E		225	225	300	300
RANGER SUPER CAB—V6 4WD—Truck Equipment Schedule T2						
XLT FX4 Off-Road 6'	R45E	25425	5075	5600	6450	9225
XLT FX4 Level II 6'	R44E	25890	4975	5475	6325	9050
REGULAR CAB PICKUP—V8—Truck Equipment Schedule T1						
F150 XL 2D 6 1/2'	F17W	21450	1650	1850	2750	4525

TRUCKS & VANS

Body Type	VIN	List	Trade-In Good	Trade-In Very Good	Pvt-Party Good	Retail Excellent
F150 XL 2D 8'	F17W	21750	1550	1750	2500	4175
F150 XL STX 6 1/2'	F17W	22445	1850	2075	3000	4900
F150 XL STX 2D 8'	F17W	22745	1700	1900	2800	4625
F150 XLT 2D 6 1/2'	F17W	24120	2075	2325	3300	5350
F150 XLT 2D 8'	F17W	24415	2000	2250	3200	5200
F150 XLT STX 6 1/2'	F17W	25115	2175	2425	3425	5525
F150 XLT STX 2D 8'	F17W	25410	2100	2350	3350	5400
4WD	8		1100	1100	1465	1465
V6, 4.2 Liter	2		(400)	(400)	(535)	(535)
V8, 5.4 Liter	L		175	175	235	235
V8, Flex Fuel, 5.4 Liter	Z		175	175	235	235
REGULAR CAB PICKUP—V8 Supercharged—Truck Equipment Schedule T1						
F150 Lightning	F073	33255	7275	7900	8800	11750
SUPER CAB PICKUP—V8—Truck Equipment Schedule T1						
F150 XL 4D 6 1/2'	X17W	24100	3375	3700	4500	6550
F150 XL 4D 8'	X17W	24400	3100	3400	4175	6075
F150 XL STX 6 1/2'	X17W	25095	3425	3750	4575	6625
F150 XL STX 4D 8'	X17W	25395	3225	3550	4325	6300
F150 XLT 4D 6 1/2'	X17W	26965	3575	3900	4875	7050
F150 XLT 4D 8'	X17W	27265	3400	3725	4550	6600
F150 XLT STX 6 1/2'	X17W	29250	3625	3950	4950	7150
F150 XLT STX 8'	X17W	28260	3450	3775	4600	6675
F150 Heritage 6 1/2'	X17W	28165	3600	3925	4900	7100
F150 Lariat 6 1/2'	X17W	28690	3800	4125	5150	7425
F150 King Ranch 4D	X07W	31660	5000	5400	6625	9450
4WD	8		1100	1100	1465	1465
V6, 4.2 Liter	2		(400)	(400)	(535)	(535)
V8, 5.4 Liter	L		175	175	235	235
SUPERCREW PICKUP—V8—Truck Equipment Schedule T1						
F150 XLT 4D 6 1/2'	W076	28965	5175	5575	6775	9625
F150 Lariat 4D 6 1/2'	W076	31055	6225	6675	8325	11800
F150 King Ranch 4D	W076	33115	6625	7100	8825	12500
4WD	8		1100	1100	1465	1465
V8, 5.4 Liter	L		175	175	235	235
SUPERCREW PICKUP—V8 Supercharged—Truck Equipment Schedule T1						
F150 Harley 5 1/2'	W073	37295	8550	9250	9975	13100
SUPER DUTY REGULAR CAB PICKUP—V8—Truck Equipment Schedule T1						
F250 XL 4D 8'	F20L	23335	2150	2400	3125	4775
F250 XLT 4D 8'	F20L	26590	2650	2975	3700	5525
F350 XL 4D 8'	F30L	23790	2500	2775	3475	5175
F350 XLT 4D 8'	F30L	27395	2825	3150	3900	5800
4WD	1		1100	1100	1465	1465
V8, Turbo Diesel, 6.0L	P		2725	2725	3620	3620
V8, Turbo Diesel, 7.3L	F		3100	3100	4135	4135
V10, 6.8 Liter	S		325	325	430	430
SUPER DUTY SUPER CAB PICKUP—V8—Truck Equipment Schedule T1						
F250 XL 4D 6 3/4'	X20L	25520	3700	4100	5075	7375
F250 XL 4D 8'	X20L	25720	3400	3775	4725	6975
F250 XLT 4D 6 3/4'	X20L	29510	3975	4375	5375	7800
F250 XLT 4D 8'	X20L	29710	3775	4175	5150	7475
F250 Lariat 4D 6 3/4'	X20L	31630	4150	4575	5575	8075
F250 Lariat 4D 8'	X20L	31830	3925	4325	5325	7725
F350 XL 4D 6 1/2'	X30L	26310	3900	4300	5300	7675
F350 XL 4D 8'	X30L	26510	3775	4175	5150	7475
F350 XLT 4D 6 1/2'	X30L	30655	4200	4625	5650	8150
F350 XLT 4D 8'	X30L	30855	3875	4275	5250	7625
F350 Lariat 4D 6 1/2'	X30L	32630	4400	4825	5875	8450
F350 Lariat 4D 8'	X30L	32830	4250	4675	5700	8225
4WD	1		1100	1100	1465	1465
V8, Turbo Diesel, 6.0L	P		2725	2725	3620	3620
V8, Turbo Diesel, 7.3L	F		3100	3100	4135	4135
V10, 6.8 Liter	S		325	325	430	430
SUPER DUTY CREW CAB PICKUP—V8—Truck Equipment Schedule T1						
F250 XL 4D 6 1/2'	W20L	26930	4575	5025	6075	8750
F250 XL 4D 8'	W20L	30005	4350	4775	5800	8375
F250 XLT 4D 6 1/2'	W20L	31430	5275	5775	6875	9800
F250 XLT 4D 8'	W20L	31630	5075	5550	6650	9500
F250 Lariat 4D 6 1/2'	W20L	33850	5325	5800	7125	10150
F250 Lariat 4D 8'	W20L	34050	5200	5675	6800	9700
F250 King Ranch 6'	W20L	36460	5600	6100	7425	10550
F250 King Ranch 8'	W20L	36660	5375	5850	7175	10200
F350 XL 4D 6 1/2'	W30L	27590	4800	5250	6350	9100
F350 XL 4D 8'	W30L	27790	4775	5225	6300	9050

Body Type	VIN	List	Trade-In Good	Trade-In Very Good	Pvt-Party Good	Retail Excellent
F350 XLT 4D 6 1/2'	W30L	32440	**5350**	**5825**	**7125**	**10150**
F350 XLT 4D 8'	W30L	32640	**5250**	**5725**	**7025**	**10000**
F350 Lariat 4D 6 1/2'	W30L	34715	**6650**	**7200**	**8400**	**11650**
F350 Lariat 4D 8'	W30L	34915	**6525**	**7075**	**8275**	**11500**
F350 King Ranch 6'	W30L	37325	**6025**	**6550**	**7925**	**11200**
F350 King Ranch 8'	W30L	37525	**5800**	**6300**	**7650**	**10850**
4WD	1,3		**1100**	**1100**	**1465**	**1465**
V8, Turbo Diesel, 6.0L	P		**2725**	**2725**	**3620**	**3620**
V8, Turbo Diesel, 7.3L	F		**3100**	**3100**	**4135**	**4135**
V10, 6.8 Liter	S		**325**	**325**	**430**	**430**

2004 FORD—(1or2)F(B,MorT)—(U021)—4—#

ESCAPE—V6—Truck Equipment Schedule T1

Body Type	VIN	List	Trade-In Good	Trade-In Very Good	Pvt-Party Good	Retail Excellent
XLS Sport Utility 4D	U021	20890	**1575**	**1750**	**2575**	**4000**
4WD			**550**	**550**	**735**	**735**
4-Cyl, 2.0 Liter	B		**(375)**	**(375)**	**(515)**	**(515)**

ESCAPE 4WD—V6—Truck Equipment Schedule T1

Body Type	VIN	List	Good	Very Good	Good	Excellent
XLT Sport Utility 4D	U931	24770	**2725**	**3025**	**4075**	**6050**
Limited Sport Util	U941	26830	**3225**	**3550**	**4725**	**7000**
2WD	0		**(550)**	**(550)**	**(735)**	**(735)**

EXPLORER 4WD—V6 Flex Fuel—Truck Equipment Schedule T1

Body Type	VIN	List	Good	Very Good	Good	Excellent
XLS Utility 4D	U72K	29620	**2050**	**2325**	**3375**	**5225**
XLS "Sport" SUV	U72K	30795	**2300**	**2600**	**3650**	**5625**
XLT Sport Utility 4D	U73K	32360	**2500**	**2825**	**3950**	**6050**
XLT "Sport" 4D	U73K	33535	**2600**	**2950**	**4075**	**6250**
NBX Sport Utility	U73K	33535	**2700**	**3050**	**4200**	**6425**
Eddie Bauer Spt Util	U74K	36435	**3250**	**3625**	**4900**	**7450**
Third Row Seat			**300**	**300**	**400**	**400**
2WD	6		**(900)**	**(900)**	**(1190)**	**(1190)**
AWD	8		**0**	**0**	**0**	**0**
V8, 4.6 Liter	W		**175**	**175**	**235**	**235**

EXPLORER 4WD—V8—Truck Equipment Schedule T1

Body Type	VIN	List	Good	Very Good	Good	Excellent
Limited Sport Util	U75W	37645	**3550**	**3975**	**5450**	**8225**
2WD	6		**(900)**	**(900)**	**(1190)**	**(1190)**
AWD	8		**0**	**0**	**0**	**0**
V6, Flex Fuel, 4.0 Liter	K		**(150)**	**(150)**	**(215)**	**(215)**

EXPLORER SPORT TRAC 4WD—V6 Flex Fuel—Truck Equipment Schedule T1

Body Type	VIN	List	Good	Very Good	Good	Excellent
XLS Utility Pickup	U77K	26460	**3725**	**4150**	**5650**	**8475**
XLT Spt Util Pickup	U77K	28185	**4775**	**5125**	**7175**	**10450**
Adrenalin Util Pkup	U77K	27380	**4925**	**5300**	**7400**	**10800**
2WD	6		**(900)**	**(900)**	**(1190)**	**(1190)**

EXPEDITION—V8—Truck Equipment Schedule T1

Body Type	VIN	List	Good	Very Good	Good	Excellent
XLS Sport Utility	U15W	32735	**1825**	**2050**	**3000**	**4600**
XLT Sport Utility	U15W	34560	**2400**	**2700**	**3700**	**5600**
Third Row Seat			**400**	**400**	**535**	**535**
4WD	4,6,8		**550**	**550**	**735**	**735**
V8, 5.4 Liter	L		**200**	**200**	**265**	**265**

EXPEDITION 4WD—V8—Truck Equipment Schedule T1

Body Type	VIN	List	Good	Very Good	Good	Excellent
XLT "Sport" SUV	U16W	38485	**3425**	**3825**	**5100**	**7550**
XLT NBX Spt Util	U16W	39280	**3575**	**3975**	**5275**	**7800**
Eddie Bauer Util	U18W	42790	**4025**	**4450**	**5825**	**8550**
Third Row Seat			**400**	**400**	**535**	**535**
2WD	3,5,7		**(550)**	**(550)**	**(735)**	**(735)**
V8, 5.4 Liter	L		**200**	**200**	**265**	**265**

EXCURSION 4WD—V10—Truck Equipment Schedule T1

Body Type	VIN	List	Good	Very Good	Good	Excellent
XLS Sport Utility 4D	U41S	40485	**5350**	**5825**	**7125**	**9825**
XLT Sport Utility 4D	U41S	41795	**5900**	**6450**	**7750**	**10650**
Eddie Bauer Spt Util	U45S	44985	**7500**	**8150**	**9700**	**13300**
Limited Sport Util	U43S	46050	**7700**	**8375**	**9925**	**13600**
Third Row Seat			**400**	**400**	**535**	**535**
2WD	0,2,4		**(550)**	**(550)**	**(735)**	**(735)**
V8, 5.4 Liter	L		**(400)**	**(400)**	**(520)**	**(520)**
V8, Turbo Dsl 6.0L	P		**2975**	**2975**	**3960**	**3960**

FREESTAR—V6—Truck Equipment Schedule T2

Body Type	VIN	List	Good	Very Good	Good	Excellent
Cargo Minivan	A546	22070	**500**	**600**	**1325**	**2275**

FREESTAR—V6—Truck Equipment Schedule T1

Body Type	VIN	List	Good	Very Good	Good	Excellent
S Minivan	A506	24460	**1000**	**1150**	**1975**	**3300**
SE Minivan	A516	26930	**1200**	**1350**	**2225**	**3725**
SES Minivan	A576	28750	**1450**	**1625**	**2550**	**4225**
SEL Minivan	A522	29995	**1550**	**1750**	**2800**	**4600**
Limited Minivan	A522	33630	**2000**	**2250**	**3425**	**5550**

ECONOLINE WAGON—V8—Truck Equipment Schedule T1

Body Type	VIN	List	Good	Very Good	Good	Excellent
E150 XL Passenger	E11W	25255	**2550**	**2850**	**3400**	**5025**

TRUCKS & VANS

TRUCKS & VANS

Body Type	VIN	List	Trade-In Good	Very Good	Pvt-Party Good	Retail Excellent
E150 XLT Passenger	E11W	28095	3075	3425	4025	5875
E150 Chateau	E11W	30095	3450	3850	4600	6675
E350 XL Super Duty	E31L	27995	2950	3300	3875	5675
E350 XLT Passenger	E31L	30085	3625	4025	4800	6950
E350 Chateau	E31L	32605	4075	4500	5350	7675
E350 XL S.D. Ext	S31L	29415	3600	4000	4775	6900
E350 XLT Extended	S31L	31270	3900	4325	5150	7400
V8, 5.4 Liter (E150)	M		175	175	235	235
V8, Turbo Dsl 6.0L	P		1650	1650	2200	2200
V10, 6.8 Liter	S		400	400	535	535
ECONOLINE VAN—V8—Truck Equipment Schedule T1						
E150 Super Cargo	E14W	23060	2750	3025	3950	6075
E250 Super Cargo	E24W	24105	3000	3325	4275	6550
E250 Ext SD Cargo	S24W	25220	3625	4000	5275	8000
E350 Super Cargo	E34L	26110	3400	3750	4900	7375
E350 Ext SD Cargo	S34L	27705	4050	4450	5850	8825
Crew Van Pkg			175	175	240	240
V8, 5.4 Liter (ex E350)	L		175	175	235	235
V8, Turbo Dsl 6.0L	P		1650	1650	2200	2200
V10, 6.8 Liter	S		400	400	535	535
RANGER REGULAR CAB PICKUP—4-Cyl.—Truck Equipment Schedule T2						
XL 2D 6'	R10D	15385	1775	1975	2500	3900
XL 2D 7'	R10D	15135	1350	1500	1975	3150
Edge 2D 6'	R10D	17470	2100	2350	3000	4625
XLT 2D 6'	R10D	16850	2400	2675	3375	5175
XLT 2D 7'	R10D	18570	1900	2125	2725	4250
4WD	1,5		800	800	1065	1065
V6, 3.0 Liter	U		200	200	265	265
V6, 4.0 Liter	E		250	250	335	335
RANGER SUPER CAB PICKUP—V6—Truck Equipment Schedule T2						
XLT 2D 6'	R14U	19365	3300	3675	4500	6800
4WD	1,5		800	800	1065	1065
4-Cyl, 2.3 Liter	D		(225)	(225)	(285)	(285)
V6, 4.0 Liter	E		50	50	65	65
RANGER SUPER CAB PICKUP—V6—Truck Equipment Schedule T2						
XL 2D 6'	R14U	19120	2750	3050	3800	5800
XL 4D 6'	R44U	19405	2900	3250	4000	6075
Edge 2D 6'	R14U	19765	3475	3850	4725	7125
Edge 4D 6'	R44U	22905	3600	4000	4875	7350
Tremor 2D 6'	R14U	21055	3200	3575	4375	6625
Tremor 4D 6'	R44U	23030	3675	4075	4975	7475
4WD	1,5		800	800	1065	1065
V6, 4.0 Liter	E		250	250	335	335
RANGER SUPER CAB PICKUP 4WD—V6—Truck Equipment Schedule T2						
XLT FX4 Off-Road	R45E	25970	5775	6325	7225	10050
XLT FX4 Level II	R45E	26515	5600	6150	7025	9750
HERITAGE REGULAR CAB PICKUP—V8—Truck Equipment Sch T1						
F150 XL 2D 6 1/2'	F17W	21765	2350	2625	3450	5375
F150 XL 2D 8'	F17W	22065	1925	2175	2925	4575
F150 XL STX 6 1/2'	F17W	22260	2475	2775	3625	5600
F150 XL STX 8'	F17W	22560	2200	2475	3275	5075
F150 XLT 6 1/2'	F17W	23935	2975	3325	4250	6525
F150 XLT 8'	F17W	24235	2350	2625	3450	5375
F150 XLT STX 6 1/2'	F17W	24930	3075	3425	4375	6700
F150 XLT STX 8'	F17W	25230	2550	2850	3725	5750
Work Truck			(400)	(400)	(535)	(535)
4WD	8		1200	1200	1600	1600
V6, 4.2 Liter	2		(425)	(425)	(565)	(565)
V8, Flex Fuel, 5.4 Liter	Z		200	200	265	265
HERITAGE REGULAR CAB PICKUP—V8 Supercharged—Truck Equip Sch T1						
F150 Lightning 6 1/2'	F07J3	33560	9600	10350	11350	15000
HERITAGE SUPER CAB PICKUP—V8—Truck Equipment Schedule T1						
F150 XL 4D 6 1/2'	X17W	24415	3925	4250	5125	7200
F150 XL 4D 8'	X17W	24715	3650	3975	4800	6775
F150 XLT 4D 6 1/2'	X17W	26780	4600	4975	5900	8225
F150 XLT 4D 8'	X17W	27080	4300	4650	5550	7775
Work Truck			(400)	(400)	(535)	(535)
4WD	8		1200	1200	1600	1600
V6, 4.2 Liter	2		(425)	(425)	(565)	(565)
V8, Flex Fuel, 5.4 Liter	Z		200	200	265	265
REGULAR CAB PICKUP—V8—Truck Equipment Schedule T1						
F150 XL 2D 6 1/2'	F12W	22010	2400	2700	3525	5475
F150 XL 2D 8'	F12W	22310	2125	2375	3175	4950

0415

Body Type	VIN	List	Trade-In Good	Trade-In Very Good	Pvt-Party Good	Retail Excellent
F150 STX 4D 6 1/2'	F12W	22810	2675	3000	3875	5975
F150 XLT 4D 6 1/2'	F12W	25120	3075	3425	4375	6700
F150 XLT 4D 8'	F12W	25420	2700	3050	3900	6025
4WD		4	1200	1200	1600	1600
V8, 5.4 Liter		5	200	200	265	265
REGULAR CAB PICKUP 4WD—V8—Truck Equipment Schedule T1						
F150 FX4 4D 6 1/2'	F14W	30635	5300	5800	7600	11300
SUPER CAB PICKUP—V8—Truck Equipment Schedule T1						
F150 XL 4D 6 1/2'	X12W	24660	4000	4325	5200	7300
F150 XL 4D 8'	X12W	24960	3750	4075	4925	6925
F150 STX 4D 5 1/2'	X12W	25010	4300	4650	5550	7775
F150 XLT 4D 5 1/2'	X12W	27665	4625	5000	5925	8275
F150 Lariat 4D 5 1/2'	X12W	30395	5025	5400	6375	8875
F150 Lariat 4D 8'	X12W	30695	5075	5450	6450	8950
4WD		4	1200	1200	1600	1600
V8, 5.4 L (ex XLT 8')		5	200	200	265	265
SUPER CAB PICKUP 4WD—V8—Truck Equipment Schedule T1						
F150 STX 4D 6 1/2'	X14W	28845	5925	6350	7625	10500
F150 XLT 4D 6 1/2'	X14W	31300	6225	6675	7950	10950
2WD		2	(1525)	(1525)	(2035)	(2035)
V8, 5.4 Liter		5	200	200	265	265
SUPER CAB PICKUP 4WD—V8—Truck Equipment Schedule T1						
F150 XLT 4D 8'	X145	31600	5850	6275	7550	10400
2WD		2	(1525)	(1525)	(2035)	(2035)
V8, 5.4 Liter		5	200	200	265	265
SUPER CAB PICKUP 4WD—V8—Truck Equipment Schedule T1						
F150 XLT 4D 5 1/2'	X12W	32830	7125	7625	9025	12350
F150 FX4 4D 6 1/2'	X13W	33130	7200	7700	9100	12450
SUPERCREW PICKUP—V8—Truck Equipment Schedule T1						
F150 XLT 4D 5 1/2'	W12W	29815	5950	6400	7650	10550
4WD		4	1200	1200	1600	1600
V8, 5.4 Liter		5	200	200	265	265
SUPERCREW PICKUP 4WD—V8—Truck Equipment Schedule T1						
F150 Lariat 4D 5 1/2'	W14W	36785	8875	9475	11300	15600
2WD		2	(1525)	(1525)	(2035)	(2035)
V8, 5.4 Liter		5	200	200	265	265
SUPERCREW PICKUP 4WD—V8—Truck Equipment Schedule T1						
F150 FX4 4D 5 1/2'	W12W	35130	9325	9925	11650	15800
SUPER DUTY REGULAR CAB PICKUP—V8—Truck Equipment Schedule T1						
F250 XL 2D 8'	F20L	24430	2500	2775	3450	5100
F250 XLT 2D 8'	F20L	27015	3225	3550	4350	6400
F350 XL 2D 8'	F30L	24885	2775	3100	3725	5450
F350 XLT 2D 8'	F30L	27820	3425	3775	4575	6700
4WD		1	1200	1200	1600	1600
V8, Turbo Dsl 6.0L		P	2975	2975	3960	3960
V10, 6.8 Liter		S	350	350	465	465
SUPER DUTY SUPER CAB PICKUP—V8—Truck Equipment Schedule T1						
F250 XL 4D 6 3/4'	X20L	26615	4175	4575	5575	8025
F250 XL 4D 8'	X20L	26815	3925	4325	5125	7250
F250 XLT 4D 6 3/4'	X20L	29935	4875	5325	6400	9125
F250 XLT 4D 8'	X20L	30135	4675	5100	5825	8075
F250 Lariat 4D 6 3/4'	X20L	32105	5225	5700	6800	9675
F250 Lariat 4D 8'	X20L	32305	4375	4800	5800	8575
F350 XL 4D 6 3/4'	X30L	27405	4375	4800	5800	8300
F350 XL 4D 8'	X30L	27605	4225	4625	5525	7875
F350 XLT 4D 6 3/4'	X30L	30455	4775	5225	6275	8975
F350 XLT 4D 8'	X30L	30655	4600	5025	6075	8725
F350 Lariat 4D 6 3/4'	X30L	32480	5125	5575	6675	9525
F350 Lariat 4D 8'	X30L	32680	4950	5400	6475	9225
4WD		1	1200	1200	1600	1600
V8, Turbo Dsl 6.0L		P	2975	2975	3960	3960
V10, 6.8 Liter		S	350	350	465	465
SUPER DUTY SUPER CAB PICKUP 4WD—V8 Turbo Diesel—Truck Sch T1						
F250 Harley 6 3/4'	X20P	39890	11250	11950	13100	16950
F250 Harley 8'	X20P	40090	11050	11750	12900	16650
F350 Harley 6 3/4'	X31P	40895	11450	12150	13350	17200
F350 Harley 8'	X31P	41095	11050	11750	12900	16650
V10, 6.8 Liter		S	(400)	(400)	(490)	(490)
SUPER DUTY CREW CAB PICKUP—V8—Truck Equipment Schedule T1						
F250 XL 4D 6 3/4'	W20L	28025	5150	5600	6675	9475
F250 XL 4D 8'	W20L	28225	4850	5300	6350	9075
F250 XLT 4D 6 3/4'	W20L	32265	5650	6150	7475	10550
F250 XLT 4D 8'	W20L	32465	5550	6050	7375	10400
F250 Lariat 4D 6 3/4'	W20L	34735	6075	6600	7975	11200

Body Type	VIN	List	Trade-In Good	Very Good	Pvt-Party Good	Retail Excellent
F250 Lariat 4D 8'	W20L	34935	5750	6250	7600	10700
F250 KingRnch 6 3/4'	W20L	37350	6350	6900	8300	11650
F250 King Ranch 8'	W20L	37550	6075	6600	7975	11200
F350 XL 4D 6 3/4'	W30L	28685	5475	5975	7300	10300
F350 XL 4D 8'	W30L	33415	5375	5850	6825	9575
F350 XLT 4D 6 3/4'	W30L	33275	5950	6475	7850	11050
F350 XLT 4D 8'	W30L	33475	5850	6375	7700	10850
F350 Lariat 4D 6 3/4'	W30L	35600	7225	7825	9075	12500
F350 Lariat 4D 8'	W30L	35800	7150	7750	9000	12400
F350 KingRnch 6 3/4'	W30L	38215	6675	7250	8650	12150
F350 King Ranch 8'	W30L	38415	6350	6900	8300	11650
4WD	1		1200	1200	1600	1600
V8, Turbo Dsl 6.0L	P		2975	2975	3960	3960
V10, 6.8 Liter	S		350	350	465	465
SUPER DUTY CREW CAB PICKUP 4WD—V8 Turbo Diesel—Truck Sch T1						
F250 Harley 8'	W21P	42385	13400	14200	15600	20100
F250 Harley 8'	W21P	42585	13300	14100	15500	20000
F350 Harley 6 3/4'	W35P	43000	13600	14400	15800	20400
F350 Harley 8'	W35P	43200	13500	14300	15750	20300
V10, 6.8 Liter	S		(400)	(400)	(490)	(490)
SUPER DUTY CAB-CHASSIS—6-Cyl. Turbo Diesel—Truck Equip Sch T1						
F450 Cab-Ch DR	F46P	27830	6825	7400	8825	12450
F450 Crew Ch DR	W46P	31240	8800	9500	11200	15550
F550 Cab-Ch	F56P	30810	5950	6475	7750	10900
F550 Crew Ch	W56P	33655	9100	9800	11550	16050
4WD	7		1200	1200	1600	1600
V10, 6.8 Liter	S		(2825)	(2825)	(3775)	(3775)

Body Type	VIN	List	Trade-In Good	Very Good	Pvt-Party Good	Retail Excellent
ESCAPE 4WD—4-Cyl. Hybrid—Truck Equipment Schedule T1						
Sport Utility 4D	U96H	28595	3050	3375	4275	6100
2WD	0		(600)	(600)	(800)	(800)
ESCAPE—4-Cyl.—Truck Equipment Schedule T1						
XLS Sport Utility 4D	U02Z	19995	1675	1875	2850	4400
4WD	9		600	600	800	800
ESCAPE 4WD—4-Cyl. V6—Truck Equipment Schedule T1						
XLT Utility 4D	U931	25545	3400	3725	4725	6750
XLT "Sport" SUV	U931	26505	3625	3975	5125	7275
Limited Sport Util	U941	27145	3725	4075	5250	7450
2WD	0		(600)	(600)	(800)	(800)
4-Cyl, 2.3 Liter	Z		(425)	(425)	(555)	(555)
FREESTYLE—V6—Truck Equipment Schedule T1						
SE Sport Utility 4D	K011	25595	1650	1850	2675	4100
SEL Sport Utility 4D	K021	26995	1850	2075	3025	4525
AWD	4		975	975	1285	1285
FREESTYLE AWD—V6—Truck Equipment Schedule T1						
Limited Sport Util	K061	30895	2650	2950	4000	5925
2WD	3		(975)	(975)	(1300)	(1300)
EXPLORER 4WD—V6 Flex Fuel—Truck Equipment Schedule T1						
XLS Sport Utility 4D	U72K	29880	2425	2725	3725	5600
XLS "Sport" SUV	U72K	31135	2575	2900	4000	6050
XLT Sport Utility 4D	U73K	32520	2925	3275	4400	6625
XLT "Sport" 4D	U73K	34265	3075	3425	4600	6875
Eddie Bauer Spt Util	U74K	36995	3850	4250	5650	8300
Third Row Seat			325	325	435	435
2WD	6		(975)	(975)	(1300)	(1300)
V8, 4.6 Liter	W		200	200	265	265
EXPLORER 4WD—V8—Truck Equipment Schedule T1						
Limited Sport Util	U75W	38175	4100	4525	5975	8775
2WD	6		(975)	(975)	(1300)	(1300)
V6, 4.0 Liter	K		(175)	(175)	(235)	(235)
EXPLORER SPORT TRAC 4WD—V6 Flex Fuel—Truck Equipment Sch T1						
XLS Utility Pickup	U77K	27125	4250	4675	6125	8950
XLT Utility Pickup	U77K	28685	5975	6375	8175	11200
Adrenalin Utility	U77K	31885	6125	6525	8400	11550
2WD	6		(975)	(975)	(1300)	(1300)
EXPEDITION—V8—Truck Equipment Schedule T1						
XLS Sport Utility 4D	U135	33365	2475	2800	3625	5300
XLT Sport Utility 4D	U155	35390	3075	3425	4475	6475
Third Row Seat			450	450	600	600
4WD	0,4,6,8		600	600	800	800
EXPEDITION 4WD—V8—Truck Equipment Schedule T1						
XLT "Sport" SUV	U165	39320	4250	4650	5850	8375

Body Type	VIN	List	Trade-In Good	Trade-In Very Good	Pvt-Party Good	Retail Excellent
XLT NBX Sport Util	U165	39540	4425	4850	6050	8600
Eddie Bauer Spt Util	U185	43725	4900	5350	6825	9700
Limited Sport Util	U205	44835	4900	5350	6600	9050
King Ranch Spt Util	U185	46560	5700	6200	7550	10350
Third Row Seat	3,5,7,9		450	450	600	600
2WD	7,9		(600)	(600)	(800)	(800)
EXCURSION 4WD—V10—Truck Equipment Schedule T1						
XLS Sport Utility 4D	U41S	41395	7300	7925	9225	12350
XLT Sport Utility 4D	U41S	42385	7850	8525	9850	13150
Eddie Bauer Spt Util	U45S	45315	10100	10900	12200	16000
Limited Sport Util	U43S	46640	9800	10550	11900	15700
Third Row Seat			450	450	600	600
2WD	0,2,4		(600)	(600)	(800)	(800)
V8, 5.4 Liter	L		(425)	(425)	(565)	(565)
V8, Turbo Dsl 6.0L	P		3225	3225	4305	4305
FREESTAR—V6—Truck Equipment Schedule T2						
Cargo Minivan	A546	22295	1025	1175	1925	3125
FREESTAR—V6—Truck Equipment Schedule T1						
S Minivan	A506	24595	1350	1525	2450	3975
SE Minivan	A516	27195	1550	1750	2700	4350
SES Minivan	A576	28695	1750	1975	2950	4700
SEL Minivan	A522	29695	1950	2175	3225	5075
Limited Minivan	A582	33395	2425	2700	3850	5975
ECONOLINE WAGON—V8—Truck Equipment Schedule T1						
E150 XL Super Duty	E11W	25525	3275	3650	4675	6725
E150 XLT S.D.	E11W	28515	4075	4500	5600	7975
E150 Chateau S.D.	E11W	30515	4375	4825	5950	8450
E350 XL Super Duty	E31L	28265	3775	4175	5275	7525
E350 XLT S.D.	E31L	31220	4625	5075	6250	8850
E350 Chateau S.D.	E31L	33025	4850	5325	6725	9475
E350 XL S.D. Ext	S31L	30865	4575	5025	6200	8775
E350 XLT S.D. Ext	S31L	32490	4700	5175	6525	9225
V8, 5.4 Liter (E150)	L		200	200	265	265
V8, Turbo Dsl 6.0L	P		1800	1800	2400	2400
V10, 6.8 Liter	S		450	450	600	600
ECONOLINE VAN—V8—Truck Equipment Schedule T1						
E150 Super Cargo	E14W	23330	3325	3675	4925	7150
E250 Super Cargo	E24W	24375	3650	4025	5325	7725
E250 Extended SD	E24W	25695	4525	4950	6375	9150
E350 Super Cargo	E34L	27160	4050	4450	5775	8325
E350 Extended SD	E34L	28295	4775	5200	6925	9975
Crew Van Pkg			200	200	255	255
V8, 5.4L (E150/E250)	L		200	200	265	265
V8, Turbo Dsl 6.0L	S		1800	1800	2400	2400
V10, 6.8 Liter	S		450	450	600	600
RANGER REGULAR CAB PICKUP—4-Cyl.—Truck Equipment Schedule T2						
XL 2D 6'	R10D	15985	1850	2100	2975	4550
XL 2D 7'	R10D	17865	1275	1450	2300	3625
STX 2D 6'	R10D	16640	2075	2350	3250	4925
XLT 2D 6'	R10D	17700	2725	3075	4025	5975
XLT 2D 7'	R10D	18100	2075	2350	3250	4925
Edge 2D 6'	R10U	18050	2925	3300	4400	6500
4WD	1,5		900	900	1200	1200
V6, 3.0 Liter (ex Edge)	U		225	225	300	300
V6, 4.0 Liter	E		275	275	365	365
RANGER SUPER CAB PICKUP—V6—Truck Equipment Schedule T2						
XL 2D 6'	R14U	19110	3525	3925	5100	7475
STX 2D 6'	R14U	19680	3500	3900	5075	7425
STX 4D 6'	R44U	20845	4625	5100	6425	9275
XLT 2D 6'	R14U	19735	4000	4425	5675	8250
XLT 4D 6'	R44U	20900	4875	5375	6900	9925
Edge 2D 6'	R14U	20085	4700	5175	6500	9375
Edge 4D 6'	R44U	21250	4450	4900	6200	8975
4WD	1,5		900	900	1200	1200
V6, 4.0 Liter	E		275	275	365	365
RANGER SUPER CAB PICKUP 4WD—V6—Truck Equipment Schedule T2						
XLT FX4 Off-Road	R45E	26365	6825	7450	8625	11800
XLT FX4 Level II	R45E	26825	6750	7375	8550	11700
REGULAR CAB PICKUP—V6—Truck Equipment Schedule T1						
F150 XL 2D 6 1/2'	F122	21295	2950	3300	4375	6500
F150 STX 4D 6 1/2'	F122	22135	3250	3600	4725	7000
4WD	4		1300	1300	1735	1735
V8, 4.6 Liter	W		350	350	475	475

TRUCKS & VANS

Body Type	VIN	List	Trade-In Good	Very Good	Pvt-Party Good	Retail Excellent
V8, 5.4 Liter	5		600	600	785	785
REGULAR CAB PICKUP—V8—Truck Equipment Schedule T1						
F150 XL 2D 8'	F12W	21736	2975	3325	4400	6525
F150 XLT 4D 6 1/2'	F12W	25676	4075	4500	5875	8575
F150 XLT 4D 8'	F12W	25976	3675	4075	5400	7925
4WD	4		1300	1300	1735	1735
V6, 4.2 Liter	2		(450)	(450)	(600)	(600)
V8, 5.4 Liter	5		225	225	300	300
REGULAR CAB PICKUP 4WD—V8—Truck Equipment Schedule T1						
F150 FX4 4D 6 1/2'	F145	33086	6775	7375	9350	13400
SUPER CAB PICKUP—V8—Truck Equipment Schedule T1						
F150 XL 4D 6 1/2'	X12W	26060	4400	4775	5950	8225
F150 XL 4D 8'	X12W	26360	4100	4450	5600	7775
F150 STX 4D 5 1/2'	X12W	26410	4700	5075	6250	8550
F150 XLT 4D 5 1/2'	X12W	28285	5025	5425	6675	9175
F150 Lariat 4D 6 1/2'	X12W	31250	5525	5950	7450	10250
4WD	4		1300	1300	1735	1735
V8, 5.4 Liter	5		225	225	300	300
SUPER CAB PICKUP 4WD—V8—Truck Equipment Schedule T1						
F150 STX 4D 6 1/2'	X14W	29840	6750	7225	8875	12100
F150 XLT 4D 6 1/2'	X14W	32225	7000	7500	9225	12550
2WD			(1675)	(1675)	(2245)	(2245)
V8, 5.4 Liter	5		225	225	300	300
SUPER CAB PICKUP—V8—Truck Equipment Schedule T1						
F150 Lariat 4D 5 1/2'	X125	30950	5475	5900	7400	10150
4WD	4		1300	1300	1735	1735
SUPER CAB PICKUP 4WD—V8—Truck Equipment Schedule T1						
F150 XLT 4D 8'	X145	32505	7025	7525	9050	12150
2WD			(1675)	(1675)	(2245)	(2245)
SUPER CAB PICKUP 4WD—V8—Truck Equipment Schedule T1						
F150 FX4 4D 5 1/2'	X145	33500	8700	9275	11000	14750
F150 FX4 4D 6 1/2'	X145	33800	8800	9375	11100	14750
SUPERCREW PICKUP—V8—Truck Equipment Schedule T1						
F150 XLT 4D 6 1/2'	W12W	30185	6675	7150	8775	11950
F150 Lariat 4D 5 1/2'	W145	37760	10450	11100	13250	17850
F150 KingRnch 5 1/2'	W145	40910	12500	13250	15400	20400
4WD	4		1300	1300	1735	1735
V8, 5.4 Liter (XLT)	5		225	225	300	300
SUPER DUTY REGULAR CAB PICKUP—V8—Truck Equipment Schedule T1						
F250 XL 4D 8'	F205	25525	2225	2500	3475	5175
F350 XL 4D 8'	F305	26270	2450	2750	3725	5500
4WD	1		1300	1300	1735	1735
V8, Turbo Dsl 6.0L	P		3225	3225	4305	4305
V10, 6.8 Liter	Y		400	400	535	535
SUPER DUTY REGULAR CAB PICKUP 4WD—V8—Truck Equipment Sch T1						
F250 XLT 2D 8'	F215	28270	5000	5450	6600	9150
2WD			(1675)	(1675)	(2235)	(2235)
V8, Turbo Dsl 6.0L	P		3225	3225	4285	4285
V10, 6.8 Liter	Y		400	400	530	530
SUPER DUTY REGULAR CAB PICKUP 4WD—V8 Turbo Diesel—Truck Sch T1						
F350 XLT 2D 8'	F31P	29365	9025	9725	11350	15250
2WD	0,2		(1675)	(1675)	(2135)	(2135)
V8, 5.4 Liter	5		(3100)	(3100)	(3930)	(3930)
V10, 6.8 Liter	Y		(2725)	(2725)	(3445)	(3445)
SUPER DUTY SUPER CAB PICKUP—V8—Truck Equipment Schedule T1						
F250 XL 4D 6 3/4'	X205	27710	4100	4500	5725	8125
F250 XL 4D 8'	X205	27910	3850	4225	5300	7450
F250 XLT 4D 8'	X205	31390	4700	5125	5400	9025
F250 Lariat 4D 8'	X205	33560	4850	5300	6475	9025
F350 XL 4D 8'	X305	28990	4200	4600	5725	8000
F350 XLT 4D 8'	X305	32825	5000	5450	6600	9150
F350 Lariat 4D 8'	X305	34850	5275	5750	7100	9800
4WD	1		1300	1300	1735	1735
V8, Turbo Dsl 6.0L	P		3225	3225	4305	4305
V10, 6.8 Liter	Y		400	400	535	535
SUPER DUTY SUPER CAB PICKUP 4WD—V8—Truck Equipment Schedule T1						
F250 XLT 4D 6 3/4'	X215	31190	7325	7925	9500	12950
F350 XLT 4D 6 3/4'	X315	28790	6050	6575	7975	10950
F350 Lariat 4D 6 3/4'	X315	34650	7575	7875	9425	12850
2WD	0		(1675)	(1675)	(2190)	(2190)
V8, Turbo Dsl 6.0L	P		3225	3225	4195	4195
V10, 6.8 Liter	Y		400	400	520	520

Body Type	VIN	List	Trade-In Good	Very Good	Pvt-Party Good	Retail Excellent

SUPER DUTY SUPER CAB PICKUP 4WD—V8 Turbo Diesel—Truck Sch T1

Body Type	VIN	List	Good	Very Good	Good	Excellent
F250 Lariat 4D 6 3/4'	X21P	33560	11200	12000	13950	18750
F350 XLT 4D 6 3/4'	X31P	32625	11200	12000	13950	18750
2WD	0		(1675)	(1675)	(2160)	(2160)
V8, 5.4 Liter	5		(3100)	(3100)	(3980)	(3980)
V10, 6.8 Liter	Y		(2725)	(2725)	(3485)	(3485)

SUPER DUTY CREW CAB PICKUP—V8—Truck Equipment Schedule T1

Body Type	VIN	List	Good	Very Good	Good	Excellent
F250 XL 4D 6 3/4'	W205	29120	5225	5700	7075	9750
F250 XL 4D 8'	W205	29320	5050	5500	6675	9250
F250 XLT 4D 8'	W205	33720	5900	6425	7825	10750
F250 King Ranch 8'	W205	37305	6800	7375	8825	12050
F350 XL 4D 8'	W305	30270	5300	5775	7150	9850
F350 Lariat 4D 8'	W305	37345	7700	8325	9650	13000
4WD	1		1300	1300	1720	1720
V8, Turbo Dsl 6.0L	P		3225	3225	4270	4270
V10, 6.8 Liter	Y		400	400	530	530

SUPER DUTY CREW CAB PICKUP 4WD—V8—Truck Equipment Schedule T1

Body Type	VIN	List	Good	Very Good	Good	Excellent
F350 XLT 4D 8'	W315	35020	8725	9400	11050	15000
F350 King Ranch 8'	W315	38650	9075	9775	11500	15550
2WD			(1675)	(1675)	(2175)	(2175)
V8, Turbo Dsl 6.0L	P		3225	3225	4175	4175
V10, 6.8 Liter	Y		400	400	515	515

SUPER DUTY CREW CAB PICKUP 4WD—V8 Turbo Diesel—Truck Sch T1

Body Type	VIN	List	Good	Very Good	Good	Excellent
F350 XL 4D 6 3/4'	W30P	30070	9425	10150	11900	16100
4WD			1300	1300	1680	1680
V8, 5.4 Liter			(3100)	(3100)	(4000)	(4000)
V10, 6.8 Liter	Y		(2725)	(2725)	(3505)	(3505)

SUPER DUTY CREW CAB PICKUP 4WD—V8 Turbo Diesel—Truck Sch T1

Body Type	VIN	List	Good	Very Good	Good	Excellent
F350 XLT 4D 6 3/4'	W31P	34820	12500	13350	15300	20400
F350 Lariat 4D 6 3/4'	W31P	37145	12650	13550	15750	21100
F350 KingRnch 6 3/4'	W31P	38450	13050	14000	16200	21700
2WD	0		(1675)	(1675)	(2150)	(2150)
V8, 5.4 Liter	5		(3100)	(3100)	(3965)	(3965)
V10, 6.8 Liter	Y		(2725)	(2725)	(3475)	(3475)

SUPER DUTY CREW CAB PICKUP 4WD—V8 Turbo Diesel—Truck Sch T1

Body Type	VIN	List	Good	Very Good	Good	Excellent
F250 XLT 4D 6 3/4'	W21P	33520	11650	12450	14450	19350
F250 Lariat 4D 6 3/4'	W21P	35990	11850	12700	14650	19650
F250 Lariat 4D 8'	W21P	36190	11650	12450	14450	19350
F250 KingRnch 6 3/4'	W21P	37105	12600	13450	15500	20800
2WD	0		(1675)	(1675)	(2155)	(2155)
V8, 5.4 Liter	5		(3100)	(3100)	(3975)	(3975)
V10, 6.8 Liter	Y		(2725)	(2725)	(3480)	(3480)

SUPER DUTY CREW CAB PICKUP 4WD—V8 Turbo Diesel—Truck Sch T1

Body Type	VIN	List	Good	Very Good	Good	Excellent
F250 Harley 6 3/4'	W215	41835	15300	16150	17450	21900
F350 Harley 6 3/4'	W215	42035	15100	15950	17250	21600
F350 Harley 6 3/4'	W315	42610	15600	16450	17800	22300
F350 Harley 8'	W315	42810	15400	16250	17550	22000
V10, 6.8 Liter			(450)	(450)	(510)	(510)

ESCAPE—4-Cyl.—Truck Equipment Schedule T1

Body Type	VIN	List	Good	Very Good	Good	Excellent
XLS Sport Utility 4D	U021	20685	2475	2750	3675	5250
4WD	9		650	650	865	865

ESCAPE 4WD—V6—Truck Equipment Schedule T1

Body Type	VIN	List	Good	Very Good	Good	Excellent
XLT Utility 4D	U931	25755	4375	4750	5850	8100
XLT 'Sport' SUV	U931	26550	4975	5375	6525	8975
Limited Sport Util	U941	27295	5100	5525	6875	9425
2WD			(650)	(650)	(865)	(865)
4-Cyl, 2.3 Liter	Z		(450)	(450)	(600)	(600)

ESCAPE 4WD—4-Cyl. Hybrid—Truck Equipment Schedule T1

Body Type	VIN	List	Good	Very Good	Good	Excellent
Sport Utility 4D	U96H	29140	3375	3725	4900	7025
2WD	5		(650)	(650)	(865)	(865)

FREESTYLE—V6—Truck Equipment Schedule T1

Body Type	VIN	List	Good	Very Good	Good	Excellent
SE Sport Utility 4D	K011	25780	1825	2075	3100	4625
SEL Sport Utility 4D	K021	27180	2500	2825	3825	5500
AWD			700	700	945	945

FREESTYLE AWD—V6—Truck Equipment Schedule T1

Body Type	VIN	List	Good	Very Good	Good	Excellent
Limited Sport Utility	K061	31280	3375	3725	4900	7050
2WD	1,2,3		(650)	(650)	(865)	(865)

EXPLORER—V6—Truck Equipment Schedule T1

Body Type	VIN	List	Good	Very Good	Good	Excellent
XLS Sport Utility 4D	U62E	27175	3075	3425	4450	6375
Third Row Seat			350	350	465	465
4WD	7		1050	1050	1395	1395

TRUCKS & VANS

Body Type	VIN	List	Trade-In Good	Very Good	Pvt-Party Good	Retail Excellent
V8, 4.6 Liter	8		200	200	265	265
EXPLORER 4WD—V6—Truck Equipment Schedule T1						
XLT Sport Utility 4D	U73E	31095	4500	4950	6075	8500
Eddie Bauer Spt Util	U74E	33070	5400	5900	7375	10250
Third Row Seat			350	350	465	465
2WD	6		(1050)	(1050)	(1410)	(1410)
V8, 4.6 Liter	8		200	200	265	265
EXPLORER 4WD—V8—Truck Equipment Schedule T1						
Limited Sport Util	U75W	36585	6275	6825	8250	11300
Third Row Seat			350	350	465	465
2WD	6		(1050)	(1050)	(1410)	(1410)
V6, 4.0 Liter	E		(175)	(175)	(250)	(250)
EXPEDITION—V8—Truck Equipment Schedule T1						
XLS Sport Utility 4D	U135	34275	3450	3800	4650	6550
XLT Utility 4D	U155	36325	4225	4625	5700	7925
Third Row Seat			500	500	665	665
4WD	4		650	650	865	865
EXPEDITION 4WD—V8—Truck Equipment Schedule T1						
XLT "Sport" SUV	U165	39030	5500	5975	7350	10100
Eddie Bauer Spt Util	U185	42710	6475	7000	8475	11600
Limited Sport Util	U205	44460	6200	6700	7950	10650
King Ranch Spt Util	U185	46060	6900	7450	8925	12000
Third Row Seat			500	500	665	665
2WD	5		(650)	(650)	(865)	(865)
FREESTAR—V6—Truck Equipment Schedule T2						
Cargo Minivan	A546	20380	1250	1425	2350	3700
FREESTAR—V6—Truck Equipment Schedule T1						
SE Minivan	A516	24385	1975	2225	3250	4925
SEL Minivan	A522	27345	2500	2800	3875	5825
Limited Minivan	A582	30305	3200	3550	4725	6975
ECONOLINE WAGON—V8—Truck Equipment Schedule T1						
E150 XL Super Duty	E11W	26170	4375	4800	5825	8050
E150 XLT S.D.	E11W	28945	5175	5650	6925	9500
E150 Chateau S.D.	E11W	31015	5725	6250	7600	10400
E350 XL Super Duty	E31L	28610	4725	5175	6225	8575
E350 XLT S.D.	E31L	31415	5875	6400	7800	10650
E350 Chateau S.D.	E31L	33220	6650	7225	8650	11800
E350 XL S.D. Ext	S31L	30600	5575	6075	7350	10050
E350 XLT S.D. Ext	S31L	32460	6350	6925	8300	11300
V8, 5.4 Liter (E150)	L		200	200	265	265
V8, Turbo Dsl 6.0L	P		1950	1950	2600	2600
V10, 6.8 Liter	S		500	500	665	665
ECONOLINE VAN—V8—Truck Equipment Schedule T1						
E150 Super Cargo	E14W	23975	4350	4750	6000	8525
E250 Super Cargo	E24W	24590	4650	5075	6375	9000
E250 Extended SD	S24W	25740	5375	5850	7425	10450
E350 Super Cargo	E34L	27380	4825	5275	6775	9550
E350 Extended SD	S34L	28310	5825	6325	7950	11150
Crew Van Pkg			200	200	265	265
V8, 5.4L (E150/E250)	L		200	200	265	265
V8, Turbo Dsl 6.0L	P		1950	1950	2600	2600
V10, 6.8 Liter	S		500	500	665	665
RANGER REGULAR CAB PICKUP—4-Cyl.—Truck Equipment Schedule T1						
XL 2D 6'	R10D	16245	2100	2375	3325	4925
XLT 2D 6'	R10D	18165	3000	3350	4375	6300
4WD	1,5		1000	1000	1335	1335
V6, 3.0 Liter	U		250	250	335	335
V6, 4.0 Liter	E		300	300	400	400
RANGER REGULAR CAB PICKUP—4-Cyl.—Truck Equipment Schedule T2						
XL 2D 7'	R10D	16190	1325	1525	2450	3750
4WD	1,5		1000	1000	1335	1335
V6, 3.0 Liter	U		250	250	335	335
V6, 4.0 Liter	E		300	300	400	400
RANGER REGULAR CAB PICKUP—V6—Truck Equipment Schedule T2						
STX 2D 6'	R10U	19905	2250	2550	3500	5150
RANGER REGULAR CAB PICKUP—V6—Truck Equipment Schedule T1						
Sport 2D 6'	R10U	18870	3500	3875	4925	7050
4WD	1,5		1000	1000	1335	1335
RANGER REGULAR CAB PICKUP—V6—Truck Equipment Schedule T2						
XLT 2D 7'	R11U	17935	2725	3050	4050	5875
4WD	1,5		1000	1000	1335	1335
V6, 4.0 Liter	E		300	300	400	400

Body Type	VIN	List	Trade-In Good	Very Good	Pvt-Party Good	Retail Excellent
RANGER SUPER CAB PICKUP—4-Cyl.—Truck Equipment Schedule T1						
XL 2D 6'	R14D	18745	3825	4225	5300	7550
XLT 2D 6'	R14D	20000	4750	5200	6350	8925
4WD	1,5		1000	1000	1335	1335
V6, 3.0 Liter	U		250	250	335	335
V6, 4.0 Liter	E		300	300	400	400
RANGER SUPER CAB PICKUP—V6—Truck Equipment Schedule T1						
STX 4D 6'	R14U	19905	4150	4575	5675	8025
STX 4D 6'	R44U	21300	5400	5925	7375	10300
Sport 2D 6'	R14U	20705	5150	5650	7100	9925
Sport 4D 6'	R44U	22100	5525	6050	7500	10450
XLT 4D 6'	R44U	21600	5225	5750	7175	10000
4WD	1,5		1000	1000	1335	1335
V6, 4.0 Liter	E		300	300	400	400
RANGER SUPER CAB PICKUP 4WD—V6—Truck Equipment Schedule T2						
XLT FX4 Level II 6'	R45E	27305	7400	8050	8975	11800
RANGER SUPER CAB PICKUP 4WD—V6—Truck Equipment Schedule T1						
XLT FX4 Off-Rd 2D	R15E	26225	6700	7300	8200	10800
XLT FX4 Off-Rd 4D	R45E	27620	7600	8250	9175	12050
REGULAR CAB PICKUP—V6—Truck Equipment Schedule T1						
F150 XL 4D 6 1/2'	F122	19805	3675	4050	5175	7375
F150 STX 4D 6 1/2'	F122	22105	4025	4425	5575	7925
4WD	4		1600	1600	2135	2135
V8, 4.6 Liter	W		425	425	565	565
V8, 5.4 Liter	5		650	650	855	855
REGULAR CAB PICKUP—V8—Truck Equipment Schedule T1						
F150 XL 4D 8'	F12W	21945	3650	4025	5125	7325
F150 XLT 4D 6 1/2'	F12W	25095	5100	5550	6850	9650
F150 XLT 4D 8'	F12W	25390	4600	5025	6250	8850
4WD	4		1600	1600	2135	2135
V6, 4.2 Liter	2		(450)	(450)	(600)	(600)
V8, 5.4 Liter	5		250	250	335	335
REGULAR CAB PICKUP 4WD—V8—Truck Equipment Schedule T1						
F150 FX4 4D 6 1/2'	F14W	32020	7975	8625	10550	14600
SUPER CAB PICKUP—V8—Truck Equipment Schedule T1						
F150 XL 4D 6 1/2'	X12W	24985	5000	5375	6350	8450
F150 XL 4D 8'	X12W	25280	4700	5050	6025	8025
F150 STX 4D 6 1/2'	X12W	26300	5100	5500	6750	8950
F150 XLT 4D 5 1/2'	X12W	28735	5550	5975	7250	9600
F150 Lariat 4D 6 1/2'	X12W	31630	6350	6800	8175	10800
4WD	4		1600	1600	2115	2115
V8, 5.4 Liter	5		250	250	330	330
SUPER CAB PICKUP 4WD—V8—Truck Equipment Schedule T1						
F150 STX 4D 6 1/2'	X14W	29695	7475	7975	9375	12300
F150 XLT 4D 6 1/2'	X14W	32050	8125	8650	10100	13200
2WD	2		(2075)	(2075)	(2690)	(2690)
V8, 5.4 Liter	5		250	250	325	325
SUPER CAB PICKUP 4WD—V8—Truck Equipment Schedule T1						
F150 XLT 4D 8'	X145	32350	7900	8425	9825	12850
2WD	2		(2075)	(2075)	(2690)	(2690)
SUPER CAB PICKUP—V8—Truck Equipment Schedule T1						
F150 Lariat 4D 5 1/2'	X125	31350	6250	6700	8000	10550
F150 Harley 6 1/2'	X125	35645	10350	10950	12700	16500
4WD	4		1600	1600	2095	2095
SUPER CAB PICKUP 4WD—V8—Truck Equipment Schedule T1						
F150 FX4 4D 5 1/2'	X145	34215	9350	9925	11600	15100
F150 FX4 4D 6 1/2'	X145	34520	9450	10050	11700	15250
SUPERCREW PICKUP—V8—Truck Equipment Schedule T1						
F150 XLT 4D 5 1/2'	W12W	31335	7475	7975	9375	12300
F150 XLT 4D 6 1/2'	W14W	34500	9850	10450	12150	15800
F150 KingRnch 6 3/4'	W125	37480	10950	11650	13550	17550
4WD	4		1600	1600	2085	2085
V8, 5.4 Liter (XLT)	5		250	250	325	325
SUPERCREW PICKUP 4WD—V8—Truck Equipment Schedule T1						
F150 XLT 4D 6 1/2'	W14W	34500	9850	10450	12150	15800
F150 Lariat 4D 5 1/2'	W145	37465	11900	12600	14800	19450
F150 Lariat 4D 6 1/2'	W145	37765	11800	12500	14450	18750
F150 KingRnch 5 1/2'	W145	40630	13600	14350	16350	21000
2WD	2		(2075)	(2075)	(2640)	(2640)
SUPERCREW PICKUP 4WD—V8—Truck Equipment Schedule T1						
F150 FX4 4D 5 1/2'	W145	36510	11100	11750	13750	17950
F150 FX4 4D 6 1/2'	W145	36810	10900	11600	13500	17500

TRUCKS & VANS

Body Type	VIN	List	Trade-In Good	Trade-In Very Good	Pvt-Party Good	Retail Excellent
SUPER DUTY REGULAR CAB PICKUP—V8—Truck Equipment Schedule T1						
F250 XL 2D 6 3/4'	F205	24835	2550	2850	3800	5550
F350 XL 2D 8'	F305	25565	2750	3050	4000	5800
4WD		1	1600	1600	2135	2135
V8, Turbo Dsl 6.0L	P		3475	3475	4645	4645
V10, 6.8 Liter	Y		450	450	600	600
SUPER DUTY REGULAR CAB 4WD—V8—Truck Equipment Schedule T1						
F250 XLT 2D 8'	F215	28575	5700	6200	7425	10000
2WD		0	(2075)	(2075)	(2635)	(2635)
V8, Turbo Dsl 6.0L	P		3475	3475	4450	4450
V10, 6.8 Liter	Y		450	450	575	575
SUPER DUTY REGULAR CAB 4WD—V8 Turbo Diesel—Truck Equip Sch T1						
F350 XLT 2D 8'	F31P	29665	9325	10050	11800	15600
2WD		0	(2075)	(2075)	(2620)	(2620)
V8, 5.4 Liter	5		(3400)	(3400)	(4315)	(4315)
V10, 6.8 Liter	Y		(2975)	(2975)	(3780)	(3780)
SUPER DUTY SUPER CAB PICKUP—V8—Truck Equipment Schedule T1						
F250 XL 4D 6 3/4'	X205	26965	4725	5150	6175	8400
F250 XL 4D 8'	X205	27165	4325	4725	5725	7825
F250 XLT 4D 8'	X205	31690	5400	5875	7100	9600
F250 Lariat 4D 8'	X205	34130	5550	6025	7275	9800
F350 XL 4D 6 3/4'	X305	28025	7100	7675	9050	12100
F350 XL 4D 8'	X305	29065	4925	5350	6375	8650
F350 XLT 4D 8'	X305	33135	5700	6200	7425	10000
F350 Lariat 4D 8'	X305	35630	6025	6525	7775	10450
4WD		1	1600	1600	2060	2060
V8, Turbo Dsl 6.0L	P		3475	3475	4490	4490
V10, 6.8 Liter	Y		450	450	580	580
SUPER DUTY SUPER CAB PICKUP 4WD—V8—Truck Equipment Schedule T1						
F350 XLT 4D 6 3/4'	X215	31495	8025	8650	10050	13400
F350 Lariat 4D 8'	X315	35425	8175	8800	10250	13600
2WD		0	(2075)	(2075)	(2600)	(2600)
V8, Turbo Dsl 6.0L	P		3475	3475	4390	4390
V10, 6.8 Liter	Y		450	450	565	565
SUPER DUTY SUPER CAB 4WD—V8 Turbo Diesel—Truck Equipment Sch T1						
F350 XLT 4D 6 3/4'	X31P	32930	12250	13100	15000	19650
2WD		0	(2075)	(2075)	(2565)	(2565)
V8, 5.4 Liter	5		(3400)	(3400)	(4230)	(4230)
V10, 6.8 Liter	Y		(2975)	(2975)	(3700)	(3700)
SUPER DUTY SUPER CAB 4WD—V8 Turbo Diesel—Truck Equipment Sch T1						
F250 Lariat 4D 6 3/4'	X21P	34130	12150	13000	14900	19550
2WD		0	(2075)	(2075)	(2570)	(2570)
V8, 5.4 Liter	5		(3400)	(3400)	(4235)	(4235)
V10, 6.8 Liter	Y		(2975)	(2975)	(3705)	(3705)
SUPER DUTY CREW CAB PICKUP—V8—Truck Equipment Schedule T1						
F250 XL 4D 6 3/4'	W205	28345	6050	6550	7825	10500
F250 XL 4D 8'	W205	28540	5650	6125	7375	9950
F250 XLT 4D 8'	W205	34020	6775	7325	8625	11550
F250 King Ranch 8'	W205	40145	7475	8075	9475	12650
F350 XL 4D 8'	W305	29475	6175	6700	7950	10650
F350 Lariat 4D 8'	W305	38120	8575	9225	10500	13800
4WD		1	1600	1600	2030	2030
V8, Turbo Dsl 6.0L	P		3475	3475	4425	4425
V10, 6.8 Liter	Y		450	450	570	570
SUPER DUTY CREW CAB 4WD—V8—Truck Equipment Schedule T1						
F350 XLT 4D 8'	W315	35325	9325	10050	11800	15600
F350 King Ranch 8'	W315	41305	10100	10800	12600	16650
2WD		0,2	(2075)	(2075)	(2585)	(2585)
V8, Turbo Dsl 6.0L	P		3475	3475	4360	4360
V10, 6.8 Liter	Y		450	450	565	565
SUPER DUTY CREW CAB 4WD—V8 Turbo Diesel—Truck Equipment Sch T1						
F250 XLT 4D 6 3/4'	W21P	33825	13250	14150	16100	21100
F250 Lariat 4D 6 3/4'	W21P	36765	13650	14550	16550	21700
F250 Lariat 4D 8'	W21P	36960	13350	14250	16200	21300
F250 KingRnch 6 3/4'	W21P	39950	14150	15050	17100	22400
F350 XL 4D 6 3/4'	W30P	29275	10950	11700	13550	17850
F350 XLT 4D 6 3/4'	W31P	35130	13650	14550	16550	21700
F350 Lariat 4D 6 3/4'	W31P	37925	14050	14950	17000	22300
F350 KingRnch 6 3/4'	W31P	41110	14450	15600	17650	23100
2WD		0	(2075)	(2075)	(2560)	(2560)
V8, 5.4 Liter	5		(3400)	(3400)	(4215)	(4215)
V10, 6.8 Liter	Y		(2975)	(2975)	(3690)	(3690)

440   DEDUCT FOR RECONDITIONING

0415

Body Type	VIN	List	Trade-In Good	Very Good	Pvt-Party Good	Retail Excellent

SUPER DUTY CREW CAB PICKUP 4WD—V8 Turbo Diesel—Schedule T1
F250 Harley 6 3/4'	W21P	50780	18300	19250	20500	25400
F250 Harley 8'	W21P	50985	18100	19050	20300	25100
F350 Harley 6 3/4'	W31P	51555	18650	19650	21000	25900
F350 Harley 8'	W31P	51760	18450	19450	20800	25700

2007 FORD—(1,2or3)F(D,MorT)–(U02Z)–7–#

ESCAPE—4-Cyl.—Truck Equipment Schedule T1
| XLS Sport Utility 4D | U02Z | 20560 | 3125 | 3425 | 4275 | 5825 |
| 4WD | 5,9 | | 975 | 975 | 1315 | 1315 |
ESCAPE 4WD—4-Cyl. Hybrid—Truck Equipment Schedule T1
| Sport Utility 4D | U59H | 27925 | 4750 | 5150 | 6575 | 9250 |
| 2WD | 0 | | (700) | (700) | (935) | (935) |
ESCAPE 4WD—V6—Truck Equipment Schedule T1
XLT Sport Utility 4D	U931	25525	5050	5450	6600	8775
XLT "Sport" SUV 4D	U931	26310	5525	5950	7075	9375
Limited Sport Util	U941	27045	6125	6575	7725	10150
2WD	0		(700)	(700)	(935)	(935)
4-Cyl, 2.3 Liter	Z		(475)	(475)	(635)	(635)
EDGE—V6—Truck Equipment Schedule T1
SE Sport Utility 4D	K36C	25995	6375	6825	8150	10700
SEL Sport Utility 4D	K38C	27990	7375	7875	9300	12150
SEL Plus Sport Util 4D	K39C	29745	7925	8425	10000	13100
AWD			525	525	700	700
FREESTYLE—V6—Truck Equipment Schedule T1
| SEL Sport Utility 4D | K021 | 26245 | 2900 | 3225 | 4300 | 6100 |
| AWD | 5,6 | | 775 | 775 | 1035 | 1035 |
FREESTYLE AWD—V6—Truck Equipment Schedule T1
| Limited Sport Utility | K061 | 31405 | 3975 | 4325 | 5500 | 7675 |
| 2WD | 2,3 | | (700) | (700) | (935) | (935) |
EXPLORER 4WD—V6—Truck Equipment Schedule T1
XLT Sport Utility 4D	U73E	28290	5250	5725	6800	9050
Eddie Bauer Spt Util	U74E	31290	6800	7350	8575	11350
Third Row Seat	6		375	375	500	500
2WD	6		(1150)	(1150)	(1520)	(1520)
V8, 4.6 Liter	8		200	200	265	265
EXPLORER 4WD—V8—Truck Equipment Schedule T1
Limited Spt Util	U758	35690	8250	8875	10150	13350
Third Row Seat	6		375	375	500	500
2WD	6		(1150)	(1150)	(1520)	(1520)
V6, 4.0 Liter	E		(200)	(200)	(265)	(265)
EXPLORER SPORT TRAC—V6—Truck Equipment Schedule T1
XLT Utility Pickup	U31K	24940	8025	8500	9775	12300
4WD	5		1125	1125	1445	1445
V8, 4.6 Liter	8		200	200	255	255
EXPLORER SPORT TRAC 4WD—V6—Truck Equipment Schedule T1
Limited Util Pickup	U53K	29270	10200	10750	12150	15100
2WD	3		(1150)	(1150)	(1440)	(1440)
V8, 4.6 Liter	8		200	200	250	250
EXPEDITION 4WD—V8—Truck Equipment Schedule T1
XLT Sport Utility 4D	U165	32895	7525	8100	9275	12100
Eddie Bauer Spt Util	U185	39295	10150	10850	12150	15700
Limited Spt Util	U205	40745	10350	11050	12350	15750
Third Row Seat			550	550	735	735
2WD	3,5,7,9		(700)	(700)	(935)	(935)
EXPEDITION EL 4WD—V8—Truck Equipment Schedule T1
XLT Sport Utility 4D	K165	37345	8775	9400	10650	13850
Eddie Bauer Spt Util	K185	41945	11000	11750	13200	17100
Limited Sport Util	K205	43395	11250	12000	13400	17100
Third Row Seat			550	550	735	735
2WD	5,7,9		(700)	(700)	(935)	(935)
FREESTAR—V6—Truck Equipment Schedule T2
| Cargo Minivan | A542 | 20480 | 2100 | 2350 | 3375 | 5050 |
FREESTAR—V6—Truck Equipment Schedule T1
SE Minivan	A512	24485	2975	3275	4275	6250
SEL Minivan	A522	27445	3425	3775	4950	7175
Limited Minivan	A582	30355	4275	4650	5950	8525
ECONOLINE WAGON—V8—Truck Equipment Schedule T1
E150 XL Super Duty	E11W	28460	5650	6150	7225	9575
E150 XLT S.D.	E11W	29920	6725	7250	8475	11200
E150 Chateau S.D.	E11W	31290	8075	8675	9950	13100
E350 XL Super Duty	E31L	28485	6175	6700	7800	10350
E350 XLT S.D.	E31L	32155	7925	8525	9900	13100

TRUCKS & VANS

Body Type	VIN	List	Trade-In Good	Trade-In Very Good	Pvt-Party Good	Retail Excellent
E350 XL S.D. Ext	S31L	31190	7175	7725	8950	11800
E350 XLT Extended	S31L	32635	8900	9550	11100	14650
V8, 5.4 Liter (E150)	L		200	200	255	255
V8, Turbo Dsl 6.0L	P		2100	2100	2665	2665
ECONOLINE VAN—V8—Truck Equipment Schedule T1						
E150 Super Cargo	E14W	24250	5475	5950	7125	9575
E250 Super Cargo	E24W	24865	5825	6325	7525	10100
E250 Ext SD Cargo	E24W	26550	6900	7425	8775	11700
E350 Super Cargo	E34L	27745	6225	6725	8025	10750
E350 Ext SD Cargo	E34L	29120	7550	8125	9500	12650
Crew Van Pkg			200	200	265	265
V8, 5.4L (E150/E250)	L		200	200	265	265
V8, Turbo Dsl 6.0L	P		2100	2100	2800	2800
V10, 6.8 Liter	S		550	550	735	735
RANGER REGULAR CAB PICKUP—4-Cyl.—Truck Equipment Schedule T2						
XL 2D 7'	R10D	15700	1775	2000	2950	4350
XLT 2D 7'	R10D	16365	3075	3425	4440	6250
4WD	1,5		1100	1100	1465	1465
V6, 3.0 Liter	U		250	250	335	335
V6, 4.0 Liter	E		325	325	435	435
RANGER REGULAR CAB PICKUP—4-Cyl.—Truck Equipment Schedule T1						
XL 2D 6'	R10D	15495	2500	2800	3750	5400
XLT 2D 6'	R10D	16970	3425	3775	4800	6775
4WD	1,5		1100	1100	1465	1465
V6, 3.0 Liter	U		250	250	335	335
V6, 4.0 Liter	E		325	325	435	435
RANGER REGULAR CAB PICKUP—V6—Truck Equipment Schedule T2						
STX 2D 6'	R10U	15865	2625	2950	3900	5600
4WD	1,5		1100	1100	1465	1465
4-Cyl, 2.3 Liter	D		(250)	(250)	(335)	(335)
RANGER REGULAR CAB PICKUP—V6—Truck Equipment Schedule T1						
Sport 2D 6'	R10U	17605	3875	4250	5300	7450
4WD	1,5		1100	1100	1465	1465
V6, 4.0 Liter	E		325	325	435	435
RANGER SUPER CAB PICKUP—4-Cyl.—Truck Equipment Schedule T1						
XL 2D 6'	R14D	16805	4225	4625	5700	7950
4WD	1,5		1100	1100	1465	1465
V6, 3.0 Liter	U		250	250	335	335
V6, 4.0 Liter	E		325	325	435	435
RANGER SUPER CAB PICKUP—V6—Truck Equipment Schedule T1						
STX 2D 6'	R14U	17835	4600	5050	6325	8750
4WD	1,5		1100	1100	1465	1465
4-Cyl, 2.3 Liter	D		(250)	(250)	(335)	(335)
V6, 4.0 Liter	E		100	100	100	100
RANGER SUPER CAB PICKUP—V6—Truck Equipment Schedule T1						
XLT 2D 6'	R14U	18365	5275	5775	7175	9900
XLT 4D 6'	R44U	19820	5725	6250	7675	10550
Sport 2D 6'	R14U	19000	5550	6050	7475	10300
Sport 4D 6'	R44U	20255	6250	6800	8250	11300
STX 4D 6'	R14U	19045	6025	6550	8025	11000
4WD	1,5		1100	1100	1465	1465
V6, 4.0 Liter	E		325	325	435	435
RANGER SUPER CAB PICKUP 4WD—V6—Truck Equipment Schedule T1						
FX4 Off-Road 2D 6'	R15E	22620	8000	8650	9575	12450
FX4 Off-Road Lvl II	R45E	24950	8850	9525	10550	13700
RANGER SUPER CAB PICKUP 4WD—V6—Truck Equipment Schedule T1						
FX4 Off-Road 4D 6'	R45E	24705	9100	9800	10850	14050
REGULAR CAB PICKUP—V6—Truck Equipment Schedule T1						
F150 XL 2D 6 1/2'	F122	19200	4375	4775	5875	8100
F150 XL 2D 8'	F122	19500	3975	4375	5400	7475
4WD	4		2000	2000	2665	2665
V8, 4.6 Liter	W		450	450	610	610
V8, 5.4 Liter	5		700	700	925	925
REGULAR CAB PICKUP—V8—Truck Equipment Schedule T1						
F150 STX 4D 6 1/2'	F12W	23750	5300	5775	7125	9750
F150 XLT 4D 6 1/2'	F12W	26050	5900	6400	7825	10700
F150 XLT 4D 8'	F12W	26350	5400	5875	7250	9900
4WD	4		2000	2000	2665	2665
V6, 4.2 Liter	2		(450)	(450)	(600)	(600)
V8, 5.4 Liter	5		275	275	365	365
REGULAR CAB PICKUP 4WD—V8—Truck Equipment Schedule T1						
F150 FX4 4D 6 1/2'	F145	30750	10100	10800	12950	17550

Body Type	VIN	List	Trade-In Good	Very Good	Pvt-Party Good	Retail Excellent
SUPER CAB PICKUP—V8—Truck Equipment Schedule T1						
F150 XL 4D 6 1/2'	X12W	24295	5325	5725	6900	9050
F150 XL 4D 8'	X12W	24595	5125	5525	6700	8800
F150 STX 4D 5 1/2'	X12W	25850	5575	5975	7225	9450
F150 XLT 4D 6 1/2'	X12W	28150	6275	6700	8000	10450
4WD	4		2000	2000	2615	2615
V8, 5.4 Liter	5		275	275	360	360
SUPER CAB PICKUP 4WD—V8—Truck Equipment Schedule T1						
F150 STX 4D 6 1/2'	X14W	29150	8450	8950	10400	13450
F150 XLT 4D 6 1/2'	X14W	31450	8950	9475	10900	14100
2WD	2		(2250)	(2250)	(2890)	(2890)
V8, 5.4 Liter	5		275	275	355	355
SUPER CAB PICKUP—V8—Truck Equipment Schedule T1						
F150 Lariat 4D 5 1/2'	X125	30750	6850	7300	8625	11250
F150 Lariat 4D 8'	X125	31050	7350	7825	9200	11950
4WD	4		2000	2000	2595	2595
SUPER CAB PICKUP 4WD—V8—Truck Equipment Schedule T1						
F150 XLT 4D 8'	X145	31750	8950	9475	10900	14100
2WD	2		(2250)	(2250)	(2870)	(2870)
SUPER CAB PICKUP 4WD—V8—Truck Equipment Schedule T1						
F150 FX4 4D 5 1/2'	X145	32850	10500	11100	12700	16150
F150 FX4 4D 6 1/2'	X145	33150	10700	11350	12850	16350
SUPERCREW PICKUP—V8—Truck Equipment Schedule T1						
F150 XLT 4D 5 1/2'	W12W	30490	8600	9125	10550	13650
F150 KingRnch 6 1/2	W125	36590	11850	12550	14400	18400
F150 Harley 5 1/2	W125	37150	13000	13750	15650	20000
4WD	4		2000	2000	2580	2580
V8, 5.4 Liter (XLT)	5		275	275	355	355
SUPERCREW PICKUP 4WD—V8—Truck Equipment Schedule T1						
F150 XLT 4D 6 1/2'	W14W	33850	10900	11500	13250	17000
2WD	2		(2250)	(2250)	(2865)	(2865)
V8, 5.4 Liter	5		275	275	350	350
SUPERCREW PICKUP 4WD—V8—Truck Equipment Schedule T1						
F150 Lariat 4D 5 1/2'	W145	36220	13550	14300	16350	20900
F150 Lariat 4D 6 1/2'	W145	36450	13650	14400	16400	20900
F150 KingRnch 5 1/2	W145	39420	15050	15850	17450	21800
2WD	2		(2250)	(2250)	(2865)	(2865)
SUPERCREW PICKUP 4WD—V8—Truck Equipment Schedule T1						
F150 FX4 4D 5 1/2'	W125	35250	11950	12650	14550	18600
F150 FX4 4D 6 1/2'	W125	35550	11750	12450	14300	18300
SUPER DUTY REGULAR CAB PICKUP—V8—Truck Equipment Schedule T1						
F250 XL 2D 8'	F205	25795	3075	3400	4375	6075
F350 XL 2D 8'	F305	26525	3425	3750	4750	6550
4WD	1		2000	2000	2665	2665
V8, Turbo Dsl 6.0L	P		3750	3750	4990	4990
V10, 6.8 Liter	Y		475	475	635	635
SUPER DUTY REGULAR CAB 4WD—V8—Truck Equipment Schedule T1						
F250 XLT 2D 8'	F215	28685	6750	7275	8650	11450
2WD	0		(2250)	(2250)	(2755)	(2755)
V8, Turbo Dsl 6.0L	P		3750	3750	4595	4595
V10, 6.8 Liter	Y		475	475	585	585
SUPER DUTY REGULAR CAB 4WD—V8 Turbo Diesel—Truck Equip Sch T1						
F350 XLT 2D 8'	F31P	29775	10850	11600	13400	17450
2WD	0		(2250)	(2250)	(2670)	(2670)
V8, 5.4 Liter	5		(3700)	(3700)	(4410)	(4410)
V10, 6.8 Liter	Y		(3800)	(3800)	(4525)	(4525)
SUPER DUTY SUPER CAB PICKUP—V8—Truck Equipment Schedule T1						
F250 XL 4D 6 3/4'	X205	27925	5575	6025	7350	9825
F250 XL 4D 8'	X205	28125	5125	5550	6875	9225
F250 XLT 4D 8'	X205	31800	6525	7025	8325	11050
F250 Lariat 4D 8'	X205	34445	6750	7275	8650	11450
F350 XL 4D 6 3/4'	X315	28135	8575	9175	10750	14150
F350 XL 4D 8'	X305	29175	5675	6150	7475	9975
F350 XLT 4D 8'	X305	33245	6850	7375	8750	11600
F350 Lariat 4D 8'	X305	35740	7450	8000	9425	12450
4WD	1		2000	2000	2450	2450
V8, Turbo Dsl 6.0L	P		3750	3750	4580	4580
V10, 6.8 Liter	Y		475	475	580	580
SUPER DUTY SUPER CAB PICKUP 4WD—V8—Truck Equipment Schedule T1						
F250 XLT 4D 6 3/4'	X215	31605	9375	10000	11650	15250
F350 Lariat 4D 6 3/4'	X315	35740	9350	10000	11750	15400
2WD	0		(2250)	(2250)	(2685)	(2685)
V8, Turbo Dsl 6.0L	P		3750	3750	4480	4480

TRUCKS & VANS

Body Type	VIN	List	Trade-In Good	Very Good	Pvt-Party Good	Retail Excellent
V10, 6.8 Liter	Y		475	475	570	570
SUPER DUTY SUPER CAB 4WD—V8 Turbo Diesel—Truck Equip Sch T1						
F250 Lariat 4D 6 3/4'	X21P	34240	13900	14800	16750	21600
F350 XLT 4D 6 3/4'	X31P	33040	14150	15050	17000	22000
2WD	0		(2250)	(2250)	(2655)	(2655)
V8, 5.4 Liter	5		(3700)	(3700)	(4385)	(4385)
V10, 6.8 Liter	Y		(3800)	(3800)	(4505)	(4505)
SUPER DUTY CREW CAB PICKUP—V8—Truck Equipment Schedule T1						
F250 XL 4D 6 3/4'	W205	29305	7150	7675	9075	12000
F250 XL 4D 8'	W205	29500	6750	7275	8650	11450
F250 XLT 4D 8'	W205	33755	7900	8475	9900	13050
F250 King Ranch 8'	W205	40255	8525	9125	10750	14100
F350 XL 4D 8'	W305	30435	7200	7750	9150	12100
F350 Lariat 4D 8'	W305	38230	9825	10500	12000	15500
4WD	1		2000	2000	2470	2470
V8, Turbo Dsl 6.0L	P		3750	3750	4625	4625
V10, 6.8 Liter	Y		475	475	585	585
SUPER DUTY CREW CAB PICKUP—V8 Turbo Diesel—Truck Equip Sch T1						
F350 XL 4D 6 3/4'	W30P	30235	11700	12500	14350	18600
4WD	1		2000	2000	2380	2380
V8, 5.4 Liter	5		(3700)	(3700)	(4400)	(4400)
V10, 6.8 Liter	Y		(3800)	(3800)	(4520)	(4520)
SUPER DUTY CREW CAB PICKUP 4WD—V8—Truck Equipment Schedule T1						
F350 XLT 4D 8'	W315	35435	10950	11700	13500	17550
F350 King Ranch 8'	W315	41415	11700	12500	14350	18600
2WD	0		(2250)	(2250)	(2655)	(2655)
V8, Turbo Dsl 6.0L	P		3750	3750	4450	4450
V10, 6.8 Liter	Y		475	475	565	565
SUPER DUTY CREW CAB 4WD—V8 Turbo Diesel—Truck Equipment Sch T1						
F250 Lariat 4D 6 3/4'	W21P	33570	15400	16350	18250	23400
F250 Lariat 4D 6 3/4'	W21P	36740	15950	16900	18950	24400
F250 Lariat 4D 8'	W21P	36935	16250	16200	18200	23500
F250 KingRnch 6 3/4'	W21P	40060	16550	17600	19650	25300
F350 XLT 4D 6 3/4'	W31P	35240	15850	16850	18700	24000
F350 Lariat 4D 6 3/4'	W31P	38035	16450	17500	19550	25200
F350 KingRnch 6 3/4'	W31P	41220	17150	18200	20300	26200
2WD	0		(2250)	(2250)	(2655)	(2655)
V8, 5.4 Liter	5		(3700)	(3700)	(4385)	(4385)
V10, 6.8 Liter	Y		(3800)	(3800)	(4505)	(4505)
SUPER DUTY CREW CAB PICKUP 4WD—V8 Turbo Diesel—Schedule T1						
F250 Harley 6 3/4'	W21P	50890	21400	22400	23500	28500
F250 Harley 8'	W21P	51095	21200	22200	23300	28300
F350 Harley 6 3/4'	W31P	51665	21800	22800	24000	29100
F350 Harley 8'	W31P	51870	21600	22700	23700	28800

2008 FORD (1,2or3)F(D,MorT)—U02Z-8-#

Body Type	VIN	List	Trade-In Good	Very Good	Pvt-Party Good	Retail Excellent
ESCAPE—4-Cyl.—Truck Equipment Schedule T1						
XLS Sport Utility 4D	U02Z	20245	4400	4750	5675	7500
4WD			1075	1075	1430	1430
ESCAPE 4WD—4-Cyl. Hybrid—Truck Equipment Schedule T1						
Sport Utility 4D	U59H	27680	6850	7325	8800	11600
2WD	0,4		(750)	(750)	(1000)	(1000)
ESCAPE 2WD—V6—Truck Equipment Schedule T1						
XLT Sport Utility 4D	U931	24485	6275	6700	7925	10250
Limited Sport Util	U941	26185	8050	8575	10000	12950
2WD	0,4		(750)	(750)	(1000)	(1000)
4-Cyl, 2.3 Liter	Z		(500)	(500)	(665)	(665)
EDGE—V6—Truck Equipment Schedule T1						
SE Sport Utility 4D	K36C	26025	7150	7575	8900	11350
SEL Sport Utility 4D	K38C	28020	8175	8650	10050	12700
Limited Spt Util 4D	K39C	29775	9000	9500	11050	14050
AWD			550	550	735	735
TAURUS X—V6—Truck Equipment Schedule T1						
SEL Sport Utility 4D	K03W	27365	4125	4475	5650	7700
AWD	5,8,6		825	825	1090	1090
TAURUS X AWD—V6—Truck Equipment Schedule T1						
Eddie Bauer Spt Utl	K08W	31955	6200	6650	8275	11150
Limited Sport Util	K06W	32935	6625	7100	8775	11800
2WD	2,3,7		(750)	(750)	(1000)	(1000)
EXPLORER 4WD—V6—Truck Equipment Schedule T1						
XLT Sport Utility 4D	U73E	28785	6700	7200	8550	10400
Eddie Bauer Spt Util	U74E	31130	8350	8925	10000	12700
Third Row Seat			400	400	515	515

Body Type	VIN	List	Trade-In Good	Trade-In Very Good	Pvt-Party Good	Retail Excellent
2WD	6		(1225)	(1225)	(1570)	(1570)
AWD	8		0	0	0	0
V8, 4.6 Liter	8		200	200	255	255
EXPLORER 4WD—V8—Truck Equipment Schedule T1						
Limited Sport Util	U758	36195	9575	10200	11400	14400
Third Row Seat			400	400	510	510
2WD	6		(1225)	(1225)	(1560)	(1560)
AWD	8		0	0	0	0
V6, 4.0 Liter	E		(200)	(200)	(255)	(255)
EXPLORER SPORT TRAC—V6—Truck Equipment Schedule T1						
XLT Utility Pickup	U31K	25435	10050	10550	11700	14200
4WD	5		1225	1225	1465	1465
V8, 4.6 Liter	8		200	200	240	240
EXPLORER SPORT TRAC 4WD—V6—Truck Equipment Schedule T1						
Limited Util Pickup	U53K	29995	13400	14050	15400	18450
2WD	3		(1225)	(1225)	(1460)	(1460)
AWD			0	0	0	0
V8, 4.6 Liter	8		200	200	240	240
EXPEDITION 4WD—V8—Truck Equipment Schedule T1						
XLT Sport Utility 4D	U165	34420	8950	9525	10650	13350
Eddie Bauer Spt Util	U185	39665	12350	13100	14300	17800
Limited Sport Util	U205	41825	13500	14250	15150	18250
King Ranch Spt Util	U185	43765	13900	14650	15550	18750
Third Row Seat			600	600	755	755
2WD	5,7,9		(750)	(750)	(940)	(940)
EXPEDITION EL 4WD—V8—Truck Equipment Schedule T1						
XLT Sport Utility 4D	K165	37945	10250	10900	12000	15050
Eddie Bauer Spt Util	K185	42315	12750	13500	14800	18400
Limited Sport Util	K205	44475	14300	15100	15950	19250
King Ranch Spt Util	K185	46415	14500	15300	16250	19650
Third Row Seat			600	600	750	750
2WD	5,7,9		(750)	(750)	(940)	(940)
ECONOLINE WAGON—V8—Truck Equipment Schedule T1						
E150 XL Super Duty	E11W	26790	6950	7450	8700	11250
E150 XLT S.D.	E11W	29565	8500	9075	10200	13000
E350 XL Super Duty	E31L	30320	7600	8125	9400	12150
E350 XLT S.D.	E31L	33125	9625	10250	11500	14550
E350 XL S.D. Ext	E31L	32710	8850	9425	10750	13750
E350 XLT Extended	S31L	34470	10450	11100	12550	15950
V8, 5.4 Liter (E150)	L		200	200	245	245
V8, Turbo Dsl 6.0L	P		2250	2250	2785	2785
ECONOLINE VAN—V8—Truck Equipment Schedule T1						
E150 Cargo Van	E14W	24595	7800	8375	9400	12000
E150 Extended	S14W	25595	8650	9250	10300	13150
E250 Cargo Van	E24W	25925	8450	9050	10100	12850
E250 Extended	E24W	27075	9625	10300	11450	14550
E350 Super Cargo	E34L	28715	9000	9625	10700	13600
E350 Extended SD	E34L	29645	10250	10950	12100	15350
Crew Van Pkg			200	200	250	250
V8, 5.4L (E150/E250)	L		200	200	250	250
V8, Turbo Dsl 6.0L	P		2250	2250	2815	2815
V10, 6.8 Liter	S		600	600	750	750
RANGER REGULAR CAB PICKUP—4-Cyl.—Truck Equipment Schedule T2						
XL 2D 7'	R10D	15925	3550	3875	5000	7000
XLT 2D 7'	R10D	17505	4600	5000	6200	8550
4WD	1,5		1300	1300	1690	1690
V6, 3.0 Liter	U		250	250	325	325
V6, 4.0 Liter	E		350	350	455	455
RANGER REGULAR CAB PICKUP—4-Cyl.—Truck Equipment Schedule T1						
XL 2D 6'	R10D	15655	4150	4525	5675	7875
XLT 2D 6'	R10D	17380	4925	5350	6800	9375
4WD	1,5		1300	1300	1675	1675
V6, 3.0 Liter	U		250	250	320	320
V6, 4.0 Liter	E		350	350	450	450
RANGER REGULAR CAB PICKUP—V6—Truck Equipment Schedule T1						
Sport 2D 6'	R10U	17915	5325	5775	7225	9875
4WD	1,5		1300	1300	1655	1655
V6, 4.0 Liter	E		350	350	445	445
RANGER SUPER CAB PICKUP—4-Cyl.—Truck Equipment Schedule T1						
XL 2D 6'	R14D	17130	5925	6400	7900	10750
4WD	1,5		1300	1300	1655	1655
V6, 3.0 Liter	U		250	250	315	315
V6, 4.0 Liter	E		350	350	445	445

TRUCKS & VANS

Body Type	VIN	List	Trade-In Good	Very Good	Pvt-Party Good	Retail Excellent
RANGER SUPER CAB PICKUP—V6—Truck Equipment Schedule T1						
XLT 2D 6'	R14U	18780	6725	7250	8725	11650
4WD	1,5		1300	1300	1645	1645
4-Cyl, 2.3 Liter	D		(275)	(275)	(350)	(350)
V6, 4.0 Liter	E		350	350	445	445
RANGER SUPER CAB PICKUP—V6—Truck Equipment Schedule T1						
Sport 2D 6'	R14U	19570	7800	8375	10150	13700
Sport 4D 6'	R44U	20825	8300	8900	10700	14450
XLT 4D 6'	R44U	20235	8000	8575	10350	14000
4WD	1,5		1300	1300	1635	1635
V6, 4.0 Liter	E		350	350	440	440
RANGER SUPER CAB PICKUP 4WD—V6—Truck Equipment Schedule T2						
FX4 Off-Road 2D 6'	R15E	23145	9950	10650	11750	14950
RANGER SUPER CAB PICKUP 4WD—V6—Truck Equipment Schedule T1						
FX4 Off-Road 4D 6'	R45E	25400	10800	11500	12700	16100
REGULAR CAB PICKUP—V6—Truck Equipment Schedule T1						
F150 XL 2D 6 1/2'	F122	18570	5400	5825	7125	9525
F150 XL 2D 8'	F122	18770	5100	5500	6775	9075
4WD	4		2200	2200	2935	2935
V8, 4.6 Liter	W		500	500	655	655
V8, 5.4 Liter	5		750	750	1000	1000
REGULAR CAB PICKUP—V8—Truck Equipment Schedule T1						
F150 STX 2D 6 1/2'	F12W	25960	6850	7325	8800	11650
F150 XLT 2D 6 1/2'	F12W	26120	7375	7900	9475	12550
F150 XLT 2D 8'	F12W	26420	6850	7325	8800	11650
4WD	4		2200	2200	2935	2935
V6, 4.2 Liter	2		(450)	(450)	(600)	(600)
V8, 5.4 Liter	5		300	300	400	400
REGULAR CAB PICKUP 4WD—V8—Truck Equipment Schedule T1						
F150 FX4 2D 6 1/2'	F145	32665	11750	12500	14700	19350
SUPER CAB PICKUP—V8—Truck Equipment Schedule T1						
F150 XL 4D 6 1/2'	X12W	24365	6800	7225	8250	10300
F150 STX 4D 5 1/2'	X12W	25920	7100	7525	8575	10700
F150 XLT 4D 5 1/2'	X12W	28220	7375	7825	8950	11150
F150 XLT 60th 6 1/2'	X12W	31500	7525	7975	9100	11350
4WD	4		2200	2200	2755	2755
V8, 5.4 Liter	5		300	300	375	375
SUPER CAB PICKUP 4WD—V8—Truck Equipment Schedule T1						
F150 STX 4D 6 1/2'	X14W	29220	9775	10300	11500	14150
F150 XLT 4D 6 1/2'	X14W	31520	10550	11150	12400	15350
2WD	2		(2450)	(2450)	(3015)	(3015)
V8, 5.4 Liter	5		300	300	370	370
SUPER CAB PICKUP—V8—Truck Equipment Schedule T1						
F150 XL 4D 8'	X125	24665	6550	6975	7950	9975
F150 Lariat 4D 5 1/2'	X125	30820	8725	9225	10400	12900
F150 Lariat 4D 6 1/2'	X125	31120	8825	9325	10500	13000
4WD	4		2200	2200	2765	2765
SUPER CAB PICKUP 4WD—V8—Truck Equipment Schedule T1						
F150 XLT 4D 8'	X145	31820	10550	11150	12600	15750
2WD	2		(2450)	(2450)	(3040)	(3040)
SUPER CAB PICKUP 4WD—V8—Truck Equipment Schedule T1						
F150 FX4 4D 5 1/2'	X145	32920	11500	12100	13450	16800
F150 FX4 4D 6 1/2'	X145	33220	11600	12200	13600	16800
SUPERCREW PICKUP—V8—Truck Equipment Schedule T1						
F150 XL 4D 5 1/2'	W12W	27820	10100	10650	11950	14800
F150 XL 4D 6 1/2'	W12W	28120	9925	10450	11700	14500
F150 XLT 4D 5 1/2'	W12W	31205	11000	11600	12900	15950
F150 XLT 60th 5 1/2'	W12W	33600	11000	11600	12900	15950
F150 XLT 60th 6 1/2'	W12W	33900	10700	11300	12600	15550
4WD	4		2200	2200	2745	2745
V8, 5.4 Liter	5		300	300	375	375
SUPERCREW PICKUP 4WD—V8—Truck Equipment Schedule T1						
F150 XLT 4D 6 1/2'	W14W	33920	13200	13900	15450	19100
2WD	2		(2450)	(2450)	(3045)	(3045)
V8, 5.4 Liter	5		300	300	370	370
SUPERCREW PICKUP—V8—Truck Equipment Schedule T1						
F150 KingRnch 6 1/2'	W125	36720	13900	14600	16200	20000
4WD	4		2200	2200	2730	2730
SUPERCREW PICKUP 4WD—V8—Truck Equipment Schedule T1						
F150 Lariat 5 1/2'	W145	36220	16500	17250	19000	23400
F150 Lariat 6 1/2'	W145	36520	16300	17100	18850	23200
F150 KingRnch 5 1/2'	W14V	39420	15650	16400	18500	23200
2WD	2		(2450)	(2450)	(3055)	(3055)

Body Type	VIN	List	Trade-In Good	Very Good	Pvt-Party Good	Retail Excellent
SUPERCREW PICKUP 4WD—V8—Truck Equipment Schedule T1						
F150 FX4 4D 5 1/2'	W145	35320	14100	14800	16400	20200
F150 FX4 4D 6 1/2'	W145	35620	13950	14650	16250	20000
SUPERCREW PICKUP AWD—V8—Truck Equipment Schedule T1						
F150 Harley 5 1/2'	W145	37425	16050	16850	18550	22800
2WD			(750)	(750)	(930)	(930)
SUPER DUTY REGULAR CAB PICKUP—V8—Truck Equipment Schedule T1						
F250 XL 2D 8'	F205	24795	5075	5475	6450	8425
F350 XL 2D 8'	F305	25515	5250	5650	6825	8925
4WD	1,3		2200	2200	2815	2815
V8, Turbo Dsl 6.4L	R		4000	4000	5120	5120
V10, 6.8 Liter	Y		500	500	640	640
SUPER DUTY REGULAR CAB 4WD—V8—Truck Equipment Schedule T1						
F250 XLT 2D 8'	F215	28480	9150	9725	11150	14200
2WD	0,2		(2450)	(2450)	(3050)	(3050)
V8, Turbo Dsl 6.4L	R		4000	4000	4970	4970
V10, 6.8 Liter	Y		500	500	620	620
SUPER DUTY REGULAR CAB 4WD—V8 Turbo Diesel—Truck Equip Sch T1						
F350 XLT 2D 8'	F31R	29535	13900	14700	16500	20800
2WD	0,2		(2450)	(2450)	(3010)	(3010)
V8, 5.4 Liter	5		(4000)	(4000)	(4905)	(4905)
V10, 6.8 Liter	Y		(4000)	(4000)	(4905)	(4905)
SUPER DUTY SUPER CAB PICKUP—V8—Truck Equipment Schedule T1						
F250 XL 4D 6 3/4'	X205	26920	7775	8275	9600	12300
F250 XL 4D 8'	X205	27115	7275	7750	9050	11650
F350 XL 4D 8'	X305	28155	7875	8375	9700	12450
F350 XL 4D 8'	X305	32900	9450	10050	11450	14600
F350 Lariat 4D 8'	X305	35420	9900	10500	11950	15200
4WD	1,3		2200	2200	2745	2745
V8, Turbo Dsl 6.4L	R		4000	4000	4995	4995
V10, 6.8 Liter	Y		500	500	625	625
SUPER DUTY SUPER CAB 4WD—V8—Truck Equipment Schedule T1						
F250 XLT 4D 6 3/4'	X215	31320	12150	12850	14450	18300
F250 XLT 4D 8'	X215	34545	11850	12550	14150	17900
F250 Lariat 4D 8'	X215	35870	12100	12800	14400	18200
F350 XLT 4D 8'	X315	32705	12550	13300	14900	18800
F350 Lariat 4D 6 3/4'	X315	35220	12200	12900	14550	18400
2WD	0,2		(2450)	(2450)	(3015)	(3015)
V8, Turbo Dsl 6.4L	R		4000	4000	4910	4910
V10, 6.8 Liter	Y		500	500	615	615
SUPER DUTY SUPER CAB 4WD—V8 Turbo Diesel—Truck Equip Sch T1						
F250 Lariat 4D 6 3/4'	X21R	34200	17750	18700	20600	25900
2WD	0,2		(2450)	(2450)	(2985)	(2985)
V8, 5.4 Liter	5		(4000)	(4000)	(4865)	(4865)
V10, 6.8 Liter	Y		(4000)	(4000)	(4865)	(4865)
SUPER DUTY SUPER CAB—V8 Turbo Diesel—Truck Equipment Sch T1						
F350 XL 4D 6 3/4'	X31R	33825	15750	16600	18350	22900
4WD	1,3		2200	2200	2690	2690
V8, 5.4 Liter	5		(4000)	(4000)	(4885)	(4885)
V10, 6.8 Liter	Y		(4000)	(4000)	(4885)	(4885)
SUPER DUTY SUPER CAB 4WD—V8—Truck Equipment Schedule T1						
F250 FX4 4D 6 3/4'	X215	36040	12450	13200	14800	18700
F250 FX4 4D 8'	X215	36240	12250	12950	14550	18400
F350 FX4 4D 6 3/4'	X315	37370	12750	13500	15200	19200
F350 FX4 4D 8'	X315	30830	12650	13400	15000	19000
V8, Turbo Dsl 6.4L	R		4000	4000	4920	4920
V10, 6.8 Liter	Y		500	500	615	615
SUPER DUTY CREW CAB PICKUP—V8—Truck Equipment Schedule T1						
F250 XL 4D 8'	W205	28280	9400	10000	11400	14550
F250 King Ranch 8'	W205	40575	11250	11950	13500	17100
F350 XL 4D 8'	W305	29400	9400	10000	11400	14550
F350 XLT 4D 8'	W305	35015	11050	11700	13350	17000
F350 Lariat 4D 8'	W305	37825	12800	13550	15000	18850
4WD	1,3		2200	2200	2710	2710
V8, Turbo Dsl 6.4L	R		4000	4000	4925	4925
V10, 6.8 Liter	Y		500	500	615	615
SUPER DUTY CREW CAB 4WD—V8—Truck Equipment Schedule T1						
F250 XLT 4D 8'	W215	33755	13900	14700	16400	20600
F350 King Ranch 8'	W315	41465	14950	15750	17550	22100
2WD	0,2		(2450)	(2450)	(3010)	(3010)
V8, Turbo Dsl 6.4L	R		4000	4000	4905	4905
V10, 6.8 Liter	Y		500	500	610	610

Body Type	VIN	List	Trade-In Good	Very Good	Pvt-Party Good	Retail Excellent
SUPER DUTY CREW CAB—V8 Turbo Diesel—Truck Equipment Sch T1						
F250 XL 4D 8'	W20R	28475	13500	14250	15900	19900
F250 Lariat 4D 8'	W20R	36935	16250	17150	19000	23900
F250 XL 4D 6 3/4'	W30R	29200	14250	15050	16800	21100
4WD		1,3	2200	2200	2680	2680
V8, 5.4 Liter		5	(4000)	(4000)	(4870)	(4870)
V10, 6.8 Liter		Y	(4000)	(4000)	(4870)	(4870)
SUPER DUTY CREW CAB 4WD—V8 Turbo Diesel—Truck Equip Sch T1						
F250 XLT 4D 6 3/4'	W21R	33570	19100	20100	21900	27200
F250 Lariat 4D 6 3/4'	W21R	36745	20000	21100	23100	28900
F250 KingRnch 6 3/4'	W21R	40385	20300	21400	23400	29300
F350 Lariat 4D 6 3/4'	W31R	37635	20400	21500	23500	29500
F350 XLT 4D 6 3/4'	W31R	34830	19500	20500	22400	28000
F350 KingRnch 6 3/4'	W31R	41275	20600	21700	23700	29700
2WD		0,2	(2450)	(2450)	(2980)	(2980)
V8, 5.4 Liter		5	(4000)	(4000)	(4855)	(4855)
V10, 6.8 Liter		Y	(4000)	(4000)	(4855)	(4855)
SUPER DUTY CREW CAB PICKUP 4WD—V8—Truck Equipment Schedule T1						
F250 FX4 4D 8'	W215	38455	14250	15050	16800	21200
F350 FX4 4D 8'	W315	39255	14850	15650	17500	22000
F350 FX4 4D 6 3/4'	W315	39445	14650	15450	17250	21700
V8, Turbo Dsl 6.4L		R	4000	4000	4895	4895
V10, 6.8 Liter		Y	500	500	610	610
SUPER DUTY CREW CAB 4WD—V8 Turbo Diesel—Truck Equipment Sch T1						
F250 FX4 4D 6 3/4'	W21R	38295	19700	20800	22800	28500
V8, 5.4 Liter		5	(4000)	(4000)	(4860)	(4860)
V10, 6.8 Liter		Y	(4000)	(4000)	(4860)	(4860)
SUPER DUTY CREW CAB 4WD—V8 Turbo Diesel—Truck Equipment Schedule T1						
F250 Harley 6 3/4'	W21R	52425	27500	28700	29900	35600
F250 Harley 8'	W21R	52620	27300	28500	29700	35300
F350 Harley 6 3/4'	W31R	53075	27900	29100	30300	36100
F350 Harley 8'	W31R	53270	27700	28900	30100	35800
V10, 6.8 Liter		Y	(550)	(550)	(615)	(615)
SUPER DUTY CREW CAB—V8 Turbo Diesel—Truck Equipment Schedule T1						
F450 4D 8'	W42R	41620	20200	21200	22300	26600
F450 XLT 4D 8'	W42R	47395	21800	22800	23900	28500
F450 King Ranch 8'	W42R	53715	24900	26000	27200	32400
4WD		1,3	2200	2200	2505	2505
SUPER DUTY CREW CAB 4WD—V8 Turbo Diesel—Truck Equip Sch T1						
F450 Lariat 4D 8'	W43R	50075	25100	26200	27400	32600
2WD		0,2	(2450)	(2450)	(2800)	(2800)

2009 FORD (1,2or3)F(D,MorT)—U027-9-#

Body Type	VIN	List	Trade-In Good	Very Good	Pvt-Party Good	Retail Excellent
ESCAPE—4-Cyl.—Truck Equipment Schedule T1						
XLS Sport Utility 4D	U027	21620	5750	6150	7125	8925
4WD			1175	1175	1470	1470
ESCAPE 4WD—4-Cyl. Hybrid—Truck Equipment Schedule T1						
Sport Utility 4D	U593	30750	11300	11900	13400	16650
Limited Sport Util	U593	33080	13550	14250	15800	19350
2WD		0,4	(875)	(875)	(1075)	(1075)
ESCAPE 4WD—V6—Truck Equipment Schedule T1						
XLT Sport Utility 4D	U93G	26185	8325	8800	9875	12200
Limited Sport Util	U94G	27640	9500	10050	11200	13750
2WD		0,4	(875)	(875)	(1095)	(1095)
4-Cyl, 2.5 Liter		7	(600)	(600)	(750)	(750)
EDGE—V6—Truck Equipment Schedule T1						
SE Sport Utility 4D	K36C	26905	8525	8975	10150	12450
SEL Sport Utility 4D	K38C	29810	10150	10650	11850	14400
Limited Sport Util	K39C	32565	11000	11500	12850	15600
Sport SUV 4D	K30C	34020	13200	13800	15300	18450
AWD		4	650	650	805	805
TAURUS X—V6—Truck Equipment Schedule T1						
SEL Sport Utility	K03W	28400	5750	6150	7350	9450
AWD		5,8,6	950	950	1265	1265
TAURUS X AWD—V6—Truck Equipment Schedule T1						
Eddie Bauer Spt Utl	K08W	33310	8400	8900	10250	12950
Limited Sport Util	K06W	34305	8825	9350	10750	13550
FWD		2,3,7	(1200)	(1200)	(1585)	(1585)
EXPLORER 4WD—V6—Truck Equipment Schedule T1						
XLT Sport Utility 4D	U73E	30130	9500	10050	11200	13900
Eddie Bauer Spt Utl	U74E	33275	11500	12100	13450	16600
Third Row Seat			475	475	595	595
2WD		6	(1300)	(1300)	(1635)	(1635)

Body Type	VIN	List	Trade-In Good	Very Good	Pvt-Party Good	Retail Excellent
AWD	8	____	**0**	**0**	**0**	**0**
V8, 4.6 Liter	8	____	350	350	440	440
EXPLORER 4WD—V8—Truck Equipment Schedule T1						
Limited Sport Util	U758	38520	**12700**	**13400**	**14900**	**18350**
2WD	6	____	(1300)	(1300)	(1625)	(1625)
AWD	8	____	0	0	0	0
V6, 4.0 Liter	E	____	(250)	(250)	(310)	(310)
EXPLORER SPORT TRAC—V6—Truck Equipment Schedule T1						
XLT Utility Pickup	U31E	26810	**12600**	**13150**	**14350**	**17050**
4WD	5	____	1300	1300	1530	1530
V8, 4.6 Liter	8	____	350	350	415	415
EXPLORER SPORT TRAC 4WD—V6—Truck Equipment Schedule T1						
Limited Util Pickup	U53E	34650	**16700**	**17400**	**18700**	**22000**
2WD	3	____	(1300)	(1300)	(1525)	(1525)
AWD	8	____	0	0	0	0
V8, 4.6 Liter	8	____	350	350	410	410
FLEX—V6—Truck Equipment Schedule T1						
SE Sport Utility 4D	K51C	28995	**9175**	**9700**	**10700**	**13050**
SEL Sport Utility 4D	K52C	32770	**10200**	**10800**	**11950**	**14600**
Limited Sport Util	K53C	35405	**11600**	**12200**	**13400**	**16300**
AWD	6	____	650	650	810	810
EXPEDITION 4WD—V8—Truck Equipment Schedule T1						
XLT Sport Utility 4D	U165	36645	**12300**	**12950**	**14150**	**17200**
Eddie Bauer Spt Util	U185	41980	**16600**	**17450**	**18850**	**22800**
Limited Sport Util	U205	46140	**17800**	**18700**	**19700**	**23300**
King Ranch Spt Util	U185	46750	**18200**	**19100**	**20100**	**23800**
Third Row Seat		____	700	700	860	860
2WD	5,7,9	____	(875)	(875)	(1075)	(1075)
EXPEDITION EL 4WD—V8—Truck Equipment Schedule T1						
XLT Sport Utility 4D	K165	40170	**13450**	**14150**	**15500**	**18850**
Eddie Bauer Spt Util	K185	44630	**18000**	**18900**	**20300**	**24600**
Limited Sport Util	K205	48790	**18300**	**19200**	**20200**	**24000**
King Ranch Spt Util	K185	49400	**18800**	**19700**	**20800**	**24600**
Third Row Seat		____	700	700	860	860
2WD	5,7,9	____	(875)	(875)	(1075)	(1075)
ECONOLINE WAGON—V8—Truck Equipment Schedule T1						
E150 XL Super Duty	E11W	29145	**8450**	**8975**	**9850**	**12050**
E150 XLT S.D.	E11W	31935	**9600**	**10150**	**11250**	**13850**
E350 XL Super Duty	E31L	31505	**9250**	**9800**	**10750**	**13100**
E350 XLT S.D.	E31L	35170	**10800**	**11400**	**12650**	**15550**
E350 XL S.D. Ext	S31L	33895	**10200**	**10800**	**11950**	**14700**
E350 XLT S.D. Ext	S31L	36515	**12000**	**12650**	**13900**	**17100**
V8, 5.4 Liter (E150)	L	____	250	250	290	290
V10, 6.8 Liter	S	____	650	650	760	760
ECONOLINE VAN—V8—Truck Equipment Schedule T1						
E150 Cargo Van	E14W	26040	**10150**	**10800**	**12100**	**15200**
E150 Extended	S14W	27040	**11100**	**11800**	**13150**	**16550**
E250 Cargo Van	E24W	27075	**10850**	**11550**	**12850**	**16150**
E250 Extended	S24W	28225	**12050**	**12800**	**14200**	**17850**
E350 Super Cargo	E34L	29865	**11350**	**12100**	**13450**	**16950**
E350 SD Extended	S34L	30795	**12600**	**13400**	**14800**	**18600**
Crew Van Pkg		____	250	250	310	310
V8, 5.4L (E150/E250)	L	____	250	250	310	310
V8, Turbo Dsl 6.0L	P	____	2500	2500	3080	3080
V10, 6.8 Liter	S	____	650	650	800	800
RANGER REGULAR CAB PICKUP—4-Cyl.—Truck Equipment Schedule T2						
XL 2D 7'	R10D	18400	**4400**	**4750**	**5800**	**7750**
XLT 2D 7'	R10D	19525	**4825**	**5225**	**6450**	**8550**
V6, 4.0 Liter	E	____	425	425	520	520
RANGER REGULAR CAB PICKUP—4-Cyl.—Truck Equipment Schedule T1						
XL 2D 6'	R10D	17555	**4875**	**5275**	**6525**	**8650**
Sport 2D 6'	R10D	19145	**5975**	**6425**	**7725**	**10150**
XLT 2D 6'	R10D	18300	**5825**	**6275**	**7550**	**9950**
RANGER SUPER CAB PICKUP—4-Cyl.—Truck Equipment Schedule T1						
XL 2D 6'	R14D	19045	**6675**	**7150**	**8575**	**11200**
4WD	1,5	____	1500	1500	1825	1825
V6, 4.0 Liter	E	____	425	425	515	515
RANGER SUPER CAB PICKUP—V6—Truck Equipment Schedule T1						
XLT 2D 6'	R14E	20235	**8375**	**8925**	**10250**	**13100**
4WD	1,5	____	1500	1500	1800	1800
4-Cyl, 2.3 Liter	D	____	(300)	(300)	(360)	(360)
RANGER SUPER CAB PICKUP—V6—Truck Equipment Schedule T1						
Sport 2D 6'	R14E	21555	**8475**	**9050**	**10550**	**13650**

Body Type	VIN	List	Trade-In Good	Trade-In Very Good	Pvt-Party Good	Retail Excellent
Sport 4D 6'	R44E	22825	9225	9825	11450	14750
XLT 4D 6'	R44E	22202	9025	9600	11200	14500
4WD	1.5		1500	1500	1795	1795
RANGER SUPER CAB PICKUP 4WD—V6—Truck Equipment Schedule T2						
FX4 Off-Road 2D 6'	R15E	25255	11850	12550	13750	17050
RANGER SUPER CAB PICKUP 4WD—V6—Truck Equipment Schedule T1						
FX4 Off-Road 4D 6'	R45E	26955	12500	13250	14400	17850
REGULAR CAB PICKUP—V8—Truck Equipment Schedule T1						
F150 XL 2D 6 1/2'	F12W	22965	7875	8375	9625	12150
F150 XL 2D 8'	F12W	23265	7475	7950	9200	11600
F150 STX 2D 6 1/2'	F12W	25765	8575	9100	10400	13100
F150 XLT 2D 6 1/2'	F12W	26935	9125	9650	11050	13900
F150 XLT 2D 8'	F12W	27235	8675	9200	10500	13250
4WD	4		2600	2600	3160	3160
V8, 24V, 4.6 Liter (XL)	8		150	150	185	185
V8, 5.4 Liter	V		325	325	395	395
SUPER CAB PICKUP—V8—Truck Equipment Schedule T1						
F150 XL 4D 6 1/2'	X12W	25670	9650	10150	11350	13800
F150 STX 4D 5 1/2'	X12W	27170	9950	10450	11650	14200
F150 STX 4D 6 1/2'	X12W	27470	10250	10750	12400	15500
F150 XLT 4D 5 1/2'	X12W	29160	11050	11600	12950	15700
F150 XLT 4D 6 1/2'	X12W	29460	11150	11700	13000	15800
4WD	4		2600	2600	3105	3105
V8, 5.4 Liter	V		325	325	390	390
SUPER CAB PICKUP—V8—Truck Equipment Schedule T1						
F150 XL 4D 8'	X12V	25970	9550	10050	11250	13700
F150 XLT 4D 8'	X12V	29760	9850	10350	11950	14950
F150 Lariat 4D 5 1/2'	X12V	33160	12050	12600	14000	16950
F150 Lariat 4D 6 1/2'	X12V	33460	12150	12750	14100	17050
4WD	4		2600	2600	3110	3110
SUPER CAB PICKUP 4WD—V8—Truck Equipment Schedule T1						
F150 FX4 4D 5 1/2'	X14V	34605	14850	15550	17100	20700
F150 FX4 4D 6 1/2'	X14V	34905	15100	15800	17350	21000
SUPERCREW PICKUP—V8—Truck Equipment Schedule T1						
F150 XL 4D 5 1/2'	W12W	29380	12550	13150	14500	17550
F150 XL 4D 6 1/2'	W12W	33340	12350	12950	14300	17300
F150 XLT 4D 5 1/2'	W128	31820	13500	14150	15700	18950
4WD	4		2600	2600	3095	3095
V8, 24V, 4.6 Liter (XL)	8		150	150	180	180
V8, 5.4 Liter	V		325	325	385	385
SUPERCREW PICKUP 4WD—V8—Truck Equipment Schedule T1						
F150 XLT 4D 5 1/2'	W148	35265	16600	17350	19000	22900
2WD	2		(2650)	(2650)	(3145)	(3145)
V8, 5.4 Liter	V		325	325	385	385
SUPERCREW PICKUP—V8—Truck Equipment Schedule T1						
F150 KingRnch 6 1/2'	W12V	40115	18500	19300	21000	25300
F150 Platinum 6 1/2'	W12V	42185	18900	19700	21500	25800
4WD	4		2600	2600	3090	3090
SUPERCREW PICKUP 4WD—V8—Truck Equipment Schedule T1						
F150 Lariat 5 1/2'	W14V	38965	20400	21300	23100	27700
F150 Lariat 6 1/2'	W14V	39265	20200	21100	22900	27500
F150 KingRnch 5 1/2'	W14V	43260	22300	23200	25100	30100
F150 Platinum 5 1/2'	W14V	44560	22500	23400	25300	30400
2WD	2		(2650)	(2650)	(3140)	(3140)
SUPERCREW PICKUP 4WD—V8—Truck Equipment Schedule T1						
F150 FX4 4D 5 1/2'	W14V	37265	18500	19300	21000	25300
F150 FX4 4D 6 1/2'	W14V	37565	18300	19100	20800	25100
SUPER DUTY REGULAR CAB PICKUP—V8—Truck Equipment Schedule T1						
F250 XL 2D 8'	F205	27060	6975	7425	8625	10800
F350 XL 2D 8'	F305	27780	7275	7725	8950	11200
4WD	1.3		2600	2600	3120	3120
V8, Turbo Dsl 6.4L	R		4225	4225	5070	5070
V10, 6.8 Liter	Y		550	550	660	660
SUPER DUTY REGULAR CAB 4WD—V8—Truck Equipment Schedule T1						
F250 XLT 2D 8'	F215	30610	11750	12350	13850	17100
2WD	0,2		(2650)	(2650)	(3095)	(3095)
V8, Turbo Dsl 6.4L	R		4225	4225	4930	4930
V10, 6.8 Liter	Y		550	550	640	640
SUPER DUTY REGULAR CAB 4WD—V8 Turbo Diesel—Truck Equip Sch T1						
F350 XLT 2D 8'	F31R	31665	16800	17650	19400	23800
2WD	0,2		(2650)	(2650)	(3075)	(3075)
V8, 5.4 Liter	5		(4225)	(4225)	(4900)	(4900)
V10, 6.8 Liter	Y		(4225)	(4225)	(4900)	(4900)

Body Type	VIN	List	Trade-In Good	Very Good	Pvt-Party Good	Retail Excellent
SUPER DUTY SUPER CAB PICKUP—V8—Truck Equipment Schedule T1						
F250 XL 4D 6 3/4'	X205	29185	10100	10700	12050	14900
F250 XL 4D 8'	X205	29380	9625	10150	11500	14250
F250 Lariat 4D 8'	X215	38595	15000	15750	17450	21400
F350 XL 4D 8'	X305	30420	10000	10600	11950	14800
F350 XLT 4D 8'	X305	35030	11900	12500	14000	17300
F350 Lariat 4D 8'	X305	38145	12650	13300	14800	18250
4WD	1,3		2600	2600	3040	3040
V8, Turbo Dsl 6.4L	R		4225	4225	4945	4945
V10, 6.8 Liter	Y		550	550	645	645
SUPER DUTY SUPER CAB PICKUP 4WD—V8—Truck Equipment Schedule T1						
F250 XLT 4D 6 3/4'	X215	33450	15000	15750	17450	21400
F250 XLT 4D 8'	X215	34635	14550	15300	16950	20800
F350 XLT 4D 6 3/4'	X315	34835	15400	16150	17850	21900
F350 Lariat 4D 6 3/4'	X315	37945	15250	16000	17700	21700
2WD	0,2		(2650)	(2650)	(3085)	(3085)
V8, Turbo Dsl 6.4L	R		4225	4225	4955	4955
V10, 6.8 Liter	Y		550	550	645	645
SUPER DUTY SUPER CAB—V8 Turbo Diesel—Truck Equipment Sch T1						
F350 XL 4D 6 3/4'	X31R	40025	18000	18850	20600	25100
4WD	1,3		2600	2600	3015	3015
V8, 5.4 Liter	5		(4225)	(4225)	(4900)	(4900)
V10, 6.8 Liter	Y		(4225)	(4225)	(4900)	(4900)
SUPER DUTY SUPER CAB 4WD—V8 Turbo Diesel—Truck Equipment Sch T1						
F250 Lariat 4D 6 3/4'	X21R	36925	20600	21600	23400	28600
2WD	0,2		(2650)	(2650)	(3065)	(3065)
V8, 5.4 Liter	5		(4225)	(4225)	(4880)	(4880)
V10, 6.8 Liter	Y		(4225)	(4225)	(4880)	(4880)
SUPER DUTY SUPER CAB PICKUP 4WD—V8—Truck Equipment Schedule T1						
F250 FX4 4D 6 3/4'	X215	38720	15600	16350	18100	22200
F250 FX4 4D 8'	X215	38920	15400	16150	17850	21900
F350 FX4 4D 6 3/4'	X315	40050	16400	17250	19000	23300
F350 FX4 4D 8'	X315	40235	15850	16650	18350	22500
V8, Turbo Dsl 6.4L	R		4225	4225	4915	4915
V10, 6.8 Liter	Y		550	550	640	640
SUPER DUTY CREW CAB PICKUP—V8—Truck Equipment Schedule T1						
F250 XL 4D 6'	W205	30545	11650	12250	13700	16950
F250 King Ranch 8'	W205	43055	14650	15400	17050	20900
F350 XL 4D 8'	W305	31665	11650	12250	13700	16950
F350 XLT 4D 8'	W305	37145	13650	14350	16000	19750
F350 Lariat 4D 8'	W305	41240	15300	16050	17650	21500
4WD	1,3		2600	2600	3025	3025
V8, Turbo Dsl 6.4L	R		4225	4225	4915	4915
V10, 6.8 Liter	Y		550	550	640	640
SUPER DUTY CREW CAB PICKUP 4WD—V8—Truck Equipment Schedule T1						
F250 XLT 4D 8'	W215	35885	16800	17650	19300	23600
F350 King Ranch 8'	W315	45330	18700	19600	21400	26200
2WD	0,2		(2650)	(2650)	(3075)	(3075)
V8, Turbo Dsl 6.4L	R		4225	4225	4900	4900
V10, 6.8 Liter	Y		550	550	640	640
SUPER DUTY CREW CAB—V8 Turbo Diesel—Truck Equipment Sch T1						
F250 XL 4D 8'	W20R	30740	16400	17250	18800	22900
F250 Lariat 4D 8'	W20R	39640	19300	20200	22100	27000
F350 XL 4D 6 3/4'	W30R	31465	17400	18250	19950	24300
4WD	1,3		2600	2600	3005	3005
V8, 5.4 Liter	5		(4225)	(4225)	(4880)	(4880)
V10, 6.8 Liter	Y		(4225)	(4225)	(4880)	(4880)
SUPER DUTY CREW CAB 4WD—V8 Turbo Diesel—Truck Equipment Sch T1						
F250 XLT 4D 8'	W21R	35700	22200	23200	25000	30300
F250 Lariat 4D 6 3/4'	W21R	39470	23100	24100	26100	31800
F250 KingRnch 6 3/4'	W21R	42865	23800	24900	27000	32900
F350 XLT 4D 6 3/4'	W31R	36960	22400	23600	25400	30800
F350 Lariat 4D 6 3/4'	W31R	40360	23200	24200	26200	32000
F350 KingRnch 6 3/4'	W31R	43755	24000	25100	26800	32400
2WD	0,2		(2650)	(2650)	(3060)	(3060)
V8, 5.4 Liter	5		(4225)	(4225)	(4880)	(4880)
V10, 6.8 Liter	Y		(4225)	(4225)	(4880)	(4880)
SUPER DUTY CREW CAB 4WD—V8—Truck Equipment Schedule T1						
F250 FX4 4D 8'	W215	41175	17400	18250	20000	24500
F350 FX4 4D 6 3/4'	W315	41935	18200	19100	20900	25600
F350 FX4 4D 8'	W315	42125	17800	18650	20400	25000
V8, Turbo Dsl 6.4L	R		4225	4225	4900	4900
V10, 6.8 Liter	Y		550	550	640	640

Body Type	VIN	List	Trade-In Good	Very Good	Pvt-Party Good	Retail Excellent
SUPER DUTY CREW CAB 4WD—V8 Turbo Diesel—Truck Equipment Sch T1						
F250 FX4 4D 6 3/4'	W21R	40975	22800	23800	25700	31400
V8, 5.4 Liter	5		(4225)	(4225)	(4875)	(4875)
V10, 6.8 Liter	Y		(4225)	(4225)	(4875)	(4875)
SUPER DUTY CREW CAB 4WD—V8 Turbo Diesel—Truck Equipment Sch T1						
F250 Harley 6 3/4'	W21R	55465	31200	32800	34000	39700
F250 Harley 8'	W21R	55660	31400	32600	33800	39400
F350 Harley 6 3/4'	W31R	56310	32200	33400	34600	40400
F350 Harley 8'	W31R	56115	32000	33200	34500	40200
SUPER DUTY CREW CAB—V8 Turbo Diesel—Truck Equipment Sch T1						
F450 XL 4D 8'	W42R	43785	23900	24800	26000	30300
F450 XLT 4D 8'	W42R	48370	25700	26800	27900	32500
F450 King Ranch 8'	W42R	56005	29000	30200	31400	36600
4WD	3		2600	2600	2835	2835
SUPER DUTY CREW CAB 4WD—V8 Turbo Diesel—Truck Equipment Sch T1						
F450 Lariat 4D 8'	W43R	51810	29200	30400	31600	36800
2WD			(2650)	(2650)	(2885)	(2885)
SUPER DUTY CREW CAB 4WD—V8 Turbo Diesel—Truck Equip Sch T1						
F450 King Ranch 8'	W43R	60425	31200	32400	33600	39200

2010 FORD (1,2orN)(ForM)(0,D,MorT)–U027–A–#

Body Type	VIN	List	Trade-In Good	Very Good	Pvt-Party Good	Retail Excellent
ESCAPE—4-Cyl.—Truck Equipment Schedule T1						
XLS Sport Utility	U027	21240	7050	7475	8600	10600
4WD	9,5		1250	1250	1545	1545
ESCAPE 4WD—4-Cyl. Hybrid—Truck Equipment Schedule T1						
Sport Utility 4D	U5K3	32225	14700	15400	16700	19850
Limited Sport Util	U5K3	34735	16450	17200	18500	22000
2WD	0,4		(1000)	(1000)	(1135)	(1135)
ESCAPE 4WD—V6—Truck Equipment Schedule T1						
XLT Sport Util 4D	U9DG	25015	9900	10400	11600	14100
Limited Sport Util	U9EG	28745	11300	11900	13200	16000
2WD	0,4		(1000)	(1000)	(1210)	(1210)
4-Cyl, 2.5 Liter	7		(700)	(700)	(845)	(845)
EDGE—V6—Truck Equipment Schedule T1						
SE Sport Utility 4D	K3GC	27695	9950	10450	11700	14100
SEL Sport Utility 4D	K3JC	30695	11100	11650	13050	15750
Limited Sport Util	K3KC	33495	12550	13100	14500	17400
Sport SUV 4D	K3AC	34695	14950	15550	17200	20500
AWD	4		725	725	890	890
EXPLORER 4WD—V6—Truck Equipment Schedule T1						
XLT Sport Utility	U7DE	32015	11050	11600	12750	15350
Eddie Bauer Spt Utl	U7EE	38015	14000	14650	16050	19300
Third Row Seat			550	550	660	660
2WD	6		(1375)	(1375)	(1665)	(1665)
AWD	8		0	0	0	0
V8, 4.6 Liter	8		300	300	360	360
EXPLORER 4WD—V8—Truck Equipment Schedule T1						
Limited Sport Util	U758	40325	14400	15050	16500	19800
2WD	6		(1375)	(1375)	(1675)	(1675)
AWD	0		0	0	0	0
V6, 4.0 Liter	E		(300)	(300)	(360)	(360)
EXPLORER SPORT TRAC—V6—Truck Equipment Schedule T1						
XLT Utility Pickup	U3BE	28625	15500	16150	17350	20200
4WD	5		1375	1375	1585	1585
EXPLORER SPORT TRAC 4WD—V6—Truck Equipment Schedule T1						
Limited Util Pickup	U5DE	36005	19950	20700	21900	25300
2WD	3		(1375)	(1375)	(1590)	(1590)
AWD	2		0	0	0	0
V8, 4.6 Liter	8		300	300	345	345
FLEX—V6—Truck Equipment Schedule T1						
SE Sport Utility 4D	K5BC	29325	10750	11300	12550	15250
SEL Sport Util 4D	K5CC	32100	11900	12500	13900	16900
Limited Sport Util	K5DC	37995	13450	14100	15650	18900
AWD	6		725	725	905	905
V6, 3.5L, EcoBoost	T		1550	1550	1935	1935
EXPEDITION 4WD—V8—Truck Equipment Schedule T1						
XLT Sport Utility 4D	U1G5	38910	14300	15000	16350	19500
Eddie Bauer Spt Util	U1J5	44715	19200	20000	21500	25500
Limited Sport Util	U2A5	46485	20700	21600	22600	26400
King Ranch Spt Util	U1J5	49015	21200	22100	23100	27000
Third Row Seat			800	800	960	960
2WD	F,H,K		(1000)	(1000)	(1200)	(1200)

Body Type	VIN	List	Trade-In Good	Very Good	Pvt-Party Good	Retail Excellent
EXPEDITION EL 4WD—V8—Truck Equipment Schedule T1						
XLT Sport Utility 4D	K1G5	42435	16200	16950	18250	21700
Eddie Bauer Spt Util	K1J5	46895	20300	21100	22600	26900
Limited Sport Util	K2A5	49135	21600	22500	23500	27500
King Ranch Spt Util	K1J5	51665	21900	22800	23800	27800
Third Row Seat			800	800	950	950
2WD	F,H,K		(1000)	(1000)	(1190)	(1190)
TRANSIT CONNECT CARGO VAN—4-Cyl.—Truck Equipment Sch T2						
XL Cargo Van 4D	S6AN	21475	9575	10050	11400	13950
XLT Cargo Van 4D	S6BN	22535	10350	10900	12300	15050
TRANSIT CONNECT PASSENGER VAN—4-Cyl.—Truck Equipment Sch T1						
XL Passenger Van	S9AN	21830	9000	9475	10550	12800
XLT Passenger Van	S9BN	23045	9750	10250	11350	13700
ECONOLINE WAGON—V8—Truck Equipment Schedule T1						
E150 XL Super Duty	E1BW	28450	9725	10200	11250	13550
E150 XLT S.D.	E1BW	31145	11000	11550	12600	15150
E350 XL Super Duty	E3BL	31545	10450	11000	12050	14450
E350 XL S.D. Ext	S3BL	33850	11300	11900	13000	15650
E350 XLT S.D.	E3BL	34265	11950	12550	13700	16450
E350 XLT S.D. Ext	S3BL	35565	13150	13800	15100	18100
V8, 5.4 Liter (E150)	L		275	275	320	320
ECONOLINE VAN—V8—Truck Equipment Schedule T1						
E150 Cargo Van	E1EW	26230	11450	12150	13350	16450
E150 Extended	S1EW	27195	12450	13200	14400	17700
E250 Cargo Van	E2EW	27230	12100	12800	14050	17250
E250 Extended	S2EW	28340	13350	14150	15550	19100
E350 Super Cargo	E3EL	29920	12750	13500	14750	18100
E350 SD Extended	S3EL	30820	13900	14750	16150	19800
Crew Van Pkg			275	275	330	330
V8, 5.4L (E150/E250)	L		275	275	330	330
V8, Turbo Dsl 6.0L	P		2750	2750	3315	3315
V10, 6.8 Liter	S		675	675	815	815
RANGER REGULAR CAB PICKUP—4-Cyl.—Truck Equipment Schedule T2						
XL 2D 7'	R1AD	19445	6325	6750	7775	9800
V6, 4.0 Liter	E		500	500	585	585
RANGER REGULAR CAB PICKUP—4-Cyl.—Truck Equipment Schedule T1						
XL 2D 6'	R1AD	19160	6950	7400	8525	10750
XLT 2D 6'	R1AD	20300	8250	8750	9925	12450
RANGER SUPER CAB PICKUP—4-Cyl.—Truck Equipment Schedule T1						
XL 2D 6'	R1ED	20235	9025	9575	10850	13600
4WD	F		1700	1700	1980	1980
V6, 4.0 Liter	E		500	500	585	585
RANGER SUPER CAB PICKUP—V6—Truck Equipment Schedule T1						
XLT 2D 6'	R1EE	22300	10650	11250	12450	15450
4-Cyl, 2.3 Liter	D		(350)	(350)	(405)	(405)
RANGER SUPER CAB PICKUP—V6—Truck Equipment Schedule T1						
Sport 2D 6'	R1EE	23875	11400	12000	13500	16800
Sport 4D 6'	R4EE	24940	11800	12450	13900	17300
XLT 4D 6'	R4EE	24205	11600	12250	13700	17050
4WD	F		1700	1700	1970	1970
REGULAR CAB PICKUP—V8—Truck Equipment Schedule T1						
F150 XL 2D 6 1/2'	F1CW	22855	9175	9675	10900	13350
F150 XL 2D 8'	F1CW	22655	8975	9450	10650	13050
F150 STX 2D 6 1/2'	F1CW	25380	10400	10900	12150	14850
F150 XLT 2D 6 1/2'	F1CW	26550	11100	11650	13050	15900
F150 XLT 2D 8'	F1CW	26850	10600	11100	12350	15100
4WD			2800	2800	3380	3380
V8, 24V, 4.6 Liter	8		175	175	195	195
V8, Flex Fuel, 5.4 Liter	V		350	350	420	420
SUPER CAB PICKUP—V8—Truck Equipment Schedule T1						
F150 XL 4D 6 1/2'	X1CW	26180	11300	11800	13150	15750
F150 STX 4D 6 1/2'	X1CW	27980	11800	12300	13700	16350
4WD	E		2800	2800	3375	3375
V8, 24V, 4.6 Liter	8		175	175	195	195
V8, Flex Fuel, 5.4 Liter	V		350	350	420	420
SUPER CAB PICKUP—V8—Truck Equipment Schedule T1						
F150 XLT 4D 6 1/2'	X1C8	29970	12700	13300	14800	17650
4WD	E		2800	2800	3370	3370
V8, Flex Fuel, 5.4 Liter	V		350	350	420	420
SUPER CAB PICKUP—V8—Truck Equipment Schedule T1						
F150 XL 4D 8'	X1CV	26840	11300	11800	13150	15750
F150 XLT 4D 8'	X1CV	30270	12600	13200	14700	17550
F150 Lariat 4D 6 1/2'	X1CV	34180	14000	14650	16150	19250

TRUCKS & VANS

TRUCKS & VANS

Body Type	VIN	List	Trade-In Good	Trade-In Very Good	Pvt-Party Good	Retail Excellent
4WD	E		2800	2800	3375	3375
SUPER CAB PICKUP 4WD—V8—Truck Equipment Schedule T1						
F150 FX4 4D 6 1/2'	X1EV	36065	17900	18650	20300	24000
F150 SVT Rptr 5 1/2'	X1EV	38995	32400	33700	34000	38700
V8, 6.2 Liter	6		800	800	850	850
SUPERCREW PICKUP—V8—Truck Equipment Schedule T1						
F150 XL 4D 5 1/2'	W1CW	29590	14600	15250	16750	19950
F150 XLT 4D 5 1/2'	W1CV	32330	15200	15850	17400	20700
F150 Kng Rnch 6 1/2'	W1CV	41475	20800	21600	22300	27600
F150 Platinum 6 1/2'	W1CV	43350	21400	22200	23900	28300
F150 Harley 5 1/2'	W1CV	43665	22200	23000	24800	29300
4WD	E		2800	2800	3350	3350
V8, 24V, 4.6 Liter	8		175	175	195	195
V8, Flex Fuel, 5.4L (XL)	V		350	350	420	420
SUPERCREW PICKUP—V8—Truck Equipment Schedule T1						
F150 XL 4D 6 1/2'	W1CV	33850	14300	14950	16450	19550
4WD	E		2800	2800	3365	3365
V8, 16V, 4.6 Liter	W		(350)	(350)	(410)	(410)
V8, 24V, 4.6 Liter	8		(175)	(175)	(220)	(220)
SUPERCREW PICKUP 4WD—V8—Truck Equipment Schedule T1						
F150 XLT 4D 6 1/2'	W1EV	35775	18800	19550	21200	25100
F150 Lariat 4D 5 1/2'	W1EV	39685	22200	23000	24800	29300
F150 Lariat 4D 6 1/2'	W1EV	39985	22200	22800	24600	29000
F150 Kng Rnch 5 1/2'	W1EV	44320	24200	25100	27000	31900
F150 Platinum 5 1/2'	W1EV	46195	24800	25700	27600	32600
2WD	C		(2825)	(2825)	(3375)	(3375)
V8, 24V, 4.6 Liter	8		(175)	(175)	(220)	(220)
SUPERCREW PICKUP 4WD—V8—Truck Equipment Schedule T1						
F150 FX4 4D 5 1/2'	W1EV	38425	20500	21300	23000	27200
F150 FX4 4D 6 1/2'	W1EV	38725	20300	21100	22800	27000
SUPER DUTY REGULAR CAB PICKUP—V8—Truck Equipment Schedule T1						
F250 XL 2D 8'	F2A5	26275	9350	9850	11050	13400
F350 XL 2D 8'	F3A5	26995	9750	10250	11450	13900
4WD	1,3		2800	2800	3250	3255
V8, Turbo Dsl 6.4L	R		4450	4450	5175	5175
V10, 6.8 Liter	Y		575	575	670	670
SUPER DUTY REGULAR CAB 4WD—V8—Truck Equipment Schedule T1						
F250 XLT 2D 8'	F215	29820	14350	15000	16550	19950
2WD	0,2		(2825)	(2825)	(3270)	(3270)
V8, Turbo Dsl 6.4L	R		4450	4450	5135	5135
V10, 6.8 Liter	Y		575	575	665	665
SUPER DUTY REGULAR CAB 4WD—V8 Turbo Diesel—Truck Equip Sch T1						
F350 XLT 2D 8'	F31R	43240	19450	20300	22000	26400
2WD	0,2		(2825)	(2825)	(3255)	(3255)
V8, 5.4 Liter	5		(4450)	(4450)	(5115)	(5115)
V10, 6.8 Liter	Y		(4450)	(4450)	(5115)	(5115)
SUPER DUTY SUPER CAB PICKUP—V8—Truck Equipment Schedule T1						
F250 XL 4D 6 3/4'	X2A5	29655	12450	13050	14400	17400
F250 XL 4D 8'	X2A5	29850	12050	12650	13950	16900
F250 XLT 4D 8'	X2A5	34100	14050	14700	16200	19550
F250 Lariat 4D 8'	X2A5	40555	20700	21600	23400	28000
F350 XL 4D 8'	X3A5	30890	12550	13150	14500	17550
F350 XLT 4D 8'	X3A5	35500	14250	14900	16400	19750
F350 Lariat 4D 8'	X3A5	38615	15250	15900	17450	21000
4WD	1,3		2800	2800	3230	3230
V8, Turbo Dsl 6.4L	R		4450	4450	5135	5135
V10, 6.8 Liter	Y		575	575	665	665
SUPER DUTY SUPER CAB PICKUP 4WD—V8—Truck Equipment Schedule T1						
F350 XLT 4D 6 3/4'	X3B5	35300	18400	19200	20800	25000
F350 XLT 4D 8'	X3B5	38415	17500	18250	19900	23900
2WD	0,2		(2825)	(2825)	(3265)	(3265)
V8, Turbo Dsl 6.4L	R		4450	4450	5125	5125
V10, 6.8 Liter	Y		575	575	660	660
SUPER DUTY SUPER CAB 4WD—V8 Turbo Diesel—Truck Equipment Sch T1						
F250 XL 4D 6 3/4'	X2BR	45010	23400	24000	25800	30900
F250 Lariat 4D 6 3/4'	X2BR	37395	23800	24700	26600	31900
2WD	0,2		(2825)	(2825)	(3250)	(3250)
V8, 5.4 Liter	5		(4450)	(4450)	(5105)	(5105)
V10, 6.8 Liter	Y		(4450)	(4450)	(5105)	(5105)
SUPER DUTY SUPER CAB—V8 Turbo Diesel—Truck Equipment Sch T1						
F350 XL 4D 6 3/4'	X3BR	40005	19500	20300	22100	26600
4WD	1,3		2800	2800	3245	3245
V8, 5.4 Liter	5		(4450)	(4450)	(5155)	(5155)

Body Type	VIN	List	Trade-In Good	Very Good	Pvt-Party Good	Retail Excellent
V10, 6.8 Liter	Y		(4450)	(4450)	(5155)	(5155)

SUPER DUTY CREW CAB PICKUP—V8—Truck Equipment Schedule T1

Body Type	VIN	List	Good	Very Good	Good	Excellent
F250 XL 4D 6 3/4'	W2A5	31015	14350	15000	16550	19950
F250 King Ranch 8'	W2A5	44120	18100	18850	20500	24600
F350 XLT 4D 8'	W3A5	37615	16650	17350	19000	22800
F350 XL 4D 8'	W3A5	32135	14350	15000	16550	19950
F350 Lariat 4D 8'	W3A5	41020	18300	19100	20600	24600
4WD	1,3		2800	2800	3220	3220
V8, Turbo Dsl 6.4L	R		4450	4450	5115	5115
V10, 6.8 Liter	Y		575	575	660	660

SUPER DUTY CREW CAB PICKUP 4WD—V8—Truck Equipment Schedule T1

Body Type	VIN	List	Good	Very Good	Good	Excellent
F250 XLT 4D 8'	W2B5	36350	19350	20200	21900	26200
F350 King Ranch 8'	W3B5	45010	21400	22300	24100	28900
2WD	0,2		(2825)	(2825)	(3260)	(3260)
V8, Turbo Dsl 6.4L	R		4450	4450	5115	5115
V10, 6.8 Liter	Y		575	575	660	660

SUPER DUTY CREW CAB—V8 Turbo Diesel—Truck Equipment Sch T1

Body Type	VIN	List	Good	Very Good	Good	Excellent
F250 XL 4D 8'	W2AR	31210	19150	20000	21500	25700
F250 Lariat 4D 8'	W2AR	40130	21900	22900	24600	29500
F350 XL 4D 6 3/4'	W3AR	42980	20200	21000	22600	27000
4WD	1,3		2800	2800	3220	3220
V8, 5.4 Liter	5		(4450)	(4450)	(5120)	(5120)
V10, 6.8 Liter	Y		(4450)	(4450)	(5120)	(5120)

SUPER DUTY CREW CAB 4WD—V8 Turbo Diesel—Truck Equipment Sch T1

Body Type	VIN	List	Good	Very Good	Good	Excellent
F250 XLT 4D 6 3/4'	W2BR	47265	25000	26000	27800	33200
F250 Lariat 4D 3/4'	W21R	39940	26100	27200	29200	34900
F250 KingRnch 6 3/4'	W21R	43930	26900	28000	30000	35900
F350 XLT 4D 8'	W3BR	48300	25500	26600	28400	33800
F350 Lariat 4D 6 3/4'	W3BR	40830	25800	26900	28800	34500
F350 King Ranch 6'	W3BR	44820	27000	28100	30000	35800
2WD	0,2		(2825)	(2825)	(3255)	(3255)
V8, 5.4 Liter	5		(4450)	(4450)	(5110)	(5110)
V10, 6.8 Liter	Y		(4450)	(4450)	(5110)	(5110)

SUPER DUTY CREW CAB PICKUP 4WD—V8—Truck Equipment Schedule T1

Body Type	VIN	List	Good	Very Good	Good	Excellent
F250 CABELA'S 6'	W2B5	43630	31100	32300	33400	38400
F250 CABELA'S 8'	W2B5	43830	30700	31900	33000	38000
F350 CABELA'S 6'	W3B5	44590	31500	32700	33900	38900
F350 CABELA'S 8'	W3A5	44780	30900	32100	33200	38200
V8, Turbo Dsl 6.4L	R		4450	4450	4680	4680
V10, 6.8 Liter	Y		575	575	605	605

SUPER DUTY CREW CAB 4WD—V8 Turbo Diesel—Truck Equip T1

Body Type	VIN	List	Good	Very Good	Good	Excellent
F250 Harley 6 3/4'	W2BR	59390	34600	35900	37000	42500
F250 Harley 8'	W2BR	59585	34400	35700	36800	42300
F350 Harley 6 3/4'	W3BR	60040	35200	36500	37700	43200
F350 Harley 8'	W3BR	60235	35000	36300	37500	43000

SUPER DUTY CREW CAB—V8 Turbo Diesel—Truck Equipment Schedule T1

Body Type	VIN	List	Good	Very Good	Good	Excellent
F450 XLT 4D 8'	W4CR	45120	26200	27200	28300	32600
F450 XLT 4D 8'	W4CR	50500	28200	29300	30400	35000
F450 King Ranch 8'	W4CR	57930	31700	32900	34100	39100
4WD	D		2800	2800	2940	2940

SUPER DUTY CREW CAB 4WD—V8 Turbo Diesel—Truck Equipment Sch T1

Body Type	VIN	List	Good	Very Good	Good	Excellent
F450 Lariat 4D 8'	W4DR	53940	31800	33000	34100	39200
2WD	C		(2825)	(2825)	(2980)	(2980)

SUPER DUTY CREW CAB 4WD—V8 Turbo Diesel—Truck Equipment Sch T1

Body Type	VIN	List	Good	Very Good	Good	Excellent
F450 Harley 8'	W4DR	63785	34200	35500	36700	42100

2011 FORD (1,2orN)(ForM)(0,D,MorT)—U027–B–#

ESCAPE—4-Cyl.—Truck Equipment Schedule T1

Body Type	VIN	List	Good	Very Good	Good	Excellent
XLS Sport Util 4D	U027	21785	8800	9275	10550	12800
4WD	9		1400	1400	1670	1670

ESCAPE 4WD—4-Cyl. Hybrid—Truck Equipment Schedule T1

Body Type	VIN	List	Good	Very Good	Good	Excellent
Sport Utility 4D	U5K3	32340	15900	16550	17750	20800
Limited Sport Util	U5K3	34850	18200	18950	20000	23100
2WD	4		(1100)	(1100)	(1260)	(1260)

ESCAPE 4WD—V6—Truck Equipment Schedule T1

Body Type	VIN	List	Good	Very Good	Good	Excellent
XLT Sport Util 4D	U9DG	26525	11950	12500	13650	16100
Limited Sport Util	U9EG	28105	12800	13400	14600	17250
2WD	0		(1100)	(1100)	(1285)	(1285)
4-Cyl, 2.5 Liter	7		(800)	(800)	(935)	(935)

EDGE—V6—Truck Equipment Schedule T1

Body Type	VIN	List	Good	Very Good	Good	Excellent
SE Sport Util 4D	K3GC	28195	12100	12650	13750	16050
SEL Sport Util 4D	K3JC	30995	14750	15350	16450	19000
Limited Spt Util 4D	K3KC	34995	16400	17050	18200	21000

TRUCKS & VANS

Body Type	VIN	List	Trade-In Good	Very Good	Pvt-Party Good	Retail Excellent
Sport SUV 4D	K3AK	36995	19050	19750	21000	24200
AWD	4	------	800	800	915	915
EXPLORER 4WD—V6—Truck Equipment Schedule T1						
Sport Utility 4D	K8B8	30995	16200	16850	17800	20600
XLT Sport Utility	K8D8	33995	19150	19900	20900	24200
Limited Sport Util	K8F8	39995	21100	21900	23000	26600
Third Row Seat		------	600	600	680	680
2WD	7	------	(1475)	(1475)	(1670)	(1670)
FLEX—V6—Truck Equipment Schedule T1						
SE Sport Util 4D	K5BC	29850	12750	13300	14650	17300
SEL Sport Util 4D	K5CC	32650	14550	15150	16550	19550
Limited Sport Util	K5DC	38620	16300	17000	18400	21700
AWD	6	------	800	800	950	950
V6, EcoBoost, 3.5L	T	------	1650	1650	1950	1950
FLEX AWD—V6—EcoBoost—Truck Equipment Schedule T1						
Titanium Spt Util	K6DT	45960	20200	21000	22600	26700
2WD	5	------	(825)	(825)	(995)	(995)
V6, 3.5 Liter	C	------	(1625)	(1625)	(1935)	(1935)
EXPEDITION 4WD—V8—Truck Equipment Schedule T1						
XL Sport Utility 4D	U1G5	40485	17750	18450	19500	22500
XLT Sport Utility 4D	U1J5	42025	19400	20200	21200	24500
Limited Sport Util	U2A5	48695	23200	24100	24900	28400
King Ranch Spt Util	U1J5	49965	23700	24600	25400	29000
Third Row Seat		------	900	900	1030	1030
2WD	H	------	(1100)	(1100)	(1260)	(1260)
EXPEDITION EL 4WD—V8—Truck Equipment Schedule T1						
XL Sport Utility 4D	K1G5	43135	19800	20600	21700	25000
XLT Sport Utility 4D	K1J5	44735	20600	21400	22500	25900
Limited Sport Util	K2A5	51345	24200	25100	25900	29600
King Ranch Spt Util	K1J5	52615	24600	25500	26300	30000
Third Row Seat		------	900	900	1030	1030
2WD	H	------	(1100)	(1100)	(1260)	(1260)
TRANSIT CONNECT CARGO VAN—4-Cyl.—Truck Equipment Sch T2						
XL Van 4D	S6AN	21895	11150	11650	13000	15550
XLT Van 4D	S6BN	22955	11950	12500	13850	16600
TRANSIT CONNECT PASSENGER VAN—4-Cyl.—Truck Equipment Sch T1						
XLT Van 4D	S9DN	23745	11500	12000	13250	15800
XLT Premium Van	S9CN	23895	11700	12200	13500	16050
ECONOLINE WAGON—V8—Truck Equipment Schedule T1						
E150 XL	E1BW	28950	10650	11150	12250	14600
E150 XLT	E1BW	31405	11800	12350	13550	16150
E350 XL Super Duty	E3BL	32045	11250	11750	12950	15450
E350 XL S.D. Ext	S3BL	34350	12050	12600	13800	16450
E350 XLT S.D.	E3BL	34525	12850	13400	14650	17450
E350 XLT S.D. Ext	S3BL	35825	14050	14650	16050	19100
V8, 5.4 Liter (E150)	L	------	300	300	345	345
V10, 6.8 Liter	S	------	700	700	805	805
ECONOLINE VAN—V8—Truck Equipment Schedule T1						
E150 Cargo Van	E1EW	26820	12450	13200	14400	17500
E150 Extended	E1EW	28030	13350	14100	15500	18800
E250 Cargo Van	E2EW	27820	12950	13700	15050	18250
E250 Extended	S2EW	29175	14400	15200	16600	20100
E350 Super Cargo	E3EL	30750	13550	14300	15650	19000
E350 SD Extended	S3EL	31650	15050	15900	17350	21000
E350 Cab-Ch DR	E3FL	26800	17050	17750	19350	22900
Crew Van Pkg		------	300	300	360	360
V8, 5.4L (E150/E250)	L	------	300	300	360	360
V10, 6.8 Liter	S	------	700	700	840	840
RANGER REGULAR CAB PICKUP—4-Cyl.—Truck Equipment Schedule T2						
XL 2D 7'	R1AD	19825	7075	7500	8725	11000
V6, 4.0 Liter	E	------	550	550	610	610
RANGER REGULAR CAB PICKUP—4-Cyl.—Truck Equipment Schedule T1						
XL 2D 6'	R1AD	19655	8250	8725	10050	12600
XLT 2D 6'	R1AD	20795	9400	9925	11250	13950
RANGER SUPER CAB PICKUP—4-Cyl.—Truck Equipment Schedule T1						
XL 2D 6'	R1ED	21350	10350	10900	12400	15400
4WD	F	------	1900	1900	2135	2135
V6, 4.0 Liter	E	------	550	550	615	615
RANGER SUPER CAB PICKUP—V6—Truck Equipment Schedule T1						
XLT 2D 6'	R1EE	22415	12300	12950	14250	17350
4-Cyl, 2.3 Liter	D	------	(700)	(700)	(770)	(770)
RANGER SUPER CAB PICKUP—V6—Truck Equipment Schedule T2						
Sport 2D 6'	R1EE	24100	12400	13050	14650	18100

Body Type	VIN	List	Trade-In Good	Trade-In Very Good	Pvt-Party Good	Retail Excellent
Sport 4D 6'	R4EE	25170	**13050**	**13700**	**15400**	**18900**
4WD	F		**1900**	**1900**	**2090**	**2090**
RANGER SUPER CAB PICKUP—V6—Truck Equipment Schedule T1						
XLT 4D 6'	R4EE	24315	**13000**	**13650**	**15350**	**18900**
REGULAR CAB PICKUP—V8—Truck Equipment Schedule T1						
F150 XL 2D 6 1/2'	F1CF	23390	**11000**	**11500**	**12850**	**15500**
F150 XL 2D 8'	F1CF	23690	**10650**	**11150**	**12450**	**15000**
F150 STX 2D 6 1/2'	F1CF	27220	**12550**	**13100**	**14550**	**17550**
F150 XLT 2D 6 1/2'	F1CF	27840	**12750**	**13300**	**14800**	**17800**
F150 XLT 2D 8'	F1CF	28145	**12150**	**12700**	**14150**	**17050**
4WD	E		**3000**	**3000**	**3565**	**3565**
V6, EcoBoost, 3.5L	T		**1650**	**1650**	**1945**	**1945**
V6, Flex Fuel, 3.7 Liter	M		**(675)**	**(675)**	**(800)**	**(800)**
SUPER CAB PICKUP—V8—Truck Equipment Schedule T1						
F150 XL 4D 6 1/2'	X1CF	27215	**13800**	**14350**	**15800**	**18550**
F150 XL 4D 8'	X1CF	29390	**13700**	**14250**	**15700**	**18450**
F150 STX 4D 6 1/2'	X1CF	30005	**14950**	**15550**	**17000**	**19950**
F150 XLT 4D 6 1/2'	X1CF	30430	**15350**	**15950**	**17400**	**20400**
F150 XLT 4D 8'	X1CF	32800	**15150**	**15750**	**17200**	**20100**
F150 FX2 4D 6 1/2'	X1CF	34050	**15650**	**16250**	**17700**	**20700**
F150 Lariat 4D 6 1/2'	X1CF	35085	**16800**	**17450**	**18950**	**22200**
Luxury Pkg			**500**	**500**	**580**	**580**
4WD	E		**3000**	**3000**	**3510**	**3510**
V6, EcoBoost, 3.5L	T		**1650**	**1650**	**1915**	**1915**
V6, Flex Fuel, 3.7 Liter	M		**(675)**	**(675)**	**(790)**	**(790)**
SUPER CAB PICKUP 4WD—V8—Truck Equipment Schedule T1						
F150 FX4 4D 6 1/2'	X1EF	37800	**20500**	**21200**	**22900**	**26700**
F150 SVT Raptor 5'	X1R6	42525	**34300**	**35600**	**36100**	**40800**
Luxury Pkg			**500**	**500**	**580**	**580**
V6, EcoBoost, 3.5L	T		**1650**	**1650**	**1905**	**1905**
SUPERCREW PICKUP—V8—Truck Equipment Schedule T1						
F150 XL 4D 5 1/2'	W1CF	30755	**16600**	**17250**	**18700**	**21900**
F150 XLT 4D 5 1/2'	W1CF	34810	**16400**	**17050**	**18550**	**21700**
F150 XLT 4D 5 1/2'	W1CF	32785	**18100**	**18800**	**20300**	**23700**
F150 FX4 4D 5 1/2'	W1CF	36410	**19150**	**19900**	**21500**	**25100**
F150 FX4 4D 6 1/2'	W1CF	36710	**19000**	**19700**	**21200**	**24800**
F150 Kng Rnch 6 1/2'	W1CF	43065	**23800**	**24700**	**26400**	**30700**
F150 Platinum 6 1/2'	W1CF	44875	**23900**	**24700**	**26500**	**30900**
Luxury Pkg			**500**	**500**	**580**	**580**
4WD	E		**3000**	**3000**	**3500**	**3500**
V6, EcoBoost, 3.5L	T		**1650**	**1650**	**1910**	**1910**
V6, Flex Fuel, 3.7 Liter	M		**(675)**	**(675)**	**(790)**	**(790)**
V8, 6.2 Liter	6		**375**	**375**	**435**	**435**
SUPERCREW PICKUP 4WD—V8—Truck Equipment Schedule T1						
F150 XLT 4D 5 1/2'	W1EF	37110	**21200**	**22000**	**23600**	**27600**
F150 Lariat 4D 5 1/2'	W1EF	40590	**25000**	**25900**	**27600**	**32200**
F150 Lariat 4D 6 1/2'	W1EF	40890	**24800**	**25600**	**27400**	**32000**
F150 Kng Rnch 5 1/2'	W1EV	45910	**27000**	**28000**	**29800**	**34700**
F150 Platinum 5 1/2'	W1EF	47720	**27800**	**28800**	**30700**	**35700**
2WD	C		**(3025)**	**(3025)**	**(3510)**	**(3510)**
V6, EcoBoost, 3.5L	T		**1650**	**1650**	**1910**	**1910**
V8, 6.2 Liter	6		**375**	**375**	**435**	**435**
SUPERCREW PICKUP—V8—Truck Equipment Schedule T1						
F150 Harley 5 1/2'	W1C6	48970	**25300**	**26200**	**28000**	**32600**
4WD	E		**3000**	**3000**	**3485**	**3485**
SUPERCREW PICKUP 4WD—V8—Truck Equipment Schedule T1						
F150 Lariat Ltd 5'	W1E6	51315	**28800**	**29800**	**31800**	**37000**
2WD	C		**(3025)**	**(3025)**	**(3495)**	**(3495)**
SUPERCREW PICKUP 4WD—V8—Truck Equipment Schedule T1						
F150 FX4 4D 5 1/2'	W1EF	39960	**23200**	**24100**	**25700**	**30000**
F150 FX4 4D 6 1/2'	W1EF	40260	**23000**	**23900**	**25500**	**29800**
F150 SVT Raptor 5'	W1R6	45290	**38500**	**39800**	**40300**	**45500**
Luxury Pkg			**500**	**500**	**580**	**580**
V6, EcoBoost, 3.5L	T		**1650**	**1650**	**1905**	**1905**
SUPER DUTY REGULAR CAB PICKUP—V8—Truck Equipment Schedule T1						
F250 XL 2D 8'	F2A6	28995	**13650**	**14250**	**15400**	**18000**
F350 XL 2D 8'	F3A6	29715	**13850**	**14450**	**15600**	**18250**
4WD	B		**3000**	**3000**	**3490**	**3490**
V8, Turbo Diesel, 6.7L			**4675**	**4675**	**5440**	**5440**
SUPER DUTY REGULAR CAB 4WD—V8—Truck Equipment Schedule T1						
F250 XLT 2D 8'	F2B6	32275	**18800**	**19550**	**20800**	**24200**
2WD	A		**(3025)**	**(3025)**	**(3495)**	**(3495)**
V8, Turbo Diesel, 6.7L			**4675**	**4675**	**5420**	**5420**

TRUCKS & VANS

Body Type	VIN	List	Trade-In Good	Very Good	Pvt-Party Good	Retail Excellent
SUPER DUTY REGULAR CAB 4WD—V8 Turbo Diesel—Truck Equip Sch T1						
F350 XLT 2D 8'	F3BT	44205	24600	25500	26900	31200
2WD	E		(3025)	(3025)	(3490)	(3490)
V8, Flex Fuel, 6.2 Liter	6		(4475)	(4475)	(5185)	(5185)
SUPER DUTY SUPER CAB PICKUP—V8—Truck Equipment Schedule T1						
F250 XL 4D 6 3/4	X2A6	31120	16900	17600	18800	21900
F250 XL 4D 8'	X2A6	31315	16550	17200	18400	21400
F350 XL 4D 6 3/4	X3B6	40005	20900	21700	22900	26600
F350 XL 4D 8'	X3A6	32360	16750	17400	18600	21700
F350 Lariat 4D 8'	X3A6	40600	19300	20100	21300	24800
4WD	B		3000	3000	3475	3475
V8, Turbo Diesel, 6.7L	T		4675	4675	5420	5420
SUPER DUTY SUPER CAB PICKUP 4WD—V8—Truck Equipment Schedule T1						
F250 XLT 4D 6 3/4	X2B6	34885	22200	23000	24300	28200
F250 XLT 4D 8'	X2B6	35070	22000	22800	24100	28000
F250 Lariat 4D 6 3/4	X2B6	39380	27700	28700	30100	34900
F350 XLT 4D 8'	X3B6	36500	22600	23400	25000	29300
F350 Lariat 4D 6 3/4	X3B6	40400	22000	22800	24100	28000
2WD	A		(3025)	(3025)	(3495)	(3495)
V8, Turbo Diesel, 6.7L	T		4675	4675	5435	5435
SUPER DUTY SUPER CAB—V8—Truck Equipment Schedule T1						
F350 XLT 4D 8'	X3AT	36695	23700	24600	25800	30000
4WD	B		3000	3000	3480	3480
V8, Flex Fuel, 6.2 Liter	6		(4475)	(4475)	(5195)	(5195)
SUPER DUTY SUPER CAB 4WD—V8 Turbo Diesel—Truck Equip Sch T1						
F250 Lariat 4D 8'	X2BT	39580	31100	32300	33800	39200
2WD	A		(3025)	(3025)	(3485)	(3485)
V8, Flex Fuel, 6.2 Liter	6		(4475)	(4475)	(5175)	(5175)
SUPER DUTY CREW CAB PICKUP—V8—Truck Equipment Schedule T1						
F250 XL 4D 6 3/4	W2AT	32480	18900	19650	20900	24300
F250 King Ranch 8'	W2A6	46880	22300	23100	24400	28300
F350 XL 4D 6 3/4	W3A6	33400	19800	20600	21800	25400
4WD	B		3000	3000	3470	3470
V8, Turbo Diesel, 6.7L	T		4675	4675	5415	5415
SUPER DUTY CREW CAB PICKUP 4WD—V8—Truck Equipment Schedule T1						
F250 XLT 4D 8'	W2B6	37320	23900	24800	26200	30400
F350 XLT 4D 6 3/4	W3B6	41425	25100	26000	27600	32300
F350 KingRnch 6 3/4	W3B6	50385	26300	27200	28600	33200
2WD	A		(3025)	(3025)	(3495)	(3495)
V8, Turbo Diesel, 6.7L	T		4675	4675	5415	5415
SUPER DUTY CREW CAB—V8 Turbo Diesel—Truck Equipment Schedule T1						
F250 XL 4D 8'	W2AT	40510	23100	24000	25200	29300
F250 Lariat 4D 8'	W2AT	49950	27800	28800	30200	35000
F350 XL 4D 8'	W3AT	41435	24100	25000	26300	30600
F350 XLT 4D 8'	W3AT	38810	26200	27100	28500	33100
4WD	B		3000	3000	3475	3475
V8, Flex Fuel, 6.2 Liter	6		(4475)	(4475)	(5190)	(5190)
SUPER DUTY CREW CAB 4WD—V8 Turbo Diesel—Truck Equipment Sch T1						
F250 XLT 4D 8'	W2BT	48230	29500	30500	32000	37100
F250 Lariat 4D 6 3/4	W2BT	41925	31700	32900	34300	39800
F250 King Ranch 6'	W2BT	46690	31600	32800	34300	39800
F350 XLT 4D 6 3/4	W3BT	42815	31100	32300	33800	39200
F350 King Ranch 8'	W3BT	47670	30800	32000	33400	38800
F350 Lariat 4D 8'	W3AT	43005	27300	28300	29600	34400
2WD	A		(3025)	(3025)	(3465)	(3465)
V8, Flex Fuel, 6.2 Liter	6		(4475)	(4475)	(5140)	(5140)
SUPER DUTY CREW CAB 4WD—V8 Turbo Diesel—Truck Equip Sch T1						
F450 XL 4D 8'	W4DT	49325	30700	31700	32600	36800
F450 XLT 4D 8'	W4DT	54680	34600	35800	36600	41300
F450 Lariat 4D 8'	W4DT	58370	38200	39400	40300	45300
F450 King Ranch 8'	W4DT	63350	40300	41600	42400	47700

2012 FORD (1,2orN)(ForM)(0,D,MorT)–(U027)–C–#

Body Type	VIN	List	Trade-In Good	Very Good	Pvt-Party Good	Retail Excellent
ESCAPE—4-Cyl.—Truck Equipment Schedule T1						
XLS Sport Utility 4D	U027	21995	10150	10600	11850	14150
4WD	9		1475	1475	1800	1800
ESCAPE 4WD—4-Cyl. Hybrid—Truck Equipment Schedule T1						
Sport Utility 4D	U5K3	33145	18150	18850	19900	22900
Limited Sport Util	U5K3	35665	19800	20600	21600	24800
2WD	4		(1500)	(1500)	(1680)	(1680)
ESCAPE 4WD—V6—Truck Equipment Schedule T1						
XLT Sport Utility	U9DG	27245	13300	13850	15250	17900
Limited Sport Util	U9EG	28745	14900	15500	16600	19250

Body Type	VIN	List	Trade-In Good	Trade-In Very Good	Pvt-Party Good	Retail Excellent
2WD	0		(1500)	(1500)	(1755)	(1755)
4-Cyl, 2.5 Liter	7		(900)	(900)	(1050)	(1050)
EDGE—V6—Truck Equipment Schedule T1						
SE Sport Utility 4D	K3GC	28465	13300	13850	15300	17850
SEL Sport Utility 4D	K3JC	31770	16200	16800	18250	21100
Limited Sport Util	K3KC	35625	17700	18350	19800	22900
Sport SUV 4D	K3AK	37800	20900	21600	23100	26700
AWD	4		875	875	1025	1025
4-Cyl, EcoBoost 2.0L	9		1050	1050	1230	1230
EXPLORER—V6—Truck Equipment Schedule T1						
Sport Utility 4D	K8B8	30995	18250	18900	19750	22500
XLT Sport Utility 4D	K8D8	34805	21400	22100	23000	26100
Limited Sport Util	K8F8	40565	23600	24400	25300	28700
Third Row Seat			650	650	720	720
2WD	7		(1550)	(1550)	(1725)	(1725)
FLEX—V6—Truck Equipment Schedule T1						
SE Sport Util 4D	K5BC	29995	14000	14550	16000	18850
SEL Sport Util 4D	K5CC	32625	16300	16950	18450	21700
Limited Sport Util	K5DC	38640	18000	18650	20300	23800
Titanium Spt Util	K5DC	45980	22000	22800	24500	28700
AWD	6		875	875	1030	1030
V6, EcoBoost, 3.5L	T		1725	1725	2040	2040
EXPEDITION 4WD—V8—Truck Equipment Schedule T1						
XL Sport Utility 4D	U1G5	41270	20100	20900	22000	25200
XLT Sport Utility 4D	U1J5	42810	21800	22600	23700	27100
Limited Sport Util	U2A5	48940	25700	26600	27500	31300
King Ranch Spt Util	U1J5	50450	26900	27900	28800	32700
Third Row Seat			975	975	1110	1110
2WD	F		(1500)	(1500)	(1710)	(1710)
EXPEDITION EL 4WD—V8—Truck Equipment Schedule T1						
XL Sport Utility 4D	K1G5	43920	22200	23000	24100	27600
XLT Sport Utility 4D	K1J5	45520	22800	23600	24700	28300
Limited Spt Util 4D	K2A5	51590	27000	28000	28900	32800
King Ranch Spt Util	K1J5	53100	27500	28500	29400	33300
Third Row Seat			975	975	1105	1105
2WD	F		(1500)	(1500)	(1700)	(1700)
TRANSIT CONNECT CARGO VAN—4-Cyl.—Truck Equipment Sch T2						
XL Van 4D	S6AN	22525	12750	13250	14500	17000
XLT Van 4D	S6BN	23585	13400	13950	15350	18000
TRANSIT CONNECT PASSENGER VAN—4-Cyl.—Truck Equipment Sch T1						
XLT Van 4D	S9BN	24260	13250	13800	15100	17600
XLT Premium Van	S9CN	24410	13500	14050	15350	17900
ECONOLINE WAGON—V8—Truck Equipment Schedule T1						
E150 XL	E1BW	29165	12900	13450	14650	17150
E150 XLT	E1BW	31620	14100	14650	15950	18600
E350 XL Super Duty	E3BL	32260	13600	14150	15400	18000
E350 XL S.D. Ext	S3BL	34565	14500	15050	16350	19050
E350 XLT S.D.	E3BL	34740	14900	15450	16800	19600
E350 XLT S.D. Ext	S3BL	36040	16850	17500	18850	22000
V8, 5.4 Liter (E150)	L		325	325	360	360
V10, 6.8 Liter	S		725	725	805	805
ECONOLINE VAN—V8—Truck Equipment Schedule T1						
E150 Cargo Van	E1EW	27510	14250	15050	16200	19350
E150 Extended	S1EW	28720	15600	16450	17650	21000
E250 Cargo Van	E2EW	28510	15100	15900	17100	20400
E250 Extended	S2EW	29865	16450	17350	18550	22100
Crew Van Pkg			325	325	380	380
V8, Flex Fuel, 5.4 Liter	L		325	325	380	380
V10, 6.8 Liter	S		725	725	850	850
ECONOLINE VAN—V8—Truck Equipment Schedule T1						
E350 Super Cargo	E3EL	31555	15900	16750	17900	21300
E350 SD Extended	S3EL	32455	17500	18400	19650	23400
Crew Van Pkg			325	325	380	380
V10, 6.8 Liter	S		725	725	850	850
REGULAR CAB PICKUP—V8—Truck Equipment Schedule T1						
F150 XL 2D 6 1/2'	F1CF	24985	12500	13050	14250	16800
F150 XL 2D 8'	F1CF	25290	12300	12800	14050	16550
F150 STX 2D 6 1/2'	F1CF	28650	14250	14800	16200	19050
F150 XLT 2D 6 1/2'	F1CF	29685	15100	15650	17100	20000
F150 XLT 2D 8'	F1CF	29990	14400	14950	16350	19250
4WD	E		3200	3200	3720	3720
V6, EcoBoost, 3.5L	T		1725	1725	2010	2010
V6, Flex Fuel, 3.7 Liter	M		(750)	(750)	(870)	(870)

Body	Type	VIN	List	Trade-In Good	Trade-In Very Good	Pvt-Party Good	Retail Excellent
SUPER CAB PICKUP—V8—Truck Equipment Schedule T1							
F150 XL 4D 6 1/2'	X1CF	28810	15350	15950	17250	19900
F150 XL 4D 8'	X1CF	28110	15250	15850	17100	19700
F150 STX 4D 6 1/2'	X1CF	31435	18350	19050	20400	23500
F150 XLT 4D 6 1/2'	X1CF	32275	17350	18000	19350	22300
F150 XLT 4D 8'	X1CF	31575	17150	17800	19100	22000
F150 FX2 4D 6 1/2'	X1CF	34895	17650	18300	19650	22600
F150 Lariat 4D 6 1/2'	X1CF	36005	18750	19450	20800	23900
Luxury Pkg			500	500	570	570
4WD	E		3200	3200	3650	3650
V6, EcoBoost, 3.5L	T		1725	1725	1975	1975
V6, Flex Fuel, 3.7 Liter	M		(750)	(750)	(855)	(855)
SUPER CAB PICKUP 4WD—V8—Truck Equipment Schedule T1							
F150 FX4 4D 6 1/2'	X1EF	38475	24700	25600	27100	31100
F150 SVT Raptor 5'	X1R6	43565	37900	39200	39100	43300
Luxury Pkg			500	500	570	570
V6, EcoBoost, 3.5L	T		1725	1725	1965	1965
SUPERCREW PICKUP—V8—Truck Equipment Schedule T1							
F150 XL 4D 5 1/2'	W1CF	32470	17850	18500	19850	22900
F150 XL 4D 6 1/2'	W1CF	32685	17650	18300	19650	22600
F150 XLT 4D 5 1/2'	W1CF	34755	20000	20800	22200	25500
F150 FX2 4D 6 1/2'	W1CF	37380	21700	22500	23900	27600
F150 FX2 4D 6 1/2'	W1CF	41890	21900	22700	24100	27700
F150 Kng Rnch 6 1/2'	W1CF	43810	25900	26800	28300	32500
F150 Platinum 6 1/2'	W1CF	45620	26100	27000	28500	32700
Luxury Pkg			500	500	570	570
4WD	E		3200	3200	3650	3650
V6, EcoBoost, 3.5L	T		1725	1725	1970	1970
V6, Flex Fuel, 3.7 Liter	M		(750)	(750)	(855)	(855)
V8, 6.2 Liter	6		400	400	455	455
SUPERCREW PICKUP 4WD—V8—Truck Equipment Schedule T1							
F150 XLT 4D 5 1/2'	W1EF	38265	23200	24000	25400	29200
F150 Lariat 4D 5 1/2'	W1EF	41760	27300	28200	29800	34100
F150 Lariat 4D 6 1/2'	W1EF	42060	27000	27900	29500	33800
F150 Kng Rnch 5 1/2'	W1EF	46785	29700	30700	32400	37000
F150 Platinum 5 1/2'	W1EF	48595	30500	31500	33200	38000
2WD	C		(3200)	(3200)	(3655)	(3655)
V6, EcoBoost, 3.5L	T		1725	1725	1975	1975
V8, 6.2 Liter	6		400	400	455	455
SUPERCREW PICKUP—V8—Truck Equipment Schedule T1							
F150 Harley 5 1/2'	W1C6	49715	27800	28700	30300	34700
4WD	E		3200	3200	3635	3635
SUPERCREW PICKUP 4WD—V8—Truck Equipment Schedule T1							
F150 FX4 4D 5 1/2'	W1EF	40955	29100	30100	31800	36400
F150 FX4 4D 6 1/2'	W1EF	42855	28600	29600	31300	35800
F150 SVT Raptor 5'	W1R6	46465	41800	43100	42700	46800
Luxury Pkg			500	500	570	570
V6, EcoBoost, 3.5L	T		1725	1725	1965	1965
SUPER DUTY REGULAR CAB PICKUP—V8—Truck Equipment Schedule T1							
F250 XL 2D 8'	F2A6	29830	15800	16450	17600	20300
4WD	B		3200	3200	3685	3685
V8, Turbo Dsl, 6.7L	T		4900	4900	5645	5645
SUPER DUTY REGULAR CAB 4WD—V8—Truck Equipment Schedule T1							
F250 XLT 2D 8'	F2B6	33160	21100	21100	22300	25700
2WD	A		(3200)	(3200)	(3640)	(3640)
V8, Turbo Dsl, 6.7L	T		4900	4900	5570	5570
SUPER DUTY REGULAR CAB PICKUP—V8 Flex Fuel—Truck Equip Sch T1							
F350 XL 2D 8'	F3A6	30550	16000	16600	17750	20500
4WD	B		3200	3200	3680	3680
V8, Turbo Diesel, 6.7L	T		4900	4900	5635	5635
SUPER DUTY REGULAR CAB 4WD—V8 Turbo Diesel—Truck Equip Sch T1							
F350 XLT 2D 8'	F3BT	45090	27200	28200	29500	33900
2WD	A		(3200)	(3200)	(3670)	(3670)
V8, Flex Fuel, 6.2 Liter	6		(4750)	(4750)	(5445)	(5445)
SUPER DUTY SUPER CAB PICKUP—V8—Truck Equipment Schedule T1							
F250 XL 4D 6 3/4'	X2A6	31955	19250	19950	21200	24400
F250 XL 4D 8'	X2A6	32150	18950	19650	20900	24100
F350 XL 4D 6 3/4'	X3B6	36210	22400	23200	24500	28200
F350 XL 4D 8'	X3A6	33195	18250	18950	20200	23300
F350 Lariat 4D 8'	X3A6	41630	21200	22000	23200	26800
4WD	B		3200	3200	3680	3680
V8, Turbo Dsl, 6.7L	T		4900	4900	5635	5635

2012 FORD

Body Type	VIN	List	Trade-In Good	Very Good	Pvt-Party Good	Retail Excellent
SUPER DUTY SUPER CAB PICKUP 4WD—V8—Truck Equipment Schedule T1						
F250 XLT 4D 6 3/4'	X2B6	35770	23500	24400	25700	29600
F250 XLT 4D 8'	X2B6	35955	23400	24300	25500	29400
F250 Lariat 4D 6 3/4'	X2B6	40410	29700	30700	32200	37000
F350 XLT 4D 6 3/4'	X3B6	37385	24300	25200	26800	31100
F350 Lariat 4D 6 3/4'	X3B6	41430	24000	24900	26200	30200
2WD	A		(3200)	(3200)	(3630)	(3630)
V8, Turbo Dsl, 6.7L	T		4900	4900	5625	5625
SUPER DUTY SUPER CAB PICKUP—V8 Turbo Diesel—Truck Equip Sch T1						
F350 XLT 4D 8'	X3AT	45415	25400	26300	27700	31900
4WD	B		3200	3200	3665	3665
V8, Flex Fuel, 6.2 Liter	6		(4750)	(4750)	(5440)	(5440)
SUPER DUTY SUPER CAB 4WD—V8 Turbo Diesel—Truck Sch T1						
F250 Lariat 4D 8'	X2BT	40610	34300	35400	36900	42400
2WD	A		(3200)	(3200)	(3665)	(3665)
V8, Flex Fuel, 6.2 Liter	6		(4750)	(4750)	(5440)	(5440)
SUPER DUTY CREW CAB PICKUP—V8—Truck Equipment Schedule T1						
F250 King Ranch 8'	W2A6	48370	28000	29000	30300	34800
4WD	B		3200	3200	3665	3665
V8, Turbo Diesel, 6.7L	T		4900	4900	5615	5615
SUPER DUTY CREW CAB PICKUP 4WD—V8—Truck Equip Sch T1						
F250 XL 4D 6 3/4'	W2A6	33315	20300	21000	22200	25600
F250 XLT 4D 6 3/4'	W2B6	42055	26500	27400	28800	33100
F350 XLT 4D 6 3/4'	W3B6	42310	26800	27800	29300	33900
F350 KingRnch 6 3/4'	W3B6	51415	28600	29600	31100	35700
2WD	A		(3200)	(3200)	(3635)	(3635)
V8, Turbo Diesel, 6.7L	T		4900	4900	5565	5565
SUPER DUTY CREW CAB PICKUP—V8 Flex Fuel—Truck Equip Sch T1						
F350 XL 4D 6 3/4'	W3A6	34235	21500	22300	23600	27200
4WD	B		3200	3200	3675	3675
V8, Turbo Dsl, 6.7L	T		4900	4900	5625	5625
SUPER DUTY CREW CAB—V8 Turbo Diesel—Truck Equipment Sch T1						
F250 XL 4D 8'	W2AT	41700	24300	25200	26500	30600
F250 Lariat 4D 8'	W2AT	51440	32800	33900	35400	40600
F350 XL 4D 8'	W3AT	42625	25800	26700	28000	32200
F350 XLT 4D 8'	W3AT	47530	27800	28800	30100	34600
F350 Lariat 4D 8'	W3AT	51870	32000	33100	34600	39700
4WD	B		3200	3200	3645	3645
V8, Flex Fuel, 6.2 Liter	6		(4750)	(4750)	(5415)	(5415)
SUPER DUTY CREW CAB PICKUP 4WD—V8 Turbo Diesel—Truck Sch T1						
F250 XLT 4D 6 3/4'	W2BT	49815	31600	32700	34100	39100
F250 KngRnch 6 3/4'	W2BT	50285	41300	42600	43900	49900
F250 Lariat 4D 8'	W2BT	54520	38700	40000	41600	47700
F350 Lariat 4D 6 3/4'	W3BT	55170	36300	37500	39000	44800
F350 King Ranch 8'	W3BT	59445	34000	35100	36600	42000
2WD	A		(3200)	(3200)	(3550)	(3550)
V8, Flex Fuel, 6.2 Liter	6		(4750)	(4750)	(5270)	(5270)

2013 FORD (1,2orN)(ForM)(0,D,MorT)–(U0F7)–D–#

Body Type	VIN	List	Trade-In Good	Very Good	Pvt-Party Good	Retail Excellent
ESCAPE—4-Cyl.—Truck Equipment Schedule T1						
S Sport Utility 4D	U0F7	23295	12350	12900	14400	17150
ESCAPE 4WD—4-Cyl. EcoBoost—Truck Equipment Schedule T1						
SE Sport Utility 4D	U9GX	27645	14500	15150	16650	19600
SEL Sport Utility 4D	U9HX	30445	15550	16200	17600	20500
Titanium Sport Util	U9J9	32945	18250	18950	20400	23800
2WD	0		(1300)	(1300)	(1545)	(1545)
EDGE—V6—Truck Equipment Schedule T1						
SE Sport Utility 4D	K3GC	28350	14250	14800	16250	18850
SEL Sport Utility 4D	K3JC	31905	17850	18500	20000	23100
Limited Sport Util	K3KC	35765	18950	19650	21300	24600
Sport SUV 4D	K3AK	37935	22100	22800	24500	28300
AWD	4		950	950	1120	1120
4-Cyl, EcoBoost, 2.0L	9		450	450	530	530
EXPLORER 4WD—V6—Truck Equipment Schedule T1						
Sport Utility 4D	K8B8	31695	20000	20700	21700	24600
XLT Sport Utility 4D	K8D8	35170	23600	24300	25300	28600
Limited Sport Util	K8F8	40680	25000	25800	26900	30500
Sport SUV 4D	K8GT	41545	29800	30700	31800	36000
Third Row Seat			700	700	785	785
2WD	7		(1625)	(1625)	(1830)	(1830)
4-Cyl, EcoBoost 2.0L	9		550	550	610	610
FLEX—V6—Truck Equipment Schedule T1						
SE Sport Utility 4D	K5B8	31710	15650	16250	17500	20200

TRUCKS & VANS

TRUCKS & VANS

Body Type	VIN	List	Trade-In Good	Trade-In Very Good	Pvt-Party Good	Retail Excellent
SEL Sport Util 4D	K5C8	34050	18200	18900	20100	23100
Limited Sport Util	K5D8	40055	19900	20600	22100	25600
AWD	6		950	950	1090	1090
V6, EcoBoost, 3.5L	T		1825	1825	2090	2090
EXPEDITION 4WD—V8 Flex Fuel—Truck Equipment Schedule T1						
XL Sport Utility 4D	U1G5	40825	23100	23900	25100	28700
XLT Sport Utility 4D	U1J5	43925	24500	25400	26700	30500
Power Third Row			1050	1050	1200	1200
2WD	H		(1300)	(1300)	(1485)	(1485)
EXPEDITION 4WD—V8 Flex Fuel—Truck Equipment Schedule T1						
Limited Sport Util	U2A5	50200	28500	29500	30300	34100
King Ranch Spt Util	U1J5	51775	28900	29900	30800	34700
2WD	K		(1300)	(1300)	(1450)	(1450)
EXPEDITION EL 4WD—V8—Truck Equipment Schedule T1						
XL Sport Utility 4D	K1G5	44350	25100	26000	27300	31200
XLT Sport Utility 4D	K1J5	46635	26000	26900	28200	32100
Limited Sport Util 4D	K2A5	52850	30400	31400	32300	36300
King Ranch Spt Util	K1J5	54425	30700	31700	32600	36600
2WD	H		(1300)	(1300)	(1485)	(1485)
TRANSIT CONNECT CARGO VAN—4-Cyl.—Truck Equipment Sch T2						
XL Van 4D	S7AN	23200	13900	14400	15900	18550
XLT Van 4D	S7BN	24260	14800	15350	16850	19650
TRANSIT CONNECT PASSENGER VAN—4-Cyl.—Truck Equipment Sch T1						
XLT Van 4D	S9BN	24825	15300	15900	17100	19600
XLT Premium Van	S9CN	24975	15500	16100	17350	19900
ECONOLINE WAGON—V8—Truck Equipment Schedule T1						
E150 XL	E1BW	29925	15550	16100	17650	20600
E150 XLT	E1BW	32370	16700	17300	18850	22000
V8, 5.4 Liter	L		350	350	405	405
ECONOLINE WAGON—V8—Truck Equipment Schedule T1						
E350 XL Super Duty	E3BL	33255	16200	16800	18300	21400
E350 XL S.D. Ext	S3BL	35555	17000	17600	19200	22400
E350 XLT S.D.	E3BL	35715	17500	18100	19700	23000
E350 XLT S.D. Ext	S3BL	37015	19600	20200	21900	25600
V10, 6.8 Liter	S		750	750	865	865
ECONOLINE VAN—V8—Truck Equipment Schedule T1						
E150 Cargo Van	E1EW	27795	15050	15850	16900	19950
E150 Extended	S1EW	29010	16450	17300	18350	21600
E250 Cargo Van	E2EW	29780	15950	16800	17850	21100
E250 Extended	S2EW	31140	17800	18750	19850	23400
Crew Van Pkg			350	350	405	405
V8, Flex Fuel, 5.4 Liter	L		350	350	405	405
ECONOLINE VAN—V8 Flex Fuel—Truck Equipment Sch T1						
E350 Super Cargo	E3EL	31955	16900	17800	18900	22300
E350 SD Extended	S3EL	32855	18700	19700	20800	24500
Crew Van Pkg			350	350	405	405
V10, 6.8 Liter	S		750	750	870	870
REGULAR CAB PICKUP—V8—Truck Equipment Schedule T1						
F150 XL 2D 6 1/2'	F1CF	24665	13750	14250	15250	17500
F150 XL 2D 8'	F1CF	24965	13550	14050	15050	17250
F150 STX 2D 6 1/2'	F1CF	28180	15550	16100	17150	19650
F150 XLT 2D 6 1/2'	F1CF	29680	16300	16900	18000	20600
F150 XLT 2D 8'	F1CF	29985	15750	16300	17400	19950
4WD	E		3300	3300	3600	3600
V6, EcoBoost, 3.5L	T		1825	1825	1985	1985
V6, Flex Fuel, 3.7 Liter	M		(800)	(800)	(870)	(870)
SUPER CAB PICKUP—V8—Truck Equipment Schedule T1						
F150 XL 4D 6 1/2'	X1CF	28490	16550	17150	18650	21600
F150 XL 4D 8'	X1CF	28790	16400	17000	18500	21400
F150 STX 4D 6 1/2'	X1CF	30965	19800	20500	22100	25500
F150 XLT 4D 6 1/2'	X1CF	32270	18500	19150	20800	24000
F150 XLT 4D 8'	X1CF	32570	18300	18950	20500	23700
F150 FX2 4D 6 1/2'	X1CF	36180	20700	21400	23000	26600
F150 Lariat 4D 6 1/2'	X1CF	36830	22600	23300	25000	28900
Luxury Pkg			500	500	575	575
4WD	E		3300	3300	3800	3800
V6, EcoBoost, 3.5L	T		1825	1825	2095	2095
V6, Flex Fuel, 3.7 Liter	M		(800)	(800)	(920)	(920)
V8, 6.2 Liter	6		1100	1100	1265	1265
SUPER CAB PICKUP 4WD—V8—Truck Equipment Schedule T1						
F150 FX4 4D 6 1/2'	X1EF	39760	27900	28900	30700	35400
F150 SVT Raptor 5'	X1R6	44335	39800	41100	40600	44300
Luxury Pkg			500	500	575	575

Body Type	VIN	List	Trade-In Good	Very Good	Pvt-Party Good	Retail Excellent
V6, EcoBoost, 3.5L	T	......	1825	1825	2090	2090
SUPERCREW PICKUP 4WD—V6 EcoBoost—Truck Equipment Sch T1						
F150 Limited 5 1/2'	W1CT	53450	33400	34400	36400	41600
2WD	C	......	(3300)	(3300)	(3790)	(3790)
SUPERCREW PICKUP—V8—Truck Equipment Schedule T1						
F150 XL 4D 5 1/2'	W1CF	32150	19600	20300	21900	25300
F150 XL 4D 6 1/2'	W1CF	33365	19400	20100	21700	25000
F150 XLT 4D 5 1/2'	W1CF	34750	21100	21800	23500	27100
F150 FX2 4D 5 1/2'	W1CF	38660	22900	23600	25400	29300
F150 Kng Rnch 6 1/2'	W1CF	44810	27100	28000	29900	34400
F150 Platinum 6 1/2'	W1CF	47395	27200	28100	30000	34600
Luxury Pkg		......	500	500	575	575
4WD	E	......	3300	3300	3800	3800
V6, EcoBoost, 3.5L	T	......	1825	1825	2095	2095
V6, Flex Fuel, 3.7 Liter	M	......	(800)	(800)	(920)	(920)
V8, 6.2 Liter	6	......	400	400	460	460
SUPERCREW PICKUP 4WD—V8—Truck Equipment Schedule T1						
F150 XLT 4D 6 1/2'	W1EF	39260	24300	25100	26900	31000
F150 Lariat 4D 5 1/2'	W1EF	42585	28800	29800	31800	36600
F150 Lariat 4D 6 1/2'	W1EF	42885	28100	29100	31000	35700
F150 Kng Rnch 5 1/2'	W1EF	47785	30800	31800	33800	38900
F150 Platinum 5 1/2'	W1EF	50370	31600	32600	34700	39900
Luxury Pkg		......	500	500	575	575
2WD	C	......	(3300)	(3300)	(3790)	(3790)
V6, EcoBoost, 3.5L	T	......	1825	1825	2090	2090
V8, 6.2 Liter	6	......	400	400	460	460
SUPERCREW PICKUP 4WD—V8—Truck Equipment Schedule T1						
F150 FX4 4D 5 1/2'	W1EF	42240	30600	31600	33700	38700
F150 FX4 4D 6 1/2'	W1EF	42540	30100	31100	33200	38200
Luxury Pkg		......	500	500	575	575
V6, EcoBoost, 3.5L	T	......	1825	1825	2090	2090
V8, 6.2 Liter	6	......	400	400	460	460
SUPERCREW PICKUP 4WD—V8—Truck Equipment Schedule T1						
F150 SVT Raptor 5'	W1RF	47235	43700	45100	44600	48900
SUPER DUTY REGULAR CAB PICKUP—V8—Truck Equipment Schedule T1						
F250 XL 2D 8'	F2A6	30380	16100	16700	18200	21200
F350 XL 2D 8'	F3A6	31280	16600	17200	18700	21800
4WD	B	......	3300	3300	3775	3775
V8, Turbo Diesel, 6.7L	T	......	5100	5100	5835	5835
SUPER DUTY REGULAR CAB 4WD—V8—Truck Equipment Schedule T1						
F250 XLT 2D 8'	F2B6	37215	20400	21100	22700	26400
2WD	A	......	(3300)	(3300)	(3790)	(3790)
V8, Turbo Diesel, 6.7L	T	......	5100	5100	5855	5855
SUPER DUTY REGULAR CAB PICKUP 4WD—V8 Turbo Diesel—Truck Sch T1						
F350 XLT 2D 8'	F3BT	46032	28500	29500	31500	36600
2WD	A,C	......	(3300)	(3300)	(3715)	(3715)
V8, Flex Fuel, 6.2 Liter	6	......	(5025)	(5025)	(5660)	(5660)
SUPER DUTY SUPER CAB PICKUP—V8—Truck Equipment Schedule T1						
F250 XL 4D 6 3/4'	X2A6	32580	20100	20800	22300	25800
F250 XL 4D 8'	X2A6	32780	19750	20500	22000	25500
F350 XL 4D 8'	X3A6	33680	19150	19850	21500	25000
F350 Lariat 4D 8'	X3A6	43175	22800	23600	25300	29400
4WD	B	......	3300	3300	3765	3765
V8, Turbo Dsl, 6.7L	T	......	5100	5100	5815	5815
SUPER DUTY SUPER CAB PICKUP—V8 Turbo Diesel—Truck Sch T1						
F350 XLT 4D 8'	X3AT	45975	26800	27700	29600	34400
4WD	B,D	......	3300	3300	3720	3720
V8, Flex Fuel, 6.2 Liter	6	......	(5025)	(5025)	(5665)	(5665)
SUPER DUTY SUPER CAB PICKUP 4WD—V8—Truck Equipment Schedule T1						
F250 XL 4D 6 3/4'	X2B6	39715	24700	25500	27200	31500
F250 XL 4D 8'	X2B6	39915	24500	25300	27000	31300
F250 Lariat 4D 6 3/4'	X2B6	45265	29900	30900	33000	38300
F350 XL 4D 8'	X3B6	36480	23500	24300	26000	30300
F350 XLT 4D 6 3/4'	X3B6	40615	25700	26600	28400	33100
F350 Lariat 4D 6 3/4'	X3B6	46165	25600	26500	28300	32900
2WD	A	......	(3300)	(3300)	(3770)	(3770)
SUPER DUTY SUPER CAB PICKUP 4WD—V8 Turbo Diesel—Truck Sch T1						
F250 Lariat 4D 8'	X2BT	53425	35200	36300	38300	44200
2WD	A	......	(3300)	(3300)	(3715)	(3715)
V8, Flex Fuel, 6.2 Liter	6	......	(5025)	(5025)	(5655)	(5655)
SUPER DUTY CREW CAB PICKUP—V8 Turbo Diesel—Truck Equip T1						
F250 Lariat 8'	W2A6	52770	35200	36300	38400	44400
4WD	B	......	3300	3300	3705	3705

Body Type	VIN	List	Trade-In Good	Very Good	Pvt-Party Good	Retail Excellent
V8, Flex Fuel, 6.2 Liter	6		(5025)	(5025)	(5640)	(5640)
SUPER DUTY CREW CAB PICKUP—V8 Flex Fuel—Truck Equip Sch T1						
F250 King Ranch 8'	W2A6	50065	32600	33700	35700	41300
F350 XL 4D 6 3/4'	W3A6	35080	22900	23700	25400	29600
4WD	B		3300	3300	3715	3715
V8, Turbo Dsl, 6.7L	T		5100	5100	5740	5740
SUPER DUTY CREW CAB PICKUP—V8 Flex Fuel—Truck Equip Sch T1						
F250 XL 6 3/4'	W2B6	34465	21500	22300	24000	27900
4WD	B		3300	3300	3720	3720
V8, Turbo Dsl, 6.7L	T		5100	5100	5750	5750
SUPER DUTY CREW CAB PICKUP 4WD—V8 Flex Fuel—Truck Equip Sch T1						
F250 XLT 8'	W2B8	41815	27400	28400	30100	34800
F250 Platinum 6 3/4'	W2B6	53750	36300	37400	39600	45900
F250 Platinum 8'	W2B6	53950	36100	37200	39400	45700
2WD	A		(3300)	(3300)	(3710)	(3710)
V8, Turbo Dsl, 6.7L	T		5100	5100	5735	5735
SUPER DUTY CREW CAB PICKUP 4WD—V8 Turbo Diesel—Truck Sch T1						
F250 XLT 6 3/4'	W2BT	49575	32800	33900	35800	41200
2WD	A		(3300)	(3300)	(3715)	(3715)
V8, Flex Fuel, 6.2 Liter	6		(5025)	(5025)	(5655)	(5655)
SUPER DUTY CREW CAB—V8 Turbo Diesel—Truck Equipment Schedule T1						
F350 XL 4D 8'	W3AT	43040	27200	28100	30000	34900
F350 XLT 4D 8'	W3AT	47875	29100	30100	32100	37300
F350 Lariat 4D 8'	W3AT	53535	36600	37800	39800	46000
4WD	B,D		3300	3300	3715	3715
V8, Flex Fuel, 6.2 Liter	6		(5025)	(5025)	(5660)	(5660)
SUPER DUTY CREW CAB 4WD—V8—Truck Equipment Schedule T1						
F350 XLT 4D 6 3/4'	W3B6	42715	28100	29100	31000	36000
F350 KingRnch 6 3/4'	W3B6	54155	34200	35300	37500	43400
F350 Platinum 6 3/4'	W3B6	54850	38700	40000	42100	48600
2WD	A		(3300)	(3300)	(3715)	(3715)
V8, Turbo Dsl, 6.7L	T		5100	5100	5740	5740
SUPER DUTY CREW CAB—V8 Turbo Diesel—Truck Equipment Sch T1						
F250 XL 8'	W2BT	43555	25200	26000	27800	32300
4WD	B		3300	3300	3735	3735
V8, Flex Fuel, 6.2 Liter	6		(5025)	(5025)	(5690)	(5690)
SUPER DUTY CREW CAB 4WD—V8 Turbo Diesel—Truck Equip Sch T1						
F350 Lariat 4D 6 3/4'	W3BT	56525	40600	41900	44000	50700
F350 King Ranch 8'	W3BT	62115	39500	40800	43000	49600
F250 Lariat 6 3/4'	W2BT	55625	39600	40900	42900	49400
F250 KingRnch 6'	W2BT	61015	41900	43200	45200	51900
F350 Platinum 8'	W3BT	62810	43900	45300	47200	54200
2WD	A		(3300)	(3300)	(3725)	(3725)
V8, Flex Fuel, 6.2 Liter	6		(5025)	(5025)	(5670)	(5670)
SUPER DUTY CREW CAB 4WD—V8 Turbo Diesel—Truck Equip Sch T1						
F450 XL 4D 8'	W4DT	50580	42400	43700	45700	52200
F450 XLT 4D 8'	W4DT	55415	46800	48200	50200	57100
F450 Lariat 4D 8'	W4DT	61465	50200	51700	53900	61000
F450 King Ranch 8'	W4DT	66735	52300	53900	55700	62700
F450 Platinum 8'	W4DT	67550	53800	55400	57200	64400

2014 FORD (1,2orN)(ForM)(0,D,MorT)—(U0F7)—E—#

Body Type	VIN	List	Trade-In Good	Very Good	Pvt-Party Good	Retail Excellent
ESCAPE—4-Cyl.—Truck Equipment Schedule T1						
S Sport Utility 4D	U0F7	23595	12850	13400	15100	18050
ESCAPE 4WD—4-Cyl. EcoBoost—Truck Equipment Schedule T1						
SE Sport Utility 4D	U9GX	28195	16400	17100	18600	21800
Titanium Sport Util	U9JX	31745	18750	19500	21100	24600
2WD	0		(1400)	(1400)	(1640)	(1640)
EDGE—V6—Truck Equipment Schedule T1						
SE Sport Utility 4D	K3GC	28995	16100	16700	18250	21100
SEL Sport Utility 4D	K3JC	32195	18800	19450	21000	24200
Limited Sport Util	K3KC	35995	20500	21200	22900	26300
Sport SUV 4D	K3AK	38495	24300	25100	26800	30900
AWD			1025	1025	1205	1205
4-Cyl, EcoBoost, 2.0L	9		475	475	560	560
EXPLORER 4WD—V6—Truck Equipment Schedule T1						
Sport Utility 4D	K8B8	32495	21400	22100	23100	26100
XLT Sport Utility 4D	K8D8	35495	25100	25900	26900	30400
Limited Sport Util	K8F8	40995	26700	27500	28600	32400
Sport SUV 4D	K8GT	41675	31000	31900	33100	37400
2WD	7		(1725)	(1725)	(1920)	(1920)
4-Cyl EcoBoost 2.0L	9		575	575	640	640

Body Type	VIN	List	Trade-In Good	Very Good	Pvt-Party Good	Retail Excellent
FLEX—V6—Truck Equipment Schedule T1						
SE Sport Util 4D	K5B8	31995	16450	17050	18650	21900
SEL Sport Util 4D	K5C8	34395	19850	20500	22100	25800
Limited Sport Util	K5D8	40295	21800	22600	24400	28500
AWD	6		1025	1025	1220	1220
V6, EcoBoost, 3.5L			1900	1900	2275	2275
EXPEDITION 4WD—V8 Flex Fuel—Truck Equipment Schedule T1						
XL Sport Utility 4D	U1G5	41975	25100	25900	27200	31000
XLT Sport Utility 4D	U1J5	45075	26500	27400	28700	32700
Third Row Seat			1125	1125	1280	1280
2WD	F		(1400)	(1400)	(1595)	(1595)
EXPEDITION 4WD—V8 Flex Fuel—Truck Equipment Schedule T1						
Limited Sport Util	U2A5	51350	30300	31300	32300	36400
King Ranch Spt Util	U1J5	55610	31700	32700	33700	37900
2WD	K		(1400)	(1400)	(1565)	(1565)
EXPEDITION EL 4WD—V8 Flex Fuel—Truck Equipment Schedule T1						
XL Sport Utility 4D	K1G5	45500	27100	28000	29400	33400
XLT Sport Utility 4D	K1J5	47785	28400	29400	30700	34900
Limited Sport Util 4D	K2A5	54000	32400	33400	34300	38600
King Ranch Spt Util	K1J5	58260	33000	34100	34900	39200
2WD	F		(1400)	(1400)	(1595)	(1595)
E350 PASSENGER VAN—V8 Flex Fuel—Truck Equipment Schedule T1						
E350 XL Super Duty	E3BL	34555	17600	18200	19650	22800
E350 XL S.D. Ext	S3BL	36855	18400	19000	20400	23600
E350 XLT S.D.	E3BL	37015	18950	19600	21000	24200
E350 XLT S.D. Ext	S3BL	38315	21000	21700	23100	26700
V10, 6.8 Liter	S		775	775	890	890
E250 CARGO VAN—V8 Flex Fuel—Truck Equipment Schedule T1						
E250 Cargo Van	E2EW	30055	18300	19250	20100	23500
E250 Extended	S2EW	31415	19800	20800	21700	25300
Crew Van Pkg			375	375	425	425
V8, Flex Fuel, 5.4 Liter	L		375	375	425	425
REGULAR CAB PICKUP—V6 EcoBoost Twin Turbo—Truck Sch T1						
F150 FX2 2D 6 1/2'	1FCT	35130	22800	23500	24400	27500
REGULAR CAB PICKUP 4WD—V6 EcoBoost Twin Turbo—Truck Sch T1						
F150 FX4 2D 6 1/2'	F1ET	39245	26600	27500	28400	32000
REGULAR CAB PICKUP—V8—Truck Equipment Schedule T1						
F150 XL 2D 6 1/2'	F1CF	25310	15350	15900	16850	19150
F150 XL 2D 8'	F1CF	25610	15150	15700	16600	18850
F150 STX 2D 6 1/2'	F1CF	29040	16750	17350	18350	20900
F150 XLT 2D 6 1/2'	F1CF	30615	17500	18150	19000	21400
F150 XLT 2D 8'	F1CF	30915	16900	17500	18500	21000
4WD	E		3600	3600	3945	3945
V6, Flex Fuel, 3.7 Liter	M		(850)	(850)	(930)	(930)
V6, EcoBoost, 3.5L	T		1900	1900	2080	2080
SUPER CAB PICKUP—V8 Flex Fuel—Truck Equipment Schedule T1						
F150 XL 4D 6 1/2'	X1CF	30225	18300	18950	20400	23400
F150 XL 4D 8'	X1CF	30525	18150	18800	20200	23200
F150 STX 4D 6 1/2'	X1CF	32740	21700	22400	23900	27400
F150 XLT 4D 6 1/2'	X1CF	34315	19900	20600	22200	25500
F150 XLT 4D 8'	X1CF	34615	19600	20300	21900	25200
F150 FX2 4D 6 1/2'	X1CF	36735	22800	23500	25100	28700
F150 Lariat 4D 6 1/2'	X1CF	37920	23800	24500	26300	30200
Luxury Equip Group			500	500	570	570
4WD	E		3600	3600	4110	4110
V6, Flex Fuel, 3.7 Liter	M		(850)	(850)	(970)	(970)
V6, EcoBoost, 3.5L	T		1900	1900	2180	2180
V8, 6.2 Liter	6		1200	1200	1370	1370
SUPER CAB PICKUP 4WD—V8 Flex Fuel—Truck Equipment Sch T1						
F150 FX4 4D 6 1/2'	X1EF	40850	29300	30300	32200	36900
V6, EcoBoost, 3.5L	T		1900	1900	2185	2185
V8, 6.2 Liter	6		1200	1200	1370	1370
SUPER CAB PICKUP 4WD—V8—Truck Equipment Schedule T1						
F150 SVT Raptor 5'	X1R6	45275	42000	43300	42900	46700
SUPERCREW PICKUP—V8 Flex Fuel—Truck Equipment Schedule T1						
F150 XL 4D 5 1/2'	W1CF	34205	20800	21500	23100	26600
F150 XL 4D 6 1/2'	W1CF	34505	20600	21300	22900	26300
F150 XLT 4D 5 1/2'	W1CF	36150	22200	23000	24600	28300
F150 STX 4D 6 1/2'	W1CF	37400	23200	24000	26400	31100
F150 King Rnch 6 1/2'	W1EF	45795	28500	29400	31200	35700
F150 Platinum 6 1/2'	W1CF	48820	30200	31100	32900	37600
4WD	E		3600	3600	4120	4120
V6, EcoBoost, 3.5L	T		1900	1900	2185	2185

Body Type	VIN	List	Trade-In Good	Very Good	Pvt-Party Good	Retail Excellent
V6, Flex Fuel, 3.7 Liter	M		(850)	(850)	(975)	(975)
			400	400	455	455
V8, 6.2 Liter	6		400	400	455	455
SUPERCREW PICKUP—V8 Flex Fuel—Truck Equipment Schedule T1						
F150 FX2 4D 5 1/2'	W1CF	39570	23900	24700	26500	30600
V6, EcoBoost, 3.5L	T		1900	1900	2195	2195
V8, 6.2 Liter	6		400	400	460	460
SUPERCREW PICKUP 4WD—V6 EcoBoost—Truck Equipment Schedule T1						
F150 Limited 5 1/2'	W1ET	53830	34700	35800	37700	43000
2WD	C		(3600)	(3600)	(4110)	(4110)
SUPERCREW PICKUP 4WD—V8 Flex Fuel—Truck Equipment Schedule T1						
F150 XLT 4D 6 1/2'	W1EF	40875	25200	26000	27800	32000
F150 Lariat 4D 5 1/2'	W1EF	44185	30700	31700	33600	38400
F150 Lariat 4D 6 1/2'	W1EF	44480	31200	32100	34000	38800
F150 King Ranch 5 1/2'	W1EF	48920	32200	33200	35100	40100
F150 Platinum 5 1/2'	W1EF	51945	33300	34300	36300	41600
2WD	C		(3600)	(3600)	(4130)	(4130)
V6, EcoBoost, 3.5L	T		1900	1900	2190	2190
V8, 6.2 Liter	6		400	400	455	455
SUPERCREW PICKUP 4WD—V8 Flex Fuel—Truck Equipment Schedule T1						
F150 FX4 4D 5 1/2'	W1EF	43690	32100	33100	35000	40100
F150 FX4 4D 6 1/2'	W1EF	43985	31600	32600	34600	39600
V6, EcoBoost, 3.5L	T		1900	1900	2180	2180
V8, 6.2 Liter	6		400	400	455	455
SUPERCREW PICKUP 4WD—V8—Truck Equipment Schedule T1						
F150 SVT Raptor 5'	W1R6	48510	46000	47400	46900	51300
SUPER DUTY CREW CAB PICKUP—V8 Flex Fuel—Truck Equip Sch T1						
F250 XL 6 3/4'	W2A6	34825	22700	23500	25100	29100
F250 King Ranch 8'	W2A6	50610	36500	37600	39500	45300
F350 XL 4D 6 3/4'	W3A6	35725				
4WD	B		3600	3600	4095	4095
V8, Turbo Dsl, 6.7L	T		5300	5300	6030	6030
SUPER DUTY CREW CAB PICKUP—V8 Turbo Diesel—Truck Sch T1						
F250 XL 8'	W2AT	43340	29800	30800	32400	37100
F250 Lariat 8'	W2AT	53840	38500	39700	41700	47500
F350 XL 4D 8'	W3AT	44240				
F350 XLT 4D 8'	W3AT	49075				
F350 Lariat 4D 8'	W3AT	54735				
4WD	B		3600	3600	4025	4025
V8, Flex Fuel, 6.2 Liter	6		(5300)	(5300)	(5925)	(5925)
SUPER DUTY CREW CAB PICKUP 4WD—V8 Turbo Diesel—Truck Sch T1						
F250 XLT 6 3/4'	W2BT	50775	35700	36800	38500	44100
F250 Lariat 6 3/4'	W2BT	56825	42600	43900	45800	52500
F350 Lariat 4D 6 3/4'	W3BT	57725				
F350 King Ranch 8'	W3BT	63315				
F350 Platinum 8'	W3BT	64010				
2WD	A		(3600)	(3600)	(4045)	(4045)
V8, Flex Fuel, 6.2 Liter	6		(5300)	(5300)	(5955)	(5955)
SUPER DUTY CREW CAB PICKUP 4WD—V8 Flex Fuel—Truck Equip Sch T1						
F250 XLT 8'	W2B6	42660	29700	30700	32400	37200
F250 KingRnch 6'	W2BT	62220	46600	47000	48800	55700
F250 Platinum 6 3/4'	W2B6	54595	40700	42000	43900	50400
F250 Platinum 8'	W2B6	63110	41400	42700	44600	51100
F350 XLT 4D 8'	W3B6	43365				
F350 KingRnch 6 3/4'	W3B6	54805				
F350 Platinum 6 3/4'	W3B6	55495				
2WD	A		(3600)	(3600)	(4050)	(4050)
V8, Turbo Dsl, 6.7L	T		5300	5300	5960	5960

GMC — See CHEVROLET TRUCKS

HONDA

2000 HONDA–(JHL,2HKor4S6)(RD174)–Y–#

CR-V 4WD—4-Cyl.—Truck Equipment Schedule T2

	VIN	List	Good	Very Good	Good	Excellent
LX Sport Utility 4D	RD174	19465	1150	1325	2150	3500
EX Sport Utility 4D	RD176	20965	1550	1750	2750	4350
SE Sport Utility 4D	RD187	23015	2025	2275	3350	5250
2WD	2		(275)	(275)	(365)	(365)

PASSPORT 4WD—V6—Truck Equipment Schedule T1

	VIN	List	Good	Very Good	Good	Excellent
LX Sport Util 4D	CM58V	27515	900	1025	1850	3025

2000 HONDA

Body Type	VIN	List	Trade-In Good	Very Good	Pvt-Party Good	Retail Excellent
EX Sport Util 4D	CM58V	29465	**1350**	**1500**	**2400**	**3875**
2WD	K		**(275)**	**(275)**	**(365)**	**(365)**
ODYSSEY—V6—Truck Equipment Schedule T1						
LX Minivan 4D	RL185	23815	**700**	**825**	**1350**	**2175**
EX Minivan 4D	RL186	26415	**1100**	**1250**	**1800**	**2850**

2001 HONDA–(JHL,2HKor4S6)(RD174)–1–#

CR-V 4WD—4-Cyl.—Truck Equipment Schedule T2
Body Type	VIN	List	Good	Very Good	Good	Excellent
LX Sport Utility 4D	RD174	19590	**1500**	**1675**	**2525**	**4000**
EX Sport Utility 4D	RD176	21190	**2000**	**2250**	**3250**	**5000**
SE Sport Utility 4D	RD187	23240	**2475**	**2800**	**3800**	**5750**
2WD	2		**(300)**	**(300)**	**(400)**	**(400)**
PASSPORT 4WD—V6—Truck Equipment Schedule T1						
LX Sport Util 4D	CM58W	27740	**1200**	**1350**	**2175**	**3450**
EX Sport Util 4D	CM58W	29690	**1675**	**1875**	**2825**	**4400**
2WD	K		**(300)**	**(300)**	**(400)**	**(400)**
ODYSSEY—V6—Truck Equipment Schedule T1						
LX Minivan 4D	RL185	24340	**825**	**950**	**1525**	**2475**
EX Minivan 4D	RL186	26820	**1200**	**1350**	**1900**	**2975**

2002 HONDA–(JHL,2HKor4S6)(RD784)–2–#

CR-V 4WD—4-Cyl.—Truck Equipment Schedule T2
Body Type	VIN	List	Good	Very Good	Good	Excellent
LX Sport Utility 4D	RD784	19640	**2325**	**2600**	**3425**	**5000**
EX Sport Utility 4D	RD788	21940	**3275**	**3625**	**4475**	**6375**
2WD	2		**(375)**	**(375)**	**(500)**	**(500)**
PASSPORT 4WD—V6—Truck Equipment Schedule T1						
LX Sport Util 4D	CM58W	28040	**1650**	**1825**	**2750**	**4225**
EX Sport Util 4D	CM58W	29990	**2225**	**2475**	**3450**	**5200**
2WD	K		**(375)**	**(375)**	**(500)**	**(500)**
ODYSSEY—V6—Truck Equipment Schedule T1						
LX Minivan 4D	RL185	24690	**1000**	**1125**	**1700**	**2675**
EX Minivan 4D	RL186	27190	**1425**	**1625**	**2275**	**3550**

2003 HONDA–(Jor5)HorJL,Kor6)(YH272)–3–#

ELEMENT 4WD—4-Cyl.—Truck Equipment Schedule T2
Body Type	VIN	List	Good	Very Good	Good	Excellent
DX Sport Utility 4D	YH272	18760	**2125**	**2375**	**3225**	**4700**
EX Sport Utility 4D	YH285	21310	**3450**	**3800**	**4950**	**7075**
2WD	1		**(450)**	**(450)**	**(600)**	**(600)**
CR-V 4WD—4-Cyl.—Truck Equipment Schedule T2						
LX Sport Utility 4D	RD774	19760	**3150**	**3500**	**4250**	**6025**
EX Sport Utility 4D	RD788	22060	**4175**	**4575**	**5600**	**7850**
2WD	2		**(450)**	**(450)**	**(600)**	**(600)**
PILOT 4WD—V6—Truck Equipment Schedule T1						
LX Sport Utility 4D	YF181	27360	**2375**	**2675**	**3525**	**5175**
EX Sport Utility 4D	YF184	29730	**3150**	**3525**	**4625**	**6725**
ODYSSEY—V6—Truck Equipment Schedule T1						
LX Minivan 4D	RL185	24860	**1350**	**1525**	**2050**	**3150**
EX Minivan 4D	RL186	27360	**1775**	**2000**	**2650**	**3975**

2004 HONDA–(J,2or5)F,HorJ(K,L,Nor6)(YH183)–4–#

ELEMENT—4-Cyl.—Truck Equipment Schedule T2
Body Type	VIN	List	Good	Very Good	Good	Excellent
LX Sport Utility 4D	YH183	18990	**3000**	**3300**	**4175**	**5900**
4WD			**550**	**550**	**735**	**735**
ELEMENT 4WD—4-Cyl.—Truck Equipment Schedule T2						
DX Sport Utility 4D	YH272	17990	**2950**	**3250**	**4125**	**5825**
EX Sport Utility 4D	YH285	20790	**4300**	**4675**	**5850**	**8150**
2WD	1		**(525)**	**(525)**	**(700)**	**(700)**
CR-V 4WD—4-Cyl.—Truck Equipment Schedule T2						
LX Sport Utility 4D	RD774	19890	**3725**	**4100**	**5050**	**7050**
EX Sport Utility 4D	RD788	22240	**4875**	**5300**	**6425**	**8925**
2WD	2		**(525)**	**(525)**	**(700)**	**(700)**
PILOT 4WD—V6—Truck Equipment Schedule T1						
LX Sport Utility 4D	YF181	27590	**3200**	**3550**	**4375**	**6150**
EX Sport Utility 4D	YF184	29960	**4200**	**4625**	**5675**	**7925**
ODYSSEY—V6—Truck Equipment Schedule T1						
LX Minivan 4D	RL185	24980	**1475**	**1675**	**2325**	**3550**
EX Minivan 4D	RL186	27480	**2150**	**2400**	**3125**	**4650**

2005 HONDA–(J,2or5)F,HorJ(K,L,Nor6)(YH283)–5–#

ELEMENT—4-Cyl.—Truck Equipment Schedule T2
Body Type	VIN	List	Good	Very Good	Good	Excellent
LX Sport Utility 4D	YH283	18990	**3700**	**4050**	**4975**	**6775**

TRUCKS & VANS

Body Type	VIN	List	Trade-In Good	Very Good	Pvt-Party Good	Retail Excellent
4WD			600	600	800	800
ELEMENT 4WD—4-Cyl.—Truck Equipment Schedule T2						
EX Sport Utility 4D	YH286	20790	5125	5525	6575	8825
2WD			(600)	(600)	(800)	(800)
CR-V 4WD—4-Cyl.—Truck Equipment Schedule T2						
LX Sport Utility 4D	RD774	21710	5050	5475	6525	8950
EX Sport Utility 4D	RD788	22865	5750	6225	7550	10300
SE Sport Utility 4D	RD779	25565	6350	6850	8225	11200
2WD	6		(600)	(600)	(800)	(800)
PILOT 4WD—V6—Truck Equipment Schedule T1						
LX Sport Utility 4D	YF181	27865	4125	4525	5525	7600
EX Sport Utility 4D	YF184	30435	4950	5425	6700	9225
ODYSSEY—V6—Truck Equipment Schedule T1						
LX Minivan 4D	RL382	25510	3400	3775	4950	7300
EX Minivan 4D	RL384	28510	4100	4500	5775	8425
Touring Minivan 4D	RL388	35010	5925	6450	8175	11750

Body Type	VIN	List	Trade-In Good	Very Good	Pvt-Party Good	Retail Excellent
ELEMENT—4-Cyl.—Truck Equipment Schedule T1						
LX Sport Utility 4D	YH283	19700	4975	5350	6175	8075
4WD			650	650	850	850
ELEMENT 4WD—4-Cyl.—Truck Equipment Schedule T2						
EX-P Sport Util 4D	YH277	22920	6425	6875	8050	10450
EX Sport Utility 4D	YH286	21575	6300	6750	7900	10250
2WD	1		(650)	(650)	(845)	(845)
CR-V 4WD—4-Cyl.—Truck Equipment Schedule T2						
LX Sport Utility 4D	RD774	22145	5675	6150	7550	10200
SE Sport Utility 4D	RD779	26000	7650	8200	9750	13100
2WD	6		(650)	(650)	(865)	(865)
CR-V 4WD—4-Cyl.—Truck Equipment Schedule T1						
EX Sport Utility 4D	RD788	24300	6750	7250	8675	11600
2WD	6		(650)	(650)	(865)	(865)
PILOT 4WD—V6—Truck Equipment Schedule T1						
LX Sport Utility 4D	YF181	28745	5750	6225	7400	9800
EX Sport Utility 4D	YF184	31295	6950	7475	8650	11450
EX-L Sport Utility 4D	YF185	33640	8250	8875	10150	13400
2WD	2		(1050)	(1050)	(1410)	(1410)
ODYSSEY—V6—Truck Equipment Schedule T1						
LX Minivan 4D	RL382	25895	4275	4675	5675	7975
EX Minivan 4D	RL384	28945	4850	5300	6625	9225
Touring Minivan 4D	RL388	37145	8250	8900	10400	14150
RIDGELINE 4WD—V6—Truck Equipment Schedule T1						
RT Short Bed	YK162	28250	5925	6350	7400	9550
RTS Short Bed	YK164	30625	7000	7475	8475	10800
RTL Short Bed	YK168	32040	8650	9225	10400	13200

Body Type	VIN	List	Trade-In Good	Very Good	Pvt-Party Good	Retail Excellent
ELEMENT—4-Cyl. VTEC—Truck Equipment Schedule T1						
LX Sport Utility 4D	YH283	21695	5700	6100	7150	9225
4WD			975	975	1260	1260
ELEMENT 4WD—4-Cyl. VTEC—Truck Equipment Schedule T1						
EX Sport Utility 4D	YH287	23705	7400	7875	9100	11650
2WD			(700)	(700)	(890)	(890)
ELEMENT—4-Cyl. VTEC—Truck Equipment Schedule T2						
SC Sport Utility 4D	YH189	24090	8050	8575	9775	12450
CR-V 4WD—4-Cyl. VTEC—Truck Equipment Schedule T2						
LX Sport Utility 4D	RE483	22395	7775	8300	9750	12850
EX Sport Utility 4D	RE485	24645	8775	9350	10850	14300
EX-L Sport Utility	RE487	26635	9450	10050	11850	15650
2WD	3		(700)	(700)	(935)	(935)
PILOT 4WD—V6 VTEC—Truck Equipment Schedule T1						
LX Sport Utility 4D	YF181	28745	6900	7425	8475	10900
EX Sport Utility 4D	YF184	31540	8100	8675	9725	12450
EX-L Sport Utility 4D	YF185	33840	9375	10000	11200	14300
2WD	2		(1150)	(1150)	(1490)	(1490)
ODYSSEY—V6 VTEC—Truck Equipment Schedule T1						
LX Minivan 4D	RL382	26240	5125	5575	6400	8550
EX Minivan 4D	RL384	29290	5875	6350	7350	9750
Touring Minivan 4D	RL388	37490	9300	9975	11350	14900
RIDGELINE 4WD—V6 VTEC—Truck Equipment Schedule T1						
RT Short Bed	YK162	28395	7675	8175	9275	11750
RTX Short Bed	YK163	28895	8175	8700	9825	12400

Body Type	VIN	List	Trade-In Good	Trade-In Very Good	Pvt-Party Good	Retail Excellent
RTS Short Bed	YK164	30870	**8550**	**9075**	**10350**	**13050**
RTL Short Bed	YK165	33535	**11000**	**11600**	**13050**	**16350**

2008 HONDA—(J,2or5)(F,HorJ)(J,K,L,Nor6)YH283-8-#

ELEMENT—4-Cyl. VTEC—Truck Equipment Schedule T1
LX Sport Utility 4D	YH283	21015	**7025**	**7450**	**8475**	**10600**
4WD			**1075**	**1075**	**1360**	**1360**

ELEMENT 4WD—4-Cyl. VTEC—Truck Equipment Schedule T1
EX Sport Utility 4D	YH287	23025	**9050**	**9550**	**10700**	**13300**
2WD		1	(750)	(750)	(940)	(940)

ELEMENT—4-Cyl. VTEC—Truck Equipment Schedule T1
SC Sport Utility 4D	YH189	23410	**9675**	**10200**	**11450**	**14150**

CR-V 4WD—4-Cyl. VTEC—Truck Equipment Schedule T2
LX Sport Utility 4D	RE483	22535	**8800**	**9350**	**10550**	**13300**
EX Sport Utility 4D	RE485	24785	**9750**	**10350**	**11700**	**14850**
EX-L Sport Utility	RE487	27370	**10650**	**11250**	**12750**	**16150**
2WD		3	(750)	(750)	(970)	(970)

PILOT 4WD—V6 VTEC—Truck Equipment Schedule T1
VP Sport Utility 4D	YF182	29630	**8550**	**9100**	**10050**	**12450**
EX Sport Utility 4D	YF184	31780	**9700**	**10300**	**11300**	**14000**
EX-L Sport Utility	YF185	34080	**11200**	**11850**	**12950**	**15950**
SE Sport Utility 4D	YF183	33630	**10600**	**11250**	**12250**	**15050**
2WD		2	(1225)	(1225)	(1505)	(1505)

ODYSSEY—V6 VTEC—Truck Equipment Schedule T1
LX Minivan 4D	RL382	26495	**6150**	**6600**	**7575**	**9775**
EX Minivan 4D	RL384	29595	**7650**	**8175**	**9250**	**11850**
Touring Minivan 4D	RL388	40645	**11200**	**11850**	**13200**	**16750**

RIDGELINE 4WD—V6 VTEC—Truck Equipment Schedule T1
RT Short Bed	YK162	28635	**9175**	**9700**	**10800**	**13300**
RTX Short Bed	YK163	29135	**10250**	**10800**	**11850**	**14500**
RTS Short Bed	YK164	31060	**10850**	**11450**	**12600**	**15400**
RTL Short Bed	YK165	33725	**13150**	**13850**	**15150**	**18450**

2009 HONDA—(J,2or5)(F,HorJ)(J,K,L,Nor6)YH283-9-#

ELEMENT—4-Cyl. VTEC—Truck Equipment Schedule T1
LX Sport Utility 4D	YH283	22145	**8925**	**9400**	**10450**	**12650**
4WD			**1175**	**1175**	**1330**	**1330**

ELEMENT 4WD—4-Cyl. VTEC—Truck Equipment Schedule T1
EX Sport Utility 4D	YH287	24255	**10950**	**11500**	**12650**	**15200**
2WD		1	(875)	(875)	(995)	(995)

ELEMENT—4-Cyl. VTEC—Truck Equipment Schedule T1
SC Sport Utility 4D	YH189	24740	**11350**	**11950**	**13150**	**15850**

CR-V 4WD—4-Cyl. VTEC—Truck Equipment Schedule T2
LX Sport Utility 4D	RE483	23155	**10450**	**11050**	**12150**	**14850**
EX Sport Utility 4D	RE485	25405	**11700**	**12300**	**13650**	**16750**
EX-L Sport Utility	RE487	27955	**12650**	**13300**	**14700**	**18000**
2WD		3	(875)	(875)	(1090)	(1090)

PILOT 4WD—V6 VTEC—Truck Equipment Schedule T1
LX Sport Utility 4D	YF182	29965	**11600**	**12200**	**13100**	**15700**
EX Sport Utility 4D	YF184	32765	**12750**	**13450**	**14450**	**17300**
EX-L Sport Utility	YF185	36005	**14700**	**15450**	**16500**	**19700**
Touring Sport Util	YF183	37565	**16700**	**17750**	**18500**	**21900**
2WD		2	(1300)	(1300)	(1560)	(1560)

ODYSSEY—V6 VTEC—Truck Equipment Schedule T1
LX Minivan 4D	RL382	27025	**7350**	**7800**	**8800**	**11000**
EX Minivan 4D	RL384	30125	**9000**	**9500**	**10600**	**13150**
Touring Minivan 4D	RL388	41125	**12700**	**13350**	**14750**	**18150**

RIDGELINE 4WD—V6 VTEC—Truck Equipment Schedule T1
RT Short Bed	YK162	28870	**11450**	**12000**	**13100**	**15600**
RTS Short Bed	YK164	31975	**12950**	**13550**	**14750**	**17550**
RTL Short Bed	YK165	34850	**15500**	**16200**	**17450**	**20700**

2010 HONDA — 5(ForJ)(N,Por6)(YH2H3)-A-#

ELEMENT—4-Cyl. VTEC—Truck Equipment Schedule T2
LX Sport Util 4D	YH2H3	22485	**11750**	**12250**	**13450**	**15950**
4WD			**1250**	**1250**	**1445**	**1445**

ELEMENT 4WD—4-Cyl. VTEC—Truck Equipment Schedule T1
EX Sport Util 4D	YH2H7	23795	**13800**	**14400**	**15800**	**18700**
2WD		1	(1000)	(1000)	(1155)	(1155)

ELEMENT—4-Cyl. VTEC—Truck Equipment Schedule T1
SC Sport Utility 4D	YH1H9	24230	**14200**	**14850**	**16150**	**19000**

2010 HONDA

Body Type	VIN	List	Trade-In Good	Very Good	Pvt-Party Good	Retail Excellent
CR-V 4WD—4-Cyl.VTEC—Truck Equipment Schedule T2						
LX Sport Utility 4D	RE4H3	23505	11550	12150	13300	15950
EX Sport Utility	RE4H5	25805	12800	13450	14700	17650
EX-L Sport Utility	RE4H7	28455	14050	14700	16150	19350
2WD		3	(1000)	(1000)	(1220)	(1220)
PILOT 4WD—V6 VTEC—Truck Equipment Schedule T2						
LX Sport Utility 4D	YF4H2	30205	13950	14600	15700	18500
EX Sport Utility 4D	YF4H4	33055	15300	16000	17100	20200
EX-L Sport Utility	YF4H5	36155	17050	17800	19050	22500
Touring Sport Util	YF4H8	39355	19250	20100	21200	24800
2WD		2	(1375)	(1375)	(1625)	(1625)
ACCORD CROSSTOUR—V6 VTEC—Truck Equipment Schedule T1						
EX Sport Utility 4D	TF1H3	30570	11550	12050	13100	15400
EX-L Spt Util 4D	TF1H5	33280	12300	12850	13900	16350
4WD			1200	1200	1400	1400
ODYSSEY—V6 VTEC—Truck Equipment Schedule T1						
LX Minivan 4D	RL3H2	27515	9900	10400	11500	13950
EX Minivan 4D	RL3H4	30615	11700	12300	13500	16350
EX-L Minivan 4D	RL3H6	34115	14750	15400	16850	20300
Touring Minivan	RL3H9	41465	16750	17500	19100	23100
RIDGELINE 4WD—V6 VTEC—Truck Equipment Schedule T1						
RT Short Bed	YK1F2	29160	13100	13700	14900	17500
RTS Short Bed	YK1F4	32265	14500	15100	16350	19200
RTL Short Bed	YK1F5	35140	17350	18050	19300	22600

2011 HONDA — (5orJ)(F,HorJ)(6,L,NorP)(YH2H3)-B-#

Body Type	VIN	List	Trade-In Good	Very Good	Pvt-Party Good	Retail Excellent
ELEMENT—4-Cyl. VTEC—Truck Equipment Schedule T2						
LX Sport Util 4D	YH2H3	22855	14300	14900	16050	18550
4WD			1400	1400	1585	1585
ELEMENT 4WD—4-Cyl. VTEC—Truck Equipment Schedule T2						
EX Sport Util 4D	YH2H7	24965	16150	16800	17950	20700
2WD			(1100)	(1100)	(1245)	(1245)
CR-V 4WD—4-Cyl. VTEC—Truck Equipment Schedule T2						
LX Sport Utility	RE4H3	23725	12750	13350	14450	17000
SE Sport Utility	RE4H4	24425	13050	13650	14750	17300
EX Sport Utility	RE4H5	26025	13900	14500	15750	18500
EX-L Spt Utility	RE4H7	28675	15250	15950	17250	20300
2WD		3	(1100)	(1100)	(1295)	(1295)
PILOT 4WD—V6 VTEC—Truck Equipment Schedule T1						
LX Sport Utility 4D	YF4H2	30425	15300	15950	17000	19800
EX Sport Utility 4D	YF4H4	33275	16850	17550	18650	21700
EX-L Sport Utility	YF4H5	36375	19200	20000	21100	24500
Touring Sport Util	YF4H9	41175	20800	21600	22700	26200
2WD			(1475)	(1475)	(1690)	(1690)
ACCORD CROSSTOUR—V6 VTEC—Truck Equipment Schedule T1						
EX-L Sport Utility 4D	TF1H3	30570	12900	13450	14650	17100
EX-L Sport Utility	TF1H5	33470	13500	14100	15300	17750
4WD		2	1400	1400	1595	1595
ODYSSEY—V6 VTEC—Truck Equipment Schedule T1						
LX Minivan 4D	RL5H2	27585	12150	12650	13950	16700
EX Minivan 4D	RL5H4	30685	14000	14600	16050	19100
EX-L Minivan 4D	RL5H6	34185	17150	17850	19400	23000
Touring Minivan	RL5H9	41535	20300	21100	22800	27100
Touring Elite 4D	RL5H9	44030	22000	22900	24600	29200
RIDGELINE 4WD—V6 VTEC—Truck Equipment Schedule T1						
RT Short Bed	YK1F2	29680	15850	16450	17550	20100
RTS Short Bed	YK1F4	32385	17600	18250	19350	22200
RTL Short Bed	YK1F5	35260	20600	21300	22400	25600

2012 HONDA — (5orJ)(F,HorJ)(6,L,NorP)(RM4H3)-C-#

Body Type	VIN	List	Trade-In Good	Very Good	Pvt-Party Good	Retail Excellent
CR-V AWD—4-Cyl i-VTEC—Truck Equipment Schedule T2						
LX Sport Utility	RM4H3	24355	14800	15450	16700	19450
EX Sport Utility	RM4H5	26455	16500	17200	18650	21800
EX-L Spt Utility	RM4H7	29105	18200	18950	20500	24000
2WD		3	(1500)	(1500)	(1720)	(1720)
PILOT 4WD—V6 VTEC I-VTEC—Truck Equipment Schedule T1						
LX Sport Utility 4D	YF4H2	30880	17700	18400	19550	22500
EX Sport Utility 4D	YF4H4	33730	19400	20100	21300	24500
EX-L Sport Utility	YF4H5	36980	21900	22700	23800	27200
Touring Sport Util	YF4H9	41630	24100	25000	26000	29700
2WD		3	(1550)	(1550)	(1770)	(1770)

0415

2012 HONDA

Body Type	VIN	List	Trade-In Good	Trade-In Very Good	Pvt-Party Good	Retail Excellent
CROSSTOUR—V6 VTEC—Truck Equipment Schedule T1						
EX Sport Util 4D	TF1H3	31150	14000	14550	15800	18200
EX-L Sport Util 4D	TF1H5	33800	15550	16150	17350	20000
4WD		2	1525	1525	1745	1745
4-Cyl, i-VTEC, 2.4 Liter			(900)	(900)	(1025)	(1025)
ODYSSEY—V6 i-VTEC—Truck Equipment Schedule T1						
LX Minivan 4D	RL5H2	29035	15200	15800	17050	19800
EX Minivan 4D	RL5H4	32285	17600	18250	19550	22700
EX-L Minivan 4D	RL5H6	35685	20700	21400	22800	26400
Touring Minivan	RL5H9	41990	23700	24600	26100	30300
Touring Elite 4D	RL5H9	44485	25400	26200	27900	32400
RIDGELINE 4WD—V6 VTEC—Truck Equipment Schedule T1						
RT Short Bed	YK1F2	30060	19250	19950	21100	24000
Sport Short Bed	YK1F7	30805	19550	20300	21400	24300
RTS Short Bed	YK1F4	32765	20800	21500	22600	25700
RTL Short Bed	YK1F5	35640	22700	23500	24700	28000

2013 HONDA — (5orJ)(F,HorJ)(6,L,NorP)(RM4H3)–D–#

Body Type	VIN	List	Trade-In Good	Trade-In Very Good	Pvt-Party Good	Retail Excellent
CR-V AWD—4-Cyl. i-VTEC—Truck Equipment Schedule T2						
LX Sport Utility	RM4H3	24775	16300	16950	17950	20600
EX Sport Utility	RM4H5	26875	17750	18450	19550	22400
EX-L Sport Utility	RM4H7	29525	20000	20800	21900	25000
2WD		3	(1500)	(1500)	(1665)	(1665)
PILOT 4WD—V6 i-VTEC—Truck Equipment Schedule T1						
LX Sport Utility 4D	YF4H2	31850	20100	20800	22000	25100
EX Sport Utility 4D	YF4H4	34100	21900	22700	23800	27100
EX-L Sport Utility	YF4H5	37350	24500	25400	26500	30100
Touring Sport Util	YF4H9	42000	27100	28000	29000	32700
2WD		3	(1625)	(1625)	(1830)	(1830)
CROSSTOUR—V6 i-VTEC—Truck Equipment Schedule T1						
EX Sport Util 4D	TF1H3	31720	16250	16850	18100	20700
EX-L Sport Util 4D	TF1H5	34370	18600	19250	20400	23200
4-Cyl, i-VTEC, 2.4 Liter			(1000)	(1000)	(1130)	(1130)
4WD			1675	1675	1875	1875
ODYSSEY—V6 i-VTEC—Truck Equipment Schedule T1						
LX Minivan 4D	RL5H2	29405	17500	18100	19300	22200
EX Minivan 4D	RL5H4	32555	19850	20500	21800	25000
EX-L Minivan 4D	RL5H6	35955	22900	23700	25000	28600
Touring Minivan	RL5H9	42260	25900	26800	28200	32300
Touring Elite	RL5H9	44755	27600	28500	30000	34300
RIDGELINE 4WD—V6 VTEC—Truck Equipment Schedule T1						
RT Short Bed	YK1F2	30180	20500	21200	22400	25400
Sport Short Bed	YK1F7	30925	21500	22200	23400	26400
RTS Short Bed	YK1F4	32885	23100	23900	25100	28300
RTL Short Bed	YK1F5	35760	24500	25400	26600	30000

2014 HONDA — (5orJ)(F,HorJ)(6,L,NorP)(RM4H3)–E–#

Body Type	VIN	List	Trade-In Good	Trade-In Very Good	Pvt-Party Good	Retail Excellent
CR-V AWD—4-Cyl. i-VTEC—Truck Equipment Schedule T2						
LX Sport Utility	RM4H3	25025	17800	18500	19550	22300
EX Sport Utility	RM4H5	27125	19600	20400	21400	24400
EX-L Sport Utility	RM4H7	29775	21400	22200	23300	26600
2WD			(1500)	(1500)	(1675)	(1675)
PILOT 4WD—V6 i-VTEC—Truck Equipment Schedule T1						
LX Sport Utility 4D	YF4H2	32100	21300	22000	23100	26300
EX Sport Utility 4D	YF4H4	34350	23200	23900	25000	28400
EX-L Sport Utility	YF4H5	37600	26200	27100	28200	31900
Touring Sport Util	YF4H9	42250	28400	29400	30300	34100
2WD			(1725)	(1725)	(1925)	(1925)
CROSSTOUR—V6 i-VTEC—Truck Equipment Schedule T1						
EX Sport Utility 4D	TF1H3	31870	17900	18550	19600	22100
EX-L Sport Utility 4D	TF1H5	34520	20300	21000	21900	24500
4WD			1800	1800	1990	1990
4-Cyl, i-VTEC, 2.4 Liter			(1100)	(1100)	(1230)	(1230)
ODYSSEY—V6 i-VTEC—Truck Equipment Schedule T1						
LX Minivan 4D	RL5H2	29655	19450	20100	21300	24400
EX Minivan 4D	RL5H4	32955	21800	22600	23700	27000
EX-L Minivan 4D	RL5H6	36455	24800	25700	26900	30600
Touring Minivan	RL5H9	42710	27900	28800	30200	34300
Touring Elite	RL5H9	45280	29500	30500	31900	36300
RIDGELINE 4WD—V6 VTEC—Truck Equipment Schedule T1						
RT Short Bed	YK1F2	30405	21500	22300	23400	26400
Sport Short Bed	YK1F7	31550	23300	24100	25200	28400

Body Type	VIN	List	Trade-In Good	Trade-In Very Good	Pvt-Party Good	Retail Excellent
RTS Short Bed	YK1F4	33210	25000	25800	27000	30300
RTL Short Bed	YK1F5	35985	26200	27100	28400	32100
SE Short Bed	YK1F6	38335	26400	27300	28500	32200

HUMMER

2000 HUMMER — 137(ZA89)--Y-#

H1 4WD—V8 Turbo Diesel—Truck Equipment Sch T3

Body Type	VIN	List	Good	Very Good	Good	Excellent
Hard Top 2D	ZA89	70819	19950	21000	22400	27500
Open Top 4D	ZA90	80499	20600	21700	23100	28400
Hard Top 4D	ZA83	89496	21300	22400	23800	29300
Wagon 4D	ZA84	93414	22000	23200	24600	30200
Slantback 4D	ZA91	95850	22200	23400	24800	30500
GA Pkg			1000	1000	1260	1260
GC Pkg			1600	1600	2015	2015
Winch			400	400	505	505

2001 HUMMER — 137(ZA82)--1-#

H1 4WD—V8 Turbo Diesel—Truck Equipment Sch T3

Body Type	VIN	List	Good	Very Good	Good	Excellent
Hard Top 2D	ZA82	76862	22400	23500	24800	30300
Open Top 4D	ZA85	84608	23200	24400	25800	31500
Hard Top 4D	ZA83	91553	24100	25300	26700	32600
Wagon 4D	ZA84	95404	24800	26100	27500	33500
GA Pkg			1000	1000	1245	1245
GC Pkg			1725	1725	2145	2145
Winch			400	400	495	495

2002 HUMMER — 137(ZA85)--2-#

H1 4WD—V8 Turbo Diesel—Truck Equipment Schedule T3

Body Type	VIN	List	Good	Very Good	Good	Excellent
Open Top 4D	ZA85	98681	27200	28600	29600	35600
Wagon 4D	ZA84	109834	29100	30500	31700	38100
Winch			475	475	575	575

2003 HUMMER — 5GR-(N23U)-3-#

H2 4WD—V8—Truck Equipment Schedule T3

Body Type	VIN	List	Good	Very Good	Good	Excellent
Sport Utility 4D	N23U	50200	9325	9875	11250	14200
Third Row Seat			275	275	355	355
Adventure Pkg			175	175	210	210
Lux Pkg			175	175	210	210
Air Suspension			325	325	405	405

H1 4WD—V8 Turbo Diesel—Truck Equipment Schedule T3

Body Type	VIN	List	Good	Very Good	Good	Excellent
Open Top 4D	A903	106185	32600	34100	34700	41100
Wagon 4D	A843	117508	34500	36100	36900	43800
Winch			550	550	650	650

2004 HUMMER — 5GR-(N23U)-4-#

H2 4WD—V8—Truck Equipment Schedule T3

Body Type	VIN	List	Good	Very Good	Good	Excellent
Sport Utility 4D	N23U	51395	11450	12100	13300	16450
Limited Ed Spt Util	N23U	59840	13250	14000	15150	18550
Third Row Seat			300	300	370	370
Adventure Pkg			175	175	220	220
Lux Pkg			175	175	220	220
Air Suspension			325	325	410	410

H1 4WD—V8 Turbo Diesel—Truck Equipment Schedule T3

Body Type	VIN	List	Good	Very Good	Good	Excellent
Open Top 4D	A903	106185	37800	39500	39800	46600
Wagon 4D	ZA84	117508	40500	42300	42600	49800
Winch			600	600	695	695
Adventure Pkg			175	175	210	210

2005 HUMMER — 5GR-(N23U)-5-#

H2 4WD—V8—Truck Equipment Schedule T3

Body Type	VIN	List	Good	Very Good	Good	Excellent
Sport Utility 4D	N23U	52000	13000	13700	14950	18150
Third Row Seat			325	325	400	400
Adventure Pkg			200	200	245	245
Lux Pkg			200	200	245	245
Air Suspension			350	350	430	430

H2 SUT 4WD—V8—Truck Equipment Schedule T3

Body Type	VIN	List	Good	Very Good	Good	Excellent
Sport Utility Pickup	N22U	53055	14400	15150	16250	19550
Adventure Pkg			200	200	240	240

Body Type	VIN	List	Trade-In Good	Very Good	Pvt-Party Good	Retail Excellent
Victory Red Ltd Ed			200	200	240	240
Lux Pkg			200	200	240	240
Air Suspension			350	350	425	425

2006 HUMMER — 5G(RorT)–(N136)–6–#

H3 4WD—5-Cyl.—Truck Equipment Schedule T3
Sport Utility 4D	N136	31195	9350	9850	11000	13500
Adventure Pkg			225	225	255	255
Luxury Pkg			225	225	255	255
Off-Road Suspension			375	375	435	435

H2 4WD—V8—Truck Equipment Schedule T3
Sport Utility 4D	N23U	53855	16100	16950	18050	21600
Third Row Seat			350	350	420	420
Adventure Pkg			225	225	255	255
Limited Edition			225	225	255	255
Luxury Pkg			225	225	255	255
Air Suspension			375	375	440	440

H2 SUT 4WD—V8—Truck Equipment Schedule T3
Sport Utility Pickup	N22U	53910	17400	18250	19350	23100
Adventure Pkg			225	225	255	255
Limited Edition			225	225	255	255
Luxury Pkg			225	225	255	255
Air Suspension			375	375	435	435

H1 4WD—V8 Turbo Diesel—Truck Equipment Schedule T3
Open Top 4D	PH90	129399	69200	72100	69900	78800
Wagon 4D	PH84	140796	73400	76500	74200	83700
Winch			700	700	765	765
Adventure Pkg			225	225	235	235

2007 HUMMER — 5G(RorT)–(N13E)–7–#

H3 4WD—5-Cyl.—Truck Equipment Schedule T3
Sport Utility 4D	N13E	31640	10400	10950	12050	14600
Adventure Pkg			225	225	270	270
Luxury Pkg			225	225	270	270
H3X Pkg			225	225	270	270
Off-Road Suspension			375	375	450	450

H2 4WD—V8—Truck Equipment Schedule T3
Sport Utility 4D	N23U	54255	19200	20100	21200	25100
Third Row Seat			375	375	445	445
Adventure Pkg			225	225	275	275
Luxury Pkg			225	225	275	275
Special Edition			225	225	275	275
Air Suspension			375	375	455	455

H2 SUT 4WD—V8—Truck Equipment Schedule T3
Sport Utility Pickup	N22U	54300	20100	21100	22000	26000
Adventure Pkg			225	225	275	275
Luxury Pkg			225	225	275	275
Special Edition			225	225	275	275
Air Suspension			375	375	450	450

2008 HUMMER — 5G(RorT)–(N13E)–8–#

H3 4WD—5-Cyl.—Truck Equipment Schedule T3
Sport Utility 4D	N13E	32390	11700	12250	13300	15850
Adventure Pkg	3		250	250	290	290
Luxury Pkg	4		250	250	290	290
Off-Road Suspension			400	400	460	460

H3x 4WD—5-Cyl.—Truck Equipment Schedule T3
Sport Utility 4D	N53E	40685	14350	15000	16100	19000
Luxury Pkg	4		250	250	285	285

H3 ALPHA 4WD—V8—Truck Equipment Schedule T3
Sport Utility 4D	N63L	39260	14350	15000	16100	19000
Luxury Pkg	4		250	250	285	285
Off-Road Suspension			400	400	455	455

H2 4WD—V8—Truck Equipment Schedule T3
Sport Utility 4D	N238	56410	27000	28200	28800	33200
Third Row Seat			400	400	455	455
Adventure Pkg	7		250	250	285	285
Luxury Pkg	8		250	250	285	285
Air Suspension			400	400	455	455

H2 SUT 4WD—V8—Truck Equipment Schedule T3
Sport Utility Pickup	N928	56455	28200	29400	30000	34400
Adventure Pkg			250	250	285	285

TRUCKS & VANS

Body Type	VIN	List	Trade-In Good	Very Good	Pvt-Party Good	Retail Excellent
Luxury Pkg		0	250	250	285	285
Air Suspension			400	400	455	455

2009 HUMMER — 5G(R,TorN)-(N13E)-9-#

H3T 4WD—5-Cyl.—Truck Equipment Schedule T3
Sport Utility Pickup	N13E	33190	18350	19100	20400	23900
Adventure Pkg			300	300	350	350
Luxury Pkg			300	300	350	350
Off-Road Suspension			400	400	465	465

H3T ALPHA—V8—Truck Equipment Schedule T3
Sport Utility Pickup	N63L	36760	19450	20200	21500	25100
Adventure Pkg			300	300	345	345
Off-Road Suspension			400	400	465	465

H3 4WD—5-Cyl.—Truck Equipment Schedule T3
Sport Utility 4D	N13E	34785	14200	14850	16100	19000
Adventure Pkg			300	300	350	350
Luxury Pkg			300	300	350	350
Off-Road Suspension			400	400	470	470

H3x 4WD—5-Cyl.—Truck Equipment Schedule T3
| Sport Utility 4D | N53E | 42830 | 19050 | 19800 | 21100 | 24600 |
| H3X Pkg | | | 300 | 300 | 345 | 345 |

H3 ALPHA 4WD—V8—Truck Equipment Schedule T3
Sport Utility 4D	N63L	41405	19050	19800	21100	24600
H3X Pkg			300	300	345	345
Off-Road Suspension			400	400	460	460

H2 4WD—V8—Truck Equipment Schedule T3
Sport Utility 4D	N238	57590	35700	37100	37300	42100
Third Row Seat			475	475	525	525
Adventure Pkg			300	300	335	335
Luxury Pkg			300	300	335	335
Air Suspension			400	400	445	445

H2 SUT 4WD—V8—Truck Equipment Schedule T3
Sport Utility Pickup	N228	57635	37700	39200	39200	44100
Adventure Pkg			300	300	330	330
Luxury Pkg			300	300	330	330
Air Suspension			400	400	440	440

2010 HUMMER — 5G(R,TorN)-(NGDE)-A-#

H3T 4WD—5-Cyl.—Truck Equipment Schedule T3
Sport Util Pickup	NGDE	33390	21900	22800	23900	27500
Adventure Pkg			350	350	400	400
Luxury Pkg			350	350	400	400
Off-Road Suspension			400	400	455	455

H3T ALPHA 4WD—V8 Flex Fuel—Truck Equipment Schedule T3
| Sport Util Pickup | NKDP | 36460 | 23400 | 24300 | 25500 | 29400 |

H3 4WD—5-Cyl.—Truck Equipment Schedule T3
Sport Utility 4D	NGDE	35865	17950	18700	19850	23000
Adventure Pkg			350	350	400	400
Luxury Pkg			350	350	400	400
Off-Road Suspension			400	400	460	460

H3 ALPHA 4WD—V8—Truck Equipment Schedule T3
Sport Utility 4D	NLDP	42485	21900	22800	23900	27600
Adventure Pkg			350	350	400	400
Off-Road Suspension			400	400	455	455

HYUNDAI

2001 HYUNDAI — KM8S(B72D)-1-#

SANTA FE 4WD—V6—Truck Equipment Schedule T2
GL Sport Utility 4D	B72D	20234	250	250	825	1400
GLS Sport Utility 4D	C72D	21234	375	475	1275	2175
LX Sport Utility 4D	C72D	22434	825	975	1825	3025
2WD		8	(300)	(300)	(400)	(400)
4-Cyl, 2.4 Liter		B	(225)	(225)	(315)	(315)

2002 HYUNDAI — KM8S(B82B)-2-#

SANTA FE—4-Cyl.—Equipment Schedule T2
| Sport Utility 4D | B82B | 17694 | 425 | 525 | 1225 | 2025 |

SANTA FE—V6—Truck Equipment Schedule T2
| GLS Sport Utility 4D | C72D | 21594 | 1025 | 1200 | 1950 | 3125 |

2002 HYUNDAI

Body Type	VIN	List	Trade-In Good	Very Good	Pvt-Party Good	Retail Excellent
LX Sport Utility 4D	C72D	23794	1575	1800	2700	4225
2WD	8		(375)	(375)	(500)	(500)

2003 HYUNDAI — KM8S(B82B)-3-#

SANTA FE—4-Cyl.—Truck Equipment Schedule T2

Body Type	VIN	List	Trade-In Good	Very Good	Pvt-Party Good	Retail Excellent
Sport Utility 4D	B82B	17894	675	800	1525	2475

SANTA FE 4WD—V6—Truck Equipment Schedule T2

Body Type	VIN	List	Trade-In Good	Very Good	Pvt-Party Good	Retail Excellent
GLS Sport Utility 4D	C72D	21894	1425	1625	2400	3725
LX Sport Utility 4D	C72D	24394	2000	2275	3200	4875
2WD	8		(450)	(450)	(600)	(600)
V6, 3.5 Liter	E		325	325	435	435

2004 HYUNDAI — KM8S(B82B)-4-#

SANTA FE—4-Cyl.—Truck Equipment Schedule T2

Body Type	VIN	List	Trade-In Good	Very Good	Pvt-Party Good	Retail Excellent
Sport Utility 4D	B82B	18589	875	1000	1775	2875

SANTA FE 4WD—V6—Truck Equipment Schedule T2

Body Type	VIN	List	Trade-In Good	Very Good	Pvt-Party Good	Retail Excellent
GLS Sport Utility 4D	C72D	23089	1475	1675	2600	4100
LX Sport Utility 4D	C72E	26089	2400	2700	3825	5900
2WD	8		(525)	(525)	(700)	(700)
V6, 3.5 Liter	E		350	350	480	480

2005 HYUNDAI — KM8(SC73D)-5-#

SANTA FE 4WD—V6—Truck Equipment Schedule T2

Body Type	VIN	List	Trade-In Good	Very Good	Pvt-Party Good	Retail Excellent
GLS Sport Utility 4D	SC73D	23594	2700	3050	3900	5675
LX Sport Utility 4D	SC73E	26594	3450	3850	4925	7075
2WD	1		(600)	(600)	(800)	(800)
V6, 3.5 Liter (GLS)	E		400	400	525	525

TUCSON—4-Cyl.—Truck Equipment Schedule T1

Body Type	VIN	List	Trade-In Good	Very Good	Pvt-Party Good	Retail Excellent
GL Sport Utility 4D	JM12B	18894	1900	2125	2800	4000
4WD	6		600	600	755	755

TUCSON 4WD—V6—Truck Equipment Schedule T1

Body Type	VIN	List	Trade-In Good	Very Good	Pvt-Party Good	Retail Excellent
GLS Sport Util 4D	JN72D	22094	3325	3650	4375	6000
LX Sport Utility 4D	JN72D	23344	4175	4550	5475	7425
2WD	1		(600)	(600)	(740)	(740)

2006 HYUNDAI — KM8(SC73D)-6-#

SANTA FE 4WD—V6—Truck Equipment Schedule T2

Body Type	VIN	List	Trade-In Good	Very Good	Pvt-Party Good	Retail Excellent
GLS Sport Util 4D	SC73D	23795	3825	4225	5175	7225
Limited Sport Util	SC73E	26495	4825	5275	6400	8900
2WD	1		(650)	(650)	(865)	(865)
V6, 3.5 Liter (GLS)	E		425	425	575	575

TUCSON—4-Cyl.—Truck Equipment Schedule T1

Body Type	VIN	List	Trade-In Good	Very Good	Pvt-Party Good	Retail Excellent
GL Sport Utility 4D	JM12B	19345	2675	2950	3675	5000
4WD	7		650	650	835	835

TUCSON 4WD—V6—Truck Equipment Schedule T1

Body Type	VIN	List	Trade-In Good	Very Good	Pvt-Party Good	Retail Excellent
GLS Sport Util 4D	JN72D	22495	3900	4225	5000	6675
Limited Sport Util	JN12D	22845	4125	4475	5275	7025
2WD	1		(650)	(650)	(825)	(825)

2007 HYUNDAI — KM8(JM72B)-7-#

TUCSON 4WD—4-Cyl.—Truck Equipment Schedule T1

Body Type	VIN	List	Trade-In Good	Very Good	Pvt-Party Good	Retail Excellent
GLS Sport Util 4D	JM72B	18995	4350	4700	5475	7200
2WD	1		(700)	(700)	(895)	(895)

TUCSON—V6—Truck Equipment Schedule T1

Body Type	VIN	List	Trade-In Good	Very Good	Pvt-Party Good	Retail Excellent
Limited Sport Util	JN12D	22845	4650	5025	5850	7675
4WD	1		975	975	1265	1265

TUCSON 4WD—V6—Truck Equipment Schedule T1

Body Type	VIN	List	Trade-In Good	Very Good	Pvt-Party Good	Retail Excellent
SE Sport Utility 4D	JN72D	22995	5250	5650	6500	8500
2WD	1		(700)	(700)	(895)	(895)

SANTA FE—V6—Truck Equipment Schedule T2

Body Type	VIN	List	Trade-In Good	Very Good	Pvt-Party Good	Retail Excellent
Limited Sport Util	SH13E	26595	6350	6875	8100	10800
Third Row Seat			250	250	335	335
AWD	7		775	775	1035	1035

SANTA FE AWD—V6—Truck Equipment Schedule T2

Body Type	VIN	List	Trade-In Good	Very Good	Pvt-Party Good	Retail Excellent
GLS Sport Utility 4D	SG73D	24795	5350	5825	6925	9275
Third Row Seat			250	250	335	335
2WD	1		(700)	(700)	(935)	(935)

SANTA FE AWD—V6—Truck Equipment Schedule T2

Body Type	VIN	List	Trade-In Good	Very Good	Pvt-Party Good	Retail Excellent
SE Sport Utility 4D	SH73E	26295	5775	6250	7475	9950
Third Row Seat			250	250	335	335
2WD	1		(700)	(700)	(935)	(935)

2007 HYUNDAI

Body Type	VIN	List	Trade-In Good	Very Good	Pvt-Party Good	Retail Excellent
VERACRUZ—V6—Truck Equipment Schedule T1						
GLS Sport Util 4D	NU13C	28695	6300	6825	7625	9725
SE Sport Utility 4D	NU13C	30395	6875	7425	8200	10450
Limited Sport Util	NU73C	34695	7850	8450	9325	11900
AWD	7		525	525	655	655
ENTOURAGE—V6—Truck Equipment Schedule T1						
GLS Minivan	MC233	24495	4000	4375	5475	7725
SE Minivan	MC233	26995	4325	4725	5850	8250
Limited Minivan	MC233	29495	4950	5375	6600	9225

2008 HYUNDAI — KM8(JM12B)–8–#

Body Type	VIN	List	Trade-In Good	Very Good	Pvt-Party Good	Retail Excellent
TUCSON—4-Cyl.—Truck Equipment Schedule T1						
GLS Sport Util 4D	JM12B	20195	4825	5200	6075	7900
TUCSON—V6—Truck Equipment Schedule T1						
Limited Sport Util	JN12D	23545	5850	6275	7375	9525
4WD	7		1075	1075	1390	1390
TUCSON 4WD—V6—Truck Equipment Schedule T1						
SE Sport Utility 4D	JN72D	23645	6550	7000	8150	10500
2WD			(750)	(750)	(970)	(970)
SANTA FE—V6—Truck Equipment Schedule T2						
Limited Sport Util	SH13E	28945	7900	8450	9550	12150
Third Row Seat			250	250	325	325
AWD	7		825	825	1065	1065
SANTA FE AWD—V6—Truck Equipment Schedule T2						
GLS Sport Util 4D	SG73D	24495	6500	6975	7900	10050
SE Sport Utility 4D	SH73E	26495	7325	7850	8950	11400
Third Row Seat			250	250	325	325
2WD	1		(750)	(750)	(970)	(970)
VERACRUZ—V6—Truck Equipment Schedule T1						
GLS Sport Util 4D	NU13C	27595	7325	7825	8600	10650
SE Sport Utility 4D	NU13C	29295	8150	8700	9450	11650
Limited Sport Util	NU13C	34745	9100	9700	10550	13000
AWD	7		550	550	680	680
ENTOURAGE—V6—Truck Equipment Schedule T1						
GLS Minivan	MC233	24595	5200	5600	6625	8850
Limited Minivan	MC233	30495	5975	6425	7700	10250

2009 HYUNDAI — KM8(JM12B)–9–#

Body Type	VIN	List	Trade-In Good	Very Good	Pvt-Party Good	Retail Excellent
TUCSON—4-Cyl.—Truck Equipment Schedule T1						
GLS Sport Util 4D	JM12B	20695	6075	6475	7650	9800
TUCSON—V6—Truck Equipment Schedule T1						
Limited Sport Util	JN12D	24645	7400	7850	9250	11850
4WD	7		1175	1175	1540	1540
TUCSON 4WD—V6—Truck Equipment Schedule T1						
SE Sport Utility 4D	JN72D	24195	8050	8525	9950	12700
2WD	1		(875)	(875)	(1160)	(1160)
SANTA FE—V6—Truck Equipment Schedule T2						
Limited Sport Util	SH13E	29595	9225	9775	11000	13750
Third Row Seat			300	300	385	385
AWD	7		950	950	1215	1215
SANTA FE AWD—V6—Truck Equipment Schedule T2						
GLS Sport Util 4D	SG73D	25445	7950	8425	9525	11900
SE Sport Utility 4D	SH73E	27345	8750	9250	10400	13000
Third Row Seat			300	300	380	380
2WD	1		(875)	(875)	(1110)	(1110)
VERACRUZ—V6—Truck Equipment Schedule T1						
GLS Sport Util 4D	NU13C	27595	8900	9425	10500	12950
Limited Sport Util	NU13C	36745	10450	11050	12200	15000
AWD	7		650	650	815	815

2010 HYUNDAI — KM8(JT3AC)–A–#

Body Type	VIN	List	Trade-In Good	Very Good	Pvt-Party Good	Retail Excellent
TUCSON AWD—4-Cyl.—Truck Equipment Schedule T1						
GLS Sport Util 4D	JT3AC	20790	9300	9825	10700	12850
2WD	3		(1000)	(1000)	(1170)	(1170)
TUCSON—V6—Truck Equipment Schedule T1						
Limited Sport Util	JU3AC	25140	10700	11250	12150	14500
AWD	C		1000	1000	1160	1160
SANTA FE—Truck Equipment Schedule T2						
Limited Sport Util	SKDAG	29390	11850	12450	13750	16600
AWD	D		1000	1000	1250	1250
4-Cyl, 2.4 Liter	B		(475)	(475)	(600)	(600)

2010 HYUNDAI

Body Type	VIN	List	Trade-In Good	Very Good	Pvt-Party Good	Retail Excellent
SANTA FE AWD—4-Cyl.—Truck Equipment Schedule T2						
GLS Sport Util 4D	SGDAB	25490	10350	10850	12100	14750
2WD	3		(1000)	(1000)	(1250)	(1250)
SANTA FE AWD—V6—Truck Equipment Schedule T2						
SE Sport Util 4D	SHDAG	28690	11200	11750	13100	16000
2WD	3		(1000)	(1000)	(1250)	(1250)
VERACRUZ—V6—Truck Equipment Schedule T1						
GLS Sport Util 4D	NU4CC	30795	10550	11100	12050	14400
Limited Sport Util	NU4CC	36645	12400	13000	14050	16800
AWD	7		725	725	865	865

2011 HYUNDAI — KM8(JT3AB)—B—#

Body Type	VIN	List	Trade-In Good	Very Good	Pvt-Party Good	Retail Excellent
TUCSON AWD—4-Cyl.—Truck Equipment Schedule T1						
GL Sport Utility	JT3AB	20540	10150	10700	11700	14000
GLS Sport Util 4D	JTCAC	24290	12400	13000	14150	16850
2WD	C		(1100)	(1100)	(1290)	(1290)
TUCSON—V6—Truck Equipment Schedule T1						
Limited Sport Util	JU3AC	25490	12750	13400	14500	17250
AWD	C		1000	1000	1165	1165
SANTA FE—V6—Truck Equipment Schedule T2						
Limited Sport Util	ZK4AG	29790	13350	13950	15300	18200
AWD	D		1000	1000	1160	1160
4-Cyl, 2.4 Liter	B		(475)	(475)	(570)	(570)
SANTA FE AWD—V6—Truck Equipment Schedule T2						
GLS Sport Util 4D	ZGDAG	25490	12250	12800	14000	16600
2WD	3		(1100)	(1100)	(1285)	(1285)
4-Cyl, 2.4 Liter	B		(475)	(475)	(570)	(570)
SANTA FE AWD—V6—Truck Equipment Schedule T2						
SE Sport Util 4D	ZHDAG	28690	12800	13400	14650	17400
2WD	3		(1100)	(1100)	(1285)	(1285)
VERACRUZ—V6—Truck Equipment Schedule T1						
GLS Sport Util 4D	NU4CC	30840	12100	12650	13950	16700
Limited Sport Util	NU4CC	36690	13750	14350	15900	19000
AWD	D		800	800	980	980

2012 HYUNDAI — 5(NMorXY)orKM8(JT3AB)—C—#

Body Type	VIN	List	Trade-In Good	Very Good	Pvt-Party Good	Retail Excellent
TUCSON—4-Cyl.—Truck Equipment Schedule T1						
GL Sport Utility 4D	JT3AB	20855	11150	11700	12750	15100
TUCSON—V6—Truck Equipment Schedule T1						
Limited Sport Util	JU3AC	25705	14100	14750	15950	18850
AWD	D		1125	1125	1285	1285
TUCSON AWD—4-Cyl.—Truck Equipment Schedule T1						
GLS Sport Utility	JUCAC	24655	13600	14200	15450	18250
2WD	3		(1500)	(1500)	(1715)	(1715)
SANTA FE—4-Cyl.—Truck Equipment Schedule T2						
Limited Sport Util	ZK4AG	30035	14200	14750	16150	19050
AWD	D		1125	1125	1305	1305
V6, 3.5 Liter	G		500	500	580	580
SANTA FE AWD—V6—Truck Equipment Schedule T2						
GLS Sport Util 4D	ZGDAG	27635	13750	14300	15600	18300
2WD	3,4		(1500)	(1500)	(1725)	(1725)
4-Cyl, 2.4 Liter	B		(500)	(500)	(565)	(565)
SANTA FE AWD—V6—Truck Equipment Schedule T2						
SE Sport Util 4D	ZHDAG	28920	13700	14250	15650	18400
2WD	4		(1500)	(1500)	(1735)	(1735)
VERACRUZ—V6—Truck Equipment Schedule T1						
GLS Sport Util 4D	NU4CC	29155	14000	14550	16050	18950
Limited Sport Util	NU4CC	35305	15650	16200	17750	20900
AWD	D		875	875	1055	1055

2013 HYUNDAI — 5(NMorXY)orKM8(JT3AB)—D—#

Body Type	VIN	List	Trade-In Good	Very Good	Pvt-Party Good	Retail Excellent
TUCSON—4-Cyl.—Truck Equipment Schedule T1						
GL Sport Utility 4D	JT3AB	21070	12550	13150	14250	16750
TUCSON AWD—4-Cyl.—Truck Equipment Schedule T1						
GLS Sport Utility	JU3AC	24920	14900	15600	16750	19600
Limited Sport Util	JUCAC	27770	16300	17000	18200	21300
2WD	3		(1300)	(1300)	(1485)	(1485)
SANTA FE SPORT AWD—4-Cyl.—Truck Equipment Schedule T2						
Sport Utility 4D	ZTDLB	27025	16000	16550	17800	20600
2WD	3		(1300)	(1300)	(1480)	(1480)
SANTA FE SPORT AWD—4-Cyl. Turbo—Truck Equipment Schedule T2						
2.0T Sport Util 4D	ZUDLA	30275	18900	19550	20800	23900

TRUCKS & VANS

2013 HYUNDAI

Body Type	VIN	List	Trade-In Good	Very Good	Pvt-Party Good	Retail Excellent
2WD 3			(1300)	(1300)	(1485)	(1485)
SANTA FE AWD—V6—Truck Equipment Schedule T2						
GLS Sport Util .... SMDHF	30945	20500	21200	22000	24800
FWD 4			(1500)	(1500)	(1635)	(1635)
SANTA FE—V6—Truck Equipment Schedule T2						
Limited Sport Util SR4HF	33945	21900	22600	23300	26100
AWD .... D			1250	1250	1350	1350

2014 HYUNDAI — 5(NMorXY)orKM8(JUDAF)-E-#

Body Type	VIN	List	Trade-In Good	Very Good	Pvt-Party Good	Retail Excellent
TUCSON AWD—4-Cyl.—Truck Equipment Schedule T1						
GLS Sport Utility .... JUDAF	23805	15550	16250	17200	19850
SE Sport Utility .... JUDAG	25855	16650	17350	18200	20900
Limited Sport Util .... JUDAG	28555	18900	19700	20400	23100
2WD 3,4			(1500)	(1500)	(1680)	(1680)
SANTA FE SPORT AWD—4-Cyl.—Truck Equipment Schedule T1						
Sport Utility 4D .... ZUDLS	27385	17200	17800	19250	22300
2WD 3			(1400)	(1400)	(1610)	(1610)
SANTA FE SPORT AWD—4-Cyl. Turbo—Truck Equipment Schedule T1						
2.0T Sport Utility .... ZWDLA	33085	20300	20900	22400	25900
2WD 3			(1400)	(1400)	(1620)	(1620)
SANTA FE AWD—V6—Truck Equipment Schedule T1						
GLS Sport Util .... SMDHF	32405	21800	22500	23400	26300
FWD 4			(1500)	(1500)	(1645)	(1645)
SANTA FE—V6—Truck Equipment Schedule T1						
Limited Sport Util SN4HF	34555	24500	25300	26200	29400
AWD .... D			1375	1375	1495	1495

INFINITI

2000 INFINITI — JNR(AR05Y)-Y-#

Body Type	VIN	List	Trade-In Good	Very Good	Pvt-Party Good	Retail Excellent
QX4 4WD—V6—Truck Equipment Schedule T3						
Sport Utility 4D AR05Y	36075	2075	2350	3275	5000

2001 INFINITI — JNR(DR07Y)-1-#

Body Type	VIN	List	Trade-In Good	Very Good	Pvt-Party Good	Retail Excellent
QX4 4WD—V6—Truck Equipment Schedule T3						
Sport Utility 4D DR07Y	36075	2250	2525	3475	5250
2WD X			(650)	(650)	(860)	(860)

2002 INFINITI — JNR(DR07Y)-2-#

Body Type	VIN	List	Trade-In Good	Very Good	Pvt-Party Good	Retail Excellent
QX4 4WD—V6—Truck Equipment Schedule T3						
Sport Utility 4D DR07Y	36095	2650	2975	3850	5675
2WD X			(725)	(725)	(970)	(970)

2003 INFINITI — JNR(AS08W)-3-#

Body Type	VIN	List	Trade-In Good	Very Good	Pvt-Party Good	Retail Excellent
FX35 AWD—V6—Truck Equipment Schedule T3						
Sport Utility 4D AS08W	36245	6375	6825	7900	10200
Intelligent Cruise Ctrl			250	250	325	325
Sport Pkg			325	325	425	425
2WD .... U			(800)	(800)	(1060)	(1060)
FX45 AWD—V8—Truck Equipment Schedule T3						
Sport Utility 4D BS08W	44770	5950	6375	7600	9875
Intelligent Cruise Ctrl			250	250	335	335
QX4 4WD—V6—Truck Equipment Schedule T3						
Sport Utility 4D DR09Y	36695	3175	3525	4425	6400
2WD .... U			(800)	(800)	(1080)	(1080)

2004 INFINITI — JNR(AS08W)-4-#

Body Type	VIN	List	Trade-In Good	Very Good	Pvt-Party Good	Retail Excellent
FX35 AWD—V6—Truck Equipment Schedule T3						
Sport Utility 4D AS08W	36395	6900	7350	8475	10800
Intelligent Cruise Ctrl			275	275	355	355
Sport Pkg			350	350	455	455
2WD .... U			(900)	(900)	(1160)	(1160)
FX45 AWD—V8—Truck Equipment Schedule T3						
Sport Utility 4D BS08W	44920	6850	7300	8650	11200
Intelligent Cruise Ctrl			275	275	365	365
QX56 4WD—V8—Truck Equipment Schedule T3						
Sport Utility 4D AA08C	51080	7250	7750	8875	11600
Intelligent Cruise Ctrl			275	275	360	360
2WD			(900)	(900)	(1170)	(1170)

Body Type	VIN	List	Trade-In Good	Very Good	Pvt-Party Good	Retail Excellent
2005 INFINITI — JNR(AS08W)-5-#						
FX35 AWD—V6—Truck Equipment Schedule T3						
Sport Utility 4D	AS08W	37060	8075	8575	9675	12200
Adaptive Cruise Control			300	300	385	385
Sport Pkg			375	375	480	480
2WD	U		(975)	(975)	(1255)	(1255)
FX45 AWD—V8—Truck Equipment Schedule T3						
Sport Utility 4D	BS08W	46060	7850	8350	9700	12350
Adaptive Cruise Control			300	300	395	395
QX56 4WD—V8—Truck Equipment Schedule T3						
Sport Utility 4D	AA08C	51700	8425	8975	10250	13300
Adaptive Cruise Control			300	300	395	395
2WD			(975)	(975)	(1290)	(1290)
2006 INFINITI — JNR(AS08W)-6-#						
FX35 AWD—V6—Truck Equipment Schedule T3						
Sport Utility 4D	AS08W	40050	9375	9925	11350	14150
Adaptive Cruise Control			325	325	410	410
Sport Pkg			400	400	505	505
2WD	U		(650)	(650)	(825)	(825)
FX45 AWD—V8—Truck Equipment Schedule T3						
Sport Utility 4D	BS08W	50500	10500	11100	12650	15650
Adaptive Cruise Control			325	325	410	410
QX56 4WD—V8—Truck Equipment Schedule T3						
Sport Utility 4D	AA08C	53250	10550	11200	12500	15750
Adaptive Cruise Control			325	325	415	415
2WD	A		(650)	(650)	(825)	(825)
2007 INFINITI — JNR(AS08W)-7-#						
FX35 AWD—V6—Truck Equipment Schedule T3						
Sport Utility 4D	AS08W	40000	11050	11600	12950	15850
Adaptive Cruise Control			350	350	430	430
Sport Pkg			425	425	525	525
RWD	U		(700)	(700)	(860)	(860)
FX45 AWD—V8—Truck Equipment Schedule T3						
Sport Utility 4D	BS08W	50550	11550	12150	13700	16850
Adaptive Cruise Control			350	350	435	435
QX56 4WD—V8—Truck Equipment Schedule T3						
Sport Utility 4D	AA08C	53850	12050	12750	14000	17300
Adaptive Cruise Control			350	350	435	435
2WD	A		(700)	(700)	(870)	(870)
2008 INFINITI — JNR(AJ09E)-8-#						
EX35—V6—Truck Equipment Schedule T3						
Journey Sport Util	AJ09E	35665	10750	11400	12150	14750
Adaptive Cruise Control			375	375	440	440
AWD			825	825	955	955
EX35 AWD—V6—Truck Equipment Schedule T3						
Sport Utility 4D	AJ09F	33415	10650	11250	12050	14650
RWD			(750)	(750)	(875)	(875)
FX35 AWD—V6—Truck Equipment Schedule T3						
Sport Utility 4D	AS08W	40365	12550	13200	14400	17250
Adaptive Cruise Control			375	375	450	450
Sport Pkg			475	475	565	565
RWD	U		(750)	(750)	(895)	(895)
FX45 AWD—V8—Truck Equipment Schedule T3						
Sport Utility 4D	BS08W	50915	15150	15850	17050	20100
Adaptive Cruise Control			375	375	440	440
QX56 4WD—V8—Truck Equipment Schedule T3						
Sport Utility 4D	AA08C	56165	15850	16650	17750	21300
Adaptive Cruise Control			375	375	450	450
2WD	D		(750)	(750)	(895)	(895)
2009 INFINITI — JNR(AJ09E)-9-#						
EX35—V6—Truck Equipment Schedule T3						
Journey Sport Util	AJ09E	36865	14100	14850	15750	18700
Intelligent Cruise Ctrl			375	375	425	425
AWD	F		950	950	1080	1080
EX35 AWD—V6—Truck Equipment Schedule T3						
Sport Utility 4D	AJ09F	36065	13850	14600	15500	18400

Body Type	VIN	List	Trade-In Good	Very Good	Pvt-Party Good	Retail Excellent
RWD			(875)	(875)	(995)	(995)
FX35 AWD—V6—Truck Equipment Schedule T3						
Sport Utility 4D	AS18W	44465	17400	18100	19200	22300
Premium Pkg			725	725	820	820
Adaptive Cruise Control			375	375	430	430
RWD	U		(875)	(875)	(1005)	(1005)
FX50 AWD—V8—Truck Equipment Schedule T3						
Sport Utility 4D	BS18W	59265	21700	22600	23400	26800
Adaptive Cruise Control			375	375	425	425
Sport Pkg			525	525	595	595
QX56 4WD—V8—Truck Equipment Schedule T3						
Sport Utility 4D	AA08C	59015	19600	20400	21500	25200
Adaptive Cruise Control			375	375	435	435
2WD	D		(875)	(875)	(1020)	(1020)

2010 INFINITI — (5orJ)N(1,3or8)(AJ0HP)–A–#

Body Type	VIN	List	Trade-In Good	Very Good	Pvt-Party Good	Retail Excellent
EX35—V6—Truck Equipment Schedule T3						
Journey Sport Util	AJ0HP	36895	15800	16550	17400	20200
Intelligent Cruise Ctrl			400	400	450	450
Premium Pkg			750	750	855	855
AWD	R		1000	1000	1120	1120
EX35 AWD—V6—Truck Equipment Schedule T3						
Sport Utility 4D	AJ0HR	36065	15600	16350	17150	19900
Intelligent Cruise Ctrl			400	400	450	450
Premium Pkg			750	750	855	855
RWD	P		(1000)	(1000)	(1125)	(1125)
FX35 AWD—V6—Truck Equipment Schedule T3						
Sport Utility 4D	AS1MW	44715	20000	20800	21800	24900
Premium Pkg			750	750	865	865
Adaptive Cruise Control			400	400	455	455
RWD	U		(1000)	(1000)	(1135)	(1135)
FX50 AWD—V8—Truck Equipment Schedule T3						
Sport Utility 4D	BS1MW	59265	24900	25900	26600	30200
Adaptive Cruise Control			400	400	450	450
Sport Pkg			575	575	645	645
QX56 4WD—V8—Truck Equipment Schedule T3						
Sport Utility 4D	ZA0NE	60015	24000	25000	25900	29700
Adaptive Cruise Control			400	400	455	455
2WD	F		(1000)	(1000)	(1135)	(1135)

2011 INFINITI — (5orJ)N(1or8)(AJ0HP)–B–#

Body Type	VIN	List	Trade-In Good	Very Good	Pvt-Party Good	Retail Excellent
EX35—V6—Truck Equipment Schedule T3						
Journey Sport Util	AJ0HP	37300	18700	19450	20200	23000
Intelligent Cruise Ctrl			425	425	465	465
Premium Pkg			800	800	885	885
AWD	R		1000	1000	1090	1090
EX35 AWD—V6—Truck Equipment Schedule T3						
Sport Utility 4D	AJ0HR	36425	18400	19150	19900	22700
Intelligent Cruise Ctrl			425	425	465	465
Premium Pkg			800	800	885	885
RWD	P		(1100)	(1100)	(1210)	(1210)
FX35 AWD—V6—Truck Equipment Schedule T3						
Sport Utility 4D	AS1MW	43925	24300	25100	26100	29400
Adaptive Cruise Control			425	425	470	470
Premium Pkg			800	800	895	895
RWD	U		(1100)	(1100)	(1225)	(1225)
FX50 AWD—V8—Truck Equipment Schedule T3						
Sport Utility 4D	BS1MW	57275	28100	29200	29700	33200
Adaptive Cruise Control			425	425	465	465
Sport Pkg			625	625	685	685
QX56 4WD—V8—Truck Equipment Schedule T3						
Sport Utility 4D	AZ2NE	60665	35100	36300	36600	40800
Adaptive Cruise Control			425	425	465	465
2WD	F		(1100)	(1100)	(1205)	(1205)

2012 INFINITI — (5orJ)N(1or8)(AJ0HP)–C–#

Body Type	VIN	List	Trade-In Good	Very Good	Pvt-Party Good	Retail Excellent
EX35—V6—Truck Equipment Schedule T3						
Journey Sport Util	AJ0HP	38850	21600	22400	23000	25900
Intelligent Cruise Ctrl			450	450	490	490
Premium Pkg			850	850	930	930
AWD	R		1125	1125	1220	1220

2012 INFINITI

Body Type	VIN	List	Good	Very Good	Good	Excellent
EX35 AWD—V6—Truck Equipment Schedule T3						
Sport Utility 4D	AJ0HR	37895	21300	22100	22700	25600
Intelligent Cruise Ctrl			450	450	490	490
RWD	P		(1200)	(1200)	(1305)	(1305)
FX35 AWD—V6—Truck Equipment Schedule T3						
Sport Utility 4D	AS1MW	45795	25800	26600	27600	31000
Limited Edition	AS1MW	52445	28200	29100	30000	33600
Adaptive Cruise Control			450	450	500	500
Premium Pkg			850	850	950	950
RWD	U		(1200)	(1200)	(1330)	(1330)
FX50 AWD—V8—Truck Equipment Schedule T3						
Sport Utility 4D	BS1MW	60245	35500	36700	37000	41000
Adaptive Cruise Control			450	450	485	485
Sport Pkg			700	700	760	760
QX56 4WD—V8—Truck Equipment Schedule T3						
Sport Utility 4D	AZ2NE	62790	41100	42400	42500	46800
Adaptive Cruise Control			450	450	485	485
2WD	F		(1500)	(1500)	(1620)	(1620)

2013 INFINITI — (5orJ)N(1or8)(AL0MM)—D—#

Body Type	VIN	List	Good	Very Good	Good	Excellent
JX35 AWD—V6—Truck Equipment Schedule T1						
Sport Utility 4D	AL0MM	42500	30500	31500	32100	35900
FWD			(1300)	(1300)	(1420)	(1420)
EX37—V6—Truck Equipment Schedule T3						
Journey Sport Util	BJ0HP	39600	26400	27300	28400	32100
Intelligent Cruise Ctrl			475	475	525	525
Premium Pkg			900	900	1000	1000
AWD	F,L,R		1250	1250	1385	1385
EX37 AWD—V6—Truck Equipment Schedule T3						
Sport Utility 4D	BJ0HR	38700	25500	26300	27500	31200
Intelligent Cruise Ctrl			475	475	525	525
RWD	E,K,P		(1300)	(1300)	(1445)	(1445)
FX37 AWD—V6—Truck Equipment Schedule T3						
Sport Utility 4D	CS1MW	46700	26700	27500	28500	31900
Limited Edition	CS1MW	53700	29100	30000	31000	34600
Adaptive Cruise Control			475	475	525	525
Premium Pkg			900	900	995	995
RWD	U,N,7,P		(1300)	(1300)	(1435)	(1435)
FX50 AWD—V8—Truck Equipment Schedule T3						
Sport Utility 4D	BS1MW	61600	37400	38700	39100	43400
Adaptive Cruise Control			475	475	515	515
QX56 4WD—V8—Truck Equipment Schedule T3						
Sport Utility 4D	AZ2NE	64740	44400	45700	45900	50300
Adaptive Cruise Control			475	475	510	510
Technology Pkg			450	450	485	485
Touring Pkg			900	900	970	970
2WD	D,F		(1500)	(1500)	(1610)	(1610)

2014 INFINITI — (5orJ)N(1or8)(BJ0HR)—E—#

Body Type	VIN	List	Good	Very Good	Good	Excellent
QX50 AWD—V6—Truck Equipment Schedule T3						
Sport Utility 4D	BJ0HR	36795	27100	28000	29000	32900
RWD	P		(1400)	(1400)	(1545)	(1545)
QX50—V6—Truck Equipment Schedule T3						
Journey Sport Util	BJ0HP	38045	28100	29100	30000	33900
Premium Pkg			950	950	1045	1045
Technology Pkg			475	475	525	525
AWD	R		1375	1375	1515	1515
QX60 AWD—4-Cyl. Supercharged Hybrid—Truck Equipment Sch T3						
Sport Utility 4D	CL0MM	47495	34800	35900	36300	40300
Intelligent Cruise Ctrl			500	500	540	540
FWD	N		(1500)	(1500)	(1625)	(1625)
QX60 AWD—V6—Truck Equipment Schedule T3						
3.5 Sport Utility	AL0MM	43945	32200	33300	33800	37700
Intelligent Cruise Ctrl			500	500	545	545
Technology Pkg			475	475	520	520
Touring Pkg			950	950	1035	1035
FWD	N		(1500)	(1500)	(1630)	(1630)
QX70 AWD—V6—Truck Equipment Schedule T3						
3.7 Sport Utility	CS1MW	47395	30200	31200	32200	35900
Intelligent Cruise Ctrl			500	500	550	550
Technology Pkg			475	475	520	520
Touring Pkg			950	950	1045	1045

TRUCKS & VANS

Body Type	VIN	List	Trade-In Good	Very Good	Pvt-Party Good	Retail Excellent
QX70 AWD—V8—Truck Equipment Schedule T3						
5.0 Sport Utility	BS1MW	62495	42800	44300	44300	48900
Technology Pkg			475	475	510	510
QX80 AWD—V8—Truck Equipment Schedule T3						
Sport Utility 4D	AZ2NE	66645	52300	53800	53700	58400
Intelligent Cruise Ctrl			500	500	530	530
Technology Pkg			475	475	505	505
Deluxe Touring Pkg			950	950	1010	1010
2WD	D,F		(1500)	(1500)	(1590)	(1590)

ISUZU

2000 ISUZU — (JAC,4S2or1GG)–(M57D)–Y–#

Body Type	VIN	List	Trade-In Good	Very Good	Pvt-Party Good	Retail Excellent
AMIGO 4WD—4-Cyl.—Truck Equipment Schedule T2						
S Sport Utility 2D	M57D	20190	1075	1250	2275	3850
Hard Top			50	50	65	65
2WD	K		(275)	(275)	(365)	(365)
V6, 3.2 Liter	W		350	350	465	465
RODEO 4WD—V6—Truck Equipment Schedule T1						
S Sport Utility 4D	M58W	24935	875	1025	2050	3525
LS Sport Utility 4D	M58W	27615	1075	1225	2100	3475
LSE Sport Util 4D	M58W	31760	1625	1850	2925	4700
2WD	K		(550)	(550)	(750)	(750)
4-Cyl, 2.2 Liter	D		(300)	(300)	(400)	(400)
VEHICROSS 4WD—V6—Truck Equipment Schedule T1						
Sport Utility 2D	N57X	31045	2975	3350	4375	6525
TROOPER 4WD—V6—Truck Equipment Schedule T1						
S Sport Utility 4D	J58X	29445	825	950	1850	3125
LS Sport Utility 4D	J58X	31145	1425	1625	2775	4575
Limited Spt Utl 4D	J58X	35193	1600	1825	3025	4950
2WD			(325)	(325)	(445)	(445)
HOMBRE—4-Cyl.—Truck Equipment Schedule T2						
S Short Bed	S144	11855	1425	1575	2350	3925
XS Short Bed	S144	13355	1650	1825	2675	4450
S Spacecab	S194	14180	1800	1975	3000	4950
XS Spacecab	S194	16005	2150	2375	3550	5800
Third Door			100	100	145	145
4WD	T		400	400	535	535
V6, 4.3 Liter	W		125	125	165	165

2001 ISUZU — (JACor4S2)–(M57W)–1–#

Body Type	VIN	List	Trade-In Good	Very Good	Pvt-Party Good	Retail Excellent
RODEO SPORT 4WD—V6—Truck Equipment Schedule T2						
Soft Top 2D	M57W	20270	1675	1900	2950	4700
Hard Top 2D	M57W	20880	1750	1975	3050	4850
2WD	K		(650)	(650)	(860)	(860)
4-Cyl, 2.2 Liter	D		(300)	(300)	(400)	(400)
RODEO 4WD—V6—Truck Equipment Schedule T1						
S Sport Utility 4D	M58W	26025	1250	1425	2500	4250
LS Sport Utility 4D	M58W	27480	1300	1475	2375	3850
LSE Sport Util 4D	M58W	31950	1875	2125	3225	5100
2WD	K		(650)	(650)	(860)	(860)
4-Cyl, 2.2 Liter	D		(300)	(300)	(400)	(400)
VEHICROSS 4WD—V6—Truck Equipment Schedule T1						
Sport Utility 2D	N57X	31045	3525	3925	5050	7350
TROOPER 4WD—V6—Truck Equipment Schedule T1						
S Sport Utility 4D	J58X	29690	1075	1250	2075	3375
LS Sport Utility 4D	J58X	31285	1850	2100	3175	5025
Limited Spt Util 4D	J58X	35333	1950	2225	3450	5525
2WD			(375)	(375)	(510)	(510)

2002 ISUZU — (JACor4S2)–(M57W)–2–#

Body Type	VIN	List	Trade-In Good	Very Good	Pvt-Party Good	Retail Excellent
RODEO SPORT 4WD—V6—Truck Equipment Schedule T2						
Soft Top 2D	M57W	22655	1900	2150	3125	4825
Hard Top 2D	M57W	22380	2250	2525	3575	5500
2WD	K		(725)	(725)	(970)	(970)
4-Cyl, 2.2 Liter	D		(350)	(350)	(465)	(465)
RODEO 4WD—V6—Truck Equipment Schedule T1						
S Sport Utility 4D	M58W	25305	1475	1675	2750	4475
LS Sport Utility 4D	M58W	28355	1650	1875	2875	4500
LSE Sport Util 4D	M58W	32340	2300	2575	3675	5650
2WD	K		(725)	(725)	(970)	(970)

Body Type	VIN	List	Trade-In Good	Very Good	Pvt-Party Good	Retail Excellent
4-Cyl, 2.2 Liter	D		(350)	(350)	(465)	(465)
AXIOM 4WD—V6—Truck Equipment Schedule T1						
Sport Utility 4D	F58X	29625	1550	1750	2725	4275
XS Sport Utility 4D	F58X	31945	1925	2175	3200	4950
2WD			(725)	(725)	(970)	(970)
TROOPER 4WD—V6—Truck Equipment Schedule T1						
S Sport Utility 4D	J58X	30015	1375	1550	2400	3825
LS Sport Utility 4D	J58X	33300	2200	2475	3575	5525
Limited Spt Util 4D	J58X	37270	2400	2700	4025	6350
2WD			(425)	(425)	(575)	(575)

Body Type	VIN	List	Trade-In Good	Very Good	Pvt-Party Good	Retail Excellent
RODEO SPORT—4-Cyl.—Truck Equipment Schedule T2						
S Soft Top 2D	K57D	14624	2175	2450	3400	5125
RODEO SPORT 4WD—V6—Truck Equipment Schedule T2						
S Hard Top 2D	M57W	20040	3275	3650	4775	7075
2WD	K		(800)	(800)	(1080)	(1080)
4-Cyl, 2.2 Liter	D		(375)	(375)	(500)	(500)
RODEO 4WD—V6—Truck Equipment Schedule T1						
S Sport Utility 4D	M58W	22004	1775	2025	3200	5125
2WD	K		(800)	(800)	(1080)	(1080)
4-Cyl, 2.2 Liter	D		(375)	(375)	(500)	(500)
AXIOM 4WD—V6—Truck Equipment Schedule T1						
S Sport Utility 4D	F58X	27620	2250	2550	3450	5150
XS Sport Utility 4D	F58X	30620	2675	3025	4100	6200
2WD	E		(800)	(800)	(1080)	(1080)
ASCENDER 4WD—6-Cyl.—Truck Equipment Schedule T1						
S Sport Utility 4D	T16S	31974	1725	1950	2950	4550
LS			350	350	460	460
Limited			600	600	790	790
2WD	S		(500)	(500)	(665)	(665)
V8, 5.3 Liter	T		225	225	285	285

Body Type	VIN	List	Trade-In Good	Very Good	Pvt-Party Good	Retail Excellent
RODEO 4WD—V6—Truck Equipment Schedule T1						
S Sport Utility 4D	M58W	23479	2175	2425	3725	5875
2WD	K		(900)	(900)	(1190)	(1190)
V6, 3.5 Liter	Y		350	350	475	475
AXIOM 4WD—V6—Truck Equipment Schedule T1						
S Sport Utility 4D	F58X	28149	2975	3300	4375	6450
XS Sport Utility 4D	F58X	31149	3375	3750	5050	7425
2WD	E		(900)	(900)	(1190)	(1190)
ASCENDER 4WD—6-Cyl.—Truck Equipment Schedule T1						
S Sport Utility 4D	T16S	31849	2500	2825	3850	5775
Third Row Seat	3		675	675	915	915
LS			375	375	500	500
Limited			650	650	870	870
2WD	S		(550)	(550)	(735)	(735)
V8, 5.3 Liter	P		225	225	305	305

Body Type	VIN	List	Trade-In Good	Very Good	Pvt-Party Good	Retail Excellent
ASCENDER 4WD—6-Cyl.—Truck Equipment Schedule T1						
S Sport Utility 4D	T16S	32083	2925	3250	4250	6200
Third Row Seat	3		725	725	970	970
LS			400	400	540	540
Limited			725	725	955	955
2WD	S		(600)	(600)	(800)	(800)
V8, 5.3 Liter	M		250	250	330	330

Body Type	VIN	List	Trade-In Good	Very Good	Pvt-Party Good	Retail Excellent
i280 EXTENDED CAB PICKUP—4-Cyl.—Truck Equipment Schedule T2						
S Short Bed	S198	17649	3600	3975	4975	7000
LS Short Bed	S198	19649	4250	4650	5725	7975
i350 CREW CAB PICKUP 4WD—5-Cyl.—Truck Equipment Schedule T2						
LS Short Bed	T136	28018	5825	6325	7800	10700
ASCENDER 4WD—6-Cyl.—Truck Equipment Schedule T1						
S Sport Utility 4D	T16S	31878	3400	3750	4800	6750
Third Row Seat	3		775	775	1025	1025
LS			450	450	585	585
Limited			775	775	1035	1035
2WD	S		(650)	(650)	(865)	(865)
V8, 5.3 Liter	M		275	275	355	355

Body Type	VIN	List	Trade-In Good	Very Good	Pvt-Party Good	Retail Excellent
2007 ISUZU — (1GGor4NU)-(S199)-7-#						
i290 EXTENDED CAB PICKUP—4-Cyl.—Truck Equipment Schedule T2						
S Short Bed	S199	17674	4550	4950	5950	8150
LS Short Bed	S199	20613	5250	5700	6950	9450
i370 EXTENDED CAB PICKUP—5-Cyl.—Truck Equipment Schedule T2						
LS Short Bed	S19E	21763	6075	6575	7950	10750
i370 CREW CAB PICKUP—5-Cyl.—Truck Equipment Schedule T2						
LS Short Bed	S13E	28043	6750	7275	8725	11750
4WD	T		1100	1100	1450	1450
ASCENDER 4WD—6-Cyl.—Truck Equipment Schedule T1						
S Sport Utility 4D	T13S	28694	3925	4300	5350	7350
LS			475	475	625	625
2WD			(700)	(700)	(935)	(935)
2008 ISUZU — (1GGor4NU)-(S199)-8-#						
i290 EXTENDED CAB PICKUP—4-Cyl.—Truck Equipment Schedule T2						
S Short Bed	S199	18084	5100	5500	6725	8950
i370 EXTENDED CAB PICKUP—5-Cyl.—Truck Equipment Schedule T2						
LS Short Bed	S19E	23084	6875	7350	8725	11500
i370 CREW CAB PICKUP—5-Cyl.—Truck Equipment Schedule T2						
LS Short Bed	S13E	25214	7600	8100	9625	12650
4WD	T		1300	1300	1640	1640
ASCENDER 4WD—6-Cyl.—Truck Equipment Schedule T1						
S Sport Utility 4D	T13S	29884	4950	5325	6225	8100
LS			500	500	640	640
2WD	S		(750)	(750)	(960)	(960)

JEEP

Body Type	VIN	List	Trade-In Good	Very Good	Pvt-Party Good	Retail Excellent
2000 JEEP — 1J4-(A29P)-Y-#						
WRANGLER 4WD—4-Cyl.—Truck Equipment Schedule T2						
SE Sport Utility 2D	A29P	16305	3525	3850	5225	7450
Rear Seat			50	50	65	65
Hard Top			250	250	335	335
WRANGLER 4WD—6-Cyl.—Truck Equipment Schedule T2						
Sport Utility 2D	A49S	18995	4150	4500	6025	8550
Sahara Spt Util 2D	A59S	20925	4575	4925	6575	9300
Rear Seat			50	50	65	65
Hard Top			250	250	335	335
CHEROKEE 4WD—6-Cyl.—Truck Equipment Schedule T1						
SE Sport Utility 2D	F27S	21285	1400	1575	2600	4250
SE Sport Utility 4D	F28S	22320	1525	1700	2775	4525
Sport 2D	F47S	21860	1675	1875	3075	4975
Sport 4D	F48S	22895	1725	1925	3150	5075
Classic Spt Ut 4D	F58S	23420	1925	2150	3450	5525
Limited Spt Ut 4D	F68S	25745	2400	2650	4025	6300
2WD			(550)	(550)	(750)	(750)
4-Cyl, 2.5 Liter	P		(300)	(300)	(400)	(400)
GRAND CHEROKEE 4WD—6-Cyl.—Truck Equipment Sch T1						
Laredo Sport Util 4D	W48S	29075	1250	1425	2400	3975
2WD			(550)	(550)	(750)	(750)
V8, 4.7 Liter	N		175	175	245	245
GRAND CHEROKEE 4WD—V8—Truck Equipment Schedule T3						
Limited Spt Util 4D	258N	35950	1700	1900	3175	5250
2WD	X		(550)	(550)	(750)	(750)
6-Cyl, 4.0 Liter	S		(150)	(150)	(200)	(200)
2001 JEEP — 1J4-(A29P)-1-#						
WRANGLER 4WD—4-Cyl.—Truck Equipment Schedule T2						
SE Sport Utility 2D	A29P	16095	3625	3925	5325	7525
Rear Seat			50	50	65	65
Hard Top			250	250	335	335
WRANGLER 4WD—6-Cyl.—Truck Equipment Schedule T2						
Sport Utility 2D	A49S	19615	4450	4800	6250	8700
Sahara Spt Util 2D	A59S	22895	4975	5350	7100	9875
Hard Top			250	250	335	335
CHEROKEE 4WD—6-Cyl.—Truck Equipment Schedule T1						
SE Sport Utility 2D	F27S	21780	1900	2125	3175	4925
SE Sport Utility 4D	F28S	22815	2050	2275	3375	5200

0415

Body Type	VIN	List	Trade-In Good	Very Good	Pvt-Party Good	Retail Excellent
Sport Utility 2D	F47S	22410	2275	2525	3675	5625
Sport Utility 4D	F48S	23445	2325	2575	3725	5725
Classic Spt Ut 4D	F58S	23835	2575	2875	4075	6200
Limited Spt Ut 4D	F68S	23970	3175	3500	4750	7125
2WD	T		(650)	(650)	(860)	(860)
GRAND CHEROKEE 4WD—6-Cyl.—Truck Equipment Sch T1						
Laredo Sport Util 4D	W48S	29855	1575	1775	2675	4275
2WD	X		(650)	(650)	(860)	(860)
V8, 4.7 Liter	N		200	200	265	265
GRAND CHEROKEE 4WD—V8—Truck Equipment Schedule T3						
Limited Spt Util 4D	W58N	35870	2075	2325	3525	5575
2WD	X		(650)	(650)	(860)	(860)
6-Cyl, 4.0 Liter	S		(150)	(150)	(200)	(200)

Body Type	VIN	List	Trade-In Good	Very Good	Pvt-Party Good	Retail Excellent
WRANGLER 4WD—4-Cyl.—Truck Equipment Schedule T2						
SE Sport Utility 2D	A29P	16410	4150	4475	5625	7650
Rear Seat			75	75	100	100
Hard Top			275	275	365	365
WRANGLER 4WD—6-Cyl.—Truck Equipment Schedule T2						
X Sport Utility 2D	A49S	18995	4900	5275	6725	9075
Sport Utility 2D	A49S	20665	5275	5650	7150	9650
Sahara Spt Util 2D	A59S	24035	5900	6300	7875	10600
Hard Top			275	275	365	365
LIBERTY 4WD—V6—Truck Equipment Schedule T1						
Sport Utility 4D	L48K	21970	1500	1675	2850	4625
Limited Utility 4D	L58K	23305	2000	2225	3500	5575
Renegade Utility 4D	L38K	23855	2075	2325	3575	5675
2WD	K		(725)	(725)	(970)	(970)
4-Cyl, 2.4 Liter	1		(275)	(275)	(365)	(365)
GRAND CHEROKEE 4WD—6-Cyl.—Truck Equipment Schedule T1						
Laredo Sport Util 4D	W48S	27995	1725	1950	3025	4800
Sport Utility 4D	W38S	29140	1850	2075	3175	5025
2WD	X		(725)	(725)	(970)	(970)
V8, 4.7 Liter	N		225	225	285	285
GRAND CHEROKEE 4WD—V8—Truck Equipment Schedule T3						
Limited Spt Util 4D	W58N	33300	2425	2725	3950	6175
Overland Spt Utl 4D	W68N	37430	2500	2825	4050	6325
2WD	X		(725)	(725)	(970)	(970)
6-Cyl, 4.0 Liter	S		(225)	(225)	(300)	(300)

Body Type	VIN	List	Trade-In Good	Very Good	Pvt-Party Good	Retail Excellent
WRANGLER 4WD—4-Cyl.—Truck Equipment Schedule T2						
SE Sport Utility 2D	A291	16910	4600	4925	6075	8125
Rear Seat			100	100	135	135
Hard Top			300	300	400	400
WRANGLER 4WD—6-Cyl.—Truck Equipment Schedule T2						
X Sport Utility 2D	A39S	19295	5675	6050	7475	9900
"Sport" Spt Util 2D	A49S	21930	6275	6675	8150	10750
Sahara Spt Util 2D	A59S	24695	6600	7025	8625	11350
Rubicon Spt Utl 2D	A59S	24995	6950	7375	9000	11850
Hard Top			300	300	400	400
LIBERTY 4WD—V6—Truck Equipment Schedule T1						
Sport Utility 4D	L48K	21880	2175	2425	3525	5450
Limited Utility 4D	L58K	24045	2675	2975	4150	6350
Renegade Utility 4D	L38K	24630	2800	3100	4275	6500
2WD	K		(800)	(800)	(1080)	(1080)
4-Cyl, 2.4 Liter	1		(325)	(325)	(425)	(425)
GRAND CHEROKEE 4WD—6-Cyl.—Truck Equipment Schedule T1						
Laredo Sport Util 4D	W48S	28640	2525	2825	3775	5650
2WD	X		(800)	(800)	(1080)	(1080)
V8, 4.7 Liter	N		350	350	455	455
GRAND CHEROKEE 4WD—V8—Truck Equipment Schedule T3						
Limited Spt Util 4D	W58N	34920	3400	3750	5050	7475
Overland Spt Utl 4D	W68J	37975	3500	3850	5175	7650
2WD	X		(800)	(800)	(1080)	(1080)
6-Cyl, 4.0 Liter	S		(300)	(300)	(400)	(400)

Body Type	VIN	List	Trade-In Good	Very Good	Pvt-Party Good	Retail Excellent
WRANGLER 4WD—4-Cyl.—Truck Equipment Schedule T2						
SE Sport Utility 2D	A291	17515	4975	5325	6525	8525
Rear Seat			100	100	135	135

TRUCKS & VANS

Body Type	VIN	List	Trade-In Good	Trade-In Very Good	Pvt-Party Good	Retail Excellent
Hard Top			325	325	435	435
WRANGLER 4WD—6-Cyl.—Truck Equipment Schedule T2						
X Sport Utility 2D	A39S	19945	6450	6850	8150	10550
"Sport" SUV 2D	A49S	22755	6975	7400	8825	11400
Unlimited Util LWB	A29S	24995	7675	8125	9625	12400
Sahara Spt Util 2D	A59S	25520	7625	8075	9550	12300
Rubicon Spt Utl 2D	A69S	25695	7775	8225	9700	12500
Hard Top			325	325	430	430
LIBERTY 4WD—V6—Truck Equipment Schedule T1						
Sport Utility 4D	L48K	21855	2675	2975	4075	6125
Limited Utility 4D	L58K	24870	3050	3400	4700	6975
Renegade Utility 4D	L38K	25455	3200	3550	4850	7150
2WD			(900)	(900)	(1190)	(1190)
4-Cyl, 2.4 Liter	1		(350)	(350)	(480)	(480)
GRAND CHEROKEE 4WD—6-Cyl.—Truck Equipment Schedule T1						
Laredo Sport Util 4D	W48S	29875	3225	3575	4575	6675
2WD			(900)	(900)	(1190)	(1190)
V8, 4.7 Liter	N,J		250	250	335	335
GRAND CHEROKEE 4WD—V8—Truck Equipment Schedule T3						
Limited Spt Util 4D	W58N	35655	4100	4500	5800	8375
Overland Spt Util 4D	W68J	39920	4525	4950	6325	9100
2WD	X		(900)	(900)	(1190)	(1190)
6-Cyl, 4.0 Liter			(350)	(350)	(465)	(465)

Body Type	VIN	List	Trade-In Good	Trade-In Very Good	Pvt-Party Good	Retail Excellent
WRANGLER 4WD—4-Cyl.—Truck Equipment Schedule T2						
SE Sport Utility 2D	A291	18510	5800	6175	7225	9175
Rear Seat			100	100	125	125
6-Cyl, 4.0 Liter	S		800	800	1005	1005
WRANGLER 4WD—6-Cyl.—Truck Equipment Schedule T2						
X Sport Utility 2D	A39S	20820	7300	7750	8925	11250
"Sport" SUV 2D	A49S	24725	8400	8875	10200	12850
Unlimited Util LWB	A44S	25480	9325	9825	11200	14050
Rubicon Spt Utl 2D	A69S	27825	9350	9875	11300	14200
Rubicon LWB Util 2D	A69S	29025	11400	11950	13300	16450
Unltd Rubicon LWB	A69S	29195	8925	9500	10700	13700
Hard Top			350	350	440	440
LIBERTY 4WD—V6—Truck Equipment Schedule T1						
Sport Utility 4D	L48K	22985	3325	3675	4825	6925
Renegade Utility 4D	L38K	24920	4025	4400	5675	8075
Limited Utility 4D	L58K	25645	3950	4325	5575	7950
2WD	K		(975)	(975)	(1300)	(1300)
4-Cyl, 2.4 Liter			(400)	(400)	(540)	(540)
4-Cyl, 2.8L, Turbo Dsl	5		1475	1475	1955	1955
GRAND CHEROKEE 4WD—V6—Truck Equipment Schedule T1						
Laredo Sport Util 4D	R48K	28745	4375	4750	5950	8350
2WD	S		(975)	(975)	(1300)	(1300)
V8, 4.7 Liter	N		275	275	355	355
GRAND CHEROKEE 4WD—V8—Truck Equipment Schedule T3						
Limited Spt Util 4D	R58N	34690	5600	6050	7575	10550
2WD	S		(975)	(975)	(1300)	(1300)
V8, HEMI, 5.7 Liter	2		275	275	355	355

Body Type	VIN	List	Trade-In Good	Trade-In Very Good	Pvt-Party Good	Retail Excellent
WRANGLER 4WD—4-Cyl.—Truck Equipment Schedule T2						
SE Sport Utility 2D	A291	18730	6825	7225	8275	10250
Rear Seat			100	100	125	125
6-Cyl, 4.0 Liter	S		825	825	1025	1025
WRANGLER 4WD—6-Cyl.—Truck Equipment Schedule T2						
X Sport Utility 2D	A39S	21040	8675	9150	10250	12700
"Sport" SUV 2D	A49S	24725	9700	10250	11500	14250
Unlimited LWB Util.	A44S	25480	10300	10850	12150	14950
Rubicon Spt Utl 2D	A69S	28125	10650	11200	12550	15500
Unltd Rubicon LWB	A69S	29125	10600	11200	12400	15650
Hard Top			375	375	460	460
LIBERTY 4WD—V6—Truck Equipment Schedule T1						
Sport Utility 4D	L48K	23965	4250	4625	5750	7975
Renegade Utility 4D	L38K	25855	5000	5400	6625	9150
Limited Utility 4D	L58K	27405	4875	5300	6650	9150
2WD	K		(1050)	(1050)	(1410)	(1410)
4-Cyl, 2.8L, Turbo Dsl	5		1575	1575	2095	2095

Body Type	VIN	List	Trade-In Good	Very Good	Pvt-Party Good	Retail Excellent
COMMANDER 4WD—V6—Truck Equipment Schedule T1						
Sport Utility 4D	G48K	29985	5175	5575	6800	9000
2WD	H		(1050)	(1050)	(1410)	(1410)
V8, 4.7 Liter	N		550	550	720	720
COMMANDER 4WD—V8—Truck Equipment Schedule T1						
Limited Spt Util 4D	G58N	38900	7975	8500	9875	12900
2WD	H		(1050)	(1050)	(1410)	(1410)
V8, HEMI, 5.7 Liter	2		275	275	375	375
GRAND CHEROKEE 4WD—V6—Truck Equipment Schedule T1						
Laredo Sport Util 4D	R48K	29830	5175	5600	6900	9350
2WD	S		(1050)	(1050)	(1410)	(1410)
V8, 4.7 Liter	N		275	275	375	375
GRAND CHEROKEE 4WD—V8—Truck Equipment Schedule T3						
Limited Spt Util 4D	R58N	36700	7450	7975	9500	12750
2WD	S		(1050)	(1050)	(1410)	(1410)
V8, HEMI, 5.7 Liter	2		275	275	375	375
GRAND CHEROKEE 4WD—V8 HEMI—Truck Equipment Schedule T3						
SRT8 Sport Util 4D	R783	39995	14400	15100	16650	20400
Overland Spt Util 4D	R682	42925	8250	8825	10400	13950
2WD	S		(1050)	(1050)	(1410)	(1410)

2007 JEEP — 1J(4or8)-(F28W)-7-#

Body Type	VIN	List	Trade-In Good	Very Good	Pvt-Party Good	Retail Excellent
PATRIOT 4WD—4-Cyl.—Truck Equipment Schedule T1						
Sport Utility 4D	F28W	17785	4575	4900	6125	8175
Limited Spt Util 4D	F48W	22785	5200	5550	7175	9525
2WD	T		(1150)	(1150)	(1520)	(1520)
COMPASS 4WD—4-Cyl.—Truck Equipment Schedule T1						
Sport SUV 4D	F47W	17585	4775	5200	5975	7925
Limited Spt Util 4D	F57W	21740	5350	5800	6850	9075
2WD	T		(1150)	(1150)	(1520)	(1520)
WRANGLER 4WD—V6—Truck Equipment Schedule T2						
X Sport Utility 2D	A241	19970	9725	10250	11450	13950
Unlimited X Spt Util	A391	23235	11600	12150	13550	16450
Sahara Spt Util 2D	A541	24785	11350	11900	13150	16000
Unltd Sahara Util 4D	A591	27560	13100	13700	15150	18350
Rubicon Spt Utl 2D	A641	26750	11900	12450	13850	16850
Unltd Rubicon Util 4D	A691	29720	15000	15800	16900	20700
Hard Top			400	400	485	485
2WD	B		(1150)	(1150)	(1380)	(1380)
LIBERTY 4WD—V6—Truck Equipment Schedule T1						
Sport Utility 4D	L48K	23460	5000	5400	6600	8825
Limited Utility 4D	L58K	27045	6000	6450	7700	10200
2WD	K		(1150)	(1150)	(1520)	(1520)
COMMANDER 4WD—V6—Truck Equipment Schedule T1						
Sport Utility 4D	G48K	31080	6575	7025	8175	10500
2WD	H		(1150)	(1150)	(1520)	(1520)
V8, 4.7 Liter	N		650	650	865	865
COMMANDER 4WD—V8—Truck Equipment Schedule T1						
Limited Sport Util	G58N	39215	9200	9750	11150	14200
2WD	H		(1150)	(1150)	(1520)	(1520)
V8, HEMI, 5.7 Liter	2		300	300	400	400
COMMANDER 4WD—V8 HEMI—Truck Equipment Schedule T1						
Overland Sport Util	G682	44545	9325	9900	11200	14100
2WD	H		(1150)	(1150)	(1450)	(1450)
GRAND CHEROKEE 4WD—V6—Truck Equipment Schedule T1						
Laredo Sport Util 4D	R48K	30205	6500	6975	8175	10700
2WD	S		(1150)	(1150)	(1520)	(1520)
V8, 4.7 Liter	N		300	300	400	400
GRAND CHEROKEE 4WD—V8—Truck Equipment Schedule T3						
Limited Spt Util 4D	R58N	37890	8925	9525	11050	14450
2WD	S		(1150)	(1150)	(1520)	(1520)
V6, Turbo Dsl 3.0L	M		900	900	1200	1200
V8, HEMI, 5.7 Liter	2		300	300	400	400
GRAND CHEROKEE 4WD—V8 HEMI—Truck Equipment Schedule T3						
SRT8 Sport Util 4D	R783	40675	15700	16400	17900	21700
Overland Spt Util 4D	R682	43260	9875	10500	12050	15700
2WD	S		(1150)	(1150)	(1520)	(1520)
V6, Turbo Dsl 3.0L	M		900	900	1200	1200

2008 JEEP — 1J(4or8)-(F28W)-8-#

Body Type	VIN	List	Trade-In Good	Very Good	Pvt-Party Good	Retail Excellent
PATRIOT 4WD—4-Cyl.—Truck Equipment Schedule T1						
Sport SUV 4D	F28W	18885	5650	6000	7425	9600

2008 JEEP

Body Type	VIN	List	Trade-In Good	Very Good	Pvt-Party Good	Retail Excellent
Limited Spt Util 4D	F48W	23605	6950	7350	8925	11550
2WD	T		(1225)	(1225)	(1630)	(1630)
COMPASS 4WD—4-Cyl.—Truck Equipment Schedule T1						
Sport SUV 4D	F47W	20195	5575	6000	6900	8800
Limited Spt Util 4D	F57W	24885	6325	6775	7775	9950
2WD	T		(1225)	(1225)	(1570)	(1570)
WRANGLER 4WD—V6—Truck Equipment Schedule T2						
X Sport Utility 2D	A241	20195	11400	11950	13050	15650
Unlimited X Spt Util	A391	24115	13350	14000	15300	18250
Sahara Spt Util 2D	A541	23050	13050	13650	15000	17900
Unltd Sahara Util 4D	A591	29025	15550	16250	17650	21000
Rubicon Spt Util 2D	A641	27880	13650	14300	15600	18650
Unltd Rubicon 4D	A691	31020	16450	17250	18450	22200
Hard Top			400	400	460	460
2WD	B		(1225)	(1225)	(1405)	(1405)
LIBERTY 4WD—V6—Truck Equipment Schedule T1						
Sport Utility 4D	N28K	23425	7125	7600	8950	11550
Limited Utility 4D	N58K	26785	8575	9125	10600	13700
2WD	P		(1225)	(1225)	(1630)	(1630)
COMMANDER 4WD—V6—Truck Equipment Schedule T1						
Sport Utility 4D	G48K	30095	8000	8475	9600	11950
2WD	H		(1225)	(1225)	(1590)	(1590)
V8, 4.7 Liter	N		700	700	910	910
COMMANDER 4WD—V8—Truck Equipment Schedule T1						
Limited Sport Util	G58N	39620	10600	11200	12550	15550
2WD	H		(1225)	(1225)	(1580)	(1580)
V8, HEMI, 5.7 Liter	2		550	550	710	710
COMMANDER 4WD—V8 HEMI—Truck Equipment Schedule T1						
Overland Sport Util	G682	44545	11100	11700	13000	16050
2WD	H		(1225)	(1225)	(1520)	(1520)
GRAND CHEROKEE 4WD—V6—Truck Equipment Schedule T1						
Laredo Sport Util	R48K	31085	7950	8475	9425	11750
2WD	S		(1225)	(1225)	(1530)	(1530)
V6, Turbo Dsl 3.0L	M		2025	2025	2545	2545
V8, Flex Fuel, 4.7 Liter	N		700	700	875	875
GRAND CHEROKEE 4WD—V8 HEMI—Truck Equipment Schedule T3						
Limited Spt Util 4D	R582	39930	11200	11850	13300	16300
2WD	S		(1225)	(1225)	(1535)	(1535)
V6, Turbo Dsl 3.0L	M		250	250	315	315
V8, Flex Fuel, 4.7 Liter	N		(650)	(650)	(830)	(830)
GRAND CHEROKEE 4WD—V8 HEMI—Truck Equipment Schedule T3						
SRT8 Sport Util 4D	R783	41220	18850	19650	20900	24600
Overland Sport Util	R682	44135	13000	13700	15100	18700
2WD	S		(1225)	(1225)	(1530)	(1530)
V6, Turbo Dsl 3.0L	M		950	950	1190	1190

2009 JEEP — 1J(4or8)-(F28B)-9-#

Body Type	VIN	List	Trade-In Good	Very Good	Pvt-Party Good	Retail Excellent
PATRIOT 4WD—4-Cyl.—Truck Equipment Schedule T1						
Sport SUV 4D	F28B	20220	6650	7025	8425	10650
Limited Util 4D	F48B	24910	8125	8550	10150	12700
2WD	T		(1300)	(1300)	(1715)	(1715)
COMPASS 4WD—4-Cyl.—Truck Equipment Schedule T1						
Sport SUV 4D	F47B	21945	6775	7225	8200	10200
Limited Spt Util 4D	F57B	26305	8500	9000	10200	12700
2WD	T		(1300)	(1300)	(1655)	(1655)
WRANGLER 4WD—V6—Truck Equipment Schedule T2						
X Sport Utility 2D	A241	21385	12750	13300	14400	17000
Unlimited X Spt Util	A391	24915	15100	15750	16950	19850
Sahara Spt Util 2D	A541	27195	14600	15250	16350	19150
Unltd Sahara Util 4D	A591	29845	18050	18800	20100	23500
Rubicon Spt Utl 2D	A641	28890	15800	16450	17700	20700
Unltd Rubicon 4D	A691	32990	19100	19900	21000	24500
Hard Top			475	475	535	535
2WD	B		(1300)	(1300)	(1455)	(1455)
LIBERTY 4WD—V6—Truck Equipment Schedule T1						
Sport SUV 4D	N28K	24520	8700	9200	10600	13400
Limited Utility 4D	N58K	27625	10450	11000	12550	15800
2WD	P		(1300)	(1300)	(1735)	(1735)
COMMANDER 4WD—V6—Truck Equipment Schedule T1						
Sport Utility 4D	G48K	32140	9650	10150	11450	14000
2WD	H		(1300)	(1300)	(1635)	(1635)
V8, 4.7 Liter	P		750	750	940	940

2009 JEEP

Body Type	VIN	List	Trade-In Good	Very Good	Pvt-Party Good	Retail Excellent
COMMANDER 4WD—V8—Truck Equipment Schedule T1						
Limited Sport Util	G58P	41335	12950	13550	15150	18400
2WD	H		(1300)	(1300)	(1610)	(1610)
V8, HEMI, 5.7 Liter			650	650	805	805
COMMANDER 4WD—V8 HEMI—Truck Equipment Schedule T1						
Overland Sport Util	G68T	45940	14550	15250	16700	20100
2WD	H		(1300)	(1300)	(1585)	(1585)
GRAND CHEROKEE 4WD—V6—Truck Equipment Schedule T1						
Laredo Sport Util 4D	R48K	33200	9800	10350	11450	14000
2WD	S		(1300)	(1300)	(1590)	(1590)
V6, Turbo Dsl 3.0L	M		2150	2150	2615	2615
V8, Flex Fuel, 4.7 Liter	P		650	650	790	790
GRAND CHEROKEE 4WD—V8 HEMI—Truck Equipment Schedule T3						
Limited Spt Util 4D	R58T	41435	14600	15300	16800	20500
2WD	S		(1300)	(1300)	(1595)	(1595)
V6, Turbo Dsl 3.0L	M		225	225	285	285
V8, Flex Fuel, 4.7 Liter	P		(700)	(700)	(865)	(865)
GRAND CHEROKEE 4WD—V8 HEMI—Truck Equipment Schedule T3						
SRT8 Sport Util 4D	R78W	43745	23700	24600	25700	29600
GRAND CHEROKEE 4WD—V8 HEMI—Truck Equipment Schedule T1						
Overland Sport Util	R68T	45625	15250	16050	17400	21100
2WD			(1300)	(1300)	(1590)	(1590)
V6, Turbo Dsl 3.0L			1000	1000	1220	1220

2010 JEEP — 1J4-(F1GB)-A-#

Body Type	VIN	List	Trade-In Good	Very Good	Pvt-Party Good	Retail Excellent
PATRIOT 4WD—4-Cyl.—Truck Equipment Schedule T1						
Sport SUV 4D	F1GB	21176	8025	8450	9575	11550
Limited Spt Util 4D	F4GB	26280	9575	10050	11250	13500
2WD	T		(1375)	(1375)	(1650)	(1650)
COMPASS 4WD—4-Cyl.—Truck Equipment Schedule T1						
Sport SUV 4D	F1FB	18595	8225	8675	9850	12100
Limited SUV	F5FB	26865	9700	10200	11500	14050
2WD	T		(1375)	(1375)	(1740)	(1740)
WRANGLER 4WD—V6—Truck Equipment Schedule T2						
"Sport" SUV 2D	A2D1	22680	13800	14400	15600	18200
Unlimited "Sport" 4D	A3H1	26100	17550	18450	19450	22400
Sahara Spt Util 2D	A5D1	27770	17550	18250	19300	22200
Unltd Sahara Util 4D	A5H1	30420	20200	21000	22100	25400
Rubicon Spt Util 2D	A6D1	29525	18150	18900	19850	22800
Unltd Rubicon 4D	A6H1	33565	21300	22100	23200	26800
Hard Top			550	550	615	615
2WD	B		(1375)	(1375)	(1525)	(1525)
LIBERTY 4WD—V6—Truck Equipment Schedule T1						
Sport SUV 4D	N2GK	25609	10100	10600	11850	14350
Renegade Spt Util	N3GK	28605	11500	12100	13400	16200
Limited Spt Util 4D	N5GK	29480	12000	12600	13950	16850
2WD	P		(1375)	(1375)	(1725)	(1725)
COMMANDER 4WD—V6—Truck Equipment Schedule T1						
Sport Utility 4D	G4GK	34295	12550	13100	14300	16850
2WD	H		(1375)	(1375)	(1630)	(1630)
V8, HEMI, 5.7 Liter	T		925	925	1095	1095
COMMANDER 4WD—V8 HEMI—Truck Equipment Schedule T1						
Limited Sport Util	G5GT	43610	17700	18400	19650	22900
2WD	H		(1375)	(1375)	(1605)	(1605)
GRAND CHEROKEE 4WD—V6—Truck Equipment Schedule T1						
Laredo Sport Util	R4GK	33460	11200	11750	12950	15600
2WD	S		(1375)	(1375)	(1690)	(1690)
V8, HEMI, 5.7 Liter	T		725	725	880	880
GRAND CHEROKEE 4WD—V8 HEMI—Truck Equipment Schedule T1						
Limited Spt Util 4D	R5GT	42540	16500	17300	18750	22400
2WD	S		(1375)	(1375)	(1680)	(1680)
V6, 3.7 Liter	K		(775)	(775)	(940)	(940)
GRAND CHEROKEE 4WD—V8 HEMI—Truck Equipment Schedule T1						
SRT8 Sport Util 4D	R7GW	44105	26700	27700	28500	32400

2011 JEEP — 1J4-(F1GB)-B-#

Body Type	VIN	List	Trade-In Good	Very Good	Pvt-Party Good	Retail Excellent
PATRIOT 4WD—4-Cyl.—Truck Equipment Schedule T1						
Sport SUV 4D	F1GB	19495	9550	10000	11100	13050
Latitude X Spt Util	F4GB	25695	11050	11550	12750	14950
2WD	T		(1475)	(1475)	(1705)	(1705)
COMPASS 4WD—4-Cyl.—Truck Equipment Schedule T1						
Sport SUV 4D	F1FB	22795	10850	11350	12550	14850

SEE BACK PAGES FOR TRUCK EQUIPMENT

TRUCKS & VANS

Body Type	VIN	List	Trade-In Good	Very Good	Pvt-Party Good	Retail Excellent
Limited Spt Util 4D	F5FB	26695	12500	13050	14200	16750
2WD	T		(1475)	(1475)	(1720)	(1720)
WRANGLER 4WD—V6—Truck Equipment Schedule T2						
"Sport" SUV 2D	A2D1	23620	15200	15850	16950	19500
Unlimited "Sport" 4D	A3H1	27120	19450	20200	21200	24100
Sahara Spt Util 2D	A5D1	28820	18900	19700	20700	23600
70th Annv Spt Utl	A7D1	29805	19650	20400	21300	24300
Rubicon Spt Utl 2D	A6D1	29995	19950	20700	21700	24700
Unltd Sahara Util 4D	A5H1	31520	22100	23000	23900	27200
Unltd 70th Annv Util	A7H1	32505	22300	23200	24100	27500
Unltd Rubicon 4D	A6H1	34320	23800	24700	25500	28800
Hard Top			600	600	665	665
LIBERTY 4WD—V6—Truck Equipment Schedule T1						
Sport SUV 4D	N2GK	25610	11850	12400	13700	16350
Renegade Spt Util	N3GK	27995	12750	13350	14800	17700
Limited Util 4D	N5GK	28995	13750	14350	15750	18750
2WD	N		(1475)	(1475)	(1785)	(1785)
GRAND CHEROKEE 4WD—V6—Truck Equipment Schedule T1						
Laredo Sport Util	R4GG	32995	17800	18550	19600	22700
2WD	S		(1475)	(1475)	(1720)	(1720)
V8, 5.7 Liter	T		800	800	935	935
GRAND CHEROKEE 4WD—V6—Truck Equipment Schedule T3						
Limited Sport Util	R5GG	39600	21000	21800	23000	26700
2WD	S		(1475)	(1475)	(1725)	(1725)
V8, 5.7 Liter	T		800	800	940	940
GRAND CHEROKEE 4WD—V8—Truck Equipment Schedule T3						
Overland Sport Util	R6GT	41095	23300	24200	25200	29000
2WD	S		(1475)	(1475)	(1705)	(1705)
V6, Flex Fuel, 3.6 Liter	G		(875)	(875)	(1020)	(1020)

2012 JEEP — (1,2or3)C4-(JPBB)-C-#

Body Type	VIN	List	Trade-In Good	Very Good	Pvt-Party Good	Retail Excellent
PATRIOT—4-Cyl.—Truck Equipment Schedule T1						
Sport SUV 4D	JPBB	17875	9575	10000	11200	13250
4WD	R		1550	1550	1800	1800
PATRIOT 4WD—4-Cyl.—Truck Equipment Schedule T1						
Latitude SUV 4D	JRFB	23560	11750	12250	13550	15950
Limited SUV 4D	JRCB	26110	12200	12700	14000	16500
2WD	P		(1550)	(1550)	(1815)	(1815)
COMPASS 4WD—4-Cyl.—Truck Equipment Schedule T1						
Sport SUV 4D	JDBB	21825	11950	12450	13800	16300
Latitude Spt Util 4D	JDEB	24225	12800	13300	14650	17300
Limited Spt Util 4D	JDCB	26825	13700	14250	15800	18600
2WD	C		(1550)	(1550)	(1860)	(1860)
WRANGLER 4WD—V6—Truck Equipment Schedule T2						
Sport SUV 2D	JWAG	23970	16400	17050	18000	20500
Unlimited Sport 4D	JWDG	27470	20800	21600	22300	25000
Sahara Spt Util 2D	JWBG	29895	20400	21200	21900	24600
Rubicon Spt Utl 2D	JWCG	30795	21400	22200	23100	26200
Hard Top			650	650	730	730
Call of Duty MW3			850	850	955	955
LIBERTY 4WD—V6—Truck Equipment Schedule T1						
Sport SUV 4D	JMAK	25770	13000	13550	15000	17700
Limited Ed SUV 4D	JMCK	29155	15200	15800	17300	20400
Limited Jet Ed SUV	JMFK	29355	15950	16600	18150	21400
2WD	L		(1550)	(1550)	(1865)	(1865)
GRAND CHEROKEE 4WD—V6—Truck Equipment Schedule T1						
Laredo Sport Util	JFAG	29820	19500	20300	21300	24400
Limited Sport Util	JFBG	40120	22700	23600	24700	28300
Altitude Edition			1650	1650	1910	1910
2WD	E		(1550)	(1550)	(1795)	(1795)
V8, 5.7 Liter	T		875	875	1010	1010
GRAND CHEROKEE 4WD—V8—Truck Equipment Schedule T1						
Overland Sport Util	JFCT	42330	25400	26400	27500	31400
2WD	E		(1550)	(1550)	(1795)	(1795)
V6, Flex Fuel, 3.6 Liter	G		(925)	(925)	(1070)	(1070)
GRAND CHEROKEE 4WD—V8 HEMI—Truck Equipment Schedule T3						
SRT8 Sport Util	JFDJ	55295	37200	38500	38900	43200

2013 JEEP — (1,2or3)C4-(JRBB)-D-#

Body Type	VIN	List	Trade-In Good	Very Good	Pvt-Party Good	Retail Excellent
PATRIOT 4WD—4-Cyl.—Truck Equipment Schedule T1						
Sport SUV 4D	JRBB	18770	11600	12100	13300	15500
Latitude SUV 4D	JRFB	23805	12700	13200	14450	16850

2013 JEEP

Body Type	VIN	List	Trade-In Good	Very Good	Pvt-Party Good	Retail Excellent
Limited SUV 4D	JRCB	26355	13250	13800	15200	17700
2WD	P		(1625)	(1625)	(1910)	(1910)
COMPASS 4WD—4-Cyl.—Truck Equipment Schedule T1						
Sport SUV 4D	JDEB	23270	12700	13200	14600	17100
Latitude Spt Util 4D	JDEB	24370	13350	13850	15400	18050
Limited Spt Util 4D	JDCB	27070	14450	15200	16750	19650
2WD	C		(1625)	(1625)	(1945)	(1945)
WRANGLER 4WD—V6—Truck Equipment Schedule T2						
Sport SUV 2D	JWAG	23120	17300	18000	18900	21300
Sport S SUV 2D	JWAG	25320	18500	19200	20000	22500
Sahara Spt Util 2D	JWBG	28620	21500	22300	22900	25500
Spt Freedom 2D	JWBG	28990	21300	22000	22700	25300
Rubicon Spt Utl 2D	JWCG	31420	22500	23300	24100	27000
Rubicon 10th Anniv.	JWCG	36990	28600	29500	30200	33400
Sahara Moab 2D	JWBG	37490	24200	25000	25700	28400
Unlimited Sport 4D	JWDG	26620	21800	22600	23200	25900
Unlimited Sport S	JWDG	29020	22000	22800	23500	26400
Unltd Sahara Util	JWEG	32120	24700	25600	26400	29600
Unltd Spt Freedom	JWDG	32490	23100	23900	24500	27100
Unltd Rubicon 4D	JWFG	34920	27600	28500	29100	32200
Unltd Rubicon 10th	JWFG	40490	31000	31900	32600	36100
Unltd Sahara Moab	JWEG	37490	25800	26700	27300	30200
Hard Top			700	700	780	780
GRAND CHEROKEE 4WD—V6 Flex Fuel—Truck Equipment Schedule T1						
Laredo Sport Util	JFAG	30420	21000	21800	22800	26000
Laredo X Sport Util	JFAG	41420	24300	25200	26300	29900
Altitude Sport Util	JFAG	37220	24000	24900	25900	29500
Limited Sport Util	JFBG	40220	24000	24900	26000	29600
TrailHawk Spt Util	JFAG	41191	24400	25300	26300	30000
Overland Sport Util.	JFCG	46215	27600	28600	29700	33800
Overland Summit	JFCG	50215	28000	29100	30100	34200
2WD	E		(1625)	(1625)	(1855)	(1855)
V8, 5.7 Liter	T		950	950	1080	1080
GRAND CHEROKEE 4WD—V8 HEMI—Truck Equipment Schedule T3						
SRT8 Sport Util 4D	JFDJ	60921	39700	41100	41400	45800
SRT8 Alpine Spt Util	JFDJ	63785	41700	43100	43300	47900
SRT8 Vapor Spt Util	JFDJ	63785	41700	43100	43300	47900

2014 JEEP — (1,2or3)C4-(JPBA)-E-#

Body Type	VIN	List	Trade-In Good	Very Good	Pvt-Party Good	Retail Excellent
PATRIOT—4-Cyl.—Truck Equipment Schedule T1						
Altitude Ed Spt Util	JPBA	17385	11150	11650	13450	16350
High Altitude Ed 4D	JPFA	22185	13300	13850	15850	19100
PATRIOT 4WD—4-Cyl.—Truck Equipment Schedule T1						
Sport SUV 4D	JRBB	20290	12800	13350	15300	18400
Latitude SUV 4D	JRFB	24390	14400	15000	16900	20200
Limited Spt Util 4D	JRCB	26890	14950	15550	17400	20700
2WD	P		(1725)	(1725)	(2155)	(2155)
COMPASS—4-Cyl.—Truck Equipment Schedule T1						
Altitude Ed Spt Util	JCBA	20285	11700	12150	14100	17100
High Altitude 4D	JCEA	24685	14450	15000	17350	21100
COMPASS 4WD—4-Cyl.—Truck Equipment Schedule T1						
Sport SUV 4D	JDBB	21390	13900	14450	16350	19550
Latitude Spt Util 4D	JDEB	24990	15250	15800	17750	21100
Limited Spt Util 4D	JDCB	28090	16500	17100	18950	22300
2WD	C		(1725)	(1725)	(2125)	(2125)
WRANGLER 4WD—V6—Truck Equipment Schedule T2						
Sport SUV 2D	JWAG	23390	18600	19350	20000	22300
Sport S SUV 2D	JWAG	25790				
Willys Wheeler 2D	JWAG	26790				
Willys Wheeler W 2D	JWAG	28890				
Sahara Spt Util 2D	JWBG	28990	23000	23800	24400	27100
Freedom SUV 2D	JWAG	29090				
Rubicon Spt Utl 2D	JWCG	31890	24000	24900	25500	28400
Rubicon X Util 2D	JWCG	36090				
Unlimited Sport 4D	JWDG	26990	23000	23800	24200	26700
Unlimited Sport S	JWDG	29590				
Unltd Willys Wheeler	JWDG	30590				
Unltd Sahara Util 4D	JWEG	32590	25900	26800	27300	30300
UnltdWillysWhr W	JWDG	32690				
Unltd Freedom Ed	JWDG	32890	26000	26900	27600	30800
Unltd Rubicon X 4D	JWFG	39790	32300	33300	33500	36500
Hard Top			750	750	825	825

0415   **SEE BACK PAGES FOR TRUCK EQUIPMENT**   491

TRUCKS & VANS

Body Type	VIN	List	Trade-In Good	Trade-In Very Good	Pvt-Party Good	Retail Excellent
WRANGLER 4WD—V6—Truck Equipment Schedule T2						
Altitude Spt Util 2D	JWBG	32690				
Polar Spt Util 2D	JWBG	33490				
Unltd Rubicon 4D	JWBG	35490	28500	29400	29700	32500
Unltd Altitude 4D	JWEG	36490	29300	30300	30600	33500
Unltd Dragon 4D	JWEG	37290				
Unlimited Polar Ed	JWEG	37290				
CHEROKEE 4WD—4-Cyl.—Truck Equipment Schedule T1						
Sport SUV 4D	JMAB	25990	16600	17200	18550	21300
Latitude Sport Util	JMCB	27490	18300	18950	20200	23100
Altitude Sport Util	JMCB	27990	18500	19150	20400	23200
TrailHawk Spt Utl	JMBB	30490	22200	22900	24100	27300
Limited Sport Util	JMDB	30990	22200	22900	24100	27300
Adaptive Cruise Control			500	500	555	555
Technology Pkg			1025	1025	1145	1145
2WD	L		(1725)	(1725)	(1945)	(1945)
V6, 3.2 Liter	S		725	725	830	830
GRAND CHEROKEE 4WD—V6 Flex Fuel—Truck Equipment Schedule T1						
Laredo Spt Util 4D	JFAG	31790	22700	23600	24200	27000
Laredo E Spt Util 4D	JFAG	33490	24400	25300	26000	29000
Altitude Spt Util 4D	JFAG	38585	25200	26200	27000	30400
Limited Spt Util 4D	JFBG	38790	27300	28300	29000	32500
Overland Spt Util 4D	JFCT	49185	28800	29800	30500	34200
Summit Spt Util 4D	JFJT	54685	34200	35400	36000	40300
2WD	E		(1725)	(1725)	(1900)	(1900)
V6, EcoDiesel, 3.0T			2950	2950	3275	3275
V8, 5.7 Liter	T		1025	1025	1140	1140
GRAND CHEROKEE 4WD—V8 HEMI—Truck Equipment Schedule T3						
SRT Sport Util 4D	JFDJ	63990	47100	48600	48500	53300

KIA

2000 KIA — KNM(JA623)-Y-#

Body Type	VIN	List	Trade-In Good	Trade-In Very Good	Pvt-Party Good	Retail Excellent
SPORTAGE 4WD—4-Cyl.—Truck Equipment Schedule T2						
Sport Util Conv 2D	JA623	14945	250	250	1175	2150
Sport Utility 4D	JA723	16745	375	450	1425	2550
EX Sport Utility 4D	JA723	19045	900	1025	2175	3800
2WD	B		(275)	(275)	(365)	(365)

2001 KIA — KND(JB623)-1-#

Body Type	VIN	List	Trade-In Good	Trade-In Very Good	Pvt-Party Good	Retail Excellent
SPORTAGE 4WD—4-Cyl.—Truck Equipment Schedule T2						
Sport Util Conv 2D	JB623	15345	275	350	1250	2225
Sport Utility 4D	JB723	17245	525	625	1625	2875
EX Sport Utility 4D	JB723	19545	1100	1250	2275	3825
Limited Spt Util 4D	JB723	20090	1250	1400	2425	4050
2WD	B		(300)	(300)	(400)	(400)

2002 KIA — KND(JA623)-2-#

Body Type	VIN	List	Trade-In Good	Trade-In Very Good	Pvt-Party Good	Retail Excellent
SPORTAGE 4WD—4-Cyl.—Truck Equipment Schedule T2						
Sport Util Conv 2D	JA623	15640	425	500	1550	2800
Sport Utility 4D	JA723	18715	750	875	1925	3325
2WD	B		(375)	(375)	(500)	(500)
SEDONA—V6—Truck Equipment Schedule T1						
LX Minivan	UP131	19590	325	400	1075	1850
EX Minivan	UP131	21590	775	875	1700	2925

2003 KIA — KND(UP131)-3-#

Body Type	VIN	List	Trade-In Good	Trade-In Very Good	Pvt-Party Good	Retail Excellent
SEDONA—V6—Truck Equipment Schedule T1						
LX Minivan	UP131	19965	550	650	1325	2225
EX Minivan	UP131	22180	1050	1200	2025	3400
SORENTO 4WD—V6—Truck Equipment Schedule T1						
LX Sport Utility 4D	JC733	21795	1475	1700	2500	3875
EX Sport Utility 4D	JC733	24595	2200	2500	3525	5450
2WD			(500)	(500)	(665)	(665)

2004 KIA — KND(UP131)-4-#

Body Type	VIN	List	Trade-In Good	Trade-In Very Good	Pvt-Party Good	Retail Excellent
SEDONA—V6—Truck Equipment Schedule T1						
LX Minivan	UP131	20615	675	775	1450	2400
EX Minivan	UP131	22725	1225	1400	2200	3625

2004 KIA

Body Type	VIN	List	Trade-In Good	Trade-In Very Good	Pvt-Party Good	Retail Excellent
SORENTO 4WD—V6—Truck Equipment Schedule T1						
LX Sport Utility 4D	JC733	23290	2150	2450	3425	5225
EX Sport Utility 4D	JC733	25490	3050	3450	4625	7025
2WD	D		(550)	(550)	(735)	(735)

2005 KIA — KND(JE723)-5-#

Body Type	VIN	List	Trade-In Good	Trade-In Very Good	Pvt-Party Good	Retail Excellent
SPORTAGE 4WD—V6—Truck Equipment Schedule T2						
LX Sport Utility 4D	JE723	20290	3100	3425	4325	6175
EX Sport Utility 4D	JE723	21990	3650	4000	5125	7275
2WD	F		(600)	(600)	(800)	(800)
4-Cyl, 2.0 Liter	4		(325)	(325)	(435)	(435)
SEDONA—V6—Truck Equipment Schedule T1						
LX Minivan	UP131	20840	1125	1275	2050	3325
EX Minivan	UP131	23240	1725	1950	2950	4675
SORENTO 4WD—V6—Truck Equipment Schedule T1						
LX Sport Utility 4D	JC733	23840	3075	3450	4275	6150
EX Sport Utility 4D	JC733	26140	3600	4025	5100	7300
2WD	D		(600)	(600)	(800)	(800)

2006 KIA — KND(JE723)-6-#

Body Type	VIN	List	Trade-In Good	Trade-In Very Good	Pvt-Party Good	Retail Excellent
SPORTAGE 4WD—V6—Truck Equipment Schedule T1						
LX Sport Utility 4D	JE723	20890	3950	4300	5175	7000
2WD	F		(650)	(650)	(835)	(835)
4-Cyl, 2.0 Liter	4		(350)	(350)	(450)	(450)
SPORTAGE 4WD—V6—Truck Equipment Schedule T2						
EX Sport Utility 4D	JE723	22590	4575	4950	5875	7950
2WD	F		(650)	(650)	(835)	(835)
SEDONA—V6—Truck Equipment Schedule T1						
LX Minivan	MB233	23665	2375	2650	3775	5700
EX Minivan	MB233	26265	3125	3475	4700	7025
SORENTO 4WD—V6—Truck Equipment Schedule T1						
LX Sport Utility 4D	JC733	24470	3450	3850	4875	6925
EX Sport Utility 4D	JC733	26770	4200	4650	5750	8050
2WD	D		(650)	(650)	(865)	(865)

2007 KIA — KND(JE723)-7-#

Body Type	VIN	List	Trade-In Good	Trade-In Very Good	Pvt-Party Good	Retail Excellent
SPORTAGE 4WD—V6—Truck Equipment Schedule T1						
LX Sport Utility 4D	JE723	21790	4700	5100	5900	7750
2WD	F		(700)	(700)	(935)	(935)
4-Cyl, 2.0 Liter	4		(375)	(375)	(500)	(500)
SPORTAGE 4WD—V6—Truck Equipment Schedule T2						
EX Sport Utility 4D	JE723	23490	5575	6025	7025	9175
2WD	F		(700)	(700)	(925)	(925)
SEDONA—V6—Truck Equipment Schedule T1						
Minivan 4D	MB133	21195	2725	3050	3950	5675
LX Minivan 4D	MB233	24295	3350	3700	4700	6650
EX Minivan 4D	MB233	26895	4150	4550	5625	7925
SORENTO—V6—Truck Equipment Schedule T1						
Sport Utility 4D	JD765	20665	3650	4025	5000	6925
SORENTO 4WD—V6—Truck Equipment Schedule T1						
LX Sport Utility 4D	JC736	25265	4575	5000	5975	8150
EX Sport Utility 4D	JC736	26865	5550	6050	7200	9675
2WD	D		(700)	(700)	(935)	(935)

2008 KIA — KND(JE723)-8-#

Body Type	VIN	List	Trade-In Good	Trade-In Very Good	Pvt-Party Good	Retail Excellent
SPORTAGE 4WD—V6—Truck Equipment Schedule T1						
LX Sport Utility 4D	JE723	21970	5425	5825	6900	8900
2WD	F		(750)	(750)	(1000)	(1000)
4-Cyl, 2.0 Liter	4		(400)	(400)	(535)	(535)
SPORTAGE 4WD—V6—Truck Equipment Schedule T2						
EX Sport Utility 4D	JE723	23520	6800	7250	8425	10850
2WD	F		(750)	(750)	(1000)	(1000)
SEDONA—V6—Truck Equipment Schedule T1						
Minivan 4D	MB233	21420	3900	4225	5300	7325
LX Minivan 4D	MB233	24320	4600	4975	6100	8375
EX Minivan 4D	MB233	26920	5225	5625	7025	9575
SORENTO—V6—Truck Equipment Schedule T1						
Sport Utility 4D	JD765	21695	4575	4975	5850	7725
SORENTO 4WD—V6—Truck Equipment Schedule T1						
LX Sport Utility 4D	JC736	24895	5475	5925	7100	9375
EX Sport Utility 4D	JC736	26895	6975	7475	8700	11350
2WD	D		(750)	(750)	(995)	(995)

TRUCKS & VANS

Body Type	VIN	List	Trade-In Good	Very Good	Pvt-Party Good	Retail Excellent
2009 KIA — KND(JE723)-9-#						
SPORTAGE 4WD—V6—Truck Equipment Schedule T1						
LX Sport Utility 4D	JE723	22670	6950	7375	8275	10200
2WD	F		(875)	(875)	(1065)	(1065)
4-Cyl, 2.0 Liter	4		(475)	(475)	(580)	(580)
SPORTAGE 4WD—V6—Truck Equipment Schedule T2						
EX Sport Utility 4D	JE723	24075	8525	9000	10050	12350
2WD	F		(875)	(875)	(1070)	(1070)
SEDONA—V6—Truck Equipment Schedule T1						
Minivan 4D	MB133	21995	5225	5575	6650	8825
LX Minivan 4D	MB233	24995	5550	5925	7225	9525
EX Minivan 4D	MB233	28495	8150	8650	10200	13300
SORENTO—V6—Truck Equipment Schedule T1						
Sport Utility 4D	JD735	22295	6175	6600	7675	9775
SORENTO—V6—Truck Equipment Schedule T1						
EX Sport Utility 4D	JD736	26095	8425	8950	10200	12900
4WD	C		1175	1175	1525	1525
SORENTO 4WD—V6—Truck Equipment Schedule T1						
LX Sport Utility 4D	JC735	25395	7125	7600	8825	11200
2WD	D		(875)	(875)	(1155)	(1155)
BORREGO—V6—Truck Equipment Schedule T1						
LX Sport Utility 4D	JJ741	26995	7675	8125	9200	11400
EX Sport Utility 4D	JJ741	28745	8100	8575	9675	12000
4WD	H		1300	1300	1640	1640
V8, 4.6 Liter	2		1550	1550	1965	1965
BORREGO 4WD—V8—Truck Equipment Schedule T1						
Limited Sport Util	JH742	40745	11700	12350	13750	16950
2WD			(1300)	(1300)	(1655)	(1655)
2010 KIA — KND(KGCA3)-A-#						
SPORTAGE 4WD—V6—Truck Equipment Schedule T1						
LX Sport Utility	KGCA3	23190	9025	9500	10850	13300
2WD	3		(1000)	(1000)	(1250)	(1250)
4-Cyl, 2.0 Liter	2,4		(550)	(550)	(685)	(685)
SPORTAGE 4WD—V6—Truck Equipment Schedule T2						
EX Sport Utility	KHCA3	24190	10200	10700	12200	15050
2WD	3		(1000)	(1000)	(1260)	(1260)
SEDONA—V6—Truck Equipment Schedule T1						
Minivan 4D	MF4A3	22990	6575	6950	8225	10550
LX Minivan 4D	MG4A3	24990	7000	7400	8775	11200
EX Minivan 4D	MH4A3	29490	9500	9975	11600	14650
2011 KIA — 5XYorKND(PA3A2)-B-#						
SPORTAGE—4-Cyl.—Truck Equipment Schedule T2						
Sport Utility 4D	PA3A2	18990	10650	11150	12100	14250
SPORTAGE—4-Cyl.—Truck Equipment Schedule T2						
EX Sport Utility	PC3A2	23990	12950	13550	14700	17200
AWD	C		1000	1000	1145	1145
SPORTAGE AWD—4-Cyl.—Truck Equipment Schedule T2						
LX Sport Utility	PBCA2	22490	11900	12450	13450	15750
2WD	3		(1100)	(1100)	(1270)	(1270)
SPORTAGE AWD—4-Cyl. Turbo—Truck Equipment Schedule T2						
SX Sport Utility	PECA6	27990	15450	16150	17450	20500
2WD	3		(1100)	(1100)	(1280)	(1280)
SORENTO—4-Cyl.—Truck Equipment Schedule T1						
Sport Utility 4D	KT3A1	20790	10850	11350	12450	14850
SORENTO—V6—Truck Equipment Schedule T1						
EX Sport Utility	KU3A2	28190	13450	14050	15350	18200
AWD	C,D		1000	1000	1160	1160
4-Cyl, 2.4 Liter	1		(500)	(500)	(585)	(585)
SORENTO AWD—V6—Truck Equipment Schedule T1						
LX Sport Utility	KTCA2	27890	12250	12800	13950	16650
SX Sport Utility	KWDA2	34490	15100	15750	17100	20300
2WD	3		(1100)	(1100)	(1290)	(1290)
4-Cyl, 2.4 Liter	1		(500)	(500)	(585)	(585)
SEDONA—V6—Truck Equipment Schedule T1						
LX Minivan 4D	MG4A7	25390	8175	8600	10000	12550
EX Minivan 4D	MH4A7	29990	10750	11200	12800	15850

Body Type	VIN	List	Trade-In Good	Trade-In Very Good	Pvt-Party Good	Retail Excellent

2012 KIA — 5XYorKND(PA3A2)–C–#

SPORTAGE—4-Cyl.—Truck Equipment Schedule T2
| Sport Utility 4D | PA3A2 | 19300 | **11700** | **12200** | **13300** | **15600** |

SPORTAGE—4-Cyl.—Truck Equipment Schedule T2
| EX Sport Utility | PC3A2 | 24700 | **14400** | **15050** | **16250** | **18900** |
| AWD | C | | **1125** | **1125** | **1305** | **1305** |

SPORTAGE AWD—4-Cyl.—Truck Equipment Schedule T2
| LX Sport Utility | PBCA2 | 23100 | **12800** | **13400** | **14600** | **17050** |
| 2WD | 3 | | **(1500)** | **(1500)** | **(1750)** | **(1750)** |

SPORTAGE AWD—4-Cyl. Turbo—Truck Equipment Schedule T2
| SX Sport Utility 4D | PCCA2 | 29200 | **17050** | **17750** | **19100** | **22300** |
| 2WD | 3 | | **(1500)** | **(1500)** | **(1750)** | **(1750)** |

SORENTO—4-Cyl.—Truck Equipment Schedule T1
| Sport Utility 4D | KT3A1 | 22050 | **12300** | **12800** | **13900** | **16350** |

SORENTO—V6—Truck Equipment Schedule T1
EX Sport Utility 4D	KU3A2	28750	**15250**	**15850**	**16950**	**19650**
AWD	C,D		**1125**	**1125**	**1310**	**1310**
4-Cyl, GDI, 2.4 Liter	6		**(500)**	**(500)**	**(580)**	**(580)**

SORENTO AWD—V6—Truck Equipment Schedule T1
LX Sport Utility	KTCA1	26150	**14000**	**14550**	**15650**	**18200**
SX Sport Utility	KWDA1	35650	**17950**	**18600**	**19800**	**23000**
FWD	3		**(1200)**	**(1200)**	**(1385)**	**(1385)**
4-Cyl, GDI, 2.4 Liter	6		**(500)**	**(500)**	**(575)**	**(575)**

SEDONA—V6—Truck Equipment Schedule T1
| LX Minivan 4D | MG4A7 | 25700 | **9900** | **10350** | **11800** | **14400** |
| EX Minivan 4D | MH4A7 | 29990 | **12450** | **12950** | **14600** | **17700** |

2013 KIA — 5XYorKND(PB3A2)–D–#

SPORTAGE—4-Cyl.—Truck Equipment Schedule T2
| Sport Utility 4D | PB3A2 | 19800 | **12550** | **13100** | **14200** | **16550** |

SPORTAGE AWD—4-Cyl.—Truck Equipment Schedule T2
LX Sport Utility	PBCA2	23500	**13700**	**14300**	**15550**	**18100**
EX Sport Utility	PCCA2	26500	**16200**	**16900**	**18100**	**21000**
2WD	3		**(1500)**	**(1500)**	**(1740)**	**(1740)**

SPORTAGE AWD—4-Cyl. Turbo—Truck Equipment Schedule T2
| SX Sport Utility 4D | PCCA6 | 29200 | **18700** | **19450** | **20600** | **23700** |
| 2WD | 3 | | **(1500)** | **(1500)** | **(1710)** | **(1710)** |

SORENTO AWD—V6—Truck Equipment Schedule T1
LX Sport Utility	KTDA2	28200	**15600**	**16200**	**17300**	**20000**
EX Sport Utility	KU3A2	28750	**17450**	**18100**	**19200**	**22100**
SX Sport Utility	KWDA2	34200	**19600**	**20200**	**21500**	**24800**
FWD	3		**(1300)**	**(1300)**	**(1475)**	**(1475)**
4-Cyl, GDI, 2.4 Liter	6		**(600)**	**(600)**	**(680)**	**(680)**

2014 KIA — 5XYorKND(PBCAC)–E–#

SPORTAGE AWD—4-Cyl.—Truck Equipment Schedule 1
LX Sport Utility	PBCAC	23950	**15750**	**16400**	**17850**	**20900**
EX Sport Utility	PCCAC	27350	**17600**	**18300**	**19700**	**22800**
SX Sport Utility	PCCA4	29250	**20100**	**20900**	**22100**	**25400**
FWD	3		**(1500)**	**(1500)**	**(1775)**	**(1775)**

SORENTO AWD—V6—Truck Equipment Schedule T1
LX Sport Utility	KTDA7	28250	**17050**	**17650**	**19450**	**23100**
EX Sport Utility	KU3A7	30850	**20100**	**20800**	**22500**	**26500**
SX Sport Utility	KWDA7	37550	**22700**	**23500**	**25200**	**29600**
Limited Sport Utility 4D		40550	**24700**	**25500**	**27100**	**31500**
FWD	3,4		**(1400)**	**(1400)**	**(1690)**	**(1690)**
4-Cyl, GDI, 2.4 Liter	6		**(700)**	**(700)**	**(845)**	**(845)**

LAND ROVER

2000 LAND ROVER — SAL(TY124)–Y–#

DISCOVERY SERIES II 4WD—V8—Truck Equipment Schedule T3
SD Spt Util 4D	TY124	36725	**475**	**575**	**1575**	**2800**
SD7 Spt Util 4D	TY124	35725	**725**	**850**	**1925**	**3400**
Sport Utility 4D	TY124	36725	**725**	**850**	**1925**	**3400**
Rear Jump Seats			**200**	**200**	**265**	**265**
Air Conditioning, Rear			**100**	**100**	**135**	**135**
Dual Moon Roofs			**475**	**475**	**635**	**635**
Performance Pkg			**300**	**300**	**390**	**390**

2000 LAND ROVER

Body Type	VIN	List	Trade-In Good	Very Good	Pvt-Party Good	Retail Excellent
RANGE ROVER 4WD—V8—Truck Equipment Schedule T3						
County Spt Ut 4D	PA124	58925	**1000**	**1125**	**1800**	**2800**
4.0 Sport Util 4D	PA124	59625	**825**	**950**	**1625**	**2550**
4.0 SE Sport Util 4D	PV124	59625	**775**	**900**	**1575**	**2450**
4.6 HSK Spt Util 4D	PF164	67625	**1200**	**1350**	**2075**	**3250**
4.6 HSE Spt Util 4D	PV144	67925	**1625**	**1825**	**2725**	**4175**
4.6 Vitesse Util 4D	PF164	68625	**1925**	**2150**	**3125**	**4775**
4.6 Holland Holland	PV164	79625	**2300**	**3550**	**4425**	**6200**

2001 LAND ROVER — SAL(TY124)-1-#

Body Type	VIN	List	Trade-In Good	Very Good	Pvt-Party Good	Retail Excellent
DISCOVERY SERIES II 4WD—V8—Truck Equipment Schedule T3						
SD Sport Util 4D	TY124	33975	**725**	**850**	**1900**	**3325**
SD7 Sport Util 4D	TY124	35725	**850**	**1000**	**2125**	**3750**
LE Sport Util 4D	TY124	34975	**750**	**875**	**1975**	**3525**
LE7 Sport Util 4D	TY124	36725	**1125**	**1300**	**2500**	**4400**
SE Sport Util 4D	TY124	36975	**1450**	**1650**	**3100**	**5350**
SE7 Sport Util 4D	TY124	38725	**1025**	**1200**	**2375**	**4100**
Rear Jump Seats			**200**	**200**	**265**	**265**
Air Conditioning, Rear			**125**	**125**	**155**	**155**
Dual Moon Roofs			**500**	**500**	**665**	**665**
Performance Pkg			**325**	**325**	**445**	**445**
RANGE ROVER 4WD—V8—Truck Equipment Schedule T3						
4.6 SE Sport Util 4D	PV164	62625	**900**	**1025**	**1700**	**2625**
4.6 HSE Sport Util	PV164	68625	**1725**	**1950**	**2850**	**4350**

2002 LAND ROVER — SAL(NM222)-2-#

Body Type	VIN	List	Trade-In Good	Very Good	Pvt-Party Good	Retail Excellent
FREELANDER AWD—V6—Truck Equipment Schedule T3						
S Sport Utility 4D	NM222	25600	**250**	**250**	**1125**	**2050**
SE Sport Utility 4D	NY222	28400	**625**	**750**	**1775**	**3125**
HSE Sport Util 4D	NE222	32200	**750**	**900**	**1900**	**3275**
DISCOVERY SERIES II 4WD—V8—Truck Equipment Schedule T3						
SD Sport Util 4D	TL144	33995	**800**	**950**	**1975**	**3400**
SD7 Sport Util 4D	TK144	34995	**1300**	**1500**	**2550**	**4325**
SE Sport Util 4D	TY144	37795	**1825**	**2075**	**3400**	**5575**
SE7 Sport Util 4D	TW124	38875	**1525**	**1725**	**2950**	**4900**
Rear Jump Seats			**250**	**250**	**335**	**335**
Air Conditioning, Rear			**125**	**125**	**175**	**175**
Dual Moon Roofs			**550**	**550**	**735**	**735**
Performance Pkg			**375**	**375**	**495**	**495**
RANGE ROVER 4WD—V8—Truck Equipment Schedule T3						
4.6 HSE Sport Util	PL162	68665	**1950**	**2150**	**3050**	**4525**

2003 LAND ROVER — SAL(NM222)-3-#

Body Type	VIN	List	Trade-In Good	Very Good	Pvt-Party Good	Retail Excellent
FREELANDER AWD—V6—Truck Equipment Schedule T3						
S Sport Utility 4D	NM222	25600	**475**	**575**	**1425**	**2450**
SE3 Sport Util 2D	NY122	26995	**750**	**875**	**1775**	**3000**
SE Sport Util 4D	NY222	28400	**950**	**1100**	**2025**	**3400**
HSE Sport Util 4D	NE222	32200	**1075**	**1250**	**2225**	**3700**
DISCOVERY 4WD—V8—Truck Equipment Schedule T3						
S Sport Util 4D	TL144	34995	**1000**	**1150**	**2125**	**3550**
SE Sport Util 4D	TY144	38995	**2500**	**2825**	**4175**	**6625**
SE7 Sport Util 4D	TW124	39995	**2425**	**2750**	**4000**	**6300**
HSE Spt Util 4D	TP144	40995	**3475**	**3875**	**5425**	**8300**
HSE7 Spt Ut 4D	TR144	41995	**3575**	**3975**	**5525**	**8475**
Rear Jump Seats			**275**	**275**	**365**	**365**
Air Conditioning, Rear			**150**	**150**	**200**	**200**
Dual Moon Roofs			**575**	**575**	**765**	**765**
Suspension Pkg			**400**	**400**	**540**	**540**
RANGE ROVER 4WD—V8—Truck Equipment Schedule T3						
HSE Sport Util 4D	MB114	71865	**4100**	**4450**	**5650**	**7950**

2004 LAND ROVER — SAL(NY222)-4-#

Body Type	VIN	List	Trade-In Good	Very Good	Pvt-Party Good	Retail Excellent
FREELANDER AWD—V6—Truck Equipment Schedule T3						
SE Sport Utility 4D	NY222	25995	**1300**	**1500**	**2600**	**4275**
SE3 Spt Util 2D	NY122	28195	**1500**	**1725**	**2850**	**4625**
HSE Sport Util 4D	NE222	28995	**1400**	**1600**	**2625**	**4225**
DISCOVERY 4WD—V8—Truck Equipment Schedule T3						
S Sport Utility 4D	TL194	34995	**1625**	**1825**	**2875**	**4575**
SE Sport Utility 4D	TY194	39250	**3475**	**3875**	**5425**	**8275**
SE7 Spt Util 4D	TW194	40350	**3300**	**3675**	**5025**	**7550**
HSE Spt Util 4D	TP194	41250	**4525**	**4975**	**6475**	**9550**
HSE7 Spt Util 4D	TR194	42250	**4625**	**5075**	**6600**	**9700**

2004 LAND ROVER

Body Type	VIN	List	Trade-In Good	Very Good	Pvt-Party Good	Retail Excellent
G4 Sport Utility 4D	TL194	39995	3525	3925	5475	8350
Rear Jump Seats			300	300	400	400
Air Conditioning, Rear			175	175	235	235
Dual Moon Roofs			600	600	800	800
Suspension Pkg			450	450	595	595
RANGE ROVER 4WD—V8—Truck Equipment Schedule T3						
HSE Sport Util 4D	ME114	72250	5225	5625	6800	9125
Westminster Util	MH114	84700	8525	9100	10500	13800
Luxury Pkg			675	675	915	915

2005 LAND ROVER — SAL(NY222)-5-#

Body Type	VIN	List	Trade-In Good	Very Good	Pvt-Party Good	Retail Excellent
FREELANDER AWD—V6—Truck Equipment Schedule T3						
SE Sport Utility 4D	NY222	27495	1700	1925	3050	4825
SE3 Sport Util 2D	NM122	27495	1550	1775	2925	4700
LR3 4WD—V8—Truck Equipment Schedule T3						
SE Sport Util 4D	AD254	44995	6225	6675	7675	10000
Third Row Seat			325	325	430	430
V6, 4.0 Liter			(1175)	(1175)	(1555)	(1555)
LR3 4WD—V8—Truck Equipment Schedule T3						
HSE Sport Util 4D	AF254	49995	7000	7475	8575	11150
Third Row Seat			325	325	430	430
RANGE ROVER 4WD—V8—Truck Equipment Schedule T3						
HSE Sport Util 4D	ME114	73750	7400	7900	9100	11900
Westminster Util	MH114	86000	10650	11350	12750	16450
Luxury Pkg			750	750	1000	1000

2006 LAND ROVER — SAL(AB244)-6-#

Body Type	VIN	List	Trade-In Good	Very Good	Pvt-Party Good	Retail Excellent
LR3 4WD—V6—Truck Equipment Schedule T3						
Sport Utility 4D	AB244	38950	5650	6050	7150	9325
Third Row Seat	C,E		350	350	465	465
LR3 4WD—V8—Truck Equipment Schedule T3						
SE Sport Utility 4D	AD254	45450	6850	7325	8575	11200
Third Row Seat	C,E		350	350	465	465
LR3 4WD—V8—Truck Equipment Schedule T3						
HSE Sport Util 4D	AG254	53450	8100	8625	10150	13100
Third Row Seat	G		350	350	460	460
Luxury Pkg			400	400	515	515
RANGE ROVER SPORT 4WD—V8—Truck Equipment Schedule T3						
HSE Sport Util 4D	SF254	56750	11300	11950	13200	16500
Luxury Pkg			800	800	1020	1020
RANGE ROVER SPORT 4WD—V8 Supercharged—Truck Equipment Sch T3						
Sport Utility 4D	SD234	69750	12650	13400	14750	18450
Adaptive Cruise Control			325	325	410	410
RANGE ROVER 4WD—V8—Truck Equipment Schedule T3						
HSE Sport Util 4D	ME154	74950	11500	12150	13400	16800
Luxury Pkg			800	800	1020	1020
RANGE ROVER 4WD—V8 Supercharged—Truck Equipment Sch T3						
Sport Utility 4D	MF134	89950	16050	16900	18000	22200
Westminster 4D	MH134	98150	17100	18000	19250	23800

2007 LAND ROVER — SAL(AD244)-7-#

Body Type	VIN	List	Trade-In Good	Very Good	Pvt-Party Good	Retail Excellent
LR3 4WD—V8—Truck Equipment Schedule T3						
SE Sport Utility 4D	AD244	42150	9175	9725	10950	13750
Third Row Seat			375	375	475	475
V6, 4.0 Liter	4		(1400)	(1400)	(1760)	(1760)
LR3 4WD—V8—Truck Equipment Schedule T3						
HSE Sport Util 4D	AG254	53950	10550	11150	12500	15650
Luxury Pkg			400	400	515	515
Third Row Seat			375	375	470	470
RANGE ROVER SPORT 4WD—V8—Truck Equipment Schedule T3						
HSE Sport Util 4D	SF254	57950	13700	14450	15550	19000
Luxury Pkg			875	875	1075	1075
RANGE ROVER SPORT 4WD—V8 Supercharged—Truck Equipment Sch T3						
Sport Utility 4D	SD234	71250	14500	15250	16300	19800
Adaptive Cruise Control			350	350	425	425
RANGE ROVER 4WD—V8—Truck Equipment Schedule T3						
HSE Sport Util 4D	ME154	77250	14200	14950	16050	19600
Luxury Pkg			875	875	1075	1075
RANGE ROVER 4WD—V8 Supercharged—Truck Equipment Schedule T3						
Sport Utility 4D	MF134	92750	19050	20000	20900	25200

2008 LAND ROVER

Body Type	VIN	List	Trade-In Good	Trade-In Very Good	Pvt-Party Good	Retail Excellent
2008 LAND ROVER — SAL(FP24N)-8-#						
LR2 AWD—6-Cyl.—Truck Equipment Schedule T3						
SE Sport Utility 4D	FP24N	34700	7475	8025	9000	11400
HSE Sport Util 4D	FR24N	36150	8775	9400	10350	13000
LR3 4WD—V8—Truck Equipment Schedule T3						
SE Sport Utility 4D	AE254	49300	11100	11700	12750	15400
HSE Sport Util 4D	AG254	54800	12900	13550	14700	17800
Third Row Seat			400	400	485	485
Luxury Pkg			425	425	530	530
RANGE ROVER SPORT 4WD—V8—Truck Equipment Schedule T3						
HSE Sport Util 4D	SF254	58500	15700	16500	17450	20700
Luxury Pkg			925	925	1110	1110
RANGE ROVER SPORT 4WD—V8 Supercharged—Truck Equipment Sch T3						
Sport Utility 4D	SH234	71950	16400	17200	18150	21600
Adaptive Cruise Control			375	375	445	445
RANGE ROVER 4WD—V8—Truck Equipment Schedule T3						
HSE Sport Util 4D	ME154	77950	16650	17450	18450	21900
Luxury Pkg			925	925	1105	1105
RANGE ROVER 4WD—V8 Supercharged—Truck Equipment Schedule T3						
Sport Utility 4D	MF134	93600	21800	22800	23600	27800
Westminster Util	MH134	105600	25800	27000	27800	32600
2009 LAND ROVER — SAL(FR24N)-9-#						
LR2 AWD—6-Cyl.—Truck Equipment Schedule T3						
HSE Sport Utility 4D	FR24N	36150	10450	11050	11900	14450
LR3 4WD—V8—Truck Equipment Schedule T3						
Sport Utility 4D	AE254	46750	20600	21500	22300	25900
Third Row Seat			475	475	545	545
HSE Lux Pkg			450	450	525	525
RANGE ROVER SPORT 4WD—V8—Truck Equipment Schedule T3						
HSE Sport Util 4D	SF254	59150	19800	20600	21600	25200
Luxury Pkg			1000	1000	1165	1165
RANGE ROVER SPORT 4WD—V8 Supercharged—Truck Equipment Sch T3						
Sport Utility 4D	SH234	72600	22400	23300	24300	28300
Adaptive Cruise Control			375	375	435	435
RANGE ROVER 4WD—V8—Truck Equipment Schedule T3						
HSE Sport Util 4D	ME154	78450	22800	23700	24600	28700
Luxury Pkg			1000	1000	1165	1165
RANGE ROVER 4WD—V8 Supercharged—Truck Equipment Schedule T3						
Sport Utility 4D	MF134	94100	30000	31200	32000	36900
Autobiography Pkg			5900	5900	6745	6745
2010 LAND ROVER — SAL(FR2BN)-A-#						
LR2 AWD—6-Cyl.—Truck Equipment Schedule T3						
HSE Sport Util 4D	FR2BN	36350	14400	15100	16050	18950
LR4 4WD—V8—Truck Equipment Schedule T3						
Sport Utility 4D	AB2D4	48100	28000	29100	29600	33600
Third Row Seat			550	550	615	615
HSE Pkg			1525	1525	1700	1700
HSE Lux Pkg			3100	3100	3460	3460
RANGE ROVER SPORT 4WD—V8—Truck Equipment Schedule T3						
HSE Sport Util 4D	SF2D4	60495	26600	27600	28300	32100
Luxury Pkg			1000	1000	1125	1125
RANGE ROVER SPORT 4WD—V8 Supercharged—Truck Equipment Sch T3						
Sport Utility 4D	SH2E4	74195	31400	32500	33200	37700
Luxury Pkg			1000	1000	1120	1120
Adaptive Cruise Control			400	400	450	450
RANGE ROVER 4WD—V8—Truck Equipment Schedule T3						
HSE Sport Util 4D	ME1D4	79275	31800	32900	33600	38200
Vision Assist Pack			375	375	435	435
Adaptive Cruise Control			400	400	450	450
Luxury Pkg			1000	1000	1125	1125
RANGE ROVER 4WD—V8 Supercharged—Truck Equipment Schedule T3						
Sport Utility 4D	MF1E4	95125	41300	42700	43000	48400
Luxury Pkg			1000	1000	1105	1105
Adaptive Cruise Control			400	400	445	445
2011 LAND ROVER — SAL(FR2BN)-B-#						
LR2 AWD—6-Cyl.—Truck Equipment Schedule T3						
Sport Utility 4D	FR2BN	36550	18000	18750	19700	22800
HSE Pkg			1625	1625	1805	1805

2011 LAND ROVER

Body Type	VIN	List	Trade-In Good	Very Good	Pvt-Party Good	Retail Excellent
HSE Lux Pkg			3275	3275	3650	3650
LR4—V8—Truck Equipment Schedule T3						
Sport Utility 4D	AB2D4	48500	30500	31600	32200	36100
Third Row Seat			600	600	655	655
HSE Pkg			1625	1625	1770	1770
HSE Lux Pkg			3275	3275	3590	3590
Metropolis Black Ltd Ed			575	575	625	625
Metropolis Limited Ed			575	575	625	625
RANGE ROVER SPORT 4WD—V8—Truck Equipment Schedule T3						
HSE Sport Util 4D	SF2D4	60495	29800	30900	31700	35800
Luxury Pkg			1000	1000	1120	1120
RANGE ROVER SPORT 4WD—V8 Supercharged—Truck Equipment Sch T3						
Sport Utility 4D	SH2E4	75395	34800	36000	36700	41300
Autobiography Pkg			3300	3300	3680	3680
Luxury Pkg			1000	1000	1115	1115
Adaptive Cruise Control			425	425	475	475
RANGE ROVER 4WD—V8—Truck Equipment Schedule T3						
HSE Sport Util 4D	ME1D4	79685	36000	37200	37900	42600
Luxury Pkg			1000	1000	1115	1115
RANGE ROVER 4WD—V8 Supercharged—Truck Equipment Schedule T3						
Sport Utility 4D	MF1E4	95465	46300	47800	48100	53700
Autobiography Pkg			6600	6600	7250	7250
Luxury Pkg			1000	1000	1100	1100

2012 LAND ROVER — SAL(FR2BN)-C-#

Body Type	VIN	List	Trade-In Good	Very Good	Pvt-Party Good	Retail Excellent
LR2 AWD—6-Cyl.—Truck Equipment Schedule T3						
Sport Utility 4D	FR2BN	36550	20400	21100	22000	25100
HSE Pkg			1725	1725	1890	1890
HSE Lux Pkg			3450	3450	3810	3810
LR4—V8—Truck Equipment Schedule T3						
Sport Utility 4D	AB2D4	50600	37500	38800	39200	43500
Third Row Seat			650	650	705	705
HSE Pkg			1725	1725	1865	1865
HSE Lux Pkg			3450	3450	3760	3760
RANGE ROVER EVOQUE 4WD—4-Cyl. Turbo—Truck Equipment Sch T3						
Sport Utility 4D	VN2BG	43995	28500	29500	30100	34000
Spt Util Coupe 2D	VN1BG	44995	28900	29900	30500	34400
Dynamic Spt Util	VS2BG	58995	33900	35100	35400	39700
Dynamic Coupe 2D	VS1BG	60795	34300	35400	35700	40100
Prestige Sport Util	VU2BG	60795	35100	36200	36500	40900
Adaptive Dynamics Susp			600	600	645	645
RANGE ROVER SPORT 4WD—V8—Truck Equipment Schedule T3						
HSE Sport Util 4D	SF2D4	61745	38300	39500	40100	44600
Luxury Pkg			1000	1000	1105	1105
RANGE ROVER SPORT 4WD—V8 Supercharged—Truck Equipment Sch T3						
Sport Utility 4D	SH2E4	76945	44700	46100	46600	51800
Autobiography Pkg			3475	3475	3835	3835
Adaptive Cruise Control			450	450	495	495
RANGE ROVER 4WD—V8—Truck Equipment Schedule T3						
HSE Sport Util 4D	ME1D4	81125	47500	49000	49400	54900
Luxury Pkg			1000	1000	1100	1100
RANGE ROVER 4WD—V8 Supercharged—Truck Equipment Schedule T3						
Sport Utility 4D	MH1E4	96520	57600	59400	59500	65400
Autobiography Pkg			6950	6950	7555	7555

2013 LAND ROVER — SAL(FP28G)-D-#

Body Type	VIN	List	Trade-In Good	Very Good	Pvt-Party Good	Retail Excellent
LR2 AWD—4-Cyl. Turbo—Truck Equipment Schedule T3						
Sport Utility 4D	FP2BG	37250	22500	23300	24400	28100
HSE Sport Util 4D	FR2BG	39795	24500	25300	26500	30400
HSE LUX Spt Util	FT2BG	42395	27400	28300	29400	33700
LR4 4WD—V8—Truck Equipment Schedule T3						
Sport Utility 4D	AB2D4	49995	41600	42800	43100	47400
HSE Sport Util 4D	AF2D4	54220	43600	44900	45200	49700
HSE LUX Spt Util	AK2D4	59220	47700	49100	49100	53800
RANGE ROVER EVOQUE 4WD—4-Cyl. Turbo—Truck Equip Schedule T3						
Pure Sport Util 4D	VN2BG	41995	30800	31800	32300	36200
Pure Plus Util 4D	VP2BG	43995	31200	32100	32700	36600
Pure Plus Cpe 2D	VP1BG	44995	31500	32400	33000	37000
Pure Premium 4D	VR2BG	48195	33500	34500	35000	39200
Pure Premium 2D	VR1BG	49195	33900	34900	35400	39700
Dynamic Spt 4D	VT2BG	51695	35900	37000	37300	41600
Prestige Spt Util	VV2BG	52595	38000	39100	39300	43800

Body Type	VIN	List	Trade-In Good	Very Good	Pvt-Party Good	Retail Excellent
Dynamic Spt 2D	VT1BG	53095	37100	38200	38500	42900
RANGE ROVER SPORT 4WD—V8—Truck Equipment Schedule T3						
HSE Sport Util 4D	SF2D4	60895	45900	47300	47600	52400
HSE LUX Sport Util 4D	SK2D4	65595	47500	48900	49600	54700
GT Limited Ed 4D	SF2D4	70995	54500	56100	56300	61700
Adaptive Cruise Control			475	475	510	510
RANGE ROVER SPORT 4WD—V8 Supercharged—Truck Equipment Sch T3						
Sport Utility 4D	SH2E4	76495	59500	61300	61500	67400
Limited Ed Spt Util	SH2E4	80040	62500	64300	64300	70400
Autobiography 4D	SP2E4	87195	66900	68900	68600	75000
Adaptive Cruise Control			475	475	510	510
RANGE ROVER 4WD—V8—Truck Equipment Schedule T3						
Sport Utility 4D	GR2DF	84350	65200	67100	66900	73200
HSE Sport Util 4D	GS2DF	89350	73800	75900	75200	81900
Adaptive Cruise Control			475	475	510	510
RANGE ROVER 4WD—V8 Supercharged—Truck Equipment Schedule T3						
Sport Utility 4D	GS2EF	100800	81300	83700	82400	89400
Adaptive Cruise Control			475	475	505	505
RANGE ROVER 4WD—V8 Supercharged—Truck Equipment Schedule T3						
Autobiography 4D	GV2EF	131800	108000	111100	108500	116800

2014 LAND ROVER — SAL(FP2BG)—E–#

Body Type	VIN	List	Trade-In Good	Very Good	Pvt-Party Good	Retail Excellent
LR2 AWD—4-Cyl. Turbo—Truck Equipment Schedule T1						
Sport Utility 4D	FP2BG	37495	27200	28000	28900	32800
HSE Sport Util 4D	FR2BG	39995	29100	30000	30800	34800
HSE LUX Spt Utl	FT2BG	42595	32000	32900	33800	38100
LR4 4WD—V6 Supercharged—Truck Equipment Schedule T1						
Sport Utility 4D	AB2V6	50595	44700	46100	46000	50200
HSE Sport Util 4D	AG2V6	55495	46900	48300	48100	52400
HSE LUX Spt Util	AK2V6	60700	50700	52200	52000	56500
RANGE ROVER EVOQUE 4WD—4-Cyl. Turbo—Truck Equipment Sch T3						
Pure Sport Util 4D	VN2BG	41995	33700	34700	35200	39400
Pure Plus Util 4D	VP2BG	44995	34100	35100	35600	39800
Pure Plus Cpe 2D	VP1BG	45040	34400	35400	35900	40100
Pure Premium 4D	VR2BG	49595	36400	37400	37700	42100
Pure Premium 2D	VR1BG	50595	36800	37900	38100	42500
Prestige Spt Util	VU2BG	56295	40800	42000	42000	46600
Dynamic Spt 4D	VT2BG	57195	38800	39900	40100	44600
Dynamic Spt 2D	VT1BG	58195	39900	41100	41200	45700
Adaptive Cruise Control			500	500	535	535
RANGE ROVER SPORT 4WD—V6 Supercharged—Truck Equipment Sch T3						
SE Sport Util 4D	WJ2VF	63495	56300	58000	57900	63200
HSE Sport Util 4D	WG2VF	68495	60200	61900	61600	67100
RANGE ROVER SPORT 4WD—V8 Supercharged—Truck Equipment Sch T3						
Sport Utility 4D	WR2EF	79995	70600	72700	71600	77500
Autobiography 4D	WV2EF	93295	77100	79300	77800	84000
RANGE ROVER 4WD—V6 Supercharged—Truck Equipment Schedule T3						
Sport Utility 4D	GR2VF	83545	76300	78500	77000	83000
RANGE ROVER 4WD—V6 Supercharged—Truck Equipment Schedule T3						
HSE Sport Util 4D	GS2VF	88545	80800	83100	81300	87600
Adaptive Cruise Control			500	500	525	525
RANGE ROVER 4WD—V8 Supercharged—Truck Equipment Schedule T3						
Sport Utility 4D	GS2EF	99995	90800	93400	91000	97700
Adaptive Cruise Control			500	500	520	520
RANGE ROVER 4WD—V8 Supercharged—Truck Equipment Schedule T3						
Autobiography 4D	GV2EF	135995	120600	123900	120700	129600
AutobiographyBlk	GV3TF	185000	155100	159400	154600	165700

LEXUS

2000 LEXUS — JT6(HF10U)–Y–#

Body Type	VIN	List	Trade-In Good	Very Good	Pvt-Party Good	Retail Excellent
RX 300 4WD—V6—Truck Equipment Schedule T3						
Sport Utility 4D	HF10U	35680	2975	3300	4150	5925
2WD			(350)	(350)	(465)	(465)
LX 470 4WD—V8—Truck Equipment Schedule T3						
Sport Utility 4D	HT00W	59500	8175	8725	9950	12950

2001 LEXUS — JTJ(HF10U)–1–#

Body Type	VIN	List	Trade-In Good	Very Good	Pvt-Party Good	Retail Excellent
RX 300 4WD—V6—Truck Equipment Schedule T3						
Sport Utility 4D	HF10U	37430	3775	4150	5050	6975
Silversport Edition			125	125	175	175

500 DEDUCT FOR RECONDITIONING

0415

2001 LEXUS

Body Type	VIN	List	Trade-In Good	Very Good	Pvt-Party Good	Retail Excellent
2WD			(400)	(400)	(535)	(535)
LX 470 4WD—V8—Truck Equipment Schedule T3						
Sport Utility 4D	HT00W	61950	8900	9475	10750	13900

2002 LEXUS — JTJ(HF10U)-2-#

RX 300 4WD—V6—Truck Equipment Schedule T3						
Sport Utility 4D	HF10U	37580	4225	4625	5500	7475
Coach Edition			175	175	250	250
2WD	G		(450)	(450)	(600)	(600)
LX 470 4WD—V8—Truck Equipment Schedule T3						
Sport Utility 4D	HT00W	63051	10100	10700	12000	15300

2003 LEXUS — JTJ(HF10U)-3-#

RX 300 4WD—V6—Truck Equipment Schedule T3						
Sport Utility 4D	HF10U	38800	4550	4950	6050	8200
2WD	G		(500)	(500)	(665)	(665)
GX 470 4WD—V8—Truck Equipment Schedule T3						
Sport Utility 4D	BT20X	45500	9175	9725	11050	14100
Third Row Seat			650	650	820	820
LX 470 4WD—V8—Truck Equipment Schedule T3						
Sport Utility 4D	HT00W	63700	13350	14100	15200	18850

2004 LEXUS — JTJ(HA31U)-4-#

RX 330 AWD—V6—Truck Equipment Schedule T3						
Sport Utility 4D	HA31U	39195	8550	9125	10350	13500
Dynamic Cruise Control			275	275	365	365
Performance Pkg			1750	1750	2345	2345
2WD	G		(550)	(550)	(735)	(735)
GX 470 4WD—V8—Truck Equipment Schedule T3						
Sport Utility 4D	BT20X	45700	10450	11050	12400	15650
Third Row Seat			675	675	840	840
LX 470 4WD—V8—Truck Equipment Schedule T3						
Sport Utility 4D	HT00W	64800	16750	17600	18250	21800

2005 LEXUS — JTJ(HA31U)-5-#

RX 330 AWD—V6—Truck Equipment Schedule T3						
Sport Utility 4D	HA31U	37800	9175	9775	11200	14600
Dynamic Cruise Control			300	300	400	400
Performance Pkg			1900	1900	2540	2540
2WD	G		(600)	(600)	(800)	(800)
GX 470 4WD—V8—Truck Equipment Schedule T3						
Sport Utility 4D	BT20X	46425	12450	13100	14350	17700
Third Row Seat			700	700	845	845
LX 470 4WD—V8—Truck Equipment Schedule T3						
Sport Utility 4D	HT00W	65400	18350	19300	20200	24300

2006 LEXUS — JTJ(HA31U)-6-#

RX 330 AWD—V6—Truck Equipment Schedule T3						
Sport Utility 4D	HA31U	38420	10200	10800	11900	14950
Dynamic Cruise Control			325	325	415	415
Performance Pkg			2050	2050	2630	2630
2WD	G		(650)	(650)	(830)	(830)
RX 400h AWD—V6 Hybrid—Truck Equipment Schedule T3						
Sport Utility 4D	HW31U	49060	10550	11200	12500	15650
Dynamic Cruise Control			325	325	415	415
2WD	G		(650)	(650)	(835)	(835)
GX 470 4WD—V8—Truck Equipment Schedule T3						
Sport Utility 4D	BT20X	47185	14200	14900	16000	19300
Third Row Seat			750	750	845	845
LX 470 4WD—V8—Truck Equipment Schedule T3						
Sport Utility 4D	HT00W	67945	23800	24900	25600	30200

2007 LEXUS — JTJ(HK31U)-7-#

RX 350 AWD—V6—Truck Equipment Schedule T3						
Sport Utility 4D	HK31U	39495	11750	12400	13450	16600
Dynamic Cruise Control			350	350	435	435
Performance Pkg			2200	2200	2725	2725
2WD	G		(700)	(700)	(865)	(865)
RX 400h AWD—V6 Hybrid—Truck Equipment Schedule T3						
Sport Utility 4D	HW31U	43275	12700	13400	14650	18050
Dynamic Cruise Control			350	350	435	435

2007 LEXUS

Body Type	VIN	List	Trade-In Good	Very Good	Pvt-Party Good	Retail Excellent
2WD .... G			(700)	(700)	(865)	(865)
GX 470 4WD—V8—Truck Equipment Schedule T3						
Sport Utility 4D	BT20X	47330	15550	16300	17350	20700
Third Row Seat			775	775	885	885
LX 470 4WD—V8—Truck Equipment Schedule T3						
Sport Utility 4D	HT00W	68090	26700	27800	28500	33300

2008 LEXUS — JTJ(HK31U)-8-#

Body Type	VIN	List	Good	Very Good	Good	Excellent
RX 350 AWD—V6—Truck Equipment Schedule T3						
Sport Utility 4D	HK31U	39565	12900	13550	14700	17750
Dynamic Cruise Control			375	375	455	455
Performance Pkg			2350	2350	2845	2845
FWD	G		(750)	(750)	(905)	(905)
RX 400h AWD—V6 Hybrid—Truck Equipment Schedule T3						
Sport Utility 4D	HW31U	43345	14950	15700	16800	20200
Dynamic Cruise Control			375	375	455	455
2WD	G		(750)	(750)	(915)	(915)
GX 470 4WD—V8—Truck Equipment Schedule T3						
Sport Utility 4D	BT20X	47580	19100	19950	20900	24500
Third Row Seat			800	800	900	900
LX 570 4WD—V8—Truck Equipment Schedule T3						
Sport Utility 4D	HY00W	74565	34400	35800	36000	41100
Dynamic Radar Cruise Ctrl			375	375	410	410

2009 LEXUS — JTJ(HK31U)-9-#

Body Type	VIN	List	Good	Very Good	Good	Excellent
RX 350 AWD—V6—Truck Equipment Schedule T3						
Sport Utility 4D	HK31U	42765	16000	16700	17950	21300
Dynamic Cruise Control			375	375	440	440
Premium Pkg			725	725	835	835
Performance Pkg			2500	2500	2935	2935
FWD	G		(1200)	(1200)	(1410)	(1410)
GX 470 4WD—V8—Truck Equipment Schedule T3						
Sport Utility 4D	BT20X	48380	22900	23800	24600	28300
Third Row Seat			800	800	905	905
LX 570 4WD—V8—Truck Equipment Schedule T3						
Sport Utility 4D	HY00W	76530	37800	39200	39300	44100

2010 LEXUS — JT(Jor2)(BK1BA)-A-#

Body Type	VIN	List	Good	Very Good	Good	Excellent
RX 350 AWD—V6—Truck Equipment Schedule T3						
Sport Utility 4D	BK1BA	39025	21300	22100	23100	26600
Premium Pkg			750	750	865	865
FWD	Z		(1100)	(1100)	(1255)	(1255)
RX 450h AWD—V6 Hybrid—Truck Equipment Schedule T3						
Sport Utility 4D	BC1BA	44125	24500	25400	26400	30200
Premium Pkg			750	750	855	855
FWD	Z		(1100)	(1100)	(1240)	(1240)
GX 460 4WD—V8—Truck Equipment Schedule T3						
Sport Utility 4D	BM7FX	52845	28500	29500	30300	34200
Premium Spt Utl	JM7FX	57640	30200	31300	32000	36000
Power Third Row			800	800	885	885
LX 570 4WD—V8—Truck Equipment Schedule T3						
Sport Utility 4D	HY7AX	77280	44600	46100	46100	51300

2011 LEXUS — (JTor2T)(Jor2)(BK1BA)-B-#

Body Type	VIN	List	Good	Very Good	Good	Excellent
RX 350 AWD—V6—Truck Equipment Schedule T3						
Sport Utility 4D	BK1BA	40250	24100	24900	26000	29500
Premium Pkg			800	800	905	905
FWD	Z		(1225)	(1225)	(1370)	(1370)
RX 450h AWD—V6 Hybrid—Truck Equipment Schedule T3						
Sport Utility 4D	BC1BA	45700	27500	28400	29300	33200
Premium Pkg			800	800	895	895
FWD	Z		(1225)	(1225)	(1355)	(1355)
GX 460 4WD—V8—Truck Equipment Schedule T3						
Sport Utility 4D	BM7FX	53220	31200	32300	32900	36800
Premium Utility	JM7FX	58015	34600	35800	36300	40500
LX 570 4WD—V8—Truck Equipment Schedule T3						
Sport Utility 4D	HY7AX	78630	48400	50000	50300	55500

2012 LEXUS — (JTor2T)(Jor2)(BK1BA)-C-#

Body Type	VIN	List	Good	Very Good	Good	Excellent
RX 350 AWD—V6—Truck Equipment Schedule T3						
Sport Utility 4D	BK1BA	41350	27300	28200	29100	32700

2012 LEXUS

Body Type	VIN	List	Trade-In Good	Very Good	Pvt-Party Good	Retail Excellent
Premium Pkg	Z		850	850	945	945
FWD			(1300)	(1300)	(1430)	(1430)

RX 450h AWD—V6 Hybrid—Truck Equipment Schedule T3
Sport Utility 4D	BC1BA	47700	32300	33300	34100	38100
Premium Pkg	Z		850	850	935	935
FWD			(1300)	(1300)	(1410)	(1410)

GX 460 4WD—V8—Truck Equipment Schedule T3
| Sport Utility 4D | BM7FX | 54120 | 35100 | 36200 | 36900 | 40900 |
| Premium Spt Util | JM7FX | 58915 | 38900 | 40200 | 40600 | 44800 |

2013 LEXUS — (JTor2T)(Jor2)(BK1BA)—D-#

RX 350 AWD—V6—Truck Equipment Schedule T3
| Sport Utility 4D | BK1BA | 41585 | 31600 | 32600 | 33500 | 37300 |
| FWD | Z | | (1350) | (1350) | (1485) | (1485) |

RX 350 F SPORT AWD—V6—Truck Equipment Schedule T3
| Sport Utility 4D | BK1BA | 47875 | 34700 | 35800 | 36500 | 40500 |

RX 450h AWD—V6 Hybrid—Truck Equipment Schedule T3
| Sport Utility 4D | BC1BA | 48185 | 36600 | 37700 | 38400 | 42500 |
| FWD | Z | | (1350) | (1350) | (1475) | (1475) |

GX 460 4WD—V8—Truck Equipment Schedule T3
| Sport Utility 4D | BM7FX | 54320 | 37900 | 39100 | 39500 | 43400 |
| Premium Spt Util | JM7FX | 59115 | 41900 | 43200 | 43600 | 47900 |

LX 570 AWD—V8—Truck Equipment Schedule T3
| Sport Utility 4D | HY7AX | 81805 | 61000 | 62800 | 62800 | 68800 |

2014 LEXUS — (JTor2T)(Jor2)(BK1BA)—E-#

RX 350 AWD—V6—Truck Equipment Schedule T3
Sport Utility 4D	BK1BA	43170	35100	36200	36800	40500
Comfort Pkg			500	500	525	525
Luxury Pkg			500	500	525	525
Dynamic Cruise Control			500	500	525	525
FWD	Z		(1425)	(1425)	(1495)	(1495)

RX 350 F SPORT AWD—V6—Truck Equipment Schedule T3
| Sport Utility 4D | BK1BA | 48360 | 39400 | 40600 | 40900 | 44900 |

RX 450h AWD—V6 Hybrid—Truck Equipment Schedule T3
Sport Utility 4D	BC1BA	49820	41100	42300	42500	46500
Comfort Pkg			500	500	520	520
Luxury Pkg			500	500	520	520
Premium Pkg			950	950	985	985
Dynamic Cruise Control			500	500	520	520
FWD	Z		(1425)	(1425)	(1485)	(1485)

GX 460 4WD—V8—Truck Equipment Schedule T3
| Sport Utility | BM7FX | 49995 | 43500 | 44800 | 44800 | 48900 |
| Premium Pkg | | | 1800 | 1800 | 1920 | 1920 |

GX 460 4WD—V8—Truck Equipment Schedule T3
| Luxury Sport Util | JM7FX | 61625 | 48100 | 49600 | 49800 | 54400 |
| Driver Support Pkg | | | 1175 | 1175 | 1250 | 1250 |

LX 570 AWD—V8—Truck Equipment Schedule T3
Sport Utility 4D	HY7AX	82690	72300	74400	73500	79600
Sensing Cruise Control			500	500	530	530
Luxury Pkg			500	500	530	530

LINCOLN

2000 LINCOLN — 5LM-(U28A)-Y-#

NAVIGATOR 4WD—V8—Truck Equipment Schedule T3
Sport Utility 4D	U28A	46500	975	1125	1900	3075
Air Conditioning, Rear			100	100	135	135
2WD	7		(350)	(350)	(465)	(465)

2001 LINCOLN — 5LM-(U28A,R)-1-#

NAVIGATOR 4WD—V8—Truck Equipment Schedule T3
| Sport Utility 4D | U28A,R | 48085 | 1175 | 1350 | 2200 | 3575 |
| 2WD | 7 | | (400) | (400) | (535) | (535) |

2002 LINCOLN — 5LM-(U28R)-2-#

NAVIGATOR 4WD—V8—Truck Equipment Schedule T3
| Sport Utility 4D | U28R | 48680 | 1500 | 1700 | 2825 | 4625 |
| 2WD | 7 | | (450) | (450) | (600) | (600) |

2002 LINCOLN

Body Type	VIN	List	Trade-In Good	Very Good	Pvt-Party Good	Retail Excellent
BLACKWOOD—V8—Truck Equipment Schedule T3						
Sport Util Pickup 4D	W05A	52500	**8175**	**8875**	**9700**	**12950**

2003 LINCOLN — 5LM—(U88H)–3–#

AVIATOR AWD—V8—Truck Equipment Schedule T3						
Sport Utility 4D	U88H	42945	**2500**	**2825**	**3725**	**5550**
2WD	6		**(500)**	**(500)**	**(665)**	**(665)**
NAVIGATOR 4WD—V8—Truck Equipment Schedule T3						
Sport Utility 4WD	U28R	52425	**3175**	**3550**	**4650**	**6900**
2WD			**(500)**	**(500)**	**(665)**	**(665)**

2004 LINCOLN — 5LM—(U88H)–4–#

AVIATOR AWD—V8—Truck Equipment Schedule T3						
Sport Utility 4D	U88H	43400	**3250**	**3625**	**4575**	**6700**
2WD	6		**(550)**	**(550)**	**(735)**	**(735)**
NAVIGATOR 4WD—V8—Truck Equipment Schedule T3						
Sport Utility 4D	U28R	52775	**4300**	**4725**	**5900**	**8375**
2WD			**(550)**	**(550)**	**(735)**	**(735)**

2005 LINCOLN — 5LM—(U88H)–5–#

AVIATOR AWD—V8—Truck Equipment Schedule T3						
Sport Utility 4D	U88H	44150	**3975**	**4375**	**5300**	**7400**
2WD	6		**(600)**	**(600)**	**(800)**	**(800)**
NAVIGATOR 4WD—V8—Truck Equipment Schedule T3						
Sport Utility 4D	U285	53985	**4625**	**5050**	**6400**	**8925**
2WD	7		**(600)**	**(600)**	**(800)**	**(800)**

2006 LINCOLN —5L(MorT)–(W165)–6–#

MARK LT 4WD—V8—Truck Equipment Schedule T3						
Super Crew Pickup	W165	43595	**11900**	**12700**	**13950**	**17800**
2WD	6		**(2075)**	**(2075)**	**(2540)**	**(2540)**
NAVIGATOR 4WD—V8—Truck Equipment Schedule T3						
Sport Utility 4D	U285	53075	**6800**	**7325**	**8500**	**11250**
Limited Edition			**300**	**300**	**405**	**405**
2WD	7		**(650)**	**(650)**	**(865)**	**(865)**

2007 LINCOLN — 5L(MorT)–(U68C)–7–#

MKX AWD—V6—Truck Equipment Schedule T3						
Sport Utility 4D	U68C	36445	**8875**	**9375**	**10550**	**12950**
Elite Pkg			**325**	**325**	**390**	**390**
FWD			**(600)**	**(600)**	**(720)**	**(720)**
MARK LT—V8—Truck Equipment Schedule T3						
Super Crew 6 1/2'	W165	42395	**11550**	**12300**	**13600**	**17150**
4WD	8		**2000**	**2000**	**2365**	**2365**
MARK LT 4WD—V8—Truck Equipment Schedule T3						
Super Crew 5 1/2'	W165	42095	**14500**	**15450**	**16800**	**21100**
2WD	6		**(2250)**	**(2250)**	**(2645)**	**(2645)**
NAVIGATOR 4WD—V8—Truck Equipment Schedule T3						
Sport Utility 4D	U285	49475	**10450**	**11150**	**12400**	**15700**
Elite Pkg			**325**	**325**	**420**	**420**
2WD	7		**(700)**	**(700)**	**(905)**	**(905)**
NAVIGATOR L 4WD—V8—Truck Equipment Schedule T3						
Sport Utility 4D	L285	52475	**12100**	**12900**	**14150**	**17750**
Elite Pkg			**325**	**325**	**415**	**415**
2WD	7		**(700)**	**(700)**	**(895)**	**(895)**

2008 LINCOLN — 5L(MorT)–(U68C)–8–#

MKX AWD—V6—Truck Equipment Schedule T3						
Sport Utility 4D	U68C	37845	**10400**	**10950**	**12200**	**14800**
Limited Edition			**350**	**350**	**415**	**415**
FWD	6		**(675)**	**(675)**	**(820)**	**(820)**
MARK LT—V8—Truck Equipment Schedule T3						
Super Crew 6 1/2'	W165	39565	**15350**	**16150**	**17250**	**20900**
4WD	8		**2200**	**2200**	**2535**	**2535**
MARK LT 4WD—V8—Truck Equipment Schedule T3						
Super Crew 5 1/2'	W165	42365	**18500**	**19450**	**20600**	**24900**
2WD	6		**(2450)**	**(2450)**	**(2820)**	**(2820)**
NAVIGATOR 4WD—V8—Truck Equipment Schedule T3						
Sport Utility 4D	U285	51555	**14000**	**14800**	**15700**	**18950**
Elite Pkg			**350**	**350**	**410**	**410**
2WD	7		**(750)**	**(750)**	**(900)**	**(900)**

TRUCKS & VANS

504   DEDUCT FOR RECONDITIONING   0415

Body Type	VIN	List	Trade-In Good	Trade-In Very Good	Pvt-Party Good	Retail Excellent
NAVIGATOR L 4WD—V8—Truck Equipment Schedule T3						
Sport Utility 4D	L285	54555	15500	16350	17300	20900
Elite Pkg			350	350	415	415
2WD	7		(750)	(750)	(905)	(905)

2009 LINCOLN — 5L(MorT)–(U68C)-9-#

MKX AWD—V6—Truck Equipment Schedule T3						
Sport Utility 4D	U68C	40035	12450	13000	14250	17000
Limited Edition			350	350	435	435
FWD	6		(725)	(725)	(860)	(860)
NAVIGATOR 4WD—V8—Truck Equipment Schedule T3						
Sport Utility 4D	U285	56265	18150	19000	19850	23400
Elite Pkg			350	350	415	415
2WD	7		(875)	(875)	(1010)	(1010)
NAVIGATOR L 4WD—V8—Truck Equipment Schedule T3						
Sport Utility 4D	L285	57955	20600	21600	22300	26100
Elite Pkg			350	350	410	410
2WD	7		(875)	(875)	(995)	(995)

2010 LINCOLN — (2or5)LM–(J6JC)–A-#

MKX AWD—V6—Truck Equipment Schedule T3						
Sport Utility 4D	J6JC	41045	14900	15600	16800	19550
Limited Edition			375	375	445	445
FWD	6		(775)	(775)	(890)	(890)
MKT—V6—Truck Equipment Schedule T3						
Sport Utility 4D	J5FR	44995	14000	14600	15900	18650
AWD	A		725	725	845	845
MKT AWD—V6 EcoBoost Twin Turbo—Truck Equipment Sch T3						
Sport Utility 4D	J5AT	49995	15300	15950	17400	20500
NAVIGATOR 4WD—V8—Truck Equipment Schedule T3						
Sport Utility 4D	J2J5	58225	20100	21000	21800	25300
Elite Pkg			375	375	435	435
2WD	H		(1000)	(1000)	(1145)	(1145)
NAVIGATOR L 4WD—V8—Truck Equipment Schedule T3						
Sport Utility 4D	J3J5	60390	22300	23200	24000	27700
Elite Pkg			375	375	430	430
2WD			(1000)	(1000)	(1130)	(1130)

2011 LINCOLN — (2or5)LM–(J6JK)–B-#

MKX AWD—V6—Truck Equipment Schedule T3						
Sport Utility 4D	J6JK	41845	18100	18800	19950	22900
Limited Edition			400	400	465	465
FWD	6		(1000)	(1000)	(1175)	(1175)
MKT—V6—Truck Equipment Schedule T3						
Sport Utility 4D	J5FR	44995	17550	18250	19600	22700
AWD	A		800	800	925	925
MKT AWD—V6 EcoBoost Twin Turbo—Truck Equipment Schedule T3						
Sport Utility 4D	J5AT	49995	18700	19450	21000	24500
NAVIGATOR 4WD—V8—Truck Equipment Schedule T3						
Sport Utility 4D	J2J5	60980	24100	25000	25800	29500
2WD	H		(1100)	(1100)	(1235)	(1235)
NAVIGATOR L 4WD—V8—Truck Equipment Schedule T3						
Sport Utility 4D	J3J5	63145	26200	27200	27900	31700
2WD	H		(1100)	(1100)	(1225)	(1225)

2012 LINCOLN — (2or5)LM–(J6JK)–C-#

MKX AWD—V6—Truck Equipment Schedule T3						
Sport Utility 4D	J6JK	42140	21100	21900	23100	26400
Limited Edition			400	400	455	455
FWD	6		(1075)	(1075)	(1235)	(1235)
MKT—V6—Truck Equipment Schedule T3						
Sport Utility 4D	J5FR	45095	18650	19350	20500	23500
AWD	A		875	875	970	970
MKT AWD—V6 EcoBoost Twin Turbo—Truck Equipment Schedule T3						
Sport Utility 4D	J5AT	47090	21100	21900	23100	26300
NAVIGATOR 4WD—V8—Truck Equipment Schedule T3						
Sport Utility 4D	J2J5	61670	27800	28800	29600	33400
2WD	H		(1500)	(1500)	(1670)	(1670)
NAVIGATOR L 4WD—V8—Truck Equipment Schedule T3						
Sport Utility 4D	J3J5	63835	30700	31800	32400	36400
2WD	H		(1500)	(1500)	(1655)	(1655)

Body Type	VIN	List	Trade-In Good	Very Good	Pvt-Party Good	Retail Excellent

2013 LINCOLN — (2or5)LM–(J6JK)–D–#

MKX AWD—V6—Truck Equipment Schedule T3

Sport Utility 4D	J6JK	42270	25000	25900	26900	30300
Elite Pkg			400	400	445	445
Limited Edition Pkg			400	400	445	445
FWD		6	(1100)	(1100)	(1205)	(1205)

MKT—V6—Truck Equipment Schedule T3

Sport Utility 4D	J5FK	46160	20500	21300	22400	25400
AWD	N,L		950	950	1050	1050

MKT AWD—V6 EcoBoost Twin Turbo—Truck Equipment Schedule T3

Sport Utility 4D	J5AT	48175	25100	26000	27200	30900

NAVIGATOR 4WD—V8 Flex Fuel—Truck Equipment Schedule T3

Sport Utility 4D	J2J5	61670	30600	31600	32700	36900
2WD	H		(1300)	(1300)	(1460)	(1460)

NAVIGATOR L 4WD—V8 Flex Fuel—Truck Equipment Schedule T3

Sport Utility 4D	J3J5	63835	34400	35500	36300	40800
2WD	H		(1300)	(1300)	(1445)	(1445)

2014 LINCOLN — (2or5)LM–(J8JK)–E–#

MKX AWD—V6—Truck Equipment Schedule T3

Sport Utility 4D	J8JK	41420	28500	29500	30200	33800
Adaptive Cruise Control			500	500	550	550
Elite Pkg			400	400	440	440
Limited Edition Pkg			400	400	440	440
FWD		6	(1100)	(1100)	(1200)	(1200)

MKT—V6—Truck Equipment Schedule T3

Sport Utility 4D	J5FK	46180	25600	26500	27300	30500
AWD	L,N		1025	1025	1080	1080
4-Cyl, EcoBoost, 2.0L	9		475	475	500	500

MKT AWD—V6 EcoBoost Twin Turbo—Truck Equipment Schedule T3

Sport Utility 4D	J5AT	48175	28800	29000	29800	33300

NAVIGATOR 4WD—V8 Flex Fuel—Truck Equipment Schedule T3

Sport Utility 4D	J2J5	59845	35200	36300	37200	41700
2WD	H		(1400)	(1400)	(1555)	(1555)

NAVIGATOR L 4WD—V8 Flex Fuel—Truck Equipment Schedule T3

Sport Utility 4D	J3J5	62010	38100	39300	40000	44800
2WD	H		(1400)	(1400)	(1545)	(1545)

MAZDA

2000 MAZDA–(JM3,4F2or4F4)–(LW28)–Y–#

MPV—V6—Truck Equipment Schedule T1

DX Minivan 4D	LW28	20475	550	675	1350	2350
LX Minivan 4D	LW28	22530	850	1000	1700	2900
ES Minivan 4D	LW28	26030	1100	1275	2025	3450

B2500 PICKUP—4-Cyl.—Truck Equipment Schedule T2

SX Short Bed	R12C	12005	875	975	1625	2750
SE Short Bed	R12C	14315	1275	1425	2200	3700
SE Cab Plus 2D	R16C	16505	1700	1875	2825	4725

B3000 PICKUP—V6—Truck Equipment Schedule T2

SX Short Bed	R12V	12400	1075	1200	1925	3225
SE Short Bed	R12V	14710	1275	1425	2200	3700
SE Cab Plus 2D	R16V	16975	1875	2075	3200	5300
SE Cab Plus 4D	R16V	17965	2025	2225	3425	5675
TroyLee Cb Plus 4D	R16V	19120	2200	2425	3700	6125

B3000 PICKUP 4WD—V6—Truck Equipment Schedule T2

SE Short Bed	R13V	18235	1775	1975	3050	5075
SE Cab Plus 4D	R17V	20970	2400	2650	3950	6425

B4000 PICKUP—V6—Truck Equipment Schedule T2

SE Cab Plus 4D	R16X	21390	2675	2950	4425	7250

B4000 PICKUP 4WD—V6—Truck Equipment Schedule T2

SE Cab Plus 4D	R17X	23300	2725	3025	4500	7375
TroyLee Cb Plus 4D	R17X	24150	2900	3200	4775	7800

2001 MAZDA–(JM3,4F2or4F4)–(U061)–1–#

TRIBUTE 4WD—V6—Truck Equipment Schedule T1

DX Sport Utility 4D	U061	21055	750	875	1775	3000
LX Sport Utility 4D	U081	22535	1150	1325	2300	3800
ES Sport Utility 4D	U081	23540	1450	1650	2650	4325

2001 MAZDA

Body Type	VIN	List	Trade-In Good	Trade-In Very Good	Pvt-Party Good	Retail Excellent
2WD						
4-Cyl, 2.0 Liter	B		(400)	(400)	(535)	(535)
			(225)	(225)	(305)	(305)
MPV—V6—Truck Equipment Schedule T1						
DX Minivan 4D	LW28	21155	775	925	1575	2600
LX Minivan 4D	LW28	23280	1100	1300	1975	3250
ES Minivan 4D	LW28	26760	1425	1675	2475	4050
B2300 PICKUP—4-Cyl.—Truck Equipment Schedule T2						
SX Short Bed	R12D	12930	1300	1425	2025	3275
SE Short Bed	R12D	15130	1675	1850	2625	4225
B2500 PICKUP—4-Cyl.—Truck Equipment Schedule T2						
SX Short Bed	R12C	12785	1200	1325	1900	3075
SE Short Bed	R12C	15130	1675	1825	2525	4050
B3000 PICKUP—V6—Truck Equipment Schedule T2						
SE Short Bed	R12U	15575	1850	2025	2875	4575
Dual Spt Short Bed	R12U	15315	1875	2050	2900	4625
SE Cab Plus 4D	R16U	17810	2325	2550	3550	5600
SE Cab Plus 4D	R16U	18180	2525	2775	3825	6025
Dual Spt Cab + 2D	R16U	17735	2600	2850	3925	6175
B3000 PICKUP 4WD—V6—Truck Equipment Schedule T2						
4WD SE Short Bed	R13U	15575	2200	2400	3325	5225
SE Cab Plus 2D	R13U	20615	2725	3000	4175	6625
B4000 PICKUP—V6—Truck Equipment Schedule T2						
Dual Sport Cab + 4D	R17X	19935	2950	3250	4400	6900
B4000 PICKUP 4WD—V6—Truck Equipment Schedule T2						
SE Cab Plus 4D	R17X	22780	3275	3575	4850	7575

2002 MAZDA—(JM3,4F2or4F4)—(U061)—2—#

Body Type	VIN	List	Trade-In Good	Trade-In Very Good	Pvt-Party Good	Retail Excellent
TRIBUTE 4WD—V6—Truck Equipment Schedule T1						
DX Sport Utility 4D	U061	22575	1175	1325	2125	3425
LX Sport Utility 4D	U081	23225	1625	1825	2750	4400
ES Sport Utility 4D	U081	24455	1975	2200	3250	5050
2WD						
4-Cyl, 2.0 Liter	B		(450)	(450)	(600)	(600)
			(275)	(275)	(365)	(365)
MPV—V6—Truck Equipment Schedule T1						
LX Minivan 4D	LW28	22770	1450	1675	2500	4050
ES Minivan 4D	LW28	27712	2000	2300	3225	5150
B2300 PICKUP—4-Cyl.—Truck Equipment Schedule T2						
Short Bed	R12D	13240	1650	1825	2500	3900
B3000 PICKUP—V6—Truck Equipment Schedule T2						
Dual Spt Short Bed	R12U	15870	2350	2575	3425	5275
Dual Spt Cab + 2D	R16U	18290	3250	3550	4625	7000
B3000 PICKUP 4WD—V6—Truck Equipment Schedule T2						
Cab Plus 2D	R13U	20775	3425	3750	4850	7350
B4000 PICKUP—V6—Truck Equipment Schedule T2						
Dual Spt Cab + 4D	R17E	20085	3475	3800	4925	7450
B4000 PICKUP 4WD—V6—Truck Equipment Schedule T2						
Cab Plus 4D	R17E	22830	3700	4050	5375	8125

2003 MAZDA—(JM3,4F2or4F4)—(Z92B)—3—#

Body Type	VIN	List	Trade-In Good	Trade-In Very Good	Pvt-Party Good	Retail Excellent
TRIBUTE 4WD—4-Cyl.—Truck Equipment Schedule T1						
DX Sport Utility 4D	Z92B	20440	1275	1450	2225	3525
2WD	0		(500)	(500)	(665)	(665)
TRIBUTE 4WD—V6—Truck Equipment Schedule T2						
LX Sport Utility 4D	Z941	22125	2000	2225	3225	4925
ES Sport Utility 4D	Z961	24885	2350	2600	3675	5600
2WD	0		(500)	(500)	(665)	(665)
MPV—V6—Truck Equipment Schedule T1						
LX S-V Minivan 4D	LW28A	21895	1650	1900	2625	4125
LX Minivan 4D	LW28A	23120	1975	2275	3050	4725
ES Minivan 4D	LW28A	26520	2525	2900	3725	5700
B2300 PICKUP—4-Cyl.—Truck Equipment Schedule T2						
Short Bed	R12D	13740	2200	2425	3075	4600
SE Cab Plus	R16D	17960	3200	3500	4325	6375
B3000 PICKUP—V6—Truck Equipment Schedule T2						
Dual Spt Short Bed	R12U	16590	2975	3275	4050	5975
Dual Spt Cab + 2D	R16V	18700	3900	4250	5350	7825
SE Cab Plus 4D	R46V	18935	3850	4200	5300	7750
B4000 PICKUP—V6—Truck Equipment Schedule T2						
Dual Spt Cab + 4D	R17E	20495	4150	4500	5675	8275
B4000 PICKUP 4WD—V6—Truck Equipment Schedule T2						
Cab Plus 2D	R17X	20260	4075	4425	5575	8125
SE Cab Plus 2D	R17X	21705	4400	4775	6000	8725

Body Type	VIN	List	Trade-In Good	Very Good	Pvt-Party Good	Retail Excellent
SE Cab Plus 4D	R17X	23240	**4575**	**4950**	**6200**	**9025**

2004 MAZDA—(JM3,4F2or4F4)—(Z92B)—4—#

Body Type	VIN	List	Trade-In Good	Very Good	Pvt-Party Good	Retail Excellent
TRIBUTE 4WD—4-Cyl.—Truck Equipment Schedule T2						
DX Sport Utility 4D	Z92B	21087	**1300**	**1475**	**2275**	**3550**
2WD	0		**(550)**	**(550)**	**(735)**	**(735)**
TRIBUTE 4WD—V6—Truck Equipment Schedule T1						
LX Sport Utility 4D	Z941	23972	**2250**	**2500**	**3525**	**5300**
ES Sport Utility 4D	Z961	25562	**2650**	**2950**	**4000**	**6000**
2WD	0		**(550)**	**(550)**	**(735)**	**(735)**
MPV—V6—Truck Equipment Schedule T1						
LX Minivan 4D	W28A	23780	**2625**	**3000**	**3750**	**5600**
ES Minivan 4D	W28A	28750	**3200**	**3650**	**4575**	**6775**
B2300 PICKUP—4-Cyl.—Truck Equipment Schedule T2						
Short Bed	R12D	14840	**2825**	**3125**	**3800**	**5575**
SE Cab Plus	R16D	18980	**3875**	**4200**	**5225**	**7550**
B3000 PICKUP—V6—Truck Equipment Schedule T2						
Dual Sport 6'	R12U	17915	**3600**	**3925**	**4900**	**7075**
Dual Sport Cab + 2D	R16V	19871	**4850**	**5225**	**6425**	**9225**
SE Cab Plus 4D	R46V	20140	**4950**	**5325**	**6550**	**9400**
B4000 PICKUP—V6—Truck Equipment Schedule T2						
Dual Sport Cab + 4D	R17E	21865	**5150**	**5550**	**6800**	**9725**
B4000 PICKUP 4WD—V6—Truck Equipment Schedule T2						
Cab Plus 2D	R17X	20850	**5075**	**5450**	**6700**	**9600**
SE Cab Plus 2D	R17X	22350	**5325**	**5725**	**7225**	**10300**
SE Cab Plus 2D	R17X	24090	**5550**	**5975**	**7500**	**10700**

2005 MAZDA—(JM3,4F2or4F4)—(Z02Z)—5—#

Body Type	VIN	List	Trade-In Good	Very Good	Pvt-Party Good	Retail Excellent
TRIBUTE—4-Cyl.—Truck Equipment Schedule T1						
i Sport Utility 4D	Z02Z	20515	**1375**	**1525**	**2475**	**3950**
4WD			**600**	**600**	**800**	**800**
TRIBUTE 4WD—V6—Truck Equipment Schedule T1						
s Sport Utility 4D	Z941	24980	**2625**	**2925**	**3825**	**5550**
2WD			**(600)**	**(600)**	**(800)**	**(800)**
MPV—V6—Truck Equipment Schedule T1						
LX-SV Minivan 4D	W28A	22665	**2950**	**3325**	**4125**	**6125**
LX Minivan 4D	W28A	23485	**3325**	**3750**	**4725**	**6950**
ES Minivan 4D	W28J	29050	**4225**	**4725**	**5800**	**8450**
B2300 PICKUP—4-Cyl.—Truck Equipment Schedule T2						
Short Bed	R12D	15935	**3225**	**3525**	**4400**	**6175**
B3000 PICKUP—V6—Truck Equipment Schedule T2						
Extended Cab 4D	R46U	19480	**5150**	**5575**	**7025**	**9700**
Dual Sport 6'	R12U	20120	**4250**	**4625**	**5750**	**8000**
Dual Sport Ext 4D	R46U	21870	**5650**	**6100**	**7600**	**10500**
B4000 PICKUP 4WD—V6—Truck Equipment Schedule T2						
Extended Cab 4D	R47E	22220	**5500**	**5925**	**7425**	**10250**
SE Extended Cab 4D	R47E	26765	**7000**	**7500**	**9275**	**12700**

2006 MAZDA—(JM1or3,4F2or4)—(CR293)—6—#

Body Type	VIN	List	Trade-In Good	Very Good	Pvt-Party Good	Retail Excellent
MAZDA5—4-Cyl.—Truck Equipment Schedule T1						
Sport Minivan 4D	CR293	18895	**3200**	**3575**	**4475**	**6575**
Touring Minivan 4D	CR193	20410	**3625**	**4000**	**5100**	**7400**
TRIBUTE—4-Cyl.—Truck Equipment Schedule T1						
i Sport Utility 4D	Z02Z	21525	**1775**	**1975**	**2875**	**4200**
4WD	9		**650**	**650**	**865**	**865**
TRIBUTE 4WD—V6—Truck Equipment Schedule T1						
s Sport Utility 4D	Z941	25290	**3675**	**4025**	**5050**	**7050**
2WD			**(650)**	**(650)**	**(865)**	**(865)**
MPV—V6—Truck Equipment Schedule T1						
LX-SV Minivan 4D	W28A	22675	**3775**	**4200**	**5325**	**7800**
LX Minivan 4D	W28A	23510	**4275**	**4750**	**5925**	**8625**
ES Minivan 4D	W28J	29075	**5125**	**5675**	**7150**	**10350**
B2300 PICKUP—4-Cyl.—Truck Equipment Schedule T2						
Short Bed	R12D	15690	**4075**	**4425**	**5400**	**7375**
B3000 PICKUP—V6—Truck Equipment Schedule T2						
Extended Cab 4D	R46U	19510	**6425**	**6900**	**8375**	**11300**
Dual Sport 6'	R12U	20145	**5475**	**5900**	**7200**	**9725**
Dual Sport Ext 4D	R46U	21900	**7000**	**7500**	**9050**	**12150**
B4000 PICKUP 4WD—V6—Truck Equipment Schedule T2						
Extended Cab 4D	R47E	22515	**6825**	**7300**	**8825**	**11900**
SE Extended Cab 4D	R47E	27060	**8850**	**9425**	**11200**	**15000**

Body Type	VIN	List	Trade-In Good	Very Good	Pvt-Party Good	Retail Excellent

2007 MAZDA–(JM1or3,4F2or4)(CR193)–7–#

MAZDA5—4-Cyl.—Truck Equipment Schedule T1
Sport Minivan 4D	CR193	19130	3900	4300	5350	7575
Touring Minivan 4D	CR193	20645	4600	5050	6150	8675
Grand Touring 4D	CR193	21895	4800	5250	6375	8950

CX-7—4-Cyl. Turbo—Truck Equipment Schedule T1
"Sport" SUV 4D	ER293	26010	3975	4325	5275	7150
Touring Sport Util	ER293	27760	4350	4725	5775	7825
AWD			525	525	700	700

CX-7 AWD—4-Cyl. Turbo—Truck Equipment Schedule T1
| Grand Touring Util | ER293 | 28560 | 4950 | 5350 | 6400 | 8600 |
| FWD | | | (600) | (600) | (795) | (795) |

CX-9—V6—Truck Equipment Schedule T1
"Sport" SUV 4D	TB28Y	30830	6250	6800	7675	9950
Grand Touring Util	TB28Y	34470	7900	8525	9500	12400
AWD	3		525	525	695	695

CX-9 AWD—V6—Truck Equipment Schedule T1
| Touring Sport Util | TB38Y | 32930 | 7500 | 8100 | 9025 | 11700 |
| FWD | | | (600) | (600) | (795) | (795) |

B2300 PICKUP—4-Cyl.—Truck Equipment Schedule T2
| Short Bed | R12D | 16170 | 4950 | 5325 | 6225 | 8200 |

B3000 PICKUP—V6—Truck Equipment Schedule T2
Extended Cab 4D	R46U	19675	7600	8100	9450	12300
Dual Sport 6'	R12U	20310	6550	7025	8275	10800
Dual Sport Ext 4D	R46U	22065	8450	9000	10400	13500

B4000 PICKUP 4WD—V6—Truck Equipment Schedule T2
| Extended Cab 4D | R47E | 22680 | 7975 | 8500 | 9875 | 12850 |
| SE Extended Cab 4D | R47E | 27225 | 10350 | 11000 | 12650 | 16400 |

2008 MAZDA–(JM1or3,4F2or4)(CR293)–8–#

MAZDA5—4-Cyl.—Truck Equipment Schedule T1
Sport Minivan 4D	CR293	19580	5100	5525	6625	8900
Touring Minivan 4D	CR293	21245	5925	6400	7525	10050
Grand Touring 4D	CR293	23000	6100	6575	7725	10300

TRIBUTE—4-Cyl. Hybrid—Truck Equipment Schedule T1
| HEV Touring | Z49H | 28535 | 6500 | 6950 | 8175 | 10600 |
| 4WD | | | 1075 | 1075 | 1430 | 1430 |

TRIBUTE 4WD—4-Cyl. Hybrid—Truck Equipment Schedule T1
| HEV Grand Touring | Z59H | 31045 | 9400 | 9975 | 11600 | 15000 |
| 2WD | | | (750) | (750) | (1000) | (1000) |

TRIBUTE—4-Cyl.—Truck Equipment Schedule T1
i Sport Utility 4D	Z02Z	20910	3900	4225	5150	6825
i Grand Touring Util	Z02Z	23875	5875	6300	7500	9775
4WD	9		1075	1075	1430	1430

TRIBUTE 4WD—4-Cyl.—Truck Equipment Schedule T1
| i Touring Spt Util | Z92Z | 23435 | 5625 | 6025 | 7225 | 9425 |
| 2WD | 0 | | (750) | (750) | (1000) | (1000) |

TRIBUTE—V6—Truck Equipment Schedule T1
s Sport Utility 4D	Z961	23900	5775	6175	7400	9625
s Touring Spt Util	Z961	24675	6075	6500	7725	10000
s Grand Touring Util	Z961	26865	7250	7725	9150	11900
2WD	0		(750)	(750)	(1000)	(1000)

CX-7—4-Cyl. Turbo—Truck Equipment Schedule T1
"Sport" SUV 4D	ER293	24345	4725	5075	6000	7875
Touring Sport Util	ER293	26095	5275	5675	6800	8850
AWD			550	550	735	735

CX-7 AWD—4-Cyl. Turbo—Truck Equipment Schedule T1
| Grand Touring Util | ER293 | 28595 | 5675 | 6075 | 7250 | 9400 |
| FWD | | | (675) | (675) | (900) | (900) |

CX-9—V6—Truck Equipment Schedule T1
"Sport" SUV 4D	TB28A	29995	7875	8475	9075	11200
Grand Touring Util	TB28A	33950	9425	10100	10750	13250
AWD			550	550	665	665

CX-9 AWD—V6—Truck Equipment Schedule T1
| Touring Sport Util | TB38A | 32930 | 9025 | 9675 | 10350 | 12750 |
| FWD | | | (675) | (675) | (825) | (825) |

B2300 PICKUP—4-Cyl.—Truck Equipment Schedule T2
| Short Bed | R12D | 16170 | 5875 | 6300 | 7350 | 9450 |

B4000 PICKUP 4WD—V6—Truck Equipment Schedule T2
| Extended Cab 4D | R47E | 22680 | 9525 | 10100 | 11500 | 14600 |
| SE Extended Cab 4D | R47E | 27225 | 12050 | 12700 | 14350 | 18200 |

Body Type	VIN	List	Trade-In Good	Very Good	Pvt-Party Good	Retail Excellent
2009 MAZDA–(JM1or3,4F2or4)(CR293)-9-#						
MAZDA5—4-Cyl.—Truck Equipment Schedule T1						
Sport Minivan 4D	CR293	19775	5700	6125	7175	9350
Touring Minivan 4D	CR293	21590	6800	7275	8375	10850
Grand Touring 4D	CR293	23345	7175	7675	8850	11450
TRIBUTE—4-Cyl. Hybrid—Truck Equipment Schedule T1						
HEV Touring	Z493	28845	8950	9475	10600	13050
4WD			1175	1175	1455	1455
TRIBUTE 4WD—4-Cyl. Hybrid—Truck Equipment Schedule T1						
HEV Grand Touring	Z593	33195	11250	11900	13200	16250
2WD			(875)	(875)	(1095)	(1095)
TRIBUTE—4-Cyl.—Truck Equipment Schedule T1						
i Sport Utility 4D	Z027	22460	5250	5625	6625	8375
i Grand Touring Util	Z027	25290	7975	8450	9500	11750
4WD	9		1175	1175	1480	1480
TRIBUTE 4WD—4-Cyl.—Truck Equipment Schedule T1						
i Touring Spt Util	Z927	25360	7825	8275	9350	11550
2WD	0		(875)	(875)	(1100)	(1100)
TRIBUTE 4WD—V6—Truck Equipment Schedule T1						
s Sport Utility 4D	Z96G	23605	7575	8025	9075	11200
s Touring Spt Util	Z96G	26620	8275	8750	9825	12100
s Grand Touring Util	Z96G	28305	9550	10100	11250	13850
2WD	0		(875)	(875)	(1100)	(1100)
CX-7—4-Cyl. Turbo—Truck Equipment Schedule T1						
"Sport" SUV 4D	ER293	24550	5475	5850	7000	8925
Touring Sport Util	ER293	26450	6400	6800	8000	10150
AWD			650	650	860	860
CX-7 AWD—4-Cyl. Turbo—Truck Equipment Schedule T1						
Grand Touring Util	ER293	29050	6975	7400	8775	11200
FWD			(725)	(725)	(955)	(955)
CX-9—V6—Truck Equipment Schedule T1						
"Sport" SUV 4D	TB28A	30490	9100	9675	10450	12900
Grand Touring Util	TB28A	34475	11100	11800	12650	15450
AWD	3		650	650	790	790
CX-9 AWD—V6—Truck Equipment Schedule T1						
Touring Sport Util	TB38A	33785	10650	11300	12100	14850
2WD			(725)	(725)	(870)	(870)
B2300 PICKUP—4-Cyl.—Truck Equipment Schedule T2						
Short Bed	R12D	16780	7100	7550	8625	10750
SE-5 Pkg			125	125	145	145
B4000 PICKUP 4WD—V6—Truck Equipment Schedule T2						
Extended Cab 4D	R47E	22870	10900	11450	12850	15900
2010 MAZDA–(JM1or3,4F2or4)(CR293)-A-#						
MAZDA5—4-Cyl.—Truck Equipment Schedule T1						
Sport Minivan 4D	CR293	18745	7275	7725	8675	10800
Touring Minivan 4D	CR293	22000	8675	9200	10200	12650
Grand Touring 4D	CR293	23755	9000	9550	10600	13150
TRIBUTE—4-Cyl.—Truck Equipment Schedule T1						
i Sport Utility 4D	Y0C7	22880	6250	6650	7800	9775
i Grand Touring Util	Y0C7	25985	8400	8875	10050	12350
4WD	9		1250	1250	1565	1565
TRIBUTE 4WD—4-Cyl.—Truck Equipment Schedule T1						
i Touring Spt Util	Y9C7	25780	8250	8725	9900	12150
2WD	0		(1000)	(1000)	(1230)	(1230)
TRIBUTE 4WD—V6—Truck Equipment Schedule T1						
s Grand Touring	Y9GG	29350	10050	10600	11800	14350
2WD	0		(1000)	(1000)	(1210)	(1210)
CX-7—4-Cyl.—Truck Equipment Schedule T1						
i SV Sport Util 4D	ER2W5	22480	8775	9250	10600	13150
i Sport SUV 4D	ER2W5	22300	8575	9025	10400	12900
CX-7—4-Cyl. Turbo—Truck Equipment Schedule T1						
s Grand Touring	ER2W3	33815	10250	10800	12300	15250
AWD			725	725	925	925
CX-7 AWD—4-Cyl. Turbo—Truck Equipment Schedule T1						
s Touring Spt Util	ER4W3	28250	10050	10600	12050	14900
FWD	2		(775)	(775)	(970)	(970)
CX-9—V6—Truck Equipment Schedule T1						
"Sport" SUV 4D	TB28A	29385	11300	11900	13100	16000
Grand Touring Util	TB28A	33395	12900	13600	14900	18200
AWD	3		725	725	895	895

2010 MAZDA

Body Type	VIN	List	Trade-In Good	Very Good	Pvt-Party Good	Retail Excellent
CX-9 AWD—V6—Truck Equipment Schedule T1						
Touring Sport Util	TB38A	32705	12650	13350	14550	17750
FWD			(775)	(775)	(945)	(945)

2011 MAZDA — (4F2orJM3)–(Y0C7)–B–#

Body Type	VIN	List	Trade-In Good	Very Good	Pvt-Party Good	Retail Excellent
TRIBUTE—4-Cyl.—Truck Equipment Schedule T1						
i Sport Utility 4D	Y0C7	23225	7875	8300	9450	11500
i Grand Utility Util	Y0C7	26330	10150	10650	11700	13850
4WD	9		1400	1400	1675	1675
TRIBUTE 4WD—4-Cyl.—Truck Equipment Schedule T1						
i Touring Spt Util	Y9C7	26125	10000	10500	11550	13700
2WD	0		(1100)	(1100)	(1285)	(1285)
TRIBUTE 4WD—V6—Truck Equipment Schedule T1						
s Grand Touring	Y9GG	29695	12800	13400	14600	17250
2WD	0		(1100)	(1100)	(1280)	(1280)
CX-7—4-Cyl.—Truck Equipment Schedule T1						
i SV Sport Utility	ER2A5	22785	9975	10450	11700	14000
i Sport Utility	ER2B5	23590	10650	11200	12300	14650
i Touring Sport Util	ER2C5	27185	11750	12350	13500	16000
CX-7—4-Cyl. Turbo—Truck Equipment Schedule T1						
s Grand Touring	ER2D3	32435	13200	13800	15150	17900
AWD	4		800	800	935	935
CX-7 AWD—4-Cyl. Turbo—Truck Equipment Schedule T1						
s Touring Spt Util	ER4C3	28750	12500	13100	14300	16900
FWD	2		(1000)	(1000)	(1190)	(1190)
CX-9—V6—Truck Equipment Schedule T1						
"Sport" SUV 4D	TB2BA	31320	13300	13950	15050	17900
Touring Sport Util	TB2CA	33240	15000	15750	16650	19550
Grand Touring Util	TB2DA	35330	17250	18050	18950	22300
FWD	2		(1000)	(1000)	(1140)	(1140)

2012 MAZDA — 4F(2or3)JM(2or3)–(W2BL)–C–#

Body Type	VIN	List	Trade-In Good	Very Good	Pvt-Party Good	Retail Excellent
MAZDA5—4-Cyl.—Truck Equipment Schedule T1						
Sport Minivan 4D	W2BL	20990	9600	10100	11150	13500
Touring Minivan 4D	W2CL	21990	10900	11450	12500	15050
Grand Touring 4D	W2DL	24670	11500	12050	13200	15900
CX-7—4-Cyl.—Truck Equipment Schedule T1						
i SV Sport Utility	ER2A5	22985	11550	12100	13350	15750
i Sport Utility	ER2B5	23790	12400	13000	14200	16750
i Touring Sport Util	ER2C5	27385	14050	14650	16000	18800
CX-7—4-Cyl. Turbo—Truck Equipment Schedule T1						
s Grand Touring	ER2D3	32635	16200	16850	18200	21300
AWD	4		875	875	1015	1015
CX-7 AWD—4-Cyl. Turbo—Truck Equipment Schedule T1						
s Touring Spt Util	ER4C3	28950	15100	15750	17100	20100
FWD	2		(1075)	(1075)	(1255)	(1255)
CX-9 AWD—V6—Truck Equipment Schedule T1						
"Sport" SUV 4D	TB2BA	31570	15900	16600	17700	20800
Touring Sport Util	TB2CA	33490	17150	17950	18900	22100
Grand Touring Util	TB2DA	35580	20200	21100	22100	25700
FWD	2		(1075)	(1075)	(1220)	(1220)

2013 MAZDA — 4F(2or3)JM(2or3)–(CW2BL)–D–#

Body Type	VIN	List	Trade-In Good	Very Good	Pvt-Party Good	Retail Excellent
MAZDA5—4-Cyl.—Truck Equipment Schedule T1						
Sport Minivan 4D	CW2BL	21735	10750	11300	12750	15650
Touring Minivan	CW2CL	22865	11950	12500	14100	17300
Grand Touring 4D	CW2DL	25265	12650	13250	14850	18200
CX-5—4-Cyl. SKYACTIV—Truck Equipment Schedule T1						
Sport SUV 4D	KE2BE	22890	14000	14600	15950	18600
Touring Sport Util	KE2CE	24690	15700	16350	17700	20500
Grand Touring	KE2DE	27840	18100	18800	20200	23500
AWD	4		950	950	1095	1095
CX-9 AWD—V6—Truck Equipment Schedule T1						
"Sport" SUV 4D	TB3BA	32170	16800	17500	18750	22000
Touring Sport Util	TB3CA	34615	18200	18950	20100	23400
Grand Touring Util	TB3DA	37170	21400	22300	23100	26700
FWD	2		(1100)	(1100)	(1230)	(1230)

2014 MAZDA — 4F(2or3)JM(2or3)–(CW2BL)–E–#

Body Type	VIN	List	Trade-In Good	Very Good	Pvt-Party Good	Retail Excellent
MAZDA5—4-Cyl.—Truck Equipment Schedule T1						
Sport Minivan 4D	CW2BL	21935	11500	12050	13500	16500
Touring Minivan	CW2CL	23065	12900	13450	15100	18350

TRUCKS & VANS

Body Type	VIN	List	Trade-In Good	Very Good	Pvt-Party Good	Retail Excellent
Grand Touring 4D	CW2DL	25465	15100	15750	17250	20700
CX-5—4-Cyl. SKYACTIV—Truck Equipment Schedule T1						
Sport SUV 4D	KE2BE	23390	15800	16450	17600	20300
Touring Sport Util	KE2CY	25410	17550	18250	19350	22200
Grand Touring	KE2DY	28415	20200	21000	22300	25600
AWD	4		1025	1025	1160	1160
CX-9 AWD—V6—Truck Equipment Schedule T1						
"Sport" SUV 4D	TB3BA	32370	17450	18200	19250	22400
Touring Sport Util	TB3CA	34865	19250	20100	21000	24300
Grand Touring Util	TB3DA	37420	23200	24200	24900	28500
FWD	2		(1100)	(1100)	(1230)	(1230)

MERCEDES-BENZ

2000 MERCEDES-BENZ — 4JG(AB54E)-Y-#

ML-CLASS 4WD—V6—Truck Equipment Schedule T3						
ML320 Spt Utl 4D	AB54E	36895	1450	1600	2600	4025
Third Row Seat			150	150	205	205
ML-CLASS 4WD—V8—Truck Equipment Schedule T3						
ML430 Spt Utl 4D	AB72E	44345	2050	2250	3375	5100
ML55 Spt Utl 4D	AB74E	65495	1850	2050	3350	5250
Third Row Seat			150	150	205	205

2001 MERCEDES-BENZ — 4JG(AB54E)-1-#

ML-CLASS 4WD—V6—Truck Equipment Schedule T3						
ML320 Spt Utl 4D	AB54E	38045	1675	1875	2850	4300
Sport Pkg			375	375	495	495
Third Row Seat			175	175	225	225
designo Edition			475	475	625	625
ML-CLASS 4WD—V8—Truck Equipment Schedule T3						
ML430 Spt Utl 4D	AB72E	44845	2675	2975	4075	5975
ML55 Spt Utl 4D	AB74E	66545	2800	3075	4500	6700
Sport Pkg			375	375	495	495
Third Row Seat			175	175	225	225
designo Edition			475	475	625	625

2002 MERCEDES-BENZ — WDCor4JG(AB54E)-2-#

ML-CLASS 4WD—V6—Truck Equipment Schedule T3						
ML320 Spt Utl 4D	AB54E	36945	2150	2375	3250	4675
designo Edition			525	525	685	685
Third Row Seat			175	175	245	245
Sport Pkg			425	425	555	555
ML-CLASS 4WD—V8—Truck Equipment Schedule T3						
ML500 Spt Utl 4D	AB75E	45595	3000	3300	4325	6175
ML55 Spt Utl 4D	AB74E	66545	3825	4150	5675	8200
Sport Pkg			425	425	555	555
Third Row Seat			175	175	245	245
designo Edition			525	525	685	685
G-CLASS 4WD—V8—Truck Equipment Schedule T3						
G500 Sport Util 4D	YR49E	73145	14600	15450	17100	21700
designo Edition			525	525	655	655

2003 MERCEDES-BENZ — WDCor4JG(AB54E)-3-#

ML-CLASS 4WD—V6—Truck Equipment Schedule T3						
ML320 Spt Utl 4D	AB54E	40315	2675	2925	3925	5625
ML350 Spt Utl 4D	AB57E	40665	3375	3675	4750	6750
Sport Pkg			475	475	615	615
Inspiration Edition			425	425	555	555
designo Edition			550	550	745	745
Third Row Seat			200	200	265	265
ML-CLASS 4WD—V8—Truck Equipment Schedule T3						
ML500 Spt Utl 4D	AB75E	46015	3700	4025	5325	7525
ML55 Spt Utl 4D	AB74E	66565	6150	6575	8225	11100
Sport Pkg			475	475	615	615
Inspiration Edition			425	425	555	555
designo Edition			550	550	745	745
Third Row Seat			200	200	265	265
G-CLASS 4WD—V8—Truck Equipment Schedule T3						
G500 Spt Util 4D	YR49	74265	17000	17900	19700	24800
G55 Spt Util 4D	YR46	90565	22300	23400	24700	30400

TRUCKS & VANS

Body Type	VIN	List	Trade-In Good	Trade-In Very Good	Pvt-Party Good	Retail Excellent
designo Edition			550	550	695	695

2004 MERCEDES-BENZ — WDCor4JG(AB57E)-4-#

ML-CLASS 4WD—V6—Truck Equipment Schedule T3

Body Type	VIN	List	Trade-In Good	Trade-In Very Good	Pvt-Party Good	Retail Excellent
ML350 Sport Util	AB57E	39720	4000	4325	5500	7550
Inspiration Edition			450	450	605	605
designo Edition			600	600	805	805
Third Row Seat			225	225	300	300

ML-CLASS 4WD—V8—Truck Equipment Schedule T3

ML500 Spt Util 4D	AB75E	46470	4400	4725	5975	8200
Inspiration Edition			450	450	605	605
designo Edition			600	600	805	805
Third Row Seat			225	225	300	300

G-CLASS 4WD—V8—Truck Equipment Schedule T3

G500 Sport Util	YR49	76870	20500	21600	22900	28100
G55 Sport Util	YR46	93420	28200	29600	30500	36700
designo Edition			600	600	700	700

2005 MERCEDES-BENZ — WDCor4JG(AB57E)-5-#

M-CLASS 4WD—V6—Truck Equipment Schedule T3

ML350 Sport Util	AB57E	40370	5125	5500	6800	9025
Special Edition			500	500	655	655
designo Edition			650	650	865	865
Third Row Seat			250	250	335	335

M-CLASS 4WD—V8—Truck Equipment Schedule T3

ML500 Sport Util 4D	AB75E	47120	5525	5925	7250	9625
Special Edition			500	500	655	655
designo Edition			650	650	865	865
Third Row Seat			250	250	335	335

G-CLASS 4WD—V8—Truck Equipment Schedule T3

G500 Sport Util 4D	YR49E	78420	27400	28700	29400	34900
G500 Grand Ed Util.	YR49C	80420	28700	30000	30800	36600
designo Edition			650	650	735	735

G-CLASS 4WD—V8 Supercharged—Truck Equipment Schedule T3

G55 Spt Util 4D	YR46E	100620	32600	34100	34500	40600
G55 Grand Ed Util	YR43720	34000	35600	35900	42300

2006 MERCEDES-BENZ — 4JG(BB86E)-6-#

M-CLASS 4WD—V6—Truck Equipment Schedule T3

ML350 Spt Util 4D	BB86E	40525	8475	8975	10350	13250
Premium Pkg			675	675	880	880
Sport Pkg			600	600	785	785

M-CLASS 4WD—V8—Truck Equipment Schedule T3

ML500 Spt Util 4D	BB75E	49275	8725	9225	10950	13950
Premium Pkg			675	675	880	880
Sport Pkg			600	600	785	785

G-CLASS 4WD—V8—Truck Equipment Schedule T3

G500 Sport Util 4D	YR49E	78420	31600	33000	33600	39600

G-CLASS 4WD—V8 Supercharged—Truck Equipment Sch T3

G55 Sport Util 4D	YR71E	100620	35300	36900	37400	44000

R-CLASS AWD—V6—Truck Equipment Schedule T3

R350 Sport Wagon	CB65E	48775	6700	7150	8025	10200
Premium Pkg			675	675	860	860
Sport Pkg			450	450	580	580

R-CLASS AWD—V8—Truck Equipment Schedule T3

R500 Sport Wagon	CB75E	56275	7450	7950	9075	11650
KEYLESS-GO			200	200	255	255
Premium Pkg			675	675	880	880
Sport Pkg			450	450	595	595

2007 MERCEDES-BENZ — 4JG(BB22E)-7-#

M-CLASS 4WD—V6 Turbo Diesel—Truck Equipment Schedule T3

ML320 CDI Spt Util.	BB22E	44455	13000	13700	15000	18250
Adaptive Cruise Control			350	350	420	420
P1 Pkg			300	300	360	360
P2 Pkg			300	300	360	360
P3 Pkg			500	500	600	600
Sport Pkg			650	650	785	785

M-CLASS 4WD—V6—Truck Equipment Schedule T3

ML350 Spt Utl 4D	BB86E	43455	10250	10850	12050	14700
Adaptive Cruise Control			350	350	420	420
P1 Pkg			300	300	360	360

Body Type	VIN	List	Trade-In Good	Very Good	Pvt-Party Good	Retail Excellent
P2 Pkg			300	300	350	350
P3 Pkg			500	500	605	605
Sport Pkg			650	650	785	785
M-CLASS 4WD—V8—Truck Equipment Schedule T3						
ML500 Spt Util 4D	BB75E	49975	11700	12300	13600	16550
Adaptive Cruise Control			350	350	420	420
P1 Pkg			300	300	360	360
P2 Pkg			300	300	350	350
P3 Pkg			500	500	605	605
Sport Pkg			650	650	785	785
M-CLASS 4WD—V8—Truck Equipment Schedule T3						
ML63 Spt Util 4D	BB77E	86275	17050	17850	19200	23100
G-CLASS 4WD—V8—Truck Equipment Schedule T3						
G500 Sport Util 4D	YR49E	81675	33700	35100	35700	41700
G-CLASS 4WD—V8 Supercharged—Truck Equipment Sch T3						
G55 Spt Util 4D	YR71E	105275	42000	43800	43900	50800
GL-CLASS 4WD—V6 Turbo Diesel—Truck Equipment Schedule T3						
GL320 CDI Spt Util	BF22E	53175	16800	17650	18950	22700
Adaptive Cruise Control			350	350	425	425
Premium Pkg			675	675	835	835
GL-CLASS 4WD—V8—Truck Equipment Schedule T3						
GL450 Spt Util 4D	BF71E	55675	13350	14050	15300	18400
Adaptive Cruise Control			350	350	425	425
Premium Pkg			675	675	840	840
R-CLASS 4WD—V6 Turbo Diesel—Truck Equipment Schedule T3						
R320 CDI Spt Wag	CB22E	44775	9675	10250	11700	14800
Adaptive Cruise Control			350	350	455	455
Premium Pkg 1			300	300	390	390
Premium Pkg 2			300	300	375	375
R-CLASS 4WD—V6—Truck Equipment Schedule T3						
R350 Sport Wagon	CB65E	43775	7525	8000	9150	11650
Adaptive Cruise Control			350	350	460	460
Premium Pkg 1			300	300	395	395
Premium Pkg 2			300	300	380	380
Sport Pkg			500	500	655	655
R-CLASS 4WD—V8—Truck Equipment Schedule T3						
R500 Sport Wagon	CB75E	51275	8950	9475	10700	13550
KEYLESS-GO			200	200	260	260
Adaptive Cruise Control			350	350	455	455
Premium Pkg 1			300	300	390	390
Premium Pkg 2			300	300	380	380
Sport Pkg			500	500	655	655
R-CLASS 4WD—V8—Truck Equipment Schedule T3						
R63 Sport Wagon	CB77E	88175	24300	25400	25900	30700
KEYLESS-GO			200	200	235	235
Adaptive Cruise Control			350	350	410	410

2008 MERCEDES-BENZ — 4JG(BB22E)-8-#

Body Type	VIN	List	Trade-In Good	Very Good	Pvt-Party Good	Retail Excellent
M-CLASS 4WD—V6 Turbo Diesel—Truck Equipment Schedule T3						
ML320 CDI Spt Utl	BB22E	45425	15400	16100	17250	20400
KEYLESS-GO			200	200	230	230
Adaptive Cruise Control			375	375	435	435
Premium Pkg 1			300	300	350	350
Premium Pkg 2			300	300	360	360
Premium Pkg 3			500	500	580	580
M-CLASS 4WD—V6—Truck Equipment Schedule T3						
ML350 Spt Util 4D	BB86E	44425	12600	13250	14300	16950
KEYLESS-GO			200	200	230	230
Adaptive Cruise Control			375	375	435	435
Premium Pkg 1			300	300	350	350
Premium Pkg 2			300	300	360	360
Premium Pkg 3			500	500	580	580
M-CLASS 4WD—V8—Truck Equipment Schedule T3						
ML350 Edition Utl	BB86E	52705	13850	14500	15600	18400
M-CLASS 4WD—V8—Truck Equipment Schedule T3						
ML550 Spt Util 4D	BB72E	53175	16200	16900	18000	21200
KEYLESS-GO			200	200	230	230
Adaptive Cruise Control			375	375	435	435
Premium Pkg 1			300	300	350	350
Premium Pkg 2			300	300	360	360
Premium Pkg 3			500	500	580	580
M-CLASS 4WD—V8—Truck Equipment Schedule T3						
ML63 Spt Util 4D	BB77E	87425	21700	22600	23800	28000

Body Type	VIN	List	Trade-In Good	Trade-In Very Good	Pvt-Party Good	Retail Excellent
KEYLESS-GO			200	200	235	235
G-CLASS 4WD—V8—Truck Equipment Schedule T3						
G500 Sport Util 4D	YR49E	86975	41600	43200	43400	49500
G-CLASS 4WD—V8 Supercharged—Truck Equipment Sch T3						
G55 Spt Util 4D	YR71E	110675	48400	50200	50400	57400
GL-CLASS 4WD—V6 Turbo Diesel—Truck Equipment Schedule T3						
GL320 CDI Spt Utl	BF22E	55975	18250	19100	20400	24100
KEYLESS-GO			200	200	235	235
Adaptive Cruise Control			375	375	445	445
Premium Pkg 1			300	300	355	355
Premium Pkg 2			300	300	370	370
GL-CLASS 4WD—V8—Truck Equipment Schedule T3						
GL450 Spt Util 4D	BF71E	58475	15700	16450	17650	20900
KEYLESS-GO			200	200	235	235
Adaptive Cruise Control			375	375	445	445
Premium Pkg 1			300	300	355	355
Premium Pkg 2			300	300	370	370
GL-CLASS 4WD—V8—Truck Equipment Schedule T3						
GL550 Spt Util 4D	BF86E	77850	18650	19500	20800	24600
KEYLESS-GO			200	200	240	240
R-CLASS 4WD—V6 Turbo Diesel—Truck Equipment Schedule T3						
R320 CDI Spt Wag	CB22E	46175	13350	14050	15250	18400
KEYLESS-GO			200	200	245	245
Distronic Cruise Control			375	375	455	455
P1 Pkg			300	300	365	365
P2 Pkg			300	300	380	380
P3 Pkg			500	500	610	610
R-CLASS 4WD—V6—Truck Equipment Schedule T3						
R350 Sport Wagon	CB65E	45175	9400	9900	10950	13400
KEYLESS-GO			200	200	245	245
Distronic Cruise Control			375	375	465	465
P1 Pkg			300	300	370	370
P2 Pkg			300	300	385	385
P3 Pkg			500	500	620	620
2WD	56		(750)	(750)	(930)	(930)

2009 MERCEDES-BENZ — 4JG(BB25E)-9-#

Body Type	VIN	List	Trade-In Good	Trade-In Very Good	Pvt-Party Good	Retail Excellent
M-CLASS 4WD—V6 Turbo Diesel—Truck Equipment Schedule T3						
ML320 BLUETEC	BB25E	48125	18150	18900	19900	23100
KEYLESS-GO			200	200	225	225
Full Leather			250	250	285	285
Premium Pkg 1			350	350	400	400
Premium Pkg 2			325	325	375	375
M-CLASS 4WD—V6—Truck Equipment Schedule T3						
ML350 Sport Util	BB86E	46625	15700	16350	17300	20000
KEYLESS-GO			200	200	225	225
Full Leather			250	250	285	285
Premium Pkg 1			350	350	400	400
Premium Pkg 2			325	325	375	375
2WD			(1050)	(1050)	(1205)	(1205)
M-CLASS 4WD—V8—Truck Equipment Schedule T3						
ML550 Sport Util	BB72E	55325	19200	20000	21000	24300
KEYLESS-GO			200	200	225	225
Full Leather			250	250	285	285
Premium Pkg 1			350	350	395	395
Premium Pkg 2			325	325	375	375
M-CLASS 4WD—V8—Truck Equipment Schedule T3						
ML63 Sport Util	BB77E	89225	28500	29500	30500	35100
G-CLASS 4WD—V8—Truck Equipment Schedule T3						
G550 Sport Utility	YR36E	101125	49000	50800	51000	57400
G-CLASS 4WD—V8 Supercharged—Truck Equipment Schedule T3						
G55 Sport Utility	YR71E	120325	55500	57400	57500	64600
GL-CLASS AWD—V6 Turbo Diesel—Truck Equipment Schedule T3						
GL320 BLUETEC	BF25E	59755	23200	24100	25200	29100
KEYLESS-GO			200	200	230	230
Premium Pkg 1			350	350	405	405
Premium Pkg 2			325	325	380	380
GL-CLASS AWD—V8—Truck Equipment Schedule T3						
GL450 Sport Util	BF71E	60755	20700	21500	22500	26000
KEYLESS-GO			200	200	230	230
Premium Pkg 1			350	350	405	405
Premium Pkg 2			325	325	380	380

Body Type	VIN	List	Trade-In Good	Very Good	Pvt-Party Good	Retail Excellent
M-CLASS AWD—V8—Truck Equipment Schedule T3						
GL550 Sport Util	BF86E	80375	24000	24900	26000	30000
R-CLASS 4WD—V6 Turbo Diesel—Truck Equipment Schedule T3						
R320 BLUETEC	CB25E	48825	16600	17350	18300	21400
KEYLESS-GO			200	200	230	230
Premium Pkg 1			350	350	400	400
Premium Pkg 2			325	325	380	380
R-CLASS 4WD—V6—Truck Equipment Schedule T3						
R350 Sport Wagon	CB65E	47325	14550	15200	16150	18850
KEYLESS-GO			200	200	230	230
Premium Pkg 1			350	350	400	400
Premium Pkg 2			325	325	380	380

2010 MERCEDES-BENZ — (4JGorWDC)(GG5GB)–A–#

Body Type	VIN	List	Trade-In Good	Very Good	Pvt-Party Good	Retail Excellent
GLK-CLASS—V6—Truck Equipment Schedule T3						
GLK350 Spt Util	GG5GB	37225	16500	17200	18200	21000
KEYLESS-GO			200	200	230	230
Full Leather			575	575	660	660
Appearance Pkg			125	125	135	135
Multimedia Pkg			425	425	485	485
Premium Pkg 1			825	825	930	930
GLK-CLASS 4MATIC AWD—V6—Truck Equipment Schedule T3						
GLK350 Spt Util	GG8HB	39225	17700	18400	19400	22400
KEYLESS-GO			200	200	230	230
Full Leather			575	575	660	660
Appearance Pkg			125	125	135	135
Multimedia Pkg			425	425	485	485
Premium Pkg 1			825	825	935	935
M-CLASS AWD—V6 Turbo Diesel—Truck Equipment Schedule T3						
ML350 BLUETEC	BB2FB	50575	22200	23000	24000	27500
KEYLESS-GO			200	200	225	225
Full Leather			575	575	650	650
Premium Pkg 1			400	400	450	450
Premium Pkg 2			350	350	395	395
M-CLASS—V6—Truck Equipment Schedule T3						
ML350 Sport Util	BB5GB	46575	17800	18500	19550	22400
KEYLESS-GO			200	200	225	225
Full Leather			575	575	650	650
Premium Pkg 1			400	400	450	450
Premium Pkg 2			350	350	395	395
M-CLASS 4MATIC AWD—V6—Truck Equipment Schedule T3						
ML350 Sport Util	BB8GB	49075	19600	20300	21400	24500
KEYLESS-GO			200	200	225	225
Full Leather			575	575	650	650
Premium Pkg 1			400	400	450	450
Premium Pkg 2			350	350	395	395
M-CLASS—V6 Hybrid—Truck Equipment Schedule T3						
ML450 Sport Util	BB9FB	55875	23900	24800	25900	29600
KEYLESS-GO			200	200	225	225
Full Leather			575	575	650	650
Premium Pkg 1			400	400	450	450
Premium Pkg 2			350	350	395	395
Distronic Cruise Control			400	400	450	450
M-CLASS AWD—V8—Truck Equipment Schedule T3						
ML550 Spt Util 4D	BB7CB	57625	23300	24200	25300	28900
KEYLESS-GO			200	200	225	225
Full Leather			575	575	650	650
Premium Pkg 1			400	400	450	450
Premium Pkg 2			350	350	395	395
M-CLASS AWD—V8—Truck Equipment Schedule T3						
ML63 AMG SUV	BB7HB	91925	36700	38000	38400	43000
R-CLASS 4MATIC AWD—V6 Turbo Diesel—Truck Equipment Sch T3						
R350 BLUETEC	CB2FE	51675	20700	21500	22400	25700
KEYLESS-GO			200	200	225	225
Premium Pkg 1			400	400	450	450
Premium Pkg 2			350	350	395	395
R-CLASS 4MATIC AWD—V6—Truck Equipment Schedule T3						
R350 Sport Wagon	CB6FE	50175	18700	19450	20300	23300
KEYLESS-GO			200	200	225	225
Premium Pkg 1			400	400	450	450
Premium Pkg 2			350	350	395	395
GL-CLASS AWD—V6 Turbo Diesel—Truck Equipment Schedule T3						
GL350 BLUETEC	BF2FB	62725	28000	29100	30000	34100

2010 MERCEDES-BENZ

Body Type	VIN	List	Trade-In Good	Very Good	Pvt-Party Good	Retail Excellent
KEYLESS-GO			200	200	225	225
Premium Pkg 1			400	400	450	450
Premium Pkg 2			350	350	390	390
GL-CLASS AWD—V8—Truck Equipment Schedule T3						
GL450 Spt Util 4D	BF7BB	63725	25200	26200	26900	30600
KEYLESS-GO			200	200	225	225
Premium Pkg 1			400	400	450	450
Premium Pkg 2			350	350	390	390
GL-CLASS AWD—V8—Truck Equipment Schedule T3						
GL550 Spt Util 4D	BF8GB	83725	30500	31700	32400	36600
G-CLASS AWD—V8—Truck Equipment Schedule T3						
G550 Sport Util 4D	YC3HF	104875	58000	59900	59800	66500
G-CLASS AWD—V8 Supercharged—Truck Equipment Schedule T3						
G55 Sport Util	YC7BF	123575	62100	64100	63900	70900

2011 MERCEDES-BENZ — (4JGorWDC)(GG5GB)-B-#

Body Type	VIN	List	Trade-In Good	Very Good	Pvt-Party Good	Retail Excellent
GLK-CLASS—V6—Truck Equipment Schedule T3						
GLK350 Spt Util	GG5GB	36375	19400	20100	21000	23900
KEYLESS-GO			200	200	225	225
Full Leather			600	600	670	670
AMG Styling Pkg			500	500	560	560
Appearance Pkg			125	125	140	140
Multimedia Pkg			450	450	495	495
Premium Pkg 1			850	850	960	960
GLK-CLASS 4MATIC AWD—V6—Truck Equipment Schedule T3						
GLK350 Spt Util	GG8HB	38375	20300	21000	22000	25100
KEYLESS-GO			200	200	225	225
Full Leather			600	600	670	670
AMG Styling Pkg			500	500	560	560
Appearance Pkg			125	125	140	140
Multimedia Pkg			450	450	495	495
Premium Pkg 1			850	850	960	960
M-CLASS AWD—V6 Turbo Diesel—Truck Equipment Schedule T3						
ML350 BLUETEC	BB2FB	53145	25500	26400	27500	31100
KEYLESS-GO			200	200	225	225
Full Leather			600	600	670	670
Premium Pkg 1			450	450	505	505
Premium Pkg 2			375	375	415	415
designo Edition			875	875	980	980
Distronic Cruise Control			425	425	475	475
M-CLASS—V6—Truck Equipment Schedule T3						
ML350 Sport Util	BB5GB	49145	21800	22600	23500	26600
KEYLESS-GO			200	200	225	225
Full Leather			600	600	670	670
Premium Pkg 1			450	450	505	505
Premium Pkg 2			350	350	395	395
designo Edition			875	875	980	980
Distronic Cruise Control			425	425	475	475
M-CLASS 4MATIC AWD—V6—Truck Equipment Schedule T3						
ML350 Sport Util	BB8GB	51645	23300	24100	25100	28400
KEYLESS-GO			200	200	225	225
Full Leather			600	600	670	670
Premium Pkg 1			450	450	505	505
Premium Pkg 2			350	350	395	395
designo Edition			875	875	980	980
Off-Road Pkg			375	375	415	415
Distronic Cruise Control			425	425	475	475
M-CLASS AWD—V6 Hybrid—Truck Equipment Schedule T3						
ML450 Sport Util	BB9FB	58445	28500	29400	30500	34500
KEYLESS-GO			200	200	225	225
Full Leather			600	600	670	670
Premium Pkg 1			450	450	505	505
Premium Pkg 2			350	350	395	395
designo Edition			875	875	980	980
M-CLASS AWD—V8—Truck Equipment Schedule T3						
ML550 Spt Util 4D	BB7CB	60245	27900	28900	29900	33900
KEYLESS-GO			200	200	225	225
Full Leather			600	600	675	675
Premium Pkg 1			450	450	505	505
Premium Pkg 2			350	350	395	395
designo Edition			875	875	980	980
Off-Road Pkg			375	375	415	415
Distronic Cruise Control			425	425	475	475

2011 MERCEDES-BENZ

Body Type	VIN	List	Trade-In Good	Very Good	Pvt-Party Good	Retail Excellent
M-CLASS AWD—V8—Truck Equipment Schedule T3						
ML63 AMG SUV	BB7HB	93465	42400	43700	44200	49100
Distronic Cruise Control			425	425	450	450
R-CLASS 4MATIC AWD—V6 Turbo Diesel—Truck Equipment Sch T3						
R350 BLUETEC	CB2FE	52615	25700	26600	27600	31300
KEYLESS-GO			200	200	220	220
Premium Pkg 1			450	450	500	500
Premium Pkg 2			375	375	410	410
R-CLASS 4MATIC AWD—V6—Truck Equipment Schedule T3						
R350 Sport Wagon	CB6FE	51115	23700	24600	25600	29000
KEYLESS-GO			200	200	220	220
Premium Pkg 1			450	450	500	500
Premium Pkg 2			375	375	410	410
GL-CLASS AWD—V6 Turbo Diesel—Truck Equipment Schedule T3						
GL350 BLUETEC	BF2FE	63755	31700	32900	33800	38200
KEYLESS-GO			200	200	225	225
Full Leather			350	350	395	395
Premium Pkg 1			450	450	510	510
Premium Pkg 2			375	375	415	415
Distronic Cruise Control			425	425	480	480
GL-CLASS AWD—V8—Truck Equipment Schedule T3						
GL450 Spt Util 4D	BF7BE	64755	28200	29300	30200	34200
KEYLESS-GO			200	200	225	225
Full Leather			350	350	390	390
Premium Pkg 1			450	450	505	505
Premium Pkg 2			375	375	415	415
Off-Road Pkg			375	375	415	415
Distronic Cruise Control			425	425	475	475
GL-CLASS AWD—V8—Truck Equipment Schedule T3						
GL550 Spt Util 4D	BF8GE	85325	37200	38500	39100	43800
Full Leather			350	350	390	390
Off-Road Pkg			375	375	410	410
G-CLASS AWD—V8—Truck Equipment Schedule T3						
G550 Sport Util 4D	YC3HF	106625	60200	62100	62200	68800
G-CLASS AWD—V8 Supercharged—Truck Equipment Schedule T3						
G55 Sport Utility	YC7BF	125325	69700	71900	71400	78600

2012 MERCEDES-BENZ — (4JGorWDC)(GG5HB)-C-#

Body Type	VIN	List	Trade-In Good	Very Good	Pvt-Party Good	Retail Excellent
GLK-CLASS—V6—Truck Equipment Schedule T3						
GLK350 Spt Util	GG5HB	36775	22200	23000	23900	26900
KEYLESS-GO			200	200	220	220
Full Leather			625	625	690	690
AMG Styling Pkg			525	525	580	580
Appearance Pkg			125	125	145	145
Multimedia Pkg			450	450	500	500
Premium Pkg 1			900	900	995	995
GLK-CLASS 4MATIC AWD—V6—Truck Equipment Schedule T3						
GLK350 Spt Util	GG8HB	38755	23100	23900	24900	28100
KEYLESS-GO			200	200	220	220
Full Leather			625	625	690	690
AMG Styling Pkg			525	525	580	580
Appearance Pkg			125	125	145	145
Multimedia Pkg			450	450	500	500
Premium Pkg 1			900	900	995	995
M-CLASS 4MATIC AWD—V6 Turbo Diesel—Truck Equipment Sch T3						
ML350 BLUETEC	DA2EB	51365	35600	36700	37200	41100
KEYLESS-GO			200	200	210	210
DISTRONIC PLUS			450	450	475	475
Driver Assistance Pkg			625	625	665	665
Premium Pkg 1			500	500	530	530
Premium Pkg 2			400	400	415	415
designo Edition			900	900	955	955
M-CLASS 4MATIC AWD—V6—Truck Equipment Schedule T3						
ML350 Sport Util	DA5HB	49865	32500	33500	34100	37700
KEYLESS-GO			200	200	210	210
DISTRONIC PLUS			450	450	480	480
Driver Assistance Pkg			625	625	665	665
Premium Pkg 1			500	500	530	530
Premium Pkg 2			400	400	415	415
designo Edition			900	900	960	960
M-CLASS 4MATIC AWD—V8 Twin Turbo—Truck Equip Sch T3						
ML550 Spt Util 4D	DA7DB	58465	38200	39400	39800	44000
KEYLESS-GO			200	200	210	210

2012 MERCEDES-BENZ

Body Type	VIN	List	Trade-In Good	Very Good	Pvt-Party Good	Retail Excellent
DISTRONIC PLUS	-------	-------	450	450	480	480
Driver Assistance Pkg	-------	-------	625	625	665	665
Premium Pkg 1	-------	-------	500	500	530	530
Premium Pkg 2	-------	-------	400	400	415	415
designo Edition	-------	-------	900	900	955	955
M-CLASS 4MATIC AWD—V8—Truck Equipment Schedule T3						
ML63 AMG SUV	DA7EB	95865	56800	58500	58700	64500
DISTRONIC PLUS	-------	-------	450	450	470	470
AMG Performance Pkg	-------	-------	3900	3900	4085	4085
Driver Assistance Pkg	-------	-------	625	625	655	655
R-CLASS 4MATIC AWD—V6 Turbo Diesel—Truck Equipment Sch T3						
R350 BLUETEC	CB2FE	54715	30000	31000	31900	35700
KEYLESS-GO	-------	-------	200	200	215	215
DISTRONIC Cruise	-------	-------	450	450	490	490
Premium Pkg 1	-------	-------	500	500	545	545
Premium Pkg 2	-------	-------	400	400	425	425
R-CLASS 4MATIC AWD—V6—Truck Equipment Schedule T3						
R350 Sport Wagon	CB5HE	53565	27800	28700	29600	33100
KEYLESS-GO	-------	-------	200	200	215	215
DISTRONIC Cruise	-------	-------	450	450	490	490
Premium Pkg 1	-------	-------	500	500	540	540
Premium Pkg 2	-------	-------	400	400	425	425
GL-CLASS AWD—V6 Turbo Diesel—Truck Equipment Schedule T3						
GL350 BlueTEC	BF2FE	63320	36300	37600	38200	42700
KEYLESS-GO	-------	-------	200	200	220	220
DISTRONIC Cruise	-------	-------	450	450	490	490
Premium Pkg 1	-------	-------	500	500	545	545
Premium Pkg 2	-------	-------	400	400	425	425
GL-CLASS AWD—V8—Truck Equipment Schedule T3						
GL450 Spt Util 4D	BF7BE	64320	31500	32600	33300	37300
KEYLESS-GO	-------	-------	200	200	220	220
DISTRONIC Cruise	-------	-------	450	450	490	490
Premium Pkg 1	-------	-------	500	500	545	545
Premium Pkg 2	-------	-------	400	400	425	425
Off-Road Pkg	-------	-------	400	400	425	425
GL-CLASS AWD—V8—Truck Equipment Schedule T3						
GL550 Spt Util 4D	BF8GE	87050	43200	44700	44800	49700
Off-Road Pkg	-------	-------	400	400	420	420
G-CLASS AWD—V8—Truck Equipment Schedule T3						
G550 Sport Util 4D	YC3HF	107975	68100	70100	70300	77400

2013 MERCEDES-BENZ — (4JGorWDC)(GG0EB)-D-#

Body Type	VIN	List	Trade-In Good	Very Good	Pvt-Party Good	Retail Excellent
GLK-CLASS 4MATIC AWD—4-Cyl. Turbo Diesel—Truck Equip Sch T3						
GLK250 BlueTec	GG0EB	39495	25600	26500	27600	31000
KEYLESS-GO	-------	-------	200	200	220	220
DISTRONIC PLUS	-------	-------	475	475	525	525
AMG Styling Pkg	-------	-------	550	550	610	610
Appearance Pkg	-------	-------	125	125	150	150
Driver Assistance Pkg	-------	-------	650	650	720	720
Multimedia Pkg	-------	-------	475	475	520	520
Premium Pkg 1	-------	-------	900	900	1000	1000
GLK-CLASS—V6—Truck Equipment Schedule T3						
GLK350 Spt Util	GG5HB	37995	24200	25000	26100	29200
KEYLESS-GO	-------	-------	200	200	220	220
DISTRONIC PLUS	-------	-------	475	475	525	525
AMG Styling Pkg	-------	-------	550	550	605	605
Appearance Pkg	-------	-------	125	125	150	150
Driver Assistance Pkg	-------	-------	650	650	715	715
Multimedia Pkg	-------	-------	475	475	520	520
Premium Pkg	-------	-------	900	900	995	995
GLK-CLASS 4MATIC AWD—V6—Truck Equipment Schedule T3						
GLK350 Spt Util	GG8JB	39995	26000	26900	27900	31400
KEYLESS-GO	-------	-------	200	200	220	220
DISTRONIC PLUS	-------	-------	475	475	525	525
AMG Styling Pkg	-------	-------	550	550	610	610
Appearance Pkg	-------	-------	125	125	150	150
Driver Assistance Pkg	-------	-------	650	650	720	720
Multimedia Pkg	-------	-------	475	475	520	520
Premium Pkg	-------	-------	900	900	995	995
M-CLASS—V6—Truck Equipment Schedule T3						
ML350 Sport Util	DA5JB	48175	34600	35700	36000	39400
KEYLESS-GO	-------	-------	200	200	210	210
DISTRONIC PLUS	-------	-------	475	475	495	495

SEE BACK PAGES FOR TRUCK EQUIPMENT

2013 MERCEDES-BENZ

Body Type	VIN	List	Trade-In Good	Very Good	Pvt-Party Good	Retail Excellent
Driver Assistance Pkg			650	650	675	675
Premium Pkg 2			900	900	935	935
M-CLASS 4MATIC AWD—V6 Turbo Diesel—Truck Equipment Schedule T3						
ML350 BLUETEC	DA2EB	52175	39500	40800	40900	44800
KEYLESS-GO			200	200	205	205
DISTRONIC PLUS			475	475	495	495
Driver Assistance Pkg			650	650	675	675
designo Edition			900	900	935	935
Premium Pkg 1			900	900	935	935
M-CLASS 4MATIC AWD—V6—Truck Equipment Schedule T3						
ML350 Sport Util	DA5HB	50675	36100	37200	37400	41000
KEYLESS-GO			200	200	205	205
DISTRONIC PLUS			475	475	495	495
Driver Assistance Pkg			650	650	675	675
designo Edition			900	900	935	935
M-CLASS 4MATIC AWD—V8 Twin Turbo—Truck Equip Sch T3						
ML550 Sport Util	DA7DB	59705	42500	43800	43900	48000
KEYLESS-GO			200	200	205	205
Driver Assistance Pkg			650	650	675	675
designo Edition			900	900	935	935
Premium Pkg			900	900	935	935
M-CLASS 4MATIC AWD—V8—Truck Equipment Schedule T3						
ML63 AMG SUV	DA7EB	97005	69200	71200	70500	76700
GL-CLASS 4MATIC AWD—V6 Turbo Diesel—Truck Equipment Sch T3						
GL350 BlueTEC	DF2EB	63275	49700	51400	51400	56400
KEYLESS-GO			200	200	215	215
DISTRONIC PLUS			475	475	505	505
Bang & Olufsen Sound			2875	2875	3070	3070
Premium Pkg 1			550	550	590	590
GL-CLASS 4MATIC AWD—V8 Twin Turbo—Truck Equipment Sch T3						
GL450 Spt Util 4D	DF7CB	64775	46100	47600	47400	52100
KEYLESS-GO			200	200	215	215
Bang & Olufsen Sound			2875	2875	3075	3075
Driver Assistance Pkg			650	650	695	695
Premium Pkg 1			550	550	590	590
GL-CLASS 4MATIC AWD—V8 Twin Turbo—Truck Equipment Schedule T3						
GL550 Spt Util 4D	DF7DB	87775	59000	60900	60300	65900
Bang & Olusfsen Sound			2875	2875	3045	3045
GL-CLASS 4MATIC AWD—V8 Twin Turbo—Truck Equipment Schedule T3						
GL63 AMG Spt Utl	DF7EE	117800	96400	99100	96300	103200
Bang & Olufsen Sound			2875	2875	2975	2975
DISTRONIC PLUS			475	475	490	490
G-CLASS 4MATIC AWD—V8—Truck Equipment Schedule T3						
G550 Sport Utility	YC3HF	113905	77000	79200	78900	86400
G63 AMG Sport Util	YC7DF	135205	102800	105700	104100	112600

2014 MERCEDES-BENZ — (4JGorWDC)(GG0EB)-E-#

Body Type	VIN	List	Trade-In Good	Very Good	Pvt-Party Good	Retail Excellent
GLK-CLASS 4MATIC AWD—4-Cyl. Turbo Diesel—Truck Equip Sch T3						
GLK250 BlueTEC	GG0EB	39905	32300	33400	34400	38400
KEYLESS-GO			200	200	220	220
DISTRONIC PLUS			500	500	550	550
Driver Assistance Pkg			675	675	745	745
Multimedia Pkg			475	475	535	535
AMG Styling Pkg			575	575	635	635
Premium Pkg 1			900	900	990	990
GLK-CLASS 4MATIC AWD—V6—Truck Equipment Schedule T3						
GLK350 Spt Util	GG5HB	38405	27100	28000	29100	32700
KEYLESS-GO			200	200	220	220
DISTRONIC PLUS			500	500	555	555
AMG Styling Pkg			575	575	640	640
Multimedia Pkg			475	475	540	540
AMG Styling Pkg			575	575	640	640
Premium Pkg 1			900	900	1000	1000
GLK-CLASS 4MATIC AWD—V6—Truck Equipment Schedule T3						
GLK350 Sport Util	GG8JB	40405	33300	34400	35600	39900
KEYLESS-GO			200	200	220	220
DISTRONIC PLUS			500	500	555	555
Driver Assistance Pkg			675	675	750	750
Multimedia Pkg			475	475	535	535
AMG Styling Pkg			575	575	635	635
Premium Pkg 1			900	900	995	995
M-CLASS—V6—Truck Equipment Schedule T3						
ML350 Sport Util	DA5JB	48715	38400	39600	39400	42600

Body Type	VIN	List	Trade-In Good	Very Good	Pvt-Party Good	Retail Excellent
KEYLESS-GO			200	200	205	205
DISTRONIC PLUS			500	500	520	520
Premium Pkg 1			900	900	935	935
M-CLASS 4MATIC AWD—V6 Turbo Diesel—Truck Equipment Schedule T3						
ML350 BlueTEC	DA2EB	52715	43200	44500	44200	47900
KEYLESS-GO			200	200	210	210
DISTRONIC PLUS			500	500	525	525
designo Edition			900	900	940	940
Premium Pkg 1			900	900	940	940
M-CLASS 4MATIC AWD—V6—Truck Equipment Schedule T3						
ML350 Sport Util	DA5HB	51215	39900	41100	40800	44200
KEYLESS-GO			200	200	205	205
DISTRONIC PLUS			500	500	520	520
designo Edition			900	900	935	935
Premium Pkg 1			900	900	935	935
M-CLASS 4MATIC AWD—V8 Twin Turbo—Truck Equip Sch T3						
ML550 Sport Util	DA7DB	60375	46400	47700	47300	51100
KEYLESS-GO			200	200	210	210
DISTRONIC PLUS			500	500	520	520
designo Edition			900	900	940	940
Premium Pkg 1			900	900	940	940
M-CLASS 4MATIC AWD—V8—Truck Equipment Schedule T3						
ML63 AMG Util	DA7EB	98175	75300	77400	76500	82900
DISTRONIC PLUS			500	500	515	515
Bang & Olufsen Sound			3000	3000	3105	3105
GL-CLASS 4MATIC AWD—V6 Turbo Diesel—Truck Equipment Sch T3						
GL350 BlueTEC	DF2EE	63925	55400	57200	56400	61200
KEYLESS-GO			200	200	210	210
DISTRONIC PLUS			500	500	525	525
Driver Assistance Pkg			675	675	710	710
Premium Pkg 1			575	575	605	605
GL-CLASS 4MATIC AWD—V8 Twin Turbo—Truck Equipment Sch T3						
GL450 Sport Util	DF7CE	65475	53400	55200	54600	59500
KEYLESS-GO			200	200	210	210
DISTRONIC PLUS			500	500	530	530
Driver Assistance Pkg			675	675	715	715
Premium Pkg 1			575	575	610	610
GL-CLASS 4MATIC AWD—V8 Twin Turbo—Truck Equipment Sch T3						
GL550 Sport Util	DF7DE	89525	69800	72100	70700	76700
Bang & Olufsen Sound			3000	3000	3170	3170
DISTRONIC PLUS			500	500	530	530
Driver Assistance Pkg			675	675	715	715
G-CLASS 4MATIC AWD—V8 Twin Turbo—Truck Equipment Sch T3						
GL63 AMG Spt Utl	DF7EE	119085	100000	102800	100500	107800
Bang & Olufsen Sound			3000	3000	3115	3115
G-CLASS 4MATIC AWD—V8—Truck Equipment Schedule T3						
G550 Sport Utility	YC3HF	115125	88500	91000	90100	98000
G-CLASS 4MATIC AWD—V8 Twin Turbo—Truck Equipment Schedule T3						
G63 AMG Spt Util	YC7DF	136625	116000	119200	116800	125800

MERCURY

2000 MERCURY — 4M2-(U86P)-Y-#

Body Type	VIN	List	Trade-In Good	Very Good	Pvt-Party Good	Retail Excellent
MOUNTAINEER AWD—V8—Truck Equipment Schedule T1						
Sport Utility 4D	U86P	30360	900	1050	1925	3225
Premier			275	275	365	365
2WD	6		(550)	(550)	(750)	(750)
4WD	7		0	0	0	0
V6, 4.0 Liter	E		(125)	(125)	(170)	(170)
VILLAGER—V6—Truck Equipment Schedule T1						
Minivan 4D	V11T	22995	700	825	1625	2825
Sport Minivan 4D	V12T	25995	1275	1475	2375	4075
Estate Minivan 4D	V14T	27695	1350	1575	2450	4225

2001 MERCURY — 4M2-(U86P)-1-#

Body Type	VIN	List	Trade-In Good	Very Good	Pvt-Party Good	Retail Excellent
MOUNTAINEER AWD—V8—Truck Equipment Schedule T1						
Sport Utility 4D	U86P	30695	1075	1225	2025	3300
Premier			325	325	420	420
2WD	6		(650)	(650)	(860)	(860)
4WD	7		0	0	0	0
V6, 4.0 Liter	E		(150)	(150)	(190)	(190)

Body Type	VIN	List	Trade-In Good	Very Good	Pvt-Party Good	Retail Excellent
VILLAGER—V6—Truck Equipment Schedule T1						
Minivan 4D	V11T	23140	925	1075	1875	3225
Sport Minivan 4D	V12T	26365	1525	1775	2750	4625
Estate Minivan 4D	V14T	27840	1600	1850	2850	4775

2002 MERCURY — 4M2-(U86W)-2-#

Body Type	VIN	List	Trade-In Good	Very Good	Pvt-Party Good	Retail Excellent
MOUNTAINEER AWD—V8—Truck Equipment Schedule T1						
Sport Utility 4D	U86W	31310	1750	2000	3100	5000
Premier			350	350	475	475
Third Row Seat			600	600	805	805
2WD	6		(725)	(725)	(970)	(970)
V6, 4.0 Liter	E		(150)	(150)	(210)	(210)
VILLAGER—V6—Truck Equipment Schedule T1						
Minivan 4D	V11T	22995	1125	1300	2025	3375
Sport Minivan 4D	V12T	24995	1875	2150	3075	4950
Estate Minivan 4D	V14T	26995	1950	2225	3175	5100

2003 MERCURY — 4M2-(U86W)-3-#

Body Type	VIN	List	Trade-In Good	Very Good	Pvt-Party Good	Retail Excellent
MOUNTAINEER AWD—V8—Truck Equipment Schedule T1						
Sport Utility 4D	U86W	32605	2175	2450	3450	5275
Premier Sport Util	U86W	34750	2475	2800	3825	5825
Third Row Seat			625	625	845	845
2WD	6		(800)	(800)	(1080)	(1080)
V6, Flex Fuel, 4.0 Liter	K		(175)	(175)	(235)	(235)

2004 MERCURY — (2MRor4M2)-(A202)-4-#

Body Type	VIN	List	Trade-In Good	Very Good	Pvt-Party Good	Retail Excellent
MONTEREY—V6—Truck Equipment Schedule T1						
Minivan	A202	29995	1675	1875	2975	4850
Premier			350	350	455	455
MOUNTAINEER AWD—V8—Truck Equipment Schedule T1						
Sport Utility 4D	U86W	32855	2825	3175	4350	6650
Premier			425	425	580	580
Third Row Seat			650	650	880	880
2WD	6		(900)	(900)	(1190)	(1190)
V6, Flex Fuel, 4.0 Liter	K		(200)	(200)	(265)	(265)

2005 MERCURY — (2MRor4M2)-(A222)-5-#

Body Type	VIN	List	Trade-In Good	Very Good	Pvt-Party Good	Retail Excellent
MONTEREY—V6—Truck Equipment Schedule T1						
Minivan	A222	29695	2100	2350	3425	5375
Premier Minivan	A222	35665	2550	2850	4000	6225
MARINER 4WD—V6—Truck Equipment Schedule T1						
Sport Utility 4D	U571	25245	3375	3700	4675	6700
2WD	6		(600)	(600)	(800)	(800)
4-Cyl, 2.3 Liter	Z		(425)	(425)	(555)	(555)
MOUNTAINEER AWD—V8—Truck Equipment Schedule T1						
Sport Utility 4D	U86W	33505	3200	3575	4875	7275
Premier Sport Util	U86W	39625	3650	4050	5425	8025
Third Row Seat			700	700	920	920
2WD	6		(975)	(975)	(1300)	(1300)
V6, Flex Fuel 4.0L	E,K		(225)	(225)	(300)	(300)

2006 MERCURY — (1,2or3)ME-(A222)-6-#

Body Type	VIN	List	Trade-In Good	Very Good	Pvt-Party Good	Retail Excellent
MONTEREY—V6—Truck Equipment Schedule T1						
Minivan	A222	29325	3175	3500	4550	6725
MARINER 4WD—4-Cyl. Hybrid—Truck Equipment Schedule T1						
Sport Utility 4D	U98H	29840	5075	5475	6650	9125
MARINER 4WD—V6—Truck Equipment Schedule T1						
Sport Utility 4D	U571	25060	4475	4850	5975	8250
Premier Sport Util	U571	27400	4725	5125	6250	8625
2WD	6		(650)	(650)	(865)	(865)
4-Cyl, 2.3 Liter	Z		(450)	(450)	(600)	(600)
MOUNTAINEER AWD—V6—Truck Equipment Schedule T1						
Sport Utility 4D	U468	31995	4900	5375	6550	9125
Third Row Seat			725	725	960	960
2WD	3		(1050)	(1050)	(1410)	(1410)
V8, 4.6 Liter	8		275	275	380	380
MOUNTAINEER AWD—V8—Truck Equipment Schedule T1						
Premier Sport Util	U38E	36145	5275	5750	7225	10050
Third Row Seat			725	725	960	960
2WD			(1050)	(1050)	(1410)	(1410)

Body Type	VIN	List	Trade-In Good	Very Good	Pvt-Party Good	Retail Excellent

TRUCKS & VANS

2007 MERCURY — (2MRor4M2)–(A222)–7–#

MONTEREY—V6—Truck Equipment Schedule T1
| Minivan | A222 | 29350 | **4150** | **4525** | **5800** | **8325** |

MARINER 4WD—4-Cyl. Hybrid—Truck Equipment Schedule T1
| Sport Utility 4D | U39H | 28615 | **6250** | **6725** | **7950** | **10450** |

MARINER 4WD—V6—Truck Equipment Schedule T1
Sport Utility 4D	U901	25420	**5150**	**5550**	**6700**	**8925**
Premier Spt Util	U901	27515	**5725**	**6150**	**7300**	**9625**
2WD	8		(700)	(700)	(935)	(935)
4-Cyl, 2.3 Liter	Z		(475)	(475)	(635)	(635)

MOUNTAINEER AWD—V6—Truck Equipment Schedule T1
Sport Utility 4D	U478	30270	**5650**	**6150**	**7250**	**9650**
Third Row Seat			750	750	1000	1000
2WD	3		(1150)	(1150)	(1520)	(1520)
V8, 4.6 Liter	8		300	300	410	410

MOUNTAINEER AWD—V8—Truck Equipment Schedule T1
Premier Spt Util	U388	34740	**6125**	**6650**	**7875**	**10450**
Third Row Seat			750	750	1000	1000
2WD	3		(1150)	(1150)	(1520)	(1520)

2008 MERCURY — (2MRor4M2)–(U39H)–8–#

MARINER 4WD—4-Cyl. Hybrid—Truck Equipment Schedule T1
| Sport Utility 4D | U39H | 28370 | **7550** | **8050** | **9475** | **12300** |
| 2WD | 2 | | (750) | (750) | (1000) | (1000) |

MARINER 4WD—V6—Truck Equipment Schedule T1
Sport Utility 4D	U911	24335	**5825**	**6250**	**7425**	**9675**
Premier Spt Util 4D	U971	26235	**6475**	**6925**	**8175**	**10600**
2WD	8		(750)	(750)	(1000)	(1000)
4-Cyl, 2.3 Liter	Z		(500)	(500)	(665)	(665)

MOUNTAINEER AWD—V6—Truck Equipment Schedule T1
Sport Utility 4D	U47E	32850	**7100**	**7625**	**8675**	**11050**
2WD	3		(1225)	(1225)	(1570)	(1570)
Third Row Seat			800	800	1030	1030

MOUNTAINEER AWD—V8—Truck Equipment Schedule T1
Premier Spt Util 4D	U488	32410	**7775**	**8325**	**9400**	**11950**
Third Row Seat			800	800	1025	1025
2WD	3		(1225)	(1225)	(1570)	(1570)
V6, 4.0 Liter	E		(300)	(300)	(385)	(385)

2009 MERCURY — (2MRor4M2)–(U393)–9–#

MARINER 4WD—4-Cyl. Hybrid—Truck Equipment Schedule T1
| Sport Utility 4D | U393 | 31195 | **9750** | **10300** | **11500** | **14100** |
| 2WD | 2 | | (875) | (875) | (1090) | (1090) |

MARINER 4WD—V6—Truck Equipment Schedule T1
Sport Utility 4D	U91G	25380	**8175**	**8650**	**9725**	**12000**
Premier Spt Util 4D	U97G	26485	**8575**	**9050**	**10150**	**12500**
2WD	8		(875)	(875)	(1095)	(1095)
4-Cyl, 2.5 Liter	7		(725)	(725)	(910)	(910)

MOUNTAINEER AWD—V6—Truck Equipment Schedule T1
Sport Utility 4D	U47E	30360	**10050**	**10600**	**11800**	**14650**
2WD	3		(1300)	(1300)	(1630)	(1630)
Third Row Seat			800	800	1000	1000

MOUNTAINEER AWD—V8—Truck Equipment Schedule T1
Premier Spt Util 4D	U388	34535	**11300**	**11900**	**13250**	**16350**
Third Row Seat			800	800	995	995
2WD	3		(1300)	(1300)	(1625)	(1625)
V6, 4.0 Liter	E		(350)	(350)	(435)	(435)

2010 MERCURY –(2MRor4M2)–(N3K3)–A–#

MARINER 4WD—4-Cyl. Hybrid—Truck Equipment Schedule T1
| Sport Utility 4D | N3K3 | 32470 | **12300** | **12900** | **14250** | **17200** |
| 2WD | 2 | | (1000) | (1000) | (1205) | (1205) |

MARINER 4WD—V6—Truck Equipment Schedule T1
Sport Utility 4D	N9BG	26510	**9700**	**10200**	**11450**	**13900**
Premier Sport Util	N9HG	28580	**10600**	**11150**	**12350**	**15000**
2WD	8		(1000)	(1000)	(1215)	(1215)
4-Cyl, 2.5 Liter	7		(800)	(800)	(970)	(970)

MOUNTAINEER AWD—V6—Truck Equipment Schedule T1
| Sport Utility 4D | N4HE | 32215 | **11350** | **11900** | **13100** | **15800** |
| 2WD | 3 | | (1375) | (1375) | (1670) | (1670) |

Body Type	VIN	List	Trade-In Good	Trade-In Very Good	Pvt-Party Good	Retail Excellent
MOUNTAINEER AWD—V8—Truck Equipment Schedule T1						
Premier Sport Util	N4J8	37995	**14200**	**14850**	**16300**	**19600**
Third Row Seat			**800**	**800**	**965**	**965**
2WD		3	**(1375)**	**(1375)**	**(1675)**	**(1675)**
V6, 4.0 Liter		E	**(400)**	**(400)**	**(485)**	**(485)**

2011 MERCURY — 4M2-(N3K3)-B-#

Body Type	VIN	List	Trade-In Good	Trade-In Very Good	Pvt-Party Good	Retail Excellent
MARINER 4WD—4-Cyl. Hybrid—Truck Equipment Schedule T1						
Sport Utility 4D	N3K3	32590	**13950**	**14550**	**15900**	**18800**
2WD		2	**(1100)**	**(1100)**	**(1290)**	**(1290)**
MARINER 4WD—V6—Truck Equipment Schedule T1						
Sport Utility 4D	N9BG	27040	**11400**	**11950**	**13200**	**15750**
Premier Sport Util	N9HG	29110	**12350**	**12950**	**14200**	**16900**
2WD		8	**(1100)**	**(1100)**	**(1310)**	**(1310)**
4-Cyl, 2.5 Liter		7	**(875)**	**(875)**	**(1040)**	**(1040)**

MITSUBISHI

2000 MITSUBISHI — JA4-(S21H)-Y-#

Body Type	VIN	List	Trade-In Good	Trade-In Very Good	Pvt-Party Good	Retail Excellent
MONTERO SPORT 2WD—V6—Truck Equipment Schedule T1						
ES Utility 4D	S21H	22982	**325**	**400**	**1100**	**1825**
MONTERO SPORT 4WD—V6—Truck Equipment Schedule T1						
LS Utility 4D	T31H	27262	**975**	**1125**	**1950**	**3250**
XLS Utility 4D	T31H	29782	**1150**	**1325**	**2175**	**3600**
Limited Utility 4D	T41R	31812	**1550**	**1800**	**2850**	**4650**
2WD		S	**(550)**	**(550)**	**(750)**	**(750)**
MONTERO 4WD—V6—Truck Equipment Schedule T1						
Sport Utility 4D	R51R	32262	**1700**	**1950**	**2875**	**4575**
Endeavor Pkg			**125**	**125**	**165**	**165**

2001 MITSUBISHI — JA4-(T21H)-1-#

Body Type	VIN	List	Trade-In Good	Trade-In Very Good	Pvt-Party Good	Retail Excellent
MONTERO SPORT 4WD—V6—Truck Equipment Schedule T1						
ES Utility 4D	T21H	25467	**750**	**900**	**1675**	**2775**
LS Utility 4D	T31H	28117	**1225**	**1425**	**2275**	**3700**
XS Sport Utility 4D	T31H	29187	**1375**	**1575**	**2475**	**4000**
XLS Utility 4D	T31H	29827	**1325**	**1525**	**2500**	**4050**
Limited Utility 4D	T41R	33297	**1850**	**2125**	**3175**	**5075**
2WD		S	**(650)**	**(650)**	**(860)**	**(860)**
MONTERO 4WD—V6—Truck Equipment Schedule T1						
XLS Spt Util 4D	W31R	31817	**1625**	**1850**	**2750**	**4325**
Limited Spt Util 4D	W51R	35817	**2175**	**2475**	**3425**	**5300**

2002 MITSUBISHI — JA4-(T21H)-2-#

Body Type	VIN	List	Trade-In Good	Trade-In Very Good	Pvt-Party Good	Retail Excellent
MONTERO SPORT 4WD—V6—Truck Equipment Schedule T1						
ES Utility 4D	T21H	25647	**1050**	**1200**	**1975**	**3200**
LS Utility 4D	T31H	28337	**1500**	**1700**	**2625**	**4150**
XLS Utility 4D	T31H	30187	**1675**	**1900**	**2850**	**4475**
Limited Utility 4D	T41R	33447	**2350**	**2650**	**3700**	**5700**
2WD		S	**(725)**	**(725)**	**(970)**	**(970)**
MONTERO 4WD—V6—Truck Equipment Schedule T1						
XLS Spt Util 4D	W31R	32247	**2025**	**2325**	**3125**	**4750**
Limited Spt Util 4D	W51R	36357	**2700**	**3075**	**3925**	**5825**

2003 MITSUBISHI — JA4-(Z31G)-3-#

Body Type	VIN	List	Trade-In Good	Trade-In Very Good	Pvt-Party Good	Retail Excellent
OUTLANDER AWD—4-Cyl.—Truck Equipment Schedule T1						
LS Sport Utility 4D	Z31G	19877	**1700**	**1925**	**2925**	**4550**
XLS Sport Utility 4D	Z41G	21370	**2125**	**2400**	**3450**	**5325**
2WD			**(500)**	**(500)**	**(665)**	**(665)**
MONTERO SPORT 4WD—V6—Truck Equipment Schedule T1						
ES Utility 4D	T21H	25802	**1450**	**1650**	**2575**	**4050**
LS Utility 4D	T21H	28362	**2000**	**2275**	**3250**	**5050**
XLS Utility 4D	T31H	30212	**2175**	**2450**	**3475**	**5350**
Limited Utility 4D	T41R	33472	**2900**	**3250**	**4375**	**6650**
2WD		S	**(800)**	**(800)**	**(1080)**	**(1080)**
MONTERO 4WD—V6—Truck Equipment Schedule T1						
XLS Spt Util 4D	W31S	33072	**2550**	**2900**	**3725**	**5550**
Limited Spt Util 4D	W51S	37182	**3200**	**3600**	**4575**	**6700**
20th Annv Ed Spt Ut	W51S	39022	**3850**	**4275**	**5325**	**7700**

Body Type	VIN	List	Trade-In Good	Very Good	Pvt-Party Good	Retail Excellent

2004 MITSUBISHI — (Jor4)A4–(Z31G)–4–#

OUTLANDER AWD—4-Cyl.—Truck Equipment Schedule T1
LS Utility Sport Utility 4D	Z31G	20692	2225	2500	3625	5550
XLS Sport Utility 4D	Z41G	22792	2675	3000	4200	6375
2WD	X		(550)	(550)	(735)	(735)

MONTERO SPORT 4WD—V6—Truck Equipment Schedule T1
LS Utility 4D	T31R	26392	2575	2900	3975	6050
XLS Utility 4D	T31R	28592	2800	3150	4250	6450
2WD	S		(900)	(900)	(1190)	(1190)

ENDEAVOR AWD—V6—Truck Equipment Schedule T1
LS Sport Utility 4D	N21S	28192	1850	2075	2950	4550
XLS Sport Utility 4D	N31S	30492	2775	3100	4125	6100
Limited Spt Utl 4D	N41S	33792	3075	3425	4500	6625
2WD	M		(900)	(900)	(1190)	(1190)

MONTERO 4WD—V6—Truck Equipment Schedule T1
Limited Spt Util 4D	W51S	35624	3925	4375	5375	7700

2005 MITSUBISHI — (Jor4)A4(LZ31F)–5–#

OUTLANDER AWD—4-Cyl.—Truck Equipment Schedule T1
LS Sport Utility 4D	LZ31F	21244	2700	3025	4050	5950
XLS Spt Utl 4D	LZ41F	23724	3350	3725	4975	7225
Limited Sport Util	LZ81F	25774	4025	4425	5725	8175
2WD	X		(600)	(600)	(800)	(800)

ENDEAVOR AWD—V6—Truck Equipment Schedule T1
LS Sport Utility 4D	MN21S	28294	2850	3175	4025	5750
XLS Sport Utl 4D	MN31S	30894	3650	4050	5125	7250
Limited Sport Util	MN41S	33794	4000	4400	5550	7800
2WD	M		(975)	(975)	(1300)	(1300)

MONTERO 4WD—V6—Truck Equipment Schedule T1
Limited Spt Utl	NW51S	36424	4950	5450	6500	8900

2006 MITSUBISHI — (Jor4)A(3,4or7)(LX41F)–6–#

OUTLANDER—4-Cyl.—Truck Equipment Schedule T1
SE Sport Utility 4D	LX41F	22624	3775	4150	5525	8000
AWD	Z		700	700	945	945

OUTLANDER AWD—4-Cyl.—Truck Equipment Schedule T1
LS Sport Utility 4D	LZ31F	22094	3650	4025	5375	7800
Limited Sport Util	LZ81F	26544	4925	5375	6975	9725
2WD	X		(650)	(650)	(865)	(865)

ENDEAVOR AWD—V6—Truck Equipment Schedule T1
LS Sport Utility 4D	MN21S	28594	3700	4050	5000	6900
Limited Sport Util	MN41S	32894	5025	5450	6575	9000
2WD	M		(1050)	(1050)	(1410)	(1410)

MONTERO 4WD—V6—Truck Equipment Schedule T1
Limited Spt Utl	MW51S	36784	6175	6750	7875	10600

RAIDER EXTENDED CAB—V6—Truck Equipment Schedule T1
LS Short Bed	HC22K	22400	2875	3150	3975	5550
4WD	T		1000	1000	1335	1335
V8, 4.7 Liter	N		350	350	465	465

RAIDER EXTENDED CAB—V8—Truck Equipment Schedule T1
DuroCross Short	HC32K	26085	4775	5150	6225	8475
4WD	T		1000	1000	1335	1335
V6, 3.7 Liter	K		(375)	(375)	(490)	(490)

RAIDER DOUBLE CAB—V6—Truck Equipment Schedule T1
LS Short Bed	HC28K	24325	4800	5175	6275	8525
DuroCross Short	HC38K	26010	4850	5250	6600	8975
4WD	T		1000	1000	1335	1335
V8, 4.7 Liter	N		350	350	465	465

RAIDER DOUBLE CAB—V8—Truck Equipment Schedule T1
XLS Short Bed	HC48K	31320	5700	6150	7550	10150
AWD	T		1000	1000	1335	1335

2007 MITSUBISHI — (Jor4)A(3,4or7)(MS31X)–7–#

OUTLANDER—V6—Truck Equipment Schedule T1
ES Sport Utility 4D	MS31X	21995	3925	4300	5300	7250
Third Row Seat			250	250	335	335

OUTLANDER 4WD—V6—Truck Equipment Schedule T1
LS Sport Util 4D	MT31X	23033	5025	5450	6575	8950
XLS Sport Util 4D	MT41X	25635	6050	6525	8000	10750
Third Row Seat			250	250	335	335
2WD	X		(700)	(700)	(935)	(935)

Body Type	VIN	List	Trade-In Good	Very Good	Pvt-Party Good	Retail Excellent
ENDEAVOR AWD—V6—Truck Equipment Schedule T1						
LS Sport Utility 4D	MN21S	29624	5025	5450	6225	8125
SE Sport Utility 4D	MN31S	31374	5800	6275	7475	9825
2WD	M		(1150)	(1150)	(1520)	(1520)
RAIDER EXTENDED CAB—V6—Truck Equipment Schedule T1						
LS Short Bed	HC22K	23665	3300	3625	4675	6500
RAIDER DOUBLE CAB—V6—Truck Equipment Schedule T1						
LS Short Bed	HC28K	24650	5500	5900	7350	9975
DuroCross Short	HC38K	27395	5975	6400	8000	10850
4WD	T		1100	1100	1465	1465
V8, 4.7 Liter	N,P		375	375	500	500
RAIDER DOUBLE CAB—V8—Truck Equipment Schedule T1						
SE Short Bed	HC28N	27355	6650	7100	8775	11850
2008 MITSUBISHI—(Jor4)A(3,4or7)(MS21W)−8−#						
OUTLANDER—4-Cyl.—Truck Equipment Schedule T1						
ES Sport Utility	MS21W	20640	4925	5300	6300	8300
SE Sport Utility	MS31W	23880	6350	6800	8150	10700
Third Row Seat			250	250	325	325
4WD			1075	1075	1400	1400
OUTLANDER 4WD—V6—Truck Equipment Schedule T1						
LS Sport Utility	MT31X	24520	7400	7900	9400	12300
XLS Sport Utility	MT41X	25760	8600	9175	10700	13850
Third Row Seat			250	250	325	325
2WD	S		(750)	(750)	(980)	(980)
ENDEAVOR AWD—V6—Truck Equipment Schedule T1						
LS Sport Utility 4D	MN21S	29724	6175	6600	7525	9500
SE Sport Utility 4D	MN31S	31524	7300	7775	8975	11450
2WD	M		(1225)	(1225)	(1550)	(1550)
RAIDER EXTENDED CAB—V6—Truck Equipment Schedule T1						
LS Short Bed	HC22K	23735	4050	4400	5375	7150
RAIDER DOUBLE CAB—V6—Truck Equipment Schedule T1						
LS Short Bed	HC28K	25795	6625	7050	8375	10950
4WD	T		1300	1300	1735	1735
2009 MITSUBISHI—(Jor4)A(3,4or7)(MS21W)−9−#						
OUTLANDER—4-Cyl.—Truck Equipment Schedule T1						
ES Sport Utility	MS21W	20905	5550	5950	6950	8775
SE Sport Utility	MS31W	24305	7350	7800	8975	11250
Third Row Seat			300	300	370	370
4WD			1175	1175	1445	1445
OUTLANDER 4WD—V6—Truck Equipment Schedule T1						
XLS Sport Util	MT31X	26325	9600	10150	11450	14250
Third Row Seat	4		300	300	365	365
2WD	L		(875)	(875)	(1070)	(1070)
RAIDER EXTENDED CAB—V6—Truck Equipment Schedule T1						
LS Short Bed	HC22K	24950	5150	5525	6775	8800
RAIDER DOUBLE CAB—V6—Truck Equipment Schedule T1						
LS Short Bed	HC28K	27010	7850	8325	9875	12700
4WD	T		1500	1500	2000	2000
2010 MITSUBISHI—(Jor4)A4(AS2AW)−A−#						
OUTLANDER—4-Cyl.—Truck Equipment Schedule T1						
ES Sport Utility	AS2AW	21580	6975	7375	8350	10250
SE Sport Utility	JS3AW	23280	8525	8975	10100	12350
Third Row Seat			350	350	415	415
4WD			1250	1250	1490	1490
OUTLANDER 4WD—V6—Truck Equipment Schedule T1						
XLS Sport Utility	JT4AX	27170	10900	11450	12700	15450
GT Sport Util 4D	JT5AX	30300	11850	12450	13850	16800
Third Row Seat			350	350	415	415
2WD	S		(1000)	(1000)	(1185)	(1185)
ENDEAVOR AWD—V6—Truck Equipment Schedule T1						
LS Sport Utility 4D	JN2AS	30239	8775	9250	10600	13100
SE Sport Utility 4D	JN3AS	32214	10050	10550	12050	14900
2WD	M		(1375)	(1375)	(1775)	(1775)
2011 MITSUBISHI—(Jor4)A4(AP3AU)−B−#						
OUTLANDER SPORT—4-Cyl.—Truck Equipment Schedule T1						
ES Sport Utility	AP3AU	20275	8625	9075	10300	12500
OUTLANDER SPORT 4WD—4-Cyl.—Truck Equipment Schedule T1						
SE Sport Utility	AR4AU	23775	10700	11150	12550	15200

2011 MITSUBISHI

Body Type	VIN	List	Trade-In Good	Very Good	Pvt-Party Good	Retail Excellent
2WD	P		(1100)	(1100)	(1370)	(1370)
OUTLANDER—4-Cyl.—Truck Equipment Schedule T1						
ES Sport Utility	AS2AW	22775	8875	9300	10500	12700
OUTLANDER—4-Cyl.—Truck Equipment Schedule T1						
SE Sport Utility	AS3AW	23775	9500	9975	11250	13600
4WD	T		1400	1400	1690	1690
OUTLANDER—V6—Truck Equipment Schedule T1						
XLS Sport Utility	JS4AX	26575	11900	12400	13900	16750
OUTLANDER 4WD—V6—Truck Equipment Schedule T1						
GT Sport Utility	JT5AX	28575	12950	13500	15150	18200
ENDEAVOR AWD—V6—Truck Equipment Schedule T1						
LS Sport Utility 4D	JN2AS	30279	10050	10500	11750	14100
SE Sport Utility 4D	JN3AS	34364	11700	12250	13550	16150
2WD	M		(1475)	(1475)	(1750)	(1750)

2012 MITSUBISHI—(4orJ)A4(AP3AU)—C—#

Body Type	VIN	List	Good	Very Good	Good	Excellent
OUTLANDER SPORT—4-Cyl.—Truck Equipment Schedule T1						
ES Sport Utility	AP3AU	20605	9375	9800	11000	13100
OUTLANDER SPORT 4WD—4-Cyl.—Truck Equipment Schedule T1						
SE Sport Utility	AR4AU	24105	11850	12350	13650	16200
2WD	P		(1500)	(1500)	(1735)	(1735)
OUTLANDER—4-Cyl.—Truck Equipment Schedule T1						
ES Sport Utility	AS2AW	23155	10250	10700	11800	13900
OUTLANDER—4-Cyl.—Truck Equipment Schedule T1						
SE Sport Utility	AS3AW	24155	10750	11250	12350	14550
4WD	T		1475	1475	1725	1725
OUTLANDER 4WD—V6—Truck Equipment Schedule T1						
GT Sport Utility	AT5AX	28705	14650	15200	16600	19400
2WD	S		(1500)	(1500)	(1745)	(1745)

2013 MITSUBISHI—(4orJ)A4(P3AU)—D—#

Body Type	VIN	List	Good	Very Good	Good	Excellent
OUTLANDER SPORT—4-Cyl.—Truck Equipment Schedule T1						
ES Sport Utility	P3AU	21195	10150	10600	11650	13700
4WD	R		1475	1475	1720	1720
OUTLANDER SPORT 4WD—4-Cyl.—Truck Equipment Schedule T1						
SE Sport Utility	R4AU	24520	13150	13650	15000	17450
LE Sport Utility	R5AU	25720	13750	14300	15650	18250
2WD	P		(1300)	(1300)	(1500)	(1500)
OUTLANDER—4-Cyl.—Truck Equipment Schedule T1						
ES Sport Utility	S2AW	23520	11100	11600	12700	14850
OUTLANDER—4-Cyl.—Truck Equipment Schedule T1						
SE Sport Utility	T3AW	24820	11750	12250	13350	15550
4WD	T		1475	1475	1740	1740
OUTLANDER 4WD—V6—Truck Equipment Schedule T1						
GT Sport Utility	T5AX	29420	15850	16450	17750	20600
2WD	S		(1300)	(1300)	(1520)	(1520)

2014 MITSUBISHI—(4orJ)A4(P3AU)—E—#

Body Type	VIN	List	Good	Very Good	Good	Excellent
OUTLANDER SPORT—4-Cyl.—Truck Equipment Schedule T1						
ES Sport Utility 4D	P3AU	21495	11700	12150	13400	15750
4WD	R		1500	1500	1725	1725
OUTLANDER SPORT 4WD—4-Cyl.—Truck Equipment Schedule T1						
SE Sport Utility 4D	R4AU	24820	15150	15700	16850	19350
2WD	P		(1400)	(1400)	(1570)	(1570)
OUTLANDER—4-Cyl.—Truck Equipment Schedule T1						
ES Sport Utility	D2A3	23820	13450	13950	15200	17600
OUTLANDER 4WD—4-Cyl.—Truck Equipment Schedule T1						
SE Sport Utility	Z3A3	25795	14550	15150	16300	18750
2WD	D		(1400)	(1400)	(1595)	(1595)
OUTLANDER 4WD—V6—Truck Equipment Schedule T1						
GT Sport Utility	Z4AX	28620	19150	19850	21000	24100

NISSAN

2000 NISSAN—(1N6,4N2,5N1orJN8)(ED28Y)—Y—#

Body Type	VIN	List	Good	Very Good	Good	Excellent
XTERRA 4WD—V6—Truck Equipment Schedule T1						
XE Sport Utility 4D	ED28Y	22019	1250	1425	2250	3625
SE Sport Utility 4D	ED28Y	26069	1775	2000	3075	4850
2WD	T		(275)	(275)	(365)	(365)
4-Cyl, 2.4 Liter			(200)	(200)	(280)	(280)

Body Type	VIN	List	Trade-In Good	Trade-In Very Good	Pvt-Party Good	Retail Excellent
PATHFINDER 4WD—V6—Truck Equipment Schedule T1						
XE Sport Utility 4D	AR05Y	28919	800	925	2000	3475
SE Sport Utility 4D	AR05Y	30869	1275	1450	2600	4400
LE Sport Utility 4D	AR05Y	31819	1525	1725	2975	5025
2WD	S		(550)	(550)	(750)	(750)
QUEST—V6—Truck Equipment Schedule T1						
GXE Minivan	XN11T	22779	1000	1175	2000	3475
SE Minivan	XN11T	24919	1500	1750	2775	4725
GLE Minivan	XN11T	26919	1800	2075	3200	5350
FRONTIER—4-Cyl.—Truck Equipment Schedule T2						
XE Short Bed	DD21S	12110	600	650	1125	1825
XE King Cab	DD26S	14060	1175	1275	1800	2775
4WD			400	400	535	535
V6, 3.3 Liter	E		125	125	165	165
FRONTIER—V6—Truck Equipment Schedule T2						
Desrt Rnr XE King	ED26S	16260	1525	1650	2200	3375
Desrt Rnr SE King	ED26S	18410	1850	2025	2725	4100
XE Crew Cab 4D	ED27S	17810	1950	2150	2850	4250
SE Crew Cab 4D	ED27S	19110	2275	2500	3250	4825
4WD	Y		400	400	535	535
FRONTIER 4WD—V6—Truck Equipment Schedule T2						
SE King Cab	DD26Y	21010	1875	2050	2750	4125

-(1N6,4N2,5N1orJN8)(ED28Y)-1-#

Body Type	VIN	List	Trade-In Good	Trade-In Very Good	Pvt-Party Good	Retail Excellent
XTERRA 4WD—V6—Truck Equipment Schedule T1						
XE Sport Utility 4D	ED28Y	22569	1450	1625	2450	3750
SE Sport Utility 4D	ED28Y	26619	2025	2275	3275	5050
2WD	T		(300)	(300)	(400)	(400)
4-Cyl, 2.4 Liter	D		(225)	(225)	(315)	(315)
PATHFINDER 4WD—V6—Truck Equipment Schedule T1						
XE Sport Utility 4D	DR07Y	30169	1250	1450	2400	3925
SE Sport Utility 4D	DR07Y	30869	1525	1750	2875	4650
LE Sport Utility 4D	DR07Y	31819	1975	2250	3500	5600
2WD	X		(650)	(650)	(860)	(860)
4WD	Y		0	0	0	0
QUEST—V6—Truck Equipment Schedule T1						
GXE Minivan	ZN15T	22959	1225	1425	2250	3850
SE Minivan	ZN16T	24419	1875	2150	3225	5350
GLE Minivan	ZN17T	27569	2150	2475	3600	5925
FRONTIER—4-Cyl.—Truck Equipment Schedule T2						
XE Short Bed	DD21S	12219	850	950	1400	2175
XE King Cab	DD26S	14169	1400	1525	2025	3100
4WD	Y		400	400	535	535
V6, 3.3 Liter	E		125	125	165	165
FRONTIER—V6—Truck Equipment Schedule T2						
Desrt Rnr XE King	ED26T	16469	1725	1875	2525	3775
Desrt Rnr SE King	ED26T	18619	2200	2400	3100	4575
XE Crew Cab 4D	ED27T	18569	2400	2625	3375	4925
SE Crew Cab 4D	ED27T	20719	2775	3025	3825	5550
4WD	Y		400	400	535	535
FRONTIER 4WD—V6—Truck Equipment Schedule T2						
SE King Cab	ED26Y	21219	2175	2375	3075	4550
FRONTIER—V6 Supercharged—Truck Equipment Schedule T2						
King Cab	MD26T	20519	2250	2450	3175	4675
Crew Cab 4D	MD27T	21969	2775	3025	3825	5550
4WD	Y		400	400	535	535

-(1N6,5N1orJN8)(ED28Y)-2-#

Body Type	VIN	List	Trade-In Good	Trade-In Very Good	Pvt-Party Good	Retail Excellent
XTERRA 4WD—V6—Truck Equipment Schedule T1						
XE Sport Utility 4D	ED28Y	22739	1925	2175	2900	4250
SE Sport Utility 4D	ED28Y	26739	2525	2850	3725	5475
2WD	T		(375)	(375)	(500)	(500)
4-Cyl, 2.4 Liter	D		(250)	(250)	(340)	(340)
XTERRA 4WD—V6 Supercharged—Truck Equipment Schedule T1						
XE S/C Spt Util 4D	MD28T	26239	2025	2275	3100	4600
SE S/C Spt Util 4D	MD28T	28039	2925	3275	4200	6175
2WD	T		(375)	(375)	(500)	(500)
PATHFINDER 4WD—V6—Truck Equipment Schedule T1						
SE Sport Utility 4D	DR07Y	29189	1875	2125	3200	5000
LE Sport Utility 4D	DR07Y	32039	2450	2775	3975	6150
2WD	X		(725)	(725)	(970)	(970)

2002 NISSAN

Body Type	VIN	List	Trade-In Good	Very Good	Pvt-Party Good	Retail Excellent
QUEST—V6—Truck Equipment Schedule T1						
GXE Minivan	ZN15T	23279	1450	1675	2525	4150
SE Minivan	ZN16T	25039	2250	2575	3550	5675
GLE Minivan	ZN17T	27689	2575	2950	3975	6300
FRONTIER KING CAB—4-Cyl.—Truck Equipment Schedule T2						
Short Bed	ED27S	13339	1675	1850	2425	3600
XE Short Bed	DD26S	14339	1725	1900	2500	3700
4WD	Y	....	550	550	735	735
V6, 3.3 Liter	E	....	150	150	200	200
FRONTIER KING CAB—V6—Truck Equipment Schedule T2						
Desert Runner XE	ED26T	16539	2150	2350	3025	4425
Desert Runner SE	ED26T	19739	2675	2950	3675	5300
FRONTIER KING CAB 4WD—V6—Truck Equipment Schedule T2						
SE Short Bed	ED26Y	22339	2700	2975	3700	5350
FRONTIER CREW CAB—V6—Truck Equipment Schedule T2						
XE Short Bed	ED27T	18739	2950	3225	4000	5750
XE Long Bed	ED27T	19299	2850	3125	3875	5600
SE Short Bed	ED27T	22239	3400	3700	4550	6500
SE Long Bed	ED27T	22799	3250	3550	4375	6250
4WD	Y	....	550	550	735	735
FRONTIER KING CAB V6 Supercharged—Truck Equipment Schedule T2						
Short Bed	MD26T	20880	2750	3025	3750	5425
4WD	Y	....	550	550	735	735
FRONTIER CREW CAB—V6 Supercharged—Truck Equipment Schedule T2						
Short Bed	MD27T	23739	3325	3625	4450	6375
Long Bed	MD27T	24299	3175	3450	4275	6125
4WD	Y	....	550	550	735	735

2003 NISSAN–(1N6,5N1orJN8)(ED28Y)–3–#

Body Type	VIN	List	Trade-In Good	Very Good	Pvt-Party Good	Retail Excellent
XTERRA 4WD—V6—Truck Equipment Schedule T1						
XE Sport Utility 4D	ED28Y	23939	2650	2950	3650	5175
SE Sport Utility 4D	ED28Y	27239	3250	3575	4425	6300
2WD	T	....	(450)	(450)	(600)	(600)
4-Cyl, 2.4 Liter	D	....	(275)	(275)	(375)	(375)
XTERRA 4WD—V6 Supercharged—Truck Equipment Schedule T1						
SE S/C Spt Util 4D	MD28T	28539	3625	4000	5025	7125
2WD	T	....	(450)	(450)	(600)	(600)
MURANO AWD—V6—Truck Equipment Schedule T1						
SL Sport Utility 4D	AZ08W	30339	3125	3475	4375	6275
SE Sport Utility 4D	AZ08W	31139	3400	3800	4825	6900
2WD	T	....	(500)	(500)	(665)	(665)
PATHFINDER 4WD—V6—Truck Equipment Schedule T1						
SE Sport Utility 4D	DR09Y	29339	2325	2600	3650	5550
LE Sport Utility 4D	DR09Y	34339	2950	3300	4450	6700
2WD	X	....	(800)	(800)	(1080)	(1080)
FRONTIER KING CAB—4-Cyl.—Truck Equipment Schedule T2						
Short Bed	ED27S	13529	2350	2550	3250	4700
XE Short Bed	DD26S	14579	2450	2675	3375	4875
4WD	Y	....	650	650	865	865
V6, 3.3 Liter	E	....	175	175	235	235
FRONTIER KING CAB—V6—Truck Equipment Schedule T2						
Desert Runner XE	ED26T	16709	2875	3125	3900	5575
Desert Runner SE	ED26T	21109	3800	4100	5175	7325
FRONTIER KING CAB 4WD—V6—Truck Equipment Schedule T2						
SE Short Bed	ED26Y	23709	3850	4150	5250	7400
FRONTIER CREW CAB—V6—Truck Equipment Schedule T2						
XE Short Bed	ED27T	18979	3575	3875	4900	6950
XE Long Bed	ED27T	19529	3475	3775	4775	6775
SE Short Bed	ED27T	22829	4450	4775	5975	8400
SE Long Bed	ED27T	23379	4275	4600	5775	8125
4WD	Y	....	650	650	865	865
FRONTIER KING CAB—V6 Supercharged—Truck Equipment Schedule T2						
Short Bed	MD26T	21359	3525	3825	4700	6650
4WD	Y	....	650	650	865	865
FRONTIER CREW CAB—V6 Supercharged—Truck Equipment Schedule T2						
Short Bed	MD27T	24329	4375	4700	5875	8275
Long Bed	MD27T	24879	4200	4525	5675	8000
4WD	Y	....	650	650	865	865

2004 NISSAN–(1N6,5N1orJN8)(ED28Y)–4–#

Body Type	VIN	List	Trade-In Good	Very Good	Pvt-Party Good	Retail Excellent
XTERRA 4WD—V6—Truck Equipment Schedule T1						
XE Sport Utility 4D	ED28Y	22940	3100	3425	4350	6100

TRUCKS & VANS

Body Type	VIN	List	Trade-In Good	Very Good	Pvt-Party Good	Retail Excellent
SE Sport Utility 4D	ED28Y	27240	3700	4075	5100	7150
2WD	T		(525)	(525)	(700)	(700)
4-Cyl, 2.4 Liter	D		(200)	(200)	(265)	(265)
XTERRA 4WD—V6—Truck Equipment Schedule T1						
SE S/C Spt Util 4D	MD28T	28540	4300	4700	5800	8100
2WD	T		(525)	(525)	(700)	(700)
MURANO AWD—V6—Truck Equipment Schedule T1						
SL Sport Utility 4D	AZ08W	30340	3900	4300	5375	7600
SE Sport Utility 4D	AZ08W	31290	4450	4875	5975	8400
2WD	T		(550)	(550)	(735)	(735)
QUEST—V6—Truck Equipment Schedule T1						
S Minivan	BV28U	24780	2750	3100	3800	5575
SL Minivan	BV28U	27280	3050	3400	4200	6175
SE Minivan	BV28U	32780	3525	3925	4900	7125
PATHFINDER 4WD—V6—Truck Equipment Schedule T1						
SE Sport Utility 4D	DR09Y	29440	3300	3675	4800	6900
LE Sport Utility 4D	DR09Y	34590	4075	4475	5750	8225
2WD	X		(900)	(900)	(1190)	(1190)
PATHFINDER ARMADA 4WD—V8—Truck Equipment Schedule T1						
SE Sport Utility 4D	AA08B	36750	5075	5450	6525	8675
SE Off-Rd Spt Utl	AA08B	39900	5900	6325	7650	10100
LE Sport Utility 4D	AA08B	41250	5900	6325	7650	10100
2WD	A		(550)	(550)	(735)	(735)
FRONTIER KING CAB—4-Cyl.—Truck Equipment Schedule T2						
Short Bed	ED27S	13830	3450	3725	4500	6325
XE Short Bed	DD26S	14880	3500	3800	4725	6600
4WD	Y		800	800	1065	1065
V6, 3.3 Liter	E		200	200	265	265
FRONTIER KING CAB—V6—Truck Equipment Schedule T2						
Desert Runner XE	ED26T	17030	3925	4225	5250	7325
FRONTIER KING CAB 4WD—V6 Supercharged—Truck Equip Sched T2						
Short Bed	MD26T	25430	4850	5200	6375	8850
FRONTIER CREW CAB—V6—Truck Equipment Schedule T2						
XE Short Bed	ED27T	19360	4925	5275	6475	8975
XE Long Bed	ED27T	19910	4800	5150	6325	8775
LE Short Bed	ED27T	24900	5475	5850	7350	10150
LE Long Bed	ED27T	25450	5450	5825	7325	10150
4WD	Y		800	800	1065	1065
FRONTIER CREW CAB—V6 Supercharged—Truck Equipment Schedule T2						
Short Bed	MD27T	24810	5475	5850	7350	10150
Long Bed	MD27T	25360	5450	5725	7200	9950
4WD	Y		800	800	1065	1065
TITAN KING CAB—V8—Truck Equipment Schedule T1						
XE Short Bed	AA06A	23050	3725	4100	4700	6525
SE Short Bed	AA06A	25050	4525	4950	5600	7700
LE Short Bed	AA06A	29450	4775	5225	5900	8075
4WD	B		1200	1200	1600	1600
TITAN CREW CAB—V8—Truck Equipment Schedule T1						
XE Short Bed	AA07A	25750	5225	5700	6400	8750
SE Short Bed	AA07A	27350	5675	6175	7100	9650
LE Short Bed	AA07A	31750	6075	6600	7550	10250
4WD	B		1200	1200	1600	1600

2005 NISSAN—(1N6,5N1orJN8)(AN08W)-5-#

Body Type	VIN	List	Trade-In Good	Very Good	Pvt-Party Good	Retail Excellent
XTERRA 4WD—V6—Truck Equipment Schedule T1						
S Sport Utility 4D	AN08W	24280	4400	4800	5800	7950
Off-Road Spt Utl	AN08W	27280	4950	5375	6425	8775
SE Spt Util 4D	AN08W	27880	5150	5600	6650	9075
2WD	T		(600)	(600)	(800)	(800)
MURANO AWD—V6—Truck Equipment Schedule T1						
S Sport Utility 4D	AZ08W	29180	3750	4125	5000	6850
SL Sport Utility 4D	AZ08W	30680	4850	5300	6200	8400
SE Sport Utility 4D	AZ08W	31630	5300	5775	6900	9300
2WD	T		(600)	(600)	(800)	(800)
QUEST—V6—Truck Equipment Schedule T1						
Minivan	BV28U	23910	2325	2600	3400	5125
S Minivan	BV28U	25110	3225	3600	4475	6600
SL Minivan	BV28U	26810	3425	3825	4875	7175
SE Minivan	BV28U	32810	4075	4500	5675	8300
PATHFINDER 4WD—V6—Truck Equipment Schedule T1						
XE Spt Util 4D	AR19W	27300	4175	4575	5625	7850
SE Spt Util 4D	AR18W	28500	4800	5225	6325	8775
SE Off-Road Utl	AR18W	31280	4900	5350	6650	9175

Body Type	VIN	List	Trade-In Good	Trade-In Very Good	Pvt-Party Good	Retail Excellent
LE Spt Utl 4D	AR18W	35400	**5650**	**6150**	**7475**	**10200**
2WD	U		**(975)**	**(975)**	**(1300)**	**(1300)**
ARMADA—V8—Truck Equipment Schedule T1						
SE Sport Utility 4D	AA08A	34670	**5850**	**6250**	**7575**	**9975**
4WD	B		**600**	**600**	**800**	**800**
ARMADA 4WD—V8—Truck Equipment Schedule T1						
SE Off-Rd Spt Utl	AA08B	40420	**7450**	**7925**	**9475**	**12400**
ARMADA 4WD—V8—Truck Equipment Schedule T1						
LE Sport Utility 4D	AA08B	42150	**7450**	**7925**	**9500**	**12500**
2WD	A		**(600)**	**(600)**	**(800)**	**(800)**
FRONTIER KING CAB—4-Cyl.—Truck Equipment Schedule T2						
XE Short Bed	BD06T	16080	**5000**	**5350**	**6375**	**8400**
FRONTIER KING CAB—V6—Truck Equipment Schedule T2						
SE Short Bed	AD06U	20130	**5725**	**6125**	**7400**	**9700**
LE Short Bed	AD06U	22880	**6975**	**7425**	**8875**	**11550**
Nismo Short Bed	AD06U	22680	**6950**	**7400**	**8850**	**11500**
4WD	W		**900**	**900**	**1140**	**1140**
FRONTIER CREW CAB—V6—Truck Equipment Schedule T2						
SE Short Bed	AD07U	22180	**6975**	**7425**	**8875**	**11550**
LE Short Bed	AD07U	24480	**7725**	**8200**	**9700**	**12600**
Nismo Short Bed	AD07U	24630	**9475**	**10000**	**11750**	**15200**
4WD	W		**900**	**900**	**1135**	**1135**
TITAN KING CAB—V8—Truck Equipment Schedule T1						
XE Short Bed	AA06A	23300	**4125**	**4525**	**5450**	**7475**
SE Short Bed	AA06A	25450	**5275**	**5750**	**6900**	**9325**
LE Short Bed	AA07B	30220	**5700**	**6200**	**7450**	**10150**
4WD	B		**1300**	**1300**	**1735**	**1735**
TITAN CREW CAB—V8—Truck Equipment Schedule T1						
XE Short Bed	AA07A	26150	**5925**	**6425**	**7625**	**10300**
SE Short Bed	AA07A	27950	**6775**	**7325**	**8600**	**11550**
LE Short Bed	AA07A	32700	**7375**	**7975**	**9325**	**12500**
4WD	B		**1300**	**1300**	**1735**	**1735**

2006 NISSAN—(1N6,5N1orJN8)(AN08W)—6-#

Body Type	VIN	List	Trade-In Good	Trade-In Very Good	Pvt-Party Good	Retail Excellent
XTERRA 4WD—V6—Truck Equipment Schedule T1						
X Sport Utility 4D	AN08W	23330	**5050**	**5450**	**6525**	**8900**
S Sport Utility 4D	AN08W	25530	**5200**	**5625**	**6975**	**9450**
Off-Rd Spt Utl	AN08W	27630	**5650**	**6100**	**7475**	**10100**
SE Spt Utl 4D	AN08W	28230	**5950**	**6425**	**7800**	**10500**
2WD	U		**(650)**	**(650)**	**(865)**	**(865)**
MURANO AWD—V6—Truck Equipment Schedule T1						
S Sport Utility 4D	AZ08W	29805	**4850**	**5275**	**6100**	**8100**
SL Sport Utility 4D	AZ08W	31355	**5700**	**6250**	**7325**	**9650**
SE Sport Utility 4D	AZ08W	32305	**6900**	**7450**	**8525**	**11150**
2WD	T		**(650)**	**(650)**	**(865)**	**(865)**
QUEST—V6—Truck Equipment Schedule T1						
Minivan	BV28U	24580	**2600**	**2925**	**3900**	**5825**
S Special Edition	BV28U	25880	**3375**	**3725**	**4675**	**6850**
SL Minivan	BV28U	27480	**4125**	**4550**	**5700**	**8225**
SE Minivan	BV28U	34080	**5050**	**5525**	**6775**	**9700**
PATHFINDER 4WD—V6—Truck Equipment Schedule T1						
S Sport Utility 4D	AR18W	27830	**5275**	**5725**	**6900**	**9200**
SE Spt Utl 4D	AR18W	29080	**5925**	**6425**	**7575**	**10000**
SE Off-Road Util	AR18W	31880	**6875**	**7400**	**8525**	**11250**
LE Spt Utl 4D	AR18W	36130	**7400**	**7975**	**9175**	**12050**
2WD	U		**(1050)**	**(1050)**	**(1410)**	**(1410)**
ARMADA—V8—Truck Equipment Schedule T1						
SE Spt Utl 4D	AA08A	35435	**6875**	**7325**	**8625**	**11150**
4WD	B		**650**	**650**	**865**	**865**
ARMADA 4WD—V8—Truck Equipment Schedule T1						
SE Off-Road Util	AA08W	41505	**8850**	**9375**	**11050**	**14150**
LE Spt Utl 4D	AA08W	43270	**8300**	**8800**	**10400**	**13500**
2WD	A		**(650)**	**(650)**	**(865)**	**(865)**
FRONTIER KING CAB—4-Cyl.—Truck Equipment Schedule T2						
XE Short Bed	BD06T	16480	**5425**	**5800**	**7025**	**9175**
FRONTIER KING CAB—V6—Truck Equipment Schedule T1						
SE Short Bed	AD06U	20730	**6350**	**6775**	**8150**	**10600**
Nismo Short Bed	AD06U	23030	**8875**	**9400**	**11000**	**14150**
4WD	W		**1000**	**1000**	**1270**	**1270**
FRONTIER KING CAB—V6—Truck Equipment Schedule T2						
LE Short Bed	AD06T	23230	**8975**	**9500**	**10800**	**13600**
4WD	Y		**1000**	**1000**	**1225**	**1225**

TRUCKS & VANS

TRUCKS & VANS

Body Type	VIN	List	Trade-In Good	Very Good	Pvt-Party Good	Retail Excellent
FRONTIER CREW CAB—V6—Truck Equipment Schedule T1						
SE Short Bed	AD07U	22580	9075	9600	11250	14500
4WD	W		1000	1000	1265	1265
FRONTIER CREW CAB—V6—Truck Equipment Schedule T2						
LE Short Bed	AD07T	24930	9575	10100	11800	15200
Nismo Short Bed	AD07U	25080	10000	10600	12350	15850
4WD	Y		1000	1000	1270	1270
TITAN KING CAB—V8—Truck Equipment Schedule T1						
XE Short Bed	AA06A	23920	4400	4800	5800	7900
SE Short Bed	AA06A	26070	5325	5775	7100	9600
LE Short Bed	BA06A	31085	6000	6500	7850	10550
4WD	B		1600	1600	2135	2135
TITAN CREW CAB—V8—Truck Equipment Schedule T1						
XE Short Bed	AA07A	26770	6125	6625	8000	10750
SE Short Bed	AA07A	28570	7100	7650	9100	12200
LE Short Bed	BA07A	33555	8200	8800	10350	13800
4WD	B		1600	1600	2135	2135

2007 NISSAN–(1N6,5N1 or JN8)(AN08W)-7-#

Body Type	VIN	List	Trade-In Good	Very Good	Pvt-Party Good	Retail Excellent
XTERRA 4WD—V6—Truck Equipment Schedule T1						
X Sport Utility 4D	AN08W	23505	6475	6950	8075	10450
S Sport Utility 4D	AN08W	25755	6925	7425	8550	11050
Off-Road Spt Utl	AN08W	27805	7425	7950	9075	11700
SE Spt Utl 4D	AN08W	28555	7675	8225	9350	12050
2WD	U		(700)	(700)	(915)	(915)
MURANO AWD—V6—Truck Equipment Schedule T1						
S Sport Utility 4D	AZ08W	30000	6200	6675	7575	9625
SL Sport Utility 4D	AZ08W	31550	7325	7875	8750	11100
SE Sport Utility 4D	AZ08W	32500	8425	9025	10000	12750
2WD	T		(700)	(700)	(895)	(895)
QUEST—V6—Truck Equipment Schedule T1						
Minivan	BV28U	25350	3450	3825	4775	6800
S Minivan	BV28U	26300	4225	4650	5650	7950
SL Minivan	BV28U	28500	5050	5500	6850	9525
SE Minivan	BV28U	35300	7225	7800	9425	13000
PATHFINDER 4WD—V6—Truck Equipment Schedule T1						
S Sport Utility 4D	AR18W	26300	6675	7200	8300	10750
SE Sport Utility	AR18W	29500	7375	7925	9075	11750
SE Off-Rd Util	AR18W	32300	8250	8850	10000	12900
LE Spt Utl 4D	AR18W	36650	8900	9525	10650	13600
2WD	U		(1150)	(1150)	(1505)	(1505)
ARMADA—V8—Truck Equipment Schedule T1						
SE Sport Utility 4D	AA08W	35695	8950	9450	10750	13550
4WD	W		975	975	1275	1275
ARMADA 4WD—V8—Truck Equipment Schedule T1						
LE Sport Utility 4D	AA08B	43785	10200	10750	12400	15650
2WD	A		(700)	(700)	(910)	(910)
FRONTIER KING CAB—4-Cyl.—Truck Equipment Schedule T2						
XE Short Bed	BD06T	16700	5950	6350	7500	9600
FRONTIER KING CAB—V6—Truck Equipment Schedule T1						
SE Short Bed	AD06U	20785	7100	7550	8825	11200
Nismo Short Bed	AD06U	23305	9900	10450	11950	15150
4WD			1100	1100	1350	1350
FRONTIER KING CAB—V6—Truck Equipment Schedule T2						
LE Short Bed	AD06U	23550	9250	9775	11250	14250
4WD			1100	1100	1365	1365
FRONTIER CREW CAB—V6—Truck Equipment Schedule T1						
SE Short Bed	AD07U	22555	9750	10300	11800	14950
SE Long Bed	AD09U	23355	9525	10050	11550	14600
4WD	W		1100	1100	1355	1355
FRONTIER CREW CAB—V6—Truck Equipment Schedule T2						
LE Short Bed	AD07U	25250	10400	11000	12500	15750
LE Long Bed	AD09U	25750	10350	10950	12450	15700
Nismo Short Bed	AD07U	25300	11300	11950	13600	17150
4WD	W		1100	1100	1350	1350
TITAN KING CAB—V8—Truck Equipment Schedule T1						
XE Short Bed	AA06A	24435	4675	5075	6025	8075
SE Short Bed	AA06A	26585	5925	6400	7675	10150
LE Short Bed	BA06A	31395	6525	7025	8325	10950
4WD	B		2000	2000	2665	2665
TITAN CREW CAB—V8—Truck Equipment Schedule T1						
XE Short Bed	AA07A	27285	6700	7225	8525	11350
SE Short Bed	AA07A	29085	7900	8475	9875	12950

TRUCKS & VANS

Body Type	VIN	List	Trade-In Good	Very Good	Pvt-Party Good	Retail Excellent
LE Short Bed	BA07A	35855	9000	9625	11150	14550
4WD	B		2000	2000	2660	2660

2008 NISSAN—(J,1or5)N(1,6or8)(AS58V)—8—#

ROGUE AWD—4-Cyl.—Truck Equipment Schedule T1
S Sport Utility 4D	AS58V	21195	7075	7575	8325	10300
SL Sport Utility 4D	AS58V	22615	7950	8475	9275	11500
2WD	T		(750)	(750)	(880)	(880)

XTERRA 4WD—V6—Truck Equipment Schedule T1
X Sport Utility 4D	AN08W	24725	8525	9050	10050	12450
S Sport Utility 4D	AN08W	26425	8875	9425	10350	12850
Off-Road Spt Utl	AN08W	27075	9250	9825	10900	13500
SE Spt Utl 4D	AN08W	29375	9550	10150	11200	13850
2WD	U		(750)	(750)	(920)	(920)

QUEST—V6—Truck Equipment Schedule T1
Minivan	BV28U	25725	4125	4500	5275	7050
S Minivan	BV28U	27545	5175	5625	6675	8925
SL Minivan	BV28U	30325	6900	7425	8550	11250
SE Minivan	BV28U	35825	8475	9075	10400	13650

PATHFINDER 4WD—V6—Truck Equipment Schedule T1
S Sport Utility 4D	AR18B	28405	8525	9075	10100	12600
SE Sport Utility 4D	AR18B	31705	9275	9850	10950	13650
SE Off-Road Util	AR18B	34605	9975	10600	11700	14550
LE Sport Utility 4D	AR18B	37705	10800	11450	12600	15650
2WD	A		(1225)	(1225)	(1525)	(1525)
V8, 5.6 Liter	B		250	250	310	310

ARMADA—V8—Truck Equipment Schedule T1
| SE Sport Utility 4D | AA08B | 36075 | 10250 | 10750 | 12100 | 14900 |
| 4WD | B | | 1075 | 1075 | 1325 | 1325 |

ARMADA 4WD—V8—Truck Equipment Schedule T1
| LE Sport Utility 4D | AA08C | 45295 | 12000 | 12550 | 14050 | 17250 |
| 2WD | D | | (750) | (750) | (925) | (925) |

FRONTIER KING CAB—4-Cyl.—Truck Equipment Schedule T2
| XE Short Bed | BD06T | 16895 | 6900 | 7350 | 8350 | 10400 |

FRONTIER KING CAB—V6—Truck Equipment Schedule T1
SE Short Bed	AD06U	20705	8275	8750	9900	12300
Nismo Short Bed	AD06U	23305	10850	11400	12750	15750
4WD	W		1300	1300	1610	1610
4-Cyl. 2.5 Liter	B		(225)	(225)	(285)	(285)

FRONTIER KING CAB—V6—Truck Equipment Schedule T2
| LE Short Bed | AD06U | 24095 | 10250 | 10800 | 12100 | 14950 |
| 4WD | W | | 1300 | 1300 | 1615 | 1615 |

FRONTIER CREW CAB—V6—Truck Equipment Schedule T1
SE Short Bed	AD07U	29555	10800	11350	12700	15650
SE Long Bed	AD09U	23355	10550	11100	12400	15350
4WD	W		1300	1300	1610	1610

FRONTIER CREW CAB—V6—Truck Equipment Schedule T2
LE Short Bed	AD07U	25795	11150	11750	13150	16250
LE Long Bed	AD09U	26295	11000	11600	13050	16100
Nismo Short Bed	AD07U	25495	12250	12900	14300	17600
4WD	W		1300	1300	1615	1615

TITAN KING CAB—V8—Truck Equipment Schedule T1
XE Short Bed	AA06A	25135	6200	6625	7600	9650
XE Long Bed	AA06E	25545	6050	6475	7450	9450
SE Short Bed	AA06A	27395	7600	8100	9200	11650
SE Long Bed	AA06E	27805	7500	8000	9125	11550
LE Short Bed	BA06A	33365	8200	8725	9850	12450
LE Long Bed	AA06E	33775	8100	8625	9775	12350
4WD	C,F		2200	2200	2795	2795

TITAN KING CAB 4WD—V8—Truck Equipment Schedule T1
| Pro-4X Short Bed | AA06C | 32725 | 10300 | 10900 | 12200 | 15350 |

TITAN CREW CAB—V8—Truck Equipment Schedule T1
XE Short Bed	AA07D	28065	8600	9150	10300	13000
XE Long Bed	AA07G	28475	8450	9000	10150	12800
SE Short Bed	AA07D	29965	9825	10450	11700	14750
SE Long Bed	BA07A	30385	9625	10250	11500	14450
LE Short Bed	BA07A	35935	11100	11800	13150	16550
4WD	C,F		2200	2200	2785	2785

TITAN CREW CAB 4WD—V8—Truck Equipment Schedule T1
| LE Long Bed | AA07B | 39275 | 13750 | 14550 | 16150 | 20200 |
| 2WD | A | | (2450) | (2450) | (3095) | (3095) |

TITAN CREW CAB 4WD—V8—Truck Equipment Schedule T1
| Pro-4X Short Bed | BA07B | 34925 | 13200 | 14000 | 15600 | 19500 |

TRUCKS & VANS

Body Type	VIN	List	Trade-In Good	Very Good	Pvt-Party Good	Retail Excellent
Pro-4X Long Bed	BA07B	35525	12850	13600	15200	19000
2009 NISSAN—(J,1or5)N(1,6or8)(AS58V)-9-#						
ROGUE AWD—4-Cyl.—Truck Equipment Schedule T1						
S Sport Utility 4D	AS58V	22200	8175	8650	9500	11550
SL Sport Utility 4D	AS58V	23790	8975	9500	10400	12600
2WD	T		(875)	(875)	(1025)	(1025)
XTERRA 4WD—V6—Truck Equipment Schedule T1						
X Sport Utility 4D	AN08W	25940	10600	11200	12300	14900
S Sport Utility 4D	AN08W	27640	10900	11500	12550	15200
Off-Rd Spt Utl	AN08W	30120	11450	12050	13050	15750
SE Spt Utl 4D	AN08W	30120	11700	12300	13400	16250
2WD	U		(875)	(875)	(1045)	(1045)
MURANO AWD—V6—Truck Equipment Schedule T1						
S Sport Utility 4D	AZ18W	28675	10200	10800	11750	14200
SL Sport Utility 4D	AZ18U	30225	11150	11750	12750	15400
LE Sport Utility 4D	AZ18U	36655	11700	12300	13400	16200
2WD	U		(875)	(875)	(1065)	(1065)
QUEST—V6—Truck Equipment Schedule T1						
Minivan	BV28U	26370	5700	6125	7100	9150
S Minivan	BV28U	27430	6900	7375	8450	10850
SL Minivan	BV28U	31330	9075	9675	10850	13800
SE Minivan	BV28U	36430	11150	11850	13200	16700
PATHFINDER 4WD—V6—Truck Equipment Schedule T1						
S Sport Utility 4D	AR18B	29990	11300	11900	13050	15850
SE Sport Utility 4D	AR18B	33290	12100	12750	13900	16850
SE Off-Road Util	AR18B	36190	12700	13350	14650	17700
LE Sport Utility 4D	AR18B	39290	13700	14400	15550	18650
2WD	A		(1300)	(1300)	(1615)	(1615)
V8, 5.6 Liter	B		300	300	365	365
ARMADA—V8—Truck Equipment Schedule T1						
SE Sport Utility 4D	AA08D	36910	12150	12700	14100	16950
4WD	D		1175	1175	1385	1385
ARMADA 4WD—V8—Truck Equipment Schedule T1						
LE Sport Utility 4D	AA08C	47525	14550	15200	16800	20200
2WD	D		(875)	(875)	(1045)	(1045)
FRONTIER KING CAB—4-Cyl.—Truck Equipment Schedule T2						
XE Short Bed	BD06T	18240	8100	8575	9475	11450
FRONTIER KING CAB—V6—Truck Equipment Schedule T1						
SE Short Bed	AD06W	22190	10000	10550	11600	14000
4WD	W		1500	1500	1790	1790
4-Cyl, 2.5 Liter	B		(250)	(250)	(290)	(290)
FRONTIER KING CAB—V6—Truck Equipment Schedule T1						
LE Short Bed	AD06U	25620	11500	12100	13300	16000
4WD	W		1500	1500	1790	1790
FRONTIER KING CAB 4WD—V6—Truck Equipment Schedule T1						
Pro-4X Short Bed	AD06W	28410	14300	15000	16350	19650
2WD	U		(2200)	(2200)	(2625)	(2625)
FRONTIER CREW CAB—V6—Truck Equipment Schedule T1						
SE Short Bed	AD07U	24040	11900	12500	13700	16500
SE Long Bed	AD09U	24840	11800	12400	13600	16350
LE Short Bed	AD07U	27320	12700	13350	14550	17500
LE Long Bed	AD09U	27820	12600	13250	14450	17400
4WD	W		1500	1500	1785	1785
FRONTIER CREW CAB 4WD—V6—Truck Equipment Schedule T2						
Pro-4X Short Bed	AD07W	29760	15550	16350	17800	21400
2WD	U		(2200)	(2200)	(2630)	(2630)
TITAN KING CAB—V8—Truck Equipment Schedule T1						
XE Short Bed	AA06A	26930	8150	8650	9700	11950
XE Long Bed	AA06E	27530	7950	8425	9475	11650
SE Short Bed	AA06A	28930	9800	10350	11500	14150
SE Long Bed	AA06E	29530	9600	10150	11300	13850
LE Short Bed	BA06A	34405	10500	11050	12250	15050
4WD	C,F		2600	2600	3085	3085
TITAN KING CAB 4WD—V8—Truck Equipment Schedule T1						
Pro-4X Short Bed	AA06C	34460	12500	13150	14600	17900
TITAN CREW CAB—V8—Truck Equipment Schedule T1						
XE Short Bed	AA07D	29480	10650	11200	12500	15300
XE Long Bed	AA07G	30080	10550	11100	12350	15150
SE Short Bed	BA07D	31130	12000	12650	13950	17100
SE Long Bed	BA07G	31505	11800	12450	13750	16850
LE Short Bed	BA07D	36605	13500	14200	15700	19200
4WD	C,F		2600	2600	3075	3075

2009 NISSAN

Body Type	VIN	List	Trade-In Good	Very Good	Pvt-Party Good	Retail Excellent
TITAN CREW CAB 4WD—V8—Truck Equipment Schedule T1						
LE Long Bed	AA07C	39905	16400	17200	18800	22900
2WD	D		(2650)	(2650)	(3130)	(3130)
TITAN CREW CAB 4WD—V8—Truck Equipment Schedule T1						
Pro-4X Short Bed	BA07C	36435	15800	16550	18150	22100
Pro-4X Short Bed	BA07C	37035	15400	16150	17700	21600

2010 NISSAN—(J,1or5)N(1,6or8)(AS5MV)−A−#

Body Type	VIN	List	Trade-In Good	Very Good	Pvt-Party Good	Retail Excellent
ROGUE AWD—4-Cyl.—Truck Equipment Schedule T1						
S Sport Utility	AS5MV	22340	9725	10250	11400	13800
SL Sport Utility	AS5MV	23930	10700	11200	12400	15000
S Krom Ed Util	AS5MV	22340	11000	11550	12700	15350
2WD	T		(1000)	(1000)	(1225)	(1225)
XTERRA 4WD—V6—Truck Equipment Schedule T1						
X Sport Utility 4D	AN0NW	26100	11800	12400	13400	15850
S Sport Utility 4D	AN0NW	28270	12150	12750	13750	16300
Off-Road Spt Util	AN0NW	31200	12750	13350	14400	17050
SE Sport Util 4D	AN0NW	31200	12900	13500	14650	17350
2WD	N,U		(1000)	(1000)	(1180)	(1180)
MURANO AWD—V6—Truck Equipment Schedule T1						
S Sport Utility 4D	AZ1MW	30450	11850	12400	13600	16300
SL Sport Utility	AZ1MW	32000	13100	13750	14950	17900
LE Sport Utility	AZ1MW	38980	13950	14600	15950	19050
2WD	N,U		(1000)	(1000)	(1215)	(1215)
PATHFINDER 4WD—V6—Truck Equipment Schedule T1						
S Sport Util 4D	AR1NB	30240	13500	14150	15200	17900
SE Sport Util 4D	AR1NB	33410	14300	15000	16050	18900
LE Sport Util 4D	AR1NB	39910	16550	17300	18400	21600
2WD	N		(1375)	(1375)	(1635)	(1635)
V8, 5.6 Liter	B		350	350	410	410
ARMADA—V8—Truck Equipment Schedule T1						
SE Sport Util 4D	AA0ND	38310	15900	16550	17850	20800
Titanium Spt Util	BA0ND	43240	16750	17450	18800	21900
4WD	C,E		1250	1250	1445	1445
ARMADA 4WD—V8—Truck Equipment Schedule T1						
Platinum Spt Util	AA0NC	52970	19950	20700	22100	25700
2WD	D,P		(1000)	(1000)	(1145)	(1145)
FRONTIER KING CAB—4-Cyl.—Truck Equipment Schedule T2						
XE Short Bed	BD0CT	18340	9150	9650	10550	12550
FRONTIER KING CAB—V6—Truck Equipment Schedule T1						
SE Short Bed	AD0CU	22290	11650	12250	13250	15700
4WD	V,W		1700	1700	1950	1950
4-Cyl, 2.5 Liter	B		(250)	(250)	(295)	(295)
FRONTIER KING CAB—V6—Truck Equipment Schedule T2						
LE Short Bed	AD0CU	25720	12950	13600	14650	17300
4WD	V,W		1700	1700	1955	1955
FRONTIER KING CAB 4WD—V6—Truck Equipment Schedule T2						
Pro-4X Short Bed	AD0CW	28510	16200	16950	18250	21600
2WD	R,U		(2200)	(2200)	(2525)	(2525)
FRONTIER CREW CAB—V6—Truck Equipment Schedule T1						
SE Short Bed	AD0EU	24140	13450	14150	15300	18100
SE Long Bed	AD0FU	24940	13350	14050	15200	18000
4WD	V,W		1700	1700	1955	1955
FRONTIER CREW CAB—V6—Truck Equipment Schedule T2						
LE Short Bed	AD0EU	27420	14400	15150	16350	19300
LE Long Bed	AD0FU	27920	14300	15050	16200	19150
4WD	V,W		1700	1700	1955	1955
FRONTIER CREW CAB 4WD—V6—Truck Equipment Schedule T2						
Pro-4X Short Bed	AD0EW	29860	17450	18300	19550	23100
2WD	R,U		(2200)	(2200)	(2525)	(2525)
TITAN KING CAB—V8—Truck Equipment Schedule T1						
XE Short Bed	AA0CA	27120	9400	9900	11000	13300
SE Short Bed	AA0CA	29120	11100	11700	12900	15550
4WD	C,J		2800	2800	3185	3185
TITAN KING CAB 4WD—V8—Truck Equipment Schedule T1						
Pro-4X Short Bed	AA0CC	34850	14850	15500	16950	20300
TITAN CREW CAB—V8—Truck Equipment Schedule T1						
XE Short Bed	AA0ED	29670	12100	12700	13950	16750
SE Short Bed	AA0ED	31320	13400	14000	15400	18500
SE Long Bed	AA0FD	31770	13200	13800	15200	18200
LE Short Bed	AA0ED	37220	15100	15800	17250	20600
4WD	C,J		2800	2800	3165	3165

TRUCKS & VANS

Body Type	VIN	List	Trade-In Good	Trade-In Very Good	Pvt-Party Good	Retail Excellent
TITAN CREW CAB 4WD—V8—Truck Equipment Schedule T1						
Pro-4X Short Bed	AA0EC	37050	18250	19100	20600	24600
2011 NISSAN–(J,1or5)N(1,6or8)(AF5MV)–B–#						
JUKE —4-Cyl. Turbo—Truck Equipment Schedule T1						
S Sport Util 4D	AF5MV	21260	10050	10550	11450	13500
SV Sport Util 4D	AF5MV	23060	10400	10900	11800	13850
SL Sport Util 4D	AF5MV	25350	10900	11400	12150	14100
AWD	V		1025	1025	1135	1135
ROGUE AWD—4-Cyl.—Truck Equipment Schedule T1						
S Sport Utility 4D	AS5MV	22860	11300	11800	12850	15050
SV Spt Util 4D	AS5MV	25270	12550	13100	14150	16550
S Krom Ed Util	AS5MV	26460	12250	12800	13900	16350
2WD	T		(1100)	(1100)	(1250)	(1250)
XTERRA 4WD—V6—Truck Equipment Schedule T1						
X Sport Utility 4D	AN0NW	26700	14000	14650	15750	18350
S Sport Utility 4D	AN0NW	28690	14200	14850	16000	18700
Pro-4X Spt Util	AN0NW	30900	15200	15850	17000	19800
2WD	N,U		(1100)	(1100)	(1295)	(1295)
MURANO AWD—V6—Truck Equipment Schedule T1						
S Sport Util 4D	AZ1MW	30900	13400	13950	15150	17700
SV Sport Util 4D	AZ1MW	34310	14900	15550	16700	19550
SL Sport Util 4D	AZ1MW	37850	16200	16900	18100	21100
LE Sport Util 4D	AZ1MW	39940	17350	18050	19350	22700
2WD	N,U		(1100)	(1100)	(1280)	(1280)
QUEST—V6—Truck Equipment Schedule T1						
S Minivan	AE2KU	28550	11500	12100	13150	15850
SV Minivan	AE2KU	31700	12950	13600	14750	17750
SL Minivan	AE2KU	35150	14950	15700	16950	20400
LE Minivan	AE2KU	42150	16850	17700	19050	22900
PATHFINDER 4WD—V6—Truck Equipment Schedule T1						
S Sport Utility 4D	AR1NB	30640	14950	15600	16700	19450
SV Sport Util 4D	AR1NB	33990	15750	16450	17550	20500
Silver Ed Spt Util	AR1NB	38290	17200	17900	19100	22200
LE Sport Utility	AR1NB	40470	18000	18750	19950	23200
2WD	N		(1475)	(1475)	(1725)	(1725)
V8, 5.6 Liter	B		400	400	470	470
ARMADA—V8—Truck Equipment Schedule T1						
SL Spt Util 4D	AA0ND	43835	19250	19950	21200	24300
4WD	C,E		1400	1400	1600	1600
ARMADA 4WD—V8—Truck Equipment Schedule T1						
SV Spt Util 4D	AA0NC	44460	18500	19150	20300	23300
Platinum Spt Util	AA0NC	53840	22800	23600	24800	28300
2WD	D		(1100)	(1100)	(1265)	(1265)
FRONTIER KING CAB—4-Cyl.—Truck Equipment Schedule T2						
S Short Bed	BD0C7	19600	10250	10800	11700	13850
FRONTIER KING CAB—V6—Truck Equipment Schedule T1						
SV Short Bed	AD0CU	23370	12700	13350	14350	16900
4WD	V,W		1900	1900	2200	2200
4-Cyl, 2.5 Liter	B		(275)	(275)	(315)	(315)
FRONTIER KING CAB 4WD—V6—Truck Equipment Schedule T1						
Pro-4X Short Bed	AD0CW	29670	18800	19650	20900	24600
2WD	R,U		(2800)	(2800)	(3245)	(3245)
FRONTIER CREW CAB—V6—Truck Equipment Schedule T1						
S Short Bed	AD0EU	23610	13250	13900	15050	17700
SV Short Bed	AD0EU	25040	14500	15200	16350	19250
4WD	V,W		1900	1900	2200	2200
FRONTIER CREW CAB—V6—Truck Equipment Schedule T2						
SV Long Bed	AD0FU	25040	14400	15100	16250	19050
SL Short Bed	AD0EU	29230	16100	16850	18050	21200
SL Long Bed	AD0FU	29730	15800	16550	17750	20900
4WD	V,W		1900	1900	2195	2195
FRONTIER CREW CAB 4WD—V6—Truck Equipment Schedule T1						
Pro-4X Short Bed	AD0EW	30410	20100	21000	22400	26300
2WD	R,U		(2800)	(2800)	(3245)	(3245)
TITAN KING CAB—V8—Truck Equipment Schedule T1						
S Short Bed	BA0CD	27815	11150	11700	12850	15250
4WD	C,J		3000	3000	3460	3460
TITAN KING CAB 4WD—V8—Truck Equipment Schedule T1						
SV Short Bed	AA0CC	32665	16050	16750	18100	21400
2WD	D,K		(3025)	(3025)	(3470)	(3470)
TITAN KING CAB—V8—Truck Equipment Schedule T1						
Pro-4X Short Bed	AA0CC	35500	17400	18100	19550	23100

2011 NISSAN

Body Type	VIN	List	Trade-In Good	Very Good	Pvt-Party Good	Retail Excellent
TITAN CREW CAB—V8—Truck Equipment Schedule T1						
S Short Bed	AA0ED	30320	13800	14400	15750	18600
SV Short Bed	BA0ED	32015	15400	16050	17450	20600
SV Long Bed	BA0FD	32465	15200	15850	17200	20300
SL Short Bed	BA0ED	37915	17600	18300	19750	23300
4WD	C		3000	3000	3460	3460
TITAN CREW CAB 4WD—V8—Truck Equipment Schedule T1						
Pro-4X Short Bed	AA0EC	37700	20700	21500	23100	27100

2012 NISSAN—(J,1or5)(NorB)(1,6,8orZ)(AF5MU)—C—#

Body Type	VIN	List	Trade-In Good	Very Good	Pvt-Party Good	Retail Excellent
JUKE—4-Cyl. Turbo—Truck Equipment Schedule T1						
S Sport Utility 4D	AF5MU	20530	11300	11800	12750	14800
SV Sport Utility	AF5MU	22340	11750	12250	13200	15300
SL Sport Utility	AF5MU	24660	12350	12900	13750	15850
AWD	V		1075	1075	1205	1205
ROGUE AWD—4-Cyl.—Truck Equipment Schedule T1						
S Sport Utility 4D	AS5MV	23590	13350	13900	15000	17350
SV Sport Utility	AS5MV	26030	14450	15050	16200	18700
2WD	T		(1500)	(1500)	(1700)	(1700)
XTERRA 4WD—V6—Truck Equipment Schedule T1						
X Sport Utility 4D	AN0NW	27120	15200	15850	17050	19800
S Sport Utility 4D	AN0NW	29110	15600	16250	17450	20300
Pro-4X Spt Util	AN0NW	31530	16650	17350	18550	21500
2WD	N,U		(1500)	(1500)	(1765)	(1765)
MURANO AWD—V6—Truck Equipment Schedule T1						
S Sport Util 4D	AZ1MW	31700	15400	16000	17150	19800
SV Sport Utility	AZ1MW	35270	16700	17350	18500	21400
SL Sport Util 4D	AZ1MW	38810	18400	19100	20200	23300
LE Sport Util 4D	AZ1MW	40710	20000	20700	22000	25300
CrossCabriolet 2D	AZ1FW	45350	19300	20000	21100	24300
2WD	N,P,U		(1500)	(1500)	(1710)	(1710)
QUEST—V6—Truck Equipment Schedule T1						
S Minivan	AE2KU	28560	12750	13350	14350	17050
SV Minivan	AE2KU	31860	14400	15100	16250	19300
SL Minivan	AE2KU	35310	16800	17550	18850	22500
LE Minivan	AE2KU	42160	18450	19250	20600	24500
PATHFINDER 4WD—V6—Truck Equipment Schedule T1						
S Sport Utility 4D	AR1NB	31380	16250	16850	18000	20800
SV Sport Utility	AR1NB	34730	17000	17650	18800	21700
Silver Ed Spt Util	AR1NB	38720	18650	19350	20500	23700
LE Sport Utility	AR1NB	42530	19150	19850	21100	24400
2WD	N		(1550)	(1550)	(1820)	(1820)
V8, 5.6 Liter	B		425	425	495	495
ARMADA—V8—Truck Equipment Schedule T1						
SL Sport Utility	AA0ND	44935	21600	22300	23600	26800
4WD	C,E		1475	1475	1680	1680
ARMADA 4WD—V8—Truck Equipment Schedule T1						
SV Sport Utility	AA0NC	45065	20500	21200	22500	25700
Platinum Spt Util	AA0NC	54925	26400	27300	28300	31900
2WD	D,F		(1500)	(1500)	(1720)	(1720)
NV1500 CARGO VAN—V6—Truck Equipment Schedule T1						
S Van 3D		26045	14000	14600	15800	18550
SV Van 3D		27645	15650	16350	17600	20700
NV2500 CARGO VAN—V6—Truck Equipment Schedule T1						
S Van 3D		27045	15150	15800	17000	19950
SV Van 3D		28645	16400	17100	18400	21600
High Ceiling Roof			1475	1475	1710	1710
V8, 5.6 Liter			525	525	610	610
NV3500 CARGO VAN—V8—Truck Equipment Schedule T1						
S Van 3D		29645	17200	17950	19250	22600
SV Van 3D		31245	18600	19350	20600	24100
High Ceiiling Roof			1475	1475	1720	1720
NV3500 PASSENGER VAN—V8—Truck Equipment Schedule T1						
S Van 3D	AF0AA	33585	19450	20200	21400	24900
SV Van 3D	AF0AA	35785	21400	22300	23400	27200
V6, 4.0 Liter	B		(625)	(625)	(710)	(710)
NV3500 PASSENGER VAN—V8—Truck Equipment Schedule T1						
SL Van 3D	AF0AA	38385	23200	24100	25300	29400
FRONTIER KING CAB—4-Cyl.—Truck Equipment Schedule T2						
S Short Bed	BD0CT	20075	11050	11600	12750	15100
FRONTIER KING CAB—V6—Truck Equipment Schedule T1						
SV Short Bed	AB0CU	23845	13900	14600	15700	18400
4WD	V,W		2200	2200	2585	2585

TRUCKS & VANS

Body Type	VIN	List	Trade-In Good	Very Good	Pvt-Party Good	Retail Excellent
4-Cyl, 2.5 Liter	B		(275)	(275)	(335)	(335)
FRONTIER KING CAB 4WD—V6—Truck Equipment Schedule T1						
Pro-4X Short Bed	AD0CW	30130	19550	20400	21700	25300
FRONTIER CREW CAB—V6—Truck Equipment Schedule T1						
S Short Bed	AD0EU	24085	14600	15300	16450	19250
SV Short Bed	AD0EU	25095	15950	16700	17900	20900
4WD	V,W		2200	2200	2580	2580
FRONTIER CREW CAB—V6—Truck Equipment Schedule T2						
SV Long Bed	AD0FU	25500	15800	16550	17700	20600
SL Short Bed	AD0EU	29690	17050	17800	19050	22200
SL Long Bed	AD0FU	30190	16500	17300	18450	21500
4WD	V,W		2200	2200	2580	2580
FRONTIER CREW CAB 4WD—V6—Truck Equipment Schedule T1						
Pro-4X Short Bed	AD0EW	29820	21000	21900	23200	27100
TITAN KING CAB—V8—Truck Equipment Schedule T1						
S Short Bed	BA0CA	28405	13300	13850	15100	17550
4WD	C,J		3200	3200	3585	3585
TITAN KING CAB 4WD—V8—Truck Equipment Schedule T1						
SV Short Bed	AA0CC	33255	18150	18850	20100	23300
2WD	A		(3200)	(3200)	(3580)	(3580)
TITAN KING CAB 4WD—V8—Truck Equipment Schedule T1						
Pro-4X Short Bed	AA0CC	36115	19150	19850	21200	24500
TITAN CREW CAB—V8—Truck Equipment Schedule T1						
S Short Bed	AA0ED	30935	16500	17150	18350	21300
SV Short Bed	BA0ED	32805	17450	18150	19400	22500
SV Long Bed	BA0FD	33055	17250	17950	19200	22300
SL Short Bed	AA0ED	38485	19650	20400	21700	25100
4WD	C		3200	3200	3580	3580
TITAN CREW CAB 4WD—V8—Truck Equipment Schedule T1						
Pro-4X Short Bed	AA0ED	38315	22200	23000	24400	28200

—(J,1or5)(NorB)(1,6,8orZ)(AF5MR)–D–#

Body Type	VIN	List	Trade-In Good	Very Good	Pvt-Party Good	Retail Excellent
JUKE—4-Cyl. Turbo—Truck Equipment Schedule T1						
S Sport Utility 4D	AF5MR	20770	12150	12650	13850	16200
SV Sport Utility	AF5MR	22890	12750	13250	14550	16900
NISMO Spt Util	AF5MR	23780	13450	13950	15200	17600
SL Sport Utility	AF5MR	25780	13750	14250	15500	17950
AWD	V		1125	1125	1245	1245
ROGUE AWD—4-Cyl.—Truck Equipment Schedule T1						
S Sport Utility 4D	AS5MV	24435	14000	14550	15900	18450
SV Sport Utility	AS5MV	26875	15300	15850	17350	20100
2WD			(1300)	(1300)	(1510)	(1510)
XTERRA 4WD—V6—Truck Equipment Schedule T1						
X Sport Utility 4D	AN0NW	25835	16400	17050	18250	21100
S Sport Utility 4D	AN0NW	27745	16750	17450	18650	21500
PRO-4X Spt Util	AN0NW	31335	18250	19000	20100	23100
MURANO AWD—V6—Truck Equipment Schedule T1						
S Sport Util 4D	AZ1MW	32955	16650	17250	18450	21200
SV Sport Util 4D	AZ1MW	35305	18100	18750	19950	22900
SL Sport Util 4D	AZ1MW	40115	20700	21400	22500	25700
LE Sport Util 4D	AZ1MW	41955	22500	23300	24600	28200
CrossCabriolet 2D	AZ1FW	45385	22900	23700	24600	27800
2WD	U,N,P		(1500)	(1500)	(1705)	(1705)
QUEST—V6—Truck Equipment Schedule T1						
S Minivan	AE2KP	26835	16050	16750	17750	20800
SV Minivan	AE2KP	30585	18250	19000	20100	23400
SL Minivan	AE2KP	34365	20200	21000	22200	26000
LE Minivan	AE2KP	43485	21900	22800	23900	28000
PATHFINDER 4WD—V6—Truck Equipment Schedule T1						
S Sport Utility 4D	AR2MM	30695	18500	19200	20300	23200
SV Sport Utility	AR2MM	33955	19300	20000	21200	24200
SL Sport Utility	AR2MM	36895	21200	21900	23100	26400
Platinum Spt Util	AR2MM	41595	22000	22700	23900	27400
2WD	N,P		(1625)	(1625)	(1895)	(1895)
ARMADA 4WD—V8—Truck Equipment Schedule T1						
SL Sport Utility	AA0NC	46995	23700	24500	25700	29100
SV Sport Utility	AA0NC	47205	22900	23700	24900	28100
Platinum Spt Util	AA0NC	57175	29000	29900	31000	34700
2WD	D,F		(1500)	(1500)	(1680)	(1680)
NV200—4-Cyl.—Truck Equipment Schedule T2						
S Van 4D	CM0KN	20850	13100	13650	14700	17100
SV Van 4D	CM0KN	21840	13700	14250	15350	17850

2013 NISSAN

Body Type	VIN	List	Trade-In Good	Very Good	Pvt-Party Good	Retail Excellent
NV1500 CARGO VAN—V6—Truck Equipment Schedule T1						
S Van 3D		26415	**14950**	**15550**	**16600**	**19250**
SV Van 3D		28055	**16650**	**17300**	**18350**	**21200**
NV2500 HD CARGO VAN—V6—Truck Equipment Schedule T1						
S Van 3D		27415	**16150**	**16800**	**17800**	**20500**
SV Van 3D		29055	**17700**	**18400**	**19450**	**22400**
High Ceiling Roof			1550	1550	1785	1785
V8, 5.6 Liter			550	550	635	635
NV3500 HD CARGO VAN—V8—Truck Equipment Schedule T1						
S Van 3D		30015	**18600**	**19300**	**20400**	**23500**
SV Van 3D		31655	**19600**	**20300**	**21600**	**25000**
High Ceiling Roof			1550	1550	1805	1805
NV3500 HD PASSENGER VAN—V8—Truck Equipment Schedule T1						
S Van 3D	AF0AA	33885	**20600**	**21300**	**22300**	**25500**
SV Van 3D	AF0AA	36085	**22500**	**23400**	**24300**	**27800**
SL Van 3D	AF0AA	38685	**24300**	**25100**	**26100**	**29900**
V6, 4.0 Liter	B		**(650)**	**(650)**	**(715)**	**(715)**
FRONTIER KING CAB—4-Cyl.—Truck Equipment Schedule T2						
S Short Bed	BD0CT	20835	**12200**	**12800**	**14250**	**17100**
FRONTIER KING CAB—V6—Truck Equipment Schedule T2						
SV Short Bed	AD0CU	23885	**15100**	**15800**	**17200**	**20300**
Desert Runner	AD0CU	24605	**15950**	**16650**	**18350**	**21900**
4WD	V,W		2500	2500	2875	2875
4-Cyl, 2.5 Liter	B		**(300)**	**(300)**	**(345)**	**(345)**
FRONTIER KING CAB 4WD—V6—Truck Equipment Schedule T2						
Pro-4X Short Bed	AD0CW	31375	**20800**	**21700**	**23400**	**27700**
FRONTIER CREW CAB—V6—Truck Equipment Schedule T2						
S Short Bed	AD0EU	23925	**16000**	**16750**	**18300**	**21700**
SV Short Bed	AD0EU	24835	**17200**	**18000**	**19550**	**23100**
SV Long Bed	AD0FU	25555	**17000**	**17750**	**19300**	**22900**
Desert Runner 5'	AD0EU	25855	**16850**	**17600**	**19350**	**23100**
SL Short Bed	AD0EU	31435	**18850**	**19700**	**21300**	**25100**
SL Long Bed	AD0FU	31935	**18400**	**19200**	**20700**	**24400**
4WD	V,W		2500	2500	2860	2860
FRONTIER CREW CAB 4WD—V6—Truck Equipment Schedule T2						
Pro-4X Short Bed	AD0EW	31065	**21700**	**22700**	**24500**	**29000**
TITAN KING CAB—V8—Truck Equipment Schedule T1						
S Short Bed	AA0CA	29815	**14850**	**15450**	**17200**	**20500**
4WD	C,J		3300	3300	3725	3725
TITAN KING CAB 4WD—V8—Truck Equipment Schedule T1						
SV Short Bed	AA0CC	35095	**20000**	**20700**	**22800**	**26900**
2WD	A,H		**(3300)**	**(3300)**	**(3720)**	**(3720)**
TITAN KING CAB 4WD—V8—Truck Equipment Schedule T1						
Pro-4X Short Bed	AA0CC	38035	**20900**	**21600**	**23700**	**28000**
TITAN CREW CAB—V8—Truck Equipment Schedule T1						
S Short Bed	AA0ED	32365	**17600**	**18250**	**20200**	**23900**
SV Short Bed	AA0ED	34445	**19200**	**19900**	**21900**	**25900**
SV Long Bed	AA0FD	34895	**19000**	**19650**	**21700**	**25600**
SL Short Bed	AA0ED	41035	**20900**	**21600**	**23700**	**28000**
4WD	C,J		3300	3300	3720	3720
TITAN CREW CAB 4WD—V8—Truck Equipment Schedule T1						
Pro-4X Short Bed	AA0EC	40235	**23700**	**24500**	**26800**	**31600**

2014 NISSAN—(J,1or5)(NorB)(1,6,8orZ)(AF5MR)–E–#

Body Type	VIN	List	Trade-In Good	Very Good	Pvt-Party Good	Retail Excellent
JUKE—4-Cyl. Turbo—Truck Equipment Schedule T1						
S Sport Utility 4D	AF5MR	19800	**12800**	**13300**	**14600**	**17000**
SV Sport Utility	AF5MR	22850	**13500**	**14050**	**15250**	**17700**
NISMO Sport Util	AF5MR	23800	**14200**	**14750**	**15950**	**18400**
SL Sport Utility	AF5MR	25100	**14500**	**15050**	**16200**	**18700**
NISMO RS 4D	DF5MR	26930	**16450**	**17100**	**18150**	**20700**
AWD	V		1200	1200	1320	1320
ROGUE SELECT AWD—4-Cyl.—Truck Equipment Schedule T1						
S Sport Utility 4D	AS5MV	22200	**14200**	**14750**	**16000**	**18400**
FWD	L,T		**(1400)**	**(1400)**	**(1525)**	**(1525)**
ROGUE AWD—4-Cyl.—Truck Equipment Schedule T1						
S Sport Utility 4D	AT2MV	24700	**16650**	**17250**	**18350**	**20900**
SV Sport Utility	AT2MV	26440	**18800**	**19450**	**20400**	**23000**
SL Sport Utility	AT2MV	30280	**20100**	**20800**	**21700**	**24300**
FWD	T		**(1400)**	**(1400)**	**(1515)**	**(1515)**
XTERRA 4WD—V6—Truck Equipment Schedule T1						
X Sport Utility 4D	AN0NW	26020	**17200**	**17850**	**19050**	**21900**
S Sport Utility 4D	AN0NW	27930	**18000**	**18700**	**19800**	**22700**
2WD	U		**(1500)**	**(1500)**	**(1745)**	**(1745)**

TRUCKS & VANS

Body Type	VIN	List	Trade-In Good	Trade-In Very Good	Pvt-Party Good	Retail Excellent
XTERRA 4WD—V6—Truck Equipment Schedule T1						
PRO-4X Spt Util	AN0NW	31950	19100	19850	20900	23900
MURANO AWD—V6—Truck Equipment Schedule T1						
S Sport Util 4D	AZ1MW	31090	17550	18150	19450	22500
SV Sport Util 4D	AZ1MW	33990	19300	20000	21300	24500
SL Sport Util 4D	AZ1MU	37850	21700	22500	23600	26900
LE Sport Util 4D	AZ1MW	40340	23800	24600	25900	29600
FWD	U		(1500)	(1500)	(1710)	(1710)
MURANO AWD—V6—Truck Equipment Schedule T1						
CrossCabriolet 2D	AZ1FY	42840	23900	24700	25600	28900
PATHFINDER 4WD—4-Cyl. Supercharged Hybrid—Truck Equipment Sch T1						
SV Sport Utility	CR2MM	37570	24300	25100	26300	29900
SL Sport Utility	CR2MM	40510	26300	27100	28400	32200
Platinum Spt Util	CR2MM	45210	28100	29000	30100	34100
2WD	N		(1725)	(1725)	(1950)	(1950)
PATHFINDER 4WD—V6—Truck Equipment Schedule T1						
S Sport Utility 4D	AR2MM	31145	20800	21500	22600	25600
SV Sport Utility	AR2MM	34405	21200	21900	23100	26300
SL Sport Utility	AR2MM	37345	24400	25200	26400	29900
Platinum Spt Util	AR2MM	42045	25500	26400	27400	31100
2WD	N		(1725)	(1725)	(1975)	(1975)
ARMADA—V8—Truck Equipment Schedule T1						
SL Sport Utility	AA0ND	43175	26400	27300	28400	31900
4WD	C,E		1500	1500	1650	1650
ARMADA 4WD—V8—Truck Equipment Schedule T1						
SV Sport Utility	AA0NE	43385	25600	25800	26900	30300
Platinum Spt Util	AA0NE	53355	31100	32100	33000	36700
2WD	D,F		(1500)	(1500)	(1665)	(1665)
NV200—4-Cyl—Truck Equipment Schedule T1						
S Van 4D	CM0KN	21100	14750	15300	16300	18750
SV Van 4D	CM0KN	22090	15350	15950	16900	19500
NV1500 CARGO VAN—V6—Truck Equipment Schedule T1						
S Van 3D	BF0KL	26665	15950	16550	17550	20200
SV Van 3D	BF0KL	27655	17750	18400	19400	22300
NV2500 CARGO VAN—V6—Truck Equipment Schedule T1						
S Van 3D	BF0KX	27665	17300	17950	18900	21700
SV Van 3D	BF0KX	28655	18850	19600	20600	23600
High Ceiling Roof	A		1625	1625	1860	1860
V8, 5.6 Liter	N		575	575	660	660
NV3500 HD CARGO VAN—V8—Truck Equipment Schedule T1						
S Van 3D	AF0KX	30565	19550	20300	21300	24500
SV Van 3D	AF0KX	31555	20600	21300	22500	26000
High Ceiling Roof	A		1625	1625	1880	1880
FRONTIER KING CAB—4-Cyl—Truck Equipment Schedule T1						
S Pickup 2D 6'	BD0CT	21130	13600	14250	15700	18600
FRONTIER KING CAB—V6—Truck Equipment Schedule T2						
SV Pickup 2D 6'	AD0CU	24060	16550	17300	18650	21900
Desert Runner 6'	AD0CU	24780	16950	17750	19400	23100
4WD	B		2800	2800	3225	3225
4-Cyl, 2.5 Liter			(300)	(300)	(345)	(345)
FRONTIER KING CAB 4WD—V6—Truck Equipment Schedule T2						
PRO-4X Pickup 6'	AD0CW	31900	22300	23200	24800	29200
FRONTIER CREW CAB—V6—Truck Equipment Schedule T2						
S Pickup 4D 5'	AD0ER	24220	17200	18000	19500	23000
SV Pickup 4D 5'	AD0ER	25320	18700	19550	21000	24600
SV Pickup 4D 6'	AD0FTR	26040	18550	19350	20800	24400
Desert Runner 5'	AD0ER	26100	18650	19500	21100	25000
SL Pickup 4D 5'	AD0ER	31830	19950	20800	22300	26200
SL Pickup 4D 6'	AD0FR	32330	19400	20300	21700	25400
4WD	V,W		2800	2800	3245	3245
FRONTIER CREW CAB 4WD—V6—Truck Equipment Schedule T2						
PRO-4X Pickup 5'	AD0EV	31660	22800	23700	25500	30000
TITAN KING CAB—V8—Truck Equipment Schedule T1						
S Short Bed	AA0CH	30265	16400	17000	18700	22000
4WD	C		3600	3600	4015	4015
TITAN KING CAB 4WD—V8—Truck Equipment Schedule T1						
SV Short Bed	AA0C4	35545	21500	22300	24200	28500
2WD			(3600)	(3600)	(4025)	(4025)
TITAN KING CAB 4WD—V8—Truck Equipment Schedule T1						
Pro-4X Short Bed	AA0C4	38485	22400	23200	25200	29600
TITAN CREW CAB—V8—Truck Equipment Schedule T1						
S Short Bed	AA0ED	31815	19050	19750	21600	25400
SV Short Bed	AA0ED	34895	20700	21400	23300	27400

Body Type	VIN	List	Trade-In Good	Very Good	Pvt-Party Good	Retail Excellent
SV Long Bed	AA0FD	35345	**20500**	21200	23100	27100
SL Short Bed	AA0ED	41485	**22400**	23200	25200	29600
4WD	C,J		**3600**	3600	4025	4025
TITAN CREW CAB 4WD—V8—Truck Equipment Schedule T1						
PRO-4X Short Bed	AA0EC	40685	**25300**	26100	28300	33200

OLDSMOBILE

2000 OLDSMOBILE — 1GH-(X03E)-Y-#

SILHOUETTE—V6—Truck Equipment Schedule T1

Body Type	VIN	List	Trade-In Good	Very Good	Pvt-Party Good	Retail Excellent
GL Extended	X03E	25530	**1075**	1225	1950	3225
GLS Extended	X03E	29220	**1450**	1650	2425	3975
Premiere Extended	X03E	32130	**1575**	1800	2700	4375
BRAVADA AWD—V6—Truck Equipment Schedule T3						
Sport Utility 4D	T13W	31923	**850**	1000	2700	5125

2001 OLDSMOBILE — 1GH-(X03E)-1-#

SILHOUETTE—V6—Truck Equipment Schedule T1

Body Type	VIN	List	Trade-In Good	Very Good	Pvt-Party Good	Retail Excellent
GL Extended	X03E	26920	**1425**	1625	2325	3750
GLS Extended	X03E	31055	**1850**	2100	2975	4700
Premiere Extended	X03E	33855	**2000**	2275	3175	4975
BRAVADA AWD—V6—Truck Equipment Schedule T3						
Sport Utility 4D	T13W	32335	**1100**	1275	2875	5275

2002 OLDSMOBILE — 1GH-(X23E)-2-#

SILHOUETTE—V6—Truck Equipment Schedule T1

Body Type	VIN	List	Trade-In Good	Very Good	Pvt-Party Good	Retail Excellent
GL Extended	X23E	27560	**1825**	2050	2850	4450
GLS Extended	X03E	31635	**2325**	2625	3500	5375
Premiere Extended	X13E	33535	**2475**	2775	3675	5625
AWD	V		**300**	300	400	400
BRAVADA AWD—6-Cyl.—Truck Equipment Schedule T3						
Sport Utility 4D	T13W	34967	**1500**	1725	2675	4275
2WD	S		**(725)**	(725)	(970)	(970)

2003 OLDSMOBILE — 1GH-(X23E)-3-#

SILHOUETTE—V6—Truck Equipment Schedule T1

Body Type	VIN	List	Trade-In Good	Very Good	Pvt-Party Good	Retail Excellent
GL Extended	X23E	28510	**2375**	2675	3600	5525
GLS Extended	X03E	32175	**2925**	3300	4300	6500
Premiere Extended	X13E	34225	**3225**	3600	4675	7050
AWD	V		**350**	350	465	465
BRAVADA AWD—6-Cyl.—Truck Equipment Schedule T3						
Sport Utility 4D	T13S	35145	**2125**	2425	3575	5625
2WD	S		**(800)**	(800)	(1080)	(1080)

2004 OLDSMOBILE — 1GH-(X23E)-4-#

SILHOUETTE—V6—Truck Equipment Schedule T1

Body Type	VIN	List	Trade-In Good	Very Good	Pvt-Party Good	Retail Excellent
GL Extended	X23E	28790	**3150**	3525	4350	6350
GLS Extended	X03E	32450	**3225**	3625	4575	6675
Premiere Extended	X13E	34510	**3600**	4025	5025	7275
AWD	V		**400**	400	515	515
BRAVADA AWD—6-Cyl.—Truck Equipment Schedule T3						
Sport Utility 4D	T13S	36245	**2775**	3125	4200	6350
2WD	S		**(900)**	(900)	(1190)	(1190)

PLYMOUTH — See DODGE TRUCKS

PONTIAC

2000 PONTIAC — 1GM-(U03E)-Y-#

MONTANA—V6—Truck Equipment Schedule T1

Body Type	VIN	List	Trade-In Good	Very Good	Pvt-Party Good	Retail Excellent
Minivan	U03E	24255	**675**	800	1400	2300
Extended Minivan	X03E	25365	**925**	1075	1725	2800

2001 PONTIAC — (1GMor3G7)-(A03E)-1-#

AZTEK—V6—Truck Equipment Schedule T1

Body Type	VIN	List	Trade-In Good	Very Good	Pvt-Party Good	Retail Excellent
Sport Utility 4D	A03E	21995	**550**	650	1575	2675

Body Type	VIN	List	Trade-In Good	Very Good	Pvt-Party Good	Retail Excellent
GT Sport Utility 4D	A03E	24995	975	1125	2150	3650
AWD	B		375	375	485	485
MONTANA—V6—Truck Equipment Schedule T1						
Minivan 4D	U03E	24810	975	1125	1825	3025
Ext Minivan 4D	X03E	27150	1400	1600	2375	3900

2002 PONTIAC — (1GMor3G7)–(A03E)-2-#

Body Type	VIN	List	Trade-In Good	Very Good	Pvt-Party Good	Retail Excellent
AZTEK—V6—Truck Equipment Schedule T1						
Sport Utility 4D	A03E	20545	950	1075	2000	3350
AWD	B		400	400	520	520
MONTANA—V6—Truck Equipment Schedule T1						
Minivan 4D	U03E	24990	1200	1375	2100	3450
Ext Minivan 4D	X03E	27390	1525	1750	2625	4225

2003 PONTIAC — (1GMor3G7)–(A03E)-3-#

Body Type	VIN	List	Trade-In Good	Very Good	Pvt-Party Good	Retail Excellent
AZTEK—V6—Truck Equipment Schedule T1						
Sport Utility 4D	A03E	20870	1275	1450	2375	3850
AWD	B		425	425	555	555
MONTANA—V6—Truck Equipment Schedule T1						
Minivan 4D	U03E	24845	1500	1700	2425	3875
Ext Minivan 4D	X03E	26645	1950	2200	3100	4875
AWD	V		700	700	945	945

2004 PONTIAC — (1GMor3G7)–(A03E)-4-#

Body Type	VIN	List	Trade-In Good	Very Good	Pvt-Party Good	Retail Excellent
AZTEK—V6—Truck Equipment Schedule T1						
Sport Utility 4D	A03E	21595	1625	1825	2925	4625
AWD	B		450	450	595	595
MONTANA—V6—Truck Equipment Schedule T1						
Minivan 4D	U03E	23845	1850	2075	2975	4650
Ext Minivan 4D	X03E	26220	2350	2625	3625	5600
AWD	V		775	775	1025	1025

2005 PONTIAC — (1GMor3G7)–(A03E)-5-#

Body Type	VIN	List	Trade-In Good	Very Good	Pvt-Party Good	Retail Excellent
AZTEK—V6—Truck Equipment Schedule T1						
Sport Utility 4D	A03E	22060	2150	2400	3400	5125
AWD	B		475	475	630	630
MONTANA—V6—Truck Equipment Schedule T1						
Ext Minivan 4D	V23E	26755	2825	3175	4100	6125
MONTANA SV6 AWD—V6—Truck Equipment Schedule T1						
Minivan 4D	X23L	28415	2800	3175	4100	6150
5-Passenger Seating			(325)	(325)	(435)	(435)
FWD	U		(800)	(800)	(1055)	(1055)

2006 PONTIAC — (1GMor3G7)–(L63F)-6-#

Body Type	VIN	List	Trade-In Good	Very Good	Pvt-Party Good	Retail Excellent
TORRENT—V6—Truck Equipment Schedule T1						
Sport Utility 4D	L63F	22990	3425	3800	4925	7025
AWD	7		575	575	780	780
MONTANA SV6 AWD—V6—Truck Equipment Schedule T1						
Minivan 4D	X23L	28760	3050	3425	4525	6675
4-Passenger Seating			(350)	(350)	(465)	(465)
FWD			(550)	(550)	(735)	(735)

2007 PONTIAC — (1GMor3G7)–(L63F)-7-#

Body Type	VIN	List	Trade-In Good	Very Good	Pvt-Party Good	Retail Excellent
TORRENT—V6—Truck Equipment Schedule T1						
Sport Utility 4D	L63F	24395	4000	4375	5375	7400
AWD	7		625	625	825	825

2008 PONTIAC — (1GMor3G7)–(L33F)-8-#

Body Type	VIN	List	Trade-In Good	Very Good	Pvt-Party Good	Retail Excellent
TORRENT—V6—Truck Equipment Schedule T1						
Sport Utility 4D	L33F	23470	4100	4450	5500	7400
GXP Sport Utility 4D	L537	27995	5075	5475	6300	8175
AWD	4,7		650	650	875	875

2009 PONTIAC — (1GMor3G7)–(L33F)-9-#

Body Type	VIN	List	Trade-In Good	Very Good	Pvt-Party Good	Retail Excellent
TORRENT—V6—Truck Equipment Schedule T1						
Sport Utility 4D	L33F	24740	5475	5850	6625	8150
GXP Sport Utility 4D	L537	29340	6600	7025	7775	9525
AWD	4,6		700	700	795	795

TRUCKS & VANS

Body	Type	VIN	List	Trade-In Good	Very Good	Pvt-Party Good	Retail Excellent

PORSCHE

2003 PORSCHE — WP1-(AB29P)-3-#

CAYENNE AWD—V8—Truck Equipment Schedule T3
S Sport Utility 4D		AB29P	56665	**5675**	**6075**	**7325**	**9675**

CAYENNE AWD—V8 Turbo—Truck Equipment Schedule T3
Sport Utility 4D		AC29P	89665	**7525**	**8025**	**9175**	**11750**

2004 PORSCHE — WP1-(AA29P)-4-#

CAYENNE AWD—V6—Truck Equipment Schedule T3
Sport Utility 4D		AA29P	43665	**6325**	**6750**	**7975**	**10400**

CAYENNE AWD—V8—Truck Equipment Schedule T3
S Sport Utility 4D		AB29P	56665	**7200**	**7650**	**8950**	**11650**

CAYENNE AWD—V8 Twin Turbo—Truck Equipment Schedule T3
Sport Utility 4D		AC29P	89665	**8650**	**9175**	**10450**	**13400**

2005 PORSCHE — WP1-(AA29P)-5-#

CAYENNE AWD—V6—Truck Equipment Schedule T3
Sport Utility 4D		AA29P	44995	**7275**	**7725**	**8975**	**11500**

CAYENNE AWD—V8—Truck Equipment Schedule T3
S Sport Utility 4D		AB29P	57195	**8375**	**8875**	**10200**	**13050**

CAYENNE AWD—V8 Twin Turbo—Truck Equipment Schedule T3
Sport Utility 4D		AC29P	90195	**9775**	**10350**	**11750**	**14950**

2006 PORSCHE — WP1-(AA29P)-6-#

CAYENNE AWD—V6—Truck Equipment Schedule T3
Sport Utility 4D		AA29P	46015	**8375**	**8875**	**10100**	**12700**
SportDesign				**1175**	**1175**	**1535**	**1535**
Off-Road Tech				**1175**	**1175**	**1535**	**1535**
Off-Road Design				**1175**	**1175**	**1535**	**1535**

CAYENNE AWD—V8—Truck Equipment Schedule T3
S Sport Utility 4D		AB29P	58015	**10450**	**11050**	**12600**	**15750**
S Titanium Spt Util		AB29P	65715	**16850**	**17700**	**18950**	**23100**
SportDesign				**1175**	**1175**	**1520**	**1520**
Off-Road Tech				**1175**	**1175**	**1520**	**1520**
Off-Road Design				**1175**	**1175**	**1520**	**1520**

CAYENNE AWD—V8 Twin Turbo—Truck Equipment Schedule T3
Sport Utility 4D		AC29P	91015	**14000**	**14700**	**16050**	**19600**
S Sport Utility 4D		AC29P	112415	**23400**	**24500**	**25700**	**30800**
SportDesign				**1175**	**1175**	**1410**	**1410**
Off-Road Tech				**1175**	**1175**	**1410**	**1410**
Off-Road Design				**1175**	**1175**	**1410**	**1410**

2007 PORSCHE — No Production

2008 PORSCHE — WP1(AA29P)-8-#

CAYENNE AWD—V6—Truck Equipment Schedule T3
Sport Utility 4D		AA29P	47295	**14150**	**14800**	**15900**	**18850**
SportDesign				**1300**	**1300**	**1510**	**1510**
Off-Road Tech				**1300**	**1300**	**1510**	**1510**

CAYENNE AWD—V8—Truck Equipment Schedule T3
S Sport Utility 4D		AB29P	58795	**16500**	**17250**	**18400**	**21700**
GTS Sport Util 4D		AD29P	73195	**23900**	**24900**	**25800**	**30000**
SportDesign				**1300**	**1300**	**1505**	**1505**
Off-Road Tech				**1300**	**1300**	**1505**	**1505**

CAYENNE AWD—V8 Twin Turbo—Truck Equipment Schedule T3
Sport Utility 4D		AC29P	94595	**27300**	**28400**	**29200**	**33800**
SportDesign				**1300**	**1300**	**1455**	**1455**
Off-Road Tech				**1300**	**1300**	**1455**	**1455**

2009 PORSCHE — WP1(AA29P)-9-#

CAYENNE AWD—V6—Truck Equipment Schedule T3
Sport Utility 4D		AA29P	48975	**17950**	**18700**	**19750**	**22900**
Full Leather				**550**	**550**	**615**	**615**
SportDesign				**1375**	**1375**	**1540**	**1540**
Off-Road Tech				**1375**	**1375**	**1540**	**1540**

CAYENNE AWD—V8—Truck Equipment Schedule T3
S Sport Utility 4D		AB29P	60295	**20400**	**21300**	**22300**	**25900**

Body Type	VIN	List	Trade-In Good	Very Good	Pvt-Party Good	Retail Excellent
GTS Sport Util 4D	AD29P	75575	30000	31100	31900	36400
Full Leather			550	550	615	615
SportDesign			1375	1375	1540	1540
Off-Road Tech			1375	1375	1540	1540
CAYENNE AWD—V8 Twin Turbo—Equipment Schedule T3						
Sport Utility 4D	AC29P	98595	34900	36200	37100	42500
S Sport Utility 4D	AC29P	124495	44600	46200	46400	52300
Full Leather			550	550	595	595
SportDesign			1375	1375	1490	1490
Off-Road Tech			1375	1375	1490	1490

2010 PORSCHE — WP1(AA2AP)–A–#

Body Type	VIN	List	Trade-In Good	Very Good	Pvt-Party Good	Retail Excellent
CAYENNE AWD—V6—Truck Equipment Schedule T3						
Sport Utility 4D	AA2AP	49475	21000	21800	22800	26000
Full Leather			575	575	635	635
SportDesign			1425	1425	1590	1590
Off-Road Tech			1425	1425	1590	1590
CAYENNE AWD—V8—Truck Equipment Schedule T3						
S Sport Utility 4D	AB2AP	61675	25100	26000	27000	30800
GTS Sport Util 4D	AD2AP	76375	35200	36500	37100	41900
Full Leather			575	575	635	635
SportDesign			1425	1425	1590	1590
Off-Road Tech			1425	1425	1590	1590
CAYENNE AWD—V8 Twin Turbo—Truck Equipment Schedule T3						
Sport Utility 4D	AC2AP	100875	45500	47000	47300	53000
S Sport Utility 4D	AC2AP	127275	55200	57000	57000	63300
Full Leather			575	575	615	615
SportDesign			1425	1425	1540	1540
Off-Road Tech			1425	1425	1540	1540

2011 PORSCHE — WP1(AA2A2)–B–#

Body Type	VIN	List	Trade-In Good	Very Good	Pvt-Party Good	Retail Excellent
CAYENNE AWD—V6—Truck Equipment Schedule T3						
Sport Utility 4D	AA2A2	49475	31800	32900	33500	37400
Full Leather			600	600	655	655
Adaptive Cruise Control			425	425	465	465
Premium Pkg			1600	1600	1735	1735
Premium Pkg Plus			2525	2525	2740	2740
Convenience Pkg			1275	1275	1390	1390
CAYENNE AWD—V6 Supercharged Hybrid—Truck Equipment Sch T3						
S Sport Utility 4D	AE2A2	68675	40900	42300	42700	47600
Full Leather			600	600	650	650
Adaptive Cruise Control			425	425	460	460
Convenience Pkg			1275	1275	1380	1380
Premium Pkg			1600	1600	1730	1730
Premium Pkg Plus			2525	2525	2725	2725
CAYENNE AWD—V8—Truck Equipment Schedule T3						
S Sport Utility 4D	AB2A2	64675	38300	39600	40100	44800
Full Leather			600	600	650	650
Adaptive Cruise Control			425	425	460	460
Convenience Pkg			1275	1275	1385	1385
Premium Pkg			1600	1600	1730	1730
Premium Pkg Plus			2525	2525	2730	2730
CAYENNE AWD—V8 Twin Turbo—Truck Equipment Schedule T3						
Sport Utility 4D	AC2A2	105775	52500	54200	54700	60800
Adaptive Cruise Control			425	425	455	455
Premium Pkg Plus			2525	2525	2685	2685
Sport Pkg			1300	1300	1390	1390

2012 PORSCHE — WP1(AA2A2)–C–#

Body Type	VIN	List	Trade-In Good	Very Good	Pvt-Party Good	Retail Excellent
CAYENNE AWD—V6—Truck Equipment Schedule T3						
Sport Utility 4D	AA2A2	49175	37200	38400	38700	42700
Full Leather			625	625	675	675
25 Years Exclusive			925	925	1005	1005
Convenience Pkg			1350	1350	1455	1455
Premium Pkg			1675	1675	1790	1790
Premium Plus Pkg			2600	2600	2810	2810
SportDesign Pkg			1350	1350	1455	1455
CAYENNE AWD—V6 Supercharged Hybrid—Truck Equipment Sch T3						
S Sport Utility 4D	AE2A2	69975	47900	49400	49900	55000
Full Leather			625	625	670	670
Adaptive Cruise Control			450	450	485	485
25 Years Exclusive			925	925	1005	1005

Body Type	VIN	List	Trade-In Good	Very Good	Pvt-Party Good	Retail Excellent
Convenience Pkg			1350	1350	1455	1455
Premium Pkg			1675	1675	1790	1790
Premium Plus Pkg			2600	2600	2810	2810
SportDesign Pkg			1350	1350	1455	1455
CAYENNE AWD—V8—Truck Equipment Schedule T3						
S Sport Utility 4D	AB2A2	65975	45600	47000	47200	52000
Full Leather			625	625	670	670
Adaptive Cruise Control			450	450	485	485
25 Years Exclusive			925	925	1005	1005
Convenience Pkg			1350	1350	1455	1455
Premium Pkg			1675	1675	1790	1790
Premium Plus Pkg			2600	2600	2810	2810
SportDesign Pkg			1350	1350	1455	1455
CAYENNE AWD—V8 Twin Turbo—Truck Equipment Schedule T3						
Sport Utility 4D	AC2A2	108075	64900	66800	66700	73300
Adaptive Cruise Control			450	450	475	475
25 Years Exclusive			925	925	990	990
Premium Plus Pkg			2600	2600	2765	2765
Sport Pkg			1350	1350	1430	1430
SportDesign Pkg			1350	1350	1430	1430

2013 PORSCHE — WP1(AA2A2)–D–#

Body Type	VIN	List	Trade-In Good	Very Good	Pvt-Party Good	Retail Excellent
CAYENNE AWD—V6—Truck Equipment Schedule T3						
Sport Utility 4D	AA2A2	49825	42500	43800	43700	47700
Full Leather			650	650	695	695
Convenience Pkg			1425	1425	1525	1525
Premium Pkg			1725	1725	1850	1850
Premium Pkg Plus			2700	2700	2895	2895
SportDesign Pkg			1425	1425	1525	1525
CAYENNE AWD—V6 Diesel—Truck Equipment Schedule T3						
Sport Utility 4D	AF2A2	56725	48200	49600	49200	53400
Full Leather			650	650	690	690
Adaptive Cruise Control			475	475	505	505
Convenience Pkg			1425	1425	1515	1515
Premium Pkg			1725	1725	1840	1840
Premium Pkg Plus			2700	2700	2880	2880
SportDesign Pkg			1425	1425	1515	1515
CAYENNE AWD—V6 Supercharged Hybrid—Truck Equipment Sch T3						
S Sport Utility	AE2A2	70825	58000	59700	59000	63700
Full Leather			650	650	685	685
Adaptive Cruise Control			475	475	500	500
Convenience Pkg			1425	1425	1500	1500
Premium Pkg			1725	1725	1825	1825
Premium Pkg Plus			2700	2700	2850	2850
SportDesign Pkg			1425	1425	1500	1500
CAYENNE AWD—V8—Truck Equipment Schedule T3						
S Sport Utility 4D	AB2A2	66825	55300	56900	56400	60900
Full Leather			650	650	685	685
Adaptive Cruise Control			475	475	500	500
Convenience Pkg			1425	1425	1505	1505
Premium Pkg			1725	1725	1825	1825
Premium Pkg Plus			2700	2700	2855	2855
SportDesign Pkg			1425	1425	1505	1505
CAYENNE AWD—V8—Truck Equipment Schedule T3						
GTS Sport Utility	AD2A2	83025	66400	68300	67300	72500
Sensing Cruise Control			475	475	500	500
CAYENNE AWD—V8 Twin Turbo—Truck Equipment Schedule T3						
Sport Utility 4D	AC2A2	109725	79700	81900	81200	88500
Full Leather			650	650	685	685
Adaptive Cruise Control			475	475	500	500
Premium Pkg Plus			2700	2700	2845	2845
Sport Pkg			1400	1400	1470	1470
SportDesign Pkg			1425	1425	1500	1500

2014 PORSCHE — WP1(AA2A2)–E–#

Body Type	VIN	List	Trade-In Good	Very Good	Pvt-Party Good	Retail Excellent
CAYENNE AWD—V6—Truck Equipment Schedule T3						
Sport Utility 4D	AA2A2	50575	45600	47000	46600	50600
Full Leather			525	525	555	555
Premium Pkg			1800	1800	1910	1910
Premium Pkg Plus			2800	2800	2970	2970
SportDesign Pkg			1500	1500	1590	1590
Ceramic Brakes			4100	4100	4350	4350

Body Type	VIN	List	Trade-In Good	Very Good	Pvt-Party Good	Retail Excellent
CAYENNE AWD—V6 Diesel—Truck Equipment Schedule T3						
Sport Utility 4D	AF2A2	57575	51700	53200	53000	57500
Full Leather			525	525	555	555
Adaptive Cruise Control			500	500	530	530
Premium Pkg			1800	1800	1905	1905
Premium Plus Pkg			2800	2800	2960	2960
SportDesign Pkg			1500	1500	1585	1585
Ceramic Brakes			4100	4100	4335	4335
CAYENNE AWD—V6 Supercharged Hybrid—Truck Equipment Sch T3						
S Sport Utility 4D	AE2A2	71875	62700	64500	63500	68500
Adaptive Cruise Control			500	500	525	525
Premium Pkg			1800	1800	1895	1895
Premium Plus Pkg			2800	2800	2945	2945
SportDesign Pkg			1500	1500	1580	1580
Ceramic Brakes			4100	4100	4315	4315
CAYENNE AWD—V8—Truck Equipment Schedule T3						
S Sport Utility 4D	AB2A2	67775	59700	61400	60700	65500
Adaptive Cruise Control			500	500	525	525
Premium Pkg			1800	1800	1895	1895
Premium Plus Pkg			2800	2800	2945	2945
SportDesign Pkg			1500	1500	1575	1575
Ceramic Brakes			4100	4100	4310	4310
CAYENNE AWD—V8—Truck Equipment Schedule T3						
GTS Sport Utility	AD2A2	84275	71500	73600	72200	77700
Adaptive Cruise Control			500	500	525	525
Ceramic Brakes			4100	4100	4300	4300
CAYENNE AWD—V8 Twin Turbo—Truck Equipment Schedule T3						
Sport Utility 4D	AC2A2	111375	93700	96300	94700	102600
S Sport Utility	AC2A2	146975	103900	106800	105000	113300
Adaptive Cruise Control			500	500	520	520
Premium Plus Pkg			2800	2800	2925	2925
Sport Pkg			1450	1450	1515	1515
SportDesign Pkg			1500	1500	1565	1565
Ceramic Brakes			4100	4100	4285	4285

RAM

2011 RAM — (1or3)D7–(E2BK)–B–#

Body Type	VIN	List	Trade-In Good	Very Good	Pvt-Party Good	Retail Excellent
DAKOTA EXTENDED CAB PICKUP—V6—Truck Equipment Schedule T1						
ST 4D 6 1/2'	E2BK	23850	10300	10950	11800	14150
Big Horn/Lone Star	E3BK	24725	11600	12300	13250	15900
4WD	W		1900	1900	2260	2260
V8, Flex Fuel, 4.7 Liter	P		800	800	950	950
DAKOTA CREW CAB PICKUP—V6—Truck Equipment Schedule T1						
Big Horn/Lone Star	E3GK	27420	14250	15050	16150	19300
Laramie 4D 5 1/4'	E5GK	31275	14650	15500	17000	20800
4WD	W		1900	1900	2255	2255
V8, Flex Fuel, 4.7 Liter	P		800	800	950	950
DAKOTA CREW CAB PICKUP 4WD—V8—Truck Equipment Schedule T1						
TRX 4D 5 1/4'	W7BP	32460	15650	16500	17600	21000
RAM REGULAR CAB PICKUP—V8—Truck Equipment Schedule T1						
1500 ST 2D 6 1/3'	B1EP	21510	9400	9850	10900	13000
1500 ST 2D 8'	B1EP	22185	9000	9425	10500	12500
1500 SLT 2D 6 1/3'	B1EP	25755	10650	11150	12200	14500
1500 SLT 2D 8'	B1EP	26055	10050	10500	11600	13750
4WD	K		3000	3000	3530	3530
V6, 3.7 Liter			(675)	(675)	(795)	(795)
V8, HEMI, 5.7 Liter			1025	1025	1205	1205
RAM REGULAR CAB PICKUP—V8 HEMI—Truck Equipment Schedule T1						
1500 Sport 2D 6 1/3'	B1ET	31440	12300	12850	14050	16600
2500 ST 2D 8'	P2ET	28495	14500	15150	16150	18700
2500 SLT 2D 8'	P2ET	31275	15300	15950	17000	19700
4WD	V		3000	3000	3525	3525
6-Cyl, Turbo Dsl 6.7L	L		5475	5475	6125	6125
RAM REGULAR CAB PICKUP—6-Cyl. Turbo Diesel—Truck Equip Sch T1						
3500 ST 2D 8' DR	M4EL	36070	21700	22600	23500	26900
3500 SLT 2D 8' DR	M4EL	39245	23900	24800	25800	29600
4WD	Y		3000	3000	3285	3285
RAM QUAD CAB PICKUP—V8—Truck Equipment Schedule T1						
1500 ST 4D 6 1/3'	B1GP	25940	13350	13950	15300	18050
1500 SLT 4D 6 1/3'	B1GP	29835	13900	14550	15850	18700

2011 RAM

Body Type	VIN	List	Trade-In Good	Trade-In Very Good	Pvt-Party Good	Retail Excellent
4WD	V		3000	3000	3510	3510
V6, 3.7 Liter	K		(675)	(675)	(790)	(790)
V8, HEMI, 5.7 Liter	T		1025	1025	1200	1200
RAM QUAD CAB PICKUP—V8—Truck Equipment Schedule T1						
1500 Sport 4D 6 1/3'	B1GT	34800	16100	16750	18150	21400
1500 Laramie 6 1/3'	B1GT	37580	17000	17700	19150	22600
4WD			3000	3000	3515	3515
RAM CREW CAB PICKUP—V8—Truck Equipment Schedule T1						
1500 ST 4D 5 1/2'	B1CP	29910	15250	15900	17300	20400
1500 SLT 4D 5 1/2'	B1CP	32490	17200	17900	19350	22800
4WD			3000	3000	3515	3515
V8, HEMI, 5.7 Liter	T		1025	1025	1200	1200
RAM CREW CAB PICKUP—V8 HEMI—Truck Equipment Schedule T1						
1500 Sport 4D 5 1/2'	B1CT	36955	19650	20400	21900	25800
1500 Laramie 4D 5'	B1CT	39340	21000	21800	23400	27500
1500 Laramie Lghrn	B1CT	43160	21200	22100	23600	27700
2500 ST 4D 6 1/3'	P2CT	31980	18650	19400	20300	23300
2500 ST 4D 8'	P2CT	32180	18250	19000	19900	22900
2500 SLT 4D 6 1/3'	P2CT	36135	19950	20700	21700	25000
2500 SLT 4D 8'	P2CT	36335	19450	20200	21600	25300
2500 Laramie 6 1/3'	P2CT	40770	21700	22600	23500	26900
2500 Laramie 8'	P2CT	40970	21300	22100	23000	26400
2500 Lrmie Lghrn 6'	P2CT	45420	26500	27500	28500	32600
2500 Lrmie Lghrn 8'	P2CT	45620	26700	27700	28600	32800
4WD	V		3000	3000	3500	3500
6-Cyl, Turbo Dsl 6.7L	L		5475	5475	6030	6030
RAM CREW CAB PICKUP 4WD—V8 HEMI—Truck Equipment Sch T1						
2500 Power Wagon 6'	T2CT	45930	27000	28000	29000	33200
RAM CREW CAB PICKUP—6-Cyl. Turbo Diesel—Truck Equipment Sch T1						
3500 ST 4D 6 1/3'	M3CL	39990	25400	26400	27300	31300
3500 ST 4D 8' DR	M3CL	40190	25200	26200	27200	31200
3500 SLT 4D 6 1/3'	M3CL	44765	26100	27100	28200	32400
3500 SLT 4D 8' DR	M3CL	44965	25800	26800	27900	32100
3500 Laramie 6 1/3'	M3CL	48780	28200	29300	30200	34600
3500 Laramie 8' DR	M3CL	48980	27800	28800	29800	34100
3500 Lrmie Lghn 6'	M3CL	53380	32500	33700	34700	39700
3500 Lrmie Lghn 8'	M3CL	53580	32200	33400	34400	39400
4WD			3000	3000	3280	3280
RAM MEGA CAB PICKUP—V8 HEMI—Truck Equipment Schedule T1						
2500 SLT 4D 6 1/3'	P2HT	36835	23300	24200	25100	28700
2500 Laramie 6 1/3'	P2HT	41470	24700	25700	26600	30500
2500 Laramie Lghrn	P2HT	46120	27300	28300	29300	33500
4WD	T		3000	3000	3280	3280
6-Cyl, Turbo Dsl 6.7L	T		5475	5475	5990	5990
RAM MEGA CAB PICKUP—6-Cyl. Turbo Diesel—Truck Equipment Sch T1						
3500 SLT 6 1/3'	M3HL	45465	30000	31100	32100	36800
3500 Laramie 6 1/3'	M3HL	49480	30600	31700	32700	37500
3500 Laramie Lghrn	M3HL	55480	34200	35400	36400	41700
4WD	Y		3000	3000	3275	3275

2012 RAM — (1,2or3)C6-(DGAG)-C-#

Body Type	VIN	List	Trade-In Good	Trade-In Very Good	Pvt-Party Good	Retail Excellent
RAM C/V—V6—Truck Equipment Schedule T2						
Van 4D	DGAG	23975	9900	10350	12150	15050
RAM REGULAR CAB PICKUP—V8—Truck Equipment Schedule T1						
1500 ST 2D 6 1/3'	D6AP	22470	11750	12250	13450	15850
1500 ST 2D 8'	D6DP	22820	11250	11750	12950	15250
1500 Outdrsman 6'	D6BP	29245	15050	15650	17000	19950
1500 Outdrsman 8'	D6EP	29545	14750	15300	16700	19550
1500 SLT 2D 6 1/3'	D6BP	26650	12800	13350	14550	17100
1500 SLT 2D 8'	D6EP	26950	12200	12750	13950	16400
RamBox			475	475	560	560
4WD	7		3200	3200	3795	3795
V6, 3.7 Liter	K		(750)	(750)	(890)	(890)
V8, HEMI, 5.7 Liter	T		1275	1275	1515	1515
RAM REGULAR CAB PICKUP—V8 Flex Fuel—Truck Equipment Schedule T1						
1500 Tradesman 6'	D6AT	23335	13200	13750	15050	17700
1500 Tradesman 8'	D6DT	23635	12950	13500	14700	17300
4WD	7		3200	3200	3785	3785
RamBox			475	475	560	560
V8, HEMI, 5.7 Liter	T		1275	1275	1510	1510
RAM REGULAR CAB PICKUP—V8—Truck Equipment Schedule T1						
2500 ST 2D 8'	D4AT	29425	16100	16750	17700	20300
2500 Outdrsman 8'	D4BT	34900	19950	20700	21700	24800

TRUCKS & VANS

TRUCKS & VANS

Body Type	VIN	List	Trade-In Good	Very Good	Pvt-Party Good	Retail Excellent
2500 SLT 2D 8'	D4BT	32205	17750	18450	19450	22300
4WD	5		3200	3200	3570	3570
6-Cyl, Turbo Dsl, 6.7L	L		5700	5700	6355	6355
RAM REGULAR CAB PICKUP—V8 HEMI—Truck Equipment Schedule T1						
1500 Express 6 1/3'	D6AT	24075	13450	14000	15350	18050
1500 Tradesman HD	D4RT	29900	16050	16700	18050	21100
1500 Sport 2D 6 1/3'	D6CT	32335	15400	16000	17400	20300
RamBox			475	475	560	560
4WD	7		3200	3200	3775	3775
RAM REGULAR CAB PICKUP—6-Cyl. Turbo Diesel—Truck Equip Sch T1						
3500 ST 2D 8' DR	DPAL	37795	22500	23300	24200	27500
3500 SLT 2D 8' DR	DPBL	40570	25000	25900	26800	30500
4WD	R		3200	3200	3520	3520
RAM QUAD CAB PICKUP—V8—Truck Equipment Schedule T1						
1500 ST 6 1/3'	D6FP	26645	15000	15600	16950	19850
1500 Tradesman 6'	D6FP	27630	14500	15050	16500	19350
1500 SLT 4D 6 1/3'	D6GP	30865	15700	16300	17700	20700
1500 Outdoorsman	D6GP	33660	15550	16150	17550	20500
RamBox			475	475	560	560
4WD	7		3200	3200	3775	3775
V6, 3.7 Liter	K		(750)	(750)	(885)	(885)
V8, HEMI, 5.7 Liter	T		1275	1275	1505	1505
RAM QUAD CAB PICKUP—V8 HEMI—Truck Equipment Schedule T1						
1500 Express 6 1/3'	D6FT	29045	15500	16100	17450	20400
1500 Big Horn 6 1/3'	D6GT	33015	18850	19600	21100	24600
1500 Lone Star 61/3'	D6GT	33015	18850	19600	21100	24600
1500 Sport 4D 6 1/3'	D6HT	35830	19750	20500	22000	25600
1500 Laramie 6 1/3'	D6JT	39410	19950	20700	22200	25900
RamBox			475	475	560	560
4WD	7		3200	3200	3760	3760
RAM CREW CAB PICKUP—V8—Truck Equipment Schedule T1						
1500 Tradesman 5'	D6LP	30110	16100	16750	18150	21200
4WD	7		3200	3200	3770	3770
V8, HEMI, 5.7 Liter	T		1275	1275	1505	1505
RAM CREW CAB PICKUP—V8—Truck Equipment Schedule T1						
1500 ST 4D 5 1/2'	D6KP	30640	16600	17250	18650	21800
1500 SLT 4D 5 1/2'	D6LP	33220	18950	19700	21200	24700
1500 Outdoorsman	D6LP	35215	19350	20100	21600	25200
RamBox			475	475	560	560
4WD	7		3200	3200	3770	3770
V8, HEMI, 5.7 Liter	T		1275	1275	1505	1505
RAM CREW CAB PICKUP—V8 HEMI—Truck Equipment Schedule T1						
1500 Express 5 1/2'	D6LT	31205	17200	17850	19250	22500
1500 Big Horn 5 1/2'	D6LT	34570	20100	20800	22300	26000
1500 Lone Star 5 1/2'	D6LT	34570	19550	20300	21800	25400
1500 Sport 4D 5 1/2'	D6MT	37685	21800	22600	24200	28200
1500 Laramie 5 1/2'	D6NT	40870	25400	26300	27900	32500
1500 Laramie Lghrn	D6PT	44120	25200	26100	27700	32200
1500 Laramie Ltd	D6NT	45700	25600	26500	28200	32800
2500 ST 4D 6 1/3'	D4CT	33140	19650	20400	21200	24100
2500 ST 4D 8'	D4HT	33340	19250	19950	20800	23700
2500 SLT 4D 6 1/3'	D4HT	37295	20900	21700	22800	26100
2500 SLT 4D 8'	D4JT	37495	20800	21600	22900	26500
2500 Big Horn 6 1/3'	D4DT	39090	21900	22700	24000	27800
2500 Big Horn 8'	D4JT	39290	21700	22500	23800	27600
2500 Lone Star 6 1/3'	D4DT	39090	21700	22500	23800	27600
2500 Lone Star 8'	D4JT	39290	21900	22700	24000	27800
2500 Outdoorsmn 6 1/3'	D4DT	39990	23500	24400	25600	29600
2500 Outdoorsmn 8'	D4JT	40190	23600	24500	25900	29900
2500 Laramie 6 1/3'	D4FT	42730	25800	26700	27700	31500
2500 Laramie 8'	D4KT	42930	26200	27100	28000	31700
2500 Lrmie Lghrn 6'	D4GT	46925	29100	30100	31100	35200
2500 Lrmie Lghrn 8'	D4LT	47125	29300	30300	31300	35400
2500 LtdLrmLghn 6	D4GT	47980	30100	31100	32100	36300
2500 LtdLrmLghn 8	D4LT	48180	30200	31200	32200	36500
RamBox			475	475	560	560
4WD	7		3200	3200	3750	3750
6-Cyl, Turbo Dsl 6.7L	L		5700	5700	6270	6270
RAM CREW CAB PICKUP 4WD—V8 HEMI—Truck Equipment Sch T1						
2500 Power Wagon 6'	D5ET	46790	32000	33100	34000	38500
RAM 3500 CREW CAB PICKUP—6-Cyl. Turbo Diesel—Truck Equip Sch T1						
ST 4D 6 1/3'	D2CL	42265	27400	28400	29200	33100
ST 4D 8' DR	DPGL	42890	27200	28200	29200	33200

TRUCKS & VANS

Body Type	VIN	List	Trade-In Good	Very Good	Pvt-Party Good	Retail Excellent
SLT 4D 6 1/3'	D2DL	47040	29200	30200	31300	35600
SLT 4D 8' DR	DPHL	47665	28900	29900	31000	35300
Big Horn 4D 6 1/3'	D2DL	48135	30200	31200	32200	36500
Big Horn 4D 8'	DPHL	48760	30900	32000	32900	37300
Lone Star 4D 6 1/3'	D2DL	48135	30200	31200	32200	36500
Lone Star 4D 8'	DPHL	48760	30900	32000	32900	37300
Outdoorsman 4D 6'	D2DL	49335	31400	32500	33400	37900
Outdoorsman 4D 8'	D2HL	48665	30800	31900	32800	37200
Laramie 4D 6 1/3'	D2EL	51855	32300	33400	34300	38900
Laramie 4D 8' DR	DPJL	52480	31700	32800	33700	38200
Laramie Longhorn 6'	D2FL	54630	34600	35700	36700	41500
Lrmie Longhorn 8'	DPKL	55255	34300	35400	36400	41200
Lrmie Lnghrn Ltd 6'	D2FL	56535	37800	39000	39900	45200
Lrmie Lnghrn Ltd 8'	DPKL	57460	38000	39200	40100	45400
RamBox			475	475	520	520
4WD	3		3200	3200	3520	3520
RAM 2500 MEGA CAB PICKUP—V8 HEMI—Truck Equipment Schedule T1						
SLT 4D 6 1/3'	D4MT	38065	24300	25200	26100	29700
Big Horn 4D 6 1/3'	D4MT	39860	23000	23800	24800	28300
Lone Star 4D 6 1/3'	D4MT	39860	23000	23800	24800	28300
Outdoorsman 6 1/3'	D4MT	40760	25300	26200	27100	30800
Laramie 4D 6 1/3'	D4NT	43500	28900	29900	30900	35000
Lrmie Lnghrn Ltd 6'	D4PT	48780	31100	32100	33100	37500
RamBox			475	475	520	520
4WD	5		3200	3200	3520	3520
6-Cyl. Turbo Dsl 6.7L	L		5700	5700	6275	6275
RAM 3500 MEGA CAB PICKUP—6-Cyl. Turbo Diesel—Truck Equip Sch T1						
SLT 4D 6 1/3' DR	D2LL	48465	31600	32700	33600	38100
Outdoorsman 6 1/3'	D2LL	49465	32000	33100	34000	38500
Big Horn 4D 6 1/3'	D2LL	49560	32100	33200	34100	38600
Lone Star 4D 6 1/3'	D2LL	49560	32100	33200	34100	38600
Laramie 4D 6 1/3'	D2ML	53280	32600	33700	34600	39200
Lrmie Longhorn 6'	D2NL	56055	35500	36700	37600	42500
Lrmie Lnghrn Ltd 6'	D2NL	57960	38400	39700	40600	46000
Lrmie Lnghrn Ltd 8'	DPKL	57460	38000	39200	40100	45400
RamBox			475	475	520	520
4WD	3		3200	3200	3520	3520

2013 RAM — (1,2or3)C6–(RGAG)–D–#

Body Type	VIN	List	Trade-In Good	Very Good	Pvt-Party Good	Retail Excellent
RAM C/V TRADESMAN—V6—Truck Equipment Schedule T2						
Van 4D	RGAG	23460				
RAM REGULAR CAB PICKUP—V6 Flex Fuel—Truck Equipment Sch T1						
1500 HFE 2D 6 1/3'	R6RG	29195	15900	16500	18000	21100
RAM REGULAR CAB PICKUP—V8—Truck Equipment Schedule T1						
1500 Tradesman 6'	R6AP	23585	14550	15100	16550	19400
1500 Tradesman 8'	R6DP	23970	14250	14800	16250	19000
1500 SLT 2D 6 1/3'	R6BP	28445	15500	16100	17600	20600
1500 SLT 2D 8'	R6EP	28745	15000	15600	17100	20000
4WD	7		3300	3300	3800	3800
V6, Flex Fuel, 3.6 Liter	G		(800)	(800)	(920)	(920)
V8, HEMI, 5.7 Liter	T		1275	1275	1480	1480
RAM REGULAR CAB PICKUP—V8 HEMI—Truck Equipment Schedule T1						
1500 Express 6 1/3'	R6AT	25820	15000	15600	17100	20000
4WD	7		3300	3300	3800	3785
RAM REGULAR CAB PICKUP—V8 HEMI—Truck Equipment Schedule T1						
1500 R/T 2D 6 1/3'	R6CT	33930	20300	21000	22600	26400
RAM REGULAR CAB PICKUP 4WD—V8 HEMI—Truck Equip Sch T1						
1500 Sport 2D 6 1/3'	R7CT	36850	20700	21500	23100	27000
RAM REGULAR CAB PICKUP—V8 HEMI—Truck Equipment Schedule T1						
2500 SLT 2D 8'	R4BT	33895	18750	19400	20800	24100
2500 Tradesman 8'	R4AT	30215	15450	16050	17600	20700
4WD	5		3300	3300	3665	3665
6-Cyl Turbo Diesel 6.6L	M		5900	5900	6550	6550
RAM REGULAR CAB PICKUP—6-Cyl. Turbo Diesel—Truck Equip Sch T1						
3500 ST Trdsmn 8	R2AL	39195	23500	24300	25800	29800
3500 SLT 2D 8'	R2BL	42905	26600	27500	29100	33600
4WD	3,R		3300	3300	3580	3580
V8, HEMI, 5.7 Liter	T		(5900)	(5900)	(6400)	(6400)
RAM QUAD CAB PICKUP—V8 Flex Fuel—Truck Equipment Schedule T1						
1500 Tradesman 6'	R6FP	28180	15850	16450	17950	21000
1500 SLT 4D 6 1/3'	R6GP	31900	17800	18450	20000	23400
RamBox			500	500	575	575
4WD	7		3300	3300	3785	3785

Body Type	VIN	List	Trade-In Good	Very Good	Pvt-Party Good	Retail Excellent
V6, Flex Fuel, 3.6 Liter	G		(800)	(800)	(915)	(915)
V8, HEMI, 5.7 Liter	T		1275	1275	1475	1475
RAM QUAD CAB PICKUP—V6 Flex Fuel—Truck Equipment Sch T1						
1500 Outdoorsman	R6GG	34555	17900	18550	20100	23500
RamBox	7		3300	3300	3780	3780
V8, HEMI, 5.7 Liter	T		1275	1275	1470	1470
RAM QUAD CAB PICKUP—V8 HEMI—Truck Equipment Schedule T1						
1500 Express 6 1/3'	R6FT	30740	17000	17600	19150	22400
1500 Big Horn 6 1/3'	R6GT	34205	20100	20800	22400	26100
1500 Lone Star 6 1/3'	R6GT	34205	20600	21300	22900	26700
1500 Sport 4D 6 1/3'	R6HT	37425	20900	21700	23300	27200
1500 Laramie 6 1/3'	R6JT	39610	21200	22000	23600	27600
RamBox	7		500	500	575	575
4WD	7		3300	3300	3785	3785
RAM CREW CAB PICKUP—V6 Flex Fuel—Truck Equipment Schedule T1						
1500 Outdrsman 5'	R6LG	36710	21200	22000	23600	27600
RamBox	7		500	500	575	575
4WD	7		3300	3300	3780	3780
V8, HEMI, 5.7 Liter	T		1275	1275	1470	1470
RAM CREW CAB PICKUP—V8 HEMI—Truck Equipment Schedule T1						
1500 Tradesman 5'	R6KP	30760	17800	18450	19950	23300
1500 Tradesman 6'	R6SP	31370	17400	18000	19550	22800
1500 SLT 4D 5 1/2'	R6LP	34515	20700	21400	23100	26900
RamBox	7		500	500	570	570
4WD	7		3300	3300	3780	3780
V6, Flex Fuel, 3.6 Liter	G		(800)	(800)	(915)	(915)
V8, HEMI, 5.7 Liter	T		1275	1275	1470	1470
RAM CREW CAB PICKUP—V8 HEMI—Truck Equipment Schedule T1						
1500 Express 5 1/2'	R6KT	32870	20100	20800	22500	26300
1500 Big Horn 5 1/2'	R6LT	36360	22100	22900	24600	28700
1500 Big Horn 6'	R6TT	37220	21100	21900	23600	27500
1500 Lone Star 5 1/2'	R6LT	36360	20800	21600	23200	27100
1500 Lone Star 6 1/3'	R6TT	37220	20800	21600	23200	27100
1500 Outdrsmn 6'	R6TT	37570	20800	21600	23200	27100
1500 Sport 4D 5 1/2'	R6MT	39280	24700	25500	27300	31800
1500 Sport 4D 6 1/3'	R6UT	39890	24500	25300	27100	31600
1500 SLT 4D 6 1/3'	R7TT	40045	25100	25900	27700	32300
1500 Laramie 5 1/2'	R6NT	41465	28300	29300	31200	36300
1500 Laramie 6 1/3'	R6VT	42075	26000	26900	28800	33400
1500 Lrmie Lghrn 5'	R6PT	45270	27900	28900	30800	35700
1500 Lrmie Lghrn 6'	R6WT	45880	27600	28500	30400	35300
1500 Laramie Ltd 5'	R6PT	48675	28400	29400	31300	36300
1500 Laramie Ltd 6'	R6WT	48975	28100	29100	31000	35900
RamBox	7		500	500	575	575
4WD	7		3300	3300	3790	3790
RAM CREW CAB PICKUP—V8 HEMI—Truck Equipment Schedule T1						
2500 Tradesman 6'	R4CT	33640	18650	19300	20800	24200
2500 Tradesman 8'	R4HT	33840	18800	19500	21000	24400
2500 SLT 4D 6 1/3'	R4DT	37715	22200	23000	24500	28500
2500 SLT 4D 8'	R4JT	37915	22400	23200	24700	28500
2500 Big Horn 6 1/3'	R4DT	39550	23900	24800	26300	30400
2500 Lone Star 6 1/3'	R4DT	39550	23700	24500	26100	30200
2500 Big Horn 8'	R4JT	39750	23700	24500	26100	30400
2500 Lone Star 8'	R4JT	39750	23900	24800	26300	30400
2500 Laramie 6 1/3'	R4FT	43490	27200	28100	29700	34300
2500 Laramie 8'	R4KT	43690	27400	28300	30000	34600
2500 Lrmie Lghrn 6'	R4GT	48785	31300	32400	34200	39400
2500 Lrmie Lghrn 8'	R4LT	48985	31500	32600	34400	39600
2500 LrmLghnLtd 6'	R4GT	53675	35500	36700	38500	44400
2500 LrmLghnLtd 8	R4LT	53875	35700	36900	38700	44600
RamBox			500	500	550	550
4WD	5		3300	3300	3645	3645
6-Cyl Turbo Diesel 6.7L	L		5900	5900	6515	6515
RAM 2500 CREW CAB PICKUP 4WD—V8 HEMI—Truck Equipment Sch T1						
Power Wagon 6'	R5ET	47750	33400	34500	36300	41700
Trdsmn Pwr Wag 6'	R5CT	50200	32100	33200	35000	40300
Laramie Power Wag	R5FT	59530	36700	37900	39800	45800
RamBox			500	500	535	535
RAM CREW CAB PICKUP 4WD—V8 HEMI—Truck Equipment Sch T1						
2500 Outdrsman 6'	R5DT	43855	27500	28400	30100	34700
2500 Outdoorsman 8'	R5JT	44055	27700	28700	30300	34900
RamBox			500	500	540	540
6-Cyl Turbo Diesel, 6.7L	L		5900	5900	6350	6350

Body Type	VIN	List	Trade-In Good	Trade-In Very Good	Pvt-Party Good	Retail Excellent
RAM 3500 CREW CAB—6-Cyl. Turbo Diesel—Truck Equip Sch T1						
ST Tradesman 6'	R2CL	43300	27100	28000	29600	34200
ST Tradesman 4D 8'	R2GL	43500	27200	28100	29700	34300
SLT 4D 6 1/3'	R2DL	47615	31000	32000	33600	38800
SLT 4D 8'	R2HL	47815	31000	32000	33800	39000
Big Horn 4D 6 1/3'	R2DL	48750	31700	32800	34500	39800
Big Horn 4D 8'	R2HL	48950	31900	33000	34800	40100
Lone Star 4D 6 1/3'	R2DL	48750	31700	32800	34500	39800
Lone Star 4D 8'	R2HL	48950	31900	33000	34800	40100
Laramie 4D 6 1/3'	R2EL	53590	36100	37300	39200	45100
Laramie 4D 8'	R2JL	53790	36200	37400	39300	45200
Laramie Lnghrn 6'	R2FL	59145	38400	39600	40600	45700
Laramie Longhorn 8'	R2KL	59345	38200	39400	40400	45500
Lrme Lnghrn Ltd 6'	R2FL	62240	42500	43800	44600	50000
Lrme Lnghrn Ltd 8'	R3KL	62280	42700	44000	44800	50200
RamBox			500	500	545	545
4WD	3		3300	3300	3590	3590
V8, HEMI, 5.7 Liter	T		(5900)	(5900)	(6420)	(6420)
RAM MEGA CAB PICKUP—V8 HEMI—Truck Equipment Schedule T1						
2500 SLT 4D 6 1/3'	R4MT	38715	25100	26000	27600	31800
2500 Big Horn 6 1/3'	R4MT	40550	24500	25400	26900	31100
2500 Lone Star 6 1/3'	R4MT	40550	24500	25400	26900	31100
2500 Laramie 6 1/3'	R4NT	44685	29700	30700	32500	37400
2500 Laramie Lghrn	R4PT	50025	31400	32500	34300	39500
2500 LrmLnghrnLtd	R4PT	54915	33300	34400	36200	41700
RamBox			500	500	535	535
4WD	5		3300	3300	3610	3610
6-Cyl Turbo Diesel, 6.7L			5900	5900	6455	6455
RAM MEGA CAB PICKUP—6-Cyl. Turbo Diesel—Truck Equip Sch T1						
3500 SLT 6 1/3' DR	R2LL	48615	32700	33800	35400	40500
3500 Big Horn 6 1/3'	R2LL	49750	32700	33800	35100	40000
3500 Lone Star 6 1/3'	R2LL	49750	32700	33800	35100	40000
3500 Laramie 6'	R2ML	53440	34500	36100	41400	
3500 Lrmie Lnghrn 6	R2NL	60145	39200	40400	41400	46700
3500 LrmLnghrnLtd	R2NL	60245	42200	43500	44700	50700
RamBox			500	500	545	545
4WD	3,R		3300	3300	3610	3610
V8, HEMI, 5.7 Liter	T		(5900)	(5900)	(6450)	(6450)

2014 RAM — (1,2or3)C6—(RGAG)—E—#

Body Type	VIN	List	Trade-In Good	Trade-In Very Good	Pvt-Party Good	Retail Excellent
RAM QUAD CAB PICKUP—V8 HEMI—Truck Equipment Schedule T1						
1500 Tradesman 6'	R6FT	31140	18700	19350	20800	24100
1500 Sport 4D 6 1/3'	R6HT	38835				
RamBox			525	525	595	595
4WD	7		3600	3600	4090	4090
V6, Flex Fuel, 3.6 Liter	G		(850)	(850)	(965)	(965)
V6, Turbo Diesel, 3.0L	M		2950	2950	3350	3350
RAM QUAD CAB PICKUP—V6 Flex Fuel—Truck Equipment Sch T1						
1500 Outdoorsman 6'	R6GG	35365	20400	21100	22600	26200
RamBox			525	525	590	590
4WD	7		3600	3600	4065	4065
V6, Turbo EcoDsl, 3.0L	M		2950	2950	3330	3330
V8, HEMI, 5.7 Liter	T		1300	1300	1460	1460
RAM QUAD CAB PICKUP—V8 HEMI—Truck Equipment Schedule T1						
1500 Express 6 1/3'	R6FT	31800	18600	19250	20800	24200
1500 SLT 4D 6 1/3'	R6GT	34320	19500	20200	21700	25200
1500 Big Horn 6 1/3'	R6GT	35515	20800	21500	23100	26800
RamBox			525	525	585	585
4WD	7		3600	3600	4015	4015
V6, Turbo EcoDsl, 3.0L	M		2950	2950	3290	3290
V6, Flex Fuel, 3.6 Liter	G		(850)	(850)	(950)	(950)
RAM CREW CAB PICKUP—V6 Flex Fuel—Truck Equipment Schedule T1						
1500 Outdrsman 5'	R6LG	37670	22300	24100	25700	29800
1500 Tradesman 5'	R6KG	33620	20700	21400	22800	26300
1500 SLT 4D 5 1/2'	R6LG	37790	22300	23100	24700	28700
1500 Big Horn 5 1/2'	R6LG	36670	22900	23600	25400	29500
1500 Lone Star 5 1/2'	R6LG	36670	22900	23600	25300	29300
RamBox			525	525	610	610
4WD	7		3600	3600	4195	4195
V6, Turbo, EcoDsl, 3.0L	M		2950	2950	3440	3440
V8, HEMI, 5.7 Liter	T		1300	1300	1505	1505
RAM CREW CAB PICKUP—V8 HEMI—Truck Equipment Schedule T1						
1500 Tradesman 6'	R6ST	33080	20300	21100	22500	26000

Body Type	VIN	List	Trade-In Good	Trade-In Very Good	Pvt-Party Good	Retail Excellent
1500 Express 5 1/2'	R6KT	34280	21000	21700	23400	27200
1500 SLT 4D 6 1/3'	R6TT	37425	26200	27000	28900	33500
1500 Big Horn 6 1/3'	R9TT	38620	23800	24600	26100	30200
1500 Lone Star 6 1/3'	R6TT	38620	23800	24600	26100	30200
1500 Outdrsman 6'	R6TT	39620	22800	23600	25200	29300
1500 Sport 4D 5 1/2'	R6MT	40690	27500	28400	30000	34500
1500 Sport 4D 6'	R6UT	40990	27300	28200	29900	34400
1500 Laramie 5 1/2'	R6NT	42875	28900	29900	31900	37100
1500 Laramie 6 1/3'	R6VT	43175	26700	27600	29800	35000
1500 Lrmie Lnghrn 5'	R6PT	46680	30800	31800	33700	38900
1500 Lrmie Lnghrn 6'	R6WT	46980	30500	31500	33300	38400
1500 Lrmie Ltd 5 1/2'	R6PT	49175	31400	32400	34200	39400
1500 Lrmie Ltd 6 1/3'	R6WT	49475	31100	32100	33900	39000
RamBox			525	525	605	605
4WD	7		3600	3600	4150	4150
V6, Turbo, EcoDsl, 3.0L	M		2950	2950	3325	3325
RAM CREW CAB PICKUP—V8 HEMI—Truck Equipment Schedule T1						
2500 Tradesman 6'	R4CT	34265				
2500 Tradesman 8'	R4HT	34465				
2500 SLT 4D 6 1/3'	R4DT	38740	24200	25000	27000	31400
2500 SLT 4D 8'	R4JT	38940	24000	24800	26700	31100
2500 Big Horn 6 1/3'	R4DT	40575	26000	26900	28700	33300
2500 Lone Star 6 1/3'	R4DT	40575				
2500 Big Horn 8'	R4JT	40775	25800	26700	28500	33100
2500 Lone Star 8'	R4JT	40775				
2500 Laramie 6 1/3'	R4FT	44460	32200	33200	34700	39600
2500 Laramie 8'	R4KT	44660	32300	33300	34900	39800
2500 Lrmie Lghrn 6'	R4GT	49875				
2500 Lrmie Lghrn 8'	R4LT	50075				
2500 Laramie Ltd 6'	R4GT	52170				
2500 Laramie Ltd 8'	R4LT	51870				
RamBox			525	525	580	580
4WD	5		3600	3600	3980	3980
6-Cyl Turbo Diesel 6.7L	L		6100	6100	6745	6745
V8, CNG, HEMI 5.7L	2		0	0	0	0
V8, HEMI, 6.4 Liter	J		575	575	640	640

SAAB

2005 SAAB — 5S3E(T13S)-5-#

9-7X AWD—6-Cyl.—Truck Equipment Schedule T3

Linear Sport Util 4D	T13S	38990	2050	2300	3275	4900

9-7X AWD—V8—Truck Equipment Schedule T3

Arc Sport Utility 4D	T13M	40990	2750	3075	4100	6025

2006 SAAB — 5S3-(T13S)-6-#

9-7X AWD—6-Cyl.—Truck Equipment Schedule T3

4.2i Sport Utility 4D	T13S	39240	2975	3300	4150	5850

9-7X AWD—V8—Truck Equipment Schedule T3

5.3i Sport Utility 4D	T13M	41240	3750	4125	5150	7125

2007 SAAB — 5S3-(T13S)-7-#

9-7X AWD—6-Cyl.—Truck Equipment Schedule T3

4.2i Sport Utility 4D	T13S	39735	3750	4125	5075	6925

9-7X AWD—V8—Truck Equipment Schedule T3

5.3i Sport Utility 4D	T13M	41735	4850	5275	6225	8325

2008 SAAB — 5S3-(T13S)-8-#

9-7X AWD—6-Cyl.—Truck Equipment Schedule T3

4.2i Sport Utility 4D	T13S	39935	5000	5400	6325	8250

9-7X AWD—V8—Truck Equipment Schedule T3

5.3i Sport Util 4D	T13M	42035	6825	7275	8600	11200
Aero Sport Utility 4D	T23H	45750	8550	9100	10250	13000

2009 SAAB — 5S3-(T13S)-9-#

9-7X AWD—6-Cyl.—Truck Equipment Schedule T3

4.2i Sport Utility 4D	T13S	41710	6875	7300	8175	10000

9-7X AWD—V8—Truck Equipment Schedule T3

5.3i Sport Util 4D	T13M	44440	9050	9575	10650	13100
Aero Sport Util 4D	T13H	48200	10850	11450	12550	15250

Body Type	VIN	List	Trade-In Good	Very Good	Pvt-Party Good	Retail Excellent

2011 SAAB — 3G0-(NREY)-B-#

9-4X AWD—V6—Truck Equipment Schedule T3

Sport Utility	NREY	36700	16000	16650	17850	20900
Prem Sport Utility	NTEY	41070	19500	20300	21500	25100

9-4X AWD—V6 Turbo—Truck Equipment Schedule T3

Aero Sport Utility	NUE6	48835	21000	21800	23100	26900

SATURN

2002 SATURN — 5GZ-(Z23D)-2-#

VUE—4-Cyl.—Truck Equipment Schedule T1

Sport Utility 4D	Z23D	17775	475	575	1575	2825
AWD			400	400	520	520
V6, 3.0 Liter	B		250	250	345	345

2003 SATURN — 5GZ-(Z23D)-3-#

VUE—4-Cyl.—Truck Equipment Schedule T1

Sport Utility 4D	Z33D	18295	750	875	1975	3500
AWD	4,6		425	425	555	555
V6, 3.0 Liter	B		275	275	375	375

2004 SATURN — 5GZ-(Z23D)-4-#

VUE—4-Cyl.—Truck Equipment Schedule T1

Sport Utility 4D	Z33D	19135	1125	1275	2400	4125
AWD	4,6		450	450	595	595
V6, 3.5 Liter	B		300	300	405	405

2005 SATURN — 5GZ-(Z23D)-5-#

VUE—4-Cyl.—Truck Equipment Schedule T1

Sport Utility 4D	Z23D	21190	1650	1875	2925	4625
AWD			475	475	630	630
V6, 3.5 Liter	4		325	325	435	435

RELAY—V6—Truck Equipment Schedule T1

2 Minivan	V03L	24485	1850	2075	2850	4300
3 Minivan	V23L	27580	2525	2825	3750	5650
AWD	X		550	550	735	735

2006 SATURN — 5GZ-(Z23D)-6-#

VUE—4-Cyl.—Truck Equipment Schedule T1

Sport Utility 4D	Z23D	19345	2175	2450	3650	5525
AWD	4,6		500	500	665	665
V6, 3.5 Liter	4		350	350	465	465

RELAY—V6—Truck Equipment Schedule T1

2 Minivan	V03L	23590	2400	2700	3575	5200
3 Minivan	V23L	27490	3225	3575	4425	6400
AWD	X		575	575	780	780

2007 SATURN — 5GZ-(Z33Z)-7-#

VUE—4-Cyl. Hybrid—Truck Equipment Schedule T1

Sport Utility 4D	Z33Z	22995	3775	4150	5150	7150

VUE—4-Cyl.—Truck Equipment Schedule T1

Sport Utility 4D	Z23D	19770	2975	3300	4275	6050
AWD	4,6		525	525	700	700
V6, 3.5 Liter	L		375	375	500	500

RELAY—V6—Truck Equipment Schedule T1

Minivan	V531	22210	3325	3675	4525	6300
2 Minivan	V031	24540	4075	4475	5400	7475
3 Minivan	V231	28625	4825	5250	6525	9175

OUTLOOK—V6—Truck Equipment Schedule T1

XE Sport Utility 4D	R137	27990	6000	6500	7475	9750
XR Sport Utility 4D	R237	30290	6825	7375	8375	10950
AWD	V		675	675	855	855

2008 SATURN — 5GZor3GS(L03Z)-8-#

VUE—4-Cyl. Hybrid—Truck Equipment Schedule T1

Green Line Spt Util	L03Z	24795	5050	5450	6300	8175

VUE—4-Cyl.—Truck Equipment Schedule T1

XE Sport Utility 4D	L33P	21395	4675	5050	5900	7675

Body · Type	VIN	List	Trade-In Good	Very Good	Pvt-Party Good	Retail Excellent
AWD	4,7		550	550	700	700
V6, 3.5 Liter	N		400	400	510	510
VUE—V6—Truck Equipment Schedule T1						
XR Sport Utility 4D	L537	24895	5175	5575	6425	8325
Red Line Spt Util	L937	27395	7025	7525	8675	11150
AWD	4,7		550	550	700	700
OUTLOOK—V6—Truck Equipment Schedule T1						
XE Sport Utility 4D	R137	28340	7450	7975	9000	11400
XR Sport Utility 4D	R237	30640	8200	8775	9900	12600
AWD	V		725	725	885	885

2009 SATURN — 5GZor3GS(L93Z)–9–#

VUE—4-Cyl. Hybrid—Truck Equipment Schedule T1						
Sport Utility 4D	L93Z	27650	6750	7175	7950	9725
VUE—4-Cyl.—Truck Equipment Schedule T1						
XE Sport Utility 4D	L33P	22770	6325	6750	7500	9200
AWD	4,6,0		650	650	745	745
V6, 3.5 Liter	N		475	475	545	545
VUE—V6—Truck Equipment Schedule T1						
XR Sport Utility 4D	L537	26095	7350	7800	8650	10550
AWD	6		650	650	745	745
4-Cyl, 2.4 Liter	P		(575)	(575)	(660)	(660)
VUE—V6—Truck Equipment Schedule T1						
Red Line Sport Util	L137	28595	8400	8900	9725	11850
AWD	4,6,0		650	650	740	740
OUTLOOK—V6—Truck Equipment Schedule T1						
XE Sport Utility 4D	R137	31055	8375	8875	10100	12700
XR Sport Utility 4D	R237	34880	9625	10200	11500	14400
AWD	V		750	750	915	915

2010 SATURN — 5GZor3GS(LAE1)–A–#

VUE—4-Cyl.—Truck Equipment Schedule T1						
XE Sport Utility 4D	LAE1	23580	7975	8400	9525	11650
VUE—V6—Truck Equipment Schedule T1						
XR Sport Utility 4D	LEE7	26965	9150	9650	10850	13250
XR-L Sport Util	LKE7	29430	10500	11000	12300	15000
AWD	F		725	725	825	825
4-Cyl, 2.4 Liter	1		(525)	(525)	(600)	(600)
OUTLOOK—V6—Truck Equipment Schedule T1						
XE Spt Util 4D	RTED	31905	10200	10700	11850	14400
XR-L Spt Util 4D	RVED	37705	12050	12650	13950	16850
AWD	V		800	800	935	935

SUBARU

2000 SUBARU — JF1(SF635)–Y–#

FORESTER AWD—4-Cyl.—Truck Equipment Schedule T1						
L Sport Utility 4D	SF635	21390	1075	1250	1900	3000
S Sport Utility 4D	SF655	23890	1450	1650	2325	3625

2001 SUBARU — JF1(SF635)–1–#

FORESTER AWD—4-Cyl.—Truck Equipment Schedule T1						
L Sport Utility 4D	SF635	21590	1425	1625	2250	3425
S Sport Utility 4D	SF655	24190	1875	2125	2875	4300

2002 SUBARU — JF1(SF635)–2–#

FORESTER AWD—4-Cyl.—Truck Equipment Schedule T1						
L Sport Utility 4D	SF635	21625	1725	1975	2700	4075
S Sport Utility 4D	SF655	24220	2300	2600	3375	5025

2003 SUBARU–(JF1or4S4)(BorS)(G636)–3–#

FORESTER AWD—4-Cyl.—Truck Equipment Schedule T1						
X Sport Utility 4D	G636	21870	2225	2500	3275	4850
XS Sport Utility 4D	G656	24220	2800	3150	3900	5625
BAJA AWD—4-Cyl.—Truck Equipment Schedule T1						
Sport Util Pickup 4D	T61C	24520	4625	5025	5900	8225

2004 SUBARU

Body Type	VIN	List	Trade-In Good	Trade-In Very Good	Pvt-Party Good	Retail Excellent

2004 SUBARU–(JF1or4S4)(BorS)(G636)–4–#

FORESTER AWD—4-Cyl.—Truck Equipment Schedule T1
X Sport Utility 4D	G636	22245	2600	2925	3750	5475
XS Sport Utility 4D	G656	24495	3350	3725	4575	6550

FORESTER AWD—4-Cyl. Turbo—Truck Equipment Schedule T1
XT Sport Utility 4D	G696	26320	4400	4850	5825	8175

BAJA AWD—4-Cyl.—Truck Equipment Schedule T1
"Sport" SUT	T61C	22545	5550	5975	7075	9700

BAJA AWD—4-Cyl. Turbo—Truck Equipment Schedule T1
Sport Util Pickup 4D	T63C	24545	6200	6650	7825	10750

2005 SUBARU–(JF1or4S4)(BorS)(G636)–5–#

FORESTER AWD—4-Cyl.—Truck Equipment Schedule T1
X Sport Utility 4D	G636	22670	3900	4300	5300	7450
XS Sport Utility 4D	G656	25070	4550	5000	6000	8375
XS LL Bean Spt Util	G676	26970	5350	5875	6975	9550

FORESTER AWD—4-Cyl. Turbo—Truck Equipment Schedule T1
XT Sport Utility 4D	G696	27070	6100	6650	7700	10350

BAJA AWD—4-Cyl.—Truck Equipment Schedule T1
"Sport" SUT	T62C	22770	6875	7350	8475	11150

BAJA AWD—4-Cyl. Turbo—Truck Equipment Schedule T1
Sport Util Pickup 4D	T63C	24770	7650	8175	9400	12350

2006 SUBARU–(JF1or4S4)(B,SorW)(G636)–6–#

FORESTER AWD—4-Cyl.—Truck Equipment Schedule T1
X Sport Utility 4D	G636	23220	4925	5400	6225	8375
X LL Bean Spt Util	G676	27521	6375	6925	7850	10300

FORESTER AWD—4-Cyl. Turbo—Truck Equipment Schedule T1
XT Limited Spt Util	G696	29320	8725	9425	10250	13100

BAJA AWD—4-Cyl.—Truck Equipment Schedule T1
"Sport" SUT	T62C	23920	8075	8625	9700	12450

BAJA AWD—4-Cyl. Turbo—Truck Equipment Schedule T1
Sport Util Pickup 4D	T63C	26220	9150	9750	11000	14100

B9 TRIBECA AWD—H6—Truck Equipment Schedule T1
Sport Utility 4D	X82D	31320	5600	6025	7175	9400
Limited Sport Util	X82D	32910	7000	7500	8725	11350
Third Row Seat			225	225	305	305

2007 SUBARU–(JF1or4S4)(B,SorW)(G636)–7–#

FORESTER AWD—4-Cyl.—Truck Equipment Schedule T1
X Sport Utility 4D	G636	22620	5450	5925	6875	9025
Sports X Spt Util	G636	22320	5475	5950	6900	9075
X LL Bean Spt Util	G676	27320	8550	9200	10150	12900

FORESTER AWD—4-Cyl. Turbo—Truck Equipment Schedule T1
Sports XT Spt Util	G696	26620	8875	9525	10400	13100
XT Limited Spt Util	G696	29320	9875	10600	11450	14400

B9 TRIBECA AWD—H6—Truck Equipment Schedule T1
Sport Utility 4D	X82D	30620	6700	7150	8275	10550
Limited Sport Util	X82D	33120	8550	9075	10350	13250
Third Row Seat			250	250	310	310

2008 SUBARU–(JF1or4S4)(B,SorW)(G636)–8–#

FORESTER AWD—4-Cyl.—Truck Equipment Schedule T1
X Sport Utility 4D	G636	22640	6675	7150	8150	10400
Sports X Spt Util	G666	23140	8075	8625	9525	11900
X LL Bean Spt Util	G676	27340	9825	10450	11500	14350

FORESTER AWD—4-Cyl. Turbo—Truck Equipment Schedule T1
Sports XT Spt Util	G696	28640	10300	10950	12000	14950
XT Limited Spt Util	G696	29540	11550	12250	13200	16300

TRIBECA AWD—H6—Truck Equipment Schedule T1
Sport Utility 4D	X91D	30640	8050	8525	9675	12050
Limited Sport Util	X92D	33240	9300	9825	11300	14250
Third Row Seat			250	250	305	305

2009 SUBARU–(JF1or4S4)(B,SorW)(G636)–9–#

FORESTER AWD—4-Cyl.—Truck Equipment Schedule T1
X Sport Utility 4D	G636	20660	9100	9650	10700	13150
X Limited Spt Util	G636	26660	10600	11200	12300	15050
X LL Bean Spt Util	G676	26660	10550	11150	12250	15000

0415   **SEE BACK PAGES FOR TRUCK EQUIPMENT**   555

TRUCKS & VANS

2009 SUBARU

Body Type	VIN	List	Trade-In Good	Very Good	Pvt-Party Good	Retail Excellent
FORESTER AWD—4-Cyl. Turbo—Truck Equipment Schedule T1						
XT Sport Utility 4D	G696	26860	11100	11700	12850	15750
XT Limited Spt Util	G696	28860	11800	12450	13650	16700
TRIBECA AWD—H6—Truck Equipment Schedule T1						
Sport Utility 4D	X91D	30660	10700	11250	12200	14550
Limited Sport Util	X92D	33260	12150	12700	13750	16400
Third Row Seat			300	300	340	340

2010 SUBARU–(JF1or4S4)(B,SorW)(H6AC)–A–#

Body Type	VIN	List	Trade-In Good	Very Good	Pvt-Party Good	Retail Excellent
FORESTER AWD—4-Cyl.—Truck Equipment Schedule T1						
2.5X Sport Utility	H6AC	20990	10900	11450	12550	15000
2.5X Premium 4D	H6CC	23490	12250	12850	13850	16400
2.5X Limited 4D	H6DC	26690	13200	13850	14700	17400
FORESTER AWD—4-Cyl. Turbo—Truck Equipment Schedule T1						
2.5XT Premium 4D	H6EC	27190	13300	13950	15000	17750
2.5XT Limited 4D	H6FC	29190	14250	14900	15950	18850
TRIBECA AWD—H6—Truck Equipment Schedule T1						
3.6R Premium 4D	X9FD	31190	12000	12500	13600	16050
3.6R Limited 4D	X9GD	33190	13550	14150	15350	18050
3.6R Touring 4D	X9GD	36490	15450	16100	17400	20400
Third Row Seat			350	350	395	395

2011 SUBARU–(JF2or4S4)(B,SorW)(SHBAC)–B–#

Body Type	VIN	List	Trade-In Good	Very Good	Pvt-Party Good	Retail Excellent
FORESTER AWD—4-Cyl.—Truck Equipment Schedule T1						
2.5X Sport Utility	SHBAC	22420	13450	14000	15100	17600
2.5X Premium Util	HBCC	23920	14300	14900	15950	18600
2.5X Limited 4D	HBDC	27220	14950	15600	16650	19400
2.5X Touring 4D	HBHC	28720	16050	16700	17750	20600
FORESTER AWD—4-Cyl. Turbo—Truck Equipment Schedule T1						
2.5XT Premium Util	HGAC	27720	15450	16100	17150	19900
2.5XT Touring 4D	HGGC	30720	17800	18500	19500	22500
TRIBECA AWD—H6—Truck Equipment Schedule T1						
3.6R Premium 4D	X9FD	31220	14050	14650	15800	18250
3.6R Limited 4D	X9HD	33220	16600	17250	18450	21300
3.6R Touring 4D	X9GD	36520	18400	19100	20300	23400
Third Row Seat			400	400	460	460

2012 SUBARU–(JF2or4S4)(B,SorW)(SHBAC)–C–#

Body Type	VIN	List	Trade-In Good	Very Good	Pvt-Party Good	Retail Excellent
FORESTER AWD—4-Cyl.—Truck Equipment Schedule T1						
2.5X Sport Utility	SHBAC	22550	14650	15200	16300	18800
2.5X Premium Util	HBCC	24070	15700	16300	17350	19900
2.5X Limited 4D	HBEC	27220	16650	17250	18300	21000
2.5X Touring 4D	HBGC	28670	18000	18700	19550	22200
FORESTER AWD—4-Cyl. Turbo—Truck Equipment Schedule T1						
2.5XT Premium 4D	HGAC	27870	17200	17850	18750	21300
2.5XT Touring 4D	HGGC	30670	19600	20300	21300	24200
TRIBECA AWD—H6—Truck Equipment Schedule T1						
3.6R Premium 4D	X9FD	31370	18000	18650	19850	22700
3.6R Limited 4D	X9GD	33370	19650	20400	21400	24200
3.6R Touring 4D	X9GD	36670	21100	21900	22900	25900
Third Row Seat			425	425	485	485

2013 SUBARU–(JF2or4S4)(B,SorW)(GPABC)–D–#

Body Type	VIN	List	Trade-In Good	Very Good	Pvt-Party Good	Retail Excellent
XV CROSSTREK AWD—4-Cyl.						
Premium Spt Util	GPABC	23790	16550	17150	18100	20600
Limited Sport Util	GPAGC	25290	17350	17950	18900	21600
FORESTER AWD—4-Cyl.—Truck Equipment Schedule T1						
2.5X Sport Utility	SHAAC	22090	15950	16550	17650	20300
2.5X Premium Util	SHADC	25090	17050	17650	18650	21300
2.5X Limited 4D	SHAEC	27790	18000	18650	19600	22200
2.5X Touring 4D	SHAGC	29190	19400	20100	20900	23600
FORESTER AWD—4-Cyl. Turbo—Truck Equipment Schedule T1						
2.5XT Premium	SHGAC	28090	18700	19350	20300	22900
2.5XT Touring	SHGGC	30790	21000	21700	22500	25400
TRIBECA AWD—H6—Truck Equipment Schedule T1						
3.6R Limited 4D	WX9FD	33390	21600	22300	23400	26400
Third Row Seat			450	450	495	495

2014 SUBARU–(JF2or4S4)(B,SorW)(GPACC)–E–#

Body Type	VIN	List	Trade-In Good	Very Good	Pvt-Party Good	Retail Excellent
XV CROSSTREK AWD—4-Cyl.—Truck Equipment Schedule T1						
Premium Spt Util	GPACC	23820	18000	18650	19500	22100

2014 SUBARU

Body Type	VIN	List	Trade-In Good	Very Good	Pvt-Party Good	Retail Excellent
Limited Spt Util AWD	GPAGC	25320	18550	19200	20100	22800
XV CROSSTREK AWD—4-Cyl. Hybrid—Truck Equipment Schedule T1						
Sport Utility 4D	GPBKC	26820	18600	19250	20200	23000
Touring Sport Util	GPBKC	30120	19200	19900	20800	23600
FORESTER AWD—4-Cyl.—Truck Equipment Schedule T1						
2.5i Sport Utility	SJAAC	23820	17900	18500	19600	22400
2.5i Premium Util	SJACC	24320	19150	19800	20700	23400
2.5i Limited 4D	SJAHC	28820	20100	20700	21600	24300
2.5i Touring 4D	SJALC	30820	21700	22400	23200	26000
FORESTER AWD—4-Cyl. Turbo—Truck Equipment Schedule T1						
2.0XT Premium 4D	SJGDC	28820	20800	21500	22100	24700
2.0XT Touring 4D	SJGLC	33820	23900	24700	25300	28200
TRIBECA AWD—H6—Truck Equipment Schedule T1						
3.6R Ltd Spt Util	WX9FD	34920	24700	25600	26700	30100

SUZUKI

2000 SUZUKI — (Jor2)S3(TC03C)-Y-#

Body Type	VIN	List	Good	Very Good	Good	Excellent
VITARA—4-Cyl.—Truck Equipment Schedule T2						
JS Convertible 2D	TC03C	13939	600	700	1650	2850
JS Hard Top 4D	TE52V	15949	675	800	1750	3025
JLS Convertible 2D	TC52C	15439	775	900	1900	3275
JLS Hard Top 4D	TE52V	16749	900	1050	2100	3600
VITARA 4WD—4-Cyl.—Truck Equipment Schedule T2						
JX Convertible 2D	TA03C	15739	625	750	1675	2900
JX Hard Top 4D	TD52V	17549	825	950	1975	3400
JLX Convertible 2D	TA52C	17239	900	1050	2100	3600
JLX Hard Top 4D	TD52V	18349	1000	1150	2225	3850
GRAND VITARA—V6—Truck Equipment Schedule T1						
JLS Hard Top 4D	TE62V	19749	275	350	1125	1975
Ltd Hard Top 4D	TE62V	22149	725	850	1775	3075
GRAND VITARA 4WD—V6—Truck Equipment Schedule T1						
JLX Hard Top 4D	TD62V	20749	525	625	1500	2600
Ltd Hard Top 4D	TD62V	23149	875	1025	1975	3425

2001 SUZUKI — (Jor2)S3(TC03C)-1-#

Body Type	VIN	List	Good	Very Good	Good	Excellent
VITARA—4-Cyl.—Truck Equipment Schedule T2						
JS Convertible 2D	TC03C	14369	925	1050	1975	3325
JS Hard Top 4D	TE52V	16079	1000	1150	2075	3500
JLS Convertible 2D	TC52C	15869	925	1050	1975	3325
JLS Hard Top 2D	TE52V	16869	1200	1350	2375	3975
JLS Hard Top 4D	TE52V	17079	1225	1400	2400	4025
VITARA 4WD—4-Cyl.—Truck Equipment Schedule T2						
JX Convertible 2D	TA03C	15969	950	1075	2025	3400
JX Hard Top 4D	TD52V	17579	1150	1300	2300	3850
JLX Convertible 2D	TA52C	17469	1200	1350	2375	3975
JLX Hard Top 2D	TD52V	18469	2175	2425	3550	5525
JLX Hard Top 4D	TD52V	18579	1250	1425	2425	4075
GRAND VITARA—V6—Truck Equipment Schedule T1						
JLS Hard Top 4D	TE62V	19879	375	475	1250	2150
Ltd Hard Top 4D	TE62V	22279	925	1075	2000	3400
GRAND VITARA 4WD—V6—Truck Equipment Schedule T1						
JLX Hard Top 4D	TD62V	21079	725	875	1725	2950
Ltd Hard Top 4D	TD62V	23479	1125	1300	2275	3850
XL-7 4WD—V6—Truck Equipment Schedule T1						
Sport Utility 4D	TX92V	21499	425	500	1200	1925
Plus Sport Util 4D	TX92V	23999	675	775	1525	2475
Touring Spt Utl 4D	TX92V	24999	900	1025	1800	2900
Limited Spt Utl 4D	TX92V	26499	1150	1300	2100	3350
2WD	Y		(650)	(650)	(860)	(860)

2002 SUZUKI — (Jor2)S3(TC52C)-2-#

Body Type	VIN	List	Good	Very Good	Good	Excellent
VITARA—4-Cyl.—Truck Equipment Schedule T2						
JLS Convertible 2D	TC52C	16089	1300	1500	2450	4000
JLS Hard Top 4D	TE52V	17299	1600	1825	2975	4800
VITARA 4WD—4-Cyl.—Truck Equipment Schedule T2						
JLX Convertible 2D	TA52C	17489	1625	1850	3025	4875
JLX Hard Top 4D	TD52V	18699	1625	1850	3025	4875
GRAND VITARA—V6—Truck Equipment Schedule T1						
JLS Hard Top 4D	TE62V	19099	750	875	1650	2750
Ltd Hard Top 4D	TE62V	22299	1375	1575	2475	4050

SEE BACK PAGES FOR TRUCK EQUIPMENT 557

TRUCKS & VANS

2002 SUZUKI

Body Type	VIN	List	Trade-In Good	Very Good	Pvt-Party Good	Retail Excellent
GRAND VITARA 4WD—V6—Truck Equipment Schedule T1						
JLX Hard Top 4D	TD62V	20299	1150	1325	2175	3575
Ltd Hard Top 4D	TD62V	23499	1550	1775	2800	4550
XL-7 4WD—V6—Truck Equipment Schedule T1						
Sport Utility 4D	TX92V	22319	550	650	1375	2200
Plus Spt Util 4D	TX92V	23819	800	925	1725	2775
Touring Spt Utl 4D	TX92V	25319	1050	1200	2025	3250
Limited Spt Util 4D	TX92V	26519	1300	1475	2325	3725
2WD	Y		(725)	(725)	(970)	(970)

2003 SUZUKI — (Jor2)S3(TA52C)–3–#

Body Type	VIN	List	Trade-In Good	Very Good	Pvt-Party Good	Retail Excellent
VITARA 4WD—4-Cyl.—Truck Equipment Schedule T2						
Convertible 2D	TA52C	17509	2175	2450	3550	5475
Hard Top 4D	TD52V	18719	2275	2550	3700	5675
2WD	C,E		(450)	(450)	(600)	(600)
GRAND VITARA 4WD—V6—Truck Equipment Schedule T1						
Hard Top 4D	TD62V	20319	1775	2025	2950	4600
2WD	E		(450)	(450)	(600)	(600)
XL-7 4WD—V6—Truck Equipment Schedule T1						
Touring Spt Utl 4D	TX92V	22339	1150	1300	2150	3450
Limited Spt Util 4D	TX92V	25399	1375	1550	2450	3850
Third Row Seat			200	200	270	270
2WD	Y		(800)	(800)	(1080)	(1080)

2004 SUZUKI — (Jor2)S3(TD52V)–4–#

Body Type	VIN	List	Trade-In Good	Very Good	Pvt-Party Good	Retail Excellent
VITARA 4WD—V6—Truck Equipment Schedule T2						
LX Hard Top 4D	TD52V	17999	2625	2950	3950	5900
2WD	E		(525)	(525)	(700)	(700)
GRAND VITARA—V6—Truck Equipment Schedule T1						
LX Hard Top 4D	TE62V	18999	1800	2050	3000	4650
4WD	D		550	550	735	735
GRAND VITARA 4WD—V6—Truck Equipment Schedule T1						
EX Hard Top 4D	TD62V	22499	2900	3275	4525	6975
2WD	E		(525)	(525)	(700)	(700)
XL-7 4WD—V6—Truck Equipment Schedule T1						
LX Sport Utility 4D	TX92V	22899	2325	2600	3600	5400
EX Sport Utility 4D	TY92V	23699	1625	1825	2725	4200
Third Row Seat			300	300	400	400
2WD	Y		(900)	(900)	(1190)	(1190)

2005 SUZUKI — JS3(TE62V)–5–#

Body Type	VIN	List	Trade-In Good	Very Good	Pvt-Party Good	Retail Excellent
GRAND VITARA—V6—Truck Equipment Schedule T1						
LX Hard Top 4D	TE62V	19994	2425	2725	3575	5325
4WD	D		600	600	800	800
GRAND VITARA 4WD—V6—Truck Equipment Schedule T1						
EX Hard Top 4D	TD62V	23194	3650	4050	5325	7825
2WD	E		(600)	(600)	(800)	(800)
XL-7 4WD—V6—Truck Equipment Schedule T1						
LX Sport Utility 4D	TX92V	25394	3000	3350	4150	5925
EX Sport Utility 4D	TY92V	24694	2525	2850	3600	5150
Third Row Seat			325	325	435	435
2WD	Y		(975)	(975)	(1300)	(1300)

2006 SUZUKI — JS3(TE944)–6–#

Body Type	VIN	List	Trade-In Good	Very Good	Pvt-Party Good	Retail Excellent
GRAND VITARA—V6—Truck Equipment Schedule T1						
XSport Spt Util 4D	TE944	21694	3350	3725	4525	6275
4WD	D		650	650	865	865
GRAND VITARA 4WD—V6—Truck Equipment Schedule T1						
Sport Utility 4D	TD941	21794	3625	4025	4750	6525
Premium Sport Util.	TD943	22894	3925	4325	5175	7125
Luxury Sport Util	TD947	25194	4875	5350	6225	8525
2WD	E		(650)	(650)	(865)	(865)
XL-7 4WD—V6—Truck Equipment Schedule T1						
Sport Utility 4D	TX92V	25494	3275	3625	4550	6350
Premium Spt Util	TX92V	27294	3825	4225	5200	7200
Third Row Seat			350	350	465	465
2WD	Y		(1050)	(1050)	(1410)	(1410)

2007 SUZUKI — (2orJ)S3(TE944)–7–#

Body Type	VIN	List	Trade-In Good	Very Good	Pvt-Party Good	Retail Excellent
GRAND VITARA—V6—Truck Equipment Schedule T1						
XSport Spt Util 4D	TE944	22119	3700	4075	4875	6625

2007 SUZUKI

Body Type	VIN	List	Trade-In Good	Trade-In Very Good	Pvt-Party Good	Retail Excellent
4WD	D		975	975	1315	1315
GRAND VITARA 4WD—V6—Truck Equipment Schedule T1						
Sport Utility 4D	TD941	22519	4025	4425	5125	6875
Luxury Sport Util	TD947	25649	5225	5700	6775	9125
2WD			(700)	(700)	(935)	(935)
XL7 4WD—V6—Truck Equipment Schedule T1						
Sport Utility 4D	DA217	26584	4075	4450	5375	7325
Special Sport Util	DA117	27999	4175	4575	5500	7475
Luxury Sport Util	DA517	28199	4275	4675	5600	7625
Limited Sport Util	DA717	30199	4875	5300	6275	8475
Third Row Seat			375	375	500	500
2WD	B		(1150)	(1150)	(1520)	(1520)

2008 SUZUKI — (2orJ)S3(TE944)-8-#

Body Type	VIN	List	Trade-In Good	Trade-In Very Good	Pvt-Party Good	Retail Excellent
GRAND VITARA—V6—Truck Equipment Schedule T1						
XSport Util 4D	TE944	22999	4425	4825	5800	7850
4WD			1075	1075	1430	1430
GRAND VITARA 4WD—V6—Truck Equipment Schedule T1						
Sport Utility 4D	TD341	23099	4400	4800	5450	7075
2WD	E		(750)	(750)	(965)	(965)
XL7—V6—Truck Equipment Schedule T1						
Sport Utility 4D	DB117	22294	2775	3075	3850	5300
XL7 4WD—V6—Truck Equipment Schedule T1						
Premium Sport Util	DA217	25499	4550	4950	5925	7900
Luxury Sport Util	DA317	27444	5100	5525	6550	8725
Limited Sport Util	DA717	29844	5675	6150	7350	9725
Third Row Seat			400	400	535	535
2WD			(1225)	(1225)	(1630)	(1630)

2009 SUZUKI — (2orJ)S3(TE041)-9-#

Body Type	VIN	List	Trade-In Good	Trade-In Very Good	Pvt-Party Good	Retail Excellent
GRAND VITARA—4-Cyl.—Truck Equipment Schedule T1						
Sport Utility 4D	TE041	20649	4600	4975	5675	7225
GRAND VITARA 4WD—4-Cyl.—Truck Equipment Schedule T1						
Premium Sport Util	TD041	22499	5900	6350	7200	9075
2WD			(875)	(875)	(1075)	(1075)
GRAND VITARA—4-Cyl.—Truck Equipment Schedule T1						
XSport Util 4D	TE144	22799	5175	5575	6425	8125
4WD	D		1175	1175	1430	1430
V6, 3.2 Liter	1,B		575	575	695	695
GRAND VITARA 4WD—V6—Truck Equipment Schedule T1						
Luxury Sport Util	TD149	27349	8650	9225	10250	12800
2WD	E		(875)	(875)	(1070)	(1070)
4-Cyl, 2.4 Liter	0,A		(475)	(475)	(595)	(595)
XL7 4WD—V6—Truck Equipment Schedule T1						
Sport Utility 4D	DA217	27995	7050	7575	8500	10650
Luxury Sport Util	DA317	29829	8400	8975	9875	12250
Limited Spt Util	DA717	30430	8750	9350	10250	12700
Third Row Seat			475	475	615	615
FWD	B		(1300)	(1300)	(1695)	(1695)
EQUATOR EXTENDED CAB—4-Cyl.—Truck Equipment Schedule T2						
Short Bed	BD09U	17995	6075	6475	7275	8975
Prem Short Bed	BD09U	22450	7975	8450	9400	11500
EQUATOR EXTENDED CAB—V6—Truck Equipment Schedule T2						
Sport Short Bed	AD09U	23670	8475	8975	9925	12150
4WD			1500	1500	1855	1855
EQUATOR CREW CAB—V6—Truck Equipment Schedule T2						
Short Bed	AD07U	23985	8675	9175	10150	12400
Sport Short Bed	AD07U	25150	10000	10550	11650	14200
Sport Long Bed	AD09U	25500	9825	10350	11400	13950
4WD			1500	1500	1850	1850
EQUATOR CREW CAB 4WD—V6—Truck Equipment Schedule T2						
RMZ Short Bed	AD07W	29325	11950	12600	13800	16850

2010 SUZUKI — (2orJ)S3or5Z6(TE0D1)-A-#

Body Type	VIN	List	Trade-In Good	Trade-In Very Good	Pvt-Party Good	Retail Excellent
GRAND VITARA—4-Cyl.—Truck Equipment Schedule T1						
Sport Utility 4D	TE0D1	19794	4800	5175	5825	7275
GRAND VITARA 4WD—4-Cyl.—Truck Equipment Schedule T1						
Premium Spt Util	TD0D2	22794	6975	7450	8100	9800
2WD	E		(1000)	(1000)	(1130)	(1130)
GRAND VITARA—4-Cyl.—Truck Equipment Schedule T1						
XSport Util 4D	TE1D8	23244	6300	6750	7400	8975
4WD			1250	1250	1420	1420

0415   **SEE BACK PAGES FOR TRUCK EQUIPMENT**   559

TRUCKS & VANS

Body Type	VIN	List	Trade-In Good	Very Good	Pvt-Party Good	Retail Excellent
V6, 3.2 Liter			**600**	**600**	**680**	**680**
GRAND VITARA 4WD—V6—Truck Equipment Schedule T1						
Limited Sport Util	TD1D9	27794	**9000**	**9525**	**10300**	**12400**
2WD		0	**(1000)**	**(1000)**	**(1135)**	**(1135)**
4-Cyl, 2.4 Liter		E	**(550)**	**(550)**	**(625)**	**(625)**
EQUATOR EXTENDED CAB—4-Cyl.—Truck Equipment Schedule T2						
Pickup 2D 6'	2D0CT	18315	**7150**	**7575**	**8425**	**10200**
Premium 2D 6'	2D0CT	22870	**9175**	**9700**	**10650**	**12850**
EQUATOR EXTENDED CAB—V6—Truck Equipment Schedule T2						
Sport 2D 6'	1D0CT	24040	**9725**	**10250**	**11250**	**13550**
4WD		V	**1700**	**1700**	**2030**	**2030**
EQUATOR CREW CAB—V6—Truck Equipment Schedule T2						
Sport 4D 5'	1D0EU	25570	**11350**	**11950**	**13000**	**15600**
Sport 4D 6'	1D0FU	25920	**11000**	**11600**	**12650**	**15200**
4WD			**1700**	**1700**	**2030**	**2030**
EQUATOR CREW CAB 4WD—V6—Truck Equipment Schedule T2						
RMZ 4D 5'	1D0EV	29645	**13300**	**14000**	**15250**	**18250**

Body Type	VIN	List	Good	Very Good	Good	Excellent
GRAND VITARA—4-Cyl.—Truck Equipment Schedule T1						
SVE Sport Util	TE0D1	19794	**5150**	**5500**	**5975**	**7200**
Sport Util	TE0D1	19994	**5225**	**5600**	**6425**	**7900**
GRAND VITARA 4WD—4-Cyl.—Truck Equipment Schedule T1						
Premium Spt Util	TD0D2	23244	**7900**	**8375**	**9050**	**10750**
Limited Sport Util	TD0D7	25644	**9750**	**10300**	**11050**	**13100**
2WD		E	**(1100)**	**(1100)**	**(1220)**	**(1220)**
EQUATOR EXTENDED CAB—4-Cyl.—Truck Equipment Schedule T2						
Pickup 2D 6'	2D0CT	18390	**8300**	**8750**	**9575**	**11400**
Premium 2D 6'	2D0CT	23174	**10350**	**10850**	**11800**	**14000**
EQUATOR EXTENDED CAB 4WD—V6—Truck Equipment Schedule T2						
Sport 2D 6'	1D0CV	26514	**10900**	**11450**	**12350**	**14650**
EQUATOR CREW CAB—V6—Truck Equipment Schedule T2						
Sport 4D 5'	1D0EU	25874	**12550**	**13150**	**14150**	**16750**
EQUATOR CREW CAB 4WD—V6—Truck Equipment Schedule T2						
Sport 4D 6'	1D0FW	28874	**12200**	**12800**	**13800**	**16350**
RMZ 4D 5'	1D0EW	29745	**14450**	**15150**	**16300**	**19250**

Body Type	VIN	List	Good	Very Good	Good	Excellent
GRAND VITARA—4-Cyl.—Truck Equipment Schedule T1						
Sport Utility 4D	TE0D1	20314	**5975**	**6325**	**7425**	**9225**
Ultimate Advntr	TE0D3	23114	**9650**	**10150**	**11600**	**14250**
GRAND VITARA 4WD—4-Cyl.—Truck Equipment Schedule T1						
Premium Spt Util	TD0D2	23664	**8875**	**9350**	**10550**	**12950**
Limited Sport Util	TD0D7	26064	**10950**	**11500**	**13000**	**15900**
2WD		E	**(1500)**	**(1500)**	**(1810)**	**(1810)**
EQUATOR EXTENDED CAB—4-Cyl.—Truck Equipment Schedule T2						
Pickup 2D 6'	2D0CT	18714	**9000**	**9475**	**10450**	**12400**
Comfort 2D 6'	2D0CT	20114	**9500**	**10000**	**10950**	**13000**
Premium 2D 6'	2D0CT	23614	**11050**	**11550**	**12650**	**14950**
EQUATOR EXTENDED CAB 4WD—V6—Truck Equipment Schedule T2						
Sport 2D 6'	1D0CW	27114	**11800**	**12350**	**13450**	**15950**
EQUATOR CREW CAB—V6—Truck Equipment Schedule T2						
Sport 4D 5'	1D0EU	26514	**13700**	**14300**	**15550**	**18400**
EQUATOR CREW CAB 4WD—V6—Truck Equipment Schedule T2						
Sport 4D 6'	1D0FW	29514	**13200**	**13800**	**15050**	**17800**
RMZ 4D 5'	1D0EW	30365	**16200**	**16900**	**18200**	**21400**

Body Type	VIN	List	Good	Very Good	Good	Excellent
GRAND VITARA—4-Cyl.—Truck Equipment Schedule T1						
Sport Utility 4D	TE0D5	20799	**7675**	**8100**	**9175**	**11150**
GRAND VITARA 4WD—4-Cyl.—Truck Equipment Schedule T1						
Premium Spt Util	TD0D6	24649	**10350**	**10850**	**12100**	**14550**
Limited Sport Util	TD0D7	26799	**12100**	**12700**	**14150**	**17100**
2WD		E	**(1500)**	**(1500)**	**(1690)**	**(1690)**

TOYOTA

Body Type	VIN	List	Good	Very Good	Good	Excellent
RAV4 4WD—4-Cyl.—Truck Equipment Schedule T2						
Sport Utility 4D	HP10V	18558	**1750**	**1950**	**2800**	**4200**

560   DEDUCT FOR RECONDITIONING

Body Type	VIN	List	Trade-In Good	Very Good	Pvt-Party Good	Retail Excellent
2WD	G,X		(350)	(350)	(465)	(465)
4RUNNER 4WD—4-Cyl.—Truck Equipment Schedule T1						
Sport Utility 4D	HM84R	26046	2075	2325	3075	4475
2WD	G		(550)	(550)	(750)	(750)
4RUNNER 4WD—V6—Truck Equipment Schedule T1						
SR5 Sport Util 4D	HN86R	29786	2875	3200	4050	5800
Limited Spt Ut 4D	HN87R	36948	3425	3775	4850	6900
2WD	G		(550)	(550)	(750)	(750)
LAND CRUISER 4WD—V8—Truck Equipment Schedule T3						
Sport Utility 4D	HT05J	51308	6925	7350	8950	11850
Third Row Seat			225	225	305	305
SIENNA—V6—Truck Equipment Schedule T1						
CE Minivan	ZF19C	23338	1475	1650	2325	3500
LE Minivan	ZF13C	25378	1800	2000	2725	4075
XLE Minivan	ZF13C	27414	2275	2525	3325	4950
Second Sliding Door			50	50	60	60
TACOMA—4-Cyl.—Truck Equipment Schedule T2						
Short Bed	NL42N	12208	1900	2100	2650	3975
Xtra Cab	VL52N	14458	2775	3075	3675	5400
PreRunner Short	NM92N	14298	2725	3025	3625	5325
PreRunner Xtra	SM92N	17418	3400	3725	4550	6575
4WD			400	400	535	535
V6, 3.4 Liter	N		100	100	135	135
TACOMA 4WD—V6—Truck Equipment Schedule T2						
Limited Xtra Cab	WN74N	24758	4350	4725	5650	8100
TUNDRA—V6—Truck Equipment Schedule T2						
Long Bed	JN321	15475	1400	1575	2375	3950
TUNDRA—V8—Truck Equipment Schedule T2						
SR5 Long Bed	KT441	23190	2750	3100	4000	6250
V6, 3.4 Liter	N		(300)	(300)	(415)	(415)
TUNDRA—V8—Truck Equipment Schedule T2						
SR5 Access Cab 4D	RT341	22730	3100	3475	4575	7050
Ltd Access Cab 4D	RT381	24975	3700	4125	5300	8075
4WD	4		650	650	865	865
V6, 3.4 Liter	N		(300)	(300)	(415)	(415)

2001 TOYOTA—(4,5orJ)T(3,B,DorE)(HH20V)-1-#

Body Type	VIN	List	Trade-In Good	Very Good	Pvt-Party Good	Retail Excellent
RAV4 4WD—4-Cyl.—Truck Equipment Schedule T2						
Sport Utility 4D	HH20V	19175	2475	2775	3550	5100
2WD			(400)	(400)	(535)	(535)
HIGHLANDER—V6—Truck Equipment Schedule T1						
Sport Utility 4D	GF21A	25605	3275	3575	4300	5775
AWD	H		600	600	815	815
4-Cyl, 2.4 Liter	D		(225)	(225)	(305)	(305)
HIGHLANDER 4WD—V6—Truck Equipment Schedule T1						
Limited Spt Util 4D	HF21A	30445	3925	4250	5175	6900
2WD			(650)	(650)	(860)	(860)
4-Cyl, 2.4 Liter	D		(225)	(225)	(305)	(305)
4RUNNER 4WD—V6—Truck Equipment Schedule T1						
SR5 Sport Util 4D	HN86R	29375	3175	3525	4450	6250
Limited Spt Ut 4D	HN87R	38085	3875	4250	5275	7350
2WD	G		(650)	(650)	(860)	(860)
SEQUOIA—V8—Truck Equipment Schedule T1						
SR5 Sport Util 4D	ZT34A	31330	2300	2575	3225	4575
4WD	B,4		600	600	815	815
SEQUOIA 4WD—V8—Truck Equipment Schedule T1						
Limited Spt Util 4D	BT48A	42755	3025	3375	4325	6200
2WD			(650)	(650)	(860)	(860)
LAND CRUISER 4WD—V8—Truck Equipment Schedule T3						
Sport Utility 4D	HT05J	53375	8325	8825	10400	13500
Third Row Seat			275	275	345	345
SIENNA—V6—Truck Equipment Schedule T1						
CE Minivan	ZF19C	24385	1625	1800	2575	3975
LE Minivan	ZF13C	26235	1950	2150	3000	4550
XLE Minivan	ZF13C	28916	2425	2675	3600	5450
TACOMA—4-Cyl.—Truck Equipment Schedule T2						
Short Bed	NL42N	12325	2225	2450	2950	4325
Xtra Cab	VL52N	14965	3225	3525	4125	5900
PreRunner Short	NM92N	14215	3100	3400	3975	5700
PreRunner Xtra	SM92N	16815	3875	4225	5025	7100
PreRunner 4D	GM92N	18335	5225	5625	6775	9250
PreRunner Ltd 4D	GM92N	22690	6025	6450	7675	10450
4WD			400	400	530	530

2001 TOYOTA

Body Type	VIN	List	Trade-In Good	Very Good	Pvt-Party Good	Retail Excellent
V6, 3.4 Liter	N		100	100	130	130
TACOMA—V6—Truck Equipment Schedule T2						
S-Runner Xtra Cab	VN52N	18385	3325	3650	4225	6050
TACOMA 4WD—V6—Truck Equipment Schedule T2						
Limited Xtra Cab	WN74N	24895	5150	5575	6500	9100
Double Cab 4D	HN72N	22345	6625	7075	8375	11350
Ltd Double Cab 4D	HN72N	25840	7075	7550	8975	12100
4-Cyl, 2.7 Liter	M		(225)	(225)	(305)	(305)
TUNDRA—V6—Truck Equipment Schedule T2						
Long Bed	JN321	16085	1600	1800	2600	4250
TUNDRA 4WD—V8—Truck Equipment Schedule T2						
SR5 Long Bed	KT441	23885	2925	3275	4175	6450
TUNDRA—V8—Truck Equipment Schedule T2						
SR5 Access Cab 4D	RT341	23455	3525	3925	5025	7600
Ltd Access Cab 4D	RT381	26205	4075	4500	5550	8250
4WD	4		750	750	1000	1000
V6, 3.4 Liter	4		(325)	(325)	(445)	(445)

2002 TOYOTA—(4,5orJ)T(3,B,DorE)(HH20V)-2-#

Body Type	VIN	List	Trade-In Good	Very Good	Pvt-Party Good	Retail Excellent
RAV4 4WD—4-Cyl.—Truck Equipment Schedule T2						
Sport Utility 4D	HH20V	19485	3050	3375	4225	6025
2WD	G		(450)	(450)	(600)	(600)
HIGHLANDER—V6—Truck Equipment Schedule T1						
Sport Utility 4D	GF21A	25970	3900	4225	5225	7025
Limited Spt Utl 4D	GF21A	29905	4600	4950	6025	8025
4WD	H		700	700	940	940
4-Cyl, 2.4 Liter	D		(275)	(275)	(365)	(365)
4RUNNER 4WD—V6—Truck Equipment Schedule T1						
SR5 Sport Util 4D	HN86R	29385	3675	4025	4900	6750
Limited Spt Utl 4D	HN87R	36615	4475	4875	5825	7950
2WD	G		(725)	(725)	(970)	(970)
SEQUOIA—V8—Truck Equipment Schedule T1						
SR5 Spt Util 4D	ZT34A	31780	3125	3450	4250	6025
4WD	B,4		700	700	940	940
SEQUOIA 4WD—V8—Truck Equipment Schedule T1						
Limited Spt Utl 4D	BT48A	43235	4025	4425	5525	7900
2WD	Z		(725)	(725)	(970)	(970)
LAND CRUISER 4WD—V8—Truck Equipment Schedule T3						
Sport Utility 4D	HT05J	53105	8875	9400	11300	14850
SIENNA—V6—Truck Equipment Schedule T1						
CE Minivan	ZF19C	24415	1825	2025	2875	4400
LE Minivan	ZF13C	26265	2200	2450	3350	5075
XLE Minivan	ZF13C	28522	2700	3000	3950	5925
TACOMA—4-Cyl.—Truck Equipment Schedule T2						
Short Bed	NL42N	12410	2575	2825	3350	4825
Xtra Cab	VL52N	15050	3625	3975	4725	6675
PreRunner Short	NM92N	14400	3550	3875	4625	6550
PreRunner Xtra	SM92N	17000	4375	4750	5575	7825
PreRunner 4D	GM92N	18620	6725	7175	8500	11450
4WD			550	550	735	735
V6, 3.4 Liter	N		175	175	230	230
TACOMA—V6—Truck Equipment Schedule T2						
S-Runner Xtra Cab	VN52N	18570	3725	4075	4825	6825
PreRunner Ltd 4D	GM92N	23000	7525	8025	9500	12800
TACOMA 4WD—V6—Truck Equipment Schedule T2						
Limited Xtra Cab	WN72N	23655	5900	6375	7525	10450
Double Cab 4D	HN72N	22630	7600	8100	9575	12900
Ltd Double Cab 4D	HN72N	26150	8750	9300	10900	14600
TUNDRA—V6—Truck Equipment Schedule T2						
Long Bed	JN321	16115	2225	2475	3175	4925
TUNDRA 4WD—V8—Truck Equipment Schedule T2						
SR5 Long Bed	KT441	23915	3475	3850	4775	7150
TUNDRA—V8—Truck Equipment Schedule T2						
SR5 Access Cab 4D	RT341	23485	4175	4600	5625	8325
Ltd Access Cab 4D	RT381	27230	4850	5325	6300	9125
4WD	4		900	900	1200	1200
V6, 3.4 Liter	N		(350)	(350)	(475)	(475)

2003 TOYOTA—(4,5orJ)T(B,DorE)(HH20V)-3-#

Body Type	VIN	List	Trade-In Good	Very Good	Pvt-Party Good	Retail Excellent
RAV4 4WD—4-Cyl.—Truck Equipment Schedule T2						
Sport Utility 4D	HH20V	19515	3650	4000	5050	7050
2WD	G		(500)	(500)	(665)	(665)

2003 TOYOTA

Body Type	VIN	List	Trade-In Good	Very Good	Pvt-Party Good	Retail Excellent
HIGHLANDER—V6—Truck Equipment Schedule T1						
Sport Utility 4D	GF21A	26000	4425	4775	5950	8025
Limited Spt Utl 4D	GF21A	29935	5075	5450	6700	8975
AWD	H		800	800	1060	1060
4-Cyl, 2.4 Liter	D		(325)	(325)	(425)	(425)
4RUNNER 4WD—V6—Truck Equipment Schedule T1						
SR5 Sport Util 4D	BU14R	29990	5450	5875	6975	9325
Sport SUV 4D	BU14R	31785	6050	6500	7675	10250
Limited Spt Ut 4D	BU17R	36190	6725	7225	8425	11200
2WD	Z		(800)	(800)	(1080)	(1080)
V8, 4.7 Liter	T		200	200	255	255
SEQUOIA—V8—Truck Equipment Schedule T1						
SR5 Spt Util 4D	ZT34A	32170	3900	4275	5225	7250
4WD	B,4		800	800	1060	1060
SEQUOIA 4WD—V8—Truck Equipment Schedule T1						
Limited Spt Util 4D	BT48A	44030	4725	5175	6450	9000
2WD	Z		(800)	(800)	(1080)	(1080)
LAND CRUISER 4WD—V8—Truck Equipment Schedule T3						
Sport Utility 4D	HT05J	53915	13000	13650	15350	19250
SIENNA—V6—Truck Equipment Schedule T1						
CE Minivan	ZF19C	24415	2425	2675	3425	4975
LE Minivan	ZF13C	26265	2850	3125	3925	5650
XLE Minivan	ZF13C	28522	3400	3725	4700	6725
TACOMA PICKUP—4-Cyl.—Truck Equipment Schedule T2						
Short Bed	NL42N	12610	2950	3250	3800	5400
Xtra Cab	VL52N	15250	4075	4425	5225	7300
PreRunner Short	NM92N	14525	3925	4275	5050	7075
PreRunner Xtra	SM92N	17200	5125	5525	6425	8900
PreRunner 4D	GM92N	18820	7225	7700	9050	12050
4WD	P		650	650	865	865
V6, 3.4 Liter	N		250	250	330	330
TACOMA PICKUP—V6—Truck Equipment Schedule T2						
PreRunner Ltd 4D	GN92N	23430	8175	8675	10100	13350
TACOMA PICKUP 4WD—V6—Truck Equipment Schedule T2						
Limited Xtra Cab	WN72N	24085	6850	7350	8600	11850
Double Cab 4D	HN72N	22830	8625	9150	10650	14100
Ltd Double Cab 4D	HN72N	26580	9525	10100	11700	15500
TUNDRA—V6—Truck Equipment Schedule T2						
Long Bed	JN321	17308	2900	3225	3750	5450
TUNDRA 4WD—V8—Truck Equipment Schedule T2						
SR5 Long Bed	KT441	24265	4175	4600	5350	7650
TUNDRA—V8—Truck Equipment Schedule T2						
SR5 Access Cab 4D	RT341	23865	4975	5425	6350	9075
Ltd Access Cab 4D	RT381	27465	5300	5800	6850	9650
4WD	B,4		1100	1100	1465	1465
V6, 3.4 Liter	N		(375)	(375)	(505)	(505)

2004 TOYOTA–(5orJ)T(B,DorE)(HD20V)–4–#

Body Type	VIN	List	Trade-In Good	Very Good	Pvt-Party Good	Retail Excellent
RAV4 4WD—4-Cyl.—Truck Equipment Schedule T2						
Sport Utility 4D	HD20V	19940	4675	5050	6250	8650
2WD	G		(550)	(550)	(735)	(735)
HIGHLANDER—V6—Truck Equipment Schedule T1						
Sport Utility 4D	GP21A	25680	5225	5600	6975	9225
Limited Spt Util 4D	GP21A	30520	6175	6575	8025	10600
Third Row Seat			300	300	400	400
AWD	E,H		875	875	1175	1175
4-Cyl, 2.4 Liter	D		(350)	(350)	(480)	(480)
4RUNNER 4WD—V6—Truck Equipment Schedule T1						
SR5 Sport Util 4D	BU14R	29985	6575	7075	8250	10900
Sport SUV 4D	BU14R	31225	7125	7625	8900	11750
Limited Spt Util	BU17R	36260	8225	8775	10050	13150
Third Row Seat			200	200	280	280
2WD	Z		(900)	(900)	(1190)	(1190)
V8, 4.7 Liter	T		200	200	270	270
SEQUOIA—V8—Truck Equipment Schedule T1						
SR5 Spt Util 4D	ZT34A	32170	5000	5425	6300	8525
4WD	B,4		875	875	1175	1175
SEQUOIA 4WD—V8—Truck Equipment Schedule T1						
Limited Spt Util 4D	BT48A	44760	6775	7325	8650	11700
2WD	Z		(900)	(900)	(1190)	(1190)
LAND CRUISER 4WD—V8—Truck Equipment Schedule T3						
Sport Utility 4D	HT05J	54765	15650	16400	17850	21800

TRUCKS & VANS

TRUCKS & VANS

Body Type	VIN	List	Trade-In Good	Very Good	Pvt-Party Good	Retail Excellent
SIENNA—V6—Truck Equipment Schedule T1						
CE Minivan	ZA23C	23495	3425	3750	4800	6875
LE Minivan	ZA23C	24800	3900	4250	5350	7625
XLE Minivan	ZA22C	28800	5075	5475	6950	9775
XLE Limited	ZA22C	35020	5825	6275	7825	10950
AWD			400	400	535	535
TACOMA PICKUP—4-Cyl.—Truck Equipment Schedule T2						
Short Bed	NL42N	12800	3825	4175	4900	6850
Xtra Cab	VL52N	15460	5425	5850	6950	9575
PreRunner Short	NM92N	14715	5100	5500	6400	8825
PreRunner Xtra	SM92N	17410	6800	7300	8425	11450
PreRunner 4D	GM92N	19030	8600	9125	10300	13300
4WD	W,H		800	800	1030	1030
V6, 3.4 Liter	N		325	325	415	415
TACOMA PICKUP—V6—Truck Equipment Schedule T2						
S-Runner Xtra Cab	VN52N	20700	5850	6300	7350	10050
PreRunner Ltd 4D	GN92N	23640	8950	9475	10850	14100
TACOMA PICKUP 4WD—V6—Truck Equipment Schedule T2						
Limited Xtra Cab	WN72N	24295	9550	10150	11900	16150
Double Cab 4D	HN72N	23040	10450	11050	12400	15950
Ltd Double Cab 4D	HN72N	26790	10850	11450	12850	16550
TUNDRA—V6—Truck Equipment Schedule T2						
Long Bed	JN321	17335	3400	3750	4150	5800
TUNDRA 4WD—V8—Truck Equipment Schedule T2						
SR5 Long Bed	KT441	24415	4725	5175	5800	8000
TUNDRA—V8—Truck Equipment Schedule T2						
SR5 Access Cab 4D	RN341	23995	4875	5325	5875	8025
Ltd Access Cab 4D	RT381	27615	5825	6350	7300	10100
SR5 Double Cab 4D	ET341	26185	6225	6775	7550	10200
Ltd Double Cab 4D	BT481	33140	10450	11250	12300	16450
4WD	B,4		1200	1200	1600	1600
V6, 3.4 Liter	N		(400)	(400)	(535)	(535)

2005 TOYOTA—(5orJ)T(B,DorE)(HD20V)—5—#

Body Type	VIN	List	Trade-In Good	Very Good	Pvt-Party Good	Retail Excellent
RAV4 4WD—4-Cyl.—Truck Equipment Schedule T1						
Sport Utility 4D	HD20V	21565	5375	5800	6825	8925
2WD	G		(600)	(600)	(765)	(765)
HIGHLANDER—V6—Truck Equipment Schedule T1						
Sport Utility 4D	GP21A	25705	5950	6325	7500	9600
Limited Spt Util 4D	DP21A	30545	7100	7525	8825	11200
Third Row Seat			325	325	420	420
AWD	E,H		975	975	1250	1250
4-Cyl, 2.4 Liter	D		(400)	(400)	(525)	(525)
4RUNNER 4WD—V6—Truck Equipment Schedule T1						
SR5 Sport Util 4D	BU14R	30335	7750	8275	9350	12050
Sport SUV 4D	BU14R	31605	8750	9325	10450	13400
Limited Spt Util	BU17R	36610	9175	9775	11000	14150
Third Row Seat			225	225	290	290
2WD	Z		(975)	(975)	(1255)	(1255)
V8, 4.7 Liter	T		225	225	275	275
SEQUOIA—V8—Truck Equipment Schedule T1						
SR5 Spt Util 4D	ZT34A	33035	6450	6950	7950	10450
4WD	B,4		975	975	1215	1215
SEQUOIA 4WD—V8—Truck Equipment Schedule T1						
Limited Spt Util 4D	BT48A	45525	9050	9700	10900	14150
2WD	Z		(975)	(975)	(1230)	(1230)
LAND CRUISER 4WD—V8—Truck Equipment Schedule T3						
Sport Utility 4D	HT05J	55590	17100	17900	19150	23100
SIENNA—V6—Truck Equipment Schedule T1						
CE Minivan	ZA23C	23790	4125	4475	5375	7375
LE Minivan	ZA23C	25295	4675	5050	6000	8175
XLE Minivan	ZA22C	29590	6100	6550	7800	10550
XLE Limited	ZA22C	35860	8850	9450	11050	14750
AWD	B		450	450	600	600
TACOMA PICKUP—4-Cyl.—Truck Equipment Schedule T2						
Short Bed	NX22N	14880	4900	5300	6125	8125
Access Cab	UX42N	17925	8025	8575	9850	12900
PreRunner Short	NX62N	14850	5550	5950	7000	9250
4WD	P,4		900	900	1195	1195
V6, 4.0 Liter	U		400	400	525	525
TACOMA PICKUP—V6—Truck Equipment Schedule T2						
PreRunner Access	TU62N	20515	9250	9850	11250	14700
4-Cyl, 2.7 Liter	M		(475)	(475)	(625)	(625)

Body Type	VIN	List	Trade-In Good	Trade-In Very Good	Pvt-Party Good	Retail Excellent
TACOMA PICKUP—V6—Truck Equipment Schedule T2						
X-Runner Access	TU22N	23650	9750	10400	11800	15400
PreRunner Dbl 5'	JU62N	22240	8800	9325	10700	13650
PreRunner Dbl 6'	KU72N	22740	8700	9225	10600	13500
TACOMA PICKUP 4WD—V6—Truck Equipment Schedule T2						
Double Cab 5'	LU42N	22240	11600	12250	13850	17500
Double Cab 6'	MU52N	25815	11700	12350	13950	17600
TUNDRA—V6—Truck Equipment Schedule T2						
Long Bed	JU321	17360	3825	4200	4925	6725
TUNDRA—V8—Truck Equipment Schedule T2						
Work Truck Long	JT321	18995	4125	4525	5150	6875
SR5 Access Cab 4D	RT341	24700	6750	7325	8150	10700
Ltd Access Cab 4D	RT381	27640	6600	7150	8075	10700
SR5 Double Cab 4D	ET341	26685	8225	8900	9825	12850
Ltd Double Cab 4D	DT481	33640	11300	12150	13250	17250
4WD	4		1300	1300	1715	1715
V6, 4.0 Liter	T		(425)	(425)	(555)	(555)

Body Type	VIN	List	Trade-In Good	Trade-In Very Good	Pvt-Party Good	Retail Excellent
RAV4 4WD—4-Cyl.—Truck Equipment Schedule T1						
SUV 4D	BD33V	22345	6375	6825	7925	10250
Sport SUV 4D	BD32V	23920	7475	7975	9075	11650
Limited SUV 4D	BD31V	24600	8150	8675	9875	12700
Third Row Seat			225	225	295	295
2WD	Z		(650)	(650)	(815)	(815)
V6, 3.5 Liter	K		575	575	730	730
HIGHLANDER—V6—Truck Equipment Schedule T1						
SUV 4D	GP21A	26235	6300	6700	7850	9875
Limited SUV 4D	DP21A	31105	8525	8975	10300	12900
Third Row Seat			350	350	450	450
AWD	E,H		1050	1050	1350	1350
4-Cyl, 2.4 Liter	D		(450)	(450)	(585)	(585)
HIGHLANDER 4WD—V6—Truck Equipment Schedule T1						
Sport SUV 4D	HD21A	29840	8025	8475	9750	12250
Limited SUV 4D	DP21A	31105	8525	8975	10300	12900
Third Row Seat			350	350	455	455
2WD	D,G		(1050)	(1050)	(1370)	(1370)
4-Cyl, 2.4 Liter	D		(450)	(450)	(585)	(585)
HIGHLANDER 4WD—V6 Hybrid—Truck Equipment Sch T1						
SUV 4D	EW21A	34995	6625	7025	8450	10950
Limited SUV 4D	EW21A	39855	8325	8800	10450	13450
Third Row Seat			350	350	465	465
2WD	D,G		(1050)	(1050)	(1410)	(1410)
4RUNNER 4WD—V6—Truck Equipment Schedule T1						
SR5 Sport Util 4D	BU14R	30475	9350	9925	11100	13950
Sport SUV 4D	BU14R	32815	10150	10750	11950	15000
Limited Spt Util	BU17R	37190	10850	11500	12600	15700
Third Row Seat			225	225	295	295
2WD	Z		(1050)	(1050)	(1310)	(1310)
V8, 4.7 Liter	T		225	225	280	280
SEQUOIA—V8—Truck Equipment Schedule T1						
SR5 Spt Util 4D	ZT34A	33465	8075	8650	9525	12150
4WD	B,4		1050	1050	1280	1280
SEQUOIA 4WD—V8—Truck Equipment Schedule T1						
Limited Spt Util 4D	BT48A	45875	10550	11250	12450	15850
2WD			(1050)	(1050)	(1295)	(1295)
LAND CRUISER AWD—V8—Truck Equipment Schedule T3						
Sport Utility 4D	HT05J	56680	20800	21800	22900	27200
SIENNA—V6—Truck Equipment Schedule T1						
CE Minivan	ZA23C	24190	4775	5175	6325	8500
LE Minivan	ZA23C	25695	5275	5700	6875	9200
XLE Minivan	ZA22C	29990	8825	9400	10750	14000
XLE Limited	ZA22C	36445	10200	10850	12350	16150
AWD	B		500	500	665	665
TACOMA PICKUP—4-Cyl.—Truck Equipment Schedule T1						
Short Bed	NX22N	15325	5275	5675	6700	8825
4WD	P,4		1000	1000	1295	1295
TACOMA PICKUP—4-Cyl.—Truck Equipment Schedule T2						
PreRunner Short	NX62N	15215	5975	6400	7500	9850
TACOMA PICKUP 4WD—4-Cyl.—Truck Equipment Schedule T2						
Access Cab	UX42N	21660	9925	10550	12000	15600
2WD	T,2		(1125)	(1125)	(1430)	(1430)
V6, 4.0 Liter	U		475	475	610	610

TRUCKS & VANS

Body Type	VIN	List	Trade-In Good	Very Good	Pvt-Party Good	Retail Excellent
TACOMA PICKUP—V6—Truck Equipment Schedule T1						
PreRunner Access	TU62N	20920	10450	11100	12550	16300
4-Cyl, 2.7 Liter	X		(600)	(600)	(765)	(765)
TACOMA PICKUP—V6—Truck Equipment Schedule T2						
X-Runner Access	TU22N	24110	11050	11700	13300	17200
PreRunner Dbl 5'	JU62N	22605	11000	11600	12750	15700
PreRunner Dbl 6'	KU72N	23105	10900	11500	12700	15600
TACOMA PICKUP 4WD—V6—Truck Equipment Schedule T1						
Double Cab 5'	LU42N	25760	13750	14450	15850	19450
TACOMA PICKUP 4WD—V6—Truck Equipment Schedule T2						
Double Cab 6'	MU52N	26180	13400	14100	15450	19000
TUNDRA—V6—Truck Equipment Schedule T1						
Long Bed	JU321	17640	4600	5025	5750	7675
TUNDRA—V8—Truck Equipment Schedule T1						
SR5 Access Cab 4D	RT341	24957	7675	8300	9375	12350
4WD	B,4		1600	1600	2050	2050
V6, 4.0 Liter	U		(450)	(450)	(575)	(575)
TUNDRA—V8—Truck Equipment Schedule T2						
Work Truck Long	JT321	19195	4725	5175	6075	8100
Ltd Access Cab 4D	RT381	27820	7425	8025	9100	12000
SR5 Double Cab 4D	ET341	27185	9075	9750	10950	14350
Darrell Waltrip Ed	ET341	30260	9225	9925	11100	14550
4WD	4		1600	1600	2070	2070
TUNDRA 4WD—V8—Truck Equipment Schedule T1						
Ltd Double Cab 4D	DT481	34220	12250	13150	14650	19050
2WD	E,3		(2075)	(2075)	(2630)	(2630)

Body Type	VIN	List	Trade-In Good	Very Good	Pvt-Party Good	Retail Excellent
RAV4 4WD—4-Cyl.—Truck Equipment Schedule T2						
SUV 4D	BD33V	22855	7125	7600	8700	10150
Sport SUV 4D	BD32V	24470	8225	8725	9900	12550
Limited SUV 4D	BD31V	25110	8825	9350	10650	13500
Third Row Seat			250	250	305	305
2WD	Z		(700)	(700)	(860)	(860)
V6, 3.5 Liter	K		625	625	765	765
FJ CRUISER 4WD—V6—Truck Equipment Schedule T1						
Sport Utility 2D	BU11F	24150	13800	14550	15350	18000
TRD Special Edition			1125	1125	1275	1275
2WD	Z		(1150)	(1150)	(1300)	(1300)
HIGHLANDER—V6—Truck Equipment Schedule T1						
SUV 4D	GP21A	26585	7725	8150	9450	11850
Limited SUV 4D	DP21A	31455	10100	10600	12150	15250
Third Row Seat			375	375	495	495
AWD	E		1125	1125	1490	1490
4-Cyl, 2.4 Liter	4		(475)	(475)	(625)	(625)
HIGHLANDER 4WD—V6—Truck Equipment Schedule T1						
Sport SUV 4D	HD21A	30190	9550	10050	11600	14500
Third Row Seat			375	375	495	495
2WD	D,G		(1150)	(1150)	(1500)	(1500)
HIGHLANDER 4WD—V6 Hybrid—Truck Equipment Schedule T1						
Sport Utility 4D	EW21A	34495	8725	9200	10550	13150
Limited Utility 4D	EW21A	36615	10150	10650	12200	15200
Third Row Seat			375	375	480	480
2WD	D,G		(1150)	(1150)	(1460)	(1460)
4RUNNER 4WD—V6—Truck Equipment Schedule T1						
SR5 Sport Util 4D	BU14R	30515	11300	11950	12950	15900
Sport SUV 4D	BU14R	32855	11700	12350	13500	16600
Limited Spt Util	BU17R	37230	12800	13500	14600	17950
Third Row Seat			250	250	300	300
2WD	Z		(1150)	(1150)	(1360)	(1360)
V8, 4.7 Liter	T		250	250	285	285
SEQUOIA—V8—Truck Equipment Schedule T1						
SR5 Spt Util 4D	ZT34A	33805	9775	10400	11450	14400
4WD	B,4		1125	1125	1360	1360
SEQUOIA 4WD—V8—Truck Equipment Schedule T1						
Limited Spt Util 4D	BT48A	46265	12800	13600	14800	18500
2WD	Z		(1150)	(1150)	(1365)	(1365)
LAND CRUISER AWD—V8—Truck Equipment Schedule T3						
Sport Utility 4D	HT05J	56820	23500	24500	25500	29900
SIENNA—V6—Truck Equipment Schedule T1						
CE Minivan	ZK23C	24800	5800	6225	7175	9350
LE Minivan	ZK23C	26325	6275	6725	7775	10100
XLE Minivan	ZK23C	30770	9875	10450	11700	15000

Body Type	VIN	List	Trade-In Good	Very Good	Pvt-Party Good	Retail Excellent
XLE Limited	ZK22C	36110	11150	11800	13200	16850
AWD	B	....	525	525	685	685
TACOMA PICKUP—4-Cyl.—Truck Equipment Schedule T1						
Short Bed	NX22N	15665	5950	6375	7450	9700
4WD	P4	....	1100	1100	1405	1405
TACOMA PICKUP—4-Cyl.—Truck Equipment Schedule T2						
PreRunner Short	NX62N	15555	6550	7000	8200	10650
TACOMA PICKUP 4WD—4-Cyl.—Truck Equipment Schedule T2						
Access Cab	TX22N	21960	10850	11500	13050	16750
2WD	T	....	(1625)	(1625)	(2065)	(2065)
V6, 4.0 Liter	U	....	550	550	700	700
TACOMA PICKUP—V6—Truck Equipment Schedule T1						
PreRunner Access	TX62N	21220	11400	12100	13700	17600
4-Cyl, 2.7 Liter	X	....	(700)	(700)	(890)	(890)
TACOMA PICKUP—V6—Truck Equipment Schedule T2						
X-Runner Access	TU22N	24450	11900	12600	14250	18300
PreRunner Dbl 5'	JU62N	22945	12100	12750	13950	16900
PreRunner Dbl 6'	KU72N	23445	12050	12650	13750	16650
TACOMA PICKUP 4WD—V6—Truck Equipment Schedule T1						
Double Cab 5'	LU42N	26100	15200	15950	17200	20700
TACOMA PICKUP 4WD—V6—Truck Equipment Schedule T2						
Double Cab 6'	MU52N	26520	14950	15700	16950	20500
TUNDRA PICKUP—V8—Equipment Schedule T1						
Short Bed	JT521	24075	8825	9450	10300	13000
Long Bed	LT521	24485	8625	9250	10050	12750
SR5 Double 6 1/2'	RT541	27495	11650	12450	13450	16950
SR5 Double 8'	ST541	27825	11150	11950	12900	16300
SR5 CrewMax 4D	ET541	42535	14200	15100	16250	20400
4WD	K	....	2000	2000	2405	2405
V6, 4.0 Liter	U	....	(475)	(475)	(570)	(570)
V8, 4.7 Liter	T	....	(475)	(475)	(570)	(570)
TUNDRA PICKUP 4WD—V8—Equipment Schedule T1						
Ltd Double Cab 4D	DV581	39235	18650	19800	20800	25900
Limited CrewMax	BV581	38185	21100	22400	23100	28500
2WD	E	....	(2250)	(2250)	(2610)	(2610)
V8, 4.7 Liter	T	....	(475)	(475)	(555)	(555)

2008 TOYOTA—(3,5orJ)T(B,D,EorM)(BD33V)—8—#

Body Type	VIN	List	Trade-In Good	Very Good	Pvt-Party Good	Retail Excellent
RAV4 4WD—4-Cyl.—Truck Equipment Schedule T2						
SUV 4D	BD33V	23185	8225	8700	9775	12100
Sport SUV 4D	BD32V	24760	9050	9575	10650	13150
Limited SUV 4D	BD31V	25440	9750	10300	11450	14150
Third Row Seat			250	250	305	305
2WD	Z	....	(750)	(750)	(920)	(920)
V6, 3.5 Liter	K	....	675	675	815	815
FJ CRUISER 4WD—V6—Truck Equipment Schedule T1						
Sport Utility 2D	BU11F	24820	15200	15900	16600	19200
2WD		....	(1225)	(1225)	(1380)	(1380)
HIGHLANDER AWD—V6—Truck Equipment Schedule T1						
SUV 4D	ES41A	29435	12000	12550	14000	16950
Sport SUV 4D	ES43A	32085	13400	14000	15800	19350
Limited SUV 4D	ES42A	34835	15300	16000	17900	21900
Third Row Seat			400	400	495	495
2WD	D	....	(1225)	(1225)	(1515)	(1515)
HIGHLANDER AWD—V6 Hybrid—Truck Equipment Schedule T1						
SUV 4D	EW41A	34385	13150	13750	15400	18700
Limited SUV 4D	EW44A	40635	15700	16400	18150	22000
Third Row Seat			400	400	495	495
4RUNNER 4WD—V6—Truck Equipment Schedule T1						
SR5 SUV 4D	BU14R	30975	13150	13800	14900	17850
Sport SUV 4D	BU14R	31010	13750	14450	15500	18600
Limited SUV 4D	BU17R	35385	14750	15450	16600	19950
Third Row Seat			250	250	285	285
2WD		....	(1225)	(1225)	(1395)	(1395)
V8, 4.7 Liter	T	....	250	250	285	285
SEQUOIA 4WD—V8—Truck Equipment Schedule T1						
SR5 Spt Util 4D	BT44A	39185	16200	17050	17800	21200
Limited Spt Util 4D	BY68A	49135	19150	20200	20900	24900
Platinum Spt Util	BY67A	56285	24400	25600	26100	30900
2WD	Z	....	(1225)	(1225)	(1425)	(1425)
LAND CRUISER 4WD—V8—Truck Equipment Schedule T3						
Sport Utility 4D	HY05J	63885	34400	35700	36000	40900

TRUCKS & VANS

Body Type	VIN	List	Trade-In Good	Very Good	Pvt-Party Good	Retail Excellent
SIENNA—V6—Truck Equipment Schedule T1						
CE Minivan	ZK23C	25025	7000	7450	8475	10750
LE Minivan	ZK23C	26550	7800	8300	9350	11850
XLE Minivan	ZK22C	30210	11300	11950	13250	16650
XLE Limited	ZK22C	36150	12650	13350	14700	18450
AWD	B		550	550	690	690
TACOMA PICKUP—4-Cyl.—Truck Equipment Schedule T1						
Short Bed	NX15980		6725	7175	8250	10500
4WD	P.4		1300	1300	1645	1645
TACOMA PICKUP—4-Cyl.—Truck Equipment Schedule T1						
PreRunner Short	NX22N	18835	7275	7750	8925	11350
TACOMA PICKUP 4WD—4-Cyl.—Truck Equipment Schedule T2						
Access Cab	UX42N	22240	12050	12700	14250	18000
2WD	T.2		(1650)	(1650)	(2075)	(2075)
V6, 4.0 Liter	U		600	600	755	755
TACOMA PICKUP—V6—Truck Equipment Schedule T1						
PreRunner Access	TU62N	21500	12750	13400	15000	18950
4-Cyl, 2.7 Liter	X		(800)	(800)	(1005)	(1005)
TACOMA PICKUP—V6—Truck Equipment Schedule T2						
X-Runner Access	TU22N	24750	12900	13600	15350	19350
PreRunner Dbl 5'	JU62N	23225	13600	14250	15450	18400
PreRunner Dbl 6'	KU72N	23725	13400	14050	15200	18150
TACOMA PICKUP 4WD—V6—Truck Equipment Schedule T1						
Double Cab 5'	LU42N	26415	16550	17300	18500	22000
TACOMA PICKUP 4WD—V6—Truck Equipment Schedule T2						
Double Cab 6'	MU52N	26800	16200	16950	18200	21600
TUNDRA PICKUP—V8—Truck Equipment Schedule T1						
Short Bed	JT521	24115	9500	10100	10900	13350
Long Bed	LT521	24445	9250	9825	10650	13050
Double 6 1/2'	RU541	25545	11500	12200	13050	15950
SR5 Double 6 1/2'	RT541	27535	12700	13450	14300	17450
SR5 Double 8'	ST541	27865	12100	12800	13700	16700
SR5 CrewMax 4D	ET541	30360	15350	16250	17200	20900
4WD	K,M		2200	2200	2625	2625
V6, 4.0 Liter	U		(500)	(500)	(595)	(595)
V8, 4.7 Liter	T		(500)	(500)	(595)	(595)
TUNDRA PICKUP 4WD—V8—Truck Equipment Schedule T1						
Double 8'	CV541	29910	14050	14850	15800	19200
Ltd Double Cab 4D	BV581	39570	20800	21900	22800	27600
CrewMax 4D	DV541	32735	18950	20000	20800	25000
Limited CrewMax	DV581	42870	22900	24100	25000	30300
2WD	E		(2450)	(2450)	(2855)	(2855)
V8, 4.7 Liter	T		(500)	(500)	(585)	(585)

2009 TOYOTA—(3,5orJ)T(B,D,EorM)(BF33V)—9—#

Body Type	VIN	List	Trade-In Good	Very Good	Pvt-Party Good	Retail Excellent
RAV4 4WD—4-Cyl.—Truck Equipment Schedule T1						
SUV 4D	BF33V	23585	9700	10200	11300	13600
Sport SUV 4D	BF32V	25610	10800	11350	12450	15000
Limited SUV 4D	BF31V	25840	11850	12450	13650	16400
Third Row Seat			300	300	355	355
2WD	Z		(875)	(875)	(1030)	(1030)
V6, 3.5 Liter	K		700	700	840	840
FJ CRUISER 4WD—V6—Truck Equipment Schedule T1						
Sport Utility 2D	BU11F	25710	17650	18400	19000	21600
2WD	Z		(1300)	(1300)	(1445)	(1445)
VENZA—4-Cyl.—Truck Equipment Schedule T1						
Sport Utility 4D	ZE11A	28145	11700	12350	13200	15800
AWD			650	650	755	755
V6, 3.5 Liter	K		700	700	830	830
HIGHLANDER AWD—V6—Truck Equipment Schedule T1						
SUV 4D	ES41A	29795	14150	14800	15950	18750
Sport SUV 4D	ES43A	32195	15800	16500	17900	21200
Limited SUV 4D	ES42A	35265	17900	18600	20200	23900
Third Row Seat			475	475	560	560
2WD	D		(1300)	(1300)	(1545)	(1545)
4-Cyl, 2.7 Liter			(600)	(600)	(710)	(710)
HIGHLANDER AWD—V6 Hybrid—Truck Equipment Schedule T1						
SUV 4D	EW41A	35445	15600	16300	17750	21000
Limited SUV 4D	EW44A	41765	18750	19500	21200	25100
Third Row Seat			475	475	565	565
4RUNNER 4WD—V6—Truck Equipment Schedule T1						
SR5 SUV 4D	BU14R	31660	16200	16900	17800	20700
Sport SUV 4D	BU14R	33970	16850	17600	18550	21600

2009 TOYOTA

Body Type	VIN	List	Trade-In Good	Trade-In Very Good	Pvt-Party Good	Retail Excellent
Limited SUV 4D	BU17R	38345	17850	18650	19600	22900
Third Row Seat			300	300	330	330
2WD	Z		(1300)	(1300)	(1445)	(1445)
V8, 4.7 Liter	T		300	300	330	330
SEQUOIA 4WD—V8—Truck Equipment Schedule T1						
SR5 Spt Util 4D	BT44A	39445	17450	18300	19200	22700
Limited Spt Util 4D	BY68A	49395	22100	23100	23800	27900
Platinum Spt Util	BY67A	56545	26500	27700	28400	33200
2WD	Z		(1300)	(1300)	(1505)	(1505)
LAND CRUISER 4WD—V8—Truck Equipment Schedule T3						
Sport Utility 4D	HY05J		38200	39600	39900	45100
SIENNA—V6—Truck Equipment Schedule T1						
CE Minivan	ZK23C	25225	8375	8875	9875	12250
LE Minivan	ZK23C	26750	9125	9625	10700	13250
XLE Minivan	ZK22C	30410	13400	14100	15450	19000
XLE Limited	ZK22C	36350	15300	16050	17500	21400
AWD	B		650	650	795	795
TACOMA PICKUP—4-Cyl.—Truck Equipment Schedule T1						
Short Bed	NX22N	16870	8200	8675	9750	12050
4WD	F4		1500	1500	1805	1805
TACOMA PICKUP 4WD—4-Cyl.—Truck Equipment Schedule T2						
PreRunner Short	NX62N	16800	8875	9375	10550	13000
TACOMA PICKUP 4WD—4-Cyl.—Truck Equipment Schedule T2						
Access Cab	UX42N	23840	13000	13700	15150	18600
2WD	T.2		(2200)	(2200)	(2630)	(2630)
V6, 4.0 Liter	U		700	700	835	835
TACOMA PICKUP—V6—Truck Equipment Schedule T1						
PreRunner Access	TX62N	23100	13800	14500	16000	19650
4-Cyl, 2.7 Liter	X		(900)	(900)	(1075)	(1075)
TACOMA PICKUP—V6—Truck Equipment Schedule T2						
X-Runner Access	TU22N	26030	14350	15100	16600	20300
PreRunner Dbl 5'	JU62N	24245	15500	16200	17500	20600
PreRunner Dbl 6'	KU72N	24745	15300	16000	17300	20400
TACOMA PICKUP 4WD—V6—Truck Equipment Schedule T1						
Double Cab 5'	LU42N	27375	18450	19200	20600	24300
TACOMA PICKUP 4WD—V6—Truck Equipment Schedule T2						
Double Cab 6'	MU52N	27820	18050	18800	20200	23800
TUNDRA PICKUP—V8—Truck Equipment Schedule T1						
Short Bed	JT521	24375	10600	11200	12150	14700
Long Bed	LT521	24705	10400	11000	11950	14450
Double 6 1/2'	RU541	25835	12850	13550	14600	17650
SR5 Double 6 1/2'	RT541	27795	14050	14750	15950	19250
SR5 CrewMax 4D	EV541	30620	18950	19900	21200	25400
4WD	M		2600	2600	3075	3075
V6, 4.0 Liter	U		(575)	(575)	(680)	(680)
V8, 4.7 Liter	T		(500)	(500)	(590)	(590)
TUNDRA PICKUP 4WD—V8—Truck Equipment Schedule T1						
Double 8'	CV541	30240	15700	16450	17700	21300
Ltd Double Cab 4D	BV581	39870	22600	23700	24800	29600
CrewMax 541	DV541	35085	20600	21600	22600	26900
Limited CrewMax	DV581	42405	25700	26900	28000	33200
2WD	E		(2650)	(2650)	(3060)	(3060)
V8, 4.7 Liter	T		(500)	(500)	(590)	(590)

2010 TOYOTA—(3,4,5orJ)T(D,E,ForM)(BF4DV)–A–#

Body Type	VIN	List	Trade-In Good	Trade-In Very Good	Pvt-Party Good	Retail Excellent
RAV4 4WD—4-Cyl.—Truck Equipment Schedule T2						
SUV 4D	BF4DV	23700	10900	11400	12600	15050
Sport SUV 4D	RF4DV	25400	12150	12700	13950	16600
Limited SUV 4D	DF4DV	26680	13050	13600	14900	17700
Third Row Seat			350	350	400	400
2WD	Z		(1000)	(1000)	(1145)	(1145)
V6, 3.5 Liter	K		750	750	865	865
FJ CRUISER 4WD—V6—Truck Equipment Schedule T1						
Sport Utility 2D	BU4BF	26070	20600	21500	21900	24600
2WD	Z		(1375)	(1375)	(1510)	(1510)
X-SP Pkg			625	625	680	680
Trail Team Special Ed			1150	1150	1255	1255
VENZA—4-Cyl.—Truck Equipment Schedule T1						
Sport Utility 4D	ZE11A	28475	12850	13450	14500	17050
AWD	B		725	725	845	845
V6, 3.5 Liter	K		750	750	885	885
HIGHLANDER AWD—V6—Truck Equipment Schedule T1						
SUV 4D	BK3EH	29850	15150	15750	17000	19800

TRUCKS & VANS

0415   **SEE BACK PAGES FOR TRUCK EQUIPMENT**   569

Body Type	VIN	List	Trade-In Good	Very Good	Pvt-Party Good	Retail Excellent
Sport SUV 4D	EK3EH	32250	17150	17850	19150	22400
SE SUV 4D	BK3EH	34730	18050	18750	20100	23400
Limited SUV 4D	DK3EH	35320	20200	21000	22300	26000
Third Row Seat			550	550	630	630
2WD	X,Y,Z		(1375)	(1375)	(1585)	(1585)
4-Cyl, 2.7 Liter	A		(700)	(700)	(800)	(800)
HIGHLANDER AWD—V6 Hybrid—Truck Equipment Schedule T1						
SUV 4D	BW3EH	35500	17600	18300	19650	23000
Limited SUV 4D	JW3EH	41820	21800	22600	24100	28100
Third Row Seat			550	550	640	640
4RUNNER 4WD—V6—Truck Equipment Schedule T1						
SR5 Spt Util 4D	BU5JR	43180	21300	22200	22800	25900
Trail Sport Util	BU5JR	36500	22500	23400	24000	27200
Limited Spt Util	BU5JR	40600	23700	24600	25200	28600
Third Row Seat			350	350	380	380
2WD	Z		(1375)	(1375)	(1510)	(1510)
4-Cyl, 2.7 Liter	X		(700)	(700)	(760)	(760)
SEQUOIA 4WD—V8—Truck Equipment Schedule T1						
SR5 Spt Util 4D	BY5G1	43180	21100	22100	22700	26200
Limited Spt Util	JY5G1	52665	26100	27200	27800	32000
Platinum Spt Util	DY5G1	59705	30100	31400	31900	36600
2WD			(1375)	(1375)	(1555)	(1555)
LAND CRUISER 4WD—V8—Truck Equipment Schedule T3						
Sport Utility 4D	HY7AJ	66770	43600	45100	45200	50400
SIENNA—V6—Truck Equipment Schedule T1						
CE Minivan	KK4CC	25340	10050	10600	11750	14400
LE Minivan	KK4CC	26865	10850	11400	12650	15450
XLE Minivan	YK4CC	30525	15900	16650	18100	21900
XLE Limited	YK4CC	36465	17650	18450	19850	23900
AWD	J		725	725	875	875
TACOMA PICKUP—4-Cyl.—Truck Equipment Schedule T1						
Short Bed	NX4CN	16880	9450	9950	11050	13400
4WD	U,E		1700	1700	1975	1975
TACOMA PICKUP—4-Cyl.—Truck Equipment Schedule T2						
PreRunner Short	NX4GN	16855	10300	10850	11950	14500
TACOMA PICKUP 4WD—4-Cyl.—Truck Equipment Schedule T2						
Access Cab	UX4EN	23840	14550	15250	16650	20100
2WD	T,C		(2200)	(2200)	(2550)	(2550)
V6, 4.0 Liter	U		800	800	925	925
TACOMA PICKUP—V6—Truck Equipment Schedule T1						
PreRunner Access	TU4GN	23100	15050	15800	17250	20800
4-Cyl, 2.7 Liter	X		(1000)	(1000)	(1160)	(1160)
TACOMA PICKUP—V6—Truck Equipment Schedule T2						
X-Runner Access	TU4CN	26085	15700	16450	17950	21700
PreRunner Dbl 5'	JU4GN	24800	17800	18500	19600	22500
PreRunner Dbl 6'	KU4HN	24800	17400	18050	19150	22000
TACOMA PICKUP 4WD—V6—Truck Equipment Schedule T1						
Double Cab 5'	LJ4EN	27385	20700	21500	22600	25900
TACOMA PICKUP 4WD—V6—Truck Equipment Schedule T2						
Double Cab 6'	LX4CN	27875	19900	20600	21700	24900
TUNDRA PICKUP—V8—Truck Equipment Schedule T1						
Short Bed	JM5F1	25155	13150	13800	14850	17500
Long Bed	LM5F1	25485	12850	13500	14550	17150
Double Cab 6 1/2'	RM5F1	27890	15400	16100	17200	20200
4WD	M		2800	2800	3215	3215
V6, 4.0 Liter	U		(650)	(650)	(745)	(745)
V8, 4.6 Liter	M		(500)	(500)	(575)	(575)
TUNDRA PICKUP 4WD—V8—Truck Equipment Schedule T1						
Double Cab 2'	CY5F1	30800	19250	20100	21300	25000
Ltd Double Cab 4D	BY5F1	40430	25200	26300	27300	31700
CrewMax 4D 5 1/2'	DY5F1	33625	22200	23200	24100	28000
Limited 4D 5 1/2'	HY5F1	42965	27200	28300	29300	34200
2WD	E		(2825)	(2825)	(3180)	(3180)
V8, 4.6 Liter	M		(500)	(500)	(565)	(565)

2011 TOYOTA—(2,3,4,5orJ)T(3,D,E,ForM)(BF4DV)-B-#

Body Type	VIN	List	Trade-In Good	Very Good	Pvt-Party Good	Retail Excellent
RAV4 4WD—4-Cyl.—Truck Equipment Schedule T2						
SUV 4D	BF4DV	24135	12600	13150	14400	16950
Sport SUV 4D	RF4DV	25835	13950	14550	15900	18650
Limited SUV 4D	DF4DV	27115	15000	15600	17050	20000
Third Row Seat			400	400	465	465
2WD	Z,K		(1100)	(1100)	(1280)	(1280)
V6, 3.5 Liter	K		800	800	930	930

Body Type	VIN	List	Trade-In Good	Very Good	Pvt-Party Good	Retail Excellent
FJ CRUISER 4WD—V6—Truck Equipment Schedule T1						
Sport Utility 2D	BU4BF	27690	22400	23200	23700	26400
2WD	Z		(1475)	(1475)	(1605)	(1605)
VENZA—4-Cyl.—Truck Equipment Schedule T1						
Sport Utility 4D	BA3BB	28685	13900	14500	15550	18050
AWD	B		800	800	920	920
V6, 3.5 Liter	C		800	800	920	920
HIGHLANDER AWD—V6—Truck Equipment Schedule T1						
Sport Utility 4D	BK3EH	30805	18900	19650	20600	23500
SE Spt Util 4D	BK3EH	35410	20500	21300	22300	25400
Limited Spt Util	DK3EH	37155	23600	24500	25500	29100
Third Row Seat			600	600	670	670
2WD	Y,Z		(1475)	(1475)	(1645)	(1645)
4-Cyl, 2.7 Liter	A		(800)	(800)	(895)	(895)
HIGHLANDER AWD—V6 Hybrid—Truck Equipment Schedule T1						
Sport Utility 4D	BC3EH	38100	22500	23300	24900	29100
Limited Spt Util	DC3EH	43755	26800	27800	29400	34000
Third Row Seat			600	600	680	680
4RUNNER 4WD—V6—Truck Equipment Schedule T1						
SR5 Sport Util 4D	BU5J2	31725	22300	23100	23800	26800
Trail Sport Util	BU5JR	36510	24300	25200	25900	29200
Limited Sport Util	BU5JR	40610	24700	25600	26400	29700
Third Row Seat			400	400	435	435
2WD	Z		(1475)	(1475)	(1600)	(1600)
SEQUOIA 4WD—V8—Truck Equipment Schedule T1						
SR5 Spt Util 4D	BY5G1	44405	25600	26600	27100	30700
Limited Spt Util	JY5G1	53890	31900	33200	33700	38200
Platinum Spt Util	DY5G1	60930	34900	36300	36700	41500
2WD	Z		(1475)	(1475)	(1635)	(1635)
V8, 4.6 Liter	M		400	400	445	445
LAND CRUISER 4WD—V8—Truck Equipment Schedule T3						
Sport Utility 4D	HY7AJ	68180	47100	48700	48800	54200
SIENNA—4-Cyl.—Truck Equipment Schedule T1						
Minivan 4D	KA3DC	25870	12800	13450	14400	17050
SIENNA—V6—Truck Equipment Schedule T1						
CE Minivan 4D	ZK3DC	26310	13700	14350	15350	18100
SE Minivan 4D	XK3DC	31360	19050	19850	21000	24800
LE Minivan 4D	KK3DC	29710	14600	15300	16400	19400
XLE Minivan 4D	YK3DC	32975	19150	19950	21300	25200
Limited Minivan	YK3DC	39310	21700	22600	23700	27800
AWD	J		800	800	940	940
4-Cyl, 2.7 Liter	A		(975)	(975)	(1155)	(1155)
TACOMA PICKUP—4-Cyl.—Truck Equipment Schedule T1						
Short Bed	NX4CN	18075	11000	11550	12750	15250
4WD	E,P		1900	1900	2165	2165
TACOMA PICKUP—4-Cyl.—Truck Equipment Schedule T2						
PreRunner Dbl 5'	JU4GN	24760	19750	20500	21300	23900
4WD	E,P		1900	1900	2165	2165
TACOMA PICKUP 4WD—4-Cyl.—Truck Equipment Schedule T2						
Access Cab	UX4EN	24300	16300	17050	18550	22200
2WD	C,T		(2800)	(2800)	(3155)	(3155)
V6, 4.0 Liter	U		900	900	1015	1015
TACOMA PICKUP 4WD—V6—Truck Equipment Schedule T2						
Double Cab 5'	LU4EN	26735	22700	23500	24300	27300
2WD	C,J		(1900)	(1900)	(2065)	(2065)
4-Cyl, 2.7 Liter	X		(1150)	(1150)	(1245)	(1245)
TACOMA PICKUP—V6—Truck Equipment Schedule T2						
PreRunner Access	TU4GN	23560	16800	17550	19100	22800
4-Cyl, 2.7 Liter	X		(1150)	(1150)	(1290)	(1290)
TACOMA PICKUP—V6—Truck Equipment Schedule T2						
X-Runner Access	TU4CN	26535	17600	18400	19950	23800
PreRunner Dbl 6'	KU4HN	25260	18950	19650	20400	23000
TACOMA PICKUP 4WD—V6—Truck Equipment Schedule T2						
Double Cab 6'	MU4FN	28335	21900	22700	23400	26300
TUNDRA PICKUP—V8—Truck Equipment Schedule T1						
Short Bed	JM5F1	26110	15350	16000	17000	19650
Long Bed	LY5F1	27385	15150	15800	16800	19450
Double Cab 6 1/2'	RY5F1	28640	18100	18800	19850	22900
4WD	K		3000	3000	3375	3375
V6, 4.0 Liter	U		(725)	(725)	(815)	(815)
V8, 4.6 Liter	M		(500)	(500)	(560)	(560)
TUNDRA PICKUP 4WD—V8—Truck Equipment Schedule T1						
Double Cab 8'	CY5F1	31525	21500	22300	23300	26900

TRUCKS & VANS

Body Type	VIN	List	Trade-In Good	Very Good	Pvt-Party Good	Retail Excellent
Limited Dbl Cab	BY5F1	40730	27400	28500	29500	33900
CrewMax 4D	DY5F1	34350	24600	25500	26400	30100
Limited CrewMax	HY5F1	43265	29000	30100	31200	35800
2WD	F		(3025)	(3025)	(3360)	(3360)
V8, 4.6 Liter	M		(500)	(500)	(550)	(550)

2012 TOYOTA—(3,4,5orJ)T(3,D,E,ForM)(BF4DV)–C–#

Body Type	VIN	List	Trade-In Good	Very Good	Pvt-Party Good	Retail Excellent
RAV4 4WD—4-Cyl.—Truck Equipment Schedule T2						
SUV 4D	BF4DV	24860	13950	14500	15950	18600
Sport SUV 4D	RF4DV	26560	16400	17000	18500	21500
Limited SUV 4D	DF4DV	27530	17050	17650	19200	22400
Third Row Seat			425	425	495	495
2WD	K,Z		(1500)	(1500)	(1745)	(1745)
V6, 3.5 Liter	K		800	800	930	930
RAV4–AC—Equipment Schedule T2						
EV SUV 4D	YL4DV	50610	22400	23100	25000	29100
FJ CRUISER 4WD—V6—Truck Equipment Schedule T1						
Sport Utility 2D	BU4BF	28390	23900	24800	25300	28000
2WD	Z		(1550)	(1550)	(1675)	(1675)
VENZA—4-Cyl.—Truck Equipment Schedule T1						
LE Wagon 4D	ZA3BB	29635	14800	15400	16650	19350
XLE Wagon 4D	ZA3BB	31985	16650	17300	18600	21600
AWD	B		875	875	1005	1005
V6, 3.5 Liter	K		800	800	920	920
HIGHLANDER AWD—V6—Truck Equipment Schedule T1						
Sport Utility 4D	BK3EH	31505	20800	21600	22500	25400
SE Spt Util 4D	BK3EH	36110	22600	23500	24300	27400
Limited Spt Util	DK3EH	37855	25600	26600	27500	31100
2WD	Y,Z		(1550)	(1550)	(1710)	(1710)
4-Cyl, 2.7 Liter	A		(900)	(900)	(990)	(990)
HIGHLANDER AWD—V6 Hybrid—Truck Equipment Schedule T1						
Sport Utility 4D	DC3EH	38950	24500	25400	26400	29800
Limited Spt Util	DC3EH	44605	28400	29400	30800	35100
4RUNNER 4WD—V6—Truck Equipment Schedule T1						
SR5 Sport Util 4D	BU5JR	33640	23600	24400	25300	28400
Trail Sport Util	BU5JR	37565	25700	26500	27400	30800
Limited Sport Util	BU5JR	41440	27400	28300	29100	32700
2WD			(1550)	(1550)	(1700)	(1700)
SEQUOIA 4WD—V8—Truck Equipment Schedule T1						
SR5 Spt Util 4D	BY5G1	45765	27400	28400	29100	32900
Limited Spt Util	JY5G1	55250	33500	34800	35500	40100
Platinum Spt Util	DY5G1	62790	37000	38300	38900	43700
2WD	Z		(1550)	(1550)	(1735)	(1735)
V8, 4.6 Liter	M		500	500	560	560
SIENNA—4-Cyl.—Truck Equipment Schedule T1						
Minivan 4D	KA3DC	25870	14700	15350	16350	19150
V6, 3.5 Liter	K		575	575	670	670
SIENNA—V6—Truck Equipment Schedule T1						
LE Minivan 4D	KK3DC	30510	16350	17050	18100	21100
SE Minivan 4D	XK3DC	34250	21000	21900	22900	26700
XLE Minivan 4D	YK3DC	36967	21300	22200	23400	27300
Limited Minivan	YK3DC	40110	23700	24700	25900	30100
AWD	J		875	875	1040	1040
4-Cyl, 2.7 Liter	K		(1025)	(1025)	(1230)	(1230)
TACOMA PICKUP—4-Cyl.—Truck Equipment Schedule T1						
Pickup 2D 6'	NX4CN	18585	12150	12700	13700	16150
4WD	E,P		2200	2200	2505	2505
TACOMA PICKUP 4WD—4-Cyl.—Truck Equipment Schedule T2						
Access Cab 4D 6'	UX4EN	24310	17650	18400	19600	23000
2WD	C,T		(3000)	(3000)	(3410)	(3410)
V6, 4.0 Liter	U		1000	1000	1135	1135
TACOMA PICKUP—V6—Truck Equipment Schedule T1						
PreRunner Access	TU4GN	23570	18550	19350	20600	24100
4-Cyl, 2.7 Liter	X		(1300)	(1300)	(1475)	(1475)
TACOMA PICKUP—V6—Truck Equipment Schedule T2						
X-Runner Access	TU4CN	27190	20200	21100	22300	26100
PreRunner Dbl 6'	TU4GN	25570	20400	21100	21900	24400
TACOMA PICKUP—V6—Truck Equipment Schedule T2						
PreRunner Dbl 5'	JU4GN	25070	21200	21900	22600	25300
4-Cyl, 2.7 Liter	X		(1300)	(1300)	(1415)	(1415)
TACOMA PICKUP 4WD—V6—Truck Equipment Schedule T1						
Double Cab 4D 5'	LU4EN	28645	24400	25200	26000	29000

Body Type	VIN	List	Trade-In Good	Trade-In Very Good	Pvt-Party Good	Retail Excellent
TACOMA PICKUP 4WD—V6—Truck Equipment Schedule T2						
Double Cab 4D 6'	MU4FN	28645	**23700**	**24500**	**25200**	**28100**
TUNDRA PICKUP—V8—Truck Equipment Schedule T1						
Short Bed	JM5F1	27340	**17050**	**17700**	**18700**	**21300**
Long Bed	LY5F1	28615	**16850**	**17500**	**18500**	**21100**
Double Cab 6 1/2'	RM5F1	29490	**19150**	**19850**	**20900**	**23800**
SR5			**150**	**150**	**165**	**165**
Sport Appearance			**150**	**150**	**165**	**165**
TRD Off-Road Pkg			**150**	**150**	**165**	**165**
4WD	C,U		**3200**	**3200**	**3555**	**3555**
V6, 4.0 Liter	U		**(800)**	**(800)**	**(890)**	**(890)**
V8, 4.6 Liter	M		**(500)**	**(500)**	**(555)**	**(555)**
TUNDRA PICKUP 4WD—V8—Truck Equipment Schedule T1						
Double Cab 8'	CY5F1	32365	**22400**	**23200**	**24200**	**27600**
Limited Dbl Cab	BY5F1	41620	**29300**	**30300**	**31300**	**35400**
CrewMax 4D	DY5F1	35190	**26500**	**27400**	**28300**	**31900**
Limited CrewMax	HY5F1	44155	**31700**	**32800**	**33900**	**38300**
2WD	E		**(3200)**	**(3200)**	**(3505)**	**(3505)**
V8, 4.6 Liter	M		**(500)**	**(500)**	**(550)**	**(550)**

Body Type	VIN	List	Trade-In Good	Trade-In Very Good	Pvt-Party Good	Retail Excellent
RAV4 AWD—4-Cyl.—Truck Equipment Schedule T2						
LE SUV 4D	BFREV	25545	**16700**	**17300**	**18550**	**21100**
XLE SUV 4D	RFREV	26535	**17550**	**18150**	**19450**	**22200**
Limited SUV 4D	DFREV	29255	**19250**	**19900**	**21200**	**24200**
2WD	Z		**(1500)**	**(1500)**	**(1675)**	**(1675)**
RAV4—AC Electric—Truck Equipment Schedule T2						
EV SUV 4D	YL4DV	50645	**25400**	**26200**	**28000**	**32200**
FJ CRUISER 4WD—V6—Truck Equipment Schedule T1						
Sport Utility 2D	BU4BF	29315	**25000**	**25900**	**26400**	**29300**
2WD	Z		**(1625)**	**(1625)**	**(1760)**	**(1760)**
VENZA—4-Cyl.—Truck Equipment Schedule T1						
LE Wagon 4D	ZA3BB	28510	**15800**	**16350**	**17950**	**21000**
XLE Wagon 4D	ZA3BB	32170	**19100**	**19750**	**21200**	**24300**
AWD	B		**950**	**950**	**1115**	**1115**
V6, 3.5 Liter	K		**800**	**800**	**915**	**915**
VENZA—V6—Truck Equipment Schedule T1						
Limited Wagon 4D	ZK3BB	38230	**20700**	**21400**	**23000**	**26600**
AWD	B		**950**	**950**	**1085**	**1085**
HIGHLANDER AWD—V6—Truck Equipment Schedule T1						
Sport Utility 4D	BK3EH	32540	**22100**	**22900**	**24200**	**27700**
Plus Sport Util 4D	BK3EH	33995	**22900**	**23700**	**25000**	**28600**
SE Sport Utility	BK3EH	36705	**25600**	**26500**	**27900**	**31800**
Limited Sport Util	DK3EH	40095	**28100**	**29100**	**30300**	**34400**
2WD	Z		**(1625)**	**(1625)**	**(1850)**	**(1850)**
4-Cyl, 2.7 Liter	A		**(1000)**	**(1000)**	**(1130)**	**(1130)**
HIGHLANDER AWD—V6 Hybrid—Truck Equipment Schedule T1						
Sport Utility 4D	BC3EH	40815	**27800**	**28800**	**29700**	**33400**
Limited Spt Util	DC3EH	47015	**30400**	**31400**	**32400**	**36400**
4RUNNER 4WD—V6—Truck Equipment Schedule T1						
SR5 Sport Utility	BU5JR	34060	**24800**	**25700**	**26700**	**30000**
Trail Sport Utility	BU5JR	37850	**26900**	**27800**	**28700**	**32200**
Limited Sport Util	BU5JR	41725	**29200**	**30200**	**31200**	**34900**
2WD	Z		**(1625)**	**(1625)**	**(1815)**	**(1815)**
SEQUOIA 4WD—V8—Truck Equipment Schedule T1						
SR5 Sport Util 4D	BY5G1	46175	**30900**	**32000**	**32700**	**36600**
Limited Sport Util	JY5G1	55660	**37900**	**39200**	**39800**	**44600**
Platinum Spt Util	DY5G1	63565	**41300**	**42700**	**43100**	**48100**
2WD	Z		**(1625)**	**(1625)**	**(1810)**	**(1810)**
SIENNA—V6—Truck Equipment Schedule T1						
L Minivan 4D	ZK3DC	27280	**15800**	**16500**	**17500**	**20300**
LE Minivan 4D	KK3DC	30830	**17750**	**18550**	**19500**	**22600**
SE Minivan 4D	XK3DC	34420	**22400**	**23300**	**24300**	**28200**
XLE Minivan 4D	YK3DC	34205	**22700**	**23600**	**24800**	**28800**
Limited Minivan	YK3DC	40800	**25600**	**26600**	**27700**	**32000**
AWD	B		**950**	**950**	**1100**	**1100**
LAND CRUISER 4WD—V8—Truck Equipment Schedule T3						
Sport Utility 4D	HY7AJ	78940	**52500**	**54200**	**54500**	**60200**
TACOMA PICKUP—4-Cyl.—Truck Equipment Schedule T1						
Pickup 2D 6'	NX4CN	19270	**13050**	**13650**	**14900**	**17600**
4WD	P		**2500**	**2500**	**2890**	**2890**
TACOMA PICKUP 4WD—4-Cyl.—Truck Equipment Schedule T1						
Access Cab 4D 6'	UX4EN	24995	**18700**	**19450**	**20900**	**24600**

Body Type	VIN	List	Trade-In Good	Very Good	Pvt-Party Good	Retail Excellent
2WD	T	------	(3000)	(3000)	(3465)	(3465)
V6, 4.0 Liter	U	------	1100	1100	1270	1270
TACOMA PICKUP—V6—Truck Equipment Schedule T2						
PreRunner Access	TU4GN	24255	19100	19900	21400	25100
4-Cyl, 2.7 Liter	X	------	(1400)	(1400)	(1620)	(1620)
TACOMA PICKUP—V6—Truck Equipment Schedule T2						
X-Runner Access	TU4CN	27520	21200	22000	23500	27600
PreRunner Dbl 6'	KU4HN	25855	21300	22000	22800	25400
Limited Pkg			450	450	490	490
TACOMA PICKUP—V6—Truck Equipment Schedule T2						
PreRunner Dbl 5'	JU4GN	25355	22000	22800	23600	26300
Limited Pkg			450	450	490	490
4-Cyl, 2.7 Liter	X	------	(1400)	(1400)	(1530)	(1530)
TACOMA PICKUP 4WD—V6—Truck Equipment Schedule T1						
Double Cab 4D 5'	LU4EN	28430	25400	26200	27100	30100
Limited Pkg			450	450	490	490
2WD	J	------	(2175)	(2175)	(2365)	(2365)
4-Cyl, 2.7 Liter	X	------	(1400)	(1400)	(1530)	(1530)
TACOMA PICKUP 4WD—V6—Truck Equipment Schedule T2						
Double Cab 4D 6'	MU4FN	28930	24800	25600	26400	29400
Limited Pkg			450	450	490	490
TUNDRA PICKUP—V8—Truck Equipment Schedule T1						
Short Bed	JU5F1	27550	18550	19200	20600	23800
Long Bed	LY5F1	28825	18350	19000	20400	23500
Double Cab 6 1/2'	RY5F1	29950	20800	21500	23000	26500
4WD	U	------	3300	3300	3775	3775
V6, 4.0 Liter	U	------	(875)	(875)	(1000)	(1000)
V8, 4.6 Liter	M	------	(500)	(500)	(570)	(570)
TUNDRA PICKUP 4WD—V8—Truck Equipment Schedule T1						
Double Cab 8'	CY5F1	33990	24000	24800	26400	30400
Limited Dbl Cab	BY5F1	42255	31700	32700	34300	39000
CrewMax 4D	DY5F1	35825	28600	29500	30900	35300
Limited CrewMax	HY5F1	44790	33500	34500	36000	40800
2WD	T	------	(3300)	(3300)	(3775)	(3775)
V8, 4.6 Liter	M	------	(500)	(500)	(560)	(560)

2014 TOYOTA—(3,4,5orJ)T(3,D,E,ForM)(ZFREV)–E–#

Body Type	VIN	List	Trade-In Good	Very Good	Pvt-Party Good	Retail Excellent
RAV4 AWD—4-Cyl.—Truck Equipment Schedule T1						
LE Sport Utility	ZFREV	25810	17750	18350	19400	21900
XLE Sport Utility	WFREV	27260	19800	20400	21400	24100
Limited Sport Util	YFREV	30580	21500	22200	23100	25800
2WD	Z	------	(1500)	(1500)	(1655)	(1655)
RAV4—AC Electric—Truck Equipment Schedule T2						
EV Sport Utility 4D	YL4DV	50660	28400	29300	29900	33100
FJ CRUISER AWD—V6—Truck Equipment Schedule T2						
Sport Utility 2D	BU4BF	29580	26000	26900	27200	30000
2WD	U	------	(1725)	(1725)	(1825)	(1825)
VENZA—4-Cyl.—Truck Equipment Schedule T1						
LE Wagon 4D	ZA3BB	28760	16750	17350	18900	21900
XLE Wagon 4D	ZA3BB	32620	20100	20800	22100	25300
AWD	B	------	1025	1025	1195	1195
V6, 3.5 Liter		------	800	800	930	930
VENZA—V6—Truck Equipment Schedule T1						
Limited Wagon 4D	ZK3BB	38930	22500	23200	24400	27700
AWD	B	------	1025	1025	1155	1155
HIGHLANDER AWD—V6—Truck Equipment Schedule T1						
LE Sport Util 4D	BKRFH	32840	24900	25800	27100	30800
LE Plus Sport Util	BKRFH	35060	25700	26600	27800	31600
XLE Sport Util 4D	JKRFH	38360	28500	29500	30600	34500
Limited Sport Util	DKRFH	41960	31000	32100	33000	37100
Ltd Platinum 4D	DKRFH	44810	33700	34800	35600	39700
4-Cyl, 2.7 Liter	A	------	(1100)	(1100)	(1230)	(1230)
HIGHLANDER AWD—V6 Hybrid—Truck Equipment Schedule T1						
Limited Spt Util	DCRFH	48160	34200	35400	36100	40200
Ltd Platinum 4D	DCRFH	50650	37300	38500	39000	43300
4RUNNER 4WD—V6—Truck Equipment Schedule T1						
SR5 Sport Utility	BU5JR	35775	25700	26600	27400	30500
SR5 Premium 4D	BU5JR	38475	27900	28800	29600	33000
Trail Sport Utility	BU5JR	36585	27800	28700	29500	32900
Trail Premium 4D	BU5JR	39505	28300	29300	30100	33500
Limited Sport Util	BU5JR	44260	30300	31300	32100	35600
KDSS Suspension			700	700	765	765
2WD	Z	------	(1725)	(1725)	(1880)	(1880)

2014 TOYOTA

Body Type	VIN	List	Trade-In Good	Trade-In Very Good	Pvt-Party Good	Retail Excellent
SEQUOIA 4WD—V8—Truck Equipment Schedule T1						
SR5 Sport Utility	BY5G1	47815	32800	34000	34600	38600
Limited Sport Util	JY5G1	56775	39100	40500	41100	45900
Platinum Spt Util	DY5G1	64515	43000	44500	44800	49800
2WD	Z		(1725)	(1725)	(1890)	(1890)
SIENNA—V6—Truck Equipment Schedule T1						
L Minivan 4D	ZK3DC	27780	16950	17700	18650	21600
LE Minivan 4D	KK3DC	31350	18950	19750	20700	23900
XLE Minivan 4D	YK3DC	34505	24100	25100	26100	30000
SE Minivan 4D	XK3DC	34720	23700	24700	25700	29600
Limited Minivan	YK3DC	41100	26800	27900	28900	33200
AWD	J		1025	1025	1175	1175
LAND CRUISER 4WD—V8—Truck Equipment Schedule T3						
Sport Utility 4D	HY7AJ	79750	62900	64900	64500	70600
TACOMA PICKUP—4-Cyl.—Truck Equipment Schedule T1						
Pickup 2D 6 ft	NX4CN	19635	14950	15600	16700	19450
4WD	P		2800	2800	3195	3195
TACOMA PICKUP 4WD—4-Cyl.—Truck Equipment Schedule T2						
Access Cab 4D 6'	UX4EN	25210	20600	21500	22800	26600
2WD	T		(3000)	(3000)	(3425)	(3425)
V6, 4.0 Liter	U		1200	1200	1370	1370
TACOMA PICKUP—V6—Truck Equipment Schedule T2						
PreRunner Access	TU4GN	24420	20900	21800	23100	27000
4-Cyl, 2.7 Liter	X		(1500)	(1500)	(1715)	(1715)
TACOMA PICKUP—V6—Truck Equipment Schedule T2						
PreRunner Dbl 6'	KU4HN	26020	22600	23400	24000	26600
Limited Pkg			475	475	515	515
TACOMA PICKUP—V6—Truck Equipment Schedule T2						
PreRunner Dbl 5'	JU4GN	25520	23200	24000	24600	27200
Limited Pkg			475	475	515	515
4-Cyl, 2.7 Liter	X		(1500)	(1500)	(1620)	(1620)
TACOMA PICKUP 4WD—V6—Truck Equipment Schedule T1						
Double Cab 4D 5'	LU4EN	28645	26800	27700	28400	31400
Limited Pkg			475	475	510	510
2WD	J		(2325)	(2325)	(2495)	(2495)
4-Cyl, 2.7 Liter	X		(1500)	(1500)	(1605)	(1605)
TACOMA PICKUP 4WD—V6—Truck Equipment Schedule T2						
Double Cab 4D 6'	MU4FN	29145	26000	26900	27500	30500
Limited Pkg			475	475	515	515
TUNDRA PICKUP—V8—Truck Equipment Schedule T1						
SR Long Bed	NY5F1	29460	19350	20000	21400	24500
SR Double 6 1/2'	RY5F1	30350	21800	22500	24300	28200
SR5 Double 8'	CY5F1	35340	24400	25200	27300	31900
4WD	U		3600	3600	4220	4220
V6, 4.0 Liter	U		(950)	(950)	(1115)	(1115)
V8, 4.6 Liter	M		(500)	(500)	(585)	(585)
TUNDRA PICKUP 4WD—V8—Truck Equipment Schedule T1						
SR5 Double 8'	CY5F1	33730	25000	25800	27300	31300
SR5 Double 6 1/2'	UY5F1	35010	24900	25700	27700	32200
Limited Double 6'	BY5F1	40985	32700	33700	35200	40000
SR5 CrewMax 4D	DY5F1	37755	29100	30100	32200	37200
Limited CrewMax	HY5F1	43275	33900	35000	36700	41800
1794 Pickup 5 1/2'	AY5F1	48315	37600	38700	39800	44800
Platinum CrewMax	AY5F1	48700	37800	39000	40300	45500
2WD	T		(3600)	(3600)	(4115)	(4115)
V8, 4.6 Liter	M		(500)	(500)	(585)	(585)

VOLKSWAGEN

2000 VOLKSWAGEN — WV2(KH270)-Y-#

Body Type	VIN	List	Trade-In Good	Trade-In Very Good	Pvt-Party Good	Retail Excellent
EUROVAN—V6—Truck Equipment Schedule T1						
GLS Minivan	KH270	31890	3375	3850	4750	7250
MV Minivan	MH270	33390	3575	4075	5000	7600
Weekender Pkg			7000	7000	9335	9335

2001 VOLKSWAGEN — WV2(KH470)-1-#

Body Type	VIN	List	Trade-In Good	Trade-In Very Good	Pvt-Party Good	Retail Excellent
EUROVAN—V6—Truck Equipment Schedule T1						
Minivan	KH470	26815	4075	4600	5450	8125
MV Minivan	MH470	28315	4450	5000	5900	8775
Weekender Pkg			7000	7000	9335	9335

TRUCKS & VANS

TRUCKS & VANS

Body Type	VIN	List	Trade-In Good	Very Good	Pvt-Party Good	Retail Excellent
2002 VOLKSWAGEN — WV2(KB470)-2-#						
EUROVAN—V6—Truck Equipment Schedule T1						
GLS Minivan	KB470	26815	5025	5625	6600	9700
MV Minivan	MB470	28315	5300	5925	7100	10400
Weekender Pkg			7000	7000	9335	9335
2003 VOLKSWAGEN — WV2(KB470)-3-#						
EUROVAN—V6—Truck Equipment Schedule T1						
GLS Minivan	KB470	26815	5975	6650	7625	10850
MV Minivan	MB470	28315	6425	7125	8150	11550
Weekender Pkg			7000	7000	9335	9335
2004 VOLKSWAGEN — WVG(BC67L)-4-#						
TOUAREG 4WD—V6—Truck Equipment Schedule T3						
Sport Utility 4D	BC67L	35515	2775	3125	3950	5750
4-Corner Suspension			1000	1000	1340	1340
V8, 4.2 Liter			1025	1025	1380	1380
TOUAREG 4WD—V10 Turbo Diesel—Truck Equipment Schedule T3						
TDI Sport Util 4D	GH67L	58415	8000	8675	9600	12650
2005 VOLKSWAGEN — WVG(BG77L)-5-#						
TOUAREG 4WD—V6—Truck Equipment Schedule T3						
Sport Utility 4D	BG77L	37795	4225	4650	5575	7750
4-Corner Suspension			1075	1075	1445	1445
V8, 4.2 Liter	M		1125	1125	1505	1505
2006 VOLKSWAGEN — WVG(BG67L)-6-#						
TOUAREG 4WD—V6—Truck Equipment Schedule T3						
Sport Utility 4D	BG67L	37975	5150	5625	6625	8875
4-Corner Suspension			1175	1175	1550	1550
V8, 4.2 Liter			1225	1225	1625	1625
TOUAREG 4WD—V10—Truck Equipment Schedule T3						
TDI Sport Util 4D	PT77L	68420	11500	12350	13500	17300
2007 VOLKSWAGEN — WVG(BE77L)-7-#						
TOUAREG 4WD—V6—Truck Equipment Schedule T3						
Sport Utility 4D	BE77L	38660	6450	6975	8025	10550
4-Corner Suspension			1250	1250	1635	1635
V8, 4.2 Liter			1325	1325	1730	1730
TOUAREG 4WD—V10 Turbo Diesel—Truck Equipment Schedule T3						
TDI Sport Util 4D	PT77L	59690	12700	13550	14550	18250
2008 VOLKSWAGEN — WVG(BE77L)-8-#						
TOUAREG 2 4WD—V6—Truck Equipment Schedule T3						
Sport Utility 4D	BE77L	49080	9400	9975	10800	13250
4-Corner Suspension			1325	1325	1530	1530
V8, 4.2 Liter			1400	1400	1630	1630
TOUAREG 2 4WD—V10 Turbo Diesel—Truck Equipment Schedule T3						
TDI Sport Util 4D	PT77L	69000	16150	17050	17750	21300
4-Corner Suspension			1325	1325	1485	1485
2009 VOLKSWAGEN — WVG(AV75N)-9-#						
TIGUAN—4-Cyl. Turbo—Truck Equipment Schedule T3						
S Sport Utility 4D	AV75N	24990	6825	7250	8200	10150
SE Sport Utility 4D	AV75N	29025	7750	8225	9200	11300
SEL Sport Util 4D	AV75N	31740	10300	10850	11900	14500
Manual, 6-Spd	C		(375)	(375)	(450)	(450)
TIGUAN 4MOTION 4WD—4-Cyl. Turbo—Truck Equipment Sch T3						
SE Sport Utility 4D	BV75N	29565	9700	10250	11250	13650
SEL Sport Util 4D	BV75N	33630	11150	11750	12850	15550
TOUAREG 2 4WD—V6—Truck Equipment Schedule T3						
Sport Utility 4D	BE77L	39990	12050	12700	13500	16100
4-Corner Suspension			1400	1400	1600	1600
V8, 4.2 Liter			1500	1500	1715	1715
TOUAREG 2 4WD—V6 Turbo Diesel—Truck Equipment Schedule T3						
TDI Sport Utility	AM77L	43490	18250	19100	20000	23700
4-Corner Suspension			1400	1400	1580	1580
ROUTAN—V6—Truck Equipment Schedule T3						
S Minivan	HW441	25390	5300	5725	6650	8575

Body Type	VIN	List	Trade-In Good	Trade-In Very Good	Pvt-Party Good	Retail Excellent
SE Minivan 4D	HW341	30290	6875	7350	8375	10700
SEL Minivan 4D	HW54X	33890	8175	8725	9775	12400
SEL Prem Minivan	HW64X	39250	9800	10450	11600	14650

2010 VOLKSWAGEN — WVGor2V4(CV7AX)–A–#

TIGUAN—4-Cyl. Turbo—Truck Equipment Schedule T3
S Sport Utility 4D	CV7AX	25050	9400	9875	10900	13100
SE Sport Utility 4D	AV7AX	29900	10600	11100	12200	14600
Wolfsburg Edition	AV7AX	28550	10200	10700	11750	14100
SEL Sport Util 4D	AV7AX	32015	12550	13150	14350	17200
Manual, 6-Spd	C		(375)	(375)	(460)	(460)

TIGUAN 4MOTION AWD—4-Cyl. Turbo—Truck Equipment Sch T3
S Sport Utility 4D	BV7AX	27050	10000	10500	11550	13850
SE Sport Utility 4D	BV7AX	31250	12300	12900	14050	16750
Wolfsburg Ed SUV	BV7AX	30500	11500	12050	13200	15800
SEL Sport Util 4D	BV7AX	33965	13350	14000	15400	18500

TOUAREG AWD—V6—Truck Equipment Schedule T3
| VR6 Sport Utility | BF7A9 | 41190 | 14750 | 15450 | 16450 | 19300 |

TOUAREG AWD—V6 Turbo Diesel—Truck Equipment Schedule T3
| TDI Sport Utility | AK7A9 | 44710 | 21100 | 22000 | 22600 | 25900 |
| 4-Corner Suspension | | | 1500 | 1500 | 1635 | 1635 |

ROUTAN—V6—Truck Equipment Schedule T3
S Minivan 4D	RW4D1	26650	7325	7800	8800	10950
SE Minivan 4D	RW3D1	31250	9325	9875	11050	13700
SEL Minivan 4D	RW5DX	37250	10800	11400	12700	15750
SEL Premium	RW6DX	43300	12250	12900	14300	17700

2011 VOLKSWAGEN — WVGor2V4(AV7AX)–B–#

TIGUAN—4-Cyl. Turbo—Truck Equipment Schedule T3
S Sport Utility 4D	AV7AX	25405	10250	10750	11800	13950
SE Sport Utility 4D	AV7AX	28765	11650	12200	13300	15750
SEL Sport Util 4D	AV7AX	33640	13900	14500	16000	19100
Manual, 6-Spd	C		(450)	(450)	(530)	(530)

TIGUAN 4MOTION AWD—4-Cyl. Turbo—Truck Equipment Sch T3
S Sport Utility 4D	BV7AX	27360	11000	11500	12600	14900
SE Sport Utility 4D	BV7AX	30720	13550	14150	15450	18300
SEL Sport Util 4D	BV7AX	35595	14800	15400	17000	20300

TOUAREG AWD—V6 Hybrid—Truck Equipment Schedule T3
| Sport Utility 4D | FG9BP | 61385 | 25800 | 26700 | 27600 | 31400 |

TOUAREG AWD—V6—Truck Equipment Schedule T3
VR6 Sport Util	FF9BP	45270	19700	20500	21400	24500
VR6 Lux Spt Util	FF9BP	49120	20700	21500	22400	25700
VR6 Exec Spt Utl	FF9BP	54820	24000	24900	25900	29600

TOUAREG AWD—V6 Turbo Diesel—Truck Equipment Schedule T3
TDI Sport Util	FK8BP	48770	25800	26700	27700	31600
TDI Lux Spt Util	FK9BP	52620	27800	26800	29700	33900
TDI Exec Spt Utl	FK9BP	58320	30700	31800	32800	37400
4-Corner Suspension			1600	1600	1835	1835

ROUTAN—V6—Truck Equipment Schedule T3
S Minivan 4D	RW4DG	26720	8875	9325	10150	12200
SE Minivan 4D	RW3DG	31420	11300	11850	12900	15500
SEL Minivan 4D	RW5DG	37420	12750	13350	14500	17400
SEL Premium	RW6DG	43320	14200	14850	16150	19400

2012 VOLKSWAGEN — WVGor2C4(AV7AX)–C–#

TIGUAN—4-Cyl. Turbo—Truck Equipment Schedule T3
2.0T S Sport Util	AV7AX	25210	12100	12600	13750	16150
2.0T LE Sport Util	AV7AX	25995	12050	12550	13700	16100
2.0T SE Sport Util	AV7AX	29505	14000	14550	15800	18450
2.0T SEL Spt Util	AV7AX	34845	16650	17300	18750	22000
Manual, 6-Spd	C		(425)	(425)	(495)	(495)

TIGUAN 4MOTION AWD—4-Cyl. Turbo—Truck Equipment Sch T3
2.0T S Sport Util	BV7AX	27165	13000	13550	14850	17400
2.0T SE Sport Util	BV7AX	31460	16300	16900	18250	21300
2.0T SEL Spt Util	BV7AX	36800	17750	18450	20000	23600

TOUAREG AWD—V6—Truck Equipment Schedule T3
VR6 Sport SUV 4D	FF9BP	44245	22500	23300	24300	27600
VR6 Lux Spt Util	FF9BP	50265	23400	24200	25400	28900
VR6 Exec Spt Util	FF9BP	55965	26800	27700	28700	32600

TOUAREG AWD—V6 Hybrid—Truck Equipment Schedule T3
| Sport Utility 4D | FG9BP | 62685 | 30200 | 31200 | 32100 | 36100 |

2012 VOLKSWAGEN

Body	Type	VIN	List	Trade-In Good	Very Good	Pvt-Party Good	Retail Excellent
TOUAREG AWD—V6 Turbo Diesel—Truck Equipment Schedule T3							
TDI Sport SUV 4D		FK9BP	47745	28100	29100	30400	34700
TDI Lux Spt Utl		FK9BP	53765	30100	31100	32500	37100
TDI Exec Spt Utl		FK9BP	59465	33300	34400	35800	40900
ROUTAN—V6—Truck Equipment Schedule T3							
S Minivan 4D		RVAAG	27840	11800	12300	13150	15400
SE Minivan 4D		RVABG	32830	14700	15350	16350	19150
SEL Minivan 4D		RVACG	38710	16400	17050	18100	21100
SEL Premium		RVADG	45100	17650	18400	19550	23000

2013 VOLKSWAGEN — WVGor2C4(AV7AX)-D-#

Body	Type	VIN	List	Trade-In Good	Very Good	Pvt-Party Good	Retail Excellent
TIGUAN—4-Cyl. Turbo—Truck Equipment Schedule T3							
2.0T S Sport Util		AV7AX	25525	12600	13100	14450	17050
2.0T SE Sport Util		AV7AX	29985	15350	15950	17450	20500
2.0T SEL Spt Utl		AV7AX	35690	17800	18450	20100	23500
Manual, 6-Spd		C		(475)	(475)	(560)	(560)
TIGUAN 4MOTION AWD—4-Cyl. Turbo—Truck Equipment Sch T3							
2.0T S Sport Util		BV7AX	27480	13900	14400	15900	18650
2.0T SE Sport Util		BV7AX	31940	17200	17850	19400	22600
2.0T SEL Spt Utl		BV7AX	37645	18800	19500	21200	24700
TOUAREG AWD—V6—Truck Equipment Schedule T3							
VR6 Sport SUV 4D		EF9BP	44300	23400	24200	25300	28700
VR6 Lux Spt Utl		EF9BP	50305	25200	26000	27100	30700
VR6 Exec Spt Utl		EF9BP	56030	28300	29200	30300	34200
TOUAREG AWD—V6 Hybrid—Truck Equipment Schedule T3							
Sport Utility 4D		EG9BP	62930	33200	34300	35100	39200
TOUAREG AWD—V6 Turbo Diesel—Truck Equipment Schedule T3							
TDI Sport SUV 4D		EP9BP	47800	32100	33100	34400	38900
TDI Lux Spt Utl		EP9BP	53805	34600	35600	37000	41900
TDI Exec Spt Utl		EP9BP	59530	37700	38900	40300	45600
ROUTAN—V6—Truck Equipment Schedule T3							
S Minivan 4D		RVAAG		13150	13700	14700	17150
SE Minivan 4D		RVABG		16400	17050	18100	21000
SEL Premium		RVADG		19350	20100	21300	24700

2014 VOLKSWAGEN — WVGor2C4(AV3AX)-E-#

Body	Type	VIN	List	Trade-In Good	Very Good	Pvt-Party Good	Retail Excellent
TIGUAN—4-Cyl.—Truck Equipment Schedule T3							
2.0T S Sport Util		AV3AX	26195	13800	14350	16000	19000
2.0T SE Sport Util		AV3AX	28205	16650	17300	18750	21900
2.0T SEL Spt Utl		AV3AX	33860	19500	20200	21500	24800
2.0T R-Line Spt Util		AV3AX	37745	21100	21800	23000	26300
TIGUAN 4MOTION AWD—4-Cyl. Turbo—Truck Equipment Sch T3							
2.0T S Sport Util		BV3AX	28150	15200	15750	17350	20400
2.0T SE Sport Util		BV3AX	30180	18750	19400	20800	24000
2.0T SEL Spt Utl		BV3AX	35815	20000	20700	22000	25300
2.0T R-Line Spt Util		BV3AX	39700	23600	24400	25400	28800
TOUAREG AWD—V6—Truck Equipment Schedule T3							
VR6 Sport SUV 4D		EF9BP	44905	25900	26700	27700	31200
VR6 Exec Spt Utl		EF9BP	58270	31100	32100	33100	37100
VR6 Lux Spt Utl		EF9BP	52385	28300	29200	30300	34000
VR6 R-Line Spt Util		DF9BP	55205	29800	30700	31700	35500
TOUAREG AWD—V6 Hybrid—Truck Equipment Schedule T3							
Sport Utility 4D		EG9BP	65080	36800	37900	38500	42700
TOUAREG AWD—V6 Turbo Diesel—Truck Equipment Schedule T3							
TDI Sport SUV 4D		EP9BP	51945	36400	37500	38600	43400
TDI Exec Spt Utl		EP9BP	61770	42100	43400	44600	50200
TDI Lux Spt Utl		EP9BP	55685	38900	40100	41300	46400
X Sport Utility 4D		EP9BP	57080	31000	32000	32900	36800
TDI R-Line Spt Util		DP9BP	58525	40300	41600	42700	48000

VOLVO

2003 VOLVO — YV1(CM59H)-3-#

Body	Type	VIN	List	Trade-In Good	Very Good	Pvt-Party Good	Retail Excellent
XC90 AWD—5-Cyl. Turbo—Truck Equipment Schedule T3							
Sport Utility 4D		CM59H	35760	2400	2700	3800	5825
Third Row Seat				225	225	295	295
FWD		N,Y		(800)	(800)	(1050)	(1050)
XC90 AWD—6-Cyl. Twin Turbo—Truck Equipment Schedule T3							
T6 Sport Utility 4D		CM91H	40660	2150	2425	3475	5350
Third Row Seat				225	225	295	295

Body Type	VIN	List	Trade-In Good	Very Good	Pvt-Party Good	Retail Excellent

2004 VOLVO — YV1(CM59H)-4-#

XC90 AWD—5-Cyl. Turbo—Truck Equipment Schedule T3
Sport Utility 4D	CM59H	36875	4025	4450	5500	7850
Third Row Seat	Y		250	250	315	315
FWD	N,Y		(875)	(875)	(1155)	(1155)

XC90 AWD—6-Cyl. Twin Turbo—Truck Equipment Schedule T3
| T6 Sport Utility 4D | CM91H | 41650 | 3725 | 4125 | 5150 | 7375 |
| Third Row Seat | | | 250 | 250 | 315 | 315 |

2005 VOLVO — YV1(CM592)-5-#

XC90 AWD—5-Cyl. Turbo—Truck Equipment Schedule T3
Sport Utility 4D	CM592	37300	4225	4650	5775	8200
Third Row Seat	Y		250	250	335	335
FWD	N,Y		(950)	(950)	(1260)	(1260)

XC90 AWD—6-Cyl. Twin Turbo—Truck Equipment Schedule T3
| T6 Sport Utility 4D | CM911 | 41700 | 3850 | 4250 | 5375 | 7650 |
| Third Row Seat | Y | | 250 | 250 | 335 | 335 |

XC90 AWD—V8—Truck Equipment Schedule T3
| Sport Utility 4D | CM852 | 46080 | 4725 | 5175 | 6375 | 9000 |
| Third Row Seat | Z | | 250 | 250 | 335 | 335 |

2006 VOLVO — YV1(CM592)-6-#

XC90 AWD—5-Cyl. Turbo—Truck Equipment Schedule T3
2.5T Sport Util 4D	CM592	38110	4825	5275	6275	8575
Third Row Seat	Y		275	275	360	360
FWD	N,Y		(1025)	(1025)	(1375)	(1375)

XC90 AWD—V8—Truck Equipment Schedule T3
Sport Utility 4D	CM852	46535	5975	6475	7725	10500
Ocean Race Spt Utl	CM852	50555	8575	9225	10600	14100
Third Row Seat	Z		275	275	360	360

2007 VOLVO — YV1(CN982)-7-#

XC90 AWD—6-Cyl.—Truck Equipment Schedule T3
3.2 Sport Utility 4D	CN982	36830	5650	6125	7175	9450
Third Row Seat	Y,Z		275	275	370	370
AWD	M		1125	1125	1460	1460

XC90 AWD—V8—Truck Equipment Schedule T3
Sport Utility 4D	CT852	47120	8525	9150	10300	13400
Sport SUV 4D	CZ852	49995	10050	10750	12050	15600
Third Row Seat	T,Z		275	275	365	365

2008 VOLVO — YV4(CN982)-8-#

XC90 AWD—6-Cyl.—Truck Equipment Schedule T3
3.2 Sport Utility 4D	CN982	36955	8900	9475	10400	12900
Third Row Seat	Y,Z		300	300	360	360
AWD	M		1200	1200	1430	1430

XC90 AWD—V8—Truck Equipment Schedule T3
Sport Utility 4D	CZ852	49250	13400	14200	15350	18900
Sport SUV 4D	CT852	50615	14500	15300	16450	20200
Third Row Seat	T,Z		300	300	355	355

2010 VOLVO — YV(1or4)(960DL)-A-#

XC60—6-Cyl.—Truck Equipment Schedule T3
3.2 Sport Utility 4D	960DL	33245	13750	14400	15500	18300
Adaptive Cruise Control			400	400	465	465
AWD	Z		950	950	1105	1105

XC60 AWD—6-Cyl. Turbo—Truck Equipment Schedule T3
T6 Sport Utility 4D	992DZ	38050	16400	17150	18100	21100
R-Design Sport Util	992DZ	42400	16000	16750	17800	20900
Adaptive Cruise Control			400	400	455	455

XC90—6-Cyl.—Truck Equipment Schedule T3
3.2 Sport Utility 4D	982CY	38550	14800	15450	16550	19450
AWD	Z		1000	1000	1110	1110
Third Row Seat	F,Y		400	400	445	445

XC90 AWD—6-Cyl.—Truck Equipment Schedule T3
| 3.2 R-Design SUV | 982CT | 42350 | 18200 | 19000 | 20100 | 23500 |
| FWD | F | | (1200) | (1200) | (1325) | (1325) |

XC90 AWD—V8—Truck Equipment Schedule T3
| Sport Utility 4D | 852CZ | 48350 | 21200 | 22100 | 23100 | 26900 |
| Third Row Seat | T,Z | | 400 | 400 | 440 | 440 |

Body Type	VIN	List	Trade-In Good	Very Good	Pvt-Party Good	Retail Excellent

2011 VOLVO — YV(1or4)(952DL)-B-#

XC60—6-Cyl.—Truck Equipment Schedule T3
3.2 Sport Utility	952DL	33250	16600	17250	18250	21100
3.2 R-Design Util	952DL	38900	18850	19600	20600	23900
Adaptive Cruise Control			425	425	480	480
AWD	Z		1100	1100	1240	1240

XC60 AWD—6-Cyl. Turbo—Truck Equipment Schedule T3
T6 Sport Utility	902DZ	39250	20200	21000	21900	25100
T6 R-Design Util	902DZ	42400	20600	21400	22300	25600
Adaptive Cruise Control			425	425	470	470

XC90—6-Cyl.—Truck Equipment Schedule T3
3.2 Sport Utility	982CY	39050	18400	19150	20200	23300
Third Row Seat	F,Y		450	450	495	495
AWD	Z		1100	1100	1210	1210

XC90 AWD—6-Cyl.—Truck Equipment Schedule T3
3.2 R-Design Util	952CT	42850	21700	22500	23500	27000
Third Row Seat	F,Y		450	450	490	490
FWD	F		(1200)	(1200)	(1305)	(1305)

XC90 AWD—V8—Truck Equipment Schedule T3
| Sport Utility 4D | 852CZ | 48850 | 24800 | 25800 | 26800 | 30600 |
| Third Row Seat | T,Z | | 450 | 450 | 490 | 490 |

2012 VOLVO — YV4(952DL)-C-#

XC60—6-Cyl.—Truck Equipment Schedule T3
3.2 Sport Utility 4D	952DL	33775	18900	19600	20600	23400
Adaptive Cruise Control			450	450	505	505
AWD	Z		1050	1050	1180	1180

XC60 AWD—6-Cyl. Turbo—Truck Equipment Schedule T3
T6 Sport Utility	902DZ	39825	22400	23200	24200	27600
T6 R-Design Util	902DZ	44025	23100	23900	25000	28500
Adaptive Cruise Control			450	450	505	505

XC90—6-Cyl.—Truck Equipment Schedule T3
| 3.2 Sport Utility | 952CY | 39275 | 21400 | 22100 | 23100 | 26200 |
| AWD | Z | | 1200 | 1200 | 1320 | 1320 |

XC90 AWD—6-Cyl.—Truck Equipment Schedule T3
| 3.2 R-Design Util | 952CT | 44075 | 24800 | 25600 | 26600 | 30200 |
| FWD | F | | (1200) | (1200) | (1320) | (1320) |

2013 VOLVO — YV4(952DL)-D-#

XC60—6-Cyl.—Truck Equipment Schedule T3
3.2 Sport Utility 4D	952DL	35245	20700	21400	22600	25800
3.2 Premier SUV	952DL	38195	21300	22100	23300	26800
3.2 Premier Plus	952DL	40095	22200	23000	24100	27600
3.2 Platinum SUV	952DL	42795	24400	24900	26000	29600
Sensing Cruise Control			475	475	540	540
AWD	Z		1100	1100	1250	1250

XC60 AWD—6-Cyl. Turbo—Truck Equipment Schedule T3
T6 Sport Utility 4D	902DZ	41545	23700	24500	25700	29200
T6 Premier Plus	902DZ	43445	24700	25500	26600	30200
T6 R-Design SUV	902DZ	45745	25700	26600	27700	31400
T6 Platinum SUV	902DZ	46145	26400	27300	28400	32300
T6 R-DsgnPrmr +	902DZ	47145	27200	28200	29200	33200
T6 R-Dsgn Pltnm	902DZ	49845	28300	29300	30500	34700
Sensing Cruise Control			475	475	530	530

XC90 3.2—6-Cyl.—Truck Equipment Schedule T3
Sport Utility 4D	952CY	40375	24500	25300	26200	29500
Premier Plus 4D	952CY	42875	25500	26300	27300	30800
R-Design Spt Util	952CT	43395	27100	28000	28900	32500
R-Design Premier +	952CT	43575	27200	28100	29000	32500
Platinum Spt Util	952CY	45575	27200	28100	29000	32600
R-Design Platinum	952CF	46275	27900	28800	29700	33300
AWD	Z		1200	1200	1330	1330

2014 VOLVO — YV4(952DL)-E-#

XC60—6-Cyl.—Truck Equipment Schedule T3
3.2 Sport Utility 4D	952DL	35765	24600	25400	26600	30100
3.2 Premier Spt Util	952DL	38865	25600	26500	27500	31100
3.2 Premier Plus 4D	952DL	40165	26400	27300	28300	31900
3.2 Platinum SUV	952DL	42865	28900	29800	30700	34500
Technology Pkg			650	650	715	715
AWD	Z		1200	1200	1315	1315

Body Type	VIN	List	Trade-In Good	Very Good	Pvt-Party Good	Retail Excellent
XC60 AWD—6-Cyl. Turbo—Truck Equipment Schedule T3						
T6 Sport Utility 4D	902DZ	42465	28400	29300	30100	33900
T6 Premier Plus 4D	902DZ	43765	29300	30200	31100	34900
T6 Platinum SUV	902DZ	46465	30200	31100	31900	35800
T6 R-Design SUV	902DZ	46715	30300	31200	32000	35900
T6 R-Dsgn Premr +	902DZ	48015	31000	32000	32700	36600
T6 R-Dsgn Pltnm	902DZ	50715	32200	33200	33900	37800
Technology Pkg			650	650	705	705
XC90 3.2—6-Cyl.—Truck Equipment Schedule T3						
Sport Utility 4D	952CY	40615	26600	27500	28400	31800
Premier Plus 4D	952CY	42115	27800	28700	29600	33200
R-Design Spt Util	952CF	43615	29500	30500	31300	35000
Platinum Spt Util	952CY	44815	29700	30700	31500	35200
R-Design Platinum	952CF	46315	30800	31800	32500	36200
AWD	Z		1200	1200	1325	1325

TRUCKS & VANS

TRUCKS & VANS

Equipment	00-02	03	04	05	06	07	08
MODEL PACKAGES (Truck Schedules T1 & T2)							
(Add Only If Not Listed on Individual Vehicle Listing)							
CHEVROLET/GMC:							
LTZ, SLT	300	—	—	—	—	—	—
LT, Xtreme	125	150	—	—	—	—	—
LS, SLE, ZR2 Suspension							
	100	125	150	—	—	—	—
DODGE:							
SLT, SXT	75	—	—	—	—	—	—
FORD:							
Limited, Chateau	325	385	—	—	—	—	—
Lariat, Adrenalin	150	225	300	375	—	—	—
XLT, XLT Sport, XLT NBX, FX4, Edge Plus, Amarillo							
	125	150	—	—	—	—	—
STX, EDGE	—	125	—	—	—	—	—
ALL MAKES:							
(All Other Model Packages Not Listed)							
	75	75	75	75	75	100	125
TRUCK SCHEDULE T1 (Deduct For)							
Manual Trans	(250)	(275)	(300)	(325)	(350)	(370)	(400)
TRUCK SCHEDULE T2 (Add For)							
Auto Trans	200	225	250	275	300	325	350
w/o Pwr Steering	(75)	(75)	(75)	(75)	(75)	(75)	(75)
w/o Air Cond	(175)	(200)	(200)	(200)	(200)	(200)	(200)
TRUCK SCHEDULE T3 (This Equipment Only)							
Premium Sound	75	100	125	150	150	150	150
Video/DVD	—	100	100	150	175	200	—
NavigationSystm	—	—	300	300	350	375	400
Grille Guard	50	50	50	50	50	50	50
Running Boards	200	200	200	200	200	200	200
Premium Wheels	150	175	200	225	250	275	300
Oversize Premium Wheels (20" Plus)							
	355	390	425	460	500	535	570
Towing Pkg	125	150	175	200	200	200	200
w/o Leather	(100)	(100)	(100)	(125)	(150)	(175)	(200)
OTHER OPTIONS (Truck Schedules T1 & T2)							
w/o Pwr Windows	(75)	(100)	(100)	(100)	(100)	(100)	(100)
w/o Power Locks	(50)	(50)	(50)	(50)	(50)	(50)	(50)
w/o Tilt Wheel	(50)	(75)	(75)	(75)	(75)	(75)	(75)
Premium Sound	50	50	50	50	50	50	50
Video/DVD	—	100	100	150	175	200	—
NavigationSystm	—	—	300	300	350	375	400
Leather	100	100	100	125	150	175	200

2000-2008 TRUCK FACTORY EQUIPMENT

Equipment	00-02	03	04	05	06	07	08
Quad Seating (4 Buckets)	125	150	150	150	150	150	150
Van Seating Pkgs							
(11/12 Pass)	275	300	325	350	375	400	400
(15 Passenger)	525	550	575	600	625	650	650
Privacy Glass (Vans/Wagons/Sport Utilities)							
	50	50	50	50	50	50	50
Sliding Rear Window (Pickups)							
	25	25	25	25	25	25	25
Roof Rack	25	25	25	25	25	25	25
Pickup Shell/Cap	75	100	100	100	100	100	100
Bed Liner	50	50	50	50	50	75	75
Grille Guard	50	50	50	50	50	50	50
Winch	50	50	50	75	100	125	150
Custom Bumper	50	50	50	50	50	50	50
Stepside							
(Short Bed PU)	50	75	100	125	150	150	150
(Long Bed PU)	(250)	(250)	—	—	—	—	—
Running Boards	200	200	200	200	200	200	200
Alloy Wheels	75	100	125	150	150	150	150
Premium Wheels	150	175	200	225	250	275	300
Oversize Premium Wheels (20" Plus)							
	315	390	425	460	500	535	570
Wide Tires or Oversize Off-Road Tires							
	50	50	50	50	50	75	100
Opt Fuel Tank	50	50	—	—	—	—	—
Towing Pkg	125	150	175	200	200	200	200
Dual Rear Wheels (Add Only on Models Not Listed as DR)							
(Pickups)	600	650	700	725	750	775	—
(Cab/Ch, Vans)	225	250	275	300	300	300	—
Single Rear Wheels (Deduct Only on Models Listed as DR)							
(Cab/Ch, Vans)	(225)	(250)	(275)	(300)	(300)	(300)	(300)
Snow Plow	300	375	450	525	600	675	750
Hydraulic Lift	350	350	350	350	350	350	350
Underbody Hoist/Dump Bed							
	350	350	350	350	350	350	350
Cab & Chassis Bodies							
9' Stake	450	475	500	525	550	575	600
12' Stake	500	525	550	575	600	625	650
14' Stake	550	575	600	625	650	675	700
16' Stake	600	625	650	675	700	725	750
12' x 8' Box	500	500	500	500	500	500	500
14' x 8' Box	550	550	550	550	550	550	550
16' x 8' Box	600	600	600	600	600	600	600
Utility	800	800	800	800	800	800	800
Aluminum Box	400	400	400	400	400	400	400

TRUCKS & VANS

SEE PAGE 9 FOR PVT PARTY & RETAIL EQUIPMENT

TRUCKS & VANS

Equipment	09	10	11	12	13	14
ALL MAKES:						
(All Other Model Packages Not Listed)						
	125	125	125	150	175	200
TRUCK SCHEDULE T1 (Deduct For)						
5-Spd Manual	(475)	(550)	(600)	(650)	(700)	(750)
6-Spd Manual	(300)	(350)	—	(510)	—	—
TRUCK SCHEDULE T2 (Add For)						
Auto Trans	400	450	500	550	600	650
w/o Pwr Steering	(100)	(125)	(150)	(150)	(150)	(150)
w/o Air Cond	(250)	(300)	(350)	(400)	(450)	(475)
TRUCK SCHEDULE T3 (This Equipment Only)						
Premium Sound	200	250	300	325	350	375
Video/DVD	250	275	300	325	350	375
NavigationSystm	450	475	500	525	550	575
Panorama Roof	400	450	500	550	600	650
Premium Wheels	350	375	400	425	450	475
Oversize Premium Wheels (20" Plus)						
	605	645	680	715	750	790
Grille Guard	75	75	75	75	75	75
Parking Sensors	50	75	100	125	150	175
Backup Camera	75	100	125	150	200	200
Running Boards	200	200	200	200	200	200
Power Sliding Doors (Minivan)						
Single	25	25	25	25	50	75
Dual	50	75	100	125	150	175
Towing Pkg	225	250	275	300	300	300
w/o Leather	(250)	(300)	(350)	(400)	(450)	(525)
OTHER OPTIONS (Truck Schedules T1 & T2)						
w/o Pwr Windows	(125)	(150)	(175)	(200)	(225)	(250)
w/o Power Locks	(75)	(100)	(125)	(150)	(175)	(175)
w/o Tilt Wheel	(100)	(125)	(150)	(175)	(200)	(200)
Premium Sound	100	125	150	175	200	225
Video/DVD	250	275	300	325	350	375
NavigationSystm	450	475	500	525	550	575
Leather	250	300	350	400	450	525
Quad Seating						
(4 Buckets)	200	250	300	325	350	375
Van Seating Packages						
(11/12 Pass)	450	500	550	600	—	700
(14/15 Pass)	800	950	1100	1225	1350	—
Power Sliding Doors (Minivans)						
Single	25	25	25	25	50	75
Dual	50	75	100	125	150	175
Privacy Glass (Vans/Wagons/Sport Utilities)						
	75	100	100	100	100	100

TRUCKS & VANS

Equipment	09	10	11	12	13	14
Sliding Rear Window (Pickups)						
	50	75	75	75	75	75
Power Sliding Rear Window (Pickups)						
	150	175	175	175	175	175
Roof Rack	50	75	100	100	100	100
Panorama Roof	400	450	500	550	600	650
Pickup Shell/Cap	150	175	200	225	250	275
Hard Tonneau	100	125	150	175	200	225
Bed Liner	100	100	100	125	150	175
Grille Guard	75	75	75	75	75	75
Winch	150	175	200	225	250	275
Custom Bumper	75	100	100	100	100	100
Parking Sensors	50	75	100	125	150	175
Backup Camera	75	100	125	150	200	200
Custom Paint	25	25	50	75	100	125
Two-Tone Paint	25	25	50	75	100	125
Stepside Bed	200	250	300	325	350	375
Running Boards	200	200	200	200	200	200
Alloy Wheels	175	200	225	250	275	300
Premium Wheels	350	375	400	425	450	475
Oversize Premium Wheels (20" Plus)						
	605	645	680	715	750	790
Wide Tires or Oversize Off-Road Tires						
	100	100	100	125	150	175
Towing Pkg	225	250	275	300	300	300
Dual Rear Wheels (Add Only on Models Not Listed as DR)						
(Pickups)	925	1050	1175	1300	1425	1550
(Cab/Ch, Vans)	375	450	500	550	600	650
Single Rear Wheels (Deduct Only on Models Listed as DR)						
(Cab/Ch, Vans)	(375)	(450)	(500)	(550)	(600)	(650)
Snow Plow	850	950	1050	1150	1250	1375
Hydraulic Lift	400	450	500	550	600	625
Underbody Hoist/Dump Bed						
	400	450	500	550	600	625
Cab & Chassis Bodies						
9' Stake	700	800	900	975	1050	1125
12' Stake	750	850	950	1050	1150	1225
14' Stake	800	900	1000	1100	1200	1300
16' Stake	875	1000	1100	1200	1300	1400
12' x 8' Box	575	650	700	750	800	850
14' x 8' Box	625	700	775	850	900	950
16' x 8' Box	700	775	850	925	1000	1075
Utility	900	1000	1100	1200	1300	1400
Aluminum Box	500	575	650	725	800	875

TRUCKS & VANS

TRUCKS & VANS